W9-BKA-134

DATE DUE			

Encyclopedia
of the
American Presidency

Editorial Board

Encyclopedia of the American Presidency

Editors

LEONARD W. LEVY
LOUIS FISHER

Volume 3

SIMON & SCHUSTER

A Paramount Communications Company

New York   London   Toronto   Sydney   Tokyo   Singapore

Simon & Schuster
Academic Reference Division
15 Columbus Circle
New York, New York 10023

A Paramount Communications Company

Printed in the United States of America

printing number
2   3   4   5   6   7   8   9   10

Library of Congress Cataloging-in-Publication Data

Encyclopedia of the American presidency

Leonard W. Levy, Louis Fisher, editors.
v. cm.

Includes bibliographical references and index.

1. Presidents—United States—Encyclopedias.   2.
Presidents—United States—Biography.   I. Levy, Leonard
Williams, 1923–   . II. Fisher, Louis.
JK511.E53 1994   353.03'13'03—dc20   93-13574 CIP

ISBN 0-13-275983-7 (Set)
0-13-275967-5 (Vol. 3)

The paper used in this publication meets the minimum
requirements of the American National Standard for
Information Sciences—Permanence of Paper for Printed Library
Materials ANSI Z39.48-1984.

Abbreviations Used in This Work

Ala. Alabama
Ariz. Arizona
Ark. Arkansas
Art. Article
b. born
c. circa, about, approximately
Calif. California
cf. confer, compare
chap. chapter (pl., chaps.)
CIO Congress of Industrial Organizations
Cong. Congress
Colo. Colorado
Conn. Connecticut
d. died
D Democrat, Democratic
D.C. District of Columbia
Del. Delaware
diss. dissertation
DR Democratic-Republican
ed. editor (pl., eds); edition
e.g. exempli gratia, for example
enl. enlarged
esp. especially
et al. et alii, and others
etc. et cetera, and so forth

exp. expanded
f. and following (pl., ff.)
F Federalist
Fla. Florida
Ga. Georgia
GOP Grand Old Party (Republican Party)
H.R. House of Representatives
I Independent
ibid. ibidem, in the same place (as the one immediately preceding)
Ida. Idaho
i.e. id est, that is
Ill. Illinois
Ind. Indiana
IRS Internal Revenue Service
Kan. Kansas
Ky. Kentucky
La. Louisiana
M.A. Master of Arts
Mass. Massachusetts
Me. Maine
Mich. Michigan
Minn. Minnesota

Miss. Mississippi
Mo. Missouri
Mont. Montana
n. note
N.C. North Carolina
n.d. no date
N.Dak. North Dakota
Neb. Nebraska
Nev. Nevada
N.H. New Hampshire
N.J. New Jersey
N.Mex. New Mexico
no. number (pl., nos.)
n.p. no place
n.s. new series
N.Y. New York
Okla. Oklahoma
Ore. Oregon
p. page (pl., pp.)
Pa. Pennsylvania
pt. part (pl., pts.)
R Republican
rev. revised
R.I. Rhode Island
S. Senate
S.C. South Carolina

S.Dak. South Dakota
sec. section (pl., secs.)
ser. series
ses. session
supp. supplement
Tenn. Tennessee
Tex. Texas
U.N. United Nations
U.S. United States, United States Reports
USA United States Army
USAF United States Air Force
USN United States Navy
U.S.S.R. Union of Soviet Socialist Republics
v. versus
Va. Virginia
vol. volume (pl., vols.)
Vt. Vermont
W Whig
Wash. Washington
Wis. Wisconsin
W.Va. West Virginia
Wyo. Wyoming

JACKSON, ANDREW (1767–1845), seventh President of the United States (1829–1837). Andrew Jackson was born on 15 March 1767 in the Waxhaw Settlement, South Carolina, the third son of Andrew and Elizabeth Hutchinson Jackson (Andrew's father died prior to the boy's birth). Young Andrew attended local schools, but his formal education was very limited. During the American Revolution, he abandoned school and served in a regiment that fought in the Battle of Hanging Rock. Later captured by the British, he was scarred on the hand and forehead for refusing to clean an officer's boots, imprisoned, during which time he contracted smallpox, and then rescued by his mother, who helped arrange an exchange of prisoners. His two older brothers died during the Revolution; shortly after Andrew's recovery from smallpox, his mother died of cholera while nursing American prisoners held aboard British prison ships in Charleston harbor.

Early Career. Orphaned at the age of fourteen, Andrew lived with relatives for a short time and then moved to North Carolina in 1784 to study law. He completed his training in 1787 and received his license to practice law in North Carolina. Offered the post of public prosecutor for the western district of North Carolina, Jackson migrated to what is now the state of Tennessee and settled in Nashville in 1788. He married Rachel Donelson in 1791. It was later claimed that, at the time, they did not realize that she had not been legally divorced from her first husband, Lewis Robards. After the divorce was finally granted, they married a second time. The strange circumstances of the marriage later figured prominently in the campaign of 1828, when Jackson was elected President.

An excellent public prosecutor, Jackson prospered and engaged in commercial trade and land speculation. He built several boats for AARON BURR and his companions to sail down the Mississippi River on an expedition that President Thomas Jefferson called a "conspiracy" and for which Jackson was severely criticized during the presidential election of 1828. A land deal almost landed Jackson in debtor's prison, and he subsequently developed a lifelong aversion to debt and the note-issuing practices of banks (because it encouraged land speculation). He also became a political leader of western Tennessee, thanks to his wife's family connections and the support of William Blount, the territorial governor. He was elected in 1795 to the constitutional convention that wrote Tennessee's first constitution and then became Tennessee's first representative to the U.S. House of Representatives when Tennessee was admitted to the Union in 1796. The following year he was elected to the U.S. Senate, but he did not distinguish himself in either house. He resigned from the Senate in 1798 and won election as a judge of the Superior Court of Tennessee, the state's highest court, where he served for the next six years. Very few of his decisions survive, but he apparently earned the respect and regard of the citizens of the state.

Elected a major general of the Tennessee militia in 1802 by the field officers of the militia, Jackson proved himself an excellent general during the WAR OF 1812 against Great Britain by defeating the Creek Indians, who had massacred frontier settlers at Fort Mims in 1814, and then halting a British invasion below New Orleans on 8 January 1815. The Battle of New Orleans made Jackson an American hero for the remainder of his life. His soldiers affectionately called him Old Hickory. When the Seminole Indians in Spanish Florida attacked settlers along the American frontier in 1818, President James Monroe ordered Jackson to put a stop to the attacks. Jackson not only pursued the Indians across the American border but seized Florida from Spain and executed two British subjects accused of assisting the Indians. After Spain sold Florida to the United States, Monroe appointed Jackson the territorial governor in 1821, but Jackson hated the assignment and served for only a few weeks before resigning. Nevertheless, he was credited with providing Florida with an efficient government administered by excellent men.

The Elections of 1824 and 1828. The Tennessee legislature unanimously nominated Jackson for the presidency on 20 July 1822, after which he was elected to the U.S. Senate. In addition to Jackson, candidates in the presidential election of 1824 included Secretary of State John Quincy Adams, Secretary of the Treasury WILLIAM H. CRAWFORD, and Speaker of the House of Representatives HENRY CLAY. Because of the number of candidates, no one received the constitutionally mandated majority of electoral votes. The election went to the House of Representatives, where, under the TWELFTH AMENDMENT to the Constitution, the members choose the President from the top three contenders. Jackson had a plurality of ninety-nine votes, Adams had eighty-four, Crawford forty-one, and Clay thirty-seven. Clay was automatically excluded from consideration, but, because of his powerful position and influence in the House, he was seen by the other candidates as the man who could decide the election. Unquestionably, Clay himself would have been elected had he been among the top three.

Clay decided to throw his support to Adams because the two men agreed on basic economic and political issues. Moreover, he dismissed Jackson, whom he called a "military chieftain," and Crawford, who had suffered a stroke and was not well enough to undertake the responsibilities of the presidency. In the House election in 1825, Adams was chosen on the first ballot. Adams then appointed Clay his Secretary of State, a position that traditionally led straight to the presidency. Jackson resigned his seat in the Senate and returned to his home, the Hermitage, outside Nashville, claiming that the people had been cheated by a "corrupt bargain" between Adams and Clay to deprive the electorate of its right to choose the President.

The "corrupt bargain" theme became the principal issue in the presidential election of 1828, and a number of prominent political leaders in the country joined in supporting Jackson for the top office, most notably Senator Martin Van Buren, the political wizard of New York who was sometimes called the "Little Magician" in recognition of his incomparable managerial skills. Other notable supporters included John C. Calhoun of South Carolina and Thomas Hart Benton of Missouri. Together, and with help from many other leaders around the country, they assembled an organization that subsequently called itself the DEMOCRATIC PARTY. The friends of the coalition of Adams and Clay took the name National Republicans.

The campaign of 1828 was one of the most sordid elections in American history. Jackson's marriage, his executions of soldiers, his involvement in the Burr Conspiracy, his personal habits, including gambling and cockfighting, and his general lack of statesmanlike qualities were cited against him. Adams, on the other hand, was accused of pimping, of corruption in the distribution of offices in the executive branch, and of misusing funds to decorate the White House. Jackson's personal popularity and the relatively strong organization behind him won him a tremendous victory at the polls. He garnered a total of 647,276 popular and 178 electoral votes to Adams's 508,064 popular and 83 electoral votes. Adams captured New England, New Jersey, and Delaware and took most of Maryland's and a little less than half of New York's electoral votes, while Jackson took all the rest. He swept everything south of the Potomac River and west of New Jersey.

Jacksonian Democracy. For Jackson's inauguration on 4 March 1829, some twenty thousand people crowded into the area east of the Capitol. After the ceremony a mob proceeded to the White House, where it celebrated by climbing on the sofas and chairs, breaking chinaware, and even jumping through the windows to get at the refreshments positioned on the lawn outside.

As President, Jackson claimed he wished to advance a program of what he called "reform retrenchment and economy." Specifically, he vowed to observe a policy of strict economy in government expenditures and thereby liquidate the national debt, extirpate corruption from the executive branch, open government employment to all, reduce tariff duties to a more "judicious" level, and, after the national debt had been paid, distribute the surplus in the Treasury to the states for the construction of public works and the improvement of education. His policies, he said, would always respect the rights of the states and their sovereignty to prevent further "consolidation" by the central government. His philosophy was clearly conservative in its commitment to a strict interpretation of the Constitution and to the protection of STATES' RIGHTS, its desire to check the expansion of powers by the federal government, and its determination to pay the national debt. It was democratic in its commitment to make government available to all. This democratic thrust to Jackson's thinking was expressed in virtually all his state papers. He constantly affirmed his belief that "the people are sovereign, their will is absolute." In his first message to Congress, he stated in strong, unequivocal terms that *"the majority is to govern"* [emphasis in original].

At various times during his eight years in office, Jackson's commitment to democracy was revealed by his advocacy of direct election of federal officers. He urged constitutional amendments that would eliminate the ELECTORAL COLLEGE and enable the people to elect their Presidents directly; eliminate the role of state legislatures in the election of U.S. Senators and turn their election over to the people; and end the appointment of federal judges, including Supreme Court Justices, again turning their selection over to the people. He also affirmed the right of voters to instruct their representatives on important national issues.

In opening government employment to all citizens on an equal basis, Jackson declared in an "Outline of principles" that he wrote shortly before his inauguration that he would conduct a strict examination into the operation of the executive department and remove those guilty of fraud and incompetence—he really believed that the Adams administration was riddled with corruption—and those appointed against "the manifest will of the people." "It is rotation in office that will perpetuate our liberty," he wrote. This rotation policy, called a "spoils system" by his opponents, would, in his mind, establish popular government and end a system of elitism. Too many government workers, Jackson believed, think they have a "life estate," a "vested right" to office. If a person holds an office "20 years or upwards, not only a vested right, but that it ought to descend to his children, & if no children then the next of kin—This is not the principles of our government. It is rotation in office that will perpetuate our liberty." One of the first principles of Jacksonian democracy, therefore, was the rejection of class or any other form of elitism in the operation of government. This theme resonated throughout Jackson's presidency.

The War over the Bank. The operation of the Second BANK OF THE UNITED STATES, an institution chartered by Congress establishing a central banking system in the country, troubled Jackson, and he repeatedly called on Congress to do something about it. His complaint distorted actual facts—in his first message he said that the Bank had failed to provide the country with sound currency, which was patently untrue—and masked his real objections to paper money and his suspicion that the Bank had used its funds to influence the outcome of elections. Furthermore, he was convinced that the operation of the Bank struck at the heart of democratic principles and therefore threatened the liberty of all.

When a bill to recharter the Bank—sponsored by Henry Clay in an attempt to create an issue by which he could defeat Jackson in the 1832 presidential election—passed Congress even though the Bank's present charter had another four years to run, Jackson vetoed it in one of the most important vetoes in American history. The President cited reasons for his action that had nothing to do with the bill's constitutionality, something never done before and something Clay, DANIEL WEBSTER, and other Senators regarded as improper. As part of his complaint, Jackson accused moneyed interest groups of using the government for their own greedy purposes. "It is to be regretted," the message declared, "that the rich and powerful too often bend the acts of government to their selfish purposes." Distinctions exist in society and always will, he said, but "every man is equally entitled to protection by law." When the laws attempt to add to these distinctions by granting "exclusive privileges" and "make the rich richer and the potent more powerful," then ordinary citizens have a right to complain and accuse their government of injustice. Corporate money used to control the acts of government endangers liberty, said Jackson. The government must treat everyone equally "and, as Heaven does its rains, shower its favors alike on the high and low, the rich and the poor."

The veto struck like a bombshell. Its implications went far beyond simple questions of constitutionality or ideological differences among different political factions. One of its more important implications was the suggestion that if the President could veto a bill for reasons other than its questionable constitutionality, then, as Daniel Webster contended in trying to convince the Senate to override the veto, the Chief Executive would usurp enormous legislative power. This interpretation meant that before Congress passed a bill the members would have to check with the President to make sure he did not object to the specifics of the bill, and it meant tailoring future legislation to accommodate his wishes. Gone, then, was the republican belief that the legislature constituted the centerpiece of government; in its place was the reality of the President's role as the head of government, the chief of state, the person who decides and directs national policy.

The election of 1832 did in fact focus almost solely

on the Bank issue, making it one of the few elections in American history in which the electorate was asked to decide the outcome of an important issue. If voters wanted the Bank, they could vote for Henry Clay; if they opposed it, they could vote for Jackson. Most likely the majority of the electorate voted their personal preference between the two men, not their attitude toward the Bank. They loved and trusted Andrew Jackson; many of them distrusted Clay. Jackson was therefore overwhelmingly returned to office. He then decreed the total destruction of the Bank. He ordered his Secretary of the Treasury, William J. Duane, to remove the government's deposits from the Bank and to place them in selected state banks, which the opposition called "pet banks." Duane refused, whereupon Jackson discharged him and chose ROGER B. TANEY to replace him. In the past, when Presidents had wished to rid themselves of objectionable CABINET officers, they had persuaded them to resign. It was the belief of some that since a Cabinet officer had to be confirmed by the Senate when he was appointed, he could not be removed without a similar confirmation. Jackson disposed of that theory. He announced that all personnel in the executive departments fell directly and immediately under his authority—even though the Secretary of the Treasury was required by law to report directly to Congress because he disbursed public funds that Congress exclusively controlled. Here was another instance of an action taken by Jackson that strengthened the power of the presidential office.

The Senate strongly objected to both the removal of deposits and the firing and at Clay's insistence passed resolutions on 28 March 1834 censuring Jackson, an action never taken before or since. The President responded to the censure with a protest message that accused the Senate with violating the Constitution because it had charged him with an impeachable offense and only the House of Representatives could bring impeachment charges against the President. But Jackson went further. He declared that the President is "the direct representative of the American people." Moreover, the "Chief Magistrate" is "elected by the people and responsible to them." No previous President had ever made such a claim or assumed such a direct relationship with the electorate. Jackson formally pronounced what had been implicit in many of his previous state papers, namely, that the office of the President and only the office of the President embodies the entire electorate. This was a modern concept in complete accord with his other democratic beliefs.

In an attempt to force recharter despite the outcome of the election, the Bank president, Nicholas Biddle, precipitated an economic panic in the winter of 1833–

1834, but he succeeded only in convincing the electorate that the Bank did in fact endanger liberty. The "hydra-headed monster," as Jackson called it, died a slow demeaning death, even in its state-chartered incarnation.

Fiscal Policy. Jackson's extensive use of his veto authority was an important example of his effectiveness in extending presidential power. Not only did he intrude in the legislative area by threatening a veto every time he disliked particular legislation, thereby assuming what Webster called "not the power of approval, but the primary power of originating laws," but Jackson used the power quite extensively. He vetoed more than all his predecessors combined. He was determined to pay the national debt, and therefore he struck down a number of bills that he believed jeopardized his goal. He annulled appropriations for building roads, lighthouses, and beacons, for dredging harbors, and for similar public works. He also killed a bill that called for the government to purchase stock in the Louisville and Portland Canal Company. For the government to own stock in such a corporation, he said, "is corrupting and must destroy the purity of our govt."; it is more injurious and destructive to the morales [sic] and Liberty of the people than the U. States Bank."

But his most famous veto of a bill for INTERNAL IMPROVEMENTS was his disapproval for the extension of the National Road from Maysville to Lexington in Kentucky. In the message he stated that the people have a right to expect their government to follow a "prudent system of expenditure" in order to pay the debt and keep taxes at "as low a point as . . . our national safety and independence will allow." When the debt was paid, then the surplus could be distributed to the states for improvements. These conservative considerations were further amplified in this Maysville veto by his expressed concern about the constitutionality of the bill—whether the government could lawfully appropriate funds for public works without a prior amendment to the Constitution. The "friends of liberty," he wrote, must be assured that "expedience" will not be the "rule of construction in interpreting the Constitution." Jackson stopped short of denying federal power to enact all public works, the obvious exception being the needs of national defense and safety. Such bills he would always approve.

By his close scrutiny of expenditures and his fiscal conservatism, Jackson succeeded in paying off the national debt. When he took office, the debt approximated $60 million. By 1835 it had been extinguished, not only because of the President's efforts to control spending but because of the enormous revenues brought in by the tariff and the sale of public lands. Then, under the terms of the Deposit/Distribution Act of 1836, all money in the Treasury in excess of $5 million was to be distributed in four installments to the states in proportion to their representation in Congress. The deposit feature of this bill regulated the government moneys in state (pet) banks. Because of Jackson's longtime prejudice against paper money, another provision of the bill required deposit banks to redeem all their notes in specie on demand, to issue no notes smaller than $5, and to accept no notes for less than $5 in payment of taxes owed the government. By degrees the restriction would be extended to include notes up to $10 and, by March 1837, up to $20. Jackson liked this feature of the bill because in time it would eliminate from circulation all paper money for less than $20.

To reinforce the restriction against paper, Jackson issued the Specie Circular on 11 July 1836, through the Secretary of the Treasury. The order decreed that, after August 15, nothing but gold and silver would be acceptable in payment for public land. What he hoped to do was halt the speculative land craze that had gripped the nation and that seemed to be running out of control. By this action he also hoped to restore what he called "real money" for "rag money," so that the earnings of honest citizens could not be manipulated by the "corrupt money power" in the country. Here was yet another example of Jackson's extensive use of presidential power. This Circular had the approval of neither Congress nor the Cabinet, and some had serious doubts about its legality. But because of his worry about the quantity of paper money flooding the country and threatening uncontrollable inflation, Jackson decided to act. Wisely, he waited until Congress had adjourned before issuing his order. He said he assumed full responsibility. The Congress later rescinded the Specie Circular, but Jackson pocket vetoed the bill in one of his last official acts.

Jackson's administration also revalued gold, which in relation to silver had been minted at the ratio of 15 to 1 since the Coinage Act of 1792. Actually the relation should have been 15.5 to 1, in keeping with commercial rates. As a result, the Coinage Act of 1792 tended to drive gold out of circulation. So Jackson changed the relationship by the Coinage of Act of 1834, which raised the ratio between gold and silver to 16 to 1. This action greatly increased the value of and desire for gold coins. To help substitute specie for paper even further, a "new dollar," depicting Liberty on one side and the American eagle on the other, was issued by the mint. Not since 1805 had there been a $1 coin.

Jackson's Nationalism. It is truly extraordinary that in Jackson were fused conservative views advocating fiscal restraint by the central government, hard money, and laissez-faire economics with more liberal notions about equality, liberty, and democracy. Another extraordinary fusion was that of his commitment to states' rights and his intense nationalism and increased exercise of presidential power, which necessarily augmented the authority of the central government. This seeming contradiction can be better understood by examining Jackson's policy of removal of the Indians and his reaction to South Carolina's NULLIFICATION of federal law.

Indian removal. By the time Jackson assumed the presidency, federal policy toward the Indians had simply drifted for years. Indian land was greatly desired in the area east of the Mississippi River, and the founders of the nation believed that once the Indians were "civilized" and adopted white culture, they would take their place in white society. If they did not, said President Jefferson, they must be driven to the Rocky Mountains. However, states insisted on exercising jurisdiction over the Indians within their boundaries, arguing that there could not be a sovereignty of Indian tribes within the sovereignty of the state. State laws were regularly enforced against the Cherokees, Creeks, Chickasaws, Choctaws, and Seminoles, the so-called Five Civilized Tribes, which occupied extensive territory within the southern states. These tribes argued that they had a right to self-government as foreign nations and that this right had long been recognized by the United States in its various treaties with the Indians. The government was therefore urged by some states to adopt a policy of removal. Although several Presidents considered the possibility, nothing was done—they neither proposed removal nor faced down the states that demanded it.

Jackson brought the matter to a head by formally asking Congress in his first message to enact an Indian removal bill. His life on the frontier and his military career, among other things, led him to the belief that the security of the nation and the protection of the Indians from certain annihilation required their removal beyond the Mississippi River. He was especially influenced by the Creek War, which occurred just prior to the British invasion at New Orleans in 1815. Had the Creeks synchronized their uprising with the invasion, the Battle of New Orleans might have been lost and the war might have ended differently and disastrously for the United States.

Jackson's proposal to Congress to remove the Indians generated a storm of protest, and he was compelled to bring considerable pressure on the legislature to get what he wanted. He personally arranged the membership of the House Committee on Indian Affairs; the chairmen of the House and Senate committees were both Tennesseans. Early in 1830 the two committees reported bills that were substantially similar. After extended debates in both houses, with the bill barely surviving defeat in the House, the Indian Removal Act passed, and Jackson signed it in May 1830. It appropriated $500,000 for the removal of the Five Civilized Tribes and authorized the President to exchange unorganized public land west of the Mississippi for land owned by the Indians in the east. The tribes received perpetual title to the new land and compensation for improvements on their old. The government would undertake all costs involved in the removal and provide support and subsistence for the Indians for the first year after their removal. In the execution of the law, treaties would be signed with the tribes.

During Jackson's two terms in office, approximately seventy such treaties were signed and ratified. Some 100 million acres of Indian land in the east was added to the public domain at a cost of roughly $68 million and 32 million acres of land in the new Indian Territory that later became the state of Oklahoma. As it developed, the tribes were bludgeoned, bribed, coerced, deceived, and duped into signing treaties. A few of them recognized the futility of resisting removal and headed west. The rest suffered an agony of starvation, deprivation, and death. Those who resisted were forcibly removed. The Second Seminole War broke out in Florida late in 1835 and lasted until 1842, costing millions of dollars and thousands of lives.

The Cherokees sued. In the celebrated case *Cherokee Nation v. Georgia* (1831), Chief Justice JOHN MARSHALL ruled against the contention that the Cherokees were a sovereign nation; he also ruled against Jackson's belief that they were subject to state law. The tribes were "domestic dependent nations," he declared, subject to the United States as a ward to a guardian. Then, when white missionaries defied Georgia law by entering Indian territory without a license from the state, they were arrested and sentenced to the penitentiary.

In *Worcester v. Georgia* (1832), Marshall struck down the Georgia law and all other laws by that state dealing with the Cherokees. Georgia had no intention of obeying the Court and in fact had boycotted the judicial proceedings. When he heard the decision, Jackson is said to have responded: "Well, John Marshall has made his decision: *now let him enforce it!*" It is highly unlikely that he spoke these words, even if they do sound like him, because there was nothing for the President to enforce. Marshall ordered the superior

court of Georgia to reverse its decision. Had the Georgia court refused this order, then the President might have been called upon to enforce the Supreme Court's decree. As it developed, the governor of Georgia, under pressure from Jackson and several allies, pardoned the missionaries with the understanding that they would make no further motion before the Supreme Court. The Cherokees ultimately yielded, signed a removal treaty, and headed west along what they called a "Trail of Tears." By that time Jackson had left office.

Nullification. Not only did Jackson agree in principal with Georgia about the Indians, but he had another reason for placating the state. He was presently occupied with the defiance of South Carolina in a dispute over tariff laws, and he needed to exercise extreme caution lest any action of his induce Georgia to join South Carolina against the federal government.

The dispute with South Carolina arose when Congress passed the TARIFF ACT OF 1832, which eliminated some of the so-called Abominations of the TARIFF OF ABOMINATIONS (1828) but still imposed a relatively high level of protection for domestic manufactures. The South generally disliked tariffs, and South Carolina believed they were unconstitutional because they aided one section of the country at the expense of others. Jackson's Vice President, John C. Calhoun, wrote an "Exposition and Protest" against the tariff that the legislature of South Carolina adopted without exposing the identify of the author. In the Exposition Calhoun advanced the doctrine of nullification, in which he claimed that a state could declare those federal laws that conflicted with its interests null and void within its borders. This doctrine of interposition would protect minority rights, according to Calhoun, and prevent tyranny by the majority. The idea of a state nullifying federal law horrified Jackson. To make his own position clear to the nullifiers, he offered a toast at a gathering of Democrats to celebrate the birthday of Thomas Jefferson: "Our Union," he cried. "It must be preserved." Later he allowed the inclusion of the word *federal* so that the toast would be printed as "Our Federal Union," since he claimed that he intended to use the word all along and simply forgot. But this disagreement, along with other factors, brought about a split in the relationship between Jackson and Calhoun. Some of the other factors included the revelation that Calhoun as Secretary of War in the Monroe administration had called for Jackson's censure for exceeding his orders in 1818 and seizing Florida. In addition, Calhoun and his wife were reputed to have masterminded a conspiracy against Margaret ("Peggy") Eaton, the wife of Secretary of

War John H. Eaton, to drive them both out of society in order to reduce the anti-Calhoun sentiment in Jackson's Cabinet. In place of Calhoun, Martin Van Buren was selected to run with Jackson in the presidential election of 1832. Calhoun resigned as Vice President and was elected to the Senate by the South Carolina legislature.

After the presidential election of 1832, the governor of South Carolina called a special session of the legislature, which ordered an elected convention to meet on 19 November 1832 to take appropriate action with respect to the tariff. On November 24 the convention passed an Ordinance of Nullification declaring the tariff laws of 1828 and 1832 "null, void, and no law, nor binding" on the officers or citizens of South Carolina. After 1 February 1833, no duties would be collected; if the government attempted to coerce the state into complying with the tariff, it would secede and proceed immediately to organize a separate government. Jackson responded to the nullification ordinance with a PROCLAMATION dated 10 December 1832, in which he warned the people of South Carolina of the consequences should they carry out the threat of SECESSION. He would never tolerate defiance of federal law. His oath of office made his duty clear—he must enforce the law, and the revenue must be collected. "Those who told you that you might peacefully prevent their execution deceived you. . . . Their object is disunion. But be not deceived by names. Disunion by armed force is *treason*. Are you ready to incur its guilt? If you are . . . on your unhappy State will inevitably fall all the evils of the conflict you force upon the Government of your country."

But Jackson tempered his threat with appeals to the people of his native state for sanity and reason. He tried not to sound menacing or unforgiving. The carrot and the stick approach best describes his policy. Most important, he publicly rejected nullification and secession as legitimate rights of the states. The people formed the Union, he said, not the states. They are sovereign, not the states. Their will is absolute. And the Union is perpetual. Less than thirty years later, during the secession crisis of 1860–1861, Abraham Lincoln extracted his arguments against secession from this proclamation. Jackson had provided the definitive statement for the perpetuity of the American Union. It was a dynamic and modern new reading of the nation's constitutional structure.

Jackson went to Congress on 16 January 1833 and asked for a FORCE BILL to compel South Carolina's compliance with the law. He said that Congress need only make a few modifications of an existing law that allowed the President to call out the state militia and use federal ships and troops. He wanted it passed before 1 February 1833, the cutoff date the state had set for the collection of the duties. Nullifiers called it a "bloody bill" and a "war bill." With secession and conflict likely, Henry Clay devised and steered through Congress a Compromise TARIFF ACT OF 1833, which Senator Calhoun declared acceptable to the nullifiers. This new tariff provided a ten-year truce. Rates would be slowly reduced to a uniform 20 percent ad valorem rate (rates based on an item's value), and protectionism would be abandoned. Both the Force Bill and the compromise tariff passed, and Jackson signed them on 2 March 1833. The convention in South Carolina reconvened and declared its satisfaction with the compromise tariff by repealing its Ordinance of Nullification, but it nullified the Force Bill. Jackson wisely chose to disregard this face-saving display of defiance, and the immediate crisis passed. "Nullification is dead," said the President. "The next pretext," he predicted, "will be the negro, or slavery question."

The Cabinets and the Senate. Jackson's constant quarreling with the Senate, especially during the Bank War, made it very difficult for him to win approval for his appointees to high office. Roger B. Taney's nomination as Secretary of the Treasury was defeated; Martin Van Buren's nomination as minister to Great Britain was voted down; so too the nominations of bank directors, ministers, and a number of other government officials. At one point, a majority of his Cabinet was unconfirmed. The strength of the opposition—since 1834 called the WHIG PARTY and powered by the "Great Triumvirate" of Senators Henry Clay, Daniel Webster, and John C. Calhoun—effectively blocked the confirmation in the Senate of many of Jackson's most important nominations. The Great Triumvirate, as powerfully articulate, commanding, and influential a group as ever sat in the Senate, regularly pounded Jackson for violating the Constitution and for acting like a dictator. They accused him of listening exclusively to a group of advisers who hungered for spoils. The pernicious system of party politics adopted by the administration, they said, came straight from Van Buren and his Regency henchmen in New York, one of whom, William L. Marcy, had announced on the Senate floor: "To the victor belong the spoils of the enemy." Besides Van Buren, the men surrounding Jackson and regularly offering advice to him included Taney, FRANCIS P. BLAIR, the editor of the Washington *Globe*, AMOS KENDALL, soon to be appointed Postmaster General, and William B. Lewis, a Tennessee neighbor and close friend. Senator George Poindexter of Mississippi, whom Jackson cordially disliked, published an article in a Washington newspaper in March 1832 in which he referred to this shadowy group of advisers as a KITCHEN CABINET. Four months earlier Nicholas Biddle had used the term in a private communication in which he declared that "the kitchen . . . predominate[s] over the Parlor" in advising the President in his war against the Bank. Presumably these advisers came up to Jackson's office on the second floor of the White House through the kitchen and back stairs. The "parlor" cabinet consisted of the men who headed the various departments of the government and whose nominations had been duly confirmed by the Senate. As a matter of fact, Jackson regularly met with the parlor cabinet each week, usually on Tuesdays, listened to the advice he had solicited from them, made his own decisions, and then expected them to support those decisions, at least publicly. The kitchen cabinet never really existed, at least not as it was described by the opposition. Jackson did receive advice from time to time from close friends, but their faces and number regularly changed; there was no structure to the operation of this so-called kitchen cabinet; it in no way compared to the parlor cabinet.

Not until late 1835 did the political complexion of the Senate change in Jackson's favor so that he was able to win confirmation of a long list of appointees. Connecticut, Illinois, Louisiana, and Virginia sent loyal Jackson Democrats to the upper house, and their votes won approval for the appointments of Taney as Chief Justice and of a second Justice, of Amos Kendall as Postmaster General, and of Andrew Stevenson as minister to Great Britain. There had been no confirmed minister to Great Britain in four years. Then, with their newly acquired majority, the Democrats in January 1837 followed through by expunging the censure against Jackson and Taney.

Jackson's record of appointments in high office was uniformly poor to bad, with a number of notable exceptions, one of which was his appointment of Amos Kendall as Postmaster General. The department had been atrociously run by Kendall's predecessor, William T. Barry, and both houses of Congress appointed committees to investigate its operation. Both committees reported back widespread corruption, inadequate service, and fiscal incompetence. Kendall turned the situation around completely. He reorganized the department, improved its efficiency, amassed a surplus after paying off debts, and rooted out corruption. These reforms were incorporated in the new Post Office Act of 2 July 1836.

Jackson was particularly sensitive to all charges of corruption in the government departments, and he was particularly embarrassed when Samuel Swartwout, collector of the New York customs, absconded with more than $1 million. He had been warned by Van Buren of Swartwout's reputation but disregarded the warning. From the start of his administration Jackson had emphasized "reform," and to that end he directed that all the departments undergo whatever reorganization was necessary to improve their operations. The State Department was reorganized in 1833, 1834, and 1836. The Office of Commissioner of Patents was created within the department, along with several other bureaus. All of them were administered by a chief clerk or an undersecretary who operated directly under the Secretary of State. And the War and Navy Departments were also reorganized.

Because of the intense controversy Jackson frequently sparked during his eight years in office, it is not surprising that he was the first President to be assaulted in public. The initial assault occurred on board a steamboat on 6 May 1833, when Robert B. Randolph, a former naval officer, came to Jackson's cabin and struck him in the face before being hustled off the ship. Randolph had been dismissed from the navy for theft at Jackson's specific direction. He was later tried, but Jackson, who by that time had left office, asked that, if found guilty, Randolph be pardoned by President Van Buren and any fine refunded. The second assault almost ended tragically. Jackson was attending the funeral of Representative Warren R. Davis of South Carolina at the Capitol on 30 January 1835. As he entered the rotunda of the east portico, Richard Lawrence stepped up to him and at point-blank range fired two pistols directly at the President. Although the caps discharged, thundering through the chamber, they failed to ignite the powder in the barrels of the two guns. Lawrence was later judged insane and taken to an asylum. He believed he was the rightful heir to the British throne and that Jackson had prevented his succession. Sooner or later, Jackson predicted, it would become necessary to place *a military guard around the President*" [emphasis in original].

Foreign Policy. In FOREIGN AFFAIRS Jackson pursued as vigorous a policy, if not an even more aggressive one, as he had in domestic affairs. At the start of his administration he announced his intention of demanding "fair reciprocity" from the European powers. He said he wished to settle differences wherever they existed on "the most fair & honorable terms." Basic to it all was his fierce desire to win universal recognition for the rights and sovereignty of the United States, something rarely given in the past, as evidenced by the XYZ affair, the seizure of ships, and the impressment of seamen during the Napoleonic wars. He was particularly concerned about trade with the British West Indies, which had been closed by Great Britain since the conclusion of the revolutionary war despite the best efforts of American statesmen, including President John Quincy Adams. Departing from the diplomacy of the past, Jackson repudiated Adams's botched efforts at negotiation and ultimately succeeded in gaining access to the British ports on a reciprocal basis. The British ban was lifted on 5 November 1830. Jackson followed this victory with demands that France, Russia, Denmark, Portugal, the Netherlands, and the Kingdom of the Two Sicilies pay for the commercial losses suffered by Americans during the Napoleonic wars. He demanded that foreign nations act honestly and honorably toward the United States. As he said in his annual message to Congress, his policy could be summarized thus: "to ask nothing that is not clearly right, and to submit to nothing that is wrong."

A few of the disputes, principally with Russia and Portugal, were resolved through executive agreements. Others produced treaties. Denmark signed a convention and agreed to pay $650,000; Spain agreed to $600,000; the Kingdom of the Two Sicilies had to be strong-armed but eventually paid $1,755,450. Only France reneged on its commitment, from an 1831 treaty, to pay 25 million francs, when the Chamber of Deputies failed to approve the appropriation. Jackson charged the French with bad faith and threatened retaliation. The French finally agreed to pay the debt if Jackson would offer an apology. Jackson refused, and it looked to many as though war might ensue. Fortunately, war was avoided when Jackson declared that it had not been his intention to menace or insult the French. That statement was seen in Paris as sufficient to allow payment of the debt under the terms of the original treaty. Jackson's successes in collecting these debts, estimated at $12.5 million, greatly enhanced both his popularity with the American people and his reputation as a statesman.

The President was less successful in his relations with Mexico. He made several attempts to buy Texas, but the appointment of a scoundrel, Colonel Anthony Butler, as U.S. minister to Mexico only damaged relations between the two nations. Butler resorted to bribery and any number of other dirty tricks to win Texas. Finally, the Mexicans demanded his recall. Jackson's mismanagement so discouraged the Texans that it contributed to the emergence of a war party in Texas that ultimately won independence from Mexico. The establishment of a Texas Republic again raised the possibility of annexation, but Jackson resisted proposing it to Congress. He feared its effect in Europe, on the election of his chosen successor, Martin Van Buren, and on the rising controversy throughout the nation over slavery. He left it to Congress to take appropriate action, and on 1 March 1837 the Senate recommended the formal recognition of Texas. This Jackson completed just before he retired from the presidency. Although he failed to gain Texas, Jackson did approve the admission of Arkansas as a state in the Union on 15 June 1836 and the admission of Michigan on 26 January 1837.

As part of his general reform program, Jackson decreed a new dress code for U.S. ministers. He insisted that their dress must conform to the "simplicity of our government . . . and [be] guided . . . by pure republican principles." Ministers were to wear a black dress coat with a gold star on each side of the collar, black and white "under clothes," a three-cornered "Chapeau de Bras, with a black cockade and eagle, and a steel mounted sword with white scabbard."

Retirement. Jackson's administration as President has been both admired and severely criticized. His Bank policy and the removal of the Indians have probably occasioned the greatest criticism. But as President he became a most important advocate and spokesman for democracy. Although he significantly advanced the powers of the President in several respects, he constantly worried over the danger to liberty of a strong, active, and highly centralized government. And he constantly warned against the influence of corporate power and money in controlling the operation of government. He opened government to all citizens, paid the national debt, and urged greater democracy through direct election of all federal officers. But his democracy and, indeed, the democracy of the entire antebellum period did not include women, blacks, or Indians.

Prior to his retirement as President, Jackson issued a farewell address, similar to George Washington's and written almost exclusively by Chief Justice Taney. In it Jackson, obviously speaking about slavery, warned of the dangers emanating from sectional differences that had recently arisen and that based party differences on geographical distinctions. Citizens of each state must guard against wounding "the sensibility or offend[ing] the just pride" of citizens of every other state and "frown" upon those who disturb the tranquillity of the nation, Jackson asserted. Weak men will convince themselves that their disturbances are undertaken "in the cause of humanity and . . . the rights of the human race," he said, but be not deceived: "Everyone, upon sober reflection, will see that nothing but mischief can come from these improper assaults upon the feelings and rights of others."

Jackson attended the inauguration on 4 March 1837 of his chosen successor, Martin Van Buren, and Senator Benton remarked that "for once, the rising was eclipsed by the setting sun." Chief Justice Taney swore in President Van Buren; both men had been rejected by the Senate just a few years earlier when Jackson had nominated them for lesser offices.

Jackson returned to the Hermitage, his Tennessee home, in 1837, but he continued to influence national politics, especially in helping to bring about the nomination of his protégé, James Knox Polk, for the presidency in 1844. In that election Polk defeated Henry Clay, which added to Jackson's pleasure. Old Hickory died on 8 June 1845 and was buried beside his wife in the garden adjacent to his home.

BIBLIOGRAPHY

Bassett, John Spencer. *The Life of Andrew Jackson.* 2 vols. 1911.

Belohlavk, John M. *"Let the Eagle Soar": The Foreign Policy of Andrew Jackson.* 1985.

Ellis, Richard B. *The Union at Risk: Jacksonian Democracy, States' Rights, and the Nullification Crisis.* 1987.

Freehling, William W. *Prelude to Civil War: The Nullification Movement in South Carolina, 1816–1836.* 1966.

Hofstadter, Richard. *The American Political Tradition and the Men Who Made It.* 1948. "Andrew Jackson and the Rise of Liberal Capitalism."

James, Marquis. *The Life of Andrew Jackson.* 1938.

Latner, Richard, *The Presidency of Andrew Jackson: White House Politics, 1829–1837.* 1979.

Parton, James. *Life of Andrew Jackson.* 3 vols. 1859–1860.

Remini, Robert V. *Andrew Jackson and the Course of American Empire, 1767–1821.* 1977.

Remini, Robert V. *Andrew Jackson and the Course of American Freedom, 1822–1832.* 1981.

Remini, Robert V. *Andrew Jackson and the Course of American Democracy, 1833–1845.* 1984.

Rogin, Michael Paul. *Fathers and Children: Andrew Jackson and the Subjugation of the American Indian.* 1975.

Satz, Ronald N. *American Indian Policy in the Jacksonian Era.* 1975.

Schlesinger, Arthur M., Jr. *The Age of Jackson.* 1946.

Watson, Harry L. *Liberty and Power: The Politics of Jacksonian America.* 1990.

White, Leonard. *The Jacksonians: A Study in Administrative History, 1829–1861.* 1954.

ROBERT V. REMINI

JACKSON, ROBERT (1892–1954), Solicitor General, Attorney General, and Associate Justice of the Supreme Court. Jackson was a key figure and adviser to Franklin D. Roosevelt in NEW DEAL legislation. Robert Houghwout Jackson's early New Deal experiences had less to do with politics or policy than with the practice of law. He went to Washington, D.C., in 1934 as general counsel to the Bureau of Internal Revenue, then worked as special counsel for the Securities Exchange Commission. In 1936 he moved to the Justice Department as an assistant attorney general.

While at Internal Revenue, Jackson worked closely with BENJAMIN V. COHEN and THOMAS CORCORAN in enforcement of the PUBLIC UTILITY HOLDING COMPANY ACT. This successful litigation—which continued to occupy Jackson's attention when he moved to the Justice Department—gave him his first exposure to the inner circles of the New Deal. He was active in the 1936 presidential campaign and in early 1937 gave a major speech outlining the Franklin D. Roosevelt administration's difficulties with the Supreme Court—a speech given, by coincidence, just days before the announcement of Roosevelt's plan to pack the Supreme Court. Jackson was quickly identified as a supporter of the COURT-PACKING PLAN. In reality he was equivocal, but he agreed to testify in support of the proposal.

The fight about the Court turned Jackson into a public figure and strengthened his relationship with Roosevelt. He was appointed Solicitor General in 1938 and Attorney General in 1940, becoming a key source of legal advice for the President in the critical years before America's entry into WORLD WAR II. As Attorney General he first opposed but eventually approved the DESTROYERS FOR BASES agreement, which allowed the United States to provide critical aid to Great Britain. Later he developed the administration's rationale for justifying American aid to the Allies in spite of its proclaimed neutrality.

In 1941 Roosevelt nominated Jackson to the Supreme Court. His first years as a Justice were not happy, partly because of infighting on the Court and partly because, during the war at least, he felt removed from the most central issues of the day. In 1945 Jackson agreed to serve as chief prosecutor at the Nazi war-crimes trials in Nuremberg, Germany.

On the Court, Jackson's record was mixed. He took a conservative position on several important CIVIL LIBERTIES cases but wrote a stirring opinion striking down mandatory salutes to the flag. He dissented from the Court's decision upholding the exclusion of JAPANESE AMERICANS from the West Coast during World War II and eventually was persuaded to support the Court's 1954 decision in *Brown v. Board of Education*, which outlawed segregation.

Jackson is also remembered for a concurring opinion in the 1952 case of YOUNGSTOWN SHEET & TUBE CO. V. SAWYER, in which the Court invalidated President Harry S. Truman's seizure of the nation's steel mills. There exists a "zone of twilight," he wrote, in which "congressional inertia, indifference or quiescence may sometimes, at least as a practical matter, enable, if not invite, measures of independent presidential responsibility." Jackson's opinion stands as a justification of his own opinions as Attorney General, in which he advised Roosevelt to act in the absence of a clear expression of congressional opinion, and as an important theoretical statement of the boundaries of presidential power.

BIBLIOGRAPHY

Gerhart, Eugene C. *America's Advocate: Robert H. Jackson.* 1958.
Kurland, Philip B. "Robert H. Jackson." In *The Justices of the Supreme Court 1789–1969: Their Lives and Major Opinions.* Edited by Leon Friedman and Fred L. Israel. 5 vols. 1969.

WILLIAM LASSER

JAPANESE AMERICANS, TREATMENT OF.

During WORLD WAR I, the United States indulged in xenophobic excesses against German aliens and citizens of German descent and some red-baiting and prosecutions of radicals took place. The nation was later ashamed of those episodes, and resolved not to repeat them. The atmosphere of American society remained relatively tolerant and mature during WORLD WAR II, except for the government's treatment of more than 100,000 Japanese aliens and citizens of Japanese descent in the Western Military District of the United States (Arizona, California, Oregon, and Washington). Their treatment was far worse than the abuse suffered by any German American during World War I.

For nearly fifty years, there had been a current of anti-Asian feeling on the West Coast, and a series of nativist know-nothing political movements had exploited and exacerbated this sentiment. A few weeks after PEARL HARBOR, politically significant voices began to demand that the government clear all persons of Japanese descent from the West Coast, aliens and citizens alike.

Under international law, enemy aliens can be interned or otherwise controlled in time of war, and the United States has long assumed that the Constitution does not prevent the American government from treating enemy aliens as other countries do.

Opinion in the West Coast states and elsewhere crystalized in favor of a presidential EXECUTIVE ORDER that would give the army the power to remove Japanese aliens and citizens of Japanese descent from the West Coast, and, if they could not relocate themselves elsewhere, to keep them in camps until they could be relocated in communities willing and able to receive them without risk of disorder or harm to the war effort. The movement to remove and intern Japanese Americans was led by General John L. DeWitt, Commander of the Western Military District, and backed by both the California delegation in Congress and California governor Earl Warren. Overwhelmed in the immediate aftermath of Pearl Harbor by the enormous problems of the new war, President Franklin D. Roosevelt accepted the idea of moving all people of Japanese descent from the West Coast and delegated the final decisions concerning the form and scope of the executive order to the Secretary of War, HENRY L. STIMSON, with only the injunction, "Be as reasonable as you can."

Executive Order 9066. The President signed Executive Order 9066 on 19 February 1942. Whether the policy could have been carried out by the executive order alone by virtue of the President's powers as COMMANDER IN CHIEF is a moot point, because WAR DEPARTMENT lawyers urged that a statute be obtained to back up what the President had done. The statute (56 Stat. 173 [1942]) was passed without difficulty.

The relocation policy was explained and defended on military grounds. Its advocates contended that in the war with Japan, espionage and sabotage were especially to be feared from persons of Japanese blood and that the Japanese aliens and citizens of Japanese descent on the West Coast constituted a virtual fifth column. Because of the many important ports, airfields, and manufacturing facilities in the area, they argued that simple military prudence dictated that the United States not run the risk of allowing Japanese Americans to remain free.

After Pearl Harbor and before the great American victory in the Battle of Midway on 5 June 1942, not only Hawaii and Alaska but the entire West Coast was vulnerable to naval and air attacks and even to the possibility of invasion. Proponents of removal and internment urged that there was no time for individual hearings to determine the loyalty of more than 100,000 persons. Some even claimed that the "inscrutability" of the Japanese meant that no inquiry into their loyalty could produce convincing results. Some vague rumors, later abandoned, circulated concerning reports of sabotage and of signaling by lights from the shore to Japanese submarines. But when the rumors of sabotage disappeared, the very fact that no sabotage had as yet occurred was put forward as evidence that the Japanese plan was sinister, disciplined, and subtle. Nor did those who spoke for the policy explain why exclusion orders and detention camps were needed for Japanese aliens and citizens of Japanese descent residing in the Western Military District but not for

West Coast residents of German or Italian origin, why such precautions were needed on the West Coast but not for the Japanese and Japanese Americans of Hawaii (where 32 percent of the population was of Japanese background), or why such exclusions and camps were unnecessary for German Americans, Italian Americans, and even for Japanese Americans living anywhere else in the country or in the PANAMA CANAL Zone.

Executive Order 9066 did not explicitly mention Japanese aliens or citizens of Japanese descent. Rather, it authorized the Secretary of War and the military commanders to designate specific military zones and, at their discretion, either to exclude any persons from such areas or to establish conditions under which such persons might enter, remain in, or leave the military zones. The statute simply put the sanction of criminal law behind the executive order, making it a misdemeanor for "any person to enter, remain in, leave, or commit any act in any military area or zone contrary to the prescribed restrictions applicable to that area." Among the puzzles these documents present is what they mean when they give military authorities power to prevent people from "leaving" designated military areas or power to establish the conditions of their leaving. Neither document authorizes the military to detain persons "removed" from a designated military area or to make the acceptance of detention a condition of leaving. The original goal of the program was to remove a defined class of persons from the West Coast, so how did the statute and executive order become the legal grounds for compulsory removal and detention in camps?

The first restrictions on Japanese aliens and citizens of Japanese descent in the Western Military District were imposed by the end of March 1942. At first, the goal of the policy was to encourage voluntary individual resettlement in other parts of the country. Difficulties arose. Japanese Americans were naturally afraid that troubles might develop in communities where they were not known. Starting about six weeks after Pearl Harbor, public opinion in California became strongly anti-Japanese. In the end, the evacuees were transported from relocation centers to camps operated by a new agency, the War Relocation Authority (WRA), staffed in part by social workers and social scientists. Relocation was to be carried out from those camps. Milton S. Eisenhower, a brother of General Dwight D. Eisenhower, was the WRA's first director, but he resigned shortly after meeting with the governors of the western states in Salt Lake City, Utah, on 7 April. Eisenhower's assurance to the governors that most of his charges were loyal and his request for the

governors' cooperation in plans for resettlement were met by anger and outrage. The governors wanted the evacuees kept in the camps under armed guard and refused even to consider Eisenhower's well-meaning resettlement plans.

Eisenhower was succeeded by an experienced Department of Agriculture official, Dillon S. Meyer. Meyer, like his predecessor, was a man of humane intentions put into an impossible situation, but he was emotionally less vulnerable than Eisenhower. His regulations, issued "in the best interests" of the internees, provided that internees could be released and resettled only if the War Relocation Authority found that they were "loyal"; if they had homes, jobs, and friends to go to; if the sentiment in the community where they were to settle was not unfavorable; if there had been no riots or other demonstrations of anti-Japanese feeling there; and if their relocation would not interfere with the war effort. In other words, in view of the difficulty of satisfying the conditions for release, detention was to be indefinite and probably for the duration of the war.

Legal Challenges. The legality of the internment program soon began to be challenged; the challenges reached the Supreme Court in a series of three cases decided in 1943 and 1944. These cases, decided during the war and not afterward, differ significantly from, for example, EX PARTE MILLIGAN (1866), the famous CIVIL WAR case in which the Supreme Court decided that martial law could not be declared for areas in which the civil courts were open. The *Milligan* decision, which held that such military suspension of CIVIL LIBERTIES was unconstitutional, was arrived at after victory over the Confederacy had been achieved, whereas victory over the Japanese was by no means assured in 1943 and 1944 (though the situation in the field was much more favorable to the Allied cause than it had been in the bleak days of 1941 and 1942). The Justices undoubtedly felt a natural disinclination as citizens to oppose or question the military judgment of the President or Congress while war was being waged.

Hirabayashi v. United States. The first of the cases was *Hirabayashi v. United States* (1943). Hirabayashi, a citizen and a senior at the University of Washington, had been convicted of violating two orders issued by General DeWitt under the authority of Executive Order 9066. He had failed to report on 11 May to a control station for compulsory transportation to a WRA camp, where he was to be interned. The second count was that on 9 May he had violated a curfew order by failing to remain at home after 8:00 P.M. The Supreme Court took up only the second count, upholding the constitutionality of the curfew order and the sentence imposed on the defendant. Since the lower court had made the two sentences concurrent, the Supreme Court confined its opinion to the constitutionality of the curfew order.

Under the wartime circumstances, the Court found the curfew a not-unreasonable military precaution, despite the fact that it discriminated against Japanese Americans. The Court held that the issue before it was the scope of the WAR POWER of the national government. The extent of presidential discretion was not presented as a separate issue, because the statute of 21 March 1942 and the appropriation acts under it were passed with Congress's full knowledge of the kinds of actions proposed (and later taken) by General DeWitt. Both Congress and the executive were held to have approved the curfew as a war measure that in their judgment was required because of the fear that persons of Japanese origin or descent residing on the West Coast would commit espionage or sabotage. The premise from which the Court's argument proceeded was the incontestable proposition that the war power is the power to wage war successfully.

The Court asked whether there was "reasonable ground" for those charged with the responsibility of national defense to believe that the threat was real and that the remedy would be useful. The circumstances, the Court said, afforded a sufficiently rational basis for the decision made. The "facts" that were held to "afford a rational basis for decision" were that in time of war "residents having ethnic affiliations with an invading enemy may be a greater source of danger than those of different ancestry" and that in time of war such persons could not readily be isolated and dealt with individually. This was the basic hypothesis on which the decisions in all three cases rested.

To support its opinion, the Court undertook a review of its own intuitions, without recourse either to the judicial record or to available scientific studies of the problem. Kiplingesque folklore about East and West lay close to the heart of the opinions. The Japanese, the Court said, had been imperfectly assimilated. They constituted an isolated group in the community, and their Japanese-language schools might be sources of pro-Japanese propaganda. Moreover, the discriminatory way in which the Japanese on the West Coast were treated may have contributed to Japanese solidarity, preventing their assimilation, and increasing in many instances their attachments to Japan and its institutions.

It goes without saying that the Court's hypothesis is contrary to the most basic principles of a legal system that punishes only criminal acts and that takes care not to equate states of mind with actions. But, at least in theory, *Hirabayashi* did assert the principle of protecting society against unwarranted and dictatorial military action.

Korematsu v. United States. On the other hand *Korematsu v. United States* (1944) seemed sharply to relax even the formal requirement of judicial review over military conduct. Korematsu, an American citizen of Japanese descent, was convicted of violating an order requiring his exclusion from the West Coast. The Court held that the problem of exclusion was identical with that of the discriminatory curfew presented in *Hirabayashi*. There, the Court said, it had decided that it was not unreasonable for the military to impose a curfew in order to guard against the special dangers of sabotage and espionage anticipated from the Japanese group. The military had found—and the Court refused to reject the finding—that it was impossible to bring about an immediate segregation of the disloyal from the loyal.

According to Justice Hugo L. Black, who wrote the Court's opinion in *Korematsu*, the exclusion orders arose merely from these two findings—that Japanese Americans were a dangerous lot and that there was no time to screen them individually. Actually, however, there was a new "finding" in this case that went well beyond the situation considered in the *Hirabayashi* case. The military had "found" that the curfew provided inadequate protection against the danger of sabotage and espionage. Therefore the exclusion of all Japanese, citizens and aliens alike, was thought to be a reasonable way to protect the West Coast. Black does not review even the possible foundations for such a judgment, and the *Korematsu* decision shows no attempt to demonstrate a reasonable connection between the factual situation and the program adopted to deal with it.

The Court refused to rule on the validity of the detention features of the relocation policy as raised by the case. Korematsu had not yet been taken to a camp, and the Court would not pass on the issues presented by such imprisonment. Those issues, the Court said were

> momentous questions not contained within the framework of the pleadings or the evidence in this case. It will be time enough to decide the serious constitutional issues which petitioner seeks to raise when an assembly or relocation order is applied or is certain to be applied to him, and we have its terms before us.

This is like saying that the appeal in an ordinary criminal case questions the validity of the original trial and verdict, but not of the sentence, since the defendant may be out on probation or bail. In any event, it is difficult to understand why this consideration did not apply equally to the evidence before the Court on the issue that the Court conceded *was* raised by the pleadings—that is, the decision of the general to exclude all Japanese from the defense area. On this issue there was literally no trial record or other form of evidence in the case.

Ex parte Endo. In *Ex parte Endo* (1944), the next stage in the judicial elucidation of the problem, an adjudication was finally obtained on part of the question of the validity of confining Japanese aliens and citizens in camps, although the decision was made on statutory, not constitutional, grounds. The case was a habeas corpus proceeding. Endo, an American citizen of Japanese ancestry, had been found to be loyal and sought her freedom from a War Relocation Center where she was being detained until the WRA could place her in a community where her arrival was unlikely to cause civil disorder. The Court held that the statute, as rather strenuously construed, did not authorize the detention of persons in the petitioner's situation, although temporary detention for the purpose of investigating loyalty was assumed to be valid as incidental to the program of orderly evacuation approved in the *Korematsu* case.

Aftermath. The decisions and opinions in the three Japanese-American cases gravely weaken the Constitution as an instrument for protecting the fundamental rights of the individual against the state. None of the opinions of the Court—except the dissents of Justices Owen J. Roberts and Frank Murphy—addresses the most important issue the cases present: the fact that the government removed more than 100,000 citizens from their homes solely on the basis of their race and confined them in remote, uncomfortable barracks for an indefinite period, in most cases for the duration of the war and beyond. This deprivation of liberty took place at a time when the civil courts were open and occurred without charges of a criminal act established by law, without indictment, without trial by jury or any other kind of a court trial, without internees being informed of the nature and cause of the accusation against them, and without being assured the other protections of the Fifth and Sixth Amendments.

The executive order, the statute, and the relocation program carried out in their name violate every safeguard of personal liberty provided by the Constitution, including not only the Fifth and Sixth Amendments but also the prohibition of legislative punishment through bills of attainder, the strict definition of the crime of treason, and the maintenance of the boundary between civil and military power. They in effect overrule *Ex parte Milligan*, one of the great landmarks in the history of American liberty, and, in Justice Robert Jackson's words, "leave a loaded pistol" in the armory of Constitutional law, available to anyone with a plausible case for using it.

Clearly, Secretary of War Stimson and Assistant Secretary John J. McCloy remained uneasy about the Japanese relocation program. They established the Nisei Regiments of Japanese Americans, which fought gallantly in the European theater, and they made sure that news about those regiments and their decorations was widely disseminated. Both Congress and the executive branch publicly apologized for "the errors and injustice" of the relocation program, and in 1992 Congress voted to compensate the surviving victims of the program for the losses they suffered. In 1993, a *coram nobis* suit had been filed, requesting the Supreme Court to correct its own errors by reviving and overruling the three cases. A *coram nobis* writ, which initiates an old review procedure at common law, has rarely been used, and then only for extraordinary error, but the error of the Supreme Court in these cases was truly extraordinary.

BIBLIOGRAPHY

Grodzins, Morton. *Americans Betrayed.* 1947.

Irons, Peter. *Justice at War.* 1983.

Rostow, Eugene V. "The Japanese American Cases—A Disaster." *Yale Law Journal* 54 (1945): 489.

Ten Broeck, Jacobus, et al. *Prejudice, War, and the Constitution.* 1954.

EUGENE V. ROSTOW

JAPANESE PEACE TREATY. The accord between the United States and Japan was signed by President Harry S. Truman at a fifty-two nation conference at San Francisco on 8 September 1951 and marked Japan's emergence from six years of American tutelage as a stable, democratic nation linked to the Western military alliance. Among its many provisions, the peace treaty formally ended hostilities between the two countries, restored Japanese sovereignty, ended the U.S. occupation, and furthered CONTAINMENT in the Far East by sanctioning the presence of American troops and military bases on Japanese soil and rearming Japan.

Immediately after WORLD WAR II, the United States had sought to demilitarize its defeated opponent. But as the COLD WAR intensified, the Truman administration abandoned its plan to diminish Japanese military strength and decided to rearm her instead as a bulwark against perceived Soviet expansion in East Asia. As President Truman told delegates to the San Francisco conference: "At the present time the Pacific area is gravely affected by outright aggression and by the threat of further armed attack. One of our primary concerns in making peace with Japan, therefore, is to make Japan secure against aggression." The Soviet Union bitterly criticized the peace treaty—a treaty that it had not been allowed to join and that turned Japan into a forward base of American power in the western Pacific.

Criticism of the Japanese peace treaty in the United States, on the other hand, remained negligible. Negotiated for Washington by JOHN FOSTER DULLES, a Republican, the "Peace of Reconciliation" as it was formally known, marked the last hurrah for bipartisanship in foreign affairs dating back to 1947. Hereafter, controversy arising from the fall of China, the KOREAN WAR, and McCARTHYISM made relations between Truman and his Republican opposition on matters of foreign policy tense and tempestuous.

BIBLIOGRAPHY

Cohen, B. C. *The Political Process and Foreign Policy: The Making of the Japanese Peace Settlement.* 1957.
Schaller, Michael. *The American Occupation of Japan: The Origins of the Cold War in Asia.* 1985.

BRIAN VANDEMARK

JAY, JOHN (1745–1829), diplomat, Secretary of Foreign Affairs, first Chief Justice of the United States. Though he served a term as president of the Continental Congress, John Jay exerted greater influence over American ideas of executive power through his distinguished if controversial career as a diplomat. A member of a prominent New York Huguenot family, Jay began a political career that lasted nearly a quarter-century when he was elected to the First Continental Congress in 1774. Preoccupied with New York state politics from 1776 until 1778, Jay took an active role in drafting the state constitution of 1777. Returning to the Continental Congress in December 1778, Jay was immediately elected its president. He resigned that position in September 1779 to accept appointment as U.S. minister to Spain. Subsequently named to the American peace commission, Jay played a critical role in its decision to negotiate independently of French supervision. After sailing home to America in June 1784, Jay was appointed Secretary of Foreign Affairs under the Continental Congress, a position he held until 1789. Though not a member of the Federal Convention, Jay supported ratification of the Constitution and contributed five essays to THE FEDERALIST.

In 1789 President George Washington nominated Jay to be the first Chief Justice of the United States.

Five years later, Washington entrusted a second crucial task to Jay when he dispatched him as a special envoy to Britain to resolve a major quarrel arising from British seizures of American ships and other issues. In 1795 Jay stepped down from the Court to assume the governorship of New York, his last major position in public life.

From the start of his Revolutionary career, Jay was aligned with those moderate leaders who believed that victory against Britain required effective government as well as popular enthusiasm. Although the evidence is not conclusive, Jay has traditionally been regarded as the principal author of the New York state constitution of 1777—a document of special importance because the governorship it created served as a prototype for the presidency that the CONSTITUTIONAL CONVENTION designed ten years later. The constitutions previously adopted by other states had radically reduced the power of the executive and made governors politically dependent on the legislatures. By contrast, the New York governor would be elected by the same propertied voters who chose state senators and, among other powers, would hold a limited veto over legislation (in conjunction with a Council of Revision consisting of the state chancellor and supreme court). (The Constitutional Convention also drew significantly on the governorship designed for the Massachusetts constitution of 1780, primarily written by Jay's congressional and diplomatic colleague, John Adams.)

The presidency of the Continental Congress was not an executive office but rather a position equivalent to that of a speaker of legislative house. Jay occupied the presidency at a time of intense fractional conflict over foreign policy; far from rising above the debate, he was actively involved with a coalition of delegates from the mid-Atlantic and southern states who favored pursuing close collaboration with France. But from this experience and his subsequent career as diplomat and Secretary of Foreign Affairs, Jay gradually came to believe that the national government could never operate effectively until its executive functions were clearly separated from the deliberative responsibilities of Congress. During the debates of 1779 and again in 1781, Congress divided sharply over the definition of its terms of peace. When the time came to negotiate peace with Britain in 1782 (which led to the Treaty of Paris) however, Jay was the first American commissioner to recognize that there was more to be gained by treating directly with Britain than by honoring the instructions of Congress to defer to the supervision of France. Diplomacy was clearly one area in which the proverbial executive virtues of secrecy, dispatch, and initiative had to be allowed to operate.

After the war Jay attempted to apply the same lesson while serving as Secretary of Foreign Affairs under the Confederation. When his efforts to negotiate a commercial treaty with a Spanish envoy reached deadlock in 1786, Jay asked Congress to revise his instructions so that the United States would abjure its claims for free navigation of the Mississippi for a period of twenty years in order to secure the desired treaty. Jay succeeded only in provoking a sharp split in Congress because southern delegates believed he wished to sacrifice their region's interests in western expansion to benefit his own mercantile constituents in northern cities. From this experience and other frustrations, Jay concluded that the national government could never operate efficiently so long as all its powers—executive, judicial, and legislative—were vested in a single Congress.

Jay accordingly welcomed the Constitution's establishment of an independent executive with substantial authority over foreign affairs. Yet when Jay examined this subject in *Federalist* 64, he took a moderate position. Far from suggesting that the President commanded a preponderant share of authority in treaty making, Jay provided a careful analysis that stressed that the benefits of executive agency in conducting negotiations would be complemented by the deliberative abilities the Senate would provide in setting the basic objects of negotiation.

After 1789, Jay helped shape American ideas of executive power in two ways. In 1793 when President Washington asked the Supreme Court to issue an advisory opinion touching on a number of points of international law, Chief Justice Jay led the Court in declining the invitation on the grounds that it would improperly violate the SEPARATION OF POWERS. But Jay was less scrupulous the next year when Washington asked him to undertake the delicate diplomatic mission as special envoy to Britain, which Jay did without resigning from the Court. No formal advice from the Senate accompanied Jay on his mission to Britain; he went there strictly as an agent of the administration. Indeed, because the treaty he negotiated was so controversial, the President was reluctant to present it to the Senate, much less to disclose the instructions under which Jay had acted—which Secretary of the Treasury ALEXANDER HAMILTON, for reasons of his own, had betrayed to Britain. In the ensuing debate the Senate narrowly approved JAY'S TREATY. But the ongoing public controversy over both the treaty and the foreign policy it embodied played a crucial role in arousing public opinion and assuring that the presidential election of 1796 would be contested by the standard-bearers of two rival parties: Vice President John Adams for the Federalists and Thomas Jefferson for the Democratic-Republicans.

BIBLIOGRAPHY

Morris, Richard B. *The Peacemakers: The Great Powers and American Independence*. 1965.

Morris, Richard B. *Witnesses at the Creation: Hamilton, Madison, Jay, and the Constitution*. 1985.

JACK N. RAKOVE

JAY'S TREATY. As a symbol of the first major foreign-policy and political crisis of George Washington's presidency, Jay's Treaty is the most notorious in American history. It arose mainly out of difficulties maintaining NEUTRALITY during the war between Britain and France that began in February 1793 and out of the opposing international perspectives of the emerging national political parties.

The war permitted Americans to build a flourishing commerce with France's Caribbean colonies. In seeking to destroy that commerce, Britain's navy seized American ships, confiscated their cargoes, and impressed or imprisoned American seamen. These indignities, with their whipping up of anti-British sentiment, presented the President with a dilemma. His charted policy of neutrality in effect favored Britain. But the United States, as an ally of France, had committed itself to free trade in time of war as well as peace. The President and his FEDERALIST PARTY advisers assumed that attempted enforcement of that principle against Britain would trigger war. Democratic-Republicans thought differently. In general they regarded the British captures as unconscionable and believed that acquiescence in them would violate treaty obligations to France.

At the same time in the Old Northwest, American and British forces confronted each other in hostility. The British suspected that an army under Gen. Anthony Wayne sent north to subdue INDIANS also intended to take their forts and threaten Canada. In February 1794 Canada's governor-general, Lord Dorchester, even lined up Indian allies for a possible war against the United States.

The frontier disputes and the Caribbean humiliations enraged Americans. Talk of war became common. Congress voted a trade embargo directed against Britain and passed bills for mustering militia and building defenses. Federalist leaders feared that the crisis would destroy their foreign and economic policy based on a close relationship with Britain. On ALEXANDER HAMILTON's advice Washington chose JOHN JAY, the Chief Justice, for a special mission to London to avert hostilities.

While Jay's instructions allowed considerable discretion, they bound him not to contravene the alliance with France. He was to win recognition of American neutral rights, obtain compensation for the maritime seizures, reconcile other differences, and conclude a trade agreement. Britain made one important concession, the commercial treaty itself, which was signed on 19 November 1794. The treaty ignored impressment, said nothing about tampering with Indians, and accepted British confiscation of enemy property on American ships if London paid for the noncontraband goods. Other issues were to go to arbitral commissions.

Outrage characterized the American public's reaction to Jay's treaty. Mobs burned Jay in effigy and Democratic-Republicans condemned his handiwork as a sellout. Most Federalists, however, were pleased. With not a vote to spare, they blocked Democratic-Republican efforts in the Senate to defeat the treaty. During this turmoil, Washington's "opinion respecting the treaty," in his words, was "not favorable to it." He reversed himself after he became convinced that EDMUND RANDOLPH, his second Secretary of State, had betrayed him in dealings with the French. On 14 August 1795, the President signed the treaty. He immediately lost much of his bipartisan esteem, becoming increasingly the target for political abuse. Even after ratifications were exchanged, Democratic-Republicans in the House of Representatives attacked him and tried to kill the treaty by withholding funds for its implementation. They failed.

Despite the treaty's unpopularity, the President's support saved it and probably prevented a war that might have split the still fragile Union. He also obtained British evacuation of the northwest posts. These benefits came at the risk of angering the French, who claimed that Jay's concessions to Britain on neutral trade were incompatible with French treaty rights. The QUASI-WAR WITH FRANCE stemmed from this resentment. Fortunately it was less divisive than the quarrel with Britain. In all, Washington's decisions to send Jay to London and to accept his flawed treaty in the long run served the nation well.

BIBLIOGRAPHY

Bemis, Samuel Flagg. *Jay's Treaty: A Study in Commerce and Diplomacy.* Rev. ed. 1957.

Bowman, Albert Hall. *The Struggle for Neutrality: Franco-American Diplomacy during the Federalist Era.* 1947.

Combs, Jerald A. *The Jay Treaty: Political Battleground of the Founding Fathers.* 1970.

DeConde, Alexander. *Entangling Alliance: Politics and Diplomacy under George Washington.* 1958.

Perkins, Bradford. *The First Rapprochement: England and the United States, 1795–1805.* 1955.

ALEXANDER DECONDE

JEFFERSON, THOMAS (1743–1826), third President of the United States (1801–1809). The leading American exemplar of the Enlightenment, Thomas Jefferson brought to the presidency a versatility of genius never equaled by any other American Chief Executive. As a political philosopher, Jefferson in the eloquent prose of the Declaration of Independence proclaimed the core values of liberty, equality, and natural rights at the heart of the American experiment in self-government. As the author of the Virginia Statute for Religious Freedom, he championed the pattern of complete religious liberty through strict separation of church and state that subsequently prevailed throughout the United States. As a Democratic-Republican leader, he helped to found what has since become the world's oldest political party (the DEMOCRATIC PARTY). As a leading man of science, he wrote *Notes on the State of Virginia*, a pioneering work in natural history, and served as president of the American Philosophical Society for almost twenty years. As the foremost American architect of his day, he sparked the revival of classical architecture in the United States by designing his home, the majestic Palladian villa MONTICELLO, as well as the Virginia state capitol and the University of Virginia. As an educator, he was the primary founder of the University of Virginia. As a bibliophile, he accumulated an extraordinary library of almost seven thousand books, covering all fields of knowledge, that served as the nucleus of the restored Library of Congress after the British burned Washington in 1814. And as a lifelong religious seeker, he became the first practitioner of higher biblical criticism in America. It was with good reason that President John F. Kennedy hailed a group of visiting Nobel laureates as the "most extraordinary collection of talents that has ever been gathered together at the White House, with the possible exception of when Thomas Jefferson dined alone."

Jeffersonian Republicanism. The central theme of Jefferson's remarkable career—and an essential key to understanding his presidency—was his almost religious commitment to the establishment of an enduring republican social and political order in the United States. Jeffersonian republicanism was a dynamic blend of Lockean liberalism and civic humanism that entailed the rejection of all vestiges of monarchy and hereditary privilege. Instead, it sought to promote liberty, advance enlightenment, and unleash the creative energies of the American people within the framework of limited government, popular sovereignty, and an agrarian society guided by a natural aristocracy based on virtue and merit rather than birth and wealth. In keeping with the precepts of Lockean liberalism, Jefferson eloquently defended the philosophy of natural rights and the contractual theory of government. To ensure that government respected the natural rights of man and guaranteed free men the fruits of their labor, he believed that its powers must be sharply limited and made strictly accountable to the people by means of written constitutions, CHECKS AND BALANCES among the different branches of government, and frequent elections. With government thus checked with the liberties of the people secure, Jefferson looked forward with hope to a general expansion of freedom, enlightenment, and prosperity.

But for Jefferson the survival of republicanism in America depended less on the structure of the American government than on the character of the American people. In accordance with the ideological presuppositions of civic humanism, Jefferson believed that in the last resort a republic could survive only among a virtuous people who were independent, frugal, temperate, industrious, ready to take up arms in defense of liberty, and willing when necessary to subordinate their private interests to the public good. The pursuit of republican virtue required personal independence, and the firmest guarantee of personal independence was the ownership of property: hence Jefferson's idealization of yeomen farmers as the backbone of American republicanism. Fearful that the growth of manufacturing and increased urbanization would create increasing webs of economic and social dependence that would undermine republican virtue and thus destroy the Republic itself, Jefferson sought to maintain the agrarian nature of American society indefinitely by seeking foreign markets to absorb surplus agricultural production and by supporting the westward advance of American settlement in the belief that expansion across space would delay the corruption to which republics were invariably subject over time.

Jefferson's presidency marked an epochal period in American history. His election signified the first transition of power from one political party to another in the United States, and he himself was the first of two American Presidents whose election was determined by the House of Representatives. Aided in no small measure by the temporary restoration of peace in Europe between France and its antagonists, Jefferson enjoyed a triumphal first administration. He firmly established the ascendancy of the Democratic-Republican Party, consigning the FEDERALIST PARTY to a political limbo from which it was never really able to emerge. He dramatically reversed the centralizing policies of the Federalists, redirecting the flow of power from the federal government to the states in an effort to give free play to the creative energies of the Amer-

ican people. He doubled the size of the United States through the LOUISIANA PURCHASE, confident that he had thereby guaranteed the long-term dominance of agriculture in the American economy, and he brought about the first American exploration of the vast lands west of the Mississippi.

The frustrations of Jefferson's second administration stood in stark contrast to the successes of his first. With the renewal in 1803 of the momentous struggle for mastery in Europe between England and France, Jefferson's second term was dominated by his unsuccessful efforts to vindicate American NEUTRALITY rights in the face of massive violations of those rights by the two mighty belligerents. Lacking effective military or naval power to support his diplomacy, in the end Jefferson sought to defend American neutrality rights through the EMBARGO ACTS. The Embargo, an extreme form of economic coercion, required an unprecedented array of federal enforcement mechanisms that ran counter to the basic libertarian thrust of Jeffersonian republicanism, and its ultimate failure was an important link in the chain of events leading to the WAR OF 1812.

Jefferson's two terms in office were also a crucial stage in the development of the American presidency. As the first party leader to serve as CHIEF EXECUTIVE, Jefferson abandoned the passive, patriot-king style of presidential leadership followed by George Washington and John Adams and adopted a more activist, popular style of leadership. In contrast to his two predecessors, who in effect viewed themselves as republicanized patriot-kings governing above political parties and through CABINET ministers in pursuit of the common good, Jefferson was the first President to govern through an organized political party in the interests of the people [see PARTY LEADER, PRESIDENT AS]. Jefferson significantly enhanced the power of the presidency by uniting the constitutional authority granted to the President by the fundamental law of the land with the popular support that flowed from his leadership of the Democratic-Republican Party. However, like Washington and Adams, Jefferson ultimately wished to eliminate political parties. He never accepted the Federalists as a legitimate political opposition and sought to rid the country of institutionalized conflict between contending parties by enticing most Federalists to support the Democratic-Republican cause. It remained for Andrew Jackson, who combined the roles of President and party leader with an acceptance of the legitimacy of the party system, to complete the transition Jefferson had begun.

Early Career. Jefferson was born into the Virginia gentry in Albemarle County, then on the western fringes of colonial settlement. His father, Peter Jefferson, was a planter and surveyor who served as a local justice of the peace and a member of the House of Burgesses, and his mother, Jane Randolph Jefferson, came from one of the most prominent families in Virginia. Jefferson attended the College of William and Mary in Williamsburg and studied law with George Wythe, the most distinguished jurist in Virginia. Before Jefferson retired from the bar in 1775, he enjoyed a successful legal practice in Virginia. An ineffective public speaker, Jefferson owed his political success to his power to move men through the force of his character and the eloquence of his prose. Jefferson was one of the wealthiest Virginia planters of his time, and it was the greatest irony of his life that his career as a defender of republican liberty was based on an economic system in which his own prosperity depended on the servitude of black men, women, and children.

Jefferson's conviction that British efforts to reorganize the empire after 1763 were part of a systematic conspiracy to destroy American liberties propelled him into a political career that lasted forty years and left a decisive mark on American history. His pamphlet *A Summary View of the Rights of British America* (1774) denied that Parliament had any authority over the colonies and argued that they were only bound to Britain by their allegiance to the king. This work spread Jefferson's fame beyond the boundaries of Virginia and led to his selection as a delegate to the Continental Congress in 1775. During his service in this body, Jefferson made his greatest contribution to the revolutionary cause through his authorship of the Declaration of Independence.

The decision for American independence and the rejection of the hierarchical monarchical order that this entailed led Jefferson to turn his attention to the task of laying secure foundations for the emerging republican order. After three years as a reforming member of the Virginia House of Delegates, Jefferson was elected governor of Virginia in 1779. He proved to be a capable administrator during his two terms as governor. But, lacking the necessary fiscal and military resources, he dealt ineffectively with two British invasions of Virginia in 1781, and the criticism he thereby incurred drove him to retire to private life in June of that year.

The tragic death of Martha Wayles Skelton, Jefferson's wife, in 1782, just four months after giving birth to the last of their six children, shattered his dream of spending the remainder of his life at Monticello surrounded by his family and pursuing his scientific interests. Before this devastating loss Jefferson had characteristically put his first period of retirement to good use by writing his first and only book, *Notes on the State of Virginia* (1785). He then resumed his public career as a member of the Confederation Congress. During his congressional service from 1783 to 1784, he made a profoundly important contribution to the future development of the new American nation with a report on a plan of government for the largely unsettled territory north of the Ohio River—a document that served as the basis for the better-known Northwest Ordinance of 1787. By applying the principles of republican government to the Northwest Territory, Jefferson provided procedures for the admission of new states into the Union on the basis of equality with the original thirteen states that had broken away from the British Empire in 1776, thus promoting rapid American settlement of the West.

Jefferson's congressional service catapulted him from the national to the international scene for the first time in his career. In 1784, Congress appointed Jefferson to serve in Paris with John Adams and Benjamin Franklin on a commission to negotiate commercial treaties with various European powers. When Franklin resigned as American minister to France in 1785, Jefferson became his successor. Jefferson's experience during his five-year mission to France convinced him that in order to achieve its foreign policy objectives the United States needed a stronger central government to replace the moribund Articles of Confederation. He generally approved the Constitution of 1787 from his vantage point in Paris, but he criticized its lack of a bill of rights. He returned to America in 1789 believing that France was the only ally on whom the United States could rely as an effective counterweight to the overweening power of Britain. He clung to this belief during the ensuing decade until the rise of Napoleon Bonaparte persuaded him that, under the Corsican despot's rule, France was no longer a fit diplomatic partner for the American republic.

Party Leader and Vice President. Despite his aversion to political parties, Jefferson became one of the chief architects of the Democratic-Republican Party during his tenure as Washington's first Secretary of State from 1790 to 1793. By 1791 Jefferson feared that his vision of a virtuous agrarian republic was being jeopardized by Secretary of the Treasury ALEXANDER HAMILTON's grand design of creating a strong central government on the basis of the support of public creditors and what Jefferson regarded as British forms of social and political corruption. In Hamilton's advocacy of a funded debt, a national bank, an excise, federal encouragement of manufactures, and loose construction of the Constitution, Jefferson discerned nothing less than a settled Federalist design to anglicize American society, monarchize American government, and accentuate American dependence on Britain. He was especially alarmed by the success of the Hamiltonian system in spawning what he perceived to be a corrupt, monied interest in Congress made up of directors of the BANK OF THE UNITED STATES, owners of its stock, and holders of the public debt—the instruments, he believed, by which Hamilton corrupted Congress and made it subservient to the alleged Federalist plan to restore monarchical government to America. Jefferson's fears of a Federalist monarchical conspiracy escalated later in the 1790s in response to the adoption of a foreign policy by the Washington and Adams administrations that appeased aristocratic Britain while affronting revolutionary France, the use of military force to suppress the WHISKEY REBELLION, the creation of a large standing army in the wake of the XYZ affair [see QUASI-WAR WITH FRANCE], and the attempt to crush the Democratic-Republican opposition through the ALIEN AND SEDITION ACTS.

Acting on his perception that Hamiltonian finance constituted a grave threat to republican liberty, Jefferson joined with James Madison as early as 1791 in forming an opposition to the Secretary of the Treasury and his policies. The two Virginians sought to generate popular opposition to Hamilton's program, to end his allegedly corrupt influence over Congress by creating a countervailing Democratic-Republican interest in that body, and to persuade Washington that dismissing Hamilton from office and modifying his policies were necessary to prevent the further degeneration of American republicanism. After working with Jefferson to establish the *National Gazette* in Philadelphia to promote the Democratic-Republican cause, Madison assumed the lead in organizing Republicans in Congress, while Jefferson opposed Hamilton in the Cabinet and in a remarkable series of private communications to Washington during 1792 in which he tried to convince the skeptical President that Hamilton and his program were undermining republicanism. Early in 1793 an increasingly desperate Jefferson made a final attempt to turn Washington against Hamilton by covertly inciting an effort by House Democratic-Republicans to censure Hamilton's administration of public finances. The failure of this maneuver forced Jefferson to rely on the Democratic-Republican Party as the only effective check on the Treasury Secretary's policies. But, even though Jefferson played a more active role in party affairs for the remainder of his tenure as Secretary of State, his weariness of political strife led him to retire to private life at the end of 1793.

The imperatives of party politics reluctantly drew Jefferson back into the political arena three years later. Frustrated by congressional failure to approve the program of commercial retaliation against Britain that he, as Secretary of State, had recommended in his Report on Commerce near the end of 1793, Jefferson had also lost confidence in Washington after the President's denunciation of the Democratic Societies in the wake of the Whiskey Rebellion. Jefferson also viewed JAY'S TREATY as a craven surrender of vital American national interests to the British. Unsuccessful in his efforts to persuade Madison to stand as Democratic-Republican candidate for President in 1796, Jefferson reluctantly allowed the Democratic-Republican Party to cast him in this role after Washington announced that fall that he would not be a candidate for reelection. Taking no active part in the campaign, Jefferson received sixty-eight electoral votes, the highest number after John Adams, who received seventy-one; under the electoral system of the time, this resulted in Jefferson's becoming Vice President.

As Vice President, Jefferson assumed the role of chief Democratic-Republican Party leader and made a lasting contribution to the orderly conduct of legislative business. After the failure of his brief effort to collaborate with President Adams, who headed the Federalists' moderate wing, Jefferson quickly emerged as the leader of the Democratic-Republican opposition to Washington's successor. He favored a more conciliatory policy toward France than that pursued by Adams, and he viewed the Alien and Sedition Acts as a transparent effort to crush the Democratic-Republican Party as well as a danger to freedom of speech and association. In order to energize the Democratic-Republican opposition, he formulated legislative strategy with congressional Democratic-Republicans, corresponded with a wide range of Democratic-Republican leaders in various states, and encouraged Democratic-Republican journalists to keep up a drumbeat of criticism of Federalist policies. Most dramatically, in 1798, in reaction to the Alien and Sedition Acts, he secretly drafted the Kentucky Resolutions, which asserted the right of the states to nullify any federal law they regarded as contrary to the Constitution [see NULLIFICATION]. In the midst of presiding over the Senate and leading the Democratic-Republican opposition, Jefferson still found time to compile and publish his *Manual of Parliamentary Procedure*, a handbook of precedents that continues to guide the conduct of legislative business in the Senate today.

First Term. Jefferson's intensifying conviction that the centralizing policies of the Federalists posed a mortal threat to the survival of republican liberty led him to stand as the Democratic-Republican presidential candidate in 1800. In accordance with the electoral customs of the time, Jefferson refrained from campaigning. Behind the scenes, however, he was deeply involved in the campaign, encouraging Democratic-Republican pamphleteers and journalists to articulate the party's position, circulating Democratic-Republican tracts, coordinating strategy with Democratic-Republican Party organizations, and enunciating through extensive correspondence with Democratic-Republican leaders a campaign platform stressing the themes of limited government, states' rights, strict construction of the Constitution, and noninvolvement in European affairs. After a vicious campaign in which Federalists denounced him as an atheist, an unworldly philosopher, and a Jacobin fanatic, Jefferson defeated Adams, getting seventy-three to Adams's sixty-five electoral votes. But since Jefferson and his running mate, AARON BURR, received the same number of electoral votes, the final outcome was decided in the House of Representatives [*see* ELECTION, PRESIDENTIAL, 1800]. To prevent the recurrence of a similar electoral crisis, the TWELFTH AMENDMENT, ratified shortly before Jefferson stood for reelection in 1804, provided that presidential electors would henceforth cast separate electoral votes for President and Vice President.

Presidential leadership. Jefferson's understanding of the significance of his election impelled him to assume an activist, popular style of presidential leadership. He frequently referred to his first presidential election victory as the "Revolution of 1800," by which he meant that it represented a decisive repudiation of centralizing Federalist policies. Convinced that nothing less than the future of republican liberty in the United States and throughout the world was at stake, Jefferson abandoned the Washington and Adams patriot-king style and combined the formal authority bestowed on the President by the Constitution with the political power he enjoyed as leader of the Democratic-Republican Party to forge a highly effective, popular form of presidential leadership. Whereas his two predecessors had governed above parties, Jefferson governed through the Democratic-Republican Party, in the process significantly enhancing both the power of the presidency and the fortunes of his party.

As President, Jefferson was fully in command as a policymaker and as an administrator. He set basic administration policies in a collegial manner, in full consultation with his Cabinet, with an exquisite respect for the prerogatives of Congress, and with a firm insistence on upholding the rightful constitutional authority of the presidency, especially in the conduct of FOREIGN AFFAIRS. He handled all the paperwork of the presidency, personally drafting hundreds of state papers and writing more than five thousand letters in response to the more than thirteen thousand he received during his terms in office. Each day he reviewed the substantive work of his Cabinet in order to keep himself informed about the details of the public business for which he was ultimately responsible. His indefatigable work habits and passionate attention to detail kept Jefferson firmly in charge of the executive branch.

Jefferson transformed the Cabinet into an effective instrument of presidential leadership. All his Cabinet officers were Democratic-Republican activists, all but one had served in Congress, and with one exception they all remained in office during his eight years as President. Through regular review of their work, periodic consultations with them on vital public issues, his own persuasive powers, and his prestige as party leader, Jefferson retained the loyalty of his Cabinet and ensured that its members remained in harmony with his goals and faithfully executed his policies. In these ways he avoided the serious ideological and policy differences that had riven Washington's Cabinet and the outright disloyalty that had marred Adams's.

Jefferson also developed an effective working relationship with the steadily increasing Democratic-Republican majorities in Congress. Because of Democratic-Republican suspicions of executive power, he relied more on his role as party leader than on his formal authority as President to exert control over Congress. While carefully respecting the constitutional prerogatives of Congress, he utilized a number of informal methods of persuasion to secure its support for his legislative proposals. He personally lobbied key Democratic-Republican Congressmen and secretly drafted bills for his congressional supporters to propose. He authorized influential Democratic-Republicans to act as administration spokesmen in Congress and regularly entertained legislators of both parties at the White House, both to promote Democratic-Republican cohesion and to disarm Federalist suspicions of him. He directed members of his Cabinet to draft legislation for Congress and to advise congressional committees on pending bills—invaluable assistance in an age when Congress had no staff of its own. Through these means Jefferson exercised such extensive influence over the Democratic-Republican majorities in Congress that one Federalist complained, "Never were a set of men more blindly devoted to the will of a *prime Mover* or *Minister* than the majority of both Houses to the will and wishes of the Chief Magistrate."

Jefferson further enhanced the power of the presidency by symbolically representing the core republican values of liberty and equality. He walked to his first inaugural ceremony without the traditional elaborate presidential escort, and he submitted written annual messages to Congress instead of personally addressing it because he believed that the latter practice was too reminiscent of the king's opening address to Parliament. He dressed simply and each day rode unescorted through the nation's capital. He abolished birthday balls and the weekly levees at the White House, receptions that had tended to attract the social elite. Twice a year, on New Year's Day and the Fourth of July, he opened the President's house to the general public. He abandoned formal protocol at White House functions and carried on an extensive private correspondence with Americans from all walks of life on a wide variety of subjects. By thus emphasizing his rejection of Federalist pomp and ceremony and affirming his adherence to the values of republican liberty and equality, he enhanced his image as a man of the people and solidified his popular support.

Finally, Jefferson expanded the scope of his presidential power and influence by attending to his duties as Democratic-Republican Party leader. He corresponded extensively with Democratic-Republican leaders throughout the nation to generate support for his policies. He took advantage of formal addresses and memorials to the President from various groups to make public responses that articulated basic Democratic-Republican principles. He urged his supporters in various states to set up newspapers to promote the Democratic-Republican cause, and he himself helped to secure the establishment in Washington of the *National Intelligencer* to serve as his administration's recognized journalistic organ. By refusing to allow his executive responsibilities to deflect him from his party responsibilities, Jefferson contributed to the growing power of Democratic-Republicans in all sections of the country during his tenure and thereby immeasurably strengthened his presidency.

Domestic policy. Jefferson's overriding domestic priority was to reverse the Federalist's centralizing policies by paying off the national debt and reducing the federal government to what he regarded as its proper constitutional limits. Jefferson secured the enactment of his basic reform program during the 1801–1802 session of Congress. The centerpiece of this program was a bold plan, devised by Secretary of the Treasury ALBERT GALLATIN, to retire the national debt of $82 million in sixteen years. Whereas Hamiltonians viewed a funded debt as an effective instrument for creating a strong nation-state by attaching public creditors to the central government, Jeffersonians regarded it as the source of a corrupt, monied interest that encouraged dangerous speculative habits among and imposed burdensome taxes on the agrarian majority. Gallatin proposed abolishing all internal taxes and dedicating $7.3 million of the government's remaining annual revenue of about $10 million from import duties, public lands, and the postal service to the retirement of the entire national debt by 1817. Largely owing to a tremendous trade boom, Jefferson managed substantially to reduce the national debt by the time he left office. But because of lost revenues resulting from the Embargo (see below) and the expenses incurred by the Louisiana Purchase and the War of 1812, Jefferson's dream of completely eliminating the national debt was not realized until the Jackson administration.

The adoption of Gallatin's debt-elimination plan was accompanied by a sharp reduction in government expenditures. In accordance with the Jeffersonian emphasis on avoiding foreign entanglements, the President closed American embassies in Portugal, the Netherlands, and Prussia, leaving the United States with ministerial diplomatic representation only in London, Paris, and Madrid. With the abolition of internal taxes came the elimination of four hundred tax-collector jobs. But Jefferson and his party achieved their greatest savings in the area of national defense. The army was reduced to three thousand men and the navy from thirteen to seven ships. Jefferson and his supporters had long feared a standing army as one of the greatest threats to republican liberty, and henceforth Jefferson expected the militia to be the nation's first line of defense in the event of foreign invasion or domestic insurrection.

Jefferson's efforts to eliminate the national debt and to decentralize government power coincided with his success in republicanizing the federal bureaucracy. When Jefferson assumed power no Democratic-Republican held an appointive federal office. Democratic-Republican radicals clamored for a wholesale removal of Federalist incumbents, while Federalists asserted that no federal official should be dismissed for purely partisan reasons. To satisfy his Democratic-Republican supporters while pursuing his goal of detaching rank-and-file Federalists from their leaders, Jefferson followed a moderate course with respect to appointments and removals. He automatically dismissed only those Federalists who were appointed after John Adams's electoral defeat had become clear, who were guilty of negligence or undue partisanship, or who were serving as federal district attorneys or marshals. He filled these offices and all others that fell vacant during his administration exclusively with Democratic-Republicans, arguing that this was necessary to compensate for the former Federalist ban on Democratic-Republican appointees. In general, Jefferson preferred to appoint educated and respectable men to federal office, in line with his belief in the need to foster a natural aristocracy of virtue and talent to guide the fortunes of the American republic. Unlike his two predecessors, however, Jefferson's appointees included significant numbers of westerners and men of ordinary birth and middling social status. In 1803 Jefferson estimated that half of all presidentially appointed officials were then Democratic-Republicans, and by the time he left office in 1809 this figure had climbed to 70 percent.

Jefferson enjoyed considerably less success in republicanizing the federal judiciary. Jefferson viewed the complete Federalist monopoly of the federal judiciary that existed when he took office as a potentially serious obstacle to republican reform. While conceding that the rule of law was an essential safeguard for republican liberty, Jefferson regarded it as incompatible with republican principles for judges to be beyond effective popular control, and he particularly resented the partisan zeal many Federalist judges had displayed in enforcing the Sedition Act against the Democratic-Republican opposition. Jefferson himself adhered to the so-called tripartite school of constitutional interpretation, which held that each branch of the federal government had the right to decide for itself the constitutionality of actions taken by the other two branches, although as President he did little to propagate this view. In 1802, however, he did strike a blow against this last remaining bulwark of Federalism when he secured the repeal of the Judiciary Act passed in the waning days of John Adams's presidency, along with the sixteen new judgeships and the new circuit court system that it had created. But his effort to use the blunt instrument of impeachment to discipline excessively zealous Federalist judges came to grief in 1805, when the Senate failed to convict Supreme Court Justice Samuel Chase of high crimes or misdemeanors after he delivered an intemperate charge to a grand jury criticizing certain Democratic-Republican political reforms in Maryland. Thereafter, an uneasy truce generally prevailed between Jefferson and the Federalist-dominated judiciary.

Foreign affairs. Despite his wish to isolate the United States from foreign entanglements, Jefferson confronted two serious international crises during his first administration, one of which he partially resolved and the other of which dramatically changed the face of the new American nation.

Soon after Jefferson took office, a long-simmering problem in American relations with the Barbary States of northern Africa came to a boil. With the loss of British naval protection after independence, the United States was obliged to follow the custom of various European powers and pay an annual tribute to Algiers, Morocco, Tripoli, and Tunis to protect American merchant ships trading in the Mediterranean from capture by Barbary pirates. Since his tenure as minister to France in the 1780s Jefferson had regarded this practice as an affront to national honor and had advocated the use of naval force against the Barbary States to end it. Consequently, in May 1801, on learning of increased aggression by Tripoli against American shipping in the Mediterranean, Jefferson dispatched a naval squadron to protect American commerce in that area. There ensued four years of naval warfare with Tripoli that ended in 1805 with a peace treaty in which the United States was exempted from paying further tribute to Tripoli [*see* BARBARY WAR]. But under Jefferson the United States continued to pay tribute to the other Barbary States, a practice that went on until 1815, when James Madison dispatched another naval squadron to the Mediterranean.

The war with Tripoli was far overshadowed by the Louisiana Purchase, the crowning achievement of Jefferson's presidency. Spain's secret retrocession of Louisiana to Napoleonic France in 1800, which did not take effect for another two years, posed a grave threat to vital American interests as well as to Jefferson's vision of a continental "empire of liberty" in North America. The proposed restoration of a reinvigorated French colonial empire in Louisiana endangered America's right to navigate the Mississippi, which was of paramount importance to the prosperity of western farmers, and threatened to halt the westward sweep of American expansion.

Jefferson's response to the Louisiana crisis was a triumph of pragmatic statesmanship. On the one hand, Jefferson notified France that the United States viewed with extreme displeasure the prospective return of French rule to Louisiana and threatened to conclude an alliance with the British if it came about. On the other hand, in reaction to the Spanish revocation of the American right of deposit at New Orleans late in 1802, an action widely attributed to French influence, Jefferson dispatched James Monroe on a special mission to France to negotiate the purchase of New Orleans and the two Florida provinces that Jefferson mistakenly assumed the Spanish had ceded to the French. In the end, as so often in the past, American diplomacy profited from Europe's distress. Unable to subjugate the slave rebellion in the strategic

Caribbean colony of Saint-Domingue (Haiti), facing the prospect of an imminent renewal of war with England, and plagued by a depleted treasury, Napoleon in April 1803 agreed to a treaty selling all of Louisiana to the United States for $15 million. Because the Constitution did not explicitly authorize the U.S. acquisition of foreign territory, the strict constructionist Jefferson at first thought that a constitutional amendment would be necessary to sanction the purchase. But Secretary of the Treasury Gallatin argued that such an acquisition was an essential attribute of sovereignty, and when Jefferson learned that Napoleon was having second thoughts about the sale of Louisiana, he suppressed his constitutional qualms and submitted the treaty to the Senate, which promptly ratified it in October 1803. By this stroke, Jefferson doubled the size of the United States, and even though critics then and later taxed him with abandoning his basic principle of constitutional interpretation, in this case he clearly decided that remaining true to strict constructionism was less important than guaranteeing the perpetuation of his vision of a virtuous agrarian republic.

Besides acquiring Louisiana, Jefferson also promoted its exploration. As early as 1802, well before he had even an inkling that the United States might acquire Louisiana, he began to make preparations for the expedition mounted by Meriwether Lewis and William Clark to explore the trans-Mississippi West and find an all-water route to the Pacific. While conclusively proving the nonexistence of the long-sought Northwest Passage, the historic Lewis and Clark expedition, which lasted from 1803 to 1806, greatly expanded American geographical and scientific knowledge of the vast regions beyond the Mississippi. Jefferson also launched lesser expeditions to explore the southern boundary of Louisiana.

Second Term. The course Jefferson pursued during his first administration won the overwhelming approval of the American electorate. As the defender of basic republican values who had preserved the peace, lowered taxes, and doubled the size of the national domain, Jefferson easily won reelection with a new running mate, Governor GEORGE CLINTON of New York. Together they defeated their Federalist opponents, CHARLES COTESWORTH PINCKNEY and RUFUS KING, by the decisive margin of 162 electoral votes to 14, with only Connecticut, Delaware, and two Maryland electors supporting the Federalist ticket.

Domestic affairs. In at least one area Jefferson during his second term adopted a more expansive view of the obligations of the federal government. Faced with the prospect of a surplus of government revenues,

Jefferson suggested in his second inaugural address that Congress pass a constitutional amendment authorizing the distribution of this money among the states for INTERNAL IMPROVEMENTS. In the following year, however, under the influence of Secretary of the Treasury Gallatin, who convinced him that this was more properly a federal responsibility, Jefferson asked Congress for a constitutional amendment empowering the federal government to construct a national system of roads and canals to cement the bonds of union. But Congress contented itself with soliciting a comprehensive report on the subject from Gallatin, and even though after his retirement Jefferson continued to support a national system of internal improvements, he still insisted that the federal government needed a constitutional amendment to undertake it—hence his later hostility to HENRY CLAY's AMERICAN SYSTEM and the doctrine of IMPLIED POWERS on which it rested.

Jefferson enjoyed greater success in bringing about the legal abolition of the African slave trade. Jefferson believed that slavery violated the natural rights of blacks to freedom and hoped that it would one day be abolished. Yet he could not overcome his own racial prejudice, and therefore he invariably insisted that abolition had to be accompanied by the colonization of freed black slaves, preferably in Africa or the West Indies. He remained a slaveholder throughout his life and freed only seven of the several hundred bondsmen he owned. Nevertheless, he was long revolted by the inhumanity of the African slave trade, and he took advantage of his annual message to Congress in December 1806 to recommend passage of legislation implementing the constitutional prohibition on American participation in this commerce after the first day of 1808. After a deeply divisive debate along sectional lines, Congress passed a law in 1807 outlawing the African slave trade after the constitutionally mandated day, though in practice this prohibition proved easy to evade for many years after Jefferson left office.

The most serious domestic problem Jefferson confronted during his second administration was Burr's Conspiracy. Because of his suspicion that Aaron Burr in 1801 had plotted with House Republicans to bring about his own election as President, Jefferson had remained aloof from his first Vice President, and Burr's subsequent effort to arrest his political decline by running for governor of New York in 1804 had ended in electoral defeat and his famous duel with Alexander Hamilton. In response to these setbacks, Burr devised a plan that, depending upon the circumstances, would have involved detaching the western states from the Union and creating an independent empire, or conquering Mexico, or both. Justifiably convinced of the basic loyalty of westerners to the Union, Jefferson thwarted Burr's conspiratorial designs without resorting to the use of massive military force, only to see Burr obtain a highly equivocal acquittal at his 1807 trial for treason thanks to Chief Justice JOHN MARSHALL's stringent legal requirements for proof of this offense.

Foreign affairs. Jefferson faced two frustratingly difficult foreign policy issues during his second term, neither of which he resolved and one of which led to the War of 1812. He expended much of his diplomatic energy in pursuing a dubious American claim to the Spanish province of West Florida. Jefferson insisted that West Florida was part of the Louisiana Purchase, but Spain and France denied this—a denial supported by the overwhelming weight of the historical evidence. Jefferson secured passage of the Mobile Act of 1804 embodying the American claim to West Florida, but he was never able to make good on it. He offered to relinquish certain American monetary claims on Spain in return for this province; he resorted to threats of military force against Spain; and he sought to enlist French diplomatic support—but all in vain. Spain insisted on the validity of its title to the disputed province, and France refused to assist the United States against Spain, which was not allied with Napoleon. It remained for Madison to achieve Jefferson's goal of adding West Florida to the United States.

The dispute over West Florida was far outweighed, however, by the controversy over escalating British and French violations of American neutrality rights. While Britain and France each tried to prevent neutral ships from trading with the other, France's lack of naval power meant that the French affected American shipping far less than did the British, with their awesome maritime power. Britain further aggravated relations with the United States by impressing seamen from American ships, patroling American harbors in search of violators of British neutrality policy, and striving to prevent American trade with the British or French West Indies. Failing to achieve a diplomatic settlement of these issues with the British, Jefferson faced the issue of peace or war in the starkest form when H.M.S. *Leopard* attacked the American warship *Chesapeake* off Norfolk, Virginia, in June 1807 and boarded the ship to remove four alleged British deserters.

Although a massive wave of war fever swept over the country in the wake of the *Chesapeake* affair, Jefferson chose economic coercion over war. Jefferson was not a pacifist, and if all else failed he was willing as a last resort to go to war to vindicate American national honor. But in this instance, circumstances and republican ideology restrained him from resorting to the sword. Besides the fact that Congress had recently ignored his request to reform the militia system and expand the navy, leaving him without credible military or naval power, Jefferson was also reluctant to go to war because he feared that this would seriously impede his effort to pay off the national debt and because he was convinced that Britain's dependence on American foodstuffs made that nation peculiarly vulnerable to American economic pressure.

Therefore, in December 1807, Jefferson prevailed upon Congress to approve the first Embargo Act, a total interdiction of American exports to all other countries. Though initially popular, the Embargo soon generated widespread economic hardship and popular resistance. To enforce it Jefferson resorted to an unprecedented exertion of federal authority and infringements of civil rights that ran directly counter to his basic libertarianism. Unsuccessful in securing concessions from Britain or France, the Embargo was replaced shortly before Jefferson left office in March 1809 by the Non-Intercourse Act, which continued the ban on trade with these two nations while allowing American commerce with the rest of the world. The failure of the Jeffersonian policy of economic coercion to resolve the neutrality crisis set the stage for the War of 1812.

Retirement. Despite widespread Democratic-Republican pleas that he run for a third term, Jefferson returned to private life in March 1809. He had decided soon after his reelection in 1804 to follow Washington's example and serve only two terms. He believed that it was necessary to establish a binding precedent that would repair what he regarded as a serious flaw in the Constitution—its failure to limit the number of terms a President could serve, therefore allowing for the possibility of a lifetime Chief Executive [*see* TWO-TERM TRADITION]. During the seventeen years he spent in retirement at Monticello, Jefferson carried on a rich correspondence, became reconciled with his old friend and onetime antagonist, John Adams, and took the lead in establishing the University of Virginia. He also grew increasingly pessimistic over the future prospects of American republicanism as growing sectional differences over slavery and incipient signs of accelerated urbanization, commercialization, and industrialization endangered his vision of a virtuous agrarian republic. In the end, however, hope characteristically triumphed over fear, and in his last surviving letter, written only ten days before his death on 4 July 1826—the fiftieth anniversary of the Declaration of Independence—he expressed his republican faith that that noble document would "be to the world, what

I believe it will be, (to some parts sooner, to others later, but finally to all,) the signal of arousing men to burst the chains under which monkish ignorance and superstition had persuaded them to bind themselves, and to secure the blessings and security of self-government."

BIBLIOGRAPHY

Adams, Henry. *History of the United States during the Administrations of Jefferson and Madison.* 9 vols. 1889–1891.
Banning, Lance. *The Jeffersonian Persuasion: Evolution of a Party Ideology.* 1978.
Cunningham, Noble. *In Pursuit of Reason: The Life of Thomas Jefferson.* 1987.
Levy, Leonard. *Jefferson and Civil Liberties: The Darker Side.* 1963.
Malone, Dumas. *Jefferson and His Time.* 6 vols. 1948–1981.
McDonald, Forrest. *The Presidency of Thomas Jefferson.* 1976.
Peterson, Merrill. *Thomas Jefferson and the New Nation.* 1970.
Tucker, Robert W., and David C. Hendrickson. *Empire of Liberty: The Statescraft of Thomas Jefferson.* 1990.

EUGENE R. SHERIDAN

JEFFERSONIAN REPUBLICAN PARTY. For discussion of the Republican Party of the first decades of the United States, also called the Democratic-Republican Party, see DEMOCRATIC PARTY.

JOHNSON, ANDREW (1808–1875), seventeenth President of the United States (1865–1869). No President before or since rose from a lower social and educational depth to reach the height of that office than did Andrew Johnson. Born on 29 December 1808 in Raleigh, North Carolina, the youngest son of illiterate tavern servants, he never attended school and at the age of thirteen became an apprentice tailor. In 1826 he migrated to eastern Tennessee where the following year he established a tailor shop in Greeneville and married Eliza McCardle. While an apprentice he had learned to read at a rudimentary level and his wife taught him to write and cipher. In time he acquired a good basic knowledge of history and the standard English classics and developed into a fluent speaker, but rarely wrote anything in his own hand.

Early Career. As soon as he was old enough to vote he became active in politics and would remain so literally to the end of his life. Starting as an alderman and mayor in Greeneville, he moved on to the state legislature, was a member of the U.S. House of Representatives from 1843 to 1853, served two terms as governor of Tennessee, and in 1857 secured election to the U.S. Senate. A Democrat, he owed his success to his championing of what he called the "plebeians"—

the small farmers and tradesmen—in opposition to the wealthy, slave-owning planters, whom he denounced as "stuck-up aristocrats."

Then came the SECESSION crisis of 1860–1861. Although he owned a few slaves and was a staunch advocate of STATES' RIGHTS, Johnson opposed secession, declaring that it was a conspiracy by the aristocrats to obtain total power in the South for themselves. Initially most Tennesseans supported his stand, but following the outbreak of the CIVIL WAR in April 1861, Tennessee joined the Confederacy and Johnson had to flee for his life to the North, where his struggle against secession had made him a hero and the leading representative of Southern Unionism.

Early in 1862, following the occupation of Nashville by Northern forces, President Abraham Lincoln appointed Johnson military governor of Tennessee, in which capacity he endeavored to establish a pro-Union civil government in that state. Next, desiring to attract prowar Democrats and border state Unionists, Lincoln selected Johnson as his running mate in the 1864 presidential campaign. On 4 March 1865, Johnson took office as Vice President in a ceremony that was marred when, having drunk some whiskey to overcome a feeling of faintness occasioned by a recent illness, he delivered a maudlin, incoherent inaugural address. Owing to the disgrace of this performance, it seemed that Johnson no longer would play a major role in national affairs.

On the night of 14 April 1865, Johnson heard knocking on the door of his Washington hotel room. It was a friend who had come to notify him that Lincoln had been shot at Ford's Theater. The following morning Johnson took the oath of office as President of the United States. Suddenly he had become the most important man in the nation.

Johnson's Reconstruction Program. He faced one of the most difficult tasks ever to confront a President. The Civil War had defeated the Confederacy's attempt to establish its independence and destroyed black chattel SLAVERY. Still to be decided, though, were the two great issues of RECONSTRUCTION: By what process and under what terms would the rebel states return to the Union, and what would be the future status of blacks now that they were free? How Johnson responded to these issues would determine the course of Reconstruction and the success or failure of his presidency.

Many Republicans, in particular the so-called RADICAL REPUBLICANS, welcomed Johnson's presence in the White House. They believed, on the basis of statements by him urging stern punishment of "traitors," that he would be more sympathetic to their views on

Reconstruction than Lincoln had been. By the same token Southerners, who looked upon Johnson as a renegade, feared the worse from him.

Both groups were mistaken. When Johnson spoke of punishing traitors, he had in mind the Southern aristocrats whom he blamed for secession and war. His main objectives when it came to Reconstruction were to restore the ex-Confederate states to the Union as quickly as possible, put political power in the South in the hands of the "plebeians," and bring about the formation of a new political party that would unite Northern and Southern moderates, thus promoting reconciliation between the sections and enabling him to win election to the presidency in his own right in 1868. As to the blacks, his states' rights ideology and perception of Southern racial attitudes, which he shared, led him to conclude that their future not only should be but would be determined by the Southern states.

On 29 May 1865, Johnson set forth his Reconstruction program in two proclamations. One, the Amnesty Proclamation, restored the political and property rights of all rebels who took an oath of allegiance to the United States save those who had held high positions in the Confederacy or possessed more than $20,000 in taxable property. Those thus excluded could regain their rights by applying for and receiving a presidential pardon.

The other proclamation pertained to North Carolina but set the pattern for all states undergoing Reconstruction. Under it, these states were to hold constitutional conventions for the purpose of forming new governments, following which they would return to the Union. Only men who had been eligible to vote in 1861 and who took the loyalty oath could participate in the conventions and the elections thereof, which meant that blacks as well as unpardoned rebels were banned from the polls. Subsequently Johnson also required the reconstructed states, as a condition for readmission, to repeal their secession ordinances, to repudiate their Confederate war debts, and to ratify the Thirteenth Amendment abolishing slavery throughout the nation.

Southerners were pleased with Johnson's program: it was unexpectedly mild and promised a speedy return to the Union and to control over their own state affairs. Most Northerners, eager for an end to sectional strife, likewise expressed approval, with only a few Radicals grumbling about the omission of civil and political rights for blacks. But then, as the program was implemented during the summer and fall of 1865, more and more Northerners, and in particular Republicans, grew increasingly concerned, even alarmed, over what was happening—and not happening—in the South.

There, in spite of the disfranchisement provisions of the Amnesty Proclamation, most of the men being elected to state offices and Congress were prominent secessionists and Confederates. Furthermore these provisions became meaningless as Johnson, finding that his plan to transfer power to the plebeians was politically unfeasible, began granting pardons wholesale. Worst of all, the new state governments, while according blacks some rudimentary legal rights, made no move whatsoever to give them even the most limited civil and political rights. Instead they enacted laws known as black codes, which had the intent and effect of reducing blacks to a subordinate condition that in some ways resembled slavery, and at the same time did little or nothing to protect blacks against the numerous acts of terrorism that were being perpetrated against them.

Congressional Reconstruction. By December Northerners in general and Republicans in particular felt that Johnson's Reconstruction program was inadequate and that it must be supplemented by further measures in order to preserve the results of the war against an intransigent South. Hence when Congress, which had been adjourned since March, reconvened that month, the Republican majority denied seats to the newly elected Southern delegations and appointed a Joint Committee of Fifteen on Reconstruction to investigate conditions in the South and propose new legislation. These actions gave a clear signal that Congress intended to share in the Reconstruction process, but it was one that Johnson chose to ignore.

Early in 1866 congressional Republicans moved to deal with the most pressing problems besetting blacks in the South by passing a bill extending the tenure and powers of the FREEDMEN'S BUREAU, an agency established toward the end of the war to provide much-needed aid to the liberated slaves. To their surprise and anger, for they thought that he had indicated a willingness to accept it, Johnson on 19 February vetoed it as unnecessary and unconstitutional. An attempt to override the veto, however, failed when enough Senate Republicans, hoping to avoid a total break with the President, voted with the Democrats to sustain it. On 22 February, Washington's Birthday, Johnson celebrated his victory with a vulgar harangue from a White House balcony to a crowd of supporters, thereby further alienating many Northerners.

In March Congress passed, with unanimous Republican backing, a civil rights bill [see CIVIL RIGHTS ACT OF 1866]. Essentially a response to the black codes, it declared that blacks were United States citizens entitled to equal protection of the laws and provided the federal government with broad enforcement powers. Again the Republicans had the impression that Johnson would not stand in their way, again they found themselves deceived. On 27 March he vetoed the bill, alleging that it violated states' rights and discriminated against whites. This time virtually all Republicans voted to override the veto, with the result that the bill became law on 9 April. The override marked the beginning of open war between Johnson and the Republicans.

The next and in some ways decisive battle in this war began in June 1866 when Congress adopted the Fourteenth Amendment. Drafted by the Joint Committee on Reconstruction and intended to make permanent the rights and protections contained in the Civil Rights Act, the amendment's key provision stated that all persons born or naturalized in the United States are citizens and that states cannot "deprive any person of life, liberty, or property, without due process of law" or "deny to any person . . . the equal protection of the law." Through informal statements Republican leaders indicated that if the Southern states ratified the amendment, thereby demonstrating an acceptance of civil rights for blacks, they would be readmitted to the Union as full-fledged members, but if they rejected it they would be subjected to much more drastic Reconstruction measures.

All the former Confederate states except Tennessee either rejected the amendment or took no action on it. They did so with the encouragement of Johnson. Like the vast majority of Southern whites he found the prospect of black civil equality repugnant. He also believed, as did they, that Northerners would not impose on their fellow whites of the South something that most of their own states denied.

Thus the 1866 congressional elections became a referendum on Reconstruction. Should the Republicans maintain their domination of Congress, this would mean that the North supported them in upholding black rights in the South. Should they lose it or have it substantially reduced, then they would stand repudiated and Johnson would be vindicated.

Johnson attempted to achieve the latter outcome in two main ways. One was to promote the organization of Johnson Clubs and the formation of a National Union Party. Unfortunately for him, most of the participants in these movements were either COPPERHEADS or Confederates, with the result that he lost support rather than gained it. The other took the form of a speaking tour in the late summer of 1866 during which he traveled by special train north to upstate New York, west to Chicago, south to St. Louis, and back to Washington through the Ohio Valley. A skilled stump orator, Johnson believed that if he could talk directly to the people they would rally behind his Reconstruction policies. However, at each stop he delivered basically the same speech; soon his audiences knew what he was going to say before he said it. Also, on several occasions hecklers caused him to lose his temper and act in a manner that lent credence to Republicans charges (false) that he was a drunkard. In sum, the "swing around the circle" was a political and personal fiasco.

In the elections the Republicans not only maintained their already large majority in Congress but increased it. With this mandate from the North, they proceeded to scrap the existing Reconstruction program and to put into effect a new one by passing in late February 1867 the Military Reconstruction Act. This divided the ten Southern states still outside the Union (Tennessee had been readmitted because of its ratification of the Fourteenth Amendment) into five military districts, each under a general empowered to govern by martial law; provided for the holding of constitutional conventions in each of the ten states; stipulated that once a state had ratified its new constitution and the Fourteenth Amendment it would be eligible for congressional representation; and gave the right to vote to all adult black males while at the same time disfranchising all persons guilty of voluntary participation in the rebellion, thereby giving blacks the majority of votes in most Southern states. It was, and it remains, the most extreme law ever enacted by Congress, for it obliterated state governments, deprived hundreds of thousands of men of the right to vote, and enfranchised a race that hitherto had been excluded from voting in all except a few New England states where it constituted a minuscule minority.

The Clash with Congress. Congress also moved to curtail Johnson's powers as President. First it amended the Army Appropriations Act of 1867 so as to require him to convey all instructions to military commanders through the commanding general of the army, Ulysses S. Grant—initially a moderate on Reconstruction, Grant had become alienated by Johnson's conduct and so could be counted on to block any attempt by him to interfere with the administration of the Military Reconstruction Act. Next Congress passed the TENURE OF OFFICE ACT, which prohibited the President from removing any official appointed by him with the consent of the Senate without that body's concurrence. Its purpose was to prevent Johnson from replacing Republican officeholders with his own adherents.

Johnson vetoed both the Military Reconstruction Act and the Tenure of Office Act, calling the first revolutionary and the second an unconstitutional intrusion by the legislative on the executive branch. Needless to say, Congress promptly overrode the vetoes, as it did his vetoes of supplementary military Reconstruction acts designed to close loopholes in the original one. By the time Congress adjourned in the summer of 1867 it seemed that Johnson had been rendered officially and politically impotent.

Again appearances proved deceptive. In spite of all of his frustrations and humiliations, Johnson remained confident that eventually the North would reject the imposition of bayonet rule and black suffrage on the South, a confidence that grew when several Northern states overwhelmingly defeated proposals to give blacks the vote. Also Johnson had high hopes that the Supreme Court, which in its EX PARTE MILLIGAN decision of 1866 had ruled that military tribunals lacked jurisdiction in areas where the regular courts were functioning, would declare military Reconstruction unconstitutional, and if given the opportunity would do the same to the Tenure of Office Act. Hence, during the late summer and fall of 1867, he launched a counteroffensive against the Republicans and their Reconstruction policies, with the climactic action being his suspension from office of Secretary of War EDWIN M. STANTON, who long had been collaborating with Congress in violation of his obligation to serve the President. To replace Stanton, he appointed Grant as acting secretary of war, hoping thereby to enhance the chance of the Senate, when Congress reconvened, approving Stanton's dismissal—or, should that fail to occur, of opening the way for a court test of the Tenure of Office Act.

It was a clever scheme—in fact, too clever, for its success required a greater adroitness than Johnson possessed. The Republicans realized that if Johnson were allowed to dismiss Stanton he then would be able to select a permanent Secretary of War who would assist him sabotaging military Reconstruction, something he already was attempting to do by various other means. Accordingly on 11 January 1868 the Senate refused to concur in Stanton's removal and declared that he still was Secretary of War.

Impeachment. This meant that Johnson now would have to resort to the courts. In anticipation of that, he had asked Grant not to relinquish the Secretary of War's office without prior notice, thus giving Johnson an opportunity to appoint another person to the post so as to make it necessary for Stanton to try to regain it by legal action. Grant had promised to do this, or at least had permitted Johnson to think that he had so promised. Instead, on the morning of 14 January, following the Senate's rejection of Stanton's dismissal,

Grant went to the War Department, locked the Secretary of War's office, and gave the key to a military aide who in turn handed it over to Stanton, thus enabling him to occupy the office. Johnson, on learning of what had happened, accused Grant of betraying him and it is possible that his accusation is valid. Even so, it was foolish of Johnson to expect Grant, the prospective Republican presidential candidate for 1868, to ruin that prospect by cooperating with him in his war with Congress.

Johnson climaxed his maladroit handling of the Stanton affair by naming Adjutant General Lorenzo P. Thomas Secretary of War and sending him to make what turned out to be a ludicrously futile attempt to gain possession of the office. All this did was to provide the Republicans with something that many of them had been seeking for a long time—a plausible excuse to impeach the President. On 24 February 1868 the House of Representatives passed, by a 126 to 47 vote, a resolution impeaching Johnson for "high crimes and misdemeanors," and on 2–3 March it adopted eleven articles of impeachment, most of them being variations of the charge that he had violated the Tenure of Office Act by trying to supplant Stanton with Thomas [see IMPEACHMENT OF ANDREW JOHNSON].

Johnson's trial, at which he was not required to be present, began on 30 March before the Senate sitting as a court of impeachment, with Chief Justice Salmon P. Chase presiding. The President's defense attorneys contended that the Tenure of Office Act was unconstitutional, and that even if it were not, it did not apply to Stanton because he had been appointed by Lincoln rather than Johnson; in addition, because IMPEACHMENT is a judicial and not a political process, Johnson could not be guilty of "high crimes and misdemeanors" because all he did was try to test the constitutionality of a law. The prosecution, which consisted of a committee from the House of Representatives, replied that the Tenure of Office Act was constitutional and that impeachment is and must be political in nature.

On 16 May the Senate voted on the eleventh impeachment article, which, because it combined the ten preceeding charges, seemed to offer the best chance of conviction. Thirty-five Senators declared Johnson guilty, nineteen voted to acquit. Ten days later votes on two other impeachment articles produced the same outcome. Since the Constitution specifies that at least two-thirds of the Senators present and voting must vote guilty in order to convict a President in an impeachment trial, Johnson escaped removal from office by the narrowest possible margin.

Seven Republicans joined with the Senate's ten Democrats and two nonparty conservatives to support acquittal. The seven recusants, as they were called, doubted the legal justification of impeachment, feared that deposing a President ultimately would hurt the REPUBLICAN PARTY and disliked the prospect of the ultra-Radical Senator Benjamin Wade of Ohio replacing Johnson, as he would have under the presidential succession law of that time owing to his being president pro tem of the Senate. In addition, during the trial Johnson let it be known that if allowed to remain in office he would cease his efforts to sabotage military Reconstruction and appoint a political neutral in place of Stanton, who had stated that he would resign if impeachment failed.

Most historians and legal experts agree that Johnson was innocent of the charges brought against him, a view confirmed by the Supreme Court in 1926 when it did what Johnson desired it to do in 1868—pronounce the Tenure of Office Act unconstitutional. On the other hand it is unlikely that Johnson's removal would have permanently weakened the presidency and even more unlikely that his acquittal left Presidents immune to congressional action. The same factors that produced the IMPERIAL PRESIDENCY of the twentieth century would have operated regardless of the outcome of Johnson's trial, and the fate of Richard M. Nixon demonstrates that a President guilty of flagrant misconduct can escape removal only by resigning first.

Evaluation. On 4 March 1869, Johnson left the White House without attending, as is customary, the inauguration of his successor. Manifestly his presidency had been a failure as regards its paramount concern, Reconstruction. Yet it did achieve two historically important successes in the field of foreign policy, the conduct of which Johnson left largely to Secretary of State WILLIAM H. SEWARD. One was compelling the French government, through a combination of diplomacy and tacit military pressure, to abandon its intervention in Mexico, thereby bringing an end to the greatest violation of the MONROE DOCTRINE until nearly a hundred years later when the Soviet Union attempted to turn CUBA into a missile base. The other was the purchase of Alaska from Russia in 1867 for $7,200,000 [see ALASKA PURCHASE TREATY], a transaction that proved extremely profitable and also expelled from the North American continent a potentially troublesome foreign presence. In addition, Johnson's administration saw the beginning of the reservation system for the INDIANS of the trans-Mississippi West, a system that in spite of serious defects probably was the most practicable one that could have been instituted at the time, given the unstoppable western surge of the American people. After returning to Tennessee, Johnson made several unsuccessful bids for a House seat before, in January 1875, winning election to the United States Senate—the sole former President ever to do so. Again becoming a member of the body that had almost expelled him from the White House gave Johnson a sense of satisfaction and vindication that was all the stronger because by then it was evident that the North had become disillusioned with Republican Reconstruction policies and that the South was achieving what Johnson in effect had given it in 1865—home rule and white supremacy. He did not, however, enjoy his triumph long. On 28 July, while visiting a daughter in Tennessee, he suffered a stroke and three days later died. He was buried in Greeneville, his body wrapped in a United States flag and with his copy of the Constitution beneath his head.

Johnson sought political power throughout his entire adult life. Ironically for him, and tragically for the nation, when he acquired, as a result of an assassin's bullet, the power of the presidency, he proved incapable of using it in a positive and effective fashion. Although he possessed great courage and determination, sincere and strong convictions, and considerable natural ability, he lacked most of the other qualities of a true statesman, notably tact, flexibility, and insight and foresight. Consequently he failed greatly in meeting the great challenge that faced him in dealing with Reconstruction. He was the wrong man in the wrong place at the wrong time.

BIBLIOGRAPHY

Brock, William R. *An American Crisis: Congress and Reconstruction, 1865–1867*. 1963.

Castel, Albert. *The Presidency of Andrew Johnson*. 1979.

DeWitt, David Miller. *The Impeachment and Trial of Andrew Johnson*. 1903. Reprint 1967.

McKitrick, Eric L. *Andrew Johnson and Reconstruction*. 1960.

Milton, George Fort. *The Age of Hate: Andrew Johnson and the Radicals*. 1930.

Trefousse, Hans L. *Andrew Johnson: A Biography*. 1989.

ALBERT CASTEL

JOHNSON, LADY BIRD (b. 1912), First Lady, wife of Lyndon Baines Johnson. A political wife for nearly three decades by the time she became FIRST LADY, Claudia Alta (Lady Bird) Taylor Johnson brought considerable Washington experience to the job. She had run her husband's congressional office briefly during World War II, been active as a Senator's wife and, as spouse of the Vice President, filled in frequently for JACQUELINE KENNEDY.

Lady Bird Johnson enlarged the First Lady's staff and filled it with particularly skilled people, including a newspaperwoman, Elizabeth Carpenter, as chief of staff. Active in promoting many items on her husband's domestic agenda, including Head Start, Lady Bird Johnson headed her own drive to limit highway advertising by law, encourage people to clean up unsightly areas, and plant trees where they were needed. Her staff called their work a beautification program, although she was not entirely comfortable with that description. In 1964 when her husband faced considerable opposition in the South because of his stand on civil rights, she campaigned on her own through seven states, traveling by a train known as the Lady Bird Special, thus opening the way for women to work independently for their husbands' election.

BIBLIOGRAPHY

Carpenter, Liz. *Ruffles and Flourishes*. 1969.
Gould, Lewis L. *Lady Bird Johnson and the Environment*. 1988.
Johnson, Lady Bird. *A White House Diary*. 1970.

BETTY BOYD CAROLI

JOHNSON, LYNDON B. (1908–1973), thirty-sixth President of the United States (1963–1969). Lyndon Baines Johnson was born on 27 August 1908 near Stonewall, Texas, in the Perdinales Valley, which would be the wellspring of his political career and was the setting he delighted to return to for physical and emotional replenishment.

Early Life. In this rural Texas world, Johnson grew up. His father, who had served in the Texas legislature, had lost money in cotton speculation, and while the family never suffered acute poverty—and was never as poor as Lyndon Johnson later would say it had been—the boy was sensitized to the ups and downs in the lives of ordinary people. Johnson's mother, Rebekah Baines, hailed from Fredericksburg, Texas. Her father, Joseph Baines, had held the seat in the Texas lower house that Sam Johnson later occupied. Rebekah early displayed a rare love of learning that persuaded her parents to send her to Baylor College at Belton.

Johnson grew up in the latter part of the Progressive era. He was also influenced by his close contact with Mexican Americans, and through those relationships he internalized the need for a more pluralistic America he would come later to recognize and foster.

Johnson was also shaped by the Texas oil and cattle booms that were creating immense wealth for a handful of people. He could imagine himself a rich man, not only to enjoy the better things of life but also to help bring succor to the less fortunate. But getting rich was only one of his ambitions. The other was to be a politician. As a boy of eleven, when his father won back his old seat in the Texas legislature, Lyndon often visited legislative sessions with the elder Johnson and later found himself aping his father's mannerisms and style—including especially his eagerness to listen to constituents and serve their needs.

In 1927, Lyndon Johnson enrolled in Southwest Texas State Teachers College. He took a job teaching at a "Mexican" school in Cotulla, Texas, and there he came to understand the extent of the poverty that was the lifelong lot of so many Mexican Americans. His acceptance in the Chicano community would eventually help him to carry Texas for the Kennedy-Johnson ticket in 1960. By the time Johnson graduated from college in 1930, the depression had struck. He taught at Sam Houston High School in Houston, where he made a lasting reputation for his labors in teaching public speaking and debate. Still, he kept his eye on the main chance. It came with an opportunity to help elect Richard Kleberg to the U.S. House of Representatives. Dick Kleberg was the son of the owner of the King Ranch—the largest ranch in the world. At one stroke, Johnson was in politics and in the orbit of great wealth.

When Kleberg went to Washington in 1932, he took Johnson along as his private secretary. In a short time, Johnson's almost manic energy had become one of the wonders of Capitol Hill. Johnson's herculean labors on behalf of Kleberg's constituents and his almost instinctive grasp of the intricacies of legislative politics was phenomenal—the envy of countless other members of Congress and their staffs. In 1934, Johnson married twenty-one-year-old Claudia Alta Taylor of Karnak, Texas. When she was an infant a nursemaid had describer her as "pretty as a ladybird," and the nickname stuck [see LADY BIRD JOHNSON]. Johnson was intrigued that his initials and Lady Bird's were the same, and they made sure their children, their dogs, and even their ranch had the same initials. Their daughter Lynda Bird Johnson was born in 1944, and Luci Baines Johnson three years later. Johnson only gradually came to recognize how much Lady Bird stabilized his frenetic life and how much he owed to her extraordinary ability to judge people.

Washington Career. Washington, quite as much as Texas, became the Johnsons' home. Johnson drew inspiration from the uncommon popularity of President Franklin D. Roosevelt. Roosevelt's mastery of the radio as a tool of leadership and his determination to enlist the federal government on behalf of society's less fortunate were altering the national political landscape. Johnson could see that plugging into the broad disbursement of federal monies would provide an avenue to political power. In 1937 he was elected to the U.S. House of Representatives. Unlike many of his peers, Johnson was not a lawyer (although he attended Georgetown University Law School in 1934) but he had an uncanny nose for the people who could help him up the political ladder. The most important of them was fellow Democrat and Texan Sam Rayburn, the Speaker of the House. A bachelor, Rayburn often enjoyed the Johnsons' hospitality. A born sycophant, Johnson took worshipful counsel from Rayburn, even as he seemed to many people to take advantage of Rayburn's loneliness. Rayburn responded to the flattery by coming to regard Johnson almost as a son and made him a Capitol Hill insider, which his junior status in Congress did not entitle him to be. Johnson was reelected to the House five times, serving until 31 December 1948.

In June 1940, Johnson had become a special duty officer with naval intelligence in the United States Naval Reserve. After PEARL HARBOR he went on active duty (the first member of the House to do so) with the rank of lieutenant commander. In 1942 he was awarded the Silver Star for gallantry in action. Critics have maintained that his political prominence was more important than his personal bravery in his receiving this decoration, which ever afterward he wore in his lapel. After six months in the service, Johnson responded to President Roosevelt's request that members of Congress return from the military and resume their legislative duties.

Johnson had made an unsuccessful bid for a Senate seat in 1941, but in 1948, running against Coke Stevenson, he was the victor by eighty-seven votes. Ever afterward opponents delighted in referring to him derisively as "Landslide Lyndon." Comfortably reelected in 1954, Johnson meanwhile became a mover and shaker in the upper house. In turn, he was elected Democratic whip (1951) and Democratic leader (1953). Then, as Majority Leader (from 1956 to 1960), he earned national standing by helping Republican President Dwight D. Eisenhower pursue important bipartisan initiatives. Johnson's reputation as a legislative statesman helped to balance his other reputation—that of being a legislative wheeler-dealer and arm-twister.

In 1955 Johnson suffered a severe heart attack ("the worst you could have and still survive," he would say) that took a greater toll than the public realized. Aware that his father had died young, he seemed more than ever in a hurry to reach his goals. He would thereafter carry around with him a copy of his latest electrocardiogram—constantly concerned that he would suffer a recurrence.

Long aiming for the presidency and convinced that the office was not necessarily closed to a national figure from south of the Mason-Dixon line, he presented himself in 1960 as a man of experience who knew how to navigate the legislative shoals.

Vice Presidency. At the Democratic national convention held in the Los Angeles from 11 to 15 July 1960, Johnson's name was placed in nomination for the presidency by his old friend Sam Rayburn. Johnson received only 409 of the 1,521 votes, however, and John F. Kennedy, with 806, won on the first ballot. Deeply disappointed in the outcome, Johnson accepted the offer of the vice presidential place from Kennedy, knowing that many in the Kennedy camp opposed the choice. The ticket barely defeated the Republican nominees, Richard M. Nixon of California and Henry Cabot Lodge of Massachusetts with 50.08 percent to 49.92 percent of the popular vote and 303 electoral votes to 219.

Kennedy consulted Vice President Johnson on major matters, but, understandably, Johnson did not like being merely Vice President. His frustration seemed to enlarge certain outward traits of his personality: his fervent physical embraces of people, which some observers believed showed an unrequited desire to be loved, and his ready use of scatological language, which suggested to some that he had a feeling of inferiority that, despite his physical size (he stood six feet, three inches tall and usually weighed more than two hundred pounds) he seemed never able to overcome. After years of being at the center of the political action in Washington, Johnson concluded that the Kennedy brothers were simply shunting him aside. Still, he served on the NATIONAL SECURITY COUNCIL and chaired both the National Aeronautics and Space Council and the President's Committee on Equal Employment Opportunity. Although he met the leaders of the world, including President Konrad Adenauer of West Germany and Charles de Gaulle of France, he was also sent on minor missions (to the Middle East, Greece, Italy and the Vatican, and Scandinavia) that he could only think of as make-work activity. This role added to the awkwardness Johnson felt in an administration shaped by the elegance and poise of a presidential couple whose style he both envied and resented. What rankled most of all was that the administration seemed to be studiously ignoring his renowned knowledge of Congress despite the President's patent inability to push through his legislative program.

The assassination of President Kennedy in Dallas, Texas, on 22 November 1963 was one of the transforming events of modern American history. Johnson, who had persuaded Kennedy to travel to Texas, was riding in the motorcade behind the President when the fatal bullets struck. Johnson was sworn in shortly afterward aboard *Air Force One* as it stood at Dallas's Love Field before its return to Washington bearing Kennedy's remains as well as the shattered presidential party. The oath of office was administered by federal district judge Sarah Tilghman Hughes in the presence, among others, of Lady Bird Johnson and JACQUELINE KENNEDY. One of the new President's first acts was the appointment of a commission to investigate and report on the assassination. Headed by Chief Justice Earl Warren, it concluded in 1964 that LEE HARVEY OSWALD had acted alone in assassinating Kennedy [*see* WARREN COMMISSION].

The Great Society. In assuming office, Johnson felt generally comfortable with the Cabinet he inherited, which more than once he would say was his choicest legacy from Kennedy. The glaring exception was Attorney General ROBERT F. KENNEDY, brother of the late President, whom Johnson viewed as the putative inheritor of John Kennedy's mantle and charisma, and therefore a rival base of power. Bobby had quickly become for millions of his brother's worshipful admirers the living symbol of the Camelot that had been lost. As such, his continuation in the Cabinet was a bone in the throat for Johnson who knew—to his unspeakable anguish—that many Americans considered their new President to be somehow a "usurper," wrongfully sitting in the slain hero's chair. Nevertheless, for Johnson to have fired the Attorney General would have been politically disastrous. Kennedy finally resigned in 1964 to run for the Senate from New York.

Johnson found himself especially relying on Secretary of State Dean Rusk, Secretary of Defense ROBERT S. McNAMARA, and the Assistant to the President for National Security Affairs, McGeorge Bundy, in dealing with increasingly nettlesome issues of war and peace. But these matters did not immediately come to the fore.

On his own now, Johnson exhibited a spate of energy that had not been seen in the White House since the early days of Franklin Roosevelt. Johnson's aides liked to think of him as having "extra glands," for despite the fact that the new President took a nap every afternoon, he was endlessly on the telephone cajoling and imprecating for the domestic goals of his administration. And whenever he returned to the White House he brought along what he called his "night reading" to prepare for the next day. Johnson was not a student of history: he regarded history as the work of the famous people he had met and known. Still, he was determined to out-Roosevelt Roosevelt and enter the pages of history as one of the great Chief Executives. In a self-conscious way, he frequently spoke in public and in private of being "your President," as if he was

burdened by the office as well as glorying in it. In his first address to Congress on 27 November 1963, Johnson resolved to continue the work begun under his predecessor and to make the passage of the civil rights bill a monument to Kennedy's memory.

Johnson's efforts to turn the bill into law involved his performing the most earnest presidential lobbying of Congress in the country's history—the more remarkable because he was the first president from the South since Woodrow Wilson. All of the techniques that Johnson had learned and perfected in his days on Capitol Hill he now drew upon. Kennedy's bill, which had been made stronger by amendments, passed the House early in February 1964. There followed a filibuster in the Senate that lasted eighty-three days but was finally broken by a cloture resolution. The bill passed on 2 July 1964. Its enactment swiftly and profoundly changed the United States. Later, contemplating his achievement, Johnson would say that he had brought the bill into law at the cost of "eleven states and twenty-two men"—that is, the states that had once made up the Confederacy and their Senators in Washington. The CIVIL RIGHTS ACT OF 1964 forbade discrimination on account of race in places of public accommodation; it prohibited discrimination by labor unions and prospective employers on account of color or sex; it contained fresh guarantees of African Americans' VOTING RIGHTS; and it established the Equal Employment Opportunity Commission to monitor enforcement of the law. To speed up school desegregation, it empowered the DEPARTMENT OF JUSTICE to institute court challenges against alleged discriminatory practices in local school districts.

While this powerful law was the centerpiece of Johnson's legislative achievement, it also represented the completion of the Kennedy inheritance. At least fifty other bills were on Johnson's own agenda, as he placed himself in the tradition of the liberal Democrats who had come to power in 1933 and crafted first the NEW DEAL and then, under Harry S. Truman, the FAIR DEAL. Johnson's successor program would bear the name the GREAT SOCIETY—a Texas-size version of what Progressives had long ago envisioned as the Good Society. Johnson defined it thus: "The Great Society rests on abundance and liberty for all. It demands an end to poverty and injustice, to which we are totally committed in our time." To achieve it, Johnson drove himself and his staff relentlessly, sometimes fearing as he gathered material for his STATE OF THE UNION MESSAGES that he would run out of ideas for new programs. Yet Johnson refused to label himself precisely. He had said a few years earlier: "I am a free man, an American, a United States Senator, and a Democrat, in that order. I am also a liberal, a conservative, a consumer, a parent, a voter . . . all those things in no fixed order."

The most important of the Great Society legislation was the Economic Opportunity Act, the first cannon shot in his War on Poverty, a struggle at the heart of what he called "my hope for America" (the title he gave to a campaign book published over his byline in 1964). Signed in August 1964, the far-reaching law, funded with an appropriation of almost a billion dollars, created the Office of Economic Opportunity (OEO) as part of the White House and authorized several major initiatives. One was VISTA (Volunteers in Service to America), a kind of domestic Peace Corps marshaled to work in depressed areas of the country. Another was the Job Corps, which aimed to retrain the hard-core unemployed. Reputedly one of the most successful Great Society programs was Head Start, designed to help disadvantaged preschool-age children, mostly in the inner cities, to overcome their cultural deprivation. Johnson's plea for Medicare health insurance for the elderly finally culminated in the passage of a satisfactory bill, which the President signed on 30 July 1965 in the presence of Harry Truman, one of the concept's original supporters. In October 1965 Johnson journeyed to the Statue of Liberty to sign a new immigration bill that eliminated the national origins quota. With no less zeal, Johnson, who longed to be known as "the education president," signed his education bill, which provided $1.5 billion in aid to elementary and secondary schools; the venue he chose for the signing was the little Texas schoolhouse that he had attended as a boy.

Johnson's apparent zeal for reform, which more than matched that of his mentor, Franklin Roosevelt, failed—to Johnson's everlasting dismay—to generate popularity and enthusiasm in the public mind. Possibly the country had developed legislative muscle fatigue, after the long generation of reforms under successive Democratic Chief Executives. Perhaps the use of television to dramatize and publicize his work had overexposed Johnson to public scrutiny. Or maybe Johnson's own hard-driving personality failed to mesh with the people's notion of what a President should be. Some Americans thought it unseemly for Johnson to display for photographers the scar that had resulted from the surgical removal of his gall bladder in October 1965; others could not forget the picture of him lifting his pet beagle by the ears. These were small matters, but they were enlarged by the media. Johnson's inclination sometimes to dissimulate in answering questions at PRESS CONFERENCES opened the way for cynical critics to aver that this "cowboy President" hailed from a place in the Southwest called "Credibility Gap." Johnson's penchant for uncommon confidentiality in his dealings added to the impression that he had the style of a riverboat gambler. He often talked to people nose-to-nose, a manner that some, particularly political opponents, took to be intimidating. (Johnson's arm-around-the-shoulders gesture, combined with words whispered into the ear, may have been an accommodation to his considerable deafness, which he was bent on hiding from the public as well as his colleagues.)

Election of 1964 and Vietnam. No one could sensibly doubt that Johnson would receive the Democratic nomination when the party convened in Atlantic City, New Jersey, in August 1964. Much attention was focused on the choice of a vice presidential nominee. Johnson played the role of interested suitor with several candidates and finally settled on Senator Hubert H. Humphrey of Minnesota, who had entered the Senate with him in 1948. Humphrey, a warm, gracious, and garrulous man with a long record of support for civil rights legislation, would be kept under tight control by Johnson. (When Humphrey himself ran for President in 1968, Johnson pettily refused him access to the "idea folder"—the collection of possible proposals for new legislation assembled by Johnson's staff for state of the union messages.) Meanwhile, a month earlier the Republicans had nominated the conservative Senator from Arizona, Barry Goldwater, on the first ballot at their convention in San Francisco. Goldwater's running mate was the New York congressman William Miller. The Republican Party, long dominated by its eastern, liberal wing, had been taken over by its right wing, centered in the South and West. The American people, its leaders said, would now have "a choice, not an echo." Republican easterners— among them the runners-up William W. Scranton of Pennsylvania and Nelson A. Rockefeller of New York—aimed to tone down the extremists in the party, but in his acceptance address Goldwater hurled down the gauntlet, proclaiming, "Extremism in the defense of liberty is no vice!" Already the long-festering civil war in Vietnam was heating up, and the public was becoming wary of the increasing involvement of the United States in Southeast Asia. Goldwater's remark to a reporter that, if he could, he would "drop a low-yield atomic bomb on Chinese supply lines in Vietnam" was not reassuring to voters. The Johnson campaign made skillful use of a television commercial that showed the detonation of a nuclear device, capitalizing on the public's fear of a nuclear exchange with the communist world.

Johnson campaigned as a temperate, experienced candidate who could be counted upon to be prudent and thoughtful. The theme was that no one should mistake his Texas accent for the tone of a provincial man: he was well aware that there was a world out there with which the United States had to deal. He had met other nations' leaders, not only through his travels as Vice President but also on the sad occasion of the Kennedy funeral, and he felt he was on easy terms with them.

In July 1964, even before the campaign got underway, Johnson dispatched five hundred more American troops to Vietnam. There were already about seventeen thousand on duty there, some having first been sent as "advisers," under President Dwight D. Eisenhower in 1954 and the buildup having continued through the Kennedy administration. The new shipment of troops did not seem exceptional, nor did the public seem aroused or distressed by a supposed attack, on 4 August 1964, on U.S. destroyers by North Vietnamese gunboats in the Gulf of Tonkin off the coast of North Vietnam. The President reported the incident in a television address and announced that the United States would carry out retaliatory air strikes against North Vietnam.

The public was generally satisfied when Congress, at Johnson's behest, passed the GULF OF TONKIN RESOLUTION, which authorized the President to take "all necessary measures to repel any armed attack against the forces of the United States and to prevent further aggression." The vote on the measure, which would prove the basis for Johnson's increasing involvement in the VIETNAM WAR, was overwhelming: 416 to 0 in the House and 88 to 2 in the Senate. Johnson did not reveal that only hours before the alleged attack, South Vietnamese patrol boats had bombarded North Vietnamese coastal islands.

Even as the United States was fatefully escalating its involvement in Vietnam, Johnson was trying to make it clear to the American electorate that he did not seek a broader war. In memorable words he declared, "We are not about to send American boys nine or ten thousand miles from home to do what Asian boys ought to be doing for themselves." The 1964 election meanwhile came to its expected conclusion: the Johnson-Humphrey ticket received the largest percentage of the popular vote in the history of presidential canvasses—61 percent. In the Electoral College Johnson won 486 votes to Goldwater's 52. As 1965 began, the Democrats had a 36-seat majority in the Senate and a 118-seat majority in the House. There would be no struggle with the Hill over Johnson's programs. At his triumphant inauguration on 20 January Johnson—President at last in his own right—took the oath of office with Lady Bird holding the Bible: the

first time that a President's wife had participated in the ceremony. Mrs. Johnson's ardent campaign to restore the scenic beauty of the United States was a pioneering effort to deal with the degradation of the environment. The First Lady was a force at the White House Conference on Natural Beauty held in May 1965, as well as in achieving passage of the Highway Beautification Act of 1965, which established a fund to eliminate roadside billboards and create scenic easements. Her work underscored her role as a savvy political adviser and partner of the President.

By the end of 1964, the fighting in Vietnam had drawn twenty-three thousand Americans into the fray. When, in February 1965, Viet Cong units attacked an American barracks at Pleiku, Johnson ordered raids against North Vietnamese supply lines and military installations. Shortly afterward, U.S. ground units went into action. Johnson and his advisers miscalculated, thinking that the overwhelming power of the United States would erode North Vietnam's willingness and ability to carry on the struggle. He was also smitten by the idea that if South Vietnam fell under Communist control a "domino effect" would quickly drop all of Southeast Asia into the communist camp. This view was strengthened by his memory of how Hitler had been appeased at Munich in 1938, an event that he constantly called to mind. He came to regard Ho Chih Minh, the leader of North Vietnam, as a rival politician with whom he could eventually make a deal, and he believed that keeping the pressure on Ho would eventually force him to halt the war. Johnson's apparent affection for the use of military force had been shown in the spring of 1965, when he sent U.S. Marines into the DOMINICAN REPUBLIC, a move that caused some commentators to denounce him as the "gendarme of the world counter-revolution."

By mid 1966, 265,000 American military men and women were in Vietnam, yet the struggle went on. Johnson was soon caught between hawks and doves: the hawks urging that the full U.S. military be deployed against North Vietnam; the doves arguing that the United States had no business in Vietnam and that the operation ought to be stopped. Johnson feared that attempting to destroy North Vietnam would bring China into the fray, as it had entered the KOREAN WAR. But he could not pull out because he did not want to be "the first President to lose a war." So Johnson and his aides slowly increased the troop commitment, confident that there was "light at the end of the tunnel."

Despite numerous efforts to bring about a negotiated settlement, including a gigantic "peace offensive" at Christmastime 1965, the fierce guerrilla war continued. The relentless struggle was made more treacherous for the American and South Vietnamese forces by the need to fight not only the North Vietnamese troops, who came down from the North along the Ho Chih Minh Trail in an endless stream, but also their allies, the Viet Cong. These irregulars were South Vietnamese communists skilled at tormenting their enemies by stealth while seeming to be part of the general population. By the end of 1967, almost half a million Americans under arms were on duty in Vietnam. They soon confronted North Vietnam's Tet Offensive during the Vietnamese New Year, when, traditionally, a truce had been observed by both sides. Enemy troops under General Vo Nguyen Giap launched simultaneous attacks on thirty South Vietnamese cities. While the communists paid heavily for the offensive, which was eventually contained, the costly battles deeply influenced American opinion. The administration, shocked and embarrassed, underwent close scrutiny from the Senate Foreign Relations Committee in televised hearings that began in March 1968. General William C. Westmoreland, who had consistently issued optimistic reports, was relieved of his command. Westmoreland later complained in his book, *A Soldier Reports*, that "press and television had created an aura not of victory but of defeat, and timid officials in Washington listened more to the media than to their representatives on the scene."

Johnson now knew he must get out of the war, especially after he was told that another 206,000 troops would have to be sent to the tormented land in order, as he liked to say, to "nail the coonskin to the wall." Meanwhile, the home front was boiling as college students, taking the lead in opposing the war, marched and held teach-ins on the subject. The highly charged atmosphere stimulated resistance to the draft and a hostility to the military that included opposition to universities housing scientific research that might have a national defense purpose. At countless colleges and universities, student rallies were punctuated with the cruel chant, "Hey, hey, LBJ, how many kids did you kill today?" (The American death toll was reaching five hundred a week as 1967 came to a close; the total number of American dead for the entire war would eventually reach fifty-three thousand.) Johnson had made the war a personal matter often speaking of "my planes" and "my troops" as he and aides planned military steps almost every Tuesday at lunch in the President's private dining room. The intimate gatherings of the so-called Tuesday Cabinet no doubt held Johnson and his people together in a tight bond of mutual loyalty and dependence strengthened by their increasing sense of beleaguerment.

Early in January 1968, Senator EUGENE J. MCCARTHY of Minnesota, a strong foe of the Vietnam War, announced that he would seek the Democratic presidential nomination. Such an affront to a sitting President of the same party was almost unheard of. Entering the New Hampshire primary, McCarthy startled the nation by winning 42 percent of the vote—a return that was read everywhere as a defeat for Johnson. Almost immediately, ROBERT F. KENNEDY, a brother of the slain President and now a Senator from New York, also threw his hat into the ring. This candidacy was salt in the wound for Johnson, whose nightmare was that he would be remembered as the President who had been sandwiched between two Kennedys, who, he thought, both considered him an inferior person. Johnson was determined now to open negotiations to end the war, although he emphasized that the outcome could not be "peace at any price." On 31 March, in a nationally televised address, Johnson announced another plan to "Vietnamize" the war. Near the end of the speech he dropped a bombshell: he would not run for reelection lest "the Presidency become involved in the partisan divisions that are developing in this political year." Later in his memoirs, *The Vantage Point* (1971), Johnson said that he had decided in January 1965 that he would not seek another term in the White House. In the meantime, he appointed CLARK CLIFFORD—a longtime adviser to Presidents going back to Truman, an honored insider, and a known hawk—to be the Secretary of Defense and to find the formula for ending the fighting. Peace talks opened in Paris in May 1968, but they went nowhere, for the North Vietnamese insisted that the United States cease all acts of war against them as a condition for negotiating. Many people, including Johnson himself, held the opinion that North Vietnam would wait the short while for the presidency to change hands in expectation of reaching a more advantageous settlement.

Even as the war and the associated events at home ate into Johnson physical and political health, racial conflict was convulsing America's cities. It reached a high point with the assassination of the Reverend Martin Luther King, Jr., on 4 April 1968, which touched off riots in cities all over the country. Despite Johnson's herculean efforts to win and extend civil rights legislation (the CIVIL RIGHTS ACT OF 1968 aimed to end discrimination in public housing), Johnson's relations with the black community had been damaged by the war, which was widely viewed as a war against nonwhite people. Moreover, although the cost of the war was paid for by borrowing rather than taxation (for Johnson believed it was possible to have both guns and butter), most African Americans did not share in the general prosperity. The resulting resentment in the inner cities, coupled with the gradual disappearance of jobs for unskilled workers, which had long served as entry-level jobs for school dropouts, produced marked unrest in the urban centers. City after city experienced long, hot summers, possibly in part because the emphasis by some African American leaders had shifted from a call for integration to one for black power. Finally, the long neglect of the needs of the black poor, in the face of the unsuccessful war that weakened respect for government leaders, now came to the fore. In 1965 the Watts district of Los Angeles blew up in ferocious disorder; Cleveland burst into flames in 1966; Newark and Detroit in 1967; and Washington in 1968—the fires and bedlam clearly visible from the White House, where soldiers patrolled the grounds.

The unprecedented racial turmoil led Johnson in 1967 to appoint a National Advisory Commission on Civil Disorders. Headed by Governor Otto D. Kerner of Illinois, it warned in its report, issued the following year, that the United States was turning into two societies, one black, one white—"separate and unequal." The report polarized the country between those who agreed that profound social changes were needed and those who believed that tougher law enforcement supplied the necessary answer.

The assassination of Robert Kennedy in Los Angeles in June 1968 stunned the nation, which was already reeling from the effects of King's slaying. When the Democrats gathered for their convention in Chicago in August, it was clear that the great domestic and international issues generated by the Johnson administration would be thoroughly aired. Antiwar advocates championed either McCarthy or GEORGE McGOVERN, Senator from South Dakota, and expected to win a plank in the party platform calling for the withdrawal of American forces from Vietnam. The supporters of Humphrey, backed the administration's policy of holding talks and refusing to withdraw unless North Vietnam did so as well. In the end only 40 percent of the convention delegates voted against the Humphrey position, and Humphrey went on to win the nomination. Meanwhile, outside the convention hall, antiwar demonstrators, irate at the proceedings, pelted the unsympathetic Chicago police with bottles and bricks. Goaded by the perceived abuse, the police struck back. The ensuing melee, seen by millions on television, seemed sure proof that the republic was in deep trouble, if not tottering. Unable to free himself from Johnson's position on the war, which he had faithfully upheld for years, Humphrey could not win the election, although it has often been said that if the campaign had run a week or two longer he might have

caught up with his Republican opponent, Richard Nixon. Humphrey broke with Johnson's policy by calling for an end to the bombing of North Vietnam, to Johnson's unbounded annoyance. Then a month later, only a week before the election, Johnson announced an end to all air, naval, and artillery bombardment. It was too late to help Humphrey, who would remain embittered by Johnson's treatment of him during the campaign.

The Administration Unravels. The powerful events of the late 1960s blunted the development of the Great Society, and its programs failed to fulfill their promise of putting an end to poverty. But in 1967 Johnson had obvious pleasure in appointing Thurgood Marshall to a vacancy on the Supreme Court, the first African American so honored. This great-grandson of a slave would in time be a bulwark of the liberal wing of the Court and would give voice to some of Johnson's deeply felt and often frustrated desires for a better America.

Johnson's other appointment to the High Court—in October 1965—had been ABE FORTAS, an old friend from Texas, later a prominent lawyer in Washington. A reluctant appointee, Fortas became a cause célèbre when Johnson chose to elevate him to become Chief Justice upon Earl Warren's retirement in 1968. Amid cries and charges of cronyism and improper conduct, which Fortas refused to fight, Fortas withdrew his name—a defeat which only added to the sense of popular rejection that hurt Johnson so deeply.

Johnson had suffered another humiliation in January 1968, on the eve of the Tet offensive, when the USS *Pueblo*, an intelligence-gathering vessel on patrol off the North Korean city of Wonsan, was seized by North Korean gunboats and the crew of eighty men interned. In a fury, Johnson called fifteen thousand air and navy reservists to active duty and ordered the aircraft carrier *Enterprise* to patrol the Korean coast. While Johnson may have been protecting the honor of the navy and demonstrating that the United States was not paralyzed by the stalemate in Vietnam, the crew and ship were not returned until eleven months later, after a painful admission by the United States—later repudiated—that the vessel had indeed been wrongly positioned.

Johnson's experiences abundantly demonstrated the truth of John Kennedy's observation that to judge a President, one must know "what he had going for him." Even his dream of going to Moscow to help negotiate a treaty limiting antiballistic missiles—a counterpiece to his War on Poverty—was shattered by events. Long planned for the beginning of October, the journey was canceled just as the tumultuous Democratic convention was getting underway in August 1968, after 200,000 Soviet and Warsaw Pact troops invaded Czechoslovakia to suppress a movement aimed at liberating the country from communism.

But for this egregious Soviet action, the Strategic Arms Limitations (SALT) would have begun during Johnson's presidency—a delay that pained Johnson to the quick. He had always hoped fervently that he might play a significant role in thawing the COLD WAR.

To this end, the administration had long been endeavoring to bring under control the design, manufacture and deployment of antiballistic missiles. Johnson was keenly conscious, as he wrote Soviet premier Aleksey N. Kosygin on 27 January 1967, that unrestrained ABM competition with the Soviet Union would incur "on both sides colossal costs without enhancing the security of our own peoples or contributing to the prospects for a stable peace in the world." Again in May Johnson wrote Kosygin urging serious discussions.

Kosygin played Hamlet. When he decided to attend a UNITED NATIONS session in late June, he agreed to sit down with the President. Yet Johnson would not travel to New York for the purpose. Kosygin, unwilling to meet in Washington or at Camp David, lest he offend the Arabs, North Vietnamese, and Chinese, finally agreed to a get-together with the President held in the little college town of Glassboro, New Jersey, on 23–26 June. Although Kosygin seemed impressed by the logic of Johnson's arguments for arms reduction, the Soviet leader seemed unable to make a commitment, likely because of policy disagreement in the Kremlin. Johnson would write: "I left Glassboro . . . with mixed feelings—disappointment that we had not solved any major problem but hope that we had moved to a better understanding of our differences."

On 1 July 1968 the United States and the Soviet Union finally signed the Treaty on the Nonproliferation of Nuclear Weapons that had been in negotiation since 1964. The Senate did not ratify it until March 1969, when Johnson was gone from the White House. Johnson's frustration in dealing with the Soviet Union can be measured in light of his confidence that he was highly skilled in the art of diplomacy and of his overweening desire to depart office with success on something other than Vietnam.

As Johnson prepared to leave the Presidency, he was aware that despite his brilliance (a sharp Senate critic of his had once said, "Gosh, he must have an IQ of 200") and the intense fire in his belly to attain his lofty goals, his administration had come at the wrong point in the historical cycle. The age of reform in which he had grown up politically was ending, and world communism was already beginning to retreat on its own. Laboring against the tide, as he had in his quest for the Great Society, he would in the end aver, "We tried to do too much too quickly."

Postpresidential Years. Fulfilling his boyhood goal of becoming rich, Johnson had used his increasing political power in Texas to gain advantages that might be more carefully scrutinized today, building up a multimillion-dollar fortune in real estate and television stations, which Lady Bird Johnson helped to manage. Mrs. Johnson had inherited thirty-eight hundred acres of land in Alabama, and while Johnson was Vice President he had acquired fifteen thousand acres of Texas land. He and a partner had bought a ranch from Texas Christian University for half a million dollars. But his pride and joy was the LBJ Ranch, although it was not really a "spread" on the order of the ones owned by the barons whose wealth he had once envied. (It consisted of the Johnson house and two hundred adjoining acres.) He donated it to the National Park Service, with the stipulation that Mrs. Johnson could use it as long as she lived.

Returning to private life on 20 January 1969, Johnson was increasingly hobbled by declining health. He grew more gaunt, his hair turned white, and his breathing became labored. His weight, always a problem, ballooned, and he took up cigarette smoking again, having once broken the habit. Ever conscious that the men in his family had died prematurely, he worked feverishly on the Lyndon Baines Johnson Library and Museum on the campus of the University of Texas at Austin; it was dedicated in May 1971. He also helped prepare his memoirs. But his heart condition, whose ravages had been a constant concern in the White House although the fact was kept hidden from the American people, was disabling him. (Constantly afraid of being laid up and unable to perform his duties, Johnson had been reassured somewhat by the ratification in 1967 of the TWENTY-FIFTH AMENDMENT, which sets forth a process for dealing with presidential disability.)

In one of his last public appearances, Johnson spoke feelingly, despite his considerable physical distress, at a memorable symposium on civil rights held at his library. Stricken fatally a few weeks later, he died in Austin on 22 January 1973. His body was flown to Washington to lie in state in the Capitol. Following the funeral in the National City Christian Church, Johnson's remains were returned to Texas and buried in the family cemetery on the LBJ Ranch.

Johnson died painfully aware that the Vietnam War has been the dark side of his moon. With all his might he wished he could have retraced the steps he had taken down the slippery path that had led to the shattering of his presidency. Still, he relied on historians to be kinder to him than so many of his contemporaries had been, and he expected to be remembered for his massive contribution to the causes of racial justice and a more equitable society.

BIBLIOGRAPHY

Bornet, Vaughn Davis. *The Presidency of Lyndon B. Johnson.* 1983.

Califano, Joseph A., Jr. *The Triumph and Tragedy of Lyndon Johnson.* 1991.

Caro, Robert A. *The Years of Lyndon Johnson: The Path to Power.* 1982.

Caro, Robert A. *The Years of Lyndon Johnson: Means of Ascent.* 1990.

Dallek, Robert. *Lone Star Rising: Lyndon Johnson and His Times, 1908–1960.* 1991.

Dugger, Ronnie. *The Politician: The Life and Times of Lyndon Johnson, The Drive for Power—from the Frontier to Master of the Senate.* 1982.

Graff, Henry F. *The Tuesday Cabinet: Deliberation and Decision on Peace and War under Lyndon B. Johnson.* 1970.

Johnson, Lady Bird. *A White House Diary.* 1970.

Johnson, Lyndon Baines. *The Vantage Point: Perspectives of the Presidency, 1963–69.* 1971.

Kearns, Doris. *Lyndon Johnson and the American Dream.* 1976.

Miller, Merle. *Lyndon: An Oral Biography.* 1980.

Steinberg, Alfred. *Sam Johnson's Boy.* 1968.

HENRY F. GRAFF

JOHNSON, RICHARD M. (1780–1850), Senator, ninth Vice President of the United States (1837–1841). A Jeffersonian and Jacksonian Democrat, Richard Mentor Johnson was born in 1780 in a frontier region near Louisville, Kentucky. He possessed little formal education, other than reading law in law offices. Johnson began practicing as a lawyer in 1802 and two years later he entered state politics.

Elected to Congress in 1807 (he would remain there until 1819), Johnson became a Jeffersonian and a nationalist. A supporter of Jefferson's embargo, Johnson spoke for war against Great Britain in 1812. At the outbreak of the WAR OF 1812, he left Congress (though not resigning his seat) to fight. Serving as an officer under General William Henry Harrison, Johnson distinguished himself at the Battle of the Thames. He allegedly killed Chief Tecumseh. The Tecumseh story, like Andrew Jackson's defeat of the British at New Orleans in 1815, became a part of DEMOCRATIC PARTY lore, later used in electioneering against William Henry Harrison in 1836 and 1840.

Johnson returned to Washington a war hero and played an important role in postwar economic policy-making. He favored a qualified program of INTERNAL IMPROVEMENTS, proposed compensation for war veterans, but opposed the establishment of the second BANK OF THE UNITED STATES. Sitting on the congressional committee on war, Johnson alone condoned Andrew Jackson's campaign in Florida. In 1816, he led a controversial congressional salary bill through Congress.

Johnson resigned from Congress in 1819 and entered the Kentucky state legislature. As had been many other western states, Kentucky was hard hit by the panic of 1819. The hasty contraction of the money supply by the Bank of the United States caused a run on several western state banks. Johnson emerged as Kentucky's chief spokesman against the bank and tight money. He led passage of a state bill abolishing imprisonment for debt; he would later argue for the same bill at the national level.

Johnson became a Senator in 1819, a post he would keep until 1829. A pro-Union nationalist, he favored the MISSOURI COMPROMISE OF 1820. In presidential politics, he supported HENRY CLAY in 1824. Increasingly, however, Johnson drifted towards a more egalitarian stance. He became an early member of the Democratic Party, joining the Jackson coalition in 1829. The move was natural. Johnson had played an important role in assisting AMOS KENDALL, a fellow Kentuckian, newspaper editor, and later Jackson Cabinet member.

Returned to the House of Representatives in 1829, Johnson developed a cordial relationship with the new President. Although not a strident economic liberal, Johnson agreed with Jackson's tariff reforms. Johnson originally voted for the Maysville road appropriations, but accepted Jackson's veto. He later supported Jackson's attack on the bank. Johnson also worked to repair the differences between the President and John C. Calhoun.

In 1831, Johnson became one of the Democrats' chief choices to replace Calhoun as the party's vice presidential nominee. A war hero like Jackson, Johnson possessed several distinct political assets: he was a well-liked westerner who could potentially balance Jackson rival Henry Clay's influence; and his position on debt relief and his egalitarian rhetoric appealed to the emerging eastern workingmen's parties. Congressional rejection of Martin Van Buren's appointment as minister to Britain, however, changed the political situation. Jackson seized on this rejection and decided to use it as an anticongressional weapon in 1832. At the first Democratic convention in 1832, the party chose Van Buren over Johnson and Philip Barbour as the vice presidential candidate.

Four years later, however, Johnson became Van Buren's running mate, choice made by retiring President Jackson himself. Johnson did not receive a majority of electoral votes for the vice presidency; the Senate subsequently elected him. Johnson played no appreciable role in the Van Buren administration. He made no lasting contributions to the momentous issues at stake during Van Buren's tenure, refraining from speaking out about the panic of 1837 or the congressional gag rule on abolitionist petitions.

In the election of 1840, Johnson proved to be a liability to the Democratic ticket. He had spent much of his adult life living openly with a mulatto mistress and had two children by her. The Whigs condemned Johnson, and the question of Johnson's personal morality became particularly significant in the South. After defeat in 1840, he retired to Kentucky and involved himself in several charitable concerns and local universities. He died in 1850.

BIBLIOGRAPHY

Latner, Richard B. *The Presidency of Andrew Jackson.* 1979.
Meyer, Leland W. *The Life and Times of Colonel Richard M. Johnson of Kentucky.* 1967.
Wilson, Major. *The Presidency of Martin Van Buren.* 1984.

JOHN F. WALSH

JOINT CHIEFS OF STAFF. The concept of a Joint Chiefs of Staff, to coordinate the military services, is a twentieth-century development. During the eighteenth and nineteenth centuries the army and the navy were wholly independent in terms of plans and, usually, operations. Inadequacies revealed in the SPANISH-AMERICAN WAR led to the first effort to improve coordination, the Joint Board, created in 1903. However, interservice cooperation remained uneven.

The requirements and pressures of planning for WORLD WAR II—including the need for a U.S. group to meet regularly with the British Chiefs of Staff—underscored the need for better coordination. In February 1942, the heads of the military services (Army Chief of Staff General GEORGE MARSHALL, Chief of Naval Operations Admiral Ernest King, Army Air Force Commander General Henry Arnold) constituted themselves as the Joint Chiefs of Staff (JCS), albeit without any formal charter or approval. Admiral William Leahy joined when he was named by President Franklin Roosevelt as Chief of Staff to the COMMANDER IN CHIEF. The JCS served as a unified strategic planning unit and commanded all U.S. forces throughout the world.

Toward the end of the war various plans surfaced for overhauling the entire national security structure, emerging finally as the 1947 NATIONAL SECURITY ACT. This act separated the air force from the army and formally created the JCS as "the principal military advisers" to both the President and new Secretary of Defense. In 1949, the position of a nonvoting chairman was created.

Relations between Presidents and the JCS have varied greatly, but are always dominated by the concept of civilian control of the military. Running somewhat counter to this is the provision of law allowing JCS members to dissent publicly from official policy—a right that has rarely been used to its full extent.

Presidential interaction with the JCS was most intense during the height of the COLD WAR, roughly from 1947 through 1975, the end of the VIETNAM WAR. President Harry S. Truman relied heavily on the first Chairman, General Omar Bradley. Truman sought JCS concurrence before relieving General Douglas MacArthur in 1951. Truman also relieved Chief of Naval Operations Admiral Louis Denfeld in 1949 after the so-called "revolt of the admirals" over the future of air power and a dispute with the air force about service "roles and missions." President Dwight D. Eisenhower, given his military background, felt better qualified to make defense decisions in a proper policy context than his JCS, and continually worried about JCS pleas for additional resources. Eisenhower also objected to public JCS dissents, believing they should simply comply with the Commander in Chief's decisions.

President John F. Kennedy felt he had been mislead by both the CENTRAL INTELLIGENCE AGENCY and the JCS on planning for the ill-fated BAY OF PIGS INVASION against Fidel Castro and failed to reappoint any incumbent JCS members when their current terms expired. Kennedy's Secretary of Defense, ROBERT S. MCNAMARA, was always skeptical of JCS and CIA estimates of Soviet capabilities, believing they largely served to promote increased U.S. defense spending. McNamara also kept very tight control over JCS dissents. President Lyndon B. Johnson got involved in a very detailed level of operational planning during the Vietnam War, and relied heavily on Chairman General Earle Wheeler. During President Richard M. Nixon's term, there was a certain degree of tension between the JCS and NATIONAL SECURITY ADVISER Henry Kissinger, especially over ARMS CONTROL with the U.S.S.R.

In 1986 Congress passed the Goldwater-Nichols Act, which increased the authority (and visibility) of the Chairman within the JCS and made him, rather than the corporate group, the President's principal military adviser.

Finally, in 1990, during the Operation Desert Shield build-up before the GULF WAR, President George Bush relieved Air Force Chief of Staff General Michael

Chairmen of the Joint Chiefs of Staff

President	Chairman, Joint Chiefs of Staff
33 Truman	Gen. Omar N. Bradley, USA, 1949–1953
34 Eisenhower	Adm. Arthur W. Radford, USN, 1953–1957 Gen. Nathan F. Twining, USAF, 1957–1960 Gen. Lyman L. Lemnitzer, USA, 1960–1961
35 Kennedy	Gen. Lyman L. Lemnitzer, USA, 1961–1962 Gen. Maxwell D. Taylor, USA, 1962–1963
36 L. B. Johnson	Gen. Maxwell D. Taylor, USA, 1963–1964 Gen. Earle G. Wheeler, USA, 1964–1969
37 Nixon	Gen. Earle G. Wheeler, USA, 1969–1970 Adm. Thomas H. Moorer, USN, 1970–1974
38 Ford	Adm. Thomas H. Moorer, USN, 1974 Gen. George S. Brown, USAF, 1974–1977
39 Carter	Gen. George S. Brown, USAF, 1977–1978 Gen. David C. Jones, USAF, 1978–1981
40 Reagan	Gen. David C. Jones, USAF, 1981–1982 Gen. John W. Vessey, Jr., USA, 1982–1985 Adm. William J. Crowe, Jr., USN, 1985–1989
41 Bush	Gen. Colin L. Powell, USA, 1989–1993
42 Clinton	Gen. Colin L. Powell, USA, 1993 Gen. John M. Shalikashvili, USA, 1993–

Abbreviations: USA, United States Army; USAF, United States Air Force; USN, United States Navy.

Dugan for revealing to the press the likely parameters of an air campaign against Iraq.

BIBLIOGRAPHY

Betts, Richard K. *Soldiers, Statesmen, and Cold War Crises.* 1977.
Joint Chiefs of Staff (Historical Division). *History of the Joint Chiefs of Staff.* Edited by Robert J. Watson. Vols. I–VI. 1979–1992.
Office of the Secretary of Defense (Historical Office). *History of the Office of the Secretary of Defense.* Edited by Alfred Goldberg. Vol. I: *The Formative Years.* 1984. Vol. II: *The Test of War.* 1988.

MARK M. LOWENTHAL

JUDGES, APPOINTMENT OF. The CONSTITUTIONAL CONVENTION of 1787 adopted the compromise recommendation of a special committee of eleven delegates, which suggested that federal jurists be appointed "by and with the ADVICE AND CONSENT of the Senate." This recommendation evolved to become Article II, Section 2, clause 2 of the Constitution, which states, "The President . . . shall have Power, by and with the Advice and Consent of the Senate, to . . . nominate . . . Judges of the Supreme Court, and all other Officers of the United States, whose Appointments are not herein otherwise provided for, and which shall be established by Law." Under the terms of these provisions Presidents have nominated, and a majority of the Senate has confirmed, thousands of judges at all levels of the federal judiciary. (In 1992, there were eleven hundred active or senior federal judges, not including bankruptcy and administrative law judges, commissioners, and magistrates.)

The President's responsibility to nominate federal judges has often been largely delegated to the ATTORNEY GENERAL and the Deputy Attorney General. This was noticeably true during the later years of the administration of President Dwight D. Eisenhower, when the selection of members of the federal judiciary was left almost exclusively to Attorney General William P. Rogers and Deputy Attorney General Lawrence E. Walsh. On the other hand, President Lyndon B. Johnson gave John C. Macy, Jr., Chairman of the U.S. Civil Service Commission and a trusted fellow Texan, the crucial role in the judicial selection process. During the administration of Ronald Reagan a formal committee was established, chaired by the President's counsel, Fred F. Fielding, and including the Attorney General plus seven other Department of Justice and White House officials. That committee reviewed recommendations for vacancies, submitted these to checks by the FEDERAL BUREAU OF INVESTIGATION and judgments by the American Bar Association (ABA), and then forwarded its recommendation to the President.

The Senate's Role in Selecting Nominees. Whichever mode a President employs for selecting candidates for federal judgeships, three crucial factors enter into the decision making. First is the obvious need to consult with the U.S. Senator(s) and possibly with other powerful political figures in the home state of the candidate for judicial office, provided these political figures are of the same party as the President. Care must be taken that the appointee not be "personally obnoxious" to a home-state Senator, on pain of having the latter invoke the age-old, almost invariably honored, custom of senatorial courtesy—an almost certain death knell to confirmation by the Senate. The custom is based on the assumption that the President will, as a matter of political patronage, practice, and courtesy, engage in such consultation prior to the nominee's designation. If the President fails to adhere to this custom, the aggrieved Senator's colleagues will almost certainly support his or her call for the nominee's defeat.

Sometimes, powerful Senators of a President's political party will insist not only on the right of prior approval of presidential candidates but will demand the right to designate particular candidates of their own. This was the case in 1974–1975, when Republican Senator Lowell P. Weicker, Jr., of Connecticut insisted that Connecticut's ex-governor, Thomas J. Meskill, be nominated to the federal appellate bench.

Meskill was confirmed by the Senate by a vote of 54 to 36 despite the American Bar Association's unanimous "not qualified" rating. This tendency of some Senators to insist on the nomination of candidates of dubious merit has been offset, somewhat, since the establishment of President Jimmy Carter's Circuit Judge Nomination Commission in 1977 (abolished in 1981), coupled with Carter's Executive Order 12097 (1978), which established guidelines and stipulated qualification standards for individuals nominated to federal judgeships. The late 1970s witnessed a burgeoning—in states such as Virginia, Pennsylvania, Iowa, Georgia, Florida, Colorado, and New York—of Senator-created merit advisory groups and commissions charged with recommending nominees to the federal bench to the Senators. By early 1984, fifty Senators in thirty-five states had agreed to choose federal district judges on a merit basis only, aided by commission recommendations. Other Senators, however, had categorically declined to do so, among them Democrats Adlai E. Stevenson (Ill.), Thomas F. Eagleton (Mo.), Paul S. Sarbanes (Md.), and Lloyd M. Bentsen (Tex.); Bentsen went so far as to say, "I am the merit commission for Texas." Yet more than one-half of Reagan's 290 federal district court appointees emerged from selection panels voluntarily sponsored by Senators.

ABA Evaluation. A second factor that has played an increasingly significant role in the federal judiciary appointment process, especially since the last months of the Truman administration, is the American Bar Association's fifteen-member Committee on Federal Judiciary. This committee, established in 1946, was widely utilized at the pre-formal-nomination stage during Eisenhower's term, a practice continued under all subsequent Presidents, although Richard M. Nixon, following the ABA committee's disapproval of his 1970–1971 list of dubiously qualified candidates, refused to submit nominees' names to it until after he had selected and publicized them. The committee's work has generally produced good results and is understandably popular with the legal profession—although there is no unanimity on that evaluation. There are those who deeply believe that the selection of members of the federal judiciary must rest, in fact as well as in name, with the executive branch, its head being specifically charged to do so under Article III of the Constitution. For such critics, the apparent delegation of important aspects of the President's authority (i.e., approval of, or at least judgment on, candidates) to a private body, no matter how qualified or representative, is at best questionable and at worst a dereliction of duty. Nor is the bar free from political or personal biases, as the committee's handling of the Supreme

Court nominations of ABE FORTAS and Clement Haynsworth in 1969 and those of Robert Bork in 1987 and Clarence Thomas in 1991 demonstrated. To cite an earlier case, had President Woodrow Wilson heeded the ABA's advice, Justice Louis D. Brandeis—one of the nation's greatest jurists—would never have been nominated. Furthermore, as Joel Grossman's intriguing study of the committee's activities over a period of two decades demonstrated rather convincingly, its membership was initially dominated by the "legal establishment."

The ABA committee has become a powerful and generally respected vehicle in the vital initial stage of the nominating process—at least below the Supreme Court level. It does not generate names for judicial vacancies but rather evaluates the qualifications of actual or potential nominees. After an investigation, customarily lasting from six to eight weeks, it reports to the Justice Department on the qualifications of the nominee and rates him or her as well qualified (WQ), qualified (Q), or not qualified (NQ). (Similar, but not identical labels are provided for Supreme Court nominees.) Its final report is a one-sentence judgment by the full membership. In a number of cases the consideration of nominees for the federal bench has been dropped after the ABA committee found them not qualified, and no NQs were approved between 1965 and 1975. Moreover, its reports have enabled the Justice Department to rule out certain names recommended by home-state Senators—though "senatorial courtesy" may prevail in the end. It should be noted that the committee also sends its ratings independently to the Senate Judiciary Committee, and does not route them through the Justice Department.

No alert and prudent Chief Executive would nowadays attempt to designate members of the judiciary purely on the basis of political considerations. Too much is at stake, and the ABA is a powerful factor in the selection process. Yet, granting the trend to make appointments on the basis of overall merit and excellence, political pressures must nevertheless be reckoned with and are disregarded only at the appointing authority's peril. Moreover, a federal judgeship is viewed as a "plum" by all concerned, in that it represents a potent patronage-whip in the hands of the executive vis-à-vis state politicians as well as Congress.

Supreme Court's Role in Selecting Nominees. There is a third crucial factor in selecting federal bench nominees: the unquestionably significant influence that sitting and retired members of the Supreme Court, especially the Chief Justice, have on nominations to the Supreme Court itself. Among Chief Justices, William Howard Taft, CHARLES EVANS HUGHES,

Supreme Court Justices[a]

President	Justice	State from which Apptd	Birth Date	Service Dates	Death Date
1 Washington, F	**1 John Jay, F**	N.Y.	1745	1789–1795	1829
	2 John Rutledge, F[b]	S.C.	1739	1789–1791	1800
	3 William Cushing, F	Mass.	1732	1789–1810	1810
	4 James Wilson, F	Pa.	1742	1789–1798	1798
	5 John Blair, Jr., F	Va.	1732	1789–1796	1800
	6 James Iredell, F	N.C.	1751	1790–1799	1799
	7 Thomas Johnson, F	Md.	1732	1791–1793	1819
	8 William Paterson, F	N.J.	1745	1793–1806	1806
	9 John Rutledge, F	S.C.	1739	1795[c]	1800
	10 Samuel Chase, F	Md.	1741	1796–1811	1811
	11 Oliver Ellsworth, F	Conn.	1745	1796–1800	1807
2 Adams, F	12 Bushrod Washington, F	Va.	1762	1798–1829	1829
	13 Alfred Moore, F	N.C.	1755	1799–1804	1810
	14 John Marshall, F	Va.	1755	1801–1835	1835
3 Jefferson, DR	15 William Johnson, DR	S.C.	1771	1804–1834	1834
	16 Henry B. Livingston, DR	N.Y.	1757	1806–1823	1823
	17 Thomas Todd, DR	Ky.	1765	1807–1826	1826
4 Madison, DR	18 Gabriel Duval, DR	Md.	1752	1811–1835	1844
	19 Joseph Story, DR	Mass.	1779	1811–1845	1845
5 Monroe, DR	20 Smith Thompson, DR	N.Y.	1768	1823–1843	1843
6 J. Q. Adams, DR	21 Robert Trimble, DR	Ky.	1777	1826–1828	1828
7 Jackson, D	22 John McLean, D	Ohio	1785	1829–1861	1861
	23 Henry Baldwin, D	Pa.	1780	1830–1844	1844
	24 James M. Wayne, D	Ga.	1790	1835–1867	1867
	25 Roger B. Taney, D	Md.	1777	1836–1864	1864
	26 Philip P. Barbour, D	Va.	1783	1836–1841	1841
	27 John Catron, D[d]	Tenn.	1786	1837–1865	1865
8 Van Buren, D	28 John McKinley, D	Ala.	1780	1837–1852	1852
	29 Peter V. Daniel, D	Va.	1784	1841–1860	1860
9 Harrison, W					
10 Tyler, W	30 Samuel Nelson, D	N.Y.	1792	1845–1872	1873
11 Polk, D	31 Levi Woodbury, D	N.H.	1789	1846–1851	1851
	32 Robert C. Grier, D	Pa.	1794	1846–1870	1870
12 Taylor, W					
13 Fillmore, W	33 Benjamin R. Curtis, W	Mass.	1809	1851–1857	1874
14 Pierce, D	34 John A. Campbell, D	Ala.	1811	1853–1861	1889
15 Buchanan, D	35 Nathan Clifford, D	Maine	1803	1858–1881	1881
16 Lincoln, R	36 Noah H. Swayne, R	Ohio	1804	1862–1881	1884
	37 Samuel F. Miller, R	Iowa	1816	1862–1890	1890
	38 David Davis, R	Ill.	1815	1862–1877	1886
	39 Stephen J. Field, D	Calif.	1816	1863–1897	1899
	40 Salmon P. Chase, R	Ohio	1808	1864–1873	1873
17 A. Johnson, D					
18 Grant, R	41 William Strong, R	Pa.	1808	1870–1880	1895
	42 Joseph P. Bradley, R	N.J.	1813	1870–1892	1892

[a] Chief Justices are shown in bold face. The Justices' party designations are nominal party affiliations at appointment. States from which Justices were appointed are usually, but not necessarily, the Justices' birth states. For a list of nominees who were not approved by the Senate, or whose nominations were withdrawn, see the table accompanying Supreme Court Justices not confirmed.

[b] Resigned without sitting.

[c] Unconfirmed recess appointment, rejected by Senate, December 1795.

[d] Nominated by Jackson, but not confirmed until after Van Buren had become President.

[e] Though many consider Brandeis a Democrat, he was a registered Republican when nominated.

Abbreviations: D, Democrat; DR, Democratic-Republican; F, Federalist; I, Independent; R, Republican; W, Whig.

*Associate Justice promoted to Chief Justice.

Prepared by Henry J. Abraham.

Continued on next page.

President	Justice	State from which Apptd	Birth Date	Service Dates	Death Date
	43 Ward Hunt, R	N.Y.	1810	1872–1882	1886
18 Grant, R	**44 Morrison R. Waite, R**	Ohio	1816	1874–1888	1888
19 Hayes, R	45 John M. Harlan, I, R	Ky.	1833	1877–1911	1911
	46 William B. Woods, R	Ga.	1824	1880–1887	1887
20 Garfield, R	47 Stanley Matthews, R	Ohio	1824	1881–1889	1889
21 Arthur, R	48 Horace Gray, R	Mass.	1828	1881–1902	1902
	49 Samuel Blatchford, R	N.Y.	1820	1882–1893	1893
22 Cleveland, D	50 Lucius Q. C. Lamar, D	Miss.	1825	1888–1893	1893
	51 Melville W. Fuller, D	Ill.	1833	1888–1910	1910
23 Harrison, R	52 David J. Brewer, R	Kans.	1837	1889–1910	1910
	53 Henry B. Brown, R	Mich.	1836	1890–1906	1913
	54 George Shiras, Jr., R	Pa.	1832	1892–1903	1924
	55 Howell E. Jackson, D	Tenn.	1832	1893–1895	1895
24 Cleveland, D	56 Edward D. White, D	La.	1845	1894–1910	1921
	57 Rufus W. Peckham, D	N.Y.	1838	1895–1909	1909
25 McKinley, R	58 Joseph McKenna, R	Calif.	1843	1898–1925	1926
26 T. Roosevelt, R	59 Oliver Wendell Holmes, Jr., R	Mass.	1841	1902–1932	1935
	60 William R. Day, R	Ohio	1849	1903–1922	1923
	61 William H. Moody, R	Mass.	1853	1906–1919	1917
27 Taft, R	62 Horace H. Lurton, D	Tenn.	1844	1909–1914	1914
	63 Charles E. Hughes, R	N.Y.	1862	1910–1916	1948
	64 *Edward D. White, D	La.	1845	1910–1921	1921
	65 Willis Van Devanter, R	Wyo.	1859	1911–1937	1941
	66 Joseph R. Lamar, D	Ga.	1857	1911–1916	1916
	67 Mahlon Pitney, R	N.J.	1858	1921–1922	1924
28 Wilson, D	68 James C. McReynolds, D	Tenn.	1862	1914–1941	1946
	69 Louis D. Brandeis, R[e]	Mass.	1856	1916–1939	1941
	70 John H. Clarke, D	Ohio	1857	1916–1922	1945
29 Harding, R	**71 William H. Taft, R**	Conn.	1857	1921–1930	1930
	72 George Sutherland, R	Utah	1862	1922–1938	1942
	73 Pierce Butler, D	Minn.	1866	1922–1939	1939
	74 Edward T. Sanford, R	Tenn.	1865	1923–1930	1930
30 Coolidge, R	75 Harlan F. Stone, R	N.Y.	1872	1925–1941	1946
31 Hoover, R	**76 *Charles E. Hughes, R**	N.Y.	1862	1930–1941	1948
	77 Owen J. Roberts, R	Pa.	1875	1930–1945	1955
	78 Benjamin N. Cardozo, D	N.Y.	1870	1932–1938	1938
32 F. D. Roosevelt, D	79 Hugo L. Black, D	Ala.	1886	1937–1971	1971
	80 Stanley F. Reed	Ky.	1884	1938–1957	1980
	81 Felix Frankfurter, I	Mass.	1882	1939–1962	1965
	82 William O. Douglas, D	Conn.	1898	1939–1975	1980
	83 Frank Murphy, D	Mich.	1890	1940–1949	1949
	84 James F. Byrnes, D	S.C.	1879	1941–1942	1972
	85 *Harlan F. Stone, R	N.Y.	1872	1941–1946	1946
	86 Robert H. Jackson, D	N.Y.	1892	1941–1954	1954
	87 Wiley B. Rutledge, D	Iowa	1894	1943–1949	1949
33 Truman, D	88 Harold H. Burton, R	Ohio	1888	1945–1958	1965
	89 Fred M. Vinson, D	Ky.	1890	1946–1953	1953
	90 Tom C. Clark, D	Texas	1899	1949–1967	1977
	91 Sherman Minton, D	Ind.	1890	1949–1956	1965
34 Eisenhower, R	**92 Earl Warren, R**	Calif.	1891	1953–1969	1974
	93 John M. Harlan, II, R	N.Y.	1899	1955–1971	1971
	94 William J. Brennan, Jr., D	N.J.	1906	1956–1990	
	95 Charles E. Whittaker, R	Mo.	1901	1957–1962	1973

Supreme Court Justices (Continued)

President	Justice	State from which Apptd	Birth Date	Service Dates	Death Date
	96 Potter Stewart, R	Ohio	1915	1958–1981	1985
35 Kennedy, D	97 Byron R. White, D	Colo.	1917	1962–1993	
	98 Arthur J. Goldberg, D	Ill.	1908	1962–1965	1990
36 L. B. Johnson, D	99 Abe Fortas, D	Tenn.	1910	1965–1969	1982
	100 Thurgood Marshall, D	N.Y.	1908	1967–1991	1993
37 Nixon, R	**101 Warren E. Burger, R**	Va.	1907	1969–1986	
	102 Harry A. Blackmun, R	Minn.	1908	1970–1994	
	103 Lewis F. Powell, Jr., D	Va.	1907	1972–1987	
	104 William H. Rehnquist, R	Ariz.	1924	1972–1986	
38 Ford, R	105 John Paul Stevens, R	Ill.	1920	1975–	
39 Carter, D					
40 Reagan, R	106 Sandra Day O'Connor, R	Ariz.	1930	1981–	
	107 *William H. Rehnquist, R	Va.	1924	1986–	
	108 Antonin Scalia, R	Va.	1936	1986–	
	109 Anthony M. Kennedy, R	Calif.	1936	1988–	
41 Bush, R	110 David Souter, R	N.H.	1939	1990–	
	111 Clarence Thomas, R	Va.	1948	1991–	
42 Clinton, D	112 Ruth Bader Ginsburg, D	D.C.	1933	1993–	
	113 Stephen G. Breyer, D	Mass.	1938	1994–	

aChief Justices are shown in bold face. The Justices' party designations are nominal party affiliations at appointment. States from which Justices were appointed are usually, but not necessarily, the Justices' birth states. For a list of nominees who were not approved by the Senate, or whose nominations were withdrawn, see the table accompanying SUPREME COURT JUSTICES NOT CONFIRMED.

ᶜ Though many consider Brandeis a Democrat, he was a registered Republican when nominated.

Abbreviations: D, Democrat; DR, Democratic-Republican; F, Federalist; I, Independent; R, Republican; W, Whig.

*Associate Justice promoted to Chief Justice.

Prepared by Henry J. Abraham.

Harlan Stone, Frederick M. Vinson, Earl Warren, and Warren Burger and, among Associate Justices, the first John M. Harlan, Samuel F. Miller, Willis Van Devanter, Louis D. Brandeis, and FELIX FRANKFURTER have all been involved in consultations with Presidents and Attorneys General in selecting Supreme Court nominees. Taft's participation in the selection process was the most open and active of all—followed at some distance by Stone, Hughes, Harlan, and Miller (in that order). Taft's role in President Warren G. Harding's nomination of Pierce Butler is a classic example of the Chief Justice's influence: Harding's Attorney General, HARRY M. DAUGHERTY, told Henry Taft (William's brother) that "the President would not approve anybody for appointment who was not approved by the Chief Justice."

Judicial Terms and Salaries. At the federal level, all judges of the constitutional courts—that is, those appointed under the provisions of Article III of the Constitution (the judicial article)—hold their position during "good behavior," which in effect means for life or until they choose to retire. The other federal judges—those of legislative courts created under a provision of Article I (the legislative article)—occupy their positions for whatever period Congress may have prescribed at the time it established the court or in subsequent legislation. In some instances this has meant "good behavior" tenure for them, too, or, frequently, terms of office ranging between four and fifteen years. The constitutional judges have the additional safeguard, stated in Article III, that their "compensation . . . shall not be diminished during their continuance in office." Hence, although their salaries may be increased during their incumbency, they may not be lowered, short of constitutional amendment.

Judicial salaries, although perhaps not commensurate with the responsibilities and prestige of the offices and often lower than comparable positions in private enterprise, are adequate. In 1991 the annual salary range was from $125,000 for district court judges to $160,000 for the Chief Justice of the United States, with the Associate Justices receiving $7,000 less. But people hardly aspire to high judicial office for financial gain.

To enable aging jurists to step down from the bench with dignity and, concurrently, to render their replacement by younger personnel more palatable, Congress in 1937 enacted a vastly improved retirement statute. Under its provisions, federal judges may retire outright on full pay equal to their last year's salary at the age of seventy after having served ten years on the federal bench or at sixty-five after having served fifteen. These requirements are waived in the presence of physical disability, in which case retirement pay is computed in accordance with length of service. A more financially advantageous arrangement, of which many retirees have availed themselves, is to opt for a "senior judge" status upon retirement. That status assumes a judge's ability to serve when called on (although only about 20 to 25 percent actually do serve), but it also means an increase in the judge's pension whenever the sitting members of any federal court receive a raise. A deceased jurist's surviving spouse and dependents receive an annual purse equivalent to 37.5 percent of the judge's average salary—if the jurist elected to participate in a contributory judicial survivor's annuity plan.

Qualifications for Nomination. Today, there is only one standard prerequisite for qualification as a federal judge—an LL.B. or J.D. degree. The possession of a law degree is neither a constitutional nor a statutory requirement for appointment, yet custom would automatically exclude from consideration anyone who did not have one, and the legal profession would remonstrate so determinedly were a nonlawyer nominated that the appointing authority would surely acquiesce. Historically, however, only 58 of the 106 Justices on the U.S. Supreme Court attended law school, and it was not until 1922 that a majority of the sitting Justices were law school graduates and not until 1957 that every sitting Justice was a law school graduate.

Theoretically, any graduate of an accredited law school may hope for an eventual appointment to the federal judiciary—provided that he or she is politically "available" and acceptable to the executive, legislative, and private forces that determine the selection, nomination, and appointment process. In the final analysis, it is the President and his immediate advisers—usually the Attorney General and Deputy Attorney General—who take the crucial step of submitting the nominee's name to the Senate. All Presidents except William Henry Harrison, Zachary Taylor, Andrew Johnson, and Jimmy Carter have succeeded in seeing at least one nominee attain membership on the highest court of the land. Of these four exceptions, the first two were removed too quickly by death; Johnson was the victim of congressional machinations that successfully prevented him from filling several Supreme Court vacancies; and fate simply never presented Carter with an opportunity to make a nomination. The 106 individual Justices who had served on the Court as of the end of the 1991–1992 term provided thirty-six Presidents (counting Cleveland only once) with 110 successful appointments (four Associate Justices were promoted to Chief Justice).

In view of the minimal basic need of a law degree, it is hardly astonishing that many newly appointed jurists lack practical judicial experience. This has been especially true of Supreme Court designees; those of the court level immediately below, the Court of Appeals, have often had some lower court experience in federal district court. Of the 106 Justices who served on the Supreme Court between 1789 and the end of 1991, only twenty-four (not counting the prior service of E. D. White, Hughes, Stone, and Rehnquist, Associate Justices who were promoted to Chief Justices) had had ten or more years of previous judicial experience on any lower level, federal or state, at the time of their appointment, and forty-two had no judicial experience whatsoever. The list of the totally inexperienced, however, contains many of the most illustrious names in the judicial history of the United States, including five Chief Justices—ROGER B. TANEY, SALMON P. CHASE, Morrison R. Waite, Melville W. Fuller, and Earl Warren—and notable Associate Justices Miller, Brandeis, Frankfurter, Joseph Story, Joseph P. Bradley, William O. Douglas, and Lewis F. Powell, Jr., to name a few. (Before his appointment, the great Chief Justice John Marshall had spent a mere three years in the very minor city hustings court of Richmond, Virginia.)

The only person who knows with certainty why someone is appointed is the President of the United States. The record indicates, however, that four basic reasons have been the most important in selecting nominees: objective merit, personal friendship, balancing representativeness on the Court, and political and ideological compatibility. Of the four reasons, the desire to balance representation of religion, geography, race, and sex was by the 1990s playing the major role in presidential choice of nominees. The emphases on gender and racial balance, especially, are here to stay, no matter how controversial they may be.

Political and ideological compatibility often strongly influence presidential choices for the Supreme Court. Among the points a President is almost certain to consider are whether or not the choice will be popular with influential interest groups, whether the nominee has been a loyal member of the President's party, whether the nominee favors presidential programs and policies, whether the nominee is acceptable to his or her home-state Senators, whether the nominee's judicial record (if any) meets the President's criteria of constitutional construction, whether the President is indebted to the nominee for past political services, and finally, whether the President feels "good" or "comfortable" about the nominee.

A comparison of the 106 people who, up to 1992, had sat on the U.S. Supreme Court yields the following "average" profile: a Supreme Court Justice is likely to be native-born (only six Justices, including Frankfurter, originally an Austrian, and George Sutherland, from England, were born outside the United States), male (Sandra Day O'Connor was, by the early 1990s, the only woman to have served on the Court; Ruth Bader Ginsburg was nominated in 1993), white (with Thurgood Marshall and Clarence Thomas the only exceptions), of Anglo-Saxon ethnic stock (all but fifteen), Protestant (there had been only eight Catholic and five Jewish Justices), fifty to fifty-five years of age at the time of appointment, firstborn (fifty-six, or 62 percent), of upper-middle to high social and economic status, reared in a nonrural (but not necessarily urban) environment, civic-minded and politically active (or at least politically aware), possessing a B.A. and a law degree (one-third from Ivy League institutions) with an excellent academic record, and having held some type of public office.

Confirmation Process. That the Senate has taken its confirmation role seriously is documented by its refusal to confirm 40 of the 143 Supreme Court nominees forwarded to it over more than two centuries of U.S. history. Eleven of these nominees were not rejected per se, but their nominations were not acted on by the Senate. True, even counting the Senate's refusal to vote in the Fortas promotion, only five nominees were formally voted down during the twentieth century (and two others not acted upon); but, as the experiences of the Nixon, Reagan, and Bush administrations demonstrate, the possibility is ever present. A return to the nineteenth-century record of one rejection or refusal to act for every three nominees would, however, appear to be highly unlikely.

Among the more prominent reasons for the forty rejections have been the following: senatorial opposition to the nominating President; the nominee's involvement with a contentious issue of public policy; opposition to the record of the incumbent Court, which the nominee was presumed to have supported; senatorial courtesy (closely linked to the consultative nominating process); a perceived "political unreliability" of the nominee; the evident lack of qualifications or limited ability of the nominee; concerted, sustained opposition by interest or pressure groups; and fear that the nominee would dramatically alter the Court's jurisprudential philosophical "lineup." Often, several reasons have figured in the rejection of a nominee.

In general, opposition to the confirmation of a federal jurist, especially a Supreme Court nominee, seems to reflect the existence of deep-seated concern in the nation. In the early years of the Court's history, relatively little interest was shown in the potentially unfortunate effects of judges of uncertain—or certain—convictions. Such interest became more frequent and noticeable as the influence of the judiciary grew. By the 1980s and 1990s, when there were so many issues with which large numbers of people were deeply concerned, almost every nominee was made to run the gauntlet. The nomination and confirmation procedure had become a battleground on which large issues were fought out before the public eye. [See SUPREME COURT NOMINEES NOT CONFIRMED.]

Impeachment. Involuntary removal of federal judges can be effected only by the process of IMPEACHMENT and conviction. It has long been legal, however, for the judicial council of a U.S. circuit to discipline a judge by stripping him or her of duties and authority while permitting the retention of both title and salary, and in 1980 Congress enacted the Judicial Councils Reform and Judicial Conduct and Disability Act, which gave the judicial councils of the thirteen circuits authority to discipline for misconduct all federal judges except those of the Supreme Court. (Judicial councils cannot, however, remove judges from office.) In accordance with constitutional requirements, impeachment for "Treason, Bribery, or other high Crimes and Misdemeanors" may be voted by a simple majority of the House of Representatives, there being a quorum on the floor. Trial is then held in the Senate, which may convict by a vote of two-thirds if a quorum is present.

As of early 1992 the House of Representatives had initiated a total of sixteen impeachment proceedings, of which thirteen were directed against federal judges. (Nine other judges resigned before formal charges were lodged against them.) Of the thirteen impeachment proceedings involving federal judges, eleven went to trial. (U.S. District Court Judge Mark H. Delaney, who was impeached in 1873 by voice vote, resigned before the articles of impeachment were prepared for Senate action, and, in the other case that did not go to trial, George W. English (a district court judge impeached in 1926) resigned before the Senate could vote.) Of the eleven cases that progressed to trial, four resulted in acquittals and seven in removals. The four acquittals are headed, both chronologically and in importance, by the only impeachment trial (as of early 1993) involving a Justice of the Supreme Court— that of Associate Justice Samuel Chase in 1804–1805.

BIBLIOGRAPHY

Abraham, Henry J. *The Judicial Process*. 6th ed. 1993.
Abraham, Henry J. *Justices and Presidents*. 3rd ed. 1992.

Bronner, Ethan. *Battle for Justice: How the Bork Nomination Shook America.* 1989.

Grossman, Joel B. *Lawyers and Judges: The ABA and the Process of Judicial Selection.* 1965.

Harris, J. P. *The Advice and Consent of the Senate.* 1953.

Massaro, John. *Supremely Political: The Role of Ideology and Presidential Management in Unsuccessful Supreme Court Nominations.* 1991.

Schmidhauser, John R. *Judges and Justices.* 1979.

Twentieth Century Task Force on Judicial Selection. *Judicial Roulette.* 1988.

HENRY J. ABRAHAM

JUDICIARY, FEDERAL. A coequal branch of the national government, the federal judiciary is independent of the President yet is also dependent on the CHIEF EXECUTIVE for the recruitment of its personnel and the enforcement of its rulings. Occasionally, federal courts and the executive branch have been embroiled in major conflicts—as in the 1930s, when the federal judiciary, led by the Supreme Court, struck down progressive economic legislation and much of Democratic President Franklin D. Roosevelt's early NEW DEAL program. But the federal courts more often offer Presidents opportunities to advance their own legal policy agenda through litigation and the President's power to appoint federal judges.

Article III of the Constitution vests the judicial power "in one supreme Court, and in such inferior Courts as the Congress may from time to time ordain and establish." Besides guaranteeing federal judges basically lifetime tenure (subject only to IMPEACHMENT), Article III extends the judicial power to all cases in law and equity arising under the Constitution and the laws of the United States.

Though it set out the Supreme Court's original jurisdiction and authorized Congress to establish its appellate jurisdiction, the Constitution was silent concerning the structure of the federal judiciary and the power of judicial review.

Structure. It was left to the First Congress to establish the federal judiciary and to define its power. The Judiciary Act of 1789 authorized five Associate Justices and one Chief Justice of the Supreme Court and created two "inferior" courts: district courts, which serve as the trial courts in the federal judicial system, and circuit courts of appeals, which are located in different geographical regions. Along with thirteen district judgeships the Judiciary Act of 1789 required members of the Supreme Court to ride circuit twice a year and to sit with district judges to hear appeals in the circuit courts instead of providing for additional appellate court judges. Although members of the Supreme Court complained about their workload throughout the nineteenth century, there were no permanent appellate court judges until after the passage of the Circuit Court of Appeals Act in 1891.

As the country expanded westward and grew in population, the size of the federal bench gradually grew as well. The number of Justices and circuits grew from three in 1789, to nine in 1837, and then to ten in 1863. During RECONSTRUCTION, Congress's antagonism toward President Andrew Johnson led it to reduce the number of Justices from ten to seven in order to deny Johnson the opportunity to make appointments to the Court. After Ulysses S. Grant was elected President, Congress in 1869 again authorized nine Justices—the number that has since prevailed.

From the original 19 federal judges, the number grew to more than 1,000 in 1992, including 709 full-time judges and another 340 who have senior status but continue to hear cases. In 1992 there were ninety-four district courts, with at least one or more in each state, depending on caseloads. District judges sit alone and preside over trials, with or without juries, and over other criminal and civil proceedings. They also approve plea bargains, supervise settlements, monitor remedial decrees, and manage the processing of cases. The number of federal circuit courts of appeals has grown to thirteen. Eleven geographical regions, or circuits, have one appellate court each, with general appellate jurisdiction over appeals from the district courts, rulings by independent regulatory commissions, and appeals of federal administrative agencies' enforcement decisions. In addition, the Court of Appeals for the District of Columbia Circuit has general jurisdiction over federal cases, but by statute also handles most challenges to federal agencies' regulations. In 1982 Congress added the Court of Appeals for the Federal Circuit, which is also located in the District of Columbia and primarily hears tax, patent, and international trade cases and appeals. Unlike district courts, federal appellate courts have twenty or more judges who hear cases in rotating three-judge panels. Occasionally, in important or especially divisive cases (particularly cases that present issues on which two or more three-judge panels have reached opposite results in similar cases), the entire circuit court sits as a panel, or *en banc*, to reach a decision and resolve conflicting interpretation of the law within the circuit.

Along with the increasing number of federal judges, there has been a significant growth in the number of law clerks, secretaries, support staff, magistrate and bankruptcy judges, and probation and pretrial workers—that is, in the size of the entire judicial branch. In 1900 the federal judiciary had 2,770 employees; by 1960, 4,992 employees; in 1980, 14,500; and more than 24,600 in 1991.

Role. These changes in the size and complexity of the judiciary reflect the increasing flow of litigation into the federal courts and magnify basic tensions in the highly decentralized, three-tiered judicial system. In 1991 federal district courts faced more than 200,000 civil cases and more than 45,000 criminal cases, while federal appellate courts handled more than 42,000 civil and criminal appeals. Because the bulk of federal litigation takes place in district courts and only about 10 percent of their decisions are appealed, district courts function as courts of both first and last resort for the overwhelming majority of federal cases. Moreover, as the size and caseloads of federal courts of appeals grew after World War II, there has been a greater propensity for more intracircuit conflicts (conflicts over the law among three-judge panels within each circuit) and for more intercircuit conflicts among the appellate courts around the country. Together, these trends push toward greater discretionary justice in the district courts, with less supervision and error correction by appellate courts, and indicate a pull away from uniformity, stability, and certainty in national public law and policy.

The increased amount of federal litigation has also affected the Supreme Court's role in the federal judicial system and diminished its capacity for appellate review of the lower federal courts. Whereas in 1920 there were just 565 cases on the Court's docket, the number has grown incrementally during each decade since World War II, from 1,300 in 1950 to more than 2,300 cases by 1960, 4,200 by 1970, 5,300 in 1980, and more than 6,000 cases by 1990. In response to these increases in the size of the docket, Congress expanded the Court's discretionary jurisdiction, giving it the power to deny review to the vast majority of cases and thereby enabling it not only to manage the docket but to set the Court's substantive policy agenda as well. As a result, the Supreme Court reviews only about 140 cases annually (less than 3 percent of the cases arriving on its docket) and takes only those cases that pose major questions of national importance. The present-day Court thus no longer serves primarily to supervise or correct the errors of lower courts. Instead, the Court functions as a "superlegislature," reviewing major issues of public law and policy of interest to the President, Congress, the national government, and the states.

No less significant than the growth in caseload has been the changing nature of the business coming into federal courts. Broad social and economic forces continue to affect the business of the federal courts, but so do the legal policy goals and priorities of the President and administration. The district courts, for example, have gradually taken on fewer criminal cases and more civil litigation. In the late nineteenth century, 61 percent of the work of federal trial courts involved criminal cases, which dominated dockets until the mid-1930s. The filing of criminal cases rapidly increased during the 1920s and early 1930s, when it leveled off. Another surge occurred in the late 1960s, followed by a decline from 1975 on. In 1980, criminal cases amounted to only 15 percent of federal district courts' caseload; this percentage declined farther, to less than 1 percent by 1991, due to a dramatic increase in civil litigation. Despite not keeping pace with the increasing rate of civil litigation, the number of criminal cases did steadily climb throughout the 1980s—the number of drug-related criminal cases alone more than doubled between 1981 and 1991.

The changing nature of the business coming before the Supreme Court further underscores how the federal judiciary's role in shaping national public law and policy grew more significant in the twentieth century. During much of the early nineteenth century, more than 40 percent of the Court's business consisted of admiralty and prize cases; matters of common law accounted for approximately 50 percent. By the 1880s admiralty cases dropped to less than 4 percent. While common law disputes and jurisdictional questions continued to account for almost 40 percent of the Court's business by the 1880s, more than 43 percent involved issues of statutory interpretation and only about 4 percent concerned matters of constitutional law. This change registered the federal government's assertion of powers to regulate interstate commerce and the executive branch's enforcement of antitrust laws and other kinds of new economic regulation. In the twentieth century, the trend toward a Court that principally decides issues of national importance for federal law and public policy continued. In the 1980s, about 47 percent of the cases annually decided by the Court raised questions of constitutional law, 38 percent dealt with the interpretation of congressional statutes, and the remaining 15 percent involved controversies over federal taxation, administrative law, and federal agencies' regulations.

The Judiciary and the Presidency. The executive branch thus plays a large role in determining the business of the federal judiciary and of the Supreme Court in particular. The litigation strategies of the executive branch, moreover, register the changing social- and economic-policy agendas of Presidents. During the administration of Democratic President Jimmy Carter, for instance, the Department of Justice promoted AFFIRMATIVE ACTION by bringing litigation in the federal courts aimed at forcing businesses and state and local governments to hire African Americans and women. That litigation policy was reversed when

Republican President Ronald Reagan was elected. Reagan's Department of Justice attacked the constitutionality of affirmative action programs in federal courts and aimed to return power to state and local governments, as well as to cut back on the enforcement of antitrust law and other economic regulation.

The Department of Justice is uniquely positioned to advance a President's social and economic policies in the federal courts. The department not only decides what kinds of litigation to pursue, but it also may relitigate issues in different federal courts. If one circuit court rejects the government's interpretation of a statute or regulation, the Department of Justice may relitigate the issue in another case in another appellate court. The department's relitigation policy foments intercircuit conflicts among the federal appellate courts and thereby creates a basis for appealing a case (and the policy issue it embodies) to the Supreme Court, which tends to hear cases posing intercircuit conflicts and deemed by the government to present "substantial questions of federal law."

Within the Department of Justice, the office of the SOLICITOR GENERAL is responsible for screening all appeals and petitions to the Supreme Court by federal agencies (except for those made by the Interstate Commerce Commission). The Solicitor General decides which cases should be taken to the Court and advances the substantive legal-policy agenda of the President in petitions, briefs, and oral arguments before the Court. Because the Solicitor General screens out a large number of federal cases that might be appealed to the Court and has earned a reputation for high-quality work, the Justices are predisposed to hear cases in which the Solicitor General participates.

Although the federal judiciary generally supports the executive branch and has served to legitimate the legal policies of the President, federal courts have not invariably done so. Democratic President Harry S. Truman, for instance, claimed an inherent power to seize the nation's steel mills in order to avert a nationwide strike that, he argued, threatened the country's effort in the KOREAN WAR. But his claim was rejected by a federal district court and a majority of the Supreme Court in YOUNGSTOWN SHEET & TUBE CO. V. SAWYER (1952). Likewise, Republican President Richard M. Nixon's claim of EXECUTIVE PRIVILEGE to withhold confidential White House communications from disclosure in a criminal trial was rebuffed in UNITED STATES V. NIXON (1974). Although Truman and Nixon disagreed with the Court's rulings, they nonetheless respected the federal judiciary's independence and complied with the rulings.

At times in the history of U.S. politics, Presidents have attacked the federal judiciary in speeches and campaigns. In the early 1930s, President Roosevelt campaigned against the Court's conservative economic philosophy and overturning of early New Deal legislation. After his landslide reelection in 1936, Roosevelt proposed a judicial reform that would have expanded the number of Supreme Court Justices from nine to fifteen, thus enabling him to secure a majority favorable to his social and economic programs. But, while the Senate was debating his COURT-PACKING PLAN, the Court abruptly upheld major pieces of New Deal legislation, and Roosevelt's proposal was eventually defeated in the Senate. Thirty years later, President Nixon attacked the liberal social philosophy and decisions of the Warren Court and promised to appoint only conservative "strict constructionists" to the federal bench. In the 1980s President Reagan repeatedly attacked the legitimacy of the Court's rulings upholding a woman's constitutional right to ABORTION, and his Solicitor General took cases to the Court that enabled him to ask the Justices to overturn their rulings on abortion.

While Presidents and their administrations may either enforce or attempt to thwart compliance with controversial rulings of the federal judiciary, in the long run their major influence over the federal courts remains contingent on their appointments to the federal bench. Although Roosevelt's Court-packing plan failed, he and his successor, Harry Truman, appointed more than 80 percent of the federal bench. The federal judiciary in turn became gradually more liberal in the areas of civil liberties and the rights of the criminally accused. In the 1970s, Republican Presidents Nixon and Gerald Ford were moderately successful with their judicial appointments in moving the federal courts back to more conservative directions. In the 1980s and 1990s, Reagan and George Bush achieved even greater success, filling more than 80 percent of the federal bench and strongly carrying their conservative social and economic philosophy into the federal courts.

The size, business, and role of the federal judiciary have evolved along with changes in the national government and American politics. Although an independent branch of the national government, the federal courts have (with some exceptions as in the 1930s) generally served to legitimize the legal policies of the executive branch and to strengthen presidential power. The ideological swing of presidential elections and the President's power to appoint federal judges have generally tended to keep the federal courts in line with the dominant political coalition and to make them democratically accountable.

BIBLIOGRAPHY

Bator, Paul, Paul J. Mishkin, David L. Shapiro, and Herbert Wechsler, *Hart and Wechsler's The Federal Courts and the Federal System.* 1981.

Caplan, Lincoln. *The Tenth Justice: The Solicitor General and the Rule of Law.* 1987.

Carp, Robert A., and C. K. Rowland. *Policymaking and Politics in the Federal District Courts.* 1983.

Goldman, Sheldon, and Austin Sarat, eds. *American Court Systems.* 2d rev. ed. 1989.

Howard, J. Woodford, Jr. *Courts of Appeals in the Federal Judicial System.* 1981.

O'Brien, David M. *Storm Center: The Supreme Court in American Politics.* 3d rev. ed. Forthcoming.

Posner, Richard. *The Federal Courts: Crisis and Reform.* 1985.

DAVID M. O'BRIEN

JUSTICE, DEPARTMENT OF. The executive branch department with primary responsibility for handling the legal work of the federal government, including the enforcement of federal law, is the Department of Justice. The department was created by the Judiciary Act of 1870 and is headed by the U.S. ATTORNEY GENERAL, whose office has existed since 1789.

The department is composed of the offices of the Attorney General, Deputy Attorney General, Associate Attorney General, Inspector General, and SOLICITOR GENERAL. The Attorney General, in addition to serving as department head, is also a member of the CABINET and a presidential adviser. The Deputy Attorney General is the second-highest position in the department, although the Associate Attorney General, created in 1977, is often considered on par. The deputy and associate divide departmental administrative responsibilities, including both lawyering and nonlawyering functions. The Inspector General conducts internal audits of the Department's programs and investigates allegations of misconduct by the Department's employees. The Solicitor General's office conducts government litigation before the Supreme Court.

Organization. The government's legal business has been divided into six subject areas, with an Assistant Attorney General heading each division. The assistants handle litigation below the Supreme Court level. The oldest, with roots going back to 1868, is the Civil Division. It represents the interests of the federal government in civil claims. The Environment and Natural Resources Division, organized in 1910 as the Land and Natural Resources Division and reorganized twenty years later, handles civil actions that relate to acquiring, owning, and managing public land and natural resources. The Criminal Division was formed in 1928 to enforce federal criminal statutes. Five years later, the Tax Division was added to specialize in civil and criminal tax litigation. That same year, 1933, the Antitrust Division was established to oversee enforcement of antitrust laws. In 1957, the Civil Rights Division was created to enforce federal civil rights law.

An Assistant Attorney General also heads the OFFICE OF LEGAL COUNSEL (OLC), created in 1933 to assist the Attorney General in preparing formal and informal legal opinions for government agencies and departments. The office's biggest client, according to one recent OLC head, is the President, usually through the WHITE HOUSE COUNSEL's office. Under some administrations, the OLC has communicated directly with the White House without going through the Attorney General.

The Justice Department is also responsible for the ninety-five U.S. attorneys and their staffs, although by tradition they operate with some independence and autonomy. Each federal judicial district has a U.S. attorney, appointed by the President and confirmed by the Senate to a four-year term. The U.S. Marshals Service, with ninety-five marshals and their deputies, also comes under the Justice Department. Two investigative units reside at Justice as well: the FEDERAL BUREAU OF INVESTIGATION (FBI) and the Drug Enforcement Administration (DEA). The FBI grew out of a small detective staff formed in 1908; after a bureau scandal, it was reorganized in 1924 under the directorship of a young lawyer named J. EDGAR HOOVER, who served as its director for the next forty-eight years. The FBI director is appointed to a ten-year term by the President with senatorial confirmation. The bureau is the largest unit in Justice. The DEA, which investigates illicit manufacturing and trafficking in controlled substances, was added to the department in 1973.

In addition to the more traditional lawyering and investigatory activities, the Justice Department houses several nonlawyering offices. Among them is the Immigration and Naturalization Service (INS), which enforces laws that relate to admission, exclusion, removal, and naturalization of non–U.S. citizens. The quasi-judicial Board of Immigration Appeals, independent of the INS, also operates out of the department through the Executive Office for Immigration Review. Also part of the Department of Justice are the Bureau of Prisons, which administers the federal prison system; the U.S. Parole Commission, which grants or revokes paroles for federal prisoners and sets parole policies; and the Office of Pardon Attorney, which makes recommendations on clemency to the President.

Other Justice Department programs include the

Office of Justice Programs, which supports research in criminal justice, particularly on the state level; the Office of Policy and Communication, which assesses the entire system of justice and makes recommendations for change; and the Community Relations Service, which provides mediation and technical assistance to handle local problems that arise under federal civil rights laws. The Executive Office for United States Trustees operates out of the department as well, providing a nationwide network to handle the administrative processing of bankruptcies. The Office of Intelligence Policy and Review represents the government before the Foreign Intelligence Surveillance Court, and the Interpol–U.S. National Central Bureau serves as a communications conduit with other Interpol member nations.

The housekeeping responsibilities of the department rest primarily with the Justice Management Division, which develops budget requests, handles personnel matters, and oversees department finances. Other internal duties are handled by the Office of Public Information and the Office of Legislative Affairs. The Office of Professional Responsibility investigates charges of misconduct of Justice employees.

Origins and Growth. While the Judiciary Act of 1789 created the office of Attorney General, no department was formally attached to that office until 1870, after the CIVIL WAR had brought a tremendous growth in government litigation. EDMUND RANDOLPH, the first Attorney General, attempted to centralize the nation's legal affairs when he requested legislation to bring the U.S. attorneys under his control, which, he argued, would help him secure the government's legal interests. The U.S. district attorneys and marshals had been created by the Judiciary Act of 1789, and statutorily they were under presidential supervision, but in reality they operated with few checks. The legislation recommended by Randolph failed to pass, however.

Debates over the establishment of a formal law department began as early as 1829, when President Andrew Jackson sent a proposal to Congress to increase the Attorney General's responsibilities and salary. The bill's supporters claimed that the current system allowed incompetent U.S. district attorneys—who were without adequate federal supervision—to injure financial interests of the country. But there was considerable congressional resistance to the legislation. The opposition was led by the famous orator DANIEL WEBSTER, who asserted that the bill would make the Attorney General into "a half accountant, a half lawyer, a half clerk, in fine, a half everything and not much of any thing" (U.S. Senate, *Register of Debates*, 26 March, 13 April, and 30 April 1830). Webster succeeded in replacing Jackson's plan with his own, which created the post of Solicitor of the Treasury.

Presidents James K. Polk and Franklin Pierce also battled Congress in an effort to extend the Attorney General's authority and to increase his salary and staff. Polk recommended the formation of a justice department in 1845, but Congress did not respond. Eight years later, Pierce won a salary increase and two more clerk positions for his Attorney General. In 1861, the U.S. attorneys and marshals were nominally brought under the Attorney General's control. Later, two Assistant Attorneys General were added, along with a law clerk. But the trend in Congress was toward fragmenting, not consolidating, legal offices within the government. Law posts were added to the Internal Revenue Service, War Department, Navy, and Post Office. Other executive departments soon agitated for legal staffs of their own and for the right to supervise their own litigation.

Despite the lack of a formal justice department, Attorneys General began to speak of themselves as heading a "law department": this is how, for example, the office was described by Attorney General CALEB CUSHING in 1856. Finally, in the years following the Civil War, the need for a larger, consolidated law department became apparent. The war had brought a monumental increase in government litigation, with cases involving questions ranging from property titles to personal rights. The federal government had to be represented in courts all across the country. The Attorney General's office did not have the staff to handle the demand, nor did it have adequate supervision over the U.S. attorneys. Instead, outside counsel had to be hired by the various executive departments at prevailing professional rates. The enormous costs incurred—estimated at close to half a million dollars over four years from 1862 to 1866—came to the notice of the Thirty-ninth Congress. Legislation to establish a department of justice was introduced in the following two Congresses. Proponents argued for it as a cost-cutting measure and as a resolution to a problem that had long plagued the nation's legal affairs—that of contradictory opinions being issued by the law officers of different departments. The bill was finally passed on 20 June 1870, and the Department of Justice came into existence on 1 July 1870. The staff was increased by two assistants and a Solicitor General, whose responsibility was to share with the Attorney General the duty of conducting cases for the United States before the Supreme Court. The act also gave the Attorney

General a positive grant of authority over the U.S. attorneys and marshals.

Legislative fiat alone, however, could not create a department, especially given two seemingly minor congressional oversights. The first was the failure to provide the department with centralized office space. Without such space, the law officers of the other departments—nominally transferred to Justice—remained located at their respective departments, where they continued in much the same manner as before. The other oversight was the failure to repeal the old statutes that had originally established and defined these law officers' positions.

Further pleas to Congress in 1903 and 1909 failed to alter the divided control of and multiple responsibility for the nation's legal system. By 1915, solicitors who were largely independent of Justice operated in State, Treasury, Interior, Commerce, Labor, Agriculture, Navy, Post Office, and Internal Revenue. Each one claimed the right to conduct litigation; each rendered legal advice to his department. With WORLD WAR I, President Woodrow Wilson issued an EXECUTIVE ORDER that required all government law officers to operate under the supervision and control of the Department of Justice. He also reiterated the binding nature of the Attorney General's opinions on executive officers. Through the war, departmental law officers could continue to render advice for their departments, but they had to leave litigation to the Department of Justice. As the emergency ended, however, the authority of the executive order lapsed and the old system reemerged. Chaos had returned by the 1920s. The consolidation of the government's legal work began again in 1933 under Attorney General HOMER CUMMINGS, when President Franklin D. Roosevelt issued another executive order. Department heads, however, continued to resist.

Role. The practice of executive departments maintaining their own law offices continues today. A department's attorneys are generally restricted to rendering legal advice on matters of concern to that department alone. Most of the government's litigation is now placed under Justice Department control, although the department may choose to recognize the litigating authority of particular agencies in particular cases. Independent agencies, such as the Tennessee Valley Authority, continue to maintain their right to conduct their own litigation if they so choose. Although the Justice Department is widely recognized as the appropriate representative for the federal government in court, conflicts do arise. One potential source of conflict exists when executive departments take opposing positions in a case. The Solicitor General and Attorney General must then decide which departmental position will be defended. Occasionally, departments challenge their authority to make this determination, and the issue must be resolved by the President. More serious conflicts can occur when the White House challenges the position taken by the Justice Department before the Supreme Court. Attorneys General recognize that constitutional authority rests with the President, yet on occasion they have resisted White House instructions to switch positions on a case.

In the nineteenth century, congressional fragmentation of the nation's law business derived in part from many states' long-standing fear of a centralized national law office. Many in Congress were suspicious of a strong Attorney General serving a strong President. This concern is evident in the debates over the Justice Department in 1866 and 1870: some members questioned the Attorney General's independence from the President, charging that law officers were mere tools of the White House and that they manipulated their legal advice to advance their Presidents' political agendas. This charge continued to be leveled at Attorneys General, including ROBERT JACKSON for justifying Franklin Roosevelt's DESTROYERS FOR BASES deal with Britain during WORLD WAR II, and ROBERT F. KENNEDY for describing, contrary to international law, the Cuban quarantine during the 1962 CUBAN MISSILE CRISIS as an act short of war. The criticism resurfaced during JOHN MITCHELL's tenure, particularly regarding the Richard M. Nixon administration's response to domestic dissent and civil rights enforcement.

To address this concern, Congress has occasionally considered removing the Department of Justice from presidential control, most recently in 1974, when the Senate Judiciary Committee held hearings on a bill sponsored by Senator Sam J. Ervin. Opponents, though sympathetic to Ervin's goals, argued that the Attorney General must be held accountable by an elected chief executive, who has the constitutional responsibility to "take care that the laws be faithfully executed." The bill did not pass. But Congress and the WATERGATE AFFAIR special prosecution force in 1975 stressed the necessity of removing politics from the administration of justice. Partly in response to concern about the politicization of Justice, Congress created the Office of Independent Counsel by the Ethics in Government Act of 1978.

BIBLIOGRAPHY

Baker, Nancy V. *Conflicting Loyalties: Law and Politics in the Attorney General's Office, 1789–1990.* 1992.

Bell, Griffin. *Taking Care of the Law*. 1982.

Clayton, Cornell. *The Politics of Justice: The Attorney General and the Making of Legal Policy*. 1992.

Cummings, Homer, and Carl McFarland. *Federal Justice: Chapters in the History of Justice and the Federal Executive*. 1937; rpt. 1970.

Harris, Richard. *Justice: The Crisis of Law, Order, and Freedom in America*. 1970.

Huston, Luther. *The Department of Justice*. 1967.

Langeluttig, Albert. *The Department of Justice of the United States*. 1927.

Learned, Henry B. *The President's Cabinet*. 1912.

Meador, Daniel J. *The President, the Attorney General, and the Department of Justice*. 1980.

NANCY V. BAKER

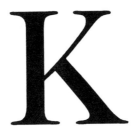

K

KANSAS-NEBRASKA ACT (1854). The act provided for the organization and government of the Kansas and Nebraska territories. Because it intensified the differences between North and South, the law proved a turning point on the road to the CIVIL WAR.

When STEPHEN A. DOUGLAS, chair of the Senate Committee on Territories, introduced the bill, he hoped to organize the last remaining portion of the LOUISIANA PURCHASE north of the 36° 30′ line. By employing the principle of "popular sovereignty," he also hoped to make the status of SLAVERY in the territories merely a local matter. Douglas believed that, if successful, he would not only settle the dangerous issue of slavery in the territories but would also become the acknowledged leader of the DEMOCRATIC PARTY, with the likely prospect of election to the presidency in 1856 or 1860 by a grateful party and nation.

Douglas's proposal, however, ran into massive trouble. By conceding to the South a division of the original Nebraska territory into Kansas and Nebraska as well as the repeal of the MISSOURI COMPROMISE of 1820, which had prohibited slavery north of 36° 30′, Douglas provoked hostile reaction in the North. The repeal of the Missouri Compromise was condemned because it opened up to slavery areas from which it had previously been excluded. Meanwhile, a coalition of those opposed to the Kansas-Nebraska Act, consisting of Free Soilers, dissatisfied Democrats, and Whigs, organized for the 1854 congressional elections and formed the basis for a new political party, the REPUBLICAN PARTY. Douglas's bill had become the catalyst for the most fateful party realignment in American history.

In the attempt to organize Kansas, the besieged policy underwent further trial. For the next four years, supporters and opponents of slavery fought for the upper hand in "Bleeding Kansas." Kansas went through a series of governors as the Democratic administration of James Buchanan committed itself to producing a state that was likely to be Democratic and proslavery.

Meanwhile, Douglas deplored the haste and fraud in the statehood process as well as Buchanan's efforts to determine the outcome; he therefore disavowed the experiment as a travesty of the doctrine of "popular sovereignty" and in 1858 opposed the admission of Kansas under the proslavery Lecompton constitution. His action produced a split in the Democratic Party that persisted into the 1860 election. With the repeal of the Missouri Compromise and the debacle over "popular sovereignty," the upshot of the Kansas-Nebraska Act was to eliminate the two moderate formulas for resolving the question of slavery in the territories, leaving only the extreme sectional approaches that required congressional intervention either to protect or to prohibit slavery's expansion.

BIBLIOGRAPHY

Johannsen, Robert W. *Stephen A. Douglas.* 1973.
Potter, David M. *The Impending Crisis, 1848–1861.* 1976.
Rawley, James A. *Race and Politics: "Bleeding Kansas" and the Coming of the Civil War.* 1969.

MICHAEL PERMAN

KATZENBACH, NICHOLAS deB. (b. 1922), Attorney General. A graduate of Yale Law School and a Rhodes scholar, Nicholas deBelleville Katzenbach played a major role in enforcing civil rights in the Kennedy and Johnson administrations. He was appointed Assistant Attorney General under President

John F. Kennedy in 1961. He moved up to Deputy Attorney General in 1962 and was appointed Attorney General by President Lyndon Baines Johnson in 1965. He served until 1966, when Johnson named him Under Secretary of State, a post he held until 1969.

While Deputy Attorney General, Katzenbach led the Justice Department team dispatched to the University of Mississippi in 1962 to cope with the unrest over civil rights that followed the admission of the first black student. In 1963 he confronted Governor GEORGE WALLACE of Alabama on the steps of the University of Alabama, personally escorting the first black students to enroll there. Katzenbach continued his advocacy of civil rights while Attorney General. He was the chief negotiator in the long struggle to pass the CIVIL RIGHTS ACT OF 1964 and played a similar role in the drafting of the VOTING RIGHTS ACT of 1965. His name appears in a key Supreme Court decision, *Katzenbach v. McClung* (1964), upholding the Civil Rights Act.

Katzenbach's other accomplishments at the Justice Department include the resolution of a lengthy controversy over the ownership of General Aniline and Film Corporation, which had been seized by the government in 1942; the completion of a brief defending the John F. Kennedy administration's blockade of CUBA during the 1962 CUBAN MISSILE CRISIS; and the negotiation of a prisoner exchange with Cuba following the BAY OF PIGS INVASION.

As Undersecretary of State, Katzenbach was intimately involved with the VIETNAM WAR. He was an early advocate of halting or limiting American bombing of North Vietnam in the hopes of fostering peace and of reducing the United States' role in the war.

BIBLIOGRAPHY

"Katzenbach, Nicholas deB." *Current Biography 1965*. 1965. Pp. 212–215.

WILLIAM LASSER

KATZ v. UNITED STATES 389 U.S. 347 (1967). Until 1967, the Supreme Court held that ELECTRONIC SURVEILLANCE of communications was not a search or seizure of tangible things subject to Fourth Amendment constraints. The government did not need a court order to engage in this activity so long as it did not physically trespass on private property. The Court abandoned that view in *Katz*. [*See* OLMSTEAD v. UNITED STATES.]

The defendant was charged with interstate transmission of gambling information. Evidence had been obtained from an electronic device that the govern-

ment attached to the outside of a telephone booth used by the defendant. Because of the Court's previous emphasis on protecting property interests, the defendant argued that the telephone booth was a constitutionally protected area and that, while inside, he had a right of privacy under the Fourth Amendment. The Court rejected that approach, however, explaining that almost every government investigative action interferes to some degree with privacy and that whether the telephone booth was a constitutionally protected area was irrelevant, since the Fourth Amendment "protects people, not places." Activities knowingly exposed to the public cannot be protected, but those that are sought to be kept private may be.

The government argued that the glass walls of the booth prevented any privacy claim, but the Court recognized that it was the uninvited ear, not the eye, of government agents that the defendant intended to shut out. By closing the door to the booth, he was entitled to assume that his conversation would not be broadcast to the entire world. Reading the Constitution more narrowly, said the Court, would ignore the central role of the telephone in facilitating private conversations.

Thus, the Court announced that property rights would no longer form the boundaries for government searches and seizures. Since the focus of the Fourth Amendment was now on persons, not locations, its reach could no longer be determined by whether or not the government had intruded into an enclosure of some kind; prior precedent would have to be overruled.

Writing for a 7 to 2 majority, Justice John Harlan explained the new standard for applying the Fourth Amendment. In the future, the Court would ask two questions to determine whether a "reasonable expectation of privacy existed." First, did the persons involved demonstrate through their actions an actual, or subjective, expectation that their activities would be private? Second, if such an expectation had been demonstrated, was society prepared to accept that expectation as reasonable in the circumstances? If both questions could be answered affirmatively, the Fourth Amendment's limits on government action would come into play.

Justice Byron White wrote a concurring opinion that raised an additional point, and one important in the development of electronic-surveillance law. He underlined the importance of the majority's explicit refusal to extend its decision to warrantless electronic surveillance for NATIONAL-SECURITY purposes. Justice White noted that such activities had been authorized by a succession of Presidents and stated that no judicial warrant should be required in advance in this area so long as the President or the ATTORNEY GENERAL considered the matter and found the surveillance to be reasonable in the circumstances.

Congress reacted to *Katz* by adopting, as part of the Omnibus Crime Control and Safe Streets Act of 1968, a procedure for prior judicial approval of electronic surveillance for law-enforcement, but not national-security, purposes. The scope of permissible, warrantless, national-security surveillance was narrowed by the Supreme Court in 1972 in UNITED STATES v. UNITED STATES DISTRICT COURT. In 1978, Congress enacted the FOREIGN INTELLIGENCE SURVEILLANCE ACT, establishing a special court to review and grant authority for national-security-related electronic surveillance in the United States. Abroad, such activities are still authorized by the Attorney General, when directed against a person protected by the Fourth Amendment, acting under a delegation of presidential power in Executive Order 12333 (46 Fed. Reg. 59941 [1981]).

BIBLIOGRAPHY

"Executive Order 12333: An Assessment of the Validity of Warrantless National Security Searches." Note. *Duke Law Journal* (1983): 611.
"The Foreign Intelligence Surveillance Act: Legislating a Judicial Role in National Security Surveillance." Note. *Michigan Law Review* 78 (1980): 1116.
"From Private Places to Personal Privacy: A Post-Katz Study of Fourth Amendment Protection." Note. *New York University Law Review* 43 (1968): 968.
"Privacy and Political Freedom: Application of the Fourth Amendment to 'National Security' Investigations." Comment. *U.C.L.A. Law Review* 17 (1970): 1205.
Theoharis, Athan G., and Elizabeth Meyer. "The 'National Security' Justification for Electronic Eavesdropping: An Elusive Exception." *Wayne Law Review* 14 (1968): 749.

AMERICO R. CINQUEGRANA

KEEP COMMISSION. President Theodore Roosevelt expanded the capacity of his office by creating six commissions to study specific public problems. The Keep Commission was the second of these. Created by Roosevelt in June 1905 and formally titled the Commission on Departmental Methods, it was popularly known as the Keep Commission after its chairman, Assistant Secretary of the Treasury Charles H. Keep. It had four other members: James R. Garfield, the Commissioner of the Bureau of Corporations; Frank H. Hitchcock, the First Assistant Postmaster General; Lawrence O. Murray, the Assistant Secretary of Commerce and Labor; and Gifford Pinchot, Chief Forester. In his letter creating the commission, Roosevelt

charged it with conducting investigations of administration to secure "an improvement in business methods" in government, specifying particularly the need for more expert knowledge in decision making, better personnel policy, improved accounting, and elimination of excess paperwork. Roosevelt sought $25,000 to support the commission's work, but Congress appropriated only $5,000.

The commission was the first systematic effort at administrative reform initiated by a President. Its method of investigation began with a survey questionnaire of federal bureaus and followed up with investigations by subcommittees, each headed by a commission member. Working into 1909, the commission conducted extensive investigations and made recommendations in several different areas—for example, recommending improvements in federal accounting, record keeping, paperwork management, and the distribution of government publications.

Two areas of distinctive innovation by the commission deserve to be highlighted: personnel policy and interagency coordination. The commission was the first federal reform effort to devise a government-wide classification and salary system, uniform work rules, and a pension system. It also represented the first effort at designing means for coordinating related activities among executive-branch agencies.

The Keep Commission's presidential orientation explains its effort at achieving increased uniformity and coherence in the executive branch. But it served President Roosevelt in more immediate ways. Roosevelt used the commission as an investigative arm of his office when politically sensitive scandals occurred in administrative agencies, first in the Government Printing Office and later in the Department of Agriculture. A third indication of the commission's close identification with the President was Congress's hostility. Congress viewed the commission as a presidential incursion on congressional prerogatives. For all their farsightedness, the commission's recommendations were rejected by Congress, and Congress expressed its hostility to the commission even more aggressively in the Tawney Amendment to the Sundry Civil Appropriation Act of 1909, when it forbade the expenditure of public money for any commission investigating administration, unless its creation was authorized by Congress.

BIBLIOGRAPHY

Kraines, Oscar. "The President versus Congress: The Keep Commission, 1905–1909." *Western Political Quarterly* 23 (March 1970): 5–54.
Skowronek, Stephen. *Building a New American State.* 1982.

PERI E. ARNOLD

KELLOGG-BRIAND PACT. On 27 August 1928 fifteen major nations signed a treaty in Paris designed to outlaw war "as an instrument of national policy." Soon nearly every nation in the world had added its assent to this agreement informally named after its two principal sponsors, French Premier Aristide Briand and American Secretary of State Frank Kellogg. The Kellogg-Briand Pact originated with Briand's 1927 request for a treaty commitment from the United States guaranteeing French security. Kellogg and President Calvin Coolidge opposed the idea, however, fearing that it would reverse the long-standing American resistance to military alliances with foreign countries. Instead Kellogg enlisted the aid of American peace activists who had been pressing for international stipulations outlawing war. The Secretary of State replied to the French that the United States would be willing to join in a multilateral agreement opposing the use of force in resolving international disputes. The resulting treaty would have the effect of providing the security guarantee the French wanted without involving the United States in a military commitment.

The Kellogg-Briand Pact soon proved ineffectual in preventing war. In the 1930s it did not stop Japan's aggression against China in 1931 and 1937, Italy's against Ethiopia in 1935, or Germany's against Poland in 1939. Yet the United States did refer to the pact when it condemned these uses of military force. After Japan invaded Manchuria in 1931, President Herbert Hoover and Secretary of State HENRY L. STIMSON proposed that the United States would not recognize changes in frontiers resulting from the use of force. Before and during WORLD WAR II the administration of Franklin D. Roosevelt often referred to Germany's, Japan's, and Italy's violations of their promises made in the Kellogg-Briand Pact to renounce war. After World War II the United States included violations of the promise to avoid war as one of the charges against German and Japanese leaders tried for war crimes. The United States furthermore included the Kellogg-Briand Pact's opposition to war in the charter of the new UNITED NATIONS organization. Despite such references Presidents since World War II believed that the pact had only rhetorical force. Presidents Harry S. Truman and Dwight D. Eisenhower replaced reliance on the pact and the collective-security provisions of the United Nations charter with a series of multilateral and bilateral military alliances with countries in Asia, Europe, the Middle East, and the Western Hemisphere.

BIBLIOGRAPHY

Ferrell, Robert. *Peace in Their Time: The Origins of the Kellogg-Briand Pact.* 1952.
Leffler, Melvyn. *The Elusive Quest: The American Pursuit of European Stability and French Security, 1919–1933.* 1979.
Kneeshaw, Stephen. *In Pursuit of Peace: The American Reaction to the Kellogg-Briand Pact, 1928–1929.* 1991.

ROBERT D. SCHULZINGER

KENDALL, AMOS (1789–1869), Postmaster General. Amos Kendall was born in Dunstable, Massachusetts, on 16 August 1789. Graduating from Dartmouth College in 1811, Kendall moved to Kentucky in 1814. First a tutor in HENRY CLAY's household, he moved to Frankfort, Kentucky, in 1816 and became editor of the *Argus of the West* newspaper, with help from his friend RICHARD M. JOHNSON. A highly successful political commentator known for his antinational bank and prodebt relief views, Kendall first supported Clay in national politics, but broke with Clay for Andrew Jackson.

With Jackson's election, Kendall moved to Washington and became a crucial Jackson adviser. During Jackson's administrations, Kendall played a preeminent role in knitting the various local and state pro-Jackson interests into a cohesive mass-based political party, the DEMOCRATIC PARTY. Serving officially as an auditor in the DEPARTMENT OF THE TREASURY from 1828 to 1836, he was a member of the famous KITCHEN CABINET. Unofficially Kendall served as Jackson's publicist and speech writer. He had a hand in many of the President's annual messages and wrote much of Jackson's celebrated veto message against the rechartering of the BANK OF THE UNITED STATES. Kendall also assisted his friend Francis Blair establish the *Globe* newspaper, the national party's organ. Kendall wrote extensively for the *Globe*.

During his second administration, Jackson named Kendall POSTMASTER GENERAL. Debt-ridden and poorly managed, the post office was an embarrassment to the Democrats' policy of rotation of office. Under Kendall, the post office was transformed into an efficient, self-sustaining institution, with clear lines of administrative hierarchy. In the late 1830s, Kendall directed the post office to cease carrying abolitionist mails to the South. The national government, he insisted, should have no hand in delivering inflammatory political material.

After Martin Van Buren's defeat in 1840, Kendall remained in Washington, carving out a rather meager career as a journalist. By the mid 1840s, Kendall turned to law and business, representing claimants against the United States government. He became Samuel F. B. Morse's agent, protecting Morse's legal interests against patent abuse and helping to set up the telegraph industry.

During the CIVIL WAR, Kendall remained a Democrat but spoke out against SECESSION. He criticized the prorreconciliationist wing of the party. Later Kendall argued against the Republican's punitive RECONSTRUCTION policy.

BIBLIOGRAPHY

Latner, Richard B. *The Presidency of Andrew Jackson.* 1979.
McCormick, Richard. *The Second Party System.* 1966.
Marshall, Lynn. "The Early Career of Amos Kendall." Ph.D. diss., University of California, Berkeley. 1968.
Remini, Robert. *Andrew Jackson and the Bank War.* 1967.

JOHN F. WALSH

KENDALL v. UNITED STATES

KENDALL v. UNITED STATES 37 U.S. 524 (1838). The *Kendall* case, involving the POST OFFICE, was part of the struggle between Congress and the President for control of executive-branch departments. The struggle was particularly intense during the presidency of Andrew Jackson. Jackson's Postmaster General, AMOS KENDALL, established an inspection office to supervise private contractors who delivered mail. Two contractors, Stockton and Stokes, submitted claims that Kendall believed were fraudulent. At first he refused to pay them anything. Congress then passed a law directing the Postmaster General to pay the contractors whatever sum the Treasury Department's solicitor thought was due. The solicitor concluded that the contractors were entitled to $161,563. With Jackson's concurrence, Kendall refused to pay more than $122,563.

The contractors argued in court that the statute made the payment a nondiscretionary (ministerial) act. Kendall countered that any payments made by the department constituted a discretionary, executive act. In constitutional law the distinction between ministerial and executive duties dates back to MARBURY V. MADISON (1803). In his opinion for the Supreme Court, Chief Justice John Marshall had drawn a distinction between the political powers of the President, "in the exercise of which he is to use his own discretion, and is accountable only to his country," and the legal obligation of the President's subordinates to carry out nondiscretionary duties assigned to them by law.

The decision of the circuit court for the District of Columbia in *Kendall*, relying on the Court's reading of *Marbury*, held that the President had "no other control over the officer than to see that he acts honestly, with proper motives," but had "no power to construe the law and see that the executive action conforms to it." The Supreme Court did not construe the President's superintendence so narrowly. Justice Smith Thompson drew a distinction between the executive power of the President, which can be used to enforce discretionary actions by officials, and "mere ministerial acts" of those officials, which are controlled by law and which neither the Postmaster General "nor the President had any authority to deny or control." The Court held that officials of the departments are not "under the exclusive direction of the President." Their political duties are controlled by him, but the Court added that "it would be an alarming doctrine, that Congress cannot impose upon any executive officer any duty they may think proper, which is not repugnant to any rights secured and protected by the constitution." In such cases, "the duty and responsibility grow out of and are subject to the control of the law, and not to the direction of the President." The Court upheld the district court's order of mandamus, ruling that the duty of the Postmaster General was a MINISTERIAL DUTY—he was simply to pay out the monetary amount awarded the contractors by the Treasury Department solicitor.

Emboldened by his victory, Stokes then sued Kendall for damages (the interest on the delayed payments) and his court costs. A jury composed of anti-Jackson Whigs awarded damages of $12,000, and in a second trial Kendall was again found liable. Congress then unanimously passed a private bill to pay Kendall's counsel's fees and court costs. Finally, in *Kendall v. Stokes* (1845), Stokes's decision was overturned by the Supreme Court, which dismissed his suit on the ground that he had already exhausted all his legal remedies in the first case.

The significance of *Kendall* is that it held that the President does not have plenary authority over officials in the departments. Though federal courts will not issue writs unless the duties of officials are clearly and solely ministerial, the Supreme Court in *Decatur v. Paulding* (1840) refused to grant a writ against Martin Van Buren's Secretary of the Navy on the grounds that the act in question was executive. But the District of Columbia federal courts have issued writs of mandamus against heads of departments in other cases in which acts are considered ministerial, such as the obligation to spend funds appropriated by Congress. Federal courts, following *Kendall*, are expected to uphold the law at the expense of the presidential directive if an aggrieved party can demonstrate that a ministerial law is not being obeyed.

BIBLIOGRAPHY

Kendall, Amos. *Autobiography.* 1872. Repr. 1949.
U.S. House of Representatives. Report 122, 21st Cong. 1st sess. (26 January 1830).
Warren, Charles. *The Supreme Court in United States History.* 1926.

White, Leonard D. *The Jacksonians: A Study in Administrative History, 1829–1861*. 1954.

RICHARD M. PIOUS

KENNEDY, JACQUELINE (1929–1994), First Lady, wife of John F. Kennedy. Although Jacqueline Bouvier Kennedy generally distanced herself from politics while her husband was Senator and took little part in the 1960 campaign, she became one of the more popular FIRST LADIES in history. Her youthfulness, fashion flair, ability in languages, and familiarity with the arts won her admirers in the United States and abroad and augmented her husband's following.

Before moving into the WHITE HOUSE, she announced her intention to make it a showcase for the finest in American furnishings and arts, and she enlisted the aid of curators and fund-raisers in the project. With her help, a law was passed in 1961 making White House property inviolable—it could not be removed by future residents—and she brought in, on loan, a curator from the Smithsonian Institution to begin cataloging the mansion's contents. She conducted a televised tour of the executive mansion and initiated a program to pay for upgrading the White House interior by selling guidebooks featuring its occupants and collections, thus helping solidify the public perception of the First Lady's responsibility for the presidential residence. In 1968 she married Aristotle Onassis.

BIBLIOGRAPHY

Baldrige, Letitia. *Of Diamonds and Diplomats*. 1968.
Thayer, Mary Van Rensselaer. *Jacqueline Kennedy: The White House Years*. 1967.
Watson, Mary Ann. "An Enduring Fascination: The Papers of Jacqueline Kennedy." In *Modern First Ladies: Their Documentary Legacy*. Edited by Nancy Kegan Smith and Mary C. Ryan. 1989.

BETTY BOYD CAROLI

KENNEDY, JOHN F. (1917–1963), thirty-fifth President of the United States (1961–1963). John Fitzgerald Kennedy was the second child and the second son of Joseph P. Kennedy, and Rose Fitzgerald Kennedy, who in all had nine children.

Kennedy's maternal grandfather, John ("Honey Fitz") Fitzgerald, had been a member of the Massachusetts senate and of the U.S. House of Representatives and was the first Irish-Catholic mayor of Boston. Rose was his favorite and he doted on her children, particularly Jack. Shortly before his death, Fitzgerald told his grandson, "You are my namesake. You are the one to carry on our family name. And mark my word, you will walk on a far larger canvas than I."

Joseph Kennedy, while a graduate of the Boston Latin School and of Harvard University and enormously wealthy and powerful, carried a deep wound: the Protestant Brahmins of Boston did not accept him because he was an Irish-Catholic. He resolved that they would have to accept his children, particularly his first-born, Joe, Jr., who, he was determined, would be elected to high office, even the presidency.

The son seemed to hold the world in his hand. He was handsome, outgoing, bright, athletic, popular, and his parents' favorite. During the war he became a navy pilot and made dangerous flights out of England. In 1945 he volunteered for a secret mission on a PB4Y to take out the bunkers from which Hitler's V-1 rockets were aimed at Britain. He was killed in the air in a giant explosion.

Now John was the oldest Kennedy son. He had been overshadowed by his brother and was reserved, bookish, and sickly. Nevertheless, he assumed the family role as a political aspirant. Further, he was a celebrity as a decorated war hero for commanding a PT boat in a sea battle in the Solomon Islands.

Between 1946 and 1958 Kennedy ran for the U.S. House of Representatives three times and for the Senate twice, always successfully. His father provided money and important connections in politics, business, and the media. His brother, ROBERT F. KENNEDY managed both Senate campaigns. His mother and sisters staged the celebrated Kennedy teas around the state to win the women's vote.

In 1960, when Kennedy ran for President against Vice President Richard M. Nixon, Robert again was campaign manager. Younger brother Edward was in charge of the Rocky Mountain region. Stephen Smith, sister Jean's husband, handled the schedule. R. Sargent Shriver, sister Eunice's husband, was responsible for minorities. After the election Shriver would head the team to find people to staff the new Kennedy administration.

Nomination and Election. In 1958, Kennedy began running seriously for the 1960 Democratic nomination. He delivered about two hundred speeches around the country, receiving extensive and favorable coverage in the press. In the 1952 Senate race, Kennedy had narrowly defeated Henry Cabot Lodge. In his Senate reelection bid he wanted to win a big majority, perhaps 200,000 to 250,000 votes. In fact, Kennedy won by an amazing 874,608 votes. While 1958 was a splendid year for Democrats, Kennedy won by the largest margin ever in his state, the biggest of any senatorial candidate in the nation, and the greatest percentage of the vote in any major senatorial contest. Millions of Democrats concluded that they had a winner.

On 2 January 1960, Kennedy announced his candidacy for President. After having talked with Democrats in all the states, he said, "I can win both the nomination and the election." On 14 January in a notable address to the National Press Club in Washington, D.C., on his concept for the presidency, Kennedy excoriated President Dwight D. Eisenhower for having failed to fulfill the eloquent hopes that he had voiced. Eisenhower's "detached limited concept" was fitting for the 1950s when the nation needed time to "draw breath," Kennedy declared, but the United States was entering "the challenging and revolutionary sixties." The new President "must place himself in the thick of the fight [and] . . . care passionately." Kennedy aligned himself with his eminent activist Democratic predecessors—Woodrow Wilson, Franklin D. Roosevelt, and Harry S. Truman. The President "must above all be the Chief Executive in every sense of the word." He must make vital foreign-policy decisions take the lead in proposing needed domestic legislation to the Congress.

There were three and one-half other Democratic candidates: Senator HUBERT H. HUMPHREY of Minnesota, Senate Majority Leader Lyndon B. Johnson of Texas, Senator Stuart Symington of Missouri, and, offstage, the two-time unsuccessful candidate ADLAI E. STEVENSON. Kennedy entered the primaries to demonstrate his popularity and to show up those who hoped for a deadlocked convention—Johnson, Symington, and Stevenson—and to confront his deepest concern, the religion issue and his Catholic faith. Only Humphrey opposed him in two critical primaries.

Wisconsin was Humphrey country. He was almost as well known as in his own state. Humphrey had long cultivated liberals, labor, and farmers in historically progressive Wisconsin—the Lutherans concentrated in the northwest along the Minnesota border, the Catholics in the southeast in Milwaukee and the nearby industrial towns. The format of the primary was potentially damaging to Kennedy: delegates were awarded by congressional district. Thus, he might carry the state and remain saddled with the religious issue. He campaigned furiously everywhere in Wisconsin and his family was out in full force.

For Kennedy the results were mixed. He won the primary with 56 percent of the vote and he carried six of the ten districts. Though Humphrey had not mentioned religion, the press and, more important, the voters, gave it heavy weight. Kennedy took the Catholic southeast and Humphrey swept the Protestant western districts. While this factor was not decisive in Wisconsin, it was threatening to Kennedy for the nation as a whole because there were many more Protestants than Catholics in the country.

West Virginia, an even bigger challenge, was 95 percent Protestant. The rich and glamorous Kennedy family would be a liability in that extremely poor state. Franklin D. Roosevelt, Jr., came to help, flashing his father's smile and reminding West Virginians of their former friend in the White House. Campaigning there made a great impression on Kennedy. As he learned about conditions, he spoke increasingly of policies to assist depressed areas. But he could not escape the burden of religion and tried to deal with it. In a speech to the American Society of Newspaper Editors he pledged that he would neither take orders nor bow to influence from his church. Dean Francis B. Sayre, Jr., of Washington's Episcopal National Cathedral sent a n open letter signed by prominent Protestant clergymen urging every Protestant minister in West Virginia to preach against religious bigotry.

Kennedy scored an amazing victory, winning 61 percent of the vote and all but seven of West Virginia's fifty-five counties. Humphrey, discouraged and broke, abandoned his quest for the presidency. Kennedy swept the remaining primaries and rode the bandwagon to the Democratic convention in Los Angeles, which opened on 11 July 1960.

That gathering had two dramatic moments, but the already-decided nomination for President was not among them. A total of 761 votes were needed. Wyoming was the last state to be called and by that time Kennedy had 750. He counted on 8½ of Wyoming's 15 votes. He knew that 2½ and more would come from the Virgin Islands, Puerto Rico, the Canal Zone, and the District of Columbia. When Kennedy, watching on television, saw his brother Teddy in the Wyoming delegation with a big grin on his face he knew that it was wrapped up. Wyoming delivered all 15 to clinch the nomination on the first ballot.

The first dramatic event was a tumultuous, emotional, and nostalgic tribute to Adlai Stevenson, who was extremely popular in southern California. His supporters packed the galleries and thousands marched outside. But the enormous demonstration on the floor had no impact on the voting.

Far more important for the future was Kennedy's choice of a running mate, Lyndon B. Johnson. The details of Kennedy's offer and Johnson's acceptance would become the subject of controversy, and the selection provoked strong opposition from many liberals as well as from Robert Kennedy. John Kennedy's reasoning was clear: his Catholicism crippled him in the South, which he needed to win, particularly Texas. Johnson, a powerful campaigner, was the only man who could deliver these states.

Kennedy in his acceptance speech proposed a program that he called the NEW FRONTIER. With that phrase he identified himself with the visions of his illustrious predecessors—Wilson's NEW FREEDOM, Roosevelt's NEW DEAL, and Truman's FAIR DEAL.

The Republicans nominated Vice President Nixon for President and Henry Cabot Lodge, whom Kennedy had defeated in the 1952 Senate race, for Vice President. Both Kennedy and Nixon were young, energetic, and experienced campaigners.

Kennedy could not rid himself of the religious issue, which was especially damaging in the Baptist South. On 12 September 1960, therefore, he confronted the issue directly in a speech on religion to the Houston Ministerial Association. He called for an "America where the separation of church and state is absolute." No priest, minister, or rabbi should instruct any candidate for office on how he should vote and no voter should decide how to cast his ballot because of his faith. He asked the ministers to support him not for the "church I believe in, for that should be important only to me, but what kind of America I believe in." The address and Kennedy's masterly handling of the questions won wide praise, but his religion remained an issue.

The 1960 campaign was the first in which the candidates debated on television [see DEBATES, PRESIDENTIAL] in four debates between 26 September and 21 October. Nixon, who could have declined the contest, assumed the risk. He was much better known than Kennedy. Eisenhower and other Republicans advised Nixon to sidestep the hazard. But he fancied himself an outstanding debater and a master of television. Only the first debate, on domestic policy, was significant and it was said to have attracted 70 million viewers. Kennedy seemed at ease, on top of the questions and the facts, and precise in his language. Nixon appeared unsure of himself, poorly informed, and inexact in his use of words. The image Kennedy projected—good looks, grace, and wit—won handily. Eisenhower was right; Kennedy closed the gap.

Kennedy's most dramatic campaign proposal was to establish a "peace corps" in which young Americans would assist the poor in less developed countries. He introduced the idea on 14 October at the student union of the University of Michigan. It caught on so quickly that he delivered a major address on the topic at the Cow Palace in San Francisco on 2 November.

The 1960 election was one of the closest in history. Of the 68.8 million ballots cast, Kennedy won by only 119,450—49.7 percent to Nixon's 49.6, with 0.7 per cent going to minor parties. The margin in the ELECTORAL COLLEGE was more comfortable; Kennedy won 303 to 219, with 15 cast from Alabama and Mississippi for Senator Harry Byrd of Virginia. The Kennedy-Johnson ticket carried seven states of the old Confederacy—Alabama, Arkansas, Georgia, Louisiana, North and South Carolina, and, most important, Texas. The Republicans won only Florida, Tennessee, and Virginia, while Mississippi voted for segregationist candidates.

On balance his religion damaged Kennedy severely. While it helped in Catholic districts, it hurt in the much more numerous Protestant areas. An informed estimate was that, if there had been no religious issue, Kennedy would have carried the popular vote 54 to 46 percent and would have won by a small landslide in the Electoral College.

Kennedy had no coattails. Democratic candidates for Congress ran well ahead of him with 55 percent of the national vote. But the Democrats lost 2 seats in the Senate and 21 in the House. While they retained margins of 64 to 36 and 262 to 175 respectively, they were fictional majorities. The historic coalition of southern Democrats and Republicans on domestic issues would continue to rule Congress. Kennedy would face formidable legislative roadblocks to the New Frontier.

Kennedy's appointments, based in large part on the Shriver team's talent search, were of unusually high quality. Later, however, he would make several poor judicial appointments to the lower courts in the South. Among the luminaries named at the outset: Secretary of Defense ROBERT S. MCNAMARA, Secretary of the Treasury C. Douglas Dillon, Attorney General Robert F. Kennedy and several of his subordinates, particularly NICHOLAS DEB. KATZENBACH, Secretary of the Interior STEWART UDALL, Secretary of Labor Arthur J. Goldberg, Chairman of the Council of Economic Advisers Walter W. Heller, Assistant Secretary of Health, Education, and Welfare Wilbur J. Cohen, White House chief of congressional relations Lawrence F. O'Brien, and Shriver himself as director of the PEACE CORPS.

Foreign Policy. Kennedy had long had a deep interest in FOREIGN AFFAIRS. When WORLD WAR II broke out and his father was ambassador to Great Britain, he had written his senior honors thesis at Harvard on British rearmament, published under the title *Why England Slept*. In the Senate he yearned for a seat on the Foreign Relations Committee and eventually got it. He traveled abroad frequently and extensively and spoke to important leaders. Like all politicians of his time, he inhabited a bipolar world ruled by the COLD WAR, but his anti-Soviet views were tempered by a profound concern for peace and a healthy skepticism of the doctrines and efficiency of the military.

At no time were cold war issues hotter than during the Kennedy presidency. The great conflicts involved the Soviet Union and its allies, CUBA and East Germany. The major events were the Bay of Pigs, Berlin, the Cuban missile crisis, and the nuclear test ban treaty.

Bay of Pigs. The BAY OF PIGS INVASION may have been the most harebrained and inept venture in the history of American foreign policy. Following the success of Fidel Castro's revolution in 1959–1960, a stream of Cuban exiles of all political shades poured into Miami. On 17 March 1960, President Eisenhower directed the CENTRAL INTELLIGENCE AGENCY to recruit and train a Cuban force capable of waging guerilla warfare. The agency established a secret training base on a coffee plantation in the Guatemalan mountains. But the CIA soon changed its mind and began training for an invasion of Cuba by only small force, on the assumption that the Cuban people would rise in support of the attempt to overthrow Castro.

On 29 November 1960 Allen Dulles, director of the CIA, briefed Kennedy. The President-elect told him to go forward with the training. The CIA plan was for an amphibious landing at the thinly populated Bay of Pigs on the south coast.

Once in office, Kennedy struggled over whether to go forward with the invasion. The affirmative reasons were the following: Castro, anticipating the landing, was receiving a heavy flow of Soviet arms and the CIA reported that a delay would be fatal. If Kennedy scrubbed the attack, fourteen hundred embittered Cubans along with the Cuban community in Miami would accuse him of betrayal. The Republicans would brand him soft on communism. The Guatemalans were pressing to rid their country of the Cuban brigade. If the plan succeeded, Kennedy would have gotten rid of Castro without using American forces, a remarkable feat. On the other side, the military soundness of the plan was extremely questionable. In early April 1961 he approved it reluctantly but only on condition that U.S. units would not be directly involved.

The brigade sailed from Nicaragua in seven small ships and made a landing at the Bay of Pigs on 17 April. Castro's forces wiped them out in three days, capturing more than eleven hundred prisoners. The military plan was ridiculous. The force was much too small; the landing site could hardly have been worse; there was no route of escape; the Cuban people did not

rise to support the exiles. Kennedy, swearing silently at those who had given him atrocious advice, took full responsibility for the disaster. As is customary, the American people rallied to their President in a crisis and his Gallup poll approval rating rose from 72 percent in the week of 10 February to 83 percent in the week of 28 April 1961. But this did not mask the fact that the President and the nation had suffered a severe blow.

Berlin. On 3–4 June 1961, less than two months after the failed invasion, Premier Nikita Khrushchev warned Kennedy at the Vienna summit that East Germany might cut off West Berlin and that, if the West responded with force, the East would do the same. Convinced that the city was the linchpin of the NATO alliance, Kennedy determined to be ready. He studied the Berlin problem intensively, beefed up conventional forces, asked Congress for an extra $3.2 billion for defense, and consulted the NATO allies. In fact, East Germany did not close off Berlin, though it did build a wall starting on 13 August 1961 to prevent the flight of its citizens to the western part of the city.

In June 1963, Kennedy made a triumphal tour of Europe climaxed by a speech to a stupendous and delirious crowd in Rudolf Wilde Platz in West Berlin. Here he delivered the memorable words, "Ich bin ein Berliner."

Cuban missile crisis. The CUBAN MISSILE CRISIS of October 1962 was the most dangerous confrontation of the cold war. A routine U-2 overflight of western Cuba on 29 August revealed SAM missile installations. By mid October the photographs conclusively proved that the Soviets were mounting missiles that could reach targets in a great arc from Hudson's Bay to Peru.

On 16 October, Kennedy brought his top advisers together as a crisis team that would be in continuous session for thirteen days. Since it was vital that the Soviets not learn that the United States knew, Kennedy continued with his scheduled routine, including campaigning for Democratic candidates.

The basic problem was to get the missiles out of Cuba without a nuclear war. Many options were examined and two came to the top: a naval blockade, later called a quarantine, including searching merchant vessels approaching the island, or a "surgical" air strike to take out the missile sites. On 20 October the President chose the blockade for several reasons: if it failed, he would have the other as the next option; bombing was not a precise instrument; and he wanted Khrushchev to have multiple options—an air strike might force him to choose nuclear war. Dean Acheson was sent with the U-2 photographs to inform the British (who had already figured it out), the French, and the

Germans. Senegal and Guinea, which had the only airfields in West Africa from which Soviet aircraft could reach Cuba, agreed to deny them landing rights, if asked. American forces mobilized in the Caribbean.

On 22 October, the President addressed the world, but specifically the Soviet leadership and the American people. The Soviet action, he said, is "deliberately provocative" and "cannot be accepted by this country, if our courage and commitments are ever to be trusted again by either friend or foe." A missile launched from Cuba "against any nation in the Western Hemisphere would be considered as an attack by the Soviet Union on the United States, requiring a full retaliatory response upon the Soviet Union. . . . All ships of any kind bound for Cuba from whatever nation or port will, if found to contain cargoes of offensive weapons, be turned back." He would immediately ask the Organization of American States (OAS) to invoke the Rio Treaty and the United Nations Security Council to demand that the Soviet Union remove its missiles. Kennedy then turned to Khrushchev, demanding that he "halt and eliminate this clandestine, reckless and provocative threat to world peace."

The OAS quickly voted 19 to 0 to support the blockade. Despite valiant efforts by U.N. Ambassador Adlai Stevenson, the Security Council became ensnarled in a bitter and prolonged debate.

On 24 October the U.S. Navy's Second Fleet took up stations in a great circle five hundred miles from the eastern tip of Cuba. Twenty-five Soviet ships were en route to the island. That afternoon a dozen changed course or stopped and later turned back to Soviet ports, presumably because they were carrying incriminating cargoes. The United States deliberately chose a neutral vessel as the first ship to be stopped and searched; its cargo proved to be innocent.

The Kremlin seemed to be taken completely by surprise and Khrushchev's first two letters to Kennedy were extremely confusing. At Robert Kennedy's suggestion, the President treated part of one as lucid and dispatched a three-point reply: the Soviet Union must remove its weapons and halt further missile introduction, both under U.N. supervision; the U.S. would terminate the blockade; and the United States would pledge not to invade Cuba. On 28 October Khrushchev accepted and began pulling his missiles out of Cuba. The crisis, which brought the world to the brink of nuclear war, ended without the firing of a shot.

The outcome was a triumph for the United States and for Kennedy. Prime Minister Harold Macmillan of Great Britain, the most concerned of world leaders about nuclear war, wrote in his diary that "President Kennedy conducted this affair with great skill, energy, resourcefulness, and courage." His approval rating in the Gallup poll shot up from 62 percent in the week of 20 September to 74 percent in the week of 16 November 1962.

Nuclear testing. International concern over nuclear testing emerged with the detonation of the U.S. hydrogen bomb BRAVO at Bikini Atoll on 1 March 1954. Over the next nine years there were long and fruitless talks in Geneva looking toward a test ban treaty. The Eisenhower administration was not interested because it considered a ban by itself a danger to the nation's security.

As a Senator, Kennedy had criticized Eisenhower's policy and had advocated a comprehensive ban or, failing that, a limitation to underground testing. During the latter part of 1961 and 1962 the United States and the Soviet Union engaged in a nuclear-testing race, including the explosion of extremely large weapons in the atmosphere. Further, because of Chinese advances, there was a growing concern over nuclear proliferation. If this madness had any virtue, it was to convince Kennedy that it must be stopped. On 24 April 1963 he and Macmillan jointly asked Khrushchev for a comprehensive test ban. While the response was churlish, Khrushchev did agree to receive emissaries on 15 July. This was the opening for Kennedy.

In a powerful address at American University on 10 June he had called on the Soviets to join in a test ban and pledged that "the United States does not propose to conduct nuclear tests in the atmosphere so long as other states do not do so." This speech rang loud in the Kremlin. Further, Khrushchev was delighted with the American emissary, the old Russia hand W. Averell Harriman.

Kennedy's hope for a comprehensive ban was soon dashed. The Soviets were firmly opposed. U.S. defense forces, particularly the air force, had relied on the Soviets to kill any test ban; now, with a treaty in the offing, they insisted on a continuation of underground testing. Moreover, it seemed that a comprehensive treaty could not win the sixty-seven votes needed for ratification by the Senate. But Andrei Gromyko of the Soviet Union, Harriman, and Lord Hailsham of Britain forged ahead and on 25 July 1963 initialed the Treaty Banning Nuclear Weapons Tests in the Atmosphere, Outer Space, and Under Water. Bipartisan support in the Senate yielded ratification by a vote of 80 to 19.

"No other accomplishment . . . ," Theodore Sorensen wrote, "gave Kennedy greater satisfaction." Glenn T. Seaborg, who, as chairman of the Atomic Energy Commission was deeply involved in the negotiations, gave the main credit to Kennedy for his "persistence," "skilled leadership," and "sensitive and patient diplomacy."

Domestic Policy. In the fifteen years between the end of World War II and Kennedy's election, American society was transformed by an immense increase in population due mainly to the baby boom as well as a sharp rise in the number of old people, a massive movement of rural southern blacks to northern cities along with a flight of whites to the suburbs, the emergence of a powerful civil rights movement, and extraordinary economic growth slowed by recessions and unemployment, particularly in the late 1950s.

The Democratic agenda, which emerged by 1960, embraced a wide range of policies of which four were fundamental: a comprehensive civil rights act, a Keynesian full-employment policy, federal aid for education at all levels, and health insurance for the aged under Social Security, known as Medicare. These policies, along with others of lesser significance, became planks in the 1960 Democratic platform. When Kennedy won the nomination, he endorsed these proposals.

As President his challenge was to push these policies through a hostile Congress. Inevitably, the political process would be painfully slow. The results of the 1962 congressional elections, basically a standoff, did not help him. Thus, Kennedy's first two years yielded only modest gains.

Civil rights. At the outset Kennedy made the political decision not to ask Congress for a comprehensive civil rights act. He reasoned that it would divide the country, shatter the DEMOCRATIC PARTY, and be rejected by Congress. While correct politically, this policy was condemned then and later on moral grounds by civil rights advocates. For two years Kennedy limited action to the executive branch. Federal agencies were ordered to hire blacks and to desegregate their facilities; by EXECUTIVE ORDER he established the Committee on Equal Employment Opportunity to promote fair employment in the federal service and among government contractors; the Interstate Commerce Commission made segregation illegal in interstate transportation; the Department of Justice filed suits to protect the right of blacks to vote in the Deep South; discrimination in public housing was prohibited; after serious violence, the University of Mississippi was compelled to admit a black student, James Meredith [*see* MEREDITH CASE]; in the face of even greater violence Birmingham was pressed to take its first halting steps toward desegregation; and, despite Governor GEORGE WALLACE, the University of Alabama was forced to enroll its first black students.

The confrontations in Birmingham and Tuscaloosa convinced Kennedy that executive action alone was not enough. In a notable televised address on 11 June 1963, therefore, he came out strongly for an omnibus civil rights act. By doing so, he transformed the politics of civil rights. Kennedy lost the southern Democrats in Congress. He needed the Republicans to create a two-thirds margin to impose cloture against filibuster in the Senate and for simple majorities in both houses on substance. The bill cleared the House Judiciary Committee on 20 November 1963, two days before the President's assassination. While it still had to go to the Rules Committee in the House and to the floor in both chambers, cloture in the Senate notwithstanding, the signs were favorable.

Employment policy. The Keynesian employment policy took the form of tax reduction. As in the case of civil rights, there were two years of delay and debate followed by a policy commitment in 1963. Congress had little interest in cutting taxes and it took time to bring the key legislator, Wilbur Mills, chairman of the House Ways and Means Committee, around. Further, the administration was divided. The COUNCIL OF ECONOMIC ADVISERS, headed by Walter Heller, pressed vigorously for tax reduction. But Secretary of the Treasury C. Douglas Dillon was lukewarm and insisted on linking lower taxes to tax reform, which, while much needed to plug loopholes, was extremely complex and took a long time to work out.

The President committed himself to the Keynesian analysis in his commencement address at Yale University on 11 June 1962. But he spent the rest of that year with only middling success trying to move Mills and Dillon. In a special message to Congress on 24 January 1963 he proposed a $13.6 billion across-the-board tax cut, $11 billion for individuals and $2.6 billion for corporations, to take effect over three years. But the measure included a great number of proposed reforms. The Ways and Means Committee held extensive hearings and in its executive sessions it responded to the lobbies and sliced away most of the reforms. The bill that the House passed on 25 September 1963 was substantially the administration's proposal on reduction with only a handful of reforms. The Senate Finance Committee opened its hearings in October and recessed on 22 November because of the assassination. But there was little doubt that the Senate would go along early in 1964.

Education. The flood of children pouring into the schools and colleges imposed an insuperable financial burden on state and local governments. Federal money was desperately needed and Kennedy strongly agreed. But at the primary and secondary levels this idea was fouled by a poisonous controversy over the church-state issue.

The Roman Catholic church operated parochial school system with 5 million students. The church, hard-pressed to finance its system, argued that government funds for public schools should also be given to private schools. Many Catholic members of Congress supported this position. A large number of Protestants and Jews thought this a dangerous and unconstitutional intrusion of the church in secular matters. Kennedy's Catholicism and his commitments during the campaign crippled his ability to resolve this bitter controversy. Further, at the outset the people he named to manage the program in the Department of Health, Education, and Welfare and the Office of Education were ineffective. While the Senate passed the bill on 25 May 1961, the administration could not even pry it loose from the House Rules Committee. Nor was anything accomplished the next year.

Once again, the tide turned in 1963. In large part this was because Francis Keppel, the distinguished dean of Harvard's School of Education, had become Commissioner of Education. The administration introduced an omnibus bill, which, as Kennedy and Keppel anticipated, Congress broke into separate bills, seven of which were enacted that year. The most important was the Higher Education Facilities Act, which provided matching grants and loans for the construction of college buildings and for the development of community colleges. But direct assistance to primary and secondary education along with scholarships for college students were laid over. Political momentum was now established and there was good reason to believe that these measures would follow in 1964 or 1965.

Medicare. Medicare proved the toughest part of Kennedy's program to enact because the American Medical Association waged a massive, expensive, and bitter campaign to prevent its passage. The critical event was Senate defeat of the bill by a narrow margin on 17 June 1962. While there was no legislative progress during 1963, in November 1963, Wilbur Mills, whose support was indispensable, reached agreement with the administration on a financing formula.

At a press conference on 14 November 1963, Kennedy was asked about his legislative program. He predicted that all of it would be enacted by 1965. Obviously, he expected to be overwhelmingly reelected in 1964 and to bring with him a more liberal Congress. There can be little doubt that this would have occurred. Kennedy, in fact, was so confident that during 1963 he directed Heller to develop a program to combat poverty.

Many important issues of lesser significance were also concerns of Kennedy: redevelopment of distressed areas, manpower training, a higher minimum wage with extended coverage for workers, federal sector collective bargaining, the education legislation for college construction, the health professions, and the mental health system, the Peace Corps, and the first steps towards WOMENS' RIGHTS.

Assassination. On 22 November 1963 LEE HARVEY OSWALD, acting alone, assassinated President Kennedy in Dallas. This was an extraordinary event, historically significant for several reasons. No other incident, possibly excepting the assassination of President Lincoln in 1865, can match it in public impact. The fact that it played instantly on television, moreover, involved the American people directly. It produced enormous public grief and a shaken faith in the very basis for government and the institutions of society.

The assassination raised questions that for many Americans have never been answered. Did Oswald act alone? Or, was he merely a hit man for right-wingers, for the CIA, for the Soviets, for Cuba? The idea of conspiracy emerged at once and has never died. Hoping to forestall speculation about the assassination, President Lyndon B. Johnson created a commission of distinguished public figures headed by Chief Justice Earl Warren to investigate the assassination and to report its conclusions. The WARREN COMMISSION made an exhaustive investigation and found no evidence of conspiracy. Nor, over the succeeding decades, has anyone produced any evidence to challenge the conclusion that Oswald acted alone.

The assassination, by cutting down the President just as he was reaching full stride, has made it impossible to make a conclusive evaluation of Kennedy's performance in office. He did not have the time to move beyond the test ban in his search for a formula to end the cold war, to work out a solution to the thorny problem of Vietnam, to get the Big Four enacted, to launch his poverty program. From this many have concluded that, because many of his programs were not enacted, his was a failed presidency. But others are convinced that he was on the road to an exceptional presidency with notable accomplishments had he been given the time.

BIBLIOGRAPHY

Bernstein, Irving. *Promises Kept: John F. Kennedy's New Frontier.* 1991.

Brauer, Carl M. *John F. Kennedy and the Second Reconstruction.* 1977.

Burns, James MacGregor. *John Kennedy: A Political Profile.* 1959.

Galbraith, John Kenneth. *Ambassador's Journal: A Personal Account of the Kennedy Years.* 1969.

Giglio, James N. *The Presidency of John F. Kennedy.* 1991.

Goodwin, Doris Kearns. *The Fitzgeralds and the Kennedys: An American Saga*. 1987.

Hamilton, Nigel. *JFK: Reckless Youth*. 1992.

Parmet, Herbert S. *Jack: The Struggles of John F. Kennedy*. 1980.

Parmet, Herbert S. *JFK: The Presidency of John F. Kennedy*. 1983.

Schlesinger, Arthur M., Jr. *A Thousand Days: John F. Kennedy in the White House*. 1965.

Sorensen, Theodore C. *Kennedy*. 1965.

Sundquist, James L. *Politics and Policy: The Eisenhower, Kennedy, and Johnson Years*. 1968.

Warren Commission. *Report of the President's Commission on the Assassination of President Kennedy*. 1964.

Wofford, Harris. *Of Kennedys and Kings*. 1980.

IRVING BERNSTEIN

KENNEDY, ROBERT F. (1929–1968), Attorney General, Senator, presidential candidate. The son of Ambassador Joseph P. Kennedy and the brother of President John F. Kennedy, Robert Francis Kennedy was destined for a life of power and controversy. He had early training in the rough-and-tumble world of politics, as the manager of his brother's 1952 Senate campaign and as a staff member on Senator Joseph McCarthy's infamous investigative committee (a position Kennedy secured through his father's connections with McCarthy). Later he worked as the committee's minority counsel and as counsel for the Senate Rackets Committee, where his long-standing feud with Teamsters Union president James (Jimmy) Hoffa commenced.

In 1959 Kennedy took the job of organizing his brother's presidential bid. By 1960 he had an established reputation for extraordinary zeal as both a prosecutor and politician, and it was for this reason, even more than the nepotism charge, that his appointment as Attorney General was controversial. His record as Attorney General is still a matter of dispute: he surrounded himself with outstanding legal talents, continued his fight against organized crime, and pursued other liberal causes, but his record on civil rights and CIVIL LIBERTIES was mixed at best, and he never reined in FEDERAL BUREAU OF INVESTIGATION (FBI) chief J. EDGAR HOOVER. Perhaps his most important role was to serve as his brother's chief confidant and adviser.

After President Kennedy's assassination Robert Kennedy was elected to the Senate from New York, and increasingly turned to the left politically. Eventually he broke with the Lyndon Baines Johnson administration over the VIETNAM WAR. (Whether Kennedy's conversion stemmed from principle or ambition is another matter of dispute.) He ran a strong race as an antiwar candidate in the Democratic presidential primaries of 1968. His own assassination on 5 June 1968 after winning the California primary (he died on 6 June) made him something of a liberal martyr, a legacy that overshadowed his earlier reputation as a zealous and ambitious political operative.

BIBLIOGRAPHY

Lasky, Victor. *Robert F. Kennedy: The Myth and the Man*. 1968.

Schlesinger, Arthur M., Jr. *A Thousand Days: John F. Kennedy in the White House*. 1965.

WILLIAM LASSER

KINFOLK, PRESIDENTIAL. Americans have been slow to accept the fact that the Presidents' kin are political players in their own right. Innoculated against the idea of a royal family, conditioned to think of women as concerning themselves primarily with the household, and taught to believe that strong men act alone, Americans have been reluctant to acknowledge that members of Presidents' families—particularly their wives—have played substantive and symbolic roles in the country's political life.

Since about 1960, in fact since the beginning of the Republic, some men and some women closely related to the Chief Executive have had an impact on public affairs. The wife of the second President of the United States, ABIGAIL ADAMS, is an excellent case in point. Not content to confine herself to hearth and home, she served as John Adams's closest confidante during his tenure as President. Mrs. Adams offered her advice freely and persistently on both domestic and foreign affairs, and vigorously pressed her husband's case before the public. Not surprisingly, her visible hand aroused antipathy. Sneered one Republican senator: "The President would not dare to make a nomination without her approbation."

Perhaps more mistrusted as an influential spouse was Woodrow Wilson's second wife, EDITH WILSON. Recently married to the President when he suffered an incapacitating stroke, she became "the first woman President of the United States." It was supposedly the President's doctor who urged that all work be directed to her due to his debility. As a result Mrs. Wilson ran the White House virtually singlehandedly. "The only decision that was mine," she wrote in *My Memoir*, "was what was important and what was not, and the *very* important decision of when to present matters to my husband."

Another First Lady whose impact both on her husband and on the American public is impossible to overestimate is ELEANOR ROOSEVELT. Almost immediately after his election she began to serve as the eyes and ears of her crippled husband. She broke precedent by holding press conferences in the White House; she had her own radio show; she lectured widely; she wrote a column for the newspapers; and she penned her autobiography, which became both a critical and commercial success. Above all, hers was a politics of conscience. As Joseph Lash observed, "In a Washington crowded with rebels and reformers her rigorous effort to live by the Golden Rule moved her into the vanguard of those who wanted the New Deal to mean a new, better, order."

Another example of influential kin was Dwight D. Eisenhower's brother Milton. While Ike was a newcomer to politics, Milton was well acquainted with Washington politics. Milton described his relationship with the Chief Executive as characterized by "an unusually strong affection." As a consequence, while he eschewed his brother's offer of an appointment to the Cabinet, Milton remained a faithful servant. As he put it: "I knew President Eisenhower found it helpful to reveal his innermost thoughts and plans to one who was not subservient to him, was not an advocate of special interests, had no selfish purpose to serve, and would raise questions and facts solely to help the President think through his problems without pressing for a particular decision."

While some of the Presidents' kin have been of consequence throughout American history, since the early 1960s there has been a marked change in the frequency and level of their participation in the political arena. It is significant that since then almost all the Presidents' wives, parents, siblings, and children have become involved in presidential politics. Why this change has taken place may be explained by several factors. The influence of political parties has declined, thereby requiring personal rather than party organization; the number and importance of primaries has increased, which compels candidates to rely on surrogates to help campaign; diminishing importance of traditional advisory groups outside the White House such as the Cabinet has enhanced the importance of counsel from those close to the President; the use of television, which, as a means of communication, has demanded the image of a happy, stable family and has provided presidential kin with welcome publicity; and finally, the changing culture has allowed previously sheltered groups, especially women, to participate actively in presidential politics.

The precise nature of the roles family members play depends on who they are; on what they are ready, willing, and able to do; and on what the candidate or President actually needs. Thus JACQUELINE KENNEDY and Amy Carter lent their own charm and appeal to John Kennedy and Jimmy Carter respectively. The four children of Gerald Ford on the other hand, were hardly stars in their own right. Yet during the 1976 campaign, they served as their father's sometime surrogates and as such proved themselves considerable political assets. Rose Kennedy and Lillian Carter, for their part, brought to their sons a humanity that might otherwise have eluded them.

And then there are kin who play more substantive roles. LADY BIRD JOHNSON was her complicated husband's indefatigable and uncomplaining helpmate. Under the most dismal of circumstances—the WATERGATE AFFAIR—Julie Nixon Eisenhower was the only family member to repeatedly and persuasively take a public stand on Richard Nixon's behalf. As to ROBERT KENNEDY, ROSALYNN CARTER, and NANCY REAGAN, they were no less than "alter egos" to the Presidents they served. Because each was the Chief Executive's partner, it must be said of them that they had an immeasurably great impact on the domestic and foreign affairs of the United States. HILLARY RODHAM CLINTON gives every evidence of playing a role similar to that of Robert Kennedy and Rosalynn Carter, who were in every way their partners' equal.

To be sure, presidential kin are by no means assets all the time. For example, Presidents Johnson, Nixon, and Carter each had brothers who often fell short of public expectation, and George Bush's son Neil cast a brief shadow on his father's administration by his involvement in the SAVINGS AND LOAN DEBACLE. These, nevertheless, are the exceptions. In general, presidential kin are often highly influential in the political and public life of the President.

BIBLIOGRAPHY

Kellerman, Barbara. *All the President's Kin.* 1980.
Lash, Joseph P. *Eleanor and Franklin.* 1971.
Withey, Lynne. *Dearest Friend: A Life of Abigail Adams.* 1981.

BARBARA KELLERMAN

KING, RUFUS (1755–1827), delegate to the Constitutional Convention, Senator, diplomat, Federalist vice presidential nominee in 1804 and 1808, presidential candidate in 1816. Turning from the law to politics, King represented Newburyport in the Massachusetts house of representatives (1783–1784) and was a Massachusetts delegate to the Confederation Congress (1784–1787). As a Massachusetts delegate to the Philadelphia CONSTITUTIONAL CONVENTION of 1787, he favored an executive elected by popularly chosen electors from each state. He argued for a strong executive with an absolute veto and eligibility for reelection. Asserting that "an extreme caution in favor of liberty might enervate the government," he relied on "the vigor of the executive as a great security for the public liberties." He preferred a relatively long term of office, though in suggesting twenty years he may have meant it as a caricature in order to defeat proposals of eleven and fifteen years. If the executive served for a limited term, King believed, he should not be impeachable. He considered as unnecessary a proposed special council to advise the executive on appointments.

As a Federalist, King worked effectively for acceptance of the constitution in the Massachusetts ratifying convention in 1788, but he soon moved to New York, where the legislature elected him to the United States Senate in 1789. He was a bulwark of the Washington administration and supported Hamilton's financial program. In 1796, after King's reelection, Washington appointed him as minister to England. King was on good terms with John Adams who, as President, retained him in office; and King remained in England throughout the Adams administration and part of Jefferson's. He later resigned in 1802, when he became convinced that he carried no weight in the Jefferson administration. Returning to the United States in 1803, he then preferred retirement to active political leadership.

In February 1804 the Federalists named CHARLES COTESWORTH PINCKNEY and King as candidates for President and Vice President to oppose Jefferson and GEORGE CLINTON. The TWELFTH AMENDMENT, effective in September, provided for separate balloting for President and Vice President, and in the election King received only 14 electoral votes to Clinton's 162. In 1808 the Federalists again nominated Pinckney and King to oppose Madison and Clinton. King received 47 votes for Vice President to Clinton's 113.

King regarded President Jefferson as an impractical ideologue and blamed him for allowing a quarrelsome, inexperienced Congress to take the initiative. He did not believe that Jefferson could force the British to abandon the impressment of American seamen or to pay for continued seizures of American ships. Condemning the embargo as a visionary experiment, he considered its tenacious enforcement a provocation of war with England. He characterized Jefferson's foreign policy as dictated by French efforts to pressure the United States into war with Britain. He was equally contemptuous of Madison's administration, believing at first that the President merely wished to remain in power and drift along without breaking relations with either France or England.

In 1812 King regarded the presidential contest as less important than the need to revise the Constitution by changing the apportionment of representation and defining more precisely the mechanism of presidential elections; such changes would not occur while Madison was President, however. During the WAR OF 1812, despite what King called the "incapacity of the Executive Government," he favored vigorous prosecution of a war he had earlier opposed, and he disapproved of Federalist separatism in New England.

King was elected in 1813 to the United States Senate and three years later was defeated for governor of New York. He was the Federalist candidate for President in 1816, an unofficial candidacy without sanction of a party caucus. As he anticipated, he was defeated by James Monroe with 183 electoral votes to King's 34 (Massachusetts, Connecticut, and Delaware). His defeat as the last Federalist candidate for the presidency symbolized the end of an era. Reelected to the Senate in 1819, he denounced the congressional caucus and undertook a final mission to England in 1825.

BIBLIOGRAPHY

Ernst, Robert. *Rufus King: American Federalist.* 1968.

King, Charles R., ed. *Life and Correspondence of Rufus King.* 7 vols. 1894–1900.

ROBERT ERNST

KING, WILLIAM RUFUS (1786–1853), thirteenth Vice President of the United States (1853). Born in North Carolina, the son of a successful planter and local political figure, Rufus King graduated from the University of North Carolina in 1803. After several years of law practice, he was elected as a Jeffersonian Republican to the state legislature in 1808 and to the United States Congress two years later. In Congress he sided with the War Hawks of 1812 and supported the second BANK OF THE UNITED STATES.

In 1816 King resigned from Congress and served as a diplomat abroad. After two years in Europe, he returned to the United States, settling in Alabama, which he represented in the United States Senate. As a Democrat, King supported the program of Andrew Jackson.

In 1836 King was elected president pro tempore of the Senate, a post he held with distinction until 1841. He defended the slave system and blamed northern interference for sectional tension. King favored the ANNEXATION OF TEXAS and in 1844 was appointed minister to France with instructions to prevent Franco-British interference with Texas annexation. While King was in France, his old friend James Buchanan was named Secretary of State. King advised settling the Oregon dispute by extending the boundary along the forty-ninth parallel. He also urged France not to oppose the American war against Mexico. In 1846 he returned home, and in 1848 Alabama sent him back to the Senate.

King's election in a close race placed him in debt to the strong STATES' RIGHTS faction of the DEMOCRATIC PARTY. As Senator, King supported land grants for railroad construction and chaired the Senate Foreign Relations Committee. He broke with his friend Buchanan in leading administration forces favoring ratification of the CLAYTON-BULWER TREATY with Great Britain. He participated in the debates over HENRY CLAY's compromise proposal, taking a moderate prosouthern position. In 1850, when Millard Fillmore became President, King was again chosen by unanimous vote of both parties to be president pro tempore of the Senate. As acting Vice President, he presided over heated discussions with fairness to all factions.

King voted for most of the compromise measures and approved the moderate Nashville Convention resolutions. He opposed both the northern Free Soilers and the extremist southern groups. In 1851 he wrote a friend: "Moderation on both sides and forbearing to denounce each other can alone produce harmony and concert of action. I trust the good sense of the country will see this and act accordingly."

King's friendship with James Buchanan went back to 1837 when the two had been roommates. King supported a Buchanan candidacy for President as early as the 1840s and also boosted him as a possible vice presidential candidate. To appease the Buchanan faction, the 1852 Democratic convention chose King to run with Franklin Pierce. King, who had been plagued with ill health for years, campaigned mostly by correspondence, assuring southerners that Pierce was safe for the South, and the ticket went on to win the election. After attending the December 1852 session of the Senate, King resigned, having served longer in that body than anyone else up to that time.

After contracting tuberculosis, King went to CUBA in February 1853 in an attempt to regain his health. Special legislation enabled him to take the oath of office there, and he returned to his Alabama home, where he died on 18 April 1853. King was a faithful party member, serving as presiding officer of the Senate during much of his time there, yet he never served in the highest office to which he was elected. His death left the nation without a Vice President during the Pierce presidency.

BIBLIOGRAPHY

Biographical Dictionary of the American Congress, 1774–1949. 1950.

Dameron, Edward Samuel Williamson. "William Rufus King." *University of North Carolina Magazine* 20 (1903): 317–322.

Martin, John Milton. "William Rufus King: Southern Moderate." Ph.D. dissertation, University of North Carolina, 1955.

Obituary of William Rufus King. *The Mobile Daily Register.* April 20, 1853.

Siousset, St. George Leakin. "James Buchanan" and "John Caldwell Calhoun." In *The American Secretaries of State and Their Diplomacy.* 17 vols. Edited by Samuel Flagg Bemis et al. 1927–1967.

LARRY GARA

KISSINGER, HENRY (b. 1923), national security adviser, Secretary of State. The German-born Henry Kissinger became the principal architect of U.S. foreign policy from 1969 to 1976. An expert on nuclear strategy and U.S.–European relations in the 1950s and 1960s while a professor at Harvard University, Kissinger served as a part-time foreign policy consultant to the administrations of John F. Kennedy and Lyndon B. Johnson. He also provided foreign policy advice to New York Governor NELSON A. ROCKEFELLER in his unsuccessful bids for the Republican presidential nomination in 1960, 1964, and 1968. After Richard M. Nixon was elected President in 1968, he selected Kissinger as his NATIONAL SECURITY ADVISER. Kissinger's appointment proved highly popular with the press and the members of the so-called foreign policy establishment, who considered the Harvard professor one of their own.

Kissinger and Nixon formed what *Time* characterized as an "improbable partnership" between the suspicious anticommunist California President and the urbane Ivy League professor. Together they concentrated foreign authority in the White House, excluding in the process nearly all the foreign affairs bureaucracy. Kissinger used his domination of the instruments of foreign policy to direct attention away from U.S. involvement in the VIETNAM WAR, and toward DETENTE with the Soviet Union, and the opening of relations with the People's Republic of China. Kissinger spent two years negotiating a cease-fire in the war in Vietnam, announced on the eve of the election of 1972 and signed in Paris on 23 January 1973. His secret, so-called backchannel communications with Chinese and Soviet leaders paved the way for Nixon's visit to China in February 1972 and for the Nixon-Brezhnev summit of May 1972. The former meeting commenced a partnership between Washington and Beijing, while the latter signaled an era of détente, or relaxation of tensions, between the two nuclear superpowers.

Kissinger's theatrical diplomatic triumphs won him vast public acclaim at the beginning of 1973. As Nixon's public standing slipped with the unfolding of the

W ATERGATE AFFAIR, the President appointed Kissinger Secretary of State in September 1973. Shortly thereafter, Kissinger's public approval soared upon receiving the Nobel Peace Prize for his role in arranging the Vietnam cease-fire. At the beginning of 1974 he seemed to overshadow Nixon as he arranged a disengagement between Israeli and Egyptian and Israeli and Syrian forces in the aftermath of the October 1973 Middle East war. Kissinger was lauded as indispensable during the paralysis that gripped the presidency in the summer of 1974.

Kissinger remained Secretary of State in the administration of Gerald R. Ford. His reputation suffered a sharp decline as the cease-fire with Vietnam disintegrated and many critics began to consider détente with the Soviet Union much more advantageous to Soviet than to U.S. interests. Kissinger's handling of foreign relations became a major issue in the 1976 presidential campaign. On the Republican side, conservative challenger Ronald Reagan charged that Kissinger's emphasis on détente had weakened the U.S. military. The Democratic candidate, Jimmy Carter, accused Kissinger of undermining American values by his indifference to HUMAN RIGHTS and the secrecy and manipulation with which he conducted foreign affairs.

BIBLIOGRAPHY

Hersh, Seymour M. *The Price of Power: Kissinger in the Nixon White House.* 1983.
Kissinger, Henry. *White House Years.* 1979.
Kissinger, Henry. *Years of Upheaval.* 1982.
Schulzinger, Robert D. *Henry Kissinger: Doctor of Diplomacy.* 1989.

ROBERT D. SCHULZINGER

KITCHEN CABINET. This was the contemptuous label that Andrew Jackson's political opponents gave to the small group of personal advisers who served him, particularly in the early years of his presidency, and who were seen by his enemies as a powerful, secret government, beholden to no one. Jackson came to office in 1829 at the head of a broad coalition of often disagreeing factions, united largely in their determination to defeat the incumbent President, John Quincy Adams. Jackson's Cabinet reflected these factions. He needed, therefore, a group of loyal aides to advise him, report on political conditions outside the White House, draft letters and speeches, and follow through on the administration's political and policy initiatives. They were not unlike a modern presidential staff of close aides directly and personally serving the President in the full range of his functions.

The kitchen cabinet was never a formal body, nor did it meet in the White House kitchen. Its member-

ship varied over time. At first, it included people drawn from the Nashville Central Committee that had overseen Jackson's 1828 election campaign: John Eaton and William Lewis. They were joined by a number of newspaper editors, AMOS KENDALL, FRANCIS PRESTON BLAIR, and briefly, Duff Green, as the administration took hold. Sometimes Cabinet members such as Martin Van Buren, or lesser government officials and future Cabinet members such as ROGER B. TANEY, became part of the informal circle. As time passed, the Jacksonian coalition became more unified and the members of the kitchen cabinet became more visible, many of them holding public office. Nevertheless, some, such as Kendall and Taney, continued to carry out behind-the-scenes chores for the President.

The kitchen cabinet played a significant political role in the growing rift between Jackson and JOHN C. CALHOUN in 1830 and 1831, its changing membership reflecting the alienation of the President and his Vice President and the coming together of Jackson and Van Buren as the election of 1832 approached. Programmatically, the kitchen cabinet played a crucial role in supporting the President in the tariff, NULLIFICATION, and the BANK OF THE UNITED STATES battles that defined his presidency. Institutionally, its presence and role illuminates the evolving needs of an activist President for a personal support staff in order to carry out his functions.

BIBLIOGRAPHY

Latner, Richard B. *The Presidency of Andrew Jackson: White House Politics, 1829–1837.* 1979.
Remini, Robert. *Andrew Jackson.* 3 vols. 1977–1984.

JOEL H. SILBEY

KNOW-NOTHING (AMERICAN) PARTY. Growing out of a quasi-political secret order called the Supreme Order of the Star Spangled Banner, the Know-Nothing Party was dedicated to stopping foreign, especially Roman Catholic, immigration. When asked about their organization, members of the secret order declared they "knew nothing," hence the popular name of the political party. In 1854 and 1856, Know-Nothings ran candidates under the banner of the American Party.

The Know-Nothing Party flared into prominence because of the failure of the second party system and the collapse of the WHIG PARTY following the disastrous Whig defeat in 1852. In 1854 most Whigs as well as many antislavery Democrats voted Know-Nothing, leading to victories in Massachusetts, New York, and California. In Kentucky and Maryland former Whigs joined some disaffected Democrats to elect Know-Nothing candidates. In 1854 the Know-Nothings in Massachusetts won all but three seats in the state house, all the state senate seats, all the congressional seats, and the governorship. In 1856 Massachusetts Know-Nothing Congressman Nathaniel Banks, a former Democrat who had broken with his party over SLAVERY, became Speaker of the House of Representatives.

In 1856 Banks rejected the American Party nomination for President and joined the antislavery REPUBLICAN PARTY. The American Party ran Millard Fillmore, a former Whig President. Fillmore, who personally had no enthusiasm for the nativist aspects of the party, carried only Maryland, a stronghold of anti-Catholic know-nothingism. Nevertheless, nationally Fillmore won 21.53 percent of the popular vote, a record for a THIRD PARTY unsurpassed until Theodore Roosevelt's PROGRESSIVE (BULL MOOSE) PARTY in 1912. Southern Whigs supported the American Party because the only alternatives were the DEMOCRATIC PARTY and the new, antislavery Republican Party, which was not even on the ballot in most of the South. In the North, conservative former Whigs and nativists supported the party.

In 1856 southern Whigs stayed with the party, as did northerners who were not concerned with the slavery and free-soil issues raised by the Republican Party. After 1856 the party collapsed, with most of its northern adherents becoming Republicans and most of its southern followers either becoming Democrats, clinging to the remnants of the virtually dead Whig Party, or, in 1860, voting for the Constitutional Union Party.

In the North the Republicans were happy to accept Know-Nothing voters, but the Republicans rejected their anti-immigrant and anti-Catholic views. Indeed, Republicans like Abraham Lincoln and SALMON P. CHASE, both from states with large immigrant constituencies, went to great lengths to separate themselves from the nativism of their new supporters.

BIBLIOGRAPHY

Gienapp, William. *Origins of the Republican Party, 1852–1856.* 1987.

PAUL FINKELMAN

KNOX, PHILANDER (1853–1921), Attorney General, Senator, Secretary of State. Philander Chase Knox, a Pittsburgh lawyer who was chief counsel for the Carnegie interests, served as Attorney General in the Cabinets of both William McKinley and Theodore Roosevelt. Believing that trusts should be regulated but not "busted," he vigorously revived enforcement of the SHERMAN ANTITRUST ACT, which had lain in desuetude after RICHARD OLNEY lost the so-called sugar trust case (*United States v. E. C. Knight*) in 1895. Knox's greatest victories came in *Northern Securities v. United States* (1904), a case against a holding company that controlled a combination of railroads, and in *Swift v. United States* (1905), known as the beef trust case. Knox was responsible for the argument that local commerce could so affect interstate commerce that Congress could constitutionally regulate the entire "stream of commerce." Knox was also responsible for the creation of the antitrust division of the DEPARTMENT OF JUSTICE, but he never instituted a criminal prosecution of offenders of the Sherman Act. After 1904, when he became a United States Senator, he was instrumental in developing rate regulation legislation.

In 1909 Knox became William Howard Taft's Secretary of State, a position from which he vigorously protected American financial interests abroad. DOLLAR DIPLOMACY was Knox's forte, first in Asia and subsequently in Central America. After Woodrow Wilson's election, Knox returned to corporate law, but he was later reelected to the Senate, where he served from 1917 to 1923 and where he was one of the chief opponents of Wilson's foreign policies. The rejection of the TREATY OF VERSAILLES and the LEAGUE OF NATIONS owed much to Knox's objections. Wilson vetoed the "Knox resolutions" for a separate American peace with Germany, but under Warren G. Harding, Knox's policies triumphed.

BIBLIOGRAPHY

Cummings, Homer, and Carl McFarland. *Federal Justice.* 1937.
Wright, Herbert F. "Philander C. Knox." In vol. 9 of *The American Secretaries of State.* Edited by Samuel F. Bemis. 10 vols. 1927–1929.

LEONARD W. LEVY

KOREAN WAR. The Korean War was a military conflict fought on the Korean peninsula from June 1950 to July 1953. The war began on 25 June 1950, when large and well-equipped North Korean forces crossed the thirty-eighth parallel separating North from South Korea and quickly drove the much smaller and ill-prepared South Korean forces down the peninsula.

At the time of the invasion, it was widely assumed that the North Koreans acted at the behest of the Soviet Union and with the approval of the People's Republic of China. More recent scholarship has indicated, however, that while the Soviets anticipated an invasion sometime in August, North Korea attacked South Korea in June without the U.S.S.R.'s knowledge and that its motives had largely to do with internal Korean politics north and south of the thirty-eighth parallel. Considerable civil strife south of the thirty-eighth parallel and increased opposition to South Korea's president, Syngman Rhee, persuaded North Korea's leader, Kim Il Sung, that the time was opportune for him to unite the two parts of Korea under his leadership.

Viewing the North Korean attack as part of a global effort at communist expansionism under Soviet leadership, however, President Harry S. Truman committed American troops to the conflict on 30 June. But before the North Koreans could be stopped, the Americans and South Koreans had been pushed back to a small perimeter around the southern port city of Pusan, extending about eighty miles from north to south and fifty miles from east to west.

American reinforcements were able to hold onto this small area, however, and on 15 September 1950 General Douglas MacArthur, who had been appointed supreme commander of UNITED NATIONS forces in Korea (officially, American troops were part of a U.N. command that had been established soon after the war began), launched a brilliant amphibious invasion behind enemy lines, striking at the port city of Inchon on South Korea's west coast, about twenty-five miles west of the capital, Seoul. In a coordinated move, U.N. forces broke out of the Pusan perimeter. The North Koreans were quickly routed and forced above the parallel.

President Truman then made a fateful decision. Sensing an opportunity actually to roll back communist expansion, the President approved orders for U.N. forces to cross the thirty-eighth parallel and to push the enemy above the Yalu River, which separates North Korea from Manchuria. In agreeing to continue the offensive above the thirty-eighth parallel, Truman assumed that neither the Soviet Union nor the People's Republic of China would intervene in the conflict. But, were they to do so, the JOINT CHIEFS OF STAFF instructed MacArthur to continue his advance as long as he believed it had a reasonable chance of success.

Despite repeated warnings by the Chinese, including a statement transmitted to the United States through India that China would not "sit back with folded hands and let the Americans come to the border," American troops crossed the thirty-eighth parallel on 7 October. By 25 October 1950, U.N. forces had reached the Yalu River. That day Chinese "volunteers" struck at South Korean and American forces at the Chosin Reservoir in northeast Korea and inflicted heavy casualties. Two weeks later, they suddenly cut off their attack. China's intrusion into the war had clearly been meant as a warning that it would not permit U.N. troops to proceed unmolested to the Yalu River.

China's warnings were ignored. On 25 November, General MacArthur began his "home by Christmas" offensive. Two days later, the Chinese invasion tore MacArthur's advance apart and led to an entirely different kind of war. Instead of a conflict that had as its purpose the reunification of Korea under U.N. auspices, the war became a holding action to contain the communist advance. The Chinese were able to drive U.N. forces below the thirty-eighth parallel, but because of inadequate logistics, an overextension of their supply lines, and their vastly inferior fire power, they were unable to press their advantage. In January 1951, U.N. forces launched a counteroffensive that took them within range of the thirty-eighth parallel. There the war stalemated for two years, until an armistice agreement was signed in 1953.

The armistice talks themselves had begun in July 1951, after the communists (Chinese and Korean) indicated that they were prepared to negotiate an end to the war. But a dispute over the repatriation of prisoners of war delayed an agreement for more than two years. Not until a new President, Dwight D. Eisenhower, took office and hinted that he might use NUCLEAR WEAPONS against the Chinese was an armistice finally signed in July at the town of Panmunjom, on the thirty-eighth parallel. Meanwhile, U.N. forces engaged mainly in a series of probing actions, known as the active defense, consisting mostly of routine patrol duty and occasional forays against strategically located enemy positions in the vicinity of the existing military line, which, except for some minor adjustments, became the final armistice line.

Nevertheless, there continued to be periods of heavy fighting. Although the communists did not have the capacity to sustain another major offensive, they were able to dig and fortify a growing complex of trenches, bunkers, and caves, which made even the United Nations' "active defense" strategy very costly. Some of the heaviest and bloodiest fighting of the war occurred in March and April 1953 in the Old Baldy–Porkchop area, a complex of hills on the western front about twelve miles west of the town of Chorwon above the thirty-eighth parallel. In the three years of conflict, 33,000 Americans were killed in combat. Another 21,000 died from other war-related causes, and 105,000 were wounded, while the South Koreans sustained 415,000 dead. Chinese and North Korean casualties have been estimated as high as two million dead and wounded.

BIBLIOGRAPHY

Cumings, Bruce. *The Origins of the Korean War.* 2 vols. 1981, 1990.

Foot, Rosemary. *A Substitute for Victory: The Politics of Peacemaking at the Korean Armistice Talks.* 1990.

Foot, Rosemary. *The Wrong War: American Policy and the Dimensions of the Korean Conflict.* 1985.

Kaufman, Burton I. *The Korean War: Challenges in Crisis, Credibility, and Command.* 1986.

MacDonald, Callum A. *Korea: The War before Vietnam.* 1986.

Max, Hastings. *The Korean War.* 1987.

Whelan, Richard. *Drawing the Line: The Korean War, 1950–1953.* 1990.

BURTON KAUFMAN

KU KLUX KLAN. There are at least three distinct periods of Ku Klux Klan activity: in the late 1860s and early 1870s; from 1921 through 1926; and least important, during the civil rights era in the 1950s and 1960s. Always a racist and secret organization dedicated to turning back the clock to an America that in its members' fantasies would parallel nirvana, they influenced presidential politics twice: in 1868 and in 1924.

Originally founded in Pulaski, Tennessee, in 1867, the Klan used terrorist methods to keep African Americans in a subordinate position and to intimidate them against trying to exercise the franchise. Klansmen wore masks and brutalized their victims, blacks as well as whites who challenged Klan positions or values. The first Ku Klux Klan exerted enormous control in some of the southern states in the 1868 presidential campaign. That year the loose agglomeration of local Klan groups dedicated themselves to helping Democrats recapture the White House. If elected, the Democrats had promised that they would restore self-governing rights to all southern states, abolish the FREEDMEN'S BUREAU, and do nothing further about aiding African Americans who wanted to vote. Therefore the Klan exerted whatever pressure it could in intimidating opponents, especially in the states of Georgia and Louisiana, where it succeeded in getting Republicans to abandon their efforts. And throughout the South, especially where large numbers of African Americans dwelled, Klansmen not only prevented blacks from voting but even stopped polls from opening. Eleven Georgia counties with black majorities recorded no votes at all for the Republican presidential candidate, Ulysses S. Grant, while the Klan's effectiveness was also dramatic in middle Tennessee, northern Alabama, and upcountry South Carolina, where anticipated Republican strength fell off sharply.

The heyday for the second Klan, which was virulently anti-Catholic, occurred in the early 1920s. Depressed agricultural conditions in rural areas and a strong desire to keep the nation a stronghold for Protestant values allowed two clever publicists, Edward J. Clarke and Mrs. Elizabeth Tyler, to build up a nationally based organization. By 1923 the Klan claimed a membership total of 4 million and virtually dominated politics in the states of Texas, Oklahoma, Arkansas, and Indiana, while exercising considerable influence, as well, in Ohio, Oregon, Maine, Connecticut, and New Jersey. Generally, Klan influence was seen in the DEMOCRATIC PARTY in the South and in the REPUBLICAN PARTY elsewhere. In 1924, the peak year of Klan political influence, Klansmen hoped to choose the Democratic presidential candidate.

The 1924 Democratic convention met in New York City's Madison Square Garden on 24 June and lasted until 10 July, the longest political convention in American history. For several days the platform committee debated whether there should be a specific denunciation of secret political organizations, although all the members claimed to be opposed to the Klan's philosophy of religious bigotry and intolerance. The party stalwart, WILLIAM JENNINGS BRYAN, argued against such a plank as "superfluous and harmful" to Democratic unity. A bare majority of the platform committee agreed with him and the issue came before the whole convention, which sided with that position by the slender margin of 543 3/20 votes to 542 7/20 votes.

Intense and bitter division in the party over whether to censure the Klan ended all hopes of Democratic victory that year. The two leading candidates for the presidential nomination, former Treasury Secretary William McAdoo of California and Governor ALFRED E. SMITH of New York, represented the rural and urban factions, respectively. McAdoo did not endorse the Klan although he quietly cultivated its support. Observers noted that those who opposed censoring the Klan backed McAdoo overwhelmingly while Smith, a Roman Catholic, found his champions among those who wanted to denounce the Klan.

The rural-urban split and the fight over whether to criticize the Klan directly hung over the entire convention. An almost equal division showed itself again in the selection of a nominee. It took 103 ballots before two-thirds of the delegates, the minimum number required by party rules, chose JOHN W. DAVIS of West Virginia as the party's standard bearer. By that time, however, it mattered not one whit who got the worthless nomination. For the first time that year, the presidential nominating conventions were broadcast on the radio, so the whole nation listened to Democrats tearing themselves apart. During the election campaign Davis came under pressure from many northern and western members of the party who wanted him to speak out against the Klan. In an August speech at Sea Girt, New Jersey, he distanced himself in a gingerly fashion:

If any organization, no matter what it chooses to be called, whether Ku Klux Klan or by any other name, raises the standard of racial and religious prejudice or attempts to make racial origins or religious beliefs the test of fitness for public office, it does violence to the spirit of American institutions and must be condemned.

President Calvin Coolidge, the Republican candidate, made no comments about the Klan.

Although Davis lost, it is unlikely that any Democrat could have defeated Coolidge in the 1924 campaign. The spectacle over whether the party should have denounced the Klan during the convention, however, shattered any hopes for even a competitive race. State and local election results in November demonstrated why so many Democrats, and most Republicans, shied away from criticizing the Ku Klux Klan that year. Klan-backed candidates won impressive victories for a variety of offices in Maine, Colorado, Indiana, Oklahoma, Kansas, Iowa, Illinois, Ohio, Michigan, and New York. Only in Texas, where anti-Klan Democrat Miriam K. Ferguson defeated her Klan-backed Republican opponent in the gubernatorial race, did Klansmen suffer a major setback. As *The Christian Century* observed in November 1924, "the nominees whom the Klan endorsed stood a preferred chance of election, and the men who unquestionably denounced the Klan generally went to defeat."

After 1926 factionalism, disputes over the distribution of funds, and the conviction of a major Indiana Klan leader, David C. Stephenson, for assaulting and causing the death of a young woman resulted in the quick demise of the Klan. In the next several decades, little was heard about the Klan. During the civil rights crusade in the 1950s and 1960s, however, many white opponents of integration joined forces with new Klansmen in some rural areas of the South. In the 1990s the organization probably numbered fewer than one thousand members.

BIBLIOGRAPHY

Chalmers, David M. *Hooded Americanism: The History of the Ku Klux Klan.* 3d ed. 1987.

Foner, Eric. *Reconstruction.* 1988.

Levine, Lawrence W. *Defender of the Faith.* 1987.

Trelease, Allen W. *White Terror: The Ku Klux Klan Conspiracy and Southern Reconstruction.* 1971.

LEONARD DINNERSTEIN

LABOR, DEPARTMENT OF. The Department of Labor was born on 4 March 1913, the day President Woodrow Wilson took office. It was a product of the progressive movement and of a half-century campaign by organized labor for a voice in the CABINET. In the words of its organic law, the department's main purpose is "to foster, promote, and develop the welfare of working people."

From Wilson to Hoover. In many ways the history of the department is the history of its secretaries. William B. Wilson, the first Secretary of Labor, had been secretary-treasurer of the United Mine Workers of America and later a Congressman who led the legislative drive to create the Department of Labor. Initially the department consisted of the preexisting bureaus of Labor Statistics, Immigration, and Naturalization, and the Children's Bureau, plus a new Conciliation Division for labor disputes. Most staff and resources, however, were devoted to immigration functions.

During WORLD WAR I the department administered the national war-labor program. Secretary Wilson molded a labor policy that included an eight-hour day, grievance mechanisms, and collective bargaining. The department maintained industrial peace, placed 4 million people in jobs, raised living standards, and improved working conditions. Its war programs provided many ideas and models for the NEW DEAL. One immediate by-product was the Women's Bureau, a successor to one of the few wartime agencies to survive into peacetime.

In the Republican era from 1921 to 1933 the department reflected the isolationism and xenophobia of the times and the desire of three administrations for less

government. James J. Davis, secretary from 1921 to 1930, was of working-class origins and had become a fund-raiser for the Moose order. Under Davis, administration of tough new immigration laws became the primary activity of the department. At the same time, the Children's Bureau led an unsuccessful fight for a constitutional amendment to protect CHILD LABOR that paved the way for federal legislation. After the start of the Great Depression, William Doak, of the Brotherhood of Railroad Trainmen, replaced Davis and served from 1930 to 1933. Davis was elected to the United States Senate and, with the cooperation of Secretary Doak, helped enact the Davis-Bacon Act, which prevented wage-slashing on federal construction projects by setting wages at the prevailing local rates.

The New Deal. President Franklin D. Roosevelt appointed FRANCES PERKINS, who had served as New York State Commissioner of Labor while he was governor, to succeed Doak. She was the first woman Cabinet member and served until 1945. Perkins, one of the most creative of Roosevelt's counselors, believed strongly that government had a major role to play in regulating the economic order to promote social justice.

Perkins was a prime shaper of the New Deal. The SOCIAL SECURITY law, enacted in 1935, was to a large extent a product of her efforts. She had accepted her post on the condition that the President would back her in seeking this goal. Her other main contribution was the FAIR LABOR STANDARDS ACT of 1938. Administered by the department, the act set a minimum wage of twenty-five cents per hour and required time-and-a-half after forty hours a week for most, though not all, workers. Perkins supported the National Labor Relations Act of 1935, which sanctioned the right of workers to organize and bargain collectively. She resigned shortly after Roosevelt's death to serve on the Civil Service Commission.

In 1945, President Harry S. Truman appointed Lewis B. Schwellenbach, a former Senator and a committed New Dealer. A massive wave of strikes broke out as unions sought catch-up gains after wartime wage freezes. This contributed to the passage of the antiunion TAFT-HARTLEY ACT, which separated the Conciliation Service from the department and created the independent Federal Mediation and Conciliation Service. Congress also ordered crippling cuts in the department's budget because it was considered pro-union. When Schwellenbach died in office in June 1948, Truman appointed Maurice J. Tobin, governor of Massachusetts, to fill the vacancy. The department's fortunes quickly turned around. Truman was re-elected, the new Democratic Congress raised the minimum wage, and the budget cuts were largely restored.

From Eisenhower to Nixon. In January 1953, President Dwight D. Eisenhower surprised many by appointing Martin P. Durkin, a Democrat and president of the International Brotherhood of Boilermakers. Durkin surprised few when he resigned in September 1953 over a disagreement on labor policy, but in his brief tenure he started a process that led to stronger centralized control within the department. Eisenhower replaced him with James P. Mitchell, a labor-relations executive. Prodded by COLD WAR concerns, Mitchell set up a research office to develop policies for increasing the country's supply of trained workers. These efforts laid the basis for later employment and training programs. Under Mitchell, known as the "conscience" of the Eisenhower administration, the department began to study the problem of employment discrimination against women, minorities, and the handicapped.

In 1961, President John F. Kennedy appointed Arthur J. Goldberg, special counsel to the AFL-CIO. Secretary Goldberg mediated labor disputes involving the transportation and aerospace industries, and even settled a strike at New York's Metropolitan Opera. He worked to protect the rights of African Americans and vigorously enforced an executive order on equal employment opportunity. Two new laws gave the department an increased role in employment and training: the Area Redevelopment Act (ARA) of 1961 and the Manpower Development and Training Act (MDTA) of 1962. Under the ARA the department provided retraining and allowances in areas of high unemployment. The MDTA gave the department broader re-

SECRETARIES OF LABOR[a]

	President	Secretary of Labor
28	Wilson	William B. Wilson, 1913–1921
29	Harding	James J. Davis, 1921–1923
30	Coolidge	James J. Davis, 1923–1929
31	Hoover	James J. Davis, 1929–1930 William N. Doak, 1930–1933
32	F. D. Roosevelt	Frances Perkins, 1933–1945
33	Truman	Frances Perkins, 1945 Lewis B. Schwellenbach, 1945–1948 Maurice J. Tobin, 1948–1953
34	Eisenhower	Martin P. Durkin, 1953 James P. Mitchell, 1953–1961
35	Kennedy	Arthur J. Goldberg, 1961–1962 W. Willard Wirtz, 1962–1963
36	L. B. Johnson	W. Willard Wirtz, 1963–1969
37	Nixon	George P. Shultz, 1969–1970 James D. Hodgson, 1970–1973 Peter J. Brennan, 1973–1974
38	Ford	Peter J. Brennan, 1974–1975 John T. Dunlop, 1975–1976 Willie J. Usery, Jr., 1976–1977
39	Carter	Ray Marshall, 1977–1981
40	Reagan	Raymond J. Donovan, 1981–1985 William E. Brock III, 1985–1987 Ann D. McLaughlin, 1987–1989
41	Bush	Elizabeth H. Dole, 1989–1991 Lynn Martin, 1991–1993
42	Clinton	Robert B. Reich, 1993–

[a] The Department of Labor was formed in 1913 when the Department of Commerce and Labor was divided into the Department of Commerce and the Department of Labor. For Secretaries of Commerce and Labor, see COMMERCE, DEPARTMENT OF.

sponsibilities for identifying labor shortages and providing training.

When Goldberg resigned in 1962, Under Secretary W. Willard Wirtz, a politically active labor law professor from Illinois, succeeded him. Wirtz believed in the Johnson administration's GREAT SOCIETY and under him the department developed a wide range of education and training programs to help high school drop-outs, other unemployed youths, older people, and the hard-core adult unemployed. The most important single program was the Neighborhood Youth Corps (NYC), which enabled needy unemployed youths to earn income while completing high school. By 1968 over 1.5 million young people had benefitted from NYC. After the passage of the CIVIL RIGHTS ACT OF 1964 an Office of Federal Contract Compliance was established to promote equal treatment of minorities.

A succession of five secretaries served short terms during the Nixon and Ford administrations: George

Shultz, a labor economist, James D. Hodgson, a corporate personnel executive, Peter Brennan, a trade unionist, John Dunlop, an economist and government adviser on labor, and Willie Usery, a unionist and labor mediator. The department's budget and responsibilities increased in this period and many programs to protect the physical and economic welfare of workers were added or expanded by Congress, though others were cut. The Comprehensive Employment and Training Act (CETA) of 1973 replaced existing programs with block grants to local government. The Emergency Employment Act of 1971 provided 170,000 temporary public service jobs. The Job Corps was shifted to the department, though half of the training centers were closed. The department began enforcement of the Occupational Safety and Health Act of 1970. To promote equal job opportunity in the construction industry the department set minority hiring goals under the controversial PHILADELPHIA PLAN. The Employee Retirement Income Security Act (ERISA) of 1974 gave the department the responsibility of protecting retirement plans.

From Carter to Bush. In 1977, President Jimmy Carter appointed Ray Marshall, an activist labor economist. Marshall played a major role in planning the administration's economic stimulus program and the department received $8 billion for CETA programs and public service jobs. Workers' safety and health programs were redirected by a new policy of "Common Sense Priorities" that focused on eliminating serious health hazards. In 1978, Congress transferred mine safety and health enforcement from the DEPARTMENT OF THE INTERIOR to the Department of Labor. Like Wirtz, Marshall minimized his involvement in labor-management disputes, and he promoted more cooperative relations between labor and management. Marshall also worked with Congress to raise the minimum wage to $3.35 an hour.

President Ronald Reagan appointed Raymond J. Donovan, a construction company executive active in Republican politics, in 1981 to help carry out his economic recovery and "regulatory relief" programs. Regulations and enforcement were curtailed to reduce the compliance burden on businesses. CETA authorizations were cut sharply. It expired in 1983 and was replaced by the more limited Job Training and Partnership Act. The department also expanded on Carter administration efforts to promote better labor-management relations.

In 1985, Secretary Donovan resigned and was replaced by William E. Brock, a former Senator then serving as U.S. Trade Representative. Brock emphasized improving manufacturing productivity through education and training programs. He also strengthened enforcement of regulatory programs within the constraints of regulatory relief. When Brock resigned in 1987, Ann Dore McLaughlin, a public relations expert with experience in private industry and government, served until the Bush administration came in. She continued Brock's policies and added efforts to deal with family issues such as child day care.

President George Bush continued Reagan's conservative approach to government and made few major changes at the department. He appointed Elizabeth Hanford Dole, a former Cabinet officer with extensive government experience, as Secretary. When a departmental commission called for government action to improve workers' skills, Dole supported legislation to implement the commission's recommendations. Under her, the department stepped up development and enforcement of job safety and health regulations, worked to improve protection of private employer pension plans, and attempted to deal with the "glass ceiling" faced by women trying to advance into executive positions in private industry. When Dole left in 1990, Lynn Martin, a former U.S. Representative, became Secretary and served until the end of the Bush administration in January 1993. Martin continued most of Secretary Dole's policies, but in 1992 regulatory programs were restrained by a presidentially ordered moratorium on development of federal rules [see RULE-MAKING POWER].

[See also LABOR POLICY.]

BIBLIOGRAPHY

Grossman, Jonathan. *The Department of Labor.* 1973.

Lombardi, John. *Labor's Voice in the Cabinet.* 1942.

MacLaury, Judson. *The U.S. Department of Labor: The First 75 Years, 1913-1988.* 1988.

Martin, George. *Madam Secretary, Frances Perkins.* 1976.

U.S. Department of Labor. *The Anvil and the Plough: A History of the United States Department of Labor.* 1963.

JUDSON MACLAURY

LABOR POLICY. For most of the first century of United States history, the President and the executive branch of the federal government rarely participated in shaping labor policy. Under prevailing constitutional interpretations, labor issues remained within the jurisdiction of the separate states. An economy largely local or regional in structure, moreover, militated against federal involvement in labor disputes. A rare exception to such noninvolvement occurred in 1834 when President Andrew Jackson dispatched federal troops to suppress rioting among Irish immigrant workers building the Chesapeake and Ohio Canal, an incident that fell within federal jurisdiction under the interstate commerce clause of the Constitution.

The Nineteenth Century. The Jacksonian precedent carried into the second half of the nineteenth century, when other Presidents used federal troops to restrain rioting during labor disputes. Citing his WAR POWERS, Abraham Lincoln sent troops to the anthracite district of Pennsylvania during the CIVIL WAR, simultaneously to combat draft resistance and strikes. Rutherford B. Hayes used the regular army to police the nation's railroads during the strikes of 1877; Benjamin Harrison ordered troops to Idaho in 1892 to restore order during a strike by silver miners; Grover Cleveland assigned federal marshals and troops to enforce judicial injunctions issued during the PULLMAN STRIKE boycott of 1894; and William McKinley sent the army to Idaho in 1899 in response to another strike by the state's miners. As these examples suggest, executive actions affecting labor tended to be episodic and limited to instances that involved interstate commerce (the railroads) or in which state governors requested federal assistance to suppress violent threats to republican government. Otherwise, the judiciary proved to be the most active branch of government in dealing with labor questions, acting under its equity power, the INTERSTATE COMMERCE ACT, and the SHERMAN ANTITRUST ACT to issue injunctions curtailing the right of workers to strike and to picket.

As large corporations grew increasingly important in the late nineteenth century and industrial conflicts wracked the nation, both the legislative and the executive branches of government sought to develop and implement a new set of labor policies. In 1883 Congress appointed a committee to investigate the relations between labor and capital. A year later, in 1884, Congress established a Bureau of Labor Statistics within the DEPARTMENT OF THE INTERIOR to gather reliable data on wages, living standards, employment levels, and strikes. Congress and the President also sought alternatives to the use of judicial injunctions and troops when strikes erupted, preferring mediation and arbitration. In 1898 Congress enacted and President McKinley signed the Erdman Act, which legitimated unionism on the railroads, outlawed employer antiunion devices, and promoted arbitration to avert strikes. Then, in 1899, McKinley and Congress united to appoint an industrial commission that undertook an elaborate investigation of relations between employers and employees. The commission's final report, presented in 1902 in nineteen volumes, foreshadowed the federal government's increasingly active role in the arena of labor policy.

The Beginnings of Labor Policy. Between 1900 and 1920 the federal government and its executive branch began to shape a national labor policy. President Theodore Roosevelt, for example, intervened in the anthracite coal strike of 1902, using his influence to compel mineowners to accept the recommendations of a special presidential commission. Instead of sending troops to restore order and to break a strike, Roosevelt deployed federal power to promote responsible trade unionism and legitimate collective bargaining. He also suggested that the federal judiciary's power to issue antistrike injunctions be curtailed and that the government consider enacting laws to regulate CHILD LABOR, protect women workers, and promote the health and welfare of working people. Under his successor, William Howard Taft, few dramatic breakthroughs occurred in the realm of labor policy. Yet the Taft administration began two initiatives that came to fruition in the administration of Woodrow Wilson. First, in response to a number of violent strikes and the urging of influential social reformers, Taft recommended the appointment of a Commission on Industrial Relations to investigate fully the relations between employers and workers. Second, Taft endorsed the establishment of a Cabinet-level DEPARTMENT OF LABOR to represent the interests of working people.

Not until Wilson entered office in March 1913, however, were the industrial commission and the Labor Department established. Wilson selected Rep. William B. Wilson of Pennsylvania, a former official of the United Mine Workers union, as the first Secretary of Labor. Secretary Wilson turned his department into a strong voice for trade unionism and collective bargaining. The industrial commission, whose members were all appointed by Wilson, investigated industrial relations between 1913 and 1915 (it held widely publicized public hearings and sponsored scholarly research studies into many aspects of the "labor question") and issued a series of final reports in 1916 that presaged the more radical social and economic reforms of the NEW DEAL. By then, President Wilson had built a firm political alliance between the American Federation of Labor and the DEMOCRATIC PARTY, a coalition that manifested itself in legislative action mandating rights for merchant seamen, granting an eight-hour day to operating railroad workers, and outlawing child labor.

The entry of the United States into WORLD WAR I in April 1917 magnified the federal government's role in making labor policy. In order to free able-bodied men for service in the military while maintaining uninterrupted industrial production, the Wilson administration regulated labor markets and industrial relations.

Various federal executive agencies managed industrial relations on the nation's railroads and in its mines, shipyards, and packinghouses. When a wave of strikes threatened to curtail production, the President in April 1918 created a National War Labor Board (NWLB) to regulate labor relations in all sectors of the economy not covered by special commissions. Under the leadership of cochairs Frank P. Walsh, an attorney and left-wing Democrat, and former President William Howard Taft, the NWLB promoted the eight-hour day for all workers; equal pay for equal work; the right of workers to unionize free from employer interference; the principle of collective bargaining; and the concept of industrial democracy. Under the aegis of the NWLB and other wartime federal labor agencies, the trade union movement nearly doubled its membership between 1917 and 1920. Never before in United States history had an administration done so much to benefit trade unions and working people, nor had the AFL linked itself so closely to the national state and a political party.

In the aftermath of the war, relations between workers and employers worsened, precipitating in 1919 a massive wave of strikes necessitating further federal intervention. The Wilson administration involved itself in a national steel strike, a strike by coal miners, and disputes on the railroads and along the waterfront. The President convened industrial conferences in Washington in 1919 and again in 1920 in an effort to forge amity between employers and labor leaders. By then, however, Wilsonian reforms were on the wane, the REPUBLICAN PARTY on the rise, and trade unionism in retreat.

The 1920s, a decade of Republican political supremacy and business hegemony, saw continued federal intervention in the labor arena. Under the leadership of Commerce Secretary Herbert Hoover, the Republican administrations sought to implement policies through which employers, union leaders, and public officials cooperated voluntarily to promote full employment, high productivity, high wages, and high consumption. Several times Hoover intervened in disputes between coal mine operators and the miners' union to promote their peaceful resolution. In 1922, President Warren G. Harding, in a manner reminiscent of Grover Cleveland in the Pullman boycott of 1894, used the full power of the government to end a national strike by railroad shopmen. By and large, however, the Republicans preferred to build cooperative relations with such moderate labor leaders as John L. Lewis of the Mine Workers and William Hutcheson of the Carpenters. Hence, in 1926, a Republican Congress passed the Railway Labor Act, which secured the

right to union representation and collective bargaining for many of the nation's railway employees. And in 1932, in the midst of the Great Depression, Congress enacted and President Hoover signed the Norris-LaGuardia Act, which eliminated the power of federal judges to issue injunctions in labor disputes.

The New Deal. The administration of Franklin D. Roosevelt and his New Deal transformed fundamentally the relationship between the national government and labor. As a result of congressional legislation, executive action, and judicial rulings, the federal government determined the basic legal system governing relations between workers and employers. It also regulated child labor, wage rates, and working hours.

With exceptions that diminished over time, federal labor policy overrode state regulations. An early piece of New Deal legislation, the NATIONAL INDUSTRIAL RECOVERY ACT (NIRA) of 1933, authorized the President to negotiate codes of fair competition with industry-wide groups concerning minimum wage rates, maximum hours, and limitations on child labor. It also granted workers the right to form unions of their own choosing and to bargain collectively with employers. Roosevelt created several executive agencies—the National Recovery Administration (NRA), the National Labor Board (NLB), and the first National Labor Relations Board (NLRB)—to implement the aspects of the NIRA affecting workers and unions. These reforms precipitated an upsurge in union organizing, a wave of strikes, and bitter resistance from employers, all of which made it difficult for the executive agencies to effect successful labor policies.

In 1935 the Supreme Court declared the NIRA unconstitutional because Congress had improperly ceded its legislative power to the executive. That same year, however, Congress enacted and the President signed a new national labor policy law, the WAGNER ACT (National Labor Relations Act), which guaranteed workers the right to unionize and to bargain collectively; specified as illegal most employer antiunion practices; and authorized the President to appoint a three-person NLRB to implement the new law. The preamble to the Wagner Act praised independent unionism as the best means to achieve economic prosperity, a more equitable distribution of national income, and industrial democracy.

While employers challenged the constitutionality of the law, workers and their unions used strikes and cooperation with the President to win recognition from hitherto giant antiunion corporations. Finally, in 1937, the Supreme Court declared the Wagner Act constitutional, placing the executive branch through the NLRB in charge of regulating labor relations throughout the national economy. A year later, Congress enacted the Fair Labor Standards Act, which set minimum wages and maximum hours and eliminated child labor in industries involved in interstate commerce.

A new national labor policy, one that legitimated trade unionism, collective bargaining, and protective legislation for working people, was thus firmly in place when the United States entered WORLD WAR II in December 1941. Federal labor policy during the World War II years recapitulated the experience of the previous war. Once again, presidentially created executive agencies regulated labor markets and tried to guarantee an adequate supply of trained workers to essential industries. And once again, presidentially appointed boards, first the National Defense Mediation Board (NDMB) and then the National War Labor Board (NWLB), regulated wartime labor relations. The NDMB, until its dissolution in December 1941, and then the NWLB promoted the growth of trade unionism, granted unions security in the shop in return for labor peace, and attempted to guarantee women workers equitable treatment and all workers protection against the ravages of inflation. When the wartime machinery failed to produce industrial peace, as was the case with coal miners who went on strike in 1943, the President used his executive authority to seize the mines, end the strike, and negotiate an agreement with the union. Under the aegis of the wartime executive agencies, trade unions increased their size to the highest proportionate level in history, representing nearly one-third of all civilian, nonagricultural workers.

From Truman to Reagan. After the war, the federal role in setting labor policy through executive agencies and decisions did not diminish. President Harry S. Truman played a decisive role in ending the massive postwar wave of strikes (1945–1946) through the work of a presidential commission to settle the dispute in the steel industry. Partly in response to the postwar strike wave, partly as a result of a Republican majority in Congress after the election of 1946, and partly in reaction to a rising tide of popular antiunionism, Congress in 1947 passed the TAFT-HARTLEY ACT, a series of revisions to the Wagner Act that defined certain union practices as unfair, granted employers broader powers of free speech, ceded to the separate states the right to abolish union security arrangements, outlawed the closed shop and secondary boycotts, and created a category of national emergency strikes that the President could stop through executive action.

Although the Taft-Hartley Act made it more diffi-

cult for unions to organize workers, especially in the southern states, in most ways it maintained federal dominance in labor relations and allowed the executive branch, primarily through the NLRB, to determine policy. Truman used the act to end strikes by coal miners and railroad workers. During the KOREAN WAR, Truman seized the steel industry to end a strike that he claimed threatened national security. Subsequently, the Supreme Court found that particular example of executive power to be unconstitutional. Indeed, under the terms of the Taft-Hartley Act, the federal courts came to police the labor policies of the executive branch and to determine the basic rules of the new system of "industrial pluralism."

During the decades of the 1950s and 1960s, under both Republican and Democratic administrations, few fundamental changes occurred in federal labor policy. The executive branch through presidential actions and NLRB rulings made policy, subject to a continuous process of judicial review. In response to public hearings that exposed examples of union corruption and criminal links to several trade unions, Congress in 1959 enacted the Landrum-Griffin Act, which charged the Labor Department with protecting the rights of individual union members and ensuring that unions administered their treasuries and welfare funds honestly.

Perhaps the most important change that transpired during the presidencies of Dwight Eisenhower, John F. Kennedy, Lyndon B. Johnson, and Richard M. Nixon was that increasing numbers of workers came to fall within the jurisdiction of the NLRB and under the protection of national wage and hour standards. Even as the proportion of nonagricultural workers represented by trade unions began to shrink steadily beginning in the late 1950s (although the absolute number of union members continued to rise erratically into the 1970s) and the labor movement lost political influence, the national labor relations system created during the New Deal and World War II years, as revised by Taft-Hartley, continued to operate.

In one aspect, however, federal labor policies changed substantially over the course of the postwar years. The achievements of the civil rights movement during the 1950s and the 1960s and the reemergence of the women's movement in the 1960s caused federal officials to add a new dimension to national labor policies. Congress, the courts, and the executive branch acted to eliminate racial and gender discrimination in the labor market by both employers and unions. By the decade of the 1970s, such issues had grown more important and controversial than more traditional questions of union-management relations.

The overwhelming Republican political victory in 1980 and the policies of the Reagan administration began the dissolution of the postwar labor relations regime. In a decisive early act as President, Reagan used his executive power to break a strike by the Professional Air Traffic Controllers union (PATCO) and to punish the strikers. Simultaneously he appointed as chair of the NLRB Donald Dotson, who was committed to reversing a half century of national labor policy. The new chairman declared that the Wagner Act had never intended to promote trade unionism and collective bargaining, both of which often violated fundamental principles of the free market. During the 1980s the NLRB and federal courts more frequently ruled in favor of employers and against unions and workers. So alienated from federal labor policy had many labor leaders grown that they increasingly suggested that the NLRA be repealed and that the nation return to the pre–New Deal system of labor relations under which unions and companies waged war without direct federal supervision.

BIBLIOGRAPHY

Atleson, James. *Values and Assumptions in American Labor Law.* 1983.

Eggert, Gerald G. *Railroad Labor Disputes: The Beginnings of Federal Strike Policy.* 1967.

Forbath, William E. *Law and the Shaping of the American Labor Movement.* 1991.

Millis, Harry A., and Emily C. Brown. *From the Wagner Act to Taft-Hartley, A Study of National Labor Policy and Labor Relations.* 1950.

Ross, Philip. *The Government as a Source of Union Power.* 1965.

Tomlins, Christopher L. *The State and the Unions: Labor Relations, the Law, and the Organized Labor Movement in America, 1880–1960.* 1985.

MELVYN DUBOFSKY

LA FOLLETTE, ROBERT M. (1855–1925), governor of Wisconsin, Senator, presidential candidate in 1924. Premier leader of the Progressive movement, Robert Marion La Follette became governor of Wisconsin in 1900 and was reelected in 1902 and 1904. As governor he sponsored Progressive positions such as tariff reform, conservation, and direct primary elections. In 1905 the Wisconsin legislature sent him to Washington as a United States Senator.

Championing Progressive causes and wielding Senate leadership of the Progressive insurgency within the REPUBLICAN PARTY, he pushed the "Wisconsin Idea" of reliance upon commission experts to resolve problems; he also promoted tariff reform, honest government, railroad regulation, and pure food and drug legislation. Ultimately, however, La Follette wanted to end big business's control of government. Underlying his goals was his fervent desire to be President, an ambition that eventually undermined the Progressive insurgency.

To challenge President William Howard Taft for the 1912 Republican presidential nomination, La Follette launched the National Progressive Republican League in 1911. His primary focus, however, centered not on Taft but on Theodore Roosevelt, a fellow Progressive. By late summer 1911 most Progressives expected a nomination battle between the two men.

La Follette delayed campaigning until December, spending the intervening time writing his autobiography to inform Americans of his personal struggle for the common man and for representative government against corporate power. By this time it was too late to keep Theodore Roosevelt out of the nomination race. Henceforth the contest shifted from Taft–La Follette to Roosevelt–La Follette, and the split among Progressive leaders and supporters was under way.

By February 1912, La Follette's supporters urged his withdrawal. Stubbornly refusing, he insisted on aggressively pursuing the nomination and vigorously attacking Roosevelt. Their contest wreaked havoc on local and state Progressive organizations. Ultimately, Taft won the Republican nomination, Roosevelt ran a third-party campaign on the PROGRESSIVE (BULL MOOSE) PARTY ticket, and Democrat Woodrow Wilson, with a minority of the popular vote, entered the White House. La Follette endorsed no candidate, but probably supported Wilson. The election was not the only loss, for the Republican insurgency, running high in 1911, now appeared destroyed. Moreover, La Follette no longer served as Senate leader of Progressives, for most insurgents there resented him as a bitter man. With no one to fill the void, the shaping of Progressivism fell to the White House and its new Democratic President.

Reelected to the Senate in 1916 and 1922, La Follette retained his ambition to be President and his antagonism toward big business continued unabated. His support of Wilson slackened over foreign policy issues, because he now saw foreign affairs also falling under the control of corporate power. He voted against the declaration of war in 1917, the Espionage Act, and the draft.

During the conservative 1920s La Follette opposed much of the major Republican legislation, continuing his personal campaign against corporate America. By early 1924, now willing to run as a THIRD-PARTY CANDIDATE La Follette obtained the support of Socialists, farm organizations, and labor unions under the banner of the Conference for Progressive Political Action

940 LAIRD, MELVIN R.

(CPPA). La Follette was the only person who could be standard-bearer for such disparate groups, which united only to defeat the conservative Republicans. One major group not included were the communists, whom La Follette and the CPPA publicly rejected.

Following the CPPA's enthusiastic nomination of him, La Follette unsuccessfully solicited Supreme Court Justice Louis Brandeis to be his running mate. He then selected Democratic Senator Burton K. Wheeler of Montana, who earlier had endorsed La Follette. La Follette's platform included a call for organization and collective bargaining among farmers and laborers, government ownership of railroads, repeal of the ESCH-CUMMINS TRANSPORTATION ACT of 1920, recovery of the naval oil reserves, denunciation of the tax policies of Secretary of the Treasury ANDREW W. MELLON, and a call for a constitutional amendment to limit judicial review via congressional override.

Much of the nation's press opposed him, frequently dubbing him a dangerous radical. Haunted by the rallying cry "Coolidge or Chaos," as well as employer intimidation of workers, La Follette watched his support dwindle. Most workers (La Follette's prime constituency) failed to support him because, ironically, they feared losing their jobs if he won. America in 1924 saw a more conservative work force attempting to hold onto what it had; additionally, farm prices rose for the first time in years, thereby leading many farmers to abandon their champion. President Calvin Coolidge outpolled La Follette, Democrat JOHN W. DAVIS, and all others in 1924. Often ill prior to the campaign, La Follette died on 18 June 1925.

BIBLIOGRAPHY

Greenbaum, Fred. *Robert Marion La Follette*. 1975.
Thelen, David P. *Robert M. La Follette and the Insurgent Spirit*. 1976.

NICHOLAS AHARON BOGGIONI

LAIRD, MELVIN R. (b. 1922), Secretary of Defense, presidential assistant for domestic affairs. Melvin R. Laird was born on 1 September 1922 in Omaha, Nebraska. He attended Carlton College in Minnesota where he received his B.A. in 1942. After serving in the armed forces during WORLD WAR II, he was elected a Wisconsin state senator. In 1952, Laird was elected to the United States House of Representatives where he remained until President Richard M. Nixon appointed him Secretary of Defense in 1969.

By the time Laird assumed the helm at the Department of Defense, America was embroiled in the VIETNAM WAR. There was widespread antimilitary sentiment. A major focus of this sentiment was the size of the defense budget. Congress wanted to cut substantially the growing defense expenditures. In 1969 the Nixon administration announced a $2.5 billion reduction for fiscal year 1970. Laird in congressional testimony asserted that this was part of the administration's overall anti-inflation policy. This trend was short lived, for in 1971 and 1972 Laird asked Congress for massive spending increases.

Laird was active in lobbying Congress for deployment of an antiballistic missile (ABM) system. He met with members of the North Atlantic Treaty Organization (NATO) to encourage their increased sharing of defense costs. He also supported the admission of Spain into the alliance. While Laird was instrumental in the changing of the draft to meet falling manpower requirements and modifying inequities in the 1967 draft law, he opposed AMNESTY for draft dodgers.

In November 1972, Laird announced his retirement at the end of Nixon's first term. However, he returned to the administration as presidential assistant for domestic affairs, which had been vacated by John D. Ehrlichman in the wake of the WATERGATE AFFAIR. After SPIRO T. AGNEW's resignation Laird was instrumental in the selection of Gerald R. Ford for the vacated office of Vice President. Laird resigned two months after Ford's selection stating that Congress should conclude the Watergate investigations by having an IMPEACHMENT vote.

BIBLIOGRAPHY

Osborne, John. *The Last Nixon Watch*. 1974. Chapter 18.
Rather, Dan, and Gary Paul Gates. *The Palace Guard*. 1974.

JEFFREY D. SCHULTZ

LAME-DUCK PRESIDENTS. The term "lame duck," which literally refers to a duck who is unable to fly, has been used to describe Presidents in their second term, and primarily in the last two years of that term, who have suffered a loss of political power. The principal reason for this loss of power is that second-term Presidents are not eligible for reelection. The TWENTY-SECOND AMENDMENT limits a President to a maximum of two full terms in office.

As the second term progresses, much of the enthusiasm, vitality, and new ideas of the first term dissipate. The President's party tends to be in a weak position in Congress, particularly after the midterm election in the sixth year. In addition, the quest of the next presidential nomination and election will have likely begun, with potential candidates of both parties positioning themselves on issues, distancing themselves from the unsuccessful policies and unpopular positions of the current administration, and organizing their own campaigns. All of this serves to reduce the President's political influence and decrease his ability to set the policy agenda and mobilize support for his program.

Perceptions also change during the last years of a presidential term. People, particularly Washington insiders, tend to look beyond the current administration to the personnel and policy changes that may result from the next election. The news media also begin to shift their near-exclusive focus from the incumbent President and his administration to the new candidates, their character, ideological orientations, policy positions, and to the new contest itself. They also become more critical and begin to explain the incumbent's current political difficulties within the context of his lame-duck status. This explanation contributes to the perception in Washington and to a lesser extent, within the broader national and international community, that the President is in a weaker position. Perceptions affect reality, and in this case, they contribute to a loss of political power.

Since Presidents have difficulty changing this perception, they tend to adopt strategies during their second term to minimize its effect. They usually emphasize foreign over domestic affairs because it is easier to mobilize bipartisan support for foreign policy than for most domestic issues. They also tend to rely more on their EXECUTIVE POWER and less on their legislative power to achieve their principal policy objectives. Within the legislative arena, they are less apt to propose new, controversial programs and more apt—particularly if their party does not control Congress—to exercise their veto as a means of preventing the opposition from imposing its policy preferences on them. Increasingly, during their second term Presidents rely on the symbolic accoutrements of the office to enhance their personal status, popularity, and influence.

In the end, the success Presidents have in offsetting the lame-duck effect has a lot to do with their ability to shift the public's focus and the media's agenda. This is why they tend to emphasize their largely ceremonial role as head of state rather than political role as head of government in the last two years of their presidency.

BIBLIOGRAPHY

Grossman, Michael B., Martha Joynt Kumar, and Francis E. Rourke. "Second-Term Presidencies: The Aging of Administrations." In *The Presidency and the Political System*, 3d ed. Edited by Michael Nelson. 1990.
Safire, William. *Safire's Political Dictionary*. 1978.

STEPHEN J. WAYNE

LANDON, ALFRED M. (1887–1987), governor of Kansas, Republican presidential nominee in 1936. Alfred M. Landon was born in West Middlesex, Pennsylvania, the son of an oilman who moved the family to Independence, Kansas, just as Landon finished high school. He graduated from the University of Kansas and for a while worked in banking. After saving enough capital, Landon worked as an independent oilman in Oklahoma. He maintained his close ties with Kansas, using his parents' home as a base for his oil operations. He became moderately successful in what was a risky business.

Landon was politically influenced by his father, who was closely associated with the progressive branch of the REPUBLICAN PARTY and worked as a delegate for Theodore Roosevelt's failed attempt to regain the Republican nomination in 1912. Landon maintained his liberal leanings throughout his political career and thought of himself as a progressive in a party controlled by eastern stuffed-shirts.

In 1932 he was the only Republican governor west of the Mississippi River and the only Republican governor reelected in 1934. Speculation about candidacy began early in 1934. Republican leaders in the Midwest began to circulate his name as an alternative to former President Herbert Hoover, who was aligned with the eastern, more conservative bloc of the party.

As governor of Kansas he gained the nickname of "Kansas Coolidge" because of his austere fiscal policies. While undoubtedly a progressive, Landon believed in retrenchment from the NEW DEAL expenditures, which he thought excessive. His politics blended economic conservatism—balanced budget, gold standard, and anti-inflation—and social liberalism—free speech, business regulation, and recognition of labor unions. He firmly believed that the states were the primary source of relief and had been circumvented in the New Deal legislation.

Landon did not actively seek the Republican nomination. In fact he stayed at home during the primary season in an effort to avoid the growing factionalism that he believed would doom the Republican Party in the election of 1936. He gained the early support of the influential, wealthy publisher and politico, William Randolph Hearst. Hearst's support was neither welcomed nor repudiated by Landon. As far as Landon was concerned it was free publicity. Despite not campaigning Landon had amazing electoral success. He won the Massachusetts and New Jersey primaries showing he could win in the East. He lost to Hoover in California because of the campaigning efforts of Hoover's California chairman, Earl Warren.

When the convention met in Cleveland in the summer of 1936, Landon had enough delegates to capture the nomination. The only consideration was to pick a running mate from among the various factional interests that now made up the Republican Party. The choice of Colonel Frank Knox, publisher of the *Chicago Daily News*, was in many ways a concession to the more conservative wing of the party. After his nomination Landon disappeared on a fishing trip to Colorado for the first month. National campaign chairman John Hamilton and Knox both took this time to attack the policies of Franklin D. Roosevelt.

When Landon returned from Colorado he toned down the attack in an attempt to capture the moderate anti-Roosevelt element of the DEMOCRATIC PARTY. However, his campaign suffered because his message offended both liberals and conservatives. Landon could not bring himself to mount a full-fledged assault. He supported some of the President's reforms. His major complaints were the inefficiency of administration and the growing debt. As the campaign began to take its toll and as he began his slide in the polls, Landon began to attack more vigorously the President and his policies, however, these attacks only continued to cloud his message.

By the time of the election Landon knew that he had no chance of winning. The landslide victory of Roosevelt was greater than even his most ardent supporters had predicted. In the final tally Landon won only 8 electoral votes—from Vermont and Maine; Roosevelt had 532 votes from the other forty-six states. The President had beaten Landon by more than eight million popular votes.

Landon did not completely retire from politics. As titular head of the party, he upgraded his warnings about the dangers of the New Deal and the growing dictatorial manner of Roosevelt. He opposed Roosevelt's policies and the COURT-PACKING PLAN. He attempted to form a political coalition with disaffected Democrats to defeat Roosevelt in 1940. Though never running for office again Alf Landon became one of the great elder statesmen of the Republican Party until his death in 1987.

BIBLIOGRAPHY

Bingay, Malcom. *Two Candidates: Landon and Roosevelt.* 1936.
Hinshaw, David, ed. *Landon: What He Stands For.* 1936.
McCoy, Donald R. *Landon of Kansas.* 1966.
Schlesinger, Arthur M., Jr. *The Politics of Upheaval.* 1960.

JEFFREY D. SCHULTZ

LATIN AMERICA. For discussions of U.S. policy with regard to Central America and South America, see ALLIANCE FOR PROGRESS; COLONIALISM; GUNBOAT DIPLOMACY; PANAMA CANAL. For discussions of United States relations with particular countries, see CUBA; DOMINICAN REPUBLIC; HAITI; PANAMA. See also PUERTO RICO.

LAW ENFORCEMENT. Under the Constitution, the President is the chief law enforcement official in the nation. Article II, Section 3, provides that the President "shall take Care that the Laws be faithfully executed." Pursuant to this constitutional mandate, the President controls federal law-enforcement activities through the appointment and direction of members of the CABINET. The primary responsibility for federal law enforcement rests with the ATTORNEY GENERAL of the United States, who heads the DEPARTMENT OF JUSTICE, but many other federal agencies also enforce federal laws. These activities are directed by the secretaries of the various departments of the executive branch and their sub-Cabinet-level appointees.

The Scope of Law Enforcement. As a consequence of the expanded role of the federal government in regulating social and economic affairs, the scope of federal law enforcement has increased enormously in the twentieth century. Federal banking regulations are the primary responsibility of the TREASURY DEPARTMENT, which also includes the SECRET SERVICE; the Bureau of Alcohol, Tobacco, and Firearms; and the U.S. Customs Bureau. The DEPARTMENT OF LABOR is responsible for enforcing federal wage and work-hours laws, federal occupational safety and health regulations, and compliance with federal contracts. The U.S. Postal Service enforces federal postal regulations. It has been estimated that more than one hundred separate federal agencies engage in law enforcement activities.

The enforcement of federal criminal laws is primarily the responsibility of the Department of Justice. The Attorney General, who is appointed by the President, appoints and directs ninety-four U.S. Attorneys, who handle the day-to-day business of enforcing the law in their respective jurisdictions. The SOLICITOR GENERAL represents the U.S. government in cases before the Supreme Court.

The Justice Department includes a number of major divisions. The Criminal Division has primary responsibility for criminal law enforcement. The Civil Rights Division enforces federal civil rights laws. The Anti-Trust Division is responsible for federal antitrust laws. The Tax Division enforces the federal tax laws. The principal law-enforcement investigative agency is the FEDERAL BUREAU OF INVESTIGATION (FBI). The Drug Enforcement Agency is responsible for enforcing federal laws on controlled substances. The U.S. Marshals

Service provides protection for the federal courts and transports persons in federal custody.

The enforcement of federal laws involves an important element of discretion on the part of responsible officials. This discretion has two dimensions. At the level of general policy, each President has the discretion to determine the manner in which particular laws will be enforced. These policy decisions are communicated from the President to the relevant presidential appointees. Within the limits of the general policy set by the administration, law-enforcement officials have broad discretion in whether to bring legal action against a particular party, the scope of that action, and the nature of any out-of-court settlement.

Federal crimes represent only a very small percentage of all illegal activity; state and local governments handle the vast majority of criminal-law violations. The federal government influences state and local law enforcement only indirectly through the Office of Justice Programs in the Department of Justice.

Expansion of Law Enforcement. Until the twentieth century, the law-enforcement role of the President was extremely limited, because the scope of federal regulation of social and economic affairs was so narrow. Prior to the creation of the Bureau of Investigation (later the FBI), the Department of Justice had no unit whose primary responsibilities was criminal investigation. The President, through the Attorney General, relied on the limited resources in the Attorney General's office, the U. S. Marshals Service, the Secret Service, and the Treasury Department.

President Theodore Roosevelt created the Bureau of Investigation in 1908. Congress had refused to establish the Bureau by legislation because of a long-standing American fear of a national police force and the more immediate congressional fear of granting investigative power to the executive branch. During its early years the Bureau was embroiled in scandal: for example, Bureau agents were caught opening the mail of members of Congress who had opposed the agency's creation. During WORLD WAR I the Bureau compiled files on people solely because of their opposition to the war or their political affiliations. Agents were involved in massive violations of civil liberties in the so-called PALMER RAIDS of 1919–1920, when thousands of political dissidents were arrested.

The national PROHIBITION of alcoholic beverages (1920–1933) under the Eighteenth Amendment introduced a new and troublesome aspect of federal law enforcement. Under the Volstead Act, responsibility for prohibition enforcement was given to the Treasury Department. Enforcement was characterized by widespread corruption and violations of individual rights.

At the same time, the Bureau of Investigation was implicated in scandals surrounding Attorney General HARRY M. DAUGHERTY.

The Calvin Coolidge administration cleaned up the Bureau. Attorney General Harlan Fiske Stone appointed J. EDGAR HOOVER as Director of the Bureau in 1924. Following Stone's orders, Hoover ordered an end to political spying, introduced higher personnel standards, and reduced the Bureau's size.

Herbert Hoover was the first President to take an active interest in improving the general quality of American criminal law enforcement. In 1929 he created the National Commission on Law Observance and Enforcement (Wickersham Commission), which conducted the first comprehensive study of the American criminal justice system.

In the mid 1930s J. Edgar Hoover transformed the Bureau of Investigation. At the request of President Franklin D. Roosevelt in 1935, Hoover resumed Bureau investigation of political groups. Roosevelt was concerned about possible subversion by German or Soviet agents. With the outbreak of WORLD WAR II, Roosevelt gave Hoover expanded authority to investigate subversive activities. Hoover went far beyond his formal mandate, however, and initiated a massive program of secret and illegal spying.

Hoover's program of spying had enormous consequences for presidential control of federal law enforcement. Because it was widely believed that Hoover had unflattering or scandalous information on many political figures, Presidents, Attorneys General, and members of Congress alike were unwilling to question his authority. At the same time, Hoover established a reputation as the principal bulwark against domestic communism, making Presidents and members of Congress reluctant to criticize him for fear of being accused of being soft on communism. As a result, Hoover became a virtually autonomous political force in American life, insulated from oversight by Congress or his nominal superiors, the President and the Attorney General.

The enormous independence of the FBI under Hoover hindered several aspects of federal law enforcement in the post–World War II years. Democratic Presidents thought the FBI failed to investigate violations of federal civil rights laws. President John F. Kennedy and his brother, Attorney General ROBERT F. KENNEDY, felt that the FBI ignored the problem of organized crime. Because of Hoover's independence, however, Democratic Presidents were unable to translate their law-enforcement views into policy. Following Hoover's death in 1972, Presidents reasserted control over the FBI, and Bureau policies increasingly reflected the priorities of presidential administrations.

The Issue of Crime. Presidential involvement in law enforcement issues took a dramatic new turn in the 1960s. The crime issue appeared in a presidential election campaign for the first time in 1964. Insurgent candidate GEORGE WALLACE raised the issue of "law and order," attacking the Supreme Court for a series of decisions protecting the rights of criminal suspects. President Lyndon B. Johnson responded to rising public concern about crime by creating the President's Commission on Law Enforcement and Administration of Justice in 1965. The commission surveyed American criminal justice, and its highly influential report stimulated a new era of criminal justice reform.

Johnson also established the Office of Law Enforcement Assistance (OLEA) in 1965 to support research and provide technical assistance to state and local criminal justice agencies. OLEA represented the first formal program of federal assistance in the area of criminal justice. This effort was greatly expanded under the Law Enforcement Assistance Administration (LEAA), established in 1968. LEAA (later reorganized under the Office of Justice Programs) gave Presidents a vehicle for influencing criminal justice policy at the state and local level.

Crime and law enforcement became prominent issues in virtually every presidential election between 1964 and 1988. REPUBLICAN PARTY candidates generally ran on platforms promising to reduce crime through more effective law enforcement. The principal long-term impact was on the Supreme Court. Beginning with Richard M. Nixon, Republican Presidents sought to appoint conservative justices to the Court. By the 1990s, the Court was dominated by a conservative majority that nearly always ruled in favor of expanded law-enforcement powers over the rights of individual criminal suspects.

With the advent of crime and law enforcement as issues in presidential elections, successive Presidents have focused administration efforts on particular aspects of law enforcement. President Kennedy, acting through Attorney General Robert Kennedy, increased federal law enforcement efforts against organized crime. President Johnson, through his Crime Commission, sought to improve the quality of law enforcement through research and federal financial assistance. President Nixon promised a tough law-and-order program, with a special emphasis on reducing drug use. President Jimmy Carter stressed enforcement of federal civil rights laws, with a special emphasis on misconduct by local police. President Ronald Reagan issued task force reports on violent crime and on the rights of crime victims. Both reports reiterated the conservative program of reducing crime through more effective law enforcement. Presidents Nixon, Reagan, and George Bush each promised to wage a "war" on drugs [*see* DRUG POLICY].

BIBLIOGRAPHY

Gentry, Curtis. *J. Edgar Hoover: The Man and the Secrets.* 1991.

Millspaugh, Arthur. *Crime Control by the National Government.* 1937.

National Advisory Commission on Law Observance and Enforcement. *Reports.* 14 vols. 1931.

Navasky, Victor. *Kennedy Justice.* 1971.

Poveda, Tony. *Lawlessness and Reform: The FBI in Transition.* 1990.

President's Commission on Law Enforcement and Administration of Justice. *The Challenge of Crime in a Free Society.* 1967.

Twentieth Century Fund Task Force on the Law Enforcement Assistance Administration. *Law Enforcement: The Federal Role.* 1976.

Walker, Samuel. *Popular Justice: A History of American Criminal Justice.* 1980.

SAMUEL WALKER

LEADERSHIP SKILLS. Students of leadership have historically been divided into two camps. Some consider that leadership by definition has a moral imperative. To be a leader is, ipso facto, to be a good leader—someone who takes into account the needs, wants, and wishes of followers. But to others leadership is neither more nor less than an individual's capacity to get others to go along. According to this view, Adolf Hitler deserves to be called a leader no less than does Mahatma Gandhi. The distinction between the two conceptions of leadership is important, for it inevitably colors the idea of what a presidential leadership skill actually is. Was President Ronald Reagan's capacity to communicate eloquent testimony to his skill as a political leader, or was it merely a facility squandered on behalf of ideas and policies that were not in the American interest?

For the purposes of this article the debate between the "is" and the "ought" of political leadership will be set aside in favor of a functional approach to the subject. It will be assumed that any trait that facilitates a President's capacity to induce others to follow his lead constitutes a leadership skill.

Leadership skills can be understood only in the context in which they are exercised. Moreover, they manifest themselves in a dynamic that entails at least two players—the leader and at least one follower. To appreciate the fact that the definition of what constitutes a leadership skill depends on the circumstance, it helps to break down the leadership process itself. These components enter into the analysis of the leadership skills of any American President: *context*, that is, the American experience since the beginning of the republic; *role*, that is, the office of the presidency, particularly its powers and constraints; the *leader* himself, that is, the President's persona; his *followers*, the various groups, organizations, and individuals that a President seeks to mobilize; and, finally, the *task*—the issue immediately at hand.

The Content of Leadership. Leadership skills depend on many factors, such as context, rule, constituency, and task. In particular, a given President's leadership skills cannot be understood apart from the history and ideology that comprise the inevitable backdrop for his particular performance. America's antileadership bias and its revolutionary (antiauthoritarian) history put a premium on leading without appearing to dominate. And the United States' changing role in world affairs—particularly its status as a military superpower during the second half of the twentieth century—puts a premium on the capacity to exercise leadership at the international as well as national level.

Nor can leadership skills be separated from the changing nature of the executive office. Presidents have, over time, become by far the most visible actors in the political system, and they have accrued extensive formal and informal powers to make decisions on their own initiative. Moreover the CHIEF EXECUTIVE is now responsible for the management of a very large bureaucracy, including a WHITE HOUSE STAFF that has grown exponentially since the administration of Franklin D. Roosevelt.

Clearly, a President's leadership skills also relate—indeed, are derived from— his innate proclivities and capacities and the particulars of his background and experience. A President who, like Woodrow Wilson, is an intellectual and student of government will have different skills from, say, Ronald Reagan, an instinctive politician (and a one-time Hollywood actor). An old Washington insider like Lyndon Baines Johnson will bring to the White House talents and deficits different from those of someone like Jimmy Carter, whose experience in government was limited to one term as governor of Georgia.

Since leadership is an interactive process, followers will also define what constitutes a leadership skill. If the President is trying to guide a recalcitrant Congress, one set of skills will be called for. Similarly, a face-to-face meeting with the prime minister of Israel will demand behavior different from that called for when, for example, dealing with Iraqi leader Saddam Hussein on the heels of Iraq's invasion of Kuwait. And still another set of leadership skills will come into play if the Chief Executive is addressing the country on nationwide television on the state of the economy.

Finally, what constitutes a leadership skill depends on the nature of the task and the situation immediately at hand. Is the challenge routine, or is it somehow exceptional? Is the President dealing with FOREIGN AFFAIRS or domestic policy? Is the executive's attempt to exercise leadership reactive, or is he trying to strike out in a bold new direction? Is the country safe and secure, or is it being somehow threatened from within or without? Is there an immediate crisis of some kind? Has the Chief Executive just settled into the Oval Office, or is the administration in its fourth year?

Saying that the definition of a leadership skill depends on a multiplicity of factors does not mean, however, that there are no constants. In fact, a review of the literature on the presidency suggests that, specifics notwithstanding, there are skills that Presidents would be advised to cultivate under any circumstances. This conclusion correlates with that to be drawn from the leadership literature more generally, which confirms that although leadership skills do depend on contingencies, there are some capacities that support the attempt to lead in almost all situations.

The Stages of Leadership. Presidential leadership is an extended process that can be divided into at least four stages. Each stage demands a different set of leadership skills.

In the first stage, the President who would lead must learn about the world in which he inevitably will have to operate. What are the domestic and international environments as seen from the new perspective of the Oval Office? What are the particular challenges that each presents at this particular moment in time? Skills relevant to this first stage of the leadership process include curiosity, a willingness to learn, and open-mindedness. Presidents should seek to learn more than they already know. They should meet with individuals and groups who bring messages from the full spectrum of the American public. And Presidents should be flexible—able to deviate at least slightly from previously held beliefs, attitudes, and opinions.

The second stage in developing leadership requires that the President establish a goal or set of goals that constitute a vision. Skills relevant to this task include pragmatism, managerial capacity, intelligence, decision-making competence, and a willingness to entertain some level of risk.

Pragmatism means that if a goal is unrealistic, it is by definition foolish. Goals are worth setting only if they are attainable, and leaders are worth their salt only if they establish ends for which the means at their disposal are adequate. Managerial capacity involves establishing a well-devised advisory system. As authors John Burke and Fred Greenstein have observed, a President's advisers should be geared to his style and needs so that they can be useful to him as he chooses among alternatives. When Presidents are called on to set priorities, putting certain goals at the top of their policy agenda and, hence, inevitably diminishing the importance of other goals, this whittling-down process demands intelligence and the capacity to review and analyze multiple variables.

There is an entire literature devoted to good decision making. Executives can proceed in a number of recognized ways that will enhance their chances of making smart decisions. Decision makers are advised to acquire good information, to generate an array of alternatives based on this information, to weigh carefully the consequences of each, and to guard against a decision-making process that is biased. To establish a leadership goal is, perforce, to make a decision. This puts a premium on the President's capacity to decide wisely and well. While Presidents are, of course, well advised to be prudent, to be frightened of the new and different is to turn caution into paralysis, so a willingness to take on some level of risk is also a necessary component of leadership.

The third stage requires that the President mobilize support by assuring his followers that to go along with him is in their best interest. Since American Presidents have neither the power nor the authority to compel compliance, their ability to mobilize others depends on their ability to convince them that the benefits of following will outweigh the costs. Skills relevant to this task include professional competence, that is, the President's having achieved some reasonable level of accomplishment at an earlier point in his political career; an ability to communicate and to control the news; a knowledge of, and willingness to employ, presidential resources; and a talent for interpersonal politicking.

In the television age, the capacity to communicate via the electronic media is, perhaps, of paramount importance. The executive's ability to mobilize publics both at home and abroad depends on this skill; in turn, members of elites (e.g., Congress, the press) will be swayed by PUBLIC OPINION. The ability to communicate implies skills such as the ability to articulate, educate, and convince, as well as to convey—literally or symbolically—such cherished ideals as unity, morality, and progress. Inevitably, there is a Machiavellian cast to this particular presidential skill. Yet Presidents who are unable to control the news and shape the image they convey, whose administrations are riddled with leaks, and whose team therefore seems in disarray, find themselves in an increasingly untenable position. For better or worse, Presidents must maintain some control over the messages they send. They must also understand and use the military, political, and eco-

nomic resources available to them. A President who would bring others along must know when to hold out the carrot and when the stick, when to promise and when to threaten. Followers must believe that these tools will be employed as conditions warrant. And in order to turn members of the political elite, particularly Congress, into active or at least passive followers, Presidents must be ready, willing, and able to employ a variety of interpersonal strategies. These include, but are not limited to, personal appeals and access, provision of services and amenities, use of CABINET and staff, bargaining, and compromise.

The tasks associated with the fourth stage of presidential leadership development remind us that mobilizing followers is not the be-all and end-all of the leadership process. Presidents who would realize their goals must ensure that political support is translated into action. Put another way, the President must direct those who have been charged with implementing the executive's decision. Skills relevant to this task include managerial competence in such areas as selection of staff, advance planning, building team coherence and loyalty, establishing policy control over bureaucracy, and maintaining lines of authority and accountability. They also include organizational competence over domains such as the White House staff, Cabinet, and large federal bureaucracies.

While the discussion above treats the President's leadership skills primarily from a functional perspective, it seems necessary to conclude with a note on leadership as ethical action. Is it accurate to refer to those leaders who are disposed to value the autonomy and integrity of their followers as endowed with a particular leadership "skill"? Probably not. A skill does not generally refer to a habit of the heart. Nevertheless, ethics matters. To think of leadership as a social contract entered into freely and fairly is to think in a way that is, in and of itself, of value.

BIBLIOGRAPHY

Burke, John P., and Fred I. Greenstein. *How Presidents Test Reality.* 1989.
Kellerman, Barbara. *The Political Presidency: Practice of Leadership.* 1984.
Kellerman, Barbara, and Ryan Barillieaux. *The President as World Leader.* 1991.
Neustadt, Richard. *Presidential Power and the Modern Presidents.* 1990.
Rockman, Bert. *The Leadership Question: The Presidency and the American System.* 1984.

BARBARA KELLERMAN

LEAGUE OF NATIONS. President Woodrow Wilson's statecraft culminated at the Paris Peace Conference of 1919 in the creation of the League of Nations. He regarded the Covenant, which would establish the legal framework for this new international organization, as the key feature of the TREATY OF VERSAILLES. It combined the idealism and practicality that characterized his diplomacy.

Wilson presented the first draft of the Covenant to a plenary session of the peace conference on 14 February. The League, he explained, would maintain peace primarily by organizing the public opinion of the world. Yet if public opinion failed, he anticipated the use of military force. Either of these methods might be employed to preserve the territorial integrity and political independence of the League's members, as promised in Article 10. The President did not intend to commit the United States to a new international status quo, however. Emphasizing the League's flexibility, he noted that Article 19 anticipated adjustments in the peace settlement as future circumstances might require. In short, the League appeared to Wilson to be a practical way to achieve the ideal of world peace in an era of potential war and revolution.

After minor changes in the Covenant, primarily to accommodate American criticism of Wilson's League, the United States and the Allies required Germany to accept it as part of the Treaty of Versailles. Membership in the League, however, excluded Germany at first. Nor did it include Soviet Russia. The victorious powers intended to use the League to sustain their dominance in world affairs.

Wilson prevailed on the Allies to locate the League's headquarters in Geneva, Switzerland. Through the League, as he told the U.S. Senate on 10 July 1919, he expected the United States to furnish moral leadership for the world. He viewed this new U.S. role in international politics as the nation's God-given destiny.

Unfortunately for Wilson, Republican Senators did not share his vision of U.S. involvement throughout the world. Under the leadership of Senator Henry Cabot Lodge of Massachusetts, they rejected the Treaty of Versailles in 1919, and again in 1920. Unless the President accepted their formal reservations to the treaty, which he refused, the Republicans resolved to keep the United States out of the new League.

Even before the treaty's defeat in the Senate, it was apparent that Wilson's vision of a new international order would fail. He had not made the world safe for democracy. Both Weimar Germany and Soviet Russia remained outside the League, and the Allies did not entrust their own security to it. As Wilson himself was painfully aware, the creation of the League neither transformed the world, nor inaugurated a new era of peace.

[*See also* FOURTEEN POINTS; WORLD WAR I.]

BIBLIOGRAPHY

Ambrosius, Lloyd E. *Woodrow Wilson and the American Diplomatic Tradition: The Treaty Fight in Perspective.* 1987.
Egerton, George W. *Great Britain and the Creation of the League of Nations: Strategy, Politics, and International Organization, 1914–1919.* 1978.
Widenor, William C. *Henry Cabot Lodge and the Search for an American Foreign Policy.* 1979.

LLOYD E. AMBROSIUS

LEBANESE RESOLUTION (1983). In response to President Ronald Reagan's decision to station approximately twelve hundred Marines in Beirut as part of a four-nation peacekeeping force, in October 1983 Congress adopted the Multinational Force in Lebanon Resolution (MFLR) (97 Stat. 805). Although the Reagan administration had dispatched contingents of Marines on two separate occasions, in August and September 1982, Congress did not invoke its constitutional authority until more than a year later. Passed after extensive negotiations between the White House and the Democratic leadership of the House of Representatives, Congress invoked its power under the WAR POWERS RESOLUTION of 1973 to limit the Marines' deployment to eighteen months, until April 1985. President Reagan signed the bill, but he denied that Congress had constitutional authority to prevent the COMMANDER IN CHIEF from deploying U.S. armed forces as part of an international peacekeeping force.

The MFLR authorized continued U.S. participation in the peacekeeping effort in accordance with an agreement between the governments of Lebanon and the United States, dated 25 September 1982. The resolution declared that U.S. armed forces participating in the peacekeeping force had been in hostilities since 29 August. Accordingly, the War Powers Resolution became operative on that date, requiring congressional approval for the operation. The MFLR also required the President to report periodically to Congress regarding the multinational force's activities, composition, and contribution toward national reconciliation in Lebanon and peace in the Middle East. This was the first time since passage of the War Powers Resolution in 1973 that Congress had formally invoked it, requiring congressional authorization to commit troops to hostilities or regions where such hostilities may be imminent. While President Reagan denied that hostilities were imminent, on 23 October a terrorist bomb killed 239 Marines in their headquarters at the Beirut international airport.

Congressional passage of the MFLR and President Reagan's subsequent statement marked the continuing struggle between the legislative and executive branches over the President's authority to dispatch U.S. armed forces abroad without a declaration of war or other authorization. Since 1973 American Presidents have dispatched armed forces abroad thirty-one times. These episodes vary in scope and duration from attempts to rescue American citizens, humanitarian operations, and minor military engagements to the U.S. invasion of PANAMA (1989) and the GULF WAR (1991). Usually, American Presidents have claimed that they need not invoke the War Powers Resolution because the operations were defensive rather than offensive, hostilities were neither present nor imminent, the armed forces would be withdrawn shortly, or that the operation was pursuant to a U.S. treaty commitment. After the ill-fated attempt to rescue American hostages in Teheran on 24 April 1980 during the IRANIAN HOSTAGE CRISIS, President Jimmy Carter stated that he had ample authority as Commander in Chief to rescue citizens and diplomats without prior congressional approval. When questioned about the invasion of GRENADA in 1983, Ronald Reagan said that it was unnecessary to invoke the War Powers Resolution because he would withdraw the armed forces within the sixty to ninety days that the act permitted him to conduct military operations abroad without seeking congressional authorization.

The struggle between President Reagan and Congress over the Lebanese troop deployment began in February 1983, following confrontations between U.S. and Israeli troops in Beirut. Senator James Exon (D-Neb.) confronted Secretary of Defense CASPAR W. WEINBERGER with the claim that the Marines were in greater danger than the administration had admitted. Secretary Weinberger countered by saying that hostilities were not imminent in Lebanon. Following an 18 April terrorist bombing at the U.S. Embassy that left fifty people dead, Congress demanded participation in any decision to expand or reenforce the Marine contingent. The debate intensified after two Marines were killed on 29 August.

On 31 August the Democratic floor leader, Robert C. Byrd (W.Va.), claimed that American combat forces were "involved in hostilities within the meaning of Section 4(a)(1) and that President Reagan should invoke the provision to assure the fullest possible legislative-executive cooperation." Some members of Congress such as Senator Barry Goldwater (R-Ariz.), who had criticized Reagan's decision to dispatch armed forces to Lebanon, argued that the Marines should be withdrawn. That same day, Secretary of State GEORGE SHULTZ denied that the Marines were engaged in hostilities, as defined by the War Powers Resolution.

The debate focused primarily on questions of presidential power and congressional prerogative rather than the desirability of intervening in Lebanon's civil war, in armed conflict between Israel and its neighbors, or in an increasingly unstable region of the world. During September some congressional leaders urged that President Reagan invoke the War Powers Resolution. Clement Zablocki (D-Wis.), chairman of the House Foreign Affairs Committee, claimed that President Reagan was "unnecessarily risking a confrontation with Congress . . . in trying to exclude Congress from fulfilling its constitutional responsibilities" under the War Powers Resolution. Similarly, Senator Charles Percy (R-Ill.), chairman of the Senate Foreign Relations Committee, virtually stated that hostilities were imminent.

On 4 September, President Reagan claimed that invoking the Resolution would exacerbate the situation because it would create the impression that the Marines could be withdrawn precipitously. It became increasingly difficult to argue that hostilities were not imminent as two more Marines were killed on 5 September. An additional two thousand Marines were dispatched to a naval task force off the Lebanese coast, and the President authorized Marine commanders in Lebanon to call for defensive air strikes from Mediterranean-based naval air forces.

By mid September the Senate's Democrats began to press for legislation invoking the War Powers Resolution. On 19 September Congress and the White House accepted a compromise resolution (MFLR) that established an eighteen-month limit on troop deployment. While President Reagan agreed to sign it in October, congressional leaders acknowledged that he could deny the constitutionality of the War Powers Resolution, its applicability to the current situation, and any restrictions on his authority as Commander in Chief to deploy U.S. armed forces abroad. In a statement on 12 October, President Reagan noted, "I do not and cannot cede any of the authority vested in me under the Constitution as Commander in Chief of United States Armed Forces." The President also denied that the MFLR could alter his institutional prerogatives or his course of action in Lebanon. Thus the standoff between Congress and the President ended.

While the legislative leadership could claim that Congress had asserted its power to control the commitment of armed forces to hostilities below the threshold of a declaration of war, the President could contend that he had preserved his power as Commander in Chief to use American troops to further U.S. NATIONAL

SECURITY interests. In the aftermath of the bombing at Marine headquarters on 23 October, the debate over the Marines' security overshadowed both the constitutional and foreign policy issues that the conflict precipitated. Underscoring the policy vacuum, former Secretary of State HENRY KISSINGER observed that if the Marines' security were the primary issue, they would have been better off at Camp Lejeune, North Carolina, than exposed to terrorist attacks in Beirut. Therefore, the MFLR altered neither the course of U.S. policy in the Middle East nor presidential deployment of U.S. forces abroad without prior congressional authorization.

BIBLIOGRAPHY

Hallenbeck, Ralph A. *Military Force as an Instrument of U.S. Foreign Policy: Intervention in Lebanon, August 1982–February 1984*. 1991.
Wald, Martin, "The Future of the War Powers Resolution." *Stanford Law Review* 36 (1984): 1407–1445.
"The War Powers Resolution: A Symposium," *Loyola Los Angeles Law Review* 17 (1984): 579–808.

EDWARD KEYNES

LEGISLATIVE LEADERSHIP. Near the top of any presidential job description would be "leading Congress." Since the American system of SEPARATION OF POWERS is actually one of shared powers, Presidents can rarely operate independently of Congress. If they are to succeed in leaving their stamp on public policy, much of their time in office will be devoted to trying to lead the legislature to support their initiatives.

Chief Legislator. Nowhere does the Constitution use the phrase *chief legislator*; it is strictly a phrase invented by textbook writers to emphasize the executive's importance in the legislative process. The Constitution does require that the President give a STATE OF THE UNION MESSAGE "from time to time" to Congress and instructs the President to recommend to the consideration of Congress "such Measures as he shall judge necessary and expedient." In fact, the President is a major shaper of the congressional agenda.

The Constitution also gives the President power to veto legislation. Once Congress passes a bill, the President may sign it, making it law; veto it, sending it back to Congress with the reasons for rejecting it; or let it become law after ten working days by not doing anything. Congress can pass a vetoed law, however, if two-thirds of each house vote to override the President. At one point in the lawmaking process the President has the last word: if Congress adjourns within ten days after submitting a bill, the President can simply let it die by neither signing nor vetoing it. This process is called a POCKET VETO.

The presidential veto is usually effective; only about 4 percent of all vetoed bills have become law since the nation's founding. Thus even the threat of a presidential veto can be an effective tool for persuading Congress to give more weight to Presidents' views. On the other hand, the veto is a blunt instrument. Presidents must accept or reject bills in their entirety; they cannot veto only the parts they do not like (most governors have an ITEM VETO that allows them to veto particular portions of a bill). As a result, the White House often must accept provisions of a bill it opposes in order to obtain others that it desires.

The presidential veto is an inherently negative resource. It is most useful for preventing legislation. Much of the time, however, Presidents are more interested in passing their own legislation. Here they must marshall their political resources to obtain positive support for their programs. Presidents' three most useful resources are their party leadership, public support, and their own legislative skills.

Party Leadership. No matter what other resources Presidents may have at their disposal, they remain highly dependent upon their party to move their legislative programs. Representatives and Senators of the President's party almost always form the nucleus of coalitions supporting presidential proposals and provide, year in and year out, considerably more support than do members of the opposition party. Thus party leadership in Congress is every President's principal task when seeking to counter the natural tendencies toward conflict between the executive and legislative branches inherent in the American government's system of CHECKS AND BALANCES.

If Presidents could rely on their fellow party members to vote for whatever the White House sent up to Capitol Hill, presidential leadership of Congress would be rather easy. All Presidents would have to do is to make sure members of their party showed up to vote. If their party had the majority, Presidents would always win. If their party was in the minority, Presidents would only have to concentrate on converting a few members of the other party to their side.

However, despite the pull of party ties, all Presidents experience substantial slippage in the support of their party in Congress and can count on their own party members for support no more than two-thirds of the time. Thus Presidents are forced to take an active role in party matters and to persuade as well as to mobilize members of their party.

The primary obstacle to party unity is the lack of consensus among party members on policies; this has been especially true of the DEMOCRATIC PARTY. This diversity of views often reflects the diversity of constituencies represented by party members, and members of Congress are more likely to vote with their constituents, to whom they must return for reelection, than to support the President's proposals.

The President's relationship with congressional party leaders is a delicate one. Although the leaders are predisposed to support presidential policies and typically work closely with the White House, they are free to oppose the President or lend only symbolic support, and they may be ineffective. Moreover, party leaders are not in a position to reward or discipline members of Congress on the basis of presidential support.

To promote goodwill with congressional party members, the White House provides them with many amenities, ranging from photographs with the President to rides on Air Force One. In general, however, party members consider it their right to receive benefits from the White House and are unlikely to be especially responsive to the President as a result.

The President can also withhold favors. Such withholding is rarely done. If party members wish to oppose the White House, there is little the President can do to stop them. The parties are highly decentralized and national party leaders do not control those aspects of politics that are of vital concern to members of Congress: nominations and elections. Members of Congress are largely self-recruited, gain their party's nomination by their own efforts and not the party's, and provide most of the money and organizational support needed for their elections. The President can do little to influence the results of these activities.

One way for the President to improve the chances of obtaining support in Congress is to increase the number of fellow party members in the Senate and House. Most recent studies show a diminishing connection between presidential and congressional voting, however, and few races are determined by the presidential COATTAILS EFFECT. The small change in party balance that usually occurs when the electoral dust has settled is striking. In the ten presidential elections between 1952 and 1988, the party of the winning presidential candidate gained an average of ten seats (out of 435) per election in the House. In the Senate the opposition party actually gained seats in half of the elections (1956, 1960, 1972, 1984, 1988), there was no change in 1976. The net gain for the President's party in the Senate averaged only one seat per election. The picture is even more bleak for midterm elections, those held between presidential elections. The President's party typically loses seats in these elections.

To add to these party leadership burdens, the President's party often lacks a majority in one or both houses of Congress, what is called a situation of DIVIDED GOVERNMENT. Between 1953 and 1992 there were twenty-six years in which Republican Presidents faced a Democratic House of Representatives and twenty years in which they encountered a Democratic Senate.

As a result of election returns and the lack of dependable party support, the President usually has to solicit help from the opposition party. The opposition is generally not fertile ground for seeking support. Nevertheless, even a few votes may be enough to bring the President the required majority.

Legislative Skills. Presidential legislative skills come in a variety of forms. Of these skills, bargaining receives perhaps the most attention from commentators on the presidency. There is no question that many bargains occur and that they take a variety of forms. President Ronald Reagan's Budget Director David Stockman recalled that "the last 10 or 20 percent of the votes needed for a majority of both houses on the 1981 tax cut had to be bought, period. . . . The hogs were really feeding."

Nevertheless, bargaining in the form of trading support on two or more policies or providing specific benefits for Representatives and Senators occurs less often and plays a less critical role in the creation of presidential coalitions in Congress than one might think. For obvious reasons, the White House does not want to encourage the type of bargaining Stockman describes, and there is a scarcity of resources with which to bargain, especially in an era of large budget deficits. Moreover, the President does not have to bargain with every member of Congress to receive support. On controversial issues on which bargaining may be useful, the President almost always starts with a sizable core of party supporters; some members of the opposition party may provide support on ideological or policy grounds. Others may support the President because of relevant constituency interests or strong public approval. Thus the President needs to bargain only if he does not have a majority (or two-thirds on treaties and veto overrides).

Presidents may improve their chances of success in Congress by making certain strategic moves. It is wise, for example, for a new President to be ready to send legislation to the Hill early during the first year in office in order to exploit the favorable atmosphere that typically characterizes this HONEYMOON PERIOD. Obviously, this is a one-shot opportunity.

An important aspect of presidential legislative strategy is establishing priorities among legislative proposals. The goal of this effort is to set Congress's agenda, for if Presidents are unable to focus Congress's attention on their priority programs, these programs may become lost in the complex and overloaded legislative process. Setting priorities is also important because Presidents and their staffs can lobby effectively for only a few bills at a time. Moreover, each President's political capital is inevitably limited, and it is sensible to focus it on a limited range of personally important issues. Otherwise this precious resource might be wasted.

Systematic studies have found that, once one takes into account the status of their party in Congress and their standing with the public, Presidents renowned for their legislative skills (such as Lyndon B. Johnson) are no more successful in winning votes, even close ones, or obtaining congressional support than those considered less adept at dealing with Congress (such as Jimmy Carter). The President's legislative skills are not at the core of presidential leadership of Congress. Even skilled Presidents cannot reshape the contours of the political landscape and create opportunities for change. Presidents work in a legislative environment largely beyond their control.

Exploiting Opportunities. Presidents are limited by electoral decisions (both presidential and congressional) and the public's evaluations of the chief executive's performance. Presidents are rarely in a position to augment substantially their resources. They operate at the margins as facilitators rather than as directors of change.

When the various streams of resources do converge, they create opportunities for leadership. Because a President's resource base is fragile, he must take advantage of the opportunities in his environment to facilitate change. The essential presidential skill in leading Congress is recognizing and exploiting conditions for change, not in creating them.

This can best be seen in the cases of three Presidents most often viewed as directors rather than mere facilitators of change. It is actually those Presidents who have best understood their own limitations and taken full advantage of their good fortune in having resources to exploit to embark on major shifts in public policy who have been most successful with Congress. When these resources diminished, they fell back to the more typical stalemate that usually characterizes PRESIDENTIAL-CONGRESSIONAL RELATIONS.

When Congress first met in special session in March 1933 after Franklin D. Roosevelt's inauguration, it rapidly passed at the new President's request bills to control the resumption of banking, repeal PROHIBITION, and effect government economies. This is all Roosevelt originally planned for Congress to do; he expected to reassemble the legislature when permanent and more constructive legislation was ready. Yet the President found a situation ripe for change. Roosevelt decided to exploit this favorable environment and strike repeatedly with hastily drawn legislation. This period of intense activity came to be known as the Hundred Days.

Lyndon B. Johnson also knew that his personal leadership could not sustain congressional support for his policies. He had to exploit the opportunities provided by the assassination of President John F. Kennedy and the election of 1964, and he quickly sent to Congress the enormous agenda of the GREAT SOCIETY.

The administration of Ronald Reagan realized from the beginning that it had an opportunity to effect major changes in public policy, but that it had to concentrate its focus and move quickly before the environment became less favorable. The President and his staff moved rapidly in 1981 to exploit the perceptions of a mandate and the dramatic elevation of Republicans to majority status in the Senate.

Thus, even Presidents who appeared to dominate Congress were actually facilitators rather than directors of change. They quite explicitly took advantage of opportunities in their environments and, working at the margins, successfully guided legislation through Congress. They were especially attentive to the state of PUBLIC OPINION in determining their legislative strategies. As the most volatile resource for leadership, public opinion is the factor most likely to determine whether or not an opportunity for change exists. By itself it cannot sustain presidential leadership of Congress, but it is the variable that has the most potential to turn a typical situation into one favorable for change, and, being mercurial, requires expeditious action to take advantage of it.

The facilitating skill required to exploit such opportunities is not to be underrated. Public opinion about matters of politics and policy is often amorphous. It lacks articulation and structure. It requires leadership to tap into it effectively, give it direction, and use it to bring about policy change. The President must sense the nature of the opportunity at hand, clearly associate himself and his policies with favorable public opinion in the minds of political elites, and approach Congress when conditions are most favorable for passing legislation.

It is important to depersonalize somewhat the study of presidential leadership and examine it from a broader perspective. In this way there are fewer risks of attributing to various aspects of presidential leadership consequences of factors largely beyond the President's control. Similarly, one is less likely to attribute incorrectly the failure of a President to achieve his

Directors of Legislative Affairs

President	Director, Office of Legislative Affairs
34 Eisenhower	Wilton B. Persons, 1953–1958 Bryce Harlow, 1958–1961
35 Kennedy	Lawrence F. O'Brien, 1961–1963
36 L. B. Johnson	Lawrence F. O'Brien, 1963–1965 O'Brien (now Postmaster General) supported by Henry Hall Wilson and Barefoot Sanders, Jr., 1965–1969
37 Nixon	Bryce Harlow, 1969–1970 Clark MacGregor, 1971–1972 William E. Timmons, 1972–1974
38 Ford	Max L. Friedersdorf, 1974–1977
39 Carter	Frank B. Moore, 1977–1981
40 Reagan	Max L. Friedersdorf, 1981–1982 Kenneth M. Duberstein, 1982–1983 M. B. Oglesby, Jr., 1983–1986 William L. Ball III, 1986–1988 Alan M. Kranowitz, 1988–1989
41 Bush	Frederick D. McClure, 1989–1992 Nicholas E. Calio, 1992–1993
42 Clinton	Howard Paster, 1993–

goals to his failure to lead properly. Things are rarely so simple.

[*See also* AGENDA, PRESIDENT'S; BIPARTISANSHIP, CONGRESS AND; CONGRESS, WHITE HOUSE INFLUENCE ON.]

BIBLIOGRAPHY

Bond, Jon R., and Richard Fleisher. *The President in the Legislative Arena*. 1990.
Edwards, George C., III. *At the Margins: Presidential Leadership of Congress*. 1989.
Edwards, George C., III. *Presidential Influence in Congress*. 1980.
Fisher, Louis. *Constitutional Conflicts between the Congress and the President*. 3d ed., rev. 1991.
Jones, Charles O. *The Trusteeship Presidency*. 1988.
Light, Paul C. *The President's Agenda*. Rev. ed. 1991.
Peterson, Mark A. *Legislating Together*. 1990.

GEORGE C. EDWARDS III

LEGISLATIVE VETO. Beginning in the 1930s, Congress has used the legislative veto to control the President and executive officers. A legislative veto is a condition placed on delegated authority that allows Congress to maintain control without having to pass another law. An early example of the legislative veto was in legislation in 1932 that delegated authority to the President to reorganize executive agencies; according to that legislation, either house of Congress could disapprove the President's reorganization proposal within a sixty-day review period. If neither house disapproved, the proposal took effect just as though Congress had enacted it. There are different forms of legislative veto: a *one-house veto* (which takes the form of a simple resolution passed by either house), a *two-house veto* (a concurrent resolution passed by both houses), and a *committee veto*. The defining characteristic of all these forms is that they are not presented to the President for his signature or veto.

In INS V. CHADHA (1983), the Supreme Court invalidated a one-house veto in an immigration statute because it violated both the Constitution's principle of bicameralism, which requires action by both houses of Congress, and the PRESENTATION CLAUSE which requires that all bills be presented to the President. Notwithstanding the Court's ruling, Congress continued after 1983 to put legislative vetoes (generally of the committee variety) in bills that it passed, and Presidents Reagan and Bush signed those bills into law. From the Court's decision in 1983 to the end of 1992, approximately two hundred new legislative vetoes were enacted into law. They survived because they satisfied the needs of executive officials and congressional committees. As of 1993, these new legislative vetoes had not been challenged in court.

Origins. Although the legislative veto has some precedents in the period following the CIVIL WAR, the first major legislative veto was the result of a legislative idea offered in 1929 by President Herbert Hoover. He proposed that Congress give him authority to submit reorganization plans for the executive branch subject to some form of congressional disapproval, suggesting that the President might act "upon approval of a joint committee of Congress." As incorporated in legislation enacted in 1932, Congress gave Hoover reorganization authority subject to a one-house veto that had to be exercised during a sixty-day review period. Hoover's proposals were disapproved by the House of Representatives, which preferred to leave reorganization changes to the incoming President, Franklin D. Roosevelt.

The procedure suggested by Hoover contained advantages for both branches. Congress could control delegated authority without having to pass another law subject to the President's veto, which would require a two-thirds majority in each house to override. The President benefited because his proposal would become law within a fixed number of days unless Congress stopped it. Moreover, the procedures established for the legislative veto prohibited Congress from offering any amendments to the President's proposal; members of Congress had to vote on the President's recommendation with a simple yes or no.

Finally, since the President's proposal would become law unless Congress disapproved it, it could not be buried in committee or delayed by filibuster in the Senate.

Over the next few years, Congress changed the form of the legislative veto in executive reorganization bills. It adopted a two-house veto in 1939 but returned to the one-house veto in 1949. With the reorganization statute establishing a precedent, Congress in the 1930s and 1940s extended the legislative veto to several other areas, including deportation of aliens, defense installations, and public-works projects.

In 1955, Attorney General HERBERT BROWNELL advised President Dwight D. Eisenhower that a statute requiring executive agencies to "come into agreement" with designated congressional committees was unconstitutional. Congress could not, Brownell said, force the executive branch to share administrative decisions with congressional committees. Congress responded by achieving the same result through a change in its internal procedures. It drafted legislative language that prohibited the House and Senate appropriations committees from providing funds for certain real estate transactions unless the public works committee in each house had first approved the contracts. The authorizing committee could control the appropriating committee. Brownell advised Eisenhower that this procedure was constitutional because it was internal to Congress: the public works committees were not controlling the executive branch directly. Of course they were doing so, indirectly, but form sometimes triumphs over substance.

Proliferation. In the 1970s, as Congress attempted to redress the balance of power with the executive branch, legislative vetoes began to proliferate. The WAR POWERS RESOLUTION of 1973 provided that Congress could pass a two-house veto requiring the President to withdraw troops engaged in combat. The IMPOUNDMENT CONTROL ACT of 1974 gave Congress a one-house veto over presidential proposals to delay ("defer") the spending of appropriated funds. Another statute in 1974 permitted Congress to exercise a two-house veto over arms sales proposed by the President. The National Emergencies Act of 1976 included a two-house veto to terminate EMERGENCY POWERS delegated to the President.

These proposals disturbed the executive branch, but the development that caused the greatest concern was a move to extend the legislative veto to agency rulemaking. Beginning in 1974, Congress passed legislation with one-house and two-house vetoes to control the disposition of PRESIDENTIAL PAPERS, regulations issued by the Commissioner of Education, passenger-restraint rules proposed by the National Highway Traffic Safety Administration, and regulations adopted by the FEDERAL ELECTION COMMISSION, the Federal Energy Regulatory Commission, and the Federal Trade Commission.

With these individual statutes in place, Congress next considered an omnibus bill that would have permitted Congress to exercise a legislative veto over all rules and regulations adopted by federal agencies. These congressional initiatives helped rupture the decades-long accommodation of the executive and legislative branches over the legislative veto. In 1978, President Jimmy Carter released a strong statement in opposition to legislative vetoes, concluding that they were unconstitutional and in the future would be treated as merely advisory rather than as binding on the executive branch. Even given this confrontation, however, the administration was still willing to compromise on a few fronts. At a press conference Attorney General Griffin Bell explained that the administration would agree, in a spirit of comity, to abide by any two-house vetoes that Congress exercised against arms sales proposals or military operations under the War Powers Resolution.

Supreme Court Decisions. In the midst of these legislative-executive conflicts, the federal courts were gingerly testing the constitutionality of legislative vetoes. In the early cases, the courts deliberately avoided across-the-board condemnations of the legislative veto. The courts moved case by case and statute by statute. This incremental strategy came to an abrupt halt in 1982, when the District of Columbia Circuit Court struck down a one-house veto over Federal Energy Regulatory Commission rules and a two-house veto over Federal Trade Commission rules. The breadth of those rulings made it clear that all legislative vetoes were invalid because they violated the presentation clause and that one-house or committee vetoes were also invalid because they violated the principle of bicameralism.

The case that reached the Supreme Court in 1983 involved an immigration statute. Congress had authorized the Attorney General to suspend the deportation of aliens subject to a one-house congressional veto. Following the logic of the lower court, the Supreme Court in *INS v. Chadha* decided that the one-house veto in the immigration statute violated the presentation clause and bicameralism. Chief Justice Warren Burger wrote the opinion for the Court. Justice Lewis Powell concurred in the judgment but stated that he preferred a more narrowly drawn holding that would have confined the ruling to cases like Chadha's, in which Congress tried to override adjudicatory proceedings. Justices Byron White and William Rehnquist dissented.

In response to the Court's ruling, Congress amended a number of statutes that contained legislative vetoes. In 1984 it revised the executive reorganization statute, eliminating language about congressional disapproval and requiring that presidential reorganization plans be approved by a joint resolution. This procedure complied with *Chadha*, because a joint resolution must be passed by Congress and presented to the President. The executive branch, however, was hampered by this change: under the previous law, presidential proposals were implemented unless stopped by one house of Congress, but the new law put the burden on the President to obtain the approval of both houses within a specified number of days. The Reagan administration considered this new procedure so onerous that it did not seek REORGANIZATION POWER after the new procedure expired in 1984.

For other statutes, including legislation on presidential emergency powers, home rule for the District of Columbia, federal salaries, export administration, and arms sales, Congress replaced the legislative veto with a joint resolution of disapproval. It debated repealing the two-house veto that had been included in the War Powers Resolution and replacing it with a joint resolution of disapproval, but in the end left the War Powers Resolution alone. Instead, in 1984 Congress passed a free-standing statute that authorizes an expedited procedure for adopting a joint resolution that would require the President to remove U.S. forces engaged in hostilities outside the United States.

On a number of other fronts, Congress and executive agencies fashioned a variety of accommodations that were the functional equivalents of the legislative veto. After 1983, Congress no longer passed legislation incorporating one-house or two-house vetoes; the form of control now shifted to congressional committees. Presidents Reagan and Bush signed bills containing a total of more than two hundred provisions giving congressional committees the power to approve agency decisions.

In 1984, President Reagan did object to a housing appropriations bill that contained half a dozen legislative vetoes giving congressional committees final control over certain agency actions. In signing the bill, he implied that these legislative vetoes were inconsistent with *Chadha* and would not be considered as legally binding by the administration. Agencies would be free to notify their review committees of pending decisions but would not have to seek their approval. The House Appropriations Committee read Reagan's PRESIDENTIAL SIGNING STATEMENT and proceeded to develop alternative procedures to return control over some agency actions to its subcommittees. It told agencies that it would not only repeal the committee vetoes but that at the same time it would repeal the discretionary authority it had given to agency administrators. If they wanted to transfer funds or take other discretionary actions, they would have to follow the commands of *Chadha*: pass a bill through both houses of Congress and have the bill presented to the President.

Informal Vetoes. To avoid this administrative rigidity, some agencies entered into informal agreements with the appropriations committees. For example, William Beggs, the Administrator of the National Aeronautics and Space Administration (NASA), wrote to the appropriations committees and proposed a compromise. He suggested that, instead of placing dollar ceilings in an appropriations statute and requiring NASA to obtain committee approval whenever it wanted to exceed those ceilings, the ceilings be stated in the conference report accompanying the bill. He then pledged that he would not spend any funds over the ceilings without the prior approval of the committees.

This recommendation, which moved a legislative veto from a public law to an informal, nonstatutory document, avoided problems caused by *Chadha*, which applies only to formal legislative vetoes placed in statutes, not to informal arrangements worked out between executive agencies and congressional committees. The agency's compliance with the agreement is ensured because it is understood that if it violates the agreement, Congress can retaliate by putting the ceilings back into a public law, forcing the agency to seek a separate public law whenever it needs to exceed a specific ceiling. Another informal, nonstatutory legislative veto was agreed to by the Bush administration in the 1989 BAKER ACCORD in order to provide funds to the contra rebels in Nicaragua.

Yet another level of informal legislative vetoes exists because of "reprogramming" procedures established between Congress and the executive branch. Agencies are allowed to shift funds within an appropriations account provided that they notify congressional committees and, in many cases, seek their approval. Without such an understanding, Congress would have to itemize appropriations with far greater specificity than it now does and would thereby restrict the flexibility available to agency managers. The consequence is a classic quid pro quo: Congress appropriates in lump sums, not in detail, and agencies agree to clear significant reprogrammings with their review committees.

Lower federal courts have recognized the need for informal clearance procedures between agencies and congressional committees. Although a trial court in 1983 found that *Chadha* did not permit a review procedure established between the General Services Administration and certain congressional committees, the Court of Appeals for the Federal Circuit reversed in *City of Alexandria v. United States* (1984), concluding that there was nothing unconstitutional about the decision of agencies to defer to committee objections. "Our separation of powers makes such informal cooperation much more necessary than it would be in a pure system of parliamentary government," wrote the court. Despite *Chadha*, legislative vetoes will survive (on either the statutory or the informal level) as a necessary accommodation between Congress and executive agencies.

BIBLIOGRAPHY

Craig, Barbara Hinkson. *Chadha: The Story of an Epic Constitutional Struggle.* 1988.

Elliott, E. Donald. "*INS v. Chadha:* The Administrative Constitution, the Constitution, and the Legislative Veto." *Supreme Court Review* (1983): 125–176.

Fisher, Louis. *Constitutional Conflicts between Congress and the President.* 1991.

Strauss, Peter L. "Was There a Baby in the Bathwater? A Comment on the Supreme Court's Legislative Veto Decision." *Duke Law Journal* (1985): 789–819.

Tribe, Laurence H. "The Legislative Veto Decision: A Law by Any Other Name?" *Harvard Journal on Legislation* 21 (1984): 1–27.

LOUIS FISHER

LEND-LEASE ACT (1941). The Lend-Lease Act was President Franklin D. Roosevelt's central effort to commit the United States to Hitler's defeat. In late 1939 Roosevelt made U.S. production available to the countries fighting Germany through the policy of cash-and-carry. By the time of his reelection in November 1940, however, he faced the problem of financing Britain's heavy arms purchases in the United States. On 2 December, Prime Minister Winston Churchill reminded Roosevelt that Britain's survival depended not only on increased shipments of goods but also on dollars to pay for the needed ships, planes, and munitions.

Roosevelt's answer was Lend-Lease, a program whereby Britain would receive the goods it required provided that it returned them in kind when the war was over. In a FIRESIDE CHAT in December 1940 the President assured isolationists that the country would most readily avoid war by supporting those fighting the Axis. The peoples of Europe did not ask the United States to fight for them, but to furnish the implements of war. The sole purpose of American policy, the President declared, was "to keep war away from our country and our people." While Treasury officials drafted a Lend-Lease bill, Roosevelt used his annual message of 6 January, 1941 to present his program to the American people. The inability of those fighting Hitler to pay, he declared, should not force them to surrender. Whatever they received under Lend-Lease they would repay with "similar materials, or . . . other goods of many kinds."

Four days later Democratic leaders placed the Lend-Lease bill, designated H.R. 1776, before Congress. The bill authorized the U.S. government "to sell, transfer title to, exchange, lease, lend, or otherwise dispose of . . . any defense article" to "any country whose defense the President deems vital to the defense of the United States." The bill defined in detail the defense articles covered by the act. It authorized American officials to assure, through tests and inspections, the proper performance of such articles. The terms and conditions for repayment would be those the President deemed satisfactory. The measure ruled out convoying by U.S. naval vessels or the movement of American ships into combat zones. Isolationists disputed Roosevelt's claim that the bill, by aiding the allies, would keep the country out of war. To assure passage Roosevelt accepted four restrictions on the execution of the Lend-Lease program, but the President's discretionary powers remained great. Both houses of Congress enacted the measure by large majorities. Over $50 billion was approved, nearly $40 billion for Britain and about $11 billion for the U.S.S.R.

BIBLIOGRAPHY

Dallek, Robert. *Franklin D. Roosevelt and American Foreign Policy, 1932–1945.* 1979.

Kimball, Warren F. *The Most Unsordid Act: Lend-Lease, 1939–1941.* 1969.

Langer, William L., and S. Everett Gleason. *The Undeclared War, 1940–1941.* 1953.

NORMAN A. GRAEBNER

LIBERALISM. Liberalism is a loose worldview that emphasizes individual freedom, usually defined in terms of universal rights based in divine or natural law. Its American variant originated in seventeenth- and eighteenth-century English libertarian thought, most definitively exemplified in John Locke and Protestant Dissenters from the Church of England. Rejecting the argument that man was born with sin, liberalism possessed an optimistic view of human nature as fundamentally rational and thus disposed toward tolerance and the enlightened pursuit of self-interest. In its

Dissenting form, it emphasized the ability of sinful persons to achieve redemption by their own will. Lockean liberalism, as restated by Thomas Jefferson, constituted the basis for the Declaration of Independence and the rationale for the addition of a Bill of Rights to the Constitution. (Locke had stated the three basic natural rights of "life, liberty, and property"; Jefferson retained the first two but substituted "the pursuit of happiness" for "property.")

In its early form, liberalism was largely a reaction against despotic state power. Its enumeration of rights emphasized representative government, protection against arbitrary arrest or imprisonment, and affirmation of free speech and religious belief. It advocated small, localized government close to the people and favored the legislative branch over the executive or the judicial. It stood for free economic activity, as unhindered as possible by state grants of monopoly and special privilege. Conceiving of standing armies as instruments of oppression and war as an irrational activity, liberalism from the beginning possessed an antimilitary, near-pacifist bias.

Jeffersonian Liberalism. Thomas Jefferson was the first President in the liberal tradition. In the 1790s, he and James Madison, his fellow leader of the Democratic-Republican Party, had criticized Federalist centralization and extravagance, the QUASI-WAR WITH FRANCE, and the repressive ALIEN AND SEDITION ACTS. In the Kentucky and Virginia resolutions, they had expressed the argument that the Constitution was a compact among the states, creating a federal government of limited powers, and if its acts exceeded its powers by threatening liberty, such acts were void. Envisioning small-scale agriculture as the basis of social stability, Jefferson and his disciples celebrated the agrarian way of life and deplored the possible growth of class-ridden cities. They were suspicious of capitalism and big finance. Jefferson's more ideological followers called these doctrines the Principles of 1798 and considered them moral absolutes.

Ironically, Jefferson's two terms in office demonstrated the practical limitations of his liberalism. A strong executive and party leader, Jefferson dominated Congress. Despite private misgivings about whether he had the authority to do so, he negotiated the LOUISIANA PURCHASE. Although he hoped to keep the functions of the national government to a minimum, the exigencies of a developing country led him to back limited plans for INTERNAL IMPROVEMENTS, most notably for a national road into the West. His determination to avoid war with Great Britain resulted in strong federal enforcement of a trade embargo that alienated the New England states.

Jefferson's immediate successors, Madison and James Monroe, although weaker Chief Executives, continued along the same path, Madison reluctantly pursuing the WAR OF 1812 against Britain and accepting a national central bank. Although a small group of "Old Republicans" still loyal to the Principles of 1798 criticized various manifestations of centralization and increased federal spending, such policies were so popular as to result in the demise of the FEDERALIST PARTY during Monroe's presidency.

Briefly, under the leadership of HENRY CLAY, who invested himself with the democratic ethos of the West, it seemed possible that a new liberalism might replace what had become a largely theoretical Jeffersonian creed. This one, advocated by a group calling themselves National Republicans, espoused comprehensive national development programs, protective tariffs, and a central bank. Its triumph, however, was forestalled by the political rise of Andrew Jackson and a resurgence of the Old Republicanism.

From Jackson to Bryan. By making himself the tribune of the West, Andrew Jackson displaced Clay and thus largely preempted the possibility that National Republicanism might succeed Jeffersonianism as the ideology of the people. Instead, it became identified with northeastern "aristocrats." Ideologically, Jacksonian democracy largely restated Jeffersonian principles while adding a less restrained celebration of the virtues of mass democracy.

Although he was a nationalist who defended the union against South Carolina's nullificationism, Jackson sought in most respects to reverse the centralizing tendencies he inherited. He rejected a national plan of internal improvements, forced the abandonment of tariff protectionism, and destroyed the BANK OF THE UNITED STATES. Overwhelmingly popular, Jackson drew support not simply from westerners but from all regions of the country except New England. Ideologically attuned to the needs of agrarian groups, he may also have received some backing from "workingmen" in the cities. To the extent that that was true, however, such support seems to have been based on his general appeal to the lower classes rather than on any policies aimed at "organized labor," which did not yet exist in the modern sense.

Jackson's policies hindered national development and destabilized the country financially, thus laying the basis for a financial panic and depression that began in 1837. His chosen successor, Martin Van Buren, probably more consistent and thoughtful in his ideological self-definition, lasted only one term. Thereafter, Jeffersonian-Jacksonian liberalism (increasingly defined as STATES' RIGHTS, agrarianism, and the theory of the Constitution as a compact) was largely identified with the interests of the South and the defense of SLAVERY, America's most profoundly antiliberal institution.

In the middle years of the nineteenth century, liberalism in its more authentic meaning as faith in individual freedom and natural rights was represented primarily by a growing antislavery movement that found its political identity first in the FREE-SOIL PARTY and then the REPUBLICAN PARTY. The Republicans successfully combined opposition to the extension of slavery with a program in the tradition of the old National Republicans—internal improvements, a homestead act, and a protective tariff. Their first President, Abraham Lincoln, personified in many ways the liberal ideal of universal opportunity. His rhetoric stressed the extension of natural rights to all.

The upsurge of industrialism in post-CIVIL WAR America created a society of growing cities, big business, and unequal distributions of power—all of which had the effect of making old definitions of liberalism seem unsatisfactory. Some claimants to the tradition, primarily influential patricians, argued for restoration of the old ethic of small, frugal, honest, responsible government—to be run by men very much like themselves embodied in the institution of a professional CIVIL SERVICE. They were especially visible in the Liberal Republican insurgency of 1872 and the Mugwump movement of 1884.

Other dissenters, not yet prone to use the term *liberal*, advocated a range of programs designed to aid farmers and small entrepreneurs, groups that increasingly felt themselves being pushed to the margins of society by corporate power. These programs included monetary inflation, low tariffs, antitrust legislation, farm price stabilization mechanisms, and regulation (or outright government ownership of) the railroads. They attracted a few radical intellectuals and attempted, with scant success, to make common cause with the nascent forces of organized labor.

In presidential politics they were represented by the Greenback-Labor Party of 1880 [*see* GREENBACK PARTY], the Populist Party of 1892, and the Democratic-Populist campaign of WILLIAM JENNINGS BRYAN in 1896. Scorned as radical and dangerous in much of the country, these movements pioneered the idea that urban, industrial America required new definitions of individual rights and strong government activity to provide opportunity to ordinary people.

Roosevelt and Wilson. In the early twentieth century Theodore Roosevelt (representing the NEW NATIONALISM) and Woodrow Wilson (the NEW FREEDOM) both became eloquent advocates of "progressive" programs to regulate the economy, provide rudimentary welfare benefits for the working class, protect consumers, support farmers, and curb the power of big capital [*see* PROGRESSIVE (BULL MOOSE) PARTY, 1912].

Roosevelt, as a post-Civil War Republican, envisioned himself as a product of a tradition of patrician leadership, patriotic duty, and activist government that had its origins in the Federalist and National Republican parties. He hoped to create an America in which different social groups would be brought together by an overriding sense of obligation to the nation and thus to one another.

Wilson, reared as a southern Democrat, began as a Jeffersonian liberal advocating opportunity for the small entrepreneur struggling against large corporations. In practice, however, his administration moved much more vigorously than Roosevelt's in the direction of economic regulation and social welfare. The demands of WORLD WAR I in fact led it to assume operation of the railroads and took it far toward overall management of the economy. By 1920, liberalism, or progressivism, thus had come to mean almost the opposite of its generally understood definition a century earlier.

Wilson's domestic programs had substantial support, but his decision to bring the United States into World War I in 1917 brought the surge of progressive liberalism to an end. Although war had been made unavoidable by the German submarine offensive, Wilson justified it as a crusade to make the world safe for democracy and extend liberal values around the globe. Like all utopian crusades, Wilson's was easier to launch than to consummate. Many of his liberal supporters, by nature ambivalent about war, were disillusioned by the inevitable compromises of the peace settlement. The peace controversy, domestic turmoil, and economic recession all combined to ensure a serious defeat for the Democrats, by now the primary advocates of liberal reform, in 1920.

New Deal and Great Society. The Great Depression and the Democratic return to power under Franklin D. Roosevelt provided liberalism with its greatest moment of the twentieth century. Roosevelt's NEW DEAL greatly extended the directions undertaken by Theodore Roosevelt and Woodrow Wilson. It identified liberalism more clearly than ever with labor and minority groups politically and with social democracy intellectually. It regulated business, established comprehensive price supports for farmers, supported labor's right to organize, gave massive aid to the unemployed, and founded welfare and old-age insurance systems.

Roosevelt also mobilized America for WORLD WAR II.

Carefully balancing in his rhetoric Wilsonian idealism with Theodore Roosevelt's realism, he persuaded the country that American self-interest was best expressed in the global defense of liberal ideals against totalitarian regimes. Thus many liberals later found it intellectually possible to move from the struggle against fascism to the COLD WAR against Soviet Communism (or, as some called it, Red Fascism).

From 1945 to 1963, the overriding demands of the COLD WAR and de facto conservative control of Congress made liberalism more a matter of conceptualization and proposal than of accomplishment. Roosevelt's successor, Harry S. Truman, made the cold war palatable to the liberals by linking American foreign policy to the affirmative purposes of European reconstruction and resistance to military aggression. At home, Truman pursued without much success the FAIR DEAL, an extension of Roosevelt's programs. His most important contribution to the agenda of domestic liberalism was a comprehensive civil rights program. John F. Kennedy, the next President to call himself a liberal, scored a breakthrough in the area of trade expansion. He also initiated major civil rights legislation and a tax cut bill to promote economic growth; both passed after his death.

It was Lyndon B. Johnson, however, who carried liberalism to its zenith in the 1960s and quite possibly overextended it. Johnson's GREAT SOCIETY included pathbreaking civil rights acts, a multifaceted war on poverty, and numerous spending programs, some aimed at increasing the quality of American life, others at enhancing federal benefits for large segments of the population. The Great Society, perhaps because it was aimed primarily at a narrow segment of the population (the urban poor), never developed the broad support that the New Deal had achieved. Johnson's commitment to the VIETNAM WAR also damaged his presidency and disrupted liberalism. Many liberals, supportive of the Great Society, saw the war as possessing no urgent moral purpose and serving no compelling national interest.

Beginning with the 1960s, moreover, liberals found themselves increasingly forced to deal not simply with questions of economic distribution or basic constitutional rights but also with a wide range of cultural controversies, among them black militance, feminism, homosexuality, illegal drug use, the rituals of patriotism, abortion, conflicts between government and religion, and crime and punishment. Instinctively, they leaned toward the libertarian side of such issues and in some instances believed that fundamental rights were involved. Such stances, however principled, rarely enjoyed broad public support.

The cultural controversies that began in the 1960s continued in one form or another into the 1990s, leaving liberalism, once a popular movement with mass political appeal, heavily dependent upon favorable rulings in the courts. While no President after Johnson, not even Ronald Reagan, led a successful counterrevolution against the achievements of the past, none of Johnson's successors as President were within the mainstream of the movement as it had come to be understood in the last third of the twentieth century.

BIBLIOGRAPHY

Cunningham, Noble E., Jr. *In Pursuit of Reason: The Life of Thomas Jefferson.* 1987.

Foner, Eric. *Free Soil, Free Labor, Free Men: The Ideology of the Republican Party before the Civil War.* 1970.

Goldman, Eric F. *Rendezvous with Destiny: A History of Modern American Reform.* 1952.

Hamby, Alonzo L. *Liberalism and Its Challengers: F.D.R. to Bush.* 1992.

Hofstadter, Richard. *The Age of Reform: From Bryan to F.D.R..* 1955.

Matusow, Allen J. *The Unraveling of America: A History of Liberalism in the 1960s.* 1984.

Schlesinger, Arthur M. *The Age of Jackson.* 1946.

Schlesinger, Arthur M. *The Age of Roosevelt.* 3 vols. 1957–1960.

ALONZO L. HAMBY

LIBERTY PARTY. Formed in 1839, the Liberty Party was America's first antislavery political party. It was the focus of the political opposition to SLAVERY until it was eclipsed by the FREE-SOIL PARTY in 1848. The party never gained the support of the nonpolitical abolitionists led by William Lloyd Garrison, and as a single-issue party it failed to attract mainstream citizens who opposed slavery but were also concerned about other political and economic issues. However, the party laid the groundwork for future successful antislavery political movements.

In 1840 the Liberty Party ran James Gillespie Birney for President and Francis Le Moyne for Vice President. Birney, a former slaveowner turned abolitionist, was the editor of *The Philanthropist*, a moderate antislavery paper. Le Moyne was the president of the Pennsylvania Anti-Slavery Society and a prominent physician. The party called for abolition of slavery in the District of Columbia and in all federal territories and an end to the interstate slave trade. Moderate by the standards of the Garrisonian immediatists, this was nevertheless a radical break with American presidential politics, because for the first time a candidate and a party attacked slavery. Birney won only about seven thousand votes in 1840.

In 1844 Birney ran on a ticket with Thomas Morris, a former United States Senator from Ohio. Birney won about sixty-two thousand votes, over 2 percent of all votes cast. The party received votes in four-fifths of the counties in the North, suggesting the breadth of antislavery political support. More importantly, Birney won some sixteen thousand votes in New York. James K. Polk, who won the election, carried New York by only five thousand votes. Had most of the Liberty Party votes gone to the Whig HENRY CLAY, he would have carried New York, and with it the election. Similarly, had Clay gained all Birney's votes, he would have surpassed Polk in the national popular vote. These vote totals indicate the importance of antislavery voters. There is no reason to believe, however, that people who voted for an antislavery ticket in 1844 would have supported the slaveholder Clay over the slaveholder Polk. It is just as likely they would have sat out the election.

In 1848 the Liberty Party initially appeared to be a stronger contender. However, as a result of the MEXICAN WAR the more broad-based Free-Soil Party emerged, with former President Martin Van Buren as its candidate. All but a handful of Liberty Party activists joined the Free-Soil Party in 1848 and then regrouped as part of the radical wing of the politically successful movement that appeared in 1854, the REPUBLICAN PARTY.

BIBLIOGRAPHY

Sewell, Richard H. *Ballots for Freedom: Antislavery Politics in the United States, 1837–1860.* 1976.
Smith, Theodore Clarke. *The Liberty and Free Soil Parties in the Northwest.* 1897.
Stewart, James B. *Holy Warriors.* 1976.

PAUL FINKELMAN

LIBRARIES, PRESIDENTIAL. The nation's presidential libraries serve as archival depositories for Presidents' personal papers and the official records of their administrations. Nine of the libraries are U.S. government agencies authorized by the Presidential Libraries Act of 1955 and administered by the Office of Presidential Libraries, a division of the National Archives and Records Administration (NARA). The Nixon presidential materials staff is not part of the presidential library system and is identified as a "presidential project" in accordance with special legislation passed by Congress.

When George Washington retired to Mount Vernon in 1797, he had no presidential library in which to deposit his papers. Washington took all personal and official papers with him, establishing the precedent that a President's papers are personal, not public, property. Today, the papers of Presidents Washington through Calvin Coolidge are located in the Manuscript Division of the Library of Congress.

Origins. By the late 1930s it had become evident that the sheer mass of documentation from the presidency of Franklin D. Roosevelt would overwhelm existing archival resources. On 12 December 1938, President Roosevelt invited a group of historians to a White House luncheon to discuss plans for the disposition of his presidential papers. Roosevelt wanted to establish a permanent structure to house and protect the records of his presidency. At a press conference following the luncheon, Roosevelt announced that he had decided to push for the establishment of a presidential library. The library was created as part of the National Archives by a joint resolution of Congress in 1939 (53 Stat. 1062), and it later became the first of the presidential libraries authorized by the 1955 Presidential Libraries Act (69 Stat. 695). On 4 July 1940, Roosevelt deeded sixteen acres of his family's estate in HYDE PARK, New York, for the planned library and museum. Over several months, a small group of supporters quietly solicited private funds for the facilities' construction. Roosevelt gave his papers as well as his personal library of fifteen thousand books and his extensive collections of art, stamps, and letters to the government. The President encouraged his family and friends to follow his lead and turn their materials over to the library. The museum opened to visitors on 30 June 1941 and to researchers on 1 May 1946.

While Roosevelt was responsible for the precedent-setting decision to build a library for his presidential materials, he did not differ from George Washington on the question of ownership. Roosevelt considered the papers his own—and gave them as a gift to the United States. The Roosevelt model proved satisfactory, and Presidents Harry S. Truman and Dwight D. Eisenhower followed Roosevelt's procedure. In 1955, the Presidential Libraries Act provided the legal basis for accepting presidential papers and maintaining presidential libraries. The act covered only the acceptance of papers and maintenance of facilities, not ownership (to the extent that anyone other than the President had a legitimate claim to the papers), and never addressed the issue of what a President was required to do with his papers. The 1955 act brought all libraries into the National Archives system and guaranteed that presidential materials would be professionally cared for.

Eight presidential libraries—those for Truman

Presidential Libraries

President	Location	Date Est'd	Size, Sq. Ft.	Number of Records, 1992	Annual Cost to Operate, Fiscal 1991, Dollars[a]	Number of Visitors, 1992
Hoover	West Branch, Iowa	1962	44,500	7,171,442	1,143,000	75,004
F. D. Roosevelt	Hyde Park, N.Y.	1940	40,539	17,336,454	3,196,000	168,514
Truman	Independence, Mo.	1957	60,865	24,755,624	1,881,000	139,230
Eisenhower	Abilene, Kan.	1962	81,466	21,765,808	2,024,000	93,287
Kennedy	Dorchester, Mass.	1979	71,847	29,328,463	5,091,000	213,996
Johnson	Austin, Tex.	1971	96,981	34,939,215	2,487,000	388,529
Nixon[b]	Yorba Linda, Cal.	1990	52,000	46,110,000[c]	2,650,000[d]	200,000 (est.)
Ford	Ann Arbor, Mich.	1981	35,532	19,618,929	2,252,000	981[e]
Carter	Atlanta, Ga.	1986	63,475	27,439,230	1,762,000	86,383
Reagan	Simi Valley, Cal.	1991	91,193	45,803,000	2,505,000	280,219
Bush[f]	College Station, Tex.					

[a]Annual cost to operate includes program costs, operations and maintenance, repair and alteration, recurring and nonrecurring reimbursables (building services in addition to rent), and rent.

[b]The Nixon Library is not part of the system of presidential libraries administered by the National Archieves. It is privately run.

[c]Not all these documents are yet housed in the Nixon Library.

[d]Because the Nixon Library is privately funded, its financing cannot be compared in every respect to the libraries funded by the federal government.

[e]Number of researchers. A separate museum in Grand Rapids, Mich., received 88,419 visitors in 1992.

[f]Under construction; scheduled to open in 1997 or 1998.

Prepared by Louis Fisher. Based on statistics received from the National Archives and the Nixon Library.

(1957), Herbert Hoover (1962), Eisenhower (1962), Lyndon B. Johnson (1971), John F. Kennedy (1979), Gerald Ford (1980–1981), Jimmy Carter (1986), and Ronald Reagan (1991)—have been established under the terms of the 1955 act. The act specified that presidential libraries would be built with nonfederal dollars; it allowed the President to leave his documents voluntarily with the Archivist of the United States and to set whatever restrictions he might deem appropriate. A private, nonprofit foundation is created to maximize the endowment for each library. The National Archives maintains the library, museum, and grounds, and professional archivists care for the papers.

Ownership of Presidential Materials. As of 1993, the papers of Richard M. Nixon were being stored in Alexandria, Virginia, and were the focus of ongoing litigation. The question of who owns a President's papers came to a head immediately following Nixon's resignation and centered around the disposition of materials related to the WATERGATE AFFAIR. In September 1974, former President Nixon and Arthur Sampson, the Administrator of General Services, signed an agreement giving Nixon possession of 42 million documents and materials relating to his presidency—including the infamous Watergate tapes. The result-

ing outcry subsided with passage of the Presidential Recordings and Materials Preservation Act of 1974 (88 Stat. 1695), signed by President Ford on 11 November 1974. This legislation nullified the Nixon-Sampson agreement, required Nixon to ensure complete public access to documents from his presidency, and established the National Study Commission on Records and Documents of Federal Officials to explore questions of control, ownership, disposition, and preservation of historical materials. The commission recommended that all documents made or received by public officials in discharge of their official duties should be recognized as the property of the United States. In 1978, President Jimmy Carter signed the PRESIDENTIAL RECORDS ACT. Becoming effective on 20 January 1981, the law finally settled the legal question of ownership: the public, not the President, has legal right of access and ownership of all official presidential records.

Legally, then, all presidential records created after 1981 are the property of the United States. But a new controversy arose over a secret agreement made on 19 January 1992 between Don W. Wilson, the Archivist of the United States, and President George Bush in which Bush was given "exclusive legal control" over the computerized records of his presidency. Many electronic files were erased from computer memories as a result of the Bush-Wilson agreement.

Using the Libraries. Today, each presidential library is a research center whose activities include protecting and preserving presidential materials; providing reference services; reviewing, arranging, and describing presidential materials; offering public programs, including exhibitions, lectures, symposia, and student workshops; acquiring additional historical materials and printed items; and engaging in an oral history program.

The holdings of the nine (including the Bush library) presidential libraries and the Nixon Project (*project* is the standard term used of presidential materials until they are turned over to the presidential library) include more than 260 million pages of textual material; 5 million still photographs; 13.5 million feet of motion picture film; 68,000 hours of disk, audiotape, and videotape recordings; and more than 280,000 museum-type objects. Researchers will notice a great deal of variation in the federally administered presidential libraries, primarily in the nature of their holdings and in the accessibility of materials.

Before visiting a presidential library, a researcher should write in advance to the supervisory archivist to describe his or her research project or interest and to request a list of the library's holdings and any other information the library can supply (e.g., on motels and other lodgings in the vicinity, nearby restaurants, local transportation options, library reproduction fees, etc.). The list of holdings will usually include four major categories: manuscripts, microfilms, audiovisual materials, and oral history transcripts. After receiving these materials, the researcher may want to call the library to speak with an archivist to determine the availability of documents. Some researchers begin this process one or two years in advance of their project to ensure enough time for declassification of materials.

On arrival at a presidential library, the researcher is given an orientation session with the supervisory archivist. The researcher completes a research application, receives an informal tour of the research facilities, and learns the rules governing research in the library. All the libraries have similar requirements. Researchers sign the register each day when entering the reading room. They may take blank sheets of paper, note cards, writing tablets, and handbags to desks in the reading room. Briefcases and other personal belongings that could be used to conceal documents must be left in the wardrobe in the reading room. Materials are ordered by filling out request slips, and restrictions are placed on the amount of material that can be checked out at a time. In using documents, it is important to preserve the original order within folders and boxes. Documents must not be leaned on, written on, traced, or handled in any way likely to cause damage.

To avoid misunderstanding library regulations, one must take note of the distinction between "papers" and "files." *Papers* are materials that are donated directly to the library by a person or his or her heirs; *files* are materials that are left in the White House and therefore belong to the official, publicly owned record of an administration. Files of aides to the President are not their personal property; an aide's files consist of those materials that were accumulated while he or she was at the White House and that were left there when the aide departed. An aide's papers, on the other hand, are those personal materials that the aide has given to the government, with or without restrictions on their accessibility.

While working in a presidential library, a scholar is likely to encounter withdrawal sheets at the front of some folders. These sheets list materials that have been removed and are unavailable. The withdrawal sheet gives information about classification; if it indicates that a document has been removed because of NATIONAL SECURITY classification, the researcher may request declassification. Executive Order 12356 (1982) permits researchers to ask agencies of the federal government to declassify documents that are currently closed for national-security reasons. The FREEDOM OF INFORMATION ACT (FOIA) applies to files, not to donated materials (papers). If the researcher requests declassification, the library will provide a standard mandatory-classification-review request form.

Future of Presidential Libraries. Just as surely as death follows life, presidential libraries now follow in the wake of presidential administrations. But the presidential library system has come under a great deal of scrutiny, and the future of such decentralized libraries is in doubt. Critics argue that the original presidential library legislation was intended only to establish a small library system, built with private funds and maintained at moderate cost to taxpayers. By 1993, however, the total program and maintenance cost had exceeded $20 million annually. Still, plans were being drawn for the construction of the George Bush Presidential Library and Museum, to be located on a ninety-acre site at Texas A&M University in College Station, Texas.

BIBLIOGRAPHY

Berman, Larry. "Presidential Libraries: How Not to Be a Stranger in a Strange Land." In *Studying the Presidency*. Edited by George C. Edwards III and Stephen J. Wayne. 1983. Pp. 225–256.

Kumar, Martha Joynt. "Presidential Libraries: Gold Mine, Booby
Trap, or Both?" In *Studying the Presidency*. Edited by George C.
Edwards III and Stephen J. Wayne. 1983. Pp. 199–224.

LARRY BERMAN

LIE-DETECTOR TESTS. See POLYGRAPH TESTS.

LINCOLN, ABRAHAM (1809–1865), sixteenth President of the United States (1861–1865). The romance of Lincoln's early life on the frontier, from his birth in a log cabin in Kentucky, to his youth on a hardscrabble farm in Indiana, to his rise to political prominence in Illinois, sometimes overshadows his presidency in popular imagination. Despite his inspiring self-education, honesty, and diligence, well exemplified by 1860, if Lincoln had died early in that year, almost no one today would have heard of him. His fame was secured by his accomplishments after winning the presidency in 1860.

Background. Abraham Lincoln had little preparation for the presidency except a life spent in partisan politics. He served four terms in the lower house of the Illinois legislature (1834–1841) and one in the U.S. House of Representatives (1847–1849). Although his law practice in Springfield, Illinois, was successful, the office was small, he never had more than one partner at a time, and he employed no staff. Lincoln had no administrative experience besides having run a tiny post office in New Salem, Illinois. He had no management experience. His formal education consisted of less than a year's schooling. He spoke no language but English, and he touched foreign soil only once, crossing briefly to the Canadian side when visiting Niagara Falls. Although he was a veteran, Lincoln's brief service in 1832 as a Black Hawk War volunteer who never saw a hostile Indian or fired a shot seemed so laughable that Lincoln himself made fun of it in a speech in Congress.

Lincoln turned his relative obscurity into an asset at the Republican nominating convention in Chicago in 1860. Lincoln's strategy, ably implemented at the convention by his managers, was "to give no offence to others—leave them in a mood to come to us, if they shall be compelled to give up their first love." Enough delegates came to him as their second choice to give him the nomination on the third ballot over the frontrunner, WILLIAM H. SEWARD, of New York. In the ensuing campaign, Lincoln observed custom for presidential candidates and gave not a single speech. He won the election with some 39 percent of the popular vote. In the states of the future Confederacy he won no votes save about two thousand in Virginia. As President-elect, he watched the country dissolve with the secession of seven slave states.

Because his political apprenticeship was served mainly in the WHIG PARTY, Lincoln originally held a rather restricted view of the presidency. "My political education," President-elect Lincoln said on 15 February 1861, "strongly inclines me against a very free use of [the veto, indirect influence, or recommendations] by the Executive, to control the legislation of the country." As President, he used the veto power sparingly and did little to influence Congress, which in any case was dominated by his own political party (which, by then, was the REPUBLICAN PARTY).

Yet, for a dedicated Whig, Lincoln had always held a surprising degree of admiration for Andrew Jackson. When he faced the Southern States' SECESSION in 1861, Lincoln turned to Jackson's message on NULLIFICATION as one of the principal sources for his own INAUGURAL ADDRESS. The fall of Fort Sumter, South Carolina, in the spring of 1861, and Lincoln's subsequent proclamation raising forces to put down rebellion, caused four more slave states to secede. When some citizens of Baltimore, Maryland, protested the passage of Union troops through their city to protect the nation's capital, Lincoln stormed at them: "The rebels attack Fort Sumter, and your citizens attack troops sent to the defense of the Government, . . . and yet you would have me break my oath, and surrender the Government without a blow. There is no Washington in that—no Jackson in that—no manhood nor honor in that." From Jackson's example and from his oath of office, President Lincoln devised EXECUTIVE POWER adequate to meet the crisis, and he gained experience quickly.

In the mid 1850s Lincoln's antislavery convictions and fear that Democratic measures were causing SLAVERY to spread to new areas in the United States caused him to become a Republican. He retained many of his Whiggish ideas about economics and government, however.

Lincoln's Administration. When he came to Washington after the election of 1860, Lincoln faced the task of organizing the work of government, assembling a Cabinet, and making both civilian and military appointments in an atmosphere of extreme national crisis.

The office of the presidency. The small-scale government Lincoln took over on 4 March 1861 did not require vast management experience. Lincoln's own office was tiny. He employed two private secretaries, John Nicolay and JOHN HAY, men in their twenties who read the incoming mail, screened visitors, and drafted responses to routine letters.

Lincoln's office routine stressed hard work and long hours over formality or bureaucratic procedure. To this day it is not clear what records were kept, copied, or discarded and by what rules. Lincoln was usually at work by 7:00 A.M. and held office hours from 10:00 to 1:00 on Mondays, Wednesdays, and Thursdays and from 10:00 to noon on Tuesdays and Fridays, when he met with the Cabinet, usually at midday. He also held public receptions on Friday afternoons. All of these constituted important public contacts in an era without PRESS CONFERENCES. A carriage ride at 4:00 P.M. was often his only relaxation aside from brief and spare meals, and he usually returned to work after dinner. Presidential vacations and holidays were virtually unknown. On Christmas Day 1861 Lincoln held a four-hour Cabinet meeting on the worst diplomatic crisis of the CIVIL WAR. He and his wife, MARY TODD LINCOLN, visited the wounded in hospitals on Christmas 1862, and on Christmas Day 1863 he worked on administrative plans for Southern amnesty and revised a paper on the constitutionality of military conscription. Family life inevitably suffered. His wife took vacations alone and amassed secret debts on shopping sprees. His eldest son, a student at Harvard, admitted with regret that he had "scarcely even had ten minutes quiet talk" with his father "during his Presidency, on account of his constant devotion to business."

The Cabinet. Lincoln's hard work and ability to judge character made up for his lack of executive experience. He possessed the deep self-confidence that knows no fear or envy of other strong individuals' personalities and abilities. He chose a Cabinet that included all his major rivals for the Republican nomination for President: WILLIAM H. SEWARD became Secretary of State; SALMON P. CHASE, Secretary of the Treasury; EDWARD BATES, Attorney General; and Simon Cameron, Secretary of War. Other choices included Montgomery Blair as Postmaster General; Caleb B. Smith as Secretary of the Interior; and Gideon Welles as Secretary of Navy. Lincoln chose mostly capable men who then ran their departments with some independence, but ability was not the only criterion he used to select them. Politics was important, too.

Lincoln's first Vice President, HANNIBAL HAMLIN, played little role in the administration.

Appointments. Political considerations may have been uppermost in Lincoln's mind. His training, after all, came in partisan politics, and he lived in the era, before CIVIL SERVICE REFORM, when parties worked by PATRONAGE. Party provided the only large organization

on which Lincoln could rely to govern the nation. As the first Republican President Lincoln faced a huge task: he removed 1,195 of the 1,520 government officials in place when he took office. Since federal jobs in the South were often left vacant because of the secession crisis, this was a nearly clean sweep.

Military appointments were another matter. Once war began, Lincoln understood that the fate of the nation depended on unity in the North behind the war effort. He knew that partisanship would not cease during the crisis, but he also knew that this had to be the country's, not the Republican party's, war. Therefore, he distributed generalships to men of varied party and ethnic antecedents. Lincoln refrained, as some other Republicans did not, from hectoring Democratic generals for lack of heart in fighting the South. In the case of GEORGE B. McCLELLAN, the President seems to have bent over backwards to avoid even the appearance of partisanship.

Seward and Chase. The dangers of choosing capable men of considerable personal political reputation for the Cabinet were twice revealed during the administration, first with Seward during the Fort Sumter crisis and second with Chase regarding the Treasury Secretary's own presidential ambitions in 1864. Seward's initial assumption that he must play a role analogous to prime minister behind a weak President somewhat complicated the crisis over Fort Sumter.

On 29 March 1861 Lincoln announced that he would send supplies but not reinforcements to Fort Sumter and would tell the South Carolina governor what he was about to do. Seward was the only Cabinet member opposed. On 1 April the Secretary of State sent Lincoln a memorandum entitled "Some Thoughts for the President's Consideration." Saying that the administration was "without a policy either domestic or foreign," Seward recommended evacuating Fort Sumter and suggested provoking a foreign incident to reunite the country. The President, hinted the memo, might "devolve [the execution of the policy] on some member of the Cabinet." Lincoln replied that the administration did have a policy and that if a new one had to be executed, "I must do it." On 12 April Southern guns fired on Fort Sumter; it surrendered two days later.

Commander in Chief. One of Lincoln's principal preoccupations after Sumter was his duty as COMMANDER IN CHIEF. Less tempted than his Confederate counterpart, JEFFERSON DAVIS, to take to the field himself, President Lincoln nonetheless personally directed a small campaign against Norfolk, Virginia, in May 1862 and carelessly exposed himself to fire when Confederate troops came near Washington on 12 July

1864. Usually, however, he left the fighting to others. He did not leave to others the choice of commanding generals. He consulted neither the Secretary of War nor the rest of the Cabinet on his choices. Lincoln did check with military experts on choosing generals, but he did not much want the advice of civilian politicians.

Lincoln has received high marks as Commander in Chief from many twentieth-century historians. He did have a profound grasp of fundamental strategy. William O. Stoddard's recollection of the gloomy hours in the White House after Union defeat at Fredericksburg, Virginia, is striking:

> We lost fifty per cent. more men than did the enemy, and yet there is sense in the awful arithmetic propounded by Mr. Lincoln. He says that if the same battle were to be fought over again, every day, through a week of days, with the same relative results, the army under Lee would be wiped out to its last man, the Army of the Potomac would still be a mighty host, the war would be over, the Confederacy gone, and peace would be won at a smaller cost of life than it will be if the week of lost battles must be dragged out through yet another year of camps and marches, and of deaths in hospitals rather than upon the field. No general yet found can face the arithmetic, but the end of the war will be at hand when he shall be discovered.

As for Lincoln's attempts to discover generals who could "face the arithmetic," it is difficult to judge him fast or slow. It was not until 1864 that he settled on Ulysses S. Grant, who fits the description of a general who understood the grim mathematics of war during the days before the germ theory of disease, when casualties from illness far exceeded those suffered on the field of battle. Confederate president Davis found Robert E. Lee early on but was never able to solve the problem of command in the Confederate west.

War Powers. Lincoln exercised the powers of Commander in Chief alone, and most would say he also expanded the presidency's powers considerably. As the historian Arthur M. Schlesinger, Jr., has shown, the Framers of the Constitution saw the powers of the Commander in Chief as "ministerial," amounting to the command and direction of the armed forces once war began. Declaring war, raising armies, and establishing the broad code to govern the armed forces—these were generally regarded as congressional powers.

Yet Lincoln quickly came to hold the view that the Commander in Chief possessed broad and vague powers to take measures essential for national self-preservation in an emergency. For example, he repeatedly stated that the EMANCIPATION PROCLAMATION was based on his power as Commander in Chief, though it had little to do with command and direction of the armies. Moreover, he came to believe that the executive—not

the legislature—held this WAR POWER, as he called it in his 4 July 1861 message to Congress. He argued that the power lay in the PRESIDENTIAL OATH OF OFFICE to "preserve, protect, and defend the Constitution." On 3 September 1863, he explained his view of the constitutionality of emancipation by saying to Chase (who wanted to expand its application), "The original proclamation has no constitutional or legal justification, except as a military measure." Later, in the summer of 1864, when Lincoln was fighting Congress's Wade-Davis RECONSTRUCTION bill, which would have required Southern states to abolish slavery before reentering the Union, he reportedly told Ohio Senator Zachariah Chandler, "I conceive that I may in an emergency do things on military grounds which cannot be done constitutionally by Congress." Lincoln's constitutional views could not be termed shallow or self-aggrandizing, but they did change with some rapidity. As late as 22 September 1861, in the course of explaining his revocation of JOHN C. FREMONT's emancipation proclamation in Missouri, Lincoln had suggested that Congress "might . . . with propriety pass a law, on the point, just such as General Fremont proclaimed" and admitted that he "might, . . . as a member of Congress, vote for it."

Lincoln's first action to attract considerable criticism on grounds of constitutionality was his SUSPENSION OF HABEAS CORPUS. Article I, Section 9, of the Constitution permits this "in cases of rebellion or invasion" when "the public safety may require it." But most authorities before the Civil War assumed that only Congress enjoyed such power. Lincoln first suspended the writ in certain areas on 27 April 1861; he suspended it throughout the nation, in certain cases, on 24 September 1862. Congress did not pass an act legalizing suspension until 3 March 1863. Tens of thousands of civilians were arrested by Union military authorities during the war, and more than four thousand were tried by military commissions, essentially courts-martial for civilians. After the Civil War and Lincoln's death, the U.S. Supreme Court, in a nonpartisan decision in the case of EX PARTE MILLIGAN (1866), declared unconstitutional the use of military trials when civilian courts are open.

For his part, Lincoln took the view that proscription of CIVIL LIBERTIES was a wartime necessity that would naturally cease as soon as war ended. He maintained on 3 December 1861 that he had been "unwilling to go beyond the pressure of necessity in the unusual exercise of power." It did not seem to him likely that Americans would became habituated to these "unusual" practices, and the actions of the Supreme Court after the war—as well as the restiveness over this matter of even Republicans in Congress during the war—bear him out. Nevertheless, Lincoln boldly assumed broad ground in denouncing disloyalty behind the lines and assuming executive power to combat it. As he explained in a public letter of 29 June 1863, he found the ultimate justification not so much in Article I, Section 9, as in his powers as Commander in Chief:

> The constitution contemplates the question as likely to occur for decision, but it does not expressly declare who is to decide it. By necessary implication, when Rebellion or Invasion comes, the decision is to be made, from time to time; and I think the man whom, for the time, the people have, under the constitution, made the commander-in-chief, of their Army and Navy, is the man who holds the power, bears the responsibility of making it. If he uses the power justly, the same people will probably justify him; if he abuses it, he is in their hands, to be dealt with by all the modes they have reserved to themselves in the constitution.

On 12 June he had warned protesters in another public letter:

> The man who stands by and says nothing, when the peril of his government is discussed, can not be misunderstood. If not hindered, he is sure to help the enemy. Much more, if he talks ambiguously—talks for his country with "buts" and "ifs" and "ands.". . . . I think the time not unlikely to come when I shall be blamed for having made too few arrests rather than too many.

Despite his bold assumption of executive powers and his sweeping denunciation of dissent, President Lincoln's internal security measures rarely degenerated into partisan restrictions of the loyal opposition party. Lincoln stood for reelection in 1864, as no would-be dictator would have done, and, as late as August, he thought he would lose. Lincoln's opponent, Democrat George B. McClellan, lost the election and never cried foul. "The people have decided with their eyes wide open," the defeated candidate wrote on 10 November 1864. Moreover, military arrests of civilians remained substantially free of corruption and were, in fact, used to control fraud in government procurements, to halt the sale of alcohol to soldiers, and to end profiting from illicit trade with the enemy. Nevertheless, they were far from just in many instances and included among their victims young boys and old men, civilian hostages, merchants arrested because they were Jewish, and men who were tortured when they did not admit to being deserters or bounty-jumpers.

Emancipation. Lincoln's boldness in assuming the constitutional power to suspend the writ of habeas corpus and in initiating a program of military arrests of civilians has at times appeared at odds with his protestations of constitutional inability to abolish slavery by presidential fiat. He seemed to some to be willing to go farther to save the Union than to free the slaves and was thus seen as being more nationalist than humanitarian. But calculations of the possible always guided Lincoln's decisions, and when all the factors are weighed, it is difficult to describe Lincoln as anything other than a nineteenth-century liberal nationalist.

Steps toward emancipation. He was not a reformer, though historians find it difficult to resist the temptation, after the fact, to see in Lincoln's steps toward emancipation the work of a visionary awaiting the opportunity to execute his antislavery program. Lincoln certainly did not see his career that way, and one of his most famous speeches—indeed the one Lincoln himself deemed best, the second inaugural address—provided eloquent testimony to this. In his first inaugural address, Lincoln expressed willingness not only to support a constitutional convention to solve sectional issues but also to endorse a proposed amendment "to the effect that the federal government, shall never interfere with the domestic institutions of the States, including that of persons held to service." Once war began, he was at first less willing than ever to interfere with slavery, for his assessment of population and geography led Lincoln to believe that the secession of the border slave states, even of Kentucky alone, might give the South an unconquerable power. When General Frémont issued his emancipation proclamation in Missouri in August 1861, Lincoln revoked it and explained on 22 September that such a threat to slavery would likely drive Kentucky out of the Union and that "to lose Kentucky is nearly the same as to lose the whole game."

In his annual message to Congress of 3 December 1861, Lincoln employed language that extended his promise to leave slavery where it already existed. He promised to avoid measures that might cause the current conflict to "degenerate into a violent and remorseless revolutionary struggle." He said he was obeying "the dictates of prudence, as well as the obligations of law" in questions concerning the confiscation of "property used for insurrectionary purposes," and he cautioned against "haste to determine that radical and extreme measures, which may reach the loyal as well as the disloyal, are indispensable."

Lincoln did not enter the presidency thinking there would be opportunity to free slaves or that he could create such a chance. He looked on his active entrance into antislavery politics back in 1854, with the passage of the KANSAS-NEBRASKA ACT, as an entirely defensive measure provoked by a newly aggressive proslavery assault on national policies that had seemed settled. In late 1861 he still assumed that he would leave slavery where it was. But constitutional scruple was no longer holding him back.

When Lincoln explained his unpopular revocation of Frémont's proclamation, he uncharacteristically mentioned the practical political problem—sentiment in the neighboring slaveholding state of Kentucky—last. He first pointed out that what Frémont wanted to do—not only to seize for temporary military use but also to determine for all time the legal status of slaves—was "simply 'dictatorship.'" "Can it be pretended," Lincoln asked testily in a private letter to Orville Hickman Browning, Senator from Illinois and an old friend, "that it is any longer the government of the U.S.—any government of Constitution and laws—wherein a General, or a President, may make permanent rules of property by proclamation?" Lincoln wrote the letter on 22 September 1861, one year to the day before he issued his own Emancipation Proclamation.

Lincoln's revocation of the Missouri proclamation and his lucid explanation of it forever made it impossible to interpret his actions as those of a simple-hearted "great emancipator" or as a consistent steward of the Constitution. He insisted, "You must not understand that I took my course on the [Frémont] proclamation *because* of Kentucky. I took the same ground in a private letter to General Fremont before I heard from Kentucky." In fact, though, Lincoln's 2 September 1861 letter to Frémont in regard to the generals' emancipation order, first stated, "I think there is great danger that the . . . paragraph, in relation to the confiscation of property, and the liberating slaves of traitorous owners, will alarm our Southern Union friends, and turn them against us—perhaps ruin our rather fair prospect for Kentucky.

Lincoln changed his mind on emancipation because the circumstances changed, and a close look at the Frémont episode reveals that Lincoln's constitutional views were already changing at that time. "I do not say Congress might not with propriety pass a law, on the point, just such as General Fremont proclaimed," he wrote. "I do not say I might not, as a member of Congress vote for it. What I object to, is, that I as President, shall expressly or impliedly seize and exercise the permanent legislative functions of the government." Such views revealed a new willingness to find some national-government power over slavery in the states. The Republican platform of 1860 had pledged the party to "the maintenance, inviolate, of the rights of the States, and especially the right of each State to order and control its own domestic institutions, according to its own judgment exclusively." By September 1861 Lincoln thought Congress had power over

slavery in war; by August 1862, he thought the President had such power.

Winning the war. The important change came, not in Lincoln's consistent antislavery sentiment or in his constitutional views but in his view of the practical political problem of winning the Civil War. By December 1861 Lincoln considered Maryland securely in the Union camp. He said, "Kentucky, too, for some time in doubt, is now decidedly, and, I think, unchangeably, ranged on the side of the Union." The key border states seemed politically secured, but the war still went badly for the Union forces, especially in the east, on which all eyes—those of Washington, Richmond, and the European capitals—focused. As spring approached in 1862, Lincoln began to agitate for voluntary emancipation by the border slave states. This constituted "one of the most efficient means of self-preservation" for the federal government, because the rebellious slave states could see abolition in their neighboring states as a sure sign Kentucky, Delaware, Maryland, and Missouri would never join the rebellion. Lincoln calculated how quickly "the current expenditures of this war would purchase, at fair evaluation, all the slaves" in any of the states. Masters could easily be compensated for their loss, therefore, and the abolition could be gradual. "In my judgment," the President said, "gradual, and not sudden emancipation, is better for all." Moreover, this plan set "up no claim of a right, by federal authority, to interfere with slavery within state limits." He found no takers. On 12 July, he cajoled and threatened border state representatives. "If the war continue long," Lincoln argued, "the institution in your states will be extinguished by mere friction and abrasion—by the mere incidents of the war. It will be gone, and you will have nothing valuable in lieu of it."

While Lincoln was awaiting a reply, he began exploring another policy. On a carriage ride to a funeral on 13 July, he mentioned for the first time to Seward and Gideon Welles "the subject of emancipating the slaves by Proclamation in case the Rebels did not cease to persist in their war on the Government and the Union." As Welles recalled,

> it was a new departure for the President, for until this time, in all our previous interviews, whenever the question of emancipation or the mitigation of slavery had been in any way alluded to, he had been prompt and emphatic in denouncing any interference by the General Government with the subject. This was . . . the sentiment of every member of the Cabinet, all of whom, including the President, considered it a local, domestic question appertaining to the States respectively, who had never parted with their authority over it.

Lincoln was sincere in citing military justification for

the contemplated measure from first mention to last. "The reverses before Richmond," Welles recalled,

> and the formidable power and dimensions of the insurrection ... impelled the Administration to adopt extraordinary measures to preserve the national existence. The slaves, if not armed and disciplined, were in the service of those who were, not only as field laborers and producers, but thousands of them were in attendance upon the armies in the field, employed as waiters and teamsters, and the fortifications and intrenchments were constructed by them.

The language of military necessity that always accompanied Lincoln's discussions of emancipation expressed sincere belief and was not a subterfuge for giving rein to humanitarian sentiment.

Shortly thereafter Lincoln drafted his Emancipation Proclamation, reading it to the full Cabinet on 22 July. His mind was made up, but he proved willing, on Seward's advice, to delay issuance. In the ensuing period, Lincoln gave the public several misleading clues about his intentions. He even coldly told a visiting delegation of black leaders on 14 August to take the lead in colonizing their race outside the United States. "It is better for us both," the President said, "to be separated."

The proclamation. General McClellan's failure to take Richmond in July 1862 caused Lincoln to draft the proclamation, and McClellan's success in turning back Robert E. Lee's invasion of Maryland at Antietam on 17 September 1862 provided Lincoln the favorable moment to announce the policy. He did so five days later.

American public reaction was partisan. In Great Britain the government and ruling classes expressed contempt for what they deemed a desperate invitation to slave insurrection. Lincoln, true to his original reasoning, expressed initial disappointment in the proclamations' results.

The preliminary proclamation gave states in rebellion one hundred days to end resistance to the government or else the proclamation would free their slaves. In the interim, Lincoln continued to confuse the public. In his annual message to Congress, on 1 December, he recommended a series of amendments to the Constitution offering compensation for any state agreeing to abolish slavery by 1900 and authorizing Congress to "appropriate money, and otherwise provide, for colonizing free colored persons, with their own consent." The latter provision almost certainly amounted to little more than political propaganda, as Congress had already twice appropriated money— $600,000 altogether—to colonize free blacks. (In the end, Lincoln spent only $38,000 of the appropriation on what historians agree were hopeless and miserable schemes.) Though the message of 1 December scared antislavery advocates and hopeful blacks, Lincoln issued the final proclamation on 1 January 1863, as he had threatened. It exempted certain areas already under Union control (as the argument of military necessity could not apply to them) and specifically endorsed the acceptance of freedmen in the U.S. armed forces.

When Lincoln looked back over these years in his second inaugural address in 1865, he said,

> One eighth of the whole population were colored slaves . . . localized in the Southern part [of the Union]. These slaves constituted a peculiar and powerful interest. All knew that this interest was, somehow, the cause of the war. To strengthen, perpetuate, and extend this interest was the object for which the insurgents would rend the Union, even by war; while the government claimed no right to do more than to restrict the territorial enlargement of it. Neither party expected for the war, the magnitude, or duration, which it has already attained. Neither anticipated that the *cause* of the conflict might cease with or even before, the conflict itself should cease. Each looked for an easier triumph, and a result less fundamental and astounding. Both read the same Bible, and pray to the same God; and each invokes His aid against the other. It may seem strange that any men should dare to ask a just God's assistance in wringing their bread from the sweat of other men's faces; but let us judge not that we be not judged. The prayers of both could not be answered; that of neither has been answered fully. The Almighty has His own purposes.

The fatalistic explanation and the lack of vindictiveness or self-righteousness were characteristic of Lincoln's discussions of emancipation and of his greatest state papers.

The sincerity of Lincoln's military reasons for emancipation need not call into question the sincerity of his humanitarian antislavery sentiments. He gave proof of these repeatedly in his life, but at no time more clearly than in the gloomy summer of 1864. Then, thinking his reelection unlikely and emancipation doomed if Democrats gained control of the government, Lincoln summoned the black abolitionist Frederick Douglass to the White House on 19 August. There, as Douglass recollected, the President told him, "The slaves are not coming so rapidly and so numerously to us as I had hoped." He then asked Douglass to formulate a plan to spread word of the proclamation to the slaves. The black leader later proposed sending black scouts through the lines to infiltrate Southern plantations "to warn [the slaves] as to what will be their probable condition should peace be concluded while they remain within the Rebel lines: and more especially to urge upon them the necessity of making their escape." Thus Lincoln would free as many persons as possible while he still had the opportunity. Years later

Douglass, who had no illusions about "the white man's President," nevertheless said, "I refer to this conversation [of 1864] because I think that, on Mr. Lincoln's part, it is evidence conclusive that the Proclamation, so far at least as he was concerned, was not effected merely as a 'necessity.'"

Victory, Peace, and Reconstruction. Military necessity constantly drove Lincoln. The White House had no telegraph service, and the President went to the War Department daily to read telegrams from the front. The tension must often have been excruciating. When Lee invaded Maryland in September 1862, for instance, Lincoln sent telegrams to McClellan at 10:15 A.M. on 10 September asking for news; at 6 P.M. on 11 September explaining available reinforcements; and, finally, at 4:00 A.M. on 12 September, asking, "How does it look now?"

Sometimes Lincoln interfered with commanders in their dispositions of troops; at other times, he abstained. Lincoln willingly took great risks with men on horseback. When he selected Joseph Hooker to command the Army of the Potomac early in 1863, Lincoln gave him a letter, dated 26 January, that stated in part:

> I have placed you at the head of the Army of the Potomac. Of course I have done this upon what appear to me to be sufficient reasons. And yet I think it best for you to know that there are some things in regard to which, I am not quite satisfied with you. I believe you to be a brave and a skilful soldier, which, of course, I like. I also believe you do not mix politics with your profession, in which you are right. . . . You are ambitious, which within reasonable bounds, does good rather than harm. . . . I have heard, in such a way as to believe it, of your recently saying that both the Army and the Government needed a Dictator. Of course it was not *for* this, but in spite of it, that I have given you the command. Only those generals who gain successes, can set up dictators. What I now ask of you is military success, and I will risk the dictatorship.

After General William T. Sherman presented Savannah, Georgia, to Lincoln as a Christmas gift in 1864, the President wrote the general:

> When you were about leaving Atlanta for the Atlantic coast I was anxious, if not fearful; but, feeling that you were the better judge, and remembering "nothing risked, nothing gained," I did not interfere. Now, the undertaking being a success, the honor is all yours. . . . But what next? I suppose it will be safer if I leave General Grant and yourself to decide.

He had written similarly to Grant after the fall of Vicksburg:

> When you first reached the vicinity of Vicksburg, I thought you should do what you finally did—march the troops across the neck, run the batteries with the transports, and thus go below; and I never had any faith, except a general hope that you knew

better than I, that the Yazoo Pass expedition, and the like, could succeed. When you got below, and took Port-Gibson, Grand Gulf, and vicinity, I thought you should go down the river and join Gen. Banks; and when you turned Northward East of the Big Black, I feared it was a mistake. I now wish to make the personal acknowledgment that you were right, and I was wrong.

A consistent and simple theme ran throughout all his military dispatches: go forward, attack, pursue. Lincoln once said to John Hay, "Often I who am not a specially brave man have had to sustain the sinking courage of these professional fighters in critical times."

Lincoln followed the campaigns closely, as the letters above show. He understood the purpose and methods of Sherman's famous March to the Sea. "Not only does it afford the obvious and immediate military advantages," Lincoln told Sherman on 26 December 1864, "but in showing to the world that your army could be divided, putting the stronger part to an important new service, and yet having enough to vanquish the old opposing force of the whole—[John B.] Hood's army—it brings those who sat in darkness to see a great light." When the President met with Sherman, Grant, and Adm. David P. Porter aboard the steamship *River Queen* off City Point, Virginia, late in March 1865, Lincoln, according to Sherman, "was full of curiosity about the many incidents of our great march, which had reached him officially and through the newspapers, and seemed to enjoy very much the more ludicrous parts—about the 'bummers,' and their devices to collect food and forage when the outside world supposed us to be starving." When Lincoln was shot at Ford's Theatre less than three weeks later, a newspaper clipping reprinting Sherman's orders was found in his pocket. In addition to instructions to "forage liberally on the country during the march," Sherman had enjoined "a devastation more or less relentless" in areas manifesting "local hostility."

The terms of peace. Sherman in his recollections also emphasized Lincoln's interest in lenient peace terms. Characteristically, Lincoln had shown no interest in vengeance. Sherman recalled,

> As to Jeff. Davis, he [Lincoln] was hardly at liberty to speak his mind fully, but intimated that he ought to clear out, "escape the country," only it would not do for him to say so openly. As usual, he illustrated his meaning by a story: "A man once had taken the total-abstinence pledge. When visiting a friend, he was invited to take a drink, but declined, on the score of his pledge; when his friend suggested lemonade, which was accepted. In preparing the lemonade, the friend pointed to the brandy-bottle, and said the lemonade would be more palatable if he were to pour in a little brandy; when his guest said, if he could do so 'unbeknown' to him, he would not object." From which illustration I inferred that Mr. Lincoln wanted Davis to escape, "unbeknown" to him.

From such kernels of truth, and from political interests later, arose the powerful Southern myth that at the Hampton Roads peace conference of 3 February 1865, Lincoln had told the Confederate vice president, Alexander H. Stephens, "Stephens, let me write 'Union' at the top of that page, and you may write below it whatever else you please." Since WORLD WAR II, a countervailing myth has arisen that maintains that Lincoln held out for "unconditional surrender." Neither is true. As the Civil War neared its end, Lincoln on three occasions wrote his peace terms down on paper. On 9 July 1864, he was insisting on two conditions for surrender, telling HORACE GREELEY (who was on his way to meet Confederate commissioners in Canada), "If you can find, any person anywhere professing to have any proposition of Jefferson Davis in writing, for peace, embracing the restoration of the Union and abandonment of slavery, *whatever else it embraces* . . . he may come to me with you." As Union military fortunes sank later that summer (and with them Republican hopes), Lincoln drafted a letter for *New York Times* editor Henry J. Raymond, saying, "You will propose, on behalf [of] this government, that upon the restoration of the Union and the national authority, the war shall cease at once, all remaining questions to be left for adjustment by peaceful modes." This letter, which did not make emancipation a condition of surrender, Lincoln never completed, sent, or used. Finally, on 31 January 1865, Lincoln's instructions to Seward for the Hampton Roads peace conference insisted on Union, emancipation, and, now, "No cessation of hostilities short of an end of the war, and the disbanding of all forces hostile to the government." He still said "that all propositions . . . not inconsistent with the above, will be considered and passed upon in a spirit of liberality."

Although Lincoln's preoccupation with questions of war and peace was great and his utilization of the powers of the Commander in Chief was full if not expansive, Lincoln's role in foreign policy was minimal. The United States was not a world power, and under the circumstances foreign policy focused on keeping Great Britain and France from recognizing the Confederacy's independence. Lincoln left this task to Seward, who has since been generally judged a very able Secretary of State.

Seward proved himself especially valuable in November and December 1861 in the crisis over the Confederate commissioners taken off the British steamer *Trent* by an overzealous U.S. naval officer. The next year, Lincoln followed Seward's advice on the timing of the Emancipation Proclamation and in general thought him so important for the administration that he saved him from being driven from the

Cabinet in December 1862. This event revealed that the President's political talents were of a high order.

After the Union's defeat at the battle of Fredricksburg (13 December 1862), Republican Senators decided that the Cabinet needed change and that Seward especially should be removed. Chase had evidently fueled the Senators' suspicions of Seward. Seward submitted his resignation to the President. When a delegation of Senators called on Lincoln, he defended his use of the Cabinet and his Secretary of State. When they returned the next night, 19 December, all the Cabinet members except Seward were present. When Lincoln quizzed the Cabinet about possible problems, Chase was deeply embarrassed, not being able to take the same tone amid his Cabinet colleagues as he had taken when alone with disaffected Republican Senators. The next day, Chase, too, offered to resign. Lincoln refused both resignations and preserved the image of Cabinet balance before the Republican Senators. He kept his Cabinet intact, except for Caleb Smith, who resigned to take a federal judgeship at the end of December. John P. Usher succeeded Smith.

The election of 1864. Political skills of a less intimate sort kept Lincoln in office. The most remarkable fact about the election of 1864, as the historian Harold Hyman has observed, "is that it occurred." But Lincoln had stated repeatedly that the war was "a people's contest" and a test of popular government. In his famous GETTYSBURG ADDRESS at the dedication of the national cemetery on the battlefield of Gettysburg, Pennsylvania, on 19 November 1863, Lincoln had described the rebellion as "testing whether . . . any nation" that was "dedicated to the proposition that 'all men are created equal' " could "long endure." He resolved that "this nation . . . shall have a new birth of freedom—and that government of the people, by the people, for the people, shall not perish from the earth." After the election, Lincoln pointed out the lesson: "We can not have free government without elections; and if the rebellion could force us to forgo, or postpone a national election, it might fairly claim to have already conquered and ruined us."

To Lincoln, the most remarkable fact about the election may well have been that he won it. On 23 August 1864, before the Democrats met and chose McClellan as their presidential candidate, Lincoln wrote, "This morning, as for some days past, it seems exceedingly probable that this Administration will not be re-elected. Then it will be my duty to so co-operate with the President elect, as to save the Union between the election and the inauguration; as he will have secured his election on such ground that he can not possibly save it afterwards." Lincoln folded the paper on which he wrote and then had his Cabinet sign the sheet without reading it.

Ultimately, the circumstances of military fortune preserved the administration in power, but Lincoln himself contributed to that favorable result. He avoided outright political confrontation with Chase, who hoped for the nomination early in the year but was forced out of contention by the embarrassing Pomeroy Circular, which had been sent to some Republicans to advocate Chase's candidacy and which made him look ungratefully ambitious, and by the failure of the party in Chase's home state, Ohio, to support him. On 30 June 1864, months after Chase had withdrawn, Lincoln removed him from the Cabinet. (William Pitt Fessenden succeeded Chase and was succeeded in turn by Hugh McCulloch.)

On 8 June Lincoln was renominated, and Andrew Johnson of Tennessee was made his running mate. At Lincoln's insistence, the platform urged passage of a constitutional amendment abolishing slavery. Yet Lincoln, as the tone of his blind memorandum suggests, never allowed the campaign to be waged on the issue of slavery alone; he and other Republicans much preferred to suggest that the Democrats would allow the Union to be sundered. The third-party candidacy of John C. Frémont, admired by RADICAL REPUBLICANS, dissolved on 22 September, and the next day Lincoln removed Montgomery Blair, whom the radicals hated, from the Cabinet. (He was replaced by William Dennison; James Speed replaced Bates, who resigned in ill health that autumn.)

Lincoln won the election with 55 percent of the popular vote and with the electoral vote of all the participating states except Delaware, New Jersey, and Kentucky.

Toward Reconstruction. Lincoln's political skills were taxed to their limit by the problem of Reconstruction. His Proclamation of Amnesty and Reconstruction, of 8 December 1863, had been well received by politicians as conservative as Reverdy Johnson of Maryland and had not been opposed by Republicans as liberal (or "radical") as Charles Sumner of Massachusetts. The President offered amnesty and restoration of property rights to most Confederate citizens who would take an oath to obey the U.S. Constitution and the laws and proclamations affecting slavery in the future. When 10 percent of the number who had voted in the presidential election of 1860 took the oath, they could organize a government whose representatives would be admitted to Congress.

Louisiana, in which a reconstruction process had already begun, became the focus of Lincoln's efforts. Congress, some of whose members doubted presiden-

tial authority over this question and desired a less conservative government than the new one forming in loyal Louisiana in 1864, put forward a different plan in the Wade-Davis bill of 2 July 1864. Lincoln killed the bill by POCKET VETO because it repudiated the Louisiana government he had been nurturing and because he did not believe Congress had the power to insist on the abolition of slavery in the states.

Lincoln's last speech, delivered from a balcony of the White House on 11 April 1865, dealt with Reconstruction. In it he for the first time publicly expressed personal support for conferring the franchise "on the very intelligent [blacks], and on those who serve our cause as soldiers." He otherwise defended the government he was still developing in Louisiana. On 14 April he approved the Secretary of War's suggested plan for military occupation of Virginia and North Carolina, though the President insisted that existing state boundaries not be ignored.

That night, JOHN WILKES BOOTH, a Maryland-born actor and Southern sympathizer who thought the country was made for the white and not the black race, shot Lincoln fatally in the back of the head. He died at 7:22 on the morning of 15 April.

BIBLIOGRAPHY

Basler, Roy P., et al., eds. *The Collected Works of Abraham Lincoln.* 9 vols. 1953–1955.

Beale, Howard K. *Diary of Gideon Welles: Secretary of the Navy under Lincoln and Johnson.* 2 vols. 1960.

Dennett, Tyler, ed. *Lincoln and the Civil War in the Diaries and Letters of John Hay.* 1939.

Donald, David, ed. *Inside Lincoln's Cabinet: The Civil War Diaries of Salmon P. Chase.* 1954.

Miers, Earl Schenck, ed. *Lincoln Day by Day: A Chronology, 1809–1865.* 3 vols. 1960.

Monaghan, Jay. *Lincoln Bibliography, 1839–1939.* 2 vols. 1943.

Randall, J. G., with Richard N. Current. *Lincoln the President.* 4 vols. 1945–1955.

Thomas, Benjamin P. *Abraham Lincoln: A Biography.* 1952.

MARK E. NEELY, JR.

LINCOLN, MARY TODD (1818–1882), First Lady, wife of Abraham Lincoln. Although Mary Todd Lincoln had little experience in Washington before her husband's inauguration in 1861, she attempted to make a strong imprint as a social leader. Realizing that her western origins rendered her suspect to capital "cavedwellers," she responded by overspending on personal as well as White House items. She also attempted to intervene in appointments, permitting favor seekers to come to the Executive Mansion and be introduced to the President or meet members of his staff. Her connections with the Confederacy (several close relatives fought for the South) raised doubts in people's minds about her commitment to the Union, but no charges were ever sustained to indicate disloyalty.

One of the most popular of all nineteenth-century First Ladies as a subject of biography, Mary Lincoln is generally portrayed as emotionally unstable and a worry to her husband during his presidency, especially following the death of their son Willie in 1862. Although a mother's grief might be condoned, extravagance in time of war was not. The President complained that if he approved payment of the enormous bills she ran up for the White House, it would "stink in the nostrils of the American people."

BIBLIOGRAPHY

Baker, Jean H. *Mary Todd Lincoln: A Biography.* 1987.
Turner, Justin G., and Linda Lovitt Turner. *Mary Todd Lincoln: Her Life and Letters.* 1972.

BETTY BOYD CAROLI

LINE-ITEM VETO. See VETO, ITEM.

LITERALIST PRESIDENT. Presidents are sometimes of the "literalist" school. John Adams, James Madison, James Buchanan and, to a degree, William Howard Taft and Dwight D. Eisenhower, by word or deed, illustrate this type. The mark of the literalist President is close adherence to the letter of the Constitution and to the requirements of democracy, at the sacrifice of leadership, initiative, and power. From Madison's presidency until Andrew Jackson's, most Presidents tended toward this type. Likewise in the interval between Abraham Lincoln and William McKinley, the type again dominated, most steadfastly represented by Ulysses S. Grant and Benjamin Harrison. The type is found far less in the twentieth century.

The most extensive formulation of the literalist presidency was provided by the WHIG PARTY in the 1830s. The Whigs abhorred the strong presidency of Andrew Jackson and as counterdoctrine asserted that presidential powers should be closely, even literally, construed, and that the legislature should be regarded as the dominant branch. To further legislative primacy, Presidents should, the Whigs argued, serve for only one term, shun the exertion of influence on legislators, and follow the direction of fellow party leaders. Whigs assumed that legislative power is popular and the executive monarchical. The animus

against the British monarch in the American Revolution was transferred to the President.

Like any type, the literalist President is not one who manifests the characteristics of his genre without exception. At times he may perform as a STRONG PRESIDENT, but, nonetheless, his statements and actions that fit the literalist mold are sufficiently numerous and important and give his administration its principal direction.

The literalist President's adherence to the law and spirit of the Constitution and federal statutes is best conveyed in William Howard Taft's classic statement in lectures after leaving the presidency:

> the President can exercise no power which cannot be fairly and reasonably traced to some specific grant of power or justly implied and included within such express grant as proper and necessary to its exercise. Such specific grant must be either in the Federal Constitution or in an act of Congress passed in pursuance thereof. There is no undefined residuum of power which he can exercise because it seems to him to be in the public interest.

Here Taft was arguing against his alienated mentor, Theodore Roosevelt, and his expansive STEWARDSHIP THEORY. In another comment, less motivated by Roosevelt, Taft noted that the Constitution gives the President "wide discretion and great power."

The literalist President makes little use of his independent EXECUTIVE POWERS (for example implied in the executive power clause of the Constitution and as COMMANDER IN CHIEF.) The contrast between Buchanan and his successor, Lincoln, and their treatment of Southern secession illuminates the difference between the literalist and the strong President. Secession, Buchanan said, was unconstitutional, but Congress and the President lacked power to compel a state to remain in the Union. Although South Carolina was resisting federal laws that the President was duty-bound to enforce, Buchanan declared that he could do nothing because no machinery was functioning in South Carolina to administer the laws, and no statute empowered the President to use force against South Carolina. Lincoln, in contrast, insisted from the outset of his presidency that the laws must be faithfully executed throughout the Union, and revenues of the United States collected at Southern ports. Relying on his executive powers as well as those powers centered in Congress, Lincoln imposed a blockade on the South, expanded the army, and suspended the writ of habeas corpus, among other measures.

The literalist President defers to the legislature. He prefers modest formulations of presidential power vis-à-vis Congress, in accordance with Madison's prescription in his debate with ALEXANDER HAMILTON over the two branches' respective roles in foreign policy. "The natural province of the executive magistrate," Madison wrote, "is to execute the laws, as that of the legislature is to make the laws." Sometimes deferential to Congress, Madison as President suffered a cabinet that was turned against him by congressional forces. His Vice President, encouraged by congressional recalcitrance, acted virtually independently of the President. The House speakership, the caucus, the committee system were launching sites of obstructions to the President. A President may pay dearly for his deference to Congress.

The literalist President has little inclination for innovation in social policy, often a domain of contentious politics, where interest groups are numerous and assertive. When pressures developed in Eisenhower's presidency for substantial national programs to improve schools, hospitals, and other welfare services, he stressed the responsibilities of local government and citizens, urging reliance "upon our own wisdom and industry, to bring us the good and comforting things of life."

The literalist President is more oriented to the past, which he reveres, than to the future. He readily cites the nation's past glories and achievements and considers them a sufficient foundation for the future. New problems at home and the dynamics of foreign affairs may be less clearly perceived and no more than partially responded to.

The literalist President is apt to prefer to enhance the management of the presidency and to consolidate and improve existing programs rather than to initiate new policies. Eisenhower, for example, was exceptional among Presidents in improving the management of the presidency and the executive branch, observing at the outset of his tenure that "with my training in problems involving organizations it was inconceivable to me that the work of the White House could not be better systematized than it had been during the years I had observed it." Among his innovations were a WHITE HOUSE CHIEF OF STAFF, a cabinet secretary and more structured CABINET meetings, and presidential assistants specializing in policy areas. To his department heads, he delegated broad responsibility for recognizing problems and taking initiatives. If possible, he remained distant from policy conflict, which he preferred to leave to others. In submitting a budget, normally a caldron of conflicting interests, Eisenhower promptly invited Congress to suggest "sensible reductions." In submitting a civil rights bill, he told the press he did not himself agree with all its provisions.

[See also PRESIDENTS' CONCEPTIONS OF THE PRESIDENCY.]

BIBLIOGRAPHY

Barber, James David. The Presidential Character. 3d rev. ed. 1985.
Burns, James MacGregor. Presidential Government. 1965.
Fisher, Louis. President and Congress. 1972.
Koenig, Louis W. The Chief Executive. 5th rev. ed. 1986.
Pious, Richard M. The American Presidency. 1979.

LOUIS W. KOENIG

LITTLE ROCK CRISIS. America's civil rights struggle raised profound constitutional issues involving presidential power. The Supreme Court affirmed in Brown v. Board of Education (1954) that racially segregated schools violated the equal protection clause of the Fourteenth Amendment. This decision generated controversy over the President's duty to enforce compliance. The Court's declaration the following year in Brown II that desegregation was essentially a local matter, which should progress with "deliberate speed," encouraged delay and resistance. Accordingly, the Constitution and federal law required President Dwight D. Eisenhower to enforce desegregation orders. Nevertheless, the Court's sanction of local control and the corresponding emergence of massive resistance left Eisenhower considerable discretion to decide at exactly what point executive intervention was appropriate. The most significant test of what became a cautious and vacillating policy was the Little Rock crisis.

The publicly reported events occurring in Little Rock, Arkansas, from 1957 to 1959 were dramatic. The local school board developed a step-by-step desegregation plan starting with the admittance of nine black young people to Little Rock Central High School on 3 September 1957. A few days before the school year began, however, there was a state court trial in which Governor Orval E. Faubus announced that he feared violence if the nine black youths entered Central High School. The state court's order maintaining segregation was overturned immediately by a local federal judge. However, when the "Little Rock Nine" approached Central on opening day, they were turned back by units of the Arkansas National Guard. Claiming that violence was imminent and asserting constitutional authority under vague policy powers, Faubus announced that he had ordered the guard to prevent compliance with the Supreme Court's desegregation decree.

For more than two weeks Little Rock was international front-page news as Faubus defied the federal courts and the President. In a well-publicized attempt at personal mediation, Eisenhower met with Faubus at the President's Newport, Rhode Island, home. Yet not until a local federal court found that the governor's claims of impending violence were groundless did Faubus withdraw the guard. The protracted confrontation, however, fostered a level of conflict in the city that had not existed before Faubus initiated the crisis. The nine black students entered Central, but shortly thereafter disorder erupted and they again withdrew. Finally, Eisenhower ordered units of the 101st Airborne Division to Little Rock to enforce the Supreme Court's desegregation decree. The paratroopers brought immediate compliance.

Coinciding with this public drama, however, were important secret events. During the summer of 1957, members of the school board had privately asked the Justice Department to intervene. Federal officials representing the administration explained that they would act only upon a formal request of local authorities or the local federal district court. During the same period Faubus privately discussed the same issue with federal authorities and was told the same thing. Faubus was correct in his assumption that the federal government wanted to avoid responsibility for initiating action. Even after a thoroughly documented FEDERAL BUREAU OF INVESTIGATION (FBI) report demonstrated that Faubus's claims concerning impending violence were groundless, federal officials carried on several further surreptitious exchanges with the governor. Meanwhile, unknown to the public, the Justice Department tried without success to persuade the National Association for the Advancement of Colored People (NAACP) to withdraw its suit on behalf of the nine black students who had been turned away from Central.

Ultimately, the Eisenhower administration played into Faubus's hands. Several provisions of the U.S. Code authorized presidential power to send federal authorities into a state to remove obstructions to the enforcement of federal law or court decrees. The use of this authority was discretionary, however, and Eisenhower chose instead to wait for a formal request from local authorities. Faubus pursued the strategy of defiance to force the President to act, thus removing from the governor in the popular view any onus of support for desegregation. The ensuing disturbance following Faubus's withdrawal of the guard caused the first and only significant break in the administration's cautious policy, when Eisenhower enforced desegregation with combat troops. Even the defenders of racial justice condemned this action as heavy handed; consequently, the administration returned to its more familiar course of careful moderation.

Tension again mounted during the summer of 1958. Faubus sought a third-term gubernatorial nomination, and the United States Supreme Court in a special August term considered the STATES' RIGHTS and police-power arguments that Faubus had used to justify defiance. The governor won a landslide victory and the Court decided in COOPER V. AARON against his constitutional arguments. In the wake of these events, at Faubus's instigation the city's high schools were closed. The Eisenhower administration nonetheless remained cautiously in the background, and the scope of the President's power to enforce compliance remained ambiguous. Not until local white moderates and an organized group of the city's women cooperated with blacks in winning a special school board election in the spring of 1959 supporting desegregation did the crisis finally end.

BIBLIOGRAPHY

Belknap, Michal R. *Federal Law and Social Order, Racial Violence and Constitutional Conflict in the Post-Brown South.* 1987.
Freyer, Tony. *The Little Rock Crisis.* 1984.
Williams, Juan. "Hall Monitors from the 101st, the Little Rock Story." In *Eyes on the Prize, America's Civil Rights Years, 1954–1965* by Juan Williams. 1987.

TONY FREYER

LITTLE v. BARREME 6 U.S. (2 Cranch) 170 (1804). This decision, written by Chief Justice JOHN MARSHALL, represents an early judicial constraint on presidential power. It is of special significance because the issue involved the President's use of military power in FOREIGN AFFAIRS. During the administration of John Adams, the United States fought the QUASI-WAR WITH FRANCE. Congress authorized the President to stop American ships bound for French ports. When the Secretary of the Navy issued orders a month after the law was enacted, one recipient of the those orders was Captain George Little, commander of the frigate U.S.S. *Boston*. The orders departed from the law in a key respect: they directed the seizure not only of ships bound to French ports but also those sailing from French ports. Pursuant to his instructions, Little seized the *Flying Fish*, a vessel carrying Danish papers and sailing from a French port.

The issue in court was whether the Danish owners should be awarded damages for the injuries they suffered. Little's defense was that he merely followed orders and that those orders excused him from liability. Marshall's first reaction, he confessed in the opinion, was that a judgment against Little for damage would be improper because military men must obey the orders of their superiors. He changed his mind, however, when he considered the character of Little's act: it stood in direct contravention of the will of Congress. The instructions from the Secretary of the Navy, Marshall wrote, could not "legalize an act which without those instructions would have been a plain trespass." His decision indicates that congressional authorization of a specified scope of executive action carries an implicit denial of the President of authority to order action outside that scope. This case stands for the proposition that gives it an abiding timeliness: the will of Congress controls.

Nowhere in *Little* does Marshall consider the possibility that the President's order might have fallen within independent powers the executive might enjoy as "sole organ" of the United States in its foreign relations. Yet it was none other than then-Congressman John Marshall, speaking on the floor of the House of Representatives in 1800, who coined the term. But, in that speech, far from arguing that President Adams had an "inherent" or "independent" power to order the extradition to Britain of a person charged with murder, Marshall in fact contended only that it was Adams's constitutional duty to see that JAY's TREATY was faithfully executed. It was the treaty, not the President's exclusive constitutional power, that authorized and indeed required the extradition in question. Therefore it probably never occurred to Marshall or any of his colleagues in 1804 that the President, acting within the Constitution that many of them had helped write, could disregard this congressional limitation. The argument for a royal prerogative was not one with which these Framers were unfamiliar. Marshall's opinion in *Little* saw presidential power as largely dependent upon the will of Congress.

BIBLIOGRAPHY

Glennon, Michael J. *Constitutional Diplomacy* (1990).
Glennon, Michael J. "Two Views of Presidential Foreign Affairs Power: *Little v. Barreme* or *Curtiss-Wright?*" *Yale Journal of International Law* 13 (1988): 5–20.

MICHAEL J. GLENNON

LLOYD–LA FOLLETTE ACT (1912). The Lloyd–La Follette Act (37 Stat. 555) is codified as section 6 of a comprehensive statute dealing with the organization and funding of the Post Office. In a densely packed paragraph, it conveys three new rights to postal and/or federal employees generally.

First, the act reads that "no person in the classified CIVIL SERVICE of the United States shall be removed therefrom except for such cause as will promote the efficiency of said service and for reasons given in writing, and the person whose removal is sought shall

have notice of the same and of any charges preferred against him, and. . . . [be] allowed a reasonable time for personally answering the same in writing; . . . but no examination of witnesses nor any trial or hearing shall be required except in the discretion of the officer making the removal." Although there had been some earlier executive orders limiting the causes for which federal civil servants could be dismissed, the act created the first general statutory protection of their tenure. The drafters of the CIVIL SERVICE ACT (1883) and many of the early civil-service reformers were opposed to placing comprehensive legal restrictions on the dismissal of civil servants. They generally believed that limitations on hiring under the merit system would deprive officials of any motive for firing productive employees, since it would be impossible to replace them with partisan choices. The "front door" being guarded, the reformers argued, there was no reason to protect the "back door" or foster dismissal by lawsuit. However, by 1912 there was reason to believe that dismissals had nevertheless sometimes been made on the basis of political disfavor or race.

Although the act did not provide for hearings, appeals, or other elaborate procedure, such protections eventually developed. The Veteran Preference Act of 1944 (58 Stat. 387) gave veteran-preference eligibles a right to appeal dismissals to the Civil Service Commission. Executive Order 10987 (27 Fed. Reg. 550 [1962]) required agencies to establish systems for reconsideration of adverse actions against employees, including, where practicable, one level of appeal. Section 7513 of the CIVIL SERVICE REFORM ACT of 1978 (92 Stat. 1111) repeats the Lloyd–La Follette Act's standard for dismissal but includes the right to appeal to the MERIT SYSTEMS PROTECTION BOARD.

Second, the Lloyd–La Follette Act also granted postal employees the right to join labor unions and other associations, insofar as they did not impose a duty to strike, engage in strikes, or assist strikes against the government. It prohibited dismissals or demotions for membership in such groups. However, the act did not require the Post Office to engage in collective bargaining and did not establish a system of labor relations. Although this provision applied only to postal employees, it was generally read to convey similar affiliation rights to most federal civil servants who were not supervisors or managers. A comprehensive system of labor relations in the federal service did not develop until authorized by Executive Order 10988 (27 Fed. Reg. 551 [1962]).

Third, the act provided that the right of civil servants "either individually or collectively, to petition Congress or any Member thereof, or to furnish information to either House of Congress, or to any committee or member thereof, shall not be denied or interfered with." This section was in response to notorious gag orders, which prevented federal employees from informing Congress about conditions in the federal service. It provided a rudimentary protection for WHISTLE-BLOWERS.

BIBLIOGRAPHY

Rosenbloom, David H. *Federal Service and the Constitution.* 1971.

DAVID H. ROSENBLOOM

LOBBYING WITH APPROPRIATED MONEY ACT (1919).

In 1919, Congress restricted executive agencies that had used appropriated funds to stimulate private citizens to lobby Congress. Members of Congress were offended by bureau chiefs and departmental heads who wrote letters and sent telegrams throughout the country, urging corporations and individuals to contact their Representatives and Senators in behalf of specific legislation.

The Lobbying with Appropriated Money Act, which remains part of current law (18 U.S.C. 1913), states that no part of appropriated funds shall, unless expressly authorized by Congress, be used directly or indirectly to pay for any personal service, advertisement, telegram, telephone, letter, printed or written matter, or other device, intended or designed to influence in any manner a member of Congress or to favor or oppose any legislation or appropriation by Congress. The statute does not prevent executive officers from communicating to members of Congress on the request of any member.

The statute is designed to prevent administrators from using their offices to drum up public support or opposition to pending legislation. Members of Congress do not want to be on the receiving end of constituent pressures artificially manufactured by agency phone calls and other actions. The GENERAL ACCOUNTING OFFICE and the former Budget Bureau have objected to agency publications that are proselytizing in tone and propagandistic in substance. Prosecutions are rare because the JUSTICE DEPARTMENT believes that Congress intended this statute to bar only "gross solicitations" of public support.

Congress generally tolerates lobbying by the President and his immediate staff. The White House post of public liaison deliberately orchestrates the lobbying efforts of private constituent groups, urging them to pressure Congress in support of the President's programs. Presidents are at liberty to advocate legislative measures, either through the constitutional prerogative to present to Congress information on the state of the union or by other recommendations judged to be necessary or expedient. Presidents frequently present their views through PRESS CONFERENCES, news broadcasts, and television, urging citizens to contact Congress about various matters.

Even with its limitations, the Lobbying with Appropriated Money Act remains an effective way to monitor and restrict agency activities. On a number of occasions, this statute has been invoked to prevent improper lobbying activities by the White House and executive agencies. The few judicial decisions handed down on this issue suggest that courts are inclined to defer to Congress and the President for the definition of appropriate lobbying activity by executive officials.

BIBLIOGRAPHY

Fisher, Louis. *The Politics of Shared Power: Congress and the Executive.* 3d ed. 1993.

LOUIS FISHER

LODGE-GOSSETT PLAN.

Senator Henry Cabot Lodge of Massachusetts and Congressman Ed Gossett of Texas proposed a constitutional amendment in 1950 that would abolish the ELECTORAL COLLEGE and provide for the counting of each state's electoral vote for President and Vice President in proportion to the popular vote. Electoral votes would be distributed among the states in the same manner as before. The electoral votes of a state would be automatically divided among the candidates in direct proportion to the popular vote, with the electoral vote being computed to three decimal places. Each candidate's national total would be the sum of the electoral votes scored in each state.

Proponents of the proportional plan cited two benefits. First, the office of presidential elector would be eliminated and, with it, the problem of the unfaithful elector. Second the general ticket system would be discarded and, with it, all its attendant evils: there would be no disfranchisement of nearly half the voters of a state; one-party states would be opened up to serious competition; candidates would not overly concentrate their efforts on larger states with heavily populated urban centers to the neglect of smaller, less populated states; conventions would no longer feel bound to choose their presidential candidates from the larger states exclusively; minority pressure groups in pivotal states, which had previously wielded influence far beyond their true size, would no longer exercise exaggerated sway in determining the outcome of elections; the electoral outcome would closely reflect the popular vote and would no longer be distorted by the operation of the Electoral College; and the chances of a minority President being elected would be reduced. Above all, every vote would not only be counted but would count and this system would thus promote greater democracy through greater voter participation.

Opponents of the Lodge-Gossett Plan argued that it would severely affect the prospects of a liberal to succeed to the presidency. The DEMOCRATIC PARTY, it was said, would come under the domination of its southern conservative wing. But the major indictment of the proposal was that it would encourage a multiplicity of political parties since every independent group would aspire to obtain some proportion of a state's electoral vote. Election results would be much closer and the winner would fail to obtain a decisive margin of victory.

Although the Senate voted 64 to 23 to endorse the amendment, it failed in the House of Representatives by a vote of 134 to 210.

In 1956 the Lodge-Gossett Plan resurfaced but was severely attacked by liberals. Neither house of Congress endorsed the proposal.

BIBLIOGRAPHY

Longley, Lawrence D., and Alan G. Braun. *The Politics of Electoral College Reform*. 2d ed. 1975.
Pierce, Neal R., and Lawrence D. Longley. *The People's President: The Electoral College in American History and the Direct Vote Alternative*. 1981.
Sayre, Wallace S., and Judith H. Parris. *Voting for President: The Electoral College and the American Political System*. 1970.

SHLOMO SLONIM

LOGAN ACT (1799). The Logan Act of 1799 (An Act to Prevent Usurpation of Executive Functions, 18 U.S.C. 953) makes it a criminal offense for a U.S. citizen to carry on any correspondence or intercourse with any foreign government "with intent to influence the measures or conduct of any foreign government . . . in relation to any disputes or controversies with the United States, or to defeat the measures of the government of the United States." The act does not apply to persons who act with the authority of the United States nor to citizens' efforts to obtain redress from foreign governments for their own injuries.

The circumstances that prompted the act's adoption involved Dr. George Logan, a Republican and Quaker from Philadelphia, who traveled to France in 1798 in an effort to defuse tensions between the United States (then governed by the Federalists under President John Adams) and the French revolutionary government [*see* QUASI-WAR WITH FRANCE]. Irritated by Logan's private diplomacy, the Adams administration sought and obtained legislation to prevent such unauthorized initiatives in the future.

The premise of the Logan Act is that the conduct of the foreign relations of the United States, especially the function of communicating with foreign powers, is a prerogative belonging exclusively to the U.S. government. Congress enacted the legislation on the assumption of presidential control over this function, consistent with the view that the President is the sole organ of the United States in its external relations. On the theory that unauthorized negotiations could interfere with the President's ability to advance the objectives of the nation as a whole, Congress provided for criminal penalties (a fine and up to three years' imprisonment) to deter such private ventures. If the President chooses, he may authorize private persons to negotiate for the United States; without such authorization, a private citizen may run afoul of the act (at least technically, even if prosecution is unlikely) by entering into communication with a foreign power on a matter in which the United States is interested.

In the two centuries that the Logan Act has been on the books, there have been no convictions under it. One indictment was brought in 1803 but the prosecution was not pursued; a handful of judicial opinions have made reference to the act in dicta (statements in a judicial opinion not essential to the decision and that do not establish a precedent). Despite the pattern of nonenforcement and questions about constitutionality, the law remains on the books and is sometimes mentioned as a possible source of prosecutorial authority when the executive branch has not endorsed a particular private mission to a foreign power.

It is widely believed that there would be formidable constitutional obstacles to any prosecutions under the act. Among the possible constitutional objections are that the act violates rights to free expression protected by the First Amendment and that it is so vague that it does not give fair notice of the proscribed conduct as required by the due process clause of the Fifth Amendment. Moreover, in light of almost complete nonenforcement of the act, questions about selective prosecution and desuetude would surely be raised as challenges to any potential future action. In addition to these constitutional problems, the Logan Act has been criticized as an obsolete and indeed harmful statute, since much unofficial diplomacy that would fall within its literal terms could be beneficial to U.S. interests.

Ironically, the broadly written phraseology of the

act is open to the interpretation that even members of Congress could be prosecuted for engaging in dialogue with foreign officials without the permission of the executive branch. This hypothetical possibility would entail constitutional objections going beyond the ones previously mentioned, deriving from the constitutional powers of Congress relevant to foreign affairs.

During the VIETNAM WAR and after, a number of highly publicized private initiatives in the diplomatic realm went forward, the Logan Act notwithstanding, even over the explicit disapproval of the executive branch. Private negotiations for release of hostages have been undertaken on various occasions, sometimes bringing success even where official diplomatic efforts had failed. Opponents of U.S. policies have frequently gone to the country in question (for example, during the Vietnam War or Central American conflicts) for dialogue with foreign leaders. Occasionally the executive branch has rattled the saber of potential prosecution in such instances.

Various other statutes likewise aim to prevent or regulate private conduct that might impede the President's conduct of U.S. foreign relations. These include the Neutrality Acts, which restrict involvement by U.S. citizens in foreign conflicts; the Foreign Agents Registration Act, which requires identification of persons acting for foreign powers in the United States; travel controls, which have been in effect from time to time with respect to certain countries [see TRAVEL, RIGHT TO]; and restrictions on financial transactions with specified countries.

Repeal of the Logan Act, or substantial amendment to tailor the statute more closely to its objectives and to constitutional concerns, would seem advisable.

BIBLIOGRAPHY

Tolles, Frederick B. "Unofficial Ambassador: George Logan's Mission to France, 1798." *William and Mary Quarterly* 3d ser., 7 (1950): 3–25.

U.S. Senate. *Memorandum on the History and Scope of the Laws Prohibiting Correspondence with a Foreign Government and Acceptance of a Commission.* By Charles Warren. 64th Cong., 2d sess., 1917. S. Doc. No. 696.

Vagts, Detlev. "The Logan Act: Paper Tiger or Sleeping Giant?" *American Journal of International Law* 60 (1966): 268–302.

LORI FISLER DAMROSCH

LOUISIANA PURCHASE. At the close of the Seven Years' War in 1763, France ceded Louisiana, or the western half of the Mississippi Valley, to Spain but later sought to recover it. Leaders of the new American nation, who eyed the trans-Mississippi territory as a desirable future acquisition, preferred a weak Spain as a neighbor. After the United States in 1795 concluded PINCKNEY'S TREATY with Spain, American traders flocked to New Orleans, creating friction with the populace. In October 1800 Spain secretly retroceded Louisiana to France in exchange for a kingdom in Tuscany. France's head of government, Napoleon Bonaparte, desired Louisiana as a granary for French possessions in the Caribbean.

When Thomas Jefferson became President in March 1801, he did not know that the French had regained Louisiana. Despite his francophile leanings, when he heard rumors of the exchange he called it ominous. He increased military units along the Mississippi and in April 1802 told Robert R. Livingston, the American minister to France, that the possessor of New Orleans "is our natural and habitual enemy," and that at the moment France takes possession "we must marry ourselves to the British fleet and nation." He also instructed Livingston to ascertain if France would sell Louisiana.

In October, when the Spanish authorities in New Orleans revoked the American traders' right of deposit, or the storing of goods for transshipment in oceangoing vessels, a crisis followed. Furious westerners and FEDERALIST PARTY members talked of war. The President faced a dilemma. Strong measures against France would lead to war, but inaction would play into the hands of his political opponents. He spoke of seizure through force but was willing to pay as much as $10 million for New Orleans and the Floridas. Backed by Congress, he sent James Monroe, a Democratic-Republican popular in the West, on a special mission to France to work with Livingston on the negotiations.

When Monroe arrived in Paris on 13 April 1803, the crisis had passed. Bonaparte offered to sell all of Louisiana. He did so because he had experienced difficulty in taking physical possession; had failed to subdue rebelling former slaves in Haiti, the key to his plan for empire in America; needed money to fight Britain after a period of truce; and desired to keep the province out of British hands. On 30 April he ceded Louisiana to the United States for $15,000,000; of this amount $3,750,000 went to pay France's American creditors.

This sudden opportunity extricated Jefferson from his difficulties. Yet the acquisition posed problems of conscience, principle, and politics. Bonaparte had violated an obligation to Spain not to sell, and the French constitution prohibited him from alienating national land without legislative approval. Furthermore, as a strict constructionist Jefferson believed initially that he lacked authority to buy territory because the Constitution did not enumerate that power. He thought of consummating the transaction with a constitutional amendment that specifically allowed it. Yet he had to act fast because the chance might slip away. Dismissing his doubts as "metaphysical subtleties," he went ahead without the amendment.

Some Federalists opposed the purchase as unconstitutional, but others, who were as expansionist as the Democratic-Republicans, were delighted with it. On 30 October 1803, the Senate approved the Louisiana treaties, and on 20 December the United States took formal possession of 828,000 square miles, or more than 5 million acres, west of the Mississippi, which doubled the national domain.

Despite the questionable title to the acquisition, vague boundaries, and ethical problems, Jefferson considered that he had made a "noble bargain." With it he set a precedent for acquiring territory by threat and treaty, stretched the Constitution, and paved the way for a steady expansion of EXECUTIVE POWER. None of these considerations bothered most Americans. They approved the Louisiana Purchase wholeheartedly and ever since have viewed it as the foremost accomplishment of his presidency.

BIBLIOGRAPHY

Adams, Henry. *History of the United States during the Administrations of Jefferson and Madison.* Vols. 1 and 2. *The First Administration of Thomas Jefferson, 1801–1805.* 1921; first published 1891.
DeConde, Alexander. *This Affair of Louisiana.* 1976.
Lyon, E. Wilson. *Louisiana in French Diplomacy, 1759–1804.* 1934.
Sprague, Marshall. *So Vast So Beautiful a Land: Louisiana and the Purchase.* 1974.
Whitaker, Arthur P. *The Mississippi Question, 1795–1803: A Study in Trade, Politics, and Diplomacy.* 1934.

ALEXANDER DECONDE

LOYALTY-SECURITY PROGRAMS. Loyalty-security programs or measures have been adopted periodically throughout American history to ensure that public employees are loyal to the constitutional regime and are not inclined to engage in subversive activities designed to weaken the government or aid the nation's enemies. As early as 1777, the Continental Congress sought to ferret out disloyal employees in the postal service, and in 1779 a general loyalty oath was required of all civilian and military officers employed by the Confederation. Concern with loyalty also ran high during the CIVIL WAR and WORLD WAR I. It was not until the late 1940s and early 1950s, however, that loyalty-security programs became a major feature of the federal CIVIL SERVICE.

WORLD WAR II and the COLD WAR raised apprehension throughout the government that the United States was highly vulnerable to subversion within the federal civil service. In 1948, the House Un-American Activities Committee held well-publicized "Hearings Regarding Communist Espionage in the United States Government," at which Whittaker Chambers and Elizabeth Bentley, themselves former communists, testified to the effect that communist infiltration of the federal government had been extensive and damaging. When the Chinese communists drove out the Nationalists in 1949, many in Congress believed that subversives within the State Department were partly responsible. Several State Department officials involved in Asian affairs were eventually dismissed on loyalty-security grounds. The case for extensive loyalty-security measures was brought to the public by Congressmen Martin Dies (D-Tex.), Richard M. Nixon (R-Cal.), and Senator Joseph McCarthy (R-Wis.), among others.

The loyalty-security issue received substantial airing during the presidential election of 1952, in which the Republican platform declared that "by the administration's appeasement of communism at home and abroad it has permitted communists and fellow travelers to serve in many key agencies and to infiltrate our American life." The party promised that a Republican President would only appoint persons of unquestioned loyalty. The issue peaked by 1954, when McCarthy was censured by the Senate for labeling its Select Committee to Study Censure Charges the "unwitting handmaiden," "involuntary agent," and "attorneys-in-fact" of the Communist Party.

The legal framework for the loyalty-security program consisted of the following:

First, the HATCH ACT section 9A (not to be confused with 9[a], which dealt with political neutrality) (53 Stat. 1148 [1939]) prohibited the federal employment of anyone having membership in a political party or organization advocating overthrow of the constitutional form of government.

Second, the U.S. Civil Service Commission's War Service Regulations of 1942 prohibited the appointment of any applicants if there was a reasonable doubt as to their loyalty. By 1946, 1,297 persons had been deemed unsuitable under this standard.

Third, Executive Order 9300 (8 Fed. Reg. 1701 [1943]) created an Interdepartmental Committee on Employee Loyalty Investigations to ensure the loyalty of incumbent federal civil servants. The FBI investigated some six thousand employees under its mandate, resulting in the dismissal of somewhere between one hundred and two hundred of them.

Fourth, EXECUTIVE ORDER 9835 (12 Fed. Reg. 1935

[1947]) required a loyalty investigation of every person entering the federal service. The Loyalty Order, as it was known, provided for the establishment of a national Loyalty Review Board and regional loyalty review boards within the Civil Service Commission. Originally the burden of persuasion was on the government to show that "on all the evidence, reasonable grounds exist for belief that the person involved is disloyal to the government of the United States." In 1951, as McCarthy and the Republicans generally were gaining political capital with the issue, the standard for dismissal was changed to "a reasonable doubt as to the loyalty of the person involved." Indicators of disloyalty included actual or attempted sabotage, espionage, treason; unauthorized disclosure of information; performance of duties in such a fashion as to show preference for the interests of another nation; advocacy of revolution, force, or violence to alter the constitutional form of government; and membership in or sympathetic affiliation with subversive groups. The Attorney General maintained a long list of groups designated as totalitarian, fascist, communist, or subversive, and membership in any one of them was probably the main criterion used in dismissals or disqualification of applicants. All told, 560 persons were dismissed under the Loyalty Order, and another 1,192 left the service after receiving interrogatories or charges.

Fifth, legislation in 1950 (64 Stat. 476) provided that notwithstanding other legal provisions, the heads of the Departments of State, Commerce, and Defense, the Army, the Navy, the Air Force, the Atomic Energy Commission, the National Security Resources Board, the National Advisory Committee for Aeronautics, the Department of the Treasury (with regard to the Coast Guard), and the Attorney General could suspend or dismiss any civilian officer or employee when deemed necessary or advisable in the interests of NATIONAL SECURITY. The law authorized the President to extend its coverage to other agencies as well. Between 1950 and 1953 there were about five hundred removals under that statute, which was still in force in the 1990s.

Sixth, Executive Order 10450 (18 Fed. Reg. 2489) in 1953, generally known as the Security Order, replaced the Loyalty Order. It extended the provisions of the 1950 statute throughout the government, thus making it the responsibility of department and agency heads to maintain programs to assure that the employment of anyone within their work forces was clearly consistent with the interests of national security. The order established a distinction between sensitive and nonsensitive positions and required more extensive investigations with regard to the former. As under the 1950 law, incumbent employees were afforded hearings within their departments, but no appeals to the Civil Service Commission were authorized. Nor were hearings required for the denial of employment to applicants on security grounds. In COLE v. YOUNG (351 U.S. 536 [1956]), the Supreme Court held that the Security Order's extension of the limited 1950 procedural protections to all positions, not just the sensitive ones for which they were intended, was invalid. There were about fifteen hundred removals under the Security Order between 1953 and 1956.

Seventh, legislation in 1955 (69 Stat. 624) replaced section 9A of the Hatch Act by prohibiting employee membership in organizations advocating overthrow of the constitutional form of government and requiring employees to sign affidavits indicating that they did not so belong.

Although a web of loyalty-security regulations remains in force, interest in the issue declined rapidly by the late 1950s, and investigations became increasingly perfunctory. However, the 1950 statute and the Security Order substantially expanded the potential scope of investigations and charges. Like the Loyalty Order, they provided for dismissal or denial of employment on grounds of disloyalty, but they also allowed disqualification if, for any reason, an employee's or applicant's employment would not be in the best interests of national security. In other words, carelessness with one's briefcase, excessive use of alcohol, or being especially vulnerable to blackmail could provide the basis for dismissal for reasons of security.

Among the many problems with loyalty-security programs has been the failure to specify precisely the behavior proscribed. Consequently, federal employees have been dismissed on loyalty-security grounds for activities or beliefs that generally enjoy robust constitutional protection. Loyalty-security investigations ranged broadly over such topics as employees' reading habits, religious practices, voting behavior, beliefs about racial equality, female chastity, and friends and associations. During the first Eisenhower administration, Democrats were more likely to bear the brunt of security screening than were Republicans, though there was a genuine, if severely overstated, fear of subversives. The program of the late 1940s and early 1950s also created an atmosphere of stifling caution among federal employees and undoubtedly cost the government the services of many highly talented individuals. The security investigation of J. Robert Oppenheimer, who is generally credited with effectively contributing to and coordinating the U.S. development of the atomic bomb during World War II, provided a strong symbolic example of the government's distaste for nonconformity during the early 1950s.

BIBLIOGRAPHY

Biddle, Francis. *The Fear of Freedom*. 1952

Bontecou, Eleanor. *The Federal Loyalty-Security Program*. 1953.

Brown, Ralph S., Jr. *Loyalty and Security*. 1958.

Emerson, Thomas I., and David Helfeld. "Loyalty among Government Employees." *Yale Law Journal* 58 (1948): 1–143.

Jahoda, Marie, and Stuart Cook. "Security Measures and Freedom of Thought." *Yale Law Journal* 61 (1952): 295–333.

McWilliams, Carey, *Witch Hunt*. 1950.

Rosenbloom, David H. *Federal Service and the Constitution*. 1971.

U.S. Atomic Energy Commission. *In the Matter of J. Robert Oppenheimer*. 1954.

DAVID H. ROSENBLOOM

M

MCCARRAN INTERNAL SECURITY ACT

(1950). The McCarran Act was an effort to curb the activities of the Communist Party of the United States and control "subversive activities" in the United States. It passed Congress, 23 September 1950, over the veto of President Harry S. Truman.

The act was a product of a growing concern, sometimes called the second red scare of twentieth-century America, over domestic Communist activities. Originating with the emergence of the COLD WAR, the red scare stemmed from numerous cases that revealed Soviet espionage activities, from the fall of Nationalist China, and from the Soviet atomic bomb. By mid-1950, it had reached levels of hysteria, partly because of Sen. Joseph R. McCarthy's numerous accusations of Communist influence in the government but primarily because of the KOREAN WAR.

A bill to limit Communist activities was rewritten in the Senate Internal Security Subcommittee and reported for a vote in September 1950. The subcommittee chairman, Sen. Pat McCarran of Nevada, was a conservative, anti-Communist Democrat frequently at odds with President Truman.

The McCarran bill contained several provisions aimed at the Communists: first, Communist organizations were required to register with the DEPARTMENT OF JUSTICE, disclose full information about their financing, and reveal their membership lists; second, any act that would "substantially contribute to the establishment within the United States of a totalitarian dictatorship" was a federal crime; third, Communists could not be granted passports; fourth, Communists could not be employed in defense plants; fifth, during national emergencies, persons suspected of subversive activities might be summarily arrested and interned; sixth, aliens who had been connected with Communist or other totalitarian organizations could not be granted visas to enter the United States; seventh, a Subversive Activities Control Board would be established primarily to develop a list of organizations required to register with the government.

The McCarran bill passed both houses of Congress by overwhelming margins. Nonetheless, Truman vetoed it based on his libertarian beliefs that the legislation went well beyond the bounds of legitimate security considerations into the restriction of political activities. Although Truman's administration had taken some strong domestic anti-Communist action—such as the federal loyalty program and the prosecution of the leadership of the Communist Party, indications are that he had been uncomfortable with such activities. Truman believed that the McCarran bill was a modern counterpart of the ALIEN AND SEDITION ACTS. "In a free country," he declared, "we punish men for the crimes they commit, but never for the opinions they have." Congress quickly overrode the veto, 286 to 48 in the House, and 57 to 10 in the Senate.

The administration of Dwight D. Eisenhower seems to have taken the McCarran Act rather seriously and to have attempted to enforce it. Eisenhower's Democratic successors, John F. Kennedy and Lyndon B. Johnson, treated the law with benign neglect. Most ironically, Richard M. Nixon, although cosponsor of an early version of the legislation, made no effort to resuscitate what was left of it by the time he became President; rather, he participated in the final stages of its dismantlement. By the early 1970s, the political climate had changed drastically; Congress has repealed key sections, the Supreme Court had struck down others, and the presidency was uninterested in enforcing what was left.

In practice, the McCarran Act had little impact. The Subversive Activities Control Board became little more than a sinecure for out-of-work politicians and ceased operations. Although Communists and suspected Communists were denied passports for years, the Supreme Court decision in *Aptheker v. Secretary of State* (1964) ruled the prohibition unconstitutional. The registration provisions, never effectively enforced, were repealed in 1968. The emergency detention provisions, never invoked, were repealed in 1971. Little remains of the original legislation other than a continued federal right (infrequently applied) to bar suspect alien totalitarians from the United States and the prohibition against employment of Communists in defense plants, never a real problem in the cold war era.

The rapid fading of the red scare after McCarthy's censure in 1954 and the new concerns of the 1960s had made the McCarran Act seem more a quaint, almost incomprehensible relic of a bygone era than either a menace to American freedom or a needed defense against foreign subversion.

BIBLIOGRAPHY

Caute, David. *The Great Fear.* 1978.
Donovan, Robert J. *Tumultuous Years: The Presidency of Harry S. Truman, 1949–1953.* 1982.
Latham, Earl. *The Communist Controversy in Washington: From the New Deal to McCarthy.* 1966.

ALONZO L. HAMBY

MCCARRAN-WALTER ACT (1952). This law, a major revision of the statutes affecting immigration, naturalization, and nationality, was passed by Congress over the veto of President Harry S. Truman on 27 June 1952. The act represented a culmination of seven years of debate over the fairness of the existing immigration system and the admission of "displaced persons" to the United States after WORLD WAR II. It was also one element of the controversy over communism in COLD WAR Washington, a controversy in which the act's sponsors, Sen. Pat McCarran of Nevada and Rep. Francis Walter of Pennsylvania, were major players.

The Truman administration had recommended an alteration in the immigration quota system of 1924, which discriminated in favor of northern and western Europeans [*see* IMMIGRATION ACT (1924)]. Moreover, Truman had advocated a temporary enlargement of the quotas to allow for the admission of an additional 300,000 persons over three years. The administration anticipated that these places would go to individuals displaced by the war and the subsequent cold war, which had produced a new class of political refugees from Eastern European nations within the Soviet orbit. (Legislation passed in 1948 and 1950 already had provided for the admission of approximately 405,000 displaced persons.)

As passed, however, the bill preserved the existing discriminatory quota structure largely unchanged and kept total immigration at the old limit of approximately 155,000 persons a year. For the first time in American history, however, it established small quotas for Asian countries. It also established preference in admission for alien husbands of female American citizens or resident aliens.

The cold war affected the bill in another way. In addition to giving immigration officials broad discretionary authority to bar suspected criminals (including those convicted in communist-bloc courts), the bill imposed ideological tests for entry into the United States. It excluded people who advocated either communism or some other totalitarian philosophy from entry as either immigrants seeking citizenship or as temporary visitors. Provisions directed primarily at communists or suspected communists gave the Attorney General power to deport aliens engaged in any activities deemed "prejudicial to the public interest" or "subversive to the national security." These passages largely reiterated sections of the McCARRAN INTERNAL SECURITY ACT (1950), which Truman also had vetoed.

Truman's veto message criticized the bill on three major counts. First, it continued discriminatory quotas; the President observed, for example, that it would allow only 289 Romanians a year to settle in the United States, although thirty thousand Romanian refugees had applied for entry. Second, its nonentry and deportation provisions violated individual rights. Third, it contained certain encroachments on EXECUTIVE POWER that Truman argued were inconsistent with the Constitution.

The message reflected Truman's instinctive liberalism and personal decency but also was related to a political agenda that reflected the outlook of the Democratic "presidential party"—that is, those constituencies that swung the most weight in Democratic national nominating conventions and presidential elections. These included a substantial number of northern, urban, working-class, ethnic groups with antecedents in southern and eastern Europe, anxious to achieve the symbolic recognition that a reformed quota system would bring and in many individual cases hoping to assist relatives who wanted to settle in the United States, and a growing and influential political intelligentsia that placed a high premium on the preservation and extension of civil liberties. Following the example of Franklin D. Roosevelt, the Democratic presidential party was also supportive of a strong presidency; Truman himself was personally determined to leave the institution as strong as he had found it.

The bill's passage by large majorities in a Democratic Congress, conversely, demonstrated that the Democratic "congressional party" shared some characteristics with the bulk of the opposition Republicans. Both the Democratic and Republican delegations on Capitol Hill reflected an overrepresentation of rural, small-town, white, Anglo-Saxon, Protestant America that would not change until the Supreme Court decision in *Baker v. Carr* (1962) required congressional districts to be drawn on a one-person, one-vote basis. Both delegations also demonstrated an intense public concern about communist subversion that Truman, who was not running for reelection, could ignore much more easily than many Representatives and Senators, who had to face their local voters. And most Democrats and Republicans in Congress felt that the presidency had grown too strong under Roosevelt and were disposed to curb its authority.

The Republican administration of Dwight D. Eisenhower, although it reflected a constituency predominantly satisfied with the old quota system, the politics of anticommunism, and a circumscribed presidency, nonetheless recognized the importance of the urban ethnic vote by advocating a thorough liberalization of McCarran-Walter. It was unsuccessful, however, in obtaining results and never made revision a high priority.

When the Democrats returned to the White House in 1961, the John F. Kennedy administration pushed hard for comprehensive reform, although without success. In 1965, Lyndon B. Johnson, enjoying an enormous landslide victory over BARRY GOLDWATER and a massive Democratic majority in Congress, made immigration reform part of his GREAT SOCIETY agenda. The Immigration Act of 1965 greatly liberalized the old quota system but left the McCarran-Walter provisions on entry and deportation in effect.

BIBLIOGRAPHY

Dinnerstein, Leonard. *America and the Survivors of the Holocaust.* 1982.

Hutchinson, E. P. *Legislative History of American Immigration Policy, 1789–1965.* 1981.

Le May, Michael C. *From Open Door to Dutch Door: An Analysis of U.S. Immigration Policy since 1920.* 1987.

Loescher, Gil. *Calculated Kindess: Refugees and America's Half-Open Door, 1945 to the Present.* 1986.

ALONZO L. HAMBY

MCCARTHY, EUGENE (b. 1916). Congressman, Senator, unsuccessful candidate for the Democratic presidential nomination in 1968. Eugene Joseph McCarthy was born in Minnesota in 1916. The political heir of ADLAI E. STEVENSON (1900–1965), McCarthy vehemently opposed the VIETNAM WAR. In early 1968, he emerged at the center of the antiwar movement within the DEMOCRATIC PARTY. A witty, acerbic voice for liberalism, McCarthy was never at ease with the popular movement at whose head he briefly stood. He insisted on stringent adherence to moral principle; yet his own political career demonstrated a strong desire for power and an unwillingness to forgive political rivals.

McCarthy grew up in rural Minnesota. He completed his master's degree at the University of Minnesota in 1939. He taught high school. During WORLD WAR II, he served in military intelligence. After the war, he taught economics at St. John's University.

In 1948, McCarthy won a congressional seat representing suburban Saint Paul that he would hold until 1958. An early critic of Senator Joseph McCarthy, he amassed a liberal record on migrant workers' rights, organized labor, civil rights, and aid-to-farmers issues. He also advocated congressional oversight of the CENTRAL INTELLIGENCE AGENCY. In 1958 he was elected to the Senate.

Although a supporter of the GREAT SOCIETY program, McCarthy became critical of the Johnson administration. McCarthy had voted for the GULF OF TONKIN RESOLUTION, but criticized the administration's handling of the Vietnam War. He first focused his attacks on American intelligence. By February 1967, after the American bombing of North Vietnam had begun and after the huge troop escalation, McCarthy publicly questioned the purpose of American policy. For McCarthy the Vietnam War was a moral issue, and he questioned the entire mentality of the COLD WAR.

McCarthy announced his candidacy for the Democratic nomination in late November 1967, explaining that he hoped to stem the "growing sense of alienation from politics" felt by the antiwar movement. He did not seek to create an alternative social movement; rather he sought to harness the already existing discontent for the Democratic Party. Although still an obscure figure to the nation's electorate, in early 1968 the McCarthy campaign benefitted from thousands of student volunteers, willing to "go clean for Gene." The heart of his campaign was his opposition to the war and Lyndon B. Johnson, positions the Tet offensive of 31 January 1968 made more appealing to voters. On 12 March, McCarthy polled 42 percent to Johnson's 49 percent in the New Hampshire primary. By the end of March, a badly shaken Johnson announced he would not seek renomination.

With Johnson eliminated, only McCarthy, ROBERT F. KENNEDY, and Vice President HUBERT H. HUMPHREY remained to contest the Democratic nomination. Humphrey, the party insiders' candidate who had Johnson's qualified support, remained aloof from the primaries, leaving Kennedy and McCarthy to struggle for the emerging left coalition. Although ideologically close, McCarthy and Kennedy did not like each other. McCarthy refused to step aside for the more charismatic Kennedy. Both opposed the war, but on domestic matters, they differed in their responses to the race riots of the post-1964 era. McCarthy, though sympathetic to civil rights and poverty concerns, remained largely apart from black America. His solution to race problems was a massive suburbanization of the inner cities.

Kennedy was ahead in the primaries when he was murdered on 5 June 1968, leaving the Democratic nomination campaign in complete disarray. The campaign of the emotionally distraught McCarthy never sputtered after Kennedy's death, and he appeared unwilling to take command. Even before the Democratic convention in Chicago, McCarthy had conceded defeat to insider Humphrey, advising his supporters not to attend out of fear of violence. The Chicago convention, the most disruptive in the party's history, was deeply disillusioning to McCarthy. Humphrey won the nomination.

McCarthy served out his term as Senator and did not seek reelection in 1970. He subsequently mounted campaigns for the presidency, which, however, never reached the scale or momentum of the 1968 effort.

BIBLIOGRAPHY

Eisele, Albert. *Almost to the Presidency.* 1972.
Herzog, Arthur. *McCarthy for President.* 1969.
Matusow, Allen J. *The Unraveling of America: A History of Liberalism in the 1960s.* 1984.

JOHN F. WALSH

MCCARTHYISM. On 9 February 1950, an obscure Republican Senator from Wisconsin interrupted a speech he was giving on subversion in government to hold aloft a piece of paper. "While I cannot take the time to name all of the men in the STATE DEPARTMENT who have been named as members of the Communist Party," Sen. Joseph R. McCarthy told an audience of Republican women in Wheeling, West Virginia. "I have here in my hand a list of 205 names that were known to the Secretary of State and who nevertheless are still working and shaping the policy of the State Department."

McCarthy had no list. He knew nothing about "Reds" in the State Department—or anywhere else. But the newspapers printed his charges, and the public was aroused. In the weeks before Wheeling, China had fallen to the communists and Russia had tested an atomic bomb. Alger Hiss had been found guilty of perjury, and Klaus Fuchs, a physicist on the MANHATTAN PROJECT, had confessed to funneling atomic secrets to the Soviets. Now a U.S. Senator was stepping forward with a simple explanation for America's troubles in the world. The communists were winning the COLD WAR because traitors in our own government were aiding their cause. The real enemy was not in Moscow; it was in Washington, D.C.

McCarthy was an erratic freshman Senator known mainly for his raucous behavior. Angry colleagues accused him of lying, of insulting senior colleagues, of disregarding the Senate's cherished rules. By 1950, his political career was in trouble, and his reelection chances looked grim. What he needed was a big issue to energize his faltering career. His charges about treason in high places made him an instant celebrity. The cartoonist Herblock coined a new word to describe his reckless charges—"McCarthyism"—but prominent Republicans rallied to his side. Sen. Robert Taft of Ohio shrewdly saw McCarthy as the party's new alchemist, a man who could turn fear and distrust into Republican votes.

When the KOREAN WAR pitted American troops against communist forces, McCarthy's message took on special force. In the 1950 elections, the Republicans gained five seats in the Senate and twenty-eight more in the House. As the presidential campaign of 1952 approached, McCarthy's attacks grew even bolder. He called Secretary of Defense GEORGE C. MARSHALL a traitor, mocked Secretary of State DEAN ACHESON as the "Red Dean of Fashion," and described President Harry S. Truman as a drunkard, adding, "The son of a bitch should be impeached." During the campaign itself, McCarthy falsely claimed that the Communist Party U.S.A.'s newspaper, the *Daily Worker*, had endorsed Democrat ADLAI E. STEVENSON for President. And on several occasions he made the ugly slip, "Alger . . . I mean Adlai."

McCarthy was easily reelected in the Republican landslide of 1952. With his own party now in control of

Congress, he became chairman of the Committee on Government Operations and its powerful Subcommittee on Investigations. Filling key staff positions with ex-agents of the FEDERAL BUREAU OF INVESTIGATION (FBI) and former prosecutors such as Roy M. Cohn, an abrasive young attorney from New York, McCarthy began to investigate "communist influence" in a host of federal agencies, including the Voice of America, the Government Printing Office, and the FOREIGN SERVICE. At the same time, other bodies, such as the House Committee on Un-American Activities and the Senate Internal Security Subcommittee, hunted for "subversives" in the nation's schools, churches, and labor unions.

McCarthy's hearings did not uncover any communists. They did, however, ruin numerous careers, undermine government morale, and make America look ridiculous in the eyes of the world. Republican criticism of McCarthy began to build, because he was now attacking a government controlled by his own party.

Many expected Dwight D. Eisenhower to put McCarthy in his place. But the new President was very slow to respond. He believed that a brawl with McCarthy would divide Republicans into warring camps and seriously demean the presidential office. Eisenhower changed his mind in the fall of 1953, however, when McCarthy and Cohn began to harass the U.S. Army. They falsely charged that a communist spy ring was operating at Fort Monmouth, New Jersey, headquarters of the Army Signal Corps, and they publicly humiliated a decorated general who had served under Eisenhower in WORLD WAR II, calling him "unfit to wear the uniform." At long last, McCarthy had attacked the one institution guaranteed to pit the Republican White House against him.

Early in 1954, the Senate decided to investigate the running feud between the army and McCarthy. At Eisenhower's insistence, Republican leaders agreed to televise the hearings. The cumulative impression of McCarthy—his windy speeches, his frightening outbursts, his crude personal attacks—was devastating to him. The highlight of the hearings came in June 1954, when Army Counsel Joseph Welch asked the Senator, "Have you no sense of decency, sir?" The audience burst into applause.

A few months later, the Senate censured McCarthy for bringing it "into dishonor and disrepute." The vote was 67 to 22, with only Republican conservatives opposed. Many believed that McCarthy's censure was linked to the easing of cold war tensions: the Korean War was over, the Soviet dictator Joseph Stalin was dead, and the radical right was in disarray. For McCar-

thy himself, things came apart at a wicked rate. Reporters and colleagues ignored him, and his influence disappeared. Unable to get his message across, McCarthy spent his final days drinking in private, railing against those who had deserted his cause. He died of acute alcoholism in 1957, virtually alone, at the age of forty-eight. But the word "McCarthyism" lives on as a pejorative, a reminder of the fear and repression of the early cold war years.

BIBLIOGRAPHY

Caute, David. *The Great Fear: The Anti-Communist Purge Under Truman and Eisenhower.* 1978.

Fried, Richard. *Nightmare in Red: The McCarthy Era in Perspective.* 1990.

Oshinsky, David M. *A Conspiracy So Immense: The World of Joe McCarthy.* 1983.

Whitfield, Stephen J. *The Culture of the Cold War.* 1991.

DAVID M. OSHINSKY

MCCLELLAN, GEORGE B. (1826–1885), general, Democratic presidential nominee in 1864. After graduating second in his class from West Point in 1846, George Brinton McClellan had a successful military career in the U.S. Army Corps of Engineers, seeing action during the MEXICAN WAR. He left the army to become a successful railroad executive.

When the CIVIL WAR broke out, McClellan reenlisted on the Union side. After his first assignment to supervise Ohio's state troops, he moved to a command in western Virginia where he gave the Union its first battlefield success in July 1861. Almost immediately, he was called to Washington to reorganize the federal forces after their disastrous rebuff at Bull Run. At age thirty-four, he was put in charge of the Army of the Potomac and proceeded, with great efficiency, to train it and revive its morale.

McClellan could equip an army but he proved unable to win battlefield victories. Worse, he argued endlessly with his Commander in Chief, Abraham Lincoln. The general's problem was that he was intolerant of civilian involvement in military matters and had little respect for politicians, especially those who, like Lincoln, were militarily and administratively inexperienced. He contested the President's strategic suggestions, most notably in the dispute of February 1862 over whether to advance toward Richmond from the north, as Lincoln proposed, or from the lower Chesapeake. The President yielded on this point but, in the ensuing Peninsular campaign of the spring and summer of 1862, McClellan refused to heed Lincoln's urgings to advance and take the offensive. McClellan even lectured the President on grand strategy and the nature of the war most notably in a letter of July 1862 in which the young general informed Lincoln that the war was to be quite limited in scope and objective.

Despite their increasingly divergent opinions about the war and how to fight it, Lincoln found himself unable to dispense with McClellan because he could not find a better alternative. Moreover, McClellan had considerable support from his troops and among critics of the war effort, especially Democrats who shared his approach to the war and saw him as a useful foil to Lincoln and the Republicans. Indeed, throughout 1862, Lincoln feared that removing McClellan would hand the Democrats not only an issue in 1862 but a candidate for 1864.

By fall 1862, however, the President felt able to remove the problematic McClellan from command. Having driven Lee out of Maryland, Lincoln widened the scope of the war to include emancipation, a policy to which McClellan was absolutely opposed. Knowing that the general would now be even less cooperative, the President used McClellan's failure to destroy the retreating Army of Northern Virginia as the reason to dismiss him, thereby also depriving the cocksure McClellan of the glory that Antietam, his only major battlefield victory of the war, might have given him.

Nevertheless, McClellan was regarded as the most viable presidential possibility for the Democrats in 1864. He possessed a popular appeal that persisted, remarkably, despite his military failures. Moreover, with a general as nominee, the Democrats could criticize the war and its conduct without appearing disloyal to the war effort or the soldiers in the field. McClellan encouraged the Democrats' overtures. All the same, the powerful peace forces within the party (usually referred to as the COPPERHEADS) that wanted an immediate end to the war, had to be conciliated. So the party's managers yielded the platform and the vice presidential slot (filled by George H. Pendleton of Ohio) to the Democrats who demanded peace. By contrast, McClellan stood for the defeat of the rebellion rather than peace at any price. He did, however, concur on the need to restore the Union without emancipation or RECONSTRUCTION as preconditions and to preserve the Constitution without change.

With his distaste for politicians and political maneuvering, McClellan involved himself as little in the campaign as he had in the nomination process. Because of the glaring contradictions in the Democrats' policy as well as the Union's capture of Atlanta just a day after their convention, the Democratic ticket ran very poorly, McClellan winning only three states—New Jersey, Delaware, and Kentucky—for 21 electoral votes to Lincoln's 212. McClellan also failed to take more than a fourth of the soldier vote, although he did win 45 percent of the popular vote nationwide.

BIBLIOGRAPHY

McPherson, James M. *Battle Cry of Freedom: The Civil War Era.* 1988.
Sears, Stephen W. *George B. McClellan: The Young Napoleon.* 1988.
Silbey, Joel H. *A Respectable Minority: The Democratic Party in the Civil War Era, 1860–1868.* 1977.

MICHAEL PERMAN

MCGOVERN, GEORGE (b. 1922) Congressman, Senator, Democratic presidential nominee in 1972. A former college professor with a doctorate in history, George McGovern first served in the executive branch as an assistant to President John F. Kennedy, running the Food for Peace program. McGovern was then elected to the United States Senate, where he acquired a distinguished record in the liberal wing of the DEMOCRATIC PARTY. As Senator, McGovern championed (among other proposals) "a federally guaranteed right to a pollution-free environment," an "excess profits" tax on businesses, and a federally guaranteed income of $6,500 to every American family.

In 1968, McGovern made a brief bid for the Democratic presidential nomination. He was then chosen to head a commission charged with reforming the party's process of NOMINATING PRESIDENTIAL CANDIDATES. The McGovern-Fraser Commission, as it came to be known, helped shape the Democratic Party for years to come. On the positive side, it enacted a series of procedural reforms to ensure that party caucuses and primaries would be conducted in an open and fair manner. Much more problematic was the quota system it established for the selection of delegates. According to the commission, state delegations to the national nominating convention had to reflect the percentages of youth, women, and racial minorities living in the delegations' respective states. This scheme of political affirmative action would haunt the party in future elections by further splintering the Democratic coalition.

In 1972, McGovern again sought the Democratic nomination. Considered a long-shot, he confounded the pundits and won the nomination by gaining the support of disaffected youth, antiwar protesters, racial minorities, and feminists. McGovern's primary campaign is still worth studying because of its innovative use of emerging technologies to mobilize people at the grass roots. In California, for example, thousands of McGovern volunteers visited Democratic voters to find out what issues they were interested in. This information was recorded and then entered into a computer, which produced personalized mailings to the voters that stressed the issue that concerned them most.

If McGovern's primary campaign was a notable success, his general election campaign proved to be a fiasco. Dogged by miscalculation and error, it never really hit its stride. The campaign's first blunder was the choice of Thomas Eagleton as McGovern's vice presidential running mate without an adequate background check. It was soon discovered that Eagleton had been hospitalized several times for mental illness. When McGovern wavered on whether or not to drop Eagleton from the ticket, doubts were raised about McGovern's competence as a leader.

The campaign's second major misstep was its decision to send Pierre Salinger to Paris to hold discussions with the government of North Vietnam. This trip was criticized by some as of dubious legality, especially during wartime. When the newsmedia reported on Salinger's mission, McGovern at first denied any connection to it. When he later acknowledged his role in the affair, he looked duplicitous.

Despite these gaffes, McGovern's campaign supplied the nation with one of its clearest referendums on the new liberalism. Like Ronald Reagan in 1980, McGovern in 1972 offered the country an ideologically pure vision of change. In foreign policy, he proposed substantial cuts in the defense budget, an almost immediate pullout from Vietnam, a reduced American role in international affairs, and a larger foreign policy role for Congress. He also advocated amnesty for draft dodgers. In domestic affairs, he proposed federal income guarantees to every American, government-run health insurance, and higher taxes (particularly on inheritances). Only on some of the more controversial social issues did he waffle, such as the legalization of marijuana.

McGovern's clear-cut vision failed to convince the electorate, which voted to return Richard Nixon to office by a margin 61 to 38 percent. Nixon by all accounts ran a ruthless campaign. But Theodore White is right that Nixon's tactics were not the decisive factor in the outcome: "All the DIRTY TRICKS, all the dirty money . . . were as nothing compared to the massive exposure that television and the press . . . gave to what the candidates thought, said, actually did." The people had heard McGovern's call for a more active federal role in American society, and they had rejected it—resoundingly.

After his defeat, McGovern stayed in the Senate, but he was eventually unseated in 1980 in the Reagan landslide. Since then, he has tried to rekindle the enthusiasm he ignited in 1972, running again for the Democratic presidential nomination in both 1984 and 1992.

BIBLIOGRAPHY

McGovern, George. *An American Journey: The Presidential Campaign Speeches of George McGovern.* 1974.
White, Theodore. *The Making of the President, 1972.* 1973.

JOHN G. WEST, JR.

MCKINLEY, WILLIAM (1843–1901), twenty-fifth President of the United States. McKinley is a central figure in the institutional development of the presidency. During his term of office, the power of the executive expanded because of the impact of the SPANISH-AMERICAN WAR in 1898 and because of the changes that McKinley made in how the presidency was conducted. In key respects McKinley was the first modern President; his administration anticipated innovations that were developed under Theodore Roosevelt and Woodrow Wilson.

Early Career. McKinley came to the White House on 4 March 1897 from a career in Republican Party politics that had made him a national figure. Born in Niles, Ohio, on 29 January 1843, McKinley served with distinction during the CIVIL WAR and rose to the brevet rank of major; as a politician, he was known by that title. Following the war, he studied law, began a practice in Canton, Ohio, and served as a prosecuting attorney for Stark County, Ohio. He was elected to Congress in 1876 and served in the House of Representatives until 1891.

McKinley married Ida Saxton in 1871. They had two daughters, both of whom died in infancy. The experience made Mrs. McKinley a perpetual invalid who received constant care and attention from her devoted husband. As a leader, McKinley closed off important parts of his personality from public view and was a self-contained, impassive person. Though he was only five feet, six inches in height, he dressed and stood so that he would seem taller. During the 1896 presidential campaign, a British reporter described the mature McKinley as having a "strong clean-shaven face" possessing "clear eyes, wide nose, full lips—all his features suggest[ing] dominant will and energy rather than subtlety of mind or emotion." In fact, McKinley was often subtle in his methods and skillful in human relationships. As ELIHU ROOT, his Secretary of War, later wrote of him, "He was a man of great power because he was absolutely indifferent to credit. His great desire was 'to get it done.' He cared nothing about the credit, but McKinley *always had his way.*"

During McKinley's fourteen years in the House, he rose to become Chairman of the Ways and Means Committee. He identified himself with the doctrine of the protective tariff, the central Republican economic idea. For McKinley the tariff embodied the nationalism of his party and its willingness to use government power to promote economic growth. After he secured passage of the McKinley Tariff Act in 1890, he was defeated for reelection in a year when the Democrats made national gains. In 1891 he ran successfully for governor of Ohio and was reelected in 1893. Even financial complications arising from the personal bankruptcy of a friend did not cripple his growing national popularity. His ability to carry an important midwestern state, his record as a governor, and his standing within the party made him a logical contender for the Republican presidential nomination in 1896. McKinley launched his campaign for the White House in 1895, relying on his friend Marcus (Mark) Alonzo Hanna, a Cleveland industrialist, for the organization of the campaign. He secured the nomination on the first ballot when the Republican Party held its national convention in St. Louis in June 1896. His running mate was Garret A. Hobart of New Jersey.

The Republicans expected only a modest challenge from the Democratic Party, which was divided over the policies of outgoing President Grover Cleveland. Instead, the Democrats mounted a formidable campaign, choosing William Jennings Bryan of Nebraska as their candidate. Bryan, who advocated the inflationary doctrine of "free silver" as an answer to the economic depression in which the nation was mired, also captured the nomination of the agrarian-based People's Party (Populists). He energetically conducted a whistle-stop canvass that compensated for the Democrats' lack of campaign funds.

To counter Bryan, McKinley waged a "front porch" campaign from his home in Canton, speaking to 750,000 visitors throughout the autumn. The speeches he made to these audiences stressed the dangers of inflation from free silver and argued that the protective tariff would hasten the return of prosperity. McKinley came across as a calm, dignified spokesman for financial stability, economic growth, and a sound dollar. Meanwhile, Hanna used the $4 million that the Republicans received in corporate contributions to send out 250 million pieces of literature that sounded these same campaign themes. Hanna called it a "campaign of education." The electorate responded to McKinley's promises of gradual, moderate change, and he won the election with 271 electoral votes to 176 for Bryan. The popular majority of 600,000 ballots was the largest since the victory of Ulysses S. Grant in 1872.

McKinley's Administration. At the time McKinley came to the presidency, the office still stood in the shadow of congressional supremacy. The legislative branch had dominated the executive branch throughout the nineteenth century. Most members of Congress shared the view of Sen. John Sherman (R-Ohio) that "the executive department of a republic like ours should be subordinate to the legislative department." That relationship had gradually been changing during the preceding two decades, but Cleveland's presidency had slowed the trend toward more executive power. During the depression of the 1890s, Cleveland had sought to assert presidential prerogatives in dealing with the economic crisis but was so maladroit in his dealings with Congress, the public, and his party that he reduced the esteem in which the presidential office was held.

The President's relations with the press had also suffered. Cleveland disliked reporters and tried to discourage them from gathering news. Covering Cleveland's administration, said one journalist, was done "much after the fashion in which highwaymen rob a stage-coach." The gates of the White House were often closed to the public, and Cleveland made few public appearances during the last years of his term. Even the physical structure of the White House itself seemed in jeopardy. "The perfect inadequacy of the executive offices to the present demands is apparent at a glance," said a reporter in March 1897. The President had only a small staff, with only one private secretary to manage the six clerks who dealt with the several hundred letters that arrived daily.

McKinley selected his cabinet before he took office. It was not, at the outset, a body of distinguished men. Regional factors heavily affected the President-elect's choices. John D. Long of Massachusetts was selected as Secretary of the Navy; Joseph McKenna of California became McKinley's first Attorney-General; Joseph Gary of Maryland became the Postmaster General; Lyman Gage, an Illinois banker, was named Secretary of the Treasury; and a Republican fund-raiser from New York, Cornelius N. Bliss, became Secretary of the Interior.

The cabinet had two weak spots. The Secretary of War, Russell A. Alger, was selected because his fellow Civil War veterans liked him, not because he had any executive talent. An even greater problem was McKinley's choice for Secretary of State. That appointment became involved with the ambitions of McKinley's friend Mark Hanna. Hanna would not serve as Postmaster General and wanted to be a senator from Ohio.

Though there was no "deal" per se, McKinley persuaded John Sherman to leave the Senate and become Secretary of State, creating an open Senate seat and enabling McKinley, who was still governor of Ohio, to name Hanna to fill the vacancy. The problem with the aging Sherman was that his mental faculties were slipping and he was not up to the job. To monitor Sherman's performance, McKinley appointed a friend, William R. Day, Assistant Secretary of State. Though initially a mediocre, McKinley's cabinet improved as the administration continued and more capable men were found to serve.

Among McKinley's first actions as president were gestures designed to render the White House more accessible. The sentries around the executive mansion were removed. McKinley traveled more than any President before him, and he used these trips to sound the themes of his administration. PRESS RELATIONS also improved. He gave reporters a table on the second floor of the White House, and the President's secretary, John Addison Porter, came out twice each day, at noon and 4:00 P.M., to brief the newsmen about the day's events. Reporters could not interview the President directly, and no direct quotations from him were permitted, but this did not stop McKinley from chatting informally with reporters or leaking information that he wished the public to have. The President knew reporters' names and faces, and he held an official reception to which the press corps was invited in late 1897. As a result of these policies, McKinley enjoyed a high degree of favorable press.

The organization of the White House also became more modern and bureaucratic. Porter, McKinley's first secretary, was not as efficient as McKinley wished, and he gradually gave way to another White House clerk, George B. Cortelyou. Cortelyou was the prototype of the modern White House staffer. He developed a system for releasing official statements and presidential speeches in a way that made the White House a valuable news source. Cortelyou also arranged McKinley's tours, making sure that reporters had copies of the President's remarks and comfortable quarters from which to file their stories. As McKinley's de facto chief of staff, Cortelyou also managed the flow of presidential business.

Foreign Policy. During his first year in office, McKinley advanced several initiatives in foreign and domestic policy. He summoned Congress into special session on 15 March 1897 to revise the tariff. The outcome was the DINGLEY TARIFF Act, passed on 24 July 1897. It was a protectionist measure, but at the President's insistence the act also contained wording that authorized him to negotiate reciprocal tariff treaties with foreign nations. Expanded trade became a continuing concern of McKinley's presidency.

Faithful to a campaign pledge that he would pursue international bimetallism, McKinley opened negotiations with France and Great Britain for greater use of silver in world trade. The campaign collapsed in October 1897 because of British insistence on the gold standard. With support for silver declining in the United States and abroad, the administration moved toward the policies that culminated in the enactment of the Gold Standard Act in 1900.

In foreign affairs, there were perennial problems relating to the status of Canada and of the influence of Great Britain in North America. The President agreed to a joint high commission between Canada and the United States in 1898 that discussed the hunting of fur seals, the boundary between Alaska and Canada, and the fisheries off Newfoundland. Relations with the British improved as a result.

The status of the Hawaiian Islands also engaged the McKinley administration during 1897. Sentiment in favor of acquiring the islands had grown in the United States during the 1890s, and the issue of Japanese immigration to Hawaii increased pressure for annexation. A treaty was negotiated, submitted to the Senate, and debated when Congress met for its regular session in December 1897. McKinley used the power of his office to assemble a two-thirds majority for the pact but was still short of the needed votes as the war with Spain approached.

The Spanish-American War. The crisis that defined McKinley's presidency began over the Spanish effort to subdue a rebellion in CUBA that had broken out in 1895. The resulting SPANISH-AMERICAN WAR of 1898 has frequently been portrayed as an unnecessary conflict, which could have been avoided had McKinley exercised more skillful diplomacy. Such criticism, however, fails to recognize that genuine issues were at stake. Spain believed that Cuba was an integral element of the Spanish nation and that a withdrawal from the island would have been cowardly and immoral. The Cuban rebels, on the other hand, would not accept anything but full independence from Spain.

When McKinley took office, United States policy toward Cuba, as Grover Cleveland had defined it, allowed Spain to try to suppress the rebellion. That approach was unpopular with the American people, and it also discouraged the Spanish from attempting to resolve the conflict by other than military means. McKinley adopted a different policy. The White House insisted that any outcome had to be one that the Cuban rebels would accept. McKinley's policy toward Spain involved a gradual intensification of diplomatic pressure to induce Spain to leave Cuba peacefully. Spain, for its part, made it clear that it would not sacrifice its sovereignty over Cuba.

The issue reached a climax early in 1898. A series of riots against Spain's autonomy program in Cuba convinced the President to send the battleship *Maine* to Havana harbor to monitor developments. In early February U.S. newspapers printed a letter stolen from the Spanish minister to the United States that criticized McKinley personally and indicated that Spain was stalling for time. Then, on 15 February, the *Maine* exploded in Havana harbor, killing its officers and crew. The event aroused anger against Spain, with the U.S. public regarding Madrid as responsible for the tragedy or negligent in not preventing it. In March, McKinley learned that a naval board of inquiry investigating the matter would conclude that an external explosion was the cause of the *Maine's* destruction. (Modern research has concluded that an internal explosion was to blame.) The President pressed Spain for acceptance of the United States' demand that Madrid agree either to American mediation that would culminate in independence for Cuba or grant an armistice to the rebels. Spain refused and at the end of March returned a negative response to the U.S. proposals. The President began work on a message to Congress asking for authority to intervene in Cuba.

The document that McKinley transmitted to Capitol Hill on 11 April 1898 has become very controversial. Historians have charged that Spain had already given in to the demands of the United States and that war was thus unnecessary. On 9 April, after being pressed by other European governments, Spain did accept a suspension of hostilities with the Cuban rebels. That move, however, did not involve any political recognition of the rebels. Spain was trying to buy time without yielding on the key demand of Cuban independence. Spain had not given in to McKinley's position. Accordingly, McKinley's message to Congress said that "the war in Cuba must stop."

During its deliberations, Congress adopted the Teller Amendment, which stated that the United States did not intend to control Cuba. Congress also agreed that the Cuban rebels should not be recognized. The President was authorized to intervene on 19 April and the United States and Spain were soon at war. Throughout the war, McKinley exercised his power as COMMANDER IN CHIEF in ways that further enhanced the authority of his office. Overall direction of the conflict lay with the President. He established a War Room in the White House, filled with telephone and telegraph lines, display maps, and a staff of clerks to implement his orders. The President had the capac-

ity to transmit orders to his commander in the field in Cuba that could be received within twenty minutes. McKinley functioned on the principle that he should exercise "a close personal direction, not only of the organization of the forces but of the general plan of operations."

McKinley wanted to end the war as soon as possible and to persuade Spain to come to the peace table. He fought a limited war for limited purposes, and he pursued victories that would induce Madrid to negotiate an end to the fighting. One of his most important decisions came early in the war. On 24 April, McKinley ordered Commodore George Dewey to begin operations against the Spanish in the PHILIPPINES. Despite the legend that credits Theodore Roosevelt with ensuring Dewey's presence at Manila Bay, the attack order that McKinley issued was part of a longstanding naval war plan against Spain in the Philippines.

After Dewey's victory on 1 May 1898, McKinley took other actions that broadened the United States' commitment in the Philippines. The number of troops assigned to the islands rose steadily from five thousand in early May to twenty thousand by the end of the month. In his orders to his military commander, McKinley used his WAR POWERS to set out an elaborate program of military government for those parts of the Philippines that the United States controlled. These provisions included collecting taxes, setting up a legal system, and seizing property. Army and navy officers were also instructed not to deal formally with the Philippine rebels led by Emilio Aguinaldo. In furtherance of his Asian policy, McKinley used presidential influence to persuade Congress to annex Hawaii during the summer of 1898.

The fighting in Cuba produced a victory for the United States by mid July, and Spain sought negotiations for an armistice. In those discussions, McKinley demanded that Spain relinquish possession of Cuba and PUERTO RICO and leave the fate of the Philippines to a peace conference. Spain accepted an armistice on 12 August 1898. By the time Spain gave in, the situation of the U.S. forces in Cuba was desperate because of the ravages of sickness. McKinley had the soldiers sent home rapidly. He also appointed a PRESIDENTIAL COMMISSION to probe the condition of the army and its performance in the war. The panel deflected criticism away from the President, defusing the issue in what was an election year, and laid the basis for later reform of the army. The use of presidential commissions became one of McKinley's favorite tactics.

The situation in the Philippines was McKinley's primary concern during the autumn of 1898. He named William R. Day, who had been Secretary of

State, to lead the delegation to the peace conference in Paris. Three Senators were also in the delegation (the Senate would vote on any treaty that was worked out). The President had not yet publicly announced his own position on the Philippines. He had rejected Philippine independence under a U.S. protectorate, but he knew that taking the islands would outrage the opponents of expansion, who were now calling themselves anti-imperialists. In a "nonpolitical" speaking tour of the Middle West in October, McKinley rallied support for Republican congressional candidates and also prepared the nation for acquisition of the Philippines. In an address in Iowa, he said, "We can accept no terms of peace which shall not be in the interest of humanity." In this way he set the terms of the debate that followed.

On 25 October, McKinley told the U.S. delegates to the peace conference to follow the "one plain path of duty—the acceptance of the archipelago." McKinley supposedly told some clergymen a year later that he had received divine guidance in arriving at this decision. The story is a famous one, but the evidence for it is unreliable. Instead, he was following the logical consequence of the policy he had established in May. When the peace treaty was signed on 10 December, the United States acquired the Philippines, Puerto Rico, and Guam. Spain granted Cuba independence and received a $20 million payment from the United States as a face-saving gesture for its diplomatic humiliation. To win Senate approval of the treaty, McKinley wooed Democratic senators, a key voting bloc, by making a tour of the South in December. He made patronage promises and rallied state legislatures (which at that time still elected Senators) behind his treaty. Divisions among the Democrats and the support of William Jennings Bryan further aided his cause. The Treaty of Paris was ratified by the Senate on 6 February 1899 by a vote of 57 to 27, one more vote than the necessary two-thirds margin.

By the time of the treaty's ratification, Philippine rebels, under Aguinaldo, had begun fighting U.S. troops. McKinley had sent a commission to the Philippines in January 1899 to exercise control over the archipelago, asserting that the United States harbored "no imperial designs" on the islands. In the battles that followed, the United States gained the upper hand militarily and tried to establish a civil government, but the Filipinos kept on fighting as opposition to the war increased in the United States. Facing defeat in conventional warfare, the Philippine insurgents turned to guerrilla tactics. Nonetheless, McKinley dispatched a second commission, this one headed by William Howard Taft, to carry on the work of creating a civil government. Although charges that the U.S. Army was genocidal toward the Filipinos are untrue, atrocities and violations of the rules of war were committed by U.S. forces fighting the guerrillas.

The fate of Cuba was another concern. McKinley intended to honor the Teller Amendment, but he also worried about possible interference in Cuba by European nations, especially Germany. He instituted military rule to restore Cuba's economy and to lay a basis for civil government. McKinley always intended that Cuba, even when indepedent, would have close ties to the United States. This principle was embodied in the Platt Amendment to a 1901 army appropriation bill, which prohibited Cuba from allying itself with a foreign power and gave the United States the right to intervene to preserve a stable government.

Other foreign-relations issues. Other Western Hemisphere foreign-relations issues during the McKinley administration included the controversy over the boundary between Canada and Alaska and revision of the CLAYTON-BULWER TREATY with Great Britain concerning a canal across Central America. The Alaska question was not settled during McKinley's presidency, but he and his third Secretary of State, JOHN HAY, did work out the second HAY-PAUNCEFOTE TREATY, which cleared the way for an Isthmian canal.

The most notable issue concerning Asia was the OPEN DOOR policy for China that John Hay announced in September 1899. European countries involved in China were asked to preserve United States access to Asian markets. The open door policy became an important statement of United States interest in the future of Asia.

Domestic Policy. On domestic issues, McKinley played down the race issue and stressed reconciliation of northern and southern whites. The situation of African-Americans worsened. Growing fears about the power of big business and the rise of trusts did not translate into direct presidential action during McKinley's first term; he intended to be more activist on trusts in a second administration. McKinley made some changes in the CIVIL SERVICE that limited its growth. In response to the report of the commission that investigated the army, he eased out Russell Alger as Secretary of War in the summer of 1899, replacing him with Elihu Root. Root proved to be an important and effective administrator.

With success on the battlefield and the return of prosperity, McKinley's reelection prospects looked good in 1900. One problem was the death of Vice President Hobart, who succumbed to heart disease in November 1899. McKinley put off choosing a running mate until June 1900. At the Republican national convention in Philadelphia, he accepted the selection of Theodore Roosevelt as the vice presidential nominee. In keeping with the tradition that incumbent Presidents did not campaign, McKinley let Roosevelt make the appeal for the Republicans. The President meanwhile devoted much of his time to the situation of the Americans who were trapped in Beijing, China, by the Boxer Rebellion. Using the war powers broadly, McKinley dispatched several thousand U.S. troops to take part in the European relief expedition.

The campaign of 1900 ended in a smashing victory for McKinley. He received 292 electoral votes compared to 151 for Bryan, who had headed the Democratic ticket for a second time. McKinley's margin in the popular vote increased. "I am now the President of the whole people," McKinley said proudly. During the session of Congress that met from 1900 into 1901, McKinley persuaded the lawmakers to adopt the Platt Amendment and to grant him authority to provide civil government for the Philippines. One newspaper proclaimed that "no executive in the history of the country" had shown more influence over Congress.

Death and Legacy. McKinley had broad plans for his second term. He intended to break precedent by traveling to Cuba or Puerto Rico, and he wished to engage the trust issue more directly. He also wanted to address the tariff question through a series of reciprocal-trade treaties that had been negotiated during his first term and to challenge protectionist Republicans in the Senate over the question of controlled reductions of tariff duties. He made his first speech in that effort when he appeared at the Pan-American Exposition in Buffalo, New York, on 5 September 1901. He told his audience that "the period of exclusiveness is past" and that the nation must look to expanded trade and commerce overseas.

Standing in a receiving line the next day, McKinley was shot by Leon F. Czolgosz, an anarchist. The President died of his wounds eight days later, on 14 September. With the succession of the colorful Theodore Roosevelt to the presidency, McKinley's historical reputation began to fade. The war with Spain seemed a mistake in retrospect, and critics charged that McKinley had been weak and indecisive in that crisis. Later appraisals, however, have indicated that McKinley was a strong and purposeful executive. He used the war powers expansively, improved relations with Congress, and handled public opinion skillfully. He was the first modern President, and successors such as Roosevelt and Woodrow Wilson built on his innovations.

BIBLIOGRAPHY

Dobson, John M. *Reticent Expansionism: The Foreign Policy of William McKinley.* 1988.
Gould, Lewis L. *The Presidency of William McKinley.* 1981.
Gould, Lewis L., and Craig H. Roell, *William McKinley: A Bibliography.* 1988.
Leech, Margaret. *In the Days of McKinley.* 1959.
McKinley, William. *Speeches and Addresses of William McKinley from March 1, 1897 to May 30, 1900.* 1900.
Morgan, H. Wayne. *William McKinley and His America.* 1963.
Olcott, Charles S. *The Life of William McKinley.* 1916.
Trask, David. *The War with Spain in 1898.* 1981.

LEWIS L. GOULD

MCKINLEY TARIFF ACT (1890). Benjamin Harrison construed the election of 1888 as a referendum in favor of the protective tariff. Harrison had, by the standards of his time, campaigned vigorously for protection, and tariff revision became his highest legislative priority. Harrison's plan contemplated extending the protective system. It also dealt with continuing Treasury surpluses by eliminating duties on goods not produced domestically, reducing internal taxes on tobacco and alcohol, and increasing expenditures on military pensions, river and harbor improvements, and naval armaments.

William McKinley, chairman of the House Ways and Means Committee, led the tariff effort in a House of Representatives narrowly controlled by Republicans. Ever mindful of the need to solidify support among western Republicans, McKinley sought to extend protection to American agricultural products and to place sugar on the free list. McKinley's bill also provided for increased tariffs on certain manufactures and the payment of bounties to domestic sugar producers.

While the House considered tariff revision, Secretary of State James G. Blaine was attempting to open foreign markets, particularly in Latin America, to American agricultural products. Fearing that placement of sugar on the free list would jeopardize diplomatic efforts, Blaine proposed that the free sugar provision apply selectively to nations agreeing to reciprocal tariff arrangements. McKinley, who became an ardent supporter of reciprocity during his own presidency, opposed the administration's reciprocity effort, and the House-passed bill did not include such provision. The administration was better able to influence Senate action, and the conference bill did include reciprocity. Such provision enabled the President to suspend free trade on sugar and certain other agricultural imports, on a nation-by-nation basis, without obtaining further legislative approval or Senate treaty concurrence.

Democrats seized on tariff increases in the McKinley Tariff as a critical issue in the election of 1890, regaining control of the House of Representatives by an overwhelming majority.

BIBLIOGRAPHY

Socolofsky, Homer E., and Allan B. Spetter. *The Presidency of Benjamin Harrison.* 1987.

Stanwood, Edward. *American Tariff Controversies in the Nineteenth Century.* Vol. 2. Repr. 1967.

Terrill, Tom E. *The Tariff, Politics, and American Foreign Policy 1874–1901.* 1973.

RALPH MITZENMACHER

MCNAMARA, ROBERT S. (b. 1916), Secretary of Defense. Robert Strange McNamara was born in San Francisco on 9 June 1916. He attended the University of California, Berkeley, for his undergraduate studies and then went on to earn an MBA at Harvard University in 1939. After WORLD WAR II, McNamara was among the group of young army officers known as the whiz kids who offered their managerial services to the struggling Ford Motor Company. In November 1960, McNamara was named company president. He was the first man outside the Ford family to hold that position.

However, his tenure would not last long as President John F. Kennedy appointed him Secretary of Defense in January 1961. McNamara immediately made it plain that he intended to make drastic changes in how he would run the Pentagon. He rejected the role of mediator between the armed branches in which his predecessors had served. Arguing that the branches were grossly inefficient and often duplicating work, McNamara enlarged his staff and created central controls on intelligence information, through the Defense Intelligence Agency, and supplies and acquisitions, through the Defense Supply Agency. He established the planning-programming-budgeting system (PPBS), which was an attempt to limit waste and enable more accurate comparative cost analysis. These changes were highly controversial as his decisions often went against those of powerful Congressmen and military officers, but McNamara did not think that the military should have a free hand in the development of weapons and wanted to avoid an arms race with the Soviet Union.

McNamara's plan for NUCLEAR WEAPONS defense had two prongs. The first was the development of the capability to absorb a first strike; the second was the ability to launch a second strike of devastating proportions.

McNamara was also involved in the decisions of both the Kennedy and Johnson administrations that led to the escalation of the VIETNAM WAR. In spring 1964, Senator Wayne Morse (D-Oreg.) referred to the conflict as McNamara's War, a statement in which McNamara took pride. He was caught between the military who wanted a freer hand in the execution of the war and civilian advisers who wanted to de-escalate the operation. By 1967 more than a half a million troops were involved in the conflict.

Late in 1967 McNamara retired as Secretary of Defense and was replaced by CLARK CLIFFORD. In March of 1968 he assumed the presidency of the World Bank, a post he held until June of 1981.

BIBLIOGRAPHY

Shapley, Deborah. *Promise and Power: The Life and Times of Robert McNamara.* 1993.

Trewhitt, Henry L. *McNamara.* 1971.

JEFFREY D. SCHULTZ

MADISON, DOLLEY (1768–1849), First Lady, wife of James Madison. Dolley Payne Todd Madison's long tenure at the apex of the capital's social life—she had acted as White House hostess on many occasions for Thomas Jefferson—helped pave the way for an important public role for FIRST LADIES. During her husband's presidency she made a point of calling on all congressmen's wives who came to Washington, and she opened the President's House for weekly receptions, thereby making James Madison, who was reticent in social situations, appear more accessible. Most of the furnishings she chose for the President's House were destroyed in the 1814 burning but she arranged for some items to be saved and helped establish the responsibility of the President's wife for management of the Executive Mansion. Although she did not intervene in partisan disputes, she used her social skills to promote her husband's popularity, and historians have generally judged her an asset to him, particularly in his 1812 reelection campaign. Her success, resulting from her considerable personal charm and her reputation for being as solicitous of her husband's enemies as of his friends, helped reveal the valuable contribution that a presidential spouse could make to an administration. After her husband completed two terms as President, she returned with him to live at their Virginia home (MONTPELIER) but following his death in 1836 she moved to Washington, D.C., residing on Lafayette Square near the White House. Presidents and other notables called on her often, and she played the part of tutor and social arbiter to Presidents' families until her death. In 1911, Charles Nirdlinger wrote a play about Dolley Madison, *First*

Lady of the Land, that is credited with bringing the title First Lady into general use.

BIBLIOGRAPHY

Anthony, Katharine. *Dolly Madison: Her Life and Times.* 1949.
Clark, Allen C. *Life and Letters of Dolly Madison.* 1914.
Hunt-Jones, Conover. *Dolley and the "Great Little Madison."* 1977.

BETTY BOYD CAROLI

MADISON, JAMES (1751–1836), fourth President of the United States (1809–1817). Whether James Madison is, as John F. Kennedy once said, "the most under-rated President in our history" is a judgment still in dispute. The burning of the capital buildings in 1814 left a black mark against Madison's reputation, for despite his personal heroism at the time, he is remembered as being the incumbent at a time when the nation's pride was at low ebb. Yet when he left office in 1817 Madison's personal popularity was high, and it was only in the wake of historian Henry Adams's searing appraisal of the Jefferson and Madison administrations (published in 1889–1891) that Madison's reputation suffered. But, in Adams's view, both Thomas Jefferson and Madison were mediocrities; and we have to ponder why Jefferson has been subsequently honored as one of our best Presidents, and Madison left as Adams left him, a dismal chief executive who could not make up his mind.

Madison came to the presidency with the highest credentials when elected in 1808. He was Jefferson's handpicked candidate, a judgment confirmed by the congressional caucus that nominated him after only token opposition. Despite a vociferous campaign, mainly in the Republican and Federalist newspapers, Madison easily won over the Federalist candidate, Charles Cotesworth Pinckney, and a recalcitrant James Monroe. That Madison and Monroe remained friends is a proof of Madison's magnanimity, for in their home state Madison had 14,655 votes to 3,408 for Monroe. Republicans (also called Democratic-Republicans) easily captured both branches of Congress, too, but when Madison was inaugurated in March 1809 there was no HONEYMOON PERIOD, such as Jefferson enjoyed during his first seven years in office.

Madison's Credentials. Madison had been Jefferson's Secretary of State and served during the tense years when the war between Great Britain and France challenged the NEUTRALITY of certain countries, mainly the United States. Naval blockades, impressment of Yankee seamen, and seizures of American ships and cargoes had been a severe test of the Jefferson administration's effort to stay out of the fighting. But both belligerents ignored American rights whenever convenient, and in desperation an embargo act was passed in 1807 forcing American ships into port and bringing unemployment to sailors and low prices to farmers, whose products were shut out of the world market. When long-smoldering enmity surfaced in Jefferson's last year in office, particularly in the faction-torn Senate, he delayed action and after giving up on the embargo (because of public pressure) was a mere caretaker in the White House.

Madison perceived the need for action but was under pressure from his own party's leaders who had been an embarrassment to Jefferson in the Senate. William Branch Giles, a Virginia Senator, who had once been Madison's protégé in Congress, was a spokesman for a Republican faction that would plague Madison during his White House tenure. Even before Madison took office, the fractious coterie warned him that they would defeat any cabinet nominations that did not meet their criteria.

Madison, after all, had helped create the presidency through his service at the CONSTITUTIONAL CONVENTION in 1787. Madison went to that gathering with a specific plan after he had diagnosed the flaws in the Articles of Confederation and found that the nation could not survive with such a misbegotten form of government. Madison drafted a plan (known in history as the Virginia Plan) calling for a three-branch government with an executive, judicial, and legislative system balanced by checks on each section's powers. No man exerted more influence at Philadelphia that summer, but he had been disappointed that his idea of a federal veto on state laws was dropped by his colleagues.

Madison viewed the final draft of the Constitution as far from ideal. He hoped the presidency would not blossom into a pseudomonarchy. In his Republican view the office was not more powerful than the legislative branch, but a partner in solving the nation's problems. From his own days in Congress, where he had been a kind of majority leader from 1789 to 1797, Madison realized the limitations of the legislature but had great faith in the combined wisdom of the President and Congress. He had witnessed such a partnership during Jefferson's first term, when Republican political philosophy had been translated into action. The national debt had been reduced, taxes cut, and the federal budget trimmed of diplomatic and military excesses. The Federalist opposition had howled at the cuts, but heavy Republican majorities carried Jefferson's program through, and Secretary of the Treasury ALBERT GALLATIN was able to keep the program on course, even when the embargo drastically reduced federal income from duties on imports.

Madison's Cabinet. Gallatin had been Jefferson's second in command, and Madison would have probably elevated the Swiss-born Gallatin to the post of Secretary of State, had he not encountered damaging opposition within his own party. Through Senator Giles this group of jealous, ambitious Senators (known to colleagues as the "Invisibles" because of their behind-the-scenes opposition) sent Madison a message early in 1809 that they would not accept Gallatin in the State Department. Perhaps, if Madison had shown more courage and nominated Gallatin anyway, he might have become known as a tough-minded President and prevailed. But in this first real test of his resolve, Madison backed down and made an unfortunate appointment for Secretary of State. His choice, Robert Smith, had served in Jefferson's Cabinet (as Navy Secretary) and was a brother to one of the "Invisibles." But Smith was not qualified for the post, and in time Madison had to serve as his own Secretary of State. Other Presidents have done this successfully, but Madison did not. The Smith appointment, plus several other questionable Cabinet appointments, constitute one of the blackest marks against his presidency.

Gallatin was already Secretary of the Treasury and thus was not required to be reconfirmed by the Senate. Likewise, Caesar Rodney stayed as Attorney General, a holdover from Jefferson's Cabinet. But in selecting William Eustis from New England and Paul Hamilton of South Carolina to run the War and Navy departments respectively, Madison chose men of little distinction who simply gave his Cabinet geographic balance. Gideon Granger, who had been Jefferson's Postmaster General, was retained in that patronage-dispensing position as a loyal Republican. Granger proved to be more loyal to Republican powerbrokers than he was to his boss and was finally fired by an exasperated Madison.

Diplomatic Problems. There were other mistakes in judgment, and Madison eventually paid a price. Only a month after his inauguration, Madison was halfway tricked into calling off the ban on British commerce, then suffered the embarrassment of having to restore it. This diplomatic contretemps came after Congress passed the Nonintercourse Act after the embargo was dropped in March 1809. The law allowed American ships to go anywhere except to England or France, but the President was empowered to cancel the provisions relating to either warring power if it met American demands. An enthusiastic Madison was told by the overeager British minister, David Erskine, that England was ready to cancel its anti-American regulations. Madison promptly ordered trade with Great

Britain restored, and for a time it seemed the discredited embargo had worked, for Erskine's action was based on orders from London sent before the Nonintercourse bill passed.

The joy in Washington was short-lived. Erskine's hasty action was denounced in London, and the ban on commerce was restored; after being acclaimed as a peacemaker, Madison suddenly looked like a fool. Whether this diplomatic double-talk reinforced Madison's Anglophobic attitude is not certain, but from the autumn of 1809 onward his posture toward England stiffened.

While Madison wrestled with his diplomatic problems, he found it necessary to dismiss Erskine's successor. James Francis Jackson, the new British minister, was held responsible for the bombardment of Copenhagen during the Napoleonic Wars (1807) and was transferred to Washington, so Madison thought, to intimidate Americans after he quarreled with Madison and his Secretary of State over the Erskine fiasco. Madison's New England opponents defiantly feted Jackson, who, upon returning to London, reported that "Madison is now as obstinate as a mule." A Federalist congressman told a friend that Madison had become "a mere puppet or a cypher managed by some chief of faction . . . behind a curtain."

New England Federalists insisted that Madison was trying to manipulate the country into a war with Great Britain as a lackey for Napoleon and denounced the President as a "Gallophile Democrat" whose French prejudices were manifest. Napoleon, whose navy had been raiding American shipping, made gestures indicating his willingness to work with the neutral Americans; but in actual practice the French were as aggressive as the British, although limited by the Royal Navy from doing as much damage.

Part of the American weakness stemmed from the widely held perception that Europe needed wheat, naval stores, and lumber from the United States so desperately that the fighting powers would allow Yankee ships to roam the world's sea-lanes unmolested. A student of international law, Madison argued that neutral ships could only carry neutral goods and therefore their seizure by a warring power violated international law. Neither the British or French subscribed to this viewpoint. The British had issued in 1807 their Orders in Council, regulations calling for the examination and possible seizure of all neutral ships and goods headed for continental ports. Napoleon retaliated with his Continental System, a series of decrees condemning vessels headed for British ports.

Exasperated by events in Europe, Madison found some solace in a jingoistic movement closer to home. A small band of Americans living in West Florida, galling under Spanish rule, had seized control of Baton Rouge in the summer of 1810 and begged for American annexation. Madison shared Jefferson's eagerness to see Spain out of Florida, East and West, and after scolding the freebooters the President issued a PROCLAMATION justifying American occupation of lands west of the Perdido River. Spain was too weak to do anything, but Great Britain sent a strong note of protest that Madison chose to ignore.

The actions by France and Great Britain in the sea-lanes, however, could not be ignored. By 1810 hundreds of American ships had been sold as prizes, while French and English dungeons held American sailors from the seized vessels. Congress reacted by passing a law, known to history as Macon's Bill No. 2. The act abandoned the discredited Nonintercourse Act and offered Great Britain and France full trade rights in return for their recognition of American neutrality on the high seas, thus allowing American ships to go wherever they pleased without breaking the new law; yet if one belligerent agreed to the plan and the other did not, war would probably ensue.

As the Royal Navy dominated all ocean lanes, it allowed American ships into British ports while denying Americans direct trade with France and its allies. Trouble came when Napoleon found a cheap way to force the issue. Napoleon read Macon's Bill No. 2 and pledged to withdraw all decrees affecting American commerce, but the pledge did not solve the Americans' problem; Congress was required to act against Great Britain (since its Orders in Council were still in force). The British said Napoleon was simply taking advantage of the American law, and that he was in fact still seizing Yankee cargoes. In a letter from the Duke of Cadore, Napoleon's foreign minister, to John Armstrong (the American Minister in Paris), the French all but demanded that the British repeal their Orders in Council. Napoleon had called the American bluff.

Only a devious diplomatic intriguer could have seen the flaws in the American position, for the law provided that an embargo would stay in place against one belligerent but be withdrawn against the other that made concessions. Cadore's letter, written at Napoleon's command, was a put-up-or-shut-up diplomatic ploy. Were the French decrees really called off, or was this a French bluff to counter an American one? The British reacted predictably: where was the proof that the French had stopped pillaging American commerce? To Americans touched with more than an ordinary dose of anglophobia, the British reaction smacked of arrogance. If the American President accepted the Cadore letter at face value, then that was not to be questioned by the British cabinet meeting at Whitehall.

Madison was tired of British arrogance and eager to find a reason to force the issue. For three years of his first term, Madison used every available device to negotiate a settlement. The impressment of American sailors was an old grievance, inherited from the 1790s when the Napoleonic wars had begun. Indeed, the British cabinet regarded the issue as nonnegotiable: the impressed American sailors helped keep the Royal Navy manned. The British saw no reason to allow deserters (as they claimed) to jump ship and join an American crew. Another grievance related to the American frontier, where Indians, encouraged by British from their forts on the Great Lakes, were blocking the course of western settlement.

Trouble was brewing on the southern frontier, too, as East Florida became a refuge for smugglers and runaway slaves. These provocations furnished an excuse for intervening in the region. Madison sent a token American force to the area; the Spanish subjects rebelled and declared their independence. For a moment, the situation resembled the situation in West Florida in 1810. Madison, however, decided it was not time to rattle sabers. The episode ended when the Americans withdrew; the angry American commander claimed he had been double-crossed. Spanish control, weak as it was, remained in East Florida.

Madison eschewed the role of bullying a weaker power, for that was what he was complaining about with regard to the French and British. Eventually, the impressment issue and the concerns of the western settlers led a segment of American public opinion to call for war with Great Britain. Whether the so-called warhawks in Congress were the leaders or followers of this outcry is uncertain, although they were noisy enough. The newspapers and speeches of the time confirm a distinct anti-British attitude in Ohio, Tennessee, Kentucky, and the Northwest Territories that were nearing statehood. This feeling was inflamed by the Battle of Tippecanoe in 1811, fought in the Indiana Territory between American frontiersmen and the Shawnees led by Tecumseh. After the American victory, headstrong frontier politicians talked about a quick war with England that would yield Canada to American arms and lead to vast new lands for settlement. Now seen as a jingoistic delusion, it was a widely held belief among western Americans in 1812. One optimist in Congress predicted a swift occupation of Canada and declared he was ready "to receive the Canadians as adopted brethren."

How much attention Madison paid to the war talk is conjecture. As President, Madison wanted to avoid a war and return to the halcyon days of Republican peace and prosperity (before 1807). The chief stumbling block to Madison's goal seemed to be the British, after Napoleon took advantage of Macon's Bill No. 2. Napoleon had no intention of really changing his hard line. In short, he engaged in a ruse, but one that was difficult to prove. We now know that the Cadore letter was a spurious document (the letter was window dressing, for after its date the French continued to seize American ships and sell their cargoes, oblivious of any countermanding order that forbade such actions), but Madison wanted to believe that someone in Europe was paying attention to American pleas for neutral rights.

Political Maneuvers. Madison's troubles seemed to be piling up, yet the State Department staff of four clerks was not overtaxed with work. Messages sent abroad could be unanswered for six to eight months. Madison was accustomed to this leisurely pace and had learned to live with the long intervals that made diplomacy a matter of patience, prudence, and more patience. In such circumstances, Madison had passively permitted Congress to shape foreign policy. His practice from 1809 to 1811 was to stay in the White House until Congress adjourned, then head for his retreat in the Piedmont. At MONTPELIER, his home in Orange County, Virginia, Madison turned his attention to crops and plantation duties. When in Washington, DOLLEY MADISON, his wife, dominated the social scene with her weekly levees and evening entertainment for Cabinet members, Senators, and Representatives. Most members of Congress lived in boarding houses on Capitol Hill, but they welcomed a chance to visit the President's House; and while her husband's shyness made him retreat into a corner, Dolley Madison impressed visitors. A Senator's wife observed that "there was a frankness and ease in her deportment, that won golden opinions from all." Even the Federalists had to admit that the President's wife was full of charm.

Madison needed his wife's support, for after the Erskine offer turned sour Madison was the target of much abuse in the New England press; in Washington, Congressmen thought he lacked resolve. HENRY CLAY, the Kentucky Congressman who was rising to power rapidly, wondered if Madison could stand up to Great Britain. And although Congressmen were critical of Madison's policies, they avoided legislation to increase taxes and thus kept the army and navy budgets at a caretaker's level. The BANK OF THE UNITED STATES, chartered by Congress in 1791, became a political issue. The Republican majority in Congress insisted the bank was unconstitutional and did not renew its charter.

Madison avoided the bank recharter fight, although Gallatin saw that a national bank would be needed if war came to help finance loans and serve as a federal paymaster. The "Invisibles" helped to defeat the recharter of the bank, partly because of their hatred for Gallatin, who made a public effort to save it. Meanwhile, because Robert Smith made indiscreet remarks that Madison could not tolerate, he eased Smith out of the Cabinet and had to soothe Gallatin to keep him from resigning. Madison offered the post of Secretary of State to James Monroe, his old friend who had fallen out of favor and had run against him for President in 1808. Monroe, an experienced diplomat, proved his loyalty to Madison as he rejuvenated the State Department in preparation for a confrontation with Great Britain and France.

In November 1811, Madison showed that his patience was nearing an end. The British minister who replaced Jackson was Sir Augustus Foster, a handsome bachelor who cultivated the Federalist opposition and believed their rumors that the country would not stand behind Madison. Foster told Madison that the Orders in Council issued by the British cabinet would be revoked, and American shipping left unmolested by the Royal Navy, only if the United States would resist Napoleon's naval blockades. Foster also wanted the ban on British imports lifted, for he insisted the Cadore letter was a fraud.

Madison sent a bellicose message to Congress, saying that Foster came close to delivering an ultimatum. The British, Madison told Congress, were on a wartime footing against American commerce, making demands and "trampling on rights which no Independent Nation can relinquish." That argument struck home, but when Madison asked Congress to make preparations for war he found there was reluctance in both the House and Senate.

Reports of the Battle of Tippecanoe, widely reprinted and hailed in the western states as the prelude to a war, coincided with Madison's message to Congress. Meanwhile all the news from European sealanes indicated Napoleon had not called off his attacks on American shipping. Madison dispatched Joel Barlow as a special envoy to France to learn the truth, reminding the diplomat that "the late licenciousness of the F. [French] privateers in the Baltic, the ruinous transmission of their cases to Paris, and the countenance given there to such abuses, are kindling a fresh flame here." Once in France, Barlow was lost in a bureaucratic shuffle and his fact-finding mission was a total failure.

The nit-picking in Congress finally ended in the spring of 1812 with the passage of laws reactivating part of the barnacle-ridden American fleet and expanding the regular army. Madison viewed the legislation with misgivings. He wrote Jefferson that the lawmakers thought they were enabling him as President "to step at once into Canada," if war was declared. But the niggardly legislators refused to pass domestic tax increases and instead simply authorized Gallatin to collect higher tariffs and borrow more money. The lack of harmony in Congress reflected a problem Madison felt powerless to overcome; the "Invisibles" had allies in a nondescript band in the House known as "Quids," who were led by Madison-hater John Randolph, and a third faction took its calls from self-serving Vice President GEORGE CLINTON. Speaker Clay was not a White House intimate and found it difficult to bring all the contending factions together, since their only common ground was an effort to embarrass Madison and browbeat Gallatin.

Madison lost his patience. With the spring weather making a fast passage to England possible, he dispatched the courier ship *Hornet* to learn whether Great Britain was ready to repeal the Orders in Council. Madison's enemies thought the whole point was to force the country into a war against England; one Federalist Representative said that Madison was trying to ensure his reelection but that he would fail. "I believe Madison's Presidential career will close with the 3d of March 1813," Samuel Taggard wrote a New England friend.

Meanwhile, newspapers from Boston southward trumpeted the return of the *Hornet* as a turning point in American history. Clinton's friends were said to be predicting Madison's mission would end in failure and awaited a signal to replace him as the caucus nominee for the presidential election that fall. All seemed to depend on the message from Whitehall. Would the British change their belligerent tune? Where was the *Hornet*? asked editorial writers. "Ever since her sailing the cant word has been, the *Hornet*, the *Hornet*," bemoaned a Kentucky newspaper. "What a sting she will bring on her return!" Then George Clinton died on 20 April, leaving dissenting Republicans with no genuine alternative to Madison as a candidate. The congressional caucus, though poorly attended, met and routinely renominated Madison as the Republican candidate for President. John Langdon was picked as the vice presidential nominee, but he demurred and was replaced by another New England man, ELBRIDGE GERRY. Thus the Virginia-Massachusetts ticket gave the Republicans a North-South balance party leaders considered essential.

Far from Washington, an important political step was taken when a section of the Louisiana Territory was converted into the state of Louisiana. The admission of a slave state did not worry northerners as much as the question of West Florida, where a band of American filibusterers seemed intent on ousting the Spanish garrison and proclaiming the area part of the United States. Madison wanted Florida as much as Jefferson had but was not ready to offend Spain when a war with Great Britain loomed.

At last the *Hornet* came home, and on 19 May 1812, Madison had the bad news in hand. The British were conceding nothing; as long as the war with France went on, the Orders in Council would be enforced. Moreover, France was talking one way and acting in another. Jefferson had once considered declaring war on both nations, and the thought now crossed Madison's mind. "To go to war agst. both, presents a thousand difficulties," he wrote Jefferson—and to fight only England furnished the Federalists with new ammunition against his administration. Madison agonized over his dilemma until he finally decided that Great Britain was the worse offender, for although France had hurt American commerce, England's conduct had hurt American pride. In Madison's mind, a restoration of American morale was more important than a revitalized market for American products.

Declaring War. Madison wrote his war message, which was read to Congress on 1 June. (Jefferson stopped the practice of actually going before Congress, a custom that stayed in place until Woodrow Wilson broke it.) A clerk told Congress that the President had tried to negotiate with the warring powers to no avail. France's paper blockade was a real nuisance, but the British resorted to genuine power on the oceans so that "the great staples of our Country have been cut off, from their legitimate markets, and a destructive blow aimed at our agricultural and maritime interests." In effect, Madison wrote, through a licensing system that allowed English merchants to export to European ports while denying Americans the same right, Great Britain waged war "against the lawful commerce of a friend, that she may better carry on the commerce with an enemy." In addition, the seizure of American sailors, ships, and cargoes proved that "We behold . . . on the side of Great Britain a state of War against the United States; and on the side of the United States, a state of peace towards Great Britain." Then he threw the final question to Congress for an answer: shall all these wrongs be ignored by the United States, or should Americans take up arms "in defense of their national rights?" Madison thought he knew the answer. "The decision will be worthy [of] the enlightened and patriotic councils, of a virtuous, a free and a powerful Nation."

Congress debated the question. After three days the House of Representatives voted 79 to 49 for war, and not one Federalist was with the majority. In the Senate, the Federalists mounted a powerful opposition that fought until 17 June, when the tally of 19 to 13 was for war. No one in America knew that British manufacturers had been testifying to a parliamentary committee that the Orders in Council were hurting business, and that the British cabinet had offered to rescind the obnoxious orders almost at the same time as Congress debated the war declaration. It was too little, and too late. When Madison learned of the British backdown late in the summer, he rejected the proposal.

The WAR OF 1812 was at once popular in the West and denounced in New England. From the outset, the New England governors announced that they would not authorize the use of state militiamen (as the national guard was then called) outside the borders of the union. The commanders of the United States Army were thereby denied the disposition of thousands of trained men and forced to depend on a volunteer army and the militias sent from the South and West. Boston bankers were no more inclined to support the war. As Gallatin began resorting to loans, he found a discordant message from Boston banks. A paltry amount of the United States' treasury notes were purchased in New England throughout the war; a mere $75,000 was sold in Boston when Gallatin floated a $16 million loan. But as Henry Adams recorded, while they avoided U.S. bonds, "Boston [bankers] bought freely British Treasury notes at liberal discount, and sent coin to Canada in payment of them." In modern times this is called "trading with the enemy," but in 1812–1814 the Boston financiers simply regarded British bond purchases as a good business investment.

Nothing during the war worried Madison more than the New England attitude toward the fight for American nationhood. Convinced that the United States would be a second-rate power as long as the British treated its former colonies with punitive arrogance, Madison could not fathom the opposition of New England politicians, newspapers, and voters to a vigorous prosecution of the war. He must have known that Federalists in Washington were privately assuring the British minister that New England would stay on the sidelines, hoping Madison would commit ruinous blunders. In fact, Sir Augustus Foster went to the White House on the evening of the secret Senate vote on the declaration of war, where he spoke to Mrs. Madison and then noted the President himself looked "white as a sheet."

Conduct of the War. As in most wars, the early days were full of predictions for a quick victory: Canada would be easily overrun, and the British would be forced to sue for peace or see their empire crumble. No sensible person thought the pitifully small American navy was much of a challenge for the might of British battleships and cruisers, but Madison and his Cabinet apparently believed the Atlantic moat would keep seacoast ports safe and allow American troops to carry on their sweep unmolested.

Reality struck with full force at the news of a disastrous defeat at Fort Detroit. In June, Congressman JOHN C. CALHOUN had told his colleagues "that in four weeks from the time a declaration of war is heard on our frontier, the whole of Upper Canada and part of Lower Canada will be in our power." But news reaching the capital in late August told a different story. General William Hull had surrendered on 16 August, giving up hundreds of American prisoners without having ordered a shot fired. Stunned by the news, Madison saw all dreams of a quick thrust into Canada fade.

Madison was painfully aware that the backsliding opposition in New England had "so clogged the wheels of war, that I fear the campaign will not accomplish the object of it." The stubborn New England governors persisted in keeping their men near home fires and outside the line of fire from British guns, Madison knew he could not count on many electoral votes in New England. Nominated again by the 1812 congressional caucus, Madison did no campaigning but was peeved by Democratic-Republican DeWitt Clinton's attempts to form an alliance with Federalists. Federalists toyed with the notion of nominating a candidate, but backed away with the hope that Clinton might squeeze past Madison in the Electoral College, as the lesser of two evils.

Clinton won his home state of New York but damaged his chances by talking as a peace candidate in New England while pretending to be a warhawk in the South and West. "No canvass for the Presidency was ever less creditable than that of DeWitt Clinton in 1812," Henry Adams wrote, for besides his double-talk on the war, Clinton was tainted with a bribery scandal in New York. "Clinton strove to make up a majority which had no element of union but himself and money," Adams concluded. Voters saw through Clinton's campaign veneer, and in the key state of Pennsylvania Madison won decisively. That triumph sealed his victory, although the final tabulation was not made until early December. In the Electoral College, Madison had 128 votes to Clinton's 89. The President carried on by Vermont in the northern tier of states, but Clinton gained only nine ballots in the slave-holding states.

Madison left no record of his elation over reelection, but he must have been pleased to learn that his old nemesis, John Randolph, had lost his House seat owing to his opposition to the war. Republicans still controlled both houses of Congress, but Federalists sent a noisy opposition from New England. That region, loud in its condemnation of the war, was favored by the Royal Navy blockade, imposed in 1813, that stretched from the Connecticut River to New Orleans. Within his own party, there was grumbling, too. Henry Clay, never an admirer of Madison's, told Attorney General Rodney that he believed the President was "wholly unfit for the storms of War . . . he is not fit for the rough and rude blasts which the conflicts of Nations generate."

The surrender of Detroit had rankled Americans, and just as the country was shocked by Pearl Harbor in 1941, in 1812 the nation wanted to know whom to blame for the military failures. There were American scapegoats aplenty. General Hull was court-martialed and ordered shot, but Madison pardoned the old man, wishing for a competent general rather than vengeance. General Henry Dearborn, the senior army field commander, found his invasion route to Canada blocked and seemed to be settling in for a war of attrition rather than easy conquest. A three-pronged assault on the major fortresses along Canadian rivers turned into a gigantic fiasco. Secretary of War William Eustis, who had approved the ill-fated plan, resigned; his temporary replacement was James Monroe, who was also Secretary of State. Madison searched for a permanent Secretary of War who could command the respect of his officers and men and settled on John Armstrong, who had been with Washington at Newburgh and was well connected in Republican circles. Armstrong replaced the Navy Secretary, Paul Hamilton, an incompetent and a drunkard, with William Jones.

Jones was a shipper with a knowledge of business. The United States Navy consisted of three ships of the line, thirteen smaller ships, and a handful of privateers; but Jones knew the value of commissioned privateers, which could plunder British shipping in the West Indies. By the war's end, nearly five hundred Yankee privateers were authorized to capture British merchantmen. The British dominated the Great Lakes at the outset of the war, but a flurry of shipbuilding by Americans was soon underway. Jefferson had once said that gun for gun, and ship for ship, Yankee sailors were superior to their British counterparts. A handful of American naval officers were eager to prove Jefferson right.

Good news came when the *Constitution* destroyed the HMS *Java* off the coast of Brazil and the American frigate *Wasp* captured the *Frolic* off the Delaware capes; and by the middle of 1813 the privateer *America* had outrun Royal Navy squadrons while cruising between the English Channel and the Canary Islands, capturing forty-one prizes worth over $1 million in profits. Not to be outdone, the British issued special licenses for American imports to encourage New England shippers to defy their allegiance in search of profits. Madison learned of this trafficking with the enemy and asked Congress to pass an embargo forbidding all commerce with the British. The Senate held up passage of the law until December, giving full vent to the "cupidity and treachery" Madison tried to stop. New England Federalists reacted with more denunciations of "Mr. Madison's War."

Negotiations for Peace. Napoleon's invasion of Russia changed the diplomatic climate in Europe. Tsar Alexander I hoped to gain British aid in his struggle and offered to mediate a settlement of the nettlesome military sideshow in America. By the time Madison received the tsar's offer, the President also heard of Napoleon's disastrous retreat from Moscow. "We shall endeavor to turn the good will of Russia to proper acct.," Madison told Jefferson. He lost no time in appointing Gallatin and a Federalist Congressman as the American envoys, and they headed for Saint Petersburg before being confirmed by the Senate.

An attack of "bilious fever" laid Madison low; his wife nursed him, worried for the President's life. But he survived and then had to write Gallatin that the Senate had rejected his nomination. Madison reported to Gallatin that "the Senate have mutilated the Mission to St. Petersburg," but the American envoys decided to await developments rather than return to America.

Patience in diplomacy seemed to pay dividends, but at home the public was impatient for a military victory. After another crushing defeat at River Raisin, an American offensive carried the war into Canada with victories at York and at the Battle of the Thames, where Tecumseh was killed. Captain Oliver Perry's fleet defeated a British squadron on Lake Erie, while to the south Andrew Jackson led a band of volunteers that struck the enemy's Indian allies. But a full-scale invasion of Canada sputtered as generals quarreled and procrastinated until the summer passed by without any real gains.

New England shippers were infuriated by the embargo that cut off trade with Canada and England, and New England political leaders talked of a regional protest that would threaten ties with the union. British indifference to the tsar's offer changed to mild interest, but the British cabinet wanted to give the tsar no credit. Early in 1814, a surprising offer from London suggested direct negotiations at a neutral site. Madison seized this straw, directed the American negotiators to work out a settlement, and added Henry Clay to the peace delegation that finally met in Ghent. The British army, now freed of Napoleon's threat, was ready to send seasoned veterans to the American front if necessary, and the American diplomats knew it but were not intimidated. Napoleon's fall from power opened up European ports to American commerce, which Madison recognized by calling for repeal of the embargo. But instead of a wait-and-see posture, the Royal Navy tightened its blockade and closed American ports from the Gulf of Mexico to the tip of Maine.

Madison made a trade with his Senate enemies by moving Gallatin out of the Cabinet but keeping him on the peace delegation (his renomination was approved). Gallatin's Cabinet replacement, George Campbell, pleaded for money from Congress and was rewarded with approval of another $24 million war loan. A few Congressmen wondered aloud if the Bank of the United States ought to be revived. Then Madison learned his Postmaster General had handed a political plum to one of the Invisibles without clearing it with him. Gideon Granger was fired; then obstreperous Michael Leib was defeated for reelection to the Senate, weakening the Invisibles.

Madison's relief, after Congress adjourned, was temporary as he interrupted his summer vacation when the American negotiators in Ghent sought guidance. The British had wanted a buffer state created to protect Indians in the Northwest. Madison and the Cabinet opposed that and directed the Americans "to insert [in the peace treaty] some declaration or protest . . . on the subject of impressment." While the diplomats parried outrageous demands by the British, American armies tried to reinforce their hand with some victories on the Canadian border. After recapturing Fort Erie, the Americans defeated a superior British force at the Battle of Chippewa, then fought a bloody standoff at Lundy's Lane. Secretary of War Armstrong overstepped his authority and had to be reprimanded by the Commander in Chief; but when warned that a British invading army might be headed toward the nation's capital, Armstrong hardly bestirred himself.

Through the spring and summer of 1814 newspapers carried rumors of a land-sea invasion involving four thousand Royal Marines. In fact, British admirals and generals were planning two invasion fleets for the American theater—one to strike at Washington, the other to hit the teeming port at New Orleans. The combined force headed for the capital landed at Benedict, Maryland, unopposed, bullied its way passed a demoralized militia, and marched into Washington with only token opposition on 24 August 1814. Madison and his wife had fled, but the President rode around the outer defenses and tried to find a force to rally. After placing the torch to the White House, the Capitol, and other public buildings, the British withdrew and headed toward Baltimore. There, beneath "the rocket's red glare," the American defenses held and forced the British to abandon what had been seen as an easy conquest only a few days before.

Madison fired Armstrong and dismissed suggestions that the government retreat westward. American morale was not low, he learned; instead, the people were defiant. The blackened public buildings reinforced their resolve, and messages came from South and West urging the President to press into Canada for revenge of this insult to the nation. Madison called for a special session of Congress and pondered the last instructions to the peacemakers in Ghent. Madison had told them in June to forget any claims of territory and seek a peace that left things where they stood in 1812.

Despite some angry British overtures, the American firmness at Ghent led to a rapid settlement on most of the issues but left the impressment problem untouched. Fortunately, the American fleet on Lake Champlain smashed a British squadron and gave the nation something to applaud in the wake of the August embarrassments. Meanwhile, New England Federalists called for a convention at Hartford to shape demands that would discredit Madison; they passed measures meant to diminish the South's political power and to allow states to block federal laws through interposition. Failure to grant the convention's resolutions, the Federalists warned, would mean the calling of another meeting to decide on direct action. The threat was all too clear, and former President John Adams was ashamed that his home state had supplied the main thrust for this outburst.

Before the delegates from Hartford could reach Washington to deliver their ultimatum, a dispatch ship dropped anchor and sent to the White House a message that the war was over. The TREATY OF GHENT had been signed, leaving most matters where they stood before the war. In short, nothing was changed, except that most Americans believed that they had defeated the British once again. The chagrined delegates from Hartford hung their heads and were silent. Within weeks, a courier from New Orleans carried the news that on 8 January 1815, General Andrew Jackson's men had massacred the invading British. In the space of four months, Madison's fortunes had been reversed.

Madison sent the Treaty of Ghent to the Senate for ratification, noting that the war had been "reluctantly declared . . . to assert the rights and independence of the Nation." Gallatin returned home and noticed how the people reacted. "The war has renewed and reinstated the national feelings and characters which the Revolution had given, and which were daily lessened," he noted. "The people . . . are more American, they feel and act more as a nation; and I hope the permanency of the Union is thereby better secured."

Peace and the End of a Presidency. Madison too was revitalized. After learning that an Algerian despot was holding American sailors in dungeons and demanding ransom, Madison asked Congress to declare that a state of war existed with the Algerian regency and sent a punitive naval squadron to back up the words. He reshuffled his Cabinet, sent Gallatin back to France as the American minister and shifted John Quincy Adams from Saint Petersburg to London as the nation's minister at the Court of Saint James's. Reforms in the Navy Department were set in motion. While scaffolds surrounded the charred White House, the Madisons lived nearby in a borrowed house and talked about retiring to Montpelier.

When Congress met in December 1815, Madison reported that the war had cost about $120 million but called that a low price for the good produced in terms of "national rights and independence." He implied that the United States was now a full-fledged member of the world community, and ought to act like one. Once a bitter opponent of the Bank of the United States, Madison now told Congress a recharter might be a good idea. No longer was Madison waiting for Congress to propose improvements. He talked of a protective tariff, better roads and canals built with federal assistance (perhaps, he inferred, a constitutional amendment might be needed to accomplish this), and a national university. The war had taught Madison a lesson in executive leadership.

Congress responded with bills providing for higher taxes, the first peacetime tariff that favored American manufacturers, a subsidy for the Cumberland Road of $100,000, and after a bitter fight, passed an act to recharter the second Bank of the United States. Madison signed the last in April 1816. He also nourished the presidential ambitions of James Monroe and was pleased when the caucus nominated his Cabinet member to be his successor.

In his last State of the Union message, Madison reviewed his eight years in office and asserted that the nation was strongly committed to its Republican moorings and that the people lived under a government "whose conduct . . . may bespeak the most noble of all ambitions, that of promoting peace on Earth, and good will to man." In his last months before quitting public life forever, Madison vetoed a bill that would have used dividends from the Bank of the United States for INTERNAL IMPROVEMENTS. Madison still wanted a constitutional amendment to sanction outright federal funding of internal improvements. He had blinked at funding for the Cumberland Road, but a massive program of road and canal building was too much of a constitutional stretch for this Framer of the Constitution.

Madison probably had no higher accolade than that of John Adams. The crusty former President wrote Thomas Jefferson his judgment of Madison, the President: "Notwithstanding a thousand faults and blunders, his Administration has acquired more glory, and established more Union, than all three Predecessors, Washington, Adams, and Jefferson put together."

Madison, for all his illnesses and financial problems, returned to Montpelier and lived the rest of his life as a senior statesman and country gentlemen. He served at the 1829 Virginia constitutional convention briefly, but otherwise limited himself to a vigorous correspondence with public men in defense of the Union against the Nullifiers of 1833. Pressed to set an example by freeing his slaves, Madison was unable to give the idea of emancipation little more than lip service, although he did serve as president of the American Colonization Society, which established Liberia.

BIBLIOGRAPHY

Brant, Irving. *James Madison.* 6 vols. 1941–1961.
Ketcham, Ralph. *James Madison: A Biography.* 1971.
Peterson, Merrill D. *James Madison: A Biography in His Own Words.* 1974.
Rakove, Jack N. *James Madison and the Creation of the American Republic.* 1990.
Rutland, Robert A. *The Presidency of James Madison.* 1990.
Schultz, Harold. *James Madison.* 1970.

ROBERT A. RUTLAND

MANAGERIAL PRESIDENCY. The term *managerial presidency*, or *administrative presidency*, denotes an approach to presidential power that emphasizes control of the executive branch and its bureaucracies as a major means of achieving presidential priorities. It contrasts with a *legislative strategy*, in which an administration (such as that of Lyndon Baines Johnson) seeks to achieve its goals primarily by developing and passing legislation. The managerial approach is particularly associated with Richard M. Nixon and Ronald Reagan.

The roots of the managerial presidency lie in the creation of the executive budget in the Budget and Accounting Act of 1921 and the Brownlow Committee Report of 1937. The 1921 act created the Bureau of the Budget, and the Brownlow Report provided the rationalization for and legitimation of an active White House staff. The managerial approach reflected the reality that in the latter half of the twentieth century the President presided over a huge set of bureaucracies with more than two million civilian employees.

While the President has always been the titular head of the executive branch, the separation of powers system in effect gives the bureaucracies another legitimate boss: the Congress, which passes enabling legislation and appropriates funds that allow the agencies to carry out programs. Because of this reality and the existence of a merit system in which career bureaucrats keep their jobs when new Presidents are elected, Presidents have often been suspicious of the career bureaucracies.

Nixon consciously shifted from his early strategy of focusing on legislation when he realized that he would have great difficulty in getting the Democratic Congress to do his bidding. In the latter years of his first term and the first years of his second he put much more focus on the administrative tools at his disposal, including impoundment of funds, more careful scrutiny of political appointees, a major reorganization effort, and a program to make the bureaucracy more responsive.

The Reagan administration self-consciously learned the lessons of the Nixon administration and resolved to make control of the executive branch a major priority. It was particularly effective in ensuring that all political appointees, both presidential and agency-head appointees, were loyal to the President's priorities rather than to the programs that they would be administering. The Reagan administration was also very effective in using the Office of Management and Budget (OMB) to enforce its budgetary priorities. It use Cabinet councils of White House staffers and departmental secretaries to ensure White House control over policy initiatives. Reagan also issued executive orders to give political appointees in OMB unprecedented control over regulations issued by departments and agencies.

Some scholars have argued that the President is the country's political leader and thus should not be concerned with managerial details. But there are several compelling arguments for the managerial approach. The primary argument is that for presidential priorities and campaign promises to become actualized they must be implemented by bureaucracies. Public laws are not self-implementing, and presidential management of implementation can greatly affect how a policy becomes a reality. Another argument is that if Presidents do not pay attention to what their lieutenants are doing, they may get into political trouble, as happened in the Watergate affair and the Iran-contra affair.

BIBLIOGRAPHY

Arnold, Peri E. *Making the Managerial Presidency.* 1986.
Henderson, Philip. *Managing the Presidency.* 1989.
Nathan, Richard P. *The Administrative Presidency.* 1983.
Pfiffner, James P., ed. *The Managerial Presidency.* 1991.
Waterman, Richard W. *Presidential Influence.* 1989.

JAMES P. PFIFFNER

MANHATTAN PROJECT. The 1930s were marked by momentous discoveries in the quickly developing field of nuclear physics, perhaps the most startling of which was the splitting of the uranium atom by German scientists in 1938. Prominent physicists throughout the world realized that nuclear energy could be used as a highly effective and destructive weapon of war. The belief that Nazi Germany was pursuing the development of nuclear weapons led Albert Einstein, at the behest of fellow scientists, to urge President Franklin D. Roosevelt to undertake an American atomic bomb project. Roosevelt responded in 1942 by creating the Manhattan Engineer District, otherwise known as the Manhattan Project.

The Manhattan Project, organized under the auspices of the Army Corps of Engineers, was headed by General Leslie Groves, an officer with a reputation for effective administrative skills. The goal was simply stated: create a usable atomic bomb before Germany was able to do so.

The Manhattan Project was initially financed with contingency funds allocated to the War Department, and eventually through appropriations concealed in the War Department budget. Only a few members of the executive branch and Congress knew of the project. When Vice President Harry S. Truman assumed the presidency in April 1945, he was completely unaware of the project. Total expenditures on the Manhattan Project exceeded $2 billion.

The primary scientific research for the project was done at Los Alamos, New Mexico, under the leadership of J. Robert Oppenheimer. The scientists at Los Alamos were charged with the design, testing, and manufacture of the bomb. Two separate locations, Hanford, Washington, and Oak Ridge, Tennessee, produced the necessary fuel, plutonium and uranium

235. Work also took place at various minor installations and in university laboratories throughout the nation. At its peak, the Manhattan Project employed over 129,000 people, most of whom had no idea of the project's actual goal.

On 16 July 1945, the scientists and engineers of the Manhattan Project successfully detonated the first atomic bomb, a plutonium implosion device set atop a 100-foot tower. The blast was estimated to have released more energy than 20,000 tons of TNT. The success of the test led directly to the bombing of Hiroshima and Nagasaki a few weeks later [*see* ATOMIC BOMB, USE OF]. The bombs dropped on the Japanese cities were both made at the Los Alamos laboratory of the Manhattan Project.

BIBLIOGRAPHY

Cantelon, Philip L., Richard G. Hewlett, and Robert C. Williams. eds. *The American Atom: A Documentary History of Nuclear Policies from the Discovery of Fission to the Present.* 2d ed. 1991.

Groves, Leslie R. *Now It Can Be Told.* 1962.

Stoff, Michael B., Jonathan F. Fanton, and R. Hal Williams. *The Manhattan Project: A Documentary Introduction to the Atomic Age.* 1991.

ALLAN IDES

MANIFEST DESTINY. Manifest destiny is a phrase used by contemporaries and historians to account for American expansion across the continent in the 1840s. John L. O'Sullivan, editor of the *Democratic Review*, first used the phrase in the summer of 1845. Still the notion that the United States was destined, by the uniqueness of its civilization, to become a country of political and territorial eminence had broad acceptability. That concept of destiny flowed largely from a sense of mission that the country extend the area of freedom to its less fortunate neighbors. The power to triumph rested on the presumed superiority of American institutions. "Democracy must finally reign," promised the *Democratic Review* in March 1840. "There is in man an eternal principle or progress which no power on earth may resist. Every custom, law, science, or religion, which obstructs its course, will fall as leaves before the wind." Free institutions may reflect specific historical and environmental conditions, but the proponents of manifest destiny seldom accepted such limitations to the universal extension of sound and humane government.

Such convictions of destiny came easily to the American people in the 1840s. The Republic's dramatic industrial and commercial development, its immense productivity and energy, contrasted sharply with the absence of such elements of power and success in the vast regions toward which the hand of destiny pointed. Yet national expansion across the continent required something more than convictions of destiny. The regions into which the United States eventually expanded—Texas, California, and Oregon north of the Columbia River—were under the legal jurisdiction of foreign governments that were not concerned with American notions of destiny. The acquisition of these regions required the formulation of policies that encompassed the precise definition of ends and the wielding of adequate means. Manifest destiny doctrine neglected completely the question of means; it contemplated no reliance on either power or diplomacy. Nor did it recognize any particular need to define ends.

Expansionists agreed that the country was destined to reach its natural limits. But aside from the Pacific Ocean there were none. The concept of destiny—the extension of the area of freedom—recognized no bounds. Quite typically O'Sullivan noted in the New York *Morning News* on 27 December 1845, that it had become "our manifest destiny to occupy and to possess the whole of the Continent which Providence has given us." Manifest destiny created an attractive vision for an ambitious, democratic people; it hardly explained the sweep of the United States across the continent. The actual territorial goals that the U.S. government pursued in its diplomacy with Texas, Mexico, and Great Britain between 1845 and 1848 were precise and totally unrelated to any universal concepts of destiny.

For national leaders in the 1840s the burden of policy-making lay in defining boundaries in the West, achievable at reasonable cost, that would best serve the country's anticipated needs. In Texas the Polk administration designated the Rio Grande as the national objective, claiming that river as the traditional boundary separating Texas from the north Mexican states [*see* TEXAS, ANNEXATION OF]. That boundary Mexico refused to concede peacefully. It was formally established only after the MEXICAN WAR. In Oregon the American objective had been clarified and proclaimed with consistency from the boundary dispute with Great Britain in 1818 until the Oregon settlement of 1846. That objective comprised the magnificent harbor of Puget Sound with access through the Strait of Juan de Fuca. The American demand for the extension of the forty-ninth parallel to the Pacific reflected the realization that such a settlement would convey the desired waterways to the United States [*see* OREGON TREATY].

American purposes in California, unlike those in

Oregon, were not formulated over time through public debate and diplomatic proposals. Still U.S. interests in California were no less precise than those in Oregon. They evolved slowly within the Cabinet; as in Oregon they were fashioned by the sea. Travelers and hide traders had defined what mattered on that coast—the marvelous harbors of San Francisco and San Diego. These specific objectives President Polk managed to gain through the diplomatic efforts of Nicholas P. Trist, his agent in Mexico, that concluded the Mexican War. To the extent that the rhetoric of manifest destiny created an expansive mood in the country, it contributed to the success of continental expansion. No one would deny that favorable public opinion is essential for the conduct of foreign policy in a democracy.

BIBLIOGRAPHY

Adams, Ephraim D. *The Power of Ideals in American History*. 1913.
Graebner, Norman A. *Manifest Destiny*. 1968.
Merk, Frederick. *Manifest Destiny and Mission in American History: A Reinterpretation*. 1963.
Weinberg, Albert K. *Manifest Destiny: A Study of Nationalist Expansionism in American History*. 1935.

NORMAN A. GRAEBNER

MANN-ELKINS ACT (1910).

The Mann-Elkins Act originated in the 1908 Republican campaign promises to increase railroad regulation. As originally proposed by the Taft administration, the bill would have enabled the Interstate Commerce Commission (ICC) to supervise railroad securities and suspend railroad-rate advances pending investigation, legalized traffic or pooling agreements between competitors, and created a commerce court to review ICC decisions. Opposed to pools and a commerce court, insurgent Progressives killed the original bill in committee and rallied around a new bill that Congress passed.

The Mann-Elkins Act (named for its sponsors, who were the heads of the appropriate House and Senate committees), while not mentioning legalized pooling, allowed railroads to continue to set rates by concerted action. But it also empowered the ICC to suspend them for up to ten months, pending an investigation, and required that the railroads prove the reasonableness of both proposed increases and original rates. In addition, the act strengthened the prohibition of the long-and-short-haul abuse and extended the ICC's jurisdiction to include telegraph, telephone, and cable lines. Despite the desire of President William Howard Taft, the act merely called for investigation, rather than federal supervision, of railroad finances; but, because of his wishes, it established the Commerce Court.

The Mann-Elkins Act simultaneously strengthened and weakened the ICC. The act weakened the commission by creating the Commerce Court, a superior ICC, that tended to reverse the ICC's antirailroad decisions, which were then again reversed by the Supreme Court. Congress killed the Commerce Court in 1913.

BIBLIOGRAPHY

Hoogenboom, Ari, and Olive Hoogenboom. *A History of the ICC: From Panacea to Palliative*. 1976.
Martin, Albro. *Enterprise Denied: Origins of the Decline of American Railroads, 1897–1917*. 1971.
Sharfman, I. L. *The Interstate Commerce Commission: A Study in Administrative Law and Procedure* 5 vols. 1931–1937.

ARI HOOGENBOOM and OLIVE HOOGENBOOM

MARBURY v. MADISON

1 Cranch 137 (1803). This case, the first in which the U.S. Supreme Court held an act of Congress unconstitutional, oozed politics, underscoring the conflict between President Thomas Jefferson, a Democratic-Republican, and the wholly Federalist Supreme Court under Chief Justice John Marshall.

In December 1801 the Supreme Court issued an order commanding James Madison, Jefferson's Secretary of State, to show cause why it should not issue a writ of mandamus compelling him to deliver to William Marbury his commission as a justice of the peace for the District of Columbia. Jeffersonian Republicans regarded that show-cause order as "a bold stroke against the Executive"; the majority leader of the Senate called it "the most daring attack which the annals of Federalism have yet exhibited."

In the final days of his presidency, John Adams had appointed the so-called MIDNIGHT JUDGES; all Federalists, they staffed the new circuit courts and other positions provided by two judiciary acts of 1801, including the extraordinary number of forty-two justices of the peace for the District of Columbia. President Jefferson, regarding the judiciary acts as partisan, believed that the Federalists had "retired into the judiciary as a stronghold . . . and from that battery all the works of republicanism are to be beaten down and erased." Instead of responding in kind by enlarging the size of the federal courts and packing them with Jeffersonians, the administration instructed a compliant Congress to repeal the Judiciary Act of 1801, eliminating the lifetime offices held by the circuit judges and therefore requiring Supreme Court Justices to return to circuit duty. Jefferson temperately reappointed twenty-three of Adams's justices of the peace, not including Marbury. A lame-duck Senate had previously confirmed Marbury; Adams had signed his commission, and Marshall, who was the outgoing Secretary of State, had affixed to it the seal of the United States. But Marshall left office on the night of 3 March 1801 without having had time to deliver all the commissions, which the new administration destroyed.

Although the Supreme Court Justices returned to circuit duty after revocation of the Judiciary Act of 1801, *Marbury* remained a political sensation. A few days before the Court's 1803 term began, the Senate defeated a motion requiring it to produce its confirmation records. An administration stalwart declared that the Senate would not interfere in a case that might lead to judicial impeachments that the Senate would decide. Jefferson ordered the impeachment of a federal district court judge, and all Washington knew that Justice Samuel Chase of the Supreme Court was next in line. A Jeffersonian paper, the Boston *Independent Chronicle* editorialized, "The attempt of the Supreme Court . . . by a mandamus, to control the Executive functions, is a new experiment. It seems to be no less than a commencement of war. . . . The Court must be defeated and retreat from the attack; or march on, till they incur an impeachment and removal from office."

In his 1803 opinion in *Marbury v. Madison*, Chief Justice Marshall searched for a way to speak his mind while at the same time avoiding embarrassment for his Court and possible impeachment were he to issue the writ commanding Madison to deliver the commission, which Madison would surely ignore. He cleverly exercised judicial restraint, ruling that the Court was powerless to issue the writ, but he did not reach the subject of the Court's incapacity until after he had chastised the administration for having acted as if they were Stuart tyrants, above the law, in "sporting away" Marbury's "vested legal right" to his job. Marshall saw nothing in the "exalted station" of the executive officer that should bar a citizen from asserting his legal rights in court or that should forbid a court from upholding those rights.

Marshall made an important distinction between political acts of the executive, with which the Court could not interfere, and ministerial acts that allowed no executive discretion, such as the obligation to deliver a sealed commission. A court could compel performance of a ministerial act, but in this case the Supreme Court, said Marshall, could not issue the writ because although the case had originated in the Court it did not fall within one of the two categories of cases of original jurisdiction fixed by Article III of the Constitution. Congress, Marshall declared, had unconstitutionally sought to augment the Court's original jurisdiction by Section 13 of the Judiciary Act of 1789, which authorized the Court to issue writs of mandamus. But Marshall was wrong: the act had not expressly added to the Court's original jurisdiction; it merely authorized the Court to issue the writ in cases "warranted by the principles and usages of law."

This was the first ruling by the Court that held an act of Congress to be unconstitutional, but the act was one whose constitutionality had never been questioned before the Court. The First Congress, dominated by Framers of the Constitution, had passed the act, which Oliver Ellsworth, Marshall's predecessor, had drafted.

The Court's ruling revealed political adroitness, ingenuity, and discretion. In its story on *Marbury*, a Federalist newspaper, the *New York Post,* used the headline, "Constitution Violated by the President." The report depicted Jefferson as a "hypocritical" apostle of civil liberty who had behaved in a "criminal" and "unprincipled" way to violate a man's "sacred right of private property." Jefferson chafed at *Marbury,* but Marshall had left him strait-jacketed: Madison had won the case, because the Court had denied the writ.

Marbury scarcely merits its historic reputation. Marshall's opinion for a unanimous Court was a partisan coup that involved a narrow exercise of judicial review, for the Court claimed that it could not accept an enhancement of its own jurisdiction in a matter touching the performance of its own duties. The Court claimed no broad power of judicial review and did not dare hold unconstitutional an act of Jefferson's administration. Only six days after *Marbury* the Court, in *Stuart v. Laird* (1803), sustained as constitutional an act that violated the Constitution, the Jeffersonian Judiciary Act of 1802 that repealed the life-tenure jobs of sitting circuit judges. Marshall, who knew when and how to hit and run, never again during his long tenure on the bench (which lasted until 1835) held an act of Congress to be unconstitutional.

BIBLIOGRAPHY

Clinton, Robert L. *Marbury v. Madison and Judicial Review.* 1989.

Haskins, George L., and Herbert A. Johnson. *History of the Supreme Court of the United States.* Vol. 2: *Foundations of Power: John Marshall, 1801–15.* 1981.

Van Alstyne, William W. "A Critical Guide to Marbury v. Madison." *Duke Law Journal* (1969): 1–47.

LEONARD W. LEVY

MARQUE AND REPRISAL. Since the Middle Ages sovereigns had authorized private armies to wage hostilities against other sovereigns by granting letters of marque and reprisal. By 1787 the Framers of the Constitution understood the marque-and-reprisal power to encompass authorizing a range of military hostilities below the threshold of a publicly declared war. Both James Madison and ALEXANDER HAMILTON believed that authorizing reprisals was a belligerent act that belonged exclusively to Congress. The United States Constitution grants to Congress all the power to initiate war and lesser military hostilities. Article I, Section 8, vests in Congress the power to declare war, grant letters of marque and reprisal, and make rules concerning captures on land and water. The Framers granted Congress these powers to assure that the President, as COMMANDER IN CHIEF, could not initiate hostilities without legislative authorization.

The Framers believed that Congress, as a representative institution, should control such important decisions as committing the nation's blood and treasure to foreign wars. "[W]hen the Framers granted to Congress the power to declare war," writes David Adler, "they were vesting in that body the sole and exclusive prerogative to initiate military hostilities on behalf of the American people." The Framers also believed that it should be more difficult to wage war than conclude the peace. During the CONSTITUTIONAL CONVENTION both Oliver Ellsworth and George Mason expressed the view that neither the President nor the Senate alone should be entrusted with the power to wage offensive war. As they understood, in a constitutional democracy the nation cannot wage war or hostilities without a democratic consensus.

Prior to 1787 the European powers fought numerous undeclared wars and engaged in military hostilities, some of which involved the North American colonies. Despite the Framers' familiarity with these practices, they did not provide for unilateral presidential commitment of the nation's armed forces to war, whether declared or undeclared. By vesting the marque-and-reprisal power in Congress, they acknowledged exclusive congressional power to determine the scope and duration of limited hostilities against other nations to redress grievances. With this grant of power, the Framers intended to vest limited as well as general warmaking in Congress rather than the President.

During the years 1798 to 1799 Congress enacted more than twenty laws authorizing limited naval war against France. Exercising its power of marque and reprisal as well the power to make rules concerning captures, Congress authorized taking prizes under certain conditions. In *Bas v. Tingy* (1800) the Supreme Court recognized congressional power to authorize and control limited as well as declared wars. In a concurring opinion, Justice Salmon P. Chase noted that Congress is empowered to wage limited war: "limited in place, in objects, and in time." If Congress decides to authorize limited war, its extent and operation depend on domestic statutes.

Although the marque-and-reprisal power may seem anachronistic today, U.S. support for recent covert hostilities and paramilitary forces in Afghanistan and Central America are modern parallels of the medieval practice of hiring private armies. As Jules Lobel argues, modern covert wars should be treated as functional equivalents of private, undeclared wars in the eighteenth century. Today the CENTRAL INTELLIGENCE AGENCY (CIA) employs paramilitary forces to carry out U.S. foreign policy. In Afghanistan and Central America the United States employed the Afghan mujahedin and the Nicaraguan contras as surrogate forces because it wanted to provide credible deniability of any military involvement. Because these forces are surrogates, Congress can control the decision to initiate and support covert military operations by exercising its power of marque and reprisal as well as its foreign-affairs powers.

BIBLIOGRAPHY

Adler, David. "The Constitution and Presidential Warmaking: The Enduring Debate." *Political Science Quarterly* 103 (1988): 1–36.

Keynes, Edward. *Undeclared War: Twilight Zone of Constitutional Power*. 1991.

Lobel, Jules. "Covert War and Congressional Authority: Hidden War and Forgotten Power." *University of Pennsylvania Law Review* 134 (1986): 1035–1110.

Reveley, W. Taylor, III. *War Powers of the President and Congress: Who Holds the Arrows and Olive Branch*. 1981.

Sofaer, Abraham D. *War, Foreign Affairs, and Constitutional Power: The Origins*. 1976.

EDWARD KEYNES

MARSHALL, GEORGE C. (1880–1959), U.S. Army Chief of Staff, Secretary of State, Secretary of Defense. George Catlett Marshall, Jr.'s half-century of public service coincided with the rise of the United States to global leadership. Commissioned as an army lieutenant in 1902, Marshall served in WORLD WAR I as a training and operations officer of the first U.S. division to engage in battle in France; as chief of operations of the First Army he planned the final American offensive. As the senior aide to General John J. Pershing while Pershing was U.S. Army Chief of Staff (1921–1924), Marshall became familiar with the workings of the White House and Congress.

In 1935, Pershing urged President Franklin D. Roosevelt to make Marshall a brigadier general, and a few months later Marshall had a brigade and one-star rank. He came to Washington, D.C., as Chief of War Plans in 1938, and soon became Deputy Chief of Staff. Impressed by Marshall, Roosevelt named him U.S. Army Chief of Staff in the spring of 1939, a post he assumed on 1 September, the day WORLD WAR II began in Europe. He remained in that position, one of the chief military advisers to the President, until November 1945.

As U.S. Army Chief of Staff (a role that, until after the war, included supervision of army air forces), Marshall appeared often before congressional committees to explain the President's program for expanding the army. (The number of army and army air force personnel increased during his tenure from 230,000 to more than eight million by war's end.) As a leading member of the JOINT CHIEFS OF STAFF, he accompanied the President to the great Allied Conferences on war strategy. He strongly supported Roosevelt's Europe First strategy and was the main proponent of a cross-Channel (direct) drive against the Germans as opposed to the British-backed Mediterranean (indirect) approach. In the early fall of 1943, Roosevelt let it be known that he wanted Marshall to lead the Allied forces in the invasion of Europe, but by December, in Cairo, after the date for the Normandy invasion had been pinpointed for spring 1944, Roosevelt began to ask Marshall what post he wanted. When Marshall insisted that his desires as to the command should not be considered, Roosevelt declared that he could not sleep if Marshall were out of the country. General Dwight D. Eisenhower was named to the supreme command.

After Roosevelt's death in spring 1945, the new President, Harry S. Truman, who as a Senator had worked with Marshall on army contracts, eagerly turned to him for advice. Within a week of Marshall's retirement as Chief of Staff in November, Truman asked him to head a mission to China to try to arrange a cease-fire between the Nationalists and the Communists. After a year of frustration in China, Marshall asked to be called home. Truman then named him to replace JAMES F. BYRNES as Secretary of State.

Secretary of State Marshall's first task was to attend the foreign ministers' conference in Moscow, where he found that the problem of achieving treaties with Germany and Austria was being complicated by growing tension between the Soviet Union and the West and by economic chaos in Europe. Marshall returned to the United States convinced that something must be done about Europe's collapsing economy.

In a speech at Harvard University on 5 June 1947, Marshall set forth a general strategy for solving Europe's problems. Truman named this proposal for European economic recovery the MARSHALL PLAN. Marshall's main contribution in helping to push the legislation for the plan through the Republican-controlled Congress was to work on a nonpartisan basis with moderate Republicans such as JOHN FOSTER DULLES and Senator Arthur Vandenberg of Michigan.

Kidney disease forced Marshall to return from a United Nations meeting in Paris in 1948. His kidney was removed, and he resigned a month later. While he was recuperating in 1949, Truman asked him to accept the presidency of the American Red Cross. He hardly had time to assume that position before the KOREAN WAR broke out and Truman called him to replace Louis Johnson as Secretary of Defense. The weary Marshall agreed to serve but limited his commitment to no more than one year; he also asked that Robert A. Lovett be appointed his deputy, with the understanding that Lovett would handle details and eventually take over the job. Truman used Marshall's prestige to answer criticism, rebuild the armed forces, and ensure U.N. armed support in Korea. Marshall proved most useful in his support of Truman's unpopular decision in 1951 to remove General Douglas MacArthur from command in Korea. He was the chief administration witness before the subsequent congressional inquiry, stoutly upholding the principle of civilian control of military forces. In September 1951, Secretary Marshall submitted his final resignation. Two years later he was awarded the Nobel Peace Prize.

BIBLIOGRAPHY

Cray, Ed. *George C. Marshall, Soldier Statesman*. 1990.
Marshall, George C. *The Papers of George Catlett Marshall*. Edited by Larry I. Bland with Sharon R. Ritenour. Vol. 1. 1981. Other volumes forthcoming.
Pogue, Forrest C. *George C. Marshall*. 4 vols. 1963–1987.

FORREST C. POGUE

MARSHALL, JOHN (1755–1835), Secretary of State, Chief Justice of the United States. Marshall's career paralleled seven presidencies. George Washington, an old family friend, was a major influence on Marshall. Like Washington in the 1780s, Marshall was demoralized by the tumultuousness of state politics and the national government's ineffectiveness. He strongly supported the new Constitution and emerged as a leading Virginia Federalist. He rejected overtures to run for Congress and declined Washington's offer to make him ATTORNEY GENERAL in 1795. Similarly, he refused John Adams's offer to be minister to France in 1796, although in 1797 he joined the Paris peace mission that culminated in the XYZ affair. Marshall declined Adams's offer of a Supreme Court seat in 1798; instead, he successfully ran for Congress. During his term, he broke party ranks to vote for repeal of the section of the Sedition Act that provided punishment for seditious speech [see ALIEN AND SEDITION ACTS].

In 1800, Adams prevailed on Marshall to become Secretary of State, after the Virginian had rejected appointment as Secretary of War. When Chief Justice Oliver Ellsworth resigned in December 1800, Adams quickly nominated JOHN JAY to replace him, but Jay, who had been the first Chief Justice, refused to serve again. On 20 January 1801, Adams surprised most of his party and angered the opposition by appointing Marshall. Thomas Jefferson, Marshall's kinsman, had long distrusted Marshall, complaining to Madison in 1798 of Marshall's "profound hypocrisy."

During Marshall's tenure on the Court, he conflicted with Jefferson in the landmark case of MARBURY v. MADISON (1803), yet he silently acquiesced when the Court approved the Jeffersonians' abolition of newly created circuit courts in *Stuart v. Laird* (1803). In retirement, James Madison let it be known that he agreed with Marshall's views on national power and judicial review. Marshall openly challenged President Andrew Jackson on the removal of the Georgia Cherokees, but contrary to legend, Jackson never said that "John Marshall had made his decision; now let him enforce it." With understandable pride, Adams said that "my gift of John Marshall to the people of the United States was the proudest act of my life."

BIBLIOGRAPHY

Beveridge, Albert. *The Life of John Marshall.* 4 vols. 1916–1919.
Kutler, Stanley I., ed. *John Marshall.* 1972.

STANLEY I. KUTLER

MARSHALL, THOMAS R. (1854–1925), twenty-eighth Vice President of the United States (1913–1921). Thomas Riley Marshall was, with little doubt, the wittiest person ever to serve as VICE PRESIDENT, a man who took neither himself nor his office too seriously. Ironically, his term included one of the most trying experiences any Vice President ever endured.

Marshall was born on 14 March 1854 in North Manchester, Indiana. A lawyer, Marshall never held political office until 1908 when he was narrowly elected governor of Indiana. Four years later, Marshall was considered a DARK HORSE presidential candidate and held his home state's convention votes during early ballots. Woodrow Wilson, who won the Democratic nomination on the forty-sixth ballot, preferred Rep. Oscar W. Underwood of Alabama as his running mate and dismissed Marshall as "a small-calibre man." Without informing Wilson, his associates had agreed days earlier to support Marshall for Vice President in exchange for Indiana's convention support. After a closely contested opening ballot, Marshall was nominated on the second ballot.

After some early gaffes in speeches, Marshall became an effective public speaker and a popular and skillful presiding officer of the Senate. He supported Wilson's policies and established a comfortable relationship with the Chief Executive. Although he did not normally attend Cabinet meetings, at Wilson's request he presided over several Cabinet meetings when the President went overseas, thereby becoming the first Vice President to preside over a Cabinet meeting. As Vice President, he lectured frequently around the country. Like Wilson, he opposed entry into WORLD WAR I initially although his position evolved to coincide with that of the administration. Renominated in 1916, he became the first Vice President in ninety-six years (since DANIEL D. TOMPKINS) to serve a second term with the same President and only the fifth ever elected to a second term. His disarming wit contributed to his popularity. He responded to a tribute by blaming his station on an "ignorant electorate." Memorably, he proclaimed that "what this country needs is a really good five-cent cigar."

His most pungent observations were, however, directed at his office. He observed that "[e]verything that can be done . . . is done to furnish [the Vice President] with some innocuous occupation" where "he can do no harm," positions like regent of the Smithsonian where "he has an opportunity to compare his fossilized life with the fossils of all ages." He suggested that the Vice President be addressed as "His Superfluous Excellency" and observed that "the only business of the Vice President is to ring the White House bell every morning and ask what is the state of health of the president."

Unfortunately, the state of Wilson's health became a national preoccupation during the final one and one-half years of Marshall's tenure. On 26 September 1919, Wilson suffered a debilitating stroke. Marshall was given no access to Wilson nor was he given information regarding his health. When Marshall did ring at the White House to inquire about Wilson's health two days after the stroke he was sent away uninformed. Indeed Marshall did not see or speak with

Wilson for the last one and one-half years of their term until moments before the inauguration of their successors.

A combination of factors, both constitutional and political, impeded Marshall from taking effective action during the crisis brought on by Wilson's illness. Nearly a half century before the TWENTY-FIFTH AMENDMENT was adopted, the Constitution provided neither Marshall nor the nation any guidance over what PRESIDENTIAL DISABILITY was, how it was to be determined, and whether it resulted in the permanent removal of the President or just a temporary transfer of powers. Coupled with, and related to, the constitutional uncertainties, the First Lady, EDITH WILSON, and Wilson's assistants discouraged any attempt to address the hiatus in executive leadership. They did not keep Marshall informed and rejected as disloyal suggestions by others that Wilson was disabled. Marshall refused to act "for fear some censorious sole would accuse me of a longing for [Wilson's] place." He decided he would act as President only in response to a congressional resolution and a written request from the First Lady and the President's physician. These conditions were not to occur and accordingly Marshall never acted to fill the de facto vacancy in the presidency although he did discharge ceremonial duties of the office.

Marshall was mentioned as a presidential candidate in 1920 and 1924 but made no effort to secure the nomination either year nor did his name engender much enthusiasm. After leaving office in 1921, Marshall practiced law and wrote his autobiography, surely one of the wittiest political memoirs this country has ever produced. He died on 1 June 1925.

BIBLIOGRAPHY

Feerick, John D. *From Failing Hands.* 1965.

Hansen, Richard H. *The Year We Had No President.* 1962.

Marshall, Thomas R. *Recollections of Thomas R. Marshall: A Hoosier Salad.* 1925.

Thomas, Charles M. *Thomas Riley Marshall: Hoosier Statesman.* 1939.

Young, Donald. *American Roulette: The History and Dilemma of the Vice Presidency.* 2d ed. 1972.

JOEL K. GOLDSTEIN

MARSHALL PLAN. The Marshall Plan of 1948 provided more than $12 billion of economic aid to sixteen countries in Western Europe over a four-year period. The devastation of WORLD WAR II, followed by unusually bad weather and poor crop yields, had left Europe in economic and political despair. Indeed, the Continent lay in shambles, making it an ideal breeding ground for totalitarianism. Realizing that this same type of situation had encouraged the rise of dictators after WORLD WAR I, the administration of Harry S. Truman took the lead in establishing an aid program designed to encourage Europe's reconstruction. By the time the assistance effort came to an end in 1952 and was incorporated into the military aid programs of that decade, the Marshall Plan had combined with a process of recovery already under way after the war to stabilize these countries and perhaps save them from communism.

Though the assistance program bears the name of Secretary of State GEORGE C. MARSHALL, it actually came into being through the efforts of President Truman. Marshall inspected the postwar ruins and instructed the head of the State Department's newly created Policy Planning Staff, George F. Kennan, to recommend a policy intended to provide relief and recovery. President Truman, insisting that the effort should bear the name of the more popular Secretary of State, appealed to Congress for a European aid bill and delivered several speeches outlining the totalitarian threat to Europe that would, in turn, endanger American freedoms. Stability on the Continent, he realized, was vital to American trade and the containment of communism. European nations must take the initiative by devising a mutual assistance program and informing the White House how it could promote recovery.

In his Harvard University commencement address of June 1947, Marshall had focused on the need to alleviate European troubles, and soon afterward he instructed his staff to prepare a recovery program that was initially aimed at helping any nation that specified its needs. But when the Soviet Union declined the offer and accused the United States of an imperialist conspiracy, the other Communist governments on the Continent followed suit and the line between Eastern Europe and Western Europe became clear. As tension grew, the Soviet Union negotiated defense pacts with several European countries, rigged elections in Hungary, established the Cominform, and announced the Molotov Plan, a series of bilateral pacts assuring aid to Communist regimes in Europe. These developments in mind, the United States made the assistance program double-edged in purpose: to provide humanitarian aid and to contain communism.

The key to European recovery was also the greatest source of controversy. To achieve reconstruction, it was crucial to have an integrated Western Europe that included revitalized Germany. France objected so strenuously that only under strong economic and political pressure from the Truman administration did the government in Paris finally relent. German recovery, the White House assured France, was reconcilable with French security. In April 1948, following the fears stirred up by the communist coup of the previous February in Czechoslovakia, Congress approved the Economic Cooperation Act, or Marshall Plan, which established the European Recovery Program aimed at helping members of the new Organization for European Economic Cooperation. Western Germany (those zones occupied by the United States, Great Britain, and France) was to be an integral participant in the program.

The Soviet premier Joseph Stalin, however, feared a reunified Germany and, in an effort to divide the Western allies, proclaimed a blockade of Berlin in June 1948. Soviet apprehensions had foundation, for the United States, Britain, France, Belgium, Luxembourg, and the Netherlands had just gathered in London to establish a government in West Germany. Only after a war scare and a massive Anglo-American airlift did the Soviets end the blockade in the spring of 1949.

The Marshall Plan thus set off a chain of events that both stabilized Western Europe and heightened the COLD WAR. On the one hand, the American effort doubtless contributed to the defeat of the Communist Party in the elections in both Italy and France, and it promoted the recovery of recipient nations while tightening the Western alliance. On the other hand, the assistance program helped to foment a crisis over Berlin, which, in turn, hastened the development of a European defense pact called the North Atlantic Treaty Organization (NATO) in April 1949. Out of the Marshall Plan came a clear east-west division of Germany (which Stalin wanted) and an uneasy balance of power on the Continent that somehow maintained the peace for four decades.

BIBLIOGRAPHY

Hogan, Michael J. *The Marshall Plan: America, Britain, and the Reconstruction of Western Europe, 1947–1952.* 1987.
Mee, Charles L., Jr. *The Marshall Plan: The Launching of the Pax Americana.* 1984.
Milward, Alan S. *The Reconstruction of Western Europe, 1945–51.* 1984.
Wexler, Immanuel. *The Marshall Plan Revisited: The European Recovery Program in Economic Perspective.* 1983.
Woods, Randall B., and Howard Jones. *Dawning of the Cold War: The United States' Quest for Order.* 1991.

HOWARD JONES

MAYAGUEZ CAPTURE. On 12 May 1975, the merchant ship *Mayaguez* was seized by a Cambodian patrol in waters claimed by Cambodia off the Poulo Wai Islands. Cambodia had claimed the right to stop and examine suspicious vessels, especially those with contraband, aiding enemy forces, conducting espionage, or otherwise violating such territorial waters.

Some of the facts surrounding the incident have been classified by the U.S. government and are still unavailable to Congress and the public. Through lawsuits, which were later settled, however, it was discovered that the *Mayaguez* was painted black and showing no flag at the time of its seizure, the latter being a fact that under international law would justify the stopping of any merchant vessel in claimed territorial waters or even upon the high seas. Additionally, the *Mayaguez* was actually 1.75 miles off a claimed Cambodian island and well outside any international shipping lanes. Further, the U.S. government knew of Cambodia's claims of sovereignty over the Poulo Wai Islands, although the first written claim had been made only in July 1972, and knew that Cambodian forces had actually occupied the islands at least since April of 1975. The United States also knew of hostilities in the area between Vietnamese and Cambodian forces, and that there had been seizures of other vessels in the general area by Cambodia. Also, the United States had warned that vessels were subject to search within claimed territorial waters. Sea-Land, the owners of the *Mayaguez*, had also specifically warned the master of the vessel to avoid shellfire around Poulo Wai just days before.

On board the *Mayaguez* at the time of its seizure were 274 containers, whose contents have never been disclosed. However, it is known that the *Mayaguez* left Saigon nine days before the capital of South Vietnam fell, that the captain of the *Mayaguez* destroyed a secret code upon capture, and that there was an $800 minicomputer on board in addition to radar and radio equipment. Several thirty-five-foot, twenty-five-ton containers had been picked up in Saigon under special circumstances (e.g., with escort by embassy personnel) before Saigon fell. These containers housed secret data and other material from the U.S. embassy in Saigon and were loaded on board as "administrative material." It is still not known where or when these secret containers were off-loaded or what they actually contained. During one of the lawsuits, a U.S. Attorney denied that the embassy cargo (of some 34 containers) was on board at the time. Yet in response to a request for the exact inventory of the containers on board, a U.S. Attorney stated that the information was classified and quite sensitive. Sea-Land, however, disclosed that 77 of the containers were "military cargo" bound for a U.S. airbase in Thailand, 17 of which were labeled "cannot identify." Despite the lawsuits and other investigative efforts, the identity of the secret cargo and the actual mission of the *Mayaguez* remain an intriguing mystery. It is not even known whether U.S. forces went after the cargo or the crew when they were actually sent.

What is known is that the U.S. government knew of the seizure some two hours after, but the President was not informed for another two hours. After another four-hour period, President Gerald R. Ford had a forty-five-minute meeting with the NATIONAL SECURITY COUNCIL (without expert advice on international law). He considered that the seizure occurred on the high seas and therefore was an act of piracy, assumptions that State Department lawyers openly admitted were respectively subject to controversy and "not legally correct." He instructed the State Department to demand the immediate release of the ship, and diplomatic notes conveying a twenty-four-hour ultimatum were sent through the Chinese.

On the morning after the seizure, the Cambodians began to move the crew to the mainland for questioning. The United States launched an air attack on the Cambodian naval vessels—first, firing warning shots and dropping riot control agents, then destroying three patrol craft and immobilizing four others—but the vessel carrying the *Mayaguez* crew was allowed to continue to another island.

Some fourteen hours after this attack, the United States turned for the first time to the UNITED NATIONS. Subsequently, the Secretary General appealed to Cambodia and the United States to resolve their dispute peacefully. But later that day, some two-and-one-half days after the seizure, the President abandoned pursuit of peaceful settlement options and sent Marines to Tang Island where the *Mayaguez* was known to rest; the marines landed under heavy fire. Independently, the crew had already left the mainland to return to Tang Island and the *Mayaguez* and Cambodia had broadcast on local radio that the crew and ship were being released.

During the second military operation, forty-one U.S. military were killed and some fifty were wounded, leaving many to question not merely the necessity for the American use of force and its legality under international law, but also whether the second operation was sensible.

BIBLIOGRAPHY

Friedlander, Robert A. "The *Mayaguez* in Retrospect: Humanitarian Intervention or Showing the Flag?" *Saint Louis University Law Review* 22 (1978): 601–613.

Paust, Jordan J. "Correspondence: *Mayaguez*." *Yale Law Journal* 86 (1976): 207–213.

Paust, Jordan J. "More Revelations About *Mayaguez* (and its Secret Cargo)." *Boston College International and Comparative Law Review* 4 (1981): 61–76.

Paust, Jordan J. "The Seizure and Recovery of the *Mayaguez*." *Yale Law Journal* 85 (1976): 774–806.

Rowan, Roy. *The Four Days of Mayaguez*. 1975.

Sandler, Michael David. "Correspondence: *Mayaguez*." *Yale Law Journal* 86 (1976): 203–207.

U.S. House of Representatives. Subcommittee on International Political and Military Affairs. House Committee on International Relations. *Reports of the Comptroller General on the Seizure of the Mayaguez*. 94th Cong., 2d sess., 1976.

JORDAN J. PAUST

MEDALS, PRESIDENTIAL. Medals have been used to commemorate American Presidents since 1790, when privately struck pieces were sold in Philadelphia in honor of George Washington's election the previous year. Official U.S. government medals bearing the likeness of Washington began to appear shortly thereafter. Today, the U.S. Mint's presidential series includes a medal honoring each of the nation's CHIEF EXECUTIVES.

Initially, most of the medals in the series honoring Presidents prior to 1869 (Thomas Jefferson to Andrew Johnson) were made for presentation to American INDIAN chiefs as symbols of peace, friendship, and special recognition. The Indian peace medals, as they are commonly known, bore a portrayal of the President on the obverse and the inscription "Peace and Friendship" on the reverse, with clasped hands and a crossed tomahawk and peace pipe. Presenting medals to the Indians bearing the likeness of the incumbent President was the continuation of a practice initially observed by the Spanish, the French, and the British. It was considered an extremely important part of American Indian policy. Over time, the Indian peace medals also began to be regarded as presidential medals.

Beginning with the administration of Millard Fillmore (1850–1853), the reverse sides of the medals began depicting the transformation of American culture. Although Indian peace medals continued to be produced through Benjamin Harrison's administration, they ceased to be included as part of the presidential series after Ulysses S. Grant's election in 1869. Instead, medals not made for Indians began to be struck by the Mint in honor of Presidents. The lone non-Indian medal included in the series prior to this time was a medal commemorating both Lincoln inaugurations (1861 and 1865). Subsequently, two medals modeled after the Indian peace medals were added to the series for Washington and John Adams. Bronze duplicates of the presidential medal series are currently available through the U.S. Mint.

Presidents have also been honored with a second type of medal—special inaugural medals. The first inaugural medal commemorated Thomas Jefferson's initial ceremony in 1801. It was struck by John Reich, a German-born die-maker. Twenty-four years later, a second inaugural medal was struck for John Quincy Adams' 1825 inauguration. A third medal was privately struck for Andrew Jackson's second inauguration (1833).

Between 1837 and 1853, presidential inaugural medals were produced by the U.S. Mint. For much of the remainder of the nineteenth century, inaugural medals were privately made. Since 1889, official inaugural medals have been authorized by the inaugural committee of the winning presidential candidate shortly after the quadrennial November election. On three occasions (1909, 1957, and 1973), images of Vice Presidents (James S. Sherman, Richard M. Nixon, and Spiro T. Agnew) also appeared on the medals.

Initially, these medals were attached to the cloth badges used to identify individuals involved in the various inaugural festivities. The 1901 committee was the first to have official medals struck for inaugural workers.

Since 1929, souvenir bronze replicas of the official inaugural medal have been sold to the public to help defray the expenses of the fireworks, parade, balls, and various social events sponsored by the committee. In 1953, silver replicas were offered for public purchase for the first time.

Only a limited quantity of medals were issued for the inaugurations of Herbert Hoover (1929) and Franklin D. Roosevelt (1933, 1937, 1941, 1945). Beginning with Harry S. Truman's 1949 oath taking, however, the quantity of medals produced has continued to increase as their popularity has grown.

BIBLIOGRAPHY

Failor, Kenneth M. *Medals of the United States Mint*. 1972.
MacNeil, Neil. *The President's Medal 1789–1977*. 1977.
Prucha, Francis Paul. *Indian Peace Medals in American History*. 1971.

STEPHEN W. STATHIS

MEDIA, PRESIDENT AND THE. A President of the United States performs his leadership techniques on a stage set for news organizations. A President and his advisers set this stage in the hope that news organizations will convey the images, sounds, and words that will persuade the public to endorse his initiatives. Through persuasion, a President kneads his constitutional and political resources into materials that influence the process of governing. The ability to persuade provides a President with those qualities that Woodrow Wilson described as "a dignifying and elevating sense of being trusted, together with a consciousness of being in an official station so conspicuous that no faithful discharge of duty can go unacknowledged and unrewarded."

For most of American history, as Richard Neustadt suggested, the benefit of "the power to persuade [has been] the power to bargain." Since the 1960s, as Samuel Kernell has pointed out, Presidents have used their persuasive powers in another manner. Presidents have "gone public," using the media as the channel to sell their image and their programs to the people. Persuasion is a fungible resource of the presidency. During periods of national crisis, such as those involving economic or foreign policy changes, a President may be made or destroyed by forces beyond his influence. A President needs to have established his ability to persuade the public at these times so that he can take credit for the good news and avoid long-term damage from the bad.

The White House Media Staff. White House publicity operations evolved as part of the White House bureaucracy. The President's aides developed tactics to enhance his image as portrayed by news organizations. During the fifty years beginning with Grover Cleveland's administration and ending with Herbert Hoover's, the evolving White House institutionalized a number of ad hoc roles performed by the President's secretary and other assistants into the permanent position of White House Press Secretary, whose most conspicuous role is as the President's spokesperson. In the twentieth century, the White House bureaucracy has evolved in a manner that has made it possible for a President to maintain, stabilize, and at times exploit his relations with the media.

By the twentieth century four essential features emerged that continue to affect the relationship between the President and the press. First, news about the White House was transmitted to the public by independent nonpartisan news organizations. Second, these organizations were heavily dependent on the White House staff for most of the information they received about the President's activities and policies. Third, the transition from an episodic to a regular relationship between the President and the press required the development of procedures to provide reporters with information on a regular basis. And fourth, the increase in both the amount and the diversity of White House publicity activities made it necessary for the President to seek specialized assistants with skills as promoters and with knowledge of the media.

The economic and technological expansion of publishing and broadcasting enterprises in the last decades of the nineteenth century made it possible for the media to respond to the enlarged prominence of the presidency. In the following decades the continuing expansion of the resources of both news organizations and the White House staff made the relationship between President and press a recognizable feature of the Washington landscape. White House officials decided to create a structure for news operations in response to the growing organizational and technological complexity of the news media as well as to their own ongoing publicity requirements. Since the administration of Theodore Roosevelt, an increasingly important factor in determining the success of a President's communications strategies has been the sophistication with which White House officials approached the job of creating and coordinating White House offices that have responsibilities for communicating the President's image and messages to the public.

Since 1933, Presidents have developed specific offices within the White House to provide resources that would enable them to develop and implement communications policies that would help increase the support they would receive from the political leadership and the public. The offices created between the 1930s and 1980s that exist at the end of the twentieth century include the West Wing Press Office, the Office of Media Liaison, the Office of Public Liaison, the PRESIDENTIAL SPEECHWRITERS, and special technical advisers. In the Reagan and Bush administrations a Director of Communications coordinated the activities of these offices and advised the President on how to utilize them to maximize the President's success in coordinating his political communications.

By the 1950s, the White House used news organizations as their major conduit for their political communications. JAMES HAGERTY, Press Secretary to Dwight D. Eisenhower, managed White House media relations to the benefit of his President. The pace of organizational development increased beginning with the administration of Richard M. Nixon. During the presidencies of Gerald R. Ford, Jimmy Carter, Ronald Reagan, and George Bush, the White House established institutions that administer and coordinate administration publicity, White House staff members who channel the President's message to Congress and interest groups. Throughout this period, administrations responded to fundamental changes involving press and public expectations of the presidency.

The Nixon presidency established the Office of Communications and the Office of Public Liaison. Nixon used both offices to build support for presidential programs and actions. In the following administrations, the Presidents took an organizational as well as a personal role. In order to make good appointments, a President has to understand how the operations of each office fulfills an essential part of his communications strategy. Presidents may not learn this lesson until after they are in office. For example as a candidate Jimmy Carter talked of abolishing the Office of Public Liaison, which he described as an example of the bloated White House staff. Later in his term, Carter realized that the Office of Public Liaison was essential to his ability to persuade. He then appointed Anne Wexler, a knowledgeable Washington insider, to the job. Wexler transformed the office into an effective instrument of political communications. In Ronald Reagan's and George Bush's administrations, the White House Director of Communications was given the specific charge of coordinating these activities for the President.

Relations with the Media. In the period from the administration of Franklin D. Roosevelt through that of Dwight D. Eisenhower, the relationship between the White House and news organizations was conducted with as much cooperation as conflict. In spite of occasional periods when news organizations and the White House treated the other as an enemy force, the more typical pattern of behavior could best be described as one of continuity and stability. For the thirty years since Eisenhower, many major news organizations grew in size, resources, and well-trained personnel. During the same period, technological change evolved so that news organizations are thought of as the media rather than as the press because of the new forms of rapid communications emphasizing the visual, not only in television but in print.

The President's personal relations with the media also changed after Eisenhower. From the White House perspective, the representatives of news organizations, and sometimes the organizations themselves, were regarded as the President's adversary. In contrast to what the White House expected was due to the President, favorable coverage could not be taken for granted. Instead, the administration had to fulfill the high standards and expectations of journalists who were not predisposed to present the Chief Executive or his policies as a success, who had more ability to uncover his mistakes, and who had a more receptive audience to convey their impression of the failures and contradictions of the administration. During the decade between 1965 and 1975, the years when the VIETNAM WAR and the WATERGATE AFFAIR diminished the public's approval of Presidents Johnson and Nixon, both Presidents' supporters regarded the media as an enemy. From the perspective of the White House, news organizations contributed a harsh and unflattering view of an administration, and when a President appeared to fail, their attacks seemed relentless.

An analysis of a segment of the media suggests that, in fact, although the adversarial aspects of the relationship grew throughout this period, the White House advantages were maintained except in response to the most dramatic crises and failures. A survey of White House stories from 1953 to 1978 in the *New York Times* and *Time* and from 1968 to 1978 on the CBS Evening News suggests that there has been a gradual decrease in the number of favorable stories and an increase in unfavorable stories, but that when the Vietnam-Watergate era is excluded, the change is relatively small. The percent of favorable stories in the print media declined from close to 60 percent in the Eisenhower administration to near 50 percent during Kennedy's term and the first part of Johnson's term. They fell near 40 percent for Johnson and close to 25 percent at the time of Nixon's resignation in all three media, but returned to the high 40s for Ford and the first two years of Carter. Similarly unfavorable stories increased from below 20 percent of the total for Kennedy to slightly above 20 percent for the Ford–early Carter years. However, throughout this period the news organizations surveyed continued to produce more favorable than unfavorable stories.

The major change in the approach of the President and his White House advisers to the media during the 1980s and 1990s came in response to the increased importance of television as the main channel of information and images to the public. Some writers have been touting the "rule of television" since the 1950s, but until the late 1970s, television news was a recreation of events whose importance was determined by the print media, especially major national newspapers such as the *New York Times*, the *Washington Post*, and the *Wall Street Journal*. By the 1980s, print journalism published stories that assumed that the reader had already learned of them through television. The reaction of Presidents and their advisers has been to provide "television opportunities" more frequently than news conferences.

Thus Presidents have attempted to use television to provide the appropriate public image to accompany their policies. Nixon, for example, wanted to provide the public with a clear image of his policies of opening relations with China and of détente with the Soviet Union. His trips to China and the Soviet Union in 1972 brought approval to these policies as well as a signifi-

cant boost to his status in the polls. Television became the key resource for Reagan's success as a persuader. In the last quarter of the twentieth century, the persona of the President as transmitted in his television appearances was the key factor for the public's evaluation of an administration.

BIBLIOGRAPHY

Cornwell, Elmer E., Jr. *Presidential Leadership of Public Opinion.* 1965.
Edwards, George C., III. *The Public Presidency.* 1983.
Grossman, Michael Baruch, and Martha Joynt Kumar. *Portraying the President: The White House and the Media.* 1981.
Kernell, Samuel. *Going Public: New Strategies of Presidential Leadership.* 1986.
Neustadt, Richard. *Presidential Power.* 1990.
Pollard, James E. *The President and the Press.* 1947.
Tulis, Jeffrey K. *The Rhetorical Presidency.* 1987.

MICHAEL BARUCH GROSSMAN

MEESE, EDWIN, III (b. 1931), counselor to the President, Attorney General. A former deputy district attorney, Edwin Meese served as Governor Ronald Reagan's chief of staff in California. After Reagan won the presidency in 1980, Meese became the President's chief policy adviser, and he organized and managed the administration's system of CABINET COUNCILS, where Cabinet officers and staff members prepared and refined policy proposals for subsequent action by the President.

Meese's most prominent public role, however, came when he was appointed ATTORNEY GENERAL in 1985. Meese's tenure at the JUSTICE DEPARTMENT was both active and controversial. He launched initiatives to combat domestic terrorism, illicit drugs, and hardcore pornography. He sparked a wide-ranging public debate about the Constitution by calling on judges to interpret it according to the "original intent" of its Framers. Finally, he oversaw the appointment of federal judges. While at both the White House and the Justice Department, he helped design and implement a screening process to select jurists who believed in judicial restraint. More than any other initiative, this one is likely to leave a long legacy, because President Reagan appointed nearly half of the federal judiciary during his two terms in office. These judges will influence the development of American law into the twenty-first century.

Meese was one of the most consistent and articulate conservatives in the Reagan administration, and he often became a lightning rod for administration critics. Upon his nomination as Attorney General in 1984, for example, Democrats in Congress demanded an independent counsel to investigate him for alleged breaches of ethics laws. Hoping to clear the record, Meese seconded the request. Counsel Jacob Stein eventually found "no basis with respect to any of the eleven allegations for the bringing of a prosecution against Mr. Meese for the violation of a federal criminal statute." A second independent counsel, James McKay, was appointed in 1987 to investigate other allegations against Meese. McKay's report the following year concluded that a prosecution against Meese was not warranted. Though often attacked, Meese rarely responded in kind. Indeed, his steady affability mirrored the President's own temperament, providing an admirable counterpoint to the bitter infighting that marked at least parts of the Reagan White House.

BIBLIOGRAPHY

Meese, Edwin, III. *With Reagan: The Inside Story.* 1992.
Meese, Edwin, III. *Major Statements of the Attorney General.* 1989.

JOHN G. WEST, JR.

MELLON, ANDREW W. (1855–1937), Secretary of the Treasury. Andrew Mellon first made a name for himself in banking in Pittsburgh, especially as the backer of high-cost, innovative industries. He financed Alcoa Aluminum in the 1890s, before most Americans knew anything about aluminum's value to industry. In the early 1900s Mellon and his family sank $15 million into Gulf Oil and backed Gulf's innovations in the petroleum business, including offshore drilling and the first corner gas stations.

By 1920 Mellon was worth close to a billion dollars, which ranked him with John D. Rockefeller and Henry Ford as one of the wealthiest men in America. After WORLD WAR I, Mellon's superior grasp of economics caught the attention of national political leaders, who were struggling with a stagnant economy, a rising national debt, and a crushing tax burden. Republican Warren G. Harding, winner of the 1920 presidential election, asked Mellon to be his Secretary of the Treasury and do for the American economy what he had done for aluminum and oil.

Mellon came to Washington at a crucial time in U.S. history. World War I had been a turning point in expanding the role of government in economic life. Before the war, the federal role in operating, regulating, and taxing businesses was small. The federal budget was less than a billion dollars a year. The taxes needed to run the government were low and fairly easily collected; land sales and tariffs were the major sources of revenue. In the 1910s, the passing of the income tax and the outbreak of World War I thrust government regulation and taxation into much broader areas of American life.

Consequently, as Treasury Secretary, Mellon collected and studied data on the American economy. He concluded that "high rates of taxation do not necessarily mean large revenue to the Government, and that more revenue may often be obtained by lower rates." Mellon found that high tax rates caused the investment capital needed for new industry to dry up. Instead, large investors put their money into tax-free municipal bonds, and the federal government actually received very little tax revenue from persons with large incomes. Mellon reasoned that lower tax rates would help investors put their funds back into industry—that is, into money-making ventures that would both employ workers and produce profits.

As Treasury Secretary under Harding and Calvin Coolidge, Mellon was able to get Congress to enact his tax cuts, with the surprising result that actual tax revenues soared while tax rates dropped. In 1921, when Mellon took office, the tax rate on top incomes was 73 percent. After eight years of Mellon's tax cuts this top rate was sliced by two-thirds, to 24 percent. The tax rates of those earning less were proportionally slashed even more. For example, people earning under $4,000 per year had their rates chopped from 4 to 0.5 percent; those in the $4,000-to-$8,000 bracket had their tax burden cut from 8 to 2 percent. Tax policy, Mellon argued, "must lessen, so far as possible, the burden of taxation on those least able to bear it." Millions of citizens were removed entirely from the income-tax rolls, and when Mellon further urged the repeal of federal taxes on telegrams, telephones, and movie tickets he became one of the most popular men in America. Moviegoers throughout the country cheered him when he was shown on newsreels in theaters during the 1920s.

When Mellon's policies actually helped generate increases in tax revenue, even Mellon's critics were amazed. In 1921 the income tax generated $690.2 million (in constant 1929 dollars); in 1926, with tax rates slashed, the federal revenue from income taxes rose to $710.2 million. This figure jumped to more than $1 billion in 1929. With taxes low and industry strong, the United States had a budget surplus in each year of the 1920s.

During the 1930s, Mellon fell out of favor. Presidents Herbert Hoover and Franklin D. Roosevelt both thought that raising taxes would help fight the Great Depression. Hoover eased Mellon out of the Treasury Department and into the job of ambassador to Great Britain. Mellon retired from political life in 1933. Before his death in 1937 he donated his outstanding art collection to the National Gallery of Art.

BIBLIOGRAPHY

Folsom, Burton W., Jr. *The Myth of the Robber Barons.* 1991.
Koskoff, David E. *The Mellons.* 1978.
Mellon, Andrew. *Taxation: The People's Business.* 1924.
Silver, Thomas B. *Coolidge and the Historians.* 1982.

BURTON W. FOLSOM, JR., and ANITA P. FOLSOM

MEREDITH CASE. President John F. Kennedy's enforcement of the enrollment of James Meredith in 1962 at the University of Mississippi in Oxford, Mississippi, reaffirmed presidential power as an ascendant force in federal-state relations and enabled Kennedy to assert presidential influence in the civil rights movement of the 1960s.

An air force veteran, Meredith applied as an "American-Mississippi-Negro citizen" for admission to the University of Mississippi, which had never knowingly admitted a black. Meredith's application was rejected for complicated academic reasons. Aided by the NAACP Legal Defense Fund, he filed suit, asserting that he had been rejected because of race. A federal district court decided against Meredith but was overruled by the Fifth Circuit Court of Appeals. After further legal maneuvers, Supreme Court Justice Hugo Black upheld the court of appeals. Governor Ross Barnett of Mississippi declared, "We will not surrender to the evil and illegal forces of tyranny."

When Mississippi officials defied the court rulings, the Fifth Circuit Court of Appeals found the governor and other officials guilty of contempt. When defiance continued, the judges directed the federal government to enforce the court's orders.

President Kennedy and Attorney General ROBERT F. KENNEDY were initially cautious in executing the responsibility thrust upon them. They sought to avoid the use of force and thus ennoble Governor Barnett in the eyes of the local citizens. The Kennedys dispatched U.S. Marshals and federalized the National Guard rather than deploy federal troops. The federal administration increased pressure on the governor.

Yielding, Governor Barnett proposed that Meredith be spirited onto the campus, while state police would assure Meredith's safety. The President accepted the plan since it would avoid Barnett's arrest and the involvement of federal troops. Nonetheless, the President, distrustful of the governor, prepared fallback measures.

Meredith was brought onto campus. The governor protested and the President delivered a televised address emphasizing that the federal government was merely carrying out court orders and therefore was not imposing its own will on Mississippi. But as the President spoke, a rampage of 2,500 protesters, many with guns, erupted on the campus. The marshals and guardsmen responded with tear gas. In night-long rioting, a newsman and a townsman were killed, two hundred marshals and guardsmen were injured, and widespread property damage inflicted. The marshals and the National Guard doubted they could hold out long, and, fearing that the mob might find and lynch Meredith, the President ordered federal troops into action. The mob was dispersed, some two hundred rioters were arrested, of whom twenty-four were students at the university.

James Meredith registered at the university and subsequently graduated. Kennedy rejected proposals to punish the state of Mississippi, while declaring that "this government would unravel very fast if . . . the Executive Branch does not carry out decisions of the court."

BIBLIOGRAPHY

Dorman, Michael. *We Shall Overcome.* 1965.
Lord, Walter. *The Past that Would Not Die.* 1965.
Silver, James W. *Mississippi: The Closed Society.* 1964.
Sorensen, Theodore C. *Kennedy.* 1965.

LOUIS W. KOENIG

MERIT SYSTEMS PROTECTION BOARD (MSPB). The CIVIL SERVICE REFORM ACT OF 1978 (CSRA) created the Merit Systems Protection Board to provide oversight and protection of the merit system that guides the federal CIVIL SERVICE. With the MSPB, President Jimmy Carter and his personnel advisers gave explicit recognition to the longtime tension in the Civil Service Commission. The director of that commission had served in the conflicting roles of adviser to the President on political appointments and guardian of merit procedures and rules.

The CSRA, in abolishing the Civil Service Commission, split and simplified the personnel system. The OFFICE OF PERSONNEL MANAGEMENT (OPM), directed by a presidential appointee, would advise the President and serve as the central human-resources manager for the federal government. The MSPB would assume the role of guardian of merit, hearing appeals from employees who believed that their protections under merit-system laws had been violated. The legislation also provided that the MSPB send annual reports to Congress on the extent to which the OPM was supporting the effective operation of the merit system. The Office of Special Counsel (OSC), created by the CSRA as part of the MSPB, was to serve as a legal advocate for employees. The Special Counsel was particularly responsible for protecting WHISTLE-BLOWERS who exposed wrongdoing and abuse.

The legislation also gave authority to the MSPB to conduct occasional "special studies" to examine the operations of the civil service and to report to the President and Congress whether the "public interest in a civil service free of prohibited personnel practices is adequately protected" (P.L. 95-454, chap. 12). The MSPB, therefore, would not only serve as guardian of the merit system but would analyze the effectiveness of specific components of that system, including the OPM.

The board would be composed of three members appointed by the President with the ADVICE AND CONSENT of the Senate. Only two of the members of the board could be from the same political party. Members would serve seven-year terms and could be removed by the President only for "inefficiency, neglect of duty or malfeasance in office" (P.L. 95-454, chap. 12). The Special Counsel, also appointed by the President with the advice and consent of the Senate, would serve a five-year term.

Implementation of the MSPB went smoothly. The Office of Special Counsel, on the other hand, suffered rocky times in its early years. Its major charge—protecting whistle-blowers—was difficult to define, and there was no institutional history to serve as guide. Most significantly, the relationship between the MSPB and the OSC was unclear and contentious. Leadership at the OSC was in nearly constant flux during its first four years, exacerbating the problem of finding an institutional identity. Budgetary constraints were a constant problem; in the second year of the OSC's operation, Congress rescinded nearly half its annual budget. Although protection of whistle-blowers and removal of what he termed "deadwood" from the bureaucracy had been very high priorities for Carter, that commitment was not shared by Congress, and the OSC's early budgetary problems reflected that lack of commitment. Although the office later stabilized, its early history had long-term negative effects on its effectiveness.

In one of the few evaluations of the MSPB and the OSC, Robert Vaughn reports that the organizations are "fundamentally separate, but mutually dependent" (Vaughn 1992, p.1). Vaughn notes that while the MSPB endured baptism by fire in the air traffic controllers' strike in the early 1980s, including criticism that it gave in to political pressure rather than protecting merit, its rulings have generally been supported by subsequent court decisions. (The primary criticism of the MSPB has in fact been that its decisions tend to favor management rather than employees.) Vaughn concludes, however, that the board is generally effetive as an adjudicatory body. His findings on the OSC, however, are less positive. In the early 1990s, it continued to be an ineffective organization. In fact, legislation was passed that permitted whistle-blowers to bypass the OSC completely and go directly to the MSPB.

BIBLIOGRAPHY

Ban, Carolyn. "Implementing Civil Service Reform: Structure and Strategy." In *Legislating Bureaucratic Change: The Civil Service Reform Act of 1978*. Edited by Patricia W. Ingraham and Carolyn Ban. 1984.

U.S. General Accounting Office. *Merit Systems Protection Board: Case Processing Timeliness and Participants' Views on Board Activities*. 1987.

U.S. Merit Systems Protection Board. *Annual Report*. Issued annually.

Vaughn, Robert. "The Merit Systems Protection Board." In *The Promise and Paradox of Bureaucratic Reform*. Edited by Patricia W. Ingraham and David H. Rosenbloom. 1992.

PATRICIA W. INGRAHAM

MERRYMAN, EX PARTE 17 F. Cas. 144 (C.C. Md. 1861). *Merryman* was an opinion in chambers written by Chief Justice ROGER B. TANEY in 1861. Taney had issued a writ of habeas corpus on 26 May 1861, for John Merryman, a Maryland citizen arrested for disloyalty around 2 A.M., 25 May 1861, by U.S. military authorities and imprisoned at Fort McHenry in Baltimore harbor. General George Cadwalader, the post commander, refused to produce the prisoner in Taney's circuit court in Baltimore on the grounds that President Abraham Lincoln had authorized suspension of the privilege of the writ of habeas corpus in the area [*see* HABEAS CORPUS, SUSPENSION OF]. Taney bowed to superior force and did not organize a posse to enforce his court order, but he wrote a stinging opinion and filed it with the circuit court clerk on 1 June.

"I had supposed it to be one of those points of constitutional law upon which there was no difference of opinion, and that it was admitted on all hands that the privilege of the writ could not be suspended, except by act of Congress," wrote Taney. He pointed out that the clause in the Constitution allowing suspension in case of invasion or rebellion appeared in Article I, Section 9, the part of the Constitution dealing with the powers of Congress and having "not the slightest reference to the Executive department." Taney further noted that the great American constitutional commentator, Joseph Story, thought only Congress could suspend the writ, as did the great Chief Justice John Marshall.

Taney sent a copy of his opinion to President Lincoln, who ignored it—until he delivered his message to the special session of Congress convened 4 July 1861.

In the meantime, the opinion was widely circulated in newspapers and pamphlets, and was twice printed in the latter form in the Confederacy. Taney helped to galvanize the Democratic opposition, leaderless since the death of STEPHEN A. DOUGLAS, but the party did not focus on CIVIL LIBERTIES as a major issue all over the country until 1863.

In his message to the special session of Congress convened 4 July 1861, President Lincoln replied to Taney's opinion without mentioning the case or the Chief Justice by name. Lincoln said that "some consideration was given to the questions of power, and propriety, before this matter was acted upon." Then he asked rhetorically, "are all the laws, *but one*, to go unexecuted, and the government itself go to pieces, lest that one be violated?" But he drew back quickly from such philosophical speculation, saying, "But it was not believed that this question was presented. It was not believed that any law was violated." The Constitution, Lincoln then argued, "is silent as to which [branch], or who, is to exercise the powers" of suspension, "and as the provision was plainly made for a dangerous emergency, it cannot be believed the framers . . . intended, that in every case, the danger should run its course, until Congress could be called together."

Unless *Ex parte Merryman* be construed as a ruling, the Supreme Court never ruled directly on the question of the suspension of the writ of habeas corpus. The possibility of an adverse decision worried administration officials, and Lincoln took particular care, in choosing a replacement for Taney after his death in 1864, that the new Chief Justice not be inclined to rule the suspension illegal.

BIBLIOGRAPHY

Neely, Mark E., Jr. *The Fate of Liberty: Abraham Lincoln and Civil Liberties.* 1991.

MARK E. NEELY, JR.

MEXICAN WAR. When James K. Polk began his presidency in March 1845, American expansionism presaged a war with Mexico. Repeatedly that country had warned U.S. officials that it would not tolerate the American ANNEXATION OF TEXAS—a region whose independence it had never recognized. When Polk moved to complete the process of annexation, General Juan Almonte, the Mexican minister in Washington, sailed for Vera Cruz to sever his country's relations with the United States. To defend Texas from a possible Mexican invasion, the President ordered General Zachary Taylor to advance from Fort Jessup, Louisiana, down the Gulf coast to Corpus Christi on the Nueces. What the President wanted of Mexico was its acceptance not only of the loss of Texas but also Texas's claim to the Rio Grande. Polk intended that his show of force would convince the Mexican government that it could not avoid coming to terms with the United States.

As Mexico continued to resist the loss of Texas, Polk's attention shifted to Mexican California. During the summer of 1845 Thomas O. Larkin, the American merchant at Monterey, warned Washington of apparent British and French designs on the region. Polk appointed Larkin as special agent to report British and French activities and encourage the people of California to cast their destiny with the United States. Mexican officials and editors recognized California's vulnerability to U.S. encroachments by land and sea. In November, Polk sent John Slidell to Mexico City to offer Mexico as much as $40 million for a boundary along the Rio Grande to New Mexico and westward to the Pacific [*see* SLIDELL'S MISSION]. When the Mexican government refused to recognize Slidell, U.S. editors and officials, reflecting a profound contempt for Mexico, advocated the use of force. During March 1846 Polk responded to the deadlock by ordering Taylor to occupy the disputed territory along the Rio Grande. As the crisis mounted, Polk awaited the expected Mexican firing on Taylor's forces. Finally on Saturday evening, 9 May, Polk learned of the Mexican attack; two days later he sent his war message to Congress, accusing the Mexicans of shedding American blood on American soil.

Backed by his country's vast superiority in military power, Polk set out to gain through war what he could not secure through purchase. He quickly dispatched land and naval forces to seize California while he carefully defined his precise objectives along the Pacific. Travelers and sea captains had long agreed that two harbors gave special significance to the California of the 1840s—the bays of San Francisco and San Diego. At the outset Polk determined to secure no less from the war than San Francisco and Monterey, but under prodding from New England hide merchants, Polk agreed that if the war lasted more than one month he would accept no settlement that did not include San Diego. The President could not reveal his objectives without exposing his administration to charges of aggression.

To strengthen his powers of coercion Polk required the total conquest of Mexico. Taylor, without specific orders, advanced into northern Mexico, won several minor engagements, and by late 1846 had captured Monterrey and Saltillo. Reinforced by additional forces from Texas, he now prepared for a showdown with the Mexican army. Meanwhile the President decided to transfer the main thrust of the American offensive to a direct assault on Mexico City through Vera Cruz. For this expedition he selected General WINFIELD SCOTT. He instructed Taylor to establish a defense line and hold it. Convinced that Taylor's forces could not withstand a full Mexican assault, General Antonío Lopez de Santa Anna, having recently returned to Mexico and taken command of the Mexican army, moved northward with twenty thousand men to annihilate the American forces at Saltillo. During February 1847 he struck Taylor's defenses at Buena Vista near Saltillo. After a fierce battle Santa Anna withdrew to San Luis Potosi to bring the north Mexican campaign to a close.

By early 1847 U.S. naval forces, reinforced by Stephen W. Kearney's overland expedition, had taken control of the entire California coast from San Diego to San Francisco and Sonoma. The American victories in California and northern Mexico presaged the brilliant successes of Scott's assault on central Mexico. Scott took Vera Cruz on 27 March and set out immediately on the road to Mexico City. His forces defeated Santa Anna at Cerro Gordo pass and reached Puebla on 6 May. Here Scott prepared for the final advance on Mexico City while his troops enjoyed the hospitality of the local Mexican populace. Early in August U.S. forces entered the beautiful Valley of Mexico and on 20 August demolished the Mexican forces at Contreras and Churubusco. Armistice negotiations halted Scott's advance momentarily, but on 8 September, American forces took Molino del Rey; five days later they stormed the fortress of Chapultepec. On 14 September the victorious American army entered Mexico City amid sporadic opposition.

Despite the war's general popularity, Polk faced persistent condemnation from Democrats and Whigs alike who accused him of involving the country in an unnecessary war for the purpose of annexing Mexican territory. Determined to secure an early peace, Polk, in April 1847, dispatched Nicholas P. Trist, chief clerk in the Department of State, to join Scott's army and seek some occasion for negotiating a treaty with Mexico. Trist's instructions demanded, as territorial indemnity, a boundary along the Rio Grande to New Mexico, west along the Gila and Colorado rivers to California, and from the Colorado to the Pacific along the thirty-second parallel to assure the acquisition of San Diego. For that boundary the United States would assume all claims of U.S. citizens against Mexico and pay as much as $25 million for New Mexico and Upper California. Polk soon discovered that an overwhelming military victory did not translate automatically into a satisfactory peace. Polk recalled Trist after the failed armistice of August. In the absence of any Mexican government willing to cede California, Polk could only ask Congress for additional appropriations to fight an enemy already defeated. While the President searched in vain for a solution to his dilemma, Trist, who had accepted a Mexican plea to ignore his recall and remain in Mexico, negotiated the TREATY OF GUADALUPE HIDALGO, signed on 2 February 1848, that conveyed to the United States the boundary that Polk sought. That treaty terminated the Mexican War and completed the American quest for frontage on the Pacific begun with the OREGON TREATY of 1846.

BIBLIOGRAPHY

Bauer, K. Jack. *The Mexican War, 1846–1848.* 1974.
Graebner, Norman A. *Empire on the Pacific: A Study in American Continental Expansion.* 1955.
Pletcher, David M. *The Diplomacy of Annexation: Texas, Oregon, and the Mexican War.* 1973.
Rives, George Lockhart. *The United States and Mexico, 1821–1848.* 2 vols. 1913.
Smith, Justin H. *The War with Mexico.* 2 vols. 1919.

NORMAN A. GRAEBNER

MIDNIGHT JUDGES. The Judiciary Act of 1789, which established the federal court system, did not create special circuit-court judgeships. A circuit court consisted of two Justices of the Supreme Court (later just one) sitting with a district court judge. Circuit riding imposed severe hardships on the Supreme Court Justices, who vainly implored Congress to create special circuit-court judges. For more than a decade Congress did nothing, but on 13 February 1801, in the final days of John Adams's administration, the act was signed into law, introducing a variety of worthy reforms, above all the establishment of intermediary federal judgeships. To Jeffersonian Republicans, however, the political character of the bill was manifest in its provision reducing the size of the Supreme Court to five Justices, thus preventing Thomas Jefferson, the incoming President, from making an appointment.

Adams appointed able men to the sixteen judicial posts, but without exception they were men of his party, the Federalists. Four days before his administration ended on 4 March, a bill for judgeships for the District of Columbia became law, allowing the appointment of three more circuit judges and forty-two justices of the peace, and again Adams appointed only Federalists. The unseemly rush to appoint these judges, to get Senate confirmation, and to issue their commissions kept the administration busy until its final days—hence the term of contempt, "the midnight judges." John Marshall, who had already been confirmed as Chief Justice, continued to serve Adams as Secretary of State, laboring until the final moments fixing the Great Seal of the United States to the commissions, some of which he could not deliver because of the hour.

Federalists regarded these new judgeships as being "as good to the party as an election." Republicans, who saw a menace in the statute, claimed that it made "sinecure places and pensions for thoroughgoing Federal partisans." In 1802 Congress, now controlled by Republicans, revoked the Judiciary Act of 1801 despite its necessary if belated reforms, thus wiping out the lifetime-tenure positions of all circuit judges and returning the Supreme Court Justices to arduous circuit duty.

BIBLIOGRAPHY

Turner, Kathryn. "The Midnight Judges." *University of Pennsylvania Law Review* 109 (1961): 494–523.

LEONARD W. LEVY

MILITARY-INDUSTRIAL COMPLEX.

An irony of the COLD WAR was that to maintain the peace and retain its freedom, the United States felt forced to build a huge peacetime military establishment, but the cost of building it threatened to create a garrison state in which there would be no real freedom. President Dwight D. Eisenhower was keenly sensitive to this irony and worried terribly about the cost and influence of a large standing army. Throughout his administration he tried to hold down the cost of defense spending in the face of demands from political, military, and industrial leaders that he accelerate the arms race.

Fearful that the Democrats would greatly expand defense spending when John F. Kennedy took office on 20 January 1961, Eisenhower used the occasion of his farewell address on 17 January to warn about the domestic dangers of an accelerated arms race. He recognized that "we face a hostile ideology global in scope, atheistic in character, ruthless in purpose, and insidious in method." The threat, Eisenhower said, would persist so long as the Communists ruled the Soviet Union. There would be many crises and thus many calls to find a "miraculous solution" by spending ever greater sums on new weapons. The threat had already forced the United States to create a "permanent armaments industry of vast proportions" and a large standing army in peacetime.

"This conjunction of an immense military establishment and a large arms industry is new in the American

experience," Eisenhower continued. "The total influence—economic, political, even spiritual—is felt in every city, every statehouse, every office of the federal government." Then he gave this direct warning: "In the councils of government, we must guard against the acquisition of unwarranted influence, whether sought or unsought, by the military-industrial complex. The potential for the disastrous rise of misplaced power exists and will persist." These became the most-quoted words of his presidency.

In a news conference the following morning, Eisenhower was asked what specific steps he would recommend in dealing with the problem. He replied, "It is only a citizenry, an alert and informed citizenry, which can keep these abuses from coming about." He pointed to magazine advertisements that showed a Titan missile or an Atlas rocket and said they represented "almost an insidious penetration of our own minds." Eisenhower had concluded his farewell address by saying, "Disarmament . . . is a continuing imperative." But until the 1990s, his warning went unheeded.

BIBLIOGRAPHY

Ambrose, Stephen E. *Eisenhower: The President.* 1984.
Eisenhower, Dwight D. *Waging Peace.* 1965.

STEPHEN E. AMBROSE

MILLIGAN, EX PARTE

4 Wallace 2 (1866). In October 1864, Lambdin P. Milligan, a citizen of Indiana, was arrested by federal troops, tried by a military commission, and sentenced to be hanged. Milligan was a Peace Democrat who believed the South should be allowed to leave the Union in peace. He had become a "major general" in an organization that planned to raid prisons in the Midwest and release Confederate prisoners of war. Though President Abraham Lincoln had suspended the writ of habeas corpus in the area, Milligan's counsel applied to the nearest federal court for the writ. The court's two judges, disagreeing, certified the case to the Supreme Court, which divided 5 to 4 in *Ex parte Milligan.* [See HABEAS CORPUS, SUSPENSION OF.]

For the majority, Justice David Davis wrote that the case involved "the very framework of the government and the fundamental principles of American liberty." The military commission that tried and sentenced Milligan was no part of the judicial power of the country. Milligan was denied a jury trial in a court not established by Congress and composed of judges not appointed during good behavior. In Indiana the federal courts were open to hear criminal accusations.

The Constitution "is a law for rulers and people, equally in war and in peace, and covers with the shield of its protection all classes of men, at all times, and under all circumstances. No doctrine, involving more pernicious consequences, was ever invented by the wit of man than that any of its provisions can be suspended during any of the great exigencies of government."

Chief Justice Chase for the four-judge minority agreed that Milligan must be discharged, but feared that the Court was imposing unwise limits on the government's ability to deal with insurrection by denying to Congress the power to authorize military commissions such as the one in Indiana. Chase was concerned that the regular federal courts might be "open and undisturbed" and yet "wholly incompetent to avert threatened danger." He feared that the majority opinion would be interpreted to cripple the constitutional power of the government in times of invasion or rebellion.

In fact, the majority opinion was misused in the post war period by southern states to resist the development of color-blind justice in both civil and military courts. But the long-term effect of *Milligan* was to stand as a defense of individual liberty in both civilian and military concerns, and it restored some of the prestige the Court had lost by its decision in DRED SCOTT V. SANDFORD (1857). On the entry of the United States into WORLD WAR I, President Wilson significantly cited *Ex parte Milligan* in renouncing any intention of suspending the Bill of Rights for the duration of the war, though in fact there were well known limitations on freedom of speech and press.

The restrictions on and forced relocation of American citizens of Japanese descent during WORLD WAR II approached the *Milligan* situation [*see* JAPANESE AMERICANS, TREATMENT OF]. After the attack on PEARL HARBOR Congress made it a crime for Japanese Americans to enter or remain in military zones designated by the President. Under this authority the commanding general of the West Coast region ordered all such persons to obey curfews and to report to relocation centers for internment. The curfew order was upheld unanimously in *Hirabayashi v. United States* (1943) as necessary to prevent espionage and sabotage in an area threatened by military attack. No question of martial law or military tribunals was involved. When the court finally reached the issue of forced evacuation and relocation camps in *Korematsu v. United States* (1944), the majority followed the same reasoning of military necessity and potential danger. At the same time the Court in *Ex parte Endo* (1944) made some amends by approving the release on habeas corpus of a Japanese American of established loyalty from a relocation camp.

Following the Japanese attack on Pearl Harbor, the governor of Hawaii suspended the writ of habeas corpus and placed the territory under martial law. After much delay, the Court held in *Duncan v. Kahanomoku* (1946) that the establishment of military tribunals to try civilians had been illegal. Though the military operations in Hawaii were very similar to those in Indiana, the *Duncan* opinion did not rely heavily on *Milligan*, and only Justice Murphy stood by the rigid rule of that case that military trials of civilians are unconstitutional except in an actual field of military operations.

German saboteurs who landed on the east coast of the United States in 1942 with intent to destroy defense facilities were denied access to the civil courts on capture and were tried by a military commissions on presidential order. Their defense was based on *Milligan*, but the precedent was rejected by the Supreme Court in *Ex parte Quirin* (1942).

BIBLIOGRAPHY

Kutler Stanley I. *Judicial Power and Reconstruction Politics*. 1968.
Irons, Peter. *Justice at War*. 1983.

C. HERMAN PRITCHETT

MILLS TARIFF ACT (1888). Presenting himself in 1884 as the champion of honesty and efficiency in government, Grover Cleveland assumed the presidency knowing little about tariff policy. Nevertheless, President Cleveland did inherit traditional Democratic antipathy to high tariffs and was influenced by reform-minded Mugwumps who had aided his election. In 1886, Cleveland supported unsuccessful efforts to reduce tariff rates led by Representative William Morrison, notwithstanding divisions over protectionism within his own party.

Moved little by doctrinaire approaches to free trade and protectionism, Cleveland did confront the problem of chronic government surpluses. Concerned that the accumulated Treasury surplus would restrict business credit but strongly opposed to increased spending, Cleveland took the unprecedented step of devoting his entire annual message of 1887 to tariff reform. In his message, Cleveland opposed reducing internal taxes on alcohol and tobacco. Instead, he proposed sharply lower tariffs on imported raw materials and consumer necessities. He also sought to reduce protective tariffs applicable to manufactures, characterizing protectionism as an unfair system of subsidies for business to the detriment of the working poor.

Roger Mills, chairman of the House Ways and Means Committee, led the Democratic tariff reduction effort in 1888. However, his bill provided for only mild cuts in tariff rates and was criticized for favoring southern products over northern manufactures. Nevertheless, the Mills bill received administration support and passed the House on nearly a straight party vote. The Republican-controlled Senate failed to act on the Mills bill before the 1888 election. After Cleveland's reelection bid had failed, the Senate passed its own revenue bill that would have cut internal taxes while increasing many protective tariffs. The Fiftieth Congress passed neither the Mills bill nor the Senate bill, but the tariff debate of 1888 did restore the DEMOCRATIC PARTY as the party of tariff reform.

BIBLIOGRAPHY

Nevins, Allan. *Grover Cleveland: A Study in Courage.* 1932.
Stanwood, Edward. *American Tariff Controversies in the Nineteenth Century.* Vol. 2. Repr. 1967.
Terrill, Tom E. *The Tariff, Politics, and American Foreign Policy 1874–1901.* 1973.

RALPH MITZENMACHER

MINISTERIAL DUTIES. The term *ministerial duties* describes a legal category of executive actions. The term means that law controls a particular action in a way that courts can enforce. Its genesis lies centuries ago in the law of England, as the common law courts decided that they could compel the king's officers to perform ministerial duties but not discretionary ones.

The new American Republic soon adopted this concept. In MARBURY V. MADISON (1803), the Supreme Court established the basic nature and extent of judicial control of executive action. William Marbury, whose commission to be a justice of the peace had not been delivered to him by Secretary of State James Madison, sued for a writ of mandamus to compel delivery. Chief Justice John Marshall emphasized the traditional distinction between ministerial and discretionary actions in the English law of mandamus. An act would be ministerial if a clear legal duty were owed the plaintiff. Marshall argued that courts could compel delivery of Marbury's commission, which was a ministerial act because the statute required delivery of a completed commission. (Marshall did not order delivery of the commission, however, because of his conclusion that the Supreme Court lacked proper jurisdiction of the case.) On the other hand, Marshall emphasized that the courts could not compel the Secretary of State to adopt some particular foreign policy, which would be a discretionary matter in which

the Secretary acted for the President. Thus a legal doctrine that had arisen in a constitutional monarchy came to be a central precept of a new republican government.

Federal courts, which have explicit authority to issue writs of mandamus to executive officers, still follow the ministerial-discretionary distinction. Employed correctly, the distinction does not ask whether the administrative function under challenge contains some element of discretion (almost all of them do), but whether the particular action challenged is within the discretion conferred by law.

For several reasons, presidential decisions usually escape characterization as ministerial acts. The President has independent constitutional powers that must be given full scope. Statutes delegating power to him are often drawn very broadly; functions of a clerical or routine nature are placed in subordinates. And courts, reluctant to reverse a President's judgment that an action is necessary, conclude that many high-level actions are political questions that are not reviewable in court. As other administration offices become increasingly subordinate, however, it becomes more likely that the actions of their occupants will be found to constitute ministerial duties.

The Supreme Court has never ordered a President to make a substantive decision in a particular way, although the court did order the President to produce certain records in UNITED STATES V. NIXON (1974). Thus, in MISSISSIPPI V. JOHNSON (1867), the Court dismissed an attempt by the state of Mississippi to enjoin the President from enforcing RECONSTRUCTION legislation. The decision recognized the broad grants of discretionary authority in the President's statutory duties and the consequent inappropriateness of judicial interference. One lower federal court held that President Richard M. Nixon had violated a statute by refusing to submit an alternate pay plan, but the court withheld mandamus in favor of issuing a declaratory judgment of the law, to show respect to the presidential office [*see* NATIONAL TREASURY EMPLOYEES UNION V. NIXON (1974)].

The Supreme Court has long been willing to mandate the performance of ministerial duties by subordinate officers. In KENDALL V. UNITED STATES (1838), the Court forced the Postmaster General to pay a claim for carriage of the mails that had been assessed by an arbitrator according to an explicit statutory procedure. The Court characterized the duty to pay the award as "a mere ministerial act, which neither [the Postmaster] nor the President had any authority to deny or control."

Sometimes the Court uses an order to a subordinate

officer to perform a ministerial duty as a means of controlling a President indirectly, where he has exceeded even his own broad statutory powers. In this way the rule of law is preserved, while minimizing direct confrontations between the branches of government at the highest levels. In YOUNGSTOWN SHEET & TUBE CO. V. SAWYER (1952), the Court enjoined the Secretary of Commerce from carrying out President Harry S. Truman's order to seize the steel mills, because a statute did not allow presidential seizures of industrial facilities.

BIBLIOGRAPHY

Fisher, Louis. *The Constitution between Friends.* 1978.
Shane, Porter M., and Harold H. Bruff. *The Law of Presidential Power.* 1988.
Tribe, Laurence H. *American Constitutional Law.* 2d ed. 1988.

HAROLD H. BRUFF

MISSISSIPPI v. JOHNSON 4 Wallace 475 (1867). The *Johnson* case rejected an attempt by the state of Mississippi to enjoin President Andrew Johnson from enforcing the Reconstruction Acts of 1867. In essence, the Supreme Court said it could not enjoin the President from performing an illegal act.

The Reconstruction Act of 2 March 1867 provided for the establishment and administration of military government, in the period of after RECONSTRUCTION after the CIVIL WAR, in the states that had seceded. The legislation cited the lack of adequate protection of life and property and stipulated that until loyal and republican state governments were established, the states would be divided into five military districts and undergo military rule. The President was required to assign a military commander to each district and to detail a military force to maintain order. The military regimes superseded the civil organizations that President Abraham Lincoln and Johnson had previously established to govern the former Confederacy. Johnson had declared that the "insurrection" was over and that order and civil authority prevailed. Congressional RADICAL REPUBLICANS, led by Thaddeus Stevens, however, overturned the President's reconstruction program and replaced ongoing civil governments with military rule.

The Reconstruction Act of 2 March provided that it would become inoperative when Mississippi and other Confederate states satisfied certain conditions, including the establishment of Negro suffrage. A supplementary Reconstruction Act of 23 March 1867 provided further stipulations.

President Johnson vetoed the initial Reconstruction Act, assailing it in scorching language as unconstitutional, but Congress overrode his veto. The President, believing that he had no choice but to enforce both Reconstruction Acts, despite their unconstitutionality, then prepared to execute the acts by replacing the civil governments, which had been functioning for over a year, with military rule. Mississippi requested the courts to enjoin the President from doing so. Mississippi contended that Congress in replacing civil government with military rule had no constitutional basis for doing so, and that Johnson, in moving to carry out the legislation, was violating the Constitution. In executing the Reconstruction Acts, Mississippi also contended, the President was performing "a mere ministerial duty," which the Court could suitably enjoin.

The Supreme Court, however, found that the President was not fulfilling a MINISTERIAL DUTY, which it defined as one in which nothing is left to discretion. The assignment of military commanders and defining their duties is not ministerial, but "executive and political." The Court deemed any attempt by the judicial branch to bar the President's performance of those duties "an absurd extravagance."

An allegation, the Court said, that the legislation to be executed is unconstitutional is insufficient to remove the case from the general principle that forbids judicial interference with the exercise of executive discretion. Just as it cannot be contended that the courts can restrain Congress from enacting an unconstitutional law, neither can the courts prevent the President from executing such a law.

The Court's restraint was also spurred by the lack of precedent and the possible consequences of an attempt to restrain the President. If the President refused to obey the Court, the judges would lack power to enforce the injunction process. If the President complied with the injunction, a collision between the executive and legislative branches might ensue. Conceivably, the House might impeach the President for his compliance with the injunction, and the Court might face the knotty question of whether it could restrain the Senate from sitting as a court of IMPEACHMENT.

In effect, the Court in weighing the President's duty under the Constitution to enforce the laws found that it is solely a duty of conscience that his oath imposes. Hence his obligation is moral rather than legal. The ultimate arbiter is the President's own conscience rather than a court of law.

BIBLIOGRAPHY

Castel, Albert. *The Presidency of Andrew Johnson.* 1979.
Donald, David. *The Politics of Reconstruction, 1865–1867.* 1965.

Dunning, William A. *Reconstruction Political and Economic* 1907.
Stampp, Kenneth M. *The Era of Reconstruction 1865–1877*. 1965.

LOUIS W. KOENIG

MISSOURI COMPROMISE.

Between 1819 and 1821, the first sustained confrontation over SLAVERY in the United States since the CONSTITUTIONAL CONVENTION of 1789 severely roiled the nation's political waters until resolved by a series of legislative actions by Congress. The whole controversy demonstrated the existence of powerful sectional and regional antagonisms in the United States and the persistence of partisan Federalist–Democratic-Republican hatreds as well.

When the people of Missouri applied for admission as a state in 1819, it seemed to be a routine action. Since 1789, Congress had admitted nine additional states to the Union, largely without controversy. Missouri proved to be different. Once Representative James Tallmadge, Jr., of New York, introduced an amendment to the Missouri statehood bill prohibiting slavery there and another freeing slaves born in Missouri after its admission at the age of twenty-five, both of which passed the House of Representatives, a full political confrontation occurred. Behind Tallmadge's actions were some genuine antislavery feelings as well as a great deal of political bitterness that had been building up during what President James Monroe had called an "ERA OF GOOD FEELINGS." Some opponents of slavery in Missouri feared that the presence of blacks in the area would serve as a barrier to white migration there. Still others were sensitive to any unbalancing of the equal number of slave and free states then in the Union. Other were angry over the extra power that slaves gave the South in presidential elections due to the Constitution's three-fifths clause. Southerners, in their turn, fiercely reacted against any threat to slavery's expansion, or any suggestion that the section, its people and its institutions, would be restricted in any way by federal authority. At the same time, once the controversy began, some of the few surviving Federalist congressmen tried to use the issues raised to make mischief and hurt the bisectional Democratic-Republican coalition dominating American politics and thus revive their own party's fortunes.

At first, the controversy seemed serious enough to threaten the continuation of the Union. But as it developed, compromising elements within Congress, with HENRY CLAY of Kentucky in the forefront, began looking for a formula that would settle the issue equitably. Senator Jesse Thomas of Illinois (a native Marylander) offered the proposals that were eventu-

ally adopted. Over a series of months and not until a number of potentially disabling roadblocks were overcome, Clay and his fellow compromisers finally worked out matters in a series of bills that admitted Missouri as a slave state, balanced by admitting the free state of Maine at the same time; most significantly, Congress barred slavery from the rest of the Louisiana Purchase territory above the line 36° 30′ north latitude, a line that would remain for over thirty years.

Although the dispute was largely fought out in Congress, from the first it also intruded into presidential politics. Some Federalists hoped to unite northern Democratic-Republicans with themselves in a coalition opposed to the reelection of James Monroe of Virginia. The controversy did complicate, for a time, Monroe's reelection expectations. The President himself opposed any restriction on slavery's expansion as unconstitutional but was under pressure from the restrictionists in his party as well as from his southern colleagues, as the presidential campaign season began. Monroe worked actively behind the scenes on behalf of the compromise, particularly among prickly Virginia Representatives who were loath to give way on what was to them a matter of constitutional principle, and allow any restrictions on slavery at all. Because of the anger and political complications, Monroe was hesitant at first to sign the Missouri bills but, after considering a veto, he did sign them. It brought him some grief for a time in the Democratic-Republican presidential nominating caucus in the House of Representatives, but this proved to be temporary. Since the legislative situation had been resolved, the bitter confrontation flared out, Monroe was reelected all but unanimously in the ELECTORAL COLLEGE in 1820, and the battle over slavery extension was delayed until another day.

BIBLIOGRAPHY

Ammon, Harry. *James Monroe: The Quest for National Identity*. 1971.
Dangerfield, George. *The Awakening of American Nationalism: 1815–1828*. 1965.
Moore, Glover. *The Missouri Controversy, 1819–1821*. 1953.

JOEL H. SILBEY

MISSOURI v. HOLLAND 252 U.S. 416 (1920).

Missouri v. Holland is a controversial Supreme Court opinion that examined the status of treaties under the Constitution. Part of a broader debate over the TREATY-MAKING POWER, the case may have implications for the President's use of that power.

In 1913, during the Progressive Era, Congress had passed legislation to regulate the killing of migratory birds. Lower federal courts invalidated those hunting regulations on the basis of the Tenth Amendment; the states traditionally had regulated migratory birds and wild animals, and the courts reasoned that the states had such power because it was "not delegated to the United States by the Constitution, nor prohibited by it to the States." Subsequently, however, President Woodrow Wilson made the Migratory Bird Treaty of 1916 with Great Britain (representing its commonwealth of Canada) with the Senate's ADVICE AND CONSENT. Congress enacted and President Wilson signed in 1918 bird-hunting legislation that implemented the treaty.

Although lower courts had invalidated the 1913 legislation, they upheld the 1918 enactment and validated the Migratory Bird Treaty. The state of Missouri appealed one of those cases to the United States Supreme Court, seeking to enjoin Ray P. Holland, the federal game warden, from enforcing the new law in its state. Missouri argued that if the 1913 legislation was invalid under the Tenth Amendment, then the 1918 law should also be invalid. The fact that Congress had passed the new legislation pursuant to a treaty should not change the case's outcome, since treaties and federal statutes alike are equally subject to the Tenth Amendment and other constitutional limitations. In a 7 to 2 vote, however, the Supreme Court disagreed with Missouri's argument. Writing for the majority, Justice Oliver Wendell Holmes held that the treaty did "not contravene any prohibitory words" in the Constitution and was not "forbidden by some invisible radiation from the general terms of the tenth amendment." Justice Holmes did not say whether the lower courts had incorrectly invalidated the older 1913 legislation but did suggest that the presence of a treaty in the current case made a difference in his decision. Although conceding that there may be "qualifications" on the treaty power, Holmes's opinion implies that treaties (and implementing legislation) are constitutional if made according to Article II's advice-and-consent procedures; the Constitution places fewer substantive restrictions on treaties and implementing legislation than it does on federal statutes in the absence of treaties.

Missouri v. Holland was controversial because it elevated treaties above federal statutes in the hierarchy of U.S. law and suggested a few constitutional limits on the treaty power. Congress has shown concern that Presidents would increasingly commit the nation to international compacts—both treaties and EXECUTIVE AGREEMENTS. (Engendering debate, Presidents have made executive agreements with other nations without following Article II's advice-and-consent process.)

Under Holmes's opinion, the Constitution would do little to restrain those compacts. By 1953, concerns about the treaty power superseding the legislative power gave rise to Sen. John Bricker's proposed constitutional amendment providing, in part, that "a treaty which conflicts with this Constitution shall not be of any force or effect." But the BRICKER AMENDMENT was never adopted, partly because of the Supreme Court's opinion in REID v. COVERT (1957). In that case, the Court by implication limited Holmes's earlier, broader opinion, suggesting that the Constitution more substantively restricted the treaty power and thus the President's use of that power.

BIBLIOGRAPHY

American Law Institute. *Restatement (Third) of the Foreign Relations Law of the United States §302 and Commentary.* Vol. I. 1987.
Henkin, Louis. *Foreign Affairs and the Constitution.* 1972.

KENNETH C. RANDALL

MISTRETTA v. UNITED STATES 488 U.S. 361 (1989). In *Mistretta*, the Supreme Court, by a vote of 8 to 1, upheld the constitutionality of the Sentencing Reform Act of 1984 against charges that it involved improper DELEGATION OF LEGISLATIVE POWER and violated SEPARATION OF POWERS. The case was decided seven months after MORRISON v. OLSON (1988), which had sustained the use of INDEPENDENT COUNSEL for investigating allegations of criminality by senior officials in the EXECUTIVE BRANCH, and it continued *Morrison's* retreat from the rigid and formalistic approach to separation-of-powers issues taken by the Court earlier in the 1980s. Although the Court never alluded to the issue, the decision implicitly rejected the theory of an "unitary executive," which would place all executive and administrative functions directly under the President, and again confirmed the power of Congress to create INDEPENDENT COMMISSIONS.

The Sentencing Reform Act was aimed at controlling what was described in the Senate Report accompanying the legislation as the "shameful disparity in criminal sentences" imposed by different federal judges on similar offenders who had committed similar offenses. Its constitutionality was defended in the Court by the Reagan administration. The act created the United States Sentencing Commission, an independent body statutorily declared to be in the judicial branch. The commission's seven voting members (at least three of whom are to be federal judges) are appointed by the President, with Senate confirmation, and are removable from the commission for cause. Its principal responsibility is to establish mandatory sentencing guidelines for federal judges. Ironically, since the promulgation of the commission's guidelines in 1987, they have been subject to intense and widespread criticism because their rigidity has been seen as increasing, not decreasing, the unfairness of sentencing in individual cases.

In an opinion by Justice Harry F. Blackmun, the Court, rejected the claim of improper delegation because it found that Congress had provided adequate guidance to the commission. It also rejected each of the claims alleging violation of the separation of powers, insisting on the need for a "flexible understanding" of this doctrine. It held that vesting rule-making authority in an entity located in the judicial branch was not impermissible, both because the Sentencing Commission was not a court but a pure example of an independent agency and because the judiciary could be authorized to make rules to assist in carrying out its responsibilities, including sentencing. It found no absolute constitutional bar to assigning administrative duties to federal judges, citing numerous examples of extrajudicial service from JOHN JAY to Earl Warren. Although it conceded that such service might be inadvisable, it declared that it would not violate the separation of powers unless it "undermines the integrity of the Judicial Branch." Nor would the judiciary's independence be affected by the President's power to appoint judges to the commission and to remove them, particularly since removed judges would retain judicial office and since removal would be permissible only for cause, a limitation that, as in the case of other independent commissions, assures protection against presidential control.

The only separation-of-powers issues that troubled the Court concerned the possibility that the political branches might, by coopting federal judges for service on bodies with policy-making authority, be able to capitalize on the public's respect for the judiciary to attain political ends, thus compromising judicial impartiality. It concluded, however, that judicial service here was constitutionally permissible because the commission's authority related to sentencing—a judicial responsibility—and not to the performance of executive or legislative functions.

The Court reaffirmed the standard it had articulated in NIXON V. ADMINISTRATOR OF GENERAL SERVICES (1977) and reiterated in *Morrison* for determining the constitutionality of congressional restrictions on the conduct of the executive branch, and applied this standard to separation-of-powers issues relating to the judicial branch, holding that violation of the separation requirement occurs when the affected branch is prevented "from accomplishing its constitutionally as-

signed functions." As in *Morrison*, the lone dissenter was Justice Antonin Scalia, who again argued that the separation doctrine must be strictly enforced. He maintained that an independent agency in the judicial branch was even more anomalous than an independent executive agency because only courts can exercise the judiciary's constitutional powers and that, consistently with the separation doctrine rule-making authority could not be delegated to a "junior-varsity Congress" whose only responsibility was purely legislative—the promulgation of mandatory sentencing guidelines. The majority, however, preferred its more "flexible understanding."

BIBLIOGRAPHY

Frankel, Marvin E., and Leonard Orland. "Sentencing Commissions and Guidelines." *Georgetown Law Journal* 73 (1984): 225–247.

Freed, Daniel J. "Federal Sentencing in the Wake of Guidelines: Unacceptable Limits on the Discretion of Sentencers." *Yale Law Journal* 101 (1992): 1681–1754.

Redish, Martin H. "Separation of Powers, Judicial Authority, and the Scope of Article III: The Troubling Cases of *Morrison* and *Mistretta*." *DePaul Law Review* 39 (1990): 299–319.

U.S. Senate. Committee on the Judiciary. *Comprehensive Crime Control Act of 1983*. 98th Cong., 1st sess., 1983. S. Rep. 98-225: 37–190; 792–793.

DEAN ALFANGE, JR.

MITCHELL, JOHN (1913–1988), Attorney General. John N. Mitchell, a Wall Street lawyer and Richard M. Nixon's law partner in the mid 1960s, managed Nixon's successful presidential bid in 1968. As Attorney General from 1969 to 1972, he remained on close terms with Nixon during the first two years, serving as a major adviser in foreign as well as domestic affairs. Mitchell's preeminence began to wane by 1971, as WHITE HOUSE ADVISERS H. R. Haldeman and John Ehrlichman became increasingly influential.

Some of his decisions as head of the Justice Department sparked controversy. Mitchell authorized a much broader use of ELECTRONIC SURVEILLANCE than had his predecessors. Despite some disagreement within the Justice Department, he approved prosecuting the so-called Chicago Seven for the unrest at the 1968 Democratic national convention. He also approved an indictment against Daniel Ellsberg for leaking the *Pentagon Papers* (a Defense Department study of the VIETNAM WAR) and an injunction against the *New York Times* and the *Washington Post* to stop their publication [*see* NEW YORK TIMES CO. V. UNITED STATES].

Mitchell resigned in March 1972 to head Nixon's reelection committee. After the election, reports surfaced linking Mitchell with the break-in of Democratic

National Committee headquarters and the subsequent cover-up that was at the heart of the WATERGATE AFFAIR. One former subordinate told the Senate Watergate Committee that Mitchell, while still Attorney General, had approved of the break-in and later had developed the burglars' story and helped prepare false testimony for the grand jury. Mitchell denied the allegations. According to White House transcripts, Nixon believed that Mitchell was concerned only with saving himself, not the presidency. Early in 1974, the President asked him to accept full responsibility for Watergate; Mitchell maintained his innocence.

In March 1974, a federal grand jury indicted Mitchell for conspiracy, obstruction of justice, and perjury. Found guilty on 1 January 1975 (the first Attorney General to be convicted), he served nineteen months in prison. In a separate case, he was tried and acquitted of charges of conspiracy to defraud the United States when he sought to arrange a meeting between financier Robert Vesco, a major campaign contributor, and William Casey, head of the Securities and Exchange Commission, which was investigating Vesco.

Rather, Dan, and Gary Paul Gates. *The Palace Guard.* 1974.
Seymour, Whitney North, Jr. *United States Attorney: An Inside View of "Justice" in America under the Nixon Administration.* 1975.
The Watergate Hearings: Break-In and Cover-up: Proceedings of the Senate Select Committee on Presidential Campaign Activities. Edited by the staff of the *New York Times.* 1973.

NANCY V. BAKER

MOLEY, RAYMOND (1886–1975), presidential adviser, Assistant Secretary of State, journalist. Moley was a professor of public law at Columbia University when SAMUEL ROSENMAN asked him to assemble the BRAIN TRUST, a group of academic advisers who provided much of the intellectual impetus for the NEW DEAL. After Franklin D. Roosevelt's 1932 victory, Moley stayed on to become an Assistant Secretary of State. This position was largely nominal, however; in practice Moley served Roosevelt in a variety of informal roles. He wrote speeches, drafted legislation, helped coordinate the President's growing legislative agenda, and provided political and policy advice. Moley's power was at its zenith in early 1933, as the administration prepared to take power and began instituting the New Deal.

Signs that Moley was uncomfortable within the Roosevelt administration were soon clear, especially after Moley clashed with Secretary of State CORDELL HULL at the London Economic Conference in July 1933. Moley left the government in August to become the editor of *Today* magazine, which started out as a strong advocate of nearly every New Deal program. Moley continued to write speeches for Roosevelt, though he complained that he was employed more for his skill as a wordsmith than for his contributions on policy matters. By late 1935, Moley was clearly estranged from the administration's progressive wing on both foreign and domestic policy. He later said that he realized how far apart he and Roosevelt had moved only when he heard his own words spoken in the 1936 STATE OF THE UNION MESSAGE, a rousing diatribe against "the political puppets of an economic autocracy." Moley's public break with Roosevelt came a year later, over the COURT-PACKING PLAN. Once a Roosevelt intimate, Moley saw the President only once after 1936, and he became an outspoken critic of the New Deal.

Schlesinger, Arthur M., Jr. *The Age of Roosevelt.* 3 vols. 1957–1960.

WILLIAM LASSER

MONDALE, WALTER F. (b.1928), Senator, forty-second Vice President of the United States (1977–1981), Democratic presidential nominee in 1984. A lifetime Democrat, Walter Frederick Mondale was a self-described progressive liberal in politics. Although a supporter of organized labor, educational reform and consumer interests, he was a political moderate. Mondale preferred quiet negotiation among organized leaders to direct confrontation.

Mondale grew up in rural Minnesota, the son of a Methodist minister. He graduated from the University of Minnesota in 1951, and the University of Minnesota law school in 1956. Mondale's family were partisans of the state's Democratic Farmer-Labor (DFL) Party, a coalition of left progressives, populists, and former New Dealers controlled by HUBERT H. HUMPHREY, EUGENE McCARTHY, and, in the 1950s, ORVILLE FREEMAN. Mondale never departed from these Minnesota roots and tried on the national level to forge an electoral alliance of organized labor, farm progressives, civil rights activists, and urban reformers.

Mondale became a Humphrey protégé. In 1958, he served as Governor Freeman's campaign manager. Freeman appointed Mondale state attorney general in 1960, a post to which he was subsequently elected.

Mondale attended the 1964 Democratic National Convention as a Humphrey supporter and was named to the convention's credentials committee, which faced an intractable political problem: who should sit as the delegation for the state of Mississippi? The Mississippi

Freedom Democratic Party (MFDP), a coalition of civil rights activists and black Mississippians excluded from the state's primaries, contested with the Regular Democrats, the segregationist core of the old party, on the right to represent the state. An ad hoc subcommittee, with Mondale as its chair, met to resolve the seating problem. Mondale arranged a compromise: the Regular Democrats would sit as the Mississippi delegation; but two members of the MFDP would sit as at-large delegates. The credential committee also tacitly promised that a change would take place in the rules governing primaries in Mississippi. Although the MFDP did not agree to the compromise, the convention accepted Mondale's plan and Humphrey received the vice presidential nomination.

In December 1964, Mondale was appointed to the U.S. Senate to replace Humphrey. He was subsequently reelected in 1966. A firm supporter of President Lyndon Johnson and the GREAT SOCIETY programs, Mondale built up a legislative record in domestic areas. He introduced the Fair Warning Act of 1966 which required auto makers to notify car owners of defects. In 1967, Mondale established his civil rights credentials by becoming the Johnson administration's floor leader in the Senate on the open-housing bill.

In 1968, Mondale joined Hubert Humphrey's campaign. The competition for the Democratic ticket was intense and the campaign complex. Against Humphrey stood ROBERT F. KENNEDY and fellow Minnesotan Eugene McCarthy. Humphrey won the nomination but lost the election narrowly to Richard Nixon. Mondale spent the first Nixon administration in the Senate, building up his progressive liberal credentials. Although he supported the Supreme Court's decision on busing, he sought to moderate white backlash against its provisions. As chair of the Select Committee on Equal Education Opportunity he favored increased federal funding to special projects in inner city schools.

Reelected to the Senate in 1972, at Humphrey's insistence Mondale began to prepare for the presidential nomination, creating a network of state contacts. In the wake of GEORGE McGOVERN's decisive defeat and Nixon's resignation, no true front-runner existed for either party. But in November 1974, Mondale announced that he no longer wanted the nomination, explaining that he had enough of Holiday Inns and politicking. Later, party insiders would wonder whether Mondale had the mental toughness to run a presidential campaign.

Jimmy Carter chose Mondale as his running mate for the 1976 election. Mondale did more than hold his own during the campaign, debating Robert Dole on television. As Vice President, Mondale showed signs of emerging as an important voice in the Carter administration, locating his office in the White House itself. He was a key participant in the negotiations between ISRAEL and Egypt, but the Carter administration ignored his labor and social-policy concerns. Mondale was also unable to improve the administration's relationship with Congress.

Immediately following Carter's defeat by Ronald Reagan in 1980, Mondale began to construct the machinery for the 1984 nomination bid. Now out of public office, he worked to strengthen his regional contacts and his policy positions on foreign affairs. In the Democratic primaries, Mondale faced challenges from Ted Kennedy, Gary Hart, John Glenn, and Jessie Jackson. Mondale's careful, scandal-free run in the primaries won out, in large part because of the AFL-CIO's early endorsement.

Union support in the election, however, proved ineffective. The incumbent, Ronald Reagan, warned that his opponent was the captive of the traditional Democratic special interests. Mondale's election campaign lacked creativity, save the choice of GERALDINE FERRARO, the first woman nominated for the vice presidency. Ferraro did well in her debates against George Bush, but accusations of financial impropriety against her husband made her a liability on the ticket. Mondale, temperamentally cautious, offered no clear alternative vision to Ronald Reagan. His moderate liberal credentials were insufficient to unseat an incumbent who had shifted the rhetoric of politics away from government spending to individual freedom. Mondale won only his home state of Minnesota and the District of Columbia, receiving 40.6 percent of the vote in an election in which only 53.3 percent of all registered voters voted. After the election, Mondale took up the practice of law in Washington. In 1993, President Clinton appointed him ambassador to Japan.

BIBLIOGRAPHY

Lewis, Finlay. *Mondale*. 1980.
Ranney, Austin, ed. *The Election of 1984*. 1985.

JOHN F. WALSH

MONETARY POLICY. Government actions intended to influence the level of interest rates, the rate of growth of the money supply, and related conditions in financial markets broadly constitute monetary policy. Today, it is conventional to say that U.S. monetary policy is guided by a desire to contribute to stable economic growth, price stability, and high employment.

Central to most discussions of monetary policy is a centuries-old idea that variation in the quantity of money has a powerful long-run influence on price levels. Price-level changes (inflation, deflation) can redistribute income among groups in society, so monetary policy choices are often politically charged. Changes in monetary policy also have a temporary impact on the so-called real economy—that is, employment and production. Because economic performance is central to public evaluations of presidential performance, Presidents have obvious incentives to care a great deal about the conduct of monetary policy. Not surprisingly, monetary policy has long been controversial and central to presidential politics.

Historical Overview. In the United States, many of the most profound political conflicts have been broadly related to monetary policy. An early example is the struggle over the Second BANK OF THE UNITED STATES launched by President Andrew Jackson's famous veto. The eventual outcomes were a lasting realignment of the political parties and the conclusion, at that time, that it was not acceptable to establish a central bank to regulate the U.S. economy.

The deflationary monetary policies of the post–CIVIL WAR era were associated with significant political turbulence. Important easy-money political movements, such as the Grangers, Greenbackers, and Populists, emerged during this period [see GREENBACK PARTY]. The conflict over deflation culminated in a politically decisive presidential contest in 1896, when the silver inflationists represented by WILLIAM JENNINGS BRYAN were soundly defeated.

The evident failures of monetary policy to prevent the stock market crash of 1929 and to adjust to the ensuing Great Depression directly contributed to a momentous transformation of the presidency during the NEW DEAL. The basic partisan alignments established during that time have continued to a significant degree to the present.

The New Deal period also saw significant reforms in the formal structure of the FEDERAL RESERVE SYSTEM. Since 1914, monetary policy in the United States has been conducted primarily by the Federal Reserve System, especially its component organizations, the Federal Reserve Board and the Federal Open Market Committee. The Federal Reserve is the central bank of the United States, and its institutional design—especially after the New Deal–era reforms—reflects a desire to insulate the organization from short-run domination by either elected politicians or Wall Street financiers. This formal independence is in tension with the obviously political nature of monetary policy. Thus, the relationship of the Federal Reserve and the President is of particular interest in understanding monetary policy.

Independence may give the Federal Reserve the needed scope for pursuing policies that are politically unpopular but economically necessary. If economic necessity is not clearly defined, however, independence may permit the Federal Reserve to abuse its large powers. Independence may also reduce the degree of coordination between monetary and FISCAL POLICY, to the detriment of both.

How Presidents Affect Monetary Policy. Presidents have limited but significant means to influence the conduct of monetary policy. Perhaps the most obvious and useful mechanism available to the President is the appointment process. The President nominates members of the Federal Reserve Board and its chairman (who also serves as chairman of the powerful Federal Open Market Committee), and the nominations are then subject to Senate ADVICE AND CONSENT. There is fairly strong evidence that board members appointed by Democratic Presidents are more likely to favor more stimulative policy—and by implication, higher employment—than are board members appointed by Republican Presidents.

Given the very long (fourteen-year) terms of the seven members of the Federal Reserve Board and the fact that the appointments are staggered, an average President should be able to appoint only two members during a normal four-year term. In fact, from the outset of the Federal Reserve through 1991, the median term in office of board members was only 4.4 years, and 78 percent of appointees served less than twelve years. In ten out of the seventeen four-year terms from 1921 to 1988, Presidents were able to make an average of more than four appointments (or reappointments) to the board. Thus, relatively high rates of turnover have given Presidents opportunities to significantly shape monetary policy in ways consistent with their own views.

Presidents are also able to recommend legislation to Congress to restructure the Federal Reserve and reduce both its policy independence and the bureaucratic perquisites that flow from that independence. This capability brings additional pressure to bear on the institution. This stick has been used infrequently, but the possibility of its use does affect the Federal Reserve's behavior.

Similarly, Presidents have publicly signaled their desires about the future course of monetary policy in order to shape Federal Reserve behavior. While Federal Reserve policy does appear to respond to presidential preferences, the magnitude of the response appears to be relatively small.

Finally, it is easy for Presidents to politicize the debate about monetary policy. Simply by publicly stating preferences about monetary policy, the President can encourage others to attempt to shape the direction of policy. When such presidential actions are perceived to imply future increases in the rate of inflation, they may provoke sharp, negative reactions in financial markets.

The chairman of the Federal Reserve is generally acknowledged to be the most important official in the making of monetary policy. The President, who appoints the chairman with the advice and consent of the Senate, possesses more leverage over the chairman than over the other board members because the chairman's term is relatively short (four years). Some evidence suggests that chairmen have "run for reelection" by trying to provide the kind of monetary policy the President prefers.

Consistent with evidence that Presidents have substantial means to shape monetary policy, there is evidence that monetary policy generally reflects the partisan identity of the incumbent President. Some evidence shows that most partisan impact occurs in the relatively concentrated period immediately after the presidency is transferred from one party to the other. Other evidence suggests that at least some of these policy effects are sustained throughout the period a particular President is in office.

There is far less support for the notion that Presidents usually succeed in turning monetary policy to their advantage before elections. Indeed, evidence shows that the Federal Reserve tries to "lie low" in the preelection period. It does this by reducing the frequency of highly visible actions during the election year and by stressing positive (or expansionary) actions whenever it does take action. Several accounts indicate that the Federal Reserve has declined to pursue highly restrictive policy during election years. A Fed desire to avoid apparent innovations in monetary policy (that is, by keeping interest rates stable) during election years could be the equivalent of adopting an accommodating stance toward fiscal expansions that might otherwise provoke a policy response (that is, higher interest rates).

Despite all this, Presidents have by no means been consistently able to shape monetary policy to their liking. Considerable tension has often existed between the President and the Federal Reserve over the conduct of monetary policy, sometimes reflected in overt and even bitter conflicts. Such conflicts have sometimes been resolved in ways that have redefined the relationship between these two central institutions for extended periods of time.

Monetary Policy since the 1960s. From the late 1960s to the early 1990s, monetary policy was increasingly seen as a relevant and powerful means of addressing economic problems, particularly inflation. In this period, a combination of economic shocks and structural changes heightened the importance of monetary policy in economic management. The decision to abandon fixed exchange rates for the dollar in the early 1970s, together with the explosive growth of international capital flows, significantly increased the importance of international factors in monetary policy calculations. Price shocks, especially in traded goods such as petroleum but also in domestic agricultural products, contributed to inflationary episodes that culminated in difficult periods of adjustment. In the (related) periods of high interest rates, the stresses and strains on financial institutions simultaneously resulted in financial innovation and in changes in the legal and regulatory climate, which substantially complicated the conduct of monetary policy. Finally, the persistent, large budget deficits that began during the Ronald Reagan presidency had the effect of making monetary policy the only flexible instrument of economic stabilization. The period between the mid-1970s and early 1990s is especially interesting to review.

Under Jimmy Carter. President Jimmy Carter took office in 1977 determined to reverse the conditions of "stagflation" that had dominated the 1970s. Carter initially proposed a program of economic stimulus, knowing that accommodative monetary policy would be necessary. The first year of the Carter administration, however, was marked by significant public squabbling between Federal Reserve Chairman Arthur Burns and the President. The Federal Reserve raised the discount rate in apparent defiance of White House preferences. Despite some evidence that money supply growth was, in fact, in line with White House desires during this period (the growth rate of one important measure of the money supply, M1, accelerated from about 6 to about 8 percent in 1977), Carter declined to reappoint Burns as chairman.

Around the same time, a process of financial innovation in response to high interest rates began. In particular, moneyholders began to try to shift funds out of non–interest-bearing demand deposits into interest-bearing accounts. The Federal Reserve later estimated that this changing approach to money management meant that observed money-supply figures significantly understated the actual economic effect of a given rate of growth of money supply.

Carter found a much more supportive Federal Reserve chairman in G. William Miller, a prominent and successful business executive. Money growth continued to be accommodative through 1978—growing at a rate above 8 percent for much of the year. Beginning in 1978, inflation accelerated steadily, consistent with prior monetary growth. By this point, following nearly a decade of high inflation, expectations of high inflation were well established in the population. Probably for that reason, the anti-inflation measures announced in late 1978 had little apparent effect—despite the fact that such measures would have seemed dramatic a decade earlier.

Reinforced by a second round of price hikes by the Organization of Petroleum Exporting Countries (OPEC), inflation in mid 1979 passed 11 percent—a rate twice as high as when Carter took office. Partly in response to the sense of economic crisis, Carter undertook a mid 1979 Cabinet shuffle that, instead of regenerating confidence, seemed to reflect an administration in disarray. In monetary affairs, the shift of Federal Reserve chairman Miller to the Treasury Department raised further doubts about the administration's commitment to containing inflation, and the dollar came under significant international selling pressure. The administration faced a classic confidence crisis in financial markets reinforced by stubbornly held expectations of high inflation. In these difficult circumstances, Carter recognized that he had no choice but to reassure the financial world. To do so, he nominated Paul Volcker, the president of the New York Federal Reserve Bank and a highly regarded player in the nation's financial management for nearly three decades, to the chairmanship of the Federal Reserve.

With Carter's acquiescence, the Federal Reserve in October 1979 moved dramatically to adopt new operating procedures. These procedures involved renouncing short-term control of interest rates in order to focus more on the money supply. The election year of 1980 proved to be a roller-coaster year from the perspective of monetary policy. Highly visible consumer credit controls were imposed for a few months in the first part of the year. The interbank rate exceeded 17 percent in April, plunged to around 9 percent in July, and then soared to almost 19 percent in December. After peaking in March at over 14 percent, inflation fell to about 11 percent by year's end. The rate of growth of the basic money supply fell from 8 percent in February to 4 percent in April only to reach nearly 8 percent again in October. By October, Carter, on the verge of defeat, was openly critical of the Federal Reserve—with little apparent effect.

Interestingly, 1980 was also marked by passage of legislation (the Depository Institutions Deregulation and Monetary Control Act) that reinforced the process of financial innovation already under way. The changes in financial practices made it more difficult in subsequent years to interpret the movement of at least some traditional indicators of monetary policy—exactly when monetary targeting enjoyed its greatest official acceptance.

Under Ronald Reagan. Taking office in 1981, President Reagan was generally supportive of the anti-inflation stance of the Federal Reserve. But he was also acutely aware of the challenges that high interest rates presented to the financial sector, especially the savings and loan industry. As the President was winning congressional approval for nearly revolutionary changes in taxing and spending, the Federal Reserve, determined to conquer inflation, pursued policies that created a deep recession. As the political costs of the recession fell heavily on the administration, criticism of the Federal Reserve was stepped up by administration economic spokespersons and they were joined by members of Congress.

Reagan administration officials nearly continuously criticized the Federal Reserve throughout the first term of the Reagan presidency, especially emphasizing the Fed's apparent failures to stabilize the growth rate of monetary aggregates. According to reports, Treasury Secretary Donald Regan opposed the reappointment of Volcker as chairman but ultimately yielded in the face of hostility to change from the financial community. Indeed, the rate of change in the basic money supply varied greatly during the first Reagan administration rather than stabilizing as one might have expected, given that both the Federal Reserve and the Reagan administration officially stressed the importance of controlling the money supply. The basic money supply indicator was, however, profoundly affected by financial innovation. Broader measures showed much greater monetary stability. In any case, inflation during the first Reagan term continued to fall (from around 12 percent to around 4 percent) at the same time that there was a significant increase in economic growth.

These economic improvements occurred in the context of a shift in fiscal policy toward permitting large permanent deficits. This change effectively transformed debates about fiscal policy, excluding issues of macroeconomic stabilization and shifting the emphasis to strategies for eliminating the deficit. Consequently, any prospects for macroeconomic adjustment were located in monetary policy and the Federal Reserve. At the same time, the policy mix of stimulative fiscal policy and restrictive monetary policy resulted in high real interest rates that helped to attract foreign capital inflows and keep the dollar strong.

The Reagan administration's economic leadership

changed dramatically in 1985, with a new Treasury Secretary (JAMES A. BAKER III) and an entirely new COUNCIL OF ECONOMIC ADVISERS (CEA). In 1986, President Reagan was able to appoint three new members of the Fed's Board of Governors, making a majority of board members sharing the "supply side" view favored by the administration. As Reagan's appointees became more assertive, Chairman Volcker's dominant position within the Federal Reserve was successfully challenged. Volcker's resignation in 1987 was followed by the appointment of conservative economist Alan Greenspan as chairman.

Under Greenspan's tenure, monetary policy followed a course favoring slow—if not necessarily steady—monetary growth and a renewed commitment to reducing inflation. The latter priority was enthusiastically supported by the Federal Reserve district bank presidents. Monetary policy was increasingly constrained by concerns about international financial flows, limiting the scope of policy action focused primarily on domestic economic conditions.

In a context of slowing economic growth, the Federal Reserve's course of action often conflicted with the desire of the administration for more economic stimulus. Nonetheless, President George Bush reappointed Greenspan for a second term in 1991, recognizing the importance of the financial sector's continuing confidence and the lack of any alternative consensus candidate.

BIBLIOGRAPHY

Alt, James E. "Leaning into the Wind or Ducking out of the Storm?" In *Politics and Economics in the Eighties*. Edited by Alberto Alesina and Geoffrey Carliner. 1991.

Axilrod, Stephen H. "U.S. Monetary Policy in Recent Years: An Overview." *Federal Reserve Bulletin* 71 (1985): 14–24.

Grieder, William. *Secrets of the Temple*. 1987.

Havrilesky, Thomas. "Monetary Signaling from the Administration to the Federal Reserve." *Journal of Money, Credit, and Banking* 19 (1988): 308–325.

Kettl, Donald. *Leadership at the Fed*. 1986.

Mayer, Thomas, ed. *The Political Economy of American Monetary Policy*. 1990.

Quinn, Dennis, and Robert Y. Shapiro. "Economic Growth Strategies: The Effects of Ideological Partisanship on Interest Rates and Business Taxation in the United States." *American Journal of Political Science* 35 (1991): 656–685.

Woolley, John T. *Monetary Politics: The Federal Reserve and the Politics of Monetary Policy*. 1984.

JOHN T. WOOLLEY

MONROE, JAMES (1758–1831), fifth President of the United States (1817–1825). James Monroe, the last of the revolutionary generation to hold the presidency, was born in Westmoreland County, Virginia, 28 April 1758, the son of Spence and Elizabeth (Jones) Monroe, the owners of a modest six-hundred acre plantation. Enrolled in William and Mary College in 1774, he left in 1776 to enlist in the Third Virginia Regiment, fighting in the battles of New York. He was promoted to major for bravery in the vanguard action at Trenton, where he was wounded. As an aide to Gen. William Alexander (Lord Stirling) with the rank of colonel he wintered at Valley Forge and fought at Monmouth. Returning to Virginia in 1780, he acted as a liaison with the southern army for Gov. Thomas Jefferson with whom he began to study law. Monroe formed a lifelong friendship with Jefferson who became at once his mentor and patron.

Early Career. After serving one term in the Virginia House of Burgesses, he was elected in 1783 along with Thomas Jefferson as a member of the Virginia delegation in the Confederation Congress. During his three-year term, he moved to the forefront of leadership, organizing the successful opposition to the Jay-Gardoqui proposals and drafting a plan for territorial government incorporated in the Northwest Ordinance of 1787. Before leaving for France in 1784, Jefferson introduced Monroe to James Madison, thus forging the third link in the collaboration, which was so influential in shaping the nation.

In 1786 he returned to Virginia after marrying Elizabeth Kortright, the daughter of a once wealthy New York merchant. It was a happy marriage—rarely were they separated for more than a few weeks—fitting the ideal of an age placing the highest value on family life. Monroe resumed his law practice, limited to county courts, first in Fredericksburg and then in Albemarle County where he relocated in 1789 to be closer to Jefferson. He ultimately acquired a 2,500-acre plantation, Highlands (now Ashlawn-Highland), adjacent to Jefferson's estate. (Later Monroe acquired another plantation, Oak Hill, near Leesburg, Virginia.) Since Madison lived twenty miles away, meetings between the three friends were easily arranged. Continuing his membership in the state legislature, Monroe was elected a delegate to the Virginia ratifying convention of 1788. As a member of the Continental Congress he had supported the move to strengthen the central government, but he opposed ratification of the Constitution because of excessive grants of power to the executive and the Senate.

Elected to the United States Senate in 1790, he worked with Madison (then in the House of Representatives) and Jefferson in founding the Democratic-Republican Party in opposition to the policies of President George Washington. In 1794 Washington appointed Monroe minister to France hoping that the choice of a Democratic-Republican would ease criticism at home and mollify France, where his policies were seen as pro-British. Monroe's open sympathy for the French revolutionary government led to his abrupt recall in 1796. Monroe defended himself in a book harshly criticizing the administration.

As proof that his recall had not shaken party confidence, the Democratic-Republican legislature elected Monroe governor of Virginia in 1799. During his three one-year terms he improved state administration and won praise for decisive action in containing the threatened slave uprising (Gabriel's Rebellion) in 1800. Monroe shared Jefferson's conclusion that future revolts were inevitable unless SLAVERY was eliminated—a goal best achieved by removing free blacks from the United States to encourage manumission. With legislative authorization Monroe wrote Jefferson about establishing a settlement on federally owned land. Jefferson, however, opposed a western site, preferring Africa. Without federal support the legislature dropped the project. At Jefferson's request the correspondence was kept confidential.

In 1803 Jefferson sent Monroe to France as special envoy to join the resident minister, Robert R. Livingston, in securing a port of deposit on the Mississippi, a mission rendered urgent by Spain's suspension of the right of deposit as a preliminary to the retrocession of Louisiana to France. Although empowered only to purchase a small area, Monroe and Livingston promptly accepted Napoleon's offer of all Louisiana. Popular approval of the LOUISIANA PURCHASE established Monroe's national reputation. Monroe remained in Europe as minister to Great Britain; he made an unsuccessful trip to Madrid to persuade Spain to acknowledge the cession of Louisiana. In 1806 Monroe and special envoy William Pinkney signed an agreement reducing British commercial restrictions. Jefferson did not submit the treaty for ratification, since it did not include a ban on impressment. Disappointed by the rejection of the treaty, Monroe was briefly estranged from the administration. In 1811, after Jefferson arranged a reconciliation, Madison, beset by a resurgent FEDERALISM and criticism from within his own party, appointed Monroe Secretary of State.

Monroe, who was admired for his pragmatism by the younger members of Congress (many later known as the War Hawks), was able to establish friendly working relations with Congress. He was able to win their support for defense measures, which led to a DECLARATION OF WAR in June 1812. After the British invasion of Washington in August 1814, Monroe became Secretary of War (he continued as Secretary of State) replacing John Armstrong, who was blamed for failing to provide for the defense of the capital. Monroe brought order into the tangled affairs of the department, but too late to affect the outcome of the war. Monroe drafted the instructions authorizing the peace commissioners to abandon the American position on neutral rights. He also began the negotiations that culminated in the Rush-Bagot agreement demilitarizing the Great Lakes.

After the war, as public attention shifted to politics, it was assumed that Monroe would be the Democratic-Republican presidential nominee in 1816. However, WILLIAM H. CRAWFORD (former Senator from Georgia and Monroe's replacement in the War Department) was favored by Democratic-Republicans dissatisfied with the long Virginia incumbency. Monroe and his backers were sufficiently alarmed to consider boycotting the congressional caucus. Crawford, only forty-four, was reputedly reluctant to challenge his senior colleague. His failure to withdraw formally was resented by Monroe's friends. Monroe was nominated by the caucus in March 1816 by the small margin of 65 votes to 54 for Crawford. The vice presidential candidate was DANIEL D. TOMPKINS, the wartime governor of New York. Although Tompkins served for two terms, he did not exert any influence on administration policies. In the election Monroe received 183 electoral votes to 34 cast for RUFUS KING, the Federalist candidate. This was the last appearance of the Federalists on the national scene and marked the end of the first two-party system.

The new political development was welcomed by Monroe, who accepted the widely held view (first stated by George Washington) that political parties were destructive of republican institutions. He let it be known that he intended to be the chief magistrate of the nation and not the head of a party. He publicized his commitment to the ERA OF GOOD FEELINGS (a phrase coined by a Federalist newspaper) by touring the nation—the first President to do so since Washington. Shortly after his inauguration he visited New England, where he was given a rapturous welcome as a hero of the American Revolution by Federalists and Democratic-Republicans alike. Two years later he was given an equally enthusiastic reception in the South and West. Although Andrew Jackson (among others) urged Monroe to complete the political reconciliation by appointing Federalists to high office, pressures from within the Democratic-Republican Party prevented him from following this advice.

Dynamics of the Administration. Monroe's Cabinet, the ablest since the first Washington administration, included three of the leading political figures of the day: John Quincy Adams (Department of State), JOHN C. CALHOUN (War Department), and William H. Crawford (Department of the Treasury) all of whom were regarded as likely candidates for President. Richard Rush stayed on as Attorney General (a part-time post) until he was appointed minister to Great Britain late in 1817. His successor, William Wirt, a prominent Baltimore attorney and author, had no political ambitions. All served during both terms. The Navy Department was occupied in succession by northerners of lesser stature: Benjamin Crowninshield (1817–1819); Smith Thompson (elevated to the Supreme Court in 1823); and Samuel L. Southard.

The Cabinet played an important role, meeting more frequently than it had under Jefferson or Madison. Adams, Calhoun, and Crawford were major participants in Cabinet discussions. Wirt spoke occasionally, the others rarely. As Adams's diary makes clear, Monroe conferred with the Cabinet not only for advice but to obtain a consensus, which would enable him to draw on the congressional followings of his secretaries. Monroe was also successful in using individual personal contacts to promote his interests. It was a method of leadership that was effective during his first term but eroded after 1820 as Crawford distanced himself from the administration and as the rivalry for the presidential succession intensified. Although Monroe clearly liked and confided in Adams and Calhoun, he never felt at ease with Crawford, who expected more direct support for his presidential aspirations than Monroe was prepared to give. There was also a strong bond between Adams and Calhoun, both of whom genuinely admired the President but distrusted Crawford who they felt placed personal ambition above national interests. By 1822 the tension between Monroe and Crawford was so great that Monroe considered dismissing the Secretary of the Treasury. Adams and others dissuaded him, pointing out that to do so would exacerbate the administration critics.

Character of Monroe's Presidency. At the time of his election Monroe seemed a rather old-fashioned figure usually clad in the black smallclothes of an earlier generation—a costume varied on ceremonial occasions with a buff coat and buff knee breeches reminiscent of the revolutionary uniform. Nearly six feet tall, dignified and formal in manners, he was an impressive figure, still vigorous and robust. His hair, worn long and tied in a queue with a black ribbon, had grayed. By no means handsome—his plain face with massive features had become deeply lined as a result of the strain of the war years. Contemporaries often commented upon his most distinctive feature—wide-

set gray eyes reflecting a genuine warmth and kindness confirmed by his frequent smile. He was remarkably even tempered and was able (with few exceptions) to work amicably with colleagues of vastly different temperaments. His invariable courtesy and command of practical details made him most effective in personal contacts. His letters and public statements tended to be prolix without the close reasoning characteristic of Madison or Jefferson's easy turn of phrase. He never aroused the same passionate devotion as Jefferson, but he was respected for his pragmatism and his steady attention to public affairs.

Monroe and his wife did not move into the President's House until September 1817 after the completion of renovations of the fire-scarred building, which had been burned by the British during the WAR OF 1812. Thereafter, because of the white paint used to cover the exterior, it was called the White House. At first Monroe used his own furniture until furniture, draperies, china, mantelpieces, and wall coverings ordered from France arrived. Long residence in France had given the Monroes a taste for French styles. The presidential family comprised daughter Eliza and her husband George Hay, who often acted as an informal political agent for the President; Monroe's brother, Joseph; and Mrs. Monroe's nephew Samuel L. Gouverneur, who returned to New York in 1820 after marrying Hester Maria, the Monroes' younger daughter. The wedding, the first in the White House, was attended only by family members and friends none of whom left an account of the ceremony. Both Joseph Monroe and Samuel L. Gouverneur acted as private secretaries since Congress did not provide funds for staff—the President had to use his own servants. Every day, when Congress was in session, Monroe received a constant stream of visitors in his White House office. Since most expected to be invited to dinner (then at 2:00 in the afternoon), there were often as many as twenty seated at the table. Mrs. Monroe only presided at state dinners. Monroe left office heavily in debt—his salary of $25,000 was inadequate to defray the cost of entertaining on the scale expected of a head of state.

Monroe returned to the formality of the Washington administration. Neither he nor members of his family accepted invitations from diplomats, public officials, or residents. Strict precedence was observed at dinners. Washington society was dismayed by Mrs. Monroe's announcement that in accordance with European custom she (unlike DOLLEY MADISON) would neither make nor return calls but be at home one morning each week to receive callers. During congressional sessions Monroe continued the biweekly receptions (known as drawing-rooms) open to all citizens properly dressed.

Domestic Policies. Although the role of the executive in domestic affairs was more limited than in modern times, the President used his annual messages to make recommendations to Congress. In his first inaugural address Monroe had outlined a policy of moderate nationalism continuing the direction begun by Jefferson and Madison. He indicated three areas for congressional action: the construction of coastal fortifications for more effective national defense; the adoption of a protective tariff; and the need for roads and canals to further economic development. Monroe took a particular interest in promoting measures to improve the defenses of the nation. While still in the War Department he had submitted a report to Congress recommending that the army be maintained at twenty thousand. Congress, however, reduced the army to the prewar strength of ten thousand. Until the decline in federal revenues after the Panic of 1819, Congress made substantial appropriations to construct coastal fortifications.

In discussing the need for INTERNAL IMPROVEMENTS in his first inaugural, Monroe failed to explain that he considered a constitutional amendment necessary, if Congress intended funding a federal program. He clarified his position in his first annual message in December 1817 urging Congress to propose an amendment. In taking this position Monroe hoped to resolve a dilemma created by Madison, who, just before leaving office, vetoed an appropriations bill for the extension of the Cumberland Road. Madison's veto seemed inconsistent, since Jefferson had signed bills for construction. Madison's response to Monroe's query did not clarify the issue: Jefferson, he said, signed the bills in haste without due consideration. Monroe's suggestion led to an outraged denunciation in Congress.

Not until 1822, when he vetoed a bill for the collection of tolls to repair the Cumberland Road, did Monroe have an opportunity to state his constitutional views. He considered the original appropriations constitutional because jurisdiction had been left to the states: tolls had never been collected. If Congress intended to fund a general system under national control, then the Constitution must be amended. On this basis he signed bills for repairs and for a survey (limited to utility) of a network of roads and canals. Although several amendments were introduced, sectional forces were so divided that none mustered the needed votes.

Monroe accepted the contemporary view that the Panic of 1819 had been caused by the postwar influx of cheap European manufactures, which forced new industries to close, and careless banking practices. The impact of specie redemption, the drop in cotton prices, and speculation in western lands was not then understood. Many unjustly attributed the financial distress to the policies of the second BANK OF THE UNITED STATES (rechartered in 1817), admittedly badly managed by William Jones, its first president. Monroe considered the bank essential to maintain a sound currency and regulate state banks. To moderate criticism of the bank, Monroe and Crawford persuaded the directors to replace Jones with Langdon Cheves, an abler manager.

Within accepted constraints concerning the role of government in the economy, there was little that either Congress or the executive could do to alleviate the distress caused by the depression. In his annual message in 1819, after promising to reduce federal expenditures, Monroe recommended the enactment of a tariff to protect industries most injured by imports. A moderate bill was introduced only to be defeated by a narrow margin as a result of southern opposition. In the past, in times of economic distress, states had adopted measures for debtor relief. In view of the extensive default in payments due on public lands, Monroe in 1820 recommended the adoption of some form of relief. Adopting a plan drawn up by Crawford, Congress passed a bill allowing debtors to obtain title for the portion of lands for which they had paid; a discount was granted to those paying on time. The War Department, which absorbed nearly a third of the federal budget of $25 million, was an obvious target for economizers in Congress. Calhoun had already reduced operating costs, but orthodox Democratic-Republicans (Old Republicans or Radicals, to use terms then current) had a long-standing hostility to a military establishment. Moreover, it suited Crawford's supporters to push for cuts in the War Department in order to embarrass Calhoun. In March 1821 Congress reduced the army to six thousand. Even after federal revenues improved, the reduction was made permanent. Funding for coastal fortifications, however, was partially restored in response to pressure from local interests.

Despite his apprehension that the debate in Congress during 1819 and 1820 over the banning of slavery in Missouri as a condition for statehood would split the nation into two hostile sections, Monroe, usually sensitive to public attitudes, failed to understand the intensity of northern antislavery sentiment. When the MISSOURI COMPROMISE was introduced in the Senate, he privately indicated his approval through Senator James Barbour and he sent George Hay to

Richmond to calm angry state leaders, who threatened SECESSION if the compromise were adopted. Aware of the differing views of his secretaries, Monroe never discussed the Missouri question with the Cabinet until the compromise bill passed, which gave only a qualified approval. In contrast to the furor engendered by the Missouri crisis, there was little public interest in the presidential election of 1820. Monroe and Tompkins were nominated by state legislatures; the presidential caucus, subjected to increasing criticism, did not meet. Voter turnout was smaller than in the previous election. Monroe, the only candidate for the presidency, received all but one of the electoral votes.

Foreign Affairs. Monroe's most important achievements were in foreign affairs to which he gave close attention. When he was in the capital, he conferred with Adams nearly every day. When he was away, messengers brought dispatches. Although Monroe left Adams in charge of all negotiations with resident ministers, he reviewed all dispatches, frequently making changes. The relationship between Monroe and Adams was remarkably harmonious based on diplomatic experience, which gave them a common view of American policy goals. Both realized that the end of the European wars provided an opportunity to advance national aims without relying (as Monroe felt Jefferson had done) on the support of France. Monroe believed that only through an independent course could the United States secure recognition as the major power in the Americas. Monroe developed his foreign policy in three directions: the continuation of the established policy of territorial expansion by forcing Spain to cede Florida and define the Louisiana boundary; the creation of a rapprochement with Great Britain, which would reopen the West Indian trade closed since the American Revolution; the formulation of a policy toward the revolutionary movements under way in Spain's former colonies.

Spain. Monroe directed his first policy initiative against Spain in October 1817 when he sent an expedition to occupy Amelia Island in the St. John's River, technically within Spanish jurisdiction. The island was being used as a base for pirates and privateers with dubious letters of marque from the revolutionary governments in Latin America. In December, Monroe, citing the provisions of PINCKNEY'S TREATY of 1795, authorized Gen. Andrew Jackson to pursue into Florida Indians raiding the southern frontier. Jackson's arbitrary conduct in seizing the Spanish posts and executing two British subjects raised the threat of an international crisis. However, the British did not protest and, as Monroe and Adams anticipated, Spain promptly opened negotiations. In the Adams-Onís

(Transcontinental) Treaty of 1819, Spain ceded Florida and the United States assumed $5,000,000 in claims against Spain. The treaty established the Louisiana boundary as running north from the Sabine River to the Canadian border and then west to the Rocky Mountains.

While the Adams and the Spanish minister were negotiating, a furious debate erupted in Congress over Jackson's conduct. Clay led a drive to censure Jackson for exceeding his instructions in seizing the Spanish posts. Clay alleged that Jackson had infringed on the power of Congress to declare war. The Cabinet was divided: Calhoun and Crawford insisting that Jackson be repudiated; Adams recommending full endorsement, since the general's actions had compelled Spain to negotiate. Monroe was sensitive to the constitutional issue, but he did not want to give Spain an advantage by condemning Jackson. Hitting on a middle course, Monroe informed Congress that the general had exceeded his orders but had done so on information received during the invasion, which made his actions necessary. Although Monroe checked the move to censure Jackson, the general never forgave the President for failing to endorse his conduct without qualification. Jackson insisted that his orders had implicitly conveyed ample authority to seize the posts.

The Monroe Doctrine. The formulation of a policy toward the revolutionary movements in Latin America was one of the issues confronting Monroe during his first term. In his annual messages Monroe often expressed his sympathy with the struggle in Latin America in behalf of liberty. Administration-sponsored NEUTRALITY legislation was interpreted in favor of the insurgents. In the press and in Congress there was considerable pressure to recognize the new regimes; Clay was the most outspoken. Monroe, however, held back until he was assured that stable governments had been established and until the final ratification of the Adams-Onís Treaty in 1821. In March 1822 Monroe extended recognition to the United Provinces of La Plata (Argentina), Chile, Peru, Colombia, and Mexico. The first American ministers were instructed to negotiate treaties of commerce on a most-favored-nation basis and to assure the new governments that the United States would support the development of political and economic institutions different from those of Europe. In these instructions Monroe reiterated ideas current since the Washington era.

At the time that Monroe was extending recognition to the Latin American states, it seemed likely that the European powers, spurred by France, might intervene to restore Spanish authority. The threat became an immediate concern in October 1823, when a dispatch from Benjamin Rush arrived with a proposal from the British foreign secretary, George Canning, that the United States and Great Britain jointly declare their opposition to intervention. In spite of the endorsement of Jefferson and Madison, Monroe chose an independent course. To accept would appear to make the nation subservient to a European power without increasing the American prestige. Moreover, acceptance would preclude the possibility of acquiring Cuba, then thought likely. Monroe also realized that cooperation with the nation's recent enemy would not be popular. Instead of using diplomatic channels, the President opted for a separate policy statement included in his annual message on 2 December 1823. After observing that the European political system was essentially different from that in the Americas, he declared that the United States would regard interference in the affairs of the American states as an unfriendly act. He added that the United States adhered to a policy of nonintervention in the affairs of other nations. A third principle, the work of Adams, who was concerned about Russian activities on the Pacific coast, asserted that the United States considered the Americas closed to further colonization. Monroe's declaration (not called the MONROE DOCTRINE until more than a generation later) was little noticed in Europe. When Monroe sent his message to Congress, he did not know that British opposition to intervention had curtailed any efforts in that regard by the other European powers. It was favorably commented upon in the American press, where it was understood as a reiteration of ideas long accepted as commonplace. The significance of Monroe's policy lay not in its content but in the method chosen, which established a precedent for later executive pronouncements. President Theodore Roosevelt expanded it to justify American intervention in Latin America—a policy never contemplated by Monroe.

Anglo-American relations. Monroe's rejection of Canning's proposal was not seen as an impediment to an Anglo-American rapprochement. An abortive attempt had been made in Monroe's first term, when Viscount Lord Castlereagh, the British foreign minister, had indicated an interest in developing better relations between the two nations, Monroe authorized Richard Rush, U.S. minister to Great Britain, and ALBERT GALLATIN, minister to France, to negotiate. In 1818 they concluded an agreement providing compensation for slaves removed by the British during the War of 1812 and making substantial concessions in the fisheries. The convention also defined the northwestern boundary along the forty-ninth parallel from the Lake of the Woods to the Rocky Mountains. Negotia-

tions were terminated when the British refused to consider the American demand for a formal disavowal of impressment.

When the British indicated in 1822 a willingness to negotiate, Monroe responded promptly. Following the President's instructions, Adams drafted a series of dispatches to Rush. Most dealt with long-standing issues such as the West Indian trade. One, however, contained a novel proposal involving a major change in American policy on neutral rights. Monroe sent a draft treaty committing the United States to participate in the British-sponsored international patrol for the suppression of the slave trade, if the British government would condemn the slave trade as piracy. Since the end of the war the British had pressed the United States to join the patrol. The trade was illegal under federal law, but Monroe, in spite of his sympathy with the proposal, had rejected British overtures. He felt that a departure from the American position concerning searches on the high seas would be opposed in Congress. However, by 1822 there seemed to be evidence of a shift in opinion as a result of the lobbying of the American Colonization Society. The society had been founded in 1816 to establish a settlement in Africa for free blacks as the first step in the elimination of slavery.

Charles Fenton Mercer, a friend of the President, was one of the key figures in the founding of the society. Mercer, using the hitherto unknown correspondence of 1801 between Jefferson and Monroe (discovered accidentally in the Virginia state archives) had recruited members from the politically powerful, including Crawford and Clay. The aims of the society coincided with the views expressed by Monroe and Jefferson. In 1817 Monroe had approved a bill sponsored by Mercer appropriating $100,000 for the society to resettle Africans captured from slave traders. Interpreting the bill broadly (Adams was the only objector in the Cabinet), Monroe allowed the navy to convoy ships sent by the society to transport colonists and to assist in the acquisition of Liberia (the capital gratefully named Monrovia.)

In 1822 the House of Representatives, on Mercer's initiative, approved by a large majority a resolution condemning the slave trade as piracy. Since pirates could not claim the protection of any flag, suspect vessels could be stopped and searched on the high seas. The Cabinet then approved the treaty with Great Britain; Adams dissented, insisting that any change in policy on this issue would expose the administration to criticism for yielding a basic American right. The British government promptly ratified the treaty, but when Monroe sent it to the Senate in the spring of

1824, it was subject to violent criticism primarily from Crawford's supporters. Crawford, seriously ill and paralyzed (he did not recover until late in the year), denied that he had ever approved the treaty and rejected Monroe's appeal to intervene in behalf of the treaty. In an effort to secure Senate approval, Monroe directly intervened, sending a special message reminding the Senate that the British had approved the American-sponsored agreement without alteration. The Senate ratified the treaty with such restrictive amendments that the British Cabinet refused to reconsider it, thus closing the door on the rapprochement Monroe had sought. The President was truly disappointed at the failure of a measure in which he took such a personal interest.

The End of Monroe's Presidency. During Monroe's last years in office the conflict between the rival presidential candidates and the rising tide of sectionalism led to incessant attacks on the administration often over petty issues such as the management of the fund for refurnishing the White House. Diplomatic and military appointments were subjected to endless objections. Monroe's attempt to honor existing Cherokee treaties involved the administration in a bitter conflict with the Georgia delegation. Although supporters of Jackson and Clay joined in these forays, Crawford's backers were the primary agents. Crawford and his friends felt that Monroe, who remained neutral concerning the presidential race, owed Crawford a debt for not opposing Monroe for the nomination in 1816. Calhoun, who withdrew early in 1824, and Adams usually managed to restrain their supporters. The tariff was the only issue that overrode partisan conflict. In 1823, in his annual message, Monroe had again recommended a protective tariff. Rival presidential factions found it convenient to put through a bill primarily beneficial to the middle states.

Exhausted by the strain of his final years in office, Monroe was relieved to relinquish the presidency to Adams in March 1825 and retire to Oak Hill and the life of a farmer, which he so much loved. He avoided the political squabbles of the day, in spite of efforts to involve him. He made frequent trips to Albemarle for reunions with Madison and to attend the meetings of the Board of Visitors of the University of Virginia. His last public service was as a member of the Virginia constitutional convention of 1829. He was chosen president but was too feeble to preside. Heavily in debt he disposed of Highlands and applied to Congress for $50,000 in compensation for expenses during past diplomatic service—his accounts have never been fully settled. Although many felt that his claim for interest on the unpaid balance was excessive, opposition to the grant came from Jacksonians and Crawfordites. Not until shortly before his death did Congress authorize the payment of $30,000. Prostrated by grief over his wife's death in 1830, and too ill to remain at Oak Hill, he moved to New York to live with his daughter and died there on 4 July 1831. Throughout the nation his death was commemorated as the passing of one of the last heroes of the American Revolution. Originally buried in New York, he was reinterred in Richmond in 1858.

BIBLIOGRAPHY

Ammon, Harry. *James Monroe: The Quest for National Identity.* Rev. ed. 1990.

Ammon, Harry, ed. *James Monroe: A Bibliography.* 1991.

Bemis, Samuel Flagg. *John Quincy Adams and the Foundations of American Foreign Policy.* 1949.

Brooks, Philip Coolidge. *Diplomacy and the Borderlands: The Adams-Onis Treaty of 1819.* 1939.

Dangerfield, George. *Era of Good Feelings.* 1952.

Perkins, Dexter. *The Monroe Doctrine, 1823–1826.* 1927.

Remini, Robert. *Martin Van Buren and the Making of the Democratic Party.* 1970.

Rothbard, Murray N. *The Panic of 1819: Reactions and Policies.* 1962.

Whitaker, Arthur P. *The United States and the Independence of Latin America, 1800–1830.* 1941.

HARRY AMMON

MONROE DOCTRINE. The Monroe Doctrine, proclaimed by President James Monroe in his annual message of December 1823, expressed a national interest long recognized by the country's early leaders—that the United States should protect its predominance in Western Hemispheric affairs by discouraging European intrusion. As long as Spain maintained its New World empire the responsibility for limiting European encroachments in Latin America lay in Madrid. During the Napoleonic wars Spain's imperial reach began to recede before a well-led independence movement. By 1822 the United States had recognized the new countries of the region. The Monroe administration did not contest Great Britain's commercial dominance of Latin America. But the collapse of Spanish power in the New World, followed by the overthrow of the Spanish monarchy, challenged British complacency. The Holy Alliance of Russia, Austria, and Prussia denounced Spanish liberalism; at the Congress of Verona in 1822 they encouraged France to dispatch an army to Spain to restore the king. The British foreign minister George Canning had no interest in Spanish republicanism but suspected that the French might use their influence in Madrid to lay the foundation of a French empire in Latin America. Canning's fears led directly to the Monroe Doctrine.

Canning and Rush. In mid August 1823 Canning informed Richard Rush, the American minister in London, that Britain intended to counter any French effort to lay hands on the Spanish colonies in America. He inquired whether the United States would make a public declaration that it also opposed a French invasion of Spanish America. On 20 August, Canning formalized this suggestion in a letter to Rush. After arguing that U.S. interests in Latin America conformed to those of Great Britain, he recommended that the two countries issue a joint declaration, warning France and other continental powers to stay out of the New World while assuring Spain that neither country had any designs on the Spanish Empire. Rush forwarded Canning's letter to Secretary of State John Quincy Adams. Impressed by Canning's constant attention, Rush, on 28 August, agreed to act without specific instructions if the British government would recognize the independence of the Latin American states.

Canning not only refused to budge on the question of recognition but also dropped the subject of the joint declaration. Rush reported to Washington on 10 October: "The termination of the discussion between us may be thought somewhat sudden, not to say abrupt, considering how zealously as well as spontaneously it was started on his side. As I did not commence it, it is not my intention to revive it." Not until 24 November did Canning explain to him that the British government, convinced that it would gain nothing from the United States, delivered a warning directly to the French ambassador in London, the Prince de Polignac. The French government, desiring to avoid trouble with Britain, responded to the ultimatum with the secret "Polignac Memorandum," which assured London that France had no intention of dispatching an expedition to the New World. Canning, through unilateral action, had neutralized Europe's challenge to British interests in the New World.

Adams's Three Principles. Meanwhile Canning's initial offer had set the Monroe Cabinet in motion. Rush's long communication of August reached Washington on 9 October. The question it raised was fundamental. Did the country's opposition to further European encroachment require a projection into European politics or could the the United States entrust hemispheric independence to the protections afforded by the Atlantic Ocean, the British navy, and Latin American resistance? Monroe harbored a profound distrust of British monarchy but he believed that Britain's economic interests in Latin America were driving that country toward a more promising relationship with the United States. Before accepting

the British offer Monroe sought the advice of Thomas Jefferson and James Madison. Jefferson, in quiet retirement at Monticello, responded with a classic reiteration of his concept of two spheres. For him it was imperative that the United States, if it desired to maintain the status quo in the Western Hemisphere, accept, like Britain, the existing order in Europe. He, like Madison, urged Monroe to accept the British overture.

France's involvement in Spain did not trouble Secretary of State Adams. He feared instead that Spain might cede CUBA to Britain as the price of an Anglo-Spanish alliance. In April 1823 he sent a long note to Hugh Nelson, the American minister in Madrid, warning the Spanish government that the United States would oppose the transfer of Cuba to any European power. Thus Adams reasserted the American doctrine of no-transfer. When Canning assured Washington that Britain had no intention of acquiring the island, Monroe suggested to the Cabinet that the United States also issue a statement of self-denial. Adams objected; for him there was no reason for the United States to bind itself permanently against the possibility that Cuba might one day solicit union with the United States.

When Monroe returned to Washington with the opinions of Jefferson and Madison corroborating his own, Russia created a crisis that demanded a further definition of America's hemispheric interests. Baron de Tuyll, the Russian minister, informed Adams that the tsar would not recognize the new governments of Latin America and that, unless the United States remained neutral, Russia might support a European invasion of the former Spanish Empire. Adams refused to be frightened. He doubted that France intended armed intervention in Latin America; moreover, the British navy was powerful enough to prevent it. When the Cabinet met on 7 November, Adams proposed that the United States decline the British overture and take its stand against the Holy Alliance unilaterally. "It would be more candid, as well as more dignified," he said, "to avow our principles explicitly to Russia and France, than to come in as a cock-boat in the wake of the British man-of-war." Adams favored an overall American policy that would combine a letter to Russia with one to France in a single statement of intent. To this Monroe agreed.

A week later Adams delivered his note to the Russian minister. In moderate language he explained that the United States was a republic and thus was attracted to the Latin American states by those very principles that repelled the tsar. He hoped that Russia would maintain a policy of neutrality. But Russia quickly created further alarm when another note reminded the administration of the Holy Alliance's success in putting down revolutions in Europe and its obligation to guarantee tranquility everywhere, including Latin America. As gloom settled over the Potomac, Adams told the Cabinet:

> My purpose would be in a moderate and conciliatory manner, but with a firm and determined spirit, to declare our dissent from the principles avowed in those communications; to assert those upon which our own Government is founded, and while disclaiming all . . . interference with the political affairs of Europe, to declare our expectation and hope that the European powers will equally abstain from the attempt to spread their principles in the American hemisphere, or to subjugate by force any part of these continents to their will.

Adams thus formulated the principle of "hands-off." Monroe accepted it and decided to proclaim this new American purpose toward the Western Hemisphere in his December message to Congress.

On 21 November Monroe read a preliminary draft of his forthcoming message to the Cabinet. Adams was troubled by the belligerent tone, especially the President's apparent determination to take up the cause of revolution in Spain and Greece, two areas in which he had no intention of acting. Greece and Spain, Adams asserted, were exclusively European issues; for thirty years Europe had been in convulsions while the United States looked on from a safe distance and disavowed any intention to interfere. Monroe's phraseology, Adams warned, had the air of open defiance to all Europe. "[I]f we must come to an issue with Europe," Adams concluded, "let us keep it off as long as possible. Let us use all possible means to carry the opinion of the nation with us, and the opinion of the world."

Adams considered it essential that Monroe not antagonize the Holy Alliance needlessly. If the Holy Alliance really intended to restore the colonies to Spain, which Adams doubted, the United States had been too hasty in recognizing South American independence. Arguing against any U.S. involvement in European affairs, Adams summarized his views before the Cabinet: "The ground that I wish to take is that of earnest remonstrance against the interference of the European powers by force with South America, but to disclaim all interference on our part with Europe; to make an American cause, and adhere inflexibly to that." Adams had added to hands-off his principle of abstention.

Monroe's Declaration. This fundamental concept of two worlds Monroe embodied in his celebrated message to Congress on 2 December 1823. The so-called Monroe Doctrine declared specifically that the American continents were no longer open to European colonization and that the United States would regard any effort of the European powers to extend their government to any portion of the Western Hemisphere as a threat to its peace and safety. On the other hand, Monroe assured the nations of the Old World that the United States would not interfere with their dependencies in the New World or involve itself in matters purely European. On the day that Monroe delivered his message to Congress newspapers from England reported that an expedition of twelve thousand men was assembling in Cadiz to restore Colombia to the Spanish crown. Monroe and much of Washington responded with the customary alarm. Again it was Adams who argued that European intervention was unlikely. During subsequent days Adams prepared documents to send to Britain and Russia. He assured Canning that the United States intended to pursue separate, but parallel, policies toward Latin America. Thereby Adams and Monroe wedded the America's status-quo policies in the Atlantic to the British navy. The United States had only one warship on active duty in the Atlantic. Adams's message to Russia concluded with a strong warning against European interference in the affairs of the Western Hemisphere.

Some continental diplomatists found the Monroe Doctrine distasteful because of its assumption that the political institutions of the New World were in some measure superior to those of the Old. Indeed, some Americans eventually viewed the Monroe Doctrine as a broad declaration of liberal principles. They believed that the United States, in defying the Holy Alliance, had not sought to defend its interests but rather the liberty of Latin America. For Austria's Prince Metternich such claims to political virtue were nothing less than arrogant. His condemnation of American attitudes toward the upheavals of Latin America and elsewhere was profound. "The United States of America," he wrote, "have cast blame and scorn on the institutions of Europe most worthy of respect. . . . In permitting themselves these unprovoked attacks, in fostering revolutions wherever they show themselves, . . . they lend new strength to the apostles of sedition and reanimate the courage of every conspirator." Baron de Tuyll passed similar judgment on the Monroe Doctrine: "The document in question enunciates views and pretensions so exaggerated, it establishes principles so contrary to the rights of the European powers that it merits only the most profound contempt."

British leaders accepted the Monroe Doctrine as a statement of American interests, nothing more. Canning took some credit for Monroe's announcement. In

1826 he boasted to Parliament: "I called the New World into existence to redress the balance of the Old." In practice the United States regarded the Monroe Doctrine as policy, not principle. Subsequent administrations judged events in Latin American in terms of U.S. interests, not by the imperative that it oppose every European action in the New World whether it touched U.S. interests or not. President James K. Polk in 1845 attempted to reaffirm the superior claims of the United States to Oregon and California by appealing to the Monroe Doctrine. The *Times* of London, on 27 December 1845, denied that the Monroe Doctrine conveyed any special rights to the United States, even in North America. Polk, declared the *Times*, had claimed a heavenly sanction without revealing any divine authentication. America had no more reason to "segregate itself from the universal system and universal code, than any other quarter [of the globe]." European governments, the *Times* advised, would deal with the North American states in accordance with their treaty arrangements.

When Polk, in the spring of 1848, moved to defend the government of Yucatan under the Monroe Doctrine, JOHN C. CALHOUN, a member of Monroe's Cabinet, dismissed the doctrine as irrelevant to U.S. relations with Latin America. Monroe, he said, had no power to establish a settled policy for the country. During the CIVIL WAR Secretary of State WILLIAM H. SEWARD, calculating the interests of the United States, refused to contest the French defiance of the Monroe Doctrine in Mexico, relying on the capacity of the Mexican government to drive the French from Mexican soil. In 1879 some Americans, in defense of the Monroe Doctrine, demanded that the United States prevent the French firm of Ferdinand de Lesseps from building a canal across PANAMA in agreement with the Colombian government. Gustave Koerner, the noted German American, retorted that the true Monroe Doctrine was the interest of the country, and that interest did not require any interference in the sovereign rights of Colombia.

Not until Theodore Roosevelt proclaimed his corollary of the Monroe Doctrine in 1904 did Monroe's declaration of 1823 rationalize U.S. intervention in the Caribbean. Roosevelt saw clearly that European creditors would challenge the political sovereignty of financially irresponsible Caribbean states unless the United States assumed responsibility for their financial behavior. Under his corollary, Roosevelt established U.S. control of the customs administration of Santo Domingo [*see* DOMINICAN REPUBLIC]. President Woodrow Wilson, largely under the Roosevelt Corollary, placed marines in HAITI and Santo Domingo in 1915 and 1916 to establish order and financial stability in those countries. Not until 1928 did J. Reuben Clark, Under Secretary of State, repudiate U.S. interventionism under the Roosevelt Corollary in his *Memorandum on the Monroe Doctrine*. By 1933 Presidents Herbert Hoover and Franklin D. Roosevelt, in their GOOD NEIGHBOR POLICY, had withdrawn all U.S. marines from Latin America. From the beginning the central objective of the Monroe Doctrine—that of preventing further European encroachment in the Western Hemisphere—triumphed without war because it reflected the genuine elements of power and interest that governed international relations in the Atlantic world.

BIBLIOGRAPHY

Bemis, Samuel Flagg. *John Quincy Adams and the Foundations of American Foreign Policy*. 1949.
May, Ernest R. *The Making of the Monroe Doctrine*. 1975.
Perkins, Bradford. *Castlereagh and Adams: England and the United States, 1812–1823*. 1964.
Perkins, Dexter. *The Monroe Doctrine, 1823–1826*. 1927.
Perkins, Dexter. *The Monroe Doctrine, 1826–1867*. 1933.
Tatum, Edward H., Jr. *The United States and Europe, 1815–1823: A Study in the Background of the Monroe Doctrine*. 1936.

NORMAN A. GRAEBNER

MONTICELLO. Monticello, the home of Thomas Jefferson, third President of the United States, is located in Albemarle County, Virginia, southeast of Charlottesville. Jefferson designed and fashioned the estate to suit his personal needs and interests. A unique creation of an American President, it is one of the great achievements of American architecture.

During the eight years of his presidency (1801–1809), Jefferson made the three-day trip home from the capital twice a year. In the spring, at the end of the congressional session, he would visit for three weeks. During the late summer, when he believed the swampy District of Columbia to be unhealthy, he would spend from eight to twelve weeks at Monticello.

Although Monticello served as a presidential retreat, he did not consider himself on vacation there. He maintained his daily routine of public business, spending long hours with correspondence and state papers brought from Washington by courier. CABINET officers and other public officials visited him, but more for social purposes than reasons of state. He always asked his daughters and their families to be there when he was.

Building at Monticello was a lifetime passion of Jefferson's. He began planning his home after he came of age in 1764 and inherited the 1,000-acre tract that included the "little mountain" that gives Monticello its name. A mountaintop setting for the house was unconventional and reflected Jefferson's appreciation of natural beauty rather than the needs of a working plantation.

The first version of the house was based on the drawings of the Italian Renaissance architect Palladio. Construction took place during the 1770s, even as the American Revolution developed. Before Jefferson completed his project, however, the death of his wife in 1782 and his subsequent service in France changed his mind about what he wanted to create. In 1794, after he left his job as Secretary of State in the Washington administration, he returned to Monticello and began major renovations, choosing a French-Roman neoclassical design for the house. When he returned to public life as Vice President and President, construction continued. The house remained in an unfinished state until 1809, and he never completed all his plans for the grounds.

Jefferson's financial situation deteriorated during his last years, and after he died in 1826 the family had to sell the estate. In 1923 the Thomas Jefferson Memorial Foundation was formed, which purchased Monticello and has preserved it as a national monument.

[*See also* HOMES, PRESIDENTIAL.]

BIBLIOGRAPHY

McLaughlin, Jack. *Jefferson and Monticello: The Biography of a Builder.* 1988.

Malone, Dumas. *Jefferson and His Time.* 6 vols. 1948–1981.

Nichols, Frederick D., and James A. Bear, Jr. *Monticello: A Guidebook.* 2d ed. 1982.

STEVEN H. HOCHMAN

MONTPELIER. A plantation in Orange County, Virginia, Montpelier was acquired by James Madison, Sr., around 1755, when his oldest son was four years old. In time, the plantation included several farms covering nearly five thousand acres. The Virginia Piedmont region, with the Blue Ridge Mountains in the distance, consists of red soil, which was cultivated for the main crop—tobacco. The elder Madison began construction on the main house in 1755, and in 1760 he moved his family into the brick dwelling that was named, as was the custom in colonial Virginia, Montpelier.

The home was finished in 1765, remodeled by James Madison, Jr., in 1797–1800, and again in 1809–1812. The architecture was typical of the region, with a central hallway flanked by large, high-ceiling rooms

with fireplaces. The first additions added some thirty feet to the south end and made the structure conform to the popular neoclassical style. The later remodeling added a rear colonnade and a front portico, with the work done by artisans recommended by Thomas Jefferson. One-story wings were added at each end, along with the addition of a garden temple on the front lawn. Numerous outbuildings provided living quarters for slaves, stables, sheds for a blacksmith and wheelwright, and other farm uses.

During Madison's presidency, the home was a summer retreat with a variety of visitors who commented on DOLLEY MADISON's lavish meals and warm hospitality. After retiring in 1817, Madison remained at Montpelier for the remaining nineteen years of his life and rarely left the plantation's boundaries.

Pressed by creditors, Dolley Madison was forced to sell Montpelier and the property passed through several hands until purchased by William DuPont near the end of the century. The estate remained in the family's hands until 1983, when DuPont's daughter died and left Montpelier to the National Trust. In 1992 efforts were in train to make Montpelier into a restored presidential residence of a dimension similar to Mount Vernon and Monticello.

BIBLIOGRAPHY

Hunt-Jones, Conover. *Dolley and the "Great Little Madison."* 1977.

ROBERT A. RUTLAND

MONUMENTS, PRESIDENTIAL. American Presidents are memorialized in hundreds of historic sites, ranging from the unassuming to the awe-inspiring. Some commemorate places where Presidents were born, worked, lived, and are buried. Others focus on significant milestones, unique INAUGURATIONS, memorabilia and personal papers, and locales that they visited. These tributes represent the efforts of federal, state, and local governments, as well as private historical societies and foundations.

A rich tradition of preserving presidential residences affords abundant opportunities to experience the varying lifestyles of America's Chief Executives [see HOMES, PRESIDENTIAL]. The stately mansions of George Washington (MOUNT VERNON), Thomas Jefferson (MONTICELLO), James Madison (MONTPELIER), Andrew Jackson (The Hermitage), Theodore Roosevelt (Sagamore Hill), and Franklin D. Roosevelt (Springwood at HYDE PARK, New York) are enduring testaments of their residents' character and personality. John Adams and John Quincy Adams, the only father and son to occupy the presidency, are remembered in part through their old House in Quincy, Massachusetts.

Lawnfield, the suburban Cleveland, Ohio mansion of James A. Garfield; Lindenwald, the thirty-six-room home of Martin Van Buren in Kinderhook, New York; and James Buchanan's Wheatland near Lancaster, Pennsylvania, provide striking contrasts to the more humble homes in Abilene, Kansas, and Dixon, Illinois, where Dwight D. Eisenhower and Ronald Reagan respectively spent their boyhoods. Other presidential homes are found in California, Georgia, Illinois, Indiana, Iowa, Kentucky, Massachusetts, Missouri, New Hampshire, New Jersey, New York, North Carolina, North Dakota, Ohio, Pennsylvania, Tennessee, Texas, Vermont, Virginia, and the District of Columbia, and on Campobello Island in Canada.

At least thirty national parks, national monuments, and national historic sites pay tribute to Presidents. Among the best-known are the Washington Monument, the Jefferson and Lincoln Memorials, and the John F. Kennedy Center for the Performing Arts in Washington, D.C., and Mount Rushmore in South Dakota. Abraham Lincoln's assassination is captured for posterity at Ford's Theater in Washington; Andrew Johnson's tailor shop is preserved in Greenville, Tennessee; and Theodore Roosevelt's 14 September 1904 inauguration is celebrated in the Buffalo, New York, house where he took the oath of office.

Thomas Jefferson's role in America's territorial expansion is recognized with the Jefferson National Expansion Memorial at Saint Louis. Theodore Roosevelt Island, an eighty-eight-acre wilderness preserve located in the Potomac River near Washington, D.C., memorializes Roosevelt's contributions as a conservationist. The Theodore Roosevelt National Memorial Park near Medora, North Dakota, attempts to capture many of those experiences on the open range that sharpened and refined his interests in conserving nature.

As a tribute to the nation's thirty-third President, Congress established the Harry S. Truman Scholarship Foundation, which annually awards four-year undergraduate scholarships to one student from each state and the District of Columbia who is preparing for a career in public service. Through the Woodrow Wilson Center for Scholars, Congress created "a living institution" that brings distinguished scholars from around the world to Washington.

Memorial grave sites at Arlington National Cemetery mark the final resting place of William Howard Taft and John F. Kennedy. Memorial tombs honor Ulysses S. Grant in New York City; Abraham Lincoln in Springfield, Illinois; William McKinley in Canton, Ohio; and James Monroe in Richmond, Virginia.

PRESIDENTIAL LIBRARIES, maintained by the National Archives and Records Administration, preserve sizable collections of artifacts, memorabilia, records, and public papers of nine Presidents—Herbert Hoover, Franklin D. Roosevelt, Harry S. Truman, Dwight D. Eisenhower, John F. Kennedy, Lyndon B. Johnson, Gerald R. Ford, Jimmy Carter, and Ronald Reagan. The three main buildings of the Library of Congress bear the names of the second (Adams), third (Jefferson), and fourth (Madison) Presidents. The state of Ohio maintains the Rutherford B. Hayes Library in Fremont. The Richard Nixon Library in Yorba Linda, California, is privately run.

BIBLIOGRAPHY

Blodgett, Bonnie, and D. J. Tice. *At Home with the Presidents.* 1988.
U.S. National Park Service. *The Presidents: From the Inauguration of George Washington to the Inauguration of Gerald R. Ford: Historic Places Commemorating the Chief Executives of the United States.* 1976.

STEPHEN W. STATHIS

MORGENTHAU, HENRY, JR. (1891–1967), Secretary of the Treasury. Henry Morgenthau, Jr., was born in 1891 into a wealthy New York family of German-Jewish heritage. As a gentleman farmer in Dutchess County, New York, he met and became the life-long friend of his neighbor, Franklin D. Roosevelt. After Roosevelt's election as governor in 1928, he appointed Morgenthau to several posts. Upon assuming the presidency, Roosevelt appointed Morgenthau as Secretary of the Treasury, where he continued throughout the NEW DEAL years as one of Roosevelt's most trusted policy advisers.

Morgenthau was seen by many of the New Dealers as one of the more conservative of Roosevelt's advisers. During the early New Deal, however, Morgenthau carried out Roosevelt's wish to devalue the currency and initiate a mild inflation of commodity prices of manipulating the gold content of the dollar, and he consistently supported many other progressive policies, including adequate unemployment relief spending. Once recovery was underway, though, Morgenthau argued for a balanced budget, believing that full recovery could be achieved only by encouraging and reassuring the business community. He became the leading opponent of the school of New Dealers who insisted that only deficit spending could generate full employment.

During the crucial period before American entry into WORLD WAR II Morgenthau supported Roosevelt's policies of extending all possible aid to Britain and applying economic sanctions against Japan. In 1944 he strongly urged severe treatment of postwar Germany by the Allies. The Morgenthau Plan proposed dismemberment of Germany and the destruction or removal of most of its heavy industry. Accepted briefly by Churchill and Roosevelt as the basis for Allied policy toward a defeated German, it was later set aside. Morgenthau briefly served in Truman's CABINET after Roosevelt's death, but resigned in July 1945 and retired from public life.

BIBLIOGRAPHY

Blum, John M. *From the Morgenthau Diaries.* 3 vols. 1959-1967.

ROBERT F. HIMMELBERG

MORMONS. Members of The Church of Jesus Christ of Latter-day Saints (commonly known as the Mormon Church) have had both religious and practical reasons to show particular interest in the federal government, including the office of President. The religious reasons relate to their reverence for the Constitution, which, Church founder Joseph Smith declared, was divinely inspired. The practical considerations have been related to changing political and historical circumstances.

Martin Van Buren was the first President with whom the Mormons had any direct contact. Driven by their persecutors from Missouri to Illinois in the winter of 1838–1839, they failed to convince Missouri courts that the state should compensate them for their lost property. Joseph Smith went to Washington, D.C., demanding federal intervention in Missouri, but Van Buren and others took the position that the federal government had no constitutional authority for such intervention. Outraged, Smith began to advance a strongly nationalistic interpretation of the Constitution, and in 1844 he announced his own candidacy for the presidency. In June, however, he was murdered by a mob in Carthage, Illinois.

During the next few years Mormon relations with the President were generally amicable. Brigham Young led the Mormons westward just as the MEXICAN WAR was beginning, and when they pressured the federal government for assistance, President James R. Polk responded by allowing five hundred Mormon volunteers to join the Army of the West. In 1850 President Millard Fillmore appointed Young as first governor of the territory of Utah.

For the rest of the century the relationship between the Mormons and the presidency was usually strained, as the President responded to persistent efforts to bring about reform among the Mormons. The major issues were: growing American concern over the practice of plural marriage (the result of what Mormons believed was a divine revelation to Joseph Smith); the close relationship between church and state in Utah; and continuing Mormon efforts to gain statehood for Utah, which, it turned out, could not be achieved until the former two issues were resolved.

In 1856 the Mormon question became involved in presidential politics when the newly formed REPUBLICAN PARTY declared in its platform that polygamy and SLAVERY were "twin relics of barbarism." The following year Democrat James Buchanan became the first President to antagonize the Mormons by direct action when he appointed a non-Mormon governor and also sent the federal army to put down a fancied rebellion in Utah. In the end, Mormons actually got along well with the President's appointee, and the Utah Expedition was ridiculed in the American press as "Buchanan's Blunder."

President Abraham Lincoln had the respect of the Mormons for his efforts at impartiality, but he signed into law the Morrill Anti-Bigamy Act that outlawed plural marriage in Utah. He also appointed a governor whose policies and conduct were so antagonistic to the Mormons that they successfully petitioned the President for his removal.

Mormon lobbyists tried to persuade the President and Congress that plural marriage was protected under their constitutional right to freedom of religion, but got nowhere. President Ulysses S. Grant, for example, distinguished the Mormons' right to worship from violation of the law and called for the "ultimate extinguishment of polygamy." In 1882, President Chester A. Arthur signed into law the Edmunds Act that, for the first time, put teeth into antibigamy legislation. Successful prosecution of Mormon polygamists proceeded rapidly and loopholes in the law were plugged by the Edmunds-Tucker Act, signed in 1887 by President Grover Cleveland. The law also allowed for confiscation of Church property. In addition, Cleveland urged restrictions on Mormon immigration from other countries.

In September 1890, Church president Wilford Woodruff announced that he had received a divine revelation requiring him to act for the "temporal salvation of the Church." The result was a proclamation, known as the "Manifesto," that announced the abandonment of the practice of plural marriage. Almost immediately the barriers to statehood fell, and in 1894 Grover Cleveland signed the Utah Enabling Act. Utah officially became a state on 4 January 1896.

The early twentieth century was a time of accommodation as the Mormons involved themselves more fully in the mainstream of American political, social, and economic life. In Utah, the traditional Mormon versus non-Mormon political camps were replaced by national parties, and Church officials urged Mormons to vote their consciences, free from religious constraints. Individual leaders, however, continued to make their personal preferences known, and it was sometimes charged that this unduly influenced the Utah electorate. In both 1908 and 1912 Joseph F. Smith, president of the Mormon Church and a Republican, openly favored the election of William Howard Taft. In 1918 a Democrat, Heber J. Grant, became president of the Church, and he supported Woodrow Wilson, especially in his campaign to take the United States into the LEAGUE OF NATIONS. This brought Grant into open disagreement with Republican Reed Smoot, a member of the Church's Council of the Twelve Apostles who was also a United States Senator and one of Wilson's chief antagonists. In 1932, however, Grant publicly endorsed Herbert Hoover. Significantly, that year Utah voters disagreed and overwhelmingly supported Franklin D. Roosevelt.

In dramatic contrast to the nineteenth century, relations between the Latter-day Saints and the American President in the twentieth century have been characterized by mutual respect and cooperation, and numerous Mormons have been appointed to responsible positions in the executive branch. Perhaps the most prominent was Ezra Taft Benson, a member of the Council of the Twelve Apostles, who served as Secretary of Agriculture under Dwight D. Eisenhower. In 1985 Benson became president of the Church.

BIBLIOGRAPHY

Alexander, Thomas G. *Mormons in Transition: A History of the Latter-day Saints, 1890–1930*. 1986.

Allen, James B., and Glen M. Leonard. *The Story of the Latter-day Saints*. 1976.

Benson, Ezra Taft. *Crossfire: The Eight Years with Eisenhower*. 1962.

Fox, Frank W. *J. Reuben Clark: The Public Years*. 1980.

Lyman, Leo. *Political Deliverance: The Mormon Quest for Statehood*. 1986.

Schapsmeier, Edward L., and Fredrick H. Schapsmeier. *Ezra Taft Benson and the Politics of Agriculture: The Eisenhower Years, 1953–1961*. 1975.

JAMES B. ALLEN

MORRILL LAND GRANT ACT (1862). The act granted each loyal state 30,000 acres of federal land per member of Congress for the purpose of endowing state colleges to support education in agriculture and mechanic arts. Sponsored by Justin S. Morrill of Vermont, the act (like the HOMESTEAD ACT earlier that year) represented a major Republican victory following long political struggle. Years of often bitter controversy over the act gave way to fairly easy passage, with secessionist Southerners out of Congress. Subsequent land grants totaled 17,430,000 acres. Combined with the Homestead Act, it would facilitate the rapid development of the northern prairies and plains regions.

Support was widespread throughout the North, including labor unions, the press, farm organizations, reformers generally, and educators specifically. Opposition came from those who argued that the government could not afford such a grant and that it needed what money it might raise from land sales. Southern opposition reflected that region's fear of northern expansion and its free-soil ramifications. Additionally, Southern planters tended to mine their soil by excessive cotton crops and were little interested in the advancement of so-called scientific agriculture, the primary purpose of the land grant. A constitutional question also emerged, with opponents claiming that the grant violated STATES' RIGHTS and would lead to further centralization. Finally, representatives of public land states such as Wisconsin and Kansas worried that too much of their land would go to outsiders.

President Abraham Lincoln and the REPUBLICAN PARTY supported the act for much the same reasons that they supported the Homestead Act: it reflected the party's pledge during the 1860 campaign to open the West to settlement under the banner of free soil and free labor. Indeed, in an 1859 address to the Wisconsin State Agricultural Society, Lincoln stressed the importance of combining labor and learning where "every blade of grass is a study."

The Morrill Act, a natural corollary to the Homestead Act, would strengthen the Republican Party's political position in part by expanding its base, by fulfilling its promises, and by providing the necessary credibility and economic confidence required to wage war successfully against the South. Ultimately, both acts fulfilled Lincoln's vision of American democracy composed of small farmers and skilled workers. The Morrill Act also revealed the struggle within the educational community between the elitism of classical study and an open and broader curriculum, better representing American democracy.

BIBLIOGRAPHY

Nevins, Allan. *The Origins of the Land-Grant Colleges and State Universities: A Brief Account of the Morrill Act of 1862 and Its Results*. 1962.

Nevins, Allan. *The State Universities and Democracy*. 1962.

NICHOLAS AHARON BOGGIONI

MORRILL TARIFF ACT (1861). The year 1857 witnessed a further Democratic reduction of tariffs and, following the panic of late summer, a dramatic decline in imports and tariff revenues. President James Buchanan—Pennsylvanian and moderate protectionist—urged Congress, in his annual messages of 1858 and 1860, to increase tariffs and to substitute specific duties in place of ad valorem duties to protect revenues in times of falling prices.

Introduced by Congressman Justin Morrill, Republican of Vermont, the Tariff Act of 1861 was principally a revenue measure to remedy governmental funding shortfalls after the 1857 depression. Intended to reverse the 20 percent reduction in rates passed in 1857 and thereby to reimplement tariff levels in effect after 1846, the act also adopted Buchanan's suggestion that specific duties be substituted for many ad valorem rates (rates calculated on an item's value). The new specific duties imposed on certain items—most notably iron and wool—increased effective protection as compared to that afforded by the Tariff Act of 1846. The act was first passed by the House of Representatives in May of 1860, adopted by the Senate in February of 1861, and signed by Buchanan on 2 March 1861.

Congressional Republicans, constituting a plurality in the House by 1860, used the act as an electioneering device in the forthcoming presidential election. Their support of increased tariffs was intended to appeal to manufacturing interests in Pennsylvania and wool growers in the West. Republicans walked a fine line in seeking increased protection in 1860, striving to hold within the newly formed Republican coalition many Northern Democrats and Know-Nothings who were free traders. Although the Republican platform adopted in 1860 endorsed protective tariffs—a plank absent from the party platform of 1856—it did so only in mild terms. Abraham Lincoln, thoroughly Whiggish in his past support of protective tariffs, downplayed his protectionist leanings in the 1860 election.

BIBLIOGRAPHY

Foner, Eric. *Free Soil, Free Labor, Free Men: The Ideology of the Republican Party before the Civil War.* 1970.
Oates, Stephen B. *With Malice toward None: The Life of Abraham Lincoln.* 1977.
Stanwood, Edward. *American Tariff Controversies in the Nineteenth Century.* Vol. 2. Repr. 1967.

RALPH MITZENMACHER

MORRIS, GOUVERNEUR (1752–1816), a Framer of the Constitution. Morris, an aristocratic New Yorker, was known for his wit, elegance, zest, and arrogance. After graduating from King's College (now Columbia University), he became a lawyer. He assisted in the framing of New York's first constitution, which provided for a comparatively strong executive. A signer of the Articles of Confederation, Morris also served as the Confederation's deputy superintendent of finance, in which role he sought to expand national powers. As a newcomer to Philadelphia, he was elected a member of Pennsylvania's strong delegation to the CONSTITUTIONAL CONVENTION in 1787. William Pierce of Georgia, another delegate, described him as "one of those geniuses in whom every species of talent combine to render him conspicuous and flowing in public debate." Similarly, James Madison referred to Morris's "brilliance of genius."

Morris spoke more often and at greater length than any other member of the convention. He vigorously supported Madison and JAMES WILSON in their nationalist proposals. Morris advocated "an Executive with sufficient vigor to pervade every part" of the United States, one who "should be the guardian of the people" and "the general Guardian of the National interests." He favored an unqualified executive veto power, a long tenure, and eligibility for reelection. Initially he thought that the President should not be impeachable.

Vehemently opposed to selection of the President by Congress, Morris preferred that "he ought to be elected by the people at large, by the freeholders of the Country," but he subsequently supported indirect election through the ELECTORAL COLLEGE. Morris was a member of the committee that devised that institution and that recommended that the powers of making appointments and treaties be given to the President, subject to the ADVICE AND CONSENT of the Senate. As a member of the Committee on Style, Morris wrote the final draft of the Constitution, work for which he was praised by Madison, who said, "The *finish* given to the style and arrangement of the Constitution fairly belongs to the pen of Mr. Morris. . . . A better choice could not have been made, as the performance of the task proved." Morris was responsible for the felicitous Preamble to the Constitution and its opening words, "We the people of the United States." Although Morris served briefly in the Senate and as a diplomat, his public life after 1787 was not notable.

BIBLIOGRAPHY

Roosevelt, Theodore. *Gouverneur Morris.* 1888.
Swiggett, Howard. *The Extraordinary Mr. Morris.* 1952.

LEONARD W. LEVY

MORRISON v. OLSON 487 U.S. 654 (1988). In *Morrison*, the Supreme Court upheld the INDEPENDENT COUNSEL provisions of the Ethics in Government Act of 1978—in particular, the conditions under which independent counsels are appointed, supervised, and may be discharged. Congress created the independent counsel system in the wake of the WATERGATE AFFAIR to mitigate conflicts of interest in the investigation and possible criminal prosecution of high-level executive officers and presidential campaign officials accused of serious offenses. The Court's opinion, authored by Chief Justice William Rehnquist, was a major victory for proponents of congressional power to limit the President's control over administrators who are not directly involved in assisting in the President's discharge of core presidential functions.

Morrison arose from allegations that Theodore B. Olson, a former Assistant Attorney General, had misled Congress concerning his role in withholding certain documents from congressional committees. The documents had been subpoenaed during an investigation of Environmental Protection Agency (EPA) enforcement of the so-called Superfund provisions of the Comprehensive Environmental Response, Compensation, and Liability Act of 1980. President Ronald Reagan offered a formal claim of EXECUTIVE PRIVILEGE to resist the subpoena, based on his asserted authority to maintain the confidentiality of open law-enforcement files.

The Reagan administration ultimately did release the documents after evidence emerged that the EPA program administrator, Rita Lavelle, had perjured herself and that the program had engaged in political favoritism in targeting its enforcement efforts. Following the resolution of the records dispute, however, the House Judiciary Committee published a multivolume study of the episode, which alleged that Olson had testified falsely concerning the EPA's position on the need to withhold the files for law enforcement purposes. Following a preliminary investigation required by the Ethics in Government Act, Attorney General EDWIN MEESE III petitioned the U.S. Court of Appeals for the District of Columbia Circuit to appoint an independent counsel for the Olson case. After the resignation of its first appointee, James McKay, the court appointed Alexia Morrison, a prominent Washington, D.C., practitioner, to continue the investigation.

Although the independent counsel ultimately determined that the facts did not support Olson's prosecution, Olson first challenged the constitutionality of the independent-counsel mechanism on three grounds: first, that federal courts could not constitutionally appoint criminal prosecutors; second, that Morrison's statutory job security interfered with the President's powers to execute the laws; and third, that the statute as a whole violated the constitutionally mandated SEPARATION OF POWERS. Over the solo dissent of Justice Antonin Scalia and with one Justice not participating, the majority rejected each of these arguments.

On the appointments issue, the Court held that the judicial appointment of independent counsel was expressly authorized by the appointments clause in Article II of the Constitution. That article permits Congress to vest the authority to appoint "inferior" officers of the United States in "courts of law." The majority concluded that an independent counsel's limited mission and tenure made the office "inferior," as did the officer's susceptibility to discharge for good cause by the Attorney General. The majority indicated that the judicial appointment of some officers, because of their functions, might be constitutionally "incongruous," but there was no institutional incongruity in the judicial selection of a prosecuting attorney.

The Court likewise found no difficulty with the statutory provision permitting the Attorney General to discharge an independent counsel solely for "good cause, physical disability, mental incapacity, or . . . other condition that substantially impairs the performance of such independent counsel's duties." Olson argued that independent counsels perform the executive function of criminal prosecution, and that the President, as the constitutional repository of executive authority, was entitled to discharge such counsel at will. The Court, however, repudiated language in earlier decisions that seemed to rest the permissibility of restrictions on presidential REMOVAL POWER on whether the officer so protected was "executive" or not. "[T]he real question," the Court said, "is whether the removal restrictions are of such a nature that they impede the President's ability to perform his constitutional duty. . . ." The Court did "not see how the President's need to control the exercise of [an independent counsel's policy-making] discretion is so central to the functioning of the Executive Branch as to require as a matter of constitutional law that the counsel be terminable at will by the President." Finally, the Court rejected all claims that an independent counsel's powers, taken together, either impermissibly aggrandized the role of Congress in executing the laws or trammeled upon the President's constitutionally assigned role.

Justice Scalia dissented vigorously from the majority's view on all points. Most significantly, he accused the majority of permitting Congress to subvert the Constitution's intended separation of powers by creating a powerful institution through which Congress could undermine an unpopular (but not impeachable) President. The split between Rehnquist and Scalia is a striking feature of the case because each, as Assistant Attorney General in charge of the Justice Department's OFFICE OF LEGAL COUNSEL, had shouldered the task of defending the President's constitutional prerogatives against legislative encroachment.

To appreciate the full significance of *Morrison*, it is necessary to recall that an independent counsel is but one sort of administrative officer appointed under limited conditions of removability. More familiar are the heads of the many so-called independent regulatory agencies, all of whom, like independent counsels, are protected against presidential discharges based solely on policy disagreements. Executive-branch lawyers have long argued that such restrictions on presidential removal authority are constitutionally suspect and that all administrative officers are subject to direct policy supervision by the President.

The Court could have reached the same judgment it pronounced in *Morrison* based on narrow grounds, just to avoid that larger debate. The majority, for example, could have limited the reach of its analysis by relying on the particular institutional history of criminal prosecutors, who represent a form of public officer that was well known when the Constitution was framed. The available historical evidence makes it highly unlikely that in the late eighteenth century criminal prosecution was understood to be "inherently executive" in the constitutional sense; therefore, limiting the President's direct control of such prosecutors would not disturb any original constitutional understanding. Or the Court could have said that, whatever the merits of Olson's analysis in a run-of-the-mill case, Congress's well-founded conflicts-of-interest concerns after Watergate justified the Ethics in Government Act, even if it were accepted for the sake of argument that the act represented a limited intrusion on executive power.

The Court, however, chose a far broader rationale: the President need not be permitted plenary removal power over any official unless that restriction would unduly impede the discharge of the President's own Article II functions. Thus, if an administrator is lawfully implementing delegated authority that is not within the scope of the President's inherent constitutional powers, then any discretion the President has to discharge that officer depends on congressional permission. By clear implication, that rationale extends beyond independent counsel to other "independent" administrators engaged, for example, in domestic economic, health, and safety regulation. It seems unlikely

that Congress, after *Morrison*, would rush to transfer a significant number of administrative authorities from administrators whom the President may fire at will to "independent" administrators, but the decision whether to do so is, according to *Morrison*, clearly a legislative one.

BIBLIOGRAPHY

Bruff, Harold. "Independent Counsel and the Constitution." *Willamette Law Journal* 24 (1988): 539–563.
Carter, Stephen. "The Independent Counsel Mess." *Harvard Law Review* 102 (1988): 105–141.
"Independent Counsel Symposium." *American Criminal Law Review* 25 (1987): 167–318.
"A Symposium on *Morrison v. Olson*: Addressing the Constitutionality of the Independent Counsel Statute." *American University Law Review* 38 (1989): 255–393.
"Symposium: Separation of Powers and the Executive Branch: The Reagan Era in Retrospect." *George Washington Law Review* 57 (1989): 401–703.

PETER M. SHANE

MORTON, LEVI PARSONS (1824–1920), twenty-second Vice President of the United States (1889–1893). Born in Shoreham, Vermont, Morton received only an elementary school education, began working when fourteen years old, and had his own dry goods firm in New York by 1855. By the 1870s, Morton had moved on and become a leading New York banker.

Morton did not begin a political career until 1876. As the Republican candidate for the House of Representatives in a Manhattan district, Morton lost by fewer than five hundred votes. Over the next two decades, however, he became an important figure in the REPUBLICAN PARTY. In 1878, Morton won in the same congressional district by some seven thousand votes. As one of the most influential bankers in the nation, he eloquently defended the gold standard against any attempt to establish the unlimited use of silver currency. At the Republican national convention of 1880, Morton sided with the powerful New York machine, the Stalwart wing of the party, supporting Ulysses S. Grant's bid for a third presidential nomination. Although the delegates nominated James A. Garfield, Morton agreed to raise funds for the campaign.

Garfield, who owed his nomination to the Half-Breed wing of the party that had opposed Grant, wanted Morton, a Stalwart, as his running mate. Morton refused the offer. Disgruntled New York Republican leaders had pressured Morton to refuse, but they then expected that President-elect Garfield would ask Morton to become Secretary of the Treasury. It was Garfield's turn to refuse. He believed that it would be too controversial to appoint a very wealthy Wall Street banker to head the Treasury. Meanwhile, though Morton had won a second term in Congress, he had lost a bid to win a seat in the Senate when the legislature chose instead Thomas C. Platt, the future boss of the Republicans in New York. Garfield then offered Morton a consolation prize, asking him to join the Cabinet as Secretary of the Navy. Morton politely informed Garfield that he preferred to serve the nation in a diplomatic capacity, and Garfield appointed him as minister to France.

Morton remained in France for four uneventful years. He switched to the Half-Breed wing of the party when he supported JAMES G. BLAINE for the presidential nomination in 1884, alienating President Chester A. Arthur, Blaine's most serious rival for the nomination. Morton then failed to win a seat in the Senate in 1885 when President Arthur supported William M. Evarts, former Secretary of State, and the New York legislature chose Evarts. Morton lost a third and final attempt to win a Senate seat in a three-man contest in 1887.

The delegates to the Republican national convention of 1888 chose Benjamin Harrison of Indiana as their presidential candidate and picked Morton as his running mate on the first ballot. Harrison and Morton won the election with 233 electoral votes.

Morton at last had gained a place in the Senate, serving as its presiding officer, but he angered many powerful Republicans in 1891 when he refused to cut off debate on Rep. Henry Cabot Lodge's controversial Elections Bill, dubbed the Force Bill, an attempt to protect the right of former slaves in the South to vote. At the Republican national convention of 1892, the delegates ignored Morton and nominated another New Yorker, Whitelaw Reid, for Vice President. Morton's political career had not come to an end, however. In 1894, he became the first Republican governor of New York in twelve years. Morton, seventy-two years old by 1896, did not seek a second term as governor that year, but he received fifty-eight votes for the presidential nomination as New York's favorite son. He then returned to the business world, founding the Morton Trust Company in 1899 and reluctantly merging with J. P. Morgan's financial empire in 1909. Morton died on his ninety-sixth birthday in 1920.

BIBLIOGRAPHY

Marcus, Robert. *Grand Old Party: Political Structure in the Gilded Age, 1880–1896.* 1971.

McElroy, Robert. *Levi Parsons Morton: Banker, Diplomat and Statesman.* 1930.

Morgan, H. Wayne. *From Hayes to McKinley: National Party Politics, 1877–1896.* 1969.

ALLAN SPETTER

MOUNT RUSHMORE. Carved into the fabled Black Hills near Keystone, South Dakota, is one of the nation's most awesome tributes to the American presidency. Mount Rushmore National Memorial, which pays tribute to Presidents George Washington, Thomas Jefferson, Abraham Lincoln, and Theodore Roosevelt, is one of the most popular and well-known tourist attractions in the United States. The four faces are an average of sixty-feet high. Their noses are twenty feet long, mouths eighteen feet wide, and eyes eleven feet across.

The idea of a Black Hills sculpture originated in 1923 with Doane Robinson, secretary and historian of the South Dakota Historical Society. Robinson originally wanted to carve the images of several romantic western heroes on a granite formation known as the Needles. A year later, Robinson sought the advice of John Gutzon Borglum, a well-known sculptor and mountain carver, who while enthusiastic about the project, was only interested in carving figures of national significance. Ultimately, the original site was abandoned and Borglum selected Mount Rushmore, named after a New York lawyer, Charles E. Rushmore, who had made several trips to South Dakota to inspect mining claims. Borglum chose Rushmore because it had smooth-grained granite suitable for accurate cutting, it dominated the surrounding terrain, and the sun would shine on its most carvable surface most of the day.

Despite considerable opposition by South Dakota newspapers and others, both the U.S. Congress and the South Dakota legislature passed laws to allow construction on the memorial to go forward. By mid 1925, Borglum had chosen the four Presidents to be depicted. Although Theodore Roosevelt's selection prompted considerable controversy, President Calvin Coolidge, among others, was influential in settling the issue. There have been suggestions to add other faces since the inception of the memorial but the quality of the granite made it difficult even to fit four.

On 10 August 1927, President Coolidge officially dedicated Mount Rushmore as a National Memorial and Borglum began his sculpture. During the next fourteen years, through numerous interruptions due to lack of funds and bad weather, more than 360 men at various times helped Borglum carve the mountain granite. Borglum traveled to Washington, D.C., on several occasions to lobby for funds to complete the memorial, which cost $989,992, federal appropriations accounting for $836,000. After Borglum died in March 1941, just a few days before his seventy-fourth birthday, work continued on Mount Rushmore under the direction of his son Lincoln, until funds were exhausted that fall. No additional carving has been done since.

BIBLIOGRAPHY

Fite, Gilbert C. *Mount Rushmore*. 1952.
Smith, Rex Alan. *The Carving of Mount Rushmore*. 1985.
St. George, Judith. *The Mount Rushmore Story*. 1985.

STEPHEN W. STATHIS

MOUNT VERNON. The estate of George Washington on the Potomac River, sixteen miles from Washington, D.C., came into the possession of the Washington family in the late seventeenth century. Washington inherited the estate and the mansion house in 1761 from his brother Lawrence's estate. Mount Vernon, then consisting of approximately 2,100 acres, not only provided the base for Washington's growing political and military stature in the colony but soon became his obsession as well. His marriage in 1759 to the wealthy Martha Dandridge Custis brought him increased resources to expend on the decoration and expansion of the mansion house and on the acquisition of adjacent land. By the time of his death in 1799, he had increased the estate's holdings to some eight thousand acres.

During the Revolution, Washington largely abandoned any attempt to deal with the estate's wartime problems, leaving the management of the plantation during his eight-year absence to his kinsman Lund Washington. When he returned to Mount Vernon after the war, he found the estate in chaos and spent much of the 1780s in an attempt—mainly unsuccessful—to restore its economic viability. For his absences during his presidency, Washington followed a different course. During his two terms in office he received—and replied to in detail—weekly reports from his managers on every aspect of labor and production on the estate. And although by no means an absentee President, he made frequent trips home—(fifteen in all)—to oversee personally the management of the estate and his business affairs, remaining at Mount Vernon anywhere from a few days to several months. For the period of his absences, he usually left detailed instructions for the operation of the government and maintained a steady correspondence with members of his Cabinet on day-to-day administration.

Unlike John Adams's journeys to Braintree, Washington's absences from the seat of government seem to have elicited little public disapproval. In the years after the Revolution and during Washington's presidency, Mount Vernon had already become a national symbol: few prominent Americans and foreign visitors did not make the pilgrimage to Washington's home, together with a steady stream of ordinary Americans, many of them unknown to the President.

After Washington's death, the estate—which was left to his nephew, Supreme Court Justice Bushrod Washington—fell into disrepair and by midcentury was little more than a ruin. In 1858 it was acquired and restored by the newly formed Mount Vernon Ladies' Association of the Union. Under their auspices, it has become the most-visited historic house in America.

BIBLIOGRAPHY

Jackson, Donald, and Dorothy Twohig, eds. *The Diaries of George Washington*. 6 vols. 1976–1979.
Mount Vernon: An Illustrated Handbook. 1974.
Wilstach, Paul. *Mount Vernon, Washington's Home and the Nation's Shrine*. 1927.

DOROTHY TWOHIG

MOVIES, PRESIDENTS IN. See FILM, PRESIDENTS IN.

MUTUAL-SECURITY TREATIES. See TREATIES, MUTUAL-SECURITY.

MYERS v. UNITED STATES 272 U.S. 52 (1926). This Supreme Court case, about which Chief Justice William Howard Taft said, "I never wrote an opinion that I felt to be so important in its effect," recognized the President's power to remove officers of the United States whose appointments had been consented to by the Senate. In its decision the Court explicitly overturned two recent precedents. In *Shurtleff v. United States* (1903) it had recognized a concurrent REMOVAL POWER—that is, that the President retained a residual constitutional removal power in the absence of statutory provisions restricting grounds for removal. In *Wallace v. United States* (1922), Taft had held that "in the absence of restrictive legislation" the President could remove officers of the United States." But what if Congress had legislated on the removal power? Would that negate the presidential power? This was the issue with which Taft dealt in *Myers*.

The facts in *Myers* are as follows. In 1876, Congress had passed a statute providing that postmasters of the first, second, and third classes were to be "appointed and may be removed by the President by and with the advice and consent of the Senate and shall hold their offices for four years unless sooner removed or suspended according to law." On 21 July 1917, President Woodrow Wilson appointed Frank S. Myers to be a postmaster of the first class in Portland, Oregon, for a term of four years. Myers had been active in DEMOCRATIC PARTY politics and in Wilson's second campaign for the presidency. But he had alienated important

Democratic leaders in Oregon, and on 2 February 1920, the Postmaster General removed Myers at the direction of the President. Wilson did not consult the Senate, as laid down by the 1876 statute.

On 25 April 1921, Myers sued in the Court of Claims for his salary from the date of his removal to the end of his term, 21 July 1921. The Court of Claims refused to rule on the constitutional issue and dismissed the suit on the grounds that he had delayed too long in filing the case. Myers died shortly thereafter. His widow, as executrix of his estate, appealed to the Supreme Court, arguing that his removal violated the 1876 statute.

The case presented the constitutional issue squarely: could the presidential removal power be qualified by congressional statute, or did the President have the exclusive constitutional power of removing executive officers of the United States whom he had previously appointed by and with the ADVICE AND CONSENT of the Senate? The Court rejected Myers's widow's argument by a vote of 6 to 3.

Writing for the majority (which also included Justices Willis Van Devanter, Pierce Butler, George Sutherland, Edward T. Sanford, and Harlan F. Stone), Chief Justice Taft held that the power to remove officers of the United States appointed by the President and confirmed by the Senate "is vested in the President alone" as part of the EXECUTIVE POWER. It is not subject to the consent of the Senate nor can it be made so by statute. The President, Taft reasoned, had to have a removal power in order to exercise his executive discretion and to ensure that his subordinates remained accountable. Taft's opinion is based on a reading of the congressional DECISION OF 1789. He argued that the First Congress vested the removal power in the President and that this decision had been acquiesced in by Congress for seventy-three years until had it passed the TENURE OF OFFICE ACT of 2 March 1867. Taft took much of the decision of 1789 out of context. The First Congress's debate on the removal power involved the Secretary of Foreign Affairs, an official acknowledged to be under the President's direct supervision. James Madison had argued, however, that some officials, such as the Comptroller of the Treasury, might have quasi-legislative and quasi-judicial duties and that their tenure could therefore be protected by Congress.

Justices James C. McReynolds, Louis D. Brandeis, and Oliver Wendell Holmes dissented from the *Myers* decision. McReynolds argued that throughout American history Congress had passed statutes that had limited the presidential removal power, including power to remove officials in the CIVIL SERVICE, the Comptroller General of the GENERAL ACCOUNTING OFFICE, and members of independent regulatory agencies, the FEDERAL RESERVE BOARD, the Tariff Commission, the Federal Farm Loan Board, the Railroad Labor Board, and the Board of Tax Appeals. "Congress has long and vigorously asserted its right to restrict removals," McReynolds concluded, "and there has been no common executive practice based on a contrary view." To adopt such a view, McReynolds argued, would be "revolutionary."

Justice Brandeis, in a forty-one-page dissent, described how Congress had often fixed the tenure of inferior officers and had limited the presidential removal power. In a three-paragraph dissent Justice Holmes pointed out that Congress had the power to create offices and abolish them, establish terms of office and pay scales, and legislate department regulations.

The significance of *Myers* did not rest in the high court's recognition of a presidential removal power (it had already done that in *Shurtleff*) but rather in its flat denial of *any* congressional power to qualify the power of the President to remove officers of the United States for whose appointment the consent of the Senate had been required. *Myers* invalidated the provisions of a number of statutes. In the aftermath of the decision, Congress stopped legislating removal provisions for new agencies such as the Federal Power Commission (in 1930) and the Securities and Exchange Commission (in 1934).

But Taft's decision went too far, in spite of warnings by Justice Stone that it should be limited to inferior officers in purely executive departments. After trenchant criticism by legal scholars such as Edward S. Corwin in *The President's Removal Power under the Constitution* (1927), the Supreme Court later cut back the reach of *Myers*, deciding in HUMPHREY'S EXECUTOR V. UNITED STATES (1935) that Congress does have the power to limit the President's removal power over commissioners with quasi-legislative and quasi-judicial powers—thus preserving the independence of commissioners of regulatory agencies, even when located inside departments. In WIENER V. UNITED STATES (1958) the Court further ruled that such officials are insulated from arbitrary removal even in the absence of a statutory provision regarding their tenure in office, and in *Nader v. Bork* (1973) a lower federal court held that the President and/or his subordinates must follow agency due process in dismissing officials.

BIBLIOGRAPHY

Corwin, Edward S. *The President's Removal Power under the Constitution.* 1927.

Hart, James. *Tenure of Office under the Constitution: A Study in Law and Public Policy.* 1930.

Loss, Richard, ed. *Corwin on the Constitution.* Vol. 1. 1981.

Mason, Alpheus T. *Harlan Fiske Stone: Pillar of the Law.* 1956.

U.S. Senate. *The Power of the President to Remove Federal Officers.* 69th Cong., 2d sess., 1926. S. Doc. No. 174.

RICHARD M. PIOUS

NATIONAL COMMITMENTS RESOLUTION

NATIONAL COMMITMENTS RESOLUTION (1969). The National Commitments Resolution (S. Res. 85, 91st Cong., 1st sess.) reflected the Senate's concern that Congress's role in making foreign policy had diminished since the beginning of WORLD WAR II. Several events, including the KOREAN WAR, had raised the question whether troops could be sent abroad without congressional authorization. In addition, the frequent justification of military action in the VIETNAM WAR on the grounds that it was necessary to fulfill American commitments had brought debate on what constitutes a national commitment and how such a commitment is made. Senator J. William Fulbright (D-Ark.), Chairman of the Senate Foreign Relations Committee, introduced the original version of the resolution on 31 July 1967, during the Presidency of Lyndon B. Johnson. Shortly before, on 17 July 1967, Senator Fulbright had cited to the Subcommittee on Separation Powers of the Judiciary Committee a number of instances in which the executive branch alone, "ignoring both the treaty power of the Senate and the war power of the Congress" had taken actions leading to a "constitutional imbalance." The Vietnam War was not his only stimulus; his examples included actions by every postwar President to that time: the YALTA CONFERENCE agreement by President Franklin D. Roosevelt, the Korean War under President Harry S. Truman, the sending of Marines to Lebanon by President Dwight D. Eisenhower, the CUBAN MISSILE CRISIS under President John F. Kennedy, and the intervention in the DOMINICAN REPUBLIC by President Johnson. Senator Fulbright was especially dismayed that after the Cuban missile crisis of 1962 and the Dominican intervention of 1965 he had been criticized for his dissent from the President's plans. The Foreign Relations Committee amended and reported Fulbright's proposed resolution favorably, but the Senate did not vote on it during the 90th Congress.

On 4 February 1969, with President Richard M. Nixon in the White House, Senator Fulbright reintroduced the resolution. The Nixon administration, like the Johnson administration, opposed the resolution, contending it was inconsistent with the allocation of powers under the Constitution. After amending the original version to define a "national commitment," the Senate adopted the resolution on 25 June 1969 by a vote of 70 to 16—a bipartisan move in the sense that a majority of Senators of both parties supported it.

As adopted, the National Commitments Resolution declared

> That (1) a national commitment for the purpose of this resolution means the use of the Armed Forces of the United States on foreign territory, or a promise to assist a foreign country, government, or people by the use of the Armed Forces or financial resources of the United States, either immediately or upon the happening of certain events, and (2) it is the sense of the Senate that a national commitment by the United States results only from affirmative action taken by the executive and legislative branches of the United States Government by means of a treaty, statute, or concurrent resolution of both Houses of Congress specifically providing for such commitment.

The National Commitments Resolution articulated an important principle, but it was nonbinding, and members of Congress soon began an effort to develop binding legislation, culminating in the WAR POWERS RESOLUTION of 1973.

BIBLIOGRAPHY

"National Commitments." *Congressional Record* 115, pt. 13 (1969): 17214–17246.

ELLEN C. COLLIER

NATIONAL ECONOMIC COUNCIL (NEC). Shortly after assuming office in January 1993, President Bill Clinton established by Executive Order 12835 the National Economic Council. The tasks of the council are to coordinate the economic-policy-making process with respect to domestic and international economic issues, to coordinate economic-policy advice to the President, to ensure that economic-policy decisions and programs are consistent with the President's stated goals, and to monitor implementation of the President's economic-policy agenda.

The council includes the President; the Vice President; the Secretaries of State, Treasury, Agriculture, Commerce, Labor, Housing and Urban Development, Transportation, and Energy; the Administrator of the Environmental Protection Agency; the Chair of the Council of Economic Advisers (CEA); the Director of the Office of Management and Budget (OMB); the United States Trade Representative; the Assistant to the President for Economic Policy; the Assistant to the President for Domestic Policy; the National Security Adviser; the Assistant to the President for Science and Technology Policy; and such other officials of EXECUTIVE DEPARTMENTS and agencies as the President may from time to time designate. The President serves as the chairman of the council, with the Vice President or Assistant to the President for Economic Policy presiding in his absence.

In making these changes in the policy-making process, the executive order also outlines and reaffirms the roles to be played by the key members of the President's economic team. The Secretary of the Treasury will continue to be the senior economic official in the executive branch and the President's chief economic spokesperson. The Director of OMB will continue to be the President's principal spokesperson on budget matters. The CEA will continue its traditional analytic, forecasting, and advisory functions. Under previous administrations, economic policy was largely developed and coordinated by the so-called troika (the Secretary of the Treasury, the Director of OMB, and the Chairman of the CEA). Another high-ranking official has been added to the President's policy team: the Assistant to the President for Economic Policy. It remains to be seen how this appointment and the establishment of the NEC will affect the manner in which economic advice is given to the President and economic policies are formulated and implemented by the administration.

BIBLIOGRAPHY

Carnegie Endowment for International Peace. Institute for International Economics. *Memorandum to the President-elect: Harnessing Process to Purpose.* 1992.

Cuomo Commission on Competitiveness. *America's Agenda: Rebuilding Economic Strength.* 1992.

EDWARD KNIGHT

NATIONAL EMERGENCIES ACT (1976). With executive branch cooperation, Congress developed and approved the National Emergencies Act of 1976 (90 Stat. 1255) to return most of the activated statutory provisions of emergency law to a dormant state, to make adjustments in the body of federal emergency law, and to establish a procedure by which future declarations of a national emergency, as well as related accounting and reporting requirements, would be made by the President.

From the earliest days of the republic, Presidents had from time to time declared the existence of a national emergency and used constitutional and statutory authority to address the crisis at hand. Some of these statutory powers were delegated to the President by Congress and existed on a stand-by basis, remaining dormant until a formal declaration of emergency was issued.

Until the crisis of WORLD WAR I, American Presidents utilized EMERGENCY POWERS at their own discretion. During the war and thereafter, however, Presidents had a growing body of stand-by emergency law available to them. Furthermore, presidential failure to terminate some emergency declarations resulted in stand-by law assuming an unanticipated permanency. Congressional concern about the President's discretion to invoke, use, and continue delegations of stand-by emergency authority became acute during the era of the VIETNAM WAR. A Special Committee on the Termination of the National Emergency was created by the Senate in 1972 to examine the legal and policy effects of an unterminated 1950 emergency declaration and to study the emergency-powers situation. Its work became more complex and demanding when it was discovered that four emergency declarations were outstanding, which also necessitated a remandating and renaming of the panel as the Special Committee on National Emergencies and Delegated Emergency Powers. After holding open hearings and producing several studies on emergency powers, the

Special Committee offered a draft reform bill in its May 1976 final report.

From this draft came the National Emergencies Act. Outstanding emergencies of 1933 (48 Stat. 1689), 1950 (64 Stat. A454), 1970 (84 Stat. 2222), and 1971 (85 Stat. 926) were effectively ended. Provisions of stand-by emergency law were selectively continued, made especially available, or terminated. According to the procedural provisions of the statute, the President, when declaring a national emergency, must specify the stand-by authorities he is activating. Congress may negate this action with a resolution disapproving the emergency declaration or the activation of a particular statutory power. The act was amended in 1985 (99 Stat. 448) to require the use of a joint resolution in this regard, which must be approved through the constitutionally provided legislative process. Originally, a so-called LEGISLATIVE VETO could be effected with a concurrent resolution approved by both chambers of Congress. Any national-emergency declaration that is not previously terminated by the President or Congress expires automatically on the anniversary of the declaration, unless the President, within the ninety-day period prior to each anniversary date, gives notice to Congress and in the *Federal Register* that the emergency is to continue in effect. In practice, Congress did not find it necessary to rescind the national emergencies subsequently declared by Presidents Jimmy Carter, Ronald Reagan, and George Bush.

[*See also* EMERGENCY POWERS].

BIBLIOGRAPHY

Fuller, Glenn E. "The National Emergency Dilemma: Balancing the Executive's Crisis Powers with the Need for Accountability." *Southern California Law Review* 52 (1979): 1453–1511.

U.S. Senate. Committee on Government Operations and Special Committee on National Emergencies and Delegated Emergency Powers. *The National Emergencies Act (Public Law 94–412)—Source Book: Legislative History, Texts, and Other Documents.* 94th Cong., 2d sess., 1976. Committee Print.

HAROLD C. RELYEA

NATIONAL HOUSING ACT (1934). Housing construction declined precipitously after 1925, foreshadowing the general economic collapse of the 1930s. Herbert Hoover's response was indirect, involving aid to housing lenders through the Reconstruction Finance Corporation and the Federal Home Loan Banks. But these measures did not solve a problem that grew to calamitous proportions by 1933. Millions of families, urban and rural alike, faced foreclosure, and others lacked funds to maintain deteriorating residences. New construction continued to dwindle, adding to the crushing burden of unemployment. Mortgage lenders, unable to collect on old loans and fearful for the future, were unwilling to make new loans.

Franklin Roosevelt ushered in a new age of direct assistance to housing in 1933 when, under the Emergency Farm Mortgage Act and the Home Owners' Loan Act, the federal government refinanced mortgages to permit defaulting homeowners to retain their residences. But more was needed to rebuild construction activity and employment, and Roosevelt proposed more sweeping reform of mortgage markets in May 1934. Congress responded promptly, passing the National Housing Act in June. This multifaceted measure created the Federal Housing Administration to provide federal insurance for new mortgage loans, authorized federal incorporation of national mortgage associations to buy and sell housing loans to provide liquidity to mortgage markets, established the Federal Savings and Loan Insurance Corporation to extend deposit insurance to savings and loan institutions, and encouraged new lending for housing renovation as well as new construction.

As Roosevelt recognized, the National Housing Act principally supported the functions of the private sector to service middle-class housing needs. As such, the expanding role of the FHA during the late 1930s—by 1940, approximately 40 percent of housing starts in a rebounding housing industry were supported by the new mortgage-insurance program—received political support from real estate industry groups that were traditionally conservative. But those same groups bitterly opposed Roosevelt's efforts to expand low-income public housing programs, denouncing his efforts as socialist.

[*See also* HOUSING POLICY.]

BIBLIOGRAPHY

Keith, Nathaniel S. *Politics and the Housing Crisis since 1930.* 1973.

Leuchtenburg, William E. *Franklin D. Roosevelt and the New Deal, 1932–1940.* 1963.

Schlesinger, Arthur M., Jr. *The Coming of the New Deal.* 1958.

RALPH MITZENMACHER

NATIONAL INDUSTRIAL RECOVERY ACT (1933). President Franklin D. Roosevelt signed the National Industrial Recovery Act (NIRA) on 16 June 1933, creating the National Recovery Administration (NRA) and calling it "the most important and far-reaching legislation ever enacted by the American Congress." Its purpose was to suspend temporarily the antitrust laws and use industrial codes to control prices, set production levels, and negotiate labor practices, while alleviating unemployment through a public works program, all to halt the downward spiral of the faltering economy.

Despite Roosevelt's high expectations, this bold attempt at national economic planning proved to be a short-lived failure. The President, and the NRA's director Hugh S. Johnson, seemed to have in mind a planning process by which the state would force industrialists to set prices and wages more wisely than the rigged marketplace of the 1920s. The NRA proposed that competitors should divide the market into equal shares and set prices at agreed-upon levels, allowing business to escape the hazards of excessive competition. Many businessmen believed that if prices could be held near or just above production costs, the small profit could sustain industry until recovery came. In return for suspending antitrust laws, business reluctantly conceded to labor higher wages, maximum hours, and the right to collective bargaining.

Even if such a scheme had merit, the NRA failed by trying to achieve too much. During the busy summer of 1933 Hugh S. Johnson pushed through 557 codes, covering virtually all aspects of American business, and encouraged compliance through the Blue Eagle campaign, which prompted business to assure its customers that "We Do Our Part." Had the NRA pursued a less ambitious path, focusing on just a few major industries, many problems might have been avoided, although Johnson, a colorful yet somewhat unstable director, made success even less likely. The task was more than Johnson and his staff could manage, and industry itself had to supply the officials to write and implement the codes. This gave business the upper hand over both labor and the consumer. The result was cartelization and higher prices in most industries, perpetuating the overproduction and underconsumption cycle of the depression.

On 27 May 1935 the Supreme Court terminated the problems of the NRA. In SCHECHTER POULTRY CORP. v. UNITED STATES the Court decided that the NRA's code system unconstitutionally delegated legislative authority to an executive agency, violating the separation of powers. Furthermore, the Court ruled that even Congress did not have the power to enforce such codes since they required an expansion of congressional authority in regulating interstate commerce.

The NRA left a mixed legacy. It certainly never achieved its goals of industrial recovery and became what Roosevelt termed an "awful headache" well before the Supreme Court issued its *Schechter* ruling. Yet, while the ambitious scheme of industrial planning that

Roosevelt and others envisioned was beyond the capacity of the American state in the 1930s, the NRA nevertheless marked a milestone in labor-management relations. Section 7-a of the act, rewritten into future congressional legislation, officially recognized labor unions and made collective bargaining national policy, and each NRA code included a clause abolishing child labor.

The verdict of most historians is that NRA could not have achieved its larger economic hopes even had Roosevelt named a less mercurial director or confined the agency to a few leading industrial sectors. Yet some see evidence that NRA's civil servants were improving their performance just as the Supreme Court ended the experiment, and credit NRA labor standards with helping to bring the southern labor market more in line with national trends. Roosevelt never completely abandoned the planning ideas embodied in NRA, and was talking of them even as the NEW DEAL was pushed aside by war.

BIBLIOGRAPHY

Bellush, Bernard. *The Failure of NRA.* 1975.
Brand, Donald R. *Corporatism and the Rule of Law: A Study of the National Recovery Administration.* 1988.
Hawley, Ellis. *The New Deal and the Problem of Monopoly: A Study in Economic Ambivalence.* 1966.
Himmelberg, Robert F. *The Origins of the National Recovery Administration: Business, Government, and the Trade Association Issue, 1921–1933.* 1976.
Johnson, Hugh S. *The Blue Eagle from Egg to Earth.* 1935.

OTIS L. GRAHAM, JR. and ELIZABETH KOED

NATIONAL ORIGINS ACT (1924). By 1900 disparate groups sought to limit drastically or stop completely the flow of immigrants into the United States. The movement to "close the gates" culminated with the National Origins Act of 1924, also known as the Johnson-Reed Act. Building on existing anti-immigration legislation and fueled by postwar antiradicalism and its red scare, this act aimed not only to reduce the number of persons entering the country, but to control the ethnic and racial makeup of those who did.

Nativists and racists aimed to preserve the nation's supposedly Nordic character; organized labor wanted to reduce the labor pool and raise wages; and business leaders (although earlier against more restrictions) chose not to resist new legislation, because mechanization, as well as increased production and profits, diminished their will to fight. Business's retreat from a legislative battle allowed fairly easy passage of the act.

Moreover, the Harding and Coolidge administrations, reflecting the country's mood and the REPUBLICAN PARTY's conservative agenda, fully supported new legislation.

With conservative Republicans in ascendancy, the early 1920s witnessed a high level of anti-immigration activity. On 19 May 1921 President Warren Harding, strongly supporting restriction, signed the Emergency Quota Act, aimed at reducing immigration by nationality. A one-year act, it was later extended to 1924. Its results, however, disappointed restrictionists by allowing in too many persons, specifically those from southern and eastern Europe. Prior to his death, Harding expressed support for more restrictive legislation. President Calvin Coolidge's 1923 state of the union address called for further immigration restrictions.

The resulting National Origins Act of 1924 reduced the 1921 quota to 164,000 and limited immigration from any one country annually to 2 percent of its 1890 American population. Effectively, this worked to reduce the quota of southern and eastern Europeans and favored northern and western Europeans. After 1927 the quota would drop to 150,000 and be determined in ratio to the distribution of national origins in the white population of the United States in 1920. From 1925 to 1930 total annual immigration levels dropped to 300,000; during the subsequent decade levels averaged 50,000 per year.

Opposing the act's ban on Japanese immigration for foreign policy reasons, President Coolidge, along with Secretary of State CHARLES EVANS HUGHES, engaged in a determined effort to delete that aspect of the bill, favoring a restrictive treaty instead. Despite his failure, Coolidge signed the bill. "America," he said, "must be for Americans." Feeling betrayed by his supporters in Congress, however, he also issued a public statement attempting to minimize Japanese anger. The Japanese, nevertheless, responded with nationwide protests and a national Humiliation Day.

The immigration policies of Congress, Harding, and Coolidge reflected the widespread postwar nationalism and nativism that led to the end of an era of virtually unlimited immigration; indeed, not only were the gates closed, but many Americans seemingly abandoned the idea that the United States formed a melting pot for the world's "huddled masses."

BIBLIOGRAPHY

Hicks, John D. *Republican Ascendancy: 1921–1933*. 1963.
Higham, John. *Strangers in the Land: Patterns of American Nativism, 1860–1925*. 1955.
Olson, James S. *The Ethnic Dimension in American History*. 1979.

NICHOLAS AHARON BOGGIONI

NATIONAL RECOVERY ADMINISTRATION.
See NATIONAL INDUSTRIAL RECOVERY ACT.

NATIONAL SECURITY. In the American political and governmental experience, *national security* is a term, concept, or symbol of varying meaning, understanding, and definition. In its simplest sense, the expression involves the protection of the United States from major threats to its territorial, political, or economic well-being. Other explanations, nonetheless, have been offered from time to time.

During the past few decades, particularly during the COLD WAR, the use of national security in political parlance, policy, and law appears to have become more frequent and visible. A perusal of the federal statutes, however, indicates that national security suddenly began to appear quite often as an undefined term in laws enacted around the time of U.S. involvement in WORLD WAR I. Then, with the return to peace, its use in new legislation tapered off over the next decade. In the aftermath of WORLD WAR II, the term again became prominent in official pronouncements, presidential directives, statutes, and agency regulations.

Although the concept of national security has not been defined in statutory law and has not been given very definite meaning in other policy instruments, its imprecise and general nature can provide considerable flexibility for governmental action. Indeed, in many policy contexts, the term may prompt or facilitate presidential resort to EXECUTIVE PREROGATIVE or use of EMERGENCY POWERS.

Vagueness, however, also may render the expression senseless or subject to accidental or willful misinterpretation, resulting in ventures that are detrimental to other rights and privileges of the polity. Consequently, an important consideration is who interprets national security to determine public policy. All three federal branches produce written instruments in this regard, usually through prescribed procedures that allow varying points of view to be expressed, if not reconciled. Such deliberations in the executive branch also are frequently cloaked in official secrecy.

More troublesome interpretations often appear to occur with sudden, unilateral, presidential actions in the name of national security. There is no one statutory check on the President in these situations, and various laws, such as the NATIONAL EMERGENCIES ACT (1976) or the WAR POWERS RESOLUTION (1973), may have relevance. Other checks include congressional power of the purse and oversight of the executive, public opinion, and, possibly, judicial restraints, although the federal courts have largely shown a reluctance to question presidential action when national security has been said to be involved.

The conflicts experienced by Congress with the President over national-security actions, however, do not seem to have deterred the continued, undefined use of the term in legislation. Furthermore, in the aftermath of the cold war, there appears to be an effort within government to broaden the national-security concept. In a classified November 1992 national-security directive on overhauling the federal intelligence structure, President George Bush reportedly envisioned an expansion of intelligence gathering to include natural resource shortages, global health problems, and environmental conditions, which previously have not been considered central to insuring national security. Thus, moving beyond the cold war, the national-security concept continues to have great importance, significance, and influence in American government.

BIBLIOGRAPHY

Boll, Michael. *National Security Planning: Roosevelt Through Reagan.* 1988.
Crabb, Cecil V., and Kevin V. Mulcahy. *American National Security: A Presidential Perspective.* 1991.
Lasswell, Harold D. *National Security and Individual Freedom.* 1950.
Relyea, Harold C. "National Security and Information." *Government Information Quarterly* 4 (1987): 11–28.

HAROLD C. RELYEA

NATIONAL SECURITY ACT (1947). The NA-TIONAL SECURITY apparatus that began to emerge during WORLD WAR II and at the onset of the COLD WAR is embodied in the National Security Act of 1947. Initial impetus for the act came from a wartime request from Army Chief of Staff Gen. GEORGE C. MARSHALL to reexamine the issue of unification of the armed services, that is, bringing the army and the navy (and their respective subsidiaries, the air force and marines) into one department. Although Secretary of the Navy JAMES V. FORRESTAL opposed the concept, he realized that outright opposition was not a viable position. Gaining agreement to a postponement until the war was over, Forrestal then asked his longtime associate, Ferdinand Eberstadt, to examine the issue. Drawing heavily on the experience of World War II, in which various aspects of policy coordination were haphazard—befitting the anarchic and competitive administrative style of Franklin Roosevelt—or constantly had to be reorganized, Eberstadt recommended an overhaul of the entire national security apparatus, not just

the military: creation of a national military establishment over three military departments (army, navy, air force), headed by a Secretary of Defense; a statutory charter for the JOINT CHIEFS OF STAFF (JCS), which came into being in 1942; creation of a NATIONAL SECURITY COUNCIL (NSC) to coordinate the various aspects of national security policy; a CENTRAL INTELLIGENCE AGENCY (CIA), to coordinate intelligence activities; and a National Security Resources Board (NSRB), to coordinate economic mobilization issues.

This, in essence, was the substance of the National Security Act as signed by President Harry S. Truman in July 1947. Given the centrality of the act to shaping the U.S. national security apparatus for the cold war, it is interesting to note how little of Congress's debate was attuned to the potential implications of the act. Among the issues drawing most attention were concerns over the development of a "Prussian" general staff in a unified defense establishment; whether the Senate would have the right to approve any new statutory positions on the NSC; the propriety of having an active-duty military officer as Director of Central Intelligence; and limits to prevent the CIA from becoming an American Gestapo.

The act had a two fold effect on NATIONAL SECURITY POLICY and practice. First, it greatly improved the coordination of virtually all aspects of national security policy: diplomatic-military, intramilitary, intelligence, and economics. In part this was done by legislating greater military coordination, but more central was the creation of bodies (NSC, CIA, the short-lived NSRB) beyond the traditional EXECUTIVE DEPARTMENTS. This led to the second major effect, the passing of these various coordinative aspects more directly under the control of the President and the EXECUTIVE OFFICE OF THE PRESIDENT (of which the NSC and the subsidiary CIA became part in 1949), and a concomitant loss for the various Cabinet departments. The NSC has been most central to this process of shifting power and control. Given the extreme malleability of the NSC's role and internal structure, especially of its own staff, the act has allowed succeeding Presidents a greater ability to bend the operations of the entire national security apparatus to their particular working methods and preferences. Through successive administrations, but most noticeable under Presidents John F. Kennedy, Richard M. Nixon, Gerald Ford, and Jimmy Carter, the STATE DEPARTMENT has been the most frequent casualty of the aggrandized NSC.

Initial amendments to the act tended to continue this general thrust. In 1949, the VICE PRESIDENT was added to the NSC's statutory membership and the Secretary of Defense was given greatly enhanced authority over a more centralized and renamed DEFENSE DEPARTMENT. However, efforts by Congress to expand further NSC membership have been opposed by Presidents. This has most often centered on NSC membership for the Secretary of the Treasury. Congress passed such legislation in 1975, but it was vetoed by President Gerald Ford.

National Security Act amendments have been a main vehicle for Congress to enact changes in CONGRESSIONAL OVERSIGHT and control of intelligence activities. These came largely in reaction to revelations, first in 1975–1976, of illegal acts by the intelligence community and clear evidence of lax congressional oversight of intelligence. In 1980, Congress made statutory its right to oversee intelligence with amendments to the act; in 1985, Congress specified its role in authorizing and appropriating funds for intelligence.

But these amendments have not changed the broad nature of the act or the way in which it enhanced the control by succeeding Presidents over national security policy and their ability to control that policy more closely from the White House. Indeed, it can be argued that the act was so little changed over the course of the cold war largely because it did create an apparatus that was both viable in its own right and responsive both to the needs of Presidents and policy. Moreover, the fact that a key player in this apparatus, the NATIONAL SECURITY ADVISER, is not a statutory position subject to confirmation and has been exempt, as an assistant to the President, from providing testimony to Congress has also enhanced the ability of Presidents to use the apparatus as they see fit with a minimum of congressional oversight.

BIBLIOGRAPHY

Caraley, Demetrios. *The Politics of Military Unification.* 1966.
Lowenthal, Mark M., and Richard A. Best. *The National Security Council: An Organizational Assessment.* 1992.

MARK M. LOWENTHAL

NATIONAL SECURITY ADVISER. The national security adviser (formally the assistant to the President for National Security Affairs) is an extremely influential position in NATIONAL SECURITY POLICY and a key support for direct action in that area by the President. The national security adviser's influence derives from his role as director of the NATIONAL SECURITY COUNCIL (NSC) staff. Given the central role of the NSC in coordinating various aspects of national security policy (diplomacy, military, intelligence, economics), the importance of the national security adviser becomes evident.

Interestingly, the position is not a statutory part of the NATIONAL SECURITY ACT, which in 1947 created the NSC. The act created an executive secretary for the NSC, which is how it functioned under President Harry S. Truman. The shift away from the executive secretary came under President Dwight D. Eisenhower, who created the position of special assistant for National Security Affairs. Under varying titles, this has been what is commonly called the national security adviser.

The role of the national security adviser has varied with each President, reflecting both their individual management styles and the extreme malleability of the NSC staff structure. Eisenhower's advisers, Robert Cutler and Gen. Andrew Goodpaster, concentrated on managing the strictly delineated NSC staff under him, with its very elaborate structure and paper flow. McGeorge Bundy served both Presidents John F. Kennedy and Lyndon B. Johnson; Bundy was the first adviser to serve as a policy advocate in his own right, rather than simply a coordinator of the views brought to the NSC by the various departments and agencies. Purists have felt that this latter role, an "honest broker" among the agencies responsible for forming and executing policy, was the proper one for the national security adviser. Walt Rostow succeeded Bundy under Johnson and spent most of his tenure dealing with the VIETNAM WAR.

President Richard M. Nixon chose HENRY KISSINGER as his national security adviser. The elaborate NSC structure was much like that under Eisenhower and totally dominated by the bureaucratically adept and aggressive Kissinger, much to the discomfort of Secretary of State William Rogers. This suited Nixon, who distrusted the State Department. In 1973, Kissinger became Secretary of State while retaining his NSC role. This unique situation continued under President Gerald Ford until 1975, when Kissinger relinquished his NSC slot to Brent Scowcroft, his deputy, as part of a larger reorganization. Scowcroft never challenged Kissinger's primacy, and probably came closest to epitomizing the honest-broker role.

President Jimmy Carter took office hoping to minimize the role of the NSC. However, Zbigniew Brzezinski, his adviser, saw his role akin to Kissinger's and came into frequent conflict with Secretary of State Cyrus Vance.

President Ronald Reagan, who delegated a great deal of authority to subordinates, had six advisers in eight years. Richard Allen, who had unexpectedly lost the job to Kissinger in 1969, resigned under a financial cloud. William Clark was a Reagan confidant but national security neophyte, who never mastered the NSC staff and process. He was succeeded by his

NATIONAL SECURITY ADVISERS

	President	National Security Adviser
34	Eisenhower	Robert Cutler, 1954–1955 Dillon Anderson, 1956 Robert Cutler, 1957–1958 Gordon Gray, 1959–1961
35	Kennedy	McGeorge Bundy, 1961–1963
36	L. B. Johnson	McGeorge Bundy, 1963–1966 Walt W. Rostow, 1966–1969
37	Nixon	Henry Kissinger, 1969–1974
38	Ford	Henry Kissinger, 1974–1975 Brent Scowcroft, 1975–1977
39	Carter	Zbigniew Brzezinski, 1977–1981
40	Reagan	Richard V. Allen, 1981–1982 William P. Clark, 1982–1983 Robert C. McFarlane, 1983–1986 John M. Poindexter, 1986 Frank C. Carlucci, 1986–1987 Colin Powell, 1987–1989
41	Bush	Brent Scowcroft, 1989–1993
42	Clinton	W. Anthony Lake, 1993–

deputy, Robert McFarlane, a veteran of the Kissinger NSC; he was succeeded in turn by his deputy, Vice Admiral John Poindexter, who left office as a result of his involvement in the IRAN-CONTRA AFFAIR, a series of intelligence operations run in his NSC staff. Frank Carlucci took over and impressed many as being the best adviser since Scowcroft. Finally, Gen. Colin Powell served and received high marks as well.

Scowcroft returned to the job under President George Bush, but functioned more individually as the President's close friend and adviser, leaving his deputy to run the staff and policy process.

Critics have often commented on the conflict that has arisen between some advisers and the Secretary of State, usually decrying the loss of status. However, this ignores the fact that such rivalries can only continue with the acceptance of the President, for whatever reason. As noted, Nixon used it to cut out the State Department; in Carter's case, it reflected his inability and unwillingness to impose discipline on the system.

The national security adviser position has also posed problems for Congress. As it has no statutory basis, the Senate cannot vote for confirmation. Some believe this should be remedied, given the importance of the job. Moreover, as an assistant to the President, the adviser does not testify before Congress as do the heads of departments and agencies, although advisers have customarily made themselves available to the media for interviews. The debate over the "proper" role of the adviser is unlikely ever to be settled, the nature of the job, perhaps more so than any other position in the national security field, is defined solely by the President, and redefined with each new administration.

BIBLIOGRAPHY

Lowenthal, Mark M., and Richard A. Best. *The National Security Council: An Organizational Assessment.* 1992.
Shoemaker, Christopher C. *The NSC Staff: Counseling the Council.* 1991.

MARK M. LOWENTHAL

NATIONAL SECURITY COUNCIL (NSC). The National Security Council is a presidential agency responsible for integrating domestic, foreign, and military policies. One of the most difficult demands of NATIONAL SECURITY POLICY in the twentieth century has been the ability to coordinate, initially, its diplomatic and military aspects, and then such other facets as economics as they became important. There was no such coordination to speak of in the United States through the eighteenth and nineteenth centuries, save in the person of the President himself to the degree that he chose to do so.

Establishment of the NSC. After the SPANISH-AMERICAN WAR it became evident that better coordination was needed. In 1903, the army and navy created the Joint Board to improve inter-service coordination. Over the next few decades the military tried to include the State Department in some larger group, largely to have some access to foreign policy decisions. A military proposal in the Taft administration for such a Council of National Defense was vetoed by Secretary of State PHILANDER KNOX. Such a council was created during the Wilson administration (1916), but largely to coordinate industrial mobilization. It included the two services and the departments of the Interior, Agriculture, Commerce and Labor, but not State, and turned out to be rather ineffective even within its own field.

Concerns over Axis activities in pre-WORLD WAR II Latin America led Secretary of State CORDELL HULL to propose to President Franklin D. Roosevelt in 1938 that a Standing Liaison Committee (SLC) of State, War, and Navy's second-ranking officers be created. The SLC's work was uneven, geographically limited, and solely coordinative, but it served as a precedent. So did informal weekly wartime meetings among the three secretaries, initiated by Secretary of War HENRY STIMSON. Before the end of World War II, these had evolved into the State, War, Navy Coordinating Committee (SWNCC), made up of assistant secretaries, but with a staff and a mandate to coordinate on "politico-military matters."

The National Security Council (NSC) evolved out of a larger late war and postwar reexamination of the entire national security apparatus and a study overseen by Ferdinand Eberstadt, a protégé of Secretary of the Navy James Forrestal. Eberstadt's plans largely became the NATIONAL SECURITY ACT (1947), which created the NSC, along with a unified Defense establishment and the CENTRAL INTELLIGENCE AGENCY, which was subordinated to the NSC. The NSC was given the mandate to advise the President on integrating "domestic, foreign and military policies relating to the national security." The membership of the NSC, as designated by 1949 amendments to the act, are the President, Vice President, the secretaries of State and Defense. The JOINT CHIEFS OF STAFF (JCS) were designated the principal military advisers; this was amended in 1986, making the chairman of the JCS the principal military adviser.

Two NSC adjuncts not mentioned in legislation, but which became increasingly important were the NSC staff, largely drawn from other agencies, and the Assistant to the President for National Security Affairs (usually referred to as the NATIONAL SECURITY ADVISER), who customarily runs the staff and has become a key player in national security policy deliberations and potent rival to secretaries of State.

Reshaping the NSC. The NSC is one of the most malleable of the national security entities, its methods and activities being constantly reshaped to fit the working methods of each President. President Harry S. Truman defined the NSC's role as purely advisory, a forum for working out recommendations, but not for making policy, which remained his prerogative.

President Dwight D. Eisenhower greatly expanded the rudimentary NSC structure he inherited into an elaborate and formal committee structure. The NSC staff took on a greater role in coordinating policy among agencies, resolving differences and preparing options and implementation papers. Robert Cutler and General Andrew Goodpaster were key to making this NSC staff function as well as it did, although some felt it was overly layered and too mechanistic.

President John F. Kennedy eliminated virtually all of Eisenhower's apparatus, meeting regularly with NSC members, but not in formal session. Critics felt this system was too ad hoc. During the CUBAN MISSILE CRISIS, for example, Kennedy created an expanded group of advisers, the Executive Committee, also referred to as Ex Comm. McGeorge Bundy, Kennedy's national security adviser, had far greater say in policy deliberations than his Eisenhower predecessors and moved from their "honest broker" role among agencies to be an advocate in his own right. President Lyndon B. Johnson largely followed the same course, again relying heavily on personal meetings with Secretary of State DEAN RUSK and Secretary of Defense ROBERT S. MCNAMARA. The interagency process was controlled, albeit fitfully, by State via a Senior Interdepartmental Group and subordinate Interdepartmental Regional Groups.

President Richard M. Nixon reinvigorated the NSC, largely based on the Eisenhower model he knew well. Under national security adviser HENRY KISSINGER an elaborate committee structure again emerged for the NSC staff. Kissinger dominated the committees and the committees in turn dominated virtually all policy, much to the discomfit of Secretary of State William Rogers. In 1973, Kissinger was given Rogers's position while keeping his White House post, underscoring the personal nature of the policy process. It was in fact the relationship between Nixon and Kissinger rather than the NSC staff's role that was prominent in this process. Kissinger, even more so than Bundy, was a forceful policy advocate. Critics felt that his "dual hat" role undercut the purposes of the NSC, as its staff director could not be an honest broker if he was also a principal policymaker from one agency. This continued under President Gerald Ford until 1975. As part of a major national security shake-up, Kissinger relinquished his NSC job to his deputy, Brent Scowcroft. Scowcroft clearly could not overshadow the Secretary of State and played an exemplary role as an honest broker.

Having campaigned against the Nixon-Ford-Kissinger foreign policy, President Jimmy Carter planned to reduce the NSC staff's role. The structure was greatly reduced and simplified, going from seven committees to two. However, national security adviser Zbigniew Brzezinski was eager to play a role similar to Kissinger's. He became an intense and often successful bureaucratic rival to Secretary of State Cyrus Vance. Critics, including some in the administration, later faulted Carter for not imposing greater discipline on the process, believing that the infighting ultimately undermined policy.

Under Reagan and Bush. The Reagan administration was a tumultuous period for the NSC. President Ronald Reagan had six national security advisers (Richard Allen, William Clark, Robert McFarlane, John Poindexter, Frank Carlucci, and Colin Powell) in eight years. None ever rivaled Secretaries of State Alexander Haig or GEORGE SHULTZ, each adviser largely serving a coordinative role again. Reagan's preference was for OPTION PAPERS from which he selected his chosen policy.

But the role of the NSC staff became controversial. Much of this centered on the fact that NSC staff members were given much latitude and some became involved in policy implementation, including intelligence operations. The IRAN-CONTRA AFFAIR that broke in 1986 centered on two issues: covert support for the contra rebels in Nicaragua, despite congressional bans; and efforts to free U.S. hostages in Lebanon. NSC staffer Oliver North was central to both and the bridge between them. Poindexter was faulted for not keeping NSC members informed about policy decisions taken by Reagan; NSC members Shultz and Secretary of Defense CASPAR W. WEINBERGER were faulted for not being forceful enough about policies with which they disagreed.

Subsequent investigations revealed that arms were sold to Iran to help free hostages, with profits being used to arm the contras. A Special Review Board (the TOWER COMMISSION: former Senator John Tower; Brent Scowcroft; former Secretary of State Edmund Muskie) faulted NSC staff operations and suggested improvements, but basically supported the NSC's traditional role given its unique flexibility. Special congressional committees were harsher on the NSC staff's activities. In reaction to the Tower Commission Report, Reagan issued a national security decision directive that specifically forbade the national security adviser or NSC staff from undertaking intelligence operations.

President George Bush's NSC has been uncontroversial. Given Bush's own familiarity with national security issues, the NSC was clearly in an advisory and coordinative role again. Scowcroft returned to his old job and was a close adviser, largely based on his long friendship with Bush. Some critics said, however, that Scowcroft was less active in terms of managing the NSC staff than he was under Ford, operating more on a personal rather than institutional basis.

BIBLIOGRAPHY

Draper, Theodore. *A Very Thin Line.* 1991.
Lowenthal, Mark M., and Richard A. Best. *The National Security Council: An Organizational Assessment.* 1992.
Lowenthal, Mark M. *U.S. Intelligence: Evolution and Anatomy.* 1984.
President's Special Review Board. *Report of the President's Special Review Board.* 1987.
Senate Select Committee on Secret Military Assistance to Iran and the Nicaraguan Opposition/House Select Committee to Investigate Covert Arms Transactions with Iran. *Report of the Congressional Committees Investigating the Iran-Contra Affair.* 1987.
Shoemaker, Christopher C. *The NSC Staff: Counseling the Council.* 1991.

MARK M. LOWENTHAL

NATIONAL-SECURITY DIRECTIVES (NSDs). Presidential instruments establishing policy, directing the implementation of policy, or authorizing the commitment of government resources with regard to NA-TIONAL SECURITY have been known as national-security directives since the administration of President George Bush. They also may be issued to obtain information from federal departments and agencies, to seek recommendations from within the executive branch on a particular course of action, and to effect other housekeeping actions. Indeed, the subject matter of NSDs is diverse and on occasion, has been controversial. Largely prepared by the staff of the NATIONAL SECURITY COUNCIL, approved NSDs bear the President's signature, are sequentially numbered for identification, are usually classified for security, and are maintained in the files of the council.

NSDs are not a new development. Similar instruments were issued, under different names, by every President since the establishment of the National Security Council in 1947. Early versions, designated simply "NSC" with a sequential identification number, were policy and strategy statements; region and country situation profiles; assessments of mobilization, arms control, atomic energy, and other functional matters; and government-organization pronouncements. When President Dwight D. Eisenhower assumed office in 1953, approximately 100 of these NSC instruments were operative; another 300 of them were approved during his administration. With the arrival of John F. Kennedy at the White House, NSC policy papers were called national-security action memoranda (NSAM). When Lyndon Baines Johnson became President in 1963, he kept the NSAM designation and approximately 370 of them were produced during the Kennedy-Johnson tenure.

President Richard M. Nixon refined arrangements somewhat. His national-security position papers—often lengthy, based on contingencies, and of uneven quality—were designated national-security study memoranda. Almost 250 of these documents were produced for Nixon and his successor, Gerald Ford. Presidentially approved NATIONAL-SECURITY POLICY and action were set out in national-security decision memoranda, at least 318 of which were produced during the Nixon-Ford presidencies. When Jimmy Carter entered the Oval Office, he retained this dual system but designated his national-security instruments presidential review memoranda and presidential directives. Only 63 of these latter documents were approved.

To initiate analyses, reviews, and position papers on national security, President Ronald Reagan issued national-security study directives. Another set of instruments, national-security decision directives (NSDDs), were used to effect national-security policy and action. More than 300 NSDDs were produced during Reagan's two terms.

President Bush utilized national-security directives to mandate national-security policy and action. By October 1989, after about nine months in office, he had issued 26 NSDs. Subsequent developments in the Persian Gulf, Eastern Europe, and the Soviet Union contributed to this figure being greatly increased.

Details about these kinds of instruments—their total number, titles, and content—are often not readily available as a consequence of their officially secret status. Such directives are usually classified for security at the highest level even before they are given presidential approval. Furthermore, as a consequence of being classified, they are distributed and made accessible within the executive branch on a need-to-know basis. Only when they have ceased to be operative, have been declassified, and have been deposited at one of the PRESIDENTIAL LIBRARIES or the National Archives may the public examine them. Occasionally, unclassified versions of NSDDs or NSDs have been released to the public, or a fact sheet has been disclosed in place of the original directive. These versions, however, are not published in the *Federal Register* and must be requested in writing from the National Security Council.

In the past few years, many within Congress have been concerned about these directives. Not only are they not routinely available to members and committee staffs, but also they are often withheld on the basis of separation of powers when specifically requested by legislators. Unable to learn their content, Senators and Representatives cannot know in advance if such instruments commit the United States and its resources to a policy or a course of action contrary to the wishes of the citizenry or to law. Indeed, the possibility exists that, in some cases, the positions set forth in such directives arguably constitute an unconstitutional invasion of the prerogatives of the legislative branch. At best, the use of these instruments sometimes appears to be an attempt by the President to make a determination unilaterally about matters better decided with congressional comity.

In an independent assessment of the President's use and the restricted status of NSDDs, the GENERAL ACCOUNTING OFFICE concluded in late 1988 "that some notification to the Congress is warranted." Congress continues to seek better accountability of presidential national-security directives as well as ways to improve its own access to them.

BIBLIOGRAPHY

Relyea, Harold C. "The Coming of Secret Law." *Government Information Quarterly* 5 (1988):97–116.

U.S. General Accounting Office. *National Security: The Use of Presidential Directives to Make and Implement U.S. Policy.* GAO/NSIAD-89-31. 1988.

U.S. House. Committee on Government Operations. *Presidential Directives and Records Accountability Act.* Hearings. 100th Cong., 2d sess., 1989.

HAROLD C. RELYEA

NATIONAL-SECURITY POLICY. The term NATIONAL SECURITY came into common usage only during the latter part of WORLD WAR II and then was used often during the COLD WAR. Thus, it is difficult, if not anachronistic, to trace this concept throughout the history of the presidency. It can best be done by first defining national security: not only the assessment of potential threats to the nation's survival and the preferred U.S. role in the world, but the planning and process by which various national resources—military, diplomatic, labor, industrial, raw materials, etc.—are coordinated to meet these threats.

Before World War I. The geographic remoteness of the United States in the eighteenth and nineteenth centuries inhibited any deep exploration of what would later be called national security needs. Two documents, Washington's FAREWELL ADDRESS and the MONROE DOCTRINE, largely defined the mainstays of what might be loosely termed U.S. national security policy during this period: noninvolvement in European affairs and no permanent alliances, coupled with the closure of the Western Hemisphere to further colonization.

The CIVIL WAR, a domestic conflict, revealed some of the problems that would become part of national-security policy in the twentieth century. The Confederacy and the Union both resorted to a draft for sufficient manpower. In a prolonged war that consumed much of ongoing industrial production, economic mobilization was also important. The North's larger industrial base provided necessary matériel and continuing civilian goods, but the WAR DEPARTMENT was reorganized three times before Secretary EDWIN M. STANTON achieved a satisfactory organization.

At the end of the nineteenth century, the United States' evident power led to a strikingly more activist view of the nation's proper international role. Theodore Roosevelt, Senator Henry Cabot Lodge, and other advocates of war with Spain cited the United States' obligations as a world power as one rationale for the SPANISH-AMERICAN WAR. This view, in addition to Alfred Thayer Mahan's geopolitical theories about the importance of sea power, also supported keeping the unexpected empire in the Pacific. Secretary of State JOHN HAY's 1899 OPEN DOOR note on China also reflected a more active role overseas, as did Roosevelt's diplomatic intervention in the first Moroccan crisis (1905–1906).

A fledgling national-security organization also began after the Spanish-American War, reflecting perceived wartime inadequacies, new demands on the military, and the Progressive era's belief in organizational restructuring. Most important were Secretary of War ELIHU ROOT's army reforms, creating a chief of staff with real authority over the army's various bureaus. To achieve some level of army-navy coordination, the Joint Board was created in 1903. However, efforts during the Taft administration to take this one step further by creating a Council of National Defense that included the State Department foundered on the objections of Secretary of State PHILANDER KNOX.

With regard to the pre-WORLD WAR I period, it is difficult to discern any distinct national-security policy. Interestingly, the Joint Board, through its own planning process (the COLOR plans), identified Japan and Germany as potential threats to broadened U.S. interests. When President Woodrow Wilson discovered the existence of Plan BLACK (Germany), he ordered the Joint Board to stop this activity.

The Two World Wars. The U.S. played no role in the prewar 1914 crisis, and held to a policy of NEUTRALITY. However, by 1915–1916, Secretary of State Robert Lansing and foreign policy adviser Colonel EDWARD M. HOUSE held that a German victory in Europe in World War I would threaten U.S. interests. Wilson articulated no such view, although he belatedly supported war preparedness, largely for political reasons. In 1917, Wilson was moved to war on the fairly narrow issue of U.S. neutral rights on the high seas and the affront of Germany's unrestricted submarine warfare. Wilson's lofty FOURTEEN POINTS and the LEAGUE OF NATIONS were developed and enunciated only after the United States entered the war and thus were belated war aims.

As a wartime leader, Wilson gave tremendous latitude and independence to General John J. Pershing, commander of the American Expeditionary Force. On the home front, there was a great expansion of government intervention in all aspects of life, including a more successful draft and full-scale economic mobilization. There was also a certain impingement of CIVIL LIBERTIES in excessive patriotic zeal generated by the government.

When it came to the peace negotiations, Wilson acted independently, even ignoring Congress as a potential partner in establishing U.S. policy, much to the eventual peril of the TREATY OF VERSAILLES. Departing from the injunction of Washington's Farewell Address, Wilson severely misjudged the willingness of the American people to sustain their wartime involvement in postwar collective security. Indeed, the luster of the Great Crusade (as some termed U.S. involvement in the war) dimmed quickly, leading to disappointment over the outcome of the war in contrast to its supposedly highly idealistic and moral purposes. Wilson's physical collapse and his own adamancy doomed any chance for a compromise with Senate opposition over the Versailles Treaty.

President Warren Harding's election was interpreted as representing this desire to pull back from Wilsonian interventionism. Yet Secretary of State CHARLES EVANS HUGHES took the lead in naval disarmament, more aptly called ARMS CONTROL later in the century. The TREATY OF WASHINGTON (1921–1922) set capital ship ratios among the five major naval powers. Ironically, this treaty and its 1930 successor in London, along with the highly idealistic KELLOGG-BRIAND PACT (1928) outlawing war, all reinforced the view that the United States could remain apart from world events despite the high degree of involvement required simply to negotiate such pacts.

The United States, like the other democracies, was slow to respond to the growing threats of fascism and Japanese aggression. Japan's seizure of Manchuria in 1931–1932 resulted in Secretary of State HENRY STIMSON's doctrine of nonrecognition of changes brought about by means contrary to Kellogg-Briand. But beyond this limited step, the United States played a small role in the growing prewar crises. Indeed, various Neutrality Acts reflected the absence of congressional and public support for any such role, as well as an attempt to avoid the "mistakes" that were seen as having led to U.S. involvement in the Great War. Moreover, the United States had very limited means to be of any influence.

President Franklin D. Roosevelt was constantly aware of the very severe domestic constraints on any more interventionist U.S. foreign policy, perhaps to the point of overestimating the strength of isolationists. Roosevelt's initial support for rearmament stemmed from concerns over the Depression economy. The 1934 Vinson-Trammell Act laid the grounds for naval expansion up to treaty limits, but was also a major jobs program. However, in 1938, after the Munich debacle, Roosevelt became convinced that rapid expansion of U.S. air power would increase both U.S. influence and preparedness. Still, the United States played little role in the final prewar crisis or in the early months of World War II, despite clear sympathy for the Allies.

The Nazi blitzkrieg in May 1940 led to a revolution in U.S. national-security policy. Roosevelt evolved a policy that walked a fine line between aiding Britain and other states resisting Germany while hoping to deter U.S. intervention. However, each step—cash-and-carry aid to circumvent the arms embargo, the destroyer-base swap with Britain, lend-lease, etc.—actually narrowed his options vis-à-vis Germany, deepening the U.S. commitment to Germany's defeat. In the Pacific, forward deployment of the fleet to Hawaii was seen as an overt deterrent to Japan.

By late 1940 Roosevelt's military advisers concluded in the first place, that the United States would have to enter the war at some point; and second, that in the event of a two-front war, Germany should be defeated first, a concept that remained a guiding wartime strategy. The Joint Board crafted the RAINBOW war plans, offering a range of strategies depending on the situation and the state of U.S. preparedness. Although Roosevelt was fully aware of the plans and condoned prewar strategic planning with Britain, he never gave formal approval to them.

As a war leader, Roosevelt took a more active interest in planning and strategy than had Wilson, although—with perhaps two exceptions—he usually deferred to the views of the JOINT CHIEFS OF STAFF, created in 1942 as a counterpart to the British Chiefs of Staff Committee. However, he took on a much more active role on the international political level, staying in close touch with Prime Minister Winston Churchill and attending several wartime conferences. On the home front, Roosevelt adapted the NEW DEAL model, allowing numerous agencies to handle various aspects of total warfare mobilization. This eventually required bringing Associate Justice JAMES F. BYRNES into the White House to coordinate the ramshackle system.

As in the past, U.S. wartime strategy emphasized a rapid end to hostilities. As Roosevelt informed Joseph Stalin at Yalta (1945), he expected the United States to demobilize quickly and not to become involved in prolonged postwar occupation in Europe or Asia. Roosevelt's postwar thinking came to rely on the nascent UNITED NATIONS, albeit with few details as to how it would function internationally beyond a general recognition of the dominant role for the four Allied powers, the United States, Britain, China, and the U.S.S.R. Little attention was given to the meaning of NUCLEAR WEAPONS to national security.

The Cold War. The hiatus between Allied victory and the cold war was brief. By 1946, George Kennan warned of the need to prepare for a long diplomatic struggle with the "unscrupulous" Soviet Union. Soviet gains in Eastern Europe and Communist electoral successes in Western Europe, coupled with Britain's economic collapse in the winter of 1946–1947, led

President Harry Truman and his advisers to adopt a version of Kennan's policy of CONTAINMENT of the U.S.S.R. until Soviet internal problems caused it to ameliorate its behavior, largely embodied later in a 1950 planning document called NSC-68, authored by Paul Nitze. The immediate manifestations of this policy were the MARSHALL PLAN (1947), designed to rebuild Western Europe's economy and so relieve socioeconomic pressures for Communism, and NATO (1949), an open-ended military commitment to the defense of Western Europe. This, in turn, resulted in a large-scale, ongoing U.S. military presence in Europe.

Containment became the overarching national security policy for the next forty-five years. Truman made it bipartisan, working closely with the Republican-controlled Congress. It also had become more significant since the creation of the Soviet atom bomb in 1949 meant that, for the first time since the mid nineteenth century, the continental U.S. was subject to potentially devastating attack.

Containment was unique in that it gave coherence to virtually all aspects of defense, diplomatic, and domestic policy. It came to include a larger peacetime military and higher defense spending; a national-security apparatus—largely embodied in the 1947 NATIONAL SECURITY ACT—unified the DEPARTMENT OF DEFENSE; NATIONAL SECURITY COUNCIL to coordinate foreign and defense policy; CENTRAL INTELLIGENCE AGENCY; numerous treaty commitments (NATO, SEATO, Japan, Korea, etc.); transport (the national highway system); education (National Defense Education Act grants); science (the "space race") and occasional civil liberties problems (the excesses of MCCARTHYISM).

Although the intensity of the cold war waxed (KOREAN WAR, CUBAN MISSILE CRISIS, the VIETNAM WAR, Afghanistan) and waned (Spirit of Camp David, DETENTE, strategic arms control), it is striking how successive Presidents largely followed the containment strategy developed in the Truman administration. Broad debates over means (rollback, counterinsurgency, détente, etc.) rarely led to doubts over ends. The trauma of the Vietnam War, however, resulted in a major political realignment: Democrats became less willing to be active overseas and the Republicans became more willing. This new stance was epitomized by the Reagan administration, which pursued the most aggressive cold-war policy since the Kennedy administration.

Mikhail Gorbachev's accession in the U.S.S.R. in 1985 saw a new Soviet willingness to deal forthrightly with its own internal problems. Gorbachev, in partnership with President Ronald Reagan, greatly reduced the cold-war rivalry as a necessary precursor to internal reform, as George Kennan, the originator of containment had predicted. Halting reform efforts, however, resulted in the collapse of Communist authority and then of the Soviet Union itself in 1991.

The success of containment and the end of the cold war left the United States with a national security policy vacuum. There appeared to be no overt threats of any magnitude and no agreement on what role the United States should play in the world. Although this role has shrunk, as has the attendant cold war apparatus, there remains a debate over the degree of continued international involvement versus a desire to concentrate much more heavily on domestic needs.

BIBLIOGRAPHY

Acheson, Dean. *Present at the Creation*. 1969.
Dallek, Robert. *Franklin D. Roosevelt and American Foreign Policy, 1932–1945*. 1979.
Halle, Louis J. *The Cold War as History*. 1967.
Kreidberg, Marvin A. and Merton G. Henry. *History of Military Mobilization in the United States Army, 1775–1945*. 1955.
Link, Arthur S. *Wilson the Diplomatist*. 1957.
Lowenthal, Mark M. *Leadership and Indecision: American War Planning and Policy Process, 1937–1942*. 1988.
May, Ernest R., ed. *The Ultimate Decision: The President as Commander in Chief*. 1960.

MARK M. LOWENTHAL

NATIONAL TREASURY EMPLOYEES UNION v. NIXON 492 F.2d 587 (D.C. Cir. 1974). May a President refuse to take actions required by statutory law? The Constitution recognizes no presidential "dispensing" power, providing instead in Article II, Section 3, that the President "shall take care that the laws be faithfully executed." In the case of *National Treasury Employees Union v. Nixon* a federal appeals court ruled on arguments made by President Richard M. Nixon that he was not bound to execute provisions of one statute because it conflicted with provisions of another and that such a decision by the President was a political question not reviewable by the federal courts.

The facts of the case are as follows: under section 5305(a) of the Federal Pay Comparability Act of 1970 (FPCA), Nixon was required to compare public and private pay scales, consider recommendations of his Advisory Committee on Federal Pay, and then either implement pay adjustments for federal employees or submit an alternative plan to Congress for pay adjustments, taking into account any national emergency or relevant economic conditions. Unless either house exercised a LEGISLATIVE VETO over his plan within thirty days, a pay increase would go into effect. In the fall of

1972, Nixon neither implemented the pay increase nor submitted any alternatives to Congress by the required date, 1 September.

Nixon's failure to implement the law triggered lawsuits by two public-employee unions. A suit brought by the National Association of Internal Revenue Employees was dismissed by a federal district court on the grounds that it lacked jurisdiction. A suit brought by the National Treasury Employees Union (NTEU), however, was decided on substantive grounds by a district court in favor of the administration. The NTEU then appealed to the federal appellate court for the District of Columbia.

The Justice Department argued that because the ECONOMIC STABILIZATION ACT of 1970 and subsequent amendments allowed the President to "stabilize prices, rents, wages, and salaries," the President was justified in ignoring the provisions of the FPCA to the extent that the pay increases it mandated would exceed the increases Nixon had already granted in January 1972. Nixon therefore was exercising executive discretion in determining his obligations under two seemingly conflicting laws. If the court took jurisdiction, it would be showing a "lack of respect" for a coordinate branch of government.

The appeals court, relying on standards developed in *Baker v. Carr* (1962) for political questions, held that the case did not present a political question. Instead, it used the doctrine of SEPARATION OF POWERS to hold that the "judicial branch of the Federal Government has the constitutional duty of requiring the executive branch to remain within the limits stated by the legislative branch." If the court did not take jurisdiction, it might indicate a lack of respect for congressional legislative authority. Following Chief Justice John Marshall in MARBURY v. MADISON (1803) the court pointed out that since Nixon had argued that he was making a judgment about the relationship between two laws, it is the province of the judiciary to state the law. Therefore, a judicial resolution of the questions presented by the relationship between the two laws would better enable the President to perform his constitutional duty to see to the laws' faithful execution.

The court also argued that by deciding the case it was protecting the presidency. If the President were held immune from suit when he refused to execute the provisions of a law on the grounds that such an executive action was covered by the political questions doctrine, the court's action "would have the almost inevitable result of causing the Congress in the future not to vest in the President . . . power of execution, but rather to confer that power directly upon cabinet officers or other federal officials designated by the Congress itself." The appeals court claimed that it was preserving presidential power, not limiting it, by accepting the case.

Having established its jurisdiction and its power to issue a writ of mandamus to the President instructing him to execute the provisions of the FPCA, the appeals court decided not to exercise that authority immediately. Instead, it acted pursuant to provisions of the Federal Declaratory Judgment Act and determined that there was no conflict between the two statutes. In this way the court demonstrated "the utmost respect to the office of the presidency" and attempted "to avoid, if at all possible, direct involvement by the Courts in the President's constitutional duty faithfully to execute the laws and any clash between the judicial and executive branches of the Government." The case was remanded to the district court and the government chose to comply with the provisions of the FPCA. *National Treasury Employees Union v. Nixon* reaffirmed the principle that presidential judgments about the relationship of one set of statutory obligations to another are reviewable by the courts and that the doctrine of political questions does not apply when the President seeks to use executive judgment about statutes he is charged with faithfully executing.

BIBLIOGRAPHY

Fisher, Louis. *Constitutional Conflicts between Congress and the President.* 3d ed. 1991.
Reichley, A. James. *Conservatives in an Age of Change: The Nixon and Ford Administrations.* 1981.
Pyle, Christopher, and Richard Pious. *The President, Congress, and the Constitution.* 1984.

RICHARD M. PIOUS

NATIVE AMERICANS. See INDIANS.

NATO TREATY. The North Atlantic Treaty Organization (NATO) represented a major strategic effort by the United States, Canada, and the democratic countries of Europe to contain the political ambitions of the Soviet Union. Signed on 4 April 1949, the NATO treaty was approved by the U.S. Senate on 21 July and entered into force on 24 August. The original parties to the treaty were the United States, Belgium, Canada, Denmark, France, Iceland, Italy, Luxembourg, the Netherlands, Norway, Portugal, and the United Kingdom.

Under Article 5 of the NATO treaty, the parties agreed that an armed attack against one or more of them in Europe or North America "shall be considered an attack against them all." In the event of an armed attack, each country "will assist the Party or Parties so attacked by taking forthwith . . . such action as it deems necessary, including the use of armed force." Article 11 explains that the treaty shall be ratified "and its provisions carried out by the Parties in accordance with their respective constitutional processes." The terms of the treaty make it clear that no nation is committed to introduce its armed forces into hostilities. It may do so if it deems such action necessary, but such introduction is not required. Nor does the treaty recognize any unilateral power of the U.S. President to commit armed forces. The provisions of the treaty are to be carried out in accordance with "constitutional processes."

The day the text of the proposed NATO treaty was made public, Secretary of State DEAN ACHESON addressed the nation. The treaty, he said, "does not mean that the United States would be automatically at war if one of the nations covered by the pact is subjected to armed attack. Under our Constitution, the Congress alone has the power to declare war." Acheson reemphasized the limited scope of the NATO commitment on the first day of hearings before the Senate Foreign Relations Committee. When asked whether anything in the treaty pledged the United States to "an automatic declaration of war in any event," he replied that nothing in the treaty had that effect. The committee probed further, asking whether the decision to go to war still resided "in the discretion and judgment of the Government and the Senate." Acheson answered, "That is true." He later commented that the "constitutional processes" mentioned in the treaty "obviously mean that Congress is the body in charge of that constitutional procedure."

[*See also* WAR, DECLARATION OF.]

BIBLIOGRAPHY

Glennon, Michael J. *Constitutional Diplomacy.* 1990.
Glennon, Michael J. "United States Mutual Security Treaties: The Commitment Myth." *Columbia Journal of Transnational Law* 24 (1986): 509–552.

MICHAEL J. GLENNON

NAVY, DEPARTMENT OF THE. *See* DEFENSE, DEPARTMENT OF.

NEAGLE, IN RE 135 U.S. 1 (1890). The issue in the case of *In re Neagle* was whether the President must always be able to cite a law of the United States or a specific constitutional authorization in support of his actions or whether the broad EXECUTIVE POWER with which he is vested justifies any action he believes to be in the public interest, so long as there is no conflict with existing legislative or constitutional provisions.

The facts of the *Neagle* case were bizarre. A disgruntled Californian named David S. Terry had threatened the life of Supreme Court Justice Stephen J. Field, whose judicial circuit included California. The Attorney General assigned a federal marshal named David Neagle to protect Field while riding circuit in California. When Terry seemed about to make a physical attack on Field in a California railroad lunchroom, Neagle killed him. The marshal was arrested by local authorities and held by the state on a charge of murder. The federal government sought Neagle's release on habeas corpus, under a federal statute making the writ available to a person in custody for an act done "in pursuance of a law of the United States."

The problem was that Congress had enacted no law authorizing the President to assign marshals as bodyguards for federal justices. But the Supreme Court declined to be bound by this technicality. The Court held that the government had to be able to protect its judges and that the President was best able to perform that function. Consequently, his action in assigning the marshal was properly considered to have been done "under the authority of the United States."

The *Neagle* ruling has been cited by the Supreme Court in both supporting and rejecting presidential actions. On the one hand, a major decision supporting executive power was IN RE DEBS (1895). President Grover Cleveland, who had sent federal troops to Chicago to break the PULLMAN STRIKE, directed his Attorney General, RICHARD OLNEY, to secure a court injunction against the striking railroad workers. Though there was no explicit statutory basis for the injunction, the Supreme Court sustained it on the ground that every government was obligated and empowered to apply to the courts for the protection of the general welfare.

On the other hand, President Harry S. Truman's action in seizing the strike-threatened U. S. steel industry during the KOREAN WAR was held invalid by the Court majority in YOUNGSTOWN SHEET & TUBE CO. V. SAWYER (1952), principally on the ground that Congress had considered giving the President the seizure power by statute but had decided against it.

Perennial congressional dissatisfaction with executive military policies came to a head during the unpopular VIETNAM WAR, and resulted in adoption of the WAR POWERS RESOLUTION, over President Richard M. Nixon's veto in 1973. The resolution, which purports to set specific limits on presidential commitment of U.S. troops abroad, lends itself more to political than judicial interpretation or enforcement.

BIBLIOGRAPHY

Fisher, Louis. *Constitutional Conflicts between Congress and the President.* 3d ed. 1991.
Swisher, Carl Brent. *Stephen J. Field, Craftsman of the Law.* 1930.

C. HERMAN PRITCHETT

NEGOTIATION, POWER OF. The President's power to negotiate treaties and other international agreements with foreign sovereigns derives from the treaty clause in the Constitution. Article II, Section 2, gives the President the "Power, by and with the Advice and Consent of the Senate, to make Treaties, provided two thirds of the Senators present concur." Although the President must share most of his powers as DIPLOMAT IN CHIEF with the legislative branch (e.g., RECEIVING AND APPOINTING AMBASSADORS and regulating the armed forces), his TREATY-MAKING POWER arguably means that his power of negotiation is exclusive. Perhaps the most famous support for the President's exclusive negotiation power comes from the Supreme Court's opinion in UNITED STATES V. CURTISS-WRIGHT EXPORT CORP. (1926). Writing for the Court in broad strokes, Justice George Sutherland opined that the federal government's international authority derives not just from the Constitution, but more generally from the nation's status of sovereignty. Sutherland continued that only one branch of the federal government, the executive, could represent the sovereign internationally: "In this vast external realm, with its important, complicated, delicate and manifold problems, the President alone has the power to speak or listen as a representative of the nation." Congress, moreover, may delegate whatever international authority it has to the President, who is the nation's "sole organ" in foreign relations. Under the sole organ theory, then, the President or his representatives may unilaterally negotiate with foreign leaders and create both formal and informal agreements, though the Senate's consent is needed for treaties to come into force.

On the other hand, the treaty clause refers not only to senatorial consent, but also to the executive receiving the Senate's advice on treaties. The records of the CONSTITUTIONAL CONVENTION do not support the notion that the Senate has no role in treaty-making until after the executive branch has concluded its treaty negotiations; in fact, the executive branch would have been completely omitted from the treaty-making process under preliminary versions of the treaty clause. By neglecting to seek the Senate's advice during treaty negotiations, the President may face unreceptive and even contentious Senators by the time he finally transmits the treaty for their consent. A prominent example is the TREATY OF VERSAILLES (1919), ending WORLD WAR I and calling for the establishment of the LEAGUE OF NATIONS. President Woodrow Wilson excluded important members of the Senate from the Versailles Treaty's negotiation. The Senate thereafter refused to give its consent to the treaty, and the United States never joined the League of Nations. In certain other instances when the Senate has not given advice during treaty negotiations, the Senate has responded by placing reservations upon or revising the instrument. Whether or not constitutionally required to do so, some modern Presidents have sought senatorial input while negotiating a treaty, with the goal of eventually receiving the Senate's swift and efficient ratification of the accord. Examples of such presidential-senatorial cooperation include the negotiation of both the NATO TREATY following WORLD WAR II and the proposed United States free-trade accord with Mexico.

BIBLIOGRAPHY

Berger, Raoul. "The Presidential Monopoly of Foreign Relations." *Michigan Law Review* 71: 1, 4–33 (1972).

Fisher, Louis. *Constitutional Conflicts between Congress and the President.* 3d ed. 1991. Chapter 8.

Fisher, Louis. *The Politics of Shared Power: Congress, and the Executive.* 3d ed. 1993.

KENNETH C. RANDALL

NEUTRALITY. Since the Revolution, America has supported neutrality during foreign wars. Respect for a neutral's sovereignty includes its territory, ships at sea, and the air above that nation. The central issues include the right of trade with belligerents in *non*contraband (nonwarlike) goods, the flag's protection of noncontraband materials, and blockades that are real. More than once, the United States has attempted to abide by neutrality, only to be drawn into war.

The American Revolution provided an opportunity for the former colonists to establish respect for neutrality. Shortly after the Declaration of Independence, John Adams headed a committee instructed to prepare a "model treaty." Among its principles were "free [neutral] ships, free [neutral] goods," seizure of contraband only, and commercial pacts that did not necessarily establish political or military ties. Accordingly, the United States signed two treaties with France in 1778: the Treaty of Alliance and the Treaty of Amity and Commerce.

The new nation under President George Washington encountered its first problems regarding neutrality during the Anglo-French wars from 1793 to 1815. The administration tried to steer clear of political entanglements while maintaining commercial ties. But this effort proved impossible. Longstanding European rivalry for North America had not ended with the Revolutionary War; the Treaty of Alliance had been established "forever"; and the Treaty of Amity and Commerce permitted French vessels to sell prizes in American ports while denying this privilege to France's enemies. When France sought assistance against England, Washington insisted in the PROCLAMATION OF NEUTRALITY of 1793 (affirmed by the Neutrality Act of the next year) that the United States would stay out of European affairs. But Anglo-American relations meanwhile deteriorated due to English seizure of American goods and impressment of American seamen. In 1795 the President ratified JAY'S TREATY, which prevented war with England, though at the expense of failing to safeguard neutrality.

Washington's successor, John Adams, confronted problems with France that led to the QUASI-WAR WITH FRANCE (1797–1801). French seizures of British goods on American vessels violated the Franco-American commercial agreement of 1778. Although the two nations came close to declaring war, they chose instead to negotiate the Convention of 1800, which abrogated the Treaty of Alliance while affirming neutral rights. Recognition of these rights seemed possible, for the European war had wound down.

Five years later, however, the Anglo-French conflict broke out anew, and in 1812 President James Madison found it impossible to stay out. Thomas Jefferson had resumed American neutrality after 1805, but by the time Madison became President, England's violations of American's neutrality made war certain. Only after two and a half years of fighting did the WAR OF 1812 end in a stalemate that nonetheless preserved American honor.

A third major conflict over neutrality occurred during the CIVIL WAR, when President Abraham Lincoln faced a diplomatic crisis following England's proclamation of neutrality in 1861. Southern resistance, he declared, constituted a domestic rebellion and did not concern other countries. The British, however, insisted that the proclamation did not extend recognition to the Confederacy, although they admitted that neutrality bestowed belligerent status. Throughout the four years of the War, England maintained a neutrality that Lincoln interpreted as pro-South and that left much ill feeling.

A fourth problem regarding neutrality arose during WORLD WAR I, when President Woodrow Wilson proclaimed neutrality and insisted that belligerents respect American commerce. England, though, expanded the definition of contraband and announced a blockade of Europe that raised questions about adherence to the Declaration of London (1909) regarding neutral rights; Germany, meanwhile, resorted to unrestricted submarine warfare and began taking American lives. In April 1917, Wilson asked Congress for a DECLARATION OF WAR on Germany that would, among other objectives, sanctify neutral rights. After the war, he met with leaders of other victorious powers and drew up the covenant of the LEAGUE OF NATIONS, which (without U.S. membership) infringed upon neutral rights by prohibiting involvement with nations that violated the peace pact.

President Franklin D. Roosevelt faced similar problems in the 1930s as he sought a flexible type of American neutrality toward another war threatening in Europe. By a series of neutrality acts, he attempted to keep the United States out of the crisis, while protecting the nation's commerce and integrity. To accomplish these goals, he sought to avoid strict neutrality by seeking the right to help victims against aggressors. Congress, however, placed restrictions on rights of neutrality by forbidding travel on belligerent vessels and by prohibiting loans and arms sales to all belligerent nations.

But again the effort to maintain neutrality proved elusive. Japan's attack on PEARL HARBOR on 7 December 1941 actually brought America into WORLD WAR II, but the President had already taken a long step toward U.S. involvement by supporting the LEND-LEASE ACT and becoming party to the ATLANTIC CHARTER, which virtually created an Anglo-American alliance. By late October the United States was engaged in an undeclared war in the Atlantic with German submarines.

World War II came to a close in late 1945 and—as in the period following World War I—the winning powers worked toward a lasting peace that actually curtailed neutral rights. Led by President Harry S. Truman, they established the UNITED NATIONS, a collective security organization that permitted the Security Council to impose sanctions on aggressors.

A survey of America's attempts to maintain neutrality during foreign wars shows the policy to be impractical if not impossible; the nation's economic and political interests are too tightly interwoven with Europe to permit political isolation. Further, history shows that among the first casualties of war is respect for neutrals. Finally, the periods following both world wars demonstrate that in the interests of peace, the triumphant powers placed restrictions on neutrality. In the post-1945 era, wars have not been formally declared and the doctrine of neutral rights has not been invoked. Neutrality remains possible only when all warring nations find it in their interests to acknowledge such principles.

BIBLIOGRAPHY

DeConde, Alexander. *Entangling Alliance: Politics and Diplomacy under George Washington.* 1958.
Divine, Robert A. *The Illusion of Neutrality.* 1962.
Gilbert, Felix. *To the Farewell Address: Ideas of Early American Foreign Policy.* 1961.
Jones, Howard. *Union in Peril: The Crisis Over British Intervention in the Civil War.* 1992.
Link, Arthur S. *Wilson: The Struggle for Neutrality, 1914–1915.* 1960.

HOWARD JONES

NEW DEAL. On the cold morning of 4 March 1933, with the economy devastated by four years of depression and the entire national banking system in collapse, Franklin Delano Roosevelt took the oath of office. During the campaign the New York governor had "pledged a new deal for the American people," and the public responded by giving him a landslide victory. Yet on INAUGURATION day the details of that "new deal" were vague, since Roosevelt ran on an anti-Hoover platform, offering only sketchy details of his recovery plan. Some aspects could have been predicted: Roosevelt was a dedicated conservationist; Presidents Theodore Roosevelt and Woodrow Wilson had greatly influenced his political ideas; and as a young man he was much impressed by the wartime planning efforts of 1917–1918.

Roosevelt launched his New Deal with a burst of legislative activity in which fifteen major programs were crafted in the administration's first hundred days. Five years of reform followed that fundamentally altered American politics and political economy, a period in which some historians see patterns in the New Deal's strategic direction. In the first New Deal (1933–1935), Roosevelt pursued recovery as a first priority, proposing a partnership between government and business-agriculture, while also establishing a set of relief efforts to provide a measure of cash and in-kind payments to destitute Americans. In 1935, frustrated by conservative opposition, especially from the Supreme Court, the administration, still working toward recovery, shifted the emphasis to reform. The energies of this second New Deal ensured Roosevelt's reelection and produced major reform measures in labor-management relations, old age pensions, taxation, a revived interest in antimonopoly activity, and a more militant rhetoric on matters of economic class. Although major New Deal legislation ceased in 1938, historians now see that Roosevelt in 1937–1938 hoped to pursue a new agenda of governmental reforms—a permanent planning board, reorganization of the executive branch, a national system of regional authorities modeled on TVA—that could be called a third New Deal.

The First New Deal. In March of 1933 Roosevelt faced a daunting task. America's banks had closed their doors. Millions were hungry and desperate. One-fourth of the workforce was unemployed. "This great Nation will endure as it has endured, will revive and will prosper . . . ," a reassuring Roosevelt said at the inauguration, "let me assert my firm belief that the only thing we have to fear is fear itself." No one there could have spelled out how the President would calm that fear, but if the first step was to radiate presidential confidence, it was a good beginning.

Sensing an opportunity for more tangible action, and drawing upon ideas of an assortment of academics, lawyers, social workers, bureaucrats, and businessmen [see BRAIN TRUST], Roosevelt launched a hectic and exciting three-month burst of activity. The anti-Hoover vote had filled Congress with Democrats, and soon a stream of messages and legislative proposals flowed from the White House to Capitol Hill. Quickly, unemployment relief programs—the Federal Emergency Relief Administration (FERA), the PUBLIC WORKS ADMINISTRATION (PWA)—and new banking legislation were put in place.

The heart of the early recovery plan was the National Recovery Administration (NRA). Building upon WORLD WAR I industrial planning experience, this innovative attempt at national economic management displayed the New Deal's initial strategy of producer-oriented planning emphasizing voluntary compliance. The hope of spurring recovery through government-negotiated codes granting both higher wages and prices led instead to a tangle of complaints, but Roosevelt urged patience with the NRA experiment. Another economic concern was agriculture, one of the sectors hardest hit by the depression. The Agriculture Adjustment Administration (AAA) attempted to organize and empower farmers to control production levels collectively, thereby raising farm income and retiring submarginal land. One of the boldest New Deal agencies, and one that drew heavily from Roosevelt's own experience, was the TENNESSEE VALLEY AUTHORITY (TVA). Firmly rooted in the conservation tradition, TVA sought to transform the impoverished Tennessee Valley through a regional planning idea that ignored state boundaries. The TVA included an extensive plan of reforestation, land-use management, retirement of submarginal land, and provision of cheap and abundant hydroelectric power. These beginnings made up the core of the first New Deal, backed up by innovative agencies like the CIVILIAN CONSERVATION CORPS (CCC). The New Deal also included taking the United States off the international gold standard to restore flexibility to monetary policy and reform of stock markets and banking.

Despite the atmosphere of enthusiasm, the first New Deal was plagued with problems. The NRA met its demise at the hand of the Supreme Court, which also invalidated the AAA. The TVA's larger scheme for regional planning was soon eclipsed by a more popular objective, generation of cheap electricity. The economy did improve, the gross national product slowly climbing from $65 billion in 1933 to reach $72 billion in 1935, but 10 million Americans still filled unemployment lines that year. The depth of the depression meant that recovery would be a long, slow task. Yet Roosevelt remained supremely optimistic throughout his first term, conveying hope to the American people via a series of FIRESIDE CHATS on radio that reassured the public and further strengthened his popularity.

The Second New Deal. Not everyone liked the New Deal, however, and by 1935 Roosevelt faced opposition from both ends of the political spectrum. Mass movements sprang up, led by men who believed the administration had not gone far enough. Louisiana's governor, Huey P. Long, pledged a Share Our Wealth Plan that guaranteed a minimum standard of living. Dr. Francis E. Townsend, a California physician, organized millions in "Townsend Clubs," and promised government pensions to all Americans over sixty. NORMAN THOMAS, a Socialist, saw the New Deal as a well-meaning failure, and called for a completely new system. On the right, Republicans and members of the new American Liberty League thought the New Deal went too far—too much government intervention and too much spending. These stirrings of revolt to right and left of the New Deal seemed to threaten the President's reelection in 1936, and after a period of uncertainty, Roosevelt seized the initiative. In the summer of 1935 he urged more congressional action, beginning with an expansion of the relief and public works programs of the first New Deal, through a new Works Progress Administration (WPA), which offered jobs for construction workers, school teachers, artists and writers, even college students. Roosevelt also pushed a new agenda including progressive taxation, a collective bargaining labor law, and a new social insurance program to aid a population most vulnerable to the whims of the economy, the elderly.

In the midst of such political opposition, the New Deal faced its most powerful foe, the Supreme Court. In May of 1935 the Justices ended the NRA experiment (which Roosevelt had already referred to as an "awful headache"), and in January of 1936 invalidated key financing elements of the AAA. Angry and frustrated with the Court's opposition, Roosevelt infused more energy and determination into his new agenda. He moved away from the voluntarism and cooperation with business that marked the early programs to put the government increasingly on the side of working-class men and women, the poor, the elderly—intended beneficiaries of second New Deal reform.

The measures of 1935 were radical in tone, but moderate in outcome, usually shaped by influential Senators and special interest groups to be something less than the original conception. SOCIAL SECURITY, although the boldest move into social insurance in the nation's history, was shaped by political pressures to exclude many agricultural workers (especially southern sharecroppers), and was financed by a regressive tax. Even the National Labor Relations Act (WAGNER ACT) of 1935, hailed as the definitive statement of support for labor and despised by management, would in time be seen as stabilizing the industrial-capitalist order. Many of Roosevelt's radical critics charged that presidential caution and congressional bargaining had tamed important reforms.

For millions of Americans, however, the second New Deal was confirmation that the man in the White House was a true friend, supported by the First Lady, ELEANOR ROOSEVELT, a dedicated and determined crusader who consistently promoted important social reform, particularly human rights and the causes of African Americans. Roosevelt's support was so strong by the 1936 election that he easily buried the Republican candidate, ALFRED M. LANDON, and ended all hopes for Norman Thomas and other THIRD-PARTY CANDIDATES. Gaining a majority of over 10 million popular votes and sacrificing only eight electoral votes to Landon, Roosevelt took every state but Maine and Vermont. Regardless of its critics, obviously the vast majority of Americans approved of the New Deal.

The "Third New Deal." As Roosevelt entered his second term, the New Deal was far from complete. He still saw "one-third of a nation ill-housed, ill-clad, ill-nourished." In the next four years he hoped to extend regional development, further improve conditions for labor, and, most importantly, to overhaul the executive branch itself. Despite these hopes, however, 1937 would mark the beginning of the end of New Deal reform, for in that year Roosevelt also decided to tackle the conservative Supreme Court.

Since 1935 the Supreme Court had systematically blocked key New Deal programs. Roosevelt responded in February 1937 by proposing a fundamental restructuring of the Court itself—what the press called his COURT-PACKING PLAN. When a judge reached the age of seventy and did not retire, Roosevelt asked for the authority to appoint another, up to a total of fifteen members of the Court. This plan, not without historical precedent and supported by some sympathetic New Dealers, was a serious political mistake. It gave substantial ammunition to Roosevelt's conservative critics, who effectively used the incident to erode the President's support and hinder further reform. When a recession that same year fueled pessimism in Congress and among depression-weary Americans, the subsequent loss of support denied Roosevelt the completion of his agenda.

One of the casualties of this 1937 debacle was his renewed attempt at national planning. Almost simultaneously with the Court-packing plan, Roosevelt asked for another "seven little TVAs" to divide the continental United States into conservation regions and supplement efforts of incompetent state and local governments. He also urged governmental reform through a restructuring of the executive office, including creation of twelve Cabinet departments, an executive office with adequate staff, and a permanent national planning board. If accomplished, such a plan would shift the balance of power decisively to the executive.

This third New Deal fell victim to the political uproar over Court reform and reorganization. When the 1937 recession ended four years of steady growth, and the 1938 election brought many Republicans back to Congress, Roosevelt's plans foundered. Congress passed a weak reorganization bill that fell far short of his intended plan and did not include a permanent planning board. By 1939 the administration's attention began to shift toward the threats posed by expansionist fascist regimes abroad, and the legislative phase of the New Deal gave way to consolidation.

The Legacy of the New Deal. With the passage of the years, the limits on the New Deal's achievements have become clear. The main goal, recovery from the depression, eluded Roosevelt until wartime mobilization forced the government to undertake vast spending measures. New Deal tax measures do not seem to have redistributed wealth significantly, relief measures never reached all the unemployed, the black population received some badly needed jobs and relief but faced discrimination in most programs. Some historians have attributed these and other shortcomings to Roosevelt's ever-shifting tactics and innate caution; most historians have been impressed with the barriers to the reform aspirations of the New Dealers and have found the voters' verdict on the New Deal a fair one.

Roosevelt's legacy is much more than a string of depression-era agencies. The New Deal fundamentally altered the American political economy, making permanent the expanded role of the federal government. Millions received federal relief, labor benefited from federal supervision of collective bargaining, and farmers received federal subsidies. Banks could no longer recklessly speculate with depositors' uninsured money. The New Deal filled out the foundation for the regulatory state and set in place the American version of the welfare state. The office of the President grew in size and importance. Conservation and land-use management efforts were invigorated and broadened. A new role for the government had been created in the realm of national economic management. The war years completed the conversion of liberals to a vision of postwar full employment guaranteed by compensatory spending. Economic regulation to guard against market failures became the norm and not a crisis-oriented aberration.

Franklin D. Roosevelt entered the White House on that cold March morning not just to bring a nation back to economic prosperity but to reform a system that had failed. His reform agenda was far from achieved when the war intervened. Nevertheless, the New Deal created a governmental role that decisively shaped American politics and political economy for the next thirty years.

BIBLIOGRAPHY

Conkin, Paul. *The New Deal.* 3d ed. 1991.

Fraser, Steve, and Gary Gerstle, eds. *The Rise and Fall of the New Deal Order, 1930–1980.* 1989.

Graham, Otis L., Jr., ed. *The New Deal.* 1973.

Graham, Otis L., Jr. "Franklin Roosevelt and the Intended New Deal." In *Essays in Honor of James MacGregor Burns.* Edited by Michael R. Beschloss. 1989.

Karl, Barry D. *The Uneasy State.* 1983.

Leuchtenburg, William E. *Franklin D. Roosevelt and the New Deal.* 1963.

Schlesinger, Arthur M., Jr. *The Age of Roosevelt.* 3 vols.. 1957–1960.

Sitkoff, Harvard, ed. *Fifty Years Later: The New Deal Evaluated.* 1985.

OTIS L. GRAHAM, JR., and ELIZABETH KOED

NEW FREEDOM. The New Freedom was Woodrow Wilson's answer to Theodore Roosevelt's NEW NATIONALISM during the presidential campaign of 1912. In broad terms, it proposed the use of government regulation of the economy to restore the viability of the price and market system, that is, to clear the market of monopolistic or oligopolistic obstructions to competition and to guarantee in the marketplace "a free and fair field." Roosevelt's New Nationalism, on the other hand, accepted what many believed were the proven efficiencies of large-scale, oligopolistic private economic power, using the government to guarantee that private business power would be used in the national interest. In the words of the Wilsonians' campaign slogans, the New Nationalism proposed to regulate the trusts while the New Freedom proposed to regulate competition. "Theirs," Wilson declared, "is a program of regulation, while ours is a program of liberty."

As President, Roosevelt had sought to outline a national policy that would balance the broad prerogatives traditionally accorded to private decision-makers against the need for a governmentally determined concept of a national interest. Like most of his contemporaries, he rejected the growing force of special-interest groups in politics. After leaving the presidency, he watched his successor, William Howard Taft, fail to cope with the challenges of the contending interest groups, and in the fall of 1911 he reentered presidential politics. For a program, he took some cues from a book, *The Promise of American Life*, written in 1909 and sent to him by its author, Herbert Croly. Croly, too, was dismayed by the growth of pressure-group politics and despaired that even giving the electorate greater power through political reforms could change things. The solution was the creation of a national faith of selflessness, a "New Nationalism" that would override self-centered and parochial interests for the higher, common interest.

Roosevelt, like Croly, believed that there were no institutional remedies for the fragmentation of life and the amoral drift of modern society. He would not interfere with the concentration of private corporate power, which, he believed, made America competitive internationally and promised greater affluence through greater industrial efficiency. But he would put such power to public use. The situation required bold leadership and a government that was prepared to take on responsibility for shaping a selfless nationalism that put the public interest above individual interests, especially when such interests put the poor, the weak, and the unorganized at severe disadvantage.

Wilson saw much the same problem. He recognized that the age of individualism had passed and that individual interests had been superseded by group coalitions of like interests. He, too, saw the need for an activist government to preserve individual liberties.

"The individual," he remarked in 1912, "is caught in a great confused nexus of all sorts of complicated circumstances, and to let him alone is to leave him helpless as against the obstacles with which he has to contend." In shaping his presidential program, Wilson declared, "We are just upon the threshold of a time when the systematic life of this country will be sustained, or at least supplemented, at every point by governmental activity." But instead of giving the government a major role in pointing the power of the great corporations toward socially desirable outcomes, he put his faith in a rejuvenated market system.

Wilson won the presidential election of 1912, which gave him the opportunity to put his reform program through Congress. It included a remarkable spurt of major legislation, including passage of a free-trade tariff bill, the UNDERWOOD TARIFF ACT (1913); the Federal Reserve Act (1913); the FEDERAL TRADE COMMISSION ACT (1914); and the CLAYTON ACT (1914). Each of these measures improved market functions by reducing trade barriers, by providing a more flexible currency system, and by setting up barriers against monopolistic mergers, predatory pricing, and other forms of unfair and destructive competition. The program did little, however, to remedy injustices that market processes failed to address because of an unequal distribution of market power.

Because both Roosevelt and Wilson advocated government regulation of business in an age when serious people argued seriously against it, many historians have treated the New Nationalism and the New Freedom as small variations on the same theme. Having common adversaries, they seemed to be allies in spite of their partisan rivalry. As their contemporary, the journalist William Allen White, put it, the rival campaign slogans appeared to describe merely "Tweedledum and Tweedledee."

But when one takes the New Freedom and the New Nationalism not merely as rival campaign devices but as serious alternative visions of the good society, the contrasts stand out. The New Nationalism represented an Old World conservative's outlook, while the New Freedom represented a classical liberal's vision. For Roosevelt, good government required good leadership, and it was the responsibility of good men to gain and use power. Power must be used, moreover, not for personal gain nor even to increase a nation's wealth but to foster the greatness of a people. Roosevelt acknowledged that most people prefer business-as-usual and wish to be left alone to cultivate their own gardens, but he regarded such an outlook with scorn. Peace and tranquillity he found good, but grandeur was infinitely better. He well understood that power can be abused, but the remedy lay not in institutions or processes but in the character of the leader. For him, great events did not wait on process but on great and moral men, and neither great doings nor great men should be constrained by mere mechanisms of government.

The contrast with Woodrow Wilson can hardly be exaggerated. In the fashion of the classical liberal, Wilson distrusted men even as he harbored great hopes for Man. Consequently, Wilson put his faith in process, in elaborate mechanisms to constrain the will of great men for both good and evil purposes. More than that, he put his faith in the multitude of ordinary men pursuing their own ordinary interest in free competition with other ordinary men. He believed implicitly in the justice of marketplace decisions about the allocation of resources, rewards, and opportunities. Wilson would use government chiefly to minimize the oppressive effects of monopoly power and other forces that tended to produce privilege and deny merit. This was, as some of his critics argued, truly a "shopkeeper's vision" of the good society. "The men who understand the life of the country," he said in 1911, "are the men on the make." He designed the New Freedom to liberate the men on the make from the grip of the men already made. He saw no more noble a function of government than that.

BIBLIOGRAPHY

Cooper, John Milton, Jr. *The Warrior and the Priest: Woodrow Wilson and Theodore Roosevelt.* 1983.
Davidson, John Wells, ed. *A Crossroads of Freedom: The 1912 Campaign Speeches of Woodrow Wilson.* 1956.
Link, Arthur S. *Woodrow Wilson and the Progressive Era.* 1954.

RICHARD M. ABRAMS

NEW FRONTIER. The Democratic convention that met in Los Angeles in July 1960 nominated John F. Kennedy for President. He delivered his acceptance speech on 15 July to a very large crowd in the Los Angeles Memorial Coliseum. THEODORE SORENSEN, his counsel and speech writer, prepared the address. While Kennedy, Sorensen wrote, "generally shrank from slogans," he wanted one here to establish continuity with the programs of his illustrious activist Democratic predecessors—Woodrow Wilson's NEW FREEDOM, Franklin D. Roosevelt's NEW DEAL, and Harry S. Truman's FAIR DEAL, thus, the New Frontier.

Since the occasion hardly called for specifics, he spoke in generalities. "I stand tonight facing west on what was once the last frontier." Some would say that "there is no longer an American frontier." But, in fact, "the problems are not all solved and the battles are not all won." The nation stood on the edge of a New

Frontier that would demand "invention, innovation, imagination, decision." But what would these new departures be? Kennedy provided a clue. The convention had given him "an eloquent statement of our party's platform. . . . This is a platform on which I can run with enthusiasm and conviction."

Chester Bowles, former governor of Connecticut, ambassador to India, and now a Congressman, was chairman of the platform committee. In preparation for this task, he had read a great many of the old PARTY PLATFORMS and had found them both wretchedly written and full of promises that the winning candidates had not kept. He decided on a very short platform confined to civil rights, foreign policy, and a restatement of Roosevelt's FOUR FREEDOMS. A gifted writer, Bowles planned to compose it himself. In fact, Harris Wofford wrote a very strong civil rights plank and Bowles the rest. This became known as Part I.

James L. Sundquist, administrative assistant to Senator Joseph S. Clark, Jr., of Pennsylvania and secretary of the platform committee, was worried about the Bowles plan, a concern shared by several other staff people. They decided that Sundquist, without notifying Bowles at the outset, should write a Part II consisting of the programs the northern liberal congressional Democrats had devised in the late 1950s for which they wanted a "ringing endorsement" from the convention. The platform committee adopted both parts and Sundquist stitched them together.

As a Senator, Kennedy, had played little part in developing these domestic policies, excepting the minimum wage. But he agreed with them and did not hesitate to appropriate them. Thus, the 1960 Democratic platform was the bridge between congressional policies and the New Frontier.

The new President's agenda fell into two broad categories. The first consisted of four policies that would have an enormous impact on the nation. The "big four" were a comprehensive civil rights act, a Keynesian FULL EMPLOYMENT policy produced by a reduction in taxes, federal aid for primary, secondary, and college education, and hospital and medical insurance for the elderly under SOCIAL SECURITY, called Medicare. The 1960 Democratic platform addressed all four.

The civil rights plank was comprehensive. Congress would enact a law that would protect the right of black people to vote and eliminate literacy tests and poll taxes as conditions for suffrage. Public accommodations would be available without discrimination. In compliance with the Supreme Court decision in *Brown v. Board of Education* (1954), every school district would be required to submit an integration plan by 1963, the one hundredth anniversary of the EMANCIPATION PROC-

LAMATION. A fair employment practices commission would be established to eliminate discrimination in employment. The federal service and government contractors would be required to desegregate.

"The DEMOCRATIC PARTY," the platform asserted, "reaffirms its support of full employment as a paramount objective of national policy. . . . If recessionary trends appear, we will act promptly with counter-measures, such as public works or temporary tax cuts."

American education faced a financial crisis with a special need for more classrooms and more teachers. The platform pledged "generous Federal financial assistance."

The 16 million elderly Americans, most with low incomes, had the greatest need for health care. "The most practicable way to provide health protection for older people," the platform read, "is to use the contributory machinery of the Social Security system for insurance covering hospital bills and other high-cost medical services."

In addition, Kennedy's New Frontier consisted of a second category of measures that, while not as important as the big four, were significant new policies. Again, either explicitly or by implication, they had all been promised by the party's platform.

Depressed areas with heavy and persistent unemployment would receive federal assistance in developing new industries. Many people were out of work either because they were new entrants into the labor force or they had been displaced by automation. The government would help them with "training and retraining that equips them for jobs to be filled." Congress, the platform pledged, would raise the minimum wage to $1.25 an hour and extend coverage to several million unprotected workers. While there was no specific endorsement of federal sector collective bargaining, the platform strongly endorsed the goal of giving "all workers" the right to organize and bargain collectively. The proposal for a PEACE CORPS was made by Kennedy after the platform was written, but the idea was in the air. The plank on the underdeveloped world urged America to establish "working partnerships" with the poor nations of the world. Insofar as WOMEN'S RIGHTS were concerned, the Democrats urged the elimination of discrimination in employment based on sex, as well as on age, race, religion, and national origin.

BIBLIOGRAPHY

Bernstein, Irving. *Promises Kept: John F. Kennedy's New Frontier*. 1991.

Sorensen, Theodore C. *Kennedy*. 1965.

Sorensen, Theodore C. "Election of 1960." In vol. 4 of *History of American Presidential Elections*. Edited by Arthur M. Schlesinger, Jr., Fred L. Israel, and William P. Hansen. 1971.

Sundquist, James L. *Politics and Policy: The Eisenhower, Kennedy, and Johnson Years.* 1968.

IRVING BERNSTEIN

NEW NATIONALISM. Coined in 1910, the phrase *New Nationalism* was a slogan used by Theodore Roosevelt to represent his political philosophy. In a speech at Osawatomie, Kansas, on 31 August 1910 Roosevelt urged Americans to embrace a New Nationalism "to deal with new problems." He described the New Nationalism as putting the "national need before sectional or personal advantage." It rose above special interests and demanded efficient, unimpeded action at all levels of government, particularly by the federal government and most particularly by the President. From then on, especially after this and other 1910 campaign speeches were published as a book entitled *The New Nationalism,* the phrase became the watchword of much of Roosevelt's subsequent career. In 1912 he continued to call for a New Nationalism, first as he vied to wrest the Republican nomination from William Howard Taft, then as he bolted to the Progressive (Bull Moose) Party, and finally as he ran for President on the Progressive ticket against both Taft and the Democratic candidate, Woodrow Wilson. Roosevelt clung to the phrase and the ideas behind it as he led the Progressives until their disbandment in 1916, although he deemphasized domestic concerns after the outbreak of World War I.

Neither the words nor their political connotations were original to Roosevelt. He gladly acknowledged that he had taken them from a book by Herbert Croly, *The Promise of American Life,* published in 1909. This debt has led to the mistaken notion that Croly inspired Roosevelt to follow a new, different, and more radical political course than he would otherwise have done. For Roosevelt the only thing new about the New Nationalism was the phrase itself. The ideas he expressed and the policies he advocated in 1910 were ones he had favored for a long time, especially since the later years of his presidency. Roosevelt's beliefs in strong, centralized government, his advocacy of governmental intervention to regulate the economy, his skepticism about antitrust policies, his criticisms of the judiciary, and, above all, his vision of a transcendent national interest—these had been hallmarks of his White House tenure (1901–1909). Whatever radicalism he later espoused came with the specific measures that he embraced in response to changing political circumstances and was not influenced by Croly.

In fact, the main line of influence seems to have run in the opposite direction. Roosevelt had really served

as a model and inspiration for many of the ideas, especially about political leadership, that Croly advanced in *The Promise of American Life.* Roosevelt's liking for the book, in turn, sprang from both a deep intellectual affinity with Croly and an appreciation of the flattery involved. Nor was the New Nationalism a radical creed. Just the reverse—it was profoundly conservative. A persistent misinterpretation has held that Roosevelt and Croly wanted to marry "Hamiltonian ends with Jeffersonian means"—meaning the adaptation of strong, centralized government (Hamiltonian means) to the democratic purposes of increasing liberty and equality for common people (Jeffersonian ends). Many of Roosevelt's Progressive followers believed that that was what he was doing, and their misunderstanding of their leader led to later disappointment and disillusionment.

Both Roosevelt and Croly rejected the Jeffersonian heritage, not only for its emphasis on limited government but also for its acceptance of the self-interest of individuals and groups as a proper political goal. They accepted life and liberty as noble aims, but not the "pursuit of happiness." Rather, for Roosevelt, "the path of duty and sacrifice" and living "the strenuous life" in pursuit of great ideals constituted the one true path for individuals, groups, and nations to follow. For both Roosevelt and Croly, the New Nationalism was a prescription for the pursuit of Hamiltonian means *and* ends in a political environment previously polluted by Jeffersonian pursuit of self-interest. The prescription consisted of political evangelism of the sort that Roosevelt had practiced before, during, and after his occupancy of the Bully Pulpit of the presidency. He exhorted Americans to rise above selfishness and identification with class, region, race, religion, and ethnic group so that they might be born again through conversion to the transcendent ideals of the New Nationalism.

In practice, the New Nationalism never amounted to much. Roosevelt not only lost the 1912 election to Wilson, but he also found his creed effectively countered by Wilson's New Freedom. At first blush, the New Nationalism seemed much bolder and more reformist than the New Freedom, because of its advocacy of highly progressive taxation and a variety of expert regulatory agencies, as well as in its acceptance of big business as a fact of economic life. However, as Wilson defined the New Freedom during the campaign, he embraced nearly all of Roosevelt's specific measures (tariff protection and woman suffrage were the exceptions), and he demanded strong government action, not to break up big business, but to open opportunities for new competitors. Over all, Wilson rejected Roosevelt's call for transcendence of self-interest and upheld morally regulated pursuit of self-interest as the right route to the good society.

Essentially, Wilson did what Roosevelt was mistakenly supposed to have done—uniting Hamiltonian big government with the Jeffersonian goal of promoting common people's interests. Because Wilson enjoyed an opportunity that Roosevelt never had—that of being President at the head of an aroused, united, reformist party—he enacted one of the most impressive legislative programs in American history and thereby set much of the agenda for the DEMOCRATIC PARTY and American liberalism for the rest of the twentieth century. The New Nationalism, by contrast, stands as a political curiosity. Because Roosevelt so fervently embraced governmental power and so bitingly condemned material interests, especially those of business and the wealthy, he and his creed have excited little devotion and, in fact, hardly even any awareness among conservatives. Roosevelt and his New Nationalism remain a prophet and a creed without honor among their own kind.

BIBLIOGRAPHY

Cooper, John Milton, Jr. *The Warrior and the Priest: Woodrow Wilson and Theodore Roosevelt.* 1983.

Croly, Herbert. *The Promise of American Life.* 1909.

Forcey, Charles. *The Crossroads of Liberalism: Croly, Weyl Lippmann, and the Progressive Era, 1900–1925.* 1961.

Levy, David W. *Herbert Croly of the New Republic.* 1985.

Roosevelt, Theodore. *The New Nationalism.* 1911.

JOHN MILTON COOPER, JR.

NEW YORK TIMES CO. v. UNITED STATES

403 U.S. 713 (1971). During the contentious final years of America's military involvement in Vietnam, a major confrontation erupted between the Richard M. Nixon administration and the press that quickly led to litigation before the U.S. Supreme Court. Daniel Ellsberg, employed by the RAND Corporation, a private think tank under contract to the U.S. Department of Defense, laboriously copied and then purloined a top secret, forty-seven-volume analysis of America's involvement in the VIETNAM WAR from RAND when he left the company.

Ellsberg showed the report—which came to be known as the Pentagon Papers—to congressional leaders, who refused to do anything with it. Finally, Ellsberg presented it to the editors of the *New York Times.* After months of analyzing the material, the editors began printing excerpts on Sunday, 13 June 1971. After the *Times* had printed excerpts on three succes-

sive days, the U.S. Department of Justice sought an injunction against continued publication. President Nixon and his White House counselors, especially Secretary of State HENRY A. KISSINGER, believed that publication of the Pentagon Papers posed a grave threat to the NATIONAL SECURITY. At no time, however, did the Nixon administration show that the Papers' release would actually endanger the national security.

A temporary restraining order (TRO) was granted by a federal district judge prohibiting further publication by the *Times* until 19 June 1971. On 18 June, the *Washington Post* printed two excerpts from the Papers, and the Department of Justice went into federal district court again to try to prevent the *Post* from publishing further excerpts. Although the district court denied the request, the Court of Appeals extended the TRO to 21 June 1971. On 22 June, the Court of Appeals remanded the case to the district court to determine whether any of the material in the Pentagon Papers posed a "grave and immediate" danger to the nation's security that justified prior restraint against the newspapers. The Court of Appeals restraint on the newspapers, the very first time in the history of the nation that a newspaper was not allowed to publish because of a prior restraint in the form of a TRO, continued until 25 June 1971.

The *Times* immediately appealed to the U.S. Supreme Court. On 25 June the Court granted certiorari; on 26 June, it heard oral arguments; and on 29 June—record time for the Supreme Court—the Justices issued a per curiam order accompanied by nine separate opinions. The Court concluded, 6 to 3, that the injunction effort by the Nixon administration was in violation of the First Amendment's guarantee of freedom of speech and press.

Two sets of intimately related constitutional and political questions were raised and answered in the *New York Times* case. One had to do with the scope of the freedom of the press discussed in the First Amendment. The second concerned the meaning and scope of the IMPLIED POWERS and INHERENT POWERS of the President to address national security matters in a timely manner.

Federal judges, at the request of the Nixon administration, had silenced the *Times* and the *Post*, albeit in the form of a temporary restraining order. A fundamental premise of American democratic society had been attacked by injunction. Because a free press and open discussion of public policy are essential to a free society, there can be no prior restraint on these rights, and a major purpose of the First Amendment is to prevent all prior restraints on press and speech. The First Amendment, for Thomas Jefferson and James

Madison, stood as a fundamental safeguard against governmental wrongs. The rights guaranteed in the First Amendment, including those of speech and the press, could not be ceded away by the people to government. In *Patterson v. Colorado* (1907) the Supreme Court had noted that "speech concerning public affairs is the essence of self-government." Certainly, the Pentagon Papers contained information that concerned the public, conveying important data about the then-controversial public policy of America's involvement in Vietnam.

As COMMANDER IN CHIEF, the President has historically argued that the presidency has the inherent power to respond immediately to domestic emergencies. The Supreme Court has had occasion to react to such presidential arguments in defense of executive initiatives. But, the President is not above the constraints of the Constitution, and the Constitution is interpreted by a coordinate branch of the national government, the federal courts. In *Home Building & Loan Association v. Blaisdell* (1934), the Court noted that "while emergency does not create power, emergency may furnish the occasion for the exercise of power." The essential principle underscored by the Court, to surface again in the *New York Times* litigation, is that a President can only use the powers given to the Chief Executive by the Constitution and cannot "create" new powers when confronted by an emergency, foreign or domestic.

The *New York Times* per curiam order, a short, two-paragraph summary of the majority position, stated that "any system of prior restraints of expression comes to this Court bearing a heavy presumption against its constitutional validity. . . . The Government . . . carries a heavy burden of showing justification for the enforcement of such a restraint. . . . We agree . . . that the Government had not met that burden. The stays entered . . . are vacated." Nine separate opinions followed—six in support of the vacate order and three dissenting. Justices Hugo Black and William O. Douglas, literal interpreters of the First Amendment, maintained that the case should have been dismissed without oral argument. For Black, "every moment's continuance of the injunctions amounts to a flagrant, indefensible, and continuing violation of the First Amendment." For Douglas, there was simply "no basis for sanctioning a previous restraint on the press."

For Justice William J. Brennan, Jr., prior restraint could only be employed when the nation was at war and the information to be published would threaten national security. "Unless and until the government has clearly made out its case, the First Amendment commands that no injunction may issue," Brennan wrote. For Justices Potter Stewart and Byron White,

there was no showing of "direct, immediate, . . . substantive, grave and irreparable damage to our nation or its people" by the administration; therefore the injunction had to be set aside.

Associate Justices John M. Harlan II and Harry Blackmun and Chief Justice Warren Burger dissented from the vacate order. Harlan believed that the matter was put to rest too quickly and that, because "these are difficult questions of fact, of law, and of judgment," it warranted a much more in-depth view of significant questions associated with the scope of the First Amendment and whether "unauthorized disclosure of any of these documents would seriously impair the national security." Blackmun believed that "what is needed here is a weighing, upon properly developed standards, of the broad right of the press to print and of the very narrow right of the Government to prevent." He, too, would have remanded the case for additional analysis, maintaining that "these cases and the issues involved and the courts, including this one, deserve better than has been produced thus far." Burger, too, was concerned about the "unseemly haste" of the order to vacate and dissented in part because "we do not know the facts of this case."

BIBLIOGRAPHY

Emerson, Thomas I. "The Doctrine of Prior Restraint." *Law and Contemporary Problems* 20 (1955): 648–739.

Junger, Peter. "Down Memory Lane: The Case of the Pentagon Papers." *Case Western Reserve Law Review* 23 (1971): 3–97.

Lofton, John. *The Press as Guardian of the First Amendment*. 1980.

Shapiro, Martin, ed. *The Pentagon Papers and the Courts: A Study in Foreign Policy-Making and Freedom of the Press*. 1972.

Ungar, Sanford. *The Papers and the Papers*. 1972.

HOWARD BALL

NIXON, PAT (1912–1993), First Lady, wife of Richard M. Nixon. Although Thelma (Pat) Ryan Nixon had many years of experience in Washington as the wife of a congressman and Vice President, she maintained a distance from politics and conducted the job of FIRST LADY as a kind of nonpartisan ambassador for the President. During extensive goodwill missions and many ceremonial appearances, she spoke to groups of all ages across the United States, and she traveled abroad with the President and on her own. Her efforts to increase volunteerism, to make the WHITE HOUSE more accessible to visitors—especially the physically disabled—and to furnish it with furniture original to it or its inhabitants (rather than reproductions) have all been well documented. But neither she nor the President's staff was successful in highlighting these accomplishments in Americans' minds; therefore, Pat Nixon's personal popularity and her value to her husband's administration derive almost entirely from her reputation as his loyal supporter.

BIBLIOGRAPHY

David, Lester. *The Lonely Lady of San Clemente.* 1978.
Eisenhower, Julie Nixon. *Pat Nixon.* 1986.
Schmidt, Paul A., " 'She Deserved So Much More': The Papers of Pat Nixon." In *Modern First Ladies: Their Documentary Legacy.* Edited by Nancy Kegan Smith and Mary C. Ryan. 1989.

BETTY BOYD CAROLI

NIXON, RICHARD M. (1913–1994), thirty-seventh President of the United States (1969–1974). On 9 August 1974, as a result of the WATERGATE AFFAIR, Richard Nixon resigned during his second term, becoming the only President in history to leave office in this manner. The slightly more than two thousand days of Nixon's presidency were marked not only by significant achievements in domestic and foreign policy but also by a constitutional crisis of unprecedented proportions. His resignation culminated a political career plagued by controversy from its inception.

Early Career. Richard Milhous Nixon was born in Yorba Linda, California, on 9 January 1913. Later the family moved to Whittier. Nixon's formative years were not particularly unusual for someone growing up in two small towns near Los Angeles. His parents, Frank and Hannah Milhous Nixon, were Quakers. Because his father was neither a particularly good nor a lucky businessman, Nixon grew up as many boys of his generation did, poor but imbued with the 1920s ethos that combined hard work with the dream of unlimited opportunity. A good student and hard worker, Nixon excelled scholastically at both Whittier High School and Whittier College. After earning a scholarship to Duke University Law School in 1934, Nixon worked even harder, graduating third in his law school class. He did not, however, obtain the hoped-for offer from a prestigious law firm, so he returned to Whittier, where he practiced law from 1937 until 1942.

His 1938 meeting of Thelma Catherine (Pat) Ryan [see PAT NIXON] and their subsequent courtship and marriage in 1940 constituted one of the few memorable episodes in Nixon's life prior to his entering politics in 1946. The outbreak of WORLD WAR II found the newlyweds in Washington, D.C., where Nixon worked in the tire-rationing section of the OFFICE OF PRICE ADMINISTRATION (OPA). Quickly disillusioned with the red tape of government bureaucracy, Nixon obtained

a commission and served in the South Pacific between 1942 and 1946, rising to the rank of lieutenant commander. Nothing distinguished either his civilian or military career during these years, and those who knew him best did not perceive any political ambition. Like most American politicians since 1945, Nixon's views on government and domestic and foreign policy appear to have been more strongly influenced by his adult experiences in the Great Depression and then WORLD WAR II than by childhood crises or ideological influences that he may have experienced as a young man while going to school or establishing himself as a lawyer.

In contrast to his nondescript background, Nixon's political career prior to his assuming the presidency proved meteoric and controversial. Elected to the Eightieth Congress in 1946 at the age of thirty-three, he served two terms, then ran successfully for the Senate in 1950. By 1952, at age thirty-nine, he was elected Vice President, and he only narrowly missed being elected President in 1960, when he was forty-seven. Eight years later Nixon won the presidency in an almost equally close contest. In 1972, when he was fifty-nine years old, he was reelected by a landslide vote.

Nixon's twenty-three years as a politician before becoming President were peppered with controversy. The controversy began in 1946, when he defeated five-term liberal Democratic Congressman Jerry Voorhis, and continued in 1950, when he defeated the equally liberal Democrat Helen Gahagan Douglas for a Senate seat. In both campaigns Nixon charged his opponents with having left-wing political views. Because of the increasing conservatism of postwar America, however, he probably would have defeated Voorhis and Douglas without any red-baiting.

Under the direction of Murray Chotiner, a lawyer turned campaign consultant for such Republican luminaries as Earl Warren and William Knowland, Nixon's congressional and senatorial campaigns used political packaging techniques, complete with innuendoes about communism. In 1946 and 1950 such tactics were not as common as they later became and they immediately earned him the reputation among liberal Democrats as an opportunistic product of the COLD WAR and a "political polarizer" who would do anything to win an election. In 1948 Nixon, as a member of the House Un-American Activities Committee (HUAC), initiated the successful attempt to end the diplomatic and governmental career of Alger Hiss by exposing Hiss's connections with the Communist Party in the 1930s. In the same year he proposed the Mundt-Nixon bill, which would have required individual communists and communist organizations to register with the federal government. These actions forever identified him in the American mind as a hardline anticommunist. He was not, however, personally or professionally associated with the MCCARTHYISM of the 1950s, and he never made a single-minded pursuit of domestic communists a major goal of his public life.

Vice Presidency. During his years as Dwight D. Eisenhower's Vice President, from 1953 to 1960, Nixon campaigned widely for Republican candidates and in the process obtained the unenviable reputation of being the party hatchet man, especially because of his attacks on ADLAI E. STEVENSON (1900–1965), the Democratic presidential candidate in 1952 and 1956. As a result, elements within the press, many academics, and liberals in general found it easier to criticize the conservatism of the Eisenhower administrations—not by attacking the popular President but by concentrating on the politics and personality of his Vice President. The 1950s were relatively quiet years for the country as well as for Nixon politically, despite the fact that he later placed five of his *Six Crises* (1962) in that decade. Of these, probably only one—the 1952 charge that he had created a slush fund of more than $18,000 to further his political career—constituted a real crisis. By going on nationwide television on 23 September 1952, Nixon successfully defended himself and forced Eisenhower to keep him on the Republican ticket. In this broadcast he presented embarrassingly detailed information about his family's finances, including the fact that his wife, Pat, unlike so many Democratic politicians' wives, did not own a fur coat but only "a respectable Republican cloth coat." This speech is best remembered for Nixon's emotional insistence that his children would keep the family's dog, Checkers, even though the cocker spaniel had been a political gift.

Besides the 1952 Checkers speech, two other media events enhanced Nixon's political fortunes and popularity with the general public: the stoning of his car in Caracas, Venezuela, in 1958 and his 1959 kitchen debate with Soviet leader Nikita Khrushchev at an American economic exhibition in Moscow. These events marked the beginning of a generally successful use of television by Nixon throughout his long career, with the notable exception of his PRESIDENTIAL DEBATES with John F. Kennedy during the 1960 campaign.

Although Eisenhower gave him few formal responsibilities, Nixon permanently upgraded the office of Vice President and gave it a much more meaningful and institutionalized role than it had ever had before. In part he accomplished this through several well-publicized trips abroad on behalf of the President. The vice presidency also assumed greater importance when Eisenhower suffered a heart attack in 1955, a bout with ileitis in 1956, and a stroke in 1957. Throughout these illnesses, Nixon handled himself with considerable tact and self-effacement, while presiding over nineteen CABINET sessions and twenty-six meetings of the NATIONAL SECURITY COUNCIL (NSC). Following his stroke, President Eisenhower worked out a plan with Nixon, Secretary of State JOHN FOSTER DULLES, and Attorney General William Rogers to create the office of Acting President in the event he became incapacitated from illness. This formal agreement authorized the Vice President to govern when the President could not discharge the powers and duties of his office.

Nixon's unsuccessful presidential campaign against Kennedy in 1960 was fraught with ironies and political lessons he never forgot. The press repeatedly described Kennedy as a "youthful front runner" representing a new generation, when in fact the candidates were approximately the same age. In addition, Nixon's congressional and vice presidential records on civil rights and foreign policy were more liberal than Kennedy's, yet the press presented them as less so. Finally, Nixon learned the hard way that television would play a most significant role in the 1960 election—the closest presidential election since Grover Cleveland defeated JAMES G. BLAINE in 1884. In 1968 and 1972 Nixon perfected a television campaign style of his own in direct reaction to his "loss" of four nationally televised presidential debates with Kennedy in September and October—losses measured not by substantive points made but by style and image projected.

To his credit, Nixon did not challenge the 1960 election results (although Eisenhower urged him to do so). He lost to Kennedy by only 112,000 popular votes, and there was strong evidence that the Democrats did not win legally in either Illinois or Texas, states whose combined ELECTORAL COLLEGE tally tipped the election in the Democrats' favor, 303 to 219. Nonetheless, after 1960 Nixon resolved never again to take any preelection lead for granted—not even in 1972. All future campaigns became no-holds-barred contests for him.

Temporarily retiring to private life, in 1961 he wrote his first book (and best-seller) *Six Crises* and in 1962 decided to run for governor of California. His defeat in that election prompted his much quoted remark to reporters that they would not "have Dick Nixon to kick around anymore." This loss spurred him to move to New York, where at long last he joined the prestigious law firm of his earlier dreams and where he continued to build bridges between moderate and conservative factions within the REPUBLICAN PARTY, especially after BARRY GOLDWATER's defeat by Lyndon B. Johnson in 1964.

By 1968, Nixon was once again positioned to win his party's nomination for the presidency. This time, unlike 1960, he faced a DEMOCRATIC PARTY hopelessly divided over the VIETNAM WAR and haplessly led by HUBERT H. HUMPHREY in the wake of Johnson's unexpected refusal to run again, ROBERT F. KENNEDY's assassination, and a strong third-party bid by GEORGE WALLACE. During the 1968 campaign Humphrey, his liberal opponent, appeared to be defending past American efforts to win the war in Vietnam more than was Nixon, whom many considered to be an original cold warrior. Nixon talked more about diplomacy and less about military escalation; he therefore seemed to be stressing less use of U.S. forces in bringing about a victory in Vietnam than Humphrey was. This position left Humphrey wearing Johnson's very tattered military mantle. Had President Johnson halted the bombing of North Vietnam and renewed the Paris peace talks before the end of October, Humphrey might have been able to squeeze by Nixon, for the election results proved to be almost as close as they had been in 1960, with Nixon winning by 500,000 popular votes and receiving 301 electoral votes compared to 191 for Humphrey and 46 for Wallace. In 1972 Nixon won by a landslide, with 520 electoral votes to 17 for GEORGE McGOVERN and a margin of almost 18 million popular votes.

Presidency. After the election, Nixon surrounded himself with two types of advisers: "freethinking" outsiders, who brainstormed with the President about new ideas and comprehensive programs, and "political-broker" insiders, who worked to draft and implement Nixon's legislative and administrative priorities. The initial momentum for change in most domestic and foreign policy areas came from freethinking outsiders such as Robert Finch, Daniel Patrick Moynihan, HENRY A. KISSINGER, and, later, John Connally. All these men appealed to Nixon's preference for bold action and, with the exception of Finch, none had been closely associated with him prior to his becoming President. During Nixon's first administration, Moynihan and Kissinger influenced certain crucial details about, but not usually the broad outlines of, domestic and foreign policies. Encouraged by such advisers during his first years in office, Nixon embarked on a systematic risk-taking course in both foreign and domestic policy that attempted to update FEDERALISM through government organization and revenue sharing, to revamp the entire welfare system with the idea of a guaranteed annual income (which he preferred to

call a negative income tax), to expand dramatically spending for both environmental and social service programs. He also worked to promote a "grand design" for U.S. diplomacy based on the NIXON DOCTRINE, devaluation of the dollar and other foreign economic policies, ending (after widening) the war in Vietnam, and establishing rapprochement with the People's Republic of China and DETENTE with the Soviet Union.

The impact of the freethinking outsiders on Nixonian policies is easy to trace. Moynihan and Finch greatly influenced specific welfare legislation; Kissinger carried out the President's foreign policy, initially as NATIONAL SECURITY ADVISER and later as Secretary of State; and Connally, whom Nixon appointed Secretary of the Treasury in 1971, almost single-handedly talked the President into wage and price controls and the devaluation of the dollar. Connally also played a crucial role in two of Nixon's most innovative environmental decisions: favoring creation of the Environmental Protection Agency and a department of natural resources—both against the wishes of the farm bloc. Perhaps of all his freethinking outsider advisers, Connally most impressed Nixon, though Connally almost never figures prominently in books about the Nixon presidency. Nixon wanted Connally for his running mate in 1968, but at the time Connally was still governor of Texas and a Democrat. From the time they first met, Nixon thought Connally understood him better than any of his other political associates did, and from the time that this apostate Democrat became Secretary of the Treasury, Nixon apparently hoped that Connally would succeed him in 1976.

The political-broker insiders, however, increasingly gained ascendancy over the freethinking outsiders within the first Nixon administration, and his plans to reorganize the federal government became both more corporate in nature and more central to his plans. This second group of advisers were gray-flannel types (many of whom Nixon had known for many years) such as John D. Ehrlichman and H. R. Haldeman, the President's two closest aides; Leonard Garment, the liberal Democratic counterpart to Moynihan among Nixon's inside advisers; Arthur Burns, counselor to the President and later head of the FEDERAL RESERVE BOARD; MELVIN R. LAIRD, Secretary of Defense; JOHN MITCHELL, Attorney General; GEORGE SHULTZ, Secretary of Labor and later head of the OFFICE OF MANAGEMENT AND BUDGET (OMB); and businessman Roy Ash, chair of the President's Council on Executive Reorganization (the ASH COUNCIL). In Nixon's first years in office Ehrlichman, Garment, Laird, and Shultz became dominant insiders on policy, while Haldeman and Ash concentrated on organizational matters. For example,

Ehrlichman, aided by John Whitaker, deputy assistant to the President and later Under Secretary of the Interior Department, significantly influenced the content of Nixon's environmental legislation, especially in connection with land-use policies. Ehrlichman and Garment were instrumental in the formulation of both his civil rights and INDIAN policies. Arthur Burns became the unexpected champion of revenue sharing with the administration. Shultz confined his advice largely to economics and labor but proved surprisingly influential in desegregation matters and countering discrimination in the work force, as well. Before Kissinger's ascendancy, Laird could be seen brokering on a wide variety of topics from foreign policy to such diverse issues as the volunteer army, revenue sharing, government reorganization, and Vietnamization.

Domestic policy. Prior to the Watergate affair, journalists, scholars, and numerous politicians had predicted that Nixon would be a cautious, if not actually a "do-nothing, caretaker" President. Moreover, few listened in 1969 when he said that he intended "to begin a decade of government reform such as this nation has not witnessed in half a century." There was much scoffing in 1971 when his SPEECHWRITERS came up with the grandiose phrase "the New American Revolution" to describe his domestic programs. Contrary to these low expectations, in his first term Nixon actively pursued reform in five domestic areas: economic policy, WELFARE POLICY, CIVIL RIGHTS POLICY, ENVIRONMENTAL POLICY, and reorganization of the executive branch of government. Ultimately, these domestic programs may be remembered longer than Nixon's activities in the realm of foreign policy, and they may even minimize his negative Watergate image.

With much of the press and Congress suspicious of him, Nixon's least obstructed route to significant domestic reform was through administrative action. This approach naturally prompted criticism from those who already distrusted his policies and priorities. If he had ended the Vietnam war during his first or second year in office Nixon might have diffused some of this distrust; the ways, covert and overt, in which he expanded and prolonged the war during his first two years in office, however, simply reinforced existing suspicions about his personality and political ethics. (Significantly, liberal paranoia about his domestic programs fueled Nixon's paranoia about liberal opposition to the war, and vice versa.)

Nixon considered his success in desegregating southern schools and his Supreme Court appointments (Warren E. Burger, Harry Blackmun, Lewis Powell, and William H. Rehnquist) his most important achievements in domestic policy. He continued to insist that Clement Haynsworth, whose Supreme Court nomination was rejected by the Senate in 1970, would have been his best choice had he been approved. Nixon also included on his list of significant firsts his initiatives on the environment and space and his declared, and well-financed, wars against cancer, illegal drugs, and hunger. Nixon's closest aides usually placed revenue sharing and environmental and land-use policies higher on the list of his domestic achievements than did the former President himself. According to Ehrlichman, this continuing difference of opinion arose from the fact that Nixon paid more personal attention during his first term to those domestic issues with "political juice," such as cancer research, labor legislation, drugs, crime, taxes, desegregation, and welfare, than he did to economic matters involving revenue sharing, housing, hunger, transportation, and consumer protection, or environmental and general health concerns. On those issues that Nixon considered "potent political medicine," he became actively involved in policy formulation; the rest he delegated to others, especially Ehrlichman—even the controversial subject of how to deal with campus unrest and antiwar demonstrations.

As for his domestic mistakes, Nixon cited wage and price controls, which he later maintained he only supported at the time because it looked as though Congress would take this initiative to control inflation if the White House did not, and the automatic cost-of-living adjustments (COLAs) for SOCIAL SECURITY recipients. He later said that COLAs made sense at the time but not in light of the runaway inflation after he left office. Of course, many critics have claimed that government use of wiretaps, the creation of the plumbers' unit in the White House to plug information leaks and ultimately to conduct break-ins, administration harassment of persons on an enemies list, and even the mere consideration of the so-called Houston plan for institutionalizing surveillance of suspect persons and groups were all enormous domestic mistakes.

Although Nixon and both sets of his advisers realized that the odds were stacked against the administration's domestic programs' receiving serious attention from a Congress dominated by Democrats, at the end of his first term as President, he had taken strong action in several major domestic reform areas, especially with respect to welfare and environmental legislation, and even in the area of civil rights. Secretary Finch of Health, Education, and Welfare (HEW) was primarily responsible for obtaining Nixon's approval of the welfare plan that eventually became known as the Family Assistance Program (FAP). If FAP had succeeded in Congress it would have changed the emphasis of American welfare from providing services to providing income and would thus have replaced the Aid to Families with Dependent Children (AFDC) program, whose payments varied widely from state to state. Instead, FAP called for a guaranteed income of anywhere from $1,600 (initially proposed in 1969) to $2,500 (proposed in 1971) for a family of four. States would have been expected to supplement this amount, and all able-bodied heads of recipient families (except mothers with preschool-age children) would have been required to accept work or training. If such a parent refused to accept work or training, however, only that parent's payment would have been withheld. In essence, FAP unconditionally guaranteed children an annual income; it would have tripled the number of children then being aided by AFDC.

A fundamental switch from services to income payments proved too great a change for congressional liberals and conservatives alike, and they formed a strange alliance to vote it down. Ironically, FAP's final defeat in the Senate led to some impressive examples of incremental legislation that might not have been passed had it not been for the original boldness of FAP. For example, Supplementary Security Income (SSI), approved on 17 October 1972, constituted a guaranteed annual income for the aged, blind, and disabled. The demise of FAP also led Nixon to support the uniform application of the food stamp program across the United States, better health insurance programs for low-income families, and an automatic cost-of-living adjustment for Society Security recipients to help them cope with inflation. In every budget for which his administration was responsible (fiscal 1971 through fiscal 1975) spending on human resource programs exceeded spending for defense for the first time since before World War II. The sevenfold increase in funding for social services under Nixon made him—not Johnson—the last of the big spenders on domestic programs.

Although Nixon's aides cite his environmental legislation as one of his major domestic achievements, it was not high on his personal list of federal priorities, despite polls showing its growing importance as a national issue. White House central files released in 1986 clearly reveal that Ehrlichman was initially instrumental in shaping the President's views on environmental matters and in conveying a sense of crisis about them. Most ideas were filtered through him to Nixon. In fact Ehrlichman, whose particular expertise was in land-use policies, has been described by one forest-conservation specialist as "the most effective environmentalist since Gifford Pinchot [the first professional American forester]." Ehrlichman and Whitaker put Nixon ahead of Congress on environmental issues, especially with respect to his use of the permit authority under the Refuse Act of 1899 to begin to clean up water supplies before Congress passed any comprehensive water pollution enforcement plan.

"Just keep me out of trouble on environmental issues," Nixon reportedly told Ehrlichman. This proved impossible because Congress ignored Nixon's recommended ceilings when it finally passed (over his veto) the Federal Water Pollution Control Act amendments of 1972. Both Ehrlichman and Whitaker agreed that these amendments were "budget-busting" legislation designed to embarrass the President on a popular issue in an election year. Statistics later showed that the money appropriated could not be spent fast enough to achieve the legislation's stated goals. The actual annual expenditures in the first years after passage approximated those originally proposed by Nixon's staff.

Despite the real national crisis that existed over school desegregation, Nixon was not prepared to go beyond what he thought the Supreme Court decision in *Brown v. Board of Education* (1954–1955) had mandated, because he believed that de facto segregation could not be ended through busing or cutting off funds from school districts. Nine days after Nixon's inauguration, his administration had to decide whether to honor an HEW-initiated cutoff of funds to five southern school districts, originally scheduled to take place in the fall of 1968 but delayed until 29 January 1969. On that day Secretary Finch confirmed the cutoff but also announced that the school districts could claim funds retroactively if they complied with HEW guidelines within sixty days. This offer represented a change from the most recent set of HEW guidelines, developed in March 1968, which President Johnson had never formally endorsed by signing.

Nixon has been justifiably criticized by civil rights advocates for employing delaying tactics in the South and particularly for not endorsing busing to enforce school desegregation in the North after the 20 April 1971, Supreme Court decision in *Swann v. Charlotte-Mecklenburg Board of Education*. Despite the bitter battle in Congress and between Congress and the executive branch after *Swann*, the Nixon administration's statistical record on school desegregation is impressive. In 1968, 68 percent of all African American children in the South and 40 percent in the nation as a whole attended all-black schools. By the end of 1972, 8 percent of southern African American children and a little less than 12 percent nationwide attended all-black schools. A comparison of budget outlays is equally revealing. President Johnson spent $911 million on civil rights activities, including $75 million for

1086 NIXON, RICHARD M.

civil rights enforcement in fiscal 1969. The Nixon administration's budget for fiscal 1973 called for $2.6 billion in total civil rights outlays, of which $602 million was earmarked for enforcement through a substantially strengthened Equal Employment Opportunity Commission (EEOC).

Most important, the EEOC staff had risen from 359 in 1969 to 1,640 by 1972, and its budget had increased from $13.2 million to $29.5 million. Nixon's civil rights enforcement budget for fiscal 1973 represented an eightfold increase over Johnson's for fiscal 1969. Enforcement funds for fiscal 1974 doubled those of 1972, with the EEOC budget increasing from $20.8 million to $43 million and the budget for the Civil Rights Division of the Justice Department increasing from $10.7 million to $17.9 million. These figures confirm that the Nixon administration put money into civil rights enforcement even though its official statements were not always on the cutting edge of this controversial issue. Nixon supported the civil rights goals of American INDIANS and WOMEN'S RIGHTS with less reluctance than he did school desegregation because these groups did not pose a major political problem and he had no legal reservations about how the law should be applied to them. As President, Nixon was never able to build as positive an image for his domestic policies as he was for his foreign policies.

Foreign policy. One of the basic decisions modern Presidents since 1960 have had to make is whether to assign primary responsibility for foreign policy to the State Department or to the NATIONAL SECURITY COUNCIL (NSC). If the President chooses the latter he will try to centralize and manage policy from the White House. Conflicts between Henry Kissinger and Secretary of State William Rogers in Nixon's first term usually ended in Kissinger's favor until Rogers finally resigned in September 1973 and Kissinger replaced him while remaining special assistant for national-security affairs. Shortly after Nixon and Kissinger began working together in the fall of 1968, they created the first system for managing foreign policy fully under White House domination by reorganizing the NSC. That Nixon intended the White House to function as the State Department cannot be doubted. In the first months of his administration, when former Republican National Chairman Leonard Hall asked the President how he was getting along with the State Department, Nixon pointed in the direction of the OVAL OFFICE and said, "There's the State Department." In theory this reorganization made the NSC the principal foreign policy forum in the White House, assigning the Secretary of State responsibility for the execution of presidential decisions resulting from NSC discus-

sions. In practice Nixon's and Kissinger's personal management of foreign policy merged policy formulation and operational functions inside and outside the NSC system. This arrangement remains the greatest strength (and weakness) of the Nixonian structural legacy for conducting diplomacy.

According to his book *No More Vietnams* (1985), Nixon viewed the Indochina conflict as military, moral, and multinational in scope. Consequently, he first sought to bring military pressure to bear on the North Vietnamese in order to speed up the negotiating process. There is little indication, however, that this approach succeeded because the Vietcong correctly counted on opposition in the United States to the announced bombing and invasion of Cambodia in April 1970 and of Laos in February 1971. Likewise, Nixon's commitment to the war as a moral cause did not ring true as the carnage increased despite American troop withdrawals under the policy known as Vietnamization. Finally, the President never succeeded in convincing the country that quick withdrawal from Vietnam would "damage American strategic interests" all over the world. Ending the draft and bringing U.S. troops home did not end congressional opposition to the war (although these actions did diminish the size of antiwar demonstrations beginning in 1971) because Nixon failed to convince Congress (and many in the country at large) that the conflict in that tiny country warranted the military, moral, and multinational importance he and Kissinger attributed to it.

Instead, Nixon allowed Kissinger as head of the NSC to become egocentrically involved in secret negotiations with the North Vietnamese from 4 August 1969 to 25 January 1972 (when they were made public). As a result, the terms finally reached in January 1973 were only marginally better than those that had been agreed to in 1969, despite the widening of the war to Cambodia and Laos in 1969 and 1970, the mining of Haiphong harbor and bombing of Hanoi in May 1972, and the Christmas bombings of North Vietnam at the end of that same year. The trade-off between Hanoi's agreement in October 1972 that South Vietnamese president Nguyen Van Thieu could remain in power in return for allowing North Vietnamese troops to remain in place in South Vietnam pales when compared to the additional twenty thousand American lives lost during this three-year period—especially when the inherent weakness of the Saigon government, obvious by 1973, is taken into consideration. (The most embarrassing evidence of this weakness was seen when President Gerald Ford was forced to order an emergency evacuation of the last remaining U.S. troops from Saigon in April 1975.)

By the time Nixon became President he had decided to establish a new policy toward the People's Republic of China in several stages. First, American anti-Chinese rhetoric had to be toned down to bring about a more rational discussion than had prevailed in the previous fifteen years. Second, trade and visa restrictions would be reduced. Third, U.S. troop levels in Vietnam and at bases surrounding China would be reduced. Finally, Nixon wanted the Communist Chinese leaders to know that he would personally consider revising the rigid cold war position of the United States regarding the Nationalist government in Taiwan. All these changes in attitude and the low-level diplomatic actions that attempted to foster rapprochement initially took place quietly and without fanfare. The Chinese ignored all these private and public signals until 1970, when the stage was set for a breakthrough in Sino-American relations. It came in April 1971, after the United States terminated all restrictions on American travel to mainland China and ended the twenty-year-old embargo on trade. Following the highly publicized Ping-Pong games between Chinese and American teams in both countries at the end of that same month, the Pakistani ambassador to the United States delivered a message from Chinese premier Jou En-lai to Nixon on 27 April (replying to one from the President on 5 January), asking him to send a representative to China for direct discussions. Despite the obvious importance and success of the rapprochement with the People's Republic of China, Nixon never believed that the media gave it as much credit as he would have liked.

Although various government officials denied that Nixon courted China in order to bring pressure to bear on the Soviet Union, the President's triumphant visit to the People's Republic of China in February 1972 was clearly part of a triangularization policy. There is some indication that, after Nixon announced in July 1971 that he would visit China the next year, the possible Sino-American rapprochement made the Soviets more amenable to moving ahead with détente in the fall of 1971. The original purpose behind improved relations with both China and the U.S.S.R., however, was to bring leverage to bear on both nations to improve the situation for the United States in Vietnam. This particular attempt at linkage did not prove successful.

No direct evidence exists that because of Soviet concern over the results of Nixon's trip to China, rapprochement became indirectly linked to the success of negotiations leading to détente between the United States and the Soviet Union. The ten formal agreements between the two nations signed in Mos-

cow in May 1972 provided for prevention of military incidents at sea and in the air, scholarly cooperation and exchange in the fields of science and technology, cooperation in health research, cooperation in environmental matters, cooperation in the exploration of outer space, facilitation of commercial and economic relations, and, most important, a reduction of tensions through the Anti-Ballistic Missile Treaty, the Interim Agreement on the Limitations on Strategic Arms (SALT I), and the Basic Principles of United States–Soviet Relations. In the area of ARMS CONTROL, Nixon's détente policy contained the potential not only to replace CONTAINMENT (the standard way the United States had fought the cold war against the Soviet Union since the late 1940s) but also to transcend the procrustean ideological constraints that were at the very heart of post–World War II conflict between the two nations.

One of the most important foreign policy discussions that took place during Richard Nixon's first year as President concerned National Security Study Memorandum 2, dated 21 January 1969. This represented the first full review of U.S. Middle East policy since the 1967 Six-Day War. The long overdue full-scale NSC debate over American Middle East policy took place at an all-day session on 1 February 1969 and resulted in the approval of the Rogers plan, named after Nixon's first Secretary of State. This plan called for an American-Soviet agreement on a comprehensive peace settlement in the Middle East and for a more evenhanded public posture toward both the Israelis and the Arabs.

From the very beginning the Rogers plan was based on three untenable assumptions: one, that the Soviet Union would agree to become a joint peacemaker with the United States (by the time Moscow was willing to accept this role in 1973, Washington had abandoned the idea) and would pressure Egyptian leader Gamal Abdel Nasser into accepting a compromise peace; two, that a publicly impartial stance toward ISRAEL and the Arabs would enhance the American bargaining position with both sides in a way that previous pro-Israeli statements by the United States had not; and three, that Israel would comply with Rogers's endorsement of a substantial withdrawal from the Occupied Territories in return for a contractual peace.

Nixon waited too long to focus systematically on Middle Eastern problems: by the fall of 1973 he was preoccupied with the unfolding of the Watergate affair. Obviously, Nixon could not have equally addressed all diplomatic fronts at once, and he clearly chose to concentrate on Vietnam, China, and the U.S.S.R. during his first term in office. So it made sense for him personally to put the Middle East on a back burner until some of his other foreign policy initiatives were achieved. In October 1969 the Soviet Union officially rejected the Rogers plan, leaving the new Republican administration with no apparent positive alternative until after the Yom Kippur War of October 1973—aside, that is, from the Nixon Doctrine, represented by excessive arms sales to the Shah of Iran. From the 1970 civil war in Jordan through the 1973 Yom Kippur War, the United States appeared to pursue a policy of stalemate. The Yom Kippur War broke the stalemate, but, by the time this breakthrough occurred, the stalemate had cost the United States more than Kissinger could ever gain back, even though it freed him to pursue hopscotch diplomacy through the countries of the Middle East.

In the Middle East in particular, and the developing world in general, Nixon's foreign policy was dominated by geopolitical considerations that had little to do with the economic reality or the political and personal lives of people in already established or emerging small nations. This obliviousness to third-world concerns can be seen in such administration actions as the tilt toward Pakistan in its 1971 war with India, the misguided intervention in the Angolan civil war, the use of the CENTRAL INTELLIGENCE AGENCY (CIA) and American businesses to destabilize the democratically elected communist regime of Salvador Allende in Chile beginning in 1971 (contributing to Allende's downfall in 1973), and the refusal to aid starving Biafrans during the Nigerian civil war of 1969 to 1970.

Nixon's diplomatic legacy is weaker than he and many others maintained. For example, the pursuit of "peace and honor" in Vietnam failed; his Middle Eastern policy, because of Kissinger's shuttling, ended up being more show than substance; he had no systematic third-world policy (except regarding Vietnam); and détente with the Soviet Union soon floundered in the hands of his successors. Likewise, the Nixon Doctrine did not prevent use of U.S. troops abroad. Only rapprochement with China remained untarnished because it laid the foundation for future U.S. recognition of China, even though Nixon failed to achieve a "two China" policy in the United Nations, whereby the Chinese government headed by Chiang Kai-Shek in Taiwan would retain a seat in the U. N. General Assembly. Instead, in 1971 the United Nations expelled the Taiwanese government and admitted the People's Republic of China. This summary is not meant to discredit Nixon as a foreign policy expert either during or following his presidency. It is simply a reminder that the positive results of his diplomacy may have faded faster than some of the results of his domestic policies.

The Watergate affair. During the quarter-century following Nixon's resignation as President, the event that forced him to leave office in disgrace also dimmed in the memory of most Americans. "Watergatitis" swept the country in 1973 and 1974, grabbing the nation's attention as had no government scandal since the TEAPOT DOME SCANDAL in the 1920s. And for good reason. The cover-up by the President and his top aides of the original break-in and bugging at the Democratic national committee headquarters in Washington's Watergate complex on 17 June 1972—as well as related corrupt or criminal political activities—ultimately resulted in the indictment, conviction, and sentencing of twenty men. These included top White House aides (Ehrlichman and Haldeman), counsel to the President (John W. Dean III), a special assistant to the President (Charles Colson), one former Cabinet member (Mitchell), and others who worked for the Committee for the Re-election of the President (Nixon's 1972 campaign organization, usually referred to derogatorily as CREEP) and/or the White House Special Investigative Unit (known more commonly as the plumbers) whose members engaged in other break-ins before Watergate occurred.

Most of the men implicated in the scandal functioned as Republican Party officials or presidential advisers in whom public trust had been placed. A few of the plumbers, such as E. Howard Hunt, James McCord, and G. Gordon Liddy—all former CIA or FBI agents—were specifically employed by the White House and paid with private funds to carry out political espionage. They in turn hired the four Cubans arrested in the Watergate complex. All served time for their participation in the original crime of burglary and bugging of the national offices of the Democratic Party. Despite multiple investigations and a plethora of books, many factual questions remain unanswered about both the Watergate incident itself and its historical significance.

The arrest of James McCord, Bernard Baker, Virgilio Gonzalez, Eugenio Martinez, and Frank Sturgis after the night watchman at the Watergate discovered adhesive tape not once but twice on basement doors of the expensive office and apartment complex, set off a series of events and investigations unprecedented in U.S. history. This break-in was the culmination of a series of political DIRTY TRICKS authorized by CRP beginning in the fall of 1971, although it is still disputed whether the two Watergate break-ins were approved by Attorney General Mitchell or presidential counsel Dean. Nixon learned of the burglars' connections with CRP and White House personnel on 20 June 1972, and on 23 June he privately agreed with a recommendation (which he thought came from Mitchell and Haldeman but which, in fact, probably originated with Dean) that the CIA should prevent FEDERAL BUREAU OF INVESTIGATION (FBI) investigation of the Watergate break-in on grounds of NATIONAL SECURITY. The CIA did not comply with the President's attempt to obstruct justice in a criminal matter, and the investigation moved forward following a delay until after the 1972 presidential election.

Even before the "smoking gun" tape of 23 June 1972 (not released by the White House until 5 August 1974) revealed how early Nixon had been involved in the cover-up, the Watergate Special Prosecution Force (WSPF) headed by the Texas attorney Leon Jaworski had concluded in February 1974 that

> beginning no later than March 21, 1973, the President joined an ongoing criminal conspiracy to obstruct justice, obstruct a criminal investigation, and commit perjury (which included payment of cash to Watergate defendants to influence their testimony, making and causing to be made false statements and declarations, making offers of clemency and leniency, and obtaining information from the Justice Department to thwart its investigation) and that the President is also liable for substantive violations of various criminal statues.

All these actions had taken place in the space of two years—from the summer of 1972 to the summer of 1974. Early in 1973, federal judge John J. Sirica, using heavy-handed legal tactics, threatened the Watergate defendants with tough sentences unless they told the truth. As McCord and others began to talk about payoffs from the White House, evidence of illegal campaign contributions (not associated with the Watergate break-in) began to surface and was investigated by the WSPF. The WSPF ultimately set up five different task forces to investigate the variety of charges surfacing against the administration—ranging from the Watergate cover-up itself to illegal campaign contributions, the ITT antitrust suits, the plumbers' other break-ins, Nixon's tax returns, and the administration's involvement with federal agencies' mistreatment of demonstrators. Nixon essentially fired Haldeman, Ehrlichman, Dean, and Mitchell by formally accepting their resignations on 30 April 1973 and announced on 22 May that they had been involved in a White House cover-up without his knowledge. Dean then decided to testify before the Senate Select Committee on Presidential Campaign Activities (called the Ervin committee after its chairman, North Carolina Democratic Senator Sam Ervin), and in testimony from 25 to 29 June he accused the President of being involved. Dean's and others' testimony before the Ervin committee disclosed, among other things, the existence of a White House enemies list of promi-

nent politicians, journalists, academics, and entertainers who had been singled for various types of harassment, including unnecessary audits by the Internal Revenue Service.

In July 1973, Alexander Butterfield, a former White House assistant, revealed (in a suspiciously inadvertent way when responding to questions from staffers from the Ervin committee) that Nixon had installed a voice-activated taping system in the Oval Office in 1971. From this point forward there were attempts to obtain unedited transcripts, or the tapes themselves, from the White House. These efforts failed until 24 July 1974, when the Supreme Court ruled in UNITED STATES v. NIXON that the President could not retain subpoenaed tapes by claiming EXECUTIVE PRIVILEGE. During this year-long legal struggle, the first special prosecutor appointed to investigate Watergate, Archibald Cox, acting on behalf of a federal grand jury, also tried to gain access to the tapes. When Cox rejected a compromise proposed by Nixon, the President ordered Attorney General Elliot Richardson and Deputy Attorney General William D. Ruckelshaus to fire the special prosecutor. Refusing to do so, they resigned 20 October 1973, and acting Attorney General Robert Bork (later unsuccessfully nominated to the Supreme Court by President Ronald Reagan) finally carried out Nixon's order. The Saturday Night Massacre, as Nixon's firing of Richardson and Ruckelshaus came to be called, was subsequently ruled an illegal violation of Justice Department procedures in a lower federal court ruling in *Nader v. Bork*.

This incident also created such negative public opinion that the President agreed to turn over nine subpoenaed tapes to Judge Sirica, only to announce on 31 October that two of the tapes did not exist and on 26 November that a third had an unexplained eighteen-and-a-half-minute gap—an erasure that remains unexplained. Finally, on 30 October 1973, the House Judiciary Committee, headed by Peter W. Rodino (D-N.J.), began preliminary investigations and in April 1974 launched a full-scale IMPEACHMENT inquiry that led, on 27 July, to a vote recommending the impeachment of the President by the House of Representatives, even before the release of the smoking-gun tape on 5 August. Nixon resigned from office on 9 August rather than face almost certain conviction in a Senate impeachment trial. He was pardoned by Gerald Ford in September. More than twenty years later, reasons for the Watergate break-in remained in dispute. As with the assassination of John F. Kennedy, none of the many investigations has ever proved beyond reasonable doubt the motivation behind the original crime.

Assessment. The lingering negative perceptions regarding Nixon personally, as well as many of his international and national initiatives, went through several stages after August 1974, when he became the only U.S. President to resign from office. At first, liberals (in particular) and Democrats (in general) had a heyday castigating the former President for fulfilling their most dire prophecies about him as the most evil, venal, lying, potentially dictatorial aberration ever to occupy the White House. In the course of the 1980s, this view of Nixon, which ostracized him from mainstream politics, began to be replaced by a more nostalgic view. This nostalgia was not felt by mainstream Republicans, who became, if anything, more conservative under Reagan than Nixon had ever thought of being, but rather by some of his longstanding left-of-center opponents. Finding themselves in a state of disarray over how to combat the conservative backlash of the 1980s—the length and depth of which they had not foreseen in 1974—many liberals began openly praising Nixon's legacy of "rational and systematic pursuit of a new world order" and wishing that they had his farsighted domestic legislation, especially on welfare and environmental issues, to kick around again. In the early 1990s, Nixon's sensitivity regarding the country's domestic needs constituted one of the most positive memories of his administration.

During the 1980s Watergate also became less of a benchmark for judging his presidency for that quarter of the population that was not born when Nixon resigned in 1974. For these young Americans, Nixon was at best an oddity, at worst someone their parents either strongly opposed or supported. On these two divergent points of view—that of aging liberals and that of teenagers—rested Nixon's gradual rehabilitation, which continued to grow in phoenixlike fashion in the early 1990s. Moreover, this rehabilitation process found fertile ground for growth abroad, where his disgrace over Watergate had never been understood in constitutional terms or thought to be as important as his foreign policy record. There is a final reason for the rehabilitation of Richard Nixon. In the last decade of the twentieth century, his longevity made him one of the few politicians in the United States who could still arouse passion—for or against. Nixon remains the most controversial American political figure since World War II and one of the most important Presidents of the twentieth century.

BIBLIOGRAPHY

Ambrose, Stephen E. *Nixon.* 3 vols. 1987–1991.
Colodny, Len, and Robert Gettlin. *Silent Coup: The Removal of a President.* 1991.
Hoff, Joan. *Nixon without Watergate: A Presidency Reconsidered.* 1992.
Kissinger, Henry. *Memoirs.* 2 vols. 1979–1982.
Kutler, Stanley I. *The Wars of Watergate: The Last Crisis of Richard Nixon.* 1990.
Lukas, J. Anthony. *Nightmare: The Underside of the Nixon Years.* 1976.
Morris, Roger. *Richard Milhous Nixon: The Rise of an American Politician.* 1990.
Nixon, Richard M. *RN: The Memoirs of Richard Nixon.* 1978.
Parmet, Herbert S. *Richard Nixon and His America.* 1990.
Reichley, A. James. *Conservatives in an Age of Change: The Nixon and Ford Administrations.* 1981.
Thornton, Richard C. *The Nixon-Kissinger Years: Reshaping America's Foreign Policy.* 1989.
Wicker, Tom. *One of Us: Richard Nixon and the American Dream.* 1991.

JOAN HOFF

NIXON DOCTRINE. On a trip to Asia in the summer of 1969, President Richard M. Nixon made some casual remarks at a press conference on 25 July 1969, in Guam regarding the future of U.S. defense commitments outside the NATO area. Hoping to reduce the prominence of the VIETNAM WAR, Nixon said that the United States "must avoid that kind of policy that will make the countries of Asia so dependent on us that we are dragged into conflicts such as the one that we have in Vietnam." In his comments, he upheld current military treaties binding the United States to allies in Asia, promised a shield against threats from nuclear powers, and offered U.S. military and economic assistance. However, he stated that Asian nations themselves had to provide the soldiers for their own defense. Journalists quickly characterized these offhand observations as the Nixon Doctrine, surprising but heartening the President. Pleased at the reception of his remarks, Nixon later elaborated on the course of U.S. policy after the Vietnam War in a speech about Vietnam on 3 November 1969 and his foreign-policy report of 18 February 1970. He reiterated that the United States would uphold its treaties, would provide a shield to protect against threats from a nuclear power, and promised that "in cases involving other types of aggression we shall furnish military and economic assistance when requested and as appropriate. But we shall look to the nation directly threatened to assume the primary responsibility of providing the manpower for its defense." The practical impact of the Nixon Doctrine was a vast increase in U.S. weapons sales to regional Asian powers. Surrogates for the United States such as Indonesia, Iran, Pakistan, the Philippines, Saudi Arabia, and South Korea, purchased over $20 billion in armaments from U.S. manufacturers in the eight years after 1969.

BIBLIOGRAPHY

Kissinger, Henry. *White House Years*. 1979.
Szulc, Tad. *The Illusion of Peace: Foreign Policy in the Nixon Years*. 1979.

ROBERT D. SCHULZINGER

NIXON v. ADMINISTRATOR OF GENERAL SERVICES

NIXON v. ADMINISTRATOR OF GENERAL SERVICES 433 U.S. 425 (1977). Are all presidential papers the Chief Executive's private property, or can public papers be separated from purely private correspondence between a President and his colleagues and friends? This question first surfaced after the WATERGATE AFFAIR and the resignation of President Richard M. Nixon in 1974. After leaving the White House Nixon and the Administrator of the U.S. General Services Administration (GSA), an agency in the executive branch, signed an agreement that neither the ex-President nor the government could have access to Nixon's papers (forty-four million documents and almost nine hundred tape recordings) without the other's consent. Furthermore, after three years, the former President could withdraw from the Archives any materials except the tapes. After five years, according to the agreement, Nixon could instruct the GSA to destroy the tapes it held.

Learning of this agreement, Congress immediately passed the Presidential Recordings and Materials Preservation Act, which required the GSA to take "possession and control" of all Nixon materials. The GSA was to screen all the documents and return to Nixon only those that were private and not of "general historical interest." As written and placed into law, the statute applied only to President Nixon's papers. Because of the scandal-ridden nature of his resignation, because he had accepted a presidential pardon from his successor, Gerald Ford, and given the manner in which papers and tapes had been maintained while Nixon was President (some were lost, another tape was erased mysteriously) and because of the deal he struck with the GSA, Congress felt obliged to pass legislation to protect the public documents that existed in the Nixon material.

Nixon was concerned about the precedent such legislation might establish for future Presidents, and he believed that the legislation was unconstitutional because, by singling him out, the act violated the constitutional prohibition against bills of attainder.

Tape recordings of presidential conversations had been central in the legal and political disputes leading up to Nixon's resignation in August 1974. In the federal courts, including Supreme Court, Nixon had argued that EXECUTIVE PRIVILEGE extended to control over his presidential tapes and papers. The President's

judgment would determine whether and when they would be released. The Supreme Court, however, ordered Nixon to release sixty-four tapes in July 1974, and less than a month later he resigned. This debate over control of presidential materials continued in the *GSA* case.

Nixon brought suit in federal court, charging that the Presidential Recordings and Materials Preservation Act infringed on executive, or presidential, privilege, violated the principle of SEPARATION OF POWERS, and was an unconstitutional bill of attainder. The Supreme Court, however, over the dissents of Chief Justice Warren Burger and Justice William H. Rehnquist, validated the legislation. The majority, in an opinion written by Justice William J. Brennan, Jr., upheld the "facial validity" of the act. They concluded that the legislation did not "impermissibly undermine" the presidency nor did it "disrupt the proper balance between the coordinate branches [by] preventing the Executive Branch from accomplishing its constitutionally assigned functions."

The Court stated that the screening performed by the GSA to separate public from private materials was "a very limited intrusion by personnel in the Executive Branch sensitive to executive concerns. These very personnel have performed the identical task in each of the Presidential libraries without any suggestion that such activity has in any way interfered with executive confidentiality." The majority also concluded that Nixon's claim of executive privilege "clearly must yield to the important congressional purposes of preserving the materials and maintaining access to them for lawful governmental and historical purposes." Regarding the bill of attainder matter, the Court concluded that, in light of Nixon's problematic behavior in the past, the former President was "a legitimate class of one" that the Congress could address through legislative enactments. In his dissent, Burger argued that the principle of separation of powers was violated by the legislation because the law "intruded into the confidentiality of Presidential communications protected by the constitutionally based doctrine of presidential privilege."

BIBLIOGRAPHY

Berger, Raoul. *Executive Privilege: A Constitutional Myth*. 1978.
Chermerinsky, Erwin. "A Paradox without a Principle: A Comment on the Burger Court's Jurisprudence in Separation of Powers Cases." *Southern California Law Review* 60 (1987): 1083–1141.
Winterton, George. "The Concept of Extra-Constitutional Executive Power in Domestic Affairs." *Hastings Constitutional Law Quarterly* 7 (1979): 1–78.

HOWARD BALL

NIXON v. FITZGERALD 457 U.S. 731 (1982). Attempts to seek damages from Presidents have been very rare. Only after the Supreme Court decided in the early 1970s that federal officers could be sued for damages on claims implied from constitutional violations did the prospect of frequent suits against Presidents become meaningful.

In *Nixon v. Fitzgerald* the Supreme Court considered whether a President is immune from civil damages for his conduct of office. Ernest Fitzgerald sued the President for removing him from a civilian position in the air force, allegedly in violation both of statutes forbidding reprisals for congressional testimony and of his constitutional right of free speech. In an opinion by Justice Lewis Powell, the Court decided that the President possesses an absolute immunity from damages for acts within the "outer perimeter" of his official duties. Because the President's action could have been taken pursuant to his powers to manage the air force, the immunity protected him.

Given the breadth of the President's powers, it will be a rare action that does not receive this immunity. The Court decided *Fitzgerald* in the absence of any statute conferring or denying PRESIDENTIAL IMMUNITY. Perhaps Congress will attempt to alter the immunity, although it is not entirely clear from the Court's opinions that a statute could do so.

The Court drew the immunity from the nature of the presidency and the consequences of subjecting the President to civil actions. By relying on general concepts of SEPARATION OF POWERS, the Court implied that the immunity is safe from congressional alteration, even though the majority disclaimed that intent. The Court noted that the constitutional text grants immunity from damages to members of Congress, but not to the President. Nevertheless, members of the CONSTITUTIONAL CONVENTION had expressed some concern that Presidents should not be exposed to harassment from courts.

In a series of earlier cases, the Court had given other executive officers qualified immunity from suits for constitutional torts, which was lost if they should have known their actions were illegal. To distinguish these cases, the Court stressed the unique nature of the presidential office. It thought that the importance of the presidency and the sensitive and far-reaching decisions with which it deals created special risks of frequent civil suits from those disgruntled with the President or his policies. The negative effects could include distracting the President from his duties in order to defend prior decisions or deterring the President from vigorous conduct of the office.

Justice Powell also pointed to the existence of various other checks on the behavior of a President. First, the ultimate remedy is IMPEACHMENT, which has actually been unveiled against two Presidents. More effective everyday incentives to adhere to the rule of law exist though: a President's desire to be reelected or to maintain his reputation in history, and intense congressional and press scrutiny of the office. Finally, the Court noted that an injured individual might be able to obtain redress without suing the President, for example by pursuing his aides.

Four Justices dissented, arguing that the President should enjoy no greater immunity than do other executive officers. The majority's position, they argued, placed the President above the law. They saw no need to protect a President from damages for clearly illegal actions. Still, the dissenters recognized that the nature of a particular function of the presidential office might call for special protection.

In a companion case, *Harlow v. Fitzgerald* (1982), the Court refused to extend the President's absolute immunity from damages to his immediate aides and limited his aides to the qualified immunity that other executive officers possess. Read together, the two cases have the effect of checking a President through his aides, whose participation is usually necessary for an action that damages individuals. At the same time the cases free the CHIEF EXECUTIVE to make his weighty decisions without fear of monetary consequences.

BIBLIOGRAPHY

Carter, Stephen. "The Political Aspects of Judicial Power: Some Notes on the Presidential Immunity Decision." *University of Pennsylvania Law Review* 131 (1983): 1341–1399.

Ray, Laura K. "From Prerogative to Accountability: The Amenability of the President to Suit." *Kentucky Law Journal* 80 (1991–1992): 739–790.

Shane, Peter M., and Harold H. Bruff. *The Law of Presidential Power.* 1988.

Tribe, Laurence H. *American Constitutional Law.* 2d ed. 1988.

HAROLD H. BRUFF

NOMINATING PRESIDENTIAL CANDIDATES. The process of nominating presidential candidates is an extraconstitutional development established by America's political parties in the early nineteenth century. The nominating system has become one of America's most complex processes, falling under the shared control of the parties, the state governments, Congress, and the federal courts.

The act of nominating candidates must be distinguished from a more general objective of paring down the number of viable candidates before the final election. The latter objective was to be secured under the Constitution by the ELECTORAL COLLEGE system and the provision for a contingency run-off election in the House. Nomination, by contrast, is an internal process of decision by a political party. In order to avoid dividing the votes of its adherents among a number of presidential hopefuls, a party establishes a method in advance of the final election to agree on a single candidate.

Although nominating was begun by the parties to fulfill their own imperatives, the dominance in America of two major parties has meant that the nominating process has assumed the task of paring down the number of presidential candidates. Since 1824, party nominations have limited the number of significant candidates—and provided enough support for one of them—so that a major-party candidate has managed to win a majority of the vote of the electors in the Electoral College. As a result, the nominating system has increasingly been viewed as a quasi-constitutional process that performs the functions of screening and winnowing candidates for the presidency.

Systems of Nomination. There have been four identifiable systems of nomination in American history.

Congressional caucus. The first system, which lasted from 1800 until 1824, was by a vote of the party's membership in Congress—the congressional caucus. This system was adopted less by design than necessity. The only meetings of party leaders on a national level in the first decades were the gatherings of party members in Congress. Each party's caucus accordingly assumed the task of nominating its candidates.

An immediate effect of nominating candidates was a change in the role of presidential electors. Electors now began to be chosen by voters or state legislators on party slates on the basis of the presidential and vice presidential candidates whom they pledged to support. Tacit recognition of this fact of slatemaking was one factor leading up to a change in the formal procedures of selecting the President and Vice President, which occurred with the adoption of the TWELFTH AMENDMENT in 1804.

The congressional caucus system never fully won acceptance as a legitimate institution. The construction of so powerful a mechanism outside of the constitutional scheme came under attack as a usurpation of a public function. Critics labeled the caucus an elitist institution ("King Caucus") that removed the choice of the President from the hands of the people, and they charged that it undermined the separation of powers by making Presidents too dependent on members of Congress. In 1812, for example, President James Madison was pressured by members of his party in Congress to agree to declare war against Great Britain as a condition for his renomination for a second term.

By 1824 the congressional caucus system had collapsed. A rump session held that year nominated WILLIAM H. CRAWFORD, but the other candidates simply ignored the whole process and pursued "nominations" by meetings of citizens or by resolutions by state legislatures. The demise of the congressional caucus system was only partly a result, however, of opposition to the specific method of nomination. Equally important was that the FEDERALIST PARTY ceased to exist after 1816, leaving no compelling reason for the one remaining party—the Jeffersonian Democratic-Republicans—to decide among its different candidates. Without party competition, there was no need to nominate.

The election of 1824 convinced many prominent national leaders, chief among them Senator Martin Van Buren, of the potential dangers of holding presidential elections without party nominations. With no party mechanisms to limit the number of entrants, the general election would likely become a contest among several independent candidates, none of whom could command a majority. Unstructured electoral competition would degenerate into a politics of personal faction based on demagogic and sectional appeals. The absence of party nominations would also return the responsibility for paring down the number of candidates to the formal constitutional procedures, including the House contingency election system that proved so controversial in 1824. The difficulties of this nonpartisan system led Van Buren and his allies to seek a reinstitution of two-party competition, not only to satisfy yearnings for renewed partisanship, but also to resolve the general problems of the electoral system.

Pure convention system. The second nominating system, which accompanied the reestablishment of political parties in the 1830s, is known as the pure convention system and was in effect from 1832 through 1908. In view of the popular hostility to the congressional caucus, the parties had to discover a new method. The institution they developed was the national party convention, which had first been employed in 1831 by a THIRD PARTY (the ANTI-MASONIC PARTY). Delegates to the conventions were selected according to rules devised by the national and (mostly) by the state party organizations. This system was more broadly representative of the party rank-and-file than the congressional caucus, and it assured the independence of presidential candidates from Congress. It also provided a boost to the principle of FEDERALISM by giving more say to state party organizations and to powerful figures in state and local politics.

The extent to which this system could be called democratic depended on the specific procedures for selecting delegates adopted by the various state parties. These procedures varied greatly from one state to another and within the same state at different times. Some states had fairly open procedures, while in other states party leaders, local or statewide, controlled the selection from beginning to end. Yet whether democratic or not, the process did not generally emphasize a direct focus on national candidates at the initial stages. Rather, participants in this process were often more concerned with local and state issues than with the question of the presidential candidate. Furthermore, it was widely appreciated that the final nomination decision would have to be made at the national convention site, which meant that the delegates selected had to be granted discretion to act on their own. Much of the discretion of delegates was controlled by state party leaders, especially in the DEMOCRATIC PARTY which recognized the formal right of state parties to bind their members. Democrats also had a two-thirds rule for nomination, which remained in effect until 1936.

As for the candidates, they did not generally campaign publicly for the nomination—at least not directly. A public campaign would have been harmful, as the final decision was made by the delegates and party leaders at the convention, where decisions were typically made after several ballots. The best the candidates might do, therefore, was to position themselves to be acceptable to a widespread following within the party. The norms of the period, moreover, dictated that the party should seek the candidate. Candidates were supposed to appear reluctant, and the courtship of party members by candidates tended to be discreet. Candidates known to be genuine possibilities did not attend the conventions, opting to stay home and feign disinterest. In a forerunner of the modern media event, the convention would dispatch a delegation to the candidate to request that he accept the party's nomination.

Mixed system. The third nominating process, known as the mixed system, began to develop in 1912 as a result of the widespread belief that the conventions had become undemocratic instruments run for the benefit of PATRONAGE-hungry party bosses. Critics of the convention system, most of whom were associated with the progressive movement, sought a new method of nomination that would reduce dramatically the influence of the parties. These critics were only partly successful. Under the mixed system that slowly grew up, the nomination decision continued to be made by the national party conventions, but the process of selecting delegates changed in a number of states.

The key innovation introduced by the progressives after 1912 was the PRESIDENTIAL PRIMARY, which was important for two reasons. First, the adoption of primary laws by the states changed the legal status of

the nominating system from one that had been an internal party matter to one that was now a legitimate object of supervision and control by public authorities. No longer was the nominating system thought of as the exclusive concern of parties. Second, most primary laws sought to legislate a particular role for the delegate, which was to represent a national candidate preference. The governing idea behind this change was that the system of choosing and mandating delegates should follow the people's (meaning, the party adherents') choice of a particular leader. The effective decision on the nomination should thus normally be made not by the delegates and party leaders in a process of bargaining and deliberation, but by the public in a popular election. Candidates should accordingly abandon their posture of feigned reluctance and directly solicit the people's favor, taking their individual program before the electorate.

A transformation of the nominating system along these lines failed because progressives fell short of securing the passage of primary laws in a majority of the states. What emerged by 1920, therefore, was a system that mixed the ideas and practices of the previous convention system with some of the progressives' new objectives. The convention continued to be the main site of the nomination decision, as the candidates could not count on winning enough delegates before the convention to lock up the contest. But a candidate who managed an impressive series of primary victories could, in addition to capturing a number of delegates, put pressure on party leaders at the convention by demonstrating a broad popular following.

The mixed character of this system allowed candidates to pursue different kinds of strategies in search of the nomination. They could follow the logic of the new method of primaries, which was to take their case directly to the voters. They could proceed by the old method of making appeals to delegations chosen by party-run caucuses. Thus neither ADLAI E. STEVENSON in 1952, nor HUBERT H. HUMPHREY in 1968 entered any primaries, yet both received the Democratic Party's nomination. Finally, they could pursue a "mixed" strategy, entering a few primaries to indicate their strength in public opinion, but placing the greater part of their energy on winning over important party leaders. This method was followed by Franklin D. Roosevelt in 1932 and John F. Kennedy in 1960.

Primary-based system. The fourth nomination system, which has been in effect since 1972, is best described as a primary-based system. The nominees, though still named officially by the party conventions, are in fact chosen in the processes of delegate selection that take place before the conventions. Delegates are chosen by one of four methods: district and state party conventions (referred to now as caucus systems), automatic selection by position (in the Democratic Party only), meetings of the congressional caucus (the Democratic Party only), and primaries. Primaries, however, are by far the most important method. They account for the selection and mandating of a majority of the delegates and, what is equally important, they embody the basic idea of legitimacy of the system, which is that the nominee should be the one who wins a plurality of votes in popular contests.

The modern nominating process consists chiefly of a series of popular elections among individual candidates inside of both parties. Candidates no longer wait for the party to bestow the nomination upon them, but instead seek to capture it in open campaigns. All candidates accordingly press their courtship of the voters with an aggressiveness that would have shocked nineteenth-century political sensibilities. With the first delegate contests coming in the winter of the election year, and with the time needed to organize a campaign and raise funds, candidates often make an official declaration of their candidacy in the year preceding the general election. Each candidate establishes a personal organization independent of the official party organization to wage a primary campaign. The personal organization of the victorious candidate will form the core of the final election campaign organization, to which the regular party organization is then added.

Candidates and Conventions. The system focuses on the individual candidates, not on the collective needs of party organizations. The candidates must decide on their own basic message, create their own organizations, and devise their own electoral strategies. Still, the parties enter into the campaigns in the sense that the volunteers, interest groups, donors, and traditional voters of each party dominate that party's process from start to finish. The types of candidates selected thus far under this system have not as a rule varied from those chosen in the past, although more candidates seriously contend as outsiders who either have little national political experience or who somehow challenge the political establishment. One candidate, Jimmy Carter in 1976, succeeded in being nominated on this basis. Certain figures in modern American politics, such as Jesse Jackson and Pat Robertson, have actually made their first formal entrance into electoral politics by running for their parties' nomination.

Nomination campaigns are of two types: those in which an incumbent is being challenged and those in which no incumbent is involved. In the first case, the challenger (and there is usually only one) focuses on the incumbent's record and attempts to make the case for change. The campaigns tend to look back and focus on an existing record. The incumbent usually enjoys close ties to the national party organization and of course possesses all the advantages connected with holding the presidency. The primary system nevertheless allows for significant challenges in the case of any incumbent who has shown signs of weakness. In contests where no incumbent is involved, the race generally begins with a number of hopefuls, and the candidates vie for support on the basis of their particular program or vision, their record, and the strengths and weaknesses of their personal attributes. Some campaigns can and do involve fundamental differences among candidates about where to lead the party. Often, however, the race takes place among a number of candidates who are relatively close to one another in terms of their basic positions and thus in a sense interchangeable from the voters' perspective. Voters therefore often shift support among the candidates with surprising rapidity, according to changing perceptions of their viability, tactical blunders or strokes of brilliance, and revelations about aspects of their character. Journalistic biases as well as accidents of modern media coverage can also exercise an important influence.

Party conventions play an entirely different role than in the past. They do not make but merely ratify a decision that has been reached during the primaries. (The convention retains an auxiliary decision-making role in the event no candidate receives a plurality.) The vocabulary once used to describe convention politics has now virtually vanished, and a new one, derived from the preconvention delegate-selection contests, has taken its place. Words such as *stampede* (a sudden transfer of convention delegates to one of the candidates) and DARK HORSE (a candidate with little initial support or prominence who is nonetheless a possible choice as a compromise on a later ballot) have been replaced by terms such as *momentum* (the enthusiasm engendered by a strong primary showing that will carry over to the next set of primaries) and *outsider* (a candidate with little national prominence and few party connections who nonetheless hopes to win public favor). The main purpose of the convention is to present a picture of the party to the nation and to showcase the candidate to the American people. The major statement of the campaign is no longer the PARTY PLATFORM, but the candidate's video biography and ACCEPTANCE SPEECH.

Controlling the System. The authority to change the nominating system today is shared by the parties (national and state), the states, the Congress, and the courts. The national parties continue to run the conventions and to decide the allocation of delegates among the states. In addition, the Democratic Party from 1972 to 1984 adopted (and then continually revised) a large number of specific rules governing the selection of delegates in the states. The state parties, to the degree permitted by national party rules and state law, determine the rules of delegate selection, especially under caucus procedures. State governments decide whether to hold primaries or caucuses and when these decisions will take place, subject again to certain constraints by the national parties. Congress and the FEDERAL ELECTION COMMISSION now determine the rules for the financing of campaigns, and some look to a federal statute as the only method by which to effect a change of the entire nomination process. Finally, the federal courts have been called upon to resolve certain jurisdictional disputes among these different bodies.

The shared control over the nominating system makes it one of the most complicated of all of America's political processes. In many instances, one authority has sought to impose a change of some kind only to discover that it has been modified by the response of another authority. Partly as a result of this arrangement, the nominating system since 1972 has undergone numerous changes on many important details. Moreover, there remain many who seek not merely a modification of the current system, but its transformation. Some argue in favor of reinstating the influence of the conventions and the party organizations, while others propose a regional or national primary system governed by federal statute.

The nomination system, although it has been governed mostly by the parties and the states, serves the major constitutional functions of screening and paring down the number of presidential candidates. Because the two-party system is not itself part of the Constitution, there is always the possibility that the nominating system could lose its de facto control over these functions, whether by a proliferation of the number of parties or by the emergence of independent presidential candidacies. Should this ever become the case, the question of how to screen and winnow the candidates will have to be revisited and no doubt addressed by formal constitutional changes. Until this occurs, however, the nomination system in its various possible arrangements, while remaining in large part under the control of the parties and the states, should also be judged according to how well it promotes general constitutional objectives of assuring a high quality of candidates, guaranteeing a proper balance between stability and change, and encouraging effective governance once candidates are elected to the presidency.

BIBLIOGRAPHY

Bartels, Larry. *Presidential Primaries and the Dynamics of Public Choice.* 1988.
Ceaser, James. *Presidential Selection.* 1979.
Polsby, Nelson W., and Aaron Wildavsky. *Presidential Elections.* 1991.
Shafer, Byron. *Bifurcated Politics—Evolution and Reform in the National Party Convention.* 1988.

JAMES CEASER

NUCLEAR FREEZE. In 1980, Randall Forsberg, a former editor and writer for the Stockholm International Peace Research Institute, began promoting the idea of a joint United States-Soviet Union freeze on the testing, production, and deployment of nuclear weapons. Forsberg, in a paper entitled "Call to Halt the Nuclear Arms Race: Proposal for a Mutual U.S.–Soviet Nuclear-Weapon Freeze," argued that both nations had achieved parity in their nuclear arsenals, and that further additions to the nuclear stockpile would not increase security, but would only increase the danger of nuclear war. Forsberg began her campaign for a nuclear freeze by speaking to previously organized disarmament groups throughout the United States. Her plan was to use the activists in these groups to bring the freeze message to middle-class America, and through what would be perceived as a grass-roots movement, to force the freeze idea on political leaders. Essential to the freeze movement was the simplicity of the proposal, as well as its call for bilateral action by the United States and the Soviet Union.

Before long the idea of a nuclear freeze was being widely debated throughout the nation, and the potential effects of a nuclear war were being given broad coverage in the media. The grass-roots movement blossomed into the Nuclear Weapons Freeze Campaign, with volunteers circulating petitions throughout the country as a core of activists met and planned strategy of the campaign. Eventually, Forsberg's idea was endorsed not only by various self-styled peace groups, but also by churches, town meetings, city councils, state assemblies, and the like. Nine states put freeze referenda on the ballot in 1982, and in eight of those states the measure passed. In late 1982, the National Conference of Catholic Bishops began circulating a draft of a proposed pastoral letter in which the bishops endorsed a nuclear weapons freeze. Polls indicated that as many as two-thirds of American citizens supported some version of the freeze.

The debate over the freeze was propelled in part by claims or perceptions that the administration of President Ronald Reagan was not serious about arms-reduction talks with the Soviet Union. In response to the freeze campaign, the Reagan administration argued that the Soviet Union would only have incentive to negotiate arms reduction if the United States continued the development and modernization of the United States' nuclear arsenal. Weapons under development would be capable of targeting and destroying Soviet missiles in hardened silos, thus challenging the survivability of the Soviet nuclear forces and forcing the Soviet Union to engage in substantial arms reductions.

In 1982 the House of Representatives narrowly rejected a resolution that called for an immediate freeze on U.S. and Soviet nuclear weapons. Instead the House passed an administration substitute resolution that linked any nuclear freeze to the results of upcoming arms reduction talks with the Soviet Union. The Senate refused to endorse any version of the nuclear freeze. In the subsequent 1982 congressional elections, several nonincumbent freeze proponents were elected. In the next term, the House of Representatives again took up the freeze issue. This time the House passed a slightly watered-down version of Forsberg's concept, calling not for an immediate freeze but for negotiations leading to a freeze. The Senate again refused to endorse any freeze resolution. Ironically, and much to the dismay of freeze supporters, despite the moderate success in the House, both houses of Congress continued to appropriate money to finance the administration's nuclear weapons buildup.

In 1983 the national freeze movement created its own political action committee, Freeze Voter '84, designed to endorse and support candidates in the 1984 elections. A number of local Freeze Voter PACs were set up in various states. Freeze Voter PACs raised $3.4 million and provided over 25,000 volunteer workers. The net result of this PAC activity is difficult to estimate. The DEMOCRATIC PARTY and its presidential nominee, WALTER MONDALE, did endorse the freeze, and nuclear armaments were an important issue in the 1984 presidential race. In terms of results, however, the net impact of the freeze campaign was at best minimal, effecting approximately a dozen or so House and Senate races out of 468 contested seats. In addition, the landslide reelection of Ronald Reagan, who had been portrayed by freeze proponents as an opponent of a freeze, augured the demise of the movement, which, in the words of one participant, went underground.

One lingering question remains. Did the freeze campaign lead President Reagan to negotiate arms reductions with the Soviet Union? Freeze proponents argue that the political pressures created by the freeze movement compelled President Reagan to tone down his anti-Soviet rhetoric and to enter serious negotiations with the Soviet Union, the net result being the negotiated arms reductions mandated by the Strategic Arms Limitation Treaty. On the other side, administration sympathizers argue that it was not the freeze movement, but the deployment of new weapons systems such as the MX missile and the B-1 bomber that placed the United States in a position to negotiate successfully with the Soviet Union. As in all such debates there is a kernel of truth to both perspectives.

BIBLIOGRAPHY

Cole, Paul M., and William J. Taylor, Jr., eds. *The Nuclear Freeze Debate: Arms Control Issues for the 1980s.* 1983.
Garfinkle, Adam M. *The Politics of the Nuclear Freeze.* 1984.
Waller, Douglas C. *Congress and the Nuclear Freeze: An Inside Look at the Politics of a Mass Movement.* 1987.

ALLAN IDES

NUCLEAR REGULATORY COMMISSION. See ATOMIC ENERGY COMMISSION.

NUCLEAR TESTING. The first test of a NUCLEAR WEAPON was conducted under the authority of the Manhattan Engineer District [*see* MANHATTAN PROJECT], the United States' secret project for the development of an atomic bomb during WORLD WAR II. The test site, known as Trinity, was in a remote desert region in New Mexico. The bomb, with an estimated explosive force of 20,000 tons of T.N.T., was placed on a 100-foot metal tower and detonated in the early morning hours of 16 July 1945. The detonation vaporized the tower and the soil upon which it stood. Within seconds the fireball created by the explosion was a half-mile wide and as tall as the Empire State Building. The mushroom cloud reached a height of almost seven miles. The atomic age had begun.

Over the next five years, the United States conducted five more test firings of nuclear weapons. Four of these tests were atmospheric and one was underwater. The test sites were remote islands in the Pacific Ocean, two at the Bikini Atoll in 1946 and one each on Enjebi, Aomon, and Runit in 1948. The 1948 tests were the product of the newly created ATOMIC ENERGY COMMISSION. A primary goal of the commission was to develop an efficient, production-line atomic bomb.

The first Soviet Union test of a nuclear device took place on 29 August 1949. The site was either the Kazakh test site near Semipalatinsk or on the northeast shore of the Caspian Sea. The successful detonation of a Soviet nuclear weapon marked the beginning of the arms race.

The United States resumed testing nuclear weapons in 1951 with sixteen detonations, fifteen of which were atmospheric tests. Most of these tests took place at the new testing grounds located in the desert north of Las Vegas, Nevada. Both the United States and the Soviet Union continued atmospheric testing throughout most of the 1950s and into the early 1960s. During that time, both nations successfully detonated powerful thermonuclear weapons, the force of which were measured in megatons of T.N.T. Between 1945 and 1963, the United States and the Soviet Union detonated over 400 nuclear explosions in the atmosphere, each nation contributing roughly half the total. Significant underground testing took place during this period as well. In addition, the United Kingdom and France had each begun smaller testing programs. By August of 1963, the world had experienced an estimated total of 578 nuclear detonations.

As early as 1954, President Dwight D. Eisenhower considered imposing a moratorium on nuclear testing. Increasing anxiety over the intensity of arms race and the effects of fallout had generated concerns over the wisdom of nuclear testing, especially atmospheric testing. Initially, the moratorium was opposed by the departments of Defense and State, as well as by the Atomic Energy Commission. However, in 1958, Eisenhower ordered a halt to all United States' nuclear testing. The Soviet Union followed Eisenhower's lead, and neither nation conducted any nuclear tests in 1959 or 1960. More importantly, the United States and the Soviet Union began talks toward banning the testing of nuclear weapons.

On 5 August 1963, after five years of negotiations, the United States, the Soviet Union, and the United Kingdom signed the Treaty Banning Nuclear Weapon Tests in the Atmosphere, in Outer Space, and Under Water, known as the Limited Test-Ban Treaty. The goal of a comprehensive test ban was aborted by the Soviet refusal to permit on-site inspections. The Limited Test-Ban Treaty was approved by the Senate and proclaimed by President John F. Kennedy on 10 October 1963. The treaty, which has now been signed by 125 nations, outlaws nuclear testing in the atmosphere, underwater, or in outer space. It permits underground testing so long as any radioactive leakage does not travel beyond the territory of the testing nation. Since the signing of the treaty, the United States has engaged in underground testing only, conducting 598 such tests through 1990. The frequency of the tests has declined significantly since 1968 when there were 45 such tests; the total for 1990 was 8.

In 1974, during the administration of President Richard Nixon, the United States and the Soviet Union negotiated a Treaty on the Limitation of Underground Nuclear Tests (Threshold Test-Ban Treaty). Among other things, the treaty limits the yield of any underground test to 150 kilotons. The treaty was not ratified until 1990, during the administration of President George Bush. The eventual ratification was the result of a satisfactory agreement on verification. Despite the belated ratification, neither nation has significantly exceeded the 150 kiloton limitation since the initial document's implementation date of 31 March 1976.

In 1977, President Jimmy Carter began negotiations with the Soviet Union, later joined by the United Kingdom, on a comprehensive nuclear weapons test ban. The negotiations continued through 1980, but were not pursued after the election of President Ronald Reagan. After reaching an agreement on the Threshold Test Ban Treaty in 1990, the United States, through the administration of President Bush, announced that it would not, for the present, enter further discussions toward a comprehensive test ban.

BIBLIOGRAPHY

Cantelon, Philip L., Richard G. Hewlett, and Robert C. Williams, eds. *The American Atom: A Documentary History of Nuclear Policies from the Discovery of Fission to the Present.* 2d ed. 1991.

Cochran, Thomas M., William M. Arkin, and Milton M. Hoenig. *Nuclear Weapons Databook*, Vol. 1: *U.S. Nuclear Forces and Capabilities.* 2d ed. 1992.

Cochran, Thomas B., William M. Arkin, Robert S. Norris, and Jeffrey I. Sands, *Nuclear Weapons Databook.* Vol. 4: *Soviet Nuclear Weapons.* 1989.

Miller, Richard L., *Under the Cloud: The Decades of Nuclear Testing.* 1986.

Pogany, Istvan, ed. *Nuclear Weapons and International Law.* 1987.

Seaborg, Glenn T., with the assistance of Benjamin S. Loeb. *Kennedy, Khrushchev, and the Test Ban.* 1981.

Stockholm International Peace Research Institute. *SIPRI Yearbook 1991: World Armaments and Disarmament.* 1991.

ALLAN IDES

NUCLEAR WEAPONS. There are two general types of nuclear weapons, atomic weapons and thermonuclear weapons. Atomic weapons, such as the bombs dropped on Hiroshima and Nagasaki, rely for their explosive force upon the energy released by fission, that is, the splitting of an atomic nucleus. Thermonuclear weapons, which carry a much greater explosive force, depend on the process of fusion, that is, the union of atomic nuclei. Most nuclear weapons today are of the thermonuclear variety.

The explosive force of a nuclear weapon is rated in terms of a comparative scale with the explosive force of

T.N.T. The atomic bomb dropped on Hiroshima, for example, had an explosive force of approximately 10 to 15 kilotons (thousands of tons) of T.N.T. By contrast, modern thermonuclear weapons are sometimes measured in terms of megatons, that is, millions of tons of T.N.T. In addition to their devastating explosive force, nuclear weapons give off deadly radiation that can spread over a wide area.

Historically, the United States' nuclear arsenal has been divided into two types of weapons: strategic and theater. Strategic weapons are designed to attack an enemy at its home base or to protect the homeland. Such weapons have delivery systems designed to travel long, intercontinental distances. Theater weapons, also referred to as tactical weapons, travel shorter distances and are designed to be used within more limited geographic regions, including battlefield use. Due to the START (STRATEGIC ARMS REDUCTION TALKS) Treaty and the dissolution of the Soviet Union, the nuclear forces of the United States underwent drastic reductions beginning in the early 1990s. Indicative of this trend was the projected decrease in the number of nuclear warheads from over 20,000 to between 4,500 and 5,000, and the virtual elimination of most theater and tactical weapons systems.

Strategic Delivery Systems. The strategic nuclear forces of the United States include land-based intercontinental ballistic missiles (ICBMs), submarine-launched ballistic missiles (SLBMs), and nuclear weapons, both missiles and bombs, carried aboard long-range bombers. These three delivery systems are sometimes referred to as the strategic nuclear triad. The purpose of the triad is to counterbalance the nuclear threat from other countries and to deter attack upon the United States by ensuring the survivability of U.S. forces in the event of a nuclear first strike by an enemy. Up through 1991, the primary purpose of the triad was to deter a potential nuclear attack by the Soviet Union. Given the demise of the Soviet Union, the scaled-down triad is designed to provide a series of flexible responses to a variety of military contingencies.

Land-based systems. In 1992 the United States deployed two types of ICBMs, the Minuteman III and the MX Peacekeeper. An ICBM is a long-range missile capable of carrying one or more nuclear warheads. Such missiles have a range of between 7,000 and 8,000 miles and are directed toward their targets by the combination of a launch trajectory and the force of gravity. The most current ICBMs have an accuracy of between 300 to 400 feet circular error probable (CEP), meaning there is a 50 percent probability that the missile will strike within a radius of 300 to 400 feet of

its intended target. In terms of explosive force, the Minuteman III carries three 170- or 335-kiloton warheads, referred to as MIRVs (multiple independently targetable reentry vehicles). Each MIRV is capable of striking a separate target. The MX Peacekeeper can carry twelve MIRVs, but is currently armed with ten. The yield of each MIRVed warhead is between 300 to 475 kilotons. In 1992 there were five-hundred-ten Minuteman III and fifty MX Peacekeepers staged in silos in the United States, yielding 2,030 independently targeted warheads. Under START, the number of Minuteman III missiles will be reduced to five-hundred.

Prior to 1991 there were plans for an additional fifty MX Peacekeepers to be placed on rail-mobile launchers, and for the production of a smaller rail-mobile single-warhead ICBM. President George Bush canceled both projects in response to the dissolution of the Soviet Union. In January 1992, President Bush also proposed to the republics of the former Soviet Union, the elimination of all multiwarhead ICBMs. For the United States, this would mean the elimination of the MX Peacekeeper and the rearming of each Minuteman III missile with a single warhead.

Submarine-based systems. The second leg of the strategic triad consists of submarine-launched ballistic missiles (SLBMs). There are currently two types of SLBMs: the Trident I (or C4) and the Trident II (or D5). The Trident I, with a range of 4,600 miles, can carry ten warheads, but is equipped with eight, each of which is rated at 100 kilotons. The Trident II, the most modern of the SLBMs, with a range of 4,000 miles and a CEP of 400 feet, can carry from fifteen to seventeen nuclear warheads. As of 1992 there was discussion of the early retirement of the Trident I.

The naval fleet contains two classes of nuclear-powered submarines (SSBNs) capable of firing SLBMs: the *Ohio*-class SSBN, which carry twenty-four missile launchers, and the *Lafayette*-class SSBN, which carry sixteen launchers. Only the *Ohio*-class, sometimes referred to as the Trident submarine, is capable of launching the highly accurate Trident II. As of 1992 there were twelve *Ohio*-class SSBNs, only four of which were equipped with the Trident II, and ten pre-*Ohio*-class SSBNs, all of which were equipped with the Trident I.

Long-range bombers. The third leg of the strategic triad consists of long-range bombers armed with gravity bombs, short-range attack missiles (SRAMs), and air-launched cruise missiles (ALCMs). The advanced cruise missile (ACM) is currently in development. Cruise missiles are independently propelled, guided missiles, capable of penetrating enemy defenses more effectively than non-stealth bombers. The long-range bombers have two strategic uses: penetration and stand-off. Penetration bombers are designed to penetrate the enemy's defense and attack from within the enemy's territory. Stand-off bombers are designed to approach the enemy's territory and to fire missiles into the territory.

The United States deploys three types of heavy bombers, the B-52 (models G and H), the B-1B, and the B-2. The B-52 *Stratofortress* has been a critical part of the United States fleet since it first entered service in 1954. The current models, the B-52G and B-52H, were first deployed in 1959 and 1962 respectively, though both models have undergone substantial life extension, modernization, and defensive upgrade. Originally used as a penetration bomber, the B-52 is being converted to stand-off and conventional uses, with penetration duties being placed in the newer B-1B and B-2 models. In its stand-off role, the B-52 carries a combination of SRAMs, each with a 170 kiloton warhead, and ALCMs, each with a variable-yield 5 to 170 kiloton warhead.

The B-1B, first deployed in 1985 and now out of production, is a supersonic penetration and stand-off bomber with a range of over 8,000 miles. It has a radar signature that is $\frac{1}{1000}$ that of the B-52 and can cruise at altitudes as low as 50 feet. The B-1B carries a variety of missiles and gravity bombs, with a maximum load of thirty-eight nuclear weapons per plane. As of 1992, there were ninety-seven B-1Bs in the fleet.

The B-2, or stealth bomber, is the most recent addition to the United States' fleet. Plans in 1992 call for a maximum of twenty B-2s, but the total number to be produced is a current political issue. The stealth bomber, which is in essence a flying wing, has a range of 8,000 miles and is equipped with the most advanced antiradar features. The B-2 will carry ACMs and gravity bombs, all of which will be stored internally. The B-2 is capable of exercising both a penetration and a conventional role.

Theater and Tactical Weapons. Theater nuclear weapons are designed for use in regional conflicts. Long-range theater weapons include the *Pershing 2* ballistic missile with a range of up to 1,200 miles, an accuracy of 150-feet CEP and a variable-yield 0.3 to 80 kiloton warhead; ground-launched cruise missiles with a range up to 1,600 miles, an accuracy of 70-feet CEP and a variable-yield 0.2 to 150 kiloton warhead; and, the F-111 theater bomber with a range of 2,500 miles and the capability of carrying three nuclear bombs. Medium-range theater weapons can be carried by various attack aircraft from the air force, the marines, and the navy. Short-range theater weapons, which are also sometimes classified as tactical weapons, include the *Lance* guided missile, which can deliver a 1 to 100 kiloton nuclear warhead up to 80 miles, as well as artillery capable of firing small nuclear artillery shells short distances. In his January 1992 force reduction initiative, President Bush announced the elimination of the United States' entire arsenal of ground-launched theater nuclear weapons.

Land-based tactical nuclear weapons include the above short-range missiles and artillery as well as atomic land mines (small atomic demolition munitions) with a 1 kiloton yield. These weapons are presumably subject to President Bush's order of elimination as well. The air force and the navy also have available antiship, antisubmarine and anti-aircraft nuclear-tipped missiles, as well as a variety of aircraft capable of delivering nuclear bombs. In January 1992, President Bush ordered the withdrawal of all tactical nuclear weapons from surface ships, attack submarines, and land-based naval aircraft. The nuclear weapons normally available for these ships and aircraft will be eliminated or stored.

BIBLIOGRAPHY

Cheney, Dick. *Annual Report to the President and the Congress.* 1992.

Cochran, Thomas B., William M. Arkin, and Milton M. Hoenig. *Nuclear Weapons Databook.* Vol. 1: *U.S. Nuclear Forces and Capabilities.* 2d ed. 1992.

Collins, John M., and Dianne E. Rennack. *CRS Report for Congress: U.S. Armed Forces, Statistical Trends, 1985–1990.* 1991.

Rogers, Paul. *Guide to Nuclear Weapons.* 1988.

Semler, Eric, James Benjamin, and Adam Gross. *The Language of Nuclear War: An Intelligent Citizen's Dictionary.* 1987.

ALLAN IDES

NULLIFICATION. The "refusal of a state to recognize or enforce within its territory any act of Congress held to be an infringement upon its sovereignty" is known as *nullification*. The debate over the delicate balance of state and national powers within the new constitutional framework dominated the thought of many of the Framers. When the John Adams's Federalist administration passed the politically repressive ALIEN AND SEDITION ACTS in 1798, Democratic-Republican leaders James Madison and Thomas Jefferson responded with their own initiatives. The Virginia and Kentucky Resolutions, borrowing heavily from the philosophy of John Locke, emphasized the concept of government as social compact. According to the resolutions, when Congress passed unconstitutional measures that infringed on the people's liberties, the states could act. In the Virginia Resolutions, the more moderate Madison suggested the right of the state to "interpose" itself politically between the people and the national government. In the Kentucky Resolutions, however, Jefferson argued that a state could nullify "all assumptions of powers by others within their own limits." While most important as an articulation of STATES' RIGHTS doctrine and CIVIL LIBERTIES, the resolutions also planted the seed of nullification in the soil of American political thought.

A quarter-century later, as the South felt increasingly threatened by the centralized power of the national government, nullification took on a new and more aggressive dimension. Intersectional economic rivals debated the merits of the tariff, but the issue masked hidden tensions over the authority of the federal government to control, or eventually abolish, SLAVERY. Vice President JOHN C. CALHOUN, a South Carolinian and former nationalist, redefined the Principles of '98. His momentous Exposition and Protest (December 1828) and, later, his so-called Fort Hill letter (July 1831) depicted a broader threat to Southern liberties in the North-versus-South (industrial-versus-agricultural) struggle.

Although numerous Southerners agreed with the theory of nullification, only South Carolinians seemed willing to act on the doctrine. In the summer of 1832, Congress reduced the prohibitive tariff rates set in 1828 [see TARIFF OF ABOMINATIONS; TARIFF ACT OF 1832]. South Carolinians, however, felt the duties remained much too high and called for a Nullification Convention to meet in Columbia on 24 November. Amid talk of military resistance, the conclave voted to nullify the federal tariffs, effective on 1 February 1833. A succeeding session of the state legislature promptly framed the measure into law.

President Andrew Jackson, a native Carolinian and a supporter of states' rights within a nationalist framework, responded immediately to quash the nullifiers. His December Proclamation denied the legality of nullification and SECESSION and affirmed the belief in the inviolability of the Union. Congress followed by passing the Jackson-inspired Force Bill on 24 February 1833, giving the President the power to use the military to collect the tariff duties.

In an effort to avert possible civil war, HENRY CLAY pushed a successful compromise tariff measure through Congress in March 1833, reducing the duties to a maximum of 20 percent over a ten year period. Calmed by the compelling arguments of Calhoun, the Nullification Convention rescinded its censure of the tariff acts but maintained the principle by nullifying the Force Bill. Infrequently utilized before the CIVIL WAR, nullification and interposition reemerged as the constitutional weapons of Southern segregationist governors in the fight against civil rights in the 1950s.

BIBLIOGRAPHY

Ellis, Richard. *The Union at Risk: Jacksonian Democracy, States Rights, and the Nullification Crisis.* 1987.

Freehling, William W. *Prelude to Civil War: The Nullification Movement in South Carolina, 1816–1836.* 1966.

Freehling, William W. *The Road to Disunion: Secessionists at Bay, 1776–1854.* 1990.

Koch, Adrienne, and Harry Ammon. "The Virginia and Kentucky Resolutions: An Episode in Jefferson's and Madison's Defense of Civil Liberties." *William and Mary Quarterly* 3d ser., 5 (1958): 145–176.

Sellers, Charles G. *Andrew Jackson, Nullification and the State-Rights Tradition.* 1963.

Wiltse, Charles. *John C. Calhoun: Nullifier.* 1949.

JOHN M. BELOHLAVEK

OATH OF OFFICE, PRESIDENTIAL.

OATH OF OFFICE, PRESIDENTIAL. Article II, Section 1, clause 8, of the Constitution provides that before a President "enter on the Execution of his Office, he shall take the following Oath or Affirmation:—'I do solemnly swear (or affirm) that I will faithfully execute the Office of President of the United States, and will to the best of my Ability, preserve, protect and defend the Constitution of the United States.'" At the first INAUGURATION, George Washington added the words "so help me God" at the conclusion of the oath, a practice that has since been followed by almost every President. The oath prescribed for all other federal officials, including the VICE PRESIDENT, was approved by the First Congress.

During the CONSTITUTIONAL CONVENTION of 1787, the drafting of the President's oath generated little debate. The Committee on Detail proposed the first half of the oath on 6 August. Three weeks later, George Mason and James Madison successfully moved to add the phrase "and will to the best of my judgment and power preserve, protect and defend the Constitution of the United States" to the oath. On 15 September the delegates substituted "to the best of my abilities" for "to the best of my judgment and power" without discussion.

In 204 years (1789–1993), the presidential oath has been administered fifty-two times. On four occasions, when inauguration day fell on a Sunday, the President chose to be sworn into office privately at the White House, and then repeated the oath on Monday, at the public ceremony on Capitol Hill. Although the Constitution makes no provision regarding who shall administer the oath, the Chief Justice of the United States has sworn in every President-elect since John Adams (1797). The Chief Justice could not administer the oath at either of George Washington's inaugurations since the Supreme Court had not yet been selected in 1789, and Chief Justice JOHN JAY was out of the county in 1793.

The precedent for succeeding Vice Presidents taking the presidential oath on assuming office was begun by John Tyler in April 1841, after William Henry Harrison became the first President to die in office. Each of the eight Vice Presidents who have since assumed the presidency due to the death or resignation of the President have followed the TYLER PRECEDENT. Among the individuals administering the oath to succeeding Vice Presidents have been three Chief Justices, four federal judges, a state supreme court justice, and a local justice of the peace.

The Constitution makes no mention of the elaborate pageantry, pomp, and celebration that accompanies the swearing in of the President, which has become one of America's most significant traditions.

BIBLIOGRAPHY

Durbin, Louise. *Inaugural Cavalcade.* 1971.
The Inaugural Story, 1789–1969. 1969.
Stathis, Stephen W. "Our Sunday Inaugurations." *Presidential Studies Quarterly* 15 (Winter 1985): 12–24.

STEPHEN W. STATHIS

OFFICE FOR EMERGENCY MANAGEMENT (OEM).

OFFICE FOR EMERGENCY MANAGEMENT (OEM). A unit of the EXECUTIVE OFFICE OF THE PRESIDENT, the Office for Emergency Management was created by President Franklin D. Roosevelt to help the President deal with the emergency posed by WORLD WAR II. Roosevelt had created the Executive Office of the President in 1939 with Reorganization Plan No. 1. That office was formally organized 8 September 1939 by Executive Order 8248, which defined five operative bodies, including, "in the event of a national emergency, such office for emergency management as the President shall determine." That same day the President declared a "limited" national emergency in response to the German invasion of Poland in early September; the United States maintained a policy of official NEUTRALITY, although Britain and France declared war on Germany. Thus, conditions were set for the establishment of the Office for Emergency Management by a presidential administrative order on 25 May 1940.

The administrative order chartered the OEM to "assist the President in the clearance of information with respect to measures necessitated by the threatened emergency," to serve as a liaison between the President and other agencies involved in "meeting the threatened emergency," and "to perform such additional duties as the President may direct." The OEM was headed by one of the President's administrative assistants, known as the Liaison Officer for Emergency Management, who were successively William H. McReynolds, Wayne Coy, and JAMES F. BYRNES. On 3 November 1943, Roosevelt accepted Byrnes's resignation from this position and appointed no successor, thereby terminating the liaison functions of the OEM.

As war enveloped Europe and Asia, the OEM became the President's vehicle for U.S. mobilization. A 7 January 1941 administrative order assigned the OEM important new duties. Significantly, the order directed the OEM to advise and assist the President "in the discharge of extraordinary responsibilities imposed upon him by any emergency arising out of war, the threat of war, imminence of war, flood, drought, or other condition threatening the public peace or safety." The emergency character of the agency made it difficult for neutralists and pacifists to attack. Furthermore, with the Reorganization Act of 1939 due to expire automatically in a short time, Roosevelt needed a way to continue mobilization and knew he could not depend on Congress for it. What he chose to do was to make the OEM a holding company for various agencies presidentially created as its subunits. By the end of 1941, America was at war, and the OEM continued to provide the framework for the establishment of a number of wartime agencies, such as the Office of Production Management, the OFFICE OF PRICE ADMINISTRATION, the Office of War Information, and the Office of Economic Stabilization. By mid-1943, the OEM's administrative and coordinative activities began to be reduced and the OFFICE OF WAR MOBILIZATION, another OEM subunit, assumed a leadership role. One of the last OEM subunits to survive was the Philippine Alien Property Administration, which was terminated in 1951. By that time, the OEM had been inactive for several years; it has never been formally abolished.

BIBLIOGRAPHY

McReynolds, William H. "The Office for Emergency Management." *Public Administration Review* 1 (1941): 131–138.
U.S. Bureau of the Budget. *The United States at War.* 1946.
Wann, A.J. *The President as Chief Administrator.* 1968.

HAROLD C. RELYEA

OFFICE OF ADMINISTRATION. The White House Office of Administration was established within the EXECUTIVE OFFICE OF THE PRESIDENT (EOP) in 1977. President Jimmy Carter proposed this office, initially referred to as the Central Administrative Unit, to Congress on 15 July 1977 in section 2 of his Reorganization Plan No. 1 of 1977 (42 FR 56101). The proposal took effect on 12 December 1977 via Executive Order 12028.

Before the creation of the Office of Administration, 380 (or 22 percent) of the full-time, permanent EOP personnel performed administrative support services in the various EOP units. This dispersion resulted in a duplication of effort, uneven quality, and poor coordination of administrative support and services. Through the consolidation of administrative functions in a single office, Carter hoped to increase the efficiency of the EOP, improve services, and create a base for more effective management of the budget and planning of all EOP units.

Skeptics saw the formation of the office as an effort to respond to criticism concerning the growth of the White House staff under President Richard M. Nixon. Creating the Office of Administration enabled Carter to shift a number of employees off the White House payroll, thus appearing to reduce the size of the staff without losing support services.

Section 3 of Executive Order 12028 states that the Office of Administration "shall encompass all types of administrative support and services that may be used, or be useful to, units within the Executive Office of the President." Mandated services include personnel management services; financial management services; data processing; library, records and information services; and office services and operations. As of 1992, the Office of Administration was the third-largest unit in the EOP, with a full-time staff of 159.

The Office of Administration is headed by a director, who is appointed by, and directly responsible to, the President. The director is accountable for ensuring that the Office of Administration provides common administrative support and services to institutional units of the Executive Office of the President. The first director, Richard Harden, was appointed by President Carter on 28 December 1977.

The Office has five functional divisions: Administrative Operations, Financial Management, Information Resources Management, Library and Information Services, and Personnel Management. Each is headed by a division director. The Administrative Management Division encompasses general administrative services such as mail, messenger, printing and duplication, graphics, word processing, procurement, and supply services.

Through the Financial Management Division, the Office of Administration maintains accounts, payrolls, and budgeting for all EOP offices. Information Resources Management and Library and Information Services manage the three EOP's nonpublic libraries (general reference, reference, and law), provide data processing and information services, and maintain official records for all units. The Personnel Management Division handles the placement, transfer, and interagency detailing of all EOP staff, with the exception of presidential appointments.

The Office of Administration plays a very small role in EOP politics, as its functions are essentially those of institutional maintenance rather than policy coordination or political liaison. As John Hart points out in *The Presidential Branch*, however, the office could form a strong base for an executive-branch management unit if this responsibility were ever to be removed from the OFFICE OF MANAGEMENT AND BUDGET (OMB).

BIBLIOGRAPHY

Bonafede, Dom. "Administering the EOP." *National Journal* (31 December 1977): 2017.
Hart, John. *The Presidential Branch.* 1987.
Patterson, Bradley H., Jr. *Ring of Power.* 1988.

MARGARET JANE WYSZOMIRSKI

OFFICE OF FEDERAL PROCUREMENT POLICY (OFPP).

Within the OFFICE OF MANAGEMENT AND BUDGET (OMB), the Office of Federal Procurement Policy is the unit responsible for the coordination of policies employed by executive-branch agencies in contracting for products and services. Historically a small agency outside the glare of publicity, OFPP found itself in an important and controversial position during the 1980s, when PRIVATIZATION—the preference for the maximum use of private-sector providers of goods and services—was aggressively pursued by the

Ronald Reagan administration. Government contracting, approximately $50 billion annually in the early years of OFPP's existence, soared to over $200 billion, and that during one of the worst periods of economic decline in the nation's history.

The OFPP developed because of growing discontent with contracting practices in the late 1960s, at which time the Congress created the Commission on Government Procurement. The Procurement Commission report was delivered in 1972 and contained 149 recommendations, the first of which was to create a central office in the executive branch to provide coordination and leadership in federal procurement policy.

Senator Lawton Chiles (D-Fla.), who had served on the commission, chaired a subcommittee of the Senate Governmental Affairs Committee to pursue the commission's recommendations. Chiles's efforts produced the Office of Federal Procurement Policy Act (P.L. 93-400) in 1974. After reauthorization reviews in 1979, 1983, and 1988 produced clear consensus on the need for a central procurement policy office, Congress gave permanent authorization to OFPP. Those three reviews reflected a concern among many members of Congress, other agencies, and firms doing business with the government that the goals for which the OFPP had been created had not been accomplished, and they produced substantial modifications in OFPP authority and responsibilities.

Several problems, however, arose. The office did not have a high enough priority in OMB to obtain adequate resources or to command the respect of other large agencies in the procurement arena. The OFPP was small and became smaller just at a time when contract expenditures were escalating dramatically. Authorized to have forty-one staff, it shrank to a total of eight professionals and five support staff actually in place in 1986. OFPP was without an administrator from 1984 to 1986.

Second, federal procurement methods continued to face serious criticism from all quarters. A consultant study in 1985 concluded that while the consolidated Federal Acquisition Regulation (FAR), called for by Congress, had been implemented, there was no adequate means to ensure oversight and management of FAR. Growing criticism of military contracts brought the creation of the President's Blue Ribbon Commission on Defense Management. The Packard Commission, as it was known, recommended contracting changes, including reduction in procurement regulations that had become too complex to permit necessary flexibility.

It was also increasingly clear that OFPP was too small an office to lead large and powerful agencies such as the Department of Defense (DOD), the General Services Administration (GSA), and the National Aeronautics and Space Administration (NASA). That also placed OFPP in the middle of a variety of congressional subcommittees with interest in those other agencies.

Congress brought pressure on OMB to improve the procurement process in general and OFPP in particular. Similar pressures came through the Office of the VICE PRESIDENT, which put the subject on the agenda of the Vice President's Task Force on Regulatory Relief, which worked in conjunction with the Office of Information and Regulatory Affairs (OIRA), whose mandate included regulatory review and reduction of paperwork burdens. One result was the appointment of a former OIRA official, Robert P. Bedell, to head OFPP.

Staff and budget increases followed. In late 1987, a GENERAL ACCOUNTING OFFICE report contained criticisms of OFPP that matched some of the agency's own concerns. The OFPP was then working with Senator Chiles, the legislative founder of OFPP, to adopt new legislation to strengthen the office by giving it permanent authorization and restoring its authority to issue regulations, a power that had been removed in earlier legislation. These efforts produced the Office of Federal Procurement Policy Act Amendments of 1988 (P.L. 100-679).

Under legislation current in 1992, OFPP had several responsibilities: to provide overall coordination and leadership of federal government procurement policy; to supervise the oversight and revision of the FAR process, working through the Federal Acquisition Regulatory Council (consisting of representatives from DOD, NASA, and GSA); to improve accounting practices through its Cost Accounting Standards Board; to maintain oversight and design improvements for the Federal Procurement Data System; and to facilitate contracting efforts through its Advocate for the Acquisition of Commercial Products. Finally, it oversaw the operation of the Federal Acquisitions Institute, an organization located in GSA and responsible for providing a well-trained procurement workforce.

In performing these obligations, OFPP could issue regulations, create forms, and collect data. It issued policy letters, such as OFPP Letter 85-1, which implemented the unified procurement regulations system called for in the OFPP Act. It could participate in the revision of OMB circulars that govern contracting or assist the President by drafting executive orders such as Executive Order 12515 on the Performance of Commercial Activities (1987). The office also regu-

larly provided congressional testimony and worked with members of the legislature to draft contract-related legislation. Thus it worked to develop proposals for contracting reforms in the wake of the George Bush administration's Defense Management Review in 1989.

The need to exercise enough power to command the respect and cooperation of major businesses and agencies while fostering an image as a facilitator and mediator is a difficult challenge. The fact that OFPP must meet that challenge while protecting huge expenditures of taxpayer dollars makes the task that much more difficult.

BIBLIOGRAPHY

U.S. General Accounting Office. *Procurement: Assessment of the Office of Federal Procurement Policy.* 1987.

PHILLIP J. COOPER

OFFICE OF INFORMATION AND REGULATORY AFFAIRS (OIRA).

The Office of Information and Regulatory Affairs is a component of the President's chief supervisory entity for the federal government, the OFFICE OF MANAGEMENT AND BUDGET (OMB). OIRA, which was created by the Paperwork Reduction Act of 1980 (44 U.S.C. 3501–3520), is headed by an administrator, who is appointed by the President and confirmed by the Senate. The staff consists mostly of desk officers, who are typically young economists, lawyers, or policy analysts.

OIRA has two principal functions, which often overlap. The first, a statutory function of OMB since 1942, is the duty to review and approve paperwork requirements that agencies impose on the public. Statutes contain many reporting and record-keeping provisions for the public to follow, which are generically called "information collection requests." Under the Paperwork Reduction Act, agencies may collect information only when it is "necessary for the proper performance" of their functions. OIRA files public comments on collection requests and may disapprove them if the agency does not accept its views. The disapproval is final for executive agencies; independent agencies may override it by majority vote. In one representative year, 1988, OIRA reviewed 2,860 collection requests from federal agencies, three-quarters of which renewed existing requirements. OIRA approved all but 133 of these.

OIRA interpreted the act to allow it to disapprove collection requests even if the information involved was not primarily for government use. The Supreme Court rejected this view in *Dole v. United Steelworkers*

(1990). The Court held that the act did not authorize review of requirements that regulated industries disclose hazards of their products to affected members of the public.

OIRA's second main function, and the most controversial, has been the implementation of EXECUTIVE ORDER 12291 and EXECUTIVE ORDER 12498, which require executive agencies to adhere to cost-benefit principles when promulgating rules and to engage in a regulatory planning process that leads to formulation of a regulatory agenda for the government for each year. These orders are based on the President's constitutional powers, rather than on statutory authorization. Under the cost-benefit order, affected agencies must estimate the costs and benefits their proposed rules will create and must consult with OIRA concerning them before issuing final rules. Experience under this program demonstrated that OIRA review could delay issuance of some important rules substantially and could even cause an agency to miss a statutory deadline for rulemaking. Also, congressional concerns arose that discretion granted to agencies by statute could be transferred to OIRA. A third source of controversy has been the extent to which the review program should be performed openly. Here, the values of confidentiality that underlie EXECUTIVE PRIVILEGE can clash with the need to assure effective CONGRESSIONAL OVERSIGHT and judicial review. Moreover, any executive review program has the potential that special interests may channel policy arguments to agencies through sympathetic reviewing officers, thereby avoiding otherwise applicable requirements of administrative law that rulemaking submissions be public. After five years of experience under the program, a compromise was worked out in 1986 between the Reagan administration and congressional committees. It provided that most written communications between OIRA and the agencies be made public after the rule to which they pertain is promulgated, but that informal oral communications within the executive could remain confidential.

Notwithstanding the informal compromise of 1986, controversy has continued under the program. When OIRA's statutory authorization was expiring in 1989, efforts were made in Congress to place more rigorous record-keeping requirements for OIRA in the statute. Dispute centered on whether OIRA should be forced to summarize oral contacts with agencies and place the summaries in the public record. OIRA would also have been required to explain in writing its reasons for suggesting changes in any proposed regulation. Efforts by congressional committees and the Bush administration to reach agreement on statutory controls for OIRA were unavailing. At the close of the 102d Congress in 1992, OIRA continued to operate under temporary reauthorization, pending resolution of the impasse.

In June 1990, President George Bush created the President's COMPETITIVENESS COUNCIL chaired by Vice President DAN QUAYLE. The council, operating in secret, served as an appellate forum within the Bush administration, considering disputes between agencies and OIRA on pending rules. The operations of the council, like those of OIRA, provoked controversy and unsuccessful attempts at statutory control.

BIBLIOGRAPHY

Bruff, Harold H. "Presidential Management of Agency Rulemaking." *George Washington Law Review* 57 (1989): 533–595.
Funk, William. "The Paperwork Reduction Act: Paperwork Reduction Meets Administrative Law." *Harvard Journal on Legislation* 24 (1987): 1–78.
National Academy of Public Administration. *Presidential Management of Rulemaking in Regulatory Agencies.* 1987.
Symposium. "Cost-Benefit Analysis and Agency Decision-Making: An Analysis of Executive Order No. 12,291." *Arizona Law Review* 23 (1981): 1195–1298.

HAROLD H. BRUFF

OFFICE OF INTERGOVERNMENTAL RELATIONS (OIR). Established by President Richard M. Nixon by Executive Order 11455 on 14 February 1969, the Office of Intergovernmental Relations was created as part of Nixon's Reorganization Plan No. 2 to provide a way to strengthen relationships between the federal, state, and local governments. The office was charged with expediting the resolution of problems pertaining to intergovernmental relations and increasing local-government power over federal decisions. The location of the office in the EXECUTIVE OFFICE OF THE PRESIDENT reflected Nixon's desire to draw local-government perspectives closer to the OVAL OFFICE. The OIR's establishment early in the Nixon administration reflected the administration's priority concern with reordering matters related to FEDERALISM.

The office consisted of three people: a director, a deputy director, and an assistant director, all under the immediate supervision of Vice President SPIRO T. AGNEW. This represented one of several administrative responsibilities given to Agnew in the first months of the Nixon administration. In addition to serving as Nixon's stand-in as chair of the CABINET, Agnew was given a key administrative role in the National Aeronautics and Space Administration (NASA), the Marine Resources and Engineering Development Council, the Council on Recreation and Natural Beauty, the Rural Affairs Council, the Council on Youth Opportunity, the Indian Opportunity Council, the Cabinet Committee on Desegregation, and the Council on Physical Fitness and Sports. Agnew had, as Nixon said, a "full plate" of activities. His appointment to coordinate the OIR was considered especially appropriate because Agnew's political experience as a former county executive and governor of Maryland suited the OIR mission well.

The creation of the OIR also reflected a broader priority of the Nixon administration, labeled the New Federalism. In his order creating the OIR, Nixon said that he was seeking to move government closer to the people, reflecting his view that control over the spending of federal dollars should rest more directly at the local level than had been true during the presidency of Lyndon Baines Johnson, when much federal spending was earmarked for specific purposes defined in Washington (through categorical grants, for example). Nixon's plans for spending at the state and local levels centered on a principle of revenue sharing. As Nixon said, the office was set up to "facilitate an orderly transfer of appropriate functions to State and local government." Nixon also directed that the OIR work closely with the Advisory Commission on Intergovernmental Relations, a commission established by Congress in 1959 to improve intergovernmental cooperation and coordination. Nixon named Nils A. Boe, a former governor of South Dakota, as the OIR's first director. At the end of 1969, Congress appropriated $290,000 for the office's operation.

After more than two years of operation, the OIR was dissolved on 14 December 1972. By Executive Order 11690, Nixon transferred the functions of the OIR to the Domestic Council. According to his statement, Nixon did so on Agnew's recommendation, but the elimination of the OIR reflected two important changes in administration politics. First, it reflected Agnew's declining influence in the administration. (Before the 1972 Republican convention, for example, there had been much talk of dumping Agnew from the ticket.) Second, it reflected the administration's effort to centralize and to place greater emphasis on administrative activities to achieve policy ends—a trend labeled the ADMINISTRATIVE PRESIDENCY by the political scientist Richard P. Nathan.

BIBLIOGRAPHY

Nathan, Richard P. *The Administrative Presidency.* 1983.
Public Papers of the Presidents of the United States: Richard Nixon. 1971.
Witcover, Jules. *White Knight.* 1972.

ROBERT J. SPITZER

OFFICE OF LEGAL COUNSEL (OLC). When President Richard M. Nixon announced the appointment of William H. Rehnquist, then Assistant Attorney General, Office of Legal Counsel, to the Supreme Court, he commented: "He is, in effect, the President's lawyer's lawyer." There is no more apt description of the role of the Office of Legal Counsel.

The Judiciary Act of 1789 provided for the appointment of a "meet person, learned in the law" as ATTORNEY GENERAL. From the outset, providing legal advice and opinions to the President and the executive branch was a primary function of the Attorney General and one he performed personally, even after creation of the DEPARTMENT OF JUSTICE in 1870.

In June 1933 the appropriation act for the Department of Justice created an Assistant Solicitor General position, to be appointed by the President with the ADVICE AND CONSENT of the Senate. His primary responsibility was to prepare opinions of the Attorney General and provide legal advice to the President and the heads of executive agencies. The title was changed to Assistant Attorney General in 1951 and the staff was designated the Executive Adjudications Division. Two years later, the name was changed to Office of Legal Counsel, a more accurate description of its essential role—helping the Attorney General provide legal advice to the President and the executive branch.

The core functions of the Office of Legal Counsel have remained the same for almost sixty years: preparing opinions of the Attorney General, providing written and oral informal advice and opinions, reviewing EXECUTIVE ORDERS and PROCLAMATIONS for form and legality, and reviewing legislation for constitutionality. Other responsibilities have been assigned to the office as the demands on the Department of Justice have varied. Following enactment of the ADMINISTRATIVE PROCEDURE ACT in 1946, for example, an Administrative Law Section was established within the Office of Legal Counsel to provide guidance to agencies and to conduct studies relating to administrative law. Its foremost recommendation was the creation of the Administrative Conference of the United States, which ultimately replaced the section. Another section of the office carried out the Department of Justice role in making recommendations to the Selective Service System on the validity of conscientious objector claims. The Conscientious Objector Section was eliminated with the ending of the draft.

The President and the Attorney General have also called upon the OLC to undertake special assignments in areas of unique legal complexity. In the 1970s, for example, the office prepared several legal opinions and analyses concerning the reform of the INTELLIGENCE COMMUNITY.

While formal litigation responsibilities are assigned elsewhere in the Department of Justice, the OLC, from time to time, becomes involved in the preparation of briefs and even in the argument of cases. Usually this occurs because of the expertise of the office in areas of constitutional law, such as the SEPARATION OF POWERS doctrine. Thus, the office was directly involved in INS v. CHADHA (1983), dealing with the issue of legislative veto of executive action. Lawyers from the office were also called upon to assist the Solicitor General's Office in the preparation of the government's amicus curiae brief in *Brown v. Board of Education* (1954). The office is usually involved in any case before the Supreme Court that has a significant constitutional issue.

The President has consistently called upon the Attorney General and the Office of Legal Counsel for advice and assistance in times of crises. The opinion advising Franklin D. Roosevelt that he could enter into lend-lease arrangements with Great Britain, prior to entry of the United States into WORLD WAR II, was prepared by the Assistant Solicitor General. It was the Office of Legal Counsel that advised President Dwight D. Eisenhower he had the authority to employ troops to ensure the safe desegregation of schools during the LITTLE ROCK CRISIS. President John F. Kennedy called upon the office, as well as the Department of State, for advice on the appropriate response to the CUBAN MISSILE CRISIS. The office has long advised Presidents regarding claims of EXECUTIVE PRIVILEGE vis-à-vis Congress. The necessary proclamations and orders to impose sanctions on Iran, during the IRANIAN HOSTAGE CRISIS, were prepared by the office, and it later assisted the Attorney General in his legal arguments at the International Court of Justice on Iranian claims.

The Attorney General regularly calls upon the office to provide advice to the President that is fully candid. This advice may range from detailed recommendations on specific conflict-of-interest or other ethics issues to matters of great constitutional import. In 1973 Attorney General Elliot Richardson commissioned the office to conduct an impartial and extensive study of the law of presidential IMPEACHMENT, which was furnished to the President in 1974 and subsequently made public. President Jimmy Carter received from Attorney General Griffin Bell an opinion notifying him that his campaign promise to remove the Department of Justice from political influence by having the Attorney General appointed for a fixed term of years and removable by the President only for specific cause was unconstitutional.

When constitutional issues are pending in Congress the Office of Legal Counsel is called upon to prepare testimony, to furnish legislative analysis, and, occasionally, to testify. It provides the legal analysis on claims of executive privilege and other matters related to the separation of powers doctrine. Attorney General ROBERT F. KENNEDY's testimony on the constitutional underpinnings of the CIVIL RIGHTS ACT OF 1964 was prepared by the OLC. Testimony opposing the WAR POWERS RESOLUTION (1973) as unconstitutional and challenging constraints on the President's authority to collect intelligence and conduct foreign affairs is prepared by, or reviewed by, the office.

While the extent to which the OLC provides routine advice to the President has varied with the closeness of the Attorney General to the President and the size and preferences of the WHITE HOUSE COUNSEL's Office, major issues of EXECUTIVE PREROGATIVE and power have always been the unique responsibility of that office.

BIBLIOGRAPHY

Bell, Griffin B., with Ronald J. Ostrow. *Taking Care of the Law.* 1982.
Cummings, Homer Stille, and Carl McFarland. *Federal Justice.* 1937.
Department of Justice. *200th Anniversary of the Office of the Attorney General: 1789–1989.* 1991.
Houston, Luther A. *The Department of Justice.* 1967.
Meador, Daniel J. *The President, the Attorney General, and the Department of Justice.* 1980.

MARY C. LAWTON

OFFICE OF MANAGEMENT AND BUDGET (OMB). Responsible for advising the President on governmentwide budget and management policies, the Office of Management and Budget is generally regarded as the most institutionalized and powerful of the units in the EXECUTIVE OFFICE OF THE PRESIDENT (EOP). This prominence does not arise simply by serving the President with what is by White House and EOP standards a uniquely large and professional staff. The President's budget office is powerful because it manages a decision-making process of inescapable importance to so many people—the executive budget.

Origins. The lineage of OMB dates back to the beginning of the twentieth century. At that time federal and state government bureaus went directly to legislative committees for funds. A major plank in the Progressive reform platform was to change this process to require a unified executive budget put together by a chief executive (mayor, city manager, governor, or president) and presented as a coordinated whole for legislative consideration. In the federal govern-

Directors of Management and Budget

President	Director of Management and Budget
29 Harding	Charles E. Dawes, 1921–1922 Herbert M. Lard, 1922–1923
30 Coolidge	Herbert M. Lard, 1923–1929
31 Hoover	J. Clawson Roop, 1929–1933
32 F. D. Roosevelt	Lewis W. Douglas, 1933–1934 Daniel W. Bell, 1934–1939 Harold D. Smith, 1939–1945
33 Truman	Harold D. Smith, 1945–1946 James E. Webb, 1946–1949 Frank Pace, 1949–1950 Frederick J. Lawson, 1950–1953
34 Eisenhower	Joseph M. Dodge, 1953–1954 Rowland R. Hughes, 1954–1956 Percival F. Brundage, 1956–1958 Maurice H. Stans, 1958–1961
35 Kennedy	David E. Bell, 1961–1962 Kermit Gordon, 1962–1963
36 L. B. Johnson	Kermit Gordon, 1963–1965 Charles L. Schulze, 1965–1968 Charles J. Zwick, 1968–1969
37 Nixon	Robert P. Mayo, 1969–1970 George P. Shultz, 1970–1972 Caspar W. Weinberger, 1972–1973 Roy L. Ash, 1973–1974
38 Ford	Roy L. Ash, 1974–1975 James T. Lynn, 1975–1977
39 Carter	Thomas Bertram Lance, 1977 James T. McIntyre, Jr., 1977–1981
40 Reagan	David Stockman, 1981–1985 James C. Miller III, 1985–1988
41 Bush	Richard G. Darman, 1989–1993
42 Clinton	Leon E. Panetta, 1993–1994 Alice M. Rivlin, 1994–

ment, this movement resulted in the BUDGET AND ACCOUNTING ACT of 1921 and the creation of the Bureau of the Budget (BOB), which was renamed the Office of Management and Budget in 1970. Though located in the Treasury Department, BOB was directly responsible to the President. This 1921 reform was aimed, however, not so much at augmenting presidential power as at recognizing the inability of a pluralistic Congress to produce a coordinated budget without executive leadership. The bureau was to be nonpolitical and focused on economy and efficiency in government operations. The orienting idea was that by helping the President prepare and execute a single executive-branch budget, the professional budget staff would enhance the power of Congress to effect its will. As CHARLES G. DAWES, the first budget director, put it in 1923:

We have nothing to do with policy. Much as we love the President, if Congress in its omnipotence over appropriations and in accordance with its authority over policy passed a law that garbage should be put on the White House steps, it would be our regrettable duty, as a bureau, in an impartial, nonpolitical and nonpartisan way to advise the Executive and Congress as to how the largest amount of garbage could be spread in the most expeditious and economical manner.

The shift toward the bureau's becoming a more strictly presidential agency began in the 1930s. In 1939, President Franklin D. Roosevelt transferred the BOB to the newly created EOP. Under Directors Harold Smith (1939–1946) and James Webb (1946–1949) the bureau developed a strong esprit de corps as the main institutional arm of the presidency composed almost entirely of career civil servants. Bureau personnel in the Administrative Management Division played a major role in the organization of emergency during WORLD WAR II and the postwar implementation of the MARSHALL PLAN. From the 1930s and beyond, the bureau's Legislative Reference Division grew to become the center for determining whether or not agencies' legislative proposals were in accord with the President's program. Throughout all this history, the heart of the bureau's activity lay with its budget examiners and the detailed knowledge about programs, organizations, and people that they gained through the annual examination of all agency spending requests.

The 1960s saw the Bureau of the Budget increasingly cross-pressured between its self-conception as the institutional source of presidential advice and executive leadership, on the one hand, and demands for more immediate responsiveness to aggressive policy leadership from the White House, on the other. In seeking new ideas and quick action, John F. Kennedy and especially Lyndon Baines Johnson often bypassed the BOB in developing their NEW FRONTIER and GREAT SOCIETY programs. Distrusting the federal bureaucracy and the CIVIL SERVICE, Richard M. Nixon sought to increase presidential control over governmentwide policy management and in 1970 adopted the recommendations of the ASH COUNCIL. Under Reorganization Plan No. 2, the Bureau of the Budget was reorganized to highlight presidential management concerns and renamed the Office of Management and Budget. Since then a variety of management initiatives have occurred under different administrations, but budgeting remains the core of the OMB's power and usefulness to the President.

Organization. The Director and Deputy Director of OMB are presidential appointees subject to Senate confirmation; the Director serves as a member of the

Cabinet. Since 1970 the Director has generally functioned not only as head of the budget agency but also as a personal political adviser to the President. New positions have also been created since 1970 to give political appointees the leadership positions for managing OMB and representing its views to the outside world. In 1964 there were three noncareer positions in .BOB below the Deputy Director level and none in line-supervisory positions; by 1992 there were about forty political appointees, of whom about fifteen had supervisory responsibility over the various operating divisions (whose staffs are mainly composed of career civil servants).

Throughout the postwar period the BOB/OMB maintained its staff size at roughly five hundred to six hundred people, with the large majority devoted to various aspects of the budget-making process. Budget examiners are the backbone of the organization; they are grouped in four broad program divisions: National Security and International Affairs; Human Resources, Veterans, and Labor; Natural Resources, Energy, and Science; and Economics and Government. The subdivisions, or branches, of these four groups review the proposed budgets and their execution for each of the departments and agencies of the executive branch. A separate Budget Review Division analyzes and keeps track of the budget numbers as a whole while it develops procedures for formulating and presenting the budget.

Since 1970 the OMB staff concerned with federal management issues have successively been separated, merged, reseparated and then remerged with the budget branches. As of 1992 a separate Management Office was responsible for reorganization and management-improvement initiatives. During the administrations of Ronald Reagan and George Bush, the Management Office's size varied from about thirty-five to about seventy persons. The OMB's management activities were supplemented in 1974 with the statutory establishment of the Office of Federal Procurement Policy and in 1980 with the Office of Information and Regulatory Affairs.

The Legislative Reference Division screens executive agencies' submissions to Congress through a process known as legislative clearance. Every department's communication to Congress on proposed legislation, testimony, and reports on pending bills must be cleared through OMB. Communications thought to conflict with important aspects of the President's program will not be cleared. Proposed legislation that is cleared carries an OMB cover statement expressing the degree of presidential support. (In descending order of support, the proposed bill

may be "in accord with the President's program," or "consistent with the Administration's objectives" or cleared with "no objection.") Likewise, any pending legislation in conflict with the President's program will, when it is taken up in the House or Senate, receive an OMB statement listing the administration's objections and signaling a possible veto. For passed legislation, the Legislative Reference Division compiles the views of affected agencies, and OMB sends its recommendation to sign or veto to the President.

In addition to these units, a cluster of offices provides staff support to OMB's Director. The General Counsel handles the fifteen to twenty-five lawsuits in which OMB is involved at any one time, as well as coordinating the issuance of EXECUTIVE ORDERS and PROCLAMATIONS by the President. A Legislative Affairs staff—in operation since the late 1970s—helps the Director lobby Congress on behalf of the President's budget program. The Office of Economic Policy provides short- and long-range economic forecasts to help guide budget negotiations, assesses the effects of tax proposals, and conducts special economic analyses of various issues. Offices for public relations and for internal administration round out the OMB organization chart.

Developments in the 1980s and 1990s. Important changes occurred in OMB's operations in the 1980s. In part, these were a function of the personalities involved. Presidents Reagan and Bush seemed to care little about the agency's work except for its ability to reduce domestic spending and regulation. Directors David Stockman, James Miller, and Richard Darman responded vigorously, using the budget agency to push that agenda publicly. But changes at OMB reflected a deeper shift in the political context that went beyond questions of personality. That shift had to do with a growing concern over total government spending levels and mounting deficits. To deal with those concerns, OMB's changes expressed the fact that the budget process was an increasingly interactive and continuous bargaining process between the President and Congress, where the emphasis was on spending totals and not the details of agency programs.

Prior to the Reagan and Bush years, BOB and OMB operated according to what might be termed a modified, bottom-up budget process. The President, in making budget decisions, largely worked from spending requests put forward by the agencies. This process was combined, with broad economic guidelines that were established in the budget agency's spring preview. In this spring stage, estimates of the fiscal policy requirements for managing the economy, agency spending demands, and estimates of likely revenues were brought together by OMB staff to provide general spending ceilings to guide agency budget requests. These requests began to come in during the late summer and early fall. During the fall, OMB staff held hearings with the agencies and examined their proposed budgets in detail. At the end of this process, the Director's Review scrutinized the agency requests and the recommendations of his budget staff and settled on the figures to be proposed to the President. The recommended ("mark" or "passback") funding levels were also given to the agencies. Finally, in December or so, any agency appeals were made to the President and he decided any major outstanding issues. The President's budget proposals were then presented to the various committees of Congress as their starting point to determine the funding for the particular agencies under their jurisdiction. The annual repetition of this cycle gave spending agencies a predictable idea of what their resources would be a year in advance and gave the President's budget staff (after the hectic pace of fall budget reviews) time to pay field visits, read the policy literature, and otherwise delve into the substance of agency programs.

While these stages formally remained in place, much else began to change in the 1970s. As U.S. economic performance deteriorated and federal spending grew, the Budget Impoundment and Control Act of 1974 placed new emphasis on aggregate budget ceilings and on reconciling these totals with projected revenues. New congressional reporting deadlines on these totals were added to OMB's work load. At the end of the Jimmy Carter administration, worries in financial markets about the proposed deficit (then $16 billion) led the President quickly to withdraw what was to have been his final budget and to negotiate a new budget with congressional leaders so as to produce a more acceptable bottom line on total spending and the deficit. The bureau, through Director James T. McIntyre, Jr., and an enlarged congressional liaison staff, played a central role in these then novel negotiations.

These early changes were dramatically reinforced and amplified in the Reagan and Bush administrations. In the first place, budgeting became more of a top-down process in that the focus of most decision making—ranging from the Director's and White House's overall strategy to the work of individual budget examiners—was on aggregate spending levels. Much more attention was devoted to using the budget to attain a preferred, limited spending sum rather than to determining how the budget funded agency operations or related to their programs' merits.

Secondly, OMB staff were routinely and heavily involved in negotiating and advocating the White House budgetary position throughout all stages of the legislative process. Bills with budgetary implications were closely tracked by OMB personnel through the multiple phases of the congressional budget process. A sophisticated computer routine (the Central Budget Management System) kept score of the projected spending results as bills wended their way through Congress and as executive-legislative bargains were made and remade.

Finally, the annual budget cycle, with its neat stages, was overlaid with an OMB budget-making process that was virtually continuous. It could hardly have been otherwise, given the constant rounds of negotiations with Congress, the frequently changing signals on the state of the economy, and the ongoing reactions of the financial community to budget deals and projections. In this setting the OMB's role provided little of the predictability for agencies that it once had. Neither was there an annual rhythm that allowed budget examiners the luxury of in-depth policy and program analysis. (Their compensation was that the Director's key position in setting the overall political strategy for the Administration and its dealings with Congress added luster to their work at OMB.)

In addition to these changes, OMB has gained important powers over federal regulatory activities. Regulations have little direct impact on the budget, but they can impose significant costs elsewhere in society. The 1980 PAPERWORK REDUCTION ACT established the OFFICE OF INFORMATION AND REGULATORY AFFAIRS (OIRA) within OMB. In 1981 President Reagan through EXECUTIVE ORDER 12291 expanded the office's mandate to include review of proposed federal regulations. Thus, OIRA not only oversaw and decided on government paperwork requirements (such as reports and information forms) placed on the public, but it was also charged with reviewing each proposed government regulation and requiring agencies to show that the benefits of a regulation exceeded its costs. In response, advocacy groups increasingly used the courts to challenge OMB reviews that delayed the promulgation of particularly controversial regulations. Congress also responded by inventing new procedures that can bypass OMB and force agencies to issue timely regulations.

Enduring Debates. Certain controversies have been a perennial feature of OMB's existence. One such debate has to do with the role of a budget agency in determining management policy. Some have argued that efforts to improve governmentwide management are inevitably shortchanged and distorted by an organization that is preoccupied with the budget. In this view, management advice to the President should, at a minimum, be organized separately within OMB and, at best, be vested in a separate EOP unit or merged with the OFFICE OF PERSONNEL MANAGEMENT (OPM). Defenders contend that OMB's control of the budget process can give powerful leverage to management improvement efforts. They argue that, with the carrots and sticks available through this government-wide, action-forcing process, management initiatives have a hope of being taken seriously. Regardless of one's view of this debate, what does seem clear is that since the 1940s management improvement has been interpreted to mean centralized pressure to achieve economy rather than advice and support to help agency managers accomplish their statutory missions.

A related, long-standing debate concerns OMB's role in the budget process itself. Those mainly interested in the content of policies have warned against the tendency of the President's budget agency to become exclusively concerned with narrow concepts of economy and efficiency ("bean counting"). They contend that without detailed knowledge of agency programs and the effects of funding changes on agency operations, OMB staff will fail to offer the sitting President the deep and broad advice required or to build up the intellectual capital for advising his successor. Opponents argue that under late-twentieth-century circumstances it is only realistic for OMB to be primarily concerned with the implications of programs for the size of government, spending totals, and potential deficits. Given the immense time constraints and the need to be directly responsive to the President's central political concerns, leisurely program analysis is said to be a thing of the past for OMB.

Far and away the most prominent controversy is the question of OMB's alleged politicization. As noted earlier, leadership throughout the budget agency has become centered in the hands of temporary political appointees. Nor is there any doubt that since 1970, at an accelerating pace, OMB and its leaders have become much more politically visible in lobbying Congress, advising on political strategy in White House councils, and serving as public advocates of the President's agenda. When latter-day OMB staff invoke the agency's lore and refer to the Dawes quotation at the beginning of this article, they typically misremember it to say that OMB must smartly respond to the President's (rather than Congress's) demand that garbage be dumped on the White House steps.

Thus critics contend that on a variety of counts, OMB's growing political prominence and clout actually weaken it as an institution of the presidency. First,

this political visibility and advocacy are said to weaken OMB's credibility as a nonpartisan, impartial source of information and analysis. Since 1980, OMB's periodic use of dubious economic projections favorable to presidential promises on deficit reduction and other budget developments has reinforced those concerns. It has also strengthened the credibility of estimates issuing from the Congressional Budget Office, which contain less political "spin." Second, critics worry that a concern to be responsive to a President's immediate political needs may fail to produce the full range of critical, though loyal, advice that a President should hear. Third, they contend that by becoming so identified with advocating a particular White House political agenda, the OMB may become suspect to successor administrations, thus harming continuity and reducing institutional memory for the presidency over time. Finally, one line of argument sees the OMB's growing political role as a dangerous contribution to nonconstitutional, exclusive presidential rule, both in the public eye and within an executive branch that, after all, derives its statutory missions from Congress, not the President.

There are also strong arguments on the other side. One is that trends toward management and budget centralization and politicization simply reflect the incongruence between growing expectations on Presidents to produce results and their difficulty in meeting these expectations within the United States' system of fragmented powers. Another argument is that, in an era of heightened concern over public spending, deficits, and governmental interference in the American economy and society, the President needs OMB's help in responding to those concerns. This view would have the OMB develop a stronger profile as the advocate and negotiator of the President's political position or have it fade into the background. A faded OMB is of little use to current or future Presidents. These debates are important because the fate of OMB says much about the changing nature of the Presidency and thus of American government itself.

BIBLIOGRAPHY

Berman, Larry. *The Office of Management and Budget 1921–1979.* 1979.

Heclo, Hugh. "Executive Budget Making." In *Federal Budget Policy in the 1980s.* Edited by Gregory B. Mills and John L. Palmer. 1984.

Heclo, Hugh. "OMB and the Presidency—The Problem of Neutral Competence." *The Public Interest* 38 (1975): 80–98.

Johnson, Bruce. "From Analyst to Negotiator: The OMB's New Role." *Journal of Policy Analysis and Management* 3 (1984): 501–515.

Moe, Terry. "The Politicized Presidency." In *The New Direction in American Politics.* Edited by John E. Chubb and Paul E. Peterson. 1985.

Pfiffner, James P. "OMB: Professionalism, Politicization, and the Presidency." In *Executive Leadership in Anglo-American Systems.* Edited by Colin Campbell, S.J., and Margaret Jane Wyszomirski. 1992.

U.S. Senate. Committee on Governmental Affairs. *OMB: Evolving Roles and Future Issues.* Hearings. 100th Cong., 1st sess., 1986.

Wildavsky, Aaron. *The New Politics of the Budgetary Process.* 1988.

HUGH HECLO

OFFICE OF PERSONNEL MANAGEMENT (OPM). Reorganization Plan No. 2, which accompanied the passage of the CIVIL SERVICE REFORM ACT (CSRA) OF 1978, created the Office of Personnel Management. The act and reorganization plan were the first major overhaul of the federal personnel management system since its creation by the CIVIL SERVICE ACT of 1883 (Pendleton Act) that established the Civil Service Commission (CSC).

The commission was established as a bipartisan commission whose three members would manage and oversee the newly established CIVIL SERVICE merit system. The Pendleton Act provided that hiring for the government would be open to all and based on merit as determined by competitive examinations. It prohibited the making of personnel decisions on the basis of partisan political factors. Civil servants could thus only be fired for reasons relating to job performance. Over the next century, as more protections against political abuse were added to CSC rules and regulations, some criticized the commission for making the personnel function cumbersome and for not being responsive enough to new needs of the government and the federal workforce. The reaction against the cumulative rules that protected federal workers contributed to passage of the 1978 CSRA.

Many personnel specialists also thought that the CSC had centralized personnel recruiting and hiring too tightly. They felt that many CSC classifications were out of date and that delays in hiring caused departments and agencies to lose good job candidates who got better offers while waiting to hear from the government.

One of the major problems with the CSC lay in its conflicting functions. The commission was responsible both for providing the leadership of the executive-branch workforce and for protecting the merit system. The conflict between the two roles was personified in the chairman of the commission, who at times served as a primary adviser to the President on personnel matters while simultaneously overseeing the civil service for possible abuse of executive political power. Though no personal impropriety was alleged, the role

conflict was evident during the administration of Dwight D. Eisenhower, when Philip Young was Chairman of the CSC and at the same time was invited to Cabinet meetings and held the title of Presidential Adviser on Personnel Management. A similar potential conflict of roles was evident when John Macy was Lyndon Baines Johnson's primary staffer on presidential personnel appointments at the same time that he chaired the CSC.

When the CSC was abolished in 1978 its functions were divided among several new organizations. Most of the functions were inherited by the new Office of Personnel Management, but the watchdog function of protecting the merit system from abuse was transferred to the new MERIT SYSTEMS PROTECTION BOARD (MSPB) and to the Office of Special Counsel, a semi-independent organization within the MSPB. Two other organizations took over some CSC responsibilities: the Federal Labor Relations Authority (FLRA) took over the functions of the Federal Labor Relations Council, and the Equal Employment Opportunity Commission (EEOC) took over most of the CSC's equal employment opportunity responsibilities.

One of the purposes of the 1978 act was to make the personnel function more responsive to executive leadership. The premise was that agency personnel directors had been too insulated from agency heads and had sometimes been more concerned with abiding by the rules of the merit system than with accomplishing agency missions. Thus the structure of the personnel agency was changed from a bipartisan commission, which is necessarily semi-independent of the President, to an agency with one director reporting directly to the President. The director of OPM, as an Executive Level II presidential appointee, would now be the primary adviser to the President on personnel management matters. The new law did, however, prohibit the OPM director from being the President's political recruiter.

Besides making the personnel function more responsive to political leadership, the framers of the CSRA intended that personnel testing and recruiting would be decentralized to the agency level. The expectation was that tests could be tailor-made for each agency's special needs and that the agencies could move more quickly in hiring than the centralized CSC system. The role of OPM would primarily be to serve as an expert consultant to help agencies with their personnel systems and to monitor the general integrity of agency personnel systems.

The first OPM director, appointed by President Jimmy Carter, was Alan K. Campbell, who had been Chairman of the Civil Service Commission and Carter's main lobbyist on Capitol Hill in getting the CSRA passed. The first mission of the new OPM was to ensure that the CSRA was implemented throughout the government.

The OPM leadership intended the new agency's role to change from the CSC's twin role of overseer and enforcer of the merit system to one of actively assisting other agencies. Along with the new role came the decision to delegate many of the former CSC's functions—particularly recruitment, examination, and staffing—to individual agencies rather than keeping them in the central personnel agency. The OPM was also charged with the implementation of other provisions of the CSRA, including performance appraisal systems, merit pay, and the newly created SENIOR EXECUTIVE SERVICE (SES).

With the election of President Ronald Reagan and his appointment of Donald Devine to be director of OPM came a reorientation of the agency's mission. The previous effort to decentralize personnel powers was reversed. Devine led the OPM to concentrate on personnel fundamentals, and OPM began to recentralize control of personnel actions for the federal government. This was in line with the Reagan administration's intention to reduce federal employment on the domestic side of the government by attrition and by reductions in the workforce throughout the domestic agencies. During the early 1980s Devine reorganized OPM several times as funding for the agency was cut by 45 percent and personnel levels were reduced by 54 percent.

Devine was not renominated for a second term as OPM director, and Reagan replaced him with Constance Horner. In 1989 President George Bush appointed Constance B. Newman to direct the agency. Newman returned OPM to the task of delegating personnel functions to agencies and revitalizing federal recruitment. The OPM also moved to take federal leadership in research on productivity improvement and worker motivation.

BIBLIOGRAPHY

Ingraham, Patricia W., and Carolyn Ban. *Legislating Bureaucratic Change: The Civil Service Reform Act of 1978.* 1984.

U.S. General Accounting Office. *Managing Human Resources: Greater OPM Leadership Needed to Address Critical Challenges.* 1989.

U.S. Merit Systems Protection Board. *U.S. Office of Personnel Management and the Merit System: A Retrospective Assessment.* 1989.

JAMES P. PFIFFNER

OFFICE OF POLICY DEVELOPMENT (OPD).

Since Herbert Hoover, Presidents have established units to help them deal specifically with domestic policy. The Office of Policy Development, one link in this chain of devices for coordinating domestic policy, was created by President Ronald Reagan in 1981.

Hoover was the first President to recognize the need for coordinated domestic policy advice in the White House, and in 1929 he formed the Committee on Social Trends. This committee included economists, sociologists, and political scientists and was charged with assessing social change and development in all domestic policy areas.

The work of President Hoover's committee served as a precedent for Franklin D. Roosevelt's National Emergency Council and National Resources Planning Board as well as Dwight D. Eisenhower's Commission on National Goals. Presidents have also turned to White House assistants and experts for ad hoc domestic policy advice and assistance. Presidents Lyndon B. Johnson and Richard M. Nixon assembled issue-specific task forces for domestic policy advice. Such temporary measures proved ineffective, however, for ongoing policy development, coordination, and planning across the broad scope of domestic issues.

The Domestic Council. In 1970, Nixon created the Domestic Council (DC) in the EXECUTIVE OFFICE OF THE PRESIDENT (EOP) by Executive Order 11541, pursuant to Reorganization Plan No. 2 of 1970. It was charged with advising the President on all aspects of domestic policy and with integrating policy into a coherent whole. The DC was a two-tiered organization. The first tier, the council, was chaired by the President; its membership included the VICE PRESIDENT, the ATTORNEY GENERAL, and secretaries of CABINET departments involved in domestic policy issues. The second tier consisted of a support staff under the direction of the Assistant to the President for Domestic Affairs. John D. Ehrlichman, the first person named to this position, served from 1970 until his implication in the WATERGATE AFFAIR prompted his resignation in December 1972.

The formal role of the DC staff was to coordinate domestic policy and to follow up on the decisions of the council and the President. In practice, however, Nixon delegated to the DC staff substantial policy-making power and de facto ability to oversee and direct the performance of department and agency executives. Policy formulation and advice were coordinated through a set of issue-oriented committees. Each committee was chaired by a member of the DC staff and included representatives of relevant executive departments and agencies, who examined and recommended possible courses of administrative action. The DC staff and the Assistant for Domestic Policy himself were policy generalists, drawing on the knowledge of

Directors of Policy Development

President	Director, Office of Policy Development
37 Nixon	John D. Ehrlichman, 1970–1973
	Kenneth R. Cole, Jr., 1973–1974
38 Ford	Kenneth R. Cole, Jr., 1974–1975
	James M. Cannon, 1975–1977
39 Carter	Stuart E. Eizenstat, 1977–1981
40 Reagan	Martin Anderson, 1981–1982
	Edwin L. Harper, 1982–1983
	John A. Svahn, 1983–1986
	Gary L. Bauer, 1987–1988
	Franmarie Kennedy-Peel, 1988–1989
41 Bush	Roger B. Porter, 1989–1993
42 Clinton	Carol Rasco, 1993–

experts in the various branches to develop targeted policy information. As the DC evolved, its staff grew quickly, reaching a high of sixty in 1972.

In practice, the DC isolated Cabinet heads from the President and insulated Nixon from most interagency debate on domestic policy issues. As a result, considerable domestic policy power came to reside in the White House Assistant for Domestic Affairs. In turn, the Domestic Council's effectiveness was dependent on the assistant's access to and influence with the President.

Under President Gerald Ford, two important changes were made to the council's organization. First, the Vice President was named vice chairman of the council and given authority for the direction of the staff. This change reflected the extensive domestic policy experience of Vice President NELSON A. ROCKEFELLER. The delay in Rockefeller's confirmation as Vice President, however, allowed the development of other White House domestic policy mechanisms, which hindered Rockefeller's ability to fully realize the potential of this arrangement. Second, President Ford called for a renewed emphasis on policy planning and, to further this, divided the responsibilities for long-term and day-to-day planning between two deputy directors of the DC. Despite these changes, the DC's staff size dropped precipitously, from sixty in 1972 to a low of fifteen in 1975, as the domestic policy unit failed to find a stable role in the Ford's administration.

Carter's Reorganization. In 1977, the DC was one of the first agencies President Jimmy Carter reorganized via Reorganization Plan No. 1. Although the agency maintained its mission to manage the process that coordinated the making of domestic policy and its integration with economic policy, its structure was changed. The council-level tier was abolished, and the remaining (formerly second) tier was renamed the Domestic Policy Staff (DPS) and placed under the direction of the Assistant to the President for Domestic Affairs and Policy. DPS's role, as set out by Domestic Policy Assistant Stuart Eizenstadt, was to coordinate the presentation of views to the President rather than to screen advice from the Cabinet or other agencies. The DPS focused on advice and analysis functions in a multiphase policy coordination process that ranged from formulation to strategic planning for legislative enactment but that avoided involvement in the implementation of policy.

The DPS developed a stable staff of between forty and fifty people and an organizational structure that allowed staff members to develop substantive expertise in assigned issue areas. Director Eizenstadt had both domestic policy experience (having served as a speechwriter for Johnson, research director for the campaign of HUBERT H. HUMPHREY, and issues director for the Carter campaign) and the respect of the President and the Cabinet. He was able to serve as an honest broker between the players, representing the opinions of each to the other while also exercising an advisory role by assessing information as it passed his way.

The DPS brought together representatives from various agencies concerned with given issues areas to form interagency task forces that examined and analyzed policy options. The DPS took an active, although not always leading, role in each of these committees and coordinated their findings for presentation to President Carter. This approach enabled the DPS to play an important role as an administrator and adviser to the President.

Reagan's System. In 1981, President Reagan again reorganized the function of the domestic policy unit, renaming it the Office of Policy Development. Consistent with his declared preference for Cabinet government, President Reagan's domestic policy system aimed at fully involving department and agency heads through a system of CABINET COUNCILS. Five such councils, organized along functional lines, were originally established, each chaired by the President or, in his absence, by the Cabinet secretary who was designated as chairman pro tempore. At first, the frequent council meetings were regularly attended by six to ten Cabinet members, the Vice President, and members of the senior White House staff.

In association with two other EOP offices, the newly formed Office of Cabinet Administration (OCA) and Office of Planning and Evaluation (OPE), OPD was cast in a supporting administrative role to the councils. The OCA was charged with the task of assigning and

OFFICE OF PRESIDENTIAL PERSONNEL (OPP)   1117

tracking issues, while OPE helped on strategic planning activities; both offices reported directly to presidential counselor EDWIN MEESE III. OPD provided staff to the Cabinet councils as well as to OCA and OPE, leaving OPD itself with depleted staff resources and shifting staff assignments. Furthermore, while OPD was headed by the Assistant to the President for Domestic Policy, he did not have direct access to President Reagan but was forced to relay information through Meese. The influence of OPD was further weakened by the frequent turnover of domestic policy assistants: Martin Anderson (1980–1982), Edwin Harper (1982–1983), John Svahn (1983–1987), Gary Bauer (1987–1988), and Franmarie Kennedy-Keel (1988–1989). None of these had the access or stature of an Ehrlichman or an Eizenstadt.

During the Reagan years, other EOP units preempted aspects of the role OPD might have played in domestic affairs. OFFICE OF MANAGEMENT AND BUDGET director David Stockman was a driving intellectual force behind the domestic policy agenda of the Reagan administration, capitalizing on both the organizational resources of OMB and his close relationship with the President. Meanwhile, political advice on policy initiation was coordinated by the WHITE HOUSE CHIEF OF STAFF, JAMES A. BAKER III, through his legislative strategy council. During the second Reagan administration, Chief of Staff DONALD REGAN centralized White House power in his office, thus effectively distancing OPD from the President.

Throughout the Reagan administration, the President's commitment to Cabinet government, his conservative policy agenda, the rapid personnel turnover at OPD, and competition from other executive units limited the office's ability to play a strong role in domestic policy development, formulation, or coordination.

President George Bush continued Reagan's pattern of reliance on Cabinet officials while also assembling a team of trusted policy advisers in the White House. This team included Roger Porter, an alumnus of the Ford and Reagan policy teams, who was given the title of Assistant for Economic and Domestic Policy and, in coordination with OMB director Richard Darman, became the primary White House domestic policy adviser to Bush throughout his presidency.

Porter delegated the direction of OPD to his deputy, William Roper, a former administrator of health care financing at the Department of Health and Human Services. Although Roper took a lead role on policy in a number of health-care issues, the office was generally relegated to a supporting role in the domestic-policy hierarchy of the Bush administration, behind Porter, Darman, and domestically oriented Cabinet councils such as the Domestic Policy Council and the Economic Policy Council.

Roper was succeeded as Deputy Assistant in 1990 by Charles E. M. Kolb, a former deputy undersecretary for planning, budget, and evaluation at the DEPARTMENT OF EDUCATION. In the last year of the Bush administration, Porter took over the directorship of OPD, adding this job to his duties as domestic and economic policy assistant.

Clinton's Focus. As of April 1993, the future of the OPD under President Bill Clinton was unclear. On the positive side, the administration had an electoral mandate for action on domestic issues and the new Assistant for Domestic Policy, Carol Rasco, was a longtime Clinton aide and domestic policy adviser. However, initially, the President used a number of other administrative devices to address particular domestic policy issues. In the instance of health care reform, HILLARY RODHAM CLINTON and senior White House aide Ira Magaziner head a task force to formulate policy. In other cases, economic considerations led to the prominence of various economic policy units such as the COUNCIL OF ECONOMIC ADVISERS, the new NATIONAL ECONOMIC COUNCIL, the Office of Management and Budget, and the DEPARTMENT OF THE TREASURY. These initial policy-development experiences seemed to indicate that OPD would have considerable competition in the domestic policy realm.

Burke, John. *The Institutional Presidency*. 1992.
Cronin, Thomas E. *Presidents and Domestic Policy Advice*. 1975.
Hart, John. *The Presidential Branch*. 1987.
Wyszomirski, Margaret Jane. "The Roles of a Presidential Office of Domestic Policy: Three Models and Four Cases." In *The Presidency and Public Policy Making*. Edited by George Edwards III, Steven Shull, and Norman Thomas. 1985.

MARGARET JANE WYSZOMIRSKI

OFFICE OF PRESIDENTIAL PERSONNEL (OPP). The story of the Office of Presidential Personnel has been one of increasing size, greater professionalism, and more centralized control of political appointments in the White House. In the nineteenth century and the first third of the twentieth century, appointments to the executive branch were dominated by the political parties. But with Franklin D. Roosevelt and the beginning of the modern presidency the function of political recruitment slowly began to be taken over by the White House. The Roosevelt administration provided the beginnings of the modern

White House staff, and the EXECUTIVE OFFICE OF THE PRESIDENT (EOP) was created in 1939. Harry S. Truman was the first President to designate one member of his staff to coordinate all political personnel matters. Dwight D. Eisenhower created the position of Special Assistant to the President for Personnel Management.

John F. Kennedy brought the beginnings of a personnel recruitment system (the talent hunt) to the White House, with a small section for political patronage and another section for searching out administrative talent. Lyndon Baines Johnson brought John Macy to the White House to act as his political personnel adviser in addition to Macy's duties as Chairman of the Civil Service Commission. Macy established a computerized talent bank of two thousand names, a figure that grew to thirty thousand by the end of Johnson's term.

Richard M. Nixon's administration began with a small personnel section, but in 1970 Frederic Malek came to the White House to head the newly created White House Personnel Office (WHPO). He developed a professional executive recruitment capacity and brought in professional private-sector head hunters. In previous administrations, the selection of sub-Cabinet-level appointments, even though they technically are presidential appointments, had often been delegated to departmental secretaries. But Malek effectively centralized control of presidential appointments in the White House and carefully protected presidential prerogatives from patronage pressures from Congress. While the number of White House staffers in the two previous administrations had never exceeded twelve, Malek had more than thirty people working for him, and there were sixty in the WHPO by the end of the administration. Malek created the most sophisticated presidential recruitment operation in the White House up to that time.

President Gerald Ford distinguished his administration from Nixon's by changing the name of the WHPO to the Presidential Personnel Office (PPO) and reducing its size to about thirty-five staffers, who emphasized governmental rather then private-sector recruiting experience. Jimmy Carter began personnel recruitment planning by designating Jack Watson to set up the Talent Inventory Program (TIP) before the election in the summer of 1976. While Watson's team assembled thousands of names, much of that effort was ignored after the election, when Hamilton Jordan, who ran Carter's campaign, dominated the early personnel recruitment efforts of the administration. Carter also reversed the increasing centralization of recruitment of presidential appointees. In accord with his commitment to Cabinet government he delegated the selection of most sub-Cabinet-level appointees to Cabinet secretaries.

President Ronald Reagan assigned preelection planning for personnel recruitment to Pendleton James, a professional private-sector recruiter with experience in the Nixon administration. In a conscious decision to learn from the experience of the Nixon and Carter administrations, the Reagan administration decided to centralize in the White House all recruitment of presidential appointments requiring advice and consent of the Senate (PAS). But in a major depature from precedent they also insisted on White House control of political appointments that are technically agency-head prerogatives—for example, noncareer SENIOR EXECUTIVE SERVICE appointments and SCHEDULE C POSITIONS. As an indicator of the importance attributed to his position, James had the title of Assistant to the President for Presidential Personnel and controlled a staff of approximately one hundred workers in the early years of the administration.

Vice President George Bush designated Chase Untermeyer to begin planning his personnel operation early in his 1988 campaign for the presidency. Bush, however, stipulated that Untermeyer could not recruit any staff or set up an office until after the election so as not to appear too confident or distract attention from the campaign. With the Bush victory in 1988 some expected that many Reagan appointees would stay in their current positions since no large change in policy or direction was indicated in the campaign. But the Bush White House let it be known that it anticipated a 90 percent turnover in political appointees and that Bush loyalists would be running the new administration. Eventually the turnover approached 70 percent in a personnel transition that was more bitter than had been expected.

The presidential appointment process, and thus the work of the Office of Presidential Personnel (OPP), is becoming more elaborate and time-consuming. This is partly due to the increasing number of presidential appointees in key executive-branch positions (with about one thousand presidential appointments requiring Senate confirmation in the executive branch and about two thousand part-time PAS appointments to boards, commissions, and councils) and the increasing scope of White House control of political appointments. But it is also due to the increasingly close scrutiny of potential personnel by the FEDERAL BUREAU OF INVESTIGATION (FBI) as well as to internal political clearances in the White House. These delaying factors are exacerbated by the lengthening time that the Senate takes to confirm nominees (from seven weeks during the Johnson administration to more than fourteen weeks during the Bush administration). The combination of delays makes it difficult for a new administration to hit the ground running.

In addition to the recruitment and placement function, the OPP has in the Reagan and Bush administrations also took on the task of systematically orienting new political appointees to their positions in the federal government. Many new appointees have no federal experience, and the orientation helps to bridge more quickly the gap between the professional context in business, academia, or the law and the much more treacherous environment of a political appointment in the federal government. Congressional relations, press relations, personnel constraints, and rigid ethical strictures are all covered in these orientation sessions.

BIBLIOGRAPHY

Mackenzie, G. Calvin. *The Politics of Presidential Appointments*. 1981.

Mackenzie, G. Calvin, ed. *The In-and-Outers*. 1987.

National Academy of Public Administration, *America's Unelected Government*. 1983.

Patterson, Bradley H., Jr. *The Ring of Power*. 1988.

Pfiffner, James P. *The Strategic Presidency*. 1988.

JAMES P. PFIFFNER

OFFICE OF PRICE ADMINISTRATION (OPA).
Despite the pump-priming programs of the NEW DEAL, the U.S. economy did not fully recover from the Great Depression until it was stimulated by WORLD WAR II. As the probability of U.S. involvement in the war grew, economic advisers to President Franklin D. Roosevelt became concerned about inflation resulting from increased war production. In April 1941, eight months before PEARL HARBOR brought about the formal entry to the United States into the war, the Office of Price Administration was established to address the problem of war-induced inflation and the possibility of rationing.

Inflation occurs when the money supply expands rapidly without a corresponding increase in the goods available, driving up prices without a rise in the quality of goods. Inflation is especially problematic during wartime, since the growth in jobs and income expands the money supply. Much production output, however, is devoted to the war effort and is not available in the consumer economy. Inflationary conditions result, exacerbated by shortages of certain consumer goods due to disruptions in supplies and diversion of materials from consumption to war production.

Rather than using MONETARY POLICY to limit the stock of money in the economy during World War II by aggressively buying up U.S. bonds in the secondary bond markets, the Federal Reserve adopted a passive policy of purchasing bonds at a fixed price. As wartime activities expanded and bank deposits increased, the money supply grew substantially.

Prior to the creation of OPA, Roosevelt's pronouncements about "holding the line" on prices were viewed by Washington insiders as somewhat hypocritical exhortations to control public consumption; they had very little impact. Original planning for defense production was delegated in May 1940 to the National Defense Advisory Council (NDAC), a group headed by William Knudsen, the head of General Motors. The council's membership included private-sector corporate executives and union leaders, among them officials of Sears and Roebuck, U.S. Steel, and Burlington Lines and of the Amalgamated Clothing Workers Union, as well as farm producers. Subsequently, the NDAC was formalized into the Office of Production Management (OPM). An office for price control (initially termed OPACS) was created within NDAC, primarily to encourage voluntary arrangements to limit prices.

Voluntary arrangements to limit prices proved ineffective, however, and OPACS was superseded by OPA. Effective price control by OPA began with the General Maximum Price Regulation of March 1942, which brought many prices under control. Controls were enhanced through an April 1943 order by Roosevelt to implement a general freeze of both wages and prices. Controls continued to be vigorously applied and enforced until June 1946. During this period, controls were effective in curbing inflation, despite substantial money supply increases. Between April 1942, when controls were implemented, and June 1946, when controls were lifted, the money supply grew at an annual rate of 17.25 percent, but wholesale prices during the same period were held to an annual rate of increase of only 3.23 percent. Considerable inflationary pressures, though temporarily suppressed, built up during the period, however, and when controls were removed in 1946, prices rose rapidly, reaching their postwar peak in August 1948. OPA was dismantled when controls were lifted.

BIBLIOGRAPHY

Fehrenbach, T. R., *F.D.R.'s Undeclared War, 1939 to 1941*. 1967.

Keynes, John M., *General Theory of Employment, Interest, and Money*. 1936.

MARCIA LYNN WHICKER

OFFICE OF PUBLIC LIAISON (OPL). One of several WHITE HOUSE STAFF units established to strengthen the President's position with outside coalitions and INTEREST GROUPS, the Office of Public Liaison was created in 1974. The office is one of several aimed at long-range planning and communication. It was used in a variety of ways by Presidents Gerald Ford, Jimmy Carter, Ronald Reagan, and George Bush.

The office was created in response to changes in the political environment of the presidency. The rise of single-issue interest groups brought increasing pressure on Presidents, whose ability to formulate policy was weakened by the decline of party organization. Presidents began to use interest groups as a resource in getting programs adopted by Congress and implemented by the bureaucracy.

Historically, there had been people on the White House staff who were assigned to maintain liaison with groups important to a President's electoral coalition, but until recently those staff members had close ties to the national party committees or were senior staff with many other duties to perform. Their liaison activities were to some extent viewed as electoral duties.

The contemporary Office of Public Liaison represents the central point of contact in the White House for most interest groups. It responds to groups' requests for information and action. The office also initiates action by bringing together people it believes will prove useful to the President as he makes policy. But the office must walk a fine line: the LOBBYING WITH APPROPRIATED MONEY ACT, passed in 1919, prohibits the use of public money for lobbying. Anne Wexler, who headed the liaison office during the Carter administration, explained how they handled the dilemma: "We never ask a person to call a Congressman, [but] we will tell him when a vote is coming up or when a markup is due and give him a lot of information about it. We can say, 'This is the program and the President would like your help and these are the committee members involved.' "

The White House often has limited resources in trying to push legislation through a reluctant Congress, especially when the President and the Congress are controlled by different parties. The President needs interest groups as much as they need him: interest groups offer not only the numerical strength of their membership but also information on potential supporters that the White House can enlist. When President Reagan sought congressional approval of his tax increase proposal in 1982, the Office of Public Liaison, through Wayne Valis, the staffperson assigned to deal with business groups, worked with a steering committee of business organizations. These groups provided information on supporters and potential opponents and also sent mailings to their members. Their members, in turn, urged their Representatives and Senators to pass the legislation.

The idea of having a White House office to develop contacts with outside interest groups originated with President Richard M. Nixon, but the WATERGATE AFFAIR prevented him from formally organizing it. Shortly after Ford became President, he announced the office's creation and appointed William J. Baroody as its first head. Subsequent Presidents have almost uniformly appointed women to head the office; these women have been the highest-ranking women on the White House staff.

The office is organized along the lines of interest-group activity. Staff members have portfolios on specific issues and groups needed for a President's electoral and legislative coalition. The liaison unit emphasizes the interest groups and individuals useful for galvanizing support for a program. At its best, the office proves useful to a President in organizing outside support.

BIBLIOGRAPHY

Kumar, Martha Joynt, and Michael Baruch Grossman. "The Presidency and Interest Groups." In *The Presidency and the Political System*. Edited by Michael Nelson. 1984.

Patterson, Bradley H. *The Ring of Power: The White House Staff and Its Expanding Role in Government*. 1988.

Pika, Joseph. "Interest Groups and the White House under Roosevelt and Truman." *Political Science Quarterly* 102 (1987): 647–668.

MARTHA KUMAR

OFFICE OF SCIENCE AND TECHNOLOGY POLICY (OSTP).

The Office of Science and Technology Policy (OSTP) was formally established in 1976 within the Executive Office of the President (EOP) by the National Science and Technology Policy, Organization, and Priorities Act of 1976 (42 USC 6611). This action marked the most recent incarnation of a White House science and technology unit.

The act provides that "the office shall serve as a source of scientific and technological analysis and judgment for the president with respect to major policies, plans and programs of the Federal Government." The economy, national security, health, foreign relations, and the environment are noted as issue areas in which the OSTP could provide valuable scientific advice to the President.

As early as WORLD WAR II, it was clear that advances in aircraft, weaponry, and radar technology required that science and technology policy be a component of NATIONAL-SECURITY POLICY. The Office of Science Re-

OFFICE OF THE U.S. TRADE REPRESENTATIVE (USTR)   1121

search and Development (OSRD) provided wartime advice and support for science. The OSRD awarded contracts for federal war-related science projects and helped to determine the scope of these projects. During the same period, the Office of Naval Research (ONR) in the Department of the Navy served as a de facto national science foundation, providing contracts for general, rather than directed, research in a variety of disciplines.

In 1950 President Truman moved the ONR function into a separate, congressionally established nonmilitary agency, the National Science Foundation (NSF). The NSF was given two main responsibilities: to support basic scientific research and to act as an adviser in the formulation of a coherent national science policy for the United States.

President Truman also empaneled a Science Advisory Committee in the EOP as part of the Office of Defense Mobilization. Under President Eisenhower, this committee evolved into the Presidential Science Advisory Committee (PSAC), which gained prominence after the launch of Sputnik threatened American technological competitiveness. Eisenhower used the PSAC to provide unbiased, expert opinions on changing technologies in defense and space. The chairman of the PSAC was given the title of Special Adviser to the President on Science and Technology.

The PSAC was part of the White House establishment and, therefore, largely insulated from congressional oversight. President Kennedy changed this on the recommendation of the Senate, in his Reorganization Plan No. 2 of 1962, which created the Office of Science and Technology (OST) in the EOP and transferred the coordination and advisory roles of the NSF to this new office. Although separate from the White House staff, the OST served as SCIENCE ADVISER to the President. The influence of the science adviser on presidential decision making waned during the terms of Presidents Johnson and Nixon. At this time, the focus of science was changing from a national-security emphasis on military and space to more domestic issues involving environmental and social concerns. This meant that science was dealing with politically sensitive issues, rather than predominantly technological ones. In addition, both NASA and the NSF had developed into other sources for science information and advice.

President Nixon's quest for strong administrative control and his tendency to politicize the EOP led to the abolition of the OST in Presidential Reorganization Plan No. 1 of 1973. The advisory function of the OST was combined with that of disburser of federal research grants under the director of the NSF. The abolition of the OST provoked opposition from the scientific community, which argued that scientific advice merited more formal representation in the structure of the Executive Office.

President Ford expressed an interest in changing the presidential science advisory structure and was receptive to recommendations from Congress and from the scientific community concerning the proper function of a new science office. The 1975 legislation establishing the Office of Science and Technology Policy, provided for a single science adviser appointed by the President with the ADVICE AND CONSENT of the Senate, a small staff, and the development of "working relationships" with the OFFICE OF MANAGEMENT AND BUDGET, the National Security Council, and the Domestic Council.

The OSTP, under the terms of this legislation, is housed in the EOP. Its director once again serves as chief policy adviser to the President on science and technology. Four associate directors, responsible for life sciences, industrial technology, policy and international affairs, and physical sciences and engineering, are also appointed by the President, subject to Senate confirmation. The OSTP was originally assigned the responsibility for producing a five-year outlook and annual reports to the President and Congress. In 1977, a portion of this reporting responsibility shifted to the NSF in order to enable the OSTP to focus on advising the President.

In addition, the OSTP coordinates federal research and development efforts and assists the Office of Management and Budget with analysis of funding proposals for research and development in the budgets of all federal agencies. Frank Press, OSTP director under President Carter, also provided advice on appointments to research and development positions.

In 1981 President Reagan considered abolishing the OSTP, but the scientific community and Congress again rallied in support of the office.

Burger, Edward J., Jr. *Science at the White House: A Political Liability.* 1981.
Smith, Bruce L. R. *The Advisers: Scientists in the Policy Process.* 1992.

MARGARET JANE WYSZOMIRSKI

OFFICE OF THE U.S. TRADE REPRESENTATIVE (USTR). Established in January 1980 by President Jimmy Carter, pursuant to a reorganization plan approved by Congress, the Office of the U.S. Trade Representative is responsible for leading the federal government in international trade negotiations and in

United States Trade Representatives

President	United States Trade Representative
35 Kennedy	Christian A. Herter, 1962–1963
36 L. B. Johnson	Christian A. Herter, 1963–1967
	William E. Roth, 1967–1969
37 Nixon	Carl J. Gilbert, 1969–1972
	William D. Eberle, 1972–1974
38 Ford	William D. Eberle, 1974–1975
	Frederick B. Dent, 1975–1977
39 Carter	Robert Strauss, 1977–1979
	Reubin Askew, 1979–1981
40 Reagan	William E. Brock, III, 1981–1985
	Clayton Yeutter, 1985–1989
41 Bush	Carla A. Hills, 1989–1993
42 Clinton	Mickey Kantor, 1993–

TRADE POLICY coordination. Its head, the U.S. Trade Representative, holds both ambassadorial and Cabinet rank.

USTR is the successor to the President's Special Representative for Trade Negotiations (STR), a position created, at congressional insistence, by President John F. Kennedy in 1963. At that time, the United States was about to embark on a major round of trade talks aimed at achieving major reciprocal reductions in tariff barriers, and key Representatives and Senators feared that the State Department, which had previously led such negotiations, would be overly responsive to other nations' needs and insufficiently attentive to the circumstances facing U.S. industry and agriculture. They therefore insisted that the U.S. delegation be led by an official housed in the EXECUTIVE OFFICE OF THE PRESIDENT (EOP) and reporting directly to the President. The STR was responsible for the successful completion of the so-called Kennedy Round in 1967 and helped win congressional authorization for the Tokyo Round of talks of 1973 to 1979 and the enactment of legislation implementing the Tokyo Round agreements.

Originally a small office (about twenty-five professional staff) involved mainly in major multilateral negotiations, STR had by the mid 1970s become the lead U.S. agency for bilateral talks as well. Creation of USTR reinforced this trend. The office's permanent staff was increased in 1980 from 59 to 131 positions (by 1991 the number was 168). Staff tends to be relatively short-term (few officials spend most of their careers there) and not particularly partisan.

USTR plays a unique role as trade policy "broker." Housed in the EOP, it is unusually responsive to congressional concerns, reflecting that branch's con-

stitutional authority to "regulate Commerce . . . with foreign Nations." It also maintains balances between foreign governments and U.S. commercial interests, between American producers that benefit from trade expansion and those that suffer from import competition, and among the several executive branch agencies with strong interests in trade policy—the departments of Commerce, Agriculture, State, and Treasury; the NATIONAL SECURITY COUNCIL; and the COUNCIL OF ECONOMIC ADVISERS. USTR has consistently leaned toward a liberal, barrier-reducing stance. But it has been more pragmatic and more responsive to producer and congressional concerns than have the economic policy agencies, and it has repeatedly negotiated import-restraining arrangements for sensitive products such as automobiles, steel, textiles, and apparel.

The USTR (like its predecessor) has usually benefited from high-quality leadership from Kennedy's trade representative, former Secretary of State Christian Herter to George Bush's USTR, Carla A. Hills. Other effective Trade Representatives have included William Eberle under Richard M. Nixon and Gerald Ford, Robert Strauss under Carter, and William Brock and Clayton Yeutter under Ronald Reagan. As foreign commercial competition grew, the Trade Representative took an increasingly aggressive posture in international negotiations. In the multilateral Uruguay Round (1990s), for example, Hills insisted on substantial reductions in agricultural trade barriers imposed by the European Community, whereas in previous rounds USTRs settled for token concessions.

The USTR also exerted more pressure on other nations to open their markets unilaterally. Trade Representatives from Robert Strauss (in 1977) on have pressed Japan for major steps to reduce its formal and informal barriers to imports. In the 1980s, similar pressure was extended to newly industrialized countries such as Korea, Brazil, Taiwan, Singapore, and Thailand. The purpose was both substantive and political. Easing of these nations' import barriers could (and did) result in greater U.S. exports. This in turn broadened support in the United States for continuation of trade-expanding policies.

Throughout its existence, USTR has given priority to global, multilateral trade arrangements under the GENERAL AGREEMENT ON TARIFFS AND TRADE (GATT). But its pragmatism led the office to seek barrier reduction wherever possible. Hence, when multilateral talks stalemated in the early and mid 1980s, William Brock encouraged development of talks with Canada, resulting in the bilateral free-trade agreement signed and implemented in 1988. During the Bush administration, USTR pushed in both the GATT Uruguay Round and in talks with Mexico and Canada to establish a North American Free Trade Area (NAFTA).

As an operating agency within the President's Executive Office that is particularly responsive to Congress, USTR is an organizational anomaly. This has created problems in transitions between administrations; for example, Reagan counselor EDWIN MEESE III tried to abolish USTR in the name of organizational tidiness. The office has nonetheless flourished because of its congressional base, its key role, and the substantive and political skill of its leadership.

BIBLIOGRAPHY

Destler, I. M. *American Trade Politics.* 2d ed. 1992.
Winham, Gilbert R. *International Trade and the Tokyo Round Negotiation.* 1986.

I. M. DESTLER

OFFICE OF WAR MOBILIZATION (OWM).

Created within the OFFICE FOR EMERGENCY MANAGEMENT (OEM), the Office of War Mobilization was established by Executive Order 9347 of 27 May 1943 to bring about a "more effective coordination of the mobilization of the Nation for war." When WORLD WAR II broke out in Europe in 1939, President Franklin D. Roosevelt, with OEM assistance, sought to exercise personal supervision over American mobilization. By the end of 1942, the first full year of the country's actual involvement in war, Roosevelt realized that, due to other demands, he could not direct the mobilization agencies.

Although many thought that it was too late in the development of the administrative structure for prosecuting the war to superimpose an effective supervisory agency with overall direction of the mobilization effort, the OWM proved to be successful. Headed by JAMES F. BYRNES, a powerful Capitol Hill veteran, former associate justice of the Supreme Court, and recent director of the Office of Economic Stabilization, the OWM coordinated the plans of the war agencies. The agency largely sought to keep out of operations, exerted power by acting only in the name of the President, and adjudicated conflicts as they arose rather than through advanced planning to avoid them.

While Byrnes's OWM appointment was well received in Congress, it did not require Senate approval. It soon became apparent that the OWM director, exercising broad, discretionary powers and located in the East Wing of the White House, not far from the OVAL OFFICE, was, indeed, an "assistant president."

When the opportunity subsequently presented itself, some legislators, desiring to restore the balance of power between Congress and the President, were eager to modify the charter for the OWM and the selection of its leader.

That opportunity came with the issue of postwar demobilization and reconversion of the economy. Congressional interest in these matters was evident with the March 1943 creation of the Senate Special Committee on Postwar Economic Policy and Planning, and the January 1944 establishment of a counterpart panel in the House. Avoiding a repetition of the hasty, unplanned demobilization that occurred after WORLD WAR I was a primary concern.

While both Roosevelt and Byrnes would have preferred to pursue reconversion through presidential EXECUTIVE ORDERS rather than legislation, they cooperated with Congress in perfecting the War Mobilization and Reconversion Act (58 Stat. 785). Signed into law on 3 October 1944, the statute chartered the Office of War Mobilization and Reconversion (OWMR), made its director a presidential appointee subject to Senate confirmation with a two-year term, and consolidated certain reconversion agencies within the OWMR. The President could delegate pertinent powers to the OWMR director "for the purpose of more effectively coordinating the mobilization of the Nation for war"; the director was authorized to formulate plans for the transition to peace and to issue orders to the other agencies to facilitate the successful realization of these plans.

When signing the legislation into law, the President issued Executive Order 9488 transferring the functions, powers, duties, and resources of the OWM to the OWMR; Byrnes became the director of the new body. The OWMR was eventually abolished by Executive Order 9809 of 12 December 1946.

BIBLIOGRAPHY

Somers, Herman Miles. *Presidential Agency: OWMR.* 1950.
U.S. Bureau of the Budget. *The United States at War.* 1946.
Wann, A. J. *The President as Chief Administrator.* 1968.

HAROLD C. RELYEA

OLD EXECUTIVE OFFICE BUILDING. Originally named the State, War, and Navy Building after the three executive departments for which it was designed and built, the Old Executive Office Building (OEOB) houses the agencies that make up the EXECUTIVE OFFICE OF THE PRESIDENT. The building, erected between 1871 and 1888, replaced four Georgian-style brick buildings that by 1820 housed the War, Navy,

State, and Treasury departments, which, together with the White House, formed the executive core of government.

As the four departments expanded in step with the nation's growth, overcrowding, along with damage and loss of government documents resulting from a series of fires, made the construction of new federal buildings a high priority. In 1836 President Andrew Jackson directed Robert Mills to draw plans for a new Treasury building to replace the one that had burned in an 1833 fire and to redesign the other executive structures. The high cost of the reconstruction of the Treasury building became the focus of partisan politics and public criticism, and construction plans for the additional buildings were halted.

The escalating costs for rental space leased by the growing State, War, and Navy departments prompted the Congressional Committee on Buildings and Grounds to ask the departments to prepare designs for their own building to be located on the site west of the White House. Design competitions produced plans that, for the first time, projected the cost of a federal building's construction at $1 million. This unprecedented amount far exceeded what Congress had expected to pay and, once again, with the outbreak of the CIVIL WAR, construction was postponed.

In 1871 successful lobbying by General of the Army William Sherman and by Secretary of State HAMILTON FISH finally procured funding for the State, War, and Navy Building. Construction began that year and continued uninterrupted for the next seventeen years. By 1888 the STATE DEPARTMENT was housed in the south wing, the Navy Department was located in the east wing, and the WAR DEPARTMENT had moved into the north, west, and center wings. Colossal in size, the gray granite building was notable for its exuberant facades with protruding pavilions and tiered columns and pilasters characteristic of the Second Empire style. Equaling and rivaling its European counterparts in style and size, the State, War, and Navy Building expressed the aspirations of a nation that had withstood a terrible civil war and was now expanding across the continent.

Soon after the building's construction, its design fell into disfavor with the public, largely as a result of the popularity of the neoclassical style featured at the Chicago World's Fair in 1893, and the building was seen as dowdy and a white elephant. By 1917, the Commission of Fine Arts sought designs to remodel the building's facades in the idiom of the buildings that formed the Federal Triangle, and in 1930 Congress authorized $3 million for the renovation. Two years later, before the work could begin, funds were cut

because of the depression. Campaigns to renovate or to demolish the building continued, spurred by documented criticism of its appearance by President Taft and by President Harding, who said that the "building was the worst I ever saw." President Truman, however, took a stand in its defense, telling a reporter from the *Washington Star,* "They've been trying to tear this down for twenty years, but I don't want it torn down. I think it's the greatest monstrosity in America."

The OEOB has provided office space for two Presidents and seven men who would later become President. Theodore Roosevelt and Franklin D. Roosevelt both worked there as assistant secretaries of the Navy. William Howard Taft was Secretary of War, occupying offices in the building's west wing, when he received the news that his party had nominated him for President. Dwight Eisenhower was a military aide to Gen. Douglas MacArthur there, and later, during his administration, he held his televised news conferences from the building's Indian Treaty Room. Vice Presidents Lyndon Johnson, Gerald Ford, and George Bush all had offices in the building before moving to the Oval Office across West Executive Avenue. During his administration, President Richard Nixon maintained a sanctuary within the building where he often went for privacy. However, he was not the first sitting President to have an office in the building; Herbert Hoover moved into Gen. John Pershing's office (interrupting Pershing's twenty-six-year occupancy of the former office of the Secretary of the Navy) after a fire destroyed the West Wing on Christmas Eve in 1929.

Edwin Denby was the last Secretary of the Navy to occupy the building before it was vacated by the Navy Department at the end of WORLD WAR I. In 1938 the War Department became the second of the original departments to leave; Secretary Harry Woodring was the last of twenty-one secretaries of War to direct military campaigns and policy from this site. Finally, in 1947, the staff of the State Department moved to its current building in Foggy Bottom, vacating the quarters where many historic events, including the signing of the PANAMA CANAL Treaty and Secretary of State CORDELL HULL's confrontation with two Japanese envoys after PEARL HARBOR, had taken place.

In 1949 the building was named the Executive Office Building to designate it as the offices of the President's executive non-CABINET-level staff, known as the Executive Office of the President. In 1962 the building was renamed the OEOB to differentiate it from the New Executive Office Building, which was being built across Pennsylvania Avenue in response to the growth of the President's staff.

Today the OEOB houses the White House Office, the Office of the Vice President, and top officials of the OFFICE OF MANAGEMENT AND BUDGET, the NATIONAL SECURITY COUNCIL, the COUNCIL OF ECONOMIC ADVISERS, the COUNCIL ON ENVIRONMENTAL QUALITY, the OFFICE OF POLICY DEVELOPMENT, the OFFICE OF SCIENCE AND TECHNOLOGY POLICY, the OFFICE OF THE U.S. TRADE REPRESENTATIVE, and the WHITE HOUSE OFFICE OF ADMINISTRATION.

BIBLIOGRAPHY

Executive Office of the President. Office of Administration. *The Old Executive Office Building, A Victorian Masterpiece.* 1984.

Kohler, Sue A. *The Commission of Fine Arts, A Brief History 1910–1990.* 1990.

Lehman, Donald J. *Executive Office Building.* 1970.

Santoyo, Elsa M. *Architectural Drawings of the Old Executive Office Building, 1871–1888: Creating an American Masterpiece.* 1988.

Seale, William. *The White House.* 2 vols. 1986.

ELSA M. SANTOYO

OLMSTEAD v. UNITED STATES 277 U.S. 438

(1928). *Olmstead v. United States* was the first case in which the Supreme Court examined whether the Fourth Amendment permits the admission at a criminal trial of evidence acquired through ELECTRONIC SURVEILLANCE of communications. The Court did not agree that telephone communications were "one of the privacies of life" that should be protected from monitoring by government agents—as conversations were from eavesdropping. So long as no trespass occurred in the course of the monitoring, the Court ruled that the Fourth Amendment was not applicable.

The defendants were charged with PROHIBITION violations, not with communicating about such matters. Thus, they argued, the government could not have obtained a search warrant to seize written messages for use as evidence of the charges against them. They further argued that, since written messages could not be seized, and since the telephone increasingly substituted for such messages, telephonic communications should receive similar protection under the Fourth Amendment. Government penetration of their telephone equipment constituted as substantial a trespass upon their property interests as any other intrusion. The telephone company was prohibited from disclosing communications, and a state statute barred interception of electronic messages.

Several telephone companies and trade associations supported the defendants. They noted that wiretapping was illegal in twenty-eight states, while thirty-five states had laws prohibiting disclosure of telephone and telegraph messages. Wiretapping was a more sinister

intrusion into the user's privacy and the property interests of both the user and the telephone company than any physical search and was particularly ominous because the telephone was becoming an integral part of social and business life.

In rebuttal, the government argued that conversations passing over wires were not protected because the Fourth Amendment protected only persons, houses, papers, and effects. Although such surveillance raised ethical concerns, it did not violate the Constitution unless accompanied by an unlawful trespass.

The Court explained the developing judicial view that evidence seized in violation of the Fourth Amendment should be excluded from trials. In this case, however, there was no material evidence to be excluded, only voluntary conversations secretly overheard. No search, no seizure, no trespass, or entry onto property, had occurred, only application of the sense of hearing. Wires extending from a home or office were no more a part of those premises than were the highways along which the wires were strung. Thus, these communications were not protected by the Fourth Amendment.

By a 5-to-4 majority, the Court held that persons using telephones intended to project their words to the outside world. Any protection for such communications would have to come from Congress. If the Court were to rule otherwise and forbid the use of evidence obtained by "other than nice ethical [but not illegal] conduct," criminals would be immunized and society would suffer.

Justice Louis Brandeis, dissented and warned that the Court must protect individual rights from increasing government capabilities just as it often approved government actions that would have appeared arbitrary or oppressive to the framers of the Constitution. He saw little difference between the postal service and the telephone companies and envisioned science equipping the government someday with the means to reproduce documents in court without having to remove them from private premises.

Mail was protected, but communications were not, even though wiretapping a telephone represented a greater violation of privacy. The government's legitimate purposes made no difference to Brandeis, since the "greatest dangers to liberty lurk in insidious encroachment by men of zeal, well-meaning but without understanding."

Nonetheless, for forty years *Olmstead* was the law. Electronic surveillance did not violate personal privacy for Fourth Amendment purposes unless accompanied by an official search or seizure of persons, papers, or other tangible material, or an actual physical invasion of private property. Subsequently, the Supreme Court issued its decisions in *Nardone v. United States* (1937) and *Nardone v. United States* (1939), interpreting the Federal Communications Act of 1934 to limit the extent to which the government could disclose information acquired or derived through electronic surveillance. However, it was not until Katz v. United States in 1967 that the Court applied the Fourth Amendment fully to telephone conversations.

BIBLIOGRAPHY

Brownell, Herbert, Jr. "The Public Security and Wiretapping." *Cornell Law Quarterly* 39 (1954): 195.

"The Fourth Amendment and Judicial Review of Foreign Intelligence Wiretapping: *Zweibon v. Mitchell*." Note. *George Washington Law Review* 45 (1976): 55.

Gasque, Aubrey. "Wiretapping: A History of Federal Legislation and Supreme Court Decisions." *South Carolina Law Review* 15 (1963): 593.

Katzenbach, N. "An Approach to the Problems of Wiretapping." *Federal Rules Decisions* 32 (1963): 107.

Orfield, Lester B. "Wiretapping in Federal Criminal Cases." *Texas Law Review* 42 (1964): 983.

AMERICO R. CINQUEGRANA

OLNEY, RICHARD (1835–1917), Attorney General, Secretary of State. In three historic cases of 1895 the Supreme Court helped make the Constitution safe for plutocracy by crippling the Sherman Antitrust Act, by invalidating the Income Tax Act, and by sustaining an injunction against Eugene V. Debs and his labor union. On each of these occasions, Olney, who as Attorney General represented the United States, left his mark—the dollar sign—on the Constitution. When in 1893 President Grover Cleveland appointed the crusty Massachusetts corporate lawyer, who had devoted his career to the service of the captains of finance and industry, Olney sought and received permission to become Attorney General from the head of the railroad company that employed him as chief counsel. The company president shrewdly observed that having Olney as Attorney General was in the railroad's best interest.

When Olney had represented the whiskey trust against the government, he had argued that a monopoly in manufacturing was local in nature, not part of interstate commerce, and so was not subject to federal regulation. As Attorney General, he instituted no antitrust suits but selected as a test case a suit that allowed the Supreme Court to hold that the Sherman Act did not apply to monopolies in manufacturing. He

also construed the act to exclude railroads. Olney barely fought for the constitutionality of the income tax, which the Court voided. He was far more interested in protecting the railroads from Debs and his American Railway Union: in 1893 Olney had employed injunctions to defeat Coxey's Army, which he determined was interfering with interstate commerce and delivery of the mails, and in 1895 he masterminded the same strategy against the Pullman Strike and persuaded President Cleveland to rely on federal troops to crush the strikers. Cleveland promoted Olney to head the State Department in 1895. As secretary Olney vigorously enforced the Monroe Doctrine to diminish British influence in Venezuela. On the whole his policies were feckless.

BIBLIOGRAPHY

James, Henry. *Richard Olney and His Public Service.* 1923.

LEONARD W. LEVY

OPEN DOOR. The "open door" refers to the policy established in 1899 and 1900 by the McKinley administration for China. It committed the United States and other nations to the continuation of unrestricted access and competitive equality in Chinese ports and the preservation of China's territorial integrity and administrative authority over its territory. The open door served as American policy toward China until the 1940s, when China acquired the power to protect itself and implement its own commercial policies.

The open-door policy in China had its antecedents in the traditional American effort to secure unrestricted access to and equal treatment in ports around the globe. Previous Presidents had promoted an open-door policy in relations with Europe, but John Tyler was the first to apply it to China in the 1840s.

The United States paid relatively little attention to China until the 1890s, when many Americans concluded that the expansion of commerce with China was necessary to prevent a social revolution in the United States. They argued that the fabled China market, a supposedly limitless outlet for surplus American goods, would relieve pressure caused by overproduction that had glutted the American market and had led to periodic depressions and labor strife. When, in 1895, Japan, Great Britain, France, Germany, and Russia divided China into spheres of influence and seemed poised to colonize China and close it to American commerce, these Americans lobbied the administration of President Grover Cleveland without success to reassert America's demand for unrestricted and equal access to Chinese ports.

Following the end of the SPANISH-AMERICAN WAR and the acquisition of the PHILIPPINE Islands chiefly to facilitate commerce with China, President William McKinley adopted a more vigorous China policy. When he learned that China faced immediate bankruptcy and a serious threat of colonization, McKinley authorized Secretary of State JOHN HAY to send a series of diplomatic notes to Great Britain, France, Germany, Russia, and Japan requesting that each commit itself to preserve the open door and commercial equality in ports in its own sphere. Despite tentative and evasive responses from these nations, Hay announced that all nations had fully accepted his proposals. Japan and the European nations, unwilling to challenge the United States or enter a colonial scramble, gave formal assent.

McKinley expanded the open-door policy in 1900. When during the Boxer Rebellion foreign missionaries, merchants, and diplomats were besieged in Peking, McKinley sent an American military expedition to China to join with Japanese and European forces to rescue them. When Hay became concerned that the foreign expeditions might become occupying armies, McKinley approved dispatch of a second series of notes to Japan and the European nations announcing that the United States was committed to the preservation of China's "territorial and administrative entity." Hay did not ask other nations to agree with this policy, but they nevertheless did so for reasons of expediency. These two series of notes established the official open-door policy of the United States.

President Theodore Roosevelt relied on a balance of power among Japan, Great Britain, France, Russia, and Germany to preserve the open door. When Russia refused to evacuate its troops from northern Manchuria after the Boxer Rebellion, Japan drove the Russians out in the Russo-Japanese War of 1904–1905. Roosevelt mediated an end to the war in the Treaty of Portsmouth in 1905, for which he received the Nobel Peace Prize. His involvement reestablished a balance of power in Manchuria, preserved the open door in Manchurian ports, and saved Manchuria from Russian or Japanese political control. Russia and Japan retained their economic control, however. Roosevelt also negotiated two agreements with Japan reaffirming both nations' commitment to preserving the open door in China.

President William Howard Taft adopted a more forceful policy aimed at strengthening American power in China and more effectively containing Japan. He redefined the open door to include investment in China and through his program of DOLLAR DIPLOMACY offered American financial and railroad interests guarantees if they would invest in China. The policy ultimately failed due to foreign opposition and the reluctance of many in the business community to enter an unstable market in which protection by the United States was realistically uncertain.

President Woodrow Wilson repudiated dollar diplomacy and initially withdrew pledges to protect American investors in China. When, following the outbreak of WORLD WAR I and withdrawal of European forces from China, Japan threatened to seize control of China's foreign policy and economy, he blocked the Japanese and secured their pledge to respect the open door. At the end of his administration, however, still concerned about Japanese expansion, he attempted to revive Taft's economic policy but had little success.

In a continuing effort to preserve the open door, President Warren G. Harding convened the Washington Conference in 1921. This conference concluded the Nine-Power Treaty (TREATY OF WASHINGTON, 1921) by which all nations active in China agreed to respect the open door and Chinese territorial and administrative integrity. The agreement survived only until 1931 when Japan provoked a war with China and in 1933 established the puppet state of Manchukuo in Manchuria. President Herbert Hoover pledged continued American support for the open door and enunciated the Stimson Doctrine, by which the United States refused to recognize Manchukuo or any territory acquired by aggression.

President Franklin D. Roosevelt continued Hoover's nonrecognition policy and, when Japan resumed its war against China in 1937 and announced its plans to establish the Greater East Asia Co-Prosperity Sphere, effectively closing China to American commerce, Roosevelt denounced the Japanese action and suggested that Japan be isolated in the world community. Roosevelt applied diplomatic and economic pressure on Japan progressively until the end of 1941, when Japan attacked the United States at PEARL HARBOR. One of America's major war aims in the Pacific war was the reestablishment of the open door in China.

The United States retreated from the open-door policy during WORLD WAR II when Nationalist Chinese leader Chiang Kai-shek demanded and secured full authority in China's ports and sovereign control of its commercial policy. In 1949, Mao Tse-tung, who defeated Chiang in a civil war and established the communist People's Republic of China, further tightened Chinese control of its territory and policy. The United States, which declined to recognize the People's Republic until 1979, quietly abandoned the formal open-door policy and reverted to its original support for a universal open door.

BIBLIOGRAPHY

Cohen, Warren I. *America's Response to China: A History of Relations.* 3d ed. 1990.

Fairbank, John K. *The United States and China.* 4th ed. 1983.

Hunt, Michael H. *The Making of a Special Relationship: The United China to 1914.* 1983.

Israel, Jerry. *Progressivism and the Open Door: America and China, 1905–1921.* 1971.

Varg, Paul A. *The Closing of the Door: Sino-American Relations, 1936–1946.* 1973.

KINLEY BRAUER

OPEN SKIES TREATY. A multilateral agreement signed by President George Bush on 24 March 1992, the Open Skies Treaty provided that twenty-five participating countries (the members of NATO and the former Warsaw Pact) would allow one another to undertake relatively unrestricted aerial overflight above their national territories, take photographs (and use other types of advanced sensors) of anything they would encounter, and analyze the acquired imagery for military purposes. The Open Skies Treaty was therefore an unprecedented "confidence-building measure," augmenting other types of ARMS CONTROL agreements and promoting the relaxation of military tensions throughout Europe. The treaty itself did not require any reduction of weaponry nor impose direct constraints upon deployment or use. It did, however, promote the "transparency" of each nation's military apparatus, helping to reduce fears about a possible surprise attack by enabling observers to detect any substantial concentration or movement of troops or equipment.

The concept of open skies was first articulated by President Dwight D. Eisenhower at a summit meeting in Geneva, Switzerland, in 1955. The Soviet Union initially expressed interest, but no treaty was reached at that time, and the idea was essentially abandoned for three decades. President Bush revived it in 1989; he persuaded the heads of NATO allies to endorse it, and negotiations were reinstituted. Initially, talks proceeded on a bloc-to-bloc basis, but the dissolution of the Warsaw Pact, followed by the fracturing of the Soviet Union, complicated the structure. The negotiations, therefore, were among the first post–COLD WAR negotiations, reflecting the new era of East-West relations and promoting the reintegration of Europe. In association with the CFE (CONVENTIONAL FORCES IN EUROPE) TREATY, the Open Skies Treaty was intended to

greatly inhibit any future attempts at military aggression between its parties.

In the final version of the treaty, each country agreed to permit a specified number of unarmed overflights (the annual quota for the United States and for Russia was forty-two each; countries such as Italy, France, and Ukraine had quotas of twelve apiece; smaller countries had lower numbers) to be undertaken on short notice and with only the barest right to exclude overflight of particular areas for safety reasons. Inspecting air crews were authorized to use video and still photography, infrared sensors, synthetic aperture radars, and other devices. The resulting data was to be shared among all the participating countries but not released to the public.

BIBLIOGRAPHY

Jones, Peter. "Open Skies: A New Era of Transparency." *Arms Control Today* 22 (May 1992): 10–15.

Krepon, Michael, and Amy E. Smithson. *Open Skies, Arms Control, and Cooperative Security.* (forthcoming).

DAVID A. KOPLOW

OPTION PAPERS. The only professional and systematic method of presenting an important, complicated, and controversial proposal to a President is to put it in writing in the form of an option paper. Such a paper describes the issue, gives the background facts, sets forth alternative choices for presidential decision and the pro and con arguments for each, identifies the Cabinet and senior White House staff officers who are proponents and opponents of each alternative, and ends with a recommendation. Inasmuch as policy issues reach the President for action because they are important, complicated, and controversial, the White House has developed a technique for dealing with them.

The option-paper process works in the following way. First, the question and any subquestions to be addressed must be identified. This assignment memorandum is almost always drafted by a WHITE HOUSE STAFF officer; often it is issued over that officer's own signature. The assignment memo will typically name the primary action officer, list the CABINET or staff officers to be consulted, and specify a deadline; it may also establish an ad hoc working group.

The second step is the tedious process of drafts, meetings, redrafts, and interagency negotiations with the aim of producing a paper ready in every sense for the President's decision. Contrary to stereotype, the drafters of an option paper do not merely produce sycophantic guff, full only of good news and pandering to what they think the President's predilections are. While the policy process of the White House requires brevity and dispatch, it also demands candor and fairness. It would be egregious disservice to any President to present an option paper that is slanted, distorted, or conceals information or that is not balanced by opposing argument.

Third, the draft option paper goes back to the White House officer who made the original assignment, who will judge it to see whether the terms of the assignment have been fulfilled. The paper itself is likely to be brief, but it may also be accompanied by tabbed attachments—in the form, for example, of signed memoranda from individual cabinet officers.

A special category of option paper, called an Enrolled Bill Memorandum and drafted by the OFFICE OF MANAGEMENT AND BUDGET (OMB), accompanies every enrolled bill (i.e., a bill that has been passed by both houses of Congress) awaiting presidential action. Such an option paper (prepared within the ten-day limit) analyzes the bill, recommends signature or VETO, and always includes the views of each affected Cabinet officer.

If an option paper is particularly lengthy, complicated, or controversial, the White House officer with primary responsibility will then draw up what has been called a road map memorandum—that is, a cover note to the President. The road map memo highlights the issue, summarizes the pro and con discussions, identifies parts of the full package that the President should study carefully, warns the President of traps, points out particularly strong personal views expressed by any of the President's advisers, and alerts the President to any attempts to paper over real differences through the use of mushy compromise language. It may itself suggest compromises and may recommend one of the options for approval.

Finally the option-paper package is then sent to the Staff Secretary, who is not only the last officer to check on the coordination of the paper but is also the person who decides when it should be presented to the President. For example, it may be required just prior to the visit of some important personage or in preparation for a high-level conference.

In reviewing an option paper, some Presidents will convene meetings of the various options' protagonists to discuss the arguments therein; a few Presidents, for example, Richard M. Nixon, are uncomfortable with heated, ego-tinged debate and prefer to read option papers quietly and alone. The President's decision may appear simply as a checked box or may be put in the form of a record of action of a meeting or as a decision memorandum initialed by the President.

Presidents have been known to fill the margins of option papers with enthusiastic, angry, or even profane comments. Today, because of the problem of leaks, neither the full text of the decision memorandum nor the original paper with the President's personal comments is (ever) circulated; the decision itself is often orally conveyed down the line. The original copy of the package is put among the President's personal papers for attention by future archivists.

BIBLIOGRAPHY

Patterson, Bradley H., Jr., *The Ring of Power: The White House Staff and Its Expanding Role in Government.* 1988.

BRADLEY H. PATTERSON, JR.

OREGON TREATY. The Oregon Treaty of 1846 settled a controversy between the United States and Great Britain that had begun in 1815 involving the boundary and title to territory in the Pacific northwest. In 1816 the United States unsuccessfully attempted to draw the boundary between British North America and the United States at 49° north latitude from Lake Superior to the Pacific Ocean. Britain accepted the line only to the Continental Divide, and both nations agreed to occupy the Oregon territory jointly. In 1827, both nations agreed to continue joint occupation until either nation gave a year's notice of its intention to end the agreement.

In 1844 James K. Polk campaigned on a platform calling for the acquisition of all of the Oregon territory, which at that time included all the land from the northern boundary of California at 42° north latitude to the southern boundary of Russian Territory at 54°40′ north latitude and west of the Continental Divide. When the British minister to the United States, Richard Pakenham, rejected Polk's compromise offer of a boundary at the 49° line, Polk committed his administration to nothing less than acquisition of the entire territory. Expansionists raised the slogan, "Fifty-four forty or fight!"

Neither the British nor most Americans wanted a war over Oregon, and the British offered the United States a draft treaty accepting the 49° line to Puget Sound but reserving all of Vancouver Island for Britain. Polk, committed to the entire territory, was inclined to reject the British offer, but the MEXICAN WAR had begun. In order to end the crisis in the north without retreating from his pledge, he sent the draft treaty to the Senate, which advised acceptance by a vote of 37 to 12 on 12 June 1846 and approved the treaty 41 to 14 three days later. Peace was preserved, and Polk was free to prosecute the Mexican War, which brought the United States the immensely more valuable Mexican Cession and California.

BIBLIOGRAPHY

Jacobs, Melvin Clay. *Winning Oregon: A Study of an Expansionist Movement.* 1938.
Merk, Frederick. *The Oregon Question: Essays in Anglo-American Diplomacy and Politics.* 1967.
Pletcher, David M. *The Diplomacy of Annexation: Texas, Oregon, and the Mexican War.* 1973.

KINLEY BRAUER

ORGANIZATION OF AMERICAN STATES (OAS). The Western Hemisphere revolt against the European imperial powers and their mercantilist system, the MONROE DOCTRINE, and the quest for mutual understanding and cooperation under the guise of inter-Americanism (originally Pan-Americanism) comprise the roots of the Organization of American States. The OAS emanated from six decades of Western Hemisphere multipartite treaties, agreements, conference resolutions, declarations, and practices. It was formally established under a constitutive act in 1948, amended in 1967 and 1974. The United States has been its primary initiator, energizer, and financial supporter over the years. Although U.S. Presidents promoted its development for more than a century, major advances occurred in the late nineteenth century and during the administrations of Woodrow Wilson, Franklin D. Roosevelt, and Harry S. Truman.

The OAS was the first contemporary regional organization to possess general (as distinguished from specialized) functions. Its primary organs preexisted the negotiation of its formal charter. Its legal foundation exceeds its constitutive act in that the organization serves to implement various treaties (such as the RIO TREATY of 1947) and other legal instruments. Its functions are comprehensive, encompassing political relations, a peaceful settlement purpose, and collective security as well as cultural, economic, and social affairs, and it serves as the hub of a series of specialized and administrative agencies. All members have representation on its primary policy bodies. The OAS has served as a model for similar organizations in other geographic areas.

Whereas normally the drafting of a constitution of an international organization precedes the establishment of its machinery, the basic components of the OAS were created incrementally prior to the adoption of its charter. The charter amalgamated the following institutions: periodic Inter-American conferences (beginning in 1889), ad hoc specialized conferences, the Pan-American Union (originally the Commercial Bureau of the Americas, launched in 1890 and renamed in 1910) and its Governing Board (created in 1901), Meeting of Consultation of Ministers of Foreign Affairs (first convened in the late 1930s), and a variety of Western Hemisphere administrative agencies.

Currently, its core organization consists of the General Assembly, the Permanent Council and two functional councils, the Meeting of Consultation of Ministers of Foreign Affairs, the Inter-American Juridical Committee, the Inter-American Commission on Human Rights, the General Secretariat, and a series of affiliated specialized organizations.

Originally twenty-one American republics belonged to the OAS. After WORLD WAR II newly independent countries were admitted to membership, which now numbers thirty-two. Membership is universal and encompasses all Western Hemisphere countries except Canada, which elected not to join. Although still a member, CUBA was excluded from the inter-American system in 1962.

The inter-American system is the oldest regional arrangement. United States leadership and support commenced during the administration of Benjamin Harrison and have continued for more than a century through eighteen presidential administrations. It is likely to remain a major regional institution, in which the United States pursues its hemispheric interests and policies. The inter-American system embraces not only the OAS but also six affiliated specialized organizations and dozens of hemispheric multipartite agencies established over the years, many of which remained operative during the years following World War II.

BIBLIOGRAPHY

Organization of American States. *Organization of American States: A Handbook.* 1977.
Slater, Jerome. *The OAS and United States Foreign Policy.* 1967.
Thomas, Ann (Van Wynen), and A. J. Thomas, Jr. *The Organization of American States.* 1963.

ELMER PLISCHKE

OSWALD, LEE HARVEY (1939–1963), accused assassin of President John F. Kennedy. Oswald was accused of shooting President John F. Kennedy with a highpower rifle on 22 November 1963, in Dallas, Texas. Governor John Connally was also wounded in the motorcade attack and a Dallas police officer was killed shortly afterwards. Oswald himself was fatally shot two days later by Jack Ruby while in the custody of Dallas Police and in full view of a national television audience.

Conspiracy theories arose because of Oswald's denial of all guilt; his own murder, which prevented any lengthy interrogation; and conflicting reports surrounding the assault. Eyewitness accounts reported shots coming from a grassy knoll in front of the President's motorcade, not just from the schoolbook depository building where Oswald was employed. These controversies prompted President Lyndon B. Johnson to create the WARREN COMMISSION, which concluded that Oswald was the lone assassin seeking revenge for Kennedy's anti-Castro policies. Oswald was a member of the Fair Play for Cuba Committee and had lived in the Soviet Union, where he married a Russian woman.

Subsequent inquiries by the media and congressional committees, however, revealed that the FEDERAL BUREAU OF INVESTIGATION was deficient in investigating the possibility of a conspiracy and in sharing information with other government agencies at the time. Moreover, the CENTRAL INTELLIGENCE AGENCY (CIA) withheld valuable information from the Warren Commission, including information about CIA foreign assassination plots.

BIBLIOGRAPHY

Clarke, James W. *American Assassins: The Darker Side of Politics.* 2d rev. ed. 1990.
Melanson, Philip H. *Spy Saga: Lee Harvey Oswald and U.S. Intelligence.* 1990.
President's Commission on the Assassination of President John F. Kennedy. *Report* (1964). The report of the Warren Commission.
U.S. House of Representatives. Select Committee on Assassinations. *Findings and Recommendations.* 95th Cong., 2d Sess. 1979.

FREDERICK M. KAISER

OUTSIDE INCOME, EXECUTIVE. Officers and employees of the executive branch are limited in the amount and type of income they may accept while in the employ of the federal government. Outside income includes money and gifts received by an executive-branch employee while he or she is receiving a federal salary [*see* SALARIES, EXECUTIVE]. Those who support major revisions in policies concerning outside earned income and honoraria consistently support changes in the salary systems for federal officials as well.

The year 1989 was a watershed for the issue of ethics in government. On 25 January 1989, President George Bush issued Executive Order 12668, establishing the President's Commission on Federal Ethics Law Reform. The commission reported on 9 March. Subsequently, Executive Order 12674, issued in April

1989, banned all outside earned income by political appointees and WHITE HOUSE STAFF. In November Congress enacted the Ethics Reform Act of 1989 (P.L. 101-194). Pursuant to these efforts, all officers and employees in the executive branch have since 1991 been prohibited from accepting honoraria. An honorarium is defined (5 USC app. 505) as a "payment of money or any thing of value for an appearance, speech or article by a Member, officer or employee, excluding any actual and necessary travel expenses incurred by such individual (and one relative) to the extent that such expenses are paid or reimbursed by any other person." This ban applies to all political appointees, as well as career officials, and is in effect for legislative and judicial officers and employees, including members of Congress and Justices of the Supreme Court. It is acceptable to allow a sponsoring organization to make a donation of up to $2,000, in lieu of an honorarium, to a charitable organization, but neither the person in whose honor the donation is made nor any dependent relative may derive any financial benefit from that charitable organization.

The total ban on honoraria has proved to be more restrictive than originally intended under the Ethics Reform Act. For example, a person working as a federal employee in the lower pay scales may have been supplementing that income by submitting occasional articles or stories for publication or by performing in occasional musical or theatrical presentations. After the act's passage, income from, any such outside activity would generally be considered an honorarium and would be banned. As of 1993, remedies for these restrictions were being sought.

Besides being forbidden to receive honoraria, noncareer executive-branch officers and employees are subject to restrictions on earned outside income. Any such personnel whose basic salary level is equal to or exceeds an established base rate (120 percent of the base rate for a GS-15 pay level; GS stands for General Schedule) must honor that restriction. The limitation amounts to allowable earned income equal to or below 15 percent of the rate of base pay for Level II of the Executive Schedule pay system (Level II is equal to the rate at which members of Congress are compensated).

Generally, accepting gifts is considered inappropriate. In an effort to avoid placing federal officials and employees in compromising positions, Congress has acted to limit the value of gifts and services provided by outside interests. Provisions of the 1992 Legislative Branch Appropriations Act (P.L. 102-90), set a "minimal value" or $250 level, which is greater, as the basis for reporting tangible gifts and gifts of food, lodging, and transportation. "Minimal value" is established under the provisions of the Foreign Gifts Act. The travel reimbursement disclosure threshold is also $250 or "minimal value," whichever is greater. The Legislative Branch Appropriations Act also established $100 as the minimum value above which gifts must be disclosed, with the dollar limitation to be adjusted every three years. No gifts of any type may be solicited or received by a federal officer or employee in return for the performance of any official act.

The Office of Government Ethics, an independent organization within the executive branch, is responsible for the issuance and promulgation of rules and regulations relating to outside income.

BIBLIOGRAPHY

Hartman, Robert W., and Arnold R. Weber, eds. *The Rewards of Public Service: Compensating Top Federal Officials.* 1980.
President's Commission on Federal Ethics Law Reform. *To Serve with Honor.* 1989
U.S. House of Representatives. *Report of the Bipartisan Task Force on Ethics.* 1989.

SHARON STIVER GRESSLE

OVAL OFFICE. The original Oval Office was built in 1909 by President William Howard Taft, when he doubled the size of the Executive Office Building, known today as the West Wing. Theodore Roosevelt had built the West Wing in 1902 to house the presidential offices, which he moved from the WHITE HOUSE, where the office functions had occupied the entire east end of the second floor. The West Wing was built as a staff office in actuality, not the President's office; the chief of state merely had a "President's room" there. On an axis with the front door and in an elegant, bow-ended office was the President's secretary, seated in the dominant position in the building. All bills were signed in the White House, where Roosevelt had what he called the study.

Taft demanded a larger staff than Roosevelt and ordered the officials in charge to create a presidential office central to the West Wing. Congress authorized an expenditure of $40,000. A limited competition of selected architects gave the job to Nathan C. Wyeth; it was he who signed the first Oval Office, which may have been his idea. President Taft was involved and loved architecture, but the extent of his participation is uncertain. Wyeth's design was simplicity itself. The inspiration obviously came from the Blue Room, one of the state rooms inside the White House.

This Oval Office eventually became the main office of the President, although Taft himself signed no bills

there; such an event did not take place until 1914, with Woodrow Wilson. The West Wing and the Oval Office burned at Christmas 1929 and were reconstructed exactly within the ruins. In 1934, President Franklin D. Roosevelt needed to expand the West Wing to house a greatly enlarged presidential staff. The idea for such an expansion had been proposed by President Herbert Hoover, but after the fire, with the overpowering presence of the Depression, he had decided merely to reconstruct.

After considerable controversy among the President, the Corps of Army Engineers, the American Institute of Architects, and the Fine Arts Commission, the expansion plan emerged. Eric Gugler of New York was the architect, and he set up his drafting room in the nearby Octagon House on New York Avenue. The work was accomplished between August and November 1934. Taft's earlier office was demolished and the new Oval Office was built on the east end of the West Wing, adjacent to the Rose Garden, which it adjoined by a columned porch. It was near the new Cabinet Room, which also looked out into the garden. The interior was more flamboyant than Wyeth's Oval Office of 1909 and suggested the art moderne style then current in architecture. Gugler surmounted the doors with whimsical pediments and built niches for books, crowned with seashells.

Except for intermittent redecoration, the Oval Office is that completed by Gugler in 1934. While the remainder of the West Wing is in a state of continual rearrangement, the Oval Office has stayed architecturally the same.

BIBLIOGRAPHY

Seale, William. *The President's House: A History.* 1985.
Seale, William. *The White House: History of an American Idea.* 1992.

WILLIAM SEALE

OVERSIGHT, CONGRESSIONAL. Congressional oversight of the presidency and of the executive branch of government derives from the legitimate involvement of Congress in executive activity. The President is titular head of the executive branch and is ultimately responsible for its actions, but he is not its sole master. The President may be called the CHIEF EXECUTIVE, but he actually shares legal authority over the executive branch with Congress. The President is charged with the faithful execution of the laws as well as with the executive power, terms that are never precisely defined in the Constitution or in statutes. From these grants of legal authority emerges the conclusion that Presidents dominate the bureaucracy. What is ignored is that Congress legally determines many things about the bureaucracy.

Areas of Congressional Authority. One of the things Congress determines is the structure of the executive branch. If, for instance, there is to be a department of education, Congress has to create it. Another thing Congress determines is almost all the programs that the executive branch administers, which are created through congressional authority; SOCIAL SECURITY, agricultural subsidies, highway improvement programs, and the space program are only a few examples. In addition, the basic outlines of personnel policy in the executive branch are created by Congress through statutes. The senior CIVIL SERVICE, executive-compensation formulas, and the scope of the merit system are usually congressionally determined. Finally, the money to run the executive branch and its programs comes out of the congressional budget and appropriations process. Legally then, Congress and the President share in controlling the executive branch; exclusive presidential authority is a myth.

Congress shares power over the executive branch from a political perspective as well as a legal one. Bureaucrats realize that authority over them is divided between the President and Congress. Understandably they want to please both. Presidential and congressional constituencies differ. Different political parties can control the presidency and Congress. Historically, party control has been divided about 40 percent of the time since 1789 and about 80 percent of the time from 1968 to 1992. Bureaucrats may find it most difficult to satisfy completely both their legal and their political masters. Presidents and some members of Congress may have different priorities and emphases; if they agree on goals, they may still clash over what is the better way to achieve them. Even if there is consensus on ends and means, disputes may arise over timing—how quickly money should be spent and for which programs.

These legal and political factors provide an invitation to struggle. The outcomes of this struggle are predictably mixed. In some situations, Presidents and their close advisers may dominate executive decision making. In other areas, power may be genuinely shared.

That Congress has substantial legal and political power in dealing with the executive branch is not a matter of dispute. Through most of U.S. history the legal basis for legislative oversight has been inferred from the legal powers of Congress over the bureau-

cracy previously mentioned. In the Legislative Reorganization Act of 1946, the legal basis for legislative oversight of the bureaucracy was clearly and directly stated when each standing committee was instructed to "exercise continuous watchfulness of the execution by the administrative agencies concerned of any laws, the subject matter of which is within the jurisdiction of such committee."

This authority is quite sufficient to justify any oversight that Congress wishes to conduct. Nonetheless, Congress has periodically added to its legal authority to oversee. For example, see the Legislative Reorganization Act of 1970 and the CONGRESSIONAL BUDGET AND IMPOUNDMENT CONTROL ACT (1974). If the legal basis for legislative oversight is broad and all-embracing, its actual exercise and impact seem far more circumscribed. The general impact of legislative oversight on the presidency and the executive branch shows that authority over the bureaucracy is in fact divided. Moreover, oversight is selectively exercised, and its impact is difficult to trace because its significance varies with the situation.

Ways of Asserting Congressional Authority. Congress has a multitude of tools and techniques to influence executive behavior. Its control over structure, program, policy, personnel, and money sets the boundaries. It can exercise that control formally through official investigations, as part of serving constituents by means of casework, through required reports, and in hearings designed to determine the shape of legislation and appropriations.

Congress can exercise its power informally in discussion and negotiation. Congress, its committees, and individual members have many ways of finding out what the executive branch is doing. Committee staff persons regularly consult with relevant persons in the executive branch. A rather constant querying process takes place on the telephone, in memoranda, and over luncheon. There are also many opportunities to attempt to influence executive behavior.

By looking at what Congress does formally and why it does it, one can gain substantial insight into the problems of legislative oversight of the presidency. Probably the most visible oversight technique is that of committee and subcommittee investigations to see that executive programs are being implemented. What is most notable here is that only a small percentage of departments, agencies, and programs are regularly subject to scrutiny through investigations. What accounts for this seemingly insufficient supervision is that while the obligation to oversee the executive branch is general and inclusive, the actual efforts to do so are based less on that obligation than on more concrete motives. The pressure to oversee comes primarily from the pursuit of political advantage. Many investigations also involve a desire to promote good public policy and to create more efficient and responsible bureaucratic behavior, but political advantage is typically the sharpest spur.

An ongoing oversight technique is dealing with the complaints and inquiries from constituents that congressional offices receive on a daily basis. These concern such matters as executive action or inaction, a government check that has not been delivered, a government contract that has been delayed or awarded to another company, a form that has been lost, a permit that has not been granted, or a host of other matters involving interactions between government and individuals. Congressional offices, concerned with serving their constituents, promptly check with the relevant department or agency in the executive branch to clarify the problem or to seek remedies for it. Communications from constituents to Congress provide a vast body of evidence concerning what is going on, or is not going on that should be going on, in the executive branch. This motherlode of data is underutilized within Congress. Valiant efforts are indeed made to satisfy constituents, but mainly that is all that happens. Efforts to collect and synthesize these data as a basis for more systematic congressional action are rare. Congressional routines concerning casework are only occasionally translated into effective, broad oversight activity.

Another formal technique that members of Congress use to oversee the executive branch is to require regular reports from the President, his department, and agencies on a wide variety of topics. In 1991 more than two thousand such reports were required. This vast expenditure of executive time and energy supposedly leads to effective oversight from Congress. The correlation, however, is spurious. Most of the reports required by Congress are routinely dispatched to the circular file. Only a few become the basis for action. The gap between appearance and reality is large.

Still another technique of oversight is for congressional committees to hold hearings on proposed legislation or when appropriations are being considered. At such hearings the questions are likely to be, How have these or similar programs worked before? How much money has been spent and for what purposes? Were these expenditures worth the cost? Legislative hearings frequently deal with oversight even if their stated purpose is something else.

If one examines congressional investigations, case-

work, required reports, and hearings, few will deal explicitly with the President and his behavior. But because the bureaucracy is legally and politically under both presidential and congressional supervision and because the President as the titular head is ultimately responsible, even if he knows nothing about specific bureaucratic actions, almost all congressional oversight of the executive branch of government in some ways, mainly indirectly, affects the president.

Relatively few bureaucratic behaviors are directly subject to congressional scrutiny, and of these, even fewer involve direct presidential actions. Presidential responsibility extends far beyond presidential knowledge, and legislative authority to oversee extends far beyond congressional behavior. The direct impact of most efforts of congressional oversight on presidents is neither extensive nor substantial. Precisely what difference oversight makes for Presidents is difficult to specify partly because what impact there is is so largely indirect.

Problems in Executive-Legislative Relations. If precise impacts are difficult to measure, some of the problems in executive-legislative relations when Congress oversees the bureaucracy are easier to specify. One of these is what information concerning the executive branch Congress is entitled to seek and obtain. From the perspective of most members of Congress the answer is whatever information members of Congress want. Legislators point to their extensive legal powers over the bureaucracy and infer from these that there are few limits to the information they can rightfully obtain. From the perspective of the President, however, there are clear limits to what information members of Congress are entitled to receive. Whatever the language used to justify presidential positions, the characteristic presidential interpretation is that Presidents should provide only what information they deem to be appropriate irrespective of congressional requests. Since law seldom provides absolute answers in these disputes, political strength and bargaining tend to determine outcomes. Congressional committees and subcommittees press for what they desire; Presidents resist when they feel requests are legally excessive or politically damaging. On occasion, Presidents even invoke EXECUTIVE PRIVILEGE, that is, they claim a constitutional right to withhold sensitive information. Members of Congress rail against such executive assertions and can sometimes force the executive to back down through political pressure.

The courts studiously avoided defining executive privilege or establishing its limits until the 1970s, when President Richard M. Nixon claimed that he could withhold tape recordings made during the WATERGATE AFFAIR from Congress and the courts. The Supreme Court ruled that while Presidents did have the right of executive privilege, they could only use it subject to limits. The limit defined here was that claims to executive privilege could not stand when executive-held materials were needed as evidence in criminal proceedings. The Court seemed to be saying that while the doctrine of executive privilege has legal status, its use cannot be determined by the President alone. Although cast in legal terms, the Court decision embodied an astute political compromise.

The few examples of congressional oversight directly related to the presidency tend to be dramatic incidents. In recent years, the Watergate controversy in the Nixon administration and the IRAN-CONTRA AFFAIR during the administration of Ronald Reagan quickly come to mind.

The Iran-contra investigation reveals a great deal about congressional oversight as it relates to the presidency. When the news reached the public that the U.S. government had been selling arms to the Iranians, allegedly to build good will that would lead to the release of U.S. hostages and that the profits from these sales had been diverted to the aid of the contras in Nicaragua, Congress mounted an intense investigation. Charges of violations of U.S. policy by the executive branch and of illegal acts (Congress had banned military aid to the contras) resounded through these investigations. The gravity of what had occurred was revealed, and the public was made aware of misbehavior by the executive branch. In these senses, these hearings seemed to be an example of the fruits of diligent congressional oversight.

Limits to Congressional Oversight. The limits to this effort at congressional oversight remain obvious. Neither congressional investigations nor any other source fully established the role of President Reagan in these events. Since that answer has not been forthcoming, one can assert that these congressional attempts to oversee presidential behavior substantially failed. Also, the absence of conclusive evidence linking President Reagan to these machinations in foreign policy stands in the way of effective congressional action to remedy existing problems. If the President personally violated the law, IMPEACHMENT could have resulted. If the President had been shown to be excessively casual or careless in supervising the bureaucracy, he could have been politically condemned. If problems of bureaucratic organization had been basic, Congress could have acted to correct these, but such problems were never clearly demonstrated. The utility

of this major effort at oversight remains unclear partly because the President and the executive branch were not fully forthcoming with what they knew; in fact they could be seen as impediments to successful legislative oversight.

Efforts at legislative oversight aimed at dealing directly with presidential behavior are commonly limited by executive efforts to prevent the full disclosure of relevant facts. Banking scandals in the Reagan and Bush administrations provide another example. Few persons in or out of the executive branch gain joy in wallowing in their own errors of judgment, their failures to act expeditiously, or their apparent protection of vested interests. Other than the complexity of problems themselves, executive intransigence stands as a major barrier to successful legislative oversight.

There is, of course, a record of some successful congressional oversight of presidential behavior, but that is not the dominant theme. Mainly, Congress tries in a rather fitful manner to oversee some selected portion of presidential activities, as has been noted. The impact of these efforts is a function of specific circumstances. Perhaps the major impact can never be precisely measured. Nevertheless, Presidents have been known to reconsider what they are about to do because they anticipate that congressional oversight with a battery of questions will follow. Presidents consider how, if called upon, they will justify what they have done. No one can prove that the "law of anticipated reactions" works. Yet fragmentary evidence suggests that the process of anticipating possible reactions and preparing defensible answers may be the most significant fruit of congressional oversight.

Since the federal bureaucracy is under the supervision of both the President and Congress, efforts at congressional oversight of the executive branch are at least indirectly oversight of the presidency. The record of congressional oversight of the bureaucracy is more difficult to evaluate. Conclusions vary with perspectives. If the standard is whether Congress systematically oversees all aspects of bureaucratic behavior, then the record of accomplishment is dismal. If the standard is whether Congress looks into basic problems as they are revealed, then the record is more mixed. If the standard is whether Congress regularly checks into a vast variety of executive behavior, then the record of Congress assuredly is good. Conclusions then depend on one's frame of reference. Some would even argue that the relatively small amount of oversight that Congress performs is entirely functional. Congress, these scholars argue, does not waste its time and energy on useless routine checks but gets involved only when its attention is brought to problems of consequence.

BIBLIOGRAPHY

Aberbach, Joel D. *Keeping a Watchful Eye: The Politics of Congressional Oversight.* 1990.

Dodd, Lawrence C., and Richard L. Schott. *Congress and the Administrative State.* 1979.

Foreman, Christopher H., Jr. *Signals from the Hill: Congressional Oversight and the Challenge of Social Regulation.* 1988.

Harris, Joseph P. *Congressional Control of Administration.* 1964.

Johnson, Loch K. *A Season of Inquiry: The Senate Intelligence Investigation.* 1985.

Ogul, Morris S. *Congress Oversees the Bureaucracy: Studies in Legislative Supervision.* 1978.

Ripley, Randall B., and Grace A. Franklin. *Congress, the Bureaucracy, and Public Policy.* 5th ed. 1991.

Smist, Frank John. *Congress Oversees the United States Intelligence Community, 1947–1989.* 1990.

MORRIS S. OGUL

P

PACS (POLITICAL ACTION COMMITTEES). Campaigns for the American presidency are very probably the only American campaigns in which PACs played a smaller role in 1992 than they did in 1972. Such a singular decline is almost entirely the result of the two quite different programs of public funding the Congress created in the 1974 revision of the Federal Election Campaign Act (FECA).

The first of those programs covers the politics of NOMINATING PRESIDENTIAL CANDIDATES before the national party conventions. During the preconvention period the candidates' money comes largely from individual contributions and public funds that match any individual contribution up to $250. PACs have consequently accounted for only 1 or 2 percent of the receipts of all candidates during the selection of convention delegates, a reflection of PAC's more general reluctance to enter nomination battles. The disincentive of not having their contributions matched with public money only reinforces that customary reluctance.

After the conventions, the major party nominees may choose full public funding for their general election campaigns. With public funding comes the commitment to accept no private money for spending on the campaign. If in the future some candidate were not to accept the public money, he or she would be free to accept contributions from PACs of up to $5,000 per PAC.

There are, however, a few opportunities for PACs around the margins of presidential campaign finance. Thanks to the Supreme Court's ruling in BUCKLEY V. VALEO (1976), any PAC, other group, or individual may spend money "independently" in the presidential campaign to urge the victory or defeat of a candidate—by buying newspaper ads or television spots, for example. To be "independent" such expenditures must be made without the knowledge of the candidate. PACs have spent substantial sums of this kind in the campaigns of the 1980s: $13.7 million, $17.5 million, and $14.1 million in 1980, 1984, and 1988, respectively.

It is, however, a special breed of PAC that spends independently in presidential campaigns. They are predominantly ad hoc PACs without parent organizations, founded by entrepreneurs to raise money (largely by direct mail) for that election only. In 1990, for example, the National Security PAC (NSPAC) reported spending $8.6 million, 61 percent of all independent spending in the campaign. It is customary, moreover, for such PACs to report as expenditures many of their fund-raising costs because those mailed letters urge support for a candidate. Political spending more narrowly defined often accounts for no more than 10 or 15 percent of their receipts. NSPAC, incidentally, did pay for the infamous Willie Horton TV ads of 1988.

Finally, PACs have been involved even less directly in presidential campaigns by contributing small sums to the "compliance funds" the candidates are permitted to raise to defray accounting and legal costs. PACs in 1989–1990 contributed less than 1 percent of the $9.6 million that Bush and Dukakis raised for such purposes. PACs also contribute far larger amounts in "soft money" raised during the campaign both by the presidential candidates and national parties for uses outside of the campaign: for party-building and local campaigns in the states.

[*See also* CAMPAIGN FINANCES; PRESIDENTIAL ELECTION CAMPAIGN FUND.]

BIBLIOGRAPHY

Alexander, Herbert E., and Monica Bauer. *Financing the 1988 Election*. 1991.

Sorauf, Frank J. *Money in American Elections*. 1988.

FRANK J. SORAUF

PALMER RAIDS. Following WORLD WAR I, the United States experienced an alarming wave of racial violence, labor strife, and social unrest. These extraordinary disruptions coincided with the Bolshevik revolution in Russia and the founding of a Communist Party in the United States, comprising mainly recent immigrants from eastern Europe. The party, though small and ineffective, quickly became a scapegoat for domestic turbulence. In the spring of 1919, a series of terrorist bombings was blamed on alien "Bolsheviks."

Attorney General A. Mitchell Palmer, a man with presidential ambitions, feared that foreign influences were subverting cherished American ideals. Palmer's decision to crack down on alien radicals met no resistance from President Woodrow Wilson, whose consuming struggle over the LEAGUE OF NATIONS had all but ruined his health. In the summer of 1919 Palmer ordered the compilation of dossiers on radical groups and individuals. That autumn, federal agents began a series of round-ups of aliens, one of which allegedly uncovered some explosives. On 21 December, the government deported 249 aliens.

On 2 January 1920 federal agents carried out a second series of arrests known as the Palmer Raids. They entered homes and businesses, social clubs and political meetings, in search of alien radicals. In the end, at least four thousand people were rounded up in thirty-three major cities across the country. Though Palmer had predicted more than twenty-seven hundred deportations, the actual number turned out to be 591. The vast majority of those arrested were treated roughly, but released. Still, the raids did enormous damage to radical politics in the United States. Membership in the Communist Party dropped from seventy thousand to sixteen thousand in 1920, as the movement was forced underground.

In the following months, as the perceived threat of Bolshevism diminished, scholars, clergymen, and public officials spoke out against the raids. Many were influenced by "Illegal Practices of the U.S. Department of Justice," a pamphlet written by Harvard Law School Professors Felix Frankfurter, Zechariah Chafee, and Roscoe Pound. The war was over, the "radicals" were silent or deported, and the labor movement lay in ruins. Political dissent in the United States had suffered a blow from which it would not quickly recover.

BIBLIOGRAPHY

Coben, Stanley. *A Mitchell Palmer, Politician*. 1963.

Murphy, Paul. *The Meaning of Freedom of Speech*. 1972.

Murray, Robert. *Red Scare: A Study in National Hysteria, 1919–1920*. 1955.

DAVID M. OSHINSKY

PANAMA. Until 1903, Panama was a province of the South American nation of Colombia. Many Americans believe that it became an independent state in November of that year principally because President Theodore Roosevelt, who was infuriated by Colombia's rejection of a pending treaty to allow the United States to build a canal across the isthmus, dispatched a U.S. warship there to shield Panamanian secessionists. Panama did indeed commence its independent history as a virtual protectorate of the United States, but the nationalist sentiments identified with nineteenth-century secessionist movements remained alive. Denied self-determination by the circumstances of their independence, Panamanians struggled to realize national sovereignty. Canceling the hated 1903 PANAMA CANAL treaty and ending the U.S. administration of a separate Canal Zone with a set of treaties in 1978 offered tangible evidence of success in this national battle. Economic and cultural independence, however, has yet to be achieved.

In the Hay-Bunau-Varilla treaty of 1903, the Roosevelt administration wrested major concessions from the new republic for the construction, maintenance, and security of the Panama Canal. U.S. presence in the isthmus, expressed most tangibly in the creation of a colonial society (and accompanying racial and ethnic segregation) in the Canal Zone, reached deep into Panamanian life and national politics.

After WORLD WAR II, the Panamanian national guard began to play a more important role in national politics, just as the U.S. presence in the Canal Zone was becoming more entrenched. In 1955, Panama secured a modification of the 1903 treaty with the Dwight D. Eisenhower administration, one that granted Panama greater benefits but accomplished little toward gaining Panamanian sovereignty over the Canal Zone. Panama's political elite became more vocally anti–United States in the 1950s and 1960s. In 1959 and 1964 serious riots erupted in the Canal Zone and nearby settlements. After the 1959 outbreak, President Eisenhower (later joined by President John F. Kennedy) called for accommodation on the sovereignty issue, largely expressed through joint displays of the Panamanian and U.S. flags at designated places in the Canal Zone. In 1964, President Lyndon B. Johnson announced negotiations for a new canal treaty to replace the 1903 treaty, but Panama rejected the new proposals. In 1968, a military junta led by Col. Omar Torrijos took control of Panama.

Serious discussions for new canal treaties resumed under the Richard M. Nixon administration. When these discussions' progress was slowed because of the transition from the Nixon to the Gerald Ford administration, Torrijos dramatically renewed relations with CUBA and trumpeted Panama's case by making new treaties throughout Latin America. The signing in 1977 and, especially, congressional approval in 1978 of the canal treaties with the United States owed as much to Torrijos as to President Jimmy Carter.

After 1968, Panama became a militarized society. Torrijos knew how to deal with the United States. His successor, Manual Antonio Noriega, exploited his relationship with Washington, which tolerated his complicity in drug smuggling and his blatantly undemocratic rule until Panama exploded in civil strife in the late 1980s. The leaders of the opposition, who came from the old social elite, now began to call for U.S. intervention as Noriega taunted Washington before cheering crowds of Panama's lower classes. Noriega charged that the United States merely wanted an excuse to repudiate the 1977 treaties and restore the old Panamanian elite to power. Despite protest, he used the National Defense Forces to overturn the election of Guillermo Endara in mid 1989. In December 1989, U.S. forces invaded Panama City, causing widespread damage and many civilian deaths. Ultimately, Noriega was apprehended, taken to Miami for trial and convicted in 1992. The invasion—called Operation Just Cause—did not bring any fundamental change in the U.S. pledge to turn over the Canal to Panama. President George Bush argued that its purpose was to apprehend a drug trafficker (Noriega) and to restore the Panamanian government to civilian control. In reality, Operation Just Cause represented yet another military solution to a Latin American political and economic dilemma, a reprise of the GUNBOAT DIPLOMACY approach. Middle-class Panamanians had become thoroughly Americanized in their consumer tastes, and they remained culturally and economically dependent. But Panamanian politics continued to march to a different drum—nationalistic and defiant.

BIBLIOGRAPHY

Conniff, Michael C. *Black Labor on a White Canal: Panama, 1904–1981* (1985).

Conniff, Michael C. *Panama and the United States: The Forced Alliance.* 1992.

Knapp, Herbert, and Mary Knapp. *Red, White, and Blue Paradise: The American Canal Zone in Panama.* 1985.

LaFeber, Walter. *The Panama Canal: The Crisis in Historical Perspective.* 1979.

McCullough, David. *The Path between the Seas.* 1977.

LESTER D. LANGLEY

PANAMA CANAL. Virtually every President since John Quincy Adams has expressed an interest in, or taken a major role in the development of U.S. policy regarding a man-made waterway across Central America. With the outbreak of the SPANISH-AMERICAN WAR in 1898, the strategic importance to the United States of an isthmian canal became manifestly clear. President Theodore Roosevelt, who was first attracted to the idea of building a canal across Nicaragua, finally determined that it would be better to complete a canal that the French had begun in PANAMA. Congress approved the purchase of the French interests and the construction of the canal. By a treaty of 1903 the United States received from a dependent Panama a strip of land across the isthmus. The Panama Canal Zone was administered by a governor appointed by the President.

The canal was completed in 1914. And, over the course of the twentieth century, the history of the Panama Canal was the story of three interrelated themes in U.S. relations with Latin America.

The first of these themes was the often stormy political relationship between the United States and Panama. Panama, dependent for survival on the U.S. presence, conducted a long struggle to benefit from the canal and, ultimately, to reaffirm Panamanian sovereignty over the Canal Zone. In the 1930s the Franklin D. Roosevelt administration ended the Panamanian protectorate and gave limited concessions to Panamanian businessmen in the zone. During WORLD WAR II, the Panama Canal earned its designation as the continental lifeline. In the late 1940s and early 1950s, the national guard began to play a more important role in Panama. In 1955 the Panamanian president, José Antonio Remón, negotiated more concessions from the Dwight D. Eisenhower administration. Four years later, young Panamanian nationalists tried to raise the Panamanian flag over the zone, provoking a riot. John F. Kennedy pledged to address Panamanian grievances by permitting the Panamanian flag to fly at selected sites in the zone. Early in 1964 the Lyndon B. Johnson administration confronted a more serious outbreak of violence between Panamanians and Canal Zone residents precipitated by a flag-raising dispute at the Canal Zone high school. One outcome of this crisis was the negotiation of new canal treaties (one of which provided for a sea-level canal), but these were rejected in Panama.

The second theme is U.S. relations with Latin America. In 1968, Omar Torrijos headed up a military junta that tossed the civilian Panamanian president out of office. Torrijos succeeded in making the Panama Canal a hemispheric issue. Both the Richard M. Nixon and Gerald Ford administrations committed the United States to a new treaty to replace the hated 1903 treaty. In the mid-1970s, an influential commission declared the Panama Canal to be the most divisive issue in hemispheric relations. With much fanfare, U.S. President Jimmy Carter and Panamanian president Torrijos signed new canal treaties, but the U.S. Senate approved them only after amendments were attached reaffirming the United States' right to intervene in Panama.

The third theme is the emotional attachment North Americans retained about the canal. By the 1970s, however, the canal had become less important both economically and militarily and, as Torrijos reminded Carter, the canal was vulnerable to sabotage by angry Panamanians. The treaties were passed by the Panamanian national assembly only because Torrijos compelled the legislature to approve them. On 31 December 1999 the Panama Canal will belong to Panama. Despite problems, the implementation of the treaties proved successful. The Canal Zone ceased to exist as a distinct, U.S. administered territory; the number of Panamanians in managerial positions rose; and a joint Panamanian–North American commission operated the canal. Most of the functions not directly related to canal operations or defense, such as schools and commissaries, were phased out.

BIBLIOGRAPHY

Conniff, Michael C. *Black Labor on a White Canal: Panama, 1904–1981.* 1985.

Conniff, Michael C. *Panama and the United States: The Forced Alliance.* 1992.

Knapp, Herbert, and Mary Knapp. *Red, White, and Blue Paradise: The American Canal Zone in Panama.* 1985.

LaFeber, Walter. *The Panama Canal: The Crisis in Historical Perspective.* 1979.

McCullough, David. *The Path between the Seas.* 1977.

LESTER D. LANGLEY

PANAMA REFINING CO. v. RYAN 293 U.S. 388 (1935). This case led to a decision that for the first time invalidated legislation for improper DELEGATION OF LEGISLATIVE POWER from Congress to the President. It arose from efforts to deal with a glut of oil that in the early years of the Great Depression drove petroleum prices down to as little as four cents a barrel. In Texas and Oklahoma, governors declared martial law and ordered bayonet-armed National Guardsmen into the oil fields to shut down wells; but states, acting alone, found they could not curb the flow, especially of hot oil—oil smuggled across state lines in defiance of quotas set by state governments.

In 1933, Congress, in Section 9(c) of Title I of the NATIONAL INDUSTRIAL RECOVERY ACT, authorized the President to interdict the shipment in interstate or foreign commerce of hot oil. By a series of EXECUTIVE ORDERS, President Franklin D. Roosevelt vested enforcement of this provision in the Secretary of the Interior, HAROLD ICKES. When the Panama Refining Company sought to restrain federal officials from enforcing regulations issued by Ickes, its case was consolidated with a companion suit launched by the Amazon Petroleum Corporation. The U.S. District Court in eastern Texas granted permanent injunctions to both companies, but the Fifth U.S. Circuit Court of Appeals reversed the decision, in favor of the government.

As these cases moved toward final resolution in the U.S. Supreme Court, the Roosevelt administration was mortified when, in unrelated litigation (*United States v. Smith*), it filed criminal indictments against several Texas oil men for conspiracy to violate the NIRA oil code only to find that the pertinent provision had been inadvertently omitted when the code was revised. The SOLICITOR GENERAL had no choice but to ask the Supreme Court to dismiss the case. The government was further discomfited when, in argument on *Panama*, it had to acknowledge that there was no official publication of executive orders and hence no way that businessmen could readily know whether they were committing violations for which they could be jailed.

On 7 January 1935, the Supreme Court, in its first decision on a NEW DEAL law, invalidated Section 9(c) as an improper delegation of power from the legislative to the executive branch. The section, said Chief Justice CHARLES EVANS HUGHES, "does not state whether, or in what circumstances . . . , the President is to prohibit the transportation of petroleum. It does not require any finding by the President as a condition of his actions. . . . It gives to the President an unlimited authority to determine the policy and to lay down the prohibition, or not to lay it down, as he may see fit. And disobedience to his order is made a crime punishable by fine and imprisonment." Moreover, he noted, Roosevelt had never submitted any express finding of the grounds for his action. "We cannot regard the President as immune from these constitutional principles," the Chief Justice declared.

In dissent, Justice Benjamin Cardozo, after chiding the government for slipshod procedures, denied that the section conferred too much discretion. Scrutiny of the statute revealed that Congress had not left the President free "to roam at will among all the possible subjects of interstate transportation, picking and choosing as he pleases," but had confined him to a single commodity—oil; and had told him the only act he could perform—interdiction. "There has been no grant to the Executive," Cardozo insisted, "of any roving commission to inquire into evils and then upon discovering them, do anything he pleases," but no other Justice joined Cardozo in this dissent.

Panama had no ancestry and few progeny. Critics faulted the Court for overreaching in applying the improper delegation rubric for the first time in its nearly century and a half of existence. There was no meaningful distinction, they contended, between Section 9(c) and legislation the Court had found acceptable in the past. The Court invoked the improper delegation doctrine twice more, in 1935 and 1936, but never thereafter, though in the early 1990s there were some indications that it might be revived. The case did, however, have one important consequence. The Roosevelt administration sensed that it had come to grief in *Panama* less because of the shortcomings of Section 9(c) than because the haphazard procedures revealed in *Smith* had provoked the Court to speak out. Consequently, on 26 July 1935 Roosevelt put his name to a law inaugurating a new publication, the *Federal Register*, a compendium of government orders and regulations kept up to date systematically.

[*See also* FEDERAL REGISTER ACT.]

BIBLIOGRAPHY

Brand, Donald R. *Corporatism and the Rule of Law*. 1988.
Ickes, Harold L. *The Secret Diaries of Harold L. Ickes*. 3 vols. 1953–1954.

WILLIAM E. LEUCHTENBURG

PAPERS, PRESIDENTIAL. From the first days of the federal government, Presidents have personally authored, ordered the production of, or indirectly prompted the preparation of documentary materials. These came to be known as presidential papers. They usually bore the President's signature or initials or otherwise were generated for his use, although broader understandings of the term have prevailed from time to time.

The Era of Inattentiveness. The management and preservation of public records were generally neglected during the first century and a half of the federal experience. Inattentiveness to the maintenance of official papers prevailed within both the infant bureaucracy and the White House. While the Secretary of State bore the legal responsibility for retaining copies of the most important government documents, lesser papers, without immediate administrative significance, disappeared in a clutter, disintegrated, became otherwise lost, or were destroyed by design.

Within this atmosphere, departing Presidents had little choice with regard to the disposition of their records. There was no national archive to receive such papers, and, for reasons of etiquette or politics or both, there was reluctance to leave them behind. Thus, facing no legal restrictions, the early Chief Executives carried away their documents of office, entrusting them to their families, estate executors, and often to fate. After decades of the perils of private ownership, many collections of presidential records came to be established within state libraries, private universities, state historical societies, and the Library of Congress. Time, however, often levied a price on some caches of such documents before they came to rest in friendly institutions. Moreover, as a consequence of private ownership and family controls, their accessibility to scholars and the public was not always readily assured.

The richest and most diverse treasure of presidential papers may be found at the Library of Congress. Efforts at building this collection were begun well over a century and a half ago and involved not insignificant amounts of money. For example, the library possesses about 95 percent of President George Washington's papers, purchased from his heirs in 1834 and 1849 at a total cost of $45,000. A large number of Thomas Jefferson's documents—23,600 items—were acquired in 1848 for $20,000. In three separate purchases totaling $65,000, the library received 10,000 items from James Madison's presidency. Of the 4,200 documents from the James Monroe collection held by the library, the bulk of them was acquired in 1849 for $20,000. The Andrew Jackson collection, consisting of some 20,000 items, came mostly from purchases in 1911 and 1932 totaling $18,000. Jackson's legal and military papers were destroyed, however, when his family home burned in 1834. Flames also consumed other presidential papers. Martin Van Buren is thought to have burned all but a carefully selected set of less than 7,000 items from his presidency. An 1858 fire at the North Bend, Ohio, home of William Henry Harrison left a legacy of less than 1,000 papers. While the Library of Congress has 800 items from John Tyler's presidency, the burning of Richmond in 1865 consumed the remainder of this collection. Similarly, the torching of Zachery Taylor's family plantation during the CIVIL WAR reduced his cache of presidential materials. Such experiences eventually prompted two alternative preservation arrangements.

Publication of Presidential Papers. To safeguard the words of the Presidents, various collections of presidential papers were published. Some, of course, were commercially produced. Others were compiled, printed, and distributed by special memorial groups, such as the Thomas Jefferson Memorial Association and the United States George Washington Bicentennial Commission. Sometimes Congress gave its imprimatur to these activities, as in the case of the Washington commission, and the Government Printing Office published the resulting volumes. The first extensive compilation of the messages and papers of the Presidents, drawing largely upon the Library of Congress collection, was prepared by James D. Richardson and published under congressional authority in multiple volumes. Its coverage extended through the presidency of Calvin Coolidge. Later, the National Archives, founded in 1934, launched its PUBLIC PAPERS OF THE PRESIDENTS of the United States and contemporaneous WEEKLY COMPILATION OF PRESIDENTIAL DOCUMENTS in order to provide broader public access to, and wider dissemination of, presidential papers.

Presidential Libraries. President Franklin D. Roosevelt sought to preserve and protect presidential papers—at least, his own—and eventually make them accessible to the public through a new type of institution: PRESIDENTIAL LIBRARIES. Two prototypes were in existence when Roosevelt advanced this concept in 1938. The Rutherford B. Hayes Memorial Library in Fremont, Ohio, had been completed with state support in 1914. Built in fulfillment of obligations to receive the former chief executive's papers and memorabilia, the library came to house 67,425 items and 293 volumes of historical material. Its collections also included certain local and regional historical records apart from those of President Hayes. The state of Ohio and the Rutherford B. Hayes–Lucy Webb Hayes Foundation have jointly continued to maintain the facility.

When President Herbert Hoover completed his term in 1933, he placed his presidential papers in an institution he had established in 1919. The Hoover Library of War, Revolution, and Peace had been created through a pledge by Hoover of $50,000 to his alma mater, Stanford University, to serve as a repository for his collection of largely original documents deriving from European propaganda and pamphleteering activities of the WORLD WAR I era. Later renamed the Hoover Institution on War, Revolution, and Peace, it subsequently severed its ties to Stanford and currently maintains itself through donations and as a contract research organization. The institution

continues to hold papers resulting from Hoover's public service since 1914. Most of his presidential materials, however, were transferred to the Hoover presidential library at West Branch, Iowa, when that building was completed and turned over to the Archivist of the United States in 1964.

Taking the Hayes and Hoover libraries as models, Roosevelt developed the concept of a publicly maintained presidential library. His plan called for the organization of a corporation to collect donations for the private construction of a suitable library building to house and preserve such historical materials as he might give, bequeath, or transfer. This edifice was to be constructed on the grounds of the Roosevelt family home at HYDE PARK, New York. Upon the completion of this library, it was to be transferred, as a gift, to the United States, provided that adequate legislation was enacted for the acceptance of such property and for its permanent care and maintenance. Such legislation was enacted in 1939 (53 Stat. 1062). The Archivist of the United States, acting on behalf of the federal government, accepted the completed library on 4 July 1940. The museum portion of the facility was opened to the public approximately one year later. The presidential papers of the library initially became available for research use by the public in the spring of 1946.

No less attentive to history and the preservation of his presidential materials, Harry S. Truman began to plan for a library similar to the one created by his predecessor. By 1950, a Missouri corporation had been created to construct a suitable facility. Other significant developments, however, overtook this effort. Congress soon approved legislation providing the statutory basis for all subsequent federal presidential libraries.

Under the terms of the new Presidential Libraries Act of 1955 (69 Stat. 695), a former President was understood to have complete control over his official records, even to the point of his defining what constituted "presidential papers." These materials could be taken away by the Chief Executive when he departed office. The Presidential Libraries Act established arrangements whereby a former President could, after privately constructing a depository edifice, deed both the building and such papers as he wished to house within it to the federal government. In accepting this property—buildings, land, records, papers, and perhaps artifacts—the government agreed to abide by the terms of the deed or contract of bequest, which often meant that restrictions were temporarily set on the public availability of some presidential materials. It was also understood that security requirements and other limited common-law restrictions, such as personal privacy, would be honored as well.

Pursuant to this statute, federal presidential libraries were subsequently created for seven former Presidents. These include the Harry S. Truman library in Independence, Missouri; the Herbert Hoover library in West Branch, Iowa; the Dwight D. Eisenhower library in Abilene, Kansas; the John Fitzgerald Kennedy library in Boston, Massachusetts; the Lyndon Baines Johnson library in Austin, Texas; the Gerald R. Ford library in Ann Arbor, Michigan; and the Jimmy Carter library in Atlanta, Georgia. New laws began to emerge, however, changing both the status of presidential papers and the arrangements for future presidential libraries.

New Requirements. Press revelations, primarily in the *Washington Post*, concerning a June 1972 burglary at the Democratic national committee offices located in the Watergate apartment complex in Washington, D.C., resulted in congressional and federal inquiries into possible White House involvement in this and related matters. Eventually, IMPEACHMENT proceedings were begun in the House of Representatives by the Committee on the Judiciary, which approved three articles of impeachment against President Richard M. Nixon, who subsequently resigned from office on 9 August 1974. In order to assure the integrity and availability of White House records for federal prosecutors pursuing various aspects of the WATERGATE AFFAIR, Congress approved the Presidential Recordings and Materials Preservation Act of 1974 (88 Stat. 1695). It placed the official papers and records of President Nixon under federal custody and set requirements that these materials remain in Washington under the supervision of the Archivist of the United States. Consequently, Nixon did not have possession of his presidential papers after he left office. Disputes ensued over the legality of this statute, the regulations implementing it, and the public availability of the materials involved. Nonetheless, the situation was little changed. A privately constructed and operated Nixon presidential library located in Yorba Linda, California, was dedicated in mid July 1990. Not part of the National Archives presidential library system, its research collection includes Nixon's congressional and vice presidential records and copies of a small store of his presidential papers.

The 1974 statute also created the temporary National Study Commission on Records and Documents of Federal Officials. This public-documents panel was "to study problems and questions with respect to the control, disposition, and preservation of records and documents produced by or on behalf of Federal offi-

cials." Chaired by former Attorney General Herbert Brownell and consisting of seventeen members representing the public and all three federal branches, the commission issued its final report in March 1977.

In partial response to some of the commission's recommendations, legislation to establish the future public ownership of presidential papers and procedures governing the preservation and public availability of such materials at the end of each Chief Executive's tenure was introduced in the House of Representatives early in 1978. It was subsequently given congressional approval and was signed into law in November as the PRESIDENTIAL RECORDS ACT of 1978 (92 Stat. 2523). The statute carefully defined *presidential records* and made all such materials created on or after 20 January 1981 subject to its provisions. It effectively made presidential papers federal property that was to remain under the custody and control of the Archivist of the United States when each incumbent President left the White House. Thus, Jimmy Carter became the last occupant of the Oval Office who could freely take away his records and papers. When Ronald Reagan concluded his term, he was obligated to turn over his presidential materials to the Archivist; they were subsequently deposited at the Reagan presidential library in Simi Valley, California, which was officially opened on 4 November 1991.

Finally, in the aftermath of the Presidential Records Act, growing public and congressional concern about the increasing cost of providing benefits to the nation's former Presidents—particularly the physical size and continued maintenance of presidential libraries—resulted in the Presidential Libraries Act of 1986 (100 Stat. 495). It set certain reporting requirements, architectural and design conditions, and fiscal limitations regarding future presidential libraries, including the requirement of an operating endowment. Thus, prior to accepting any gift of land, a building, or equipment to create a federal presidential library or making any physical or material change in an existing one, the Archivist must submit a written report to Congress providing detailed information, as specified in the statute, about the transaction. Portions of the endowment requirements for new federal presidential libraries, however, were specifically made applicable "to any President who takes the oath of office as President for the first time on or after January 20, 1985." Consequently, the George Bush presidential library will be the first such facility to be subject to all of these recent reform requirements.

For the future, increased use of electronic formats and electronic information technology in the production of presidential records seemingly will present new challenges. Greater attention to the preservation of computer software and hardware may be necessary to avoid technological impediments to the accessibility of presidential information stored in electronic formats. Communications by presidential aides using online systems may be lost without the use and retention of electronic memory in these transactions. Similarly, succeeding drafts of presidential documents may disappear if modifications are made using only the electronic version contained in a personal computer. These kinds of considerations pertain to presidential records in both their active and archival phases. Moreover, they ultimately suggest a dynamic new understanding of presidential papers.

BIBLIOGRAPHY

Jones, H. G. *The Records of a Nation.* 1969.

McCoy, Donald R. *The National Archives: America's Ministry of Documents, 1934–1968.* 1978.

National Academy of Public Administration. *The Effects of Electronic Recordkeeping on the Historical Record of the U.S. Government.* 1989.

U.S. National Archives and Records Administration. *NARA and Presidential Records: Laws and Authorities and Their Implementation.* 1988.

U.S. National Study Commission on Records and Documents of Federal Officials. *Final Report.* 1977.

HAROLD C. RELYEA

PAPERWORK REDUCTION ACT (1980). Enacted to reduce the reporting and paperwork burden imposed on the public by the federal departments and agencies, the Paperwork Reduction Act of 1980 (94 Stat. 2812) also strengthened the mandate of the OFFICE OF MANAGEMENT AND BUDGET (OMB) regarding the collection and dissemination of information as well as governmentwide management of information resources. Furthermore, as the federal departments and agencies have made greater use of electronic formats in the collection, maintenance, dissemination, and use of information, efforts have been made in Congress to amend the Paperwork Act and utilize it as a vehicle for setting policy concerning various aspects of electronic information, such as inventory, public accessibility, and sale.

Concerted efforts to address the federal burden of paperwork and reporting began during the NEW DEAL and the WORLD WAR II years when government programs and services both increased and intensified. In July 1935 the Central Statistical Board, initially established by presidential order in 1933, was given a statutory charter and responsibility "to plan and promote . . . the elimination of duplication in, statistical services carried on by or subject to the supervision of

the Federal Government" (49 Stat. 498). Subsequently, in its efforts to reduce the reporting burden of American business, the board recommended that Congress adopt a definite policy of oversight on duplication reporting requirements and establish a statistical coordinating agency. In response, the Senate, in 1940, created a Special Committee to Study Problems of American Small Business. In its 1941 final report, the committee offered draft legislation for coordinating federal reporting services and minimizing the burdens of providing reports and information to federal agencies. This bill was subsequently developed and adopted as the Federal Reports Act (FRA) of 1942 (56 Stat. 1078). Setting the first federal policy for controlling government paperwork, the FRA prevailed for almost forty years.

In the late 1960s, there was growing realization in Congress that the FRA was no longer adequate for addressing new and persistent paperwork problems. Hearings by the Senate Select Committee on Small Business revealed various difficulties in this regard. To obtain a comprehensive evaluation of the many facets of the paperwork burden and expert views as to solutions, Congress established a temporary study panel, the U.S. Commission on Federal Paperwork, at the end of 1974 (88 Stat. 1789). The commission completed its work in September 1977, having produced 36 topical reports and offered 770 recommendations.

Two years later, in September 1979, the OMB reported that more than half the commission's recommendations had been implemented. A major commission proposal, upgrading the FRA through reform legislation, was not realized until the following year when the Paperwork Act was adopted.

In brief, the statute establishes within the OMB an OFFICE OF INFORMATION AND REGULATORY AFFAIRS (OIRA), which is the primary administrative unit for implementing the act. The director of the OMB and the administrator of the OIRA are made responsible for various functions, including requests for clearance for collecting information, statistical policy, records management, automatic data processing, and telecommunications. Agencies are also assigned specific responsibilities, including the designation of a senior official for managing information resources. Although the concept of information-resources management was not defined in the statute, it is generally regarded to include birth-to-grave management of agency records, data, and information products, as well as agency resources for their production, maintenance, and utilization.

In April 1982, the OMB reported that the federal

paperwork burden had been reduced by nearly 17 percent since the statute's approval. An implementing circular, A-130, issued in late December 1985, was criticized for overreaching to areas of information policy not intended by the Paperwork Act for OMB management and otherwise treating government information as an economic commodity rather than a public resource. Attempts to amend the law since its initial enactment have not been successful.

BIBLIOGRAPHY

Caudle, Sharon L. *Federal Information Resources Management: Bridging Vision and Action.* 1987.

Funk, William F. "The Paperwork Reduction Act: Paperwork Reduction Meets Administrative Law." *Harvard Journal on Legislation* 24 (1987): 1–116.

U.S. Bureau of the Budget. "Management of Federal Information Resources." *Federal Register* 50 (1985): 52730–52751.

U.S. Commission on Federal Paperwork. *History of Paperwork Reform Efforts.* 1977.

HAROLD C. RELYEA

PARDON POWER. Article II, Section 2, of the Constitution states: "The President . . . shall have Power to grant Reprieves and Pardons for Offenses against the United States, except in Cases of Impeachment." The authority to grant pardons, the roots of which are traceable to the royal prerogative of the English monarchy, is at once the most imperial and delicate of the President's powers. A presidential pardon precludes the punishment of a person who has committed an offense against the United States. In view of the fact that the IMPEACHMENT exception is the only explicit textual limitation on the exercise of the power, scholars have described the authority as unfettered and immune to the doctrine of CHECKS AND BALANCES. In dictum, the Supreme Court has characterized the power as "unlimited." The apparently untrammeled power always has carried with it a great potential for abuse. The Framers of the Constitution were steeped in English history; the king frequently used pardons as partisan indulgences for friends and supporters. In spite of their familiarity with absolutist Stuart claims and their fear of a power-hungry executive with a proclivity for usurpation, the Framers opted, by the pardon clause, to vest the President with a broad discretion to correct miscarriages of justice and to restore tranquillity in the wake of rebellion.

The Constitutional Framework. The presidential pardon power was forged by the CONSTITUTIONAL CONVENTION in light of English practice. Executive mercy, found in ancient Mosaic, Greek, and Roman law, was introduced into English jurisprudence in the seventh century, according to Blackstone, on the grounds that all offenses are committed against the king's peace, and since it is the king who is injured by fighting in his house, it is reasonable that he alone should possess the power of forgiveness. The act of mercy, then, would be dispensed by the king in his grand role as the "fountain of justice." The historical record suggests, however, that the grant of a pardon was not so much an act of grace as it was the tool of pecuniary and political aggrandizement. Pardons often were sold for fees and used as an instrument of conscription to entice convicted felons and murderers to support military adventures. Evidently, pardons were so easily obtainable for persons who had committed such crimes as homicide, larceny, and robbery that law-abiding subjects who had accused them feared retribution, a prospect that also discouraged others from making accusations. The systematic abuse of the pardon power across several centuries provoked numerous complaints from Parliament, which feared for its statutes, and eventuated in a constitutional crisis in the late seventeenth century between the House of Commons and the Crown. The bold attempt by Charles II to use the pardon power as a means to preempt the impeachment in 1678 of the earl of Danby, lord high treasurer of England, triggered a constitutional crisis that would have resounding implications for the presidential pardon power: May a royal pardon prevent an impeachment? For members of the Commons, who viewed the impeachment power as a means of bringing corrupt ministers to heel, the act of executive clemency could not be tolerated. It was feared that a pardon before trial would stifle testimony and therefore bury the facts surrounding the plot. Had the Commons acquiesced in the pardon, the pretended accountability of the ministers would have ceased, for the king would have been free to exercise the prerogative to screen them from parliamentary inquiry. Charles did not want to lose his trusted aide, but Danby was not worth another civil war. Therefore, in spite of the pardon, Danby spent five years in the Tower of London without trial. In legislation that effectuated the arguments and sentiments expressed by the Commons during the Danby affair, Parliament passed the Act of Settlement in 1700, which declared that an impeachment could not be impeded by a pardon.

English practice was constantly before the eyes of those who drafted the state constitutions during the revolutionary war period. For most states, it was the norm: a pardon may not be pleaded to ban impeachment. Exceptions to this practice were more restrictive of the pardoning authority, as reflected, for example, in the absolute denial to the governor of a pardon power, in the requirement that pardons were contingent upon approval from the legislature, or in the prohibition of preconviction pardons.

The Constitutional Convention refused to embrace these restrictions. The debate on the pardon power was framed by a proposal from Charles Pinckney of South Carolina that mirrored the English practice. The impeachment exception evoked no controversy since the Framers were familiar with the Danby affair and they had no desire to vest the President with a power that had been denied to the Crown. The convention focused principally on the question of whether the President should be empowered to grant pardons for treason, an issue that occasioned an impassioned debate. Some delegates, including ALEXANDER HAMILTON, would have permitted pardons for treason but only if the Senate approved. In rhetoric that stirred images of a presidential coup and that sharply echoed the concerns of the Commons a century before, George Mason warned that a President might issue pardons "to screen from punishment those whom he had secretly instigated to commit the crime, and thereby prevent a discovery of his own guilt." In the end, in spite of their fear of the subversion of the Republic by pardons, the Framers could not bring themselves to fashion an exception for treason. From history and first-hand experience in the form of Shays' Rebellion, the Framers were familiar with the seductive potential of a well-aimed and well-timed pardon to quell rebellions and restore tranquillity. Without such an option, rebels might just as well die on the battlefield than by the gallows. The wisdom and potential benefits of that policy, however, would not have overcome fears of presidential complicity in treasonous activities without assurances from JAMES WILSON of the availability of impeachment to curb abuse of the pardon power. In fact, every warning that a President might use the pardon power to exonerate accomplices, to forestall investigations, and generally to subvert law and government was met with assurances that the threat of impeachment would prevent such misconduct.

The debate on treason focused attention on the presidency, and not Congress, as the repository of the pardon power. Since the timing of a pardon offered to rebels was critical and since Congress was not expected to be in continuous session, there was little choice but to vest the power in the President. But the Framers' reluctance was alleviated by Wilson's reassuring remarks about the restraining impact of impeachment, and by the rationale, as explained by Hamilton in FEDERALIST 74, that the President's realization that the very fate of an individual might rest on his shoulders would assure a scrupulous exercise of the authority in order to avoid accusations of weakness or connivance.

The convention's creation of a virtually unlimited presidential pardon power has been confirmed by the judiciary. A pardon may be issued before conviction, but not before an offense has been committed, for such an act would amount to the power to dispense with the laws, the claim to which led to King James II's forced abdication. A pardon may be conferred absolutely or conditionally, provided the conditions are constitutional. However, whether a pardon may be conferred over the objections of the recipient is not clear since the acceptance of a pardon is generally considered an admission of the commission of a crime. The power to pardon also includes the authority to commute sentences, and to remit fines, penalties, and forfeitures. It has been held that the pardon power, which includes authority to issue a general AMNESTY, may not be restricted by congressional legislation, but since Congress also has authority to grant general amnesties, the exercise of its power may confer clemency in terms more generous than the President's.

While the Supreme Court has viewed the President's pardon power as virtually unfettered, it also has held that the abuse of the power is vulnerable to judicial review and impeachment. Two decisions have established a foundation, however slim, for judicial review of the pardon power, in light of considerations of due process and SEPARATION OF POWERS. In 1925, in *Ex parte Grossman*, Chief Justice William Howard Taft allowed for the possibility that excessive abuses of the pardoning power might provoke a test of its validity in federal court, but he noted that sufficient abuses had not yet occurred. In 1974, in *Schick v. Reed*, Chief Justice Warren Burger stated that under the right circumstances, conditions to pardons could be declared invalid.

Granting Pardons. Presidents have granted pardons for various offenses since the dawn of the Republic. With few exceptions, the country has been well served by exercise of the power. President George Washington initiated the use of the pardon authority in 1795 when he issued a proclamation of amnesty to participants in the WHISKEY REBELLION. Since then, pirates who have assisted United States military causes, participants in insurrections, deserters, federal officials, and polygamists, among others, have received clemency. An occasional pardon—to JEFFERSON DAVIS and the Confederate soldiers, or to Richard M. Nixon, or to VIETNAM WAR draft evaders, for example—has excited intense controversy and heightened public interest in the power; but a great many pardons have been issued without fanfare to federal prisoners who have reached the late stages of their lives and are near death. The frequency and volume of pardons granted, moreover, are perhaps greater than most Americans would suppose. During the CIVIL WAR and its aftermath, Presidents Abraham Lincoln and Andrew Jackson issued amnesties to some 200,000 persons. In 1933, President Franklin D. Roosevelt exercised the power to restore the civil rights of about 1,500 persons who had completed prison terms for violating the draft or for espionage acts during WORLD WAR I, and in 1945 he restored citizenship rights to several thousand former convicts who had served at least one year in the military and subsequently had earned an honorable discharge. In 1946, President Harry S. Truman granted pardons to more than 1,500 people who had been sentenced to prison for violating the Selective Service Act, and on Christmas Day, 1952, he restored civil rights to 9,000 people who had been convicted of desertion during peacetime. In addition to the more than 10,000 beneficiaries of the Vietnam War clemency and amnesty programs of Presidents Gerald Ford and Jimmy Carter, some 4,600 pardons and 500 commutations were granted between 1953 and 1984 by Presidents from Dwight D. Eisenhower to Ronald Reagan. Reagan issued about 380 pardons during his eight years in the White House.

Until the Civil War, the exercise of the pardoning authority had not provoked controversy or question. But the stresses of that war, the vindictive mood of many Northerners, and the desire for retribution among some in Congress raised concerns about the use of the power. Some members of Congress objected to the inconsistent consideration of requests for pardons and to the preferential treatment accorded Kentuckians; the influence peddling of pardon brokers; and the insincerity of the recipients, who were required to take a loyalty oath to the Union. Congress even undertook an examination of Johnson's bank account pursuant to allegations that he had been bribed to issue pardons. To some Americans, it seemed that the administration of the pardon power was as arbitrary as it had been in England.

The exercise of the pardon power and the consideration of its use in more recent times have perhaps excited more public dissatisfaction with and curiosity in the scope of the power and its political and legal dimensions than at any other point in our history. In particular, Americans have witnessed the possibility that President Nixon might pardon himself and more than thirty aides involved in WATERGATE AFFAIR offenses, the unconditional pardon that President Ford granted to Nixon, and in December 1992 the pretrial pardon that President George Bush issued to former

Secretary of Defense Casper Weinberger for charges stemming from his role in the IRAN-CONTRA AFFAIR. These episodes have revealed the darker ways in which a power to temper justice with mercy might be transformed into a political tool to be exploited and abused for partisan causes.

Befitting its royal heritage, the presidential pardoning power is subject to few constitutional restraints, and only then in rare and unlikely circumstances. In theory, judicial review and impeachment are available to restrain the pardon power, but in practice they are not apt to be invoked unless the President abuses the power excessively or otherwise administers it in a grossly arbitrary manner. Contrary, therefore, to Supreme Court dictum and scholarly assertions of an illimitable power to pardon, there are boundaries that fence the exercise of executive clemency. Nevertheless, it is easier to speak of abuses, as opposed to illegal uses, of the pardon authority. The principal restriction on the power remains political, to be exercised by Americans on Election Day.

BIBLIOGRAPHY

Adler, David Gray. "The President's Pardon Power." In *Inventing the American Presidency*. Edited by Thomas E. Cronin. 1989.

Corwin, Edward S. *The President: Office and Powers, 1787–1984: A History and Analysis of Practice and Opinion*. 5th rev. ed. 1984.

Dorris, Jonathan T. *Pardon and Amnesty under Lincoln and Johnson*. 1953.

Duker, William. "The President's Power to Pardon: A Constitutional History." *William and Mary Law Review* 18 (1977): 475–535.

Humbert, W. H. *The Pardoning Power of the President*. 1941.

Kurland, Philip. *Watergate and the Constitution*. 1978.

DAVID GRAY ADLER

PARKER, ALTON B. (1852–1926), Democratic presidential nominee in 1904. Alton Brooks Parker is remembered only as the colorless, unsuccessful challenger to Theodore Roosevelt who lost by a wide margin to the most exciting political figure of the early twentieth century. Selected as the careful and responsible alternative to Roosevelt's flamboyance and personal appeal, Parker proved to be a lackluster campaigner and a weak candidate.

Parker was born near Cortland, New York, educated at local schools, and graduated from Albany Law School in 1873. He served in several local positions in Ulster County, including surrogate from 1877 to 1885. He managed the gubernatorial campaign of David B. Hill in 1885, and was named to the New York supreme court a year later. He then went on to the New York court of appeals in 1889, and rose through the various levels of that court system until 1897. He won a statewide race to become chief judge of the New York court of appeals in 1897. Parker was a respected jurist and an influential lawyer within the New York Democratic Party. These qualities helped to make him a national candidate in 1904.

Following the second defeat of WILLIAM JENNINGS BRYAN in the presidential election of 1900, conservative Democrats looked to recapture their party and run a candidate in 1904 without any taint of radicalism. They regained control from the Bryan forces in several states between 1901 and 1903, but they still faced the problem of finding a candidate to make the race against Theodore Roosevelt, who had become President upon the death of William McKinley in 1901. Knowing that any Democrat could count on the electoral votes of the Solid South, party leaders wanted to find someone who could win the state of New York. If a candidate could do that, and carry the states of Connecticut, New Jersey, and Indiana, he would be within striking distance of the 240 electoral votes needed to win.

Since Parker had shown vote-getting appeal in his 1897 race with the New York electorate, he began to be mentioned in 1903 as a possible candidate. Circumstances favored Parker. With Bryan not a factor, there was no strong challenger within the agrarian wing of the Democrats. The newspaper publisher William Randolph Hearst was Parker's only serious rival, but his scandal-ridden personal life led one newspaper to call him only "a low voluptuary." By the spring of 1904, Hearst's candidacy had collapsed.

Meanwhile, Parker's fortunes strengthened. He said very little that might be divisive. When a reporter asked him to give his views on current issues, he responded: "You may be right in thinking that an expression of my views is necessary to secure the nomination. If so, let the nomination go." Parker's candidacy hinged on keeping quiet, allowing his supporters to depict him as a sane, balanced alternative to President Roosevelt. Parker was nominated on the first ballot when the Democrats held their convention in Saint Louis in July 1904. Still divided over the monetary question of the free coinage of silver, the Democrats attempted to dodge the issue in their platform. Parker sent a public telegram insisting that he regarded "the gold standard as firmly and irrevocably established." His running mate was the eighty-two year old Henry G. Davis of West Virginia.

Parker's campaign started badly. His acceptance speech was not successful, and his efforts to run a front-porch campaign from his home in Esopus, New York, were futile. He lacked the public allure of Roosevelt, and it soon became evident that the Democrats were divided and confused. As the voting neared, it seemed as if Parker would be humiliated at the polls.

In an attempt to inject life into his faltering campaign, Parker charged that Roosevelt and his campaign manager, George B. Cortelyou, were accepting campaign funds from large corporations in return for future favors. Roosevelt denied the charge vigorously, although there was some truth in it, and Parker proved unable to make the allegation stick publicly. When Americans voted, they gave Roosevelt an overwhelming popular majority and 336 electoral votes, the largest total up to that time. Parker received 140 electoral votes from the South. He never ran for public office again, and practiced law in New York until his death. As one newspaper said in 1904, Parker was an "estimable and symmetrical gentleman" who "presented to the inquiring vision all the salient qualities of a sphere." He had the misfortune to run against one of the most popular Presidents in American history, and his campaign never really had a chance of victory.

BIBLIOGRAPHY

Gould, Lewis L. *Reform and Regulation: American Politics from Roosevelt to Wilson.* 1986.
Shoemaker, Fred C. "Alton B. Parker: The Images of a Gilded Age Statesman in an Era of Progressive Politics." Master's thesis, Ohio State University, 1983.

LEWIS L. GOULD

PARLIAMENTARY SYSTEM. The parliamentary system is the major alternative to the American presidential-congressional system, when nations select a democratic form of government. The parliamentary system has flourished longest in Great Britain, a democracy without a formal constitution, having a unitary and centralized political system, and with little autonomy for local government. In contrast, the parliamentary system of Germany and other countries of Western Europe are federal in character, with important powers and functions divided between the central government and the member states. The French Fifth Republic is a hybrid of the parliamentary and presidential systems, with the principal legislative body, the National Assembly, possessing many characteristics of a parliamentary system, coupled with a powerful presidency.

In its essentials, the historic parliamentary system, as practiced by its chief progenitor, Great Britain, vests all governmental power in Parliament, a two-house legislature that combines legislative, executive, and judicial duties and powers. The structure is called officially "The Crown in Parliament" and includes the monarch and the House of Commons and the House of Lords. Both houses act on legislation, although the Commons retains legislative authority; the monarch approves legislation before it becomes law. The monarch's approval is pro forma. The Commons has 630 members, who are popularly elected from districts in which they need not reside. Members are elected for a maximum term of five years, although the prime minister, a member of Parliament, can ask the crown to call a general election at any time: Parliaments often do not last a full five years. The House of Lords has little legislative power, and the monarch is limited to ceremonial and symbolic roles. The monarch opens new sessions of Parliament in an elaborate ceremony and reads an address, which the prime minister and the cabinet prepare, which often provides an agenda for the new legislative session. The President also has ceremonial and symbolic roles. He, more than anyone, symbolizes the nation, and he awards medals and other public recognition to citizens and their acceptional achievements.

The counterpart to the President in the parliamentary system is the prime minister, who is usually the leader of the majority party in the House of Commons. The prime minister chooses the cabinet from the leaders of the majority party, who are also members of Parliament.

The cabinet, called the government, prepares all major legislation and introduces it in the Commons; with rare exception, government bills pass without difficulty. The House of Commons sometimes votes against the government on an important issue, which is regarded as a vote of no confidence, whereupon the prime minister usually resigns with the cabinet. Or, the Commons may simply adopt a vote of no confidence. Either a general election, or the formation of a new government supported by the existing House of Commons, follows. A decline in public opinion polls may weaken party support and prompt the resignation of the prime minister, who is then replaced by another leader within the ruling party. Impasse between cabinet and Parliament is short-lived, unlike DIVIDED GOVERNMENT in the United States, where the President may be of one party and another party may control one or both of the congressional houses, prompting conflict and deadlock.

In Britain, cabinet government functions according to the principle of collective responsibility. Each minister is responsible for the performance of his department, but the entire cabinet supports him and shares his responsibility. When the cabinet decides on a policy, each minister supports it in Parliament and in public even if he disagrees with it. A dissenting minister who cannot comply with this protocol is expected to resign.

The most potent weapon of the parliamentary system, the magical force that keeps it functioning with smooth assurance, is tight party discipline. When the system is functioning optimally, the prime minister's party provides the government with a majority of legislators whose voting support, with little exception, is granitic—"solid masses of steady votes," Walter Bagehot, the master political essayist, put it. The party leader, who is ordinarily the prime minister, possesses powers that far exceed those of the American President. British parties are national organizations, unlike American parties, which are chiefly state and local in character. The British party secretariat or central office is the prime minister's personal machine, since he appoints its principal officers and controls propaganda, research, and finance. No member of the House of Commons of the prime minister's party, who has crossed the floor, or sided with the opposition on a major issue, has won reelection since 1945.

In contrast, the American President may command uncertain support from his congressional party. When, for example, President Harry S. Truman proposed a legislative program of twenty-one points to aid the nation's conversion from war making to peace making, he won enactment of only two of them despite his party's majorities in both congressional houses.

Nonetheless, the prime minister suffers several vulnerabilities. If public support for the government's policies declines, if public opinion polls foreshadow a likely loss of the next election, a prime minister may be toppled, as was Margaret Thatcher in 1991. Widespread public discontent with her key policies and her enmity with several party leaders led to her failure to win reelection as party leader. That rebuff led to her departure as prime minister, and the succession of her protégé, John Major. Narrow vote margins in the House of Commons, the result of national elections that in Britain are often close, may constrain or eventually overturn a government. In 1979, the Labour government of James Callaghan lost a motion of no confidence by one vote, owing to the illness and absence of a single Labour member.

Parliamentary systems have no analogue comparable to the presidential system's use of PRESIDENTIAL PRIMARIES, state and local party conventions, and national nominating conventions. In Britain, the voters elect a new House of Commons. Following the election, the monarch requests the leader of the victorious party to form a government as prime minister, thus ratifying the electorate's preference. But the selection of the party leader prior to his or her appearance before the electorate is largely a matter of intraparty maneuver.

The American President, once elected, enjoys more stability of tenure than the British prime minister. Presidents as unpopular as James Buchanan and Herbert Hoover, persisted in office until the next inauguration, while in Britain, their departure would have been speeded long before. For more than a year, until he resigned in the face of certain IMPEACHMENT with the exposure of the WATERGATE AFFAIR, President Nixon clung to his office despite widespread public belief that he was guilty of criminal acts and despite the severe drain the crisis inflicted upon his effectiveness. In Britain, Nixon would have been ejected from office in a matter of weeks by the pressure of his parliamentary party responding to hostile public opinion.

In theory, the President is more powerful than the prime minister in legislation. Head of the executive branch, he is the coequal of Congress. In theory, the prime minister and the other cabinet ministers are a committee who serve the House of Commons, but in fact they are the premier influence in policy making. Although in theory Commons legislates, the cabinet, or the government, as it is also called, dominates the law-making process. The government plans and controls the Commons' time. The introduction of legislation is almost completely the government's monopoly. A rule requiring that all legislation involving expenditure bear the crown's or, in reality, the government's approval, endows the government with sweeping control, since virtually any legislation of significance requires money. Parliament is largely limited to influencing the government's future course: flaws exposed in legislative debate presumably will be corrected by the government.

The prime minister, unlike the President, shares power with the cabinet and other ministers who are not cabinet members. The President is free to ignore his CABINET. In choosing the cabinet, the prime minister is more restricted than the President. The prime minister is obliged to work with certain associates; the President is not. To form a Government, the prime minister must attract the support of the principal factions of his party, done by allotting cabinet seats to factional leaders. The President may consider political interests, geographical concerns, as well as friendship in choosing members of his cabinet. The prime minister's range of choice is far narrower.

Admirers of the parliamentary system are impressed with the ease and assurance with which it enacts policy. In its usual workings, prime minister and the cabinet oversee legislation, guided by public opinion expressed by interest groups, the press, and the House of Commons. Parliament has ceded administration to the government including matters such as organizational structure, programs, finance, and directing the civil service. Commons votes the funds the government requests and lacks constitutional power to exceed the government's specified sums. The contemporary parliamentary system reduces the House of Commons to a passivity wholly alien to the assertive American Congress. Commons most resembles the American ELECTORAL COLLEGE, registering the popular will in choosing a government and then ratifying the program and voting the funds it requests.

BIBLIOGRAPHY

Alexander, Andrew, and Alan Watkins. *The Making of the Prime Minister 1970.* 1970.

Carter, Byrum E. *The Office of Prime Minister.* 1956.

Jennings, Ivor. *The Queen's Government.* 1967.

King, Anthony, ed. *The British Prime Minister.* 1969.

Mackintosh, John P. *The British Cabinet.* 2d rev. ed. 1968.

Mackintosh, John P. *The Government and Politics of Britain.* 3d rev. ed. 1974.

LOUIS W. KOENIG

PARTIES, POLITICAL. For discussion of the President as leader of a political party, see PARTY LEADER, PRESIDENT AS. For discussion of particular political parties, see ANTI-MASONIC PARTY; DEMOCRATIC PARTY; FEDERALIST PARTY; FREE-SOIL PARTY; GREENBACK PARTY; KNOW-NOTHING (AMERICAN) PARTY; LIBERTY PARTY; PROGRESSIVE (BULL MOOSE) PARTY; PROGRESSIVE PARTY, 1924; PROGRESSIVE PARTY, 1948; PROHIBITION PARTY; REPUBLICAN PARTY; THIRD PARTIES; WHIG PARTY.

PARTY LEADER, PRESIDENT AS. The relationship between the presidency and the American party-system has always been a difficult one. The architects of the Constitution established a nonpartisan President who, with the support of the judiciary, was intended to play the leading institutional role in checking and controlling the virulent party conflict that the Framers feared would destroy the fabric of representative democracy. An ideal executive would stand above the "merely" political conflicts of factions and rule benevolently in the public interest.

Like most of the Framers of the Constitution, George Washington, the first CHIEF EXECUTIVE, disapproved of factions, and he did not regard himself as the leader of any political party. Washington believed that Article II of the Constitution encouraged the President to stand apart from the jarring party conflict that was inherent to the legislative body. As such, the President could provide a strong measure of unity and stability to the political system. This was a task that, by temperament and background, Washington was well suited to perform. Although he insisted on being master of the executive branch, it was contrary to his principles to try to influence congressional elections or the legislative process. The primary duty of the President, he believed, was to execute the laws.

The Origins of Parties. Washington's conception of the presidency did not survive even his own administration, however. Ultimately, disagreements among his brilliant constellation of advisers led to the demise of the nonpartisan presidency. Party conflict arose from the sharp differences between ALEXANDER HAMILTON, Secretary of the Treasury, and Thomas Jefferson, Secretary of State, differences that began during Washington's first term and became irreconcilable during the second term. Hamilton favored a strong, dynamic national government, anchored by an independent and active President; Jefferson professed not to be a friend of energetic central government. Jefferson was especially opposed to Hamilton's proposal for a national bank, which was contained in the Treasury Secretary's December 1790 report to Congress. According to Jefferson, Hamilton's plan would establish national institutions and policies that transcended the powers of Congress and the states. Furthermore, Hamilton favored domestic and international initiatives that presupposed a principal role for the President in formulating public policies and carrying them out. This view, Jefferson believed, made the more decentralizing institutions—Congress and the states—subordinate to the executive, thus undermining popular sovereignty and pushing the United States toward a British-style monarchy.

Ultimately these constitutional disagreements made inevitable an open outbreak of party conflict between the Federalists, who shared Hamilton's point of view, and the Democratic-Republicans, who shared Jefferson's. The full implications of this conflict became clear with the election of Jefferson as the third President in 1800. Jefferson's predecessor John Adams, who occupied the vice presidency during Washington's term, was clearly identified with the FEDERALIST PARTY. But he shared Washington's disdain for party leadership and any claims he might have made on his party were thwarted by Hamilton's ongoing influence. Jefferson too held an antiparty position; by the time he ascended to the presidency, however, partisan conflict and institutions had evolved to a point that demanded presidential party leadership. Moreover, party leadership offered a means by which he could lead the nation without violating the Democratic-Republican fear of executive usurpation, and thus make the executive office more democratic.

The Democratic-Republican Party [*see* DEMOCRATIC PARTY] helped to introduce and, by its example, helped to legitimize the idea of a presidential candidate as the head of a party ticket. The concept of a candidate as a party leader necessitated a formal change in the balloting arrangements of the electoral college. Originally, the ELECTORAL COLLEGE, which was conceived without political parties in mind, required presidential electors to cast a single ballot with the name of two presidential candidates on it. After the counting of the assembled ballots, the candidate with the most votes, provided the number was a majority, would become President, and the runner-up would become Vice President.

Under this procedure, the election of 1800 produced a tie. A caucus of each party's members of Congress had been held to choose nominees for President and Vice President; the caucus's decision then was coordinated with party organizations in the various states so electors were selected as instructed agents, pledged to cast their two ballots for the party's presidential and vice-presidential candidates. The party effort was too successful. Seventy-three Democratic-Republican electors were chosen (to sixty-five for the Federalists), and each voted for Jefferson and his running mate, AARON BURR. According to the Constitution, it thus fell to the lame-duck Federalist majority in the House of Representatives to decide which Democratic-Republican—Jefferson or Burr—would become President. After thirty-five ballots, the Federalist majority finally consented to the choice of Jefferson.

By 1804, the TWELFTH AMENDMENT was adopted, which implicitly acknowledged the existence of political parties and provided for separate balloting by the electors for President and Vice President. This amendment ratified a fundamental shift in the status of electors. They quickly lost the independent status envisioned by the Framers. Instead, they became instruments of party will. Moreover, the parties' dominance of presidential selection added a new, extraconstitutional presidential eligibility requirement, a party nomination. Party affiliation and nomination thus became a decisive criteria for selection, and the idea that electors should possess discretion was rejected as undemocratic.

In turn, the presence of a party's candidate at the head of a party ticket for elected offices conferred on that individual the status of party leader. Once elected, that figure assumed responsibility beyond the leadership of the executive branch. Unlike Washington and

Adams, Jefferson deemphasized the constitutional powers of the office, governing instead through the role of party leader. The Jefferson administration encouraged the development of disciplined organization in Congress, with the President relying on floor leaders in the House and Senate to advance his program. Another source of presidential influence was the party caucus: during Jefferson's tenure as President, conclaves of leaders from the executive and legislative branches formulated policy and encouraged party unity.

Despite the assumed party division during his two terms in office, Jefferson never viewed a party system, consisting of two parties contending peacefully against each other in mutual tolerance, as a solution to the constitutional challenge posed by Hamiltonianism. Instead, Jefferson, as well as his Democratic-Republican successors in the White House, James Madison (1809–1816) and James Monroe (1818–1825), hoped to overcome the Federalists at the polls and restore a nonpartisan system dedicated to popular rule, that is, joined to a more democratic executive that would be respectful of legislative power and STATES' RIGHTS.

Monroe's ascendance to the presidency in 1817 signaled the complete triumph of the Democratic-Republicans. During Monroe's first term as President, the Federalist Party disappeared as a national organization; in fact, Monroe was unopposed for reelection in 1820. With the Federalists vanquished, the 1824 election became a contest of individuals rather than parties. Rival and sectional leaders, each supported by his own organization and following, ran for President in one of the most bitter and confusing campaigns in American history.

For the second time in twenty years, an election was decided not by the voters but by the House of Representatives. WILLIAM H. CRAWFORD was the nominee of the Democratic-Republican caucus; but the party machinery had run down badly by 1824, and its support was no longer tantamount to election. Four candidates (Crawford, Andrew Jackson, John Quincy Adams, and HENRY CLAY) so divided the electoral votes that no one received the necessary majority to be President. In accordance with the Twelfth Amendment, the House of Representatives narrowly elected Adams despite the fact that Jackson had obtained the greater number of popular and electoral votes. The controversial election of 1824 ensured the demise of what had come to be called "King Caucus," thus precipitating reforms that significantly transformed the link between Presidents and their parties.

Presidents and Party Government. With Jackson's election in 1828, the confused political situation that had underlain the previous presidential campaign was replaced by a new party alignment. Jackson and JOHN C. CALHOUN, who was Vice President during Adams's administration, formed the Democratic Party, which dedicated itself to the traditional Democratic-Republican principles of states' rights and a narrow interpretation of the national government's constitutional powers. Adams and Clay, who stood for strengthening the role of the federal government, formed the opposition WHIG PARTY.

The advent of the Jackson presidency was accompanied by important party reforms that significantly enhanced the President's party leadership role. The demise of "King Caucus" left a vacuum in the presidential nominating process that was filled by the national party convention. Conventions were used by the Democrats in 1832 and were accepted by the Whigs after the presidential campaign of 1836. National convention delegates were selected by conventions in the states, which consisted in turn of local organizations of party members. Taken together, the new and elaborate Whig and Democratic organizations reached far beyond the halls of Congress and eventually penetrated every corner of the Union. Sustained by his party's far-reaching political network, Jackson became the first President in American history to appeal to the people over the heads of the legislative representatives. Meanwhile, under the astute direction of Jackson's Vice President and successor in the White House, Martin Van Buren, Jackson also implemented a system of rotation into government personnel practices, using the President's power of removal to replace federal employees for purely partisan reasons [see PATRONAGE].

Although the major elements of presidential party leadership as developed during the Jacksonian era would endure to the twentieth century, an important shift in the character of President-party relations occurred in the immediate aftermath of the CIVIL WAR. Abraham Lincoln made skillful use of his position as leader of the new REPUBLICAN PARTY (the Whigs disintegrated in the face of the SLAVERY controversy) to hold together the Union and maintain the initiative in conducting the war. But Lincoln's assertive wartime leadership surprised and disconcerted most of his partisan brethren in Congress, who acted forcefully to weaken the presidency after his assassination; thereafter, the presidential nominee was usually beholden to the party leaders, who, fortified by patronage and the strong partisan loyalties among the electorate, dominated national conventions.

The national party chairman firmly linked the President and party. The Democrats had created the first national party committee headed by a party chair in 1848 to conduct the presidential campaign and to guide the party's fortunes between conventions. With Mark Hanna's reign of the Republican national committee from 1896 to 1904, the national party chair emerged as a figure of imposing political stature. As William McKinley's national chairman for the 1896 election, Hanna transformed the Republican national committee into a formidable campaign machine, distributing 120 million pieces of campaign literature, keeping 1,400 speakers on the road, and maintaining good relations with the press. Once elected, McKinley relied heavily upon Hanna, who served as the administration's principal political strategist and patronage agent.

Yet developments were under way in the country that would soon render the Republican model of party government obsolete. Massive social and economic changes were increasing the scale and complexity of American life, producing jarring economic dislocations and intense political conflicts. In the face of change, pressures mounted for a new style of governance, one that would require a more expansive national government and a more systematic administrative of public policy. The limited, nineteenth-century polity, which could accommodate decentralized party organizations, political patronage, and a dominant Congress, began to give way to a new order that depended upon consistent and forceful presidential leadership.

Executive Leadership. The rise of the modern presidency during the first half of the twentieth century signified the emergence of the President, rather than Congress or party organizations, as the leading instrument of popular rule. Acting on this modern concept of presidential leadership, Theodore Roosevelt (1901–1909) and Woodrow Wilson (1913–1921) inaugurated the practices during the Progressive Era that strengthened the President as popular and legislative leader. It fell to Franklin D. Roosevelt, however, to consolidate or institutionalize the changes in the executive office that were initiated during the first two decades of the twentieth century. His long tenure in the White House, 1933–1945, transformed presidential-party relations, placing executive leadership at the heart of the ascendant Democratic Party's approach to politics and government. Roosevelt's NEW DEAL program, developed in response to the Great Depression, brought the welfare state to the United States, years after it had become a fixture in European nations. His extraordinary leadership in expanding the federal government to meet the domestic crisis of the 1930s, and later an international one, WORLD WAR II, effected a dramatic increase in the size and scope of the federal executive.

Roosevelt pursued a personnel policy to build up a national organization rather than allowing patronage to be used merely to build senatorial and congressional machines. Although the President followed traditional patronage practices during his first term, the recommendations of JAMES A. FARLEY, chairman of the Democratic Party, were not followed so closely after his reelection. Instead, Roosevelt turned more and more frequently to a loosely knit, but well defined group of individuals—the so-called New Dealers—whose loyalties were to the New Deal rather than the Democratic Party. As a result, many appointments in Washington went to individuals who were supporters of the President and believed in what he was trying to do but were not Democrats in many instances, and in all instances were not organization Democrats.

Moreover, whereas Presidents since Jefferson had taken care to consult with legislative party leaders in the development of their policy programs, Roosevelt relegated his party in Congress to a decidedly subordinate status. He offended legislators by his use of PRESS CONFERENCES to announce important decisions and eschewed the use of the party in Congress. Though Roosevelt used Farley and Vice President JOHN NANCE GARNER, especially during the first term, to maintain close ties with Congress, legislative party leaders complained that they were called into consultation only when their signatures were required at the bottom of the page to make the document legal.

The most dramatic moment in Roosevelt's challenge to traditional party practices was the "purge" campaign of 1938. This involved Roosevelt directly in one gubernatorial and several congressional primary campaigns in a bold effort to replace conservative Democrats with candidates who were "100 percent New Dealers." Such intervention was not unprecedented. William Howard Taft and Wilson had made limited efforts to remove recalcitrant members from their party. But Roosevelt's campaign was unprecedented in scale, and unlike previous efforts, it made no attempt to work through the regular party organization. The degree to which his action was a departure from the norm is measured by the press labeling it the "purge," a term associated with Adolf Hitler's attempt to weed out dissent in Germany's National Socialist Party and Joseph Stalin's elimination of "disloyal" party members from the Soviet Communist Party.

In the final analysis the "benign dictatorship" that Roosevelt sought to impose on the Democratic Party was more conducive to corroding the American party system than reforming it. Roosevelt, in fact, felt that a full revamping of party politics was impractical, given the obstacles to centralized party government that are so deeply ingrained in the American political experience. The immense failure of the purge reinforced this view—all but two of the Democrats whom Roosevelt opposed were renominated. Moreover, the purge campaign, which was widely condemned as an assault on the constitutional system of CHECKS AND BALANCES, galvanized the political opposition to Roosevelt, apparently contributing to the heavy losses that the Democrats sustained in the 1938 elections. Ironically, then, Roosevelt's campaign only strengthened the conservative Democrats.

As the presidency evolved into a large and active institution, it preempted party leaders in many of their significant tasks: linking the President to interest groups, staffing the executive branch, developing, and most important, providing campaign support. Presidents no longer won election and governed as head of a party but were elected and governed as the head of a personal organization they created in their own image.

The Roosevelt administration obtained legislative authority in the Ramspeck Act (1940) to extend CIVIL SERVICE protection over the New Deal loyalists who were brought to Washington to staff the newly created welfare state. Beginning with Roosevelt, Presidents came to rely on executive-branch personnel to perform many of the political and social services that had traditionally been the province of the political party.

Disengagement and Isolation. Since the 1930s, further advancements in communications technology, especially television, served to connect the President even more directly with the public. Although Dwight D. Eisenhower (1953–1961) had been the first President to appear on television regularly, it was under and because of John F. Kennedy (1961–1963) that television became an essential determinant of a President's ability to lead the nation. Kennedy's effective use of television further weakened the party's traditional position as intermediary between the President and the public. In addition and indeed in response, party loyalties in the electorate began to decline. [See TELEVISION AND PRESIDENTIAL POLITICS.]

The 1968 election and its aftermath dramatized the decay of party politics and organization. The Democratic nominee, Vice President HUBERT H. HUMPHREY, led a party that was bitterly divided by the VIETNAM WAR. Its convention in Chicago was ravaged by controversy, both within the hall and out on the streets, where antiwar demonstrators clashed violently with the Chicago police. Without entering a single primary, Humphrey was nominated by the regular party leaders, who still controlled a majority of delegates and

who preferred him to the antiwar candidate, Sen. EUGENE McCARTHY.

Humphrey's controversial nomination and the failure of his general election campaign against the Republican candidate, former Vice President Richard M. Nixon, gave rise to important institutional reforms. The rules of the Democratic Party were revised to make its presidential nominating conventions more representative. The new rules eventually caused a majority of states to change from selecting delegates in closed councils of party regulars to electing them in direct PRESIDENTIAL PRIMARIES. Although the Democrats initiated these changes, many were codified in state laws that affected the Republican Party almost as much.

The declining influence of the traditional party organizations was apparent not only in the new nominating rules but also in the perceptions and habits of the voters. The 1968 election marked the beginning of an increased tendency for voters to "split their tickets," that is, to divide their votes among the parties. The trend toward ticket splitting continued into the 1990s. The electorate has tended to place the presidency in Republican hands and Congress under the control of Democrats, an historically unprecedented pattern of DIVIDED GOVERNMENT in national politics.

Divided government profoundly affected the course of the Nixon administration, exacerbating the alienation of the White House from party politics. Nixon sought congressional support to achieve policy goals during the first two years of his presidency. But faced with few legislative achievements, he later attempted to carry out his policies through the powers and personnel of the executive branch. Nixon intensified his efforts to strengthen presidential government after 1972, reflecting the more conservative position on domestic issues that characterized his presidency during the second term.

Nixon's attempt to achieve his political and policy objectives unilaterally has been widely regarded as an unprecedented usurpation of power and, ultimately, as a direct cause of the WATERGATE AFFAIR, which forced him to resign from office. The improprieties of Nixon's personal reelection organization, the Committee to Re-elect the President (CREEP), particularly its attempt to tap telephones in the offices of the Democratic national committee and the subsequent efforts by the President and his aides to cover up the break-in, brought down the Nixon presidency.

But Nixon's approach to modern presidential leadership was not entirely new; in important respects it was a logical extension of the evolving modern presidency. CREEP's complete autonomy from the regular

Republican organization was merely the culmination of presidential preemption of the traditional responsibilities of national party committees. Nixon's attempt to concentrate managerial authority in the hands of a few White House aides and Cabinet "supersecretaries" simply extended the contemporary practice of reconstructing the executive branch to be a more formidable instrument of presidential government.

Nixon's presidency had the effect of strengthening opposition to the unilateral use of presidential power, while further attenuating the bonds that linked Presidents to the party system. The evolution of the modern presidency now left it in complete political isolation. This isolation continued during the administrations of Gerald R. Ford (1974–1977), a Republican, and Jimmy Carter (1977–1981), a Democrat, so much so that by the end of the 1970s statesmen and scholars were lamenting the demise of the presidency as well as the party system.

Presidential Parties. The erosion of old-style politics allowed a more nationalized party system to develop, forging new links between Presidents and their parties. The Republican Party, in particular, developed a strong institutional apparatus; since the 1970s, its organizational strength in national politics has been unprecedented. Because the reconstituted party system has been associated less with patronage than with political issues and sophisticated fund-raising techniques, it may not pose as much an obstacle to the personal and programmatic ambitions of Presidents as did the traditional system. Indeed, the nomination and election of Ronald Reagan in 1980 were the culmination of nearly two decades of organizational efforts by Republican conservatives. Reagan's candidacy added a firm philosophical commitment and political skill to the partisan recipe. Not only did the Republicans capture the White House, but they won a majority in the Senate for the first time since 1952.

Significantly, it was Reagan who broke with the tradition of the modern presidency and identified closely with his party. The spirit of the relationship between the party chair, Frank Fahrenkopf, and the White House was much more positive than it had been since the advent of the modern presidency. Cooperation and good will prevailed as Reagan worked hard to strengthen the Republican's organizational and popular base, surprising even his own White House political director with his total readiness to make fund-raising appearances for the party and its candidates.

Despite the recent changes in the party system, any celebration of the dawn of a new era of disciplined party government would be premature. Reagan's personal popularity never was converted into Republican control of the government. His landslide in 1984 did not prevent the Democrats from maintaining a strong majority in the House of Representatives; and despite his plea to the voters to elect Republicans in the 1986 congressional elections, the Democrats recaptured control of the Senate.

Thus, the closer ties the Reagan administration tried to forge between the modern presidency and the Republican Party did not alter the unprecedented partisan and electoral divisions that characterize the era of divided government. Furthermore, the persistence of divided government itself retards the restoration of partisanship in the presidency.

The 1988 election, in which Vice President George Bush defeated his Democratic opponent, Governor Michael Dukakis of Massachusetts, seemed to indicate that divided government had become an enduring characteristic of American politics. Indeed, never before had voters given a newly elected President fewer fellow partisans in Congress than they gave Bush. The 1988 campaign and its aftermath, moreover, confirmed the disassembling of the partisan and presidential realms in American politics.

The 1992 presidential election, in which the Democratic candidate, Gov. Bill Clinton of Arkansas, defeated the incumbent President, George Bush, seemed to underscore, if not provide an escape from, the disturbing political and constitutional developments of the previous quarter century. Lacking his predecessor's popular support and conservative convictions, Bush's term in office exposed the weakness of the Republican Party—indeed, his unhappy stay in the White House threatened the modern presidency with the same sort of isolation and drift that characterized the Ford and Carter years. The Democratic Party took surprising advantage of Bush's misfortune; mindful of how intractable factiousness had denied them control of the presidency for twelve years, the Democrats ran a rather effective campaign that not only captured the White House, but left them in control of both congressional chambers. Clinton's victory thus promised to ameliorate the partisan and electoral divisions that had prevailed since 1968.

Still, the meaning of the 1992 election was somewhat ambiguous. In a three-candidate race between Clinton, Bush, and an independent, ROSS PEROT, Clinton won a landslide in the electoral college, sweeping thirty-two states with 370 electoral votes. Yet he won only 43 percent of the popular vote, roughly the same percentage of the total vote Dukakis won in 1988.

The strong showing of Perot, who won 19 percent of the popular vote, reflected the continuing decline of the electorate's partisan loyalties. Fearful of alienating its already fragile support among a public that has very little inclination to identify with partisan causes, the Clinton administration might resort to the same sort of executive leadership, dominated by plebiscitary appeals and institutional confrontation, that have diminished the place of party in American politics.

As America approached the twenty-first century, the decline of party reopened the old problem of how to constrain presidential ambition. The "emancipation" of the President from the constrictive grip of partisan politics has been closely linked to the transformation of the executive office from an institution of modest size and authority into a formidable institution invested with formal and informal powers that short-circuit the legislative process and judicial oversight. Yet, paradoxically, this more powerful and prominent Chief Executive has been reduced to virtually complete political isolation, deprived of the stable base of popular support once provided by political parties. Presidents must now build popular support on the uncertain foundation of public opinion and a diverse, as well as demanding, constellation of interest groups. The corrosion of presidential party politics also makes the nation vulnerable to the unchecked play of ambition the Framers of the Constitution feared, risking the dangers of "image" appeals and increased divisions among different political groups, exacerbated if not created by leaders operating under weakened restraints.

Bass, Harold F., Jr. "Chief of Party." In *Guide to the Presidency*. Edited by Michael Nelson. 1989.
Ceaser, James W. *Presidential Selection: Theory and Development*. 1979.
Cronin, Thomas E. "Presidents and Political Parties" In *Rethinking the Presidency*. Edited by Thomas E. Cronin. 1982.
Harmel, Robert, ed. *Presidents and Their Parties: Leadership or Neglect?* 1984.
Ketcham, Ralph. *Presidents Above Party, 1789-1829*. 1984.
Milkis, Sidney M. "The Presidency and Political Parties." In *The Presidency and the Political System*. 3d ed. Edited by Michael Nelson. 1990.
Ranney, Austin. "The President and His Party." In *Both Ends of the Avenue: The Presidency, the Executive Branch, and Congress in the 1980s*. Edited by Anthony King. 1983.
Wattenberg, Martin P. *The Rise of Candidate-Centered Politics: Presidential Elections in the 1980s*. 1991.

SIDNEY M. MILKIS

PATRONAGE. The appointment of people to government jobs as a reward for past service and with the expectation of future political support is known as political patronage. Its widespread use in the federal government was introduced by Andrew Jackson, who argued that all government jobs were essentially simple and that incumbent government officials tended to abuse their power. Though Jackson's use of patronage did not lead to the wholesale replacement of federal workers, he did provide the rationale for the transformation of limited patronage into the spoils system and its development over the next half-century.

The Spoils System. The spoils system, in which each newly elected President replaced government workers with political supporters, flourished in the mid nineteenth century and played an important role in the development of political parties in the United States. Reformers criticized the spoils system, arguing that it led to incompetence, inefficiency, corruption, and the need to train a new cadre of compaigners to do government jobs every four years. Further, the system's critics argued that the atmosphere created by the exchange of jobs for political support discouraged the best young people from serving in the government. Rather than representing a conflict over political principles, partisan political competition was reduced to a fight between those in office and those who wanted their jobs.

The argument of the reformers was moral as well as practical. As Theodore Roosevelt said in 1895, "The spoils system was more fruitful of degradation in our political life than any other that could possible have been invented. The spoils-monger, the man who peddled patronage, inevitably bred the vote-buyer, the vote-seller, and the man guilty of misfeasance in office." Presidents complained that they were reduced to petty job-brokers and that too much presidential time was taken up in making patronage decisions. In addition, many of the positions were effectively controlled by partisans in Congress, a reality that undercut the President's control of the executive branch.

One element of the patronage system was the practice of political assessment, in which an officeholder was expected to return a portion, often a fixed percentage, of the annual pay for the position to party coffers. Patronage not only provided government jobs but often conferred other benefits, including government contracts, land grants, and franchises. The modern counterparts of these benefits include grants, contracts, military bases, demonstration projects, and other public works and expenditures.

Defenders of the spoils system argued that it was crucial to the health of political parties and, in turn, that parties were essential to democracy. They also argued that lifetime tenure in government jobs led to arrogance and that frequent turnover in official positions was essential to a republican form of government. The patronage system also performed the important function of recruiting people to work for the government at a time when there was no other practical mechanism for doing so. Contemporary defenders of patronage argue that loyalists in the executive branch are necessary to ensure that the president's policy preferences are faithfully implemented.

Civil Service Reform. The arguments of the reformers came to fruition when CHARLES GUITEAU, a disappointed office-seeker, assassinated President James A. Garfield in 1881. This act galvanized Congress to pass the CIVIL SERVICE ACT of 1883 (Pendleton Act), which created the merit system under which civil servants would be chosen on the basis of ability rather than party affiliation. The act also forbade executive-branch officials from making personnel decisions (hiring, firing, promotions, demotions) on a partisan basis. It also created the Civil Service Commission to run personnel recruitment for the government and act as a watchdog for the protection of merit principles.

Initially, the Pendleton Act covered only 10 percent of the CIVIL SERVICE, giving Presidents the option of using EXECUTIVE ORDERS to include (blanket in) other categories of workers, thus protecting their own political appointees from being dismissed by the next President. By the 1930s more than 70 percent of government workers were in the civil service, and by the 1980s well over 80 percent were covered.

The spoils system, however, continued to flourish in state and local governments, giving rise to the infamous political machines of the early twentieth century (which continued well into the century). But when federal aid became conditioned on the presence of merit criteria in state and local civil-service systems, state and local governments became much more professionalized. In the 1970s several Supreme Court cases limited the ability of political officials at the state level to remove government workers only on the basis of partisan affiliation unless it could be shown that partisanship was essential to the performance of the job.

As the merit system was extended in the twentieth century, patronage and political machines began to decline in importance. And in the mid-twentieth century political parties themselves began to decline as government began to be more professionalized. The widening scope of government's role and the increasing complexity of its functions demanded people with high levels of technical skills who were not traditional partisans. The domination of national politics by political parties was undercut by the growing importance of primary elections in the presidential nominating system. Party bosses no longer controlled presidential nominations, and the functions of organizing compaigns and raising money were taken over by individual candidate organizations and professional consultants.

White House Control. With the rise of the modern presidency the number of patronage appointments continued to shrink and the control of patronage began to shift from party organizations to the White House. This process began during the NEW DEAL but accelerated as the WHITE HOUSE STAFF expanded and took on increasingly important functions.

During the 1952 presidential campaign the REPUBLICAN PARTY hired a consulting firm to advise Dwight D. Eisenhower on filling high-level political jobs, and in 1961 President John F. Kennedy began to reach beyond partisan politics with his talent hunt. The administration of Richard M. Nixon began the real professionalization of the OFFICE OF PRESIDENTIAL PERSONNEL by bringing in professional executive recruiters from private-sector search firms.

The size of the White House personnel operation also increased, so that the job of handling patronage or political recruitment, which had been performed by a single staffperson in the Truman and Eisenhower administrations, was done by between thirty and sixty staffpeople in the Nixon administration. During the early years of the administration of Ronald Reagan, the presidential recruitment office employed about a hundred people. More than just size and degree of professionalism had changed however. The process of centralizing control of the executive branch in the White House was solidified by the policy of controlling all patronage or political appointments—agency heads as well as presidential appointments—from the White House.

The control of the government also shifted from partisan control by the Democratic or Republican Party to an emphasis on policy control. To gain policy control, competence as well as loyalty was necessary. The definition of loyalty also shifted from partisan loyalty to ideological loyalty, especially in the Reagan administration. In the administration of George Bush, personal loyalty and past service to the President were emphasized more than ideological loyalty. Under both Reagan and Bush there was also the growing realization that technical and managerial competence was also necessary for a successful presidential administration.

The increasing need for professional experts and managers to run the government constrained the use of patronage for purely political purposes. In the late twentieth century, the spoils system amounted to about two thousand honorary and part-time appointments to boards and commissions where political loyalty was a principal criterion for appointment.

At the highest level, the major political appointments available to each President include in the executive branch (including CABINET secretaries and ambassadors) about 828 presidential appointments requiring confirmation by the Senate (PAS). Other full-time PAS appointments include about 187 U.S. attorneys and marshals and 956 federal judges, though a President would probably appoint only about 200 judges during a single term, since judges hold lifetime tenure. The immediate White House staff who serve at the pleasure of the President number about 438. Part-time Presidential appointments to commissions, boards, and councils number about 2,089.

At the next level down are noncareer (political) members of the SENIOR EXECUTIVE SERVICE (SES), which was created by the CIVIL SERVICE REFORM ACT of 1978. These can number up to 10 percent of a total of seven thousand SES positions. Finally, there are about eighteen hundred SCHEDULE C POSITIONS (at GS level 15 and below) available to each presidential administration. Noncareer SES and Schedule C positions are legally agency head appointments, but in practice the White House has heavily influenced who gets these appointments in recent administrations.

Some scholars distinguish between policy-determining positions, which must be filled by the President in order to control the executive branch, and those positions that are used merely to reward political supporters. They argue that the latter political patronage positions undermine the competence and continuity of government and are thus incompatible with the needs of a modern, technocratic government. In practice, however, it is extremely difficult to distinguish the needs of executive leadership and the desire to reward political supporters. Patronage has had a long history, and despite its shrinkage in the twentieth century, it will continue to play an influential role in politics.

BIBLIOGRAPHY

Henry, Laurin L. *Presidential Transitions*. 1960.
Mackenzie, G. Calvin. *The Politics of Presidential Appointments*. 1981.
Patterson, Bradley H., Jr. *The Ring of Power*. 1988.
Tolchin, Martin, and Susan Tolchin. *To the Victor: Political Patronage from the Clubhouse to the White House*. 1971.
Van Riper, Paul P. *History of the United States Civil Service*. 1958.
White, Leonard D. *The Republican Era*. 1958.

JAMES P. PFIFFNER

PAYNE-ALDRICH TARIFF ACT (1909). Conscious of the growing public tendency to associate the protective tariff with trusts and high consumer prices, President William H. Taft believed that the DINGLEY TARIFF ACT of 1897 was excessive. He proposed, as had the Republican platform of 1908, that tariffs be lim-

ited to the difference between foreign and domestic production costs, plus a reasonable profit.

Facing a growing Treasury deficit, Taft immediately called Congress into special session to revise the tariff. The House bill, authored by Sereno Payne, chairperson of the Ways and Means Committee, was a moderate reduction measure. Senate conservatives, led by arch-protectionist Nelson Aldrich, pushed for numerous rate increases. Taft attempted to secure reductions in the tariff levels set by Payne-Aldrich, but he was only modestly successful. Despite his hint to Senate progressives that he would veto the bill, Taft signed it, even though it was only marginally less protective than the Dingley Tariff.

Taft was more successful in his efforts to increase revenues. At his urging, the act imposed a corporate income tax. Taft also secured congressional approval of the Sixteenth Amendment (income tax amendment) during the special session.

The Payne-Aldrich Tariff also granted the President discretionary authority to apply maximum tariffs (being 25 percent greater than rates otherwise applicable) to any nation that "unduly" discriminated against American products and established a Tariff Board to advise the President on tariff matters. Taft used the implicit threat of sanctions in trade negotiations, but he never imposed maximum tariffs.

Disappointed that the act did not reduce tariffs significantly, Taft nevertheless praised it as "the best tariff bill that has been passed." Progressive distaste for continued high tariffs contributed to the split within the REPUBLICAN PARTY that doomed Taft's reelection effort in 1912.

BIBLIOGRAPHY

Coletta, Paolo E. *The Presidency of William Howard Taft*. 1973.
Pringle, Henry F. *The Life and Times of William Howard Taft*. Rep. 1964.
Taussig, F. W. *The Tariff History of the United States*. 8th ed. 1931.

RALPH MITZENMACHER

PEACE CORPS. The Peace Corps was founded by President John F. Kennedy in 1961. It was established on the principle of people-to-people contact, the exchange of skills and ideas, and the hope that the individual experiences of Americans in developing countries can make the world a healthier, safer, and better place to live. Working at subsistence allowances, volunteers were to serve as teachers, health workers, community developers, agricultural advisers, childcare workers, nurses, physicians, and thirty-seven other job categories.

The actual program was presaged by a statement made on 14 October 1960 during the presidential campaign at the University of Michigan by the then Senator Kennedy. He was received enthusiastically by a student audience when he announced his intention to create a group of volunteers who would "serve a larger cause, the cause of freedom and the cause of a peaceful world. Peace Corps volunteers will demonstrate their interest in people who may live on the outside of the globe, who may live in misery but who, because of the presence of these Americans, live in hope."

Sargent Shriver, brother-in-law of the President, was appointed the director of the organization, which was initially created as an office in the White House. On 30 August 1961 the first group of American Peace Corps volunteers arrived in Ghana. Under the aegis of the Lyndon Johnson administration, the organization grew to encompass more than fifty countries with more than fifteen thousand volunteers, a number never again reached during the succeeding years. Though the organization became the single most lasting monument to the Kennedy administration, its numbers eroded considerably during the VIETNAM WAR when Americans sought other ways to express their national and patriotic sentiments.

Under Executive Order 11603 of 1 July 1971 (36 Fed. Reg. 12675), the Peace Corps was transferred to the agency created by Reorganization Plan No. 1 of 1971 and designated as ACTION by President Richard M. Nixon. The ACTION Agency was established by law under Title IV of the Domestic Volunteer Service Act of 1973. Executive Order 12137 of 16 May 1979 superseded Executive Order 11603 but continued the policy of the Peace Corps operating as an agency within ACTION. Section 601 of the International Security and Development Cooperation Act of 1981 (Public Law 97-113), in amending the Peace Corps Act, removed the Peace Corps from ACTION and established the Peace Corps as an independent agency within the executive branch, effective 29 December 1981.

In the 1990s, six thousand volunteers, including large numbers of minorities and senior citizens, continued to serve in nearly ninety countries. Upon the collapse of the Eastern bloc nations in the late twentieth century, President George Bush assigned Peace Corps volunteers to Poland, Yugoslavia, and Czechoslovakia.

BIBLIOGRAPHY

Ashabranner, Brent. *A Moment in History: The First Ten Years of the Peace Corps.* 1971.

JOSEPH F. MURPHY

PEARL HARBOR. The surprise Japanese attack on the U.S. Pacific fleet at Pearl Harbor Naval Base, Hawaii, on 7 December 1941, heavily damaged America's battleship fleet and destroyed more than 250 army, navy, and marine corps planes on airfields ashore. American casualties totaled 2,403 killed and 1,178 wounded, making Pearl Harbor the worst disaster in American naval history. This "day of infamy," as President Franklin D. Roosevelt described it, roused America from its isolationist slumber, plunged the United States into WORLD WAR II, galvanized the American people behind a massive war effort, and triggered a heated and continuing debate over presidential responsibility for the disaster.

Throughout 1940–1941, President Franklin D. Roosevelt and his advisers focused on the war in Europe while seeking to avert a showdown with Japan over its expansionist drive in East Asia and the Pacific. When U.S. economic sanctions failed and talks between Washington and Tokyo broke down in autumn 1941, Japan proceeded with plans for a preemptive strike against American forces in the Pacific, which caught the United States badly offguard and ill-prepared for the blow.

The Pearl Harbor attack simplified Roosevelt's task of political leadership by instantly uniting a U.S. public heretofore bitterly divided between interventionists and isolationists. Roosevelt and his advisers, in this sense, felt relieved that war had finally come. Yet they felt appalled at the extent of the losses and the evidence of American military unpreparedness.

Intense recriminations followed in the wake of debacle. Roosevelt's critics blamed lapses in Washington or, in more extreme cases, accused Roosevelt of foreseeing and accepting the surprise attack on Pearl Harbor as a necessary means of bringing a unified America into the European war by the Pacific back door. The administration and a major postwar congressional investigation fixed responsibility on local military commanders for errors of judgment.

Gradually, the search for scapegoats gave way to the search for a deeper and fuller understanding of how the disaster occurred. In truth, both American military and civilian leaders, by overestimating Pearl Harbor's deterrent value and underestimating Japanese capabilities, contributed to the failure to anticipate—a classic human frailty—that lay at the heart of the Pearl Harbor tragedy.

BIBLIOGRAPHY

Prange, Gordon W. *At Dawn We Slept: The Untold Story of Pearl Harbor.* 1981.

Tansill, Charles C. *Back Door to War: The Roosevelt Foreign Policy, 1933–1941.* 1952.
Wohlstetter, Roberta. *Pearl Harbor: Warning and Decision.* 1962.

                    BRIAN VANDEMARK

PERKINS, FRANCES (1880–1965), social worker, Secretary of Labor. Perkins, who was born in Boston, received her B.A. from Mount Holyoke College in 1902. After five years of teaching, she began her career in social work in 1907. She was executive secretary of the New York City Consumers' League from 1910 to 1912 and of the Committee on Safety of the City of New York, which had been formed in response to the 1911 Triangle Shirtwaist fire, from 1912 to 1917.

She married in 1913 and had two children. In 1919, New York governor ALFRED E. SMITH named her to the governing board of the state department of labor. She was responsible for drafting industry regulatory codes and hearing workmen's compensation cases. After his election as governor in 1928, Franklin D. Roosevelt named her the administrative head of the state labor department.

With his election as President in 1932, Roosevelt named Perkins Secretary of Labor—the first woman CABINET member. Because Perkins regarded protective legislation rather than unions as workers' best hope for improved conditions, her relations with organized labor were never close. She headed the committee appointed by Roosevelt in 1934 to frame plans for a comprehensive system of SOCIAL SECURITY. Along with her contribution to the resulting Social Security Act of 1935, she played a key role in the adoption of the Fair Labor Standards Act of 1938. Staying on in the Cabinet during Harry S. Truman's first months, she resigned on 1 July 1945. From 1946 to 1953, she was a member of the U. S. Civil Service Commission. She taught at Cornell University until her death in 1965.

BIBLIOGRAPHY

Martin, George. *Madame Secretary: Frances Perkins.* 1976.
Patterson, James T. *America's Struggle against Poverty, 1900–1980.* 1981.
Perkins, Frances. *The Roosevelt I Knew.* 1946.

                    JOHN BRAEMAN

PEROT, H. ROSS (b.1930), businessman, independent presidential candidate in 1992. H. Ross Perot, the Dallas-based billionaire, became a major figure in the 1992 presidential election through his forceful personality, his apparent willingness to talk about things the major-party candidates avoided, his becoming the vessel for many people's anger and frustration with the political system, and his very substantial wallet. Perot, who was born 27 June 1930, had earned his fortune largely through his computer company's success at winning contracts with the federal government for processing Medicare and Medicaid claims.

Perot had for some years been on the fringes of public policy issues. He had worked on reforming Texas's education system and its antidrug policies. But he became famous for his much-publicized efforts in 1969 to free American prisoners of war held in North Vietnam. His successful effort to free two of his company's employees who were imprisoned in Iran in 1978 was the subject of a best-selling book, *On Wings of Eagles,* and of a television miniseries. But there were some questions about Perot's version of the Iran escapade, and his persistence on the POW issue—his charges that the Reagan administration was not doing enough to help prisoners Perot believed were still being held in North Vietnam—caused fallings out between him and President Reagan and also between him and then Vice President George Bush.

Everything about Perot's candidacy was unconventional. He launched it on a television talk show in February 1992, saying that if volunteers placed his name on the ballot in fifty states, he would run for President. But his campaign began well before the ballot work was finished, in mid September, and Perot himself put substantial funds into the work of his "volunteers." The crew-cut, plain-talking, can-do Perot captured people's imagination and became the leader of a substantial movement. At the height of his popularity, in early June, Perot was running about even with Bill Clinton and George Bush in the polls and led in some. There was much speculation that Perot could carry enough states to keep either major-party candidate from winning the election outright and that the outcome would be decided, according to the Constitution, by the House of Representatives.

But there had been signs from almost the beginning that Perot was not prepared for a presidential race. His knowledge of public affairs was fragmentary, and his temperament was wrong for the rigors of electoral politics. Also, his authoritarian personality was the cause of considerable unease. When Perot suddenly withdrew from the race—because he could not take the pressure—on 16 July, the last day of the Democratic convention, he left many of his followers feeling abandoned. And Clinton won the bulk of Perot's supporters.

Perot's reentry into the race on 1 October was just as

quirky as his withdrawal had been, but he made it clear that he did not want to be declared a quitter. His thirty-minute "infomercials"—featuring Perot sitting behind a desk and pointing to various charts about the state of the economy—broke all the rules of television, and amassed huge audiences. But Perot was not as ready as he had suggested to propose hard steps to eliminate the federal deficit. Still, he helped make the deficit an issue in the election, and he also put political reform on the agenda—especially the subjects of "revolving-door" lobbyists and lobbyists for foreign countries. In doing so, he forced Clinton to make a big play for the Perot constituency, both before and after the election so that Clinton could have a governing majority and win reelection in 1996.

Two weeks before the election, Perot began to climb in the polls again; his backing got as high as about 20 percent. But then his bizarre behavior cut into his momentum. In his appearance on the television program "60 Minutes" nine days before the election, and at a press conference the following day, he showed aspects of his personality that he had kept fairly well hidden since his reentry—signs of an overly suspicious nature and his short temper. He said that he had pulled out of the race because he had been warned that the Bush campaign would try to disrupt his daughter's wedding; he also told a not-very-credible tale about an attempt on his life in 1970 by some Black Panthers—who, he said, had been sent by the North Vietnamese.

Nonetheless, his winning 19 percent of the vote representing nearly 20 million people, showed that he still had a substantial following—or that a large number of people remained unmoved by the major-party candidates.

BIBLIOGRAPHY

Perot, Ross. *United We Stand: How We Can Take Back Our Country.* 1992.

ELIZABETH DREW

PERSONAL PRESIDENT. The "personal President" is Theodore Lowi's term for the dramatic expansion of the power of the federal government through broad delegations of power to the presidency. The presidency has become the central character in the American political system, the repository of great expectations for democratic politics and effective and energetic government.

The roots of the personal President lie in the NEW DEAL and Franklin Delano Roosevelt. According to Lowi's account of the rise of the personal President, four developments occurred in the 1930s that pro-

vided the basis for expanded presidential power: First, a constitutional revolution that expanded enormously the power of the federal government and effectively eliminated any restraint on what the national government could undertake; second, a governmental revolution based on a new social contract calling for the federal government to assume primary responsibility for the economy and the public welfare; third, an institutional revolution, fueled by broad DELEGATION OF LEGISLATIVE POWER to the President and administrative agencies, that centralized power in the presidency and greatly increased the policy-making discretion of agency officials; and fourth, a political revolution in which the President displaced Congress as the primary center of political power and generated a new, mass democratic politics that bound the President and the public together.

The changes wrought in the presidency during the Democratic-dominated 1930s and 1940s were ratified by Republican Presidents in the decades that followed. The personal President has come to embrace a number of significant characteristics. It is built on broad delegations of legislative power from Congress that include virtually unlimited powers when Presidents declare the nation to be in a crisis. It relies on a vast administrative apparatus, the EXECUTIVE OFFICE OF THE PRESIDENT, that serves as the President's personal bureaucracy.

Most importantly, Lowi argues, the power of the personal President is plebiscitary in nature: much like the "Roman emperors and French authoritarians who governed on the basis of popular adoration," the personal President governs through appeals to mass democratic politics. The role of President as the only political leader with a national constituency has reshaped American democracy around the cult of the presidency. Presidents derive their power by drawing it directly from the people more than through constitutional provisions. The restraints on the exercise of governmental power inherent in constitutional democracy have been weakened; the power of the personal President is not effectively balanced and checked.

While the personal President helped energize national politics, unify a nation with major regional differences, and give direction in addressing pressing public problems, this type of presidency has ultimately victimized Presidents and the political system by creating enormous and unreasonable expectations that Presidents have not been able to satisfy. Recent Presidents have become consumed by public dissatisfaction that is rooted in expectations that greatly exceed the ability of any person to satisfy. Presidents dissipate their political support over time and often end their administrations victims of their inability to satisfy the promises they make.

The idea of the personal President makes an important contribution to understanding the American political system. In contrast to other studies of the presidency that rely on psychological and personality assessments, Lowi's analysis helps illuminate the institutional arrangements that have created the enormous power Presidents possess.

BIBLIOGRAPHY

Lowi, Theodore J. *The Personal President: Power Invested, Promise Unfulfilled.* 1985.

GARY C. BRYNER

PETERS v. HOBBY 349 U. S. 331 (1955). Several cases in the 1950s concerned the administrative procedures required to remove someone from the executive branch on grounds of disloyalty to the federal government. The constitutional challenge in this instance was raised by John P. Peters, a professor of medicine at Yale University and a specialist in the study of metabolism, whose loyalty to the United States had been questioned by several unidentified accusers. Peters had been removed and disbarred from his federal government employment as a special consultant in the U.S. Public Health Service. Authority for the removal and disbarment originated in President Harry S. Truman's EXECUTIVE ORDER 9835 of 21 March 1949, which provided the head of each executive-branch department or agency with the power "to assure that disloyal civilian officers or employees are not retained in his department or agency." The same executive order created a central Loyalty Review Board in the Civil Service Commission. A key issue in the Peters case involved the standard for removal used by the Loyalty Review Board, specifically, whether "on all the evidence, there is a reasonable doubt as to the loyalty of the person involved to the Government of the United States." In two separate hearings before an agency review board, Peters had denied under oath that he was a member of the Communist Party as well as other charges made by his unidentified accusers. The agency review board determined that there was no reasonable doubt of his loyalty. But subsequently the Loyalty Review Board conducted a "post-audit," holding an additional hearing at which Peters again testified under oath. The accusers again remained anonymous. In May 1953 the Loyalty Review Board ruled against Peters, barring him from federal service for three years.

Peters's petition argued that the action violated both Executive Order 9835 and the constitutional requirement of due process because he was prevented from confronting and cross-examining his accusers. He also argued that the constitutional prohibitions against bills of attainder and ex post facto laws were violated by the board's procedures.

The majority of the Supreme Court, in an opinion by Chief Justice Earl Warren, held that the Loyalty Review Board's additional hearing on Peters, which was not requested by either Peters or the agency review board, was an action beyond its authority under Executive Order 9835. President Dwight D. Eisenhower had issued another executive order, No. 10450, granting the Loyalty Review Board authority to intervene on its own authority in order to establish uniformity among agency loyalty procedures after a case had already been determined by the board.

The Warren Court majority limited its decision to the issue of administrative procedure and authority. Justices Hugo L. Black and William O. Douglas concurred but argued that the key constitutional issues should be confronted. Justice Stanley F. Reed, joined by Justice Harold Burton, dissented on the ground that the majority had departed from long-standing Supreme Court deference to executive-branch control of its own administrative procedures. As Reed put it, "The Executive Branch is traditionally free to handle its internal problems of administration in its own way. The legality of judicial review of such intra-executive operations as this is, for me, not completely free from doubt." Reed and Burton concluded that President Eisenhower was aware of the actions of the Loyalty Review Board and approved them. The board itself had, according to Reed, "correctly interpreted the President's intentions." Reed also argued that the Court was traditionally more restrained in treating judicial interpretations of executive orders and procedures than in its interpretation of the meaning of congressional statutes, an interesting proposition that he did not elaborate on.

[*See also* LOYALTY-SECURITY PROGRAMS.]

BIBLIOGRAPHY

Bontecou, Eleanor. *The Federal Loyalty-Security Program.* 1953.
Fisher, Louis. *The Constitution between Friends: Congress, the President, and the Law.* 1978.
Pritchett, C. Herman. *Congress versus the Supreme Court.* 1961.

JOHN R. SCHMIDHAUSER

PETS, PRESIDENTIAL. Pets are an integral part of many families, including the First Family. In most cases the presidential pets have been typical animals—horses, dogs, cats, and birds. George Washington had his horse, Nelson (his mount at the surrender at Yorktown). James and Dolley Madison had a green parrot that was often seen at diplomatic functions. Occasionally, though, First Family pets have been a bit more exotic. For a short time, John Quincy Adams kept an alligator in the East Room, while his wife raised silkworms whose silk was spun into her dresses. Some pets have run to the silly side: Benjamin Harrison had goats to pull his grandchildren's wagons—as his grandfather President William Henry Harrison had done for him. William Howard Taft had a cow named Pauline Wayne—which was the last bovine to reside at 1600 Pennsylvania Avenue. A fair number of White House pets have been gifts from political well-wishers or foreign governments.

One of the most unusual collections of animals belonged to Theodore Roosevelt. The Roosevelt White House was a menagerie with animals ranging from horses to black bears, hyenas, badgers, and a slew of reptiles. Many of these animals were ultimately donated to the Washington Zoo, now the National Zoological Park. Perhaps the most famous of the Roosevelt pets was a particularly cantankerous black bear named Jonathan after Mrs. Roosevelt's ancestor Jonathan Edwards.

The Roosevelts were not the only First Family to have a zoo. Calvin Coolidge had one of the largest White House collections of pets. Most of Coolidge's pets were of the dog and cat variety, but not all were. One pet, a mockingbird, was released by Mrs. Coolidge when she learned that owning a caged mockingbird violated District of Columbia law. President Coolidge was particularly fond of a raccoon sent him by some Mississippians. The raccoon, named Rebecca, could often be seen taking walks with the President around the White House grounds. Many of the Coolidges' exotic pets—including a couple of lion cubs, a small hippo, and a bobcat—were donated to the National Zoo.

Three of the best-known presidential pets have been dogs—an airedale named Laddie Boy, a scottish terrier named Fala, and a spaniel named Millie. While America was returning to normalcy after World War I, an airedale was capturing the hearts of the President and the country. Laddie Boy was given to President Warren G. Harding by an old friend from Ohio. The dog soon became a regular feature at Cabinet meetings, where he was provided with his own chair. Laddie Boy's image was often used in newspaper cartoons, and *The Washington Star* ran interviews with Laddie Boy on issues of the day.

In the last year of President Franklin D. Roosevelt's term, and after a series of dogs had been banned from the White House for biting, a scotty was presented to the President. He named the dog Fala, and the two became inseparable, creating security problems for the Secret Service, which thought the dog announced the presence of the President too clearly. Fala's popularity grew when he was named an army private for having donated one dollar to the war fund drive. In the 1944 campaign, Republicans attempted to turn Fala into a liability by circulating the untrue story that the dog had cost taxpayers $15,000. The President responded to the charges in a Fireside Chat that was immensely funny. [*See* Election, Presidential, 1944.]

While Laddie Boy was often interviewed about current events and Fala was made a private because of the war bond drive, President George Bush's spaniel, Millie, is the only White House pet to have written about what it is like to be part of the First Family. *Millie's Book* was part of Barbara Bush's campaign to end illiteracy in the United States. In addition to being an author, Millie reportedly spent much of the day in high-level meetings with the President.

BIBLIOGRAPHY

Bush, Barbara. *Millie's Book.* 1990.
Truman, Margaret. *White House Pets.* 1969.

JEFFREY D. SCHULTZ

PHILADELPHIA PLAN. The genesis of affirmative action in government contracting (and arguably all federal affirmative action programs) is the Philadelphia Plan. Designed to respond to the virtual exclusion of racial minorities in the industrial and craft unions participating in federally funded construction projects in the Philadelphia area, the Philadelphia Plan demanded that government contractors submit minority employment goals as part of their contracting bids. These goals were to fall within a range specified by the Department of Labor's Office of Federal Contract Compliance and based upon the following factors:

> (1) the current extent of minority group participation in the trade; (2) the availability of minority group persons for employment in such trade; (3) the need for training programs in the area and/or the need to assure demand for those in or from the existing training programs; and (4) the impact of the program upon the existing labor force.

The story of the Philadelphia Plan begins in the final months of the Johnson administration. Pursuant to President Johnson's 1965 Executive Order 11246 demand that government contractors make adequate use of minorities and women, contracts in Philadelphia and other selected cities were held up until contractors submitted pledges to hire minority workers. After the GENERAL ACCOUNTING OFFICE challenged the Philadelphia Plan as "unauthorized," the Johnson administration rescinded it. However, on 27 June 1969, the Philadelphia Plan was reintroduced by the Nixon administration.

Labor unions and Comptroller General Elmer Staats attacked the revised plan as inconsistent with antidiscrimination legislation prohibiting race-conscious decision making in employment. For example, plumbers and pipefitters were given a minority goal that escalated from a range of 5 to 8 percent in 1970 to a range of 22 to 26 percent in 1973. Labor Secretary GEORGE SHULTZ and Attorney General JOHN MITCHELL answered these charges, arguing both that numerical targets simply reflected what "might be expected" from nondiscriminatory hiring and that contractors who had "exerted good faith efforts" would not be penalized for failing to meet their hiring goals.

This dispute was settled in Congress when it considered, in the fall of 1969, legislation blocking the Philadelphia Plan. Comptroller General Staats, who initiated this challenge, did more than argue against the legality of the plan. He also contended that the ATTORNEY GENERAL sought to subordinate COMPTROLLER GENERAL authority over federal contracting procedures, thereby calling into question legislative control over federal expenditures. Although this argument prevailed in the Senate, it failed in the House and was ultimately defeated. The key to this defeat was a major White House lobbying campaign, including a threatened veto. Following the administration's victory, the Department of Labor extended the plan to nineteen other cities. In April 1971, pointing to Congress's continued funding of the Philadelphia Plan program as indicative of Congress's implicit ratification of the plan, the Third U.S. Circuit Court of Appeals upheld the plan in *Contractors Ass'n of Eastern Pa. v. Secretary of Labor* (1971).

Today the Philadelphia Plan stands as the backbone of Executive Order 11246 demands on all federal contractors. Without question, the revised Philadelphia Plan represents the Nixon administration's most significant civil rights initiative. In light of President Nixon's antibusing "southern strategy," the plan is also Nixon's most surprising civil rights initiative. The Philadelphia Plan, however, made good political sense to Nixon. First, it enabled Nixon to counterbalance his antibusing initiatives and appeal to minority voters. Second, the Philadelphia Plan created a political dilemma for the Democrats, namely, the division of

two traditional Democrat constituencies—labor unions and civil rights groups. "The NAACP wanted a tougher requirement; the unions hated the whole thing," according to Nixon's chief of staff John Ehrlichman. While these groups "were locked in combat," the Nixon administration "was located in the sweet and reasonable middle."

BIBLIOGRAPHY

Graham, Hugh Davis. *The Civil Rights Era.* 1990.
Schuwerk, Robert. "The Philadelphia Plan: A Study in the Dynamics of Executive Power." *University of Chicago Law Review* 39(1972): 723–760.

NEAL DEVINS

PHILIPPINES. Commodore George Dewey's defeat of the Spanish at the Battle of Manila Bay on 1 May 1898 signaled the end of more than three centuries of Hispanic colonialism in the Philippines [*see* SPANISH-AMERICAN WAR]. As a result of the Treaty of Paris of December 1898, the islands became the first and only American colony. After WORLD WAR II, the United States continued to maintain an armed presence in the now independent Philippines, which served as a cornerstone of American defense in the Far East. This arrangement ended only in 1992, after the Philippine Senate voted not to renew the leases for Clark Air Base and Subic Naval Base. Nevertheless, because the Philippines became a major element in American strategic thinking concerning Asia, Presidents from William McKinley to George Bush have had a Philippine policy.

President McKinley initially had sent warships to the Philippines to check Spanish power in the Pacific in the event of war with Spain. Once he became aware of Spanish weakness, he opted to acquire the archipelago, encouraged by the jingoist American press. He refused to acknowledge the existence of the independent Philippine government (1898–1902) established by a native leadership that had declared its independence from Spain. McKinley did not trust the Filipinos under President Emilio Aguinaldo to govern themselves, and he feared a serious struggle of reconquest if the Spaniards sought to reassert their authority. He was also concerned lest Japan, Germany, or France seek to fill the power vacuum left in the event of a U.S. withdrawal. At British urging, he instructed American negotiators to demand that Spain cede the whole archipelago to American control. After the Spanish departure in 1899, there followed the bloody three-year war in which U.S. forces overcame the army of Aguinaldo's Philippine Republic.

William Howard Taft served as the chief architect of colonial policy in the Philippines from 1901 to 1913. As civil governor (1901–1904), then as U.S. Secretary of War (1904–1908), and finally as President, he shaped a policy that called for collaboration in democratic governance with the native elite; the training of a native civil service; rapid improvement in public works, public health, and public education; and free trade between the United States and the Philippines. Although the other parts of Taft's program were put in place rapidly, it took until 1909 for the Republican Presidents to obtain tariff relief for Philippine goods through the PAYNE-ALDRICH TARIFF ACT. Political difficulties with Japan led Theodore Roosevelt in 1907 to refer to the Philippines as America's "heel of Achilles" in the Far East; however, long-term retention of the Philippines remained Republican policy.

From the time of the debate over the Treaty of Paris, many southern Democrats joined with anti-imperialists and agricultural interests to oppose retention of the Philippines. The first change to modify seriously the Republican program came during the administration of Woodrow Wilson. He inaugurated a rapid Filipinization of the insular civil service, established a bicameral native legislature, empowered Filipino leaders Manuel Quezon and Sergio Osmeña, and created the Philippine National Bank. While Wilson failed to get a firm date for independence, the Jones Act of 1916 stated inevitable autonomy as a matter of principle.

When the Republicans returned to office in 1921, they sought to slow the momentum toward separation and to prolong the education in democratic government. Presidents Warren G. Harding, Calvin Coolidge, and Herbert Hoover could not reverse, however, the impulse toward rapid independence favored by American Democrats and Philippine nationalists. Three factors came to the aid of the latter's cause: U.S. concern for an increasingly powerful Japan, economic worries associated with the Great Depression, and American labor's fear of competition from Filipino migrant workers. President Franklin D. Roosevelt signed the Tydings-McDuffie Act in 1934 that established the Philippine Commonwealth with a ten-year transition to independence.

Roosevelt, preoccupied with more pressing domestic and international matters, took little interest in Philippine welfare and defense, and General Douglas MacArthur's Philippine-American forces were only partially prepared for the Japanese invasion in December 1941. Despite the heroic struggle on the Bataan peninsula, Roosevelt did not have the resources to forestall a Japanese occupation that lasted until February 1945; Philippine independence followed on 4 July 1946.

President Harry S. Truman initiated Philippine recovery through the Tydings Rehabilitation act and the Bell Trade Act that renewed free trade between the two nations lasting, with extensions, until 1974. Both measures contained provisions favorable to American interests. When the KOREAN WAR broke out in 1950, Truman sent arms and advisers to help Philippine government forces suppress the leftist, peasant-based Hukbalahap (Huk) movement. Both Truman and President Dwight D. Eisenhower heavily supported Secretary of Defense, later President, Ramon Magsaysay, who was responsible for the Huk defeat.

Throughout the COLD WAR American Presidents furnished the Philippines with political and martial assistance in exchange for Filipino diplomatic cooperation and the use of the military facilities. President John F. Kennedy, for instance, augmented the counterinsurgency training of the Philippine armed forces. During the VIETNAM WAR the bases proved so valuable to the Americans that President Lyndon B. Johnson showed his appreciation with greatly increased aid. Even after free trade ended, despite growing nationalist resentment, the leases on the bases were renewed. From 1972 to 1986 Presidents Richard M. Nixon, Gerald Ford, Jimmy Carter, and Ronald Reagan found it expedient to support the martial-law regime of Ferdinand Marcos, though he became more dictatorial, corrupt, and unpopular as the years passed. Because Marcos still supported the bases agreement and American business interests, the status quo persisted.

In 1983 Benigno Aquino, Jr., Marcos's chief rival, was assassinated and resentment over this act and the failing economy caused discontent to increase. President Ronald Reagan finally abandoned Marcos in February 1986 and threw American support to Corazon Aquino, the widow of Benigno, who had just won the presidential election.

When the Philippine Senate in 1991 rejected the Philippine-American Friendship Treaty, which included an extension of the lease for the bases, President George Bush made only half-hearted efforts toward forging a new agreement. The demise of the cold war and the faltering economy in the United States made him less willing to pay for naval and air facilities in an area no longer considered vital to U.S. defense.

BIBLIOGRAPHY

Bonner, Raymond. *Waltzing with a Dictator: The Marcoses and the Making of American Policy*. 1987.

Friend, Theodore. *Between Two Empires: The Ordeal of the Philippines, 1929-1946.* 1965.

Grunder, Garel A., and William E. Livezey. *The Philippines and the United States.* 1951.

May, Glenn Anthony. *Battle for Batangas: A Philippine Province at War.* 1991.

Owen, Norman G., ed. *Compadre Colonialism: Studies on the Philippines under American Rule.* 1971.

Steinberg, David Joel. *The Philippines: A Singular and a Plural Place.* 1990.

JOHN A. LARKIN

PHOTOGRAPHER, WHITE HOUSE. See WHITE HOUSE PHOTOGRAPHER.

PIERCE, FRANKLIN (1804–1869), fourteenth President of the United States (1853–1857). Pierce was an upright man devoted to the Union and the Constitution but a weak leader. His administration helped set the nation on a course toward civil war.

Franklin Pierce was a product of New Hampshire upbringing and politics. His father, Benjamin Pierce, was an officer in the war of Independence and a loyal Democrat who served two terms as governor. Franklin, who emulated his father's military and political careers, graduated from Bowdoin College in 1824, studied and practiced law, and was elected to the New Hampshire General Court in 1829, the same year his father was reelected governor. When twenty-eight years old, he was chosen speaker of the New Hampshire legislature.

Early Career and the Election of 1852. In 1833 Pierce was elected to the first of two terms in Congress and in 1837 he went to the Senate.

In Congress, Pierce, a loyal Democrat, served without distinction but worked hard at committee assignments, especially the Senate Committee on Pensions. In 1842 he resigned his Senate seat, partly to please his wife, Jane Means Appleton Pierce, who disdained political life and its obligatory social events. Pierce was a heavy drinker and a charming party guest. Mrs. Pierce hoped her husband's departure from Washington would reduce the temptation for him to imbibe so often and so freely.

Back in New Hampshire Pierce continued to serve the Democrats and again practiced law. During the MEXICAN WAR, he served as a colonel and later as a brigadier general. He led troops through hostile territory from Veracruz to near Mexico City, where his horse, frightened by artillery fire, threw him to the ground, causing a pelvic injury and a badly wrenched knee. Next day he tried to resume his command, only to injure the same knee again and faint from the pain. Twisted accounts of his battle experience were to haunt him throughout his political career, even though his Mexican War comrades later supported his bid for the presidency.

Returning to New Hampshire, Pierce resumed his legal career and his political work as party loyalist and disciplinarian. Increasingly his legal clients were the new corporations and mill owners who found his service as lawyer and lobbyist useful. As a leading member of the Concord Cabal he strongly supported the COMPROMISE OF 1850, which included the unpopular Fugitive Slave Act. That support made him acceptable to southern Democrats. Division over the free-soil issue, coupled with the obvious ambitions of a number of leading Democrats, threatened the party's 1852 bid for the White House. New Hampshire's Levi Woodbury was viewed as a possible DARK HORSE candidate should the convention become deadlocked. Woodbury's death in the fall of 1851 led the Concord Cabal to begin behind-the-scenes campaigning for Pierce, who had merely hinted that he would accept in case of a deadlock. The convention, which could not agree on LEWIS CASS, James Buchanan, STEPHEN A. DOUGLAS, or William Marcy, finally—after forty-eight ballots—nominated Pierce. The delegates then chose Alabama's WILLIAM KING for Vice President and endorsed a platform that supported all parts of the Compromise of 1850. The Whigs, who also endorsed the compromise, nominated WINFIELD SCOTT and William A. Graham. John P. Hale got the Free-Soil nomination, running on the Free Democratic ticket.

Pierce accepted the nomination but did not campaign actively. Except for efforts of the small FREE-SOIL PARTY, the campaign was lackluster, focusing on personal characteristics rather than a discussion of issues. In the electoral vote Pierce received 254 votes to Scott's 42, though he received fewer than 50,000 more popular votes than the combined total of his opponents. The election signaled the end of the WHIG PARTY as a significant national party. Yet any joy that Pierce may have felt over his electoral triumph quickly disappeared because of a personal tragedy. Shortly before the Pierce family was to leave New Hampshire for Washington, eleven-year-old Bennie, their one remaining son, was killed before his parents' eyes in a railroad accident. It was the worst of a series of tragedies that colored the Pierce presidency. Both Mrs. Pierce and Bennie had hoped that he would not be elected, since neither wished to move to Washington. Mrs. Pierce never fully recovered from Bennie's death, which she associated with her husband's political ambitions. She also believed that he had deceived her in denying that he encouraged his nomination. She remained in mourning during their years in the White House and spent much time in her room.

Tragedy struck again, early in the Pierce administration, with the death of New Hampshire's Senator Charles G. Atherton who was to have been Pierce's lieutenant in the Senate. Now he had none. He was also without a Vice President, because William King died shortly after the inauguration. King's death made Missouri's Senator David R. Atchison president pro tem of the Senate and Pierce's successor should he die in office. Atchison was one of the most extreme pro-slavery Senators.

Domestic Affairs. Pierce hoped in vain that party unity exhibited in the campaign would carry over into his administration. Trouble started with his CABINET choices. Some would not serve, while others were unacceptable to one or another partisan faction. The final choices provided good geographical representation but lacked other important elements, including the Young America faction led by Stephen A. Douglas and the Southern unionists. William L. Marcy of New York was Secretary of State, JEFFERSON DAVIS of Mississippi was Secretary of War, James Guthrie of Kentucky was Secretary of the Treasury, and Robert McClelland of Michigan was Secretary of the Interior. James Campbell of Pennsylvania was named Postmaster General; James C. Dobbin, who had led the stampede for Pierce in the nominating convention, was Secretary of the Navy; and CALEB CUSHING was Attorney General. Most were little known except Marcy, Davis, and Cushing, who dominated Cabinet meetings but often were at odds over policy. Despite those differences there were no changes in the Cabinet during Pierce's presidential term.

At the inaugural, Pierce surprised his listeners by delivering an address without script or notes. In it he outlined traditional Democratic policy: limited, honest, and frugal government and respect for STATES' RIGHTS. He believed that passage of the Compromise of 1850, followed by his election, had settled the dispute over SLAVERY. His foreign policy would be aggressive and he hinted strongly that CUBA would be annexed before he left office.

Unfortunately, Pierce's suggestions for reform legislation to make government more efficient and economical failed to win congressional approval. The department heads dutifully prepared lengthy and persuasive arguments for lowering the tariff, modernizing the navy, eliminating the huge post office debt, reorganizing the military administration, improving the quality of the government work force, and constructing a federally funded transcontinental railroad,

a project Pierce first favored, then opposed. Most of the suggestions would have trampled on well-established special interests, which Congress was unwilling to disturb. Within bounds, however, the administration did operate without graft or corruption.

Increasingly Pierce was perceived in the North as a Doughface, a northerner with southern principles. Jefferson Davis was one of his closest advisers and a personal friend. The few INTERNAL IMPROVEMENT projects that Pierce permitted to become law were in the South, though he gave other reasons for his approval. Some Americans also saw him as incompetent and indifferent to the problems ordinary people faced. While he willingly signed bills giving land to war veterans and their widows, he consistently opposed homestead legislation for other settlers and vetoed a bill for which the prison and mental-health reformer, Dorothea Dix, had worked, a measure that would have provided land to subsidize institutions for the indigent mentally ill. The bill had strong bipartisan and popular support, but Pierce found it incompatible with states' rights.

Foreign Affairs. In no area was Pierce's ambition less realized than in foreign affairs. Because of strong support from the Young America faction of the party and the influence of Davis and other southern politicians, he became involved in a number of projects to annex territory, expand American influence abroad, and checkmate the influence of Great Britain and France. There were two notable instances of success. The treaty ending the Mexican War failed to annex to the United States land in the Southwest that was needed if there was to be a southern railroad to the Pacific. After supervising an army survey of four possible routes, Davis preferred and promoted the southern one. Pierce sent Davis's friend, James Gadsden, to Mexico to negotiate for the purchase of the right of way. After complex negotiations the resulting treaty led to the GADSDEN PURCHASE.

The other annexation involved the search for a cheaper supply of guano, Pacific island bird droppings, which were a rich source of fertilizer. In 1856, Congress passed a law providing that any U.S. citizen who discovered an unoccupied and unclaimed island containing guano could claim it in the name of the United States. Within thirty years more than seventy islands, including Midway and the Christmas Islands, were annexed under this legislation. It was the first official move of the United States to create an overseas empire.

During the Pierce administration, relations with Great Britain were often tense. The CLAYTON-BULWER TREATY of 1850 allowed for the possibility of a jointly built canal in Central America. Under American interpretation of the treaty, the British were also obligated to withdraw from Nicaragua and Honduras, something the British would not accept. James Buchanan, the American minister in London, was instructed to work out the differences between the two countries. Ultimately his efforts succeeded. An 1854 treaty gave the United States expanded fishing rights off the Canadian coast and listed numerous raw materials that both countries would admit duty free. Pierce hoped the popular treaty would pave the way for eventual annexation of Canada. During the Crimean War the British minister to the United States created a near-crisis when he engaged in illegal recruiting for his nation's army. Even though Pierce had him recalled, the British did not retaliate. In 1856, Buchanan returned to the United States, and his place was taken by GEORGE MIFFLIN DALLAS, who succeeded in negotiating a treaty that settled the Nicaragua question but left Belize (British Honduras) under British control.

Commodore Matthew C. Perry's naval expedition to open Japan to Western trade, begun under Millard Fillmore's administration, met with limited success under Pierce. Plans to annex the Sandwich Islands [see HAWAII, ANNEXATION OF] and a port in the DOMINICAN REPUBLIC failed.

The greatest frustration in foreign policy for the Pierce administration was its failure to annex CUBA. The appointment of Pierre Soulé as minister to Spain was made primarily to consummate that longtime American objective. Soulé, like Jefferson Davis, openly advocated Cuban annexation. At Marcy's request Buchanan, Soulé, and John Y. Mason, minister to France, met first in Ostend, Belgium, then at Aix-la-Chapelle, France, to work out a Cuban policy. Although Marcy still hoped for purchase, Soulé interpreted his instructions as the signal for a stronger course of action. The diplomats' secret communiqué to Marcy was leaked to the press and came to be known as the Ostend Manifesto. It clearly suggested that if Spain would not sell Cuba, the United States would be justified in taking it. The manifesto reached the American public at a time of midterm elections. In the North the communiqué was viewed as truckling to the slave power and, as one editor put it, a "manifesto of brigands." Marcy backed off, denying that he had ever intended to endorse force, and the island remained in Spanish hands.

Sectionalism and Slavery. While the Ostend Manifesto met serious opposition at home, a major reason for the defeat of Democrats in the 1854 elections was the KANSAS-NEBRASKA ACT. Senator Stephen A. Douglas had promoted the organizing of western territory both for settlement and to provide a route for a Pacific railroad originating in Chicago, his hometown. In order to get southern support for such legislation he had to include a clause declaring the Missouri Compromise "inoperative and void." Pierce reluctantly agreed to support the bill, which provided for the creation of two western territories, Kansas and Nebraska, with the issue of slavery to be decided by the settlers themselves by popular sovereignty. It was assumed that Nebraska would be free but that Kansas might be open to slavery. To many northerners the new law, which passed in May 1854, was another concession to the arrogant slave power. The response was "a hell of a storm," just as Douglas had predicted when he yielded to southern demands on the Missouri Compromise question. "Anti-Nebraska" became a political rallying cry in numerous northern communities.

Most settlers went to Kansas hoping merely to improve their own circumstances, but some were also motivated by politics. The New England Emigrant Aid Company sent settlers with the avowed intent to keep slavery out, while Missourians and other southerners were determined to make Kansas a slave state. When elections were held, Missourians infiltrated Kansas Territory and stayed just long enough to vote. The result was two territorial governments, one free, the other proslavery. Pierce consistently supported the proslavery faction as the only legitimate government. In the last half of his presidency he appointed three governors of Kansas Territory. The first, Andrew H. Reeder, was fired after a year because he became involved in land speculation schemes. He was also becoming less supportive of the proslavery faction and later became a leader of the free-state faction. Wilson Shannon, the second appointee, found Kansas impossible to govern and resigned in 1856. The national press viewed frontier violence over land claims or personal matters as part of the struggle over slavery. The sack of Lawrence, a center of free-state activity, John Brown's murder of five proslavery settlers, and a host of other violent incidents made "Bleeding Kansas" a popular slogan in parts of the North. At the same time, northern anger was roused by the use of federal troops in Boston to return the fugitive Anthony Burns to slavery and by the vicious beating of Senator Charles Sumner by the proslavery Representative Preston S. Brooks on the floor of the Senate. Pierce's third appointment as governor of Kansas Territory was John W. Geary, whose even-handed approach finally brought temporary quiet to that troubled territory.

Meanwhile, despite his growing unpopularity, Pierce was confident of another term. He could not face the fact that he had made too many enemies in his own party to be nominated again. Instead, the Democratic convention chose James Buchanan, elder statesman from Pennsylvania, who, because of his diplomatic post in London, had not been tainted by the furor over the Kansas-Nebraska Act.

The election of 1856 also brought to the national scene the first Republican presidential candidate. Widespread dissatisfaction with the Pierce policies gave strength to the new REPUBLICAN PARTY, which drew its support from antislavery Whigs and Democrats and the sudden strength of nativist groups which used anti-immigrant and anti-Catholic sentiments to form the KNOW-NOTHING (AMERICAN) PARTY. In the midterm elections of 1854 that mix of partisan elements caused a serious setback for the Democrats, who lost power in Congress and in some local offices in northern states. Know-Nothingism proved most powerful when joined with anti-Nebraska forces, but eventually that faction, too, succumbed to sectionalism and faded from the political scene. It was the Republican Party that held its ground, nominating JOHN C. FREMONT for the presidency. Although in 1856 they could not defeat Buchanan and the well-established Democratic machine, the Republicans had consolidated their strength and set the stage for eventual victory.

Assessing the Pierce Presidency. Pierce, relieved when Buchanan defeated Frémont, looked upon the Democratic victory as a vindication of his own policies. The government was in good hands, he thought, and the Constitution and respect for property, including slave property, was secure. In his final message to Congress he blamed abolitionists for all the sectional problems and warned against a party that catered to only one section's interests.

Indeed, Franklin Pierce pronounced his administration a success. At the least, he could take pride that it had been free from the taint of scandal or misuse of office for private gain. The purchase of a small section of Mexico through the Gadsden Treaty and acquisition of some Pacific guano islands were small accomplishments, though they did little to satisfy the expansionist dreams of the Young America imperialists. Pierce could also point to the fact that Congress sustained all his vetoes of internal improvement legislation and other bills that he considered unconstitutional.

Yet his administration's major legislative accomplishment, the Kansas-Nebraska Act, served only to deepen a dangerous sectional division. That legislation and its aftermath fostered a strictly northern political party and did as much as anything to set the nation's course toward division and civil war. Pierce never understood the basis and strength of the growing free-soil and antislave-power sentiment in the northern states. He was devoted to the Union as originally founded and the Constitution as originally understood, a Constitution that protected property, even property in persons.

Franklin Pierce considered abolitionists and free-soilers troublemakers who threatened the Union. Even after outbreak of the CIVIL WAR he put major blame on northern action and agitation. During the war he was falsely accused of membership in the largely fictitious, pro-Confederate Knights of the Golden Circle, a charge of disloyalty that wounded him deeply.

The 1850s were a time that would have tested severely even the most creative and assertive leadership. Pierce lacked such qualities, and he did not grow into the job. No President was more handsome or presidential in appearance than Franklin Pierce, and fewer were less qualified for the office. In SCHOLARLY RATINGS, the historian Thomas A. Bailey may have summed it up when he pronounced Pierce "less than a success, not wholly a failure." In any event, his administration left the country perched precariously on the edge of civil war, and for that it must be considered a disaster.

BIBLIOGRAPHY

Brown, Charles M. *Agents of Destiny: The Lives and Times of the Filibusters.* 1980.
Gara, Larry. *The Presidency of Franklin Pierce.* 1991.
Gienapp, William E. *The Origins of the Republican Party, 1852–1856.* 1987.
Horsman, Reginald. *Race and Manifest Destiny: The Origins of American Racial Anglo-Saxonism.* 1981.
Johannsen, Robert W. *Stephen A. Douglas.* 1973.
Malin, James C. *The Nebraska Question, 1852–54.* 1953.
Nevins, Allan. *Ordeal of the Union.* 2 vols. 1947.
Nichols, Roy Franklin. *Franklin Pierce: Young Hickory of the Granite Hills.* Rev. ed. 1958.
Nichols, Roy Franklin. "The Kansas-Nebraska Act: A Century of Historiography." *Mississippi Valley Historical Review* 43 (1956): 187–212.
Sewell, Richard. *Ballots for Freedom: Antislavery Politics in the United States, 1837–1860.* 1976.
Wolff, Gerald W. *The Kansas-Nebraska Bill: Party, Section, and the Coming of the Civil War.* 1977.

LARRY GARA

PIKE COMMITTEE. The House of Representatives set up the Pike Committee to investigate government intelligence operations. Beginning on 22 December 1974, reporter Seymour M. Hersh of the *New York*

Times published a series of articles that accused the CENTRAL INTELLIGENCE AGENCY (CIA) of "massive" spying and other illegal intelligence activities directed against activists opposed to the VIETNAM WAR as well as other dissidents. Hersh reported that the CIA had compiled files on more than ten thousand American citizens in violation of the NATIONAL SECURITY ACT OF 1947, which barred the CIA from performing security functions inside the United States. The Hersh exposés galvanized Congress into making its first major investigation of the government's intelligence services.

Each chamber of Congress created its own investigative panel. In January 1975, the Senate established the Select Committee for the Study of Government Operations with Respect to Intelligence Activities, known as the CHURCH COMMITTEE after its chairman, Frank Church (D-Idaho). A month later, the House established its own Select Committee on Intelligence, initially chaired by Lucien Nedzi (D-Mich.).

The Nedzi Committee had a short life. Chairman Nedzi drew serious criticism from House colleagues for the extremely slow place of his start-up compared to the Church Committee, which was quick to begin its investigation. Some accused Nedzi of deliberately trying to slow his committee's progress out of concern that left-leaning members of the panel might harm the INTELLIGENCE COMMUNITY through too pointed an inquiry.

During this period of delay, media reports alleged that the CIA had been involved in assassination plots against foreign leaders, and soon thereafter reporters disclosed that Nedzi himself had been aware of these plots in his earlier capacity as a member of the House Armed Services subcommittee with CIA oversight responsibilities. Nedzi reluctantly conceded the validity of these charges, discrediting his claim to objectivity. The House chose a new chairman, Otis Pike (D-N.Y.). Fourteen weeks after the creation of the Nedzi Committee, the Pike Committee finally began its inquiry.

Meeting informally, Senator Church and Representative Pike decided on a rough division of labor between their committees. Two major questions had arisen during the debate that led to the establishment of the two panels. First, what were the proper legal and ethical boundaries for intelligence operations, both at home and abroad? Second, how could the quality of intelligence-as-information be improved? The Church Committee focused on the first issue (involving warrantless mail opening, cable interceptions, assassination plots, and other questionable practices), while the Pike Committee concentrated on questions of intelligence quality—that is, how to improve

the content and timeliness of information provided to policymakers by the CIA and the other intelligence agencies. The two committees strayed across these boundaries from time to time, but generally this remained the division of labor between them.

For the rest of the year, the Pike Committee fell into a series of bitter disputes with the CIA and the other intelligence agencies, as well as with the White House (under President Gerald Ford). The first bone of contention had to do with the committee's access to information it felt it needed to conduct a thorough probe; a second conflict arose over which information the committee had the authority to release publicly without the approval of the executive branch. In one major confrontation, the Pike Committee decided to declassify on its own authority passages of selected intelligence documents. One document indicated that the intelligence community had been widely off-target regarding the outbreak of the 1973 Arab-Israeli war (the Yom Kippur War). The document contained four words that, according to media reports, revealed that the United States had the capability of intercepting Egyptian communications, despite security precautions taken by Cairo. Director of Central Intelligence William E. Colby argued that the words warranted secrecy and should be removed from the document, but a majority of committee members disagreed, opting to release the entire document. In contrast to the Church Committee, whose members were willing to negotiate with executive officials over which documents they would receive and how they would be handled, members of the Pike Committee consistently demanded free access to any documents they deemed relevant to their inquiry.

Trouble with the executive branch was only one of the tribulations the Pike Committee underwent. In January 1976, the House of Representatives voted 146 to 124 against the release of the committee's final report, on grounds that the committee had no right to disclose classified information over the objections of the executive branch. Dejected by this rebuff from their own colleagues, a majority of the Pike Committee's members decided in February to issue the panel's twenty unclassified recommendations (including a proposal to create a permanent House oversight committee for intelligence policy) and shut down its offices.

The Pike Committee's war with the executive branch was over—or so it seemed. Within twenty-four hours, however, the top-secret Pike Committee report was on the newsstands, published by the *Village Voice*, a New York City weekly. The Pike Committee investigators now found themselves the subjects of a House investigation into the source of the leak—something this inquiry was never able to determine. Despite its travails, the Pike Committee's central recommendation was adopted by the House a year later, when it created the Permanent Select Committee on Intelligence.

BIBLIOGRAPHY

"The CIA Report the President Doesn't Want You to Read: The Pike Papers." *Village Voice* (16 and 23 February 1976).

Elliff, John T. "Congress and the Intelligence Community." In *Congress Reconsidered.* 2d ed. Edited by Lawrence C. Dodd and Bruce I. Oppenheimer. 1977.

Freeman, J. Lieper. "Investigating the Executive Intelligence: The Fate of the Pike Committee." *Capitol Studies* 5 (1977): 103–117.

Johnson, Loch K. *A Season of Inquiry: Congress and Intelligence.* 1988.

Smist, Frank J., Jr. *Congress Oversees the United States Intelligence Community, 1947–1989.* 1990.

LOCH K. JOHNSON

PINCKNEY, CHARLES COTESWORTH (1746–1825), soldier, statesman, Federalist presidential nominee in 1804 and 1808.

Born into an affluent South Carolina family with extensive land holdings, Pinckney was educated in English public schools and spent a brief time studying in France. He read law at Oxford, where he heard William Blackstone lecture, and in 1764 was admitted to the bar in London's Middle Temple. Much like an English gentleman who was not quite ready for the world, Pinckney took a grand tour of Europe and did not return to America until 1769. He quickly established himself as a lawyer and rising figure in Charleston's social, business, and political circles.

Pinckney's residence and schooling in England had little effect on his political leanings, for he joined the colonists' resistance movement from the outset. After serving on various patriot committees fostering a break with England, Pinckney favored independence and once the war started he was an early volunteer for military duty. He rose rapidly in the ranks of South Carolina's First Regiment in the Continental Line (army), moving from captain to colonel until he joined George Washington's staff as an aide-de-camp. Washington was impressed with Pinckney at the battles of Germantown and Brandywine and never forgot the young southerner's battlefield demeanor.

Pinckney's wartime career was cut short when he reported for duty on the front lines in South Carolina. In 1780 he was captured at the surrender of Charleston and released on parole, but he was not free to serve until an exchange of prisoners near the war's end made him eligible for full duty. He left the army and leaped into state politics, winning a seat in the state legislature in 1782, and soon was a leading force in his native state's political scene. In 1787, Pinckney led the state delegation at the CONSTITUTIONAL CONVENTION in Philadelphia, where he was a forceful spokesman for Southern interests, particularly slavery. He sought and obtained the 1808 cutoff date for the slave trade as a concession from Northern interests, and he was an adamant proponent of the Senate's ratification of treaties as a check on the executive branch.

Under the new government, Pinckney turned down important posts offered by Washington, including command of the army and a Supreme Court justiceship, but at length accepted the minister's post to France in 1796. Revolutionary leaders in France, distrustful of Pinckney's political leanings, refused to accept his credentials. He was awaiting passage to return to America when President John Adams appointed him to serve on a commission to negotiate Franco-American differences. With John Marshall and ELBRIDGE GERRY, Pinckney served on the commission, where he is said to have rebuffed the French demand for a $250,000 bribe by exclaiming: "No, no! Not a sixpence!" In the ensuing publicity over the so-called XYZ affair, Pinckney's rejection of a corrupt bargain made him a minor hero. He was appointed a major-general in the regular army, where he served two years (1798–1800).

Federalist politicians, impressed with Pinckney's southern credentials, placed him on the 1800 ticket as the vice presidential candidate. Pinckney himself had no part in ALEXANDER HAMILTON's backstage maneuvers that called for a Southern surge of support to edge Pinckney ahead of President Adams in the electoral balloting and place him in the White House. Instead, a Democratic-Republican groundswell set the nation on a new political course as Thomas Jefferson and AARON BURR won seventy-three electoral votes each, John Adams sixty-five, and Pinckney sixty-four. Pinckney's decorum won respect from Federalists everywhere, and he was their presidential nominee in both 1804 and 1808. As was then the custom, a public figure allowed his name to be entered at presidential caucuses and in local voting, but Pinckney never wrote a campaign speech or shook a hand in seeking support. He was overwhelmed by Jefferson in 1804, as he and his running mate, RUFUS KING, won only 14 electoral votes to 162 for the Republican ticket. Against Madison in 1808 Pinckney, the southern slaveholder, won only the electoral votes of Federalists in New England and the middle states while losing in his home territory.

Pinckney's active political life was over. He retired to his plantation near Charleston and until his death Pinckney devoted his time to the affairs of the Society of the Cincinnati, the promotion of southern agriculture, and educational causes for the betterment of southern youth.

BIBLIOGRAPHY

Wallace, David D. *South Carolina: A Short History, 1520–1948.* 1961.
Zahniser, Marvin R. *Charles Cotesworth Pinckney: Founding Father.* 1967.

ROBERT A. RUTLAND

PINCKNEY'S TREATY. Since the Peace of Paris marked the conclusion of the American Revolution in 1783, the United States and Spain eyed each other suspiciously. Spain knew that American frontiersmen coveted the colonies of Florida and Louisiana. The two nations also quarreled over the use of the Mississippi River and a boundary discrepancy between Florida and the American territories in the old Southwest. Fortunately for the Spanish, the United States under the Articles of Confederation was both too militarily weak and politically divided to force any concessions from Madrid.

By the mid 1790s the Spanish minister of foreign affairs, Manuel de Godoy, sought to extricate Spain from the imbroglios of European war and and a failed frontier policy in North America. In July 1795, Spain deserted her English alliance and signed a separate peace at Basel with the French Republic. Almost simultaneously, the Washington administration dispatched Thomas Pinckney of South Carolina from his ministerial post in London to resolve outstanding Spanish-American difficulties. Thrust into the mix was the recently ratified JAY'S TREATY—a controversial Anglo-American convention whose terms may have influenced Godoy's concessions to Pinckney.

Whether motivated by fear of American aggression or British reprisals, the Spanish minister quickly surrendered on all disputed points. On 27 October 1795, the two diplomats signed the Treaty of San Lorenzo, giving the United States the southwestern territory north of 31° latitude, granting the free navigation of the Mississippi River, and legitimatizing the American claim to the east bank of the river. Although the product of Spanish weakness as much as American strength, the treaty marked the first major United States gain in territory for the constitutional republic and foreshadowed the eventual demise of the Spanish borderlands empire.

BIBLIOGRAPHY

Bemis, Samuel F. *Pinckney's Treaty: America's Advantage from Europe's Distress, 1783–1800.* 1926.
Whitaker, Arthur P. *The Spanish-American Frontier, 1783–1795.* 1927.
Young, Raymond. "Pinckney's Treaty—A New Perspective." *Hispanic American Historical Review* 43 (1963): 526–535.

JOHN M. BELOHLAVEK

PLATFORMS, PARTY. A platform is a political party's statement of its principles, record, and intended programs, but its true character is often debated. "We believe," said the Democrats on the eve of the historic NEW DEAL, "that a party platform is a covenant with the people to [be] faithfully kept by the party when entrusted with power." But according to a more cynical interpretation, "A platform is to run on, not to stand on."

American political parties have presented formal platforms since the DEMOCRATIC PARTY adopted nine policy resolutions during its presidential nominating convention in 1840. Even earlier, individual candidates or legislative caucuses had presented similar statements as "addresses to the people."

Over the history of American parties, platforms have grown in length and complexity. By 1988, the Republican platform covered thirty pages of single-spaced triple-column type; even a deliberately short Democratic platform that year comprised some five thousand words, almost ten times the length of the party's first manifesto. Platforms also reflect the passage of political time, with later entries such as ABORTION and "sociology of science" replacing earlier topics such as "saloons" and "Christian sabbath." The 1988 Republican platform shows the contemporary range, with major-section titles such as "Jobs, Growth, and Opportunity for All"; "Strong Families and Strong Communities"; and "America: Leading the World."

Writing the Platform. The adoption of a party program is now a regular feature of presidential politics, and is also usually evident in state politics. At the national level, the platforms are prepared by committees representing each of the state delegations. Originally written at the conventions themselves, they are now drafted in advance, sometimes after public hearings, and involve consultation among presidential aspirants and important interest groups. When an incumbent President is a candidate for reelection, the drafting will typically be directed from the White House. Invariably adopted before each convention's formal selection of the presidential nominee, typically on the second night of the party convention, the platform is depicted as the programmatic basis of his candidacy.

The relationship between the presidential nominee and the platform, however, is more complicated than is suggested by this sequential order. As they seek their party's leadership, candidates also present their personal programs, and the nominating contest may even center on programmatic differences. While the winning candidate will formally accept the platform, there are a few historical examples of disagreement between the candidate and the platform, for example, GEORGE B. McCLELLAN's 1864 repudiation of the Democrats' call for negotiations to end the CIVIL WAR.

At the same time, platform development is somewhat separate from the rivalry of individual aspirants and proceeds independently during the early months of the presidential election year. The winning candidate's ideas will certainly dominate the party's manifesto, particularly in cases of renomination of an incumbent President, but nominees will also offer platform concessions to broaden their support within the party.

Platforms have often been critical in presidential elections. When the Democrats championed the unlimited coinage of silver in 1896, they foreshadowed the nomination of WILLIAM JENNINGS BRYAN and the emergence of a dominant national Republican majority. When in 1936 the Democrats declared "that government in a modern civilization has certain inescapable obligations to its citizens," they established the philosophical foundation of the welfare state. When Democrats and Republicans in the 1970s and 1980s took conflicting positions on the EQUAL RIGHTS AMENDMENT and the constitutional right to abortion, they stimulated a "gender gap" in voting behavior.

Despite these historic relationships, party platforms are usually denigrated. Moisei I. Ostrogorski, a noted critic of American politics, wrote the classic condemnation of the party convention platforms a century ago:

The platform, which is supposed to be the party's profession of faith and its program of action is only a farce—the biggest farce of all the acts of this great parliament of the party. The platform represents a long list of statements relating to politics, in which everybody can find something to suit him, but in which nothing is considered as of any consequence by the authors of the document, as well as by the whole convention. . . . The platform has just as little significance and authority for Congress. Its members consider themselves in no way bound to the programs laid down in the convention, for they know perfectly well under what circumstances and with what mental reservations it has been promulgated.

Ostrogorski's attack has often been replicated. Yet if platforms are meaningless, it seems odd that they should bring, as they have, severe intraparty disagreement, not to mention the attention of interest groups, mass media, and practical politicians. Platform conflicts have occasioned convention walkouts by southern Democrats in 1948 and physical confrontations among Republican factions in 1964, and they have often provoked more controversy at the conventions than the presidential nominations themselves. The 1988 Democratic convention and the 1992 Republican convention, for example, respectively nominated MICHAEL DUKAKIS and George Bush without conflict. In contrast to this tranquillity, these same conventions respectively featured internal battles over the issues of increased taxation of the wealthy and abortion. Rather than neglect platforms, politicians seem to regard them as significant factors in the quest for voter support.

Party Coalitions. Platforms may be considered both from the viewpoint of their role within a party and as one element in the electoral relationship between a party and the voters. The platform may first be seen as a useful indicator of the nature of the party coalition. Specific interests seek to have their demands included in the party platform as much to gain a seat at the table of governmental decision as to promote any particular program. In turn, when it includes a group's agenda in the platform, the party is telling that group that it is worthy of political notice. The parties use the platform particularly to appeal to distinct, recognizable, and potentially important minorities, such as unions, governmental reformers, and African Americans.

Particular pledges may become symbolic markers of these appeals. For example, the Democratic party since 1948 has consistently promised to repeal all or part of the TAFT-HARTLEY ACT of 1947, although it is obvious even to unions that such repeal is politically impossible. The purpose of this pledge is not to forecast future legislation but to assure the organized labor movement that it will be given significant power in a future Democratic administration. Similarly, in the 1980s Republican platforms promised to protect the "right to life" of unborn fetuses, even though such action realistically can only be taken by the U.S. Supreme Court. This party promise cannot be specifically redeemed, but including it in the platform demonstrates that a Republican government will include opponents of abortion.

The party coalition includes individuals as well as groups, and the platform is a means of persuading important politicians—especially defeated presidential aspirants—to support the party nominee. Thus, in

1988, Democratic primary candidate Jesse Jackson endorsed his victorious Democratic rival, Dukakis, only after the platform was amended to include Jackson's proposals to limit defense spending and to increase school funding.

Conflicts over the party platform frequently involve not only differences over policy issues but over control of the party itself. Thus, the Democrats' adoption of a civil rights plank in 1948 meant that the party was turning from its traditional base among white southerners toward urban blacks, just as its earlier support of the repeal of PROHIBITION in 1932 marked a shift in the party toward the industrial north.

As a representation of the party, then, the platform is important, but not as an inspired gospel to which politicians resort for policy guidance. It is important because it summarizes, crystallizes, and presents to the voters the character of the party coalition. The stands taken in the platform clarify a party's positions on current controversies and reveal the nature of its support and appeals.

In analyzing the electoral significance of platforms, two important questions need to be considered: first, their content and, second, their impact. Ostrogorski and later commentators have denounced platforms as being no more than empty partisan rhetoric. Detailed contents analysis of platforms, however, provides contrary evidence.

Platform Content. Platform statements may be put in three general categories, which may be illustrated by excerpts from the 1988 Republican manifesto. First, platforms include some vague rhetoric or simple factual statements without useful political content, for example, "An election is about the future, about change." Second, and more significantly, the party statements evaluate the parties' past records, for example: "Under a Republican Administration, family incomes are growing at the fastest pace recorded in 15 years." Third, platforms make promises, varying in specificity, of future policy actions, for example: "We will fight to end the Social Security earnings limitation for the elderly."

Contrary to what critics have contended, detailed analysis shows that most platform statements fall into the latter two categories. Party manifestos are not principally vague paeans to God, mother, and country. The first category of statements, above, which includes factual statements as well as hot air, usually comprises only about one-sixth of a platform's total. In contrast, almost one-third of an average platform represents evaluation of a party's records, providing abundant material for those critical voters who cast their ballots on the basis of a President's (or party's) past performance.

The discussion of the past focuses on the action of the incumbent party in the White House—a focus that points to the central importance of the presidency in American government. The most common statements in platforms are approvals of current policy by the party in power, and the second most common are policy disapprovals by the party out of power. The debate, then, is over the record of the current Chief Executive and his party, not a drawing of contrasts between two different sets of policies argued over the previous four years. This focus on the record of the incumbents is promoted by the nature of the American political system. Presidential government and the lack of a similarly authoritative spokesperson for the other party focus attention on the Chief Executive's program. A two-party system, moreover, tends to reduce political conflict to a simple alternative of continuity or change in present policies without equal consideration of the opposition's alternatives. It is also simpler to concentrate on the known record of the incumbent than on the hypothetical performance of the opposition.

About half of the statements in party platforms are promises for the future. These pledges can also be categorized by type (in this case illustrated by excerpts from the 1988 Democratic platform). Some pledges are meaningless rhetoric, for example, the assertion that "all Americans have a fundamental right to economic justice in a stronger, surer national economy." More specifically, the party may express its concern over a particular problem, for example: "Advance notice of plant closings and major layoffs is not only fundamentally right but also economically sound." Even more precisely, the party may pledge particular actions, for example, support of "an indexed minimum wage that can help lift and keep families out of poverty."

Again, these promises are relatively meaningful. Typically, fewer than one in five platform pledges are simply rhetorical commitments to consensual values such as peace and prosperity. Even disregarding other vague and general statements, scholarly research has shown that more than half of all platform pledges are sufficiently specific to enable voters to know the parties' policy directions, and this conclusion holds not only for ordinary, lengthy platforms but also for the abbreviated program that the Democrats adopted in 1988 in an effort to avoid controversial issues. Furthermore, platform promises also become the basis of the presidential campaign. The party nominees do not forget the program after the convention adjourns. The issues that are included in the platform are also included in the electioneering of the candidates.

Pledges and Policy Guidance. Specificity in platform pledges varies according to the policy topic being addressed. Pledges by the parties are designed to encourage voting on the basis of promised group benefits, the most common criterion employed by the voters. The parties in turn construct their platforms in order to appeal to these popular interests.

The more specific pledges occur in areas such as policy toward labor, natural resources, social welfare, and agriculture—topics on which voters are likely to be relatively knowledgeable. Consequently, pledges dealing with these subjects must be specific to convince groups within the electorate. The gains to be obtained from a given foreign policy, for example, are usually cloudy, but a senior citizen is apt to have the skill of an actuary in calculating the advantage of a change in SOCIAL SECURITY law. Parties respond to these differences by being more or less explicit in their promises.

The party platform is, to be sure, a campaign document, but it is also an element of presidential government. While its characteristics originate in a party's goal of electoral victory, it also reflects the party's relationship to the voters. In order to win elections, the party must also promote, to some extent, the interests of voters, giving elections a policy significance. These documents are reasonably meaningful indications of the party's intentions. Through a platform's representations of the past and pledges for the future, a party and a President become committed to particular policies. The voter, by conferring legitimacy on these programs, intervenes significantly in the process of government. Platforms provide assistance to voters and indirect policy influences on the parties.

This significance of platforms becomes further evident in their actual impact on governmental policy. A wide variety of studies have shown that Presidents and parties do, in fact, deliver on the promises made in party platforms. The degree of program fulfillment, however, varies according to topic, with higher fulfillment on issues involving specific benefits to discrete voting groups.

Platforms have been used as standards by which parties approvingly measure their own performance and condemn that of the opposition. For a generation, Republican speeches critically compared New Deal deficit spending to the Democrats' 1932 promise to reduce federal expenditures and balance the budget. While Democrats egregiously failed to implement this pledge, they did fulfill their promises of unemployment relief, a public works program, regulation of the stock market, and protection of bank deposits.

More recently, Democrats have found their platform a source of inspiration rather than embarrassment. As President Jimmy Carter took office, his staff compiled a list of campaign promises as a guide to legislative action. The achievement of these pledges became the basis of his reelection effort. The importance of platforms has also been recognized by other policy initiators, such as the WHITE HOUSE STAFF and the OFFICE OF MANAGEMENT AND BUDGET, which use these documents as source material for legislative and executive initiatives.

One line of research has compared the emphasis given in platforms to different policy areas with the consequent spending emphases in legislation. It has found a strong relationship between these factors, so that, for example, an emphasis on military defense in the Republican platform in an election year would be followed by a significant increase in defense spending. It is, of course, critical to these relationships that a party actually win the presidential election: the party that gains control of the White House, regardless of the Congressional outcome, places its priorities on the national agenda; the loser loses not only the election but also its policy goals.

Pledges and Accomplishments. Another line of research compares specific platform pledges to actual accomplishments. The redemption of party promises takes various forms, sometimes coming through legislation (e.g., the Republican commitment to cut taxes after the election of Ronald Reagan in 1980), sometimes through executive action (e.g., the Republican promise to appoint judges opposed to abortion), and sometimes simply through promised inaction (e.g., the consistent bipartisan promises to maintain social security benefit levels).

In analyzing platform fulfillment, researchers find that usually more than half—and sometimes as many as three-fourths—of national party pledges are actually redeemed. Similar levels of accomplishment are found in regard to state party platforms and presidential campaign promises. There are higher degrees of fulfillment when the party promises are consistent with majority sentiment in public opinion polls and when the party favors the status quo rather than a change in existing policy. When both party platforms endorse a particular course of action, such bipartisan promises are highly likely to be redeemed, although relatively few issues (less than a quarter of all promises) actually receive support in both Democratic and Republican manifestos.

Control of the executive branch is critically important for a pledge's chance of redemption. In keeping with the presidency's central position in American government, the party holding the White House is far better able to redeem its promises. The party in power generally achieves more than half again as many of its program objectives as the party out of power. The most dramatic impact of presidential control has been in the area of social welfare. The President's party has

POINT FOUR PROGRAM

been able to achieve nearly two-thirds of its promises, despite their usually controversial nature, compared to fewer than half of the out-party's social welfare goals. Winning the presidency does indeed make a difference in future policies.

Much that is contained in party platforms does become public policy, but not everything. What is indicated by the degree of a platform's fulfillment in implemented programs? Is it significant that as many as three-fourths of all pledges are kept in some way? Or is it more significant that more than a quarter of all pledges are not redeemed? Whatever measurement is employed, it is notable that platforms are considered at all, for party manifestos have usually been the object of scorn. In light of conventional wisdom, it is remarkable to find any fulfillment of party pledges. There is no absolute standard with which to compare party performance. Even the promises of the Delphic Oracle were subject to interpretation, and human vows are necessarily less reliable. All married persons have solemnly pledged to "love, honor, and cherish," but more than a third of all marriages end in divorce. Should parties be more faithful?

In summary, platforms are neither simple nor simple-minded. At times, these party statements are only endorsements of undisputed values, such as motherhood and patriotism, but sometimes they deal with controversial issues such as abortion and war. Janus-like, they provide both retrospective evaluations of parties' records in office and pledges of future conduct. More often than not, parties do fulfill these promises to some extent, particularly when in control of the presidency. Platforms are certainly campaign vehicles to run on, but they also reflect and affect the meaning of the electoral race and the direction the winner will actually take.

BIBLIOGRAPHY

Budge, Ian, and Richard I. Hofferbert. "Mandates and Policy Outputs: U.S. Party Platforms and Federal Expenditures." *American Political Science Review* 84 (1990): 111–132.

David, Paul T. "Party Platforms as National Plans." *Public Administration Review* 31 (1971): 303–315.

Elling, Richard C. "State Party Platforms and State Legislative Performance: A Comparative Analysis." *American Journal of Political Science* 23 (1979): 383–405.

Johnson, Donald B. *National Party Platforms*. 2 vols. 1978.

Krukones, Michael G. *Promises and Performance: Presidential Campaigns as Policy Predictors.* 1984.

Monroe, Alan D. "American Party Platforms and Public Opinion." *American Journal of Political Science* 27 (1983): 27–42.

Pomper, Gerald M., with Susan S. Lederman. *Elections in America: Control and Influence in Democratic Politics.* 2d ed. 1980.

Wattier, Mark J. "Platform Pledges and Campaign Communica-
tions: Developing and Discussing the 1988 Democratic Platform." *Southeastern Political Science Review* 19 (1991): 170–192.

GERALD M. POMPER

POINT FOUR PROGRAM. The Point Four program, begun in 1950, during the administration of President Harry S. Truman, provided technical assistance and private investment for underdeveloped nations. The President had called for "a bold new program" to promote "the improvement and growth" of these countries as the fourth point in his inaugural address of 20 January 1949. Prior to that time, most foreign aid, including the MARSHALL PLAN, had been targeted for European reconstruction. Developing nations in Latin America, the Middle East, and Africa complained that the United States was ignoring their economic needs.

President Truman was sensitive to these complaints. In the COLD WAR atmosphere that existed at the end of the 1940s he believed that a healthy world economy was essential to prevent the spread of communism. He was also eager to gain access to the raw materials of less developed countries, which he considered essential for the United States' own industrial needs. He intended Point Four, therefore, to serve both foreign policy and domestic purposes. Although Truman had been giving consideration to a program of technical assistance for several years, the idea of including the proposal in his inaugural address came from two White House assistants, CLARK CLIFFORD and George Elsey, who adopted the theme from a State Department assistant, Ben Hardy. Truman's proposal to share America's technical advances with underdeveloped countries encountered considerable skepticism in Congress and, within the President's own administration, from officials who doubted the utility of another aid program. It took until June 1950 for Congress finally to approve the Act for International Development establishing the Technical Cooperation Administration (TCA) in the STATE DEPARTMENT. To head the agency, Truman appointed Dr. Henry Garland Bennett, president of Oklahoma A&M University.

There is still controversy as to how effective the Point Four program was before the TCA was incorporated in 1953 into the Mutual Security Act. Thirty-five countries benefited from TCA assistance, which went toward programs designed to increase the food supply, eradicate disease, improve literacy rates, build roads, and develop hydroelectric power. But the Point Four program was not successful in encouraging private investment abroad, and the total amount of assistance provided under the program was also small

($148 million in 1952 and $156 million in 1953), especially when compared to the $12 billion Marshall Plan. Furthermore, a number of countries later complained that most of the technical assistance provided by the United States promoted projects directly benefiting industrialized countries, for example, increasing the availability of raw material supplies, rather than bringing about the economic development of recipient countries.

BIBLIOGRAPHY

Lefler, Melvyn P. *Preponderance of Power: National Security, the Truman Administration, and the Cold War.* 1992.

McCoy, Donald R. *The Presidency of Harry S. Truman.* 1984.

BURTON KAUFMAN

POLICY, PRESIDENTIAL. A formal response to a specific problem that a President chooses to solve is known as *presidential policy.* Presidential policy is separated into three broad interest areas—economic, domestic, and foreign. Each policy area includes a number of specific programs administered by a variety of agencies of government.

Three Broad Categories. ECONOMIC POLICY includes policy on taxes, employment, inflation, money supply, economic development, public works and job training (which overlap the domestic policy area), TRADE POLICY (which overlaps the foreign policy area), and budget (which is sometimes separately treated as a fourth policy area). Economic policy is generally developed by three major policy-making bodies: the DEPARTMENT OF THE TREASURY, the COUNCIL OF ECONOMIC ADVISERS (CEA), and the DEPARTMENT OF COMMERCE. Other institutional players become involved in specific subareas of economic policy—for example, the FEDERAL RESERVE BOARD on MONETARY POLICY, the United States Trade Representative on trade policy, and the Secretary of Labor on employment and job-training policy.

Obviously, economic policy affects domestic and foreign policy, and vice versa. Rising unemployment may create pressure for protectionist trade policy even as it pushes health and welfare costs upward. Because such impacts are felt more directly on domestic income-support programs, economic policy is sometimes considered a subset of presidential domestic policy. However, the administrative hosts are sufficiently balkanized by professional ties and bureaucratic cultures that it is reasonable to think of economic and domestic policy as separate areas.

Even without economic policy in the mix, domestic policy represents a very broad category. In budget impact alone, domestic policy can be said to occupy almost three-quarters of the federal budget, including programs in areas as diverse as agriculture, aging, SOCIAL SECURITY (which is sometimes considered an economic-policy area), aid to families with dependent children, health (which contains strong elements of economic policy in its price controls), veterans, children and youth, education, housing, occupational health and safety, transportation, environmental protection, food and drug regulation, consumer protection, criminal justice, drug control, national forests and parks, INDIANS, and oceans.

Aside from the departments of DEFENSE, STATE, and Treasury and the parts of the Department of Commerce that are solely engaged in economic policy, virtually every other agency of government has a role in setting domestic policy, as do the White House domestic policy staff and the OFFICE OF MANAGEMENT AND BUDGET (OMB). Domestic policy also engages the largest number of federal civilian employees, with the departments of AGRICULTURE, HEALTH AND HUMAN SERVICES, VETERANS AFFAIRS, and INTERIOR being the largest providers of policy advice and administration.

Because of the breadth of domestic policy, many presidential scholars break the area down into three subsets: health policy (including veterans programs, Medicare, and Medicaid), income security policy (including all welfare programs, veterans benefits, job-training programs, and sometimes Medicaid), and natural resources policy (including many programs administered by the departments of Interior and Agriculture as well as regulations enforced by the Environmental Protection Agency and the Occupational Health and Safety Administration). This kind of grouping led Richard M. Nixon to propose a "super-cabinet" that would have condensed the then-eleven Cabinet departments into four: natural resources, human resources, economic resources, and national security (Nixon's proposal failed).

Of the three broad policy areas, foreign policy may be the easiest to define. It includes defense and NATIONAL SECURITY issues, human rights, international cooperation, foreign assistance and development, and trade. Foreign-policy programs are more neatly divided up than are those that fall under either domestic or economic policy. The lion's share of foreign-policy responsibility is located in three centers of advice and administration: the Department of Defense, the Department of State, and the NATIONAL SECURITY COUNCIL (NSC). As with economic policy, other institutional players come into the decision-making process on specific programs—for example, the CENTRAL INTELLIGENCE AGENCY (CIA) on national security policy and the

1178 POLICY, PRESIDENTIAL

National Security Agency on more specialized intelligence estimates.

As with both economic and domestic policy, overlaps are notable and frequent in the foreign-policy area. Thus, even though these three policy areas retain their descriptive value, it is important to note that the lines between the three have blurred substantially. International events have profound domestic impacts, and the solutions to domestic problems are increasingly international in reach. In addition, economic problems appear to influence virtually every decision made in either domestic or foreign policy, either because of budgetary constraints or international implications. Thus, it may be increasingly appropriate to refer to presidential policy as a singular phenomenon that, depending on the subject, will have primary impacts on one or more of the three policy areas.

Types of Programs. The three functional categories can be combined with descriptions based on the nature of the specific program or proposal in order to provide a more detailed understanding of presidential policy. As Mark Peterson argues in *Legislating Together*,

> If we are to understand fully the processes by which the President and Congress make legislative choices, and if we are to evaluate the policy-making capacity of both institutions, including giving meaning to the notion of presidential 'success,' then it is essential that careful efforts be made to distinguish among various kinds of policy initiatives.

Thus, in addition to sorting presidential policy by genus (economic, domestic, and foreign) and species (aging, national security, tax, etc.), scholars also describe policy by reference to at least seven additional categories.

First, presidential policy can be described as either *substantive* or *symbolic*. Presidents are under no obligation to solve a given problem in economic, domestic, or FOREIGN AFFAIRS with a new program, or, for that matter, to take any action at all. They can and sometimes do let history take its own course, weighing in with symbolic gestures—among which commissions, studies, and task forces are time-honored devices—in lieu of programmatic action.

Second, policy can be described by its intended effects, whether to *distribute* a set of benefits to all citizens and/or groups, *redistribute* a set of benefits from one class or group of citizens to another, or *regulate* the behavior of citizens, groups, corporations, and other actors in a given policy area through rules and the threat of sanctions. The 1983 social security reform package might be considered an example of another type of policy in which almost all citizens lost benefits, whether through reduced benefits and delays in cost-of-living adjustments for retirees or higher taxes for corporations and workers.

Third, policy can be described by its enactment mechanism—that is, whether it is to be adopted through the legislative, administrative, or judicial channel. Some presidential policies are adopted through EXECUTIVE ORDERS or another administrative strategy; others must be enacted by Congress; and still others move through the courts. Presidential domestic policy, for example, is heavily focused on Congress, since so much of the PRESIDENT'S AGENDA must be enacted to have impact.

Fourth and fifth, policy can be described by its size (large- or small-scale) and scope (is it a new, untested initiative or a modification of an old idea that already has constituents?). All presidential policies are not created equal: some programs have greater scale, others are relatively limited experiments. Ultimately, descriptions of programs' size and scope are most telling when they are combined, characterizing given proposals as large-new, large-old, small-new, or small-old. As John Campbell argues,

> Large-new decisions are the sort one reads about in cases studies and the agenda-setting literature; a good example for the aging policy area in America is Medicare. . . . At the extreme, these decisions have a large fiscal impact and they significantly alter the relations among social groups or between state and society.

Sixth, policy can be described by its implementation focus—that is, whether it is to be managed by federal, state, or local government, by the nonprofit sector, or by individuals who are required to report to government, whether as citizens who file tax returns or corporations that file hazardous waste permits. Implementation focus is particularly important for explaining who the public will hold accountable for how a certain policy fares. By devolving responsibility to state and local governments, for example, a President can distance his administration from direct responsibility while at the same time, however, losing some control over outcomes and diminishing his ability to claim credit should the program succeed.

Seventh, policy can be described by the tool it employs to achieve its desired ends. Presidents have a number of different options at their disposal—grants, tax expenditures, direct provision of services, and so on. Each tool carries both strengths and weaknesses. Cash assistance (as in welfare, for example) is easy to administer but much less attractive politically than some other tools.

Ultimately, policy is best viewed as a concrete expression of the President's goals, which can in turn be separated into three general categories: reelection, historical achievement, and good policy. In searching for policy ideas to match those goals, Presidents pay attention to a variety of different sources but rely primarily on Congress, current events, and the agencies and departments of government.

BIBLIOGRAPHY

Campbell, John. "Japanese Policy and the Old People Boom." *Journal of Japanese Policy Studies* 5(1981): 329–350.
Peterson, Mark. *Legislating Together.* 1991.
Salamon, Lester. *Beyond Privatization: The Tools of Government.* 1989.

PAUL C. LIGHT

POLITICAL ACTION COMMITTEES. See PACS (POLITICAL ACTION COMMITTEES).

POLITICAL PARTIES. For discussion of the President as leader of a political party, see PARTY LEADER, PRESIDENT AS. For discussion of particular political parties, see ANTI-MASONIC PARTY; DEMOCRATIC PARTY; FEDERALIST PARTY; FREE-SOIL PARTY; GREENBACK PARTY; KNOW-NOTHING (AMERICAN) PARTY; LIBERTY PARTY; PROGRESSIVE (BULL MOOSE) PARTY; PROGRESSIVE PARTY, 1924; PROGRESSIVE PARTY, 1948; PROHIBITION PARTY; REPUBLICAN PARTY; THIRD PARTIES; WHIG PARTY.

POLK, JAMES K. (1795–1849), eleventh President of the United States (1845–1849). In many respects, the decade of the 1840s constituted a bridge between the earlier issues of national concern (namely, economic questions of national bank, tariff, and depression) and the later dominating question of SLAVERY in the territories. James Knox Polk stood boldly on that bridge during his presidency. He effectively dealt with the economic problems left over from previous administrations, and he presided over and encouraged the territorial expansion that would cause the nation in the 1850s to rivet its attention upon the future of slavery in the West. For his actions, Polk was severely criticized by some yet lauded by others. The controversy that still seems to swirl around interpretations of his presidency indicates, among other things, that he was an effective Chief Executive and a strong leader; otherwise, there would not be much reason for the disputing analyses.

Prepresidential Career. Polk's early life offered some clues about the man who eventually would lead the nation. Born in Mecklenburg County, North Carolina at almost the end of the eighteenth century, James was the first of Samuel and Jane Knox Polk's ten children. When young James was not quite eleven, the Polks moved to the Middle Tennessee area below Nashville to enhance their economic status. Polk turned his attention to schooling and enjoyed success at two nearby academies. At the age of twenty he embarked upon collegiate studies at the University of North Carolina. He graduated in 1818 at the head of his class.

He returned to Tennessee, first to Nashville to read law at Felix Grundy's office and then to the Polk hometown of Columbia to commence the practice of law in 1820. The legal profession held few attractions for Polk, however, for a brief stint as clerk of the state senate had stirred political ambitions within him. He began his public service in 1823 with election to the state legislature and two years later he launched a fourteen-year career in the U.S. House of Representatives, four of them as Speaker. Greatly assisting his personal and public life was his marriage in January 1824 to Sarah Childress of Murfreesboro, a union that was both devoted and permanent.

With the DEMOCRATIC PARTY in great trouble in Tennessee, Polk heeded the summons of its leaders and returned in 1839 in an attempt to win the governor's chair and thereby stem the tide of Whiggery. Successful in the former but less so in the latter objective, Polk calculated that his victory boosted his chances for national office. Yet his vice presidential ambitions were thwarted in 1840, a turn of events that compelled him to seek the gubernatorial office again in 1841 and in 1843. To his dismay and that of the state Democratic Party, Polk lost both of these campaigns; yet despite such reverses, he was determined to stage a comeback.

The Campaign of 1844. Polk did not hesitate therefore to step forward in 1844 when Andrew Jackson declared that the Democratic Party needed an advocate of western expansion. At its somewhat disputatious convention, the Jacksonians decided upon Polk as the party's nominee. His devotion to hard work, his single-mindedness, and his skillful political maneuvering paid off.

When the WHIG PARTY followed its script by designating HENRY CLAY as its standard-bearer, the stage was set for the fascinating contest between rival claims about the ANNEXATION OF TEXAS. Whereas Polk took a steadfast position favoring the "re-annexation of Texas," Clay attempted to moderate his earlier outright opposition to it. With Clay shifting on the principal campaign issue, Polk needed to accomplish only two things to strengthen his chances of victory: convince John Tyler to relinquish his quixotic notion of a presidential race and defuse the tariff question in the state of Pennsylvania. After having accomplished both of these aims, the Democratic contender next had to worry about a possible threat from the LIBERTY PARTY. On election day in the state of New York that party's sixteen thousand votes created some difficulties for both of the major candidates. But Polk squeaked by with a plurality of the statewide vote (he garnered five thousand more votes than did Clay) and captured New York's critically important thirty-six electoral votes. In an extremely tight election throughout the nation, Polk failed to capture a majority of the popular vote—a pattern that characterized all but one of the subsequent presidential elections through 1860. He won a clear majority of the ELECTORAL COLLEGE votes, however, and thus commenced preparations for his inauguration as the nation's eleventh President.

Manifest Destiny. As the campaign itself had revealed, the nation was beginning to fix its attention on territorial extension. Polk could not escape that concern, and he chose to ride the crest of expansionism rather than ignore it or attempt to fight against it. Labeled MANIFEST DESTINY by one of the prominent journal editors, this set of beliefs constituted a driving force in the 1840s. It meant different things to different people, to be sure, but basically it was an endorsement of the conviction that the United States had been granted a providential imperative to extend its boundaries—perhaps all the way to the Pacific coast. Cast in this light, there was a pronounced inevitability to the argument; God had ordained expansionism and nothing could or would prevail against it. Some champions of manifest destiny maintained that the nation had the altruistic duty to carry the ideals of democracy and liberty to other regions and peoples. Yet for other advocates, economic motivations lay at the heart of their convictions; this was particularly true of northeastern merchants and shippers, who longed for access to the Pacific coast as a stimulus to continental business transactions and to the opening of Oriental trade. Farmers, worried about agricultural surpluses, looked to western expansion as a way of developing markets for their goods.

As some students of the 1840s have noted, a strong component of neo-Jeffersonianism could be found in manifest destiny. Continuing territorial extension would enhance the role and place of the agricultural sector; a nation bent on opening and farming new lands, so it was argued, would lack the impulse to seek industrial and city growth as answers to its future. Certainly this view was one with which Polk himself could readily identify, as indeed could many people from the western or southern states.

Manifest destiny also had racial undercurrents. People occupying the far western lands, according to some exponents, were inferior; therefore, they simply had

to yield to the westward pressures that would bring new cultures and traditions. Another racial angle involved the perennial slavery question; this was particularly pertinent to the Texas scene. The opening of new regions would enable southerners to move with their slaves and escape the deteriorating soil conditions of some parts of the South, thereby ensuring the future of black slavery, which might otherwise be endangered. Moreover, as some shrewd advocates of expansionism noted, the westward movement of blacks would lessen the likelihood of their moving into northern and eastern states. When the newly elected Polk contemplated the future, he did so within an environment captivated by the beckonings of manifest destiny.

Polk's Cabinet. But before he could focus on loftier matters, Polk had to wrestle with the demanding question of who would serve in his CABINET. He found that to be a much more difficult challenge than he had imagined, although he early committed himself to a geographical symmetry. There must be someone from New England, a person from New York, a representative of the Deep South, a member from Pennsylvania, someone from Virginia, and finally a friend from Tennessee.

As the situation evolved, New York presented special complications, for Polk had to navigate between its warring Silas Wright–Martin Van Buren and conservative factions. Initially, he turned to Wright with the offer of the Treasury portfolio, knowing in advance that the newly elected governor would reject it. Eventually, still attempting to placate the Van Buren forces, who had been apathetic or even hostile to Polk's candidacy, the President-elect offered the War Department to Benjamin Butler. Believing that post to be unworthy of his status, however, Butler refused the position, an action that then opened the way for Polk to award it to William L. Marcy, a conservative. Polk probably handled the vexing New York situation about as well as could be expected, but problems with the divided party there haunted him throughout his administration.

Polk was steadfast in his belief that James Buchanan of Pennsylvania should have the prestigious State Department post, although he rightly worried about Buchanan's future presidential ambitions. Since the Vice President-elect, GEORGE MIFFLIN DALLAS, was from Pennsylvania and represented a rival faction of Democrats, the Buchanan appointment became complicated. Eventually Polk turned a deaf ear to Dallas's pleading and proceeded with his original plan, though the Buchanan-Dallas rivalry would trouble the administration from time to time.

Long an admirer of George Bancroft of Massachusetts, the President-elect readily decided upon him for the post of Navy Secretary. Yet, even that relatively simple appointment caused complexities before it was finally secured. Polk knew that he wanted his longtime friend from Tennessee, Cave Johnson, in his Cabinet, and the best available spot was that of Postmaster General. Johnson eagerly accepted and served faithfully for four years as Polk's special confidant.

There were two other vacancies: Attorney General and Secretary of the Treasury. To accommodate the expectations of the Deep South states, Polk eventually turned to Robert J. Walker of Mississippi for the Treasury assignment, although that had not been his original plan for Walker. Once in Washington, however, Polk felt the pressure, from several quarters, to place Walker in an elevated post; and he shrewdly calculated the importance of Walker's Pennsylvania connections, not the least of which were family ties with Dallas. On the day before inauguration, Polk suddenly filled the Attorney General position with this college friend and former Tyler Cabinet member, John Y. Mason of Virginia. Mason's appointment enabled Polk to remain true to his geographical game plan but caused him to renege on his pledge to exclude Tyler's people.

After having organized his official family, the challenge for Polk was to keep it working together as an effective and harmonious entity. He did amazingly well, despite the obviously divisive issues that confronted the administration. As partial evidence, one need only look at the stability of personnel in the Cabinet. A year and a half after the commencement of the presidency, Polk initiated the first change when he rewarded Bancroft with the post of minister to Britain. Then Polk transferred Mason to the Navy Department, the slot Mason had earlier occupied in the Tyler Cabinet. About a month later, October 1846, the President turned to New England (always keeping in mind geographical symmetry) and offered the vacant post of Attorney General to Nathan Clifford of Maine, who accepted. Eventually in 1848 Polk tapped Clifford for a special assignment as one of the treaty commissioners to Mexico. Consequently, the President was forced to seek yet another person for Attorney General; after some initial problems, he selected Isaac Toucey of Connecticut (again the geographical consideration). When considering both the possibility of numerous personnel changes and the experience of such Presidents as Jackson and Tyler, one must credit Polk with skillful handling of his Cabinet.

Moreover, it must be recognized that the President truly utilized his executive officers, not only to administer their assigned departments but also to confer with him on all the weighty matters that burdened the administration. He made no effort to circumvent his Cabinet, as had Jackson, and declared his expectation that each member should attend the two regularly scheduled Cabinet meetings each week as well as the extra ones. Members of Polk's official family thus had an incredible opportunity to assist him in governing the nation; but there was no question that Polk was the person in charge.

The Domestic Agenda. In the rush to scrutinize the President's diplomatic policies, it is tempting to brush by the domestic agenda that he and his Cabinet pursued. From the outset Polk controlled this arena, for he seized the initiative when he identified the twin pillars of tariff reform and an INDEPENDENT TREASURY as major goals. In his long prepresidential career he had consistently embraced the low-tariff position, believing that it was best for the nation since such rates favored the agricultural rather than the manufacturing sector. He inherited the tariff question from the Tyler presidency, which had seen the passage of a protective tariff in 1842.

Tariff reform. Polk addressed tariff reform in his inaugural speech and again in his first annual message to Congress. Although advocating a lowering of the duties, he looked to the national legislature to fashion an acceptable bill. Thankfully, Treasury Secretary Walker, a staunch supporter of low tariffs, gathered data from merchants and importers and other segments of the business community in order to build a case for the reduction of rates [see WALKER TARIFF ACT]. Thus the House committee charged with responsibility for tariffs turned to Walker for assistance. It reported out its low-tariff recommendations in April 1846; but the House stalled and delayed, partly because it awaited word from Britain concerning the repeal of the Corn Laws. Moreover, Congress experienced other distractions, such as the declaration of war against Mexico and the critical negotiations with Britain over the Oregon boundary. Much to Polk's chagrin, the House did not finally vote on the proposed tariff until 3 July; but it gave him a resounding victory, primarily because of heavy Democratic support.

Gratified at this promising turn of events, Polk then looked to the Senate for its response to the House bill. Despite difficulties with three Senators in particular, the President successfully lobbied for the so-called Walker Tariff. Near the end of July, the Senate endorsed the bill, thanks to a remarkable 80 percent of Democrats' favoring it. The President rejoiced that "an immense struggle between the two great political parties of the country" had ended in victory for the low-tariff forces and thereby for the farming segment of the nation.

The Independent Treasury. Less controversy and attention accompanied the other major piece of domestic economic legislation, namely, the Independent Treasury. It simply could not compete for the limelight, given everything else that was happening in the spring and summer months of 1846. Like the tariff issue, the independent treasury question was inherited from the Tyler administration, which had seen the repeal of the earlier Van Buren scheme. Polk's thinking, much like Van Buren's, was that the only safe place for federal funds was in an independent treasury, certainly not in a national bank or even in the state banks. He made this clear in both his inaugural speech and in his first annual message.

Accordingly, with the President's urging and perhaps with Secretary Walker's direct involvement again, the House committee began consideration of the legislation to create an independent, or constitutional, treasury. Moving with disturbing slowness, the committee finally reported out the bill at the end of March and the whole House voted favorably upon it on 2 April.

If the President expected immediate reaction from the Senate, he was sorely disappointed, for the chair of the Finance Committee, Dixon H. Lewis, revealed his intentions to delay the bill indefinitely. True to his word, Lewis, despite some direct chiding from the President, sat on the bill until early June. Thereafter his committee forwarded it to the entire Senate, which then rather quickly approved it, albeit by a narrow margin.

Internal improvements. In any event, by the summer of 1846, Polk had accomplished the two major goals of his domestic economic agenda. But the battle was not entirely over, for Congress had some plans of its own, namely the passage of INTERNAL IMPROVEMENTS measures. Good Jacksonian that he was, the President made no mention of internal improvements in either his inaugural address or in his first annual message. Naturally he believed that the federal government simply could not constitutionally support such programs, except for the most restricted national defense interests.

Both sessions of the Twenty-ninth Congress, however, experienced a burgeoning attraction toward internal improvements, especially on the part of westerners, whether Whig or Democrat. In the spring of 1846, therefore, the House passed a rivers-and-harbors bill that called for $1.4 million in federal appropriations; a fourth of the Democrats supported the bill, but it was principally a Whig-backed measure. The

Senate did not deal with the legislation until July but finally approved it by a substantial margin of votes, slightly more than one-third of which came from Democrats.

Within a few days Polk sent a veto message to Congress in which he outlined his opposition primarily upon constitutional grounds but also upon the argument that it would drain the Treasury—a not unimportant point, given the outbreak of the MEXICAN WAR. Congress made an abortive attempt to override his veto.

During the next session, not surprisingly, Congress returned to internal improvements, although on a much less grandiose scale, when it endorsed appropriations of slightly over $500,000. Polk greeted the bill instantly with a pocket veto and decided to work later on a veto message that would be worthy of the Jacksonian stance against such legislation. After months of labor the President in December produced his document, which eloquently summarized the plea for a very limited central government.

For whatever reason, neither the first session (December 1847–August 1848) nor the second session (December 1848–March 1849) of the Thirtieth Congress enacted internal-improvements bills. Fearing the threat of such legislation in the second session, however, Polk prepared a veto message just in case. He waited anxiously in March 1849 for the opportune moment to spring the veto trap, but it never arrived. In a way he regretted this turn of events, because the unused veto message was, in his words, "one of the ablest papers I have ever prepared." Polk's forthright stand against internal-improvements appropriations had the desired effect, for no such legislation was enacted. Whether dealing with this challenge or with his proposals for a lower tariff and an independent treasury, the President was eminently successful.

Foreign Relations. Both success and controversy stalked Polk's path as he directed his energies to foreign relations.

Texas. To argue that he inherited the Texas question is to state the obvious; truthfully, he could not avoid it, for it was dumped in his lap by the Tyler administration. Remember first the abortive Texas annexation treaty of 1844; then recall that immediately after the November election Tyler and Sen. JOHN C. CALHOUN positioned themselves to treat the Texas matter when Congress arrived in Washington. Thus in that critical interval between Polk's election and his inauguration, events were set in motion that demanded the new President's attention.

Thanks to the insistence of Tyler and Calhoun, both houses of Congress wrestled with Texas annexation in their short session, December 1844–March 1845. The House produced a bill calling for the immediate admission of Texas as a state, while the Senate adopted Thomas Hart Benton's proposal for the appointment of treaty commissioners to negotiate a new annexation agreement. The obvious disparity between the two bills was bridged by Robert J. Walker's ingenious recommendation that the House resolution be adopted, with the Benton plan attached. Thus the President could decide between the two approaches to resolving Texas's future. Both houses consented to this unusual arrangement and one suspects that the newly arrived Polk played a conspicuous role in the compromise. In any event, in the waning moments of his presidency Tyler embraced the House version and sent word to Texas that it would be annexed immediately, if it consented. With that he made his exit and Polk entered the White House.

The new President was ready. He and his Cabinet discussed the Texas problem and Polk forwarded a message to Andrew J. Donelson, chargé d'affaires to Texas, to await further instructions. Shortly thereafter, Polk commissioned three special agents to go to Texas to facilitate a proannexation climate there. They heeded their instructions, attended annexation meetings, and made some reasonable and some not so reasonable promises to the Texans.

At any rate, in the spring and summer of 1845 they, as well as Texas officials and British and French diplomats, all participated in stirring controversy in the Lone Star Republic. Much to the relief of the Polk administration, Sam Houston became a convert to annexation after having initially resisted it. In the midst of developments in Texas, the British chargé d'affaires, Charles Elliot, went to Mexico City and eventually returned with the promise that Mexico would recognize Texas independence, provided Texas did not seek annexation to the United States. Meanwhile Polk had sent William S. Parrott as a special agent to Mexico City to encourage that country to accept Texas annexation. Not leaving anything to chance, the President also ordered troops under command of Gen. Zachary Taylor into Texas, with the avowed purpose of deterring a possible Mexican invasion in the summer months.

The president of Texas, Anson Jones, presented the annexation proposal to his congress in June; after securing that endorsement, a special convention met in July, when annexation was again approved. This conclave also devised a state constitution, which the voters eventually approved in an October referendum. All that was left was for the U.S. Congress to admit Texas as the nation's twenty-eighth state. This admission was accomplished in December 1845, an action that closed a chapter of U.S.-Texan relations but opened a new and extremely difficult chapter on U.S.-Mexican relations. Manifest destiny was on the move.

The Mexican War. How much and in what other ways expansionism would move would soon be known. The incurably optimistic Parrott sent encouraging messages to the White House and then arrived in person to repeat his prediction that Mexico was ready to negotiate. Thus while the Texas matter was still pending, Polk opted to open the larger question of expansion to the Pacific coast. In the fall of 1845, for example, he commissioned John Slidell to go to Mexico with an offer to purchase California and New Mexico and with a plea for the recognition of the Rio Grande as the boundary of Texas, in exchange for which the United States would relinquish its claims (in excess of $3 million) against Mexico. SLIDELL'S MISSION constituted Polk's first peace initiative; but when it failed by March 1846, armed conflict with Mexico took on a menacing inevitability. Slidell did not succeed because the Mexican government, rocked by turmoil and instability at this juncture, refused to deal with him. Polk was deeply disappointed that his scheme to buy the western lands outright had been rebuffed by Mexican officials; he then ordered Taylor's troops to position themselves along the Rio Grande—perhaps to deter aggression or perhaps to invite it.

Not unexpectedly, skirmishes between Mexican troops and Taylor's forces commenced in late April; but even before word of this outbreak of hostilities reached Washington, Polk and his advisers were pressing toward a DECLARATION OF WAR. Thus when the news arrived at the nation's capital on the night of 9 May, Polk and his Cabinet swung into action. The President spent the better part of the next day writing his war message; after both houses of Congress received his request, they voted overwhelmingly in favor of a declaration of war. By these actions then manifest destiny moved into a new and different phase.

Luckily, Taylor won victory after victory in the early weeks of the war (actually he continued to do so throughout the conflict), thereby buying valuable time for Polk and his administration to develop a strategy to conduct the war and also to plan for peace. The United States was woefully unprepared for war against a foreign country in 1846; yet volunteers were called for and they responded by the thousands. Although Taylor was strategically located in the field, where he was repeatedly successful, the President lacked an overall commander. He therefore turned to the best available man, WINFIELD SCOTT, but two weeks later relieved him of command after a somewhat comical series of disagreements. Meanwhile Secretary Buchanan attempted to force Polk to disavow any territorial ambitions; the President emphatically refused, however, for he fully intended that the United States would win new lands from the war with Mexico.

Meanwhile, as Taylor's troops pushed into the northern fringes of Mexico, events took place in California that would assure U.S. domination there. JOHN C. FREMONT and his troops moved into northern California and helped foment rebellion against Mexican rule. By midsummer the so-called Bear Flag Republic had been established; and with the arrival of Commodore Robert Stockton off the California coast, the tempo of events accelerated. In August, U.S. military leaders pushed into Los Angeles and proclaimed United States authority over the entire province. From that point forward, this rich plum of manifest destiny rested in the hands of the United States, but it would be a year and a half before Mexico would admit that reality.

Toward peace with Mexico. Ever mindful of the olive branch, Polk confidently launched three different peace initiatives in the summer months. Regrettably, none succeeded. In July, the President sent Alexander Mackenzie to confer with Gen. A. L. Santa Anna, temporarily exiled in Havana. The former Mexican leader gave assurances to Mackenzie that if he gained control of the government, he would approve territorial cessions and bring about peace with the United States. Under safe escort provided by U.S. ships, Santa Anna left Cuba and returned to Mexico; but once there, he betrayed the alleged understanding and became instead the new commander of Mexican troops and prolonged the war for more than a year. Ironically, the Polk administration, while pursuing a peace plan, had helped place Santa Anna in power.

With encouragement from Consul John Black in Mexico City, who believed that the government there might be receptive to a peace commission, Polk made a second effort for peace by sending a message to Mexico indicating a willingness to engage in discussions in either Mexico or Washington. But the President's badly timed offer reached Mexico just after an overthrow of the government; hence the new leaders steadfastly refused Polk's offer.

His third attempt at peace was to seek a $2 million appropriation from Congress, so that the United States might be able to purchase the coveted territories and thereby conclude the armed conflict. Although Polk secured approval in the Senate, the House balked at the request, largely because David Wilmot added his controversial WILMOT PROVISO to the measure. Wilmot insisted that Congress stipulate that no slavery would be permitted in any of the territory acquired from Mexico. Congress was unable to reach agreement before the session adjourned, thus thwarting the President's hopes. In response, Polk moved away from these peace efforts to a consideration of opening a second military front in Mexico, namely, the Vera Cruz-to-Mexico City campaign.

This military endeavor would eventually bring the elusive peace. Polk turned to Winfield Scott (there simply was no one else available) to take charge of the second front. In March 1847, after news of Scott's victory at Vera Cruz reached the President, he decided to launch his final peace effort by sending a treaty negotiator to accompany Scott. Turning to Nicholas P. Trist, chief clerk in the State Department, Polk instructed him to devise a treaty that would assure the United States of all the lands between Texas and the Pacific coast and an acceptance of the Rio Grande as the boundary of Texas. Armed with these guidelines, Trist made his way to Mexico and joined Scott's army. During troubling days of personal hostility between the two men, however, the peace process stalled, although Scott's soldiers reaped consecutive military victories. After patching up their differences, which had greatly exasperated and dismayed Polk, Scott and Trist focused upon the tedious and tricky task of negotiating peace terms with Mexican officials. No great progress was made until Scott and his men had captured Mexico City; but even then, peace talks faltered for weeks and eventually months. Certain that Trist was somehow at fault, Polk ordered him home; yet the stubborn negotiator refused the summons and eventually worked out a peace treaty in early 1848. The conquering nation paid the vanquished foes $15 million and took responsibility for the old claims against Mexico—in return for which the United States acquired New Mexico and California and the Rio Grande as the Texas boundary. Polk and manifest destiny had won the Southwest.

The Oregon question. Long before that goal had been achieved, however, the Polk administration had dealt effectively with the Northwest, where skillful diplomatic and political maneuvering yielded a remarkable Oregon boundary compromise [see OREGON TREATY]. Like many other matters that Polk confronted, he inherited this problem from the Tyler administration. It had earlier offered to draw a boundary line along the forty-ninth parallel, thereby dividing British and American portions of the vast Oregon territory; but London had rejected that proposal. Except for a last-minute flurry in Congress in early 1845 concerning possible Oregon legislation, that is where the question rested when Polk assumed office.

The new President did not hesitate to reiterate the Democratic Party position in his inaugural address when he spoke of the "clear and unquestionable" title to Oregon. Here he seemed to side with the All Oregon extremists without actually doing so—a strategy he utilized several times. The British minister, Richard Pakenham, employed the favorite device of submitting the Oregon boundary to arbitration, which Polk and Buchanan quickly rejected. The President appointed Louis McLane minister to Britain in the early summer and sent him off to London with a new proposal: the forty-ninth parallel but with free ports for the British south of that line. Shortly after McLane departed, Buchanan notified Pakenham in Washington of the new offer. Unfortunately, the British official summarily refused the Polk plan without waiting for word from his superiors in London. This move so alienated Polk that he withdrew the proposal and professed in the fall months to have no further interest in dealing with the British regarding the Oregon boundary. Only Buchanan's persistent entreaties for further conversations prevented the President from taking an even more drastic position.

As the time neared for the preparation of his first annual message, Polk contemplated his next move. He boldly decided to look John Bull "straight in the eye" by requesting Congress to give notice to Britain that the joint occupation of Oregon should be terminated. Such a statement would of necessity force the Oregon question to a showdown, because under earlier agreements both countries would have to negotiate a settlement of the dividing line. Debate raged in and out of Congress over whether the notice resolution constituted an invitation to war or a step toward peace. Apparently having no other alternative, Pakenham again recommended arbitration, which was immediately denounced by the Polk administration. In the House, the resolution passed easily and quickly by early February 1846. But Calhoun and others who feared a breakdown in relationships between the United States and Britain fretted over the notice resolution and sought to stall or perhaps even kill it. As the Senate deliberated, Polk agreed that he would submit to that body any proposal from Britain that provided for the forty-ninth parallel. Finally, Calhoun switched his position, and in April the notice resolution cleared the Senate. Both houses hammered out their differing versions and reached agreement later in the month.

Mindful of events transpiring in America, officials in London stirred themselves to respond, thanks to McLane's prodding. Therefore in mid-May they proposed that the Oregon boundary be drawn along the forty-ninth parallel with a detour south around Vancouver Island—essentially the same plan that the Tyler administration had presented three years earlier. When the formal proposal was presented to the Polk administration, the President was ready to ask the Senate for its advice. But he had not counted upon Buchanan's sudden, last-minute objections to this proposed boundary. After an exchange of strong words between the two men, Polk proceeded with his plan to seek the Senate's advice. By an overwhelming vote the Senate urged the President to accept the British proposal. Thereafter, Buchanan and Pakenham met to draw up the actual treaty which was then submitted in mid-June and won decisive approval by the Senate. Expansionism thus carried the nation to the far reaches of the Pacific Northwest and did so without armed conflict. Americans endorsed this victory by migrating to that great new piece of the continent.

An Assessment. Polk had thus accomplished his four announced goals: resolve the Oregon question, acquire California, lower the tariff, and establish an independent treasury. It was by all reckonings an impressive record; yet there were complications. Chief among these was simply that the aggressive pursuit of his objectives had stirred dissension, and his expansionist agenda produced a countervailing movement to thwart the extension of slavery in the West.

These evolving situations became readily apparent in the presidential election of 1848. The creation of the FREE-SOIL PARTY, for example, indicated that the world was being transformed—especially when that group turned to Martin Van Buren for its nominee. Probably equally disturbing to the President was the selection of his nemesis, Zachary Taylor, as the Whig candidate. The rejection of the Democratic Party by the voters in November compounded his dismay.

For whatever reason, Polk failed to comprehend his role in fostering divisions within his own party and within the nation. After all, to him expansionism should have united the country, not divided it; but the years that followed told a different story. Yet the problems of the 1850s should not be laid exclusively at his door; to do so would absolve other national leaders from blame or responsibility. Had he lived more than a few months after leaving the White House, perhaps Polk would have come to grips with the new realities. He served as an agent of change while devoutly hoping to conserve traditional views and values. It was an irony that he did not fully appreciate.

BIBLIOGRAPHY

Bauer, K. Jack. *The Mexican War, 1846–1848*. 1974.
Bergeron, Paul H. *The Presidency of James K. Polk*. 1987.

Hietala, Thomas R. *Manifest Design: Anxious Aggrandizement in Late Jacksonian America.* 1985.

Johannsen, Robert W. *To the Halls of the Montezumas: The Mexican War in the American Imagination.* 1985.

McCormac, Eugene I. *James K. Polk: A Political Biography.* 1922.

McCoy, Charles A. *Polk and the Presidency.* 1960.

Merk, Frederick. *The Monroe Doctrine and American Expansionism, 1843–1849.* 1966.

Pletcher, David M. *The Diplomacy of Annexation: Texas, Oregon, and the Mexican War.* 1973.

Schroeder, John H. *Mr. Polk's War: American Opposition and Dissent, 1846–1848.* 1973.

Sellers, Charles G. *James K. Polk: Continentalist, 1843–1846.* 1966.

PAUL H. BERGERON

POLK DOCTRINE.

President James Monroe's famed proclamation of December 1823 against further European colonization in America scarcely concerned succeeding American Presidents [*see* MONROE DOCTRINE]. But during summer 1845 President James K. Polk received rumors of British designs on California. During the autumn American expansionists demanded that the President reaffirm the superior claims of the United States to Oregon and California under the Monroe Doctrine. In his annual message to Congress in December, Polk declared the Monroe Doctrine a defense against any European encroachments on the North American continent. Polk's decision to reassert the Monroe Doctrine rested in part on Francois Guizot's speech, delivered in the French Chamber of Deputies in June 1845, which claimed a European interest in the continued independence of such regions as Texas to preserve "the balance of the Great Powers among which America is divided."

Polk responded in his December message that the United States would resist any "European interference on the North American continent . . . [at] any and all hazards." For him the European concept of balance of power could have no application to North America, especially to the United States. "We must ever maintain the principle," he said, "that the people of this continent alone have the right to decide their own destiny." The decision of any North Americans to join the United States was not Europe's concern. Repeating Monroe's noncolonization principle, Polk declared that "it should be distinctly announced to the world as our settled policy that no future European colony or dominion shall with our consent be planted or established on any part of the North American continent."

In January 1846 Senator William Allen of Ohio, chairman of the Foreign Relations Committee, introduced a resolution designed to commit the Congress to Polk's interpretation of the Monroe Doctrine. JOHN C. CALHOUN and other conservatives quickly buried the resolution by denying that the Monroe Doctrine granted the United States any special rights. The country could judge its interests in America as elsewhere and defend them if challenged. It could do nothing more.

BIBLIOGRAPHY

Graebner, Norman A. *Ideas and Diplomacy: Readings in the Intellectual Tradition of American Foreign Policy.* 1964.

Sellers, Charles. *James K. Polk: Continentalist, 1843–1846.* 1966.

NORMAN A. GRAEBNER

POLLS AND POPULARITY.

Public opinion polls of the American electorate have become the dominant way of assessing the popularity of the President of the United States. These polls are conducted regularly by news organizations such as the joint efforts of the *New York Times* and CBS News or ABC News and the *Washington Post* as well as by polling outfits such as the Gallup Organization. Typically, these polls ask Americans their general opinion of the performance of the President and often ask more specific questions about presidential performance in the realms of the domestic economy and foreign policy. For example, a *New York Times*-CBS News poll asked the following battery of questions about the popularity of President George Bush: "Do you approve or disapprove of the way George Bush is handling his job as President?" "Do you approve or disapprove of the way George Bush is handling foreign policy?" and "Do you approve or disapprove of the way George Bush is handling the economy?"

With such questions, the President's popularity rating is simply the percentage of the citizenry that approves of his performance. Other questions that have been used to measure presidential popularity include "How would you rate the job that _____ is doing as President? Excellent, good, only fair, or poor?" Here the percentage of respondents who replied "excellent" or "good" are combined to produce the measure of presidential popularity.

There are a number of points to be made about patterns and trends in presidential popularity. First, approval levels can change dramatically over a short period of time. For example, the onset of an international crisis in which the President exercises dramatic leadership, addresses the American public on television, holds a televised press conference, and the like is sometimes associated with a sharp increase in presidential popularity, an increase that often fades as the crisis ebbs. There is a marked tendency for Americans

POLYGRAPH TESTS   1187

to support the President in the face of a foreign threat or challenge.

Second, Americans may give the President good grades on one issue, yet strongly disapprove of his performance in regard to another. For example, in March 1991, during the height of the GULF WAR, Americans overwhelmingly approved of George Bush's overall performance by a margin of 88 percent to 8 percent with 4 percent unsure in a poll conducted by the *New York Times* and CBS News. Not surprisingly, 83 percent of the people polled in that same survey also approved of the President's handling of foreign policy. But when it came to the handling of the economy, 43 percent of Americans disapproved of the President's performance and only 42 percent approved. In this example, it is clear that citizens' overall evaluations of the President were determined by the issue most salient to them at the time—the Gulf War. But as the war receded in the public's consciousness and the condition of the economy became the prominent issue, the public's assessment of George Bush changed dramatically. Thus, in another *New York Times*-CBS News poll conducted a year later, the President's overall approval rating had plummeted to 39 percent (with 50 percent disapproving), his economic performance was evaluated even more negatively (21 percent approval versus 73 percent disapproval), while his handling of foreign policy still enjoyed support, though diminished (50 percent approval versus 41 percent disapproval).

Third, Americans are not homogeneous in their evaluations of Presidents. That is, different subgroups of Americans are more likely or less likely to be supportive of the President. For example, when Americans are examined according to their political party preferences, strong differences emerge. Throughout the Reagan and Bush Administrations, Americans who identified themselves as Republicans were most supportive of the President, Democrats were least supportive, and independents were somewhere in between. Other breakdowns such as by gender and race are routinely done and differences in presidential support are often observed. For example, blacks during the Reagan and Bush administrations were less supportive of the President than whites (in part because blacks are heavily Democratic in their partisan orientations) and women were less supportive than men.

While many observers welcome the opportunity that public opinion polls provide for citizens to voice their views about the performance of their leaders and their government, other observers worry that the presidential popularity polls distort politics and government in a number of ways. First, the results of the polls have become a major news story in and of themselves. This is especially worrisome since in many instances the media that report the news are also generating it through their sponsorship of polls. More attention becomes devoted to the President's political standing as measured in the polls and less is given to an analysis of the substantive activities of government. Some observers worry that the polls are too influential with respect to presidential decision making. They argue that Presidents who carry the latest polls in their pockets are more likely to govern with an eye toward what is popular rather than what is sound. They worry that the heavy emphasis on presidential popularity polls may lead administrations to be overly dependent on political ploys and gimmicks designed to increase poll ratings in the short term to the detriment of long range problem solving that may entail risks of unpopular decisions. Finally, observers worry that the polls may give a misleading portrait of the condition of the country and the performance of the President; they argue that popularity is not synonymous with successful leadership and that other indicators of performance ratings may encourage leaders to ignore that part of the American public whose dissatisfaction with the President and the government is rooted in deep and fundamental policy concerns. Despite these concerns about how surveys of presidential popularity are used and interpreted, it is clear that public opinion polling is so central to the fabric of American political life and discourse that analyses of presidential popularity will inevitably depend largely on the results provided by polls.

BIBLIOGRAPHY

Asher, Herbert B. *Polling and the Public*. 2d ed. 1992.
Kernell, Samuel. *Going Public: New Strategies of Presidential Leadership*. 1986.
Mueller, John E. *War, Presidents, and Public Opinion*. 1973.

HERBERT B. ASHER

POLYGRAPH TESTS. Polygraph tests are designed to assess truthfulness and deception in situations ranging from the screening of job applicants to the investigation of specific criminal incidents. While various testing or questioning techniques are utilized, the polygraph instrument is fairly standard. It measures at least three physiological indicators of arousal—rate and depth of respiration, blood pressure, and perspiration. Changes in these physiological indicators in response to a set of questions are taken to indicate the subject's deception or truthfulness. The examiner reviews the pattern of arousal responses and infers the subject's veracity.

Interest in using a scientific instrument as an aid to detecting lies dates from at least 1895, when an Italian criminologist, Cesare Lombroso, claimed success in determining the guilt or innocence of a criminal suspect through blood pressure fluctuation during interrogation. During WORLD WAR I, William Moulton Marston, a criminal lawyer, convinced a group of psychologists at the National Research Council that the correlation between lying and elevated blood pressure was highly reliable. They proposed that Marston be appointed a special assistant to the Secretary of War with authority to use his method in spy cases. No action was taken on the recommendation and many years passed before federal law enforcement and national defense agencies made any extensive commitment to polygraph testing.

In 1964 a House of Government Operations Committee report severely criticized the validity and widespread agency use of polygraph examinations. It recommended comprehensive research to determine the validity and reliability of polygraph tests, prohibiting their use in all but the most serious NATIONAL SECURITY and criminal cases, improving the training and qualifications of federal polygraph operators, and guaranteeing that such tests be voluntary. During the next several years, various congressional committees held hearings and issued reports criticizing a number of aspects of polygraph testing by agencies.

A 1983 report by the congressional Office of Technology Assessment concluded that "there is at present only limited scientific evidence for establishing the validity of polygraph testing." Early that year, President Ronald Reagan issued a national security decision directive (NSDD 84), which, in part, authorized agencies to require all employees to take a polygraph examination in the course of internal investigations of unauthorized disclosures of security-classified information. After much congressional protest, the Department of Justice announced a comprehensive policy on federal polygraph use. It authorized polygraph testing as a condition of initial or continuing employment with or assignment to agencies with highly sensitive responsibilities directly affecting national security, as a condition of access to highly sensitive classified information, as a means of investigating serious criminal cases, and as a means of investigating serious administrative-misconduct cases, including unauthorized disclosure of CLASSIFIED INFORMATION.

Later, congressional efforts at limiting polygraph use in private-sector employment culminated in the Employee Polygraph Protection Act of 1988 (102 Stat. 646). The statute prohibits businesses from requiring workers and job applicants to submit to polygraph tests. Federal, state, and local governments, as well as companies doing business with national security agencies or manufacturing and selling controlled drugs, are exempt from the ban. Also, polygraph examinations are allowed if an employer has "reasonable suspicion" that a worker is involved in a crime causing economic harm to the firm, such as embezzlement. However, in private employment where polygraph testing is permissible, results, or a worker's refusal to submit to such an examination, may not be used as the sole basis for dismissing or reprimanding the employee. The Secretary of Labor is authorized to enforce and investigate compliance with the statute. Employers found violating the statute may be assessed a civil penalty of not more than $10,000.

BIBLIOGRAPHY

U.S. Office of Technology Assessment. *Scientific Validity of Polygraph Testing: A Research Review and Evaluation.* 1983.

HAROLD C. RELYEA

POSTMASTER GENERAL. From 1789 until 1971 the Postmaster General was appointed by, and reported to, the President. Their relationship after 1829, when Andrew Jackson became President and made Postmaster General William T. Barry a member of his CABINET, was a close one. Not only did the Postmaster General often serve as the President's chief political adviser, he also had more jobs to award to party supporters than any other Cabinet member. Often, the person appointed Postmaster General had chaired the President's political party.

After 1836, the President directly appointed postmasters in larger post offices and the Postmaster General named postmasters of the smaller offices. Postmasters were valuable "agents for disseminating information," according to President James Buchanan. He believed in rotating postmasterships, so one position could be used to reward several supporters. Removals and resignations of postmasters sometimes took place at a dizzying rate, although a few Presidents and Postmasters General preferred to remove postmasters only for cause.

The story is told that Postmaster General John McLean was asked by the third President under which he served, Jackson, whether he objected to removing postmasters who had been active politically in the last campaign. McLean replied that he did not if the removal policy operated against Jackson's supporters

Postmasters General

President	Postmaster General
1 Washington	Samuel Osgood, 1789–1791 Timothy Pickering, 1791–1795 Joseph Habersham, 1795–1797
2 J. Adams	Joseph Habersham, 1797–1801
3 Jefferson	Joseph Habersham, 1801 Gideon Granger, 1801–1809
4 Madison	Gideon Granger, 1809–1814 Return J. Meigs, Jr., 1814–1817
5 Monroe	Return J. Meigs, Jr., 1817–1823 John McLean, 1823–1825
6 J. Q. Adams	John McLean, 1825–1829
7 Jackson	William T. Barry, 1829–1835 Amos Kendall, 1835–1837
8 Van Buren	Amos Kendall, 1837–1840 John M. Niles, 1840–1841
9 W. H. Harrison	Francis Granger, 1841
10 Tyler	Francis Granger, 1841 Charles A. Wickliffe, 1841–1845
11 Polk	Cave Johnson, 1845–1849
12 Taylor	Jacob Collamer, 1849–1850
13 Fillmore	Nathan K. Hall, 1850–1852 Samuel D. Hubbard, 1852–1853
14 Pierce	James Campbell, 1853–1857
15 Buchanan	Aaron V. Brown, 1857–1859 Joseph Holt, 1859–1861 Horatio King, 1861
16 Lincoln	Montgomery Blair, 1861–1864 William Dennison, 1864–1865
17 A. Johnson	William Dennison, 1865–1866 Alexander W. Randall, 1866–1869
18 Grant	John A. Creswell, 1869–1874 James W. Marshall, 1874 Marshall Jewell, 1874–1876 James N. Tyner, 1876–1877
19 Hayes	David M. Key, 1877–1880 Horace Maynard, 1880–1881
20 Garfield	Thomas L. James, 1881
21 Arthur	Thomas L. James, 1881 Timothy O. Howe, 1882–1883 Frank Hatton, 1883 Walter Q. Gresham, 1883–1884 Frank Hatton, 1884–1885
22 Cleveland	William F. Vilas, 1885–1888 Don M. Dickinson, 1888–1889
23 B. Harrison	John Wanamaker, 1889–1893
24 Cleveland	Wilson S. Bissell, 1893–1895 William L. Wilson, 1895–1897
25 McKinley	James A. Gary, 1897–1898 Charles E. Smith, 1898–1901
26 T. Roosevelt	Charles E. Smith, 1901–1902 Henry C. Payne, 1902–1904 Robert J. Wynne, 1904–1905 George B. Cortelyou, 1905–1907 George von L. Meyer, 1907–1909
27 Taft	Frank H. Hitchcock, 1909–1913
28 Wilson	Albert S. Burleson, 1913–1921
29 Harding	Will H. Hays, 1921–1922 Hubert Work, 1922–1923 Harry S. New, 1923
30 Coolidge	Harry S. New, 1923–1929
31 Hoover	Walter F. Brown, 1929–1933
32 F. D. Roosevelt	James A. Farley, 1933–1940 Frank C. Walker, 1940–1945
33 Truman	Frank C. Walker, 1945 Robert E. Hannegan, 1945–1947 Jesse M. Donaldson, 1947–1953
34 Eisenhower	Arthur E. Summerfield, 1953–1961
35 Kennedy	J. Edward Day, 1961–1963 John A. Gronouski, Jr., 1963
36 L. B. Johnson	John A. Gronouski, Jr., 1963–1965 Lawrence F. O'Brien, 1965–1968 W. Marvin Watson, 1968–1969
37 Nixon	Wilton M. Blount, 1969–1971

as well as Adams's. Jackson offered McLean a seat on the Supreme Court instead. McLean accepted.

During Andrew Johnson's Presidency and over his veto, the TENURE OF OFFICE ACT was passed, making it illegal to remove certain postmasters from their positions without the consent of the Senate. The act was also interpreted to mean that heads of departments should hold office during the term of the appointing President and for one month thereafter, subject to the Senate's ADVICE AND CONSENT. The act was repealed in 1869 but a postal code adopted in 1872 continued that provision for the Postmaster General. It remained in effect until the Postal Reorganization Act of 1970.

Theodore Roosevelt's presidency marked an end to the nineteenth century's postal purges, but the positions of postmasters and, later, rural carriers remained political appointments until 1969 when President Richard Nixon and Postmaster General Winton M. Blount jointly announced an end to political appointments in the Post Office Department. A year later, the Postal Reorganization Act was passed and the appointment of the Postmaster General was depoliticized.

The act removed the Postmaster General from the President's Cabinet and his appointment. Instead, the Postmaster General is selected by nine presidentially appointed postal governors, no more than half of them of the same political party, and the Postmaster General serves at the governor's discretion. To date, the governors have chosen business leaders or postal officers to serve as the chief executive officer of the nation's largest civilian organization, the UNITED STATES POSTAL SERVICE.

BIBLIOGRAPHY

Fowlser, Dorothy Ganfield. *The Cabinet Politician.* 1943.

MEGAERA HARRIS

POSTMODERN PRESIDENT. The modern presidency, epitomized by the administration of Franklin D. Roosevelt, was regarded as a powerful yet benign institution in the American political system. This categorization of the presidency was challenged both by the crises prompted by the IMPERIAL PRESIDENCIES of Lyndon B. Johnson and Richard M. Nixon as well as the relative weakness of Presidents Gerald Ford and Jimmy Carter. Although the administration of Ronald Reagan seemed to hearken back to the "modern" paradigm, significant shifts in the American political, social, and economic environment may have prompted the emergence of a new paradigm for the institution—a "postmodern" presidency.

Analysts of the presidency are divided as to how to describe the causes and defining attributes of the postmodern presidency. One approach focuses on changes that the domestic environment has wrought on the presidency; the other approach centers on the impact of changes in international relations. Ryan Barilleaux, in his book *The Post-Modern Presidency*, notes several changes in American society since the Roosevelt era to which the presidency has had to adapt: The decentralization of Congress and the decay of the party system, a rise in the power of the judiciary and of regulatory bodies, the prevalence of an adversarial relationship between the mass media and political figures, and the growing federal deficit.

The characteristics that mark the postmodern presidency, as Barilleaux defines it, are the resurgence of prerogative power, as exemplified by the President's ability to issue parallel unilateral policy declarations (PUPDs) and the location of the increasingly prominent OFFICE OF MANAGEMENT AND BUDGET (OMB) in the EXECUTIVE OFFICE OF THE PRESIDENT (EOP); the tendency of Presidents to "go public" through carefully staged media events as a means of direct persuasion of the electorate; the growth of a presidential "general secretariat," especially the OMB and the NATIONAL SECURITY COUNCIL, as a powerful political tool; the careful use of APPOINTMENT POWER for both judicial and regulatory

positions; expanded presidential contact with members of Congress to garner support for presidential programs; and the expanded role of the VICE PRESIDENT as a policy adviser. Barilleaux sees the postmodern presidency as a powerful and vital office, well equipped to take the reins of a fragmented government in a relatively hostile environment.

An alternative interpretation, presented by Richard Rose in *The Post-Modern President*, rests on the presumption that the primary changes to the presidency have been caused by America's changed international status, shifting the international role of the President from that of policy maker to that of policy negotiator. The nation's loss of international primacy also challenges the domestic image of the President, which during the modern era was tied to the nation's international leadership. The postmodern President, by this understanding, is caught in the paradox of trying to exercise world leadership without adequate resources or domestic support.

By either definition, the contemporary presidency exists in a markedly different environment than that of the 1930s. The postmodern President must maintain a very difficult juggling act to keep a positive public image, effective political performance, and international respect intact, amid conditions that provide fewer resources than, and different challenges and changed political relationships from, those that challenged the modern presidency.

BIBLIOGRAPHY

Barilleaux, Ryan. *The Post-Modern Presidency.* 1989.
Rose, Richard. *The Post-Modern President.* 1988.

MARGARET JANE WYSZOMIRSKI

POST OFFICE, DEPARTMENT OF THE. The Post Office Department traces its history to Wednesday, 28 July 1775, when the Second Continental Congress unanimously adopted a recommendation to appoint a POSTMASTER GENERAL for the United Colonies. Congress elected Benjamin Franklin to fill the position for a one-year term. Although no name was given to the organization so engendered, it became known as the General Post Office until Postmaster General John McLean renamed it the Post Office Department in 1823 by the simple expedient of printing new stationery with that heading. Congress legitimized custom in 1872, when it established the Post Office Department as an executive department.

Beginnings. By any name, the Post Office Department was the second agency (the first was Indian Affairs) created by the federal government-to-be and reflected Congress's recognition of the need for reliable communications if the colonies were to unite in fighting for independence and then to succeed as a nation.

During the American Revolution, the most important task of the post office was to carry communications between Congress and its armies. After the war, its task was to help bind the nation together, language still used in 1970 when the Postal Reorganization Act created the United States Postal Service from the Post Office Department.

The ordinance, passed on 18 October 1782, created a postal monopoly.

The ordinance gave the Postmaster General, those he authorized, and "no other person whatsoever" the right and duty to handle mail. Before this, some states had argued that, under the Articles of Confederation, Congress had the right to establish and regulate only interstate, not intrastate, post offices.

The Post Office Department continued under the Constitution, which gave Congress the power to establish post offices and post roads. In an act of 1789, Congress resolved that the regulations of the Post Office would be the same as those used prior to the new Congress and placed the Postmaster General under the direction of the President of the United States. Previously, the Postmaster General reported to the Congress. Authority to fund postal buildings and services remained with Congress through 1970.

In Great Britain, the post office was considered a source of revenue and reported to the Treasury. In the United States, the essential policy of the Post Office Department—public service before profit—was established by the time Samuel Osgood became the fourth Postmaster General, and the first whose name had been sent to the Senate by the President for confirmation. The sixth Postmaster General, John McLean, also supported "service first" but cautioned that expenses and receipts must balance over time, a concept still used.

Developing Services. During its early years, the department used its revenues to expand services and was used, in turn, by the President and the Congress to support public programs such as the establishment of roads, ostensibly for the post, into the Ohio wilderness and other territories. Eager to find faster ways to move the mail, the department also was an early paying customer on virtually every new means of transportation, thus supporting their development. Mail was carried by post riders, stagecoaches, steamboats, railroads, hot air balloons, automobiles, dogsleds, pneumatic tubes, airplanes, and mules. Cats, tried in Europe but found to be "thoroughly undisciplined," were one of the few means not harnessed.

Congress designated waterways as post roads in 1823 and railroads in 1838, after the Post Office Department had tested each. Traveling by ship, rail, ship again or stagecoach via Central America, mail from the original states could reach California in three to four weeks by the middle of the nineteenth century. However, the public wanted faster transportation.

In 1860, William H. Russell advertised for "Young, skinny, wiry fellows not over 18. Must be expert riders willing to risk death daily. Orphans preferred." The Pony Express, soon to be a contractor for the Post Office Department, had begun, and its young riders carried mail from St. Joseph, Missouri, to Sacramento, California, in ten days, faster than any other mail service. Another breakthrough in transcontinental mail service occurred in 1920, when the Post Office Department began coast-to-coast airmail service.

Prior to linking the coasts, however, the Post Office Department also helped to bring rural America into the political and commercial mainstream through the institution of rural free delivery (RFD) in 1902 and parcel post in 1913. Established in the face of strong opposition, both services were received enthusiastically by rural citizens.

Although many city dwellers had enjoyed free delivery since 1863, rural families still collected their mail from the post office at the turn of the century. The Post Office Department's proposal to deliver mail over rutted roads and through forests were denounced as impractical and expensive—but not by rural people who spent $72 million within twenty years to improve roads so that they could qualify for rural free delivery.

Originally, the Post Office Department expected parcel post to move food products from farms to consumers, but mercantile use of the service soon exceeded all others. Five years after parcel post service began on 1 January 1913, Sears Roebuck and Company tripled its revenues. Mail order businesses boomed.

Parcel rates varied by distance, a practice that continues. In 1863, however, Postmaster General Montgomery Blair eliminated distance as a factor in determining postage rates for domestic letters.

Blair also suggested that postal administrations throughout the world establish more uniform international rates. During his time, complex rate formulas resulted in postage rates ranging from five cents to $1.02 for a letter traveling to Australia, depending on the route. Delegates from the fifteen postal administrations, most of the world's mail, met in 1863 and began implementing more consistent rates. However, where some postal administrations controlled the post, telegraph, and telephone systems, American telegraph and telephone services were managed by the Postmaster General only during WORLD WAR I. After the War, their operation reverted to private enterprise.

A few years later, the airmail planes and fields developed and run by the Post Office Department were sold or transferred to local municipalities, and the Post Office Department began to contract with emerging private carriers for the transportation of mail.

The Post Office Department coped with manpower shortages during WORLD WAR II by implementing the zoning system (e.g., Cleveland 33, Ohio) to make sorting easier for new workers. It handled increased volume spurred by population growth and developments in office and computer technology by establishing transportation centers and the ZIP Code system and by beginning to develop mechanized and automated mail systems, although it encountered difficulties in planning and modernizing because it received funding from Congress and had no control over postal rates.

In 1970, Congress passed the Postal Reorganization Act. The act created the UNITED STATES POSTAL SERVICE as an independent establishment of the executive branch, authorized it to manage policy and rates under the control of nine Governors, and removed the Postmaster General from the CABINET.

BIBLIOGRAPHY

History of the U.S. Postal Service, 1775-1984. 1985.
Rich, Wesley Everett. *The History of the United States Post Office to 1829.* 1924.
Scheele, Carl H. *A Short History of the Mail Service.* 1970.

MEGAERA HARRIS

POTSDAM CONFERENCE. The meeting held at Cecilienhof Palace in the Berlin suburb of Potsdam, 17 July to 2 August 1945 marked President Harry S. Truman's first meeting with Winston Churchill, his only meeting with Josef Stalin, and the last Allied summit conference of WORLD WAR II. Major issues discussed by the Allied leaders at Potsdam included the occupation of Germany, postwar reparations, territorial boundaries in Central and Eastern Europe, the political future of recently liberated areas, the atomic bomb, and the specific timing of Russia's entry into the war against Japan.

Reluctant to attend an early conference because of his lack of experience—he had been President only three months—President Truman approached the Potsdam meeting with trepidation. As he wrote to his mother and sister before leaving Washington, "I have a briefcase all filled up with information on past conferences and suggestions on what I'm to do and say. Wish I didn't have to go, but I do and it can't be stopped now."

Once he reached Potsdam, however, Truman used the occasion to take the measure of his counterparts, Churchill and Stalin. He felt great respect and admiration for the British prime minister, whom he privately characterized as "a most charming and a very clever person." Truman formed a surprisingly warm impression of Stalin, too. The Soviet dictator, wanting to establish a relationship with the new President, exhibited his best personal behavior. Truman came away persuaded of his forthrightness, observing: "I can deal with Stalin."

Such feelings did not last long. Within a year, Truman's suspicions of Soviet behavior had intensified enormously, and the restrained cordiality of Potsdam had given way to the rising tension of the COLD WAR.

BIBLIOGRAPHY

Feis, Herbert. *Between War and Peace: The Potsdam Conference.* 1960.
Mee, Charles L., Jr. *Meeting at Potsdam.* 1975.
U.S. Department of State. *Foreign Relations of the United States, 1945, Conference of Berlin (Potsdam).* 2 vols. 1960.

BRIAN VANDEMARK

PREROGATIVE, EXECUTIVE. See EXECUTIVE PREROGATIVE.

PRESENTATION CLAUSE. The Constitution's presentation clause is one of several provisions that ensure presidential involvement in the legislative process. According to Article I, Section 7, "Every Bill which shall have passed the House of Representatives and the Senate, shall, before it becomes a Law, be presented to the President of the United States." Upon a bill's presentation, the President may either approve the bill by signing it within ten days, veto the bill and return it to the house of origin [*see* VETO, REGULAR], veto the bill by withholding the executive signature if Congress has made return impossible by adjourning in the intervening time [*see* VETO, POCKET], or, if Congress is still in session, allow the bill to become law after ten days by not signing it.

Article I, Section 7, further stipulates that "every Order, Resolution, or Vote to which the Concurrence of the Senate and House of Representatives may be necessary . . . shall be presented to the President . . . before the Same shall take Effect." This paragraph was added to avoid a situation in which Congress might seek to avoid presidential review of legislation by giving it some other name.

At the CONSTITUTIONAL CONVENTION there was general agreement that the President should retain final say over legislation. Even though the President must deal with legislation within ten days of presentation, considerable flexibility exists regarding the actual presentation process. After a bill is passed by both houses of Congress, actual presentation may be delayed if the President is out of the country or otherwise indisposed. The U.S. Court of Claims, in *Eber Bros. Wine and Liquor Corp. v. United States* (1964), ruled that during a presidential absence Congress can present bills to the President abroad, hold them for presentation until the President's return, or present bills at the White House as though the President were there.

The question of presentation played a key role in a constitutional challenge of the LEGISLATIVE VETO. The Supreme Court ruled in INS v. CHADHA (1983) that the congressional practice of using simple and concurrent resolutions to control executive-branch actions was unconstitutional. Despite the fact that legislative vetoes were previously created in bills passed through the regular legislative process, including presentation to the President, the Court held that this power unconstitutionally avoided presentation.

Presentation is not required for congressional enactments that are expressions of opinion or that involve internal administrative matters. Article V of the Constitution also avoids presentation by allowing Congress to propose constitutional amendments by a two-thirds vote in both chambers, at which point proposed amendments are sent directly to the states for ratification.

BIBLIOGRAPHY

Craig, Barbara Hinkson. *Chadha: The Story of an Epic Constitutional Struggle*. 1988.

Fisher, Louis. *Constitutional Conflicts between Congress and the President*. 3d rev. ed. 1991.

Spitzer, Robert J. *The Presidential Veto: Touchstone of the American Presidency*. 1988.

ROBERT J. SPITZER

PRESIDENCY, PRESIDENTIAL CONCEPTIONS OF THE. "Presidents define themselves through their exercise of Presidential power," according to George Bush. They form and express their conceptions of the office in much the same way, mainly through the interaction of their personalities, experiences, and the circumstances in which they serve. Thus Presidents' views on the presidency have been more evident in their deeds than in their words. This survey draws as much as possible on the Presidents' own comments on the presidency, but, also, it makes inferences from their conduct of the office.

The prevailing presidential concepts of the office fall neatly into two long periods. The first, Washingtonian, model (1789–1901) followed the constitutional-administrative model of the first incumbent. The second, or Jackson-Roosevelt, model was set by Andrew Jackson but largely suppressed by the political and social circumstances of the nineteenth century; it was revived by Theodore Roosevelt.

The Washington Period. The most important political circumstance of George Washington's presidency was the new system of government. The federal union had arisen in the shadow of its failed predecessor in a social context of incipient disorder and rudimentary national integration. The colonies had developed so separately into states, and transportation and communication among them was so difficult that national political organizations were impossible. Thus, the earliest Presidents had no national, democratic foundation on which to base political leadership.

By personality and background, the first President was ill-suited to politicize the office. Washington was an eighteenth-century colonial English country gentleman, stiff and formal, greatly valuing dignity and propriety. His highest social value was ordered liberty. His public career before the presidency had given him greatest satisfaction in military command and greatest frustration in the politics of the Continental Congress. Washington thus saw the presidency as a dignified, nonpolitical office dedicated to securing the fragile unity and independence of the nation. To promote unity, Washington said, the President should raise "a standard to which the wise and just can repair" and attract loyalty to the central government. His weekly levees in the capital and his state tours throughout the country had the express purpose of displaying his person as a rallying point for national unity. Similarly, he avoided involvement in regional or partisan causes and controversial domestic legislation.

To secure national independence, Washington assumed presidential constitutional preeminence in foreign and defense affairs. He issued the PROCLAMATION OF NEUTRALITY of 1793 without consulting Congress and expelled Edmond-Charles-Édouard Genet, the obnoxious French diplomat, despite Congressional protests. In rejecting demands for confidential information on JAY'S TREATY negotiations, Washington told the House of Representatives, "I have ever entertained but one opinion on the subject; . . . that the power of making treaties is exclusively vested in the President, by and with the advice and consent of the Senate."

Washington asserted his military authority by mobilizing troops without congressional authorization to deal with the WHISKEY REBELLION and by vetoing on policy (rather than constitutional) grounds a bill to reduce the size of the army.

John Adams did not possess Washington's national prestige and personal dignity but shared his lack of enthusiasm for politics. Social circumstances in the United States had changed little, and national unity and independence remained fragile. Adams's conception of the office was basically the same as Washington's, although his lesser leadership skills and the rise of partisan politics hindered his ability to give it comparable effect.

The inauguration of Democratic-Republican Thomas Jefferson to succeed the Federalist Adams in 1801 consummated the first peaceful transfer of national governmental power to an opposition leader in the history of modern democracy. Jefferson's conception of the presidency underwent a parallel transformation (men have often changed their view on becoming President). As Democratic-Republican leader during Federalist administrations after 1793, Jefferson had championed congressional preeminence, but as President he assumed and exercised unprecedented executive powers.

Jefferson's evolution occurred in a gradually changing political and social context. Geographic integration progressed little and national independence was insecure until the WAR OF 1812, but political unity grew as the constitutional system solidified and Federalist–Democratic Republican hostility declined. These circumstances permitted Jefferson and his Democratic-Republican successors James Madison, James Monroe, and John Quincy Adams to develop somewhat more ambitious conceptions of the office. By personality, too, the Democratic-Republicans were better suited to exercise political—as distinct from governmental—leadership, as they had more taste for elective politics.

Unlike Washington and Adams, the Democratic-Republicans embraced the President's role as party leader. Jefferson organized the Democratic-Republican Party and was its undisputed leader until he retired. As President, he added fellow-partisanship as a criterion for appointment. The Democratic-Republican Presidents were also more active legislators. Jefferson directed the Democratic-Republican congressional caucus that he had organized as Vice President and proposed domestic legislation more freely than had the Federalists. Madison and Monroe were less

assertive, but John Quincy Adams exceeded any of his predecessors in claiming legislative leadership.

The Democratic-Republicans repeatedly and consistently reaffirmed presidential preeminence in foreign and defense matters, most dramatically in the LOUISIANA PURCHASE, BARBARY WAR, and MONROE DOCTRINE. Also, Madison claimed for the Presidency the COMMANDER IN CHIEF role in substance as well as form by asserting control over military commanders during the War of 1812.

The Jacksonian Model. By the administration of Andrew Jackson (1829–1837), political and social circumstances had changed radically from the Federalist era. The early dangers to unity and independence had largely disappeared, although SLAVERY was becoming a new threat. The social change of greatest constitutional effect was the dramatic improvement in transportation, integrating the nation geographically and providing a basis for a genuine national political office. Jackson's stubborn, indomitable, domineering personality built the new presidency on that foundation.

Jackson saw the President as the "tribune of the people." To enable the people to pick their tribune, Martin Van Buren formed for Jackson the first national presidential campaign organization, which became a political party. On the basis of his election mandate, Jackson asserted unprecedented presidential control over the administration and Congress.

Jackson's army background and belligerent personality led naturally to his view of military leadership as a special presidential preserve, though the peaceful times gave him little opportunity to apply it. He also asserted presidential diplomatic leadership, especially in West Indies trade negotiations, relations with Mexico and Texas, and settling the French spoliation claims (claims by American citizens for losses incurred as a result of Napoleon's seizure of their property between 1800 and 1815).

Congressional Whigs challenged Jackson's conception of the presidency, but most of his successors—of whatever party—accepted it. Through most of the nineteenth century, however, political and social circumstances—especially pre–CIVIL WAR divisions over slavery and post–Civil War RECONSTRUCTION—inhibited their exercise of Jacksonian powers.

Martin Van Buren, Jackson's successor, had been his main ally in conceiving and constructing the political presidency. However, Van Buren's less forceful public personality and a disastrous economic depression, prevented him giving effect to its principles.

William Henry Harrison, the first Whig President, talked weak presidency while campaigning but behaved very much strong presidency during the four months between his election and his death. John Tyler had fought the Jacksonian presidency from the Senate but defended Jackson's conception of the presidency with equal tenacity from the White House, in extremely difficult circumstances. James K. Polk, a loyal Jackson protégé, consciously emulated his towering predecessor.

When Polk retired in 1849, the country was headed toward civil war. The issue of slavery was ripping the American political and social fabric and virtually paralyzing the presidency. Presidents Zachary Taylor, Millard Fillmore, Franklin Pierce, and James Buchanan seem to have been chosen for their willingness to evade the slavery issue. They deferred to Congress in most areas. Taylor declared that once a President had made a recommendation to Congress "the Executive department of the Government cannot rightfully control the decision of Congress on any subject of legislation until that decision shall have been officially submitted to the President for approval." Those who sought to assert authority usually failed. Congress overrode five of Pierce's nine vetoes, though only one veto had failed in the entire previous history of the presidency.

Abraham Lincoln was a classic Whig theorist who became Jacksonian practitioner. In Congress, Lincoln had villified Polk's forceful presidency, but President Lincoln asserted greater executive powers than any predecessor. Without Congressional authorization, he mobilized troops, requisitioned supplies, waged war by proclamation, drew treasury funds without appropriations, issued currency, suspended the right of habeas corpus [see HABEAS CORPUS, SUSPENSION OF], created courts, suppressed newspapers, arrested editors, and emancipated slaves. He commanded the military more fully and directly than his predecessors. Outside the scope of WAR POWERS, however, Lincoln adhered closely to the Whig theory.

Andrew Johnson, Ulysses S. Grant, Rutherford B. Hayes, James A. Garfield, Chester A. Arthur, Grover Cleveland, and Benjamin Harrison conceptualized the office mainly by defending the presidency's independence and coordinacy with Congress. This generation of Presidents, however, was preoccupied with domestic affairs—Reconstruction, industrialization, conquest of the West—and Congress, with its greater powers to accommodate conflicting interests, constantly thwarted their endeavors to act on their constitutional beliefs. The most notable of Congress's efforts to undermine the presidency was the IMPEACHMENT OF ANDREW JOHNSON. Congress also frustrated Grant's efforts at presidential leadership in foreign relations, and Cleveland lost two Supreme Court nominations and used 584 legislative vetoes—though only seven were overridden.

Presidents consistently claimed administrative leadership, yet under the TENURE OF OFFICE ACT, passed over Johnson's veto, they could not remove disloyal officials. Also, the emerging practice of senatorial courtesy curbed Presidential appointment powers by enabling individual Senators to control patronage from their states.

The Jackson-Roosevelt Period Begins. As the nineteenth century ended, the post–Civil War agenda had been largely exhausted. The South was reconstructed, the North industrial, and the West settled. Moreover, by population, territory, economy, and industrial base, the United States had risen to top rank among the nations of the world. Circumstances were ripe to turn from internal to external emphasis in national policies and from congressional to presidential leadership. That situation coincided with the tenure of three successive chief executives of international vision and clearly defined concepts of executive power.

William McKinley presided, reluctantly and with no clear intentions, over the opening stages of the internationalization of his office. In 1898, he was pushed into the SPANISH-AMERICAN WAR, the first significant American engagement in affairs beyond the Western Hemisphere. The same year saw the ANNEXATION OF HAWAII.

Theodore Roosevelt, McKinley's successor, suffered no such reluctance. He called the President "a steward of the people bound actively and affirmatively to do . . . anything that the needs of the Nation demanded unless such action was forbidden by the Constitution or the laws." Roosevelt used his elaborate concept of the presidency to bust trusts, promote conservation, settle labor conflicts, and propose consumer protection laws, along with many other domestic initiatives. However, his most striking addition to the institution of the presidency was his concept and practice of international leadership. He greatly enlarged the U.S. role in the Western Hemisphere by promulgating his Roosevelt Corollary to the Monroe Doctrine and by inciting rebellion in PANAMA to permit construction of the Panama Canal. Moreover, he energetically waged a well-considered, systematic campaign to extend American influence throughout the world. He arbitrated an end to the Russo-Japanese War and to a conflict between three European powers and Venezuela and cosponsored the Algeciras Conference of 1906 and the Hague Peace Conference of 1907. His naval construction program gave the United States its first global armed presence.

William Howard Taft had developed a Rooseveltian conception of the presidency while holding three high-level executive offices in Roosevelt's administration. He argued that Presidents should be dynamic, active leaders of Congress and their political parties. However, he was more judicial than executive in temperament and was less adroit politically than his flamboyant mentor. Consequently, despite their similar conceptions of the office and general policy views, Taft was less successful at applying them than Roosevelt had been. After the two men had fallen out politically and returned to private life, they debated their conceptions of the presidency. Roosevelt enunciated his STEWARDSHIP THEORY and Taft responded that the President has "no undefined residuum of power which he can exercise because it seems to him to be in the public interest." Their differences, though, were more rhetorical than substantive. Roosevelt admitted constitutional and legal restrictions on the presidency and Taft conceded that the "Constitution does give the President wide discretion and great power, and . . . calls from him activity and energy to see that within his proper sphere he does what his great responsibilities and opportunities require."

Early in his career, Woodrow Wilson had advocated a parliamentary system, but under Roosevelt's influence he touted a much more independent executive. "The President," Wilson said, is "the representative . . . of the whole people. . . . If he rightly interpret the national thought and boldly insist upon it, he is irresistible." Wilson thought that the President's control of foreign affairs, was "very absolute." "The initiative in foreign affairs, which the President possesses without any restriction whatever, is virtually the power to control them absolutely," he wrote.

The political and social circumstances of the 1920s—disillusionment with the TREATY OF VERSAILLES and mounting economic and social problems—limited presidential leadership possibilities. The personalities of the Presidents during this period and their conceptions of the office tended to fit that situation.

Warren G. Harding's few scattered comments on the presidency clearly indicated that he felt overwhelmed by its magnitude and complexity. Calvin Coolidge referred to the "appalling burden" of the office, listed its authority in expansive terms, and commented, "A power so vast in its implications has never been conferred upon any ruling sovereign." Coolidge reacted to the availability of so much power mainly by delegating authority, avoiding details, and constructing his prerogatives strictly. Yet he also claimed that the President was "truly the agent of the people" and the "champion of the rights of the whole country" against "organized minorities," and he vowed to resist any encroachment on the President's APPOINTMENT POWER. He evaded the Taft-Roosevelt debate by claiming that is was "better practice to wait to decide each question on its merits as it arises."

Herbert Hoover recorded few views on the presidency before or during his term. Later, he commented very freely on the "excessive" power wielded by his successor, Franklin D. Roosevelt, though Hoover's own conduct of the office had not reflected so passive an attitude. He had asserted firmly the President's constitutional right to the appointment and REMOVAL POWER and actively promoted a long series of laws to deal with the Great Depression, including job-creating appropriations of hundreds of millions of dollars.

From FDR to Kennedy. The depression dominated the opening years of Franklin D. Roosevelt's administration. Franklin Roosevelt generally shared his cousin Theodore's views of the presidency. As a naval official during WORLD WAR I, he had observed Wilson's leadership at close hand. He had Theodore Roosevelt's drive and dynamic personality but a more polished manner. Franklin Roosevelt saw the true function of the presidency as that of finding "among many discordant elements that unity of purpose that is best for the Nation as a whole." He called the presidency "a single, strong Chief Executive office in which was vested the entire Executive power of the national Government." This included the right to nominate and remove officials without Congressional interference and a rational control structure, provided through the Reorganization Act of 1939. As President, Roosevelt was a sort of general manager of the collective efforts of the country. During the depression, he mobilized the nation's resources for economic recovery. However, rather than claim some "undefined residuum of power," he invoked a World War I–era law to call the BANK HOLIDAY of 1933 and vowed to ask Congress for "broad Executive power to wage a war against the emergency" if ordinary measures proved inadequate. After PEARL HARBOR, he became bolder. Although he recognized "my responsibility to the Constitution," he would "use every power vested in me to accomplish defeat of our enemies." Some of his decisions during WORLD WAR II stretched the power of the presidency as greatly as had Lincoln's wartime decisions.

The crisis environment in which the presidency had operated since 1929 continued under Harry S. Truman, with the COLD WAR and KOREAN WAR. Moreover, the United States had become militarily and economically the most powerful nation in the world, inevitably enhancing opportunities for presidential leadership. Truman's conception of the office accorded well with those circumstances. His EMPLOYMENT ACT of 1946 consecrated Franklin Roosevelt's concept of the President as manager of the economy. Truman's foreign policy initiatives—the TRUMAN DOCTRINE, the MARSHALL PLAN of 1947, the NATO TREATY, and the Korean War—organized the global leadership that Roosevelt had developed pragmatically. Truman went farther than Roosevelt in his seizure of steel mills in 1951—an act that was declared unconstitutional by the Supreme Court in YOUNGSTOWN SHEET & TUBE CO. V. SAWYER (1952).

Truman also expanded the President's administrative role by securing broad congressional authority to reorganize the bureaucracy. He cultivated party and legislative leadership roles, but his pugnacious partisanship sometimes poisoned his relations with Congress. His twelve overridden vetoes tied Andrew Johnson's record.

The cold war continued unabated and the economy prospered through the next three administrations. Dwight D. Eisenhower's administration illustrated again how the presidency transforms partisan attitudes. The Republicans had criticized the "dictatorial" conduct of Democratic Presidents for twenty years, then went ahead and elected one of their own whose conception of the office differed little from his predecessors'. Eisenhower, no less than Roosevelt and Truman, saw the Presidency as a position of national and global leadership. His style was less belligerent, partisan, and public than Truman's, however, and journalists and scholars depicted him as weak and timid. Recent, more serious study shows that Eisenhower used the office very effectively, often through quiet persuasion behind the scenes. His most public battles for his conception of the presidency concerned the President's role as DIPLOMAT IN CHIEF. Eisenhower defeated attempts to curb his TREATY-MAKING POWER and intervened unilaterally to halt the Anglo-French and Israeli invasions of the Suez Canal Zone in 1956. Yet he respected congressional interest in foreign policy by securing supporting resolutions for his actions in the Quemoy-Matsu and Lebanese crises of 1958. On the domestic front, he electrified the nation by sending paratroopers to Little Rock, Arkansas, in 1957 to enforce school integration.

John F. Kennedy began his presidential campaign by criticizing Eisenhower's "detached, limited concept of the Presidency" and identifying himself with the "fast-moving, creative Presidential rule" of the preceding Democrats. He went beyond even Theodore Roosevelt's stewardship theory by proclaiming that the President "must be prepared to exercise the fullest powers of his Office—all that are specified and some that are not." Kennedy said that if "a brushfire threatens some part of the globe he alone can act, without waiting for the Congress. . . . It is the President alone who must make the major decisions of our foreign policy." Presidents, according to Kennedy's formulation, have the power "to place us in a war . . . without the consent of Congress."

Three years later, however, Kennedy was less ebullient. "The problems are more difficult than I imagined," he said. "It is much easier to make the speeches than it is to finally make the judgments. . . . It is a tremendous change to go from being a Senator to being President. . . . Congress looks more powerful sitting here than it did when I was there in Congress." Kennedy even credited former President Eisenhower with wielding more influence out of office than he had in the White House.

From Johnson to Bush. The VIETNAM WAR was the most important circumstance of Lyndon Baines Johnson's presidency. It deepened the cold war and reinforced presidential power—that is, until national consensus on the U.S. presence in Vietnam broke down. Johnson's domineering personality, with his seemingly insatiable appetite for power and unrivaled political skills, exploited every opportunity for presidential leadership, but divisive opposition to the war ultimately weakened his presidency.

Johnson spoke of the presidency mainly to emphasize the magnitude of its burdens and opportunities. He said that the "only thing that appeals to me about being President is the opportunity it provides to do some good for the country," and he called the presidency "a great institution of freedom." The closest Johnson came to having an abstract view of the office was in defining what he said was its one basic tenet: "The job of the President is to set priorities for the nation, and he must set them according to his own judgment and his own conscience."

The Vietnam War remained the defining element in the presidency of Richard M. Nixon—that is, until the WATERGATE AFFAIR. Vietnam and Watergate fueled a large body of negative opinion from those who deeply distrusted a man who had made a career of attacking conventional LIBERALISM and was undertaking to turn the ultimate liberal institution—the strong presidency—to conservative purposes. The situation was complicated by the fact that Nixon, an intensely partisan Republican, faced Democratic congressional majorities throughout his tenure. Nixon had responded to Kennedy's 1960 campaign speech, quoted above, by arguing that a strong President might not be Kennedy's "table pounder" but rather a "persuader," as Eisenhower had been. In 1968, Nixon advocated "an activist view" of the office, with the President "deeply involved in the entire sweep of America's public concerns." He called the nature of the presidency inspirational and directive, with its "moral authority" providing a platform from which to "articulate the nation's values, define its goals and marshal its will." In his memoirs, Nixon identified four roles for the President: "head of state . . . to deal with foreign affairs; . . . head of government . . . to provide domestic leadership and legislative programs; . . . COMMANDER IN CHIEF, [with] the ultimate authority and responsibility for America's armed forces; and . . . leader of [a political] Party."

The circumstances of Gerald Ford's presidency were quite different from those of his postwar predecessors. The Vietnam War had ended and the cold war had abated a bit. The Watergate scandal had tarnished the office of the President to an unprecedented extent, and Ford was the first President in history who had never faced a national electorate. By background and personality, Ford fit that situation well. The result was a less Jacksonian presidency than any since Hoover. During Ford's twenty-five years in the House of Representatives, he had advocated a better balance between the branches of the national government. While Minority Leader during the Johnson administration, Ford had spoken of the "terrifying buildup of power in the Executive," of the nation's having "come as close to one-man government . . . as at any time in our . . . history," of a need for a limitation on presidential power, and of Congress being "a pawn in the hands of the White House." After Nixon's election, however, he expressed virtually unreserved support for the presidency, admired the way the "President sets a tone for the country." His public statements while President reveal little about his concept of the office. He saw it, above all, as means to heal the political wounds the country suffered under Johnson and Nixon. In his memoirs, *A Time to Heal* (1979), Ford wrote:

> When I was in the Congress myself, I thought it fulfilled its constitutional obligations in a very responsible way, but after I became President, my perspective changed. It seemed to me that Congress was . . . determined to get its oar deeply into the conduct of FOREIGN AFFAIRS. This not only undermined the Chief Executive's ability to act, but also eroded the SEPARATION OF POWERS concept in the Constitution.

Ford also disagreed with most of his predecessors about the burdens of office. About his time as President, he wrote, "I never felt better physically. I never had a clearer mind. I never enjoyed an experience more. The truth is that I couldn't wait to start the day."

The general circumstances of the Jimmy Carter administration resembled those of the Ford years. International tensions were exacerbated by the Soviet invasion of Afghanistan and the IRANIAN HOSTAGE CRISIS. Domestically, Carter faced the energy crisis and a stagnant economy. Approaching the presidency, Carter saw it in Rooseveltian terms and characterized himself as "strong and aggressive" like Theodore Roosevelt but "maybe a good deal quieter." He believed he fit James David Barber's "active-positive" personality type that best suited the presidency. Of the President, Carter said,

> [He is] the only person who can speak with a clear voice to the American people and set a standard of ethics and morality, excellence, greatness. He can call on the American people to make a sacrifice and explain the purpose of the sacrifice, propose and carry out bold programs to protect, to expose and root out injustice and discrimination and divisions. . . . He can provide and describe a defense posture that will make our people feel secure, a foreign policy to make us proud once again.

In office, however, Carter seemed even less activist than Ford and hardly resembled even a quiet version of Theodore Roosevelt.

The cold war abated during Ronald Reagan's administration, and the economy recovered. Reagan combined Nixon's conservative activism with Franklin Roosevelt's political personality and skill. As of 1992, Reagan had not published a conceptualization of the office, but his conduct returned it squarely to the Jackson-Roosevelt mold. In domestic affairs, he and British Prime Minister Margaret Thatcher changed the way the world thought about politics by making small government a virtue. Internationally, Reagan forced the Soviets to face the reality of the bankruptcy of communism. As the presidency passed its bicentennial, the Jackson-Roosevelt concept of the office seemed well established as the norm despite wide differences in Presidents' personalities and great fluctuations in the presidency's historical context.

George Bush described "the President's role" as "guiding and directing the Nation's foreign policy," serving "as Commander in Chief of our Armed Forces," and "shaping the Nation's domestic agenda," and he said that "the real power of the Presidency lies in a President's ability to frame, through action, through example, through encouragement, what we as a nation must do." Early in his administration, the collapse of communism and the consequent emergence of an unprecedented global consensus enabled him to demonstrate—most notably in the GULF WAR—that the Jackson-Roosevelt conception of the presidency was very much alive and well as the twentieth century drew to a close.

[*See also* THEORIES OF PRESIDENCY.]

BIBLIOGRAPHY

American Heritage Book of the Presidents and Famous Americans. 1967.

DeGregorio, William A. *The Complete Book of U.S. Presidents.* 1984.

Filler, Louis, ed. *The President Speaks.* 1964.

Goldsmith, William M. *The Growth of Presidential Power: A Documented History.* 3 vols. 1974.

Graff, Henry F., ed. *The Presidents: A Reference History.* 1984.

Harnsberger, Caroline Thomas, ed. *Treasury of Presidential Quotations.* 1964.

Nelson, Michael, ed., *Congressional Quarterly's Guide to the Presidency.* 1989.

Reedy, George E., advisory ed. *The Presidency.* 1975.

Taylor, Tim. *The Book of Presidents.* 1972.

Tourtellot, Arthur Bernon. *The Presidents on the Presidency.* 1964.

In addition, presidential memoirs, which have been written by most Presidents who survived their terms, are sometimes useful sources.

WILLIAM G. ANDREWS

PRESIDENT. For discussion of the office of President of the United States, see CONSTITUTION, PRESIDENT IN; CONSTITUTIONAL REFORM; EXECUTIVE POWER. For discussion of the title "President of the United States," see the following article. For discussion of the establishment of the presidency in the early years of the Republic, see CREATION OF THE PRESIDENCY. For discussion of the President's roles in the government and the American political system, see CHIEF EXECUTIVE; COMMANDER IN CHIEF; DIPLOMAT IN CHIEF; LEGISLATIVE LEADER; PARTY LEADER, PRESIDENT AS. For discussion of how the presidency has been understood by Presidents and by political scientists, see COMMENTATORS ON THE PRESIDENCY; PRESIDENCY, PRESIDENTIAL CONCEPTIONS OF THE; THEORIES OF THE PRESIDENCY.

PRESIDENT (TITLE). At the CONSTITUTIONAL CONVENTION of 1787 the Framers wrestled with the thorny issue of creating and titling the office of CHIEF EXECUTIVE of the United States. Much attention was paid to determining the nature of the office, the manner of election, term of office, and whether the executive should be a collegial body or a single person and, if the latter, whether there should be a mandated advisory council. Little discussion was devoted to the title of the office and its incumbent.

What emerged from some sixteen weeks of deliberation (25 May–17 September) was a single executive whom the Constitution denominates as "President of the United States of America" (Article II, Section 1). This presidency is unique in that the incumbent is vested with full EXECUTIVE POWER and authority, is responsible to the people rather than to Congress, and serves as both chief of state and head of government, whereas in most other countries these are two separate offices and in democratic systems the head of government is responsible to the legislature.

In the process of designing this office, the Framers drew titular precedents from sources such as the American colonial and state governments, the Continental Congress, and the Articles of Confederation. The presiding officers of the Continental Congress and the Constitutional Convention were called presidents. At the time, however, no national executive bore this title,,and subsequently only governments that employed the American model, such as Latin American republics and the PHILIPPINES, possess a similar executive office and title.

During the deliberations of the Convention—in the Virginia Plan (29 May), the Report of the Committee of the Whole (13 June), the New Jersey Plan (15 June), and the Resolution Referred to the Committee of Detail (26 July)—the office was generically referred to as a national or federal executive, or simply as the executive. Alternative expressions suggested during these considerations and in commentary were "Supreme Executive," "Magistracy, Executive Magistracy, or Magistrate," and "Governor of the United States of America."

It was not until 6 August, when the Committee of Detail—which prepared the actual draft of the Constitution—submitted its report, that the executive was designated the "President of the United States of America" (in Article II). It appears that this title is attributable to JAMES WILSON, who prepared the draft, and that it was not debated at the Convention.

From documentation and analysis it may be inferred that the decision on this title may have been influenced by several factors. First, there was the desire to avoid any semblance of monarchism or aristocracy. Second, until late in the convention's deliberations, the collegial executive proposed may have consisted of a presiding officer, or president, and a council. Third, the emerging executive office in four states (Delaware, New Hampshire, Pennsylvania, and South Carolina) bore the title president instead of governor. Fourth, there was the precedent of the presiding officer of the Continental Congress employing the title "President of the United States of America" for certain purposes. And, finally, there was the simple fact that George Washington, who was universally expected to become the first chief executive under the Constitution, already held the title president as presiding officer of the Constitutional Convention.

In practice, the title of the presidency is expressed in three forms. It is generally specified as "the President," as evidenced by some fifteen references in the Constitution. In some cases it is formally designated as "President of the United States," as in the PRESIDENTIAL OATH OF OFFICE. When used in FOREIGN AFFAIRS, it is the "President of the United States of America," as in the presidential signing of international instruments such as the TREATY OF VERSAILLES (Woodrow Wilson, 1919), the UNITED NATIONS DECLARATION (Franklin D. Roosevelt, 1942), and certain ARMS CONTROL treaties (beginning with Richard M. Nixon, 1972) and when it is necessary to distinguish this country from other federations, such as Brazil or Mexico.

The final aspect of the presidential title is the fashion in which the President is addressed. Various forms were discussed during the Constitutional Convention and the First Congress (including "Elective Majesty," "Elective Highness" or "Serene Highness," and "Protector of the Rights of the United States"). Wilson, in his draft constitution, denominated the President as "His Excellency," but this was not included in the final version of the Constitution. As a consequence, the President is officially addressed as "Mr. President." As far as formal protocol is concerned, in correspondence the President's title is simply "The President" (or, in foreign relations, "The President of the United States of America") and orally the President is addressed as "Mr. President."

BIBLIOGRAPHY

Farrand, Max. *The Framing of the Constitution.* 1926.
Farrand, Max, ed. *The Records of the Federal Convention of 1787.* 4 vols. 1966.
Hart, James. *The American Presidency in Action, 1789.* 1948.
Rossiter, Clinton. *1787—The Grand Convention: A Study in Constitutional History.* 1948.
Thach, Charles C., Jr. *The Creation of the Presidency, 1775–1789: A Study in Constitutional History.* 1969.

ELMER PLISCHKE

PRESIDENTIAL CHARACTER.

In 1972, the political scientist James David Barber published the first edition of *The Presidential Character*, a book that was intended to bring the presidency into clearer focus by examining it through the lenses of psychology. Initially, the book excited considerable interest among scholars, many of whom accepted Barber's basic premise that the personality of the incumbent in an office as powerful as the presidency is an important object of study, and among journalists, who were impressed by his claim that the book could "help citizens and those who advise them cut through the confusion [of election campaigns] and get at some clear criteria for choosing Presidents." Within a few years, however, the psychological theory that underlay *The Presidential Character* became the subject of severe critical scrutiny. Although the book still enjoyed an audience more than twenty years after it first appeared (it was published in a fourth edition in 1992), its standing among scholars had fallen.

Barber's Theory. According to Barber, a political personality includes three components. The first, worldview, develops during adolescence and consists of "primary, politically relevant beliefs, particularly his conceptions of social causality, human nature, and the central moral conflicts of the time." (All quotations of Barber are from his book.) The second is style, that is, the "habitual way of performing three political roles: rhetoric, personal relations, and homework." Style develops during early adulthood. Character is the third component and, in Barber's view, "the most important thing to know about the president or candidate." As he defines the term, "character is the way the President orients himself toward life—not for the moment, but enduringly." It "grows out of the child's experiments in relating to parents, brothers and sisters, and peers at play and in school, as well as to his own body and the objects around it." Through these experiences, the child—and thus the adult to be—arrives subconsciously at a deep and private understanding of fundamental self-worth.

For some Presidents, this process results in high self-esteem, which Barber regards as the vital ingredient for psychological health and presidential productiveness. Others must search outside themselves for evidence of worth that at best will be a partial substitute. Depending on the source and nature of their limited self-esteem, Barber suggests, these insecure people will concentrate their search in one of three areas: the affection from others that compliant and agreeable behavior brings, the sense of usefulness that comes from performing a widely respected duty, or the deference that attends dominance and control over other people. Because politics is a vocation rich in opportunities to find all three of these things—affection from cheering crowds and backslapping colleagues, a sense of usefulness from public service in a civic cause, dominance through official power—it is not surprising that some insecure people are attracted to a political career.

These ambitions make for a problem, Barber argues. If Presidents use their office to compensate for private doubts and demons, it follows that they will not always use it for public purposes. Affection-seekers will be so concerned with preserving the goodwill of those around them that they seldom will challenge the status quo. Duty-doers will be similarly inert, although in their case inertia will result from the feeling that to be useful they must be diligent guardians of time-honored practices and procedures. Passive Presidents of both kinds may provide the nation with "breathing spells, times of recovery in our frantic political life," or even "a refreshing hopefulness and at least some sense of sharing and caring." Still, in Barber's view, their main effect is to "divert popular attention from the hard realities of politics," thus leaving the country to drift. And "what passive presidents ignore, active presidents inherit."

Power-driven Presidents pose the greatest danger to the country. They will seek psychological compensation for their low self-esteem not in inaction but in intense efforts to maintain or extend their personal sense of domination and control through public channels. When things are going well for power-driven Presidents and they feel they have the upper hand on their political opponents, problems may not arise. But when things cease to go well, as eventually they must in a democratic political system, such Presidents' responses almost certainly will take destructive forms, such as rigid defensiveness and aggression against opponents. Only those with high self-esteem will be secure enough to lead as democratic leaders must lead, with persuasion and flexibility as well as action and initiative.

The challenge to voters, in the heat and haste of a presidential campaign, is to learn what the candidates are really like. Barber proposes that the answer to the difficult question of what motivates a political leader comes from asking two easy questions: is the person active or passive ("How much energy does the man invest in his presidency?") and is the person positive or negative ("Relatively speaking, does he seem to experience his political life as happy or sad, enjoyable or discouraging, positive or negative in its main effect?")?

According to Barber, the four possible combinations of answers to these two questions turn out to be almost synonymous with the four psychological strategies that people use to enhance self-esteem.

Active-positives are the most psychologically healthy of the group. Their sense of high self-worth enables them to work hard at politics, to have fun at what they do, and thus to be fairly good at it. Of the four eighteenth- and nineteenth-century Presidents and the fifteen twentieth-century Presidents whom Barber has studied, he places Thomas Jefferson, Franklin D. Roosevelt, Harry S. Truman, John F. Kennedy, Gerald R. Ford, Jimmy Carter, and George Bush in the active-positive category.

The *passive-positives* are the affection-seekers: James

Madison, William Howard Taft, Warren G. Harding, and Ronald Reagan). Although not especially hard-working, passive-positives enjoy being President.

The *passive-negatives* neither work like the active-positives nor play like the passive-positives. They include George Washington, Calvin Coolidge, and Dwight D. Eisenhower. Duty, not pleasure or zest, gets them into politics.

Finally, there are the power-seeking *active-negatives*, who compulsively throw themselves into their presidential chores yet derive little satisfaction from their efforts. In Barber's view, active-negative Presidents John Adams, Woodrow Wilson, Herbert Hoover, Lyndon B. Johnson, and Richard Nixon all shared one important personality-rooted quality: they persisted in disastrous courses of action (Adams's repressive ALIEN AND SEDITION ACTS, Wilson's LEAGUE OF NATIONS battle, Hoover's depression policies, Johnson's VIETNAM WAR, and Nixon's WATERGATE AFFAIR) because to have conceded error would have been to lose their sense of control, something their psychological constitutions would not allow them to do.

Critical Reception. *The Presidential Character* won early praise from scholars and journalists when it was published in 1972. Presidential scholars had long taken as axiomatic that the presidency is an institution shaped in large measure by the personalities of individual Presidents. But seldom had the literature of personality theory been brought to bear on the subject. Instead, academic studies of the presidency were rife with offhand observations ("President Eisenhower was a father figure"; "the public is fickle") and benign assumptions. As the political scientist Erwin C. Hargrove wrote in 1974, "We had assumed that ideological purpose was sufficient to purify the drive for power, but we forgot the importance of character." Barber's book represented an ambitious effort to treat the subject of presidential personality in a sustained and intellectually rigorous manner.

Journalists were impressed by *The Presidential Character*'s good writing, practical applicability (the book's subtitle is *Predicting Performance in the White House*), and specific predictions concerning Richard Nixon, who was President at the time the book was published. As early as 1969, Barber had written that "Nixon [will] respond to challenges to the morality of his regime, to charges of scandal and/or corruption" with efforts "to hush it up, to conceal it, bring down the blinds. If it breaks open and Nixon cannot avoid commenting on it, there is a real setup here for another crisis." These predictions seemed borne out by Nixon's behavior during the Watergate crisis of 1973–1974.

In part despite and in part because of the initial

success of *The Presidential Character*, critical doubts eventually were voiced. Many scholars argued that Barber's theory was too simple, that his four character types did not begin to cover the full range of human complexity. At one level, this criticism was as trivial as it was true. Barber states very clearly that "we are talking about tendencies, broad directions; no individual man exactly fits a category." His typology was offered as a method for sizing up potential Presidents, not for diagnosing and treating them. Given the nature of political campaigning, little beyond a reasonably accurate shorthand device could be expected. The real question, then, involved the accuracy of Barber's shorthand device.

Barber's defense of the intellectual foundation of his character typology—that it was "long familiar in psychological research" and "appeared in nearly every study of personality"—was not convincing. He offered neither footnotes nor other references to such studies, thus leaving himself open to the withering scorn of reviewers like the political scientist Alexander George, who pointed out that personality theory is in fact a "quagmire" in which "the term 'character' in practice is applied loosely and means many different things."

Some scholars questioned not only the technical basis of Barber's psychological theory of presidential behavior but also the importance of psychological explanation itself. In their view, Barber's theory seemed to unravel even as he applied it. A healthy political personality turns out not to be the guarantor of presidential success that Barber suggested: he classed the relatively ineffectual Ford, Carter, and Bush as active-positives early in their presidencies. Nor does Barber's notion of psychological unsuitability seem to correspond to failure in office. The ranks of the most successful Presidents in recent surveys by historians include some whom Barber classified as active-positives (Jefferson, Franklin Roosevelt, and Truman) but also an equal number of active-negatives (Adams, Wilson, and Lyndon Johnson) and others whom Barber labeled as passive-negatives (Washington and Eisenhower).

Personality alone does not define the presidency. As the political scientist Jeffrey Tulis noted, Lincoln's behavior as President can be explained much better by his political philosophy and skills than by his seemingly active-negative character. Similarly, Hargrove argued, one need not resort to psychology to explain the failures of active-negatives Hoover and, in the latter years of his presidency, Lyndon Johnson. Hoover's unbending opposition to instituting federal relief in the face of the depression may have stemmed more from ideological beliefs than psychological rigidity.

Johnson's refusal to change the administration's policies in Vietnam could be interpreted as the action of a self-styled consensus leader trying to steer a moderate course between hawks who wanted full-scale military involvement and doves who wanted unilateral withdrawal. These Presidents' actions were ineffective, but not necessarily irrational.

The criticisms of *The Presidential Character* were telling; Barber's character theory soon fell into public and scholarly disfavor. But the criticisms did not obscure his major contributions: a concentration (albeit excessive) on the importance of presidential personality in explaining presidential behavior, a sensitivity to personality as a variable (power does not always corrupt, nor does the office always make the individual), and a boldness in approaching the problems voters face in predicting what candidates will be like if they are elected.

BIBLIOGRAPHY

Barber, James David. *The Presidential Character: Predicting Performance in the White House.* 1972. 4th rev. ed. 1992.

George, Alexander. "Assessing Presidential Character." *World Politics* 26 (1974): 234–282.

Hargrove, Erwin C. "Presidential Personality and Revisionist Views of the Presidency." *Midwest Journal of Political Science* 17 (1973): 819–836.

Nelson, Michael. "The Psychological Presidency." In *The Presidency and the Political System*, 3d ed. Edited by Michael Nelson. 1990. Pp. 189–212.

Tulis, Jeffrey. "On Presidential Character." in *The Presidency in the Constitutional Order*. Edited by Jeffrey Tulis and Joseph M. Bessette. 1981. Pp. 283–313.

MICHAEL NELSON

PRESIDENTIAL-CONGRESSIONAL RELATIONS. The designer of the nation's capital, Major Pierre L'Enfant, followed logic and advice when he placed the President and Congress on opposite sides of the city. Congress would occupy a single large building on Jenkins Hill, the highest promontory. On a plain a mile or so to the northwest would be the Executive Mansion. A broad avenue was planned to permit ceremonial exchanges of communication; but a bridge linking them by spanning Tiber Creek was not built until the third decade of the nineteenth century. Characteristically, the Capitol faced eastward and the Executive Mansion northward, their backs turned on each other.

Collaboration between the two branches lies at the heart of the successes—and failures—of the American form of government. The relationship has been sometimes benign but often stormy. Although cooperation is required to pass and implement policies, the two branches have different duties and serve divergent constituencies. Constitutional scholar Edward S. Corwin was referring to foreign policy when he described the Constitution as "an invitation to struggle" between the two elected branches, but the phrase applies even more to domestic policies.

The Constitutional Formula. Following history and philosophical principles, the Constitution's writers devoted Article I to the legislative branch. Congress has a breathtaking array of powers, embracing nearly all governmental functions known to eighteenth-century thinkers. Reflecting the Founders' Whig heritage, prerogatives include the historic parliamentary power of the purse, in addition to sweeping supervision over money and currency, interstate and foreign commerce, and public works and improvement projects. Congress also plays an active part in foreign and defense policies—which had traditionally been prerogatives of the British Crown. It can declare war [*see* WAR, DECLARATION OF] ratify treaties, raise and support armies and navies, and make rules governing military forces. Finally, Congress is granted the power "to make all Laws which shall be necessary and proper for carrying into Execution the foregoing Powers," the famous "elastic clause."

In working out these policies, however, the Constitution spreads authority across the two elected branches. Even though Congress is vested with "all legislative Powers herein granted" (Article I, Section 1), other provisions make it clear that these powers must be shared with the executive. Presidents can convene one or both houses of Congress in special session. Although a President cannot personally introduce legislation, he "shall from time to time give to the Congress Information of the State of the Union, and recommend to their Consideration such Measures as he shall judge necessary and expedient." In other words, Presidents can shape the legislative agenda, even if they cannot assure that their proposals will be taken seriously, much less enacted. Presidents since Franklin D. Roosevelt have taken a much more active agenda-setting role than their nineteenth-century predecessors [*see* AGENDA, PRESIDENT'S]. Presidents vary widely in legislative success, but all are now expected to submit a legislative program.

Presidents also have the power to veto congressional enactments [*see* VETO, POCKET; VETO, REGULAR]. Once a bill or resolution has passed both houses of Congress and has been presented to the President, the President must sign or return it within ten days, excluding Sundays. A two-thirds vote is required in both houses to overrule a President's veto. In addition to this regular (or return) veto, the President may "pocket veto" a bill when the adjournment of Congress prevents its return for an override vote.

The veto power makes the President a major player in legislative politics. Of more than fourteen hundred regular vetoes from President George Washington through President George Bush, only about 7 percent were overridden by Congress. (Many vetoed bills eventually resurface in another form, however.) The most powerful vetoes are those that are threatened but not employed. Lawmakers constantly look to the White House to ascertain whether or not the President is likely to sign the bill. Therefore, enactments usually embody tradeoffs between provisions desired by the President and those favored by legislators on Capitol Hill. That is the leading reason why vetoes are relatively infrequent: throughout American history, Presidents have vetoed only about 3 percent of all the measures presented to them.

Congress, by the same token, shapes the executive branch. Virtually alone among the world's national assemblies, Congress writes, processes, and refines its own legislation, relying on "in-house" staff and outside information as well as executive recommendations. Executive agencies and their programs are chartered by law. Executive and judicial officers are nominated by the President but confirmed by the Senate. Congress has the power to declare war and to raise and equip military forces. Although Presidents conclude treaties with foreign nations, these must be ratified with the ADVICE AND CONSENT of the Senate.

The resulting constitutional system is popularly known as SEPARATION OF POWERS. But James Madison (FEDERALIST 48) observed more accurately that it is a system of separate institutions sharing functions, so that "these departments be so far connected and blended as to give to each a constitutional control over the others." Interbranch relations are a product of compromise and accommodation, not of isolation or exact metes and bounds.

Growth of the "Legislative Presidency." History bears out Madison's commonsense approach to interbranch relationships. Rigid lines of demarcation between the White House and Capitol Hill have been repeatedly trespassed. ALEXANDER HAMILTON, the first Secretary of the Treasury, aggressively sought mastery over Congress, as did Thomas Jefferson as President a decade later. In turn Congress soon began delving into the details of administration—a habit, now called micromanagement, that persists to this day.

However, executive-legislative relations have expanded in volume, intensity, and formal structure. Presidents and Congresses tended to work at arm's length during the nineteenth century, although strong Presidents like Thomas Jefferson, Andrew Jackson, and Abraham Lincoln took an active part in legislation. After 1865 there ensued an era of presidential eclipse—"congressional government," President Woodrow Wilson called it—that lasted for more than a generation. Yet post-CIVIL WAR trends, including economic development, social complexity, and an expanding public sector, laid the groundwork for later legislative activism.

The modern legislative role of the President is primarily a twentieth-century phenomenon. Wilson and the two Roosevelts all took lengthy legislative agendas up to Capitol Hill. Wilson revived the practice of delivering his STATE OF THE UNION MESSAGE in person, to assure public attention and media coverage. Since the end of WORLD WAR II, everyone—Congress, the press, the public—has expected vigorous presidential leadership. Presidents who (like George Bush) neglect to present a legislative agenda, or who (like Gerald Ford) appear to defer to congressional initiatives, invite criticism that they are weak or ineffective.

Presidential Coalition-Building. If modern Presidents have no choice but to exert legislative leadership, they continue to compile widely differing records of success. More than anything else, success or failure hinges on whether the President's party controls the House and Senate, and how many votes the parties and even their factions command. Unified party control of the two branches nearly always produces higher levels of agreement than does divided party control [*see* DIVIDED GOVERNMENT]. A President's skills or popularity with the public have less impact, although they may enhance a President's legislative record.

Despite the importance of party labels, members of Congress are independent players who vote less often out of party loyalty than to advance their constituency and career interests. Viewed from the White House, no fellow partisan's support can be taken for granted; conversely, no opposition-party member can be entirely written off. Presidents and their advisers must repeatedly forge coalitions in order to achieve legislative victories. In persuading and bargaining with Congress, Presidents work on several levels: with congressional leaders (especially those of the President's own party); with the scattered committee and factional work groups on Capitol Hill; with individual members, sometimes one by one; and with Congress as a whole, through media focus and grassroots support.

Dealing with congressional leaders. Congress is organized by the political parties, and its party leaders monitor its legislative schedule. Leadership in the larger House of Representatives emerged early; the Speaker is a partisan as well as a parliamentary officer, with potent organizing and scheduling powers. The Senate's floor leadership emerged in the Wilson era, primarily (scholars have concluded) in order to coordinate Senate actions with White House initiatives.

Presidents meet frequently with House and Senate leaders from both parties. Enlisting the leaders' support is only one purpose of such meetings. Party leaders bring reports and warnings about the likely fate of presidential initiatives. They take back equally valuable information about the President's plans and intentions that can be turned into the coin of influence in dealing with their colleagues. Needless to say, formal meetings are only the tip of the iceberg. White House staff members and congressional leaders are in daily, even hourly, contact on a wide range of legislative matters.

Capitol Hill work groups. Bargaining with a few influential leaders, however, cannot ensure passage of the President's program. Congress embraces a large number of work groups—committees, subcommittees, task forces, informal caucuses. In the 102d Congress (1991–1992), there were 107 standing work groups (committees and subcommittees) in the Senate and 176 in the House. Informal voting-bloc groups outside the standing committee system also allow members to involve themselves in policies of interest to them.

On any given topic, therefore, not one but many work groups may be involved. This confronts executive agencies with a bewildering array of access points on Capitol Hill. Formerly, a White House aide or agency lobbyist could forge alliances with the handful of legislators who served on the relevant committee. Those members could be counted upon to carry the word to their colleagues. Under current practice, liaison officers from executive agencies must work with voting-bloc groups and frequently canvass large numbers of members, not excluding the most junior ones. During the thirteen months preceding implementation of the North American Free Trade Agreement (NAFTA) in August 1992, staff aides of U.S. Trade Representative (USTR) Carla A. Hills logged forty consultations with individual lawmakers and no less than 199 meetings with congressional work groups, from the House Ways and Means and the Senate Finance committees to the Northeast-Midwest Coalition and the Senate Textile Group.

Persuading individual lawmakers. Sooner or later, Presidents and their aides must retail their appeals, going individually to members of Congress in order to sell the White House position, ask for votes, and offer inducements for support. Sometimes these incentives include concessions on matters unrelated to the issue at hand—for example, approving federal projects in the member's home district, or nominating a judge supported by a given Senator.

Presidents have always had to make these personal, informal overtures. Washington dispatched Treasury Secretary Hamilton to consult with members; Jefferson socialized at the White House with congressional allies. The modern presidency, with its stress on legislative achievements, led to the assignment of White House staffers to conduct day-to-day relations with Capitol Hill. President Dwight D. Eisenhower, in spite of his modest legislative goals, set up the first separate congressional affairs office. President John F. Kennedy in 1961 expanded the staff (renamed the Office of Congressional Relations) under Lawrence F. O'Brien, who is regarded as the father of modern legislative liaison. Presidents since Kennedy have added their individual touches, but all have continued the liaison apparatus [see CONGRESS, WHITE HOUSE LIAISON WITH].

Effective congressional liaison involves granting or withholding resources in order to cultivate support on Capitol Hill. This includes not only PATRONAGE—executive and judicial posts—but also construction projects, government installations, offers of campaign support, access to strategic information, plane rides on Air Force One, White House dinners and social events, signed photographs, and countless other favors both large and small that can be traded for needed votes. Some of these services may seem petty or even tawdry, but it is out of a patchwork of such appeals that legislative majorities are sometimes built.

Some Presidents relish the persuasive challenges of their office. President Lyndon B. Johnson was known for "the treatment," a face-to-face full-court press that ranged the whole gamut of human emotions and often left its targets emotionally battered. President Ronald Reagan was known for dispensing cuff links and theater tickets along with brief homilies concerning the issue at hand. George Bush engaged in a variety of informal contacts, ranging from White House social events to mobile-phone conversations. A few Presidents, like Richard M. Nixon and Jimmy Carter, disliked asking for votes and preferred to leave the task to others.

Mobilizing public pressure. In their efforts to goad members of Congress into agreement, Presidents strive to mobilize PUBLIC OPINION. WHITE HOUSE STAFFS devote much time to gaining media attention and stimulating popular support. Presidents are better than Congress at exploiting the media, and so they assume media coverage will enhance their influence [see MEDIA, PRESIDENT AND THE]. The hope is that a FIRESIDE CHAT, a nationally televised address, a carefully planned event, or a nationwide tour might be able to tap a vast reservoir of support "outside the beltway" that members of Congress dare not defy.

Going public on an issue is not without its risks. The President may raise expectations that cannot be fulfilled, make inept appeals, lose control over the issue, alienate legislators whose support is needed, or put forward hastily conceived proposals. "Going to the country" can be a potent tactic, but overuse will dull its impact. And if the President already has overall support on Capitol Hill, such "hot-button tactics" are redundant. Cultivating public favor and support will nevertheless continue to figure prominently in White House efforts to prevail in legislative-executive struggles.

Patterns of Interbranch Control. Of all the factors that affect interbranch relations, partisan control is the most powerful. Both branches may be controlled by the same single party—a situation that might be termed party government. Or there may be divided government, placing Congress and the White House in the hands of opposing parties. A third pattern, truncated majority, leaves the President's party controlling one but not both houses of Congress. Historically this situation has been rather rare, though it remains a possible option.

Party government. Historically, the same party has tended to control the White House and both chambers of Congress. Even in the twentieth century, this has been the case during about two-thirds of all the Congresses. But this orderly state of affairs is less common than it once was: one-party control marked only nine of the twenty-four Congresses that convened between 1945 and 1992. During much of this period, tensions between White House and Capitol Hill were high.

Eras of true legislative harmony—party government in the parliamentary sense of the term—are quite atypical in the United States. There have been only three such periods in the twentieth century: Wilson's first administration (1913–1917); Franklin Roosevelt's celebrated NEW DEAL (1933–1936); and the balmiest days of Lyndon Johnson's GREAT SOCIETY (1963–1966). Flowing from rare convergences of a forceful CHIEF EXECUTIVE, an unfulfilled policy agenda, and a Congress eager to respond to presidential leadership, these periods saw frantic law making that produced landmark legislation and innovative governmental programs.

Periods of party government as productive as these three are not free of problems. The pace of law making is sometimes so rapid that political institutions require years to absorb the new programs and their costs. Succeeding generations may retrench or even reverse overambitious or ineffective programs.

Partisan control of the two branches, however, does not guarantee legislative success. Although Congress had Democratic majorities during all but four years from the late 1930s until the mid 1960s, its affairs were actually dominated by a conservative coalition of southern Democrats and Republicans. The coalition's ascendancy over domestic policy outlasted several Presidents of varying goals and skills. It succeeded in thwarting civil rights and social legislation pushed by Presidents Franklin D. Roosevelt, Harry S. Truman, and later John F. Kennedy. The later case of Jimmy Carter is more complicated; his relations with Capitol Hill were troubled, despite huge Democratic majorities in both chambers and a better-than-average legislative record.

Divided government. Divided government has become commonplace in modern times. It marked two years of the Truman presidency, all but two years of Eisenhower's, and all of Nixon's, Ford's, Reagan's, and Bush's presidencies (Reagan enjoyed six years with a Republican Senate). Under divided government, interbranch relationships range from lukewarm to hostile. During the Eisenhower administration, Democratic Congresses refrained from attacking the popular President, developing instead modest legislative alternatives and pushing them in election years. Hostility marked relations between Truman and the Republican Congress of 1947–1948, which he called the "awful Eightieth Congress" during his barnstorming 1948 reelection campaign. The same hostility marked relations between Nixon and Democratic Congresses (1969–1974).

Divided government flows from an overall decline in party identification and the rise of ticket-splitting by voters. Presidential candidates are viewed through different lenses than are legislative candidates. Politicians at all levels are led to fashion their own campaigns and organizations, bypassing partisan appeals and relying on personal factors or campaign technology.

Long dominant at state and local levels, the Democratic Party has a deep bench of attractive candidates who advocate government services desired by voters. Thus Democrats have normally won majorities of the votes cast in congressional elections. By contrast the Republicans have since the 1950s dominated the presidential sweepstakes, seven elections to three. Their successes derive not only from regional strengths reflected in the ELECTORAL COLLEGE, but from their successful identification with middle-class voters' concerns: national security, anticommunism, and conservative personal and family values. Reflecting a characteristic ambivalence toward government,

Americans at the same time vote for Presidents who promise "no new taxes" and legislators who stress constituency services and pledge to preserve desired government benefits. Public opinion surveys, moreover, indicate that people prefer having divided government so that the two branches can check each other.

Divided government does not preclude interbranch cooperation or legislative productivity. Despite divided party control, legislative activity was extraordinarily high during the Nixon and Ford presidencies and during Reagan's first year. Some scholars contend that the supposed benefits of unified party control have been exaggerated. Examining legislative productivity levels, Davidson (1991) found that they corresponded imperfectly with presidential administrations, whether with united or divided party control. Mayhew (1991) found that unified or divided control made little difference in enactment of important legislation or launching of high-profile congressional investigations of executive-branch misdeeds.

Yet divided government exacts a long-term price in terms of policy stalemate. Policy decisions may be deferred or compromised so severely that the solutions have little impact. Uncommon leadership and skillful interbranch bargaining is required to overcome divergent political stakes and resultant inertia. Frustration in achieving their policy goals psychologically wears down Presidents, legislators, and their staffs.

Assessing Presidential Success. Shifts of influence between the White House and Capitol Hill are a recurrent feature of American politics. Scholars have characterized certain eras as times of congressional government and others of presidential dominance. Certainly there is an ebb and flow of power between the two branches, but one must be cautious in making such generalizations.

Passage of presidentially supported measures is a starting point; indeed, the rates at which such measures are passed is the most common index of presidential success. In fact, however, influence over legislation is difficult to measure with certainty. Who really initiates legislation? A President can draw publicity by articulating a proposal and giving it currency, but its real origins are likely to be embedded in years of political agitation, congressional hearings, or academic discussion. What exactly is the President's program? Major proposals are trumpeted by the President; but what of minor proposals? Lyndon Johnson used to announce support for measures already assured of passage to boost his record of success. Thus, not all measures endorsed by a President ought to be given equal weight. Finally, who actually wields the decisive influence in passing a piece of legislation? Presidential lobbying may tip the scales, but no legislation passes Congress without help from many quarters. For these and other reasons, measuring White House influence over legislation is hazardous.

The legislative-executive balance of power is in constant motion. The influence of either branch can be affected by issues, circumstances, or personalities. Even when one branch is eclipsed, it may exert potent influence. Nor are legislative-executive struggles zero-sum games. If one branch gains power, it does not mean that the other necessarily loses it. Generally speaking, expanding governmental authority since World War II has augmented the authority of both branches. Their growth rates may differ and their temporary fortunes diverge, but they are unlikely to be permanently dominant or subordinate.

BIBLIOGRAPHY

Binkley, Wilfred E. *President and Congress.* 1962.
Bond, Jon R., and Richard Fleisher. *The President in the Legislative Arena.* 1990.
Chamberlain, Lawrence H. *The President, Congress, and Legislation.* 1947.
Davidson, Roger H. "The Presidency and the Three Eras of the Modern Congress." In *Divided Democracy.* Edited by James A. Thurber. 1991.
Edwards, George C., III. *At the Margins: Presidential Leadership of Congress.* 1989.
Fisher, Louis. *Constitutional Conflicts between Congress and the President.* 3d ed. 1991.
Jacobson, Gary C. *The Electoral Origins of Divided Government.* 1990.
Kernell, Samuel. *Going Public: New Strategies of Presidential Leadership.* 1986.
Mayhew, David R. *Divided We Govern: Party Control, Lawmaking, and Investigations 1946–1990.* 1991.
Wayne, Stephen J. *The Legislative Presidency.* 1978.

ROGER H. DAVIDSON

PRESIDENTIAL ELECTION CAMPAIGN FUND. The program of public grants to fund presidential campaigns is in fact two quite separate programs, one for the period before the national nominating conventions and one for the campaign after them. These programs have governed five presidential elections— 1976 through 1992—and they have colored virtually everything about both the campaigns and CAMPAIGN FINANCES. The funds come from the Presidential Election Campaign Fund (PECF), which depends on taxpayers to check a box on their federal return.

Nomination Campaigns. The public funding of nomination seekers before the conventions rests entirely on matching all individual contributions up to a maximum of $250. Those two linked sources of money thus dominate the financing of the campaigns in both the primary and the caucus states. In 1988 individual contributions—both those matched and the larger ones up to the limit of $1,000—accounted for 66 percent of all candidate receipts ($141.1 million of $213.8 million). All public matching funds ($65.7 million) accounted for another 31 percent.

In order to be eligible for such matching, however, candidates must first raise $5,000 in individual contributions of $250 or less in twenty different states. That was not a very daunting threshhold when it was adopted in 1974, and with the purchasing power of a dollar in 1992 only 37 percent of what it was in 1974, the barrier is far lower than it was originally. Indeed, all substantial Democratic and Republican contenders since 1974 have easily achieved eligibility. (One of them, Republican John Connally, chose not to achieve it in 1980.) In addition, three other candidates have qualified: Lyndon LaRouche, a self-described Democrat; Sonia Johnson of the Citizens Party; and Leonora Fulani of the New Alliance Party, in 1988 and 1992.

Public money does not come unencumbered. Candidates choosing it must accept spending limits at two levels: a $10 million overall limit for the entire preconvention campaign and a series of state-by-state limits reflecting the populations of the states in 1974. Congress here provided, however, that the limits be adjusted upward to reflect inflation as measured by the consumer price index (CPI). The overall limit thus stood at $27.6 million in 1992, with the state limits varying from $552,400 for the seventeen least-populous states to $9.8 million for California. The sum of the state limits is more than three times the overall limit.

Such an intricate system of raising and spending money for fifty separate "elections" in so short a time inevitably intrudes campaign finance into the making of political strategy. Contenders are free to establish their eligibility and raise money in the year before the presidential election, but the first pay out of federal funds comes in early January of election year, and others follow each succeeding month. From then until the end of the delegate hunt, candidates spend in order to win delegates in the states and improve their performance in national polls so that they can raise more money and win more delegates. Candidates must also plan their strategies around the spending limits, deciding which states to contest and which not to, whether to spend early and ignore the later state primaries, how to stay within the very tight spending limits of small-population but politically important states such as New Hampshire.

Financial Status of the Tax Checkoff and the Presidential Election Campaign Fund, 1973–1992

| Year[a] | Tax Checkoff | | Presidential Election Campaign Fund | |
	Amount Designated, in millions	Percent of Returns	Disbursements, in millions	Year-end Balance, in millions[b]
1973	$ 2.4	—	$ 0.0	$ 2.4
1974	27.6	—	0.0	27.6
1975	31.7	—	2.6	59.6
1976	33.7	—	69.5	23.8
1977	36.6	27.5	0.5	60.9
1978	39.2	28.6	0.006	100.3
1979	35.9	25.4	1.1	135.2
1980	38.8	27.4	101.4	73.8
1981	41.0	28.7	0.6	114.4
1982	39.0	27.0	0.001	153.5
1983	35.6	24.2	11.8	177.3
1984	35.0	23.7	120.1	92.7
1985	34.7	23.0	1.6	125.9
1986	35.8	23.0	0.006	161.7
1987	33.7	21.7	17.8	177.9
1988	33.0	21.0	158.6	52.5
1989	32.3	20.1	1.8	82.9
1990	32.5	19.8	0.002	115.4
1991	32.3	19.5	21.2	127.1
1992	29.6	17.7	153.2	4.1

[a] Year indicates the year the funds were received or disbursed from the fund; checkoff data based on tax returns for the previous year (but filed in the year indicated).

[b] Year-end balance may not be easily reconciled with other data, in part because of repayments from candidates and parties following postelection audits.

Prepared by Joseph E. Cantor, Congressional Research Service, based on IRS data as compiled by the Federal Election Commission.

General Election Finance. After the conventions meet and confirm the Democratic and Republican nominees, each may claim full public funding for the fall general election campaign. It is, in fact, the only instance of full public funding in all of American politics—"full" meaning a government grant the size of the spending limit attached to its acceptance. The sum is $20 million in 1974 dollars; its value in 1992 was $55.2 million. It comes as a lump-sum commitment against which a candidate can draw; no matching is required. Candidates thus can base their campaign plans on its availability from the very beginning; they are also freed of fund-raising burden during the campaign. Not surprisingly, perhaps, all major party candidates accepted it from 1976 through 1992.

While the Republican and Democratic candidates can claim the public money by reason by their party's having won more than 25 percent of the votes at the previous election, minor party candidates are less fortunate. They win only a portion of the indexed $20

million *after* the election, the portion being a ratio of their share of the vote in relation to the average major party candidate's, *if* their vote exceeds 5 percent. Thus, with 6.6 percent of the vote in 1980, John Anderson, an independent candidate, was paid $4.2 million after the election. Had he chosen to run in 1984, he would have been entitled to that sum up front. However troubling these arrangements for minor-party candidates were to some commentators, the Supreme Court upheld them, along with all other aspects of public funding in a 1976 decision (BUCKLEY v. VALEO). The Court's chief insistence was that public money be voluntarily chosen by candidates.

The "fullness" of public funding is, however, subject to some exceptions in the laws of 1974. The candidates themselves may spend an additional $50,000 from their personal resources. The national party committees may raise and spend 2 cents per person of voting age in 1974 pennies to support the party's presidential candidate. That limit was $9.9 million in 1992. And the candidates' campaigns may also raise and spend 10 percent above the limit to cover legal and accounting costs in complying with the statutes. Finally, as a consequence of the Supreme Court's 1976 decision, any individual or group may spend to support or oppose a presidential candidate *if* that spending is done without the knowledge of the candidate advantaged. PACS (POLITICAL ACTION COMMITTEES) do almost all of that independent spending.

Public funds, therefore, carry about 30 percent of candidates' expenses in the preconvention period. The sums vary from election year to election year, largely the result of the number of eligible candidates and the presence or absence of a President seeking a second term. The total in 1988 was the greatest in the legislation's history. In the autumn, public funds account for virtually all of the candidates' personal campaigns, and that sum is easily calculable as the year's equivalent of 1974's $20 million—multiplied by two. In addition, there are indexed subventions—$10.6 million in 1992—for each party's national nominating convention.

The Supply of Money. Whence comes the money? All of it comes from the Presidential Election Campaign Fund, an earmarked account fed by the U.S. income tax checkoff. Taxpayers may divert $1 (single filers) or $2 (joint returns) of their tax liability to the fund simply by checking a box near the top of the first page of their returns. Even though the accompanying instructions assure that checking the box does not increase one's tax liability, no more than 30 percent of taxpayers have ever done so, and in 1989 the percentage reached an all-time low: 19.8 percent. States employing the same device for their public funding programs reported similar declines.

At the same time, the balances of the PECF have dwindled to the point that they almost certainly will not be large enough to pay for the campaigns and conventions of 1996. Indeed, a shortfall for 1992 was predicted in 1991; it failed to materialize largely because the Democratic contenders raised such relatively small sums for matching in the preconvention period. While the falling rate on the checkoff has contributed to the shortfall, the problem has more fundamental roots: spending from the fund is indexed, but infusions (the sums checked off) are not. Given that anomaly, the fund was bound to run dry; declining checkoffs only hastened the day.

So, changes must be made before 1996. Early in 1992 the FEDERAL ELECTION COMMISSION (FEC), the agency overseeing the program, began a publicity campaign to try to raise the percentage of taxpayers checking off. If that fails to replenish the fund sufficiently—and many experts doubt that it will—harder choices loom. Congress might increase the size of the sums checked off; it could also appropriate money for the fund out of general tax revenues. Or the size of subsidies might be reduced, either by legislation or by prorating the available money. What is more, those decisions will have to be made at a time of increasing voter resistance to the cost of campaigns, growing Republican antipathy to the very idea of public funding, and greater competition for public money at a time of massive budgetary deficits.

Since the mid 1980s another kind of money, soft money, has come into controversy in presidential campaigns. It is money raised by candidates, party committees, or PACs governed by federal law that as contributions would violate federal law. The donors must, therefore, be steered to a state in which the money can be legally given and accepted. So, while a corporation or union is forbidden by federal law from making contributions to candidates for Congress directly from its treasury, a national party or presidential candidate may encourage it to make the contribution to a state party committee where it is a legal contribution under that state's laws. The money can, however, be used only for state or local candidates or for general party activities such as organizational overhead or voter registration drives. In the 1988 campaign the presidential candidates, George Bush and Michael Dukakis, and their respective national party committees each raised close to $25 million in soft money.

Soft money raises two key issues. It enables large contributors to win the gratitude of presidential candidates in ways the Congress thought it had stopped in 1974. And it does *indirectly* introduce new monies into the presidential campaign; while soft money cannot be spent in federal campaigns, it may free money in the hands of state and local parties which can be so used. The campaign finance reform bill of 1992, vetoed by President Bush, would have greatly limited the raising of such funds.

BIBLIOGRAPHY

Alexander, Herbert E., and Monica Bauer. *Financing the 1988 Election.* 1991.

Heard, Alexander. *The Costs of Democracy.* 1960.

Mutch, Robert E. *Campaigns, Congress, and the Courts.* 1988.

Sorauf, Frank J. *Inside Campaign Finance: Myths and Realities.* 1992.

FRANK J. SORAUF

PRESIDENTIAL GREATNESS AND CULTURAL DILEMMAS. What is the mark of a great President? Polling a panel of experts has become the accepted way of rendering history's judgment of presidential performance. The presidential greatness game began in earnest in 1948, when Arthur Schlesinger asked fifty-five prominent historians to grade past Presidents: A signified Great; B, Near Great; C, Average; D, Below Average; and E, Failure. Believing there is wisdom in numbers, subsequent surveys have expanded the panel of experts from 571 in 1970 to 953 in 1983.

The practice of evaluating presidential performance by polling historians is a curious one. Surveys are usually conducted to obtain information about respondents, either their preferences (which candidate or party do you prefer?) or their beliefs about or knowledge of the empirical world (how many members are in the House of Representatives?). We do not as a rule conduct surveys to gauge the validity of a claim. Why then do we do so with respect to presidential performance? The answer is that we lack agreed-upon criteria for making these judgments. If we had accepted criteria, surveys would be superfluous (and subject to corroboration); we would need only to check presidential performance against the established yardsticks.

While these surveys have yielded interesting information about the respondents—a 1983 poll conducted by Robert K. Murray and Tim H. Blessing, for instance, found that American historians specializing in women's history held George Washington in much lower esteem than did the sample as a whole—they are not a good tool for evaluating presidential performance. There is no reason to think the mean judgment of a thousand historians more valid than the estimate of a single scholar specializing in the past Presidents. Insofar as the aim is to compare the performances of Presidents rather than to gather information about the pollees, energies should be directed to devising appropriate criteria for evaluating performance.

The original Schlesinger survey completely sidestepped the issue of criteria for appraising presidential performance. The only instruction Schlesinger supplied was that respondents should judge a President's *"performance in office*, omitting anything done before or after." How one was to gauge the performance in office was left unspecified. In the absence of such criteria, the finding that President X ranked higher than President Y was difficult to interpret.

In *Presidential Greatness* (1966), Thomas Bailey attempted to remedy this deficiency by identifying criteria by which Presidents could be measured. He came up with forty-three yardsticks for measuring presidential greatness, including achievement, administrative capacity, appointees, blunders, eloquence, industriousness, scandals, and sensitivity. If the Schlesinger survey suffered from a lack of guidelines, the surfeit of tests devised by Bailey, including everything and excluding nothing, left the reader with a commendably broader view of the many facets of the presidency but equally helpless at evaluating presidential performance.

Often the evaluation of presidential greatness employs measures such as amount of legislation passed, activity in office, or number of objectives pursued. But these criteria create a pronounced bias toward activist Presidents. That such criteria sneak in ideological judgments about the ends of government is indicated by Schlesinger's conclusion that the 1962 survey showed that average or mediocre Presidents "believed in negative government, in self-subordination to the legislative power." Why should a contemporary activist view—the best presidencies add functions to government and/or the presidency—be a standard for scholars?

Though acutely aware of the limitations of presidential ratings as conducted at present, we do not accept Bailey's claim that "comparing eminent figures is only a game" or Curtis Arthur Amlund's assertion that "each [President] operated within a unique political environment." By taking aim at the easy target of presidential ratings, attention is deflected away from the more significant defect of wrapping each President and his times in a unique cocoon, thereby reducing the study of the presidency to political biography. The result, as James MacGregor Burns correctly pointed out in *Presidential Government* (1965), is that "We know everything about the Presidents and nothing about the Presidency." It would be both ironic and unfortunate for the best-known effort to compare presidencies to discredit the laudable, indeed essential, goal of making comparisons among administrations.

Cultural Analysis. All Presidents face cultural dilemmas, albeit of different kinds and intensities. Their ability to resolve these dilemmas provides a criterion for evaluating their performance. Our hypothesis is that presidencies can be evaluated in terms of dilemmas confronted, evaded, created, or overcome. "Great" Presidents are those who provide solutions to culturally induced dilemmas. The type of leadership preferred and feared, and the kinds of support given to leaders and the demands made on them, vary according to the political culture—individualist, egalitarian, or hierarchial.

The *individualist* regime is organized to maximize the scope of individual autonomy and thus minimize the need for authority. Following a Groucho Marx kind of logic, individualist believe that any leader strong enough to help them is too strong to be trusted. *Egalitarians* are dedicated to diminishing differences among people. Would-be egalitarian leaders are thus in trouble before they start, for authority is a prima facie case of inequality. Aspiring leaders must therefore dissemble, at once persuasive about the right course to follow and self-effacing, as if they were not leading at all. Fearing disorder, *hierarchies* shore up authority in every way they can. This means just what Alexis de Tocqueville and later political scientists have said it does: support for authority and, hence, leadership is relatively weak in America. With egalitarians rejecting authority, individualists desiring to escape from it, and hierarchical forces too weak to impose it, Presidents who seek to rely on formal authority alone are in a precarious position.

The following examples are drawn from a larger project we have undertaken to apply cultural analysis to all Presidents from Washington through Abraham Lincoln. There are two primary categories of cultural dilemmas. The first involves the President who has some blend of egalitarian and individualist cultural propensities. All Jeffersonian and Jacksonian Presidents labored to square their own and their followers' antiauthority principles with the exercise of executive authority. The second type involves the President who has hierarchical cultural propensities. All hierarchical Presidents have struggled to reconcile their, and their party's, hierarchical cultural preferences with the anti-hierarchical ethos dominant in the society and polity. This conflict animated the presidencies of Washington, John Adams, and John Qunicy Adams, and it hamstrung Whig presidential aspirants such as HENRY CLAY and DANIEL WEBSTER.

George Washington. Wherein lies Washington's greatness? How can historians' characterizations of Washington as "good," "competent," and "honest" sum up to a great President? The deepest fear of an individualist political culture is the leader who overstays his welcome. Acutely conscious of this fear, Washington continually reassured his countrymen of his desire to step down immediately after he had completed his assigned task. By voluntarily relinquishing power and spurning offers to make his leadership permanent, Washington became, according to Barry Schwartz, the paragon of the individualist political leader. In being good, Washington became great.

With severe limits on the substance of power, Washington had to make do with the appearance of power. Painfully aware of the revolutionary bias against central rule, Washington tried to enhance the government's image of competence and strength by employing federal power where it was not merely adequate to the purpose but overwhelming, as in the WHISKEY REBELLION. In the absence of public support for peace-time military preparations, which neither individualists nor egalitarians would give, Washington avoided committing American military forces to ventures that might expose the weakness beneath the carefuly cultivated appearance of strength. So successful was Washington at substituting the appearance of power for the reality that his successor, John Adams, was left with the erroneous impression that the President operated in a hierarchical political system.

Adams's son, John Quincy Adams, was no better than his father at reconciling his own hierarchical dispositions with the antiauthoritarian bias of the political system. His presidency was severely hampered by a refusal to exploit PATRONAGE to advance his policy objectives. Believing that there was a consensus on policy and that implementation was a matter of neutral competence, the younger Adams viewed his subordinates as being above or removed from politics. Consequently, he was unwilling to dismiss those whom he considered qualified, even if, as in the case of the Postmaster General John McLean, they dispensed patronage to Adams's opponents. It is no coincidence that John Qunicy Adams, like John Adams or, for that matter, Jimmy Carter, lasted only a single term in the presidency. Each of these Presidents was a hierarch without a hierarchy, that is, hierarchically disposed leaders unable or unwilling to make allowances for the antileadership nature of the American political system.

Thomas Jefferson. Jeffersonian Republicans, who fused egalitarian and individualist propensities, faced the task of reconciling their deep suspicion of authority with the exercise of executive power. Jefferson's dilemma, as Lance Banning phrases it, was "to govern in accordance with an ideology that taught that power was a monster and governing was wrong." Aware that overt displays of presidential leadership were likely to raise the cry of executive usurpation, Jefferson opted for a covert leadership style. Jefferson's biographer, Dumas Malone, finds his protagonist always making a "conscious effort to avoid all appearances of dictation." The key to Jefferson's political leadership, continues Malone, was that "he did not permit his followers to think of him as a boss at all." He led without appearing to do so, instructed while appearing only to suggest, guided while seeming to defer. According to Robert M. Johnstone, Jr., Jefferson's informal influence was carefully concealed behind a public facade of deference to Congress.

Jefferson's distaste for public confrontation was expressed by one of his favorite maxims—"take things always by their smooth handle." Like Dwight D. Eisenhower, the HIDDEN-HAND PRESIDENT he so much resembles, Jefferson would not publicly challenge even the most abusive of opponents. When John Randolph recklessly abused and villified the administration, Jefferson responded (as did Eisenhower to Senator Joseph R. McCarthy) by privately undercutting rather than publicly attacking his adversary. Jefferson's "hidden hand" leadership style resolved the dilemma of leadership in an antileadership culture for himself but failed to educate his followers on the need for leadership. Jefferson's successors, James Madison and James Monroe, who lacked his skill, stature, and luck, were consequently unable to provide much in the way of presidential leadership.

Andrew Jackson. Believing that the central government created inequalities and suppressed competition, Jacksonians attempted strictly to limit the scope of government activity. The Jacksonian aversion to central authority created the same presidential dilemma—reconciling antiauthority dispositions with the exercise of authority—that the Jeffersonians had had to face.

Andrew Jackson's greatness consisted in fusing an energetic CHIEF EXECUTIVE with a limited central government. He justified presidential activism in the name of limiting the activities of hierarchical institutions—the "Monster Bank" (the Second BANK OF THE UNITED STATES), "King Caucus," even government itself. Presidential powers were to be enlisted in the battle to remove the institutional impediments to increased equality. Public participation would be increased by extending the franchise, overthrowing the senatorial caucus system for nominating Presidents, and instituting rotation in office. Terminating the privileges conferred on private industry by government through charters and franchises would permit the unfettered operation of free enterprise and, thereby, promote equality.

Jackson portrayed the President as mandated by the people to check concentrations of political and economic power. He argued that strengthening the presidency, rather than emboldening hierarchy, would flatten the hierarchy by increasing popular control of those in positions of authority. The concept of the mandated presidency provided an effective cover under which leaders could exercise power while denying they were doing anything more than carrying out the popular will. If the President was mandated to carry out a policy, he could not be exercising personal discretion and therefore there was no reason to fear "executive usurpation." Jackson portrayed the executive REGULAR VETO, which was originally designed by the Federalists as a check upon democracy, as the people's main weapon in their battle to promote equality by limiting government.

By slaying the "Monster Bank," however, Jackson left his Democratic successors without a visible hierarchical target around which to unite individualism and egalitarianism. Even the "sly fox," as President Martin Van Buren was known, could not combat the panic of 1837 with slogans about monsters.

James K. Polk hoped that territorial expansion, like Jackson's bank war, would reunite the Democratic alliance of egalitarianism and individualism. To egalitarian Democrats, the power of slaveholders was analogous to the power of the rich—both slave power and money power demonstrated that "privilege never restrains its ambition to rule." By alienating the more egalitarian wing of his party, Polk's expansionist policies drained the DEMOCRATIC PARTY of the crusading idealism that had characterized it during the 1830s and early 1840s, giving the party an increasingly southern cast. His most conspicuous failing as a political leader was an inability to grasp that, because of SLAVERY, expansion was creating more problems than it was solving, both for the Democratic Party and the nation.

The string of failed cultural solutions, and hence failed presidencies, in the decade prior to the CIVIL WAR testifies to the extraordinary impediments to presidential leadership produced by slavery. Franklin Pierce tried to reestablish the Jacksonian coalition of individualists and egalitarians, but slavery brought to the fore the hitherto submerged tension between majority rule and the property rights of a minority. The optimistic doctrine that liberty and equality were mutally supportive, while able to soften class conflict, could not, in the end, cope with racial conflict. Millard Fillmore hoped to hold together the Whig alliance of individualism and hierarchy by removing slavery from the national agenda through the COMPROMISE OF 1850 and elevating national economic development to the forefront of the agenda. But Filmore's solution reproduced the cultural contradiction within Whiggery—for how could the WHIG PARTY laud economic development and celebrate industrial capitalism as the highest stage of civilization without looking upon the South's "peculiar institution" as anything but a blight on the economic potential of the nation? Witnessing the failure of both Pierce and Fillmore to reconstitute their old cultural coalitions, James Buchanan attempted to create a new alliance that would unite the establishment against egalitarian abolitionists. But while individualists were content to protect slavery where it already existed, the issue of the expansion of slavery into the territories forced many individualists to repudiate an establishment based on hierarchical principles.

Abraham Lincoln. A loyal aherent of the Whig Party for as long as it remained in existence, Lincoln resolved its dilemma of basing government on weak hierarchy by leading during wartime, when he could invoke the COMMANDER IN CHIEF clause, and by creating a new cultural coalition in which hierarchy was subordinated to individualism. Lincoln's political ambition—which William H. Herndon called the "little engine that knew no rest"—was thwarted by Lincoln's identification with the Whig Party. From the sobering experience of Clay's defeats in 1836 and 1844, as well as the victories of the apolitical generals William Henry Harrison in 1840 and Zachary Taylor in 1848, Lincoln learned that his own personal advancement depended on creating a party that could elevate not only war heroes but an Illinois party politician to the presidential office. He thus helped to give the majority political culture in America—individualism—the dominant place in governing the nation. The REPUBLICAN PARTY amalgam of economic individualism and social hierarchy would dominate American politics for the next half-century in the same way that Jefferson and Jackson's alliance of egalitarianism and individualism had dominated the previous half-century.

A Lincoln presidency outside the context of the Civil War is inconceivable. The firing on Fort Sumter gave Lincoln the opportunity to avoid his predecessors' fate by reconciling the dilemmas handcuffing his party. The slavery issue, which had shackled the presidency in the previous decade, now served as a means for unleashing presidential power. Lincoln's greatness consisted in demonstrating that an individualist regime could cope with large-scale crises without a transformation in its cultural identity. Lincoln's example offered hope that individualist regimes were not subject to an "inherent and fatal weakness"; such a regime could be strong enough to maintain its existence in an emergency without permanently altering internal social relations in a hierarchical direction. It turned out that temporary emergency leadership in times of total war need not inexorably lead to permanent dictatorship in peacetime.

Lincoln's solutions had limitations. By keeping his war aims ambiguous so as to attract the support of all three cultures, Lincoln left his successor, Andrew Johnson, with a lack of guidance as to how to proceed with reconstructing the Union. One wonders to what extent the IMPEACHMENT OF ANDREW JOHNSON was a judgment on Lincoln's usurpations. In resolving one set of cultural dilemmas, great Presidents may create insoluble dilemmas for their successors, and presidential greatness is thus intimately related to presidential failure. [*See also* RATINGS, SCHOLARLY.]

BIBLIOGRAPHY

Amlund, Curtis Arthur. "President-Ranking: A Criticism." *Midwest Journal of Political Science* 8 (1964): 309–315.

Bailey, Thomas A. *Presidential Greatness: The Image and the Man from George Washington to the Present.* 1966.

Burns, James MacGregor. *Presidential Government: The Crucible of Leadership.* 1965.

Ellis, Richard, and Aaron Wildavsky. *Dilemmas of Presidential Leadership: From Washington through Lincoln.* 1989.

Greenstein, Fred I. *The Hidden-Hand Presidency: Eisenhower as Leader.* 1982.

Murray, Robert K., and Tim H. Blessing. *Greatness in the White House: Rating the Presidents, Washington through Carter.* 1988

Schlesinger, Arthur M. *Paths to the Present.* 1949, 1964.

Schartz, Barry. "George Washington and the Whig Conception of Heroic Leadership." *American Sociological Review* 48(1983):18–33.

RICHARD J. ELLIS and AARON WILDAVSKY

PRESIDENTIAL LEADERSHIP. The Framers did not conceive the presidency as a locus for leadership. They planned that the President would be the administrative head of the new federal government, but even this role was left largely undefined. Under Article II of the Constitution the President would be COMMANDER IN CHIEF of the army and navy; would have powers of administrative, diplomatic, and judicial appointments [*see* APPOINTMENT POWER]; would give Congress "Information of the State of the Union" [*see* STATE OF THE UNION MESSAGE]; and should "take care that the laws be faithfully executed," along with related and lesser duties. Still, even this slender administrative writ has allowed Presidents to develop a huge bureaucratic apparatus, which in turn has allowed them to exert leadership throughout American society. Presidents have vastly extended their leadership capacities and impact in other dimensions of the presidency—legislative, party, PUBLIC OPINION, global-strategic, and moral. The expansion of these leadership roles began very early in the two-hundred-year history of the presidency.

The Presidents' View of Their Leadership Role. Although the Framers planned to put legislative power securely into the hands of Congress, within a few years George Washington's Secretary of the Treasury, ALEXANDER HAMILTON, was exerting forceful leadership over fiscal policy. Despite Thomas Jefferson's earlier fears of executive tyranny, as the first Democratic-Republican President he exerted close, though often skillfully concealed, influence over Congress. Despite a clear grant of the veto power—an executive weapon that had been widely used by royal governors of the colonies—the VETO was used only sparingly by the first six Presidents. Andrew Jackson's veto of the Maysville Road bill, however, indicated the potential of this power, which over the decades became a key instrument of presidential leadership, especially when Congress could not override vetoes. Following Abraham Lincoln's exercise of legislative power during the CIVIL WAR—even to the extent of not calling Congress into session during the war's critical early months—Presidents have had ample precedents for their role as "legislator in chief"; thereafter, their exercise of this role largely turned on their personal dispositions and political needs.

The Framers did not plan that the President would be a political leader, or certainly not in the narrower sense of party leader, for the CHIEF EXECUTIVE was to govern over and above factions, including political parties. But remorseless conflicts over ideology and issues soon forced members of Congress and the American populace into increasingly sharp divisions. As the rudiments of national parties slowly rose out of these conflicts, Washington and his successor, John Adams, took leadership of the Federalists, and Jefferson and James Madison of the Democratic-Republicans. As President, Jefferson made full use of his party support in Congress and among the voters, creating precedents that could be used by Jackson, Lincoln, and the strong presidents of the twentieth century. Presidential party leadership was buttressed by an ever enlarging pool of federal appointments, though ultimately CIVIL-SERVICE REFORM and public disapproval put some limits on PATRONAGE. The degree of party leadership exercised by the White House has also changed depending on the extent of factional and ideological differences within the legislature and the electorate. Perhaps the most important aspect of presidential leadership has been that this single, ultimately highly politicized, seat of government has become the most prized object of political parties.

While presidential leadership of public opinion has varied according to the Chief Executive's goals and communications skills, as well as the political and ideological context, the President's influence over the media has been a central tool of leadership from the start. Aside from the eras when great senatorial orators such as HENRY CLAY and DANIEL WEBSTER dominated press attention, the President has provided Washington correspondents with the key visible political actor. That the White House is a BULLY PULPIT is a description that has been much overused, but it is no less true for that. Today the President has immediate access to a massive array of electronic communication tools that allow him to overshadow every other organ of government, especially in times of crisis.

Indeed, at least in the short run, the scope and impact of the President's leadership are most enlarged in times of crisis—especially military crisis. Despite Lincoln's intellectual and political background in WHIG PARTY doctrine, which opposed executive "unsurpation," the Civil War President employed both his constitutional and extraconstitutional WAR POWERS to the hilt. Since the mid-nineteenth century, war has been the forcing house of executive leadership, as Presidents have moved more and more into the global arena, employing a wide range of economic, political, and diplomatic resources to build wartime coalitions with other powers such as Great Britain, the Soviet Union, and pre-Communist China, and ultimately gaining control of the "ultimate weapon," the U.S. nuclear arsenal.

Presidential power and leadership have by no means gone unchecked, however. The Framers seated the presidency in a matrix of CHECKS AND BALANCES that gave Congress, the judiciary, and state governments the crucial ability to limit the presidency and, indeed, one another. Congress has often been refractory and beyond the control even of its own leaders, much less the President. The federal judiciary, typically consisting of judges mostly chosen by a President's predecessors and hence without obligation to him, are sometimes actively hostile to White House policies. Presidential leadership might reach into Congress, benefiting from party unity, personal influence, and patronage, but such tools of leadership have had little force with judges holding lifetime tenure or with state and local officials such as big-city mayors, who have occupied their own political turf and exploited their independent political resources.

The moral dimension of presidential leadership has been the most indefinable of presidential powers. A role that in other democracies has been left to a monarch or to the ecclesiastical establishment has been seized by Presidents or has gravitated into their hands. Many of the speeches of, for example, Theodore Roosevelt and Franklin D. Roosevelt were as much sermons as political statements. In a narrow sense, the White House has often set the nation's moral tone in a host of ways involving, for instance, where the President goes to church, how the FIRST LADY dresses, whom the President has to dinner (as in a noted instance when Theodore Roosevelt invited a prominent black leader to his table), and whom the White House chooses to honor in the arts. But in a broader sense Presidents have assumed crucial moral leadership at decisive moments in the nation's history, as with Lincoln's EMANCIPATION PROCLAMATION, Woodrow Wilson's call for U.S. participation in the LEAGUE OF NATIONS, and John F. Kennedy's call for a renewed dedication to public service in his INAUGURAL ADDRESS.

In an opportunistic and pragmatic manner, Presidents have tried first one, then another combination of the leadership tools outlined above in seeking to realize their ends. Paradoxically, however, this intertwining of leadership resources has not stabilized the foundations or the conduct of presidential leadership but has made them unpredictable. It has also led to the further enhancement of presidential leadership efforts, drawing the chief executive into new functions. In recent years, for example, presidential leadership practices or duties have been described as agenda-shaping, coalition-building, morale-strengthening, and priority-setting. For some who fear excesses of presidential power, these activities, added to the traditional ones, make the presidency a loose cannon rolling in all directions across the heaving decks of the ship of state, threatening to crush the deckhands supposedly in charge of it.

To treat presidential leadership from an institutional and historical perspective, however valid and indispensable, is to neglect the central actors—the Presidents themselves. A number of Presidents have been remarkably forthcoming and articulate about their theories of White House leadership. Increasingly, later Presidents have shaped their own theories of leadership on not only the actions but also the spoken or written words of their predecessors. Of all the Presidents Theodore Roosevelt was the most forthcoming and significant in his defense of his energetic exercise of presidential leadership. "My view," he wrote in his autobiography, was that every high executive officer

> was a steward of the people bound actively and affirmatively to do all he could for the people. . . . I declined to adopt the view that what was imperatively necessary for the Nation could not be done by the President unless he could find some specific authorization to do it. My belief was that it was not only his right but his duty to do anything that the needs of the Nation demanded unless such action was forbidden by the Constitution or by the laws. Under this interpretation of executive power I did and caused to be done many things not previously done by the President and the heads of the departments. I did not usurp power, but I did greatly broaden the use of executive power.

Roosevelt justified his position in moral terms: "I acted for the public welfare, I acted for the common well being of all our people." As usual, he was defensive about himself. He had not "cared a rap" about those who criticized his "usurpation of power," he wrote, because that talk was "all nonsense."

William Howard Taft, who succeeded Roosevelt in 1909, flatly differed with his predecessor over the reach of presidential leadership:

> The true view of the Executive functions is . . . that the President can exercise no power which cannot be fairly and reasonably traced to some specific grant of power or justly implied and included within such express grant as proper and necessary to its exercise. Such specific grant must be either in the Federal Constitution or in act of Congress passed in pursuance thereof. There is no undefined residuum of power which he can exercise because it seems to him to be in the public interest.

His appointment as Chief Justice of the United States by President Warren G. Harding in 1921 left Taft in a position to employ this perspective in helping to decide any relevant cases that might come to the Supreme Court; Roosevelt died in 1919.

Franklin D. Roosevelt adapted his concept of presidential leadership from several presidential models, not least from his cousin Theodore. The presidency, he said on the eve of becoming President in 1933, was far more than an administrative office or an engineering job. "It is pre-eminently a place of moral leadership," he declared. "All our great presidents were leaders of thought at times when certain ideas in the life of the nation had to be clarified." Washington personified the idea of federal union. Jefferson practically originated the party system as we know it by opposing the democratic theory to the republicanism of Hamilton. The theory was reaffirmed by Jackson. Two great principles of our government were forever put beyond question by Lincoln. Grover Cleveland, coming into office following an era of great political corruption, typified rugged honesty. Theodore Roosevelt and Wilson "were both moral leaders, each in his own way and his own time, who used the presidency as pulpit. Isn't that what the office is—a superb opportunity for reapplying, applying in new conditions, the simple rules of human conduct we always go back to?" During Franklin Roosevelt's day, the technical and economic environment was changing more quickly than ever before—a trend whose importance he acknowledged: "Without leadership alert and sensitive to change, we are all bogged up or lose our way."

Having studied the presidency at Harvard and observed it at close range from Capitol Hill for almost a decade and a half, John F. Kennedy took an activist view of presidential leadership even while running for the office. According to Kennedy the people demanded

> a vigorous proponent of the national interest—not a passive broker for conflicting private interests. They demand a man capable of acting as the commander-in-chief of the Grand Alliance, not merely a bookkeeper who feels that his work is done when the numbers on the balance sheet come out even. They demand that he be the head of a responsible party, not rise so far above politics as to be invisible—a man who will formulate and

fight for legislative policies, not be a casual bystander to the legislative process. Today a restricted concept of the presidency is not enough. . . . In the decade that lies ahead—in the challenging revolutionary sixties—the American presidency will demand more than ringing manifestos issued from the rear of the battle. It will demand that the President place himself in the very thick of the fight, that he care passionately about the fate of the people he leads, that he be willing to serve them at the risk of incurring their momentary displeasure.

Later Presidents have had little new or daring to say about presidential leadership; their views have largely derived from earlier presidential pronouncements. They have shared a growing consensus that Presidents must be active leaders employing all legitimate powers and tools of their office and operating in all relevant arenas—legislative, party, opinion, moral. Since virtually all the presidents of the second half of the twentieth century were involved in major or minor ways, they embraced another consensus—that Presidents must assume extraordinarily high and conspicuous activist leadership when hostilities break out, if only to convince the populace that there is one responsible authority in charge.

In assuming wartime leadership as Commander in Chief, Presidents can use Lincolnian precedents for taking action outside usual constitutional boundaries. "Was it possible to lose the nation and yet preserve the Constitution?" the Civil War President demanded, and answered,

> By general law, life and limb must be protected, yet often a limb must be amputated to save a life, but a life is never wisely given to save a limb. I felt that measures otherwise unconstitutional might become lawful by becoming indispensable to the preservation of the Constitution through the preservation of the nation.

Lincoln variously ignored, bypassed, pressured, and cooperated with Congress. More than a century later another Republican President, George Bush, made clear that while he would solicit the backing of Congress, he would take military action without it if the situation demanded. A year after the 1991 PERSIAN GULF WAR, when asked why President Bush's foreign policy leadership appeared more impressive than his domestic leadership, Vice President DAN QUAYLE was quoted as saying, "In foreign affairs, the president decides what is in the best interests of this country, and he does it." In domestic policy, the Vice President added, he needs the "total cooperation of the Congress." Conventional wisdom about presidential WAR POWERS had become consensual thinking.

The Study of Presidential Leadership. So vast and inchoate has the presidency become as an institution, so protean its powers and responsibilities, so complex and even fragile some of the sources and tools of

presidential leadership, that scholars even more than Presidents have had difficulty coming to intellectual terms with it. The most widely used approach to the study of the presidency—and of presidential leadership—has been the biography. Biographies during the presidency's first century tended to be hagiographical in their treatment of Chief Executives such as Washington, Jefferson, and Lincoln; during the presidency's second century biographies tended to test Presidents in terms of their leadership skills. Both approaches influenced how voters felt about Presidents and how the Presidents viewed their predecessors and themselves. But the analytical and evaluative frameworks through which presidencies were interpreted varied so widely as to make these studies inadequate for defining and evaluating presidential leadership. The most common test of Presidents has been to measure PRESIDENTIAL GREATNESS; political scientists, historians, and even citizens (through sample surveys) have been asked to evaluate Chief Executives as "Great," "Near-Great," "Average," and so on—but without there being any definition of greatness. After two centuries we knew almost everything about individual Presidents but much less about the presidency.

A more sophisticated approach to understanding presidential leadership has been the analysis of presidential power. Since resources of presidential power—patronage, skill, electoral and congressional support, access to funds, and the like—can be measured and to some degree quantified, the power-analysis approach has been especially useful for transactional situations in which both presidential and nonpresidential power resources could be estimated. But it is equally apparent that "presidential power" does not easily translate, in theory or practice, into "presidential leadership" broadly construed. To understand leadership per se requires an analysis of the motivations behind the agenda of both the President and those he sought to influence, as well as analysis of the economic, social, political, and cultural context in which leadership is being exercised.

An approach to the understanding of presidential leadership that combines several perspectives may be called the biographical-institutional-power concept, with *institutional* defined as including both constitutional and extraconstitutional arrangements. From this perspective three patterns may be discerned: the Madisonian pattern, emphasizing checks and balances, minority rights (including protection against majority rule), and limited government; the Jeffersonian pattern, embracing concepts of unified party leadership, majority rule, minority opposition with protected rights, and purposeful, collegial government; and the Hamiltonian pattern, emphasizing heroic leadership, personal organizations as leadership bases, expedient use of power, and a protected but disorganized opposition. All these patterns call for presidential leadership but with markedly different dimensions and impacts.

The biographical-institutional-power approach to presidential leadership is more sophisticated if placed in a cultural context. As the models have developed over the years, the Madisonian pattern, with its emphasis on personal liberty against government, can be seen as reflecting the powerful individualistic dimensions of American thought and behavior; the Jeffersonian pattern may be viewed as representing the almost-as-powerful egalitarian concept of achieving class, gender, and racial equality through government; and the Hamiltonian pattern as embodying hierarchical arrangements and aiming primarily at the maintenance of order and stability, at least for the short run.

Other approaches to understanding presidential leadership include the psychobiographical, which heavily emphasizes the early psychological development of those who became President and character analysis, which uses both psychological and sociological explorations of pre-presidential experiences as helping to explain and even predict presidential behavior. Still another approach is the concept of transforming leadership, which examines the extent to which Presidents do not merely employ transactional methods—such as bargaining, negotiating, and brokering—to influence the behavior of others but sometimes transcend short-run and ephemeral exchanges. In so doing they mobilize followers by responding to their wants and needs; raise them through levels of aspiration, expectation, and entitlement; and, ultimately, convert followers into new leaders who put demands on the original leaders, thus producing a climate of collective leadership.

This last kind of study—that of the transforming interrelationship of leaders and followers, president and people—contributed most to the study of presidential leadership in the 1980s and 1990s. This approach will contribute to and gain from trends in social history emphasizing the dynamic role of local and communal leadership in the shaping of presidential leadership and the impact of that collective leadership, horizontal and vertical, on the economic and social grassroots. This approach will integrate well with studies of the "cobblestone leadership" that has helped transform old dictatorships into struggling democracies, and it may counterbalance overemphasis on the "great man" approach to presidential leadership.

Presidential leadership, variously benign and malign, heavy-handed and sensitive, hierarchical and participatory, egalitarian and elitist, is here to stay as an indispensable part of the American political system; the key question is whether the practitioners and the scholars together can variously comprehend its nature, exploit its power, and help a democratic electorate tame the elephant.

BIBLIOGRAPHY

Adams, John. *Defense of the Constitution of Government of the United States of America.* 1787–1788.

Barber, James David. *The Presidential Character.* 1985.

Buchanan, Bruce. *The Citizen's Presidency.* 1986.

Burns, James MacGregor. *Presidential Government.* 1973.

Cronin, Thomas E. *The State of the Presidency.* 1980.

Edwards, George C., III, and Stephen J. Wayne. *Presidential Leadership.* 1985.

Ellis, Richard, and Aaron Wildavsky, *Dilemmas of Presidential Leadership.* 1989.

Goldsmith, William M. *The Growth of Presidential Power.* 3 vols. 1974.

Hargrove, Erwin C. *The Power of the Modern Presidency.* 1974.

Kellerman, Barbara. *The Political Presidency.* 1984.

Madison, James, Alexander Hamilton, and John Jay. *The Federalist.* 1787–1788.

Seligman, Lester G., and Cary R. Covington. *The Coalitional Presidency.* 1989.

JAMES MACGREGOR BURNS

PRESIDENTIAL RECORDS ACT (1978). Traditionally, when the President left office, he took his papers with him. As the years passed, however, the propriety and wisdom of this practice came into question. Historians became alarmed that such papers were accidently destroyed, lost, and sometimes only selectively released for scrutiny. Archivists lamented the resulting omissions in the national government record. Not only were entire files carried away, but also presidential correspondence sometimes was retrieved from departmental files. The undefined concept of PRESIDENTIAL PAPERS, indeed, knew no bounds. This aspect of the practice became particularly troublesome in the aftermath of the establishment of the EXECUTIVE OFFICE OF THE PRESIDENT. Franklin D. Roosevelt created a panoply of emergency and wartime agencies within this domain, all of which closely served the President and, therefore, were regarded as producers of presidential papers. The removal of the documentary materials of such agencies constituted both a records-management problem and a difficulty of maintaining a continuity of administration.

A policy change grew out of federal inquiries into possible White House involvement in a June 1972 burglary at Democratic national committee offices located in the Watergate apartment complex in Washington, D.C. These investigations eventually led to President Richard M. Nixon resigning from office on 9 August 1974. In order to assure the integrity and availability of White House records for federal prosecutors pursuing various aspects of the Watergate affair, Congress approved the Presidential Recordings and Materials Preservation Act of 1974 (88 Stat. 1695). It placed the official papers and records of President Nixon under federal custody and established the temporary National Study Commission on Records and Documents of Federal Officials. Created "to study problems and questions with respect to the control, disposition, and preservation of records and documents produced by or on behalf of Federal officials," the panel issued a final report in March 1977.

Responding to some of the commission's recommendations, Congress, in November 1978, passed a law known as the Presidential Records Act (92 Stat. 2523). Carefully defining "presidential papers" and covering all such materials created on or after 20 January 1981, the statute effectively makes presidential papers federal property, which is to remain under the custody and control of the Archivist of the United States when each incumbent President leaves the White House. In December 1992, a federal appellate court ruled that former President Nixon had a "compensable interest" in his presidential papers. Because the 1974 statute required federal possession of the materials, Nixon was entitled to just compensation.

BIBLIOGRAPHY

U.S. National Study Commission on Records and Documents of Federal Officials. *Final Report.* 1977.

HAROLD C. RELYEA

PRESIDENTIAL STRATEGIES (VIETNAM).
The Vietnam decision-making strategies of Presidents Dwight D. Eisenhower and Lyndon B. Johnson offer a unique comparison of two Presidents confronting a similar—although not identical—national security problem, in the same region of the world, against a common adversary, and in a situation in which American-backed forces were in danger of defeat. In both instances, the President and his circle of advisers engaged in a prolonged and at times intense process of deliberation. Within each administration, opinion varied on the central question of whether the United States should intervene militarily; both Eisenhower and Johnson were exposed to views favoring intervention and opposing intervention, as well as options that

ranged between them. Each President also operated within a political environment that—at least at the start of deliberations—did not dictate or otherwise unduly determine whatever course they might choose to follow; public opinion and Congress were thus open to presidential leadership and direction at the outset of each episode.

Eisenhower and Johnson, however, differed in their ultimate policy choices. In 1954, with French colonial forces in danger of defeat by the Communist Viet Minh, especially at the beleaguered French outpost at Dien Bien Phu, Eisenhower decided not to intervene. At the Geneva peace conference held in the summer of 1954 after Dien Bien Phu had fallen, Vietnam (the most important part of what was then called Indochina) was partitioned, an outcome that probably represented the best possible solution short of an improbable victory by French or American military force. Only months later, the Indochina crisis was largely forgotten. In 1965, Lyndon Johnson took a different course, moving incrementally from 23,000 American advisory personnel at the start of that year to an authorized deployment in late July of some 200,000 American troops. In announcing his decision, Johnson left open the possibility that more might come; his commitment in the Vietnam War would soon reach some one-half million American troops, divide the nation, and undermine his presidency.

Eisenhower's Strategy. The strategies each President followed in coming to an eventual decision also differed significantly. Eisenhower relied on a decision-making process that had both a well-articulated formal structure and a lively process of informal contact and deliberation. The formal component of his advisory system was the National Security Council machinery that had been developed the year before. This consisted of a National Security Council that not only met weekly during Eisenhower's presidency but was expanded beyond its statutory membership to include, among others, the Secretary of the Treasury and the Attorney General. Meetings of the NSC were preceded by extensive staff work by the NSC Planning Board, a committee of second-level departmental officials who crafted the papers for discussion by the NSC. Meetings of the NSC were followed, in turn, by the work of the Operations Coordinating Board, which was charged with facilitating the implementation of national security decisions. The entire process was coordinated by the President's Special Assistant for National Security (Robert Cutler in 1954), who not only took an active role in the work of the Planning Board and the OCB, but acted as a managerial custodian of the NSC's deliberations: making sure discussion stayed on track, encouraging the presentation of a full range of policy views, exploring the implications and consequences of options under consideration but avoiding acting as a policy advocate. In short, Eisenhower relied on a formal advisory system that was deliberately designed to yield a range of well-explored policy options and have them fully aired at the highest reaches of his administration.

The formal NSC machinery did not stand alone, however, and was complemented by a range of informal avenues of information and advice. In 1954, these included frequent private meetings and other conversations between the President and his Secretary of State, JOHN FOSTER DULLES, as well as other persons in the President's wide network of informal confidants, in and out of government. Eisenhower also constituted ad hoc advisory groups at the outset of his deliberations, one of which was under the direction of his longtime associate, Under Secretary of State Walter Bedell Smith, and which provided him with policy advice separate from that of the NSC. Eisenhower's reliance on Dulles and the work of Smith's group were especially instrumental in the creation of, initially, an "area plan" that envisioned a region-wide solution to the crisis and, eventually, the proposal for "united action": a multilateral effort in the region that potentially threatened intervention by the Allies but may have actually been designed to bolster French resolve at Geneva and deter a complete communist takeover of the region.

Eisenhower's use of both formal and informal strategies of decision making is particularly noteworthy. The two ad hoc advisory groups provided a range of carefully reasoned advice to the President. But while they deliberated, debate continued in the NSC, some of which was directed at papers produced by the Planning Board and some triggered by unfolding events. These meetings were generally marked by lively and spirited discussion among the participants, Eisenhower included. Minutes of the NSC meetings (declassified in the mid 1980s) indicate little evidence of reticence among those present in expressing their views, even if they challenged those of the President, nor of tailoring their advice to what they perceived as the President's or the group's favored course of action.

The formal NSC process fostered vigorous policy debate, but its direct impact on Eisenhower's decisions is less clear. Many key decisions, especially Eisenhower's choice not to intervene unilaterally, were made in informal contexts and on the basis of the President's own judgments and considerable military and foreign policy expertise. But the formal NSC process did encourage Eisenhower and his advisers to rethink and

defend their policy views, thereby providing a useful check on decisions made on a more informal basis. The NSC process also provided a sounding board for Eisenhower's propensity to think out loud about possible courses of action. For example, his seeming willingness, at the start of the crisis, to consider an air strike to relieve the French troops surrounded at Dien Bien Phu and later his increasing realization that such a military effort would draw the United States further into the conflict and lead to greater levels of American involvement may have been influenced by the reactions of his associates (as well as his own recognition of the scale and difficulty of becoming enmeshed in a land war in Asia).

Eisenhower's own contributions to the decision-making process were also considerable. Not only did the President exercise his own judgment in making a final decision—there was no voting in the NSC as was commonly thought in the 1950s—but he possessed an acutely developed cognitive style that enabled him to capitalize on the information and advice before him. At key points in the 1954 episode, for example, he was able to think strategically about the events in Indochina and their relevance to American interests; his vast military experience enabled him to understand the pitfalls of American military involvement on the Asian mainland; he routinely thought in terms of the advantages and disadvantages presented by policy alternatives; he placed the question of intervention in Indochina within the larger and more comprehensive pattern of world politics; and he often cut through complexities by rendering "net judgments" that got at the core of the issue under consideration. Eisenhower's own expertise and cognitive skills thus complemented his effective use of an advisory system designed to foster an informed and rational process of policy choice.

Johnson's Strategy. Lyndon Johnson's strategy of decision making in 1965 stands in almost direct contrast with Eisenhower's. In late 1964 through early February of 1965, Johnson was initially cautious if not undecided about what course he wished to pursue in defending South Vietnam. On several occasions in 1964 he elected not to respond to communist attacks on American facilities in South Vietnam and various archival documents from this period reveal a President with mixed feelings about how and whether to use American military force in Vietnam. Although generally in agreement that the deteriorating situation required some American response, Johnson's advisers also differed about what to do. Ambassador Maxwell Taylor in Saigon favored retaliatory air strikes if not an extensive air war against the enemy. NSC adviser McGeorge Bundy and Defense Secretary ROBERT S.

McNamara became increasingly convinced of the merits of American troops in Vietnam, but Secretary of State Dean Rusk and Under Secretary of State George Ball were reluctant to involve American military force in a prolonged and active role. Johnson, for his part, had reservations about air strikes, preferring to use U.S. unconventional forces.

Although in late January 1965, Bundy informed Johnson that the administration was at a crossroads over Vietnam and that alternatives needed to be developed and argued out, no thorough review of policy was undertaken of the sort Eisenhower had ordered at the outset of the 1954 crisis. Instead, events drove decisions: an attack on an American military installation at Pleiku led to a decision to engage in retaliatory bombing of North Vietnam, which quickly slid into a policy of sustained bombing against the North—Operation Rolling Thunder. Several weeks following the attack, Johnson also authorized, with very little discussion among his advisers or by the NSC, the introduction of several Marine battalions into South Vietnam. These troops were initially sent to guard U.S. air bases, but gradually their military mission increased: the area they were authorized to patrol expanded first to ten miles around U.S. bases, then to thirty miles, and, by 1 June 1965, to fifty miles; shortly thereafter the U.S. military commander in South Vietnam, General William Westmoreland, was given authority to use U.S. forces in any way he deemed fit. The number of American forces also grew: 82,000 troops were authorized for deployment in early June, 95,000 by mid June, 125,000 by early July and almost 200,000 by late July. Yet during this period, little consideration was given to the results of increasing escalation: U.S. forces had yet to engage the enemy in a battle in which they chose to stand and fight nor was much known about the effects of the air war on the enemy's military infrastructure and morale.

Johnson's advisers held a broad spectrum of views yet the advisory process was so disorganized and Johnson's management of it so haphazard that they were never channeled into focused debate. Much of Eisenhower's formal NSC machinery had been dismantled by President John F. Kennedy: the Planning Board and OCB were gone and policy advice was now coordinated by an NSC special assistant who acted as a policy advocate not a managerial custodian. Kennedy's distrust of formal advisory processes was shared by his successor. From October 1964 until the attack at Pleiku, Johnson did not convene a single meeting of the NSC. During the Pleiku crisis a number of NSC meetings were called, but the NSC then met only four times—all briefly—between 1 April and Johnson's

announcement in late July of an open-ended commitment.

In March, Johnson shifted to a more informal forum of policy deliberation—Tuesday lunches with a small group of his top advisers. Most lunches had only six participants, and many were attended by only three top advisers—McNamara, Rusk, and Bundy. On only one occasion was Joint Chiefs of Staff Chairman Earle Wheeler in attendance. The shift away from the NSC also excluded an increasingly vocal critic of the war, Vice President Hubert H. Humphrey. The limited attendance at the Tuesday lunches narrowed the range of Johnson's policy advice, and at those meetings where only McNamara, Rusk, and Bundy were present, Johnson faced a powerful advocate of escalation (McNamara), an NSC adviser similarly inclined (Bundy), and a Secretary of State reluctant to express his views.

The procedures of the Tuesday lunches were also problematic. Absent a managerial custodian (as Robert Cutler had been in 1954) to keep the meeting on track, discussions tended to be digressive conversations rather than sharply focussed analytic exercises. No notes were kept of proceedings or decisions, and membership beyond the three main participants varied from week to week. Others in the policy process were forced to rely on whatever word of mouth reports might be transmitted to them by those who happened to attend.

Although Johnson was no Caligula, bullying his advisers into acceptance of positions he favored, his interpersonal style often tended to discourage a candid airing of views. A number of participants—of both more hawkish and dovish views—later recounted their reticence in expressing their views. When open discussion did sometimes occur, Johnson often failed to focus on matters that needed examination. Instead, he would frequently turn his attention to narrower matters, such as the selection of bombing targets, thereby failing to explore broader strategic questions, the implications and consequences of increasing American involvement, or the linkage between military involvement and the political, social, and economic reforms needed to defeat the enemy.

In contrast to Eisenhower, Johnson thus lacked both an advisory system that could aid his process of policy choice and the personal skills or interest in undertaking the kind of examination of the problem before him that might lead to its successful resolution. At best, his skills were political: retaining the loyalty of those who increasingly came to have reservations about the course he had incrementally come to accept and downplaying the significance of mounting American involvement in Vietnam to the Congress, press, and the public.

Johnson's decision-making strategy is perhaps best exemplified by the two-week period of deliberations that took place before his announcement on 28 July 1965. Although the meetings were well publicized and seemed to signal a fundamental examination of American policy in Vietnam that many felt was long overdue, Johnson's mind was essentially made up and the ostensible question of whether to engage the United States in a land war on the Asian continent had already largely been settled by the incremental escalation of the prior months. But Johnson could now claim that he had heard all sides of the issue from the country's best and brightest. Moreover, his public announcement on 28 July deliberately portrayed caution and restraint: he announced that American troop strength would only grow from 75,000 to 125,000, not the 175,000 to 200,000 that had in fact been authorized. Only in passing did he seem to acknowledge that this was only the beginning: "I have asked the Commanding General, General Westmoreland, what more he needs to meet this mounting aggression. He has told me. We will meet his needs."

BIBLIOGRAPHY

Berman, Larry. *Planning a Tragedy: The Americanization of the War in Vietnam.* 1982.

Billings-Yun, Melanie. *Decision against War: Eisenhower and Dien Bien Phu, 1954.* 1988.

Burke, John P., and Fred I. Greenstein (with Larry Berman and Richard Immerman). *How Presidents Test Reality: Decisions on Vietnam, 1954 and 1965.* 1989.

Gardner, Lloyd C. *Approaching Vietnam: From World War II through Dienbienphu, 1941–1954.* 1988.

Gelb, Leslie H. with Richard Betts. *The Irony of Vietnam: The System Worked.* 1979.

Gibbons, William C. *The U.S. Government and the Vietnam War: Executive and Legislative Roles and Relationships.* Parts 1, 2, and 3. 1986–1989.

Herring, George C. *America's Longest War: The United States and Vietnam, 1950–1975.* 2d ed. 1986.

Kahin, George McT. *Intervention: How America Became Involved in Vietnam.* 1984.

JOHN P. BURKE

PRESIDENTIAL SUCCESSION ACT (1947). The Presidential Succession Act (61 Stat. 380–381) was the product of a two-year effort by President Harry S. Truman to revise an 1886 law. After becoming President, following Franklin D. Roosevelt's death in April 1945, Truman had been particularly concerned that the nation would not have an elected VICE PRESIDENT for almost four years. Others, both inside and outside Congress, were also troubled by the prospect.

Under the Presidential Succession Law of 1886, the Secretary of State, followed by the other members of the CABINET, constituted the heirs to the presidency after the Vice President. "Since the members of the Cabinet are all presidential appointees," Truman reasoned in his *Memoirs*, "the law gave me the power to appoint my own successor until a new Vice President could be elected." He believed this was a power "no president ought to possess."

On 19 June 1945, in a special message to Congress, Truman urged a revision of the 1886 act in the interest of "orderly, democratic government." It was the Speaker of the House, he contended, "whose selection next to that of the President and Vice President, can most accurately said to stem from the people themselves." Therefore, Congress should enact legislation placing the Speaker "first in order of succession, in case of the removal, death, resignation or inability" of the President and Vice President. If the Speaker was not qualified, the presidency would then pass to the president pro tempore of the Senate. Ten days later, the House, after perfunctory consideration, gave voice-vote approval to legislation incorporating Truman's proposal. The Seventy-ninth Congress (1945–1946), however, concluded without Senate action on the bill.

The political ramifications of the plan changed dramatically in 1946 when the Republicans gained control of Congress for the first time in nearly two decades. Truman remained undaunted. On 7 February 1947, in letters to newly installed Speaker Joseph W. Martin, and President Pro Tempore Arthur H. Vandenberg, both Republicans, he again recommended congressional action.

Despite strong Democratic opposition, the Senate on 27 June approved (50 to 35) a succession bill, similar to the 1945 measure passed by the House. The House overwhelmingly (365 to 11) concurred on 10 July. Opposition derived from doubts about the bill's constitutionality.

The Presidential Succession Act of 1947, embodied virtually all Truman's suggestions. It provided that in case of the death, resignation, removal, disability, or failure of the President and Vice President to qualify, the Speaker of the House, upon resigning as Speaker and Representative, would act as President. The line of succession next passed to the president pro tempore, then to the Secretary of State and other Cabinet officers in the order of the creation of the departments. An individual exercising presidential power under these circumstances was to serve the remainder of the current presidential term except in those instances when a President-elect or a Vice President–elect, who initially failed to qualify, subsequently qualified; or when the disability of an incumbent was removed.

BIBLIOGRAPHY

Joseph E. Kallenbach. "The New Presidential Succession Act." *American Political Science Review* 41 (October 1947): 931–941.

Silva, Ruth C. "The Presidential Succession Act of 1947." *Michigan Law Review* 47 (February 1949): 451–476.

Truman, Harry S. *Memoirs: Year of Decisions.* 1955.

STEPHEN W. STATHIS

PRESIDENTS AND MORAL PHILOSOPHY.
We speak of the need for a public philosophy to explain and justify the functions of the presidency. Theodore Roosevelt introduced Americans to the concept of the BULLY PULPIT, that is, that the President is a moral teacher. Among students of the presidency a school of thought has grown up that places its main emphasis on what Jeffrey Tulis calls the *rhetorical presidency*. Tulis's central thesis is that the early presidency was a teaching presidency. The primary responsibility of the Chief Executive was to explain and defend the Constitution. From George Washington to William McKinley, the President's highest moral and political responsibility was to "speak" the Constitution.

Presidential Worldviews. Whatever the strengths of most modern Presidents, they have displayed little interest in moral philosophy or understanding of history. A consensus exists that the last American President with a developed sense of history was John F. Kennedy. Since history is the companion of philosophy and is sometimes defined as past politics or otherwise linked with the philosophy of history, the lack of a well-developed view of history suggests that for most modern Presidents moral and political philosophy are also lacking.

To the extent that Presidents and their staffs invoke the ideas of philosophy and history, they do so in rather crude and primitive terms. We have only to think of explanatory formulas such as the "Munich syndrome" or the "Vietnam syndrome." To encapsulate the complexities of history in the proposition that aggression anywhere must be resisted at its source or that opposition to a revolutionary nationalist movement's invasion of its neighbors is doomed to fail is hard to sustain. Yet the Munich view prevailed until the VIETNAM WAR and the slogan "never again Vietnam" still has its supporters while serious scholars write of "selective" resistance to aggression.

One reason presidential worldviews sound an uncertain note is the difficulty of distinguishing between Presidents and presidential SPEECHWRITERS. Historians still dispute whether the underlying philosophy of Kennedy's inaugural address reflected Kennedy's philosophy or THEODORE SORENSEN's. Whatever the qualifications of the modern speechwriting corps, a grasp of moral philosophy is generally not one of them. "Read my lips" is more typical of the language of speechwriters than is "Four score and seven years ago." Speechwriters are wordsmiths, not moral philosophers.

Not only the techniques of speechwriting but the demands and requirements of political leadership and the paths to power postwar Presidents have taken make it unlikely that modern Presidents will cultivate moral philosophy. George Bush, we were told, was not a particularly reflective man. He rallied an international coalition to prosecute the PERSIAN GULF WAR not with texts in moral philosophy but through adroit use of the telephone. Based on his experience with the TOWER COMMISSION, national security adviser Brent Scowcroft declared that Ronald Reagan was the least intellectually curious leader he had ever known. Although President Jimmy Carter claimed to have read and absorbed Reinhold Niebuhr's moral philosophy, scholars and journalists questioned his understanding of Niebuhr, finding Carter more the engineer than the philosopher. Gerald Ford is remembered for his mastery of the budget, not for his philosophy. Few would consider Richard M. Nixon or Lyndon Baines Johnson moral philosophers. Kennedy's contemporaries describe him as an activist and a pragmatist. Dwight D. Eisenhower gained public confidence because of his stature as a world leader. Harry S. Truman stands out among Presidents for his decisiveness and his policy initiatives, including the TRUMAN DOCTRINE and the MARSHALL PLAN. Franklin D. Roosevelt was an authentic political genius, but he is praised less for his worldview than for his political instincts.

According to Plato, the role of the philosopher-king is to enhance understanding and not to rule. Historically, the distinction between philosopher and ruler is that between theory and practice, a distinction that some have identified as the most fundamental issue in political philosophy. It is an issue that reappears in different political traditions, as in the assertion of the economic theorist John Maynard Keynes that behind each policy action is the work of some academic scribbler. Therefore, for those who would discover the relation between Presidents and moral philosophy the inquiry must extend beyond looking at American Presidents since World War II. The question goes to the heart of the issue of the relation of contemplation, or reflection, and action.

Sources of Moral Philosphy. If particular Presidents have not been the authors of certain visions of moral philosophy, then where do such ideas originate? Just as it would be claiming too much to argue that the political process is consistently marked by coherence and order, it is equally false to describe it as only chaos and incoherence. The Harvard political scientist Samuel H. Beer argues, "In all the furious motion of campaigns, lobbying and lawmaking, and in the vast and confusing output of statutes, policies, and programs . . . one can discern certain ideas at work." Where are we to find the sources of such ideas?

The sources are at least four in number. They include the great traditions and classics of Western moral and political thought, American writings such as THE FEDERALIST, a few extraordinary Presidents who have spoken for the ages, and major crises in our history that have evoked moral and political formulations and responses. A first, obvious source of ideas of moral philosophy is Greco-Roman and Judeo-Christian thought. The Greek idea of human fulfillment through political participation is a cornerstone idea of democracy: that, as in Aristotle's idea of the acorn realizing itself in the oak, we become what we are intended to be through life in the state. For the classical philosopher, life is eternally unfolding, and the individual in politics strives for virtue as the philosopher seeks wisdom. The core ideas of politics in the Judeo-Christian tradition are, on one hand, the sanctity and infinite worth of the individual, and, on the other, a denial of human perfectibility. From the former stems the American proposition that government derives its just powers from the consent of the governed, from the latter the need for CHECKS AND BALANCES and SEPARATION OF POWERS. The contributions of these two traditions are fundamental to the American experiment.

A second source is the writings of the Founders and the thought of leaders whose works remain central to our moral and political tradition. THE FEDERALIST remains the best textbook in democratic political theory. Its authors nourished their moral and political understanding through appropriating an inheritance of two thousand years of experience of politics and philosophy in the West. ALEXANDER HAMILTON, James Madison, and JOHN JAY were as conscious of the lessons of political experience in ancient Greece as in Britain and the colonies. From *The Federalist* to postwar thinkers such as Niebuhr and Walter Lippmann, American Presidents have had access to a body rich in moral and political thought.

The third source comprises the small group of Presidents who are exceptions to the rule that Presidents are not moral philosophers. Who can doubt that Abraham Lincoln offered the Republic a vision of faith and politics that endures to the present day? Who

but Lincoln among our Presidents could have spoken of bringing an "unnecessary and injurious" war to a conclusion? Where can one find a definition of liberty to match his analysis of contradictory perspectives: "The shepherd drives the wolves from the sheep's throat, for which the sheep thanks the shepherd as a liberator, while the wolf denounces him for the same act as the destroyer of liberty." We still turn to George Washington for understanding of national interest, to Thomas Jefferson for the reconciliation of political order and individual freedom, and to Woodrow Wilson for definitions of congressional government and a new world order. That a small handful of Presidents has joined an equally small group of reflective leaders in other countries—for example, Benjamin Disraeli, W. E. Gladstone, and Winston Churchill in modern England—suggests that all societies are similarly dependent on the rare mind that combines creative moral thought and political leadership.

Finally, the major crises in American history comprise an important source of thought that Presidents have brought to bear on issues of moral and political philosophy. The movers and shakers of the American economic and political order periodically call on one another for a restatement of national goals. Such efforts, however, seem to have negligible results. Setting aside the question of whether the participants have been intellectual figures of the highest distinction, the reasons for failure may be more fundamental. A recitation of the great moral and political statements in American history discloses that each has been linked with a major crisis or a turning point for the Republic. The Declaration of Independence was such a turning point; confronted with the challenge, leaders such as Jefferson rose to the occasion. When Washington was burned in effigy for the PROCLAMATION OF NEUTRALITY, whose critics, such as French envoy Edmond-Charles-Édouard Genet, called on the United States to come to France's assistance in its conflict with Great Britain, the first President helped the citizenry understand the relationship of treaty obligations and the imperatives of NATIONAL SECURITY. No other utterance on SLAVERY could have encompassed the moral dignity of Lincoln's EMANCIPATION PROCLAMATION, forged in the crisis of the CIVIL WAR. So, too, were Wilson's FOURTEEN POINTS the product of crisis—and of the struggle to preserve peace according to the terms of the TREATY OF VERSAILLES following WORLD WAR I. Likewise, Franklin D. Roosevelt's great moral statements—his reassurance that Americans had "nothing to fear but fear itself," the FOUR FREEDOMS, and his contributions to the Charter of the UNITED NATIONS—drew their power from the crisis of WORLD WAR II.

The great historic statements of moral and political philosophy do not emerge full-blown from the knotted brows of Presidents. They are the products of great minds caught up in the challenge of momentous events and circumstances. Some Presidents rise to the challenge, others do not. As we have seen, the majority are not at home with moral philosophy. Yet even for those few philosopher-presidents, profound moral statements have depended as much on the challenges they faced as on their capacity for response. Thus the logic of events merges with the quality of presidential utterances to give us enduring visions of moral philosophy.

BIBLIOGRAPHY

Beer, Samuel H. "In Search of a New Public Philosophy." In *The New American Political System*. Edited by Anthony King. 1978.
Harbaugh, William Henry. *The Life and Times of Theodore Roosevelt*. Rev. ed. 1963.
Hinckley, Barbara. *The Symbolic Presidency: How Presidents Portray Themselves*. 1990.
Morgenthau, Hans J., and David Hein. *Essays on Lincoln's Faith and Politics*. 1983.
Tulis, Jeffrey. *The Rhetorical Presidency*. 1987.

KENNETH W. THOMPSON

PRESIDENT'S FOREIGN INTELLIGENCE ADVISORY BOARD (PFIAB). The President's Foreign Intelligence Advisory Board is the highest-level advisory committee in the U.S. government. The PFIAB was first established in February 1956 by President Dwight D. Eisenhower and was then called the President's Board of Consultants on Foreign Intelligence Activities. Dr. James R. Killian, Jr., president of the Massachusetts Institute of Technology, was its first chairman. When John F. Kennedy was elected President in 1960, he initially decided to abolish the board as a "useless impediment." But after the fiasco of the BAY OF PIGS INVASION in April 1961 he quickly reestablished the board, giving it its current name. The President's Foreign Intelligence Advisory Board has played an important role in guiding America's intelligence policy ever since—except for the four-year hiatus after President Jimmy Carter abolished it in 1977. President Ronald Reagan, by Executive Order 12331, reestablished the board on 20 October 1981.

The board's duties and responsibilities are broad. As spelled out in the executive order establishing it, the "Board shall assess the quality, quantity, and adequacy of intelligence collection, of analysis and estimates, of counterintelligence, and other intelligence activities. The Board shall have the authority to continually review the performance of all agencies of the Government [including the Central Intelligence Agency, the Department of Defense, and the Federal Bureau of Investigation] that are engaged in the collection, evaluation, or production of intelligence or the execution of intelligence policy." The board also is given the authority to assess the "adequacy of management, personnel, and organization in the intelligence agencies."

As set forth in Executive Order 12331 the members of the board, who serve without compensation, are appointed directly by the President and are supposed to be chosen from "trustworthy and distinguished citizens outside the Government who are qualified on the basis of achievement, experience, and independence." The board reports directly to the President, although as a practical matter much of the work of the board is conducted with the President's top NATIONAL SECURITY and intelligence advisers. The board is authorized to directly "advise and make recommendations to the Director of Central Intelligence, the CIA, and other Government agencies engaged in intelligence." All members of the board have access to all information necessary to carry out its duties in the possession of any agency in the Government.

The PFIAB, like its smaller sister, the PRESIDENT'S INTELLIGENCE OVERSIGHT BOARD (PIOB), derives most of its power and influence from its ability to access highly classified information and to deal directly with the President. While it shares with the PIOB the weaknesses of not having a large investigative staff or subpoena powers, it does have a much larger membership, often twenty or more, and a substantially larger staff. Moreover, the domain of PFIAB, unlike that of PIOB, is policy, not policing. In the area of intelligence policy, a board of twenty or more highly competent people, backed by a half a dozen or so professional staff members, can be a formidable force.

During the 1980s the board included such distinguished men and women as Frank Borman, the former astronaut; W. Glenn Campbell, the director of the Hoover Institution; John B. Connally, former governor of Texas; Alan Greenspan, noted economist; Leon Jaworksi, the former director of the Office of the Watergate special prosecutor; Claire Booth Luce, former ambassador to Italy; H. Ross Perot, chairman of Electronic Data Systems Corporation; and Edward Bennett Williams, the noted lawyer.

While the work that PFIAB has done is unusually highly classified and every member is required on appointment to sign an agreement "never to reveal any classified information obtained by virtue of his or her service with the Board except to the President or to such persons as the President may designate," there have been a few published studies that give some clues concerning the type of issues and problems with which the board is concerned. Some of the things that PFIAB has dealt with in the past include control and coordination of the INTELLIGENCE COMMUNITY, particularly in the area of COVERT OPERATIONS; improved strategic warning systems of a possible nuclear attack on the United States; management of the National Security Agency; the general development and improvement of U.S. intelligence capabilities; improvement of methods of handling sensitive intelligence; more effective coordination and evaluation of covert action; review of CIA paramilitary operations; investigations into satellite reconnaissance systems; and analysis of deficiencies in the collection and analysis of intelligence from Southeast Asia.

To a certain degree the PFIAB does for U.S. intelligence what civilian control in the Department of Defense does for the military. The board is only a part-time board and it has no power of command, but its presence has proved to be a healthy one for U.S. intelligence.

The power and influence of the PFIAB has risen and fallen under different administrations. It was strong under Eisenhower. After a shaky start with Kennedy it regained its foothold and continued strong through Lyndon B. Johnson, Richard M. Nixon, and Gerald Ford. After its demise under Carter, it was resurrected by Reagan and from 1981 to 1985 it regained the kind of influence it had had under Eisenhower. But in October 1985, President Reagan, on the advice of staff, sharply reduced the membership of the board from twenty-one to fourteen, cutting its effectiveness. President George Bush, a former Director of the CIA, went even further and slashed the membership back to six people early in his first term.

The PFIAB is the classic example of an outside group of private citizens, not on the public payroll, directly advising the President on important policy matters. Such a group of outside advisers can be a bracing tonic for any President, helping him to keep from becoming insulated and isolated from the bad news that WHITE HOUSE STAFF is often reluctant to deliver. Unfortunately, outside advisory groups of private citizens are often seen as threats by the President's closest advisers, especially the insecure ones, and these advisory groups are perpetually the subject of abolition attempts.

BIBLIOGRAPHY

Anderson, Martin. *Revolution*. 1988.
Cline, Ray S. *The CIA under Reagan, Bush, and Casey*. 1981.
The President's Foreign Intelligence Advisory Board (PFIAB). 1981.

MARTIN ANDERSON

PRESIDENT'S INTELLIGENCE OVERSIGHT BOARD (PIOB). The President's Intelligence Oversight Board was first established by President Gerald Ford on 17 February 1976 by Executive Order 11905. Its creation was a direct result of a series of allegations and revelations of improper activity by elements of the U.S. intelligence community. This small, virtually unknown board of three people appointed by the President is charged with the daunting task of keeping U.S. intelligence agencies honest and operating within the law. Reporting directly to the President, the board has potential access to the most secret intelligence information. This combination of knowledge and access to the President gives the Board its potential power.

The formal duties of the Intelligence Oversight Board are to inform the President of intelligence activities that any member of the board believes are in violation of the Constitution or of the laws governing the United States, EXECUTIVE ORDERS, or presidential directives; to forward to the ATTORNEY GENERAL reports received concerning intelligence activities that the board believes may be unlawful; to review the internal guidelines of each agency within the INTELLIGENCE COMMUNITY concerning the lawfulness of intelligence activities; to review the practices and procedures of the inspectors general and general counsel of the intelligence community for discovering and reporting intelligence activities that may be unlawful or contrary to executive order or presidential directives; and to conduct such investigations as the board deems necessary to carry out its function under this order.

The idea of an independent presidential advisory group, acting as a watchdog on the U.S. intelligence community, has enjoyed broad support since its inception in 1976, even though the results have not been as desirable as hoped for. The events that led up the IRAN-CONTRA AFFAIR in the mid 1980s entirely escaped the attention of the Intelligence Oversight Board until the scandal burst into public view. In hindsight this should not have been unexpected. Although the PIOB does have the authority to request classified material of any nature and reports directly to the President, its powers do not match its responsibilities.

The PIOB operates with a tiny staff, essentially a secretary and an executive director, and does not have the administrative support to conduct thorough, comprehensive investigations on its own. Nor does it have the power to subpoena witnesses and compel testimony, even in cases of NATIONAL SECURITY. As presently constituted, the board must rely primarily on what others report and on its own judgment regarding the questions it puts to high-ranking members of the intelligence agencies. To a great degree the board relies on moral suasion and the reflected authority of the President.

BIBLIOGRAPHY

Anderson, Martin. *Revolution.* 1988.
Sciaroni, Bretton G. "The Theory and Practice of Executive Branch Intelligence Oversight." *Harvard Journal of Law & Public Policy* 12 (Spring 1989): 397–432.

MARTIN ANDERSON

PRESS AND THE PRESIDENCY, HISTORY OF. When George Washington departed for MOUNT VERNON at the end of his presidency, leaving behind him a record of antagonism, even hatred, toward the press, he canceled his subscriptions to some thirty newspapers. In retirement, he renewed most of them, and spent the last evening of his life reading a local paper and discussing the news. That has been more or less the pattern of relationships between Presidents and the press from Washington's time to the present.

The President's powers have gradually accumulated a sweeping authority. The media—press, radio, and television—have also become more powerful; constitutionally the only check on them is the libel laws. This fact has been difficult for most Presidents to accept.

The Early Republic. President Washington, like his successors, tried to manage the news whenever he could. Yet JAY'S TREATY (1794), for instance, was leaked to the press by its opponents before Congress could even consider it. In Washington's time, the press was in the hands of political parties. Newspapers were scurrilous propaganda organs; Washington was often outraged by the criticism of opposition papers.

John Adams, a more aggressive President, signed into law the infamous ALIEN AND SEDITION ACTS. The Sedition Act punished critics of the government. Adams, like so many others, believed that the press should present America in the best possible light. The FEDERALIST PARTY began to decline partly because of the opposition press; Adams never forgave the newspapers for their part in it.

President Thomas Jefferson, who was attacked as intensely as Washington and Adams had been, opposed federal power over the press but encouraged state prosecutions for seditiously libeling him and his administration. In the abstract, however, Jefferson championed the freedom of the press.

President James Madison, who had done so much to ensure the adoption of First Amendment freedoms, became a victim of press criticism, mainly due to the unpopular WAR OF 1812. The political parties began to lose control of the press, and editors became more interested in news than in party propaganda. News-

papers expressed dissent when they thought it was called for, against both the government and the party in power. In New England, the Federalist press, which opposed the war, excoriated Madison's ineffective war policies.

During the MEXICAN WAR (1846–1847), or "Mr. Polk's War," as some of the President's press critics called it, there was great dissent. President James K. Polk equated dissent with treason. Although the war was a military success, the country was divided by it. Minorities in both political parties and the opposition press did not stop it, but they did affect the outcome of the treaty (1848), the terms of which Polk would have preferred not to accept.

The Civil War and After. The first great battle between President and press, however, came with the CIVIL WAR. President Abraham Lincoln, whose nomination had been largely achieved by two Chicago newspaper editors, Joseph Medill and Charles Ray, endured more vicious criticism from the press than any President before or since. Yet Lincoln exhibited both patience and leniency in dealing with his opposition in the press. Lincoln was adept at using the newspapers as sounding boards, speaking often to reporters covering the White House. He began the presidential PRESS CONFERENCE, although on a purely informal basis.

He sought a careful balance between NATIONAL SECURITY in wartime and freedom of the press. In his zeal to save the nation, Lincoln, however, permitted widespread censorship and suppression of the press. Some COPPERHEAD editors were thrown into jail without being formally charged. Telegraph companies were censored, and generals were even allowed to suppress newspapers on their own intitiative. After Lincoln's assassination, mob censorship appeared again.

During the administration of Ulysses S. Grant, reporters exposed numerous scandals. Soon after Grant's inauguration, newspapers disclosed that he had appointed forty-eight kinsmen to PATRONAGE positions. His rich friends, the papers revealed, had showered him with expensive gifts, and his brother-in-law was involved in a conspiracy to rig the gold market. Most papers thought Grant was innocent. In his second inaugural address, Grant declared that he had been "the subject of abuse and slander scarcely ever equaled in political history."

The press then exposed Grant's Vice President and others in the administration for accepting stock in the Union Pacific Railway. In 1876, the *New York Herald* disclosed corruption in the War Department, which resulted in the impeachment of Secretary of War William W. Belknap, who was accused of taking bribes.

The *St. Louis Democrat* exposed the WHISKEY RING fraud—a conspiracy of federal revenue officials, led by a Grant appointee, to defraud the government of tax moneys. In all, two-hundred and thirty-six people were indicted, including Grant's private secretary. In his final message to Congress, Grant referred to these scandals as "errors of judgment."

Presidents continued to contend with the press. President William McKinley did his best to resist pressure from jingoistic New York publishers, William Randolph Hearst and Joseph Pulitzer, to go to war with Spain. His successor, President Theodore Roosevelt, acclaimed by the press as a trustbuster assailed the press when it turned to muckraking and exposed the corruption of some of the big business interests that supported him and the Republican Party.

Roosevelt was so incensed by the *New York World's* investigation of an alleged scandal involving PANAMA CANAL financing that he tried to get Pulitzer, the paper's publisher, indicted for libel and thrown into jail. The indictment was quashed by a federal judge, a decision upheld unanimously by the Supreme Court.

How far could the press go in criticizing a President? In the several actions resulting from this test of presidential power and government control of the press the Supreme Court on appeal ruled in effect that the federal government could not sue newspapers for criminal libel in its own courts. Roosevelt had attempted, for the first time, to assert the doctrine that the rights of the Chief Executive superseded First Amendment rights or any law that happened to interfere with presidential authority.

The Twentieth Century. Upon taking office President Woodrow Wilson declared that he believed in "pitiless publicity" for public business and instituted the first formal White House press conference. Near the end of his presidency, he confided to a friend, "Don't believe anything you read in the newspapers."

President G. Warren Harding, the only newspaper publisher ever to occupy the White House, began with the best press relations any president ever enjoyed, but by the time of his death relations with the press had deteriorated.

The advent of radio, followed by television, brought a whole new dimension to the relationship between Presidents and the press. Electronic media and their immense power were not envisioned by the Framers of the First Amendment. When the government assumed control of the new wireless telegraphy in 1912 and 1913, it intended to separate the legitimate needs of the armed forces from the uncontrolled activities of the ham operators, by assigning separate frequencies.

Congress passed the Radio Act of 1927 because the burgeoning radio industry was beseeching it to end the chaos of unregulated frequencies. The Communications Act of 1934, creating the Federal Communications Commission (FCC) was not thought of at first as anything more than further technical regulation. Slowly, however, the increasingly vital matter of news broadcasting came under the constant threat of government censorship, through the implied powers of FCC. Congress refused to take seriously the idea that First Amendment protection should be extended to broadcasting.

Presidents were quick to seize radio, and then television, as a political tool of immense influence. Franklin D. Roosevelt, with his FIRESIDE CHATS on the radio, was the first to demonstrate how a popular President could enhance his popularity. Subsequent Presidents, including John F. Kennedy, Lyndon B. Johnson, Richard M. Nixon, and Ronald Reagan, demonstrated how the power of the presidency can be used to command the simultaneous attention of millions of people for purposes of political persuasion as well as for bringing the presidency closer to the voters.

All these Presidents condemned the newspapers from time to time, as their predecessors had done before them. In the end Roosevelt, who had enjoyed the affection of most voters and was said by admiring reporters to be the best managing editor in the country, was disillusioned with his treatment by the press. As William Allen White, editor of the *Emporia Gazette*, put it, Roosevelt believed the press had "utterly misunderstood and entirely misconstrued and misconstructed the motives underlying the presentation of the news."

President Harry S. Truman shared the common presidential belief that the press did not reflect public opinion. His brushes with the press were well publicized. But like President Dwight D. Eisenhower, his personal feelings did not seriously hamper his relationships with reporters and editors. Eisenhower was so popular that he experienced minimum dissent from the press; nevertheless, he believed the press was often unfair to him and his administration and misrepresented public opinion. Yet, both of these Presidents in their press conferences got on relatively well with the media.

When John F. Kennedy became President a new era of press relations began. Kennedy manipulated the press shrewdly and used television with an adroitness not seen before. His administration first advanced the notion that the government had an inherent right to lie, if necessary, and to use the media to do it.

Presidents Johnson and Nixon utilized this notion as a modus operandi, notably during the VIETNAM WAR. From the beginning of his political life, Nixon exhibited a hostility toward the media. Ironically, before the WATERGATE AFFAIR, Nixon had had the editorial support of about 80 percent of the nation's newspapers throughout his political career. Yet he was convinced that the media, especially television, were against him.

As a former actor, President Ronald Reagan understood how to use television far more effectively than his predecessors. Although he gave relatively few press conferences, Reagan succeeded, according to some media observers, in intimidating and controlling media coverage. In addition, he used the publicity machinery of the White House, which had begun to expand in the Nixon era and had reached formidable proportions by 1980, to influence the public in ways that sometimes more than matched the media. Nonetheless, Reagan left office critical of the media.

The tension between Presidents and the media is a good thing because the adversarial relationship means that many sides of public questions will be vented.

[*See also* MEDIA, PRESIDENT AND THE; PRESS RELATIONS.]

BIBLIOGRAPHY

Lorant, Stefan. *The Presidency.* 1951.

Mott, Frank Luther. *American Journalism.* 3d ed. 1952.

Nevins, Allen, ed. *American Press Opinion, Washington to Coolidge.* 1928.

Pollard, James E. *The Presidents and the Press.* 1972

Tebbel. John. *A Compact History of the American Newspaper.* 1963.

Tebbel, John, and Sarah Miles Watts. *The Press and the Presidency.* 1985.

JOHN TEBBEL

PRESS CONFERENCES. The presidential press conference is a permanent feature of the modern presidency. It is a forum of executive presentation that has proved to be a fixed aspect of PRESIDENTIAL LEADERSHIP, yet it is flexible in that a President may choose to use it in different ways. Each President since Franklin D. Roosevelt has felt the need to publicly respond to the queries of newspeople, but Presidents have varied widely in the degree to which they have enjoyed the experience and found it a useful tool.

Both Presidents and reporters grouse about press conferences, but these events work to the advantage of both sides in Presidents' PRESS RELATIONS. Both find them useful forums for explanations of presidential policy, goals, and actions. Such forums are to the President's advantage because he can meet with the press in a place of his choosing and at a time of his liking. He can choose to answer questions as he wishes, with reporters unable to force him to respond to unwanted queries. On the other side, the news media regard news conferences as events worth covering.

Unlike many other events, the press conference is one in which news organizations play a significant role. Their reporters have the opportunity to shape the questioning without guidance or control from the White House.

Development of Press Conferences. The routine relationship between reporters and the President crystalized during the administration of Theodore Roosevelt. He set aside a room for the use of the press and spoke regularly with a select group of reporters. In the afternoons he would regularly meet with half a dozen reporters while he was being shaved by the White House barber. Roosevelt's remarks to reporters were off the record; their value lay in reporters' gaining a greater understanding of the President's policies and actions. The opportunity to query the President regularly proved useful for both sides: it produced better-informed news stories, and, from the President's viewpoint, those stories were more favorable than they might otherwise have been.

Even after the dynamic Roosevelt left office, reporters remained very interested in presidential news. If the President did not provide it, people on his staff had to. While William Howard Taft met sporadically with groups of reporters during his years in the White House, Woodrow Wilson formally established the regularly scheduled press conference. Wilson decided that he would rather direct the distribution of information than let others do it for him. In 1913 and 1914, he met with reporters on Mondays and Thursdays; in 1915, he met with them once a week, on Tuesdays. After 1915 the conferences dropped off due to increasing international tension, as evidenced by the sinking of the British luxury liner *Lusitania*.

Two central features of the format established by Wilson remain: press conferences are open to reporters who are eligible to cover the President, and the reporters lead the questioning. Present practice differs, however, in that the President can call a conference whenever he likes rather than on a predetermined day of the week. Too, press conferences are now broadcast live on television, as they have been since the John F. Kennedy administration. Obviously, at formal press conferences the President's remarks are for direct attribution. As an instrument of policy making, particularly domestic policy, which relies heavily on Congress for its enactment, the press conference has continued to be an important element of presidential leadership of PUBLIC OPINION. Press conferences have been especially important when the President is actively promoting a legislative agenda and experiencing good political weather. Thus it became a central part of Franklin Roosevelt's publicity strategies when he was pushing congressional enactment of the NEW DEAL agenda. During WORLD WAR II, however, Roosevelt's conferences fell off from their earlier twice-weekly schedule.

Roosevelt's successors have found that the press conference has become an indispensable event on the presidential calendar. The average number of press conferences per month from the administration of Franklin Roosevelt through the third year of the George Bush administration, however, fell from 6.9 (for Roosevelt) to around 2 (for Eisenhower, Kennedy, and Johnson), to a low of 0.5 (for Richard M. Nixon). Gerald Ford (1.3) and Jimmy Carter (1.2) met more frequently with the press, but Ronald Reagan matched Nixon's low. George Bush (3.3) nearly matched Harry S. Truman's frequency (3.4). While each President has felt the need to have press conferences, not all have done so on a regular basis. In the period since Eisenhower was President, when an average of two conferences were held per month, only Presidents Johnson and Bush have met that standard.

Difficulties with Press Conferences. Right from the beginning of his presidency, President Nixon was loath to hold press conferences because he and his staff believed that reporters were hostile to him and his programs. His press conferences were consistently contentious. Fed by antagonisms that had built up over the years of the VIETNAM WAR and the WATERGATE AFFAIR, when the White House was less than forthcoming with information the press sought, relations between the President and the press hit a low point that was reached in the Carter years. Reporters' questioning was viewed by officials (and by the public) as rude. Ultimately, the contentiousness lessened during President Bush's first term because of the frequency of his press conferences. Reporters knew they would be able to ask Bush questions and stopped competing for the President's attention in an indecorous manner.

Press conferences are just one strategy in a President's publicity arsenal. He chooses those forums in which he is most comfortable. President Reagan appeared best in settings that were scripted. His finest public hours were speeches in which he captured and articulated the public mood, such as the speech marking the anniversary of the Normandy landing and the speech memorializing the astronauts killed in the explosion of the *Challenger* space shuttle. His habit of summarizing programs and goals in terms of particular cases and anecdotes caused him trouble in press conferences and left his White House Press Office staff with considerable work to explain and refine his statements. Presidents Carter and Ford were quite adept at handling their press conferences, but both

avoided using them when they faced severe criticism, such as when Ford pardoned Nixon and, similarly, when Carter was criticized for his mishandling of the IRANIAN HOSTAGE CRISIS.

Advantages and Disadvantages. Even though reporters choose the questions, Presidents and their staffs are able to make fairly accurate predictions about the nature of the questions that will be posed. WHITE HOUSE STAFF members keep briefing books to make sure that the President is familiar with administration policy and actions. Before a conference, time is spent going over possible responses to the anticipated questions. Yet many Presidents regard such work a waste of time. For example, in the summer of 1979, President Carter stopped holding frequent conferences despite his proficiency in answering questions. Presidents find other disadvantages to them as well. There is always the danger that the President will misstate himself in a way that will have important policy, particularly foreign policy, implications. Presidents fear they will lose more than they gain through their appearances with reporters. They do not like being put in a position of having to deal with questions they would prefer not to.

For most Presidents, however, the advantages of press conferences outweigh the disadvantages. By scheduling and location, a President can control whether a press conference constitutes a high- or low-profile event. If a President wants to appear in command and with the full trappings of the office, as President Reagan preferred, he will schedule his conferences in the East Room of the WHITE HOUSE at an evening hour when he is most likely to get the largest audience. If, on the other hand, the President wants to make his conferences low-profile events, as President Bush chose to do in his first term, he may schedule them very frequently and hold them in the Press Room of the White House or in the auditorium in the Executive Office Building.

The press conference has served as an excellent forum for the President to command national attention. When the President wants to explain a policy or action but does not want to do so in a formal speech before Congress or to the nation, a press conference is often a suitable arena. He can explain policy in his own terms, deciding how he wants to answer questions and free from the pressure of being forced to discuss something he would rather not. He can establish the conference's agenda and, hence, to some extent, the news media's agenda for the following day. The press conference represents one important way for him to dominate the national political scene. When he calls a conference, news organizations and the public generally listen.

BIBLIOGRAPHY

Cornwell, Elmer. *Presidential Leadership of Public Opinion*. 1965.

Grossman, Michael Baruch, and Martha Joynt Kumar. *Portraying the President: The White House and the News Media*. 1981.

Kernell, Samuel. *Going Public: New Strategies of Presidential Leadership*. 1986.

Lammers, William. "Presidential Press Conference Schedules: Who Hides, and When." *Political Science Quarterly* 96 (1981): 261–278.

Maltese, John. *Spin Control: The White House Office of Communications and the Management of Presidential News*. 1992.

Manheim, Jarol. "The Honeymoon's Over: The News Conference and the Development of Presidential Style." *Journal of Politics* 41 (1979): 55–75.

Pollard, James E. *Presidents and the Press*. 1964.

Smith, Carolyn. *Presidential Press Conferences: A Critical Approach*. 1990.

MARTHA KUMAR

PRESS CORPS, WHITE HOUSE. See WHITE HOUSE PRESS CORPS.

PRESS RELATIONS. While nineteenth-century Presidents submitted themselves to occasional private interviews with friendly journalists, the White House was not a regular beat for Washington, D.C., reporters until 1896, when William Price, of the *Washington Star*, stationed himself outside the presidential mansion to interview Grover Cleveland's visitors. Price's initiative inspired imitators, and, on a winter day in 1902, Theodore Roosevelt saw reporters huddled around the north portico and invited them inside. Later that year he had a pressroom built in the new West Wing, which, historian George Juergens notes, "conferred a sort of legitimacy on their presence. . . . They were no longer there as guests of the president."

Woodrow Wilson was the first Chief Executive to hold regular PRESS CONFERENCES, initiated when 125 reporters crowded into the East Room on Saturday afternoon, 15 March 1913, eleven days after Wilson's inauguration. Joseph Tumulty, the President's secretary, also gave a daily briefing for the White House regulars, about thirty reporters from the major news organizations, just as presidential secretary William Loeb had done during Theodore Roosevelt's administration.

Roosevelt and Wilson, unlike William Howard Taft, whose term fell between theirs, both appreciated the importance of news to presidential leadership. And if activist Presidents had uses for the press, so too did the expansionist newspaper and magazine industry want energetic White House occupants who could help it sell its products.

Future Presidents might have learned from the ways Roosevelt and Wilson manipulated the press by taking advantage of the conventions and necessities of news-gathering or simply by intimidating reporters. Roosevelt was the inventor of colorful phrases ("malefactors of great wealth," "BULLY PULPIT," "my hat's in the ring"), precursors of the sound bites of the television age. He was an expert at releasing information to gain maximum attention, sometimes putting out a story on Sunday night that would gain extra coverage on Monday morning, an otherwise slow time for news. He mastered the trial balloon, a technique designed to measure support for a proposal without actually endorsing it. He used calculated leaks of previously secret information, sometimes to undercut an opponent. And he was known to restrict the access of offending reporters.

Wilson eventually stopped holding press conferences, citing national security concerns as his excuse, but Warren G. Harding, the only newspaper editor ever to have been elected President, reinstituted them, insisting, however, that reporters' questions had to be submitted in advance in writing. He also invented the term "White House spokesman" to allow him to speak without direct attribution. Calvin Coolidge and Herbert Hoover continued the written-question rule. Twice-a-week press conferences thus became institutionalized in the 1920s on terms very advantageous to Presidents.

During most of the twentieth century the history of presidential press relations was largely a history of the press conference. At one time the *New York Times* Washington bureau even hired a limousine to get its reporters back to the office, since, according to the journalist James Reston, "Many of these conferences took place near deadline, when it was hard to find a taxi." Franklin D. Roosevelt held 998 press conferences (and one private interview) during his twelve-plus years in office, and, although oral questioning was permitted, most of his answers had to be used without quoting him or on background (meaning without White House attribution) or were off the record (meaning not for publication).

If, as is often assumed, the presidency and the press are adversarially balanced, on a sort of symbolic teeter-totter, the presidency was on the upswing through the administration of Franklin Roosevelt, but it started to come down when Harry S. Truman took office. Responding to the growth of the press corps, Truman moved the sessions—reduced to one a week—out of the OVAL OFFICE, an intimate setting, and into an auditorium called the Indian Treaty Room across the street from the White House. The new format, according to the communications expert Carolyn Smith, changed the atmosphere "from conversation to competitive questioning." Moreover, writes the political scientist Elmer Cornwell, "While F.D.R. was so conspicuously in charge of the conference at all times, Mr. Truman was either disinclined or unable to exert similar control." By the end of the Truman presidency the conferences were being recorded and portions released for use on radio. The next President, Dwight D. Eisenhower, had his conferences filmed for delayed broadcast on television; his successor, John F. Kennedy, inaugurated live TV conferences.

Putting reporters into the picture did not necessarily make them more assertive; it did, however, offer that potential, which was sometimes realized by television journalists on their way to celebrity. Newspaper reporters, at the same time, were being given new freedom (perhaps because of TV competition) to go beyond the "objective" style of wire-service stories to interpretation of a President's performance.

There were various means by which Presidents might counter what they increasingly viewed as a less-than-friendly WHITE HOUSE PRESS CORPS. One way was to hold fewer news conferences. While Eisenhower met the press twice a month, Richard M. Nixon's press conferences averaged one every other month. Another way was to hold conferences with reporters in other regions of the country, who—according to the conventional wisdom of Washington—would be less challenging. A third way, perfected by Ronald Reagan's adviser Michael Deaver, was to lure TV cameras with situations and pictures so compelling that they assured favorable coverage (for example, the scene of the President at a Normandy beach on the fortieth anniversary of D-day). Yet a fourth way was to solicit expert advice and to hire more staff in addition to the White House PRESS SECRETARY and his office. Eisenhower sought the counsel of actor-director Robert Montgomery when preparing for TV appearances. Nixon created an Office of Communications, originally to coordinate governmentwide information efforts. Assistants were assigned to help journalists outside the beltway, that is, outside Washington, D.C. When Presidents were candidates for reelection, other resources were available. As Jeb Magruder, who was deputy director of Nixon's communications office, recalled, "We were seeking not only to speak through the media in the usual fashion—press releases, news conferences—but to speak around the media, much of which we considered hostile, to take our message directly to the people." By the Reagan presidency, according to Gary R. Orren, of Harvard University, approximately 25 percent of the White House senior staff were employed in public relations jobs.

Press relations—the interaction between a President and the journalists who report from the White House—are often described as if they were static. For those who see the interaction between President and press primarily as a political tug-of-war, reporters represent either a liberal or a conservative challenge to the President. Those who attack the press from the right cite evidence, mostly in the form of straw polls, showing that Washington reporters are overwhelmingly in favor of liberal Presidents, presidential policies, and presidential candidates; those who accuse the press of a conservative bias cite evidence of publishers' being overwhelmingly in favor of more conservative Presidents, policies, and candidates.

A portrait that better reflects the fluidity of the relationship, however, has been devised by Michael Baruch Grossman and Martha Joynt Kumar, among others. The Grossman-Kumar scheme shows that interaction between the President and the press goes through three phases during an administration, which Grossman and Kumar call *alliance, competition*, and *detachment*. In their judgment,

> There is a period at the beginning of an administration when the White House and news organizations appear to be allies in producing and disseminating news. This is followed by clashes over news and information so great that the two sides appear to be adversaries. In a third stage the intensity of the competition burns out and is replaced by a relationship that is more structured and less intense than that in either of the first two periods.

The start of a presidency is a time of fermentation. New people and new ideas arrive in Washington, and, from a reporter's point of view, this is a time for good stories. From the President's vantage point, these stories tend to be favorable. Then the administration has its first foreign crisis or its first domestic scandal, weaknesses in personnel begin to appear, and the novelty of new personalities wears off. These things make for good stories for reporters, but they are no longer favorable to the President. Ultimately, President and press, having mutual needs, learn to live with each other like an old married couple who can no longer surprise one another. Finally, reporters begin to look forward to the next President, when the process will start again. Thus the objective of the press to get good stories and the objective of the President to get favorable attention sometimes coincide, sometimes not.

BIBLIOGRAPHY

Cornwell, Elmer E., Jr. *Presidential Leadership of Public Opinion.* 1965.
Grossman, Michael Baruch, and Martha Joynt Kumar. *Portraying the President: The White House and the News Media.* 1981.

Juergens, George. *News from the White House: The Presidential-Press Relationship in the Progressive Era.* 1981.

Maltese, John Anthony. *Spin Control: The White House Office of Communications and the Management of Presidential News.* 1992.

Smith, Carolyn. *Presidential Press Conferences.* 1990.

STEPHEN HESS

PRESS SECRETARY, WHITE HOUSE. See WHITE HOUSE PRESS SECRETARY.

PRIMARIES, PRESIDENTIAL. While state presidential primaries are today the major determinant in deciding who will become the nominees of the major political parties for the nation's highest office, their major influence is a relatively recent development. In the first two presidential elections, in 1789 and 1792, there were no nominations separate from the general election process. The members of the political elite from the various states, acting through the mechanism of the ELECTORAL COLLEGE, chose George Washington by unanimous vote. People of different political persuasions believed that the nation's revered military leader would take the interests of all American citizens into account.

Early Nominating Procedures. Cleavages soon appeared, however, that led to the formation of two major political parties. The FEDERALIST PARTY, led by Washington and ALEXANDER HAMILTON, represented mercantile interests that favored the creation of a national bank (the BANK OF THE UNITED STATES) and created a tariff to protect our manufacturers and merchants from competition from abroad. The rival Democratic-Republicans, represented by Thomas Jefferson and James Madison, opposed the Federalist program on the grounds that it benefited only mercantile interests and not the nation's farmers, with whom they had close ties. By the mid-1790s the two blocs were voting against each other in Congress, and congressional candidates were in effect running as Federalists and Democratic-Republicans. Washington stepped down from the presidency in 1797, and party politics spread from the Congress to the nation's highest office. Since that date the major political parties have experimented with a number of mechanisms designed to nominate the presidential candidates who will run against each other in the general election.

The first such mechanism was the congressional caucus. In this mechanism, members of the national legislature from the two parties formed caucuses, each of which nominated its own presidential candidate. Already convened in the nation's capital, with a knowl-

edge of potential presidential candidates from all over the country, these caucuses provided peer review by members of Congress, who assessed the skills and abilities of persons seeking the presidency. The method had some serious faults. It violated the SEPARATION OF POWERS principle of the constitution by giving members of the legislative branch a major role in choosing the President. Moreover, a party's caucus did not represent those areas that that party had lost in the previous congressional election, not to mention excluding interested and involved citizens who participated in party activities, particularly campaigns. It became impractical for the Federalists when their congressional delegation was so reduced that it ceased to provide adequate geographical representation. The Republicans utilized it between 1800 and 1820 to nominate three Virginians—Jefferson, Madison, and James Monroe—each of whom served as President for two terms. In 1824, however, when the Democratic-Republicans (as the party was now known) attempted to nominate Secretary of the Treasury WILLIAM H. CRAWFORD three-fourths of the Democratic-Republican members of Congress who were friends of Andrew Jackson boycotted the meeting.

For a short period the nomination of presidential candidates was vested primarily in the states, where legislators and conventions chose favorite sons such as Andrew Jackson and John Quincy Adams as presidential candidates. In 1824, four candidates were nominated, and, although Jackson won more popular votes than any of the others, he did not secure a majority of the electoral votes, and the election was thrown into the House of Representatives, which chose from the top three electoral-vote winners; Jackson lost to John Quincy Adams, who benefited from a political deal with HENRY CLAY (one of the four nominees but not included in the top three electoral-vote winners) in which Clay gave his support to Adams purportedly in return for being named Secretary of State. Thus, while the congressional caucus system was too centralized to represent state and local political units properly, the method of allowing individual states to nominate candidates was too decentralized to select a common party candidate. Some method was required that would represent party interests from throughout the country and that would also produce the nomination of a single candidate from each party.

The nomination method that soon developed to meet these joint requirements was a national convention composed of party delegates from all the states. By the early 1830s it had become the means by which parties nominated their presidential and vice presidential candidates. The national convention remains in place today, but it, like the entire nomination process, has undergone major changes.

The selection of delegates to the national convention is determined by states and is also affected by decisions made by the national political parties. Three methods of selection have been used. One is selection by party leaders, such as members of the state central committee, the party chairperson, and the governor (if the party controls that office). The second is choice by state conventions composed of people who are themselves elected at party caucuses and conventions in smaller geographical areas, such as precincts, wards, counties, and congressional districts. The third method is election by the voters themselves in presidential primaries.

The Rise of State Primaries. For most of the century and a half since the institution of the national convention, selection of delegates by party leaders or by state conventions dominated the nomination process. In the early twentieth century, as part of the Progressive movement designed to take government out of the control of political bosses and to place it in the hands of the people, a number of states instituted presidential primaries. This method, unlike the *direct primary* used to vote directly for party nominees for other political offices, selects national-convention delegates, who, in turn, choose the party presidential nominees. After enjoying popularity for a brief period, the use of state presidential primaries became more limited. During the NEW DEAL period, an average of fifteen states had presidential primaries; together, they chose between 33 and 45 percent of the national-convention delegates. As late as 1968, only seventeen states used presidential primaries to select convention delegates, together constituting 38 percent of the convention total.

The acrimonious debates over the VIETNAM WAR at the 1968 Democratic national convention, together with Vice President HUBERT H. HUMPHREY's presidential nomination despite the fact that he failed to enter a single primary (party leaders favoring him dominated the delegations of caucus-convention states) led to great dissatisfaction with the nomination process. In the years that followed, a series of party commissions were appointed to work with states to change the nomination rules to make the process less dominated by party leaders and more open to the influence of rank-and-file Democrats. One of the major outcomes of the movement was a dramatic increase in the number of state presidential primaries—a trend that affected Republicans as well.

By 1980 the number of states holding primaries had more than doubled. After a small decrease in 1984 in the number of states using presidential primaries, the number rose again in 1988. During that campaign year, thirty-five Republican state primaries selected about three-fourths of that party's national convention delegates, and thirty-four Democratic primaries chose about two-thirds of Democratic convention delegates.

State primaries work in a number of different ways. For instance, the selected delegates may be required to vote for the particular candidate with whom they are associated or they may be free to vote their own presidential-candidate preferences at the national convention. Another difference has to do with candidate choice: in some primaries, a candidate's name will appear on the ballot only if he or she officially enters the contest; in others, the candidate's name may automatically be placed on the ballot if the candidacy is recognized by the national news media. A third difference concerns the selection of state delegates: they may be chosen statewide, by district, or by a combination of the two; moreover, a state may award all the delegates to the statewide or district-vote winner or they may be allocated proportionally (though not always exactly) according to the relative size of the votes for the various candidates. In addition, in some states all the delegates are chosen in the primary while in others some are chosen in the primary and some in state conventions. Yet another difference involves who may vote in a primary: the election may be closed to those who are not registered members of a particular party or open to all registered voters. Finally, state presidential primaries are held on different dates, beginning in mid February and ending in June of the presidential year. On some dates, only one primary occurs; on others several are held. In recent years, major changes have occurred in state presidential primaries. Not only have there been more primaries, but they have been scheduled earlier in the election year. New Hampshire has retained its tradition of holding the nation's first primary, but other states have moved their primaries up on the calendar so that they are conducted before mid March. The most dramatic change in this respect was the creation in 1988 of "Super Tuesday." On the first Super Tuesday, 8 March 1988, sixteen states held their presidential primaries. There was a distinctive regional cast to this development: of the sixteen Super Tuesday primaries, fourteen were in southern and border states (the other two were in Massachusetts and Rhode Island). In 1992, eight primaries were held on Super Tuesday (10 March), six of which were in southern and border states and the other two in Massachusetts and Rhode Island. Presidential primaries have thus become the dominant method of choosing delegates to the national conventions of both major political parties. In 1988, however, about one-third (about fifteen of the fifty states) used the caucus-convention system to select their delegates. Moreover, 16 percent of the Democratic convention votes were allocated to "super delegates"—that is party leaders, including Democratic governors, members of the Democratic National Committee, and about 80 percent of the Democratic members of Congress. The process of selecting delegates to the national conventions has therefore remained a mixed system.

General Nature of the Nomination Campaign. The nomination campaign is a long winnowing process in which each of the two major parties chooses a nominee from a pool of potential candidates (the pool is typically much larger in the party that is out of power). As the political scientist Austin Ranney has pointed out, the nomination phase is more important than the general election stage of the campaign because "the parties' nominating processes eliminate far more possibilities than do the voters' electing processes."

The nomination campaign is much more loosely structured than the general election campaign. Instead of contending with one known opponent representing the other major political party, an aspirant for a party's nomination typically does not know how many opponents he or she will face or who they will be. Unlike the general election campaign, which typically begins after the national conventions and accelerates around Labor Day, the nomination campaign has no set starting date. Also, once selected, a presidential nominee can use his or her party label to attract votes and has access to the help of traditional party leaders in waging the campaign; candidates for a party's nomination, however, must develop other types of political appeals to attract the support of what the political scientist Hugh Heclo has termed the "selectorate"—that is, those who take part in the nomination phase of the presidential campaign—as well as personal political organizations to advance their candidacies.

The "Invisible Primary." Although the nomination process normally does not officially start until early in the election year, political maneuvering may begin long before that time. Indeed, the journalist Arthur Hadley has called the interval between the election of one President and the first primary of the next presidential election the "invisible primary." During that time, would-be candidates test the viability of their candidacies. They try to determine, for example, whether they have the desire and stamina to endure extended absences from home and long hours on the campaign trail. (Democratic hopeful WALTER MONDALE

withdrew two years before the 1976 election when he decided he did not.) A candidate must also find out whether he or she can assemble a personal staff to plan campaign strategy and a larger group to do the advance work necessary to organize the upcoming campaign in the various states.

The media can also be an important factor for the would-be candidate. Massachusetts Senator Edward Kennedy's 1980 campaign for the Democratic nomination, for example, was severely damaged by a 1979 interview with CBS commentator Roger Mudd in which he seemed unable to explain his actions in a 1969 automobile accident in which a young woman, Mary Jo Kopechne, had drowned. In 1988, former Colorado Senator Gary Hart's quest for the Democratic nomination suffered a similar fate when the *Miami Herald* reported his extramarital affair with model and actress Donna Rice. On the other hand, candidates can take action to enhance their name-recognition and to garner favorable publicity from the media. Early in Jimmy Carter's 1976 campaign, for example, his staff recommended that he curry favor with *New York Times* columnist Tom Wicker and *Washington Post* publisher Katherine Graham by commenting favorably on their newspapers and, if possible, scheduling visits with them.

Another important factor affecting a would-be candidate's decision to run is his or her ability to raise funds for the long campaign ahead. Since the 1970s legislation has favored the raising of moneys in comparatively small amounts; there is a limit of $1,000 on individual contributions and $5,000 on those by PACS (POLITICAL ACTION COMMITTEES); moreover, only contributions of $250 or less may be matched by federal funds. In the 1988 race, nationally recognized candidates such as Republicans George Bush and Robert Dole, as well as those with access to special fund-raising constituencies (e.g., televangelist and Republican candidate Pat Robertson, whose "700 Club" TV show provided a ready-made direct-mail constituency, and Democrat MICHAEL DUKAKIS, who benefited from Greek-Americans' contributions from all over the country) were advantaged in the fund-raising process. By the end of 1987, Bush had raised $18.1 million; Robertson, $14.2 million; Dole, $13.2 million, and Dukakis, $10.2 million—funds that enabled them to compete in early primaries and caucuses.

During the period preceding the actual state contests, candidates can gather additional political support, name-recognition, and favorable publicity in other ways as well. One way is to gain the endorsement of interest groups, as Walter Mondale did in 1984, when he won the early endorsement of the AFL-CIO, the National Education Association, and the National Organization for Women. (Reacting to criticism that Mondale had been a "special interest" candidate, the Democrats in 1988 avoided such all-out endorsements so early in the campaign.) Another method is to enter contests that have no effect on the composition of the state delegations: for example, in 1979 Carter forces worked hard to defeat Kennedy in the Florida state convention straw poll. A third possibility is to engage in debates with other candidates, hoping to be declared the winner by the media.

The Official State Primaries. Whatever may transpire before the formal state contests, they are the mechanisms that actually select the delegates to the national conventions that will choose the party nominees. In recent years most major candidates have been on the ballots of all or virtually all the primaries. This does not mean, however, that each candidate will expend an equal effort in each primary.

One of the major factors determining the amount of effort a candidate will devote to a given primary is when that primary is held. Since 1952, a pledged-delegate primary in New Hampshire has been the first primary (only the Iowa caucuses have preceded it). Although the number of delegates from New Hampshire is small (in 1992, 18 of 4,288 Democratic delegates and 23 of 2,209 Republicans) a victory there focuses immediate attention on the winner—as it did for John F. Kennedy in 1960, Carter in 1976, and the two eventual nominees in 1988, Bush and Dukakis. Moreover, if a candidate loses in New Hampshire but draws a greater percentage of the votes than is expected, the media may interpret the result as a "moral" victory, a judgment that benefited Democrats EUGENE MCCARTHY in 1968 and GEORGE MCGOVERN in 1972.

As previously noted, in 1988 a number of states, primarily in the South, held their primaries in early March. These had a major effect on the nomination campaigns, particularly for the Republicans, who had winner-take-all contests. In 1988 Bush swept all sixteen Republican primaries on Super Tuesday and essentially wrapped up the nomination. In contrast, three candidates—Dukakis, Jesse Jackson, and Tennessee Senator Albert Gore—divided up the Democratic primaries, which generally used the proportional rule to award delegates.

Besides timing, other factors help determine how candidates focus their efforts. They typically enter state contests in which they expect to do well. In 1984 Mondale chose to concentrate on Pennsylvania and Illinois because both states had many Catholic, Jewish, and union voters—groups among whom the Minnesota politician had long been popular. That same year

Hart focused on Massachusetts and Wisconsin because of their academic communities, with which he shared liberal political views. At times, however, candidates may select states that are not considered advantageous to prove that they have a broader appeal than is generally thought. In 1960 Kennedy entered the West Virginia primary to demonstrate that a Catholic could win in a state that was 95 percent Protestant; in 1976 Carter chose the Pennsylvania primary to show that a Southern Baptist could do well in a northern industrial state with a large Catholic population. Both calculations were excellent and greatly advanced their respective candidacies.

The number of delegates a state has at the national convention is also a factor that determines the amount of effort expended there. In 1988, of the ten most populous states, only one, Michigan, did not hold a primary. Thus, unless the nomination has been virtually decided by the time of a large state primary, most, if not all candidates, may be expected to focus their efforts there.

Of the factors that affected presidential nominations in the 1970s, 1980s, and early 1990s, the date of the state contest was the most important. Between 1976 and 1988, every Democratic or Republican nominee won at least one of the two small states of Iowa and New Hampshire and finished no lower than third in the other. Of the two, New Hampshire appeared to be the more important. After winning the Iowa caucuses in 1980, Bush declared he had "Big Mo" (momentum), but it suddenly evaporated a week later when he lost to Ronald Reagan, the eventual nominee, in the New Hampshire primary. In 1988, Bush had the reverse experience: he lost to Dole in Iowa but recovered with a victory in New Hampshire that sent him on the way to the Republican nomination. The same was true for the Democratic contest: Missouri Representative Richard Gephardt won the 1988 Iowa caucuses but was defeated in the New Hampshire primary by Dukakis, the eventual Democratic nominee.

One final point should be made about the presidential primaries. Although the situation differs from election to election, there has been a definite trend to decide the nominations in both parties fairly early. From 1976 to 1988, the candidate who won the most delegates by mid March went on to win the party's nomination. It is significant that during the same general period presidential primaries became the dominant force in presidential nomination policies.

BIBLIOGRAPHY

Aldridge, John. *Before the Convention: A Theory of Presidential Nominations.* 1980.

Asher, Herbert. *Presidential Elections and American Politics.* 5th ed. 1992.

Bartels, Larry M. *Presidential Primaries and the Dynamics of Public Choice.* 1988.

Crotty, William, and John S. Jackson III. *Presidential Primaries and Nominations.* 1985.

Grassmuck, George, ed. *Before Nomination: Our Primary Problems.* 1985.

Greer, John. *Nominating Presidents: An Evaluation of Voters and Primaries.* 1989.

Hadley, Arthur. *The Invisible Primary.* 1976.

Kessel, John. *Presidential Campaign Politics.* 4th ed. 1992.

Schaefer, Byron E. *Quiet Revolution: The Struggle for the Democratic Party and the Shaping of Post-Reform Politics.* 1983.

Wayne, Stephen. *The Road to the White House.* 4th ed. 1992.

RICHARD A. WATSON

PRIVATE ENVOYS. A major summit practice, introduced early in U.S. history, is the President's utilization of private envoys as personal agents to represent the country abroad. Initially called secret agents, they also are known as executive agents, presidential special envoys, or personal emissaries. Private envoys are appointed without Senate confirmation (and sometimes without consulting the State Department) for particular, limited assignments. Their authority, duties, and compensation are determined by the President, and generally they are responsible only to the President and report directly to the White House.

The Envoys' Role. Such special envoys supplement traditional diplomatic missions. Besides representing the United States at state ceremonies abroad, they are commissioned to represent the President directly to foreign leaders, keep the President informed, convey official policies and positions, confer and negotiate on the President's behalf, engage in troubleshooting and mediation, and extend the President's influence abroad. They bypass established bureaucracies, elevate matters to the highest level, and expedite relations.

Today, the missions of such envoys are rarely clandestine. Originally they were commissioned only on exceptional occasions and usually for restricted periods, but over time usage was broadened to include any assignment the President elects to handle outside conventional diplomatic channels.

Approximately four hundred presidential special emissaries were appointed during the century following the Revolution, and by the time of WORLD WAR I some five to six hundred had been commissioned, evidencing that this practice had become common-place. At present more than two dozen may be accredited in a single year, and, while their total number and the quantity of their missions can only be surmised, they may well aggregate in the thousands.

Many prominent statesmen and distinguished diplomats have served as executive agents. Prior to the Constitution these included John Adams, William Carmichael, Charles Dumas, Benjamin Franklin, JOHN JAY, and Thomas Jefferson. President George Washington appointed David Humphreys, James Monroe, GOUVERNEUR MORRIS, Thomas Pinckney, and others to such assignments. The list has embraced ranking statesmen (DEAN ACHESON and John J. McCloy), professional diplomats (William C. Bullitt, Ellsworth Bunker, and Norman Davis), career Foreign Service officers (Hugh Gibson, Robert J. McCloskey, and Llewellyn E. Thompson), and a few military officers (Generals Maxwell Taylor and Vernon Walters and Colonel William Donovan).

Presidential personal emissaries may be classified according to the position they occupied prior to appointment, the nature of the tasks assigned, and the extent to which they actually represent the President. Under the first classification, they are of two types: those who otherwise occupy no official position in the government and those government agents, such as Vice Presidents, members of Congress, and the Secretary of State, who are sent abroad on special missions. The trend has been to rely more frequently on current and former government officials for these tasks.

Types of Envoys. Under the second classification, based on assignment, special envoys may be grouped in the following categories: *ceremonial agents*, such as Theodore Roosevelt, who was sent to the funeral of King Edward VII in 1910, and GEORGE C. MARSHALL, sent to the coronation of Queen Elizabeth II in 1953; *goodwill envoys*, such as Milton Eisenhower, who made visits to Latin America during the 1950s, and ROBERT F. KENNEDY, who made a globe-girdling tour in 1962; *special messengers for obtaining information and conveying presidential views*, such as Joel R. Poinsett, who made trips to South America from 1810 to 1814, several emissaries during the crises in PANAMA and the DOMINICAN REPUBLIC in the 1960s, and a series of agents promoting President Lyndon Baines Johnson's "peace offensive" during the VIETNAM WAR; *mediators*, such as Vice President HENRY A. WALLACE, General Patrick Hurley, and General George C. Marshall, who were sent by Presidents Franklin D. Roosevelt and Harry S. Truman to try to ameliorate the conflict between the Nationalist and Communist Chinese, as well as a number of Secretaries of State and other high-ranking State Department officials dispatched to deal with

Arab-Israeli and other Middle East crises (including Joseph J. Sisco, Philip Habib, and JAMES A. BAKER III); *other troubleshooters*, such as career diplomat Robert Murphy (who served Presidents Roosevelt, Truman, and Dwight D. Eisenhower) and Cyrus Vance (whom President Johnson relied on during the Cyprus, South Korean, Dominican, and Vietnam crises); *roving emissaries* such as W. Averell Harriman (appointed by Presidents Roosevelt, John F. Kennedy, and Johnson) and Secretaries of State DEAN RUSK, HENRY KISSINGER, and Baker; and, on rare occasions, a *resident emissary*, for example, Myron C. Taylor, who was commissioned resident representative to the Vatican during WORLD WAR II.

A good many emissaries have been appointed as special negotiators. A sampling includes Robert Livingston and James Monroe (LOUISIANA PURCHASE, 1803), Secretary Richard Rush (Rush-Bagot Agreement, 1817), Nicholas P. Trist (TREATY OF GUADALUPE HIDALGO ending the MEXICAN WAR, 1848), Admiral Matthew C. Perry and Townsend Harris (commercial treaties with Japan, 1854 and 1868), Secretary WILLIAM SEWARD (ALASKA PURCHASE TREATY, 1867), former Secretary William R. Day (Treaty of Paris ending the SPANISH-AMERICAN WAR, 1898), William W. Rockhill (OPEN DOOR policy for China and Peking Protocol, 1901), JOHN FOSTER DULLES (JAPANESE PEACE TREATY ending WORLD WAR II, 1951), Deputy Secretary Warren Christopher (settlement of IRANIAN HOSTAGE CRISIS, 1980–1981), and Max Kampelman (East-West arms limitation, Geneva, 1985–1987). Other twentieth-century special envoys of note include Chief Justice Fred M. Vinson (mission to Moscow, 1948), former Senator Walter F. George (special representative to NATO, 1957), and former Congressman James P. Richards (to promote the EISENHOWER DOCTRINE in the Middle East, 1957).

There are two exceptional categories of executive agents who represent the President in a special way. The first is the *ambassador-at-large*. President Franklin D. Roosevelt commissioned Norman Davis as his ambassador-at-large, sending him to several international conferences. In 1949 this office was formalized, and since then more than thirty emissaries have borne this title, including Arthur J. Goldberg, U. Alexis Johnson, George C. McGhee, and Paul Nitze. The second category embraces those who function as the intimates of the President, possess the President's personal confidence, and are accepted abroad as genuine presidential surrogates. This unique role has been filled by Woodrow Wilson's envoy Colonel EDWARD M. HOUSE; Franklin D. Roosevelt's envoy HARRY HOPKINS; W. Averell Harriman, who served several Presidents and was twice designated ambassador-at-large; and Henry Kissinger, who served Presidents Richard M. Nixon and Gerald Ford.

Constitution Questions. The appointment of presidential special agents raises both constitutional and political issues.

The practice has been held to violate the spirit, if not the letter, of the Constitution. The matter of constitutionality—including the use of members of Congress for such missions—was debated most vigorously during the period from 1880 to World War I. Aside from expediency and the fact that such envoys have been used throughout U.S. history, two considerations are used to justify their use: the legal fiction that these emissaries are "employees" rather than "officers" of the United States and that such agents on special assignments have temporary duties of limited duration.

The critical legal-political issues are whether such appointments are not overtly prohibited by the Constitution, whether they are necessary for the President to fulfill his responsibilities effectively, and whether they produce acceptable consequences. So many precedents have been set, however, that the use of such envoys may be said to be constitutional by prescriptive practice. Despite the objections raised, the President, as DIPLOMAT IN CHIEF, is ultimately accountable for the conduct of American foreign relations. So long as he is inclined to assume personal direction over diplomatic affairs, he will appoint individuals he deems able to surmount the constraints of ordinary diplomatic practice in promoting the objectives and policies of the nation.

BIBLIOGRAPHY

Burke, Lee H. *Ambassador at Large: Diplomat Extraordinary.* 1972.

Grieb, Kenneth J. "Executive Agents." In vol. 1 of *Encyclopedia of American Foreign Policy.* Edited by Alexander de Coude. 3 vols. 1978.

Plischke, Elmer. *Diplomat in Chief: The President at the Summit.* 1986. Chapter 3.

Thorpe, Francis N. "Is the President of the United States Vested with Authority under the Constitution to Appoint a Special Diplomatic Agent with Paramount Power without Advice and Consent of the Senate?" *American Law Register and Review* (April 1984): 257–264.

Waters, Maurice. "Special Diplomatic Agents of the President." *Annals of the American Academy of Political and Social Science* 307 (September 1956): 124–133.

Wriston, Henry M. *Executive Agents in American Foreign Relations.* 1929.

Wriston, Henry M. "The Special Envoy." *Foreign Affairs* 38 (1960): 219–237.

ELMER PLISCHKE

PRIVATIZATION. The term *privatization* is an umbrella term that has come to be a shorthand referent to describe a number of practices. If activities having a public character are viewed on a spectrum, with one end being a purely public function and the other a purely private function, any decision that moves an activity toward the private end of the spectrum can be described as an act of privatization. In many instances, however, the shift from the public sector may only be partial, as in contracting for a service, with residual responsibility remaining with the public sector. As a term and a concept, privatization entered the political and economic lexicon in the 1970s. It is employed internationally and is today one of the central concepts in any discussion of possible future directions for the world economy.

Objectives and Methods. While specific privatization proposals differ in their scope and method, promoters of privatization are quite clear in their objectives. In every instance, the objectives of privatization are to reverse the century-long expansion of the public sector, to decrease the intervention of the state in the economy and in private lives generally, and to promote the productivity of the unit in question through the market, where the transaction process is regulated but prices are deregulated.

There are various methods for privatizing public functions. The sale, or divestiture, by a government of an agency, corporation, or service to private ownership is the most clear-cut method of privatization; an example is the sale by the U.S. government of Conrail in 1985. Another form of divestiture is to sell some asset, such as government-held loans, to a private firm or individual. Or the government may simply give some asset away, as the federal government did when transferring land to homesteaders in the nineteenth century.

The administrative branch of government may be given responsibility for performing a function and decide that actual delivery of the service would best be provided by a third party—either another government, a nonprofit enterprise, or even a private firm under contract. Contracting-out is a privatization practice as old as the Republic and is common at all levels of government. Governments may decide to charge the users of a service a fee sufficient to cover the cost of providing the service. User fees are employed to raise revenues or to ration services for the greatest efficiency. Governments may desire that a particular service be publicly funded but not directly delivered by a governmental entity. In that case a voucher may be given by the government to a citizen to purchase this service from either a public or private provider, a good example of this was the GI Bill to provide educational benefits for veterans of World War II. Privatization, as should be evident, encompasses many variations on a theme.

Theoretical Basis. The theoretical basis for privatization derives from the free-market school of economics, which dates back to the publication of Adam Smith's *Wealth of Nations* in 1776. The classical economic liberalism espoused by Smith and his followers emphasized the marketplace as the most efficient, equitable, and salutary mechanism for the distribution of goods and services in society. In the twentieth century, the theory of market economics was challenged not only by Marxist communism but also by a less doctrinaire democratic socialism. Socialism, in its various manifestations, has emphasized the collective over the individual and the need for governmental intervention to correct alleged market imperfections and to provide for a rational redistribution of wealth and services.

From the close of World War I until the mid 1970s, the preponderence of opinion favored reliance on the public sector rather than the private market to produce prosperity. State-enterprise capitalism was portrayed as innovative because it permitted central economic planning, a necessary prerequisite, it was argued, for both developed and newly emerging national economies. Central economic planning, however, first came under attack by a new generation of free-market economists and public-choice theorists in the 1950s and later gained momentum in the 1970s and 1980s. By the early 1980s, free-market economics had displaced socialism as the dominant economic paradigm, in the process altering the political map of the world.

Great Britain under Prime Minister Margaret Thatcher took the lead in all forms of privatization. Opposition was overcome by the economic logic, empirical evidence, and the political appeal of the market approach not only in the industrial sector but in the provision of public services as well. Soon the labor governments in Spain, Australia, and even Scandinavia had accepted privatization and were vying with one another to see which could move fastest toward a full market economy.

The communist nations, with their centralized, controlled economies, fell virtually without resistance to the market economic forces and in the 1990s sought with varying degrees of success to privatize their societies. Even Argentina, long the stronghold of paternalistic government enterprises, had begun selling its mismanaged and inefficient state-owned enterprises to private bidders. The necessity to participate in the single world economic order was the driving force behind this economic revolution.

The situation in the United States was somewhat different from the rest of the world in that the federal government never owned major industries. Government policy objectives were pursued through regulation rather than equity ownership. President Ronald Reagan was a promoter of privatization, which in the United States tended to take the form of economic DEREGULATION, increased contracting-out, and greater reliance on market-based fees.

Privatization, while clearly in the ascendancy, is not a panacea to solve the economic problems of the world. It is a necessary but not sufficient basis for long-term economic growth and political freedom. The great strength of the free market is that it is based on and encourages the acquisitive nature of individuals and that it is largely self-correcting when distortions occur. But privatization does not eliminate the need for public-sector management; it merely alters the character of this management. Privatization often results in new and more sophisticated demands on public sector management (e.g., management of programs through third parties), demands that are only beginning to be fully understood. What is taking place worldwide is the emergence of a new type of administrative state, one that must simultaneously improve the international competitiveness of both its private and public sectors in an era when the very concept of the nation-state is being challenged.

BIBLIOGRAPHY

Gayee, Dennis J., and Jonathan N. Goodrich, eds. *Privatization and Deregulation in Global Perspective*. 1990.

Moe, Ronald C. "Exploring the Limits of Privatization." *Public Administration Review* 47 (1987): 453–460.

National Academy of Public Administration. *Privatization: The Management Challenge*. 1989.

Savas, Emanuel S. *Privatization: The Key to Better Government*. 1987.

U.S. President's Commission on Privatization. *Privatization: Toward More Effective Government*. 1988.

Wolf, Charles, Jr. *Markets or Governments: Choosing between Imperfect Alternatives*. 1988.

RONALD C. MOE

PRIZE CASES 2 Black 635 (1863). In the *Prize Cases*, the Supreme Court, in an opinion by Justice Robert C. Grier, upheld by a 5 to 4 vote President Abraham Lincoln's imposition of a blockade in April 1861, on the ports of Southern states that had seceded from the Union. The Court also considered whether the property of persons domiciled in those states was the proper subject of capture on the seas, as Lincoln had ordered, as "enemies' property."

The Court weighed several crucial questions in the context of Lincoln's action. Was the ongoing insurrection a war within the meaning of the Constitution? Did the President have the legal right to conduct war without a DECLARATION OF WAR as the Constitution requires? When Lincoln imposed the blockade and initiated other military actions, Congress was not in session.

The Court determined that the Southern insurrection was indeed a war within the Constitution's use of that term. It was not necessary that both parties in the conflict be acknowledged as independent or sovereign states. A war may exist if one belligerent claims sovereignty over the other. A civil war, which begins by insurrection against the lawful authority of the government, is not a declared war, but its existence is determined by the actions of those in rebellion and the government's response. When, because of the insurrection, the courts cannot be kept open, as they could not in the Southern states, war exists and hostilities may be prosecuted on the same footing as if those opposing the government were foreign enemies invading the land.

Although the Constitution empowers Congress to declare war, the Court noted, war cannot be declared against a state of the United States. Rather, it is the President who must respond to the eruption of hostilities since the Constitution confers "the whole EXECUTIVE POWER" on him, and he is bound to take care that the laws be faithfully executed. Also, Congress by previous legislation had authorized the President to repel hostilities against the United States. Under the acts of 28 February 1795 and 3 March 1807, the President was authorized to call out the militia and employ United States military forces against invasions by foreign nations and to suppress insurrection against the government of a state or of the United States.

The Court noted that if war is made by a foreign invader, the President does not initiate war but is obliged to respond without awaiting a war declaration or other legislative action. Whether armed resistance occurs to such degree that a civil war exists, warranting the status of belligerence to the enemy, is for the President to determine. In all such questions, the Court declared itself bound by decisions and acts of the political departments of the government. Accordingly, the President calculates the degree of force the crisis demands, and the proclamation of a blockade is itself conclusive evidence that a state of war existed and that recourse to such a measure is justified.

The Court noted that in 1861, subsequent to Lincoln's imposition of the blockade, Congress enacted many laws acknowledging the existence of war and approving the government's prosecution of it. The Court said that had there been a defect in what the President did in invoking the blockade, Congress's enactment of subsequent ratifying legislation would have cured it. The Court seemed to suggest that the President may commit illegal acts, beyond the scope of his authority, but if these acts are within the scope of legislative power, Congress can cover them with a cloak of legality. The *Prize* holding does not altogether imply this, and its most significant outcome is that the President was viewed as having acted within his power.

The Court, in defining the President's power to determine the nature of the property seized in the blockade, deemed it open ended. A belligerent has a right to cripple an enemy's resources, the Court declared, and the property seized does not depend on the personal allegiance of the owner, and hence it is of no consequence whether it belongs to a person in rebellion or to an ally or loyal citizen.

In a dissenting opinion, Justice Samuel Nelson, joined by three justices, noted that the acts of 1795 and 1807 did not confer on the President the power to declare war against a state of the Union nor to decide that war existed. Nor did those acts authorize the capture and confiscation of the property of every citizen of the state, wherever it was found on the waters. The legislature, not the President, has power over the business and property of a citizen by the express language of the Constitution.

Congress alone determines whether war exists, or should be declared, Justice Nelson wrote, and until Congress acts, no citizen of a state can be punished in his person or his property, unless he committed offenses against a law of Congress, passed before the offense occurred.

BIBLIOGRAPHY

Corwin, Edward S. *The President: Office and Powers.* 4th rev. ed. 1957.
Randall, J. G. *Constitutional Problems under Lincoln.* 1951.

LOUIS W. KOENIG

PROCLAMATION OF NEUTRALITY (1793).

In 1793, President George Washington announced a policy of NEUTRALITY when France declared war on England and set off a series of events that lasted until 1815 and became known as the Napoleonic Wars. Neutrality had been a difficult decision. Secretary of State Thomas Jefferson emphasized sentimental ties with the French stemming from the period of the American Revolution, whereas Secretary of the Treasury ALEXANDER HAMILTON warned that alienating the British would cut off America's commercial lifeline and draw the United States into a war that would devastate the new nation. Both men agreed, however, that the United States could not become involved.

In the spring of 1793, the French had appeared ready to invoke the Treaty of Amity and Commerce and the Treaty of Alliance of 1778. The first pact assured commercial rights and prize privileges; the second guaranteed assistance in "defensive" wars. Citizen Edmond Charles Genet was en route to the United States, authorized to commission privateers, secure advance payments on debts incurred during the revolutionary war, and negotiate a "national pact" that would convert the United States into a French base of operations against England and its ally Spain. Though he never asked the United States to enter the war, acquiescence in his demands would have established a virtual Franco-American alliance. To escape this dangerous situation, Hamilton argued that the French had declared war on England, thereby releasing the United States from its obligations under the Treaty of Alliance. Further, he insisted, treaties were between governments and not peoples; the French Revolution had toppled the throne and thereby released America from its treaty obligations. Jefferson countered with an argument for de facto recognition—that even though King Louis XVI had fallen, the French nation was still in existence. But Jefferson likewise recognized the danger of establishing ties with France. If the French sought aid under the treaties of 1778, he argued, the United States could decline because the French had not come to its assistance when the British refused to evacuate the northwest fur posts.

On 22 April 1793, President Washington urged Americans, under penalty of law, "to pursue a conduct friendly and impartial" toward the warring nations. Though the President did not mention the word neutrality in the proclamation, his meaning was clear. Congress followed with the Neutrality Act of June 1794, which made the United States a leading proponent of neutral rights. Washington's decision for neutrality kept the United States out of Europe's wars during the nation's crucial formative period.

BIBLIOGRAPHY

Ammon, Harry. *The Genet Mission.* 1973.
Bowman, Albert H. *The Struggle for Neutrality: Franco-American Diplomacy during the Federalist Era.* 1974.
DeConde, Alexander. *Entangling Alliance: Politics and Diplomacy under George Washington.* 1958.

HOWARD JONES

PROCLAMATIONS. Ever since the administration of George Washington, Presidents have issued proclamations having the force of law. These proclamations set boundaries for the behavior of private citizens as well as government officials. Despite their impact, proclamations have not been generally well understood. The confusing processes by which they have been developed, promulgated, and integrated with other policy tools as well as the controversial claims to authority on which they have sometimes been based have not made proclamations a popular subject for presidential scholars.

The Nature of Proclamations. Presidents have issued more than six thousand proclamations since George Washington's Proclamation of Neutrality of 1793. The number is approximate because, as with executive orders, there was historically no system for identifying, listing, and publishing in one authoritative location all proclamations. Even after the enactment of the Federal Register Act, in 1935, there were difficulties. First, considerable effort was required to construct a codification of proclamations and executive orders that would be comprehensive and current. The Office of the Federal Register has developed the *Codification of Presidential Proclamations and Executive Orders* but it presents only those proclamations issued since World War II. Second, apart from the general requirements for publication of new proclamations in the *Federal Register*, the only guidelines that govern their promulgation are two executive orders, E.O. 10347 (1952) and E.O. 11030 (1962), which themselves do little more than describe the process, format, and routing for the production of the documents. Since Presidents have issued the equivalent of proclamations under many titles and in many forms not covered by existing publication laws, it can be difficult to identify and integrate them into a coherent set of presidential policy statements.

Presidential proclamations issued under a proper claim of authority are legally binding. They may be ratified or nullified by legislative action after their issuance, unless they are based on a valid claim by the executive to independent constitutional authority. Legislative failure to block presidential action or the defeat of resolutions opposing White House actions are considered evidence of support. Of course, proclamations may not violate existing statutes or constitutional constraints.

Proclamations have even been used, and upheld, as the basis for criminal prosecutions. Judge James Wilson charged a grand jury that it could indict a violator of Washington's Neutrality Proclamation even though there was no statute authorizing such an indictment. A man who refused on principle to register for the draft as required by President Jimmy Carter's Proclamation 4771 was convicted and his conviction upheld.

Formally, the distinction between executive orders and proclamations is that orders are issued by the President to government agencies or officials while proclamations are directed to persons outside government. Thus, President Carter's Proclamation 4771 (1980) directed all eighteen-year-old males to register for the military draft. On the other hand, proclamations may be issued together with executive orders. For example, President Gerald R. Ford simultaneously issued Proclamation 4483 in 1973 granting pardons under certain circumstances to Vietnam War–era draft evaders and Executive Order 11967, outlining the implementation actions to be taken by the Attorney General under the program.

The Supreme Court has held that there is no legal distinction between proclamations and executive orders. The internal versus external dichotomy used to distinguish between them is not particularly helpful in practical terms, since many executive orders directing action by government agencies clearly have a major impact on those outside government. In the case of Ford's amnesty program, for example, men who had presumably violated the selective service laws could not obtain the pardon set forth in the proclamation unless the process established by the executive order determined that they were eligible for it.

In general, proclamations have been issued in a number of general categories. Most are hortatory, designating a period of recognition, celebration, or concern, like Proclamation 6407 proclaiming 1992 the Year of the American Indian. Others, like Carter's selective service proclamation, are effectively ordinances, rules of general applicability. Particularly in the area of trade and foreign policy, the President issues a third type of proclamation, which renders an authoritative finding of fact and sets forth the response triggered by the situation. Thus, President George Bush issued Proclamation 6413 (1992) finding that the Peoples' Republic of China had implemented the memorandum of understanding between the PRC and the United States on the protection of intellectual property by recognizing the copyrights of American authors. Therefore, Proclamation 6413 granted copyright protection in the United States to works produced by PRC authors. The President may also make authoritative findings of fact and announce responses in domestic matters. These are often rendered in what are found to be emergency situations such as natural disasters.

Legal Authority. Of course, presidential lawmaking by proclamation depends for its force on the legal authority that supports it. Unlike executive orders, which Presidents have often insisted can rest at least partly on the President's claim of general executive powers to supervise subordinate officials and agencies, proclamations that are directed to those outside government face a demanding challenge.

Historically, the concept of presidential proclamations derives from the crown prerogative. However, many of the Framers of the Constitution, including JAMES WILSON, James Madison, and even ALEXANDER HAMILTON, rejected the elements of the crown prerogative as the price for support in creating an effective presidency. Moreover, as the Proclamations Case of 1611 indicated, even the British king did not have unlimited powers to issue any proclamation the crown desired. When Washington issued his Neutrality Proclamation in 1793, it triggered the HELVIDIUS-PACIFICUS DEBATES over the proper range of presidential powers under the Constitution.

In most cases Presidents rely in issuing proclamations on authority specifically granted or at least implied by statute, even in matters of foreign policy and even where purely hortatory proclamations are involved. In fact, many hortatory proclamations are issued in response to calls from Congress in the form of a public law or joint resolution, as in the case of Public Law 102-188 authorizing and requesting the issuance of the Year of the American Indian.

The most important proclamations have often been issued in matters of economic policy, international trade and tariffs, NATIONAL SECURITY, or foreign policy. In these fields, Presidents have usually relied on statutes that specified their authority to make a finding that a problem exists and to respond to it. Some statutes authorize the president to undertake a decision-making process. Proclamations are then employed to implement the policy produced by that process. For example, President Carter entered into negotiations with Mexico for a trade agreement under the authority of the Trade Act of 1974. As a result of that negotiation process, the President issued Proclamation 4707 (1979) implementing concessions granted by the United States under the agreement, but, when the Mexican government was not forthcoming on mutual actions expected as part of the process, Carter suspended the U.S. concessions with his Proclamation 4792 (1980).

When Presidents rely on authority they consider to be implied by existing statutes or act under extremely broad delegations of statutory authority, there can be conflict. For example, Carter issued Petroleum Import Adjustment Program Proclamations 4744, 4748, and 4751 (1980), which imposed a 10 percent oil

import fee under authority he thought was implied by the TRADE EXPANSION ACT of 1962. His actions were later struck down in a legal challenge in which the court observed that the President had erred in attempting to use legislation for something never considered by Congress and in a manner that flew in the face of the intent with which the law was originally adopted.

However, President Richard M. Nixon fared much better in an even more dramatic exercise of power in 1971. Claiming authority from the Trade Expansion Act of 1962, and the ECONOMIC STABILIZATION ACT of 1970, the administration suspended exchange of U.S. currency, set limits on domestic spending and foreign aid, imposed a freeze on wages and prices, suspended a variety of trade-related proclamations then in force, and placed a 10 percent surcharge on all dutiable imports. Although the court that reviewed Proclamation 4074 found the legislative delegation of power to the President to be incredibly broad, possibly unwise, and even potentially dangerous, it nevertheless concluded that the President's action on the import fee fit the delegation and that the delegation was permissible in light of its intention to permit presidential response to economic emergencies.

Indeed some of the most important controversies over proclamations have arisen in situations in which Presidents have justified their actions by reference to a state of emergency, usually related to national security or economic crises. President Nixon based his actions in 1971 on the proclamation of a state of economic emergency brought on by serious deficits in balance of payments, instability in trading on the dollar, and related tariff practices that exacerbated the trade imbalance.

Where Presidents act in matters of foreign policy and national security, there is often an assertion of combined statutory and constitutional authority under the COMMANDER IN CHIEF and FOREIGN AFFAIRS powers.

Challenges to Proclamations. Because they are directed at private citizens and businesses, presidential proclamations are easier to challenge than executive orders. Since executive orders are directed to agencies or government officials, it is more difficult for citizens to meet procedural requirements and establish a proper basis for a suit that would challenge the President's authority. Still, even if a citizen is able to mount a legal challenge to a presidential proclamation, it may be very difficult to prevail in light of the tradition of deference by the judiciary to foreign policy and national security decisions.

Notwithstanding their usefulness as policy-making tools for a President, proclamations have weaknesses as well. Despite their record of success in court, proclamations may fall in a legal challenge. They are even more likely to be overturned by a later administration. The President who invests the time and energy to move legislation through the Congress is more likely to establish enduring policy than one who relies on proclamations. For example, one of the last proclamations issued by President Carter was Proclamation 4813 (1981), which extended the "Emergency Building Temperatures Restrictions" imposed by Proclamation 4667 (1979) intended to protect the U.S. against further oil crises in the light of unrest in the Middle East. Less than a month later, Ronald Reagan issued Proclamation 4820 (1981) revoking Carter's orders on grounds that his action imposed an "excessive regulatory burden" that would be achieved by "voluntary restraint and market incentives."

Presidential proclamations, like executive orders, are potentially useful tools. However, given their vulnerability as policy statements over time, the sometimes dubious authority on which they may be based, and the closed process by which they are developed and promulgated, they are limited and possibly dangerous tools for many presidential tasks.

BIBLIOGRAPHY

Friedelbaum, Stanley H. "The 1971 Wage-Price Freeze: Unchallenged Presidential Power." *Supreme Court Review* (1974): 33–80.

Hart, James. *The Ordinance Making Powers of the President of the United States.* 1925.

Office of the Federal Register. *Codification of Presidential Proclamations and Executive Orders, April 13, 1945–January 20, 1989.* 1990.

U.S. House of Representatives. Committee on Government Operations. *Executive Orders and Proclamations: A Study of a Use of Presidential Power.* 85th Cong., 1st sess., 1957. Committee Print.

U.S. Senate. Committee on Government Operations and the Special Committee on National Emergencies and Delegated Emergency Powers. *The National Emergencies Act: Sourcebook.* 94th Congress, 2d sess., 1976. Committee Print.

PHILLIP J. COOPER

PROGRESSIVE (BULL MOOSE) PARTY
(1912). When Theodore Roosevelt lost his bid for the REPUBLICAN PARTY's nomination for President in 1912, he bolted the party and, with a large number of reform-minded party insurgents, he organized the Progressive Party. A few of those insurgents, some of whom held offices they had won as Republicans, ran for office with Roosevelt on the Progressive ticket. But the Progressive Party was essentially a vehicle for Roosevelt's presidential candidacy. When Roosevelt declined to be a candidate again in 1916, the party disbanded. The chief political effect of the Progressive Party was to split the Republicans, leaving the Republican Party firmly in the grip of its right wing.

Roosevelt left the presidency in 1909, having announced on his election to a full term of office in 1904 that he would not be a candidate for reelection. He was succeeded by his own protégé, William Howard Taft, whom he correctly saw as exceptionally able and incorrectly believed would be capable of carrying forward his progressive program. Taft did support most of Roosevelt's reform objectives, but, unlike Roosevelt, he had little energy, appetite, or aptitude for politics. Also, Taft's conservative view of the law left little room for the kind of redistribution of economic and political advantages in the American polity that Roosevelt had sought. Within a year of the beginning of Taft's administration, Roosevelt's friends and a number of insurgents within the Republican Party had begun urging Roosevelt to displace Taft at the head of the party ticket in 1912.

What finally provoked Roosevelt to try to depose Taft was, ironically, Taft's determination to enforce the SHERMAN ANTITRUST ACT. Roosevelt believed that the Sherman Act was a mistake and that prudence required government to distinguish between "good" and "bad" trusts. Taft, insisting on the letter of the law, began proceedings against the United States Steel Corporation for merger activities that Roosevelt, as President, had at least tacitly approved. When the indictment was announced, Roosevelt interpreted it as a personal affront. He was thus well prepared to accept the call from those intent on Taft's replacement.

Actually, a powerful insurgency had been brewing within the Republican Party for at least a decade. It had been caused partly by a genuine idealistic commitment to democratic reform and a more equitable distribution of economic advantages. Some of it, though, was merely a rationale for outs wanting in and using popular progressive rhetoric to arm their demands. Much of the insurgency turned on impatience among relatively young Republicans who were shunted to the periphery of party power because of youth and because of geography—for example, because their constituencies were midwestern or western rather than eastern. Feeling shut out by the Old Guard of their own party, they began building local careers on an anti–Old Guard platform. Until Roosevelt announced in February 1912 that his "hat [was] in the ring" for the Republican nomination, the insurgents' preferred candidate was Sen. ROBERT M. LA FOLLETTE of Wisconsin.

Roosevelt lost the support of his conservative friends virtually on the day he announced his candidacy. He had already made them queasy with speeches he had made on a western tour in the summer of 1910. In an address at Osawatomie, Kansas, he had outlined his vision of the reforms he believed the country required. There he had called for a NEW NATIONALISM that would put "the national need before sectional or personal advantage" and would regard "the executive power as the steward of the public welfare." Conservatives such as his friend Senator Henry Cabot Lodge stayed with him until a speech in Columbus, Ohio, in February 1912, in which he declared his support for recall of state judicial decisions by popular referendum. That struck at what conservatives viewed as the most sacred of institutions defending civilization against the rising tide of populist RADICALISM. At the Republican national convention, Roosevelt's old conservative friends, notably convention chairman ELIHU ROOT, used their strategic positions to deny him the nomination. Roosevelt and many of his supporters walked out, charging that the convention had been rigged and the nomination stolen.

As the presidential nominee of the hastily organized Progressive Party (dubbed the "Bull Moose" Party because Roosevelt told his followers he was in the contest to win and was feeling fit as a bull moose), Roosevelt attracted more support from advanced progressive publicists and activists than from insurgent Republican politicians. La Follette, for example, eventually endorsed the Democratic nominee, Woodrow Wilson, while others ducked for cover. The politicians found that Roosevelt's declared sympathy for business consolidations grated against their more popular antitrust postures. More daring progressives outside politics, such as Amos Pinchot, Jane Addams, Herbert Croly, and George W. Perkins, found Roosevelt's program truly exciting. It included a call for progressive income and inheritance taxes, voter rights to initiate and pass judgment on legislation by referenda, popular recall of elected officials, and a powerful presidential office that could reconcile labor and industry and turn the great power of business corporations to public purposes.

The three-party contest in 1912 resulted in Woodrow Wilson's election with 6 million votes, only 42 percent of the popular tally. Roosevelt came in second with 4 million votes, to Taft's 3 million. Roosevelt abandoned the Progressive Party after the election, and without him it withered and died.

BIBLIOGRAPHY

Harbaugh, William H. *The Life and Times of Theodore Roosevelt*. Rev. ed. 1975.
Morison, Elting E., and John M. Blum, eds. *The Letters of Theodore Roosevelt*. 8 vols. 1951–1956.
Mowry, George E. *Theodore Roosevelt and the Progressive Movement*. 1946.

RICHARD M. ABRAMS

PROGRESSIVE PARTY (1924). The Progressive Party of 1924 emerged as a protest by a rump group of progressive reformers who were dismayed by the overwhelming dominance of national politics by conservative forces. It was fated to be as short-lived and futile as its 1912 predecessor of the same name.

The REPUBLICAN PARTY, its insurgent members mostly disarmed by the defeat of the Theodore Roosevelt wing in 1912, regained dominance of national politics with the end of WORLD WAR I. Woodrow Wilson's dream of a LEAGUE OF NATIONS that would provide collective security for democracy and worldwide economic prosperity met with defeat at the hands of ethnic animosities and critics on both the right and the left. Thousands of Irish-American voters, riled by America's association with England in the war effort, left the DEMOCRATIC PARTY, which has been their political home for generations. Conservative nationalists worried over every hint that U.S. foreign policy might be limited in any way by some supranational parliament. Social critics on the left suspected that Wilsonian internationalism would simply export the kind of statist excesses they had witnessed at home all too often during and in the aftermath of the war. In 1918, the Republicans recaptured control of Congress, and in 1920 they swept back into the White House by a near-record popular majority.

In 1922, exasperated by the Old Guard conservatives' grip on the Republican Party and by national policies that put farm-belt interests on hold, a large group of social reformers and other veterans of progressive politics met and organized the Conference for Progressive Political Action (CPPA). Two years later, with Old Guard eastern Republicans in full control of the party, and with the Democrats nominating J. P. Morgan's lawyer, JOHN W. DAVIS, for President, the CPPA founded a new Progressive Party and put forward for President the longtime darling of midwestern Republican insurgency, Sen. ROBERT M. LA FOLLETTE of Wisconsin.

The Progressive Party proposed the nationalization of railroads and other public utilities and a number of measures designed to remedy injuries felt by (especially) midwestern farmers since the close of the war. Its efforts ran up against a nation enjoying considerable prosperity; a mild, passive, and seemingly inoffensive Republican President; and a labor union movement that saw little that expressed its interests in the new party. In the end, La Follette captured the electoral votes of only his own state of Wisconsin, and President Calvin Coolidge cruised easily to victory with nearly 16 million votes over a mere 8.4 million for Democrat Davis, and 4.8 million for La Follette. La Follette died within a year, and once again a party called Progressive dissolved before a second national election came around.

BIBLIOGRAPHY

McKay, Kenneth C. *The Progressive Movement of 1924.* 1947.

RICHARD M. ABRAMS

PROGRESSIVE PARTY, 1948.

The Progressive Party was an independent political party founded by supporters of HENRY A. WALLACE as a vehicle for his presidential candidacy in the 1948 national elections. Wallace had served Franklin D. Roosevelt loyally as a member of his Cabinet (Secretary of Agriculture, 1933–1940) and as Vice President (1941–1945). A liberal New Dealer and international idealist, Wallace considered himself the true heir to FDR's domestic and foreign policies.

In 1946 President Harry S. Truman summarily dismissed Wallace from his post as Secretary of Commerce for the latter's public criticism of the administration's get-tough policy toward the Soviet Union. Wallace favored a conciliatory approach to Joseph Stalin as a means of avoiding a prolonged COLD WAR. After being fired from Truman's Cabinet, Wallace became editor of *The New Republic.* Shortly thereafter a liberal and left-wing group opposing Truman's actions formed the Progressive Citizens of America (PCA). Evolving from the PCA, the Progressive Party held its first national convention at Philadelphia 23 to 25 July 1948. It had no historical antecedents in either the PROGRESSIVE (BULL MOOSE) PARTY of 1912 or the PROGRESSIVE PARTY of 1924. The Democrats already had nominated Truman, the Republicans, THOMAS E. DEWEY, and the States Rights (Dixicrat) Party, STROM THURMOND. It appeared that the combination of bolting southerners and alienated Democratic liberals in the Progressive Party would doom Truman's election chances.

The Progressive Party chose Henry Wallace as its presidential nominee and Senator Glen Taylor (D-Idaho) as his vice presidential running mate. The party's platform was extremely critical of President Truman's foreign policy yet offered no criticism whatsoever of the Soviet Union. While the 3,240 delegates and alternates ostensibly were formulating planks from the floor in democratic fashion, a small coterie of pro-Soviet sympathizers actually controlled all aspects of the convention. Even the Vermont resolution, stating "it is not our intention to give blanket endorsement of the foreign policy of any nation," was defeated. The Communist Party of the U.S.A. also endorsed Wallace as its presidential nominee.

During the course of the ensuing campaign, Wallace was pilloried by the press. His attempts to defend the Soviet Union were negated by the Berlin blockade and the Communist coup d'état in Czechoslovakia. On election day the Wallace-Taylor ticket polled only 1,157,140 popular votes and no electoral votes. After the outbreak of the KOREAN WAR in 1950, Wallace broke with the party. Despite his moral fervor and religious idealism, his campaign had been a fiasco. It ruined his reputation and ended his political career even though he later blamed Joseph Stalin for the shooting war in Korea.

In 1952 the Progressive Party nominated Vincent Hallinan, a lawyer who championed radical causes, for the presidency and Charlotte Bass, an African American civil rights activist, as his vice presidential running mate. The ticket attracted a mere 140,023 votes, thus signaling the final demise of the Progressive Party.

BIBLIOGRAPHY

Schapsmeier, Edward L., and Frederick H. Schapsmeier. *Prophet in Politics: Henry A. Wallace and the War Years, 1940–1965.* 1971.
Schmidt, Karl M. *Henry A. Wallace: Quixotic Crusade 1948.* 1960.
Yarnell, Allen. *Democrats and Progressives: The 1948 Presidential Election as a Test of Postwar Liberalism.* 1974.

EDWARD L. SCHAPSMEIER

PROGRESSIVISM.

For discussion of the goals and programs of Progressivism—an early-twentieth-century reform movement in both the Republican and the Democratic parties—see ANTITRUST POLICY; BUSINESS POLICY; ELECTION, PRESIDENTIAL, 1912; LABOR POLICY; LA FOLLETTE, ROBERT M.; PROHIBITION; TAX POLICY; WOMEN'S RIGHTS. Progressivism influenced the policies of the Theodore Roosevelt and Wilson administrations (for discussion of these policies, see ROOSEVELT, THEODORE; WILSON, WOODROW) and inspired the formation of the PROGRESSIVE (BULL MOOSE) PARTY and the PROGRESSIVE PARTY (1924).

PROHIBITION.

An early nineteenth-century effort to encourage temperate use of alcoholic beverages turned quickly into a movement for banning their manufacture, transportation, or sale. During WORLD WAR I, prohibition gained the broad political support necessary for incorporation into the Constitution as the Eighteenth Amendment. Although the use of alcoholic beverages fell sharply, many Americans ignored the liquor ban. Growing criticism of national prohibition led to a successful campaign for its repeal in 1933.

Colonial Americans consumed large quantities of alcoholic beverages, which were often safer than impure water or milk and less expensive than coffee or tea. By the 1820s, alcohol consumption reached its all-time high, a per capita annual average of 7 gallons of alcohol, which was contained in 70 gallons of beer or cider, 39 gallons of wine, or 15½ gallons of distilled liquor. After voluntary abstinence campaigns led by physicians and Protestant ministers sharply reduced American alcohol consumption, antebellum temperance advocates began seeking legal bans on liquor to extend the benefits of abstinence. During the 1850s eleven states adopted prohibition laws. When support for prohibition declined during and after the CIVIL WAR, prohibitionists organized to promote reform. Unhappy at being ignored by the major political parties, drys founded the PROHIBITION PARTY in 1869, the Woman's Christian Temperance Union in 1874, and the Anti-Saloon League of America in 1895. From the 1880s to World War I, local option laws and statewide prohibition spread. Encouraged, an antialcohol coalition of church groups, feminists, social and political reformers, and businessmen began calling for a total, permanent national solution: constitutional prohibition.

Prohibition first affected presidential politics in 1884, when Prohibition Party candidate John St. John drew enough votes from Republican JAMES G. BLAINE to cause his loss in New York and enable Democrat Grover Cleveland to win an extremely close national contest. Despite a vague Republican temperance plank in 1888, the Prohibition Party once again became a factor in a close presidential election. Thereafter the influence of the Prohibition Party declined, and temperance reformers turned increasingly to the single-issue Anti-Saloon League to pressure major parties to support liquor bans in return for its support.

Presidential candidates and Presidents avoided the prohibition debate until Congress approved a constitutional prohibition resolution in December 1917 and legislatures in three-fourths of the states completed ratification of the Eighteenth Amendment on 16 January 1919. The national ban was to take effect one year later. In October 1919 the Congress approved the Volstead Act, providing for prohibition enforcement and defining intoxicating beverages as those containing more than one-half percent alcohol (thus banning beer and wine as well as distilled liquors). President

Woodrow Wilson, who objected to several of the bill's provisions and believed that a public allowed to drink beer would more easily give up distilled liquor, vetoed the act. Congress easily overrode the veto, further weakening the already declining political standing of the ailing President.

National prohibition sharply reduced, though it did not altogether eliminate the use of alcoholic beverages. Purchasing liquor was not only illegal, it was also very expensive. However, a sizable minority of Americans, particularly recent immigrants and the urban middle and upper classes, saw nothing wrong with drinking. A series of Presidents wrestled with the problem of prohibition enforcement. Warren G. Harding, who publicly endorsed the need to uphold the law but privately enjoyed alcoholic beverages, reflected the ambivalent American attitude. Presidents Calvin Coolidge and Herbert Hoover encouraged greater federal effort, though, like Harding, they viewed prohibition enforcement as primarily a state and local responsibility. Hoover, calling the law "an experiment noble in motive and far-reaching in purpose," defended prohibition in his 1928 presidential contest with Democrat ALFRED E. SMITH, a repeal advocate. Hoover subsequently appointed a presidential commission chaired by George Wickersham to explore ways of improving prohibition observance and enforcement. When the Wickersham Commission expressed mixed feelings about continuing prohibition, Hoover nevertheless regarded its support as an obligation.

The 1932 Democratic convention endorsed repeal of prohibition. An ambivalent Franklin D. Roosevelt resisted this until its broad popularity became evident. The November victory of Roosevelt and the Democrats was widely seen as a mandate for repeal, and less than four months later, Congress passed the Twenty-first Amendment. Roosevelt then urged modification of the Volstead Act to permit beer of 3.2 percent alcohol content. State conventions quickly ratified the amendment, bringing national prohibition to an end on 5 December 1933. Roosevelt received considerable credit for the achievement of the unprecedented and seemingly impossible reversal of a constitutional amendment, thereby enhancing his popularity and political stature during his early months as President.

BIBLIOGRAPHY

Blocker, Jack S., Jr. *American Temperance Movements: Cycles of Reform.* 1989.
Kerr, K. Austin. *Organized for Prohibition: A New History of the Anti-Saloon League.* 1985.
Kyvig, David E. *Repealing National Prohibition.* 1979.

DAVID E. KYVIG

PROHIBITION PARTY. The Prohibition Party, a significant minor political party during the 1880s, was formed in Chicago in September 1869 by temperance reformers who believed that their crusade could best be advanced by an independent national political organization. After the CIVIL WAR, the Republican example encouraged the view that a party devoted to a moral issue could gain control of the federal government. Advocating a federal income tax, woman suffrage, and direct election of Senators as well as PROHIBITION of alcohol, the Prohibition Party made little progress at first, winning for its presidential candidates only six thousand votes in 1872 and ten thousand in 1876 and 1880.

In 1884, however, the party's presidential candidate, two-term Governor John St. John of Kansas, polled 150,857 votes. St. John's 24,999 votes in New York drew enough votes from Republican JAMES G. BLAINE to cause his 1,047-vote loss. The New York result enabled Democrat Grover Cleveland to win the presidency in an extremely close national contest. Although the Republicans sought to regain prohibitionist support by adopting a vague temperance plank in 1888, the Prohibition Party won 250,122 votes that year and once again appeared to be a factor in a close presidential election.

The Prohibition Party polled 271,000 votes in 1892. Nevertheless, it was overshadowed as a broad-based reform party by the People's Party and thereafter its vote totals declined. Furthermore, never again did the Prohibition Party hold an electoral balance of power. Temperance reformers increasingly abandoned hope of achieving independent political power and turned to single-issue organizations such as the Anti-Saloon League to pressure major parties to support liquor bans in return for their support. The Prohibition Party survived only as an obscure and tiny organization, one which contributed little in the 1910s to the triumph of the national prohibition crusade.

BIBLIOGRAPHY

Blocker, Jack S., Jr. *American Temperance Movements: Cycles of Reform.* 1989.

DAVID E. KYVIG

PROTECTION OF THE PRESIDENT. The protection of the President—and of others associated with the office—became an extensive and complex permanent responsibility during the twentieth century, particularly compared to the limited and sporadic operations before then. The SECRET SERVICE, originally established as a small anticounterfeiting organization in the DEPARTMENT OF THE TREASURY in 1865, has been the lead agency in presidential security since 1894, when it first began to protect the President. In the early 1900s, however, both the army and the then-new Bureau of Investigation in the DEPARTMENT OF JUSTICE [see FEDERAL BUREAU OF INVESTIGATION] were rivals for the responsibility, since then a number of federal, state, and local agencies have assisted the Secret Service in providing security, depending upon the circumstances and the type of activity. From small beginnings, when the protective function consumed only about 10 percent of the Secret Service's few resources, it now accounts for an estimated 40 percent of its budget normally and 60 percent during presidential election years ($476 million in fiscal year 1992), when the number, extent, and duration of details escalates.

The specific statutory assignments for the Secret Service have been added piecemeal over the years, beginning in 1906 with protection for the President. These assignments in law usually ratified an ongoing duty that had been initiated by the President or another official in the executive branch in response to PRESIDENTIAL ASSASSINATIONS, assaults, threats, or other concerns about the protectee's safety: for example, for the President in 1906 following William McKinley's assassination; the President's immediate family in 1917 during WORLD WAR I; the Vice President in 1951 following the attack on BLAIR HOUSE, where President Harry S. Truman was temporarily residing; and major presidential candidates in 1968 following the assassination of ROBERT F. KENNEDY. As a related matter, assassination of the President was not a federal crime until 1965, after President John F. Kennedy's murder.

Several of the early security details authorized by executive officials—for the President, his family, and the President-elect—moreover, had violated clear statutory prohibitions on the Secret Service, which was limited to anticounterfeiting duties at the time. In most cases, the initial statutory authority appeared in an annual appropriations act and continued as such for years or even decades before it was made permanent.

The Secret Service's specific protective assignments (18 U.S.C. 3056) now include the President, Vice President, and their immediate families; the President-elect, Vice President-elect, and their immediate families; major presidential and vice presidential candidates (and their spouses within 120 days of the election); and former President's, their spouses (until remarriage), and their minor children (until the age of sixteen). Major party candidates are identified by the Secretary of the Treasury after consultation with a special bipartisan advisory committee consisting of the Speaker and minority leader of the House of Representatives, the majority and minority leaders of the Senate, and one additional person selected by these four. All protectees—except for the President, Vice President, President-elect, and Vice President-elect—may decline such protection.

The Uniformed Division of the Secret Service, which has its own separate protective assignments in law (3 U.S.C. 202), emerged in 1977; it superseded the Executive Protective Service, which had replaced the White House Police. The White House Police force was established in 1922 to protect the Executive Mansion and grounds; later, in 1962, its duties were expanded specifically to cover protection of the President and members of his immediate family, along with any building in which White House offices are located. The Uniformed Division's express statutory protective assignments are now the President, Vice President, and their immediate families; the WHITE HOUSE and any buildings in which presidential offices are located; and the Vice President's official residence.

Until the late 1800s, security was infrequent, usually confined to a military guard unit at ceremonial occasions. This could be substantial, however, as with Abraham Lincoln's inauguration in 1861, when there was a massive troop presence. Presidential protection was otherwise generally limited to occasional bodyguards and some modest precautionary measures connected with specific threats or the likelihood of violence; again, President-elect Lincoln's circuitous and secret travel to Washington in 1861 illustrates this. Finally, some early protection of the President was only part of or incidental to other, broader security arrangements. For instance, beginning in 1864, the Washington Metropolitan Police sent a detail to provide security for the White House rather than directly and formally to guard the President himself.

During the first hundred years of the presidency, protection was usually provided by military units, since the President as COMMANDER IN CHIEF could call on them without specific statutory authority. Other forces were involved, however, when circumstances dictated. A state militia provided security on at least one occasion, when President George Washington accompanied troops to put down the WHISKEY REBELLION in 1794. In addition, as noted above, the Washington Metropolitan Police set up a guard detail at the White House in 1864, because of the exigencies of the CIVIL WAR, and provided occasional security for the President when he left the grounds. Unfortunately, one of its officers left his post at Ford's Theater, giving JOHN WILKES BOOTH unimpeded access to shoot Lincoln. Private detectives and bodyguards may have also been available at times, for instance, when they traveled by train. Since Presidents did not have travel funds until the early 1900s, they frequently relied upon the largess of railroad owners, who may have had their own guards on duty.

The situation began to change in 1894, when the Secret Service for the first time provided protection for the President (Grover Cleveland) and his family, both at the White House and outside the District of Columbia. The protective details were initiated because of threats against the President, discovered by Secret Service detectives, and a possibility of kidnapping of his young children at the family vacation home in New York State. Cleveland himself was unaware of the detail at the vacation site; security had been requested by his wife, because of intruders on the property, and agreed to by his personal secretary (who, in effect, served as chief of staff). The White House fabricated a cover story to account for the agents, because the Secret Service was then prohibited from engaging in protection or any other activities that were not spelled out in its annual appropriations. Its funding, which was limited to anticounterfeiting and a few other enumerated duties, contained an injunction on the use of its funds, "for no other purpose whatever." Consequently, these early details violated the legal restrictions on the Secret Service. Later, the chief was demoted ostensibly for authorizing it, although other reasons probably accounted for his removal by a new administration.

A special account was available for presidential protection during the SPANISH-AMERICAN WAR in 1898. Because it lapsed afterwards, renewed security again violated the continuing prohibition on Secret Service funds. The chief at the time later admitted to committing a "technical perjury" in authorizing protection for President McKinley, who, knowing one of the agents personally, requested it directly. In fact, three agents were on duty in Buffalo, New York, when Mckinley was shot in 1901. Following the assassination, the third President murdered within a thirty-seven-year period, security became more routine, well coordinated, and expanded for Theodore Roosevelt, with the Secret Service as the lead agency.

In 1902, the House Judiciary Committee objected to legislation passed by the Senate that would have allowed the Secretary of War to use military personnel in civilian dress to protect the President "as unnecessary and as an encroachment upon the liberties of our people." This defeat for the military, in effect, ratified the Secret Service's primacy in the field of presidential protection. Its position was further solidified in 1906, when it was finally given explicit statutory authority for "protection of the person of the President."

Later, however, criticism of the Secret Service's investigation of land-fraud schemes indirectly led to the creation of a new Bureau of Investigation in the Justice Department. As a result, in 1910, Congress granted the ATTORNEY GENERAL the same discretionary authority to "protect the person of the President." Despite this shared formal power, the Secret Service remained preeminent in presidential security matters because of its longer experience and larger force at the time.

Express statutory authority for presidential protection continued exclusively in annual appropriations acts for four more decades. It was not until 1948—with the codification of Title 3, the Presidency—that a permanent statute for protecting the President, his immediate family members, and the President-elect was enacted. But this legislation did not designate a specific agency. Three years later, in 1951, with the codification of Title 18, the Secret Service itself was finally given permanent authority to protect the President as well as his immediate family, the President-elect, and the Vice President (at his request).

The protective responsibility also involves a number of federal, state, and local agencies, depending upon the site and circumstances surrounding the protectee as well as the type of activity. Indeed, the Secret Service is empowered to call upon other executive departments and agencies to assist it on a cost-reimbursed basis (except for the Coast Guard and Department of Defense for temporary assistance). Organizations that assist in protection include U.S. military units; the Coast Guard; national guard forces, particularly in cases of civil disorder; local and state police, for traffic and crowd control among other services; the General Services Administration, which manages federal property and, thus, has responsibility for installing security facilities and equipment at the White House and presidential offices, among other places; and federal intelligence and law enforcement agencies, including the CENTRAL INTELLIGENCE AGENCY (CIA) and the FBI, which has its own specific statutory mandate "to assist in the protection of the person of the President" (28 U.S.C. 533).

Protection also encompasses a wide variety of distinct activities. These range from providing security equipment at residences and offices to precautionary measures when protectees travel; from providing bodyguards to surveillance and interrogation of individuals identified as high risks; from advance detection of plots to prevention research into the motives and characteristics of would-be assassins; and from intelligence gathering on terrorist organizations to criminal investigations of threats and assaults.

BIBLIOGRAPHY

Bowen, Walter S., and Harry Edward Neal. *The United States Secret Service*. 1960.

Kaiser, Frederick M. "Origins of Secret Service Protection of the President." *Presidential Studies Quarterly* 18 (1988): 101–127.

Kaiser, Frederick M. "Presidential Assassinations and Assaults: Characteristics and Impact on Protective Procedures." *Presidential Studies Quarterly* 11 (1981): 545–558.

Melanson, Philip H. *The Politics of Protection: The U.S. Secret Service in the Terrorist Age*. 1984.

Sherman, Richard B. "Presidential Protection During the Progressive Era: The Aftermath of the McKinley Assassination." *The Historian* 46 (1983): 1–20.

U.S. House of Representatives. Select Committee on Assassinations. *Findings and Recommendations*. 95th Cong., 2d sess., 1979.

U.S. Institute of Medicine. *Behavioral Science and the Secret Service: Toward the Prevention of Assassination*. 1981.

U.S. President's Commission on the Assassination of President John F. Kennedy (Warren Commission). *Report*. 1964.

U.S. Secret Service. *Moments in History, 1865–1990*. 1990.

FREDERICK M. KAISER

PROTOCOL, PRESIDENTIAL. Since George Washington's day, the President, serving as both chief of state and head of government, has been the ceremonial head of the country and the operational CHIEF EXECUTIVE of the government respecting both internal and external affairs, comparable to the combined roles of foreign monarchs (and other chiefs of state) and government chief executives. The manner in which the President performs these dual responsibilities depends not only on the President's personal qualities and the temperament but also on the rules that guide his demeanor and actions. Such rules—national and international—constitute the essence of presidential protocol.

Definition of Protocol. As chief of state the President greets and plays host to foreign dignitaries and a procession of American visitors, tours the country to meet with groups of citizens, proclaims holidays, bestows medals and honors, and entertains a variety of White House guests. He is officially received by other governments, confers with their leaders, issues policy declarations, and occasionally signs treaties and agreements. These and similar actions are governed by established, sometimes mandated, procedures. As a consequence, the President has been called a one-person epitomization of America or, as President William Howard Taft put it, the personal embodiment and representative of the people's dignity and majesty.

Protocol applies to all official procedure, ceremony, precedence, and etiquette. It governs not only presidential relations with foreign chiefs of state, heads of government, and other high-level officials but also many aspects of diplomatic affairs and a variety of domestic functions. It regulates diverse features of the international treaty process, the handling of official messages to and from other governments, the accrediting of American diplomats and consuls, and the reception of envoys assigned to Washington. It also controls many national formalities and ceremonies, such as the presidential INAUGURATION and presidential messages to Congress, the signing of legislation, the issuance of presidential PROCLAMATIONS and EXECUTIVE ORDERS, and the conferral of national recognition and awards.

Defined as procedure, deportment, and courtesy, or as the "rule book" by which official relations are conducted, protocol is called a body of "social discipline," a mixture of "good manners and common sense," a set of "rules of conduct," and a prescription of "hierarchical order." Presidential protocol has its supporters and its detractors. Some hold that protocol preserves the symbolism of American sovereignty, continuity, grandeur, and dignity for the President. Others have called it a conspicuous thief of the President's precious time or a device for gaining release from the routine tasks and hard decisions required by the presidential office. Some view it as undemocratic, pretentious, patrician, and unnecessary. But those who utilize it generally regard it as useful, if not essential, in the handling of official relations.

Because of widespread sentiment that ceremonious protocol was not in keeping with the American tradition and spirit, it was not until 1893, in the last days of the Benjamin Harrison administration, that Congress permitted the appointment of American and reception of foreign diplomats accorded the rank of ambassador. Previously such emissaries had held the inferior rank of minister. Similarly, for more than a century the same sentiment precluded the designation of a State Department official to serve as master of ceremonies for official receptions, dinners, and other occasions.

Only in 1919, during the Woodrow Wilson administration, was an officer empowered to head a Ceremonial Section in the Department of State. In 1928, during the Calvin Coolidge administration, a full-fledged Division of Protocol was created, which twice (1929–1931 and 1933–1937) was amalgamated with and later separated from the Division of International Conferences. Soon after WORLD WAR II, under President Harry S. Truman, the Secretary of State elevated the Division of Protocol to the Office of the Chief of Protocol, who bears the personal status of ambassador.

The Chief of Protocol is the principal adviser to the President, Vice President, Secretary of State, and other officials on diplomatic procedure, precedence, and other matters of protocol. The Protocol Office, as officially prescribed, is responsible for arranging visits of foreign chiefs of state, heads of government, and other leaders; monitoring official White House ceremonial and other high-level functions and public events; operating the President's guest house (BLAIR HOUSE); sending delegations to represent the President at public ceremonies abroad; accrediting thousands of foreign embassy, consular, and international-organization personnel stationed in the United States; and determining entitlement to—and resolving many, sometimes thorny problems respecting—diplomatic and consular privileges and immunities. The office also compiles and publishes diplomatic, consular, and mission employee lists and prescribes ranking within them and deals with many other status, procedural, social, and related matters. In short, this office is responsible for the government's obligations relating to all aspects of national and international protocol.

Practice of Protocol. Whereas protocol was initially regulated by national and international custom and usage, many important aspects have come to be determined by international treaties, congressional statutes, executive orders, and administrative regulations. For example, the Vienna conventions on Diplomatic Relations (1961) and on Consular Relations (1963) prescribed common international principles concerning diplomatic and consular officers accredited to this country and Americans commissioned for service abroad. These treaties, subscribed to by some 150 governments, deal with the mutuality of relations; the manner of establishing, suspending, and terminating foreign missions; determining persona grata (acceptability) status of individual officers and their staffs; and setting the procedure for presenting letters of credence and official reception of diplomats and the issuing of exequaturs to consuls authorizing the performance of their duties. They also stipulate rules respecting precedence, including delineation of categories of diplomatic and consular officials and individual ranking within them; inviolability of persons, premises, and communications; privileges and immunities; the parameters of diplomatic and consular functions; and the public display of national flags, coats of arms, and emblems.

For years the precedence order of diplomats in Washington, D.C., and other capitals was founded on principles established at the congresses of Vienna (1815) and Aix-la-Chapelle (1818), which based rank on titles of individual emissaries and their personal seniority or length of service at that rank in that capital. The four ranks of diplomats, in order of priority, included ambassadors extraordinary and plenipotentiary (and papal legates or nuncios), envoys extraordinary and ministers plenipotentiary (and papal internuncios), ministers resident, and two classes of chargés d'affaires. By the Vienna Convention of 1961 this order was modified to embrace papal nuncios in Catholic countries, ambassadors extraordinary and plenipotentiary, ministers plenipotentiary, and three classes of chargés d'affaires. In each capital the dean of the diplomatic corps is the most senior foreign diplomat, the spokesperson for and representative of the entire diplomatic corps.

U.S. protocol prescribes that the President head the order of precedence, followed by the Vice President, Speaker of the House of Representatives, Chief Justice, former Presidents, Secretary of State, and foreign ambassadors accredited to Washington. Overall, there are more than forty American precedence categories comprising several hundred individuals and groups, such as CABINET secretaries, Senators, Congressmen, deputy and assistant secretaries of Cabinet departments, and state governors. Each of these categories has its own order of priority. Also included are heads of international organizations, the mayor of Washington, the Director of the Mint, the Librarian of Congress, and many others. Potentially, this order of precedence embraces some two to three thousand individuals and their spouses.

Protocol also applies to such domestic matters as ceremonies for presidential appearances before Congress, swearing in of officials, and the hosting of meetings with foreign leaders and numerous other luncheons, dinners, receptions, and social events, as well as the use of the Great Seal of the United States. It also governs the form of White House invitations and responses, individual positions in reception lines, and the shape and seating arrangements at conference and dinner tables (seating differs depending on whether the table is round, square, rectangular, or C-, E-, or U-shaped). Protocol also prescribes rules for dress (whether formal or informal attire) and forms of address: the President is simply addressed as "Mr. President," whereas other officials bear noble titles, such as "Excellency" (for ranking foreign diplomats) and "Honorable" (for Cabinet officers, Supreme Court Justices, members of Congress, governors, mayors, and American ambassadors).

Failure to recognize precedence and proper procedure may insult individuals and their governments. In inviting foreign leaders to visit the United States, and in receiving them, attention must be paid to the nature, frequency, timing, and duration of each visit in relation to the interests and expectations of other governments. Special protocol difficulties arise when a number of ranking foreign leaders come to Washington for collective ceremonies—as when seventeen attended President John F. Kennedy's funeral in 1963 and when twenty-nine—embracing one emperor, eleven presidents, and seventeen prime ministers— were welcomed by President Richard M. Nixon at a White House dinner to celebrate the United Nations' twenty-fifth anniversary in 1970. In such cases sensitivities are aroused whether precedence is based on titles and ranks of the individuals or on an alphabetical arrangement of the countries they represent.

Practicalities of Protocol. Issues of protocol have inspired many anecdotes. One joke relates how a President, boarding a naval vessel, fell overboard and in keeping with proper procedure was given a forty-three-gun salute—the customary twenty-one for boarding, twenty-one for departing, and one for "man overboard"! It has also been recounted that when President Washington undertook a coach trip to New England in 1790, he avoided Rhode Island because it had not ratified the Constitution and was therefore foreign territory.

American tradition initially eschewed the official and social pageantry common in European societies. Benjamin Franklin appeared at the Versailles court wigless, sporting an old coat and a wooden cane, but learned that it was diplomatically advantageous to adopt the customary dress. During the Franklin Pierce administration, Secretary of State William Marcy issued a dress circular advising U.S. diplomats abroad to limit themselves to the "simple dress" of American citizens, which was applauded at home but created embarrassing difficulties overseas. Since those days traditional attire for state ceremonies and diplomatic relations has transmuted from lace, satin, and buckled shoes to striped trousers, black morning coats, spats, and homburgs, and eventually to worsted and tweed working garb and occasional tuxedos and tails for special occasions. When asked his opinion of full dress at White House dinners, President Truman responded that although it posed a protocol problem, he himself would never wear tails.

When Queen Elizabeth II of Great Britain came to the United States on a formal four-day state visit in 1957, her itinerary included four state dinners, three state luncheons, four receptions, a royal investiture ceremony, an American football game, and a traditional reciprocal state dinner. President Dwight D. Eisenhower later commented that he would have fired any aide who dared devise such a schedule for him.

Years earlier ELEANOR ROOSEVELT had cautioned that state guests should be given more time to "put their feet up and relax."

Illustrating the problem of precedence, a troublesome issue was thrust into the lap of protocol experts during the Herbert Hoover administration: they were required to decide whether Vice President CHARLES CURTIS's half-sister outranked Speaker Nicholas Longworth's wife at a White House dinner. In another instance, an American ambassador stationed abroad decided to give a dinner in honor of the newly arrived ambassador of another country but was advised that he could not invite any other ambassadors because they all outranked the guest of honor. In preparing for her first official reception, Mrs. George C. Marshall sought guidance on certain protocol graces and was told always to ask the senior officer's wife to pour the coffee, not the tea, because "coffee outranks tea."

Sometimes protocol preparations are upset by unplanned and embarrassing events. In 1954, President William Tubman of Liberia, arriving at New York by ship a day ahead of schedule, had to remain at anchor in the Upper Bay for a day in order to dock at the prescribed time. When Soviet leader Nikita Khrushchev flew to Washington for a summit meeting in 1959, his plane arrived an hour late and, when it landed, its exit faced in the wrong direction, so that Khrushchev emerged on the side away from the reception party and had to crouch under the plane to be welcomed by President Eisenhower.

BIBLIOGRAPHY

Buchanan, Wiley T., Jr. *Red Carpet at the White House: Four Years as Chief of Protocol in the Eisenhower Administration*. 1964.

McCaffree, Mary Jane, and Pauline Innis. *Protocol: The Complete Handbook of Diplomatic, Official, and Social Usage*. 1989.

Miller, Hope Ridings. *Embassy Row: The Life and Times of Diplomatic Washington*. 1969.

Moreno, Salcedo L. *A Guide to Protocol*. Rev. ed. 1959.

Radlovic, I. Monte. *Etiquette and Protocol: A Handbook of Conduct in American and International Circles*. 1957.

Symington, James W. *The Stately Game*. 1971.

U.S. Department of State, Historical Office. *The Protocol Function in Unites States Foreign Relations: Its Administration and Development, 1776–1968*. Research Project no. 767. October 1968.

Wood, John R., and Jean Serres. *Diplomatic Ceremonial and Protocol: Principles, Procedures, and Practices*. 1970.

ELMER PLISCHKE

PSYCHOLOGICAL PRESIDENCY. From the broadest perspective, psychology permits us to explore the impact of cognitive processes and ego defensive characteristics on presidential decision making.

Decision makers perceive the world through images that screen, simplify, and shape reality. For political leaders, these images are often based on learning from dramatic political events experienced early in their lives. These images make action possible, but once formed may be rigidly adhered to and applied to new situations that differ considerably from the early experience. The result may be policy choices that are likely to fail. For example, America's domino theory about the spread of communism was one such image; lessons learned from the West's appeasement of Adolf Hitler were misapplied by American Presidents to revolutionary third world leaders, contributing to the American fiascoes in the VIETNAM WAR and the IRAN-CONTRA AFFAIR.

Crisis situations can lead to similarly maladaptive responses. Faced with threats to major values, a need for immediate action, and ambiguous information, Presidents will often resort to defensive avoidance tactics. These include procrastination in making a difficult choice, or the delegation of decision to a third party, and/or the bolstering of a preferred option by selective screening, rationalization, or GROUPTHINK. Harry Truman, after the Inchon landing during the KOREAN WAR, resorted to all of these techniques. Responding to domestic political pressures to cross the thirty-eight parallel, Truman dismissed Chinese threats to intervene in the Korean war as beyond their interests and capabilities and delegated to General Douglas MacArthur the authority to pace the American/U.N. advance into North Korea, only belatedly placing limits on the General, as he rushed his troops toward the Yalu River and threatened to bomb Manchuria.

Psychology also illuminates the nature of the leader's relationship to his followers. A leader has authority, as Max Weber has shown us, because people respect his constitutional and legal position, and/or are devoted to a tradition that he represents, and/or because he has charismatic appeal for them. In charismatic relationships the leader creates a strong emotional tie to his followers and is idealized by them. He is seen as having almost supernatural powers or qualities. Drawing upon the psychic repository of his people, the charismatic leader can articulate the higher interest of a people, directing their free-floating discontent into movements for constructive social change. Or he may simply manipulate their feelings to maximize his own power. In the latter case he may use demagogic appeals that encourage in his followers psychological regression and the expression of forbidden impulses. Appeals to the narcissistic needs of the people to feel superior to others and the use of outsiders as targets for aggressions are two possible tactics. In extreme cases, the demagogic leader may aspire to become a totalitarian ruler, installing himself as the source of all authority and reality testing in a political system organized around his personality.

American political culture and institutions have screened against the worst forms of political leadership suggested above. The commitment of the American elite and public to constitutional processes and the orderly transfer of power and to the political principle of democratic moderation has kept extremists and charismatic figures who would use their talent for demagogic purposes from the top of the political ladder. Other possibilities, however, have been present at one time or another. Some Presidents have shown a relative strong commitment to substantive values and democratic procedures, while others have emphasized power seeking, as shall be noted in more detail below. Transformational leaders (George Washington, Woodrow Wilson, and Franklin D. Roosevelt) have come forward during crises to transcend the prevailing order. Transactional leaders maintain the status quo during more ordinary times (Dwight D. Eisenhower, Gerald Ford). Presidents have also differed in the extent to which they have relied primarily on traditional and legal bases of authority (Herbert Hoover, Ford) as contrasted to charismatic appeal (Franklin D. Roosevelt, John F. Kennedy, Ronald Reagan).

The contemporary office of the American presidency, moreover, shapes the psyche and the behavior of its incumbents in ways not touched upon in the general leadership theories. The American President is the leader of the "free world," the symbol of the American nation, as well as CHIEF EXECUTIVE of the government. For the public as a whole, he is the unique repository of popular hopes and fantasies. College-level American government textbooks prior to Vietnam War and Watergate glorified the President, portraying him as the source of creativity and morality within the American political system. Even after the widespread disillusionments associated with the WATERGATE AFFAIR and cover-up, the public's longing for a strong and moral leader remained. Jimmy Carter's meteoric rise to power on a campaign theme suggesting that he had both extraordinary strength and virtue is evidence of that longing.

These high expectations, however, are apt to be frustrated. Institutional and legal constraints limit what the President can do, and the complexity of the economic and cultural problems he faces make it difficult to define what effective action might be. The result is "the impossible presidency" (Barger, Lowi).

The President cannot meet the unrealistic expectations placed upon him, and the public, disappointed in his real accomplishments, may become increasingly critical. Frustrated at this criticism, as well as by his failure to accomplish his goals, the President will be tempted to settle for the image of accomplishment and surround himself with aides who defer to him, flatter him, and protect him from negative feedback. The result is an impairment in reality testing in both the President and the nation.

Despite all these trends, the office, as George Reedy has argued, does not produce the same behavior in each incumbent. Rather it tends to exaggerate, for better or worse, the psychological tendencies the President had formed earlier in his career. Several possible variations in presidential character and style have been delineated in James David Barber's *Presidential Character* (1977). The active-positive Presidents (for example, Jefferson, Franklin Roosevelt, Truman, Kennedy, Ford, and Carter) are viewed as self-confident individuals who took the initiative in resolving political problems and enjoyed the exercise of power. The active-negatives (for example, John Adams, Wilson, Hoover, Lyndon Johnson, Nixon) are characterized as driven by ambition and aggression in what they saw as hostile environments. [*See* CHARACTER, PRESIDENTIAL]

In conceptualizing the differences among character, style, and world view and using comparative case studies, Barber's work was a path breaker. Moreover, like others before him, he understood that the relationships among behavior, world view, and personality are complex and that a phenomenon at one of these levels could not be simply explained by a phenomenon at another level. His classification system, however, presents certain problems. To place John Adams, Woodrow Wilson, and Richard Nixon in the negative-active category is to ignore important differences in their goals and moral values. The active-positive category, moreover, does not permit a distinction between individuals who are genuinely self-confident and certain narcissistic types who only appear to be self-confident when things are going well for them.

Classifications more directly linked to dynamic psychology may enable one to avoid some of these problems. Alexander and Juliette George, Fred Greenstein, and this author have suggested how such approaches might be utilized to understand individual political leaders. The next step will be to build a more general theory, based on empirical studies, about the relationships of psychodynamic characteristic to political behavior. Presidents may most usefully be classified in terms of ego structures (self-esteem, relations to others, reality testing), superego development (internalization of democratic and constitutional social values), and ego-defensive traits. Persons with high self-esteem are apt to have substantive goals beyond their own immediate interests and a capacity for easy and genuine relationships with others. They will have internalized social values that regulate their behavior in a nonoppressive way and they will be characterized by relatively low ego defensiveness. If they are successful politicians, they will have developed their skills in using power, but that power will be employed in the pursuit of substantive goals they share with others in the political system. When challenged, they can learn and adapt their behavior the better to achieve their goals.

Individuals with less self-esteem are more likely to focus on their own power or glory as an end, get highly defensive when challenged, and fail to learn from mistakes. Yet even these ego-defensive individuals will differ. For those with a relatively strong superego, the need for power and glory will be balanced, to some extent, by the need to see themselves as pursuing morally acceptable ends. Ego-defensive moves will not lead them into extreme, highly aggressive, or immoral or illegal behavior. For those without that kind of superego development, the concern for power and glory is relatively unmediated by substantive goals, and challenges are apt to be met with destructive and possibly illegal behavior.

Several Presidents have shown many of the attributes of high self-esteem. Franklin Roosevelt, Eisenhower, and Kennedy had substantive goals and were at ease with other people. They also trusted their political capabilities, showed relatively few ego-defensive traits, and learned from their mistakes. Other Presidents have shown a more fragile self-esteem and have become quite ego defensive when threatened with a loss of power or prestige. Woodrow Wilson, as Alexander and Juliette George have shown, became rigid and withdrew from former political friends when the projects in which he had vested his pride and moral interests were at stake (for example, American adherence to the League of Nations Covenant). Jimmy Carter's strong need to prove that he was exceptional and his difficulties in relating to political equals contributed to his problems in the presidency. Yet each of these individuals, despite some clear differences in the level of their self-esteem, pursued substantive goals and internalized a respect for law and democratic values.

Two post–World War II Presidents seem to have had more serious underlying problems of self-esteem and, when challenged, a greater proclivity to reach for extreme and morally questionable responses. Both Lyndon B. Johnson and Richard Nixon, despite their very real accomplishments, placed a relatively high priority on political power as an end in itself. This is apparent in the extent to which each shifted his programmatic goals during the climb up the political ladder and sought out expressions of his courage and honor once he was in power (Johnson in Vietnam, Nixon in his various "crises"). When threatened with political failure and criticism, both Johnson and Nixon became rigid and resorted to questionable tactics. Both men developed "credibility gaps" through repeated misleading statements to the American people on crucial issues. During the Watergate crisis, Nixon participated in actions that later led the House Judiciary Committee to conclude that he had conspired to obstruct justice.

Psychology, in short, allows us to explain more fully the processes whereby national leaders, generally, make decisions, define goals, and relate to followers. It enables us to delineate how specific institutional and cultural expectations shape the behavior of American Presidents. It sensitizes us to those variations in the character traits of individual incumbents that can lead to constructive or destructive behavior in office. In this latter type of inquiry the investigator enters into a sensitive domain in which political biases—his own, as well as those of the reviewers of his work—are apt to be mobilized. Yet it is only through such analysis that we can distinguish between persons with real self-confidence and those who only seem to possess it; between those who seek power as an end and those who seek it as a means; between those who limit themselves because they have internalized legal and moral constraints and those who are relatively unbounded by such inner constraints.

BIBLIOGRAPHY

Barger, Harold M. *The Impossible Presidency.* 1984.

George, Alexander, and Juliette George. *Woodrow Wilson and Colonel House: A Personality Study.* 1956.

Glad, Betty. *Jimmy Carter: In Search of the Great White House.* 1980.

Glad, Betty. "Political Psychology: Where Have We Been? Where Are We Going?" In *Political Science: Looking to the Future.* Edited by William Crotty. Vol. 3. 1991.

Greenstein, Fred I. "Psychological Analysis of Single Political Actors." In *Personality and Politics: Problems of Evidence, Inference, and Conceptualization.* 1969.

Kellerman, Barbara, ed. *Political Leadership: A Source Book.* 1986.

Lowi, Theodore J. *The Personal President: Power Invested, Promise Unfulfilled.* 1985.

Reedy, George E. *The Twilight of the Presidency.* 1970.

BETTY GLAD

PUBLIC OPINION. "Public sentiment is everything. With public sentiment nothing can fail; without it nothing can succeed." These words, spoken by Abraham Lincoln, pose what is perhaps the greatest challenge to any President: to obtain and maintain the public's support. Because Presidents are rarely in a position to command others to comply with their wishes, they must rely on persuasion. Public support—expressed as PUBLIC RATINGS—is perhaps the greatest source of influence a President has, for it is difficult for other power holders in the American form of democracy to deny the demands of a President who has popular backing.

Understanding Public Opinion. Understanding public opinion can be a considerable advantage to the White House in obtaining and maintaining public support. At the very least, Presidents want to avoid needlessly antagonizing the public. Thus, Presidents need reliable estimates of public reactions to the actions they are contemplating. It is equally useful for Presidents to know what actions and policies, either symbolic or substantive, the public wants. No politician wants to overlook opportunities to please constituents and, perhaps even more significant, to avoid frustrating them. By knowing what the public desires, a President may use his discretion to gain its favor when he feels the relevant actions or policies are justified.

In addition, Presidents often want to lead the public to support them and their policies. To do this they need to know the views of various segments of the public and the specific issues on which the people can be moved. Presidents usually do not want to use their limited resources on hopeless ventures. Nor do they want to be too far ahead of the public. If they are, they risk losing their followers and alienating segments of the population.

It should not be surprising, then, that the White House commissions public opinion polls regularly and that pollsters are close advisers of the President.

Going Public. Presidents are not passive followers of public opinion. The White House is a virtual whirlwind of public relations activity. John F. Kennedy, the first television President, considerably increased the rate of public appearances held by his predecessors. Kennedy's successors, with the notable exception of Richard M. Nixon, have been even more active in making public appearances. Indeed, they have averaged more than one appearance every weekday of the year.

Often the President's appearances are staged purely to obtain the public's attention. Standing in front of the Marine Corps Memorial in Arlington National Cemetery, George Bush announced his support for a constitutional amendment to prohibit FLAG DESECRATION. In cases such as these the President could have simply made an announcement, but the need for public support drives the White House to employ public

relations techniques similar to those used to publicize products.

In many democracies, the position of head of state and head of government are occupied by different people. For example, the queen is head of state in England, but she holds little power in government and politics. In America, these roles are fused. As head of state, the President is America's ceremonial leader and symbol of government. Trivial but time-consuming activities—tossing out the first baseball of the season, lighting the White House Christmas tree, meeting some extraordinary Boy Scout—are part of the ceremonial function of the presidency governed by elaborate PRESIDENTIAL PROTOCOL. Meeting foreign heads of state, receiving ambassador's credentials, and making global goodwill tours represent the international side of this role. Presidents rarely shirk these duties, even when they are not inherently important. Ceremonial activities give them an important symbolic aura and a great deal of favorable press coverage, contributing to their efforts to build public support.

The White House can also largely control the environment in which the President meets the press—in the case of Ronald Reagan having his helicopter revved up as he approached it so that he could not hear reporters' questions and give unrehearsed responses.

Policy Support. Commentators on the presidency often refer to it as a BULLY PULPIT, implying that Presidents can persuade or even mobilize the public to support their policies if only they are skilled enough communicators. Certainly Presidents frequently do attempt to obtain public support for their policies with speeches over television or radio or to large groups. All Presidents since Harry S. Truman have had media advice from experts on lighting, makeup, stage settings, camera angles, clothing, pacing of delivery, and other facets of making speeches.

Despite this aid and despite the experience that politicians have in speaking, presidential speeches aimed at directly leading public opinion have typically been rather unimpressive. In the modern era only Franklin D. Roosevelt, John F. Kennedy, and Ronald Reagan could be considered effective speakers. The rest were not, and typically did not look good under the glare of hot lights and the unflattering gaze of television cameras.

Moreover, the public is not always receptive to the President's message. Americans are not especially interested in politics and government, and so it is not easy to get their attention. Citizens also have predispositions about public policy (however ill informed) that act as filters for presidential messages. In the absence of national crises—which, fortunately, are rare—most people are unreceptive to political appeals.

The public may misperceive or ignore even the most basic facts regarding a presidential policy. As late as 1986, 62 percent of Americans did not know which side the United States supported in Nicaragua, despite extensive, sustained coverage of the President's policy in virtually all components of the media for many years.

Ronald Reagan, sometimes called the Great Communicator, was certainly interested in policy change and went to unprecedented lengths to influence public opinion on behalf of such policies as deregulation, decreases in spending on domestic policy, increases in the defense budget, and aid for the Nicaraguan contras. Nevertheless, support for regulatory programs and spending on health care, welfare, urban problems, education, environmental protection, and aid to minorities increased, not decreased, during Reagan's tenure. Support for increased defense expenditures was decidedly lower when he left office than when he was inaugurated. In the foreign policy realm, near the end of 1986, only 25 percent of the public favored the President's cherished aid to the contras in Nicaragua.

Mobilizing the Public. Sometimes merely changing public opinion is not sufficient; the President, instead, wants the public to communicate its views directly to Congress. Mobilization of the public may be the ultimate weapon in the President's arsenal of resources with which to influence Congress. When the people speak, especially when they speak clearly, Congress listens attentively.

Mobilizing the public involves overcoming formidable barriers and accepting substantial risks. It entails the double burden of obtaining both opinion support and political action from a generally inattentive and apathetic public. If the President tries to mobilize the public and fails, the lack of response speaks clearly to members of Congress.

Perhaps the most notable contemporary example of the President mobilizing public opinion to pressure Congress is Ronald Reagan's effort to obtain passage of his tax-cut bill in 1981. Shortly before the crucial vote in the House, the President made a televised plea for support of his tax-cut proposals and asked the people to let their Representatives in Congress know how they felt. Evidently Reagan's plea worked, as thousands of phone calls, letters, and telegrams poured into congressional offices. The President easily carried the day.

The Reagan administration's effort at mobilizing the public on behalf of the 1981 tax cut is significant not only because of the success of presidential leadership but also because it appears to be a deviant case—even for Ronald Reagan. In the remainder of his tenure, the President went repeatedly to the people regarding a wide range of policies, including the budget, aid to the contras in Nicaragua, and defense expenditures. Despite high levels of approval for part of that time, Reagan was never again able to arouse many in his audience to communicate their support of his policies to Congress. Most issues hold less appeal to the public than substantial tax cuts.

The President and the Press. Despite all their efforts to lead public opinion, Presidents do not directly reach the American people on a day-to-day basis. It is the mass media that provides people with most of what they know about Chief Executives and their policies. The media also interprets and analyzes presidential activities, even the President's direct appeals to the public. The press is thus the principal intermediary between the President and the public, and relations with the press are an important aspect of the President's efforts to lead public opinion.

No matter who is in the White House or who reports on presidential activities, Presidents and the press tend to be in conflict. George Washington complained that the "calumnies" against his administration were "outrages of common decency." Thomas Jefferson once declared that "nothing in a newspaper is to be believed." Presidents are inherently policy advocates. They want to control the amount and timing of information about their administration, whereas the press wants all the information that exists without delay. As long as their goals are different, PRESIDENTS AND THE MEDIA are likely to be adversaries.

Because of the importance of the press to the President, the White House monitors the media closely. President Lyndon B. Johnson installed a special television in the OVAL OFFICE so that he could watch the news on all three networks at once; near the oversized set stood news tickers from Associated Press, United Press International, and Reuters. The White house also goes to great lengths to encourage the media to project a positive image of the President's activities and policies. About one-third of the high-level White House staff members are directly involved in media relations and policy of one type or another, and most staff members are involved at some time in trying to influence the media's portrayal of the President.

Most of the news coverage of the White House comes under the heading "body watch." In other words, reporters focus on the most visible layer of Presidents' personal and official activities and provide the public with step-by-step accounts. They are interested in what Presidents are going to do, how their actions will affect others, how they view policies and individuals, and how they present themselves, rather than in the substance of policies or the fundamental processes operating in the executive branch. Since there are daily deadlines to meet and television reporters must squeeze their stories into sound bites measured in seconds, not minutes, there is little time for reflection, analysis, or comprehensive coverage.

Bias is the most politically charged issue in relations between the President and the press. A large number of studies have concluded that the news media, including the television networks and major newspapers, are not biased systematically toward a particular person, party, or ideology, as measured in the amount of favorability of coverage. The bias found in such studies is inconsistent; the news is typically characterized by careful neutrality.

Some observers believe that news coverage of the presidency often tends to emphasize the negative (although the negative stories are typically presented in a neutral manner). Stories on scandals involving presidential appointees are one example. On the other hand, one could argue that the press is inherently biased toward the White House. A consistent pattern of favorable coverage exists in all major media outlets, and the President is typically portrayed with an aura of dignity and treated with deference.

Much of the energy the White House devotes to public relations is aimed at increasing the President's public approval. The reason is simple: the higher the President stands in the polls, the easier it is to persuade others to support presidential initiatives.

Because of the connection between public support and presidential influence, the President's standing in the polls is monitored closely by the press, members of Congress, and others in the Washington political community. President watching is a favorite American pastime. For years the Gallup Poll has asked Americans this question: "Do you approve or disapprove of the way [John Kennedy, George Bush, or whoever] is handling his job as president?"

Presidents frequently do not have widespread public support, often failing to win every majority approval. Presidents Nixon, Gerald R. Ford, and Jimmy Carter did not even receive approval from 50 percent of the public on the average. Ronald Reagan, a "popular" President, had only a 52 percent approval level. George Bush began with solid public support, increased that significantly when he used armed force in the PERSIAN GULF WAR, but then saw his public support decline precipitously in 1992.

BIBLIOGRAPHY

Edwards, George C., III. *Presidential Approval*. 1990.
Edwards, George C., III. *The Public Presidency*. 1983.
Grossman, Michael B., and Martha J. Kumar. *Portraying the President*. 1981.
Kernell, Sam. *Going Public*. 1986.
Krosnick, Jon A., and Donald R. Kinder. "Altering the Foundations of Support for the President through Priming." *American Political Science Review* 84 (1990): 497–512.
Tulis, Jeffrey K. *The Rhetorical Presidency*. 1987.

GEORGE C. EDWARDS III

PUBLIC PAPERS OF THE PRESIDENTS. An annual publication series, the *Public Papers of the Presidents of the United States* contains most of the public messages, letters, memoranda, remarks, and statements of the Presidents that were released by the White House during a given year. Press releases, presidential documents published in the *Federal Register*, and presidential reports to Congress are listed in appendixes to each annual volume in the series, but their texts are not included in the contents. Thus, the series must be supplemented by such other sources as the *Federal Register*, the *Code of Federal Regulations*, the *Foreign Relations of the United States*, and similar accounts.

The series was inaugurated in 1957 by the Office of the Federal Register of the National Archives in response to a recommendation of the National Historical Publications Commission. Funds for the undertaking were congressionally approved in the Independent Offices Appropriation Act of 1957 (71 Stat. 231). The first volume, published by the Government Printing Office, was produced in 1958; it contained the public messages, speeches, and statements of President Dwight D. Eisenhower for 1957. Subsequent volumes have been released annually for Presidents Herbert Hoover, Harry S. Truman, John F. Kennedy, Lyndon B. Johnson, Richard M. Nixon, Gerald Ford, Jimmy Carter, Ronald Reagan, and George Bush.

The first extensive compilation of the messages and papers of the Presidents was prepared by James D. Richardson and published under congressional authority in multiple volumes. Its coverage extended through the presidency of Calvin Coolidge. Subsequently, various private compilations of presidential materials were published, but no systematic series resulted. The papers of President Franklin D. Roosevelt were compiled by his friend and White House counsel, SAMUEL ROSENMAN, and commercially published. The presidential public papers series begun by the National Archives built on Richardson by picking up Hoover, working around Roosevelt, and continuing with Truman and his successors.

BIBLIOGRAPHY

Reid, Warren R. "Public Papers of the Presidents." *American Archivist* 25 (1962): 435–439.

Schmeckebier, Laurence F., and Roy B. Eastin. *Government Publications and Their Use.* 2d rev. ed. 1969.

Stevens, Robert D., and Helen C. Stevens. "Documents in the Gilded Age: Richardson's Messages and Papers of the Presidents." *Government Publications Review* 1 (1974): 233–240.

HAROLD C. RELYEA

PUBLIC UTILITY HOLDING COMPANY ACT (1935). A centerpiece of the second NEW DEAL, the Public Utility Holding Company Act (PUHCA) provided the first comprehensive federal regulation of the utility industry. Written by BENJAMIN V. COHEN with assistance from THOMAS CORCORAN, James Landis, and others, the act authorized the Federal Power Commission (FPC) to regulate interstate shipments of electrical power, the Federal Trade Commission (FTC) to regulate natural gas shipments, and the Securities and Exchange Commission (SEC) to regulate the financial operations of public utility holding companies.

The PUHCA is widely regarded as the embodiment of the "evils of bigness" philosophy of Supreme Court Justice Louis D. Brandeis. Essentially it forced the breakup of power companies into smaller units—first by altogether prohibiting holding companies more than twice removed from their operating companies, and second by authorizing the SEC, after five years, to dissolve any holding company that impaired the advantages of local management, efficient operation, or effective regulation.

The latter provision was introduced by FELIX FRANKFURTER (at that time an adviser to President Franklin D. Roosevelt) as a compromise after a much stronger provision—the so-called "death penalty"—was objected to by the House of Representatives. The provisions of the act dealing with financial regulations have much in common with the Securities Act of 1934, also written largely by Cohen and Corcoran.

The Public Utility Holding Company Act—known before passage as the Wheeler-Rayburn bill—was controversial from the start. It was strongly opposed by the electric utility industry, which put up a strong lobbying effort led by WENDELL WILLKIE, chairman of Commonwealth and Southern Electric. In *Electric Bond & Share Co. v. Securities and Exchange Commission* (1938) the Supreme Court upheld the act's constitutionality.

BIBLIOGRAPHY

Funigiello, Philip J. *Toward a National Power Policy: The New Deal and the Electric Utility Industry, 1933–1941.* 1973.

WILLIAM LASSER

PUBLIC WORKS ADMINISTRATION. Founded in 1933 and led by Secretary of the Interior HAROLD ICKES, the Public Works Administration (PWA) was the primary NEW DEAL agency for funding large public projects such as buildings, bridges, roads, and dams. Between 1933 and 1939 the PWA was involved in the construction of 70 percent of the new schools in the United States, 65 percent of the country's courthouses, and 35 percent of its hospitals.

The agency's projects included the Lincoln Tunnel between New York and New Jersey, the San Francisco–Oakland Bay Bridge, and the aircraft carriers U.S.S. *Yorktown* and U.S.S. *Enterprise.* In the same period the PWA spent over $6 billion and was indirectly responsible, it was estimated, for the employment of more than ten million Americans. The agency initiated the federal government's role in public housing and created jobs for African American workers.

Jobs creation, in fact, was a principal focus of the PWA, though the agency soon faced competition from the Works Project Administration (as the WORKS PROGRESS ADMINISTRATION [WPA] was renamed in 1939) under HARRY HOPKINS. The two agencies sought the same end but with very different philosophies: PWA stressed the indirect creation of jobs through major capital projects, while WPA aimed simply at putting as many people to work as quickly as possible. Hopkins and Ickes were natural rivals for President Franklin D. Roosevelt's attention, and in the end Hopkins won; from Roosevelt's point of view, Hopkins's direct creation of jobs, even in make-work projects, was politically far more attractive than Ickes's more substantial but less efficient methods.

By 1935 the battle between Ickes and Hopkins was all but over, and the PWA was the loser. That year Congress appropriated only $313 million to the PWA (compared with over $3 billion in 1933), and though the agency received more money in 1938 its days were numbered. In 1939 the PWA was merged into the Federal Works Agency.

BIBLIOGRAPHY

Watkins, T. H. *Righteous Pilgrim: The Life and Times of Harold L. Ickes.* 1990.

WILLIAM LASSER

PUERTO RICO.

PUERTO RICO. In assessing the impact of different Presidents and their policies on Puerto Rico, three essential facts must be kept in mind. First, primary federal power over island matters rests with the U.S. Congress. Since 1898, when this Caribbean island became part of the United States as war booty following the SPANISH-AMERICAN WAR, the history of United States–Puerto Rican relations is full of seemingly important presidential statements regarding the island that have crashed against the wall of congressional indifference and conservatism. Presidential authority has played important roles at times, but in most fundamental areas and instance it had been subject to the overwhelming will of Congress, which wields power over the island far superior to that it has over States. Two episodes, one going back to the very origins of the U.S.–P.R. relationship and the other a very recent one, illustrate the point.

In 1899, when President William McKinley delivered his annual message to Congress, he alluded to Puerto Rico's economic predicament by saying:

> It must be borne in mind that since the cession Porto Rico has been denied the principal markets she had long enjoyed and our tariffs have been continued against her products as when she was under Spanish sovereignty. The markets of Spain are now closed to her products. . . . The island of Cuba, which used to buy her cattle and tobacco without custom duties, now imposes the same duties upon these products as from any country entering her ports. [Puerto Rico] has therefore lost her free intercourse with Spain and Cuba without compensating benefits in the [United States] markets.

President McKinley went on to recommend strongly the establishment of free trade between the United States and Puerto Rico, but his emphatic plea and his very sound reasons did not sway Congress, which chose temporarily to impose tariff duties upon the island's commerce.

Ninety years later, President George Bush, in his first message to Congress, stated that the time had come finally to resolve the matter of Puerto Rico's relationship with the United States. He expressed his preference for the admission of the island as a new state of the Union but clearly recognized that this was a matter for Puerto Ricans to decide, urging Congress to enact legislation to allow Puerto Ricans to make their choice. Two years later, after some important legislative action, Congress abandoned its effort to approve a bill authorizing a Puerto Rican referendum on the issue. A congressional stalemate, partly provoked by members of President Bush's own party, put an end to legislative efforts to implement Bush's policy.

The second essential fact is that the extent of presidential power changed significantly when Puerto Rico became a commonwealth of the United States in 1952. During the first five decades of U.S.–P.R. relations, the island was merely an American territory and most of its local government was named by the President with the consent of the U.S. Senate. The governor of Puerto Rico, all of the judges of its Supreme Court, the attorney general, the secretary of education and the auditor of the local government were all presidential appointees. Up to 1917 even the members of the upper chamber of the local legislature were named by the President. During this period of clear colonial tutelage, a few Presidents distinguished themselves by appointing well-intentioned albeit inexperienced officials. Generally, however, the posts were regarded as political plums for loyal friends, and mostly mediocre and paternalistic officials were appointed. With the establishment of commonwealth status, Puerto Rico, like a state, gained free rein in choosing all its own public officials, and presidential power over appointments, and indirectly over policy, was limited, as with the states of the Union, to key federal officials such as U.S. federal district court judges and regional heads of federal executive departments.

The third essential fact is that both before and after the establishment of commonwealth status, the most significant presidential policies and statements have been those dealing with the complex issue of U.S.–P.R. relations. Presidential decisions regarding run-of-the-mill matters, including short-range emergency questions such as relief for natural disasters, are frequent and important but none has the encompassing magnitude of presidential postures regarding Puerto Rico's status. In this regard, in addition to those already alluded to, two presidential policies merit special recognition.

The first one came about at the time when the newly created commonwealth status was submitted for approval to the United Nations General Assembly in 1952. The U.S. delegation there had asked that Puerto Rico be removed from the UNITED NATIONS list of non–self-governing territories. The request was largely based on a memorandum from President Harry S. Truman that dwelt at great length on the island's political development, and that recognized that Puerto Rico had entered into a "voluntary association with the United States" on the basis of "mutual consent," thus attaining a "full measure of self-government." The debate on the Puerto Rico issue lingered on as several members of the United Nations questioned whether Puerto Rico had fully exercised its right to free determination in choosing commonwealth status. The United Nations in 1953 finally adopted a resolution approving the new status. The 26 to 16 vote, with 18 abstentions, came after the U.S. delegate to the General Assembly read a message from President Dwight D. Eisenhower stating that if at any time Puerto Rico requested "more complete and even absolute independence," he would recommend that Congress grant it. This statement, known as the Eisenhower Declaration, helped carry the day, and has become one of the foundations for Puerto Rico's renewed quest for self-determination.

The other very special policy came about in July 1961. By that time doubts were rising both in Puerto Rico and the United States as to the real nature of the island's relationship with the mainland. Puerto Rican leaders were particularly concerned about the persistent notion that commonwealth status notwithstanding, the island remained a U.S. territory. President John F. Kennedy sought to dispel such doubts and did so with an EXECUTIVE ORDER issued 25 July 1961, which became established U.S. policy. The order summarized the 1952 congressional action and 1953 U.N. resolution approving commonwealth status; acknowledged the importance of Puerto Rico's special relationship with the United States; and instructed all departments, agencies, and officials of the executive branch to "faithfully and carefully observe and respect this [new] arrangement" in the relations between Puerto Rico and the United States.

Eisenhower and Kennedy's policies are, of course, not the last words on the matter, and they have not been faithfully honored by Congress or ensuing Presidents. They remain, however, in the eyes of many Puerto Ricans and others as the most enlightened of U.S. presidential policies regarding Puerto Rico.

BIBLIOGRAPHY

Morales-Carrión, Arturo. *Puerto Rico: A Political and Cultural History.* 1983.
Trias-Monge, J. *Constitutional History of Puerto Rico.* 1982.
Wells, Henry. *The Modernization of Puerto Rico.* 1969.

JAIME B. FUSTER

PULLMAN STRIKE. During the depression of 1893 the Pullman Company, which manufactured railroad cars, slashed wages. The workers struck and joined EUGENE V. DEBS's American Railway Union (ARU) in 1894. Pullman refused to negotiate with the union, which retaliated with a boycott: union members would not handle Pullman cars anywhere in the nation.

On the company's side was the General Managers' Association, twenty-four railroad corporations that collusively fixed wages and hours in the industry and assisted member companies in labor disputes. The managers, who declared that they would have to wipe out Debs and the union, counted on assistance from Attorney General RICHARD OLNEY. Olney, who had helped found the managers' association, had accepted appointment by President Grover Cleveland only after receiving assurance from the Chicago, Burlington, and Quincy Railroad Company that his acceptance was in the railroad's best interests. On recommendation from the managers, Olney appointed one of their number, Edwin Walker, as his special assistant in Chicago, which was the rail center of the nation and headquarters of the union. If smashed there, Olney said, the boycott, which affected twenty-seven states, would collapse everywhere else.

Olney instructed Walker to secure an injunction against the union on the ground that the boycott, by interfering with rail transportation, obstructed the Unites States mail and interstate commerce. Walker obtained a draconian injunction from the federal district court in Chicago. It prohibited any striker or union member from obstructing the mail, interstate commerce, or railroad properties; it prohibited any effort to persuade railroad employees to stop work; and it prohibited any union communications for any of those purposes. The union could not direct the boycott without violating the injunction. Similar injunctions were obtained in thirteen states.

Minor violence, some cooked up by the managers, offered a pretext for putting into action a prearranged plan. President Cleveland received a telegram from the federal attorney in Chicago requesting federal troops. The *Chicago Tribune* published fictitious stories headlined "Mob Is In Control" and "Mob Bent On Ruin"—stories that were copied by eastern papers. Cleveland, believing that federal troops were necessary to support the federal courts, ordered out the army, not the state militia, in disregard of city and state authorities and against their protests. The managers gloated: "It has now become a fight between the U.S. government and the American Railway Union." The presence of troops and July 4th libations altered the situation in Chicago. Rioting and sabotage began. Olney instructed Walker to swear in as many federal deputy marshals as he needed, and five thousand men—most of them chosen by the managers, were deputized; their number included thugs, provocateurs, and ex-convicts. The state militia had to be called out as well as the police. The strikers in Chicago found themselves opposed by fourteen thousand armed men. Thirteen people were killed, fifty-three wounded. There were shootings and injunctions elsewhere in the country, and Debs was arrested and convicted of obstruction of interstate commerce and interfering with the mails. Cleveland and his administration had smashed the Pullman strike and the boycott and, in the process, had aided the managers to annihilate the union. The Supreme Court assisted in the union-busting by its decision in IN RE DEBS (1895). Use of the labor injunction became common thereafter.

BIBLIOGRAPHY

Lindsey, Almont. *The Pullman Strike*. 1942.
Rich, Bennett M. *The Presidents and Civil Disorder*. 1941.

LEONARD W. LEVY

PUMP PRIMING. Pump priming, the economic concept that government may increase the overall level of economic activity by increasing its own spending, is one of several fiscal policy tools available to combat recession or depression. Government may effect pump priming through discretionary spending increases or through automatic stabilizers—spending programs, such as unemployment compensation or welfare, that increase automatically during business cycle downturns.

Nineteenth-century Presidents, when confronted with depression or panic conditions, disclaimed power and responsibility to cure the nation's economic ills. Commencing with Herbert Hoover in the early 1930s, modern Presidents have frequently employed pump priming in times of economic distress. Both Hoover and Franklin Roosevelt increased public works spending and instituted governmental credit programs for the benefit of farmers, businessmen, and homeowners. Yet neither depression-era President was fully committed to policies of unrestrained government spending, and both attempted to increase taxes and balance governmental budgets prematurely. Preparation for and the waging of WORLD WAR II proved to be the ultimate pump priming cure for the depression, not Roosevelt's peacetime spending initiatives.

Passage of the EMPLOYMENT ACT OF 1946 institutionalized government recession-management and allocated responsibility for fiscal policy to the President and the newly created COUNCIL OF ECONOMIC ADVISERS. Commencing with Harry Truman, pump priming initiatives surfaced sporadically after World War II, with spending programs often linked to tax reductions. Democratic Presidents John Kennedy and Lyndon Johnson were the most committed practitioners of such economic fine-tuning. But even Richard Nixon—who relied almost exclusively on monetary policy during the initial years of his presidency—described himself as Keynesian by 1971.

Ideological support for pump-priming techniques soured after the inflation-ridden 1970s. Policy experience of the previous twenty years suggested that interventionist administrations sometimes applied discretionary fiscal stimulus too late after the commencement of cyclical downturns, either because of economic forecasting deficiencies that did not permit adequate recession warnings or because of delays in the congressional appropriations process. Fiscal stimulus so delayed could then boost the economy too much in the recovery phase, leading to price inflation and real shortages. Many economists, therefore, abandoned ad hoc interventionism in favor of automatic stabilizers and monetary policy as preferred tools to mitigate business downturns.

Ronald Reagan, reflecting this new ideological antipathy to pump priming, disclaimed fiscal demand-side management in favor of supply-side tax policies intended to promote long-term growth rather than short-term full employment. Still, Reagan was a prolific pump primer in his own right, combining a huge military build-up, tax reductions, and ever-increasing governmental deficits to achieve the economic expansion of the 1980s. Ironically, Reagan's heritage of budgetary deficits restricted George Bush's ability to engage in a fresh round of pump priming to combat renewed recession in 1990, and Bush's hesitant response to rising unemployment was fatal to his reelection effort in 1992. As presidential transition loomed in early 1993, it remained unclear how Bill Clinton would reconcile his own campaign commitments to short-term fiscal stimulus and long-term deficit reduction.

BIBLIOGRAPHY

Boskin, Michael J. *Reagan and the Economy: The Successes, Failures, and Unfinished Agenda*. 1989.
Stein, Herbert. *Presidential Economics: The Making of Economic Policy From Roosevelt to Reagan and Beyond*. 2nd rev. ed. 1988.

RALPH MITZENMACHER

QUADRENNIAL SALARY COMMISSION.
Since 1967, there has been a statutory policy that salaries of top federal officials in each of the three branches will receive an independent review every four years. The review by the Citizens' Commission on Public Service and Compensation in fiscal 1994 was the initial salary study conducted pursuant to the provisions of the Ethics Reform Act of 1989 (103 Stat. 1716).

The Citizens' Commission is comprised of six members, two each appointed by the President, the Congress, and the judiciary, along with five members chosen by lot from registered voters from various regions of the country. The Citizens' Commission is charged with making recommendations to the President by 15 December of the year of their appointment. The President then must make his recommendations at some point during the following month. Although Congress must approve or disapprove by recorded vote the President's recommendations, it is not required to act within any given time frame. However, there must be an intervening election of the House of Representatives between the point of approval and the effective date of any salary adjustments. These provisions of the Ethics Reform Act of 1989 meet the intervening election requirement of the twenty-seventh Amendment to the Constitution, ratified in May 1992.

The salaries covered by the review are those paid to the Vice President, the Justices of the Supreme Court and other federal judges, Speaker of the House of Representatives, president pro tem of the Senate, majority and minority leaders and members of both houses of Congress, and the officials in the executive

branch who are on the executive schedule. Many other managerial and administrative positions that do not fall within the categories listed are directly linked by statute to them and, therefore, are affected by the results of the quadrennial reviews. It is estimated that as many as ten thousand salaried positions are affected.

Legislation in 1967 established the quadrennial review mechanism (81 Stat. 613). There was a general consensus that responsible personnel management within the federal system required that the rank and file salaries be established at levels comparable to those in the private sector and that salaries of high-level policymakers be reviewed on a relatively systematic basis so that two goals might be achieved: first, the officials' salaries would be removed from the direct political arena, and second, all salaries would be more in line with the marketplace. As long as Congress was responsible for legislating all salary adjustments, the system was prone to delays, inequities, and compression in the lower ranks because the upper ranks were not being adjusted.

The Commission on Executive, Legislative, and Judicial Salaries was activated six times. The commission recommendations, which uniformly were changed somewhat by each President, met with mixed results. There were significant salary adjustments pursuant to three of the seven commissions activated prior to the Ethics Reform Act of 1989. Issues other than salary concerned the commissions. For example, the 1977 adjustment was predicated on enactment of a strong code of public conduct and the 1987 adjustment came only after the fiscal 1985 commission reported that it would not make salary recommendations but did recommend action by the Congress to change the approval/disapproval process and only then to establish a special commission outside the quadrennial cycle for the purpose of recommending salaries (99 Stat. 1322).

BIBLIOGRAPHY

Hartman, Robert W., and Arnold R. Weber, eds. *The Rewards of Public Service; Compensating Top Federal Officials.* 1980.
U.S. House of Representatives. Committee on Post Office and Civil Service. *The Report of the Commission on Executive, Legislative and Judicial Salaries.* 94th Cong., 2d sess., 1976. Committee Print No. 94–27.

SHARON STIVER GRESSLE

QUADRIAD. During the John F. Kennedy administration, the Secretary of the Treasury, the director of the budget, the chairman of the COUNCIL OF ECONOMIC ADVISERS (CEA), and the chairman of the FEDERAL RESERVE BOARD, meeting together, were dubbed "the quadriad." Such meetings, often with the President, had begun at least as early as the Franklin D. Roosevelt administration (before the creation of the Council of Economic Advisers) and had become more regular during the Dwight D. Eisenhower administration as a means of coordinating economic policy. Staff proposals to routinize quadriad meetings stressed the importance of avoiding any sense of crisis that might otherwise accompany an "unusual" meeting of top economic officials. Although the name *quadriad* has been applied unevenly since the Johnson administration, the use of economic policy coordinating committees has continued.

The use and effectiveness of the quadriad has varied over time, reflecting the personality and styles of the individuals involved. Top officials in the Kennedy and Johnson administrations promoted quadriad meetings with the President because they believed the meetings had the effect of increasing Federal Reserve cooperation with administration policy.

The quadriad continued to meet in the Richard M. Nixon administration, but after Arthur Burns assumed the chairmanship of the Federal Reserve the usefulness of the quadriad as a two-way communication mechanism declined. By the Gerald Ford administration, the quadriad was little used, reflecting in large part the relatively close relationship that developed between Burns and Ford.

There were quarterly meetings of the quadriad during the Jimmy Carter years, but this proved to be no guarantee of a smooth relationship between the administration and the Federal Reserve. In the Ronald Reagan administration, the quadriad was little used; indeed, Reagan's style of reliance on a few key staff members together with his general lack of interest in MONETARY POLICY meant that he rarely participated in any meetings that involved the chairman of the Federal Reserve.

In the Bush administration, the task of coordinating economic policy was assigned to the Economic Policy Council, which sometimes met in the configuration referred to as the quadriad. Due to deteriorating relationships between Treasury Secretary Nicholas F. Brady and Federal Reserve Chairman Alan Greenspan, efforts to elicit cooperation from the Federal Reserve fell increasingly to President Bush individually.

BIBLIOGRAPHY

Bach, G. L. *Making Monetary and Fiscal Policy.* 1971.
Kettl, Donald. *Leadership at the Fed.* 1986.
Niskanen, William. *Reaganomics.* 1988.

JOHN T. WOOLLEY

QUALIFICATIONS FOR PRESIDENT. The Constitution provides that "No Person except a natural born Citizen, or a Citizen of the United States at the time of the Adoption of this Constitution, shall be eligible to the Office of President; neither shall any Person be eligible to that Office who shall not have attained to the Age of thirty five Years, and been fourteen Years a Resident within the United States." The TWENTY-SECOND AMENDMENT, which was added to the Constitution in 1951, further disqualifies any person who already has been elected to two terms as President, or who has been elected once and, through succession, has served more than half of another President's four-year term.

In the constitutional theories that prevailed during the late eighteenth century, stated qualifications for office were widely regarded as necessary to prevent certain kinds of people from even coming before the voters. Several state constitutions required that the governor meet a minimum property-owning (often land-owning) standard, the idea being that voters should be restricted to choosing among candidates with a substantial economic stake in the community. Some states specified that a profession of Christianity, or even Protestantism, was a minimum constitutional requirement for election, perhaps in accordance with the then-widespread common law rule that only Christians could be relied upon to swear to affirm a valid oath of office. Age and residency requirements for governor were less prevalent.

The Constitutional Convention. The qualifications for President that were included in the plan of government that the Framers wrote at the CONSTITUTIONAL CONVENTION of 1787 do not accord with the common theory and practice of the time. Religious qualifications were, with little debate, explicitly rejected; indeed, Article VI of the Constitution provides that "no religious Test shall ever be required as a Qualification to any Office or public Trust under the United States."

The issue of property qualifications was more vexing to the delegates. On 26 July, two months after the opening of the convention, they approved a motion that "the President of the US[,] the Judges, and members of the Legislature should be required to swear that they were respectively possessed of a clear unencumbered Estate to the amount of—— in the case of the President &c &c." But the delegates retreated from that decision when John Rutledge of South Carolina, who chaired the committee that was charged to come up with a specific figure for property ownership, confessed that he was "embarrassed by the danger on one side of displeasing the people by making them [the property qualifications] too high, and on the other of rending them nugatory by making them low."

No statement of the age, citizenship, and residency requirements that eventually were included in the Constitution was made until 7 September, when the convention, unanimously and without debate, approved a committee recommendation that the President be at least thirty-five years old, a natural-born citizen (or a citizen at the time of the Constitution's adoption), and a resident of the United States for at least fourteen years. Prior to that late date (the Convention ended just ten days later), the delegates seem to have been operating on the principle that qualifications for an office were unnecessary if qualifications for those who choose the person to fill the office already had been established. Thus, qualifications for judges and other appointed officials were never included in the Constitution because they were to be selected by other government officials for whom qualifications were stated. Conversely, because qualifications were not stated for voters, they were established for members of Congress as early as James Madison's Virginia Plan, which was proposed during the first week of the convention.

Throughout most of the Convention, the majority of delegates remained wedded to the idea that Congress, a body of constitutionally "qualified" members, would elect the President. Thus, no need was seen to include qualifications for President in the Constitution. When, in September, the delegates decided that a constitutionally "unqualified" ELECTORAL COLLEGE should choose the President, they added a presidential qualifications clause as well.

The Qualifications. Because no debate accompanied the delegates' decisions on presidential qualifications, any explanation of why they chose the age, residency, and citizenship requirements that are in the Constitution must be somewhat speculative.

Age. An age requirement of thirty-five years was included in the qualifications clause for two apparent reasons. First, the delegates presumed that age would foster maturity in a President. As George Mason of Virginia said in the debate concerning the minimum age for members of the House of Representatives, "every man carries with him in his own experience a scale for measuring the deficiency of young politicians, since he would if interrogated be obliged to declare that his political opinions at the age of twenty-one were too crude & erroneous to merit an influence on public measures." Second, it was believed, the passage of years in a candidate's life left in its wake a public record for the voters to assess. According to JOHN JAY, the author of FEDERALIST 64, the age requirement "confines the electors to men of whom the people have had time to form a judgment, and with respect to whom they will not be liable to be deceived by those brilliant appearances of genius and patriotism which, like transient meteors, sometimes mislead as well as dazzle."

Residency. The stipulation that the President must be at least fourteen years a resident of the United States was designed to eliminate from consideration both British sympathizers who had fled to England during the American Revolution and popular foreign military leaders, notably Baron Frederick von Steuben of Prussia, who had emigrated to the United States to fight in the revolution. As for the fourteen-year length of the residency requirement (which was substituted for an initial proposal of twenty-one years), it is worth noting that although the latter length would have excluded three of the delegates from eligibility to the presidency, the former excluded none.

Citizenship. The reason for requiring that the President must be a natural-born citizen was also tied to contemporary politics. Rumors had spread while the convention was meeting that the delegates were plotting to invite a European monarch to rule the United States. To refute these rumors, the delegates issued the only press release of their otherwise secret deliberations, telling the *Pennsylvania Journal* that "though we cannot, affirmatively, tell you what we are doing, we can, negatively, tell you what we are not doing—we never once thought of a king." More tangibly, they also added the natural-born citizen requirement to the

Constitution so that no critic could plausibly charge during the ratification debates that the presidency was a latent European monarchy.

Constitutional Amendments. The two-term limit on Presidents, which was established by the Twenty-second Amendment in 1951, bespoke the politics of its time as surely as the citizenship and residency requirements in the original Constitution bespoke the politics of 1787. From 1932 to 1944, Franklin D. Roosevelt, a liberal Democrat, was elected to four consecutive terms as President. The Republicans, who took control of Congress in 1947 for the first time since 1930, banded with conservative southern Democrats to enact a constitutional amendment that would disqualify any future Roosevelt from serving more than twice. Ironically, the only two Presidents whom the two-term limit has really restricted have been the Republicans Dwight D. Eisenhower and Ronald Reagan, both of whom opposed the amendment.

The TWELFTH AMENDMENT, which became part of the Constitution in 1804, applied the President's age, residency, and citizenship requirements to the VICE PRESIDENT.

Constitutional Ambiguities. A number of thorny legal questions attend the Constitution's provisions for presidential qualifications, for example, whether the residency requirement entails fourteen *consecutive* years in the United States prior to the election. Some challenged Herbert Hoover's eligibility to be President in 1929 by arguing that much of his time during the preceding fourteen years had been spent abroad. Hoover's defenders prevailed on the narrow ground that he had maintained a legal domicile in the United States throughout this period.

An even more unsettled issue is whether the "natural born Citizen" requirement disqualifies those who are born of American parents on foreign soil. As the legal scholar Charles Gordon has argued, the principle of *jus sanguinis*, "under which nationality could be transmitted by descent at the moment of birth," was more a part of the common law in 1787 than the old doctrine of *jus soli*, which determined a person's nationality according to the place of birth. But a controversial statement by Justice Horace Gray in the 1898 case of *United States v. Kim Ark* seemed to restrict natural-born citizenship to those born "within the United States." The case did not concern presidential qualifications, however, and Gray's remark was not legally binding.

The legal complexities of the citizenship requirement aside, many have criticized its wisdom. In the late 1970s, the Secretary of State HENRY A. KISSINGER, a naturalized U.S. citizen of German birth, was barred

by the presidential qualifications clause from his office's legal place in the line of succession to the presidency. In 1983, Senator Thomas Eagleton of Missouri proposed a constitutional amendment to repeal the citizenship and residency qualifications for President in favor of a requirement that the President must be a citizen for eleven years.

[*See also* CREATION OF THE PRESIDENCY.]

BIBLIOGRAPHY

Gordon, Charles. "Who Can Be President of the United States?: The Unresolved Enigma." *Maryland Law Review* 28 (Winter 1968): 1–32.
Nelson, Michael. "Constitutional Qualifications for President." In *Inventing the American Presidency*. Edited by Thomas E. Cronin. 1989. Pp. 13–32.

MICHAEL NELSON

QUASI-WAR WITH FRANCE (1798–1800). JAY'S TREATY placed severe strains on the relationship between France and the United States, resulting in a series of confiscatory French decrees that put American vessels and their cargoes at risk. In late 1796, France refused to receive the U.S. minister and ordered him out of the country. At a special session of Congress called on 16 May 1797, President John Adams explained the deteriorating conditions with France, including the suspension of diplomatic relations. While pledging to pursue negotiations toward a peaceful resolution, he urged Congress to enact legislation to strengthen America's naval power and to adopt other "effectual measures of defense."

Adams's major diplomatic effort was to send a bipartisan commission to France to negotiate a settlement. This initiative degenerated into what became known as the XYZ affair: France insisted that America offer bribes and loans, in part to compensate for Adams's criticism of French actions. Publication of this information inflamed American public opinion, inspiring the patriotic slogan, "Millions for defense, but not one cent for tribute," and prompting measures to push the country toward war.

In 1798, Congress enacted a number of laws to support military action by the President. A series of statutes granted supplemental funds for naval armament, increased the number of ships, authorized additional regiment of artillerists and engineers, reinforced the defense of ports and harbors, funded additional cannons, arms, and ammunition, empowered the President to raise a provisional army and seize French ships, and suspended commerce with France.

Congress also terminated the 1778 treaty of amity and commerce with France. Out of this war climate came the repressive ALIEN AND SEDITION ACTS of 1798 and the LOGAN ACT of 1799, which prohibited private citizens from encroaching on presidential duties by negotiating with foreign governments.

The Quasi-War represents America's first undeclared war. Although Congress did not formally declare war on France, there was never any doubt that it authorized the President to conduct war. During the debates of 1798, Congressman Edward Livingston considered the country "now in a state of war; and let no man flatter himself that the vote which has been given is not a declaration of war."

Official responsibility of naval warfare fell to Secretary of War James McHenry, widely regarded as incompetent. To remedy this deficiency, Congress enacted a separate Department of the Navy on 30 April 1798. Adams's first choice for Secretary of the Navy, George Cabot, refused to serve. His second choice, Benjamin Stoddert, accepted, and the Senate quickly confirmed him. On 2 July 1798, President Adams nominated George Washington to be COMMANDER IN CHIEF of the army to defend against invasion. Washington accepted, but he insisted that ALEXANDER HAMILTON serve as second in command. The war, however, was fought on the high seas.

Adams, who had a strong background in naval strategy, established the general policy but delegated extensive powers to Stoddert, who proved to be an able administrator. France was preoccupied with its European wars and depended largely on privateers supported by a few frigates and sloops of war to conduct its combat with American vessels. The augmented American Navy dominated the military engagements and inflicted heavy losses on the French. On 30 September 1800, a convention of peace, commerce, and navigation was concluded. The financial difficulty that France experienced in meeting its obligations under this treaty helped set the stage for the LOUISIANA PURCHASE.

The Quasi-War provoked several decisions by the Supreme Court that helped define presidential WAR POWERS and the authority of Congress to limit the President. In two rulings, the Court recognized that Congress could authorize hostilities either by a formal declaration of war or by a statute authorizing an undeclared war. As noted in *Bas v. Tingy* (1800) and *Talbot v. Seeman* (1801), military conflicts could be "limited," "partial," and "imperfect," without requiring a formal declaration. In *Talbot*, Chief Justice JOHN MARSHALL wrote for the Court, "The whole powers of war being, by the constitution of the United States,

vested in congress, the acts of that body can alone be resorted to as our guides in this inquiry." A similar judgment appears in LITTLE v. BARREME (1804), another case generated by the Quasi-War. A statute from the 1798–1800 period had authorized the President to seize vessels sailing to French ports, but President Adams issued an order directing American commanders to capture ships sailing both to and from French ports. Chief Justice Marshall decided that Adams had exceeded the authority given him by Congress. According to the ruling, presidential orders to military commanders could not be inconsistent with national policy established by Congress in a statute.

BIBLIOGRAPHY

Anderson, William G. "John Adams, the Navy, and the Quasi-War with France." *American Neptune* 30 (1970): 117–132.

Deconde, Alexander. *The Quasi-War: The Politics and Diplomacy of the Undeclared War with France, 1797–1801.* 1966.

Palmer, Michael J. *Stoddert's War: Naval Operations during the Quasi-War with France, 1798–1801.* 1987.

LOUIS FISHER

QUAYLE, DAN (b. 1947) Congressman, Senator, forty-fourth Vice President of the United States (1989–1993). James Danforth Quayle was a young rising star in the United States Senate when George Bush tapped him to be his running mate during the 1988 presidential campaign. In some ways, the choice proved unfortunate for Quayle. Virtually unknown on the national scene, he was patronized by the newsmedia and treated as if he were a political featherweight. The coverage was largely unfair. Media reports to the contrary, Quayle had already proved himself intelligent, industrious, and ambitious.

A young lawyer and newspaperman from Indiana, he had defeated a Democratic incumbent in a congressional race in 1976, the same year his party lost the presidency. Two years later, at age thirty-one, Quayle unseated the distinguished Democratic Senator Birch Bayh. Quayle's record in Congress was not flashy, but it was respectable. In the Senate, he formed a group of Republican Senators to work on defense-related issues, and he played a leading role in getting an important clarification attached to the Reagan administration's INF (INTERMEDIATE-RANGE NUCLEAR FORCES) TREATY with the Soviet Union in 1988. He was also politically astute, looking for opportunities to move ahead. In early 1988, he began a behind-the-scenes campaign to be chosen as George Bush's running mate, should Bush win the Republican Party's presidential nomination.

Philosophically conservative, Quayle was not afraid to be flexible about the uses of federal power. In the early 1980s, for example, he drafted and then pushed through Congress a major federal jobs program, the Job Training Partnership Act of 1982. Initially opposed by the Reagan administration, the act passed because Quayle was able to forge a legislative alliance with such liberal Democrats as Senator Edward Kennedy.

Quayle's first years as Vice President showed him to be hard-working but low-key. Following George Bush's example as Vice President, Quayle was the consummate team player, viewing his primary role as a champion of the President's policies. Quayle traveled extensively around the country in support of Republican candidates and around the world as a stand-in for President Bush. Equally important, Quayle served as the Bush administration's chief liaison with Congress, regularly spending two days a week on Capitol Hill lobbying and listening to his former colleagues.

Quayle also chaired the President's Council on Competitiveness and the National Space Council. The former group served as the Bush administration's de facto board of review for major new federal regulations. Analyzing regulations for their economic impact, it sought to balance the need for regulation with potential economic costs. Quayle viewed the Competitiveness Council as a necessary check on the sprawling regulatory establishment. Declaring that "the future of the country is at stake," he argued that a way had to be found to "tame" the federal bureaucracy.

Much of the council's work was unobtrusive, but it also became an idea shop for key Bush administration initiatives. In 1991, for example, it produced a list of fifty reforms of the judicial system intended to reduce the rampant growth of litigation. The Vice President unveiled the package in a widely noted speech before a hostile audience at the American Bar Association. Other major initiatives developed by Quayle through the council include the redrafting of wetlands regulations to protect property rights and proposals to streamline the approval process for new drugs used against life-threatening illnesses such as AIDS, cancer, and Alzheimer's disease.

As chairman of the National Space Council, meanwhile, Quayle spearheaded a major reorganization of the national space program, and he developed a new policy to promote the commercial uses of space. As part of his efforts at reorganization, Quayle urged the President to fire NASA chief Richard Truly, which Bush eventually did.

During the 1992 primary campaign, Quayle was assigned the role of shoring up President Bush's rela-

tions with the conservative wing of the REPUBLICAN PARTY. During the primaries, he was sent on the attack against Patrick Buchanan, who mounted a lively, if ineffectual, challenge to Bush from the right. As the primary season drew to a close, Quayle turned his attention to the theme of "traditional values," decrying the collapse of the two-parent family and attacking America's "cultural elite" for the way it despised the moral standards upon which Western civilization had been built. Quayle's evocation of this theme sparked comparisons to SPIRO T. AGNEW in Nixon's 1972 presidential campaign.

Despite his reputable performance as Vice President, Quayle continued to struggle against the early doubts that had been raised about his abilities, proving that first impressions can be hard to break.

BIBLIOGRAPHY

Broder, David S., and Bob Woodward. *The Man Who Would Be President: Dan Quayle*. 1992.
Fenno, Richard. *The Making of a Senator: Dan Quayle*. 1988.

JOHN G. WEST, JR.

QUEBEC CONFERENCE (1943). The Quebec Conference of August 1943 during WORLD WAR II enabled President Franklin D. Roosevelt and Prime Minister Winston Churchill to resolve questions of strategy following the successful Allied invasion of Sicily in July. On 25 July a bloodless coup overthrew Mussolini. Mussolini's former chief of staff, General Pietro Badoglio, succeeded him as Italy's prime minister. To avoid anarchy in Italy, Roosevelt and Churchill were inclined to recognize the Badoglio government. When the Quebec Conference opened on 17 August, Badoglio announced his intention to take Italy out of the war. Roosevelt demanded that his government declare war on Germany and issue a statement of intent to accept a popularly elected government after Germany's defeat. Stalin accused Roosevelt and Churchill of excluding the U.S.S.R. from the Italian surrender negotiations. Finally on 13 October the Badoglio government accepted Roosevelt's demands, and he and Churchill recognized Italy's cobelligerency.

Meanwhile Roosevelt had responded to Stalin's continuing demands for a second front by agreeing to OVERLORD, a cross-Channel invasion of northwest France in May 1944. The President wanted U.S. and British forces to take Italy but denied Churchill's plea for an Anglo-American venture into the Balkans. He shared Churchill's concern for Soviet expansion into the region but remained convinced that the Western powers could reach some accommodation with the

Soviets on the future of Eastern Europe. At Quebec, Roosevelt, with the aid of the American JOINT CHIEFS OF STAFF, extracted a still-qualified British commitment to OVERLORD. As the Quebec Conference ended on 24 August, Churchill cautioned against OVERLORD if Germany had more than twelve mobile divisions in northern France and if the Allies had not gained control of the air.

BIBLIOGRAPHY

Dallek, Robert. *Franklin D. Roosevelt and American Foreign Policy, 1932–1945.* 1979.

Feis, Herbert. *Churchill, Roosevelt, Stalin: The War They Waged and the Peace They Sought.* 1957.

Sherwood, Robert. *Roosevelt and Hopkins.* 1950.

NORMAN A. GRAEBNER

RADICALISM. In late-eighteenth-century America, radicalism connoted opposition to vested interests, social privilege, ascribed status, and aristocratic elites. A century later, radicalism had come to signify class consciousness, social change, and belief in an alternate economic order.

President Theodore Roosevelt established a pattern of presidential rhetoric and actions toward radicals. Regarding anarchism as "a crime against the whole human race," he proposed the exclusion of all anarchists, to which Congress agreed in 1903. He similarly condemned the Socialist Party, founded in 1901, which he felt was "far more ominous than any populist or similar movement in time past."

Roosevelt and Wilson. Roosevelt's antianarchist animus extended beyond socialists and communists to other radicals such as members of the Western Federation of Miners (WFM) and, after its founding in 1905, the Industrial Workers of the World (IWW), known as the Wobblies. In 1907, Roosevelt sent federal troops into Nevada against both unions, at the request of Governor John Sparks. For virtually all Americans, including Roosevelt, these unions were synonymous with socialism, which in turn was synonymous with anarchism and assassination.

President William Howard Taft expressed sentiments similar to Roosevelt's, and President Woodrow Wilson's election victory in 1912 brought no lessening of government hostility toward radical unions like the IWW or to radicalism generally. Even before the United States entered WORLD WAR I radicals felt the effect of federal prosecution. Wilson reacted similarly to all who failed to endorse his prewar or wartime decisions. In his third annual message to Congress,

which included an arms preparedness program, he charged that foreign-born opponents of his policy—radicals and pacifists—were "pouring the poison of disloyalty into the very arteries of our national life." Invariably Wilson questioned the patriotism of those opposing preparedness, and he condemned pacifists.

The IWW's talk about violent class warfare and the overthrow of capitalism led Wilson to approve repressive action against both its leadership and rank and file. Detesting labor radicalism, he thought the IWW was "a menace to organized society and the right conduct of industry" and sent federal troops into labor disputes in Colorado, Montana, Arizona, and the state of Washington.

Wilson did not object to mobilizing law enforcement authorities against the IWW or radicals in general. Large-scale deportation proceedings of alien radicals, primarily IWW members, were yet another string in the federal prosecutorial bow. The Bureau of Investigation—the parent of the FEDERAL BUREAU OF INVESTIGATION (FBI)—opened a nationwide investigation, raided twenty IWW offices with the help of civilian volunteers, arrested hundreds and confiscated "more than five tons" of radical literature. Indictment on conspiracy charges and violation of the 1917 Espionage Act—indeed violations of eleven different statutes and presidential proclamations—led to the conviction of 166 Wobblies in Chicago, including the entire general executive board. It was followed by local and regional trials of Wobblies elsewhere.

Considering the 1917 act a mild measure, Wilson supported its amendment, the 1918 Sedition Act, as well as the 1918 Alien Act. These statutes reinforced the national mood of hysteria, especially so when reaction to the Bolshevik revolution added a violent anti-Communist ingredient to the anti-German, anti-pacifist, anti-IWW atmosphere. Investigations affecting CIVIL LIBERTIES were undertaken by multiple federal agencies. Suspects were indicted, tried in federal court and, given the climate of wartime and postwar patriotism, quickly convicted. Wilson agreed that IWW leaders should be prosecuted for violating the Espionage Act.

Even after expressing grave doubts about the justice of suppressing certain newspapers, he wanted to have the managing editor of the *Kansas City Star* indicted for publishing a letter opposed to the war. Appeals to the White House from radicals, liberals, and civil libertarians made no impression on him, and he declared that authority to censor was "absolutely necessary to the public safety."

Peace did not bring an end to federal indictments, trials, and prison terms for radicals. Amnesty campaigns found most CABINET members as well as the President unrelenting. Wilson approved of the PALMER RAIDS, the roundup and arrests of about three thousand allegedly subversive aliens. Wilson could not forgive those who had opposed the war. He refused to consider a general amnesty or individual pardons for thousands: "In each instance I have had the matter thoroughly looked into and am in a position to contest the accuracy of any statement that the rights of a single citizen have been unjustly invaded." "I do not deem it wise to pardon EUGENE V. DEBS," the President wrote, "I will never consent to the pardon of this man." Wilson's more amiable successor, President Warren G. Harding, released Debs on Christmas Day, 1921.

Between the Wars. Deportation of alien radicals, however, continued into the Harding years. President Harding, moreover, would not offer executive clemency to Wobblies and considered political crime more of a menace than ordinary crime.

President Calvin Coolidge appointed Harlan Stone as Attorney General, a step for decency, and Stone ordered J. EDGAR HOOVER to discontinue all intelligence-gathering operations on radicals. He also unconditionally pardoned the remaining Wobblies who had languished in federal prisons (and President Franklin D. Roosevelt would pardon the last of the prisoners during his first year in office).

When communist protesters at the White House were arrested by police in December 1929, President Herbert Hoover immediately ordered their release. Hoover's Justice Department, however, pursued court cases involving denial of citizenship to a number of pacifists and radicals and authorized the army to evict the BONUS ARMY from a shantytown near the Capitol in 1932.

President Roosevelt personally authorized FBI surveillance of subversive organizations in August 1936. He authorized warrantless buggings of homes or conversations when "grave matters involving the defense of the nation" were involved and thus inadvertently gave the FBI carte blanche for a warrantless wiretap of anyone "suspected of subversive activities." [*See* ELECTRONIC SURVEILLANCE.]

Roosevelt also signed the HATCH ACT (1939), section 9A of which prohibited federal employees from being members of "any political party or organization which advocates the overthrow of our constitutional form of government"; and it became the duty of the executive branch to screen all personnel. The Civil Service Commission concluded that being a "follower" of communism raised a "strong presumption" against one's loyalty to the United States. The President also signed into law the 1940 Alien Registration Act, known as the Smith Act, notwithstanding a distaste for any assault upon rights of aliens. A peacetime sedition measure, and comparable to the 1917 Espionage Act, it embodied most of the antiradical legislation of the past twenty years. The law received its first application in 1941, when a federal grand jury handed down an indictment in Minneapolis against twenty-nine members of the Socialist Workers Party, an ineffectual and insignificant organization of Trotskyites who had been arrested and sent to jail by order of Roosevelt's Attorney General.

The Cold War Loyalty Programs. President Harry S. Truman's views were reflected in EXECUTIVE ORDER 9835, which established a comprehensive LOYALTY-SECURITY PROGRAM for all federal employees. It subjected current employees and applicants for civilian employment in the executive branch to loyalty investigation by the FBI. When "reasonable grounds" existed for belief in an employee's disloyalty, a hearing was held before the agency's loyalty board. Despite presidential assurances to the contrary, the right of the accused to due process—the right to full disclosure of charges, or to confront accusers and to cross-examine witnesses—was denied. The Attorney General supplied the agency's hearing board with a list of 275 "communist, or subversive" organizations, which went far toward sanctioning guilt by association and which made membership, affiliation, even sympathy with such groups a basis for determining disloyalty and discharge. In effect, the agency's hearing board and an appellate loyalty review board became both judge and prosecutor, and the government could deny employment or remove the employee. [*See* ATTORNEY GENERAL'S SUBVERSIVES LIST.]

In July 1948, the Truman administration indicted the top leaders of the Communist Party of the United

States (CPUSA) under the Smith Act, on charges of open advocacy of the overthrow of the government by force and violence. The McCarran-Walter Act of 1952 altered immigration law to screen out "subversives" and provided for deportation of immigrants and naturalized citizens who held to communist and "communist-front" affiliations. Truman signed this measure and boasted of the work of the FBI in national-security areas.

Truman, however, vetoed the McCarran Internal Security Act of 1950, a measure repressive to the point of hysteria. Instead, he sought to build safeguards into his loyalty-security program that would prevent an employee from being "fired without evidence" or only owing to "rumor, gossip, or suspicion," and he condemned the House Committee on Un-American Activities for its illiberalism and "red-herring" activities. But he was also convinced that "Communist infiltration [was] . . . a threat" to the United States.

President Dwight D. Eisenhower, by both action and apathy, tacitly encouraged antiradical repression during the COLD WAR. Like his predecessors', his administration was marked by tension between libertarian rhetoric and illiberal practices. The Justice Department continued to indict and prosecute Communist Party leaders. The Passport Division of the State Department denied travel abroad to, among others, the novelist Howard Fast, the playwright Arthur Miller, Justice William O. Douglas, the artist Rockwell Kent, and the singer and actor Paul Robeson.

In April 1953, Eisenhower promulgated Executive Order 10450, establishing a new federal loyalty program. More sweeping than the earlier Truman program, it made "the interests of the national security," not loyalty, the prime criterion for discharge from governmental service. All federal employees were now subject to discharge for association with any subversive organization. Eisenhower also signed the Communist Control Act of 1954, virtually outlawing the CPUSA.

Loyalty probes mounted rather than diminished, and loyalty and security considerations dominated in Washington, D.C. The Attorney General, Herbert Brownell reported in 1954 that "enforcement of laws has resulted in the conviction of 41 top Communist leaders," the indictment of 35 more, "and 105 subversive aliens have been deported."

From Vietnam to Reagan. Presidents Lyndon B. Johnson and Richard M. Nixon resented the widespread, increasingly intense protest movement against the VIETNAM WAR. COINTELPRO, the FBI's massive domestic spying program, had begun in the early 1950s and continued into the early 1970s. Nixon, according to CENTRAL INTELLIGENCE AGENCY Director

Richard Helms, authorized CIA concentration against the New Left. The CIA infiltrated antiwar groups and ran an illegal campaign of wiretaps and mail openings on some of the roughly ten thousand Americans whose names were in its files.

Nixon also approved the Huston Plan, which allowed illegal break-ins and telephone and mail surveillance to gather information on suspected subversives, antiwar dissidents, and black extremists. Later he rescinded the plan; but the CIA's Operation Chaos and the FBI's COINTELPRO as well as other covert counterintelligence operations continued, directed toward antiwar, antidraft "agitation, propaganda, or organized effort." Army agents infiltrated the antiwar moratorium marches of October and November 1969, and the army's subversive file contained more than 210,000 dossiers on organizations and 80,000 biographical files, mostly of radicals or alleged radicals. The army's Counter Intelligence Analysis Branch monitored domestic protest activity and engaged in the surveillance of the Trotskyite Young Socialist Alliance.

In the 1980s, fifty-two of the fifty-nine regional offices of the FBI remained involved in open-ended domestic-security investigations that included bugging and burglaries against radicals, pacifists, and Christian passive resistants, who opposed American involvement in Nicaragua and El Salvador. President Ronald Reagan pardoned convicted FBI officials who had authorized a series of illegal searches in their hunt for fugitive radicals. Reagan also issued a secret executive order (E.O. 12333, signed on 4 December 1981) allowing domestic surveillance and other intrusive investigative techniques, such as warrantless wiretaps, without specific suspicion of crime, by federal agencies, including the CIA. Moreover, deportation actions were initiated, such as one against a woman alien who wrote favorably about the revolutions in CUBA and Nicaragua. Reagan's administration continued to bar alien radicals from visiting the United States, a policy that continued early into the Bush presidency (under the McCarran-Walter Act of 1952), though on a lesser scale.

BIBLIOGRAPHY

Blanchard, Margaret A. *Revolutionary Sparks: Freedom of Expression in Modern America.* 1992.
Dubovsky, Melvyn. *We Shall Be All.* 1969.
Goldstein, Robert. *Political Repression in Modern America.* 1978.
Longaker, Richard. *The Presidency and Industrial Disputes.* 1963.
Murphy, Paul. *The Constitution in Crisis Times.* 1972.
Preston, William. *Aliens and Dissenters.* 1963.
Smith, James Morton. *Freedom's Fetters.* 1956.

MILTON CANTOR

RADICAL REPUBLICANS. A faction, or wing, of the REPUBLICAN PARTY in the CIVIL WAR and RECONSTRUCTION era, the Radical Republicans advocated extreme measures against the South and the system of SLAVERY. Although the terms *Radical* and *Republican* have often been treated as synonymous, the Radicals were, in fact, never a numerical majority nor the dominant element within the party. Instead, they were a vocal and forceful vanguard that pressured the Republicans into considering, and sometimes adopting, advanced positions.

When the Republican Party was formed in the 1850s, the Radicals were those most hostile to slavery. Not necessarily abolitionists, they nevertheless saw the party as an agency for crusading against slavery rather than as an end in itself. During the war, the Radicals, led by Zachariah Chandler, Benjamin F. Wade, and Charles Sumner in the Senate and Thaddeus Stevens, Henry Winter Davis, and George W. Julian in the House, urged the adoption of confiscation and emancipation as well as an aggressive military strategy against the Confederacy that would mobilize all the human and material resources available to the North. They also established the Joint Committee on the Conduct of the War.

As COMMANDER IN CHIEF and head of the executive branch, Abraham Lincoln was a primary focus of Radical criticism. Most Radicals believed him to be opposed to their far-reaching objectives, but Lincoln often arrived at the positions staked out by the Radicals, which has led many to conclude that the President was merely more deliberate and cautious than the Radical congressmen in reaching similar goals. All the same, many Radicals wanted the Republican Party to field SALMON P. CHASE, rather than Lincoln, as the presidential candidate in 1864. They also challenged the President over the shape and control of postwar policy toward the South.

After Lincoln's death, the Radicals' concern over Reconstruction intensified. In Andrew Johnson they found an implacable opponent who espoused a postwar policy even more conciliatory than Lincoln's had been. Most Radicals wanted enfranchisement for the former slaves, and some proposed the confiscation and redistribution of Southern planters' land. All Radicals concurred in the need to delay the former Confederate states' readmission to the Union until the beginnings of a new political and social order had been established in the South. For the four or so years following the passage of the Reconstruction Act of 1867 that was less radical than they had hoped, the Radicals pressured the federal government to maintain its involvement in the South and continue its support of the Republican-controlled state governments there. By the early 1870s, however, the Radical faction's energy and cohesiveness were waning, as was the North's willingness to sustain Reconstruction and protect the freedmen. As sectional issues became less salient, the reason and the occasion for Radicalism became less apparent.

BIBLIOGRAPHY

Benedict, M. Les. *A Compromise of Principle: Congressional Republicans and Reconstruction, 1863–1869.* 1974.
Foner, Eric. *Free Soil, Free Labor, Free Men: The Ideology of the Republican Party before the Civil War.* 1970.
Trefousse, Hans L. *The Radical Republicans: Lincoln's Vanguard for Racial Justice.* 1968.

MICHAEL PERMAN

RANDOLPH, EDMUND (1753–1813), a Framer of the Constitution, first Attorney General, Secretary of State. Randolph was a Virginia patrician who as governor of the state presented to the CONSTITUTIONAL CONVENTION the nationalistic Virginia Plan of Union. It scrapped the Articles of Confederation and provided for a supreme national government of three branches with broad undefined powers. The plan called for the executive to be chosen by the legislature for an unspecified term, to be ineligible for reelection, and to possess a general authority to execute national laws and exercise the executive powers vested in Congress under the Articles of Confederation. The executive, joined by members of the judiciary, would have a veto over legislative acts, national and state. Randolph favored a three-member executive on the supposition that a single executive might be "the foetus of monarchy." He adhered to these positions even after the Convention had substantially drafted the provisions of Article II on the presidency. His draft of the report of the Committee of Detail revealed his considerable impact on other matters.

Randolph refused to sign the Constitution because he believed that the ratification process required adoption or rejection in toto without the possibility of amendments that he recommended. On further reflection he decided to support the Constitution, and at the Virginia ratifying convention, the popular governor had substantial influence. He even reversed himself by affirming the wisdom of provisions of Article II.

President George Washington respected Randolph enough to appoint him the first Attorney General, a position not originally of CABINET rank. Randolph proved himself to be an able legal adviser to the

President and to the EXECUTIVE DEPARTMENTS, and he exercised control over federal attorneys and federal litigation. Washington increasingly relied on Randolph, whose moderation and judiciousness he admired. In 1792 Washington elevated the Attorney General to the Cabinet. When Thomas Jefferson resigned as Secretary of State in 1794, Randolph succeeded him for a year; he resigned after getting caught in partisan politics and making an indiscreet communication to the French minister.

BIBLIOGRAPHY

Anderson, Dice R. "Edmund Randolph." *Dictionary of American Biography* 15: 353–355.

LEONARD W. LEVY

RATINGS, PUBLIC. "President watching" is a favorite American pastime. Because of the connection between public support and WHITE HOUSE INFLUENCE ON CONGRESS, the President's standing in the polls is monitored closely by the press, members of Congress, and others in the Washington political community. The Gallup Poll alone surveyed the public about its approval of the President about seven hundred times in the period from 1953 to 1992.

The Gallup organization began asking about presidential approval in 1935. For the first three years it experimented with different wording of the question, seeking to avoid responses that represented "liking" the President. Since 1937, the approval question has read as follows: "Do you approve or disapprove of the way [President's name] is handling his job as president?" Most other polling organizations have adopted this wording as well.

Factors Affecting Approval. Much of the energy the White House devotes to public relations is aimed at increasing the President's public approval, because the higher the President stands in the polls, the easier it is to persuade others to support presidential initiatives. Yet Presidents frequently do not have widespread public support, often failing to win even majority approval. Presidents Richard M. Nixon, Gerald R. Ford, and Jimmy Carter did not even receive approval from 50 percent of the public on the average. Ronald Reagan, a "popular" President, averaged only a 52 percent approval level.

Presidential approval is the product of many factors. At the base of presidential evaluations is the predisposition of many people to support the President. Political party identification provides the basic underpinning of approval or disapproval and mediates the impact of other factors. Party identification serves as one of the fundamental orienting mechanisms in American politics.

Presidents typically receive very high support from members of their own party, and this support is usually stable over time. Republican Presidents do especially well. Members of the President's party are always more likely to approve than disapprove of his performance, usually by very large margins, while the identifiers with the opposition party are more likely to disapprove than to approve the President's handling of his job. On average, those who identify with the President's party give nearly 40 percentage points higher approval than those who identify with the opposition party (independents fall in between). Moreover, party members are not prone to approving Presidents of the other party.

Democratic Presidents face a more challenging task in obtaining approval and in minimizing disapproval from those who identify with their party, because the base of the DEMOCRATIC PARTY has been larger and more diverse than that of the REPUBLICAN PARTY, including in it most liberals and many moderates and conservatives. Nevertheless, many more Democrats approve than disapprove of Democratic Presidents.

Not only do the absolute levels of presidential approval differ for each group of partisans, they also may shift by different magnitudes or in opposite directions. In other words, Democrats, Republicans, and independents do not always react the same to the President or to the events and conditions by which they evaluate him. What Democrats see as positive, Republicans may view as quite negative and vice versa.

Despite the influence of party identification, it is only a predisposition. Perceptions that are inconsistent with party identification escape its mediating effects and influence individuals. Many members of the opposition party, for example, support the President. On the average, the President receives about a 40 percent approval rating from members of the opposition party. Party identification, then, is an influencing, not a controlling, predisposition.

The presidential HONEYMOON PERIOD is the interval between the election of a new President and the point at which substantial segments of the public, the press, and Congress begin to voice criticism of the President and his policies. The press typically treats a new chief executive favorably; thus, the cues on which the public may base its evaluations of the President are supportive of the White House. There is also a kind of bandwagon effect after an election in which people tend to view the winner more favorably than they did before the election.

Some observers believe that honeymoons are fleeting phenomena in which new occupants of the White House receive only a short breathing period from the public before beginning their inevitable descent in the polls. Declines certainly do take place, but they are neither inevitable nor swift. Throughout his two terms in office, President Ronald Reagan experienced considerable volatility in his relations with the public, but his record certainly does not indicate that the loss of public support is inexorable or that it cannot be revived or maintained. President George Bush enjoyed more public support in his third year in office than in his first year.

One factor commonly associated with someone's approval is personality. In popular usage the term *personality* refers to characteristics such as warmth, charm, and humor that may influence responses to an individual on a personal level. It is not unusual for observers to conclude that the public evaluates Presidents more on style than on substance, especially in an era in which the media and sophisticated public relations campaigns play such a prominent role in presidential politics.

Yet studies have found that substantial segments of the public may "like" the President but still not approve of the way he is handling his job. Personality is also unlikely to be a dynamic influence on presidential approval, since the President's personality does not change during his tenure in office, and the impressions the public holds of the President's personality form early and change slowly.

What is of greater influence on presidential approval and more subject to change is the way the public evaluates some of the job-related traits it attributes to the President. Assessments of characteristics such as the President's integrity, reliability, and leadership ability (as opposed to attributes such as personal warmth and charm), may change as new problems arise or in relation to the President's past performance. Certain characteristics may become more salient in response to changing conditions. Thus, views of the President's job-related characteristics may change over time, and there is evidence that the public's evaluations of them influence their approval of his performance in office.

The Political Environment. Although some factors predispose many members of the public to approve or disapprove of the President's performance, presidential approval ratings may change while predispositions remain essentially constant. To account for such alterations in the President's standing in the public requires focusing on aspects of the political environment that are more subject to change than predispositions.

Understanding presidential approval requires iden-

tifying what is on the minds of Americans. If a matter is not important to people, it is unlikely that it will play a role in their evaluation of the President. One cannot assume that all people use the same criteria in evaluating the President or that people always judge him by the same benchmarks. The importance of specific issues to the public also varies over time and is closely tied to objective conditions such as unemployment, inflation, international tensions, or racial conflict, and issues of concern will vary from group to group.

The relative weight of values and issues in evaluations of the president also varies over time. Valence, or style, issues are values such as patriotism, morality, or a strong national defense, on which there is a broad consensus in the public; such issues are more basic than a position on a specific policy. The President's articulation of valence issues, directly and in the symbols he employs in his actions and speech, can affirm the values and beliefs that define citizens' political identities. As a result, valence issues may be powerful instruments for obtaining public support, for Presidents often prefer to be judged on the basis of consensual criteria with which they can associate themselves. Ronald Reagan was especially effective in this regard.

Even if a matter, such as the economy, is important to the public, it is not likely to affect people's evaluations of the President unless they hold him responsible for it. Despite the prominence of the CHIEF EXECUTIVE, there are several reasons why people may not hold the President responsible for all the problems they face personally or for some problems that they perceive confront the country.

Most people do not politicize their personal problems, and most of those who have personal economic problems do not believe the government should come to their assistance. Some people may feel that those who preceded the President or who share power with him are to blame for important problems. Similarly, there is evidence that voters are sophisticated enough to recognize that current conditions are not necessarily reflective of either present or future economic performance. Thus, blame is not automatic for presiding over hard times.

For matters that are significant to the public and for which it holds the President accountable, the quality of the President's performance becomes a factor in presidential approval. The conventional view is that people's evaluations of the President are affected strongly by their personal economic circumstances. However, an impressive number of studies have found that people differentiate their own circumstances from those of the country as a whole and that personal economic circumstances are typically subordinated to other, broader considerations when people evaluate the President.

The question then is whether people rely on the overall performance of the economy as their criteria of evaluation of his performance or whether they employ a more general notion of how he is handling economic policy. The two criteria are related, but the latter may give the President more leeway and it seems to have the stronger relationship to overall presidential approval. The public may be less harsh in its evaluations of a President who is struggling with a difficult situation, even if he is not meeting with short-term success, as in the case of Franklin D. Roosevelt in 1933 and 1934.

Sometimes public approval of the President increases suddenly. One popular explanation for these surges of support are "rally events," which John Mueller defined as events that relate to international relations, directly involve the United States and particularly the President, and are specific, dramatic, and sharply focused. The argument is that the public will rally around the flag at such times and support the President. A classic example is the 18 percentage point rise in President George Bush's approval ratings immediately after the fighting began in the GULF WAR in 1991.

Potential rally events are more likely to show a decrease than an increase in presidential approval, however. Presidents average about one rally every year and a half, and most of the rallies that do occur are less than 7 percentage points. In addition, there are several rallies that have alternative explanations rooted in domestic politics and policies.

Even the rallies that do occur may be short-lived. For example, the famous 5 percentage point increase in approval accorded President John F. Kennedy immediately following the BAY OF PIGS INVASION was succeeded by a 6 percentage point decline in the next poll—despite the public's pride in the first manned U.S. space flight, which occurred before the last poll. Even some rallies that sustained themselves for more than one poll brought only temporary relief. Jimmy Carter's ratings rose substantially following the taking of American hostages in Iran in November 1979 (in fact he had two consecutive rallies as the IRANIAN HOSTAGE CRISIS dragged on), but his approval rating fell below 40 percent by March 1980.

BIBLIOGRAPHY

Brody, Richard A. *Assessing the President.* 1991.

Edwards, George C., III. *Presidential Approval.* 1990.

Edwards, George C., III. *The Public Presidency.* 1983.

Kinder, Donald R. "Presidents, Prosperity, and Public Opinion." *Public Opinion Quarterly* 45 (1981): 1–21.

Krosnick, Jon A., and Donald R. Kinder. "Altering the Foundations of Support for the President through Priming." *American Political Science Review* 84 (1990): 497–512.

Mueller, John E. *War, Presidents, and Public Opinion.* 1973.

GEORGE C. EDWARDS III

RATINGS, SCHOLARLY. Attempts to rate the Presidents of the United States in some comparative way date back at least to the 1920s, but the first set of presidential ratings that gained wide notice was Arthur M. Schlesinger, Sr.'s *Life* poll of fifty-five historians, published in the magazine on 1 November 1948. Schlesinger's poll divided the Presidents into the following groups: great (Lincoln, Washington, Franklin Roosevelt, Jefferson, Wilson, Jackson), near great (Theodore Roosevelt, John Adams, Polk, Cleveland), average (John Quincy Adams, Monroe, Hayes, Madison, Van Buren, Taft, Arthur, McKinley, Andrew Johnson, Hoover, Benjamin Harrison) below average (Tyler, Coolidge, Fillmore, Taylor, Buchanan, Pierce), and failures (Grant, Harding). The poll established what has become a model for categorizing the Presidents. (William Henry Harrison and James A. Garfield were excluded due to their brief tenure in office.)

The Schlesinger Poll. The 1948 Schlesinger poll also established the idea that presidential ratings by historians are more than simply parlor games reflecting historians' personal preferences. The discussion accompanying the ratings suggested that historians believed that presidential achievements exist beyond the minds of intellectual elites—that is, that some presidential actions have actually benefited the nation more than other presidential actions. The Schlesinger poll also suggested that historians evaluated Presidents both on their day-to-day achievements and the overall policies of each administration. Thus, Warren Gamaliel Harding, whose adequate records in foreign policy and legislative achievements should have earned him a rating above failing, was nevertheless relegated to the bottom category due, at least in part, to his failure to control his subordinates.

Schlesinger's conduct of his 1948 poll, however, raised serious methodological questions. Respondents had been chosen from a very limited population (mostly Ivy League professors); no attempts had been made to randomize the selection process within that population; and, though Schlesinger treated the results as though he knew what the respondents had in mind when they made their rankings, there was nothing in the survey that could have given him this assurance. In short, the survey had been conducted haphazardly and unscientifically. Schlesinger seems, in fact, to have undertaken the project on something of a whim.

Nevertheless, the 1948 poll found a ready audience. The intellectual climate of the post–World War II period encouraged the quantification of matters once seen as being primarily subjective, and students of politics were eager to find some benchmark for quantitative inquiries into the nature of leadership. The Schlesinger rankings, informal as they were, could at least be treated as though they had numerical validity. A host of studies evolved that used the Schlesinger poll as a point of departure. Chief among these were Clinton Rossiter's *The American Presidency* (1960) and Morton Borden's *America's Ten Greatest Presidents* (1961). Schlesinger, noting the attention given his original poll, readministered it in 1962 to a group of seventy-five historians. In this attempt, he tried to be somewhat more systematic; for instance, to aid his analysis he introduced seven questions that the historians were asked to apply to each chief executive, but by and large the same methodological weaknesses of design and selection that had characterized his earlier poll flawed the 1962 version. The results of this poll mirrored those of the 1948 poll. Though losing his "great" ranking, Andrew Jackson remained in sixth place, while Grover Cleveland and James K. Polk exchanged places. In the middle ranges, some random movement occurred, though the failures—Ulysses S. Grant and Harding—remained the same.

The Maranell Poll. In the atmosphere of increasing interest in quantitative analyses, however, it was only a matter of time until someone trained in survey techniques would attempt to create a methodologically rigorous rating. The most influential of the critiques of Schlesinger's method came from Stanford historian Thomas A. Bailey in his book *Presidential Greatness* (1966). Bailey pointed to a large number of biases and potential biases encouraged by Schlesinger's methodology and tried to offset the biases by creating his own ranking. Bailey's work, while thought-provoking, did not, however, solve the basic problem of nonrandom responses. Four years later, Gary M. Maranell, a sociologist at the University of Kansas, noting Bailey's remarks, created a poll based on "social-psychological scaling methods, the inclusion of additional dimensions of evaluation, the use of a much larger and less biased sample, and the use of a single professional society as a sampling frame." Although Maranell entitled his work "An Extension of the Schlesinger Polls," the piece, published in the *Journal of American History* (June 1970), broke new ground in its attempt to bring "scientific" rigor to the ranking of the Presidents.

Maranell accepted the idea that presidential ratings by historians have a basis in a reality beyond the mere opinions of individual historians, but he discarded Schlesinger's categories in favor of assigning unique scores to each President based on the deviation of their ratings from the mean score of all Presidents. He observed that Schlesinger had primarily measured presidential prestige solely, and he tried to increase the usefulness of presidential rankings by including other areas of analysis. Maranell asked his respondents to rank the Presidents on six different scales—prestige, strength of action, activeness, idealism or practicality, flexibility, and accomplishments—and added a seventh scale to measure the amount of information respondents possessed about each President.

Maranell received returns from 571 historians; the new set of rankings he established were used by researchers for the next two decades. In these rankings, Abraham Lincoln, George Washington, and Franklin D. Roosevelt maintained their positions as the greatest, second-greatest, and third-greatest Presidents. Thomas Jefferson, however, moved to fourth position, Theodore Roosevelt moved to fifth, and Woodrow Wilson fell from fourth to sixth. Maranell uncovered a major reevaluation of Harry S. Truman, who passed Jackson and Polk, moving into seventh place. Similarly, the effects of revisionism regarding the presidency of Dwight D. Eisenhower could be seen taking hold as he moved from twenty-second place to nineteenth, despite the presence, above him, of two later Presidents—John F. Kennedy, who ranked ninth, and Lyndon B. Johnson, who ranked sixteenth. Meanwhile William McKinley fell from fifteenth to twenty-second place.

Maranell's analytical framework indicated that historians based their rankings on perceptions of the Presidents' power while in office, the Presidents' level of activity, and the importance of the Presidents' accomplishments. The intangibles of flexibility and idealism seemed to have very little impact on presidential ratings. A potential confounding influence appeared, however, in a high correlation between the information a respondent possessed concerning a President and a President's eventual prestige ranking—suggesting that the more a historian knows about a President, the higher he or she is likely to rate him.

The Murray-Blessing Poll. Maranell's poll has not, as of 1993, been further elaborated. But a host of new polls emerged as the country moved away from the twin traumas of the Vietnam War and the Watergate Affair. The most detailed of these polls was developed by Robert K. Murray and Tim H. Blessing of Pennsylvania State University. Murray and Blessing created a

19-page, 383-question poll that first asked historians detailed demographic questions, then specific questions regarding the presidency in general, then for evaluations of individual Presidents on individual actions, and finally turned to the actual rating the Presidents. Unlike Maranell, the authors used the Schlesinger categories (though they added a category—"above average"—because of the negative connotation of calling a President simply "average", and they also tried to measure how discrete actions affected historians' perceptions of individual Presidents.

Their sample of 846 historians indicated that the history profession's collective rating of most Presidents had changed little since the time of Maranell. The first eight Presidents in the Murray-Blessing ranking (Lincoln, Franklin Roosevelt, Washington, Jefferson, Theodore Roosevelt, Wilson, Jackson, and Truman) remained the same as the first eight in the Maranell poll—although Franklin Roosevelt and Washington switched places, as did Truman and Jackson. Below those eight though, the effects of ongoing evaluations could be seen. Kennedy fell from ninth to thirteenth as the impact of the assassination began to fade. Lyndon Johnson moved up sharply—based almost entirely on his domestic programs—from sixteenth to tenth. The growing strength of Eisenhower revisionism boosted Ike from sixteenth to eleventh. Cleveland plummeted from twelfth to seventeenth; Polk slipped a notch to twelfth; and Ford virtually tied Carter in mediocrity as the two Presidents placed twenty-fourth and twenty-fifth, respectively. Meanwhile the number of Presidents considered failures enlarged significantly as historians apparently became more willing to condemn Presidents whom they had once been willing to tolerate. Andrew Johnson, apparently wounded badly by his failure to promote postbellum civil rights, pitched from twentieth in the Maranell poll to thirty-second in the Murray-Blessing poll. James Buchanan likewise slipped into the failing category, again apparently because of his failure to take a resolute stand against SLAVERY. Richard M. Nixon, hounded by Watergate, Vietnam, and simply being Nixon (the majority of historians indicated that Nixon's physical appearance harmed him somewhat), emerged in the failure category. Ulysses S. Grant and Harding, meanwhile, assumed their traditional places at the bottom of the poll.

The Murray-Blessing results indicated that the wounds of the CIVIL WAR had not yet healed, that the entry of larger numbers of women and minority professors into the history profession had begun to influence the collective voice of American historians (for instance, female historians sharply downgraded Washington, pushing him below Franklin Roosevelt),

and that a small part of the profession's changing perceptions of the Presidents may have been based on changing political views within the profession. The Murray-Blessing poll thus offered glimpses into the changing nature of the history profession as well as into the workings of the President and the presidency. As the poll's authors noted, though, the ratings of most Presidents cannot be expected to undergo major changes; assessments of most presidential performances apparently remain the same regardless of who does the rating.

Other Polls. A number of other polls taken during the same time period confirmed both the stability of presidential ratings and a number of the shifts noted by Murray and Blessing. In 1981, David Porter polled forty-one experts in the field of the presidency (following the Schlesinger preference for a small body of experts). The Porter poll noted the shifts downward of Wilson, Kennedy, Cleveland, and Andrew Johnson. It also confirmed the upward movement of Theodore Roosevelt, Lyndon Johnson, and Eisenhower and likewise confirmed that Buchanan had now slipped into the failing category. Porter's respondents did rank Washington higher than Franklin Roosevelt, Carter higher than Ford, and held out some hope that Grant could emerge from his traditional ranking as the second-worst president of all time as the poll moved him up three notches. Nixon, however, was again relegated to the failing category.

Steve Neal, a political reporter for the *Chicago Tribune*, again using a small (forty-nine) panel of experts, published his own list in 1982. Again, the results were not very different from either the Murray-Blessing or Porter polls. Improvements in the prestige of Theodore Roosevelt, Lyndon Johnson and Eisenhower were noted, as were the Wilson, Kennedy, and Cleveland declines. Neal, however, did not note the decline in Andrew Johnson's ratings (admittedly low to begin with) that the two other 1981–1982 polls detected. He did detect a rather dramatic rise in the prestige of McKinley (ranking him eleventh), which the other polls did not find.

Finally, in 1991, Tim H. Blessing of the Murray-Blessing study created a 19-page, 164-question poll to evaluate the position of Ronald Reagan. This poll, building on the original Murray-Blessing poll, used the statistical method of Guttman Scaling to create scores for Reagan's handling of domestic policy, economic policy, military policy, foreign policy, foreign-policy implementation, executive control, and personal and intangible attributes, By and large, the great majority of the 481 historians surveyed ranked Reagan quite low on policy and implementation measures, slightly higher on executive control, and only somewhat higher on personal attributes and intangibles. The different scales and the demographic data, however, revealed that professional opinion was deeply divided on the quality of the Reagan administration. Not too surprisingly, though, given Reagan's scale scores, the respondents to the Blessing Poll placed Reagan in the "below average" category.

Despite exceptions such as Reagan, though, more than four decades of polling have provided rankings of most Presidents that seem reasonably secure. The list below provides the "normal" ranking of most presidents; an asterisk indicates those Presidents whose rankings have shown such volatility that their "normal" rankings may not be as stable as most. Some Presidents rank near category borders and may shift from one category to another more as a result of random movement than as a result of changing evaluations. These are placed in those categories containing slashes (/).

The "normal" rankings are as follows: great (Lincoln, Washington, Franklin Roosevelt, Jefferson), great/near great (Theodore Roosevelt, Wilson), near great (Truman, Jackson*), near great/above average (John Adams, Eisenhower*, Lyndon Johnson*, Polk), above average (Kennedy, Madison, Monroe, John Quincy Adams*, Cleveland*), above average/average (McKinley, Taft), average (Van Buren, Hoover, Hayes, Arthur, Ford, Carter*, Benjamin Harrison), below average (Taylor, Reagan*, Tyler, Fillmore, Coolidge, Pierce), below average/failure (Andrew Johnson*), failure (Buchanan, Nixon*, Grant*, Harding). (William Henry Harrison and James A. Garfield were excluded due to their brief tenure in office.)

BIBLIOGRAPHY

Bailey, Thomas A. *Presidential Greatness: The Image and the Man from George Washington to the Present.* 1966.

Borden, Morton. *America's Ten Greatest Presidents.* 1961.

Maranell, Gary M. "The Evaluation of the Presidents: An Extension of the Schlesinger Polls." *Journal of American History* 57 (June, 1970).

Murray, Robert K., and Tim H. Blessing. *Greatness in the White House: Historians Rate the Presidents, Washington through Carter.* 1988.

Neal, Steve. "Our Best and Worst Presidents." *Chicago Tribune Magazine* (10 January 1982).

Pederson, William D., and Ann M. McLaurin, eds. *The Rating Game in American Politics.* 1987. The Porter poll (1981) is here included, though the original poll results in manuscript form are in the possession of the author.

Rossiter, Clinton. *The American Presidency,* rev. ed. 1960.

Schlesinger, Arthur, Sr. "Our Presidents: A Rating by 75 Historians." *New York Times Magazine* (29 July 1962).

TIM H. BLESSING

REAGAN, NANCY (b. 1921), First Lady, wife of Ronald Reagan. Although Nancy Davis Reagan had no experience as a Washington wife prior to her husband's inauguration, she made a strong impression on the capital and the nation, and she maintained this prominence through eight years. Her emphasis on stylish clothing and on refurbishing the family quarters in the White House (at a cost of $730,000 in private contributions) earned her both critics and admirers.

Initially termed a detriment to her husband's ratings because of her reputation for extravagant spending and an underdeveloped social conscience, she adopted a new project to replace the lackluster Foster Grandparents program she had headed. Her leadership of the campaign to "Just Say No" to drugs accompanied an improvement in her ratings. Both she and her husband downplayed her influence in any of his important decisions, but she was widely credited with a major role, especially in his choice of personnel and in his scheduling. Accounts written by White House insiders (after they left the administration) support this view. By the time Nancy Reagan departed from Washington, a major newspaper credited her with raising the job of FIRST LADY to the status of an "Associate Presidency."

BIBLIOGRAPHY

Anthony, Carl Sferrazza. " 'She Saves Everything': The Papers of Nancy Davis Reagan." In *Modern Ladies.* Edited by Nancy Kegan Smith and Mary C. Ryan. 1989.

Deaver, Michael. *Behind the Scenes.* 1987.

Reagan, Nancy. *My Turn.* 1989.

BETTY BOYD CAROLI

REAGAN, RONALD (b. 1911), fortieth President of the United States (1981–1989). A radio sports announcer and movie actor before he entered public life, Ronald Wilson Reagan redefined the nation's political agenda during a contradictory presidency that confounded the expectations of adherents and adversaries alike. Elected President in 1980 on a platform of increased military spending, reduced taxes, and a balanced budget, Reagan accomplished the first two goals at the expense of the third. Although Reagan had long contended that government should learn to live within its means, he never once submitted a balanced budget to Congress during his eight years in office. The United States became a debtor nation under Reagan, who bequeathed to his successor, George Bush, the largest national debt and federal budget deficit in world history. But despite limited experience in foreign policy, Reagan put aside his militant distrust of the Soviet Union to cooperate with the Soviet leader, Mikhail Gorbachev. Together they forged what Reagan called a new era in superpower diplomacy and nuclear arms reduction that led to the end of the COLD WAR.

Known widely as the Great Communicator, Reagan was famed for his television skills and an amiable manner that took the edge off his conservatism. He delighted people with self-deprecating one-liners, some scripted and others spontaneous. While he was a hero to American conservatives and led them out of the political wilderness, his popularity was not limited to those who shared his ideological views. "Reagan's solutions to problems were always the same as the guy in the bar," said Stuart K. Spencer, an adviser and friend. Certainly, Reagan tended to see himself as Everyman, or at least as every American. When asked, on the eve of his election in 1980, what it was that Americans saw in him, Reagan replied, "Would you laugh if I told you that I think, maybe, they see themselves and that I'm one of them. I've never been able to detach myself or think that I, somehow, am apart from them."

Origins. Reagan came from humble origins and followed a unique path to the presidency. Born in Tampico, Illinois, on 6 February 1911, he was the second son of Jack, an itinerant, alcoholic shoe salesman, and Nelle Reagan, a religious woman known for acts of kindness and charity. Ronald Reagan was close to his mother who raised him as a member of her Christian (Disciples of Christ) Church. Jack's drinking bouts cast a shadow over the lives of the Reagan boys, who said their mother shielded them and explained, years before this was an accepted view, that alcoholism was an illness. The nomadic Reagans moved from one small Illinois town to another before settling in Dixon, where Reagan showed an early interest in dramatics. The Reagans were impoverished by the Depression and rescued in 1933 by the Democratic administration of President Franklin D. Roosevelt. Loyal Democrat Jack Reagan was put to work distributing welfare grants to other stricken families in the Dixon area, and a place on the payroll was also found for Neal, his other son. Roosevelt became Ronald Reagan's first political hero. Long after he became a conservative Republican, Reagan remained appreciative of what Roosevelt had done for his family and admired the way he used radio to communicate his political program. Reagan closely patterned his later radio and television speeches after Roosevelt's FIRESIDE CHATS.

As a youth, Reagan demonstrated the optimism, winning personality, and self-confidence that would serve him in good stead throughout his various careers. "Life is just one grand, sweet song, so start the music," said the self-written caption beneath Reagan's picture in his high-school yearbook. He was from an early age an accomplished rote memorizer, an ability that enabled him to pass examinations with a minimum of study at Eureka College, a small Disciples of Christ college in Peoria where Reagan played football and participated in college plays. Reagan worked his way through college with odd jobs and the savings from six summers of work as a lifeguard on a dangerous section of the Rock River, where he is reputed to have saved seventy-seven persons from drowning. A businessman steered him toward a radio career. Reagan auditioned for a sports announcer's job at radio station WOC in Davenport, Iowa, by describing from memory a football game that Eureka College had lost. Characteristically, Reagan gave the game a stirring, happy ending and won the job. Later, he moved to station WHO in Des Moines, where he became widely known as sports announcer "Dutch" Reagan.

Hollywood. Encouraged by a friend, Reagan took a screen test in Hollywood in 1937 while visiting southern California. He was signed to a contract by Warner Brothers and typecast as a wholesome if sometimes naive hero whose natural goodness foiled manipulative or sinister villains. Reagan recognized when he entered politics that his many portrayals of "good guys" in the movies had also typecast him favorably with the voters. But his good-guy role was not a pose. As the author Garry Wills observed, Reagan in Hollywood most often played the "heartwarming role" of himself.

Movie career. All his early movie roles were in B-pictures that Reagan said "the studio didn't want good, it wanted them Thursday." But in 1940, aided by actor Pat O'Brien, he landed a coveted role as the doomed, rakish University of Notre Dame football star George Gipp in *Knute Rockne—All American*, and his acting career flourished. He won praise from film critics for performances in *Kings Row* (1942), *The Voice of the Turtle* (1947), and *The Hasty Heart* (1948). He met his first wife, the noted film actress Jane Wyman, on the set of *Brother Rat* (1938), in which they costarred. They married in 1940 and divorced eight years later. Reagan married Nancy Davis, another film actress, in 1952. She became one of his most influential advisers as his career turned from acting to politics.

Reagan made fifty-three films during twenty-seven years in Hollywood. Even after he became President, he considered himself an actor by occupation. In 1966, when he was running for governor of California and a reporter asked him how he would do in office, Reagan replied, "I don't know, I've never played a governor." The quip was a typical example of the self-deprecating humor that Reagan often employed effectively, but it contained more than a grain of truth. A quarter century later, shortly before he left the White House after two terms as President, Reagan was asked if he had learned anything as an actor that had been of use to him in the presidency. "There have been times in this office when I've wondered how you could do the job if you hadn't been an actor," he replied.

Reagan's friend, the columnist George Will, observed that Reagan had a heightened appreciation of the theatrical element in politics. And for much of his political career he was surrounded by aides who appreciated this quality and did much to take advantage of it. Many of Reagan's appearances, even his frequent photo opportunities with the WHITE HOUSE PRESS CORPS, were carefully staged and scripted to make a point with network news audiences. Reagan lavished attention on public performances, particularly on television. He highly valued—some say overvalued—what Theodore Roosevelt had called the BULLY PULPIT aspect of the presidency. Reagan believed that a President's function was to rally public support and perform effectively on the world stage. And he had a performer's appreciation of his audience. "I don't think you can be a performer without liking people," he said. "You like the audience. You want to please the audience."

While Reagan left Hollywood, it never left him. Throughout his political career, he drew on Hollywood experiences. Visitors to the White House, including heads of state, were regaled with Hollywood stories. On occasion, Reagan was ridiculed for quoting scenes from films as if they had occurred in real life.

Political activities. Reagan joined the U.S. Army cavalry reserve while a radio announcer because it gave him an opportunity to ride horses. He was called into the army early in WORLD WAR II but spent the war in southern California making military training films. When he left the service, he plunged into union activity in the Screen Actors Guild, which he served as president for six years. Reagan at the time was an active Democrat who made many speeches in behalf of his party's candidates. He campaigned for President Harry S. Truman in 1948 and for the actress, Representative Helen Gahagan Douglas, who was defeated by Richard M. Nixon in a 1950 Senate election after a virulent red-baiting campaign. As late as 1950, according to Frank Mankiewicz, Reagan was considered as a Democratic candidate for an open House seat by the Los Angeles County party committee but rejected because he was "too liberal."

But Reagan's political orientation had begun to shift

in response to changes in his career and economic status. The postwar years were turbulent times of technological and political change in Hollywood. As the cold war intensified, leftists and liberals came under political attack from the House Un-American Activities Committee (HUAC). Under the guise of exposing Communist influence in the movie industry, the committee conducted intimidating investigations that resulted in wholesale dismissals of studio employees and the creation of a blacklist for writers, actors, and directors who refused to cooperate. Immediately after the war, Reagan had joined two Hollywood groups that were later found to have been heavily infiltrated by Communists. Reagan quickly became disillusioned and joined an anti-Communist faction. He also cooperated with the FBI and furnished the agency information about meetings he had attended. Though Reagan was critical of HUAC's methods, as president of the Screen Actors Guild he helped implement the blacklist of actors who declined to inform on others suspected of leftist sympathies. Throughout his political career, Reagan would trace his militant anti-Communism to his Hollywood experiences.

The late 1940s were a troubled time for Reagan. His first marriage had collapsed and his movie career was in decline. He had been on the verge of stardom at the beginning of the war. A $1 million contract negotiated by the agent Lew Wasserman on the basis of *Kings Row* made Reagan one of the film community's highest-paid actors. But public attention had shifted to newer and younger stars, and Reagan found it increasingly difficult to obtain desirable roles. He also resented paying federal income taxes, which then had rates of 75 to 90 percent in the highest brackets. While still a liberal Democrat, he espoused a "human depreciation allowance" similar to the depreciation allowed oil companies. He found a more sympathetic ear among wealthy Republicans than Democrats. As much as anything, it was Reagan's feelings about taxes that pushed him on a conservative course.

Reagan's career was also influenced in a conservative direction when he became a spokesman in the 1950s for General Electric and host of its weekly television program "General Electric Theater" (1954–1962). Because he feared flying, Reagan traveled by train to widely scattered General Electric plants throughout the country, giving inspirational speeches and answering questions from his audiences. It was a valuable political apprenticeship that enabled Reagan to polish his speaking delivery and develop a patriotic and probusiness message that made effective use of anecdotes ridiculing the government. The message was basically a single talk that Reagan called The

Speech. Ultimately, it was a speech too partisan and controversial for General Electric, which fired him as the company's spokesman and television host.

By then, Reagan's metamorphosis from liberal Democrat to conservative Republican was virtually complete. He backed Nixon against John F. Kennedy in the 1960 presidential campaign. In 1962, at the age of fifty-one, Reagan changed his registration to Republican while participating in Nixon's campaign to become governor of California. Nixon lost, but Reagan was coming into demand as a speaker for conservative causes. His big moment came on 27 October 1964, when he delivered The Speech to a national television audience in behalf of the presidential candidacy of BARRY GOLDWATER. Reagan's speech brought in $1 million for Republican candidates, more money than had been raised by any political speech up to that time. David S. Broder of the *Washington Post* called it "the most successful political debut since WILLIAM JENNINGS BRYAN electrified the 1896 Democratic convention with his 'Cross of Gold' speech."

Reagan's Ascent. Goldwater was trounced by President Lyndon B. Johnson in a monumental landslide that shattered the REPUBLICAN PARTY and made Reagan the surviving hope of forlorn conservatives. Reagan was not discouraged. He sensed growing middle-class disillusion with the costs of Johnson's GREAT SOCIETY programs and the course of the VIETNAM WAR. In 1966, relying on the financial backing of a group of wealthy, self-made entrepreneurs organized by auto dealer Holmes Tuttle, Reagan ran for governor of California. Incumbent Democratic Governor Edmund G. (Pat) Brown, seeking a third term, welcomed Reagan's candidacy and believed his lack of experience and conservative views would make him easy to defeat. Brown told audiences that he had been serving the public while Reagan was making *Bedtime for Bonzo* (1951), but Reagan turned his inexperience into an asset by billing himself as a citizen-politician who would make government run more efficiently. Michael Deaver, an aide to Reagan, would later say that the recurrent underestimation of Reagan was his secret weapon. Reagan defeated Brown by nearly a million votes and served two four-year terms as governor of the nation's most populous state.

Governor. Once in office, Reagan showed little interest in day-to-day governance but displayed a pragmatic streak that belied his rhetoric. Though he had promised to "squeeze, cut, and trim" the cost of government, he embraced Democratic proposals to balance the state budget by raising taxes. Democratic legislative leaders believed that raising taxes would ruin Reagan politically, but he persuaded voters that the tax hikes were needed to cover a huge deficit that had been bequeathed to him. In fact, the taxes produced a surplus, and Reagan managed to make political points by returning a portion of it to the taxpayers. He won election to a second term in 1970, but his winning margin over former Assembly Speaker Jesse M. Unruh was only half of what it had been in 1966. During his second term he cooperated with Democrats in the legislature to achieve significant welfare and tax reforms.

Presidential hopeful. Reagan had his eye on the White House. He ran abortively for the Republican nomination for President in 1968, starting late and losing out to Nixon. After Nixon was elected, it was widely anticipated that Reagan would seek the presidency at the end of a second Nixon term in 1976. Instead, the WATERGATE AFFAIR forced Nixon from office in 1974. Reagan, who had given Nixon the benefit of every doubt during the Watergate inquiry, quickly turned against President Gerald R. Ford and opposed him for the Republican nomination in 1976.

Using the resources of White House incumbency and capitalizing on the reluctance of Republicans to see another President discarded, Ford narrowly beat back the Reagan challenge. But Reagan established himself as the conservative choice in the process. His strong showing followed by Ford's defeat at the hands of Jimmy Carter made Reagan the front-runner in a large field of Republican presidential candidates in 1980. George Bush won an upset victory in the Iowa caucuses, but Reagan regained the upper hand at a famous debate in Nashua, New Hampshire, when the moderator attempted to turn off Reagan's microphone. "I paid for this microphone," Reagan responded angrily, borrowing a remembered line from a Spencer Tracy movie. Reagan's performance nailed down a victory in the New Hampshire primary, and put him on the road to the Republican nomination. He chose Bush as his running mate.

Reagan then faced a politically damaged President in the general election. Carter had been on the defensive since 4 November 1979, a year before election day, when fifty Americans stationed at the U.S. embassy in Tehran had been taken hostage by militant followers of the Iranian Islamic fundamentalist leader, the Ayatollah Ruhollah Khomeini. Americans felt humiliated by the plight of the hostages and frustration with the Carter administration deepened after a military rescue attempt ended in disaster on 24 April 1980. But Carter may have been damaged even more by the huge increase in oil prices and subsequent inflation caused largely by an earlier cutoff of oil exports by Khomeini. With inflation soaring and interest rates rising steadily in the United States, Reagan hammered away at Carter on economic issues. In a variant of a refrain once used by Franklin Roosevelt, he asked rhetorically, "Are you better off today than you were four years ago?"

Carter's political strategists, like those of previous Reagan opponents, relished the idea of facing the former California governor. But Reagan again showed that he was an effective campaigner who could use his showmanship to prevail in a head-to-head encounter. In their only debate of the campaign, Carter pointed out that Reagan had criticized Medicare earlier in his political career, "There you go again," Reagan responded, using a phrase he had practiced during a predebate rehearsal. While not responsive to Carter's point, it proved the only memorable line of a debate that probably assured Reagan's victory. Reagan won an electoral landslide, but the independent candidacy of John B. Anderson deprived him of a majority of the popular votes.

The New President. Reagan made a strong first impression as President. He had been advised by Nixon to focus on economic recovery during his first six months in office, and the Iranian regime cooperated by releasing the hostages while Reagan was being inaugurated. Using the OFFICE OF MANAGEMENT AND BUDGET Director David A. Stockman as his point man, Reagan then launched what was called the Reagan revolution. He proposed increased military spending, reduced income-tax rates, and cutbacks in various domestic programs. Reagan's agenda was widely hailed by conservatives and denounced by liberals but relatively little attention was paid by either side to the fact that the budget he submitted to Congress was unbalanced. Reagan had been assured by his SUPPLY-SIDE ECONOMICS advisers that the income tax cuts would revive a stagnant economy and provide government with increased revenues at lower tax rates. When Republican Senators urged reductions in cost-of-living increases in SOCIAL SECURITY and other programs as a means of reducing the deficit, Reagan refused.

Two defining events occurred early in the Reagan presidency. One was an attempt on Reagan's life on 30 March 1981, by John W. Hinckley, Jr., outside a Washington hotel. The deranged Hinckley shot and wounded Reagan and his press secretary, James S. Brady, before he was overcome by SECRET SERVICE agents. The bullet that struck Reagan, then seventy, lodged within an inch of his heart, narrowly missing the vital aorta by about the same distance. With his life in the balance, Reagan was rushed to a Washington hospital where he won the admiration of Americans for his insouciance on the operating table. "Please tell me you're Republicans," he told the doctors who were preparing him for surgery.

The assassination attempt gave Reagan a political boost, as Congress rushed to pass his budget and tax bills. But it also encouraged Reagan's tendency to disengage from decision making. In the months after the assassination, partly at the insistence of Nancy Reagan, the President's work schedule was sharply limited and most of his duties were performed by aides, especially White House Chief of Staff JAMES A. BAKER III. Through a skillful orchestration of ceremonial appearances and a nationally televised speech by Reagan to Congress, White House media adviser Deaver gave the public the impression that Reagan had largely recovered from his wounds and was fully engaged. But when William P. Clark, who had been Reagan's chief of staff in Sacramento, became his national security adviser nearly ten months after the assassination attempt, he found that Reagan had been scarcely briefed on foreign policy developments during his first year in office. Because Clark understood the way Reagan assimilated information, he started showing him government movies on world trouble spots.

The other defining moment of Reagan's first year in office occurred on 3 August 1981, when thirteen thousand members of the Professional Air Traffic Controllers Organization (PATCO) walked off their jobs. The union had backed Reagan in the 1980 campaign, when labor support for the Republican nominee was rare and valued. But at the recommendation of Secretary of Transportation Drew Lewis, Reagan promptly fired the strikers. The move "showed a decisiveness and an ease with his instincts," observed Donald Rumsfeld, White House Chief of Staff under Gerald Ford. Reagan said later that his action "convinced people who might have thought otherwise that I meant what I said."

The nation sank swiftly into recession in that summer of 1981, as the FEDERAL RESERVE BOARD under its Carter-appointed chairman, Paul A. Volcker, clamped down hard on the nation's money supply. Volcker believed the move was a necessary remedy for runaway inflation, but the immediate result was massive unemployment and the nation's worst recession since the Great Depression. In the face of divided counsel within his administration, Reagan backed Volcker. Characteristically, Reagan believed that America's economic ills could be cured by a restoration of public confidence. "Stay the course," he proclaimed as his popularity sunk to a first-term low point of 35 percent in January 1983. By then, however, the harsh medicine prescribed by Volcker had succeeded in sharply reducing inflation. By spring, an economic recovery had begun that would prove the longest peacetime expansion in United States history, extending through Reagan's second term and carrying over into the first year of the Bush administration.

Reagan meanwhile pursued a cautious foreign policy despite sharp anti-Soviet rhetoric. He was reluctant to commit U.S. troops to foreign conflicts, even for objectives he favored such as stopping Communist expansion in Central America. But Reagan stumbled into a disastrous intervention in the Middle East when he sent U.S. Marines into Lebanon on an ill-defined mission as part of an international peacekeeping force. Lebanon was then a quagmire after years of violent civil war. When the Israeli government subsequently withdrew its troops from Lebanon, the U.S. Marines became sniper targets for Muslim forces. Then on 23 October 1983, a Sunday morning, a suicide bomber drove an explosives-laden truck into the marine compound at the Beirut airport. The blast killed 241 Marines, most of them in their sleep, and injured more than 100 others. While Americans were assimilating this shocking news, Reagan a day later gave the order for U.S. forces to invade GRENADA, where a bloody leftist coup had killed the prime minister and left the tiny island nation in a state of anarchy. Reagan said he acted to protect American students and at the request of other Caribbean nations. The heavily outnumbered Cuban forces on Grenada were subdued in two days with American casualties of 19 killed and 115 wounded. The Grenada invasion effectively diverted public attention from the catastrophe in Lebanon. Republican leaders, Defense Secretary CASPAR W. WEINBERGER, and members of the White House staff who feared that the Lebanese involvement would become another Vietnam then pressed Reagan to withdraw the surviving marines from Lebanon, which he did in early February 1984.

Reagan was now free to run for reelection under a banner of peace and prosperity. Using the slogan, "It's morning again in America," Reagan carried forty-nine states and won 59 percent of the popular vote in defeating WALTER F. MONDALE, who carried only his homestate of Minnesota and the District of Columbia. Perhaps the most striking feature of the election was Reagan's appeal to the nation's youngest voters, those aged eighteen to twenty-four. Reagan was the oldest President in United States history, but he had a young man's vision. "We present to the people of America a sparkling vision of tomorrow, a belief that greatness lies ahead, only waiting for us to reach out for it," he said at the Orange County, California, rally that launched his campaign. It was a recurrent and resonant theme.

The Iran-Contra Affair. Throughout this century, landslide victories have encouraged Presidents to overreach. Franklin Roosevelt attempted to pack the Supreme Court in 1937, Lyndon B. Johnson expanded the war in Vietnam in 1965, and Richard Nixon persisted in the Watergate coverup in 1973. For Reagan, the 1984 landslide was similarly a prelude to political catastrophe.

Reagan turned seventy-four shortly after his second inauguration. He had become hard of hearing and would in 1985 undergo a cancer operation. Riding high after reelection, he was convinced that his economic recovery program had put the nation permanently on the right track. It was in this confident mood that Reagan allowed experienced aides on whom he was more dependent than he realized to leave the White House. Baker, Clark, and EDWIN MEESE III, a counsellor, were awarded Cabinet posts, while Deaver quit the government. Secretary of Treasury DONALD T. REGAN, who barely knew Reagan, became WHITE HOUSE CHIEF OF STAFF. Other key posts were filled by men of even less experience and limited ability. Suddenly, an administration that had prided itself on effective use of symbolism lost its touch. A Reagan visit to a West German cemetery in Bitburg (8 May 1985) where some Nazi SS troops were buried was widely protested by Jewish groups and caused national embarrassment.

But Reagan's mistakes in the heady year after his reelection involved substance as well as symbolism. Encouraged by National Security Adviser Robert C. (Bud) McFarlane, Reagan approved a secret initiative to sell U.S. arms to Iran in an effort to free American hostages seized by Lebanese terrorists with whom Iran was believed to have influence. The initiative contradicted Reagan's promise never to deal with terrorists and U.S. public policy of opposing all arms sales to Iran or Iraq, then engaged in a deadly war of attrition. Furthermore, the initiative was strongly opposed by Reagan's leading Cabinet officers, Defense Secretary Weinberger and Secretary of State GEORGE SHULTZ. Among other things, they pointed out that trading weapons for hostages was likely to encourage additional hostage-taking. These prophetic warnings went unheeded. Though some hostages were freed in exchange for the antitank and antiaircraft missiles sent the Iranians, Lebanese terrorists compensated for their loss by kidnapping other Americans.

The arms-for-hostages deal remained a secret until November 1986, when a Lebanese magazine disclosed it along with news that McFarlane, after leaving the government, had headed a clandestine mission to Tehran. Later in the month, Attorney General Meese revealed that millions of dollars collected from the arms sales had been diverted to the Nicaraguan rebels who were trying to overthrow their nation's leftist government. These rebels, known as contras, had the ardent support of the CENTRAL INTELLIGENCE AGENCY (CIA) and of Reagan, who had called them "the moral equivalent of the Founding Fathers."

The IRAN-CONTRA AFFAIR rapidly became a crisis that threatened the existence of the Reagan administration. Reagan dismissed his National Security Adviser, Admiral John M. Poindexter, and Oliver L. North, a marine lieutenant colonel on the NATIONAL SECURITY COUNCIL staff who had masterminded the diversion. He also named a board of inquiry headed by former Senator John Tower of Texas (the TOWER COMMISSION) Congress launched its own investigation. An INDEPENDENT COUNSEL was named to investigate criminal charges. Meese said later that he was worried that Reagan might be impeached. Reagan's popularity, at stratospheric levels since the American withdrawal from Lebanon, dropped precipitously. Reagan was so shaken by the negative public reaction that he went into virtual hiding for three months.

But Reagan weathered the Iran-contra storm. Under prodding from Nancy Reagan and Tower, he reluctantly accepted responsibility for the arms sales while denying knowledge of the diversion, which Poindexter said he had approved without telling the President. Poindexter stuck to this story in the face of widespread skepticism during testimony before a congressional joint investigating committee and again in his own trial on felony charges of obstructing justice and related charges. (North and Poindexter were convicted in separate trials but their convictions reversed on grounds jurors might have been influenced by compelled congressional testimony.) The Tower Commission was stunned by Reagan's confused and changing recollections of his actions in approving the arms sales but reached no conclusion on his role, if any, in the contra diversion. Neither did the joint congressional committee, though its final report criticized the "secrecy, deception and disdain for law" it said had characterized the Iran-contra affair. Frank Carlucci, a veteran government official under five Presidents, was brought in as National Security Adviser to reform the National Security Council staff. Reagan reluctantly dismissed Chief of Staff Regan, who was blamed by the Tower board for "the chaos that descended on the White House" in the wake of the Iran-contra disclosures. He was replaced by former Senate Republican leader Howard H. Baker, Jr., of Tennessee.

Reagan gradually regained the approval he had squandered during the public airing of the scandal.

Opinion surveys suggested that a majority of Americans did not believe Reagan had told them the truth about his role in the Iran-contra affair but forgave him because they believed his principal motivation had been to free the American hostages. Baker and his successor as Chief of Staff, Kenneth M. Duberstein, restored a sense of calm and efficiency at the White House during the final two years of the Reagan presidency.

Foreign Affairs. These two years witnessed the completion of a turnaround in U.S.-Soviet relations that were a prelude to the dissolution of the Soviet Union and to far-reaching arms reduction agreements achieved during the Bush presidency. The turnaround was all the more remarkable because Reagan had been by far the most anti-Soviet President of the nuclear age. He questioned the legitimacy of the Soviet government at his first presidential news conference and in a celebrated speech (8 March 1983) called the Soviet Union the "evil empire" and "the focus of evil in the modern world." U.S.-Soviet relations were dismal throughout Reagan's first term, when Reagan's attitude and a succession of ill or geriatric Soviet leaders discouraged substantive dialogue between the superpowers. Relations reached a low point in the wake of a notorious incident (1 September 1983) in which a Soviet fighter plane shot down a Korean jumbo jet that had wandered into Soviet airspace, killing the 269 people aboard, including 61 American citizens. A war scare soon developed in the United States and Europe, and the Soviets walked out of missile talks in Geneva.

But U.S.-Soviet relations improved in Reagan's second term, particularly after the ascension to power in the Soviet Union of Mikhail Gorbachev (10 March 1985). Arms-control talks resumed. Reagan and Gorbachev held five summit meetings and on 8 December 1987, in Washington, they signed the INF (INTERMEDIATE-RANGE NUCLEAR FORCES) TREATY. The treaty was significant because it was the first such pact that reduced superpower nuclear arsenals rather than merely regulating the rate at which these arsenals would be allowed to increase. The INF Treaty also provided for the first inspection in both nations of the actual destruction of missiles.

Reagan fervently desired to rid the world of nuclear weapons. His fears of nuclear war were rooted in his acceptance of the biblical story of Armageddon as a prophecy of nuclear holocaust and in his distrust of the doctrine of nuclear deterrence to which Western leaders had subscribed since the end of World War II. According to Martin Anderson, a longtime adviser, Reagan did not learn until 31 July 1979, during a tour of the North American Aerospace Defense in Colorado, that the United States had no defense for nuclear missiles. Reagan was appalled. As President, he proposed in 1983 what he called his dream of a defensive shield that would repel incoming missiles. He called it the SDI (STRATEGIC DEFENSE INITIATIVE), but it became better known as Star Wars. The proposal was repeatedly denounced by Gorbachev and its feasibility discounted by many U.S. scientists, but research into SDI technologies concerned the Soviets and may have been a factor in promoting U.S.-Soviet negotiations.

How much credit is due Reagan (and Secretary of State George Shultz) for bringing Gorbachev to the nuclear bargaining table remains a matter of debate. Some historians believe that the U.S.-Soviet rapprochement and ultimate disintegration of the Soviet Union was determined almost entirely by conditions in the Soviet Union. Others believe that Reagan's willingness to engage in a determined military competition with the Soviets and his success in gaining congressional support for his defense buildup influenced events. Whatever the ultimate historical judgment, it is clear that Reagan came to office with the recognition that the Soviet Union was economically vulnerable to an expanded arms race, a point he made during the 1980 campaign in calling for a military buildup. Unlike some who shared his anti-Soviet views, Reagan also made it clear that he advocated the buildup as a means toward the goal of arms reduction. In addition, Reagan was one of the first American conservatives to recognize that Gorbachev, whom he liked personally, was different from his Soviet predecessors.

Reagan may have been influenced in his opinion of Gorbachev by his staunchest international ally and friend, British Prime Minister Margaret Thatcher, who held similar views. The two conservative world leaders often reinforced one another at international gatherings, and Thatcher gave Reagan high marks for speaking out early and often against Soviet adventurism and Marxist ideology. "President Reagan has achieved the most difficult of all political tasks: changing attitudes and perceptions about what is possible," Thatcher said in a tribute late in the Reagan presidency. "From the strong fortress of his convictions, he set out to enlarge freedom the world over at a time when freedom was in retreat—and he succeeded."

The final months of Reagan's presidency were marked by foreign-policy successes, notably the beginning of Soviet withdrawal from Afghanistan, where the President and Congress had cooperated in sending military aid to anti-Soviet forces. A long-sought settlement in southern Africa withdrawing foreign troops from Namibia was also achieved. Reagan finally abandoned efforts to persuade Congress to arm the contras

in Nicaragua, where a noncommunist government was elected shortly after he left office. Whether this happened in part because of military pressure from the contras or would have occurred in any event remains an open historical question. Whatever the case, Reagan had no taste for further adventures in Central America and he refused to authorize an invasion of PANAMA to oust strongman Antonio Manuel Noriega, an action subsequently taken by President George Bush. On the final day of Reagan's presidency, National Security Adviser Colin L. Powell told Reagan, "The world is quiet today, Mr. President."

The Reagan Legacy. During eight years in the White House, Reagan had learned to value the loyalty and discretion of Vice President Bush. He also recognized that the results of the 1988 election would be seen as a referendum on his own presidency, and he campaigned strenuously for Bush, whose domestic advocacies were in large part a continuation of Reagan's policies. The problems that afflicted the nation in the Bush years were also soon seen as Reagan's legacy. The deficit-financed economic boom gave way to a persistent recession. The nation was hobbled by the costs of a mammoth SAVINGS AND LOAN DEBACLE, the product of congressional relaxation of the rules governing thrifts and a tolerant attitude toward irregularities by the Reagan administration. It quickly became apparent that the plight of the cities and of the poor had worsened during the Reagan years. One out of five children, many of them black, lived in poverty at the end of Reagan's second term in office. A 1989 survey showed that the richest two-fifths of Americans had the highest share of national income (67.8 percent) and the poorest two-fifths the lowest share (15.4 percent) in the forty years the Census Bureau had been compiling such statistics.

When Reagan left office, he had appointed slightly more than half of the federal judiciary. Most of the new judges were conservative, as Reagan had promised, and most were well qualified, according to an American Bar Association study. Reagan's legacy of Supreme Court appointments was less ideological, and certainly less even, than either his supporters or foes had expected. His appointment of Sandra Day O'Connor, the first woman ever to serve on the Supreme Court, was widely hailed by moderates and liberals. But a furious battle erupted in the Senate over Reagan's effort to put the conservative constitutional scholar Robert H. Bork on the Court. Bork was rejected. After another nominee withdrew following disclosures of drug use, Reagan selected Judge Anthony Kennedy, who was confirmed, and joined O'Connor as a member of a centrist bloc on the Court.

Reagan's other Supreme Court appointment, Antonin Scalia, emerged as leader of the court's conservatives. Reagan also promoted William Rehnquist, a conservative Nixon-appointed Associate Justice, to Chief Justice.

Reagan left office in 1989, unimpressed by his reputation as the Great Communicator, a phrase often used derisively by opponents to suggest that Americans liked not what Reagan said but the way he said it. Reagan disagreed, saying that it was the content of his message that attracted people. "I wasn't a great communicator, but I communicated great things, and they didn't spring full bloom from my brow, they came from the heart of a great nation—from our experience, our wisdom and our belief in the principles that have guided us for two centuries."

The conservative coalition that Reagan had led to victory in 1980 was never the same without him. Lacking a leader and the glue of the cold war that had bound them together, conservatives began quarreling among themselves once Reagan left office. President Bush found it difficult to hold the allegiance of the so-called Reagan Democrats—conservative southern and western Democrats, ethnic blue-collar workers, and young people—who had so enthusiastically backed Reagan. The national sense of purpose that Reagan had rekindled in the early days of his presidency diminished after he departed.

Reagan is unlikely to be remembered as a great President. He had no peers in the bully-pulpit aspects of the office, but he was often a hesitant decision maker when the cameras were not rolling. Despite Iran-contra and Lebanon, he nonetheless deserves overall high marks in the foreign policy arena because of his contributions to the end of the cold war. It is his economic legacy that clouds what might otherwise be a generally positive assessment of his presidency.

That legacy, like so much else in the Reagan presidency, is mixed. For reasons not entirely of his own making, such as a glut in the world oil supply, Reagan was spectacularly successful in reducing the uncontrolled inflation that had been the bane of Americans during the Carter years. The inflation rate, which averaged 12.5 percent in the final year of the Carter presidency, averaged only 4.4 percent during Reagan's last year in office. The prime interest rate fell nearly six points. Eighteen million new jobs were created, and the unemployment rate dropped. But the nation's private wealth grew only 8 percent in the six Reagan recovery years, about a one-fourth the growth rate of the 1975–1980 period that Reagan had derided as inflation-prone and unproductive. Meanwhile, the national debt nearly tripled, to $2.684 trillion, while the trade deficit quadrupled. On balance, the nation paid a heavy price for the Reagan recovery, and the supply-side experiment did not succeed. Personal savings rates declined during the 1980s, and lower tax rates did not produce the promised additional revenues. Reagan at no time proposed a budget that raised the money needed to pay for all the programs he thought necessary, although there is no evidence he understood this. It is possible that Reagan was deceived by his rhetoric that the federal budget could be brought into balance painlessly through the elimination of "waste, fraud, extravagance and abuse."

As with any presidency, much that Reagan did is not susceptible to statistical measurement. Reagan set out to inspire his fellow Americans at a time when public confidence in government was extraordinarily low. Six months into his presidency Reagan was asked what he most wanted to accomplish. "What I'd really like to do is go down in history as the President who made Americans believe in themselves again," he replied. Even some of Reagan's critics would acknowledge that he largely succeeded in this important goal.

Reagan was an enduring repository of national characteristics and values. He believed, as he often said, in "reaching for the stars," and that Americans could accomplish anything if they set their minds and hearts to the task. "If there is one thing we are sure of, it is . . . that nothing is impossible, and that man is capable of improving his circumstances beyond what we are told is fact," he had said in the speech announcing his presidential candidacy. He never ceased to believe this. This shining optimism was the key to Reagan's character and to his broad acceptance by the American people. Reagan was undeterred by age or adversity, and he roused others to believe that the nation's best days are in the future, not the past. His greatest achievement as President may have been the intangible one of making Americans feel good about themselves.

BIBLIOGRAPHY

Adelman, Kenneth L. *The Great Universal Embrace; Arms Summitry—A Skeptic's Account.* 1989.

Anderson, Martin. *Revolution: The Reagan Legacy.* 1990.

Barrett, Laurence I. *Gambling with History; Ronald Reagan in the White House.* 1983.

Boaz, David, ed. *Assessing the Reagan Years.* 1988.

Cannon, Lou. *President Reagan: The Role of a Lifetime.* 1991.

Cannon, Lou. *Reagan.* 1982.

Cannon, Lou. *Ronnie and Jesse: A Political Odyssey.* 1969.

Niskanen, William A. *Reaganomics: An Insider's Account of the Policies and the People.* 1988.

Reagan, Ronald. *An American Life.* 1990.

Stockman, David A. *The Triumph of Politics: How the Reagan Revolution Failed.* 1986.

Wills, Garry. *Reagan's America.* 1985.

LOU CANNON

RECESS APPOINTMENTS. Under Article II, Section 2, of the Constitution, "The President shall have Power to fill up all Vacancies that may happen during the Recess of the Senate, by granting Commissions which shall expire at the End of their next Session."

The Framers empowered the President to make recess appointments, without Senate confirmation, because they anticipated long periods each year when the Congress would be in adjournment. It would have been difficult to operate the federal government had it been necessary to wait for the next session of the Senate, which might be a half year or more away, before nominations could be made and confirmed and vacancies filled.

A recess appointee may continue to hold office, without Senate confirmation, until the end of the session following the one in which the appointment was first made. Even in the 1990s, that could be a period of a year or more.

The ambiguous constitutional phrase, "Vacancies that may happen during the Recess of the Senate," was long a subject of controversy. Did it mean simply vacancies that may occur during a recess or all vacancies that happen to exist during a recess even though they may have occurred while the Senate was in session? President George Washington adopted a narrow view of this provision and employed recess appointments only when a vacancy occurred during a Senate recess. Most of his successors have taken a more expansive approach. Since President James Madison's time, despite Senate opposition, Presidents have given this language a broad construction and used recess appointments to fill any existing vacancies, even those that first occurred while the Senate was in session.

Before the lengthening of congressional sessions, Presidents often found some political leverage in the use of recess appointments and would sometimes wait until after adjournment to fill a vacancy. When the Congress returned to session, the name of the individual who had received the recess appointment would then be sent to the Senate for confirmation. By this time, however, the nominee would have accumulated months of experience on the job. This made it difficult for the Senate to oppose the nomination on the grounds of inexperience.

The principal current use of recess appointments is for the strategic purpose of circumventing the confir-

mation process. President Ronald Reagan used recess appointment powers as part of his effort to undermine the Legal Services Corporation (LSC), a government agency that provides legal assistance in civil cases for the poor. Reagan made no appointments to the board of directors of the LSC for most of his first year in office. Then, to prevent holdovers who were Jimmy Carter's appointees from determining the 1982 grants of the LSC, Reagan made seven recess appointments on the last day of 1981. Over the next few years, Reagan made several regular nominations to the LSC board, then withdrew them before a Senate confirmation decision. At the same time, he continued to fill vacancies with recess appointments. Reagan appointees were thus able to control the LSC between 1981 and 1984, even though not a single one was confirmed by the Senate.

Many of the people who served on the LSC board during these years were fundamentally hostile to its purpose and policies. Reagan himself had long sought the abolition of the LSC. But Congress was not likely to follow the President's lead on the matter of abolition, nor to confirm many of the people who received recess appointments to the board. So Reagan used recess appointments to juggle board members, and thus deny Senate control through the confirmation process, in order to impose his own restrictive view of LSC functions.

Recess appointments of federal judges have posed a special concern because they raise the possibility of litigants facing a judge who does not have a lifetime appointment and who will soon be reviewed for confirmation by the Senate. Impartiality and objectivity may be less reliable under those circumstances.

But the federal courts have upheld the President's authority to make recess judicial appointments. The U.S. Court of Appeals for the Second Circuit took that position in an important 1962 case, *United States v. Allocco.* In 1983, the full U.S. Court of Appeals for the Ninth Circuit, finding that there was no reason to favor the constitutional guarantee of lifetime tenure for judges over the constitutional language providing for recess appointments, also concluded, in the case of *United States v. Woodley,* that Presidents had constitutional authority to make recess appointments to the federal courts.

There have been fifteen recess appointments in the history of the Supreme Court to Potter Stewart, who was named in 1959. Of the fifteen, only five actually participated in the work of the Court before Senate confirmation. Of the five who did take their seats before confirmation, four were later confirmed by the Senate and one, John Rutledge, was denied confirmation by the Senate in 1795. In 1960, however, the Senate passed a sense of the Senate resolution, introduced by Senator Philip A. Hart, which stated that recess appointments should not be made to the Supreme Court "except under unusual circumstances and for the purpose of preventing or ending a demonstrable breakdown in the administration of the Court's business." The Hart Resolution is not legally binding on Presidents, but there have been no recess appointments to the Supreme Court since its passage.

As early as 1863, Congress sought to control the use of recess appointments by enacting a statute that read in part "nor shall any money be paid out of the Treasury of the United States, as salary, to any person appointed during the recess of the Senate, to fill a vacancy in any existing office . . . until such appointee shall have been confirmed by the Senate." That was a broad restriction, preventing payment of any salary to any recess appointee.

Current law applies this restriction more narrowly to any recess appointee selected to fill a vacancy that "existed while the Senate was in session and was by law required to be filled by and with the ADVICE AND CONSENT of the Senate." The restriction does not apply if the vacancy arose within thirty days before the end of the session of the Senate; or if, at the end of the session, a nomination for the office, other than the nomination of an individual appointed during a previous recess of the Senate, was pending before the Senate; or if a nomination for the office was rejected by the Senate within thirty days before the end of the session and an individual other than the one whose nomination was rejected thereafter receives a recess appointment. This does not prevent the use of recess appointments to fill vacancies that could be filled by regular appointments, but it does prevent payment of salary to the appointee under the circumstances described here.

The ambiguity of the recess appointments clause of the Constitution has left much room for subsequent—and still continuing—interpretation and debate.

BIBLIOGRAPHY

Congress and the Nation, 1981–1984. 1985.
Corwin, Edward S. The Constitution and What It Means Today. 1978.
Fisher, Louis. Constitutional Conflicts between Congress and the President. 3d ed. 1991.
Mackenzie, G. Calvin. The Politics of Presidential Appointments. 1981.

G. CALVIN MACKENZIE

RECIPROCAL TRADE AGREEMENTS. In 1934, the Congress for the first time authorized the President to engage in wholesale modification of tariff rates, a task until then performed through tariff acts by the Congress under one of its constitutional powers.

The Reciprocal Trade Agreements Act of 1934 was enacted in part as a reflection of the DEMOCRATIC PARTY's traditional support of freer trade and in part as a reaction to the highly protectionist SMOOT-HAWLEY TARIFF ACT of 1930 and its disastrous consequences for international trade. By raising U.S. tariff rates to the highest levels ever, the 1930 act had triggered retaliatory measures by other nations and contributed heavily toward a virtual collapse of international trade. By 1932, both U.S. imports and exports fell to 30 percent of their 1929 levels. The 1932 Democratic platform called for reciprocal trade agreements as a means for revitalizing international trade, but President Franklin D. Roosevelt's domestic priorities delayed such action until 1934. Secretary of State CORDELL HULL was a major force behind passage of reciprocal trade legislation.

The 1934 act authorized the President, within specified limits, "to enter into foreign trade agreements . . . and to proclaim such modifications of existing duties and other import restrictions" as were provided for in the agreements. The Congress was relieved of the cumbersome, controversial, and time-consuming task of individual tariff making, and the process acquired flexibility and ability for timely responsiveness to changed circumstances. Under the negotiating authority of the 1934 act, which was extended eleven times, the United States signed bilateral reciprocal tariff concessions agreements with twenty-eight countries, acceded to the GATT (GENERAL AGREEMENT ON TARIFFS AND TRADE) in 1947, and took part in five rounds of multilateral tariff negotiations under GATT auspices.

The President's trade-agreement authority was subsequently reenacted, expanded, and redefined. The Trade Expansion Act of 1962 for the first time authorized complete elimination of duties in limited specified circumstances. Under the 1962 act, the United States participated in the sixth (Kennedy) round of GATT multilateral negotiations from 1964 to 1967.

The Trade Act of 1974 authorized the President specifically to negotiate tariff agreements, nontariff-barrier agreements, and agreements extending most-favored-nation (MFN), nondiscriminatory status to nonmarket-economy (NME) countries, but required the latter two types of agreements to be implemented by fast-track enactment [see FAST-TRACK AUTHORITY]. Under this negotiating authority, the United States entered into and implemented a tariff agreement and fourteen other agreements (the latter agreements enacted by the Trade Agreements Act of 1979) that were concluded during the seventh (Tokyo) round of GATT multilateral negotiations from 1975 to 1979. The authority of the 1974 act has also been used since 1975 to conclude and implement MFN agreements with several NME countries.

The Trade and Tariff Act of 1984 authorized the President also to negotiate with individual countries agreements for elimination of all duties, in effect, authorizing free-trade area (FTA) agreements. Such agreements were concluded and implemented by fast-track enactment with respect to ISRAEL (effective August 1985) and Canada (January 1989).

The Omnibus Trade and Competitiveness Act of 1988 (OTCA) authorized the President, until 31 May 1993, to enter into trade agreements to modify duty rates (and implement them by proclamation) and to reduce nontariff barriers and to enter into FTA agreements (subject to fast-track enactment). The OTCA trade agreement authority applies to the negotiation and implementation of any agreements reached in the eighth (Uruguay) round of GATT multilateral negotiations and to the North American Free Trade Agreement (NAFTA).

BIBLIOGRAPHY

Haggard, Stephan. "The Institutional Foundations of Hegemony: Explaining the Reciprocal Trade Agreements Act of 1934." *International Organization* 42 (Winter 1988): 91–119.

U.S. Tariff Commission (since 1975: U.S. International Trade Commission). *Operation of the Trade Agreements Program.* 1949–.

VLADIMIR N. PREGELJ

RECOGNITION POWER. It is well established that the President as DIPLOMAT IN CHIEF has the implied power to recognize foreign nations and foreign governments. At the outset, a distinction must be made between recognizing nations and recognizing governments, although the President possesses both recognition powers. The recognition of a nation simply refers to the executive branch's affirmation that a new country has come into existence. To become a nation, an entity must have a defined territory; a permanent population; some domestic regulation or control of that population; and the ability to conduct relations with other countries. Some have argued that the executive must recognize as a new nation any entity having those attributes; but others have argued that an entity attains statehood only if the executive formally recognizes the entity as a nation. Under either theory, a nation's recognition is significant, since only nations can possess all of the sovereign rights and duties available under international law. For example, only nations can usually enter into treaties and join most international organizations. The President's recognition of a nation is the starting point of foreign affairs and is part and parcel of his control over international matters. The executive branch must determine whether to establish diplomatic relations with a new nation.

Nation or Regime? The President's recognition of a nation may overlap with his recognition of a government in that nation, but not always. When only one governmental regime claims to control a new nation, the President's recognition of that foreign state may occur simultaneously with his recognition of the governmental regime. However, when more than one government contends for a new nation's leadership, or when a revolutionary force challenges a government's control in an existing country, the President must decide which of those entities to recognize. In such instances, the President's decision whether to recognize a foreign government may be more complex and more politicized than his decision to recognize a nation. When faced with a choice between two competing forces, the President may recognize the governmental regime that is more committed to American values and democracy; during the COLD WAR, the United States and the Soviet Union each wanted to recognize and support the particular regime with which it was most compatible. The President may make his recognition decision only after seeing which of the competing regimes actually takes firm and prolonged control of the foreign country. Like the power to recognize a nation, the President's power to recognize a particular foreign government is essential to his foreign affairs authority.

The Constitution says nothing explicit about the power to recognize other nations or governments. Instead, the recognition power is said to derive impliedly from one of the President's few explicit international powers—his power of RECEIVING AND APPOINTING AMBASSADORS. Article II, Section 2, of the Constitution provides that the President "shall nominate, and by and with the Advice and Consent of the Senate, shall appoint Ambassadors, other public Ministers and Consuls." Article II, Section 3, provides that the President "shall receive Ambassadors and other public Ministers." By implication, if the President is empowered to appoint and receive ambassadors, he can determine which countries and which governments to recognize in conducting those ambassadorial relations. In other words, the President's recognition power is an implied precondition to his authority to appoint and receive ambassadors.

Exclusive Executive Power. The President's recognition power is assumed to reside exclusively in the executive branch, without senatorial oversight. Supreme Court decisions have directly and indirectly validated the President's exclusive recognition power. For example, in UNITED STATES v. BELMONT (1937), the Supreme Court upheld an agreement between the executive branch and the Soviet Union that settled and assigned monetary claims and counterclaims between the two governments. That executive agreement was made in connection with the President's recognition of the Soviet government. Justice George Sutherland's opinion clearly stated that the executive branch alone possessed the power to recognize the Soviet government: "The recognition, establishment of diplomatic relations, the assignment . . . were all parts of one transaction, resulting in an international compact between the two governments. That the negotiations . . . and agreements and understandings . . . were within the competence of the President may not be doubted." He concluded that "in respect of what was done here, the Executive had authority to speak as the sole organ of [the national] government." Although the federal courts have regularly supported the President's recognition practices, they have established a distinction between de jure recognition and de facto recognition. Even when the executive has not formally accorded recognition to a government by law (de jure recognition), the courts may give some privileges (e.g., immunity) to a government that clearly and realistically exists on a factual basis (de facto recognition).

From the early days of the Republic, the executive branch has exerted the power to recognize other nations and governments. In FEDERALIST 69, ALEXANDER HAMILTON initially doubted the significance of the executive's power to receive ambassadors. But when later debating James Madison, Hamilton argued strongly for executive supremacy in foreign affairs, including the recognition power. Hamilton reasoned: "No objection has been made to the President's having acknowledged the republic of France, by reception of its minister, without having consulted the Senate." Presidents have since recognized many countries and governments without consulting with Congress. Nevertheless, even if not constitutionally required, it may be politically prudent for the President to consult with the Congress when recognition issues arise; after all, congressional appropriations may be needed to support the President's recognition of a new country or government.

President Jimmy Carter angered the Congress when he unilaterally terminated the Mutual Defense Treaty with the Republic of China (Taiwan) and shifted the United States' recognition from Taiwan to the People's Republic of China in 1978. In so doing, President Carter contravened a congressional resolution that had sought "prior consultation between the Congress and the executive branch on any proposed policy changes affecting the continuation in force of the Mutual Defense Treaty." Members of Congress sued the politically unsavvy Carter, but the Supreme Court held the suit to be unjusticiable.

BIBLIOGRAPHY

American Law Institute. *Restatement (Third) of the Foreign Relations Law of the United States, Section 201–205*. 1987.
Corwin, Edward S. *The President*. 5th ed. 1984.
Franck, Thomas M., and Michael J. Glennon. *Foreign Relations and National Security Law*. 1987.
Henkin, Louis. *Foreign Affairs and the Constitution*. 1972.
McClure, Wallace. *International Executive Agreements*. 1967.

KENNETH C. RANDALL

RECONCILIATION BILLS. The central enforcement procedures of the federal budgetary process are known as reconciliation bills. The reconciliation process facilitates congressional action on omnibus measures that control spending, particularly in entitlement programs, and increase revenue levels. With special legislative rules governing amendments, germaneness, and timing, reconciliation bills permit Congress to expedite action on politically difficult legislative changes needed to implement comprehensive budgetary programs.

The reconciliation mechanism was established under the 1974 CONGRESSIONAL BUDGET AND IMPOUNDMENT CONTROL ACT. While intended to enforce congressional budget resolutions, reconciliation has become the primary instrument for carrying out budget agreements between the President and Congress. The first reconciliation bill was not enacted until 1980. It broadened original understandings about the purpose and scope of reconciliation, particularly by extending coverage to existing entitlements, and subsequent reconciliation efforts have produced additional extensions.

Shortly after Ronald Reagan took office in 1981, the OFFICE OF MANAGEMENT AND BUDGET (OMB) developed a sweeping program of spending reductions, and reconciliation became the mechanism for enacting the Reagan program. With Republicans controlling the Senate and the Republican minority in the House able to attract sufficient Democratic support, agreement was finally reached on an omnibus reconciliation package that contained outlay reductions of more than $130 billion for fiscal years 1982 through 1984.

The executive-dominated reconciliation effort of 1981 was not repeated, although reconciliation bills were enacted almost every year between 1981 and 1992. In addition, the reconciliation process has been formalized. The 1985 and 1987 GRAMM-RUDMAN-HOLLINGS ACTS have made reconciliation a mandatory enforcement feature of the annual budget process and confirmed reconciliation coverage over entitlements (except SOCIAL SECURITY).

The most significant reconciliation measures, however, have been based upon budget agreements reached between the White House and Congress. The 1990 Omnibus Budget Reconciliation Act and BUDGET ENFORCEMENT ACT, for example, further extended the reconciliation process. They contained discretionary spending caps for fiscal years 1991 through 1995, as well as entitlement and revenue controls, that were intended to constrain future deficits. If Congress decides to extend its deficit-reduction efforts, or must enforce the deficit-neutral constraints governing entitlement increases and revenue cuts, reconciliation will likely be used to accomplish the changes.

The scope of the reconciliation process is extremely broad, extending to entitlements, appropriations, and revenues. Its utility consists in providing for coherent, comprehensive congressional action. In addition, the President must sign any reconciliation legislation. Reconciliation requires, in sum, leadership agreement, and this translates into the practical necessity for negotiated budget pacts that bring the reconciliation process into motion.

BIBLIOGRAPHY

Collender, Stanley E. *The Guide to the Federal Budget, Fiscal Year 1992.* 1991.
Gilmour, John B. *Reconcilable Differences? Congress, the Budget Process and the Deficit.* 1990.

DENNIS S. IPPOLITO

RECONSTRUCTION. The term *Reconstruction* refers both to the period just after the CIVIL WAR, roughly 1865 to 1877 and to the policy employed by the U.S. government toward the states of the defeated Confederacy. The course that the victorious United States took in the war's aftermath was of critical importance in determining the future of the Southern states and the recently emancipated slaves as well as of the relations between the two formerly warring sections.

Reconstruction was also a critical episode for the presidency. The period began in 1865 with the assassination of Abraham Lincoln. His successor, Andrew Johnson, was impeached in 1868 but acquitted by the Senate. Finally, during the mid 1870s, the presidency of Ulysses S. Grant was rocked by financial scandals

that threatened to implicate the President himself. This decline in reputation and power came immediately after the presidency had reached a pinnacle of success and prestige under Lincoln during the war.

The problem of Reconstruction—how to reorganize the former Confederate states and reintegrate them into the nation—also played a large role in the deterioration of presidential authority. Because the formulation and implementation of postwar policy in the South was of such central importance, Congress claimed that the matter could not be left to the President alone. Reconstruction policy was therefore caught up in a jurisdictional contest between the presidency and Congress.

Lincoln's approach to Reconstruction, as outlined in a proclamation of 8 December 1863, assumed that, while the war was still raging, the executive and military authorities should organize loyal elements to form new governments in those areas of the Confederacy under federal occupation. The Republican-controlled Congress objected because the plan's standards of loyalty were too lenient and because only a small minority of the citizenry would constitute the new electorate. To stall the initiative that the President had already begun in Union-occupied Louisiana, Congress passed the Wade-Davis bill in July 1864, which laid down more stringent procedures. After Lincoln pocket-vetoed the bill, Congress denied admission to the Representative elected from Louisiana.

The impasse between Congress and President might well have been bridged had the politically astute and flexible Lincoln lived. His successor, Andrew Johnson, a border-state Union Democrat, adopted Lincoln's approach but, when Congress objected and refused to seat the Southern delegations elected under his policy, Johnson simply refused to consider any kind of negotiation or accommodation whatsoever. For the next fifteen months, from December 1865 until March 1867, Johnson confronted the Republican majority in Congress. In 1866 Congress passed the CIVIL RIGHTS ACT OF 1866 and an act to extend the life of the FREEDMEN'S BUREAU, both of which the President vetoed. Johnson also thwarted the ratification of Congress's alternative terms for Southern readmission, the Fourteenth Amendment. Finally, Congress passed the Reconstruction Act in March 1867. But Johnson vetoed it and then proceeded, after his veto was overridden, to use his authority as COMMANDER IN CHIEF to subvert its implementation in the South.

Congress was compelled not only to beat back the endless stream of vetoes but also to curb Johnson's power. The TENURE OF OFFICE ACT of March 1867 was intended to prevent him from dismissing CABINET members without congressional consent, while a clause in the Army Appropriations Act of 1867 curbed his authority to relieve military commanders who were responsible for enforcing the Reconstruction Act. Finally, when Johnson tried to remove the Secretary of War, EDWIN M. STANTON, congressional Republicans saw an opportunity for IMPEACHMENT to end Johnson's obstruction once and for all. Although they ultimately failed to secure a guilty verdict in the President's trial in the Senate, Johnson was essentially neutralized for the rest of his term, which was what most Republicans had wanted anyway [see IMPEACHMENT OF ANDREW JOHNSON].

After 1868, the objective of federal Reconstruction policy changed. The government's task was now to preserve and maintain the regimes it had set up in each Southern state under the Reconstruction laws. This responsibility fell to President Grant (1869–1877), who was not only chief executive for most of the period of Reconstruction but also presided over its collapse. On occasion, Grant used his power, as when he intervened firmly to force Georgia to ratify the Fifteenth Amendment in 1869–1870, to put down the KU KLUX KLAN in South Carolina in 1871 and 1872, and to sustain the Republicans in Louisiana from 1872 to 1875. But in many other instances, he pleaded lack of presidential authority to act, and after 1873 he generally acquiesced in the defeat of the faltering Republican governments by their Democratic enemies. Previously, he had tried to maintain Reconstruction, but he now began to realize that propping up these Southern governments was no longer popular in the North and that control of the Southern states was no longer necessary to ensure Republican success in presidential elections. Indeed, abandonment of the last three Republican states in exchange for their presidential electoral votes made it possible for the Republican Rutherford B. Hayes to become President in the disputed election of 1876. Thus, a presidential election ended Reconstruction and brought the sectional conflict to a close, just as a presidential election in 1860 had broken up the Union and precipitated the war.

BIBLIOGRAPHY

Benedict, M. Les. *A Compromise of Principle: Congressional Republicans and Reconstruction, 1863–1869.* 1974.

Foner, Eric. *Reconstruction: America's Unfinished Revolution, 1863–1877.* 1988.

Gillette, William. *Retreat From Reconstruction, 1869–1879.* 1979.

McKitrick, Eric L. *Andrew Johnson and Reconstruction.* 1960.

Perman, Michael. *The Road to Redemption: Southern Politics, 1869–1879.* 1984.

MICHAEL PERMAN

RECONSTRUCTION FINANCE CORPORATION. In December 1931, President Herbert Hoover asked Congress to create a reconstruction finance corporation to make loans to private financial institutions, which could then meet depositor demands, forestall banking panics that had closed more than five thousand banks during the 1920s, increase commercial lending, and end the depression. Hoover signed the RFC Act on 2 February 1932. The Reconstruction Finance Corporation (RFC) could also make railroad loans. Many roads could not meet their bonded debt payments. When they defaulted, the financial institutions holding such asserts were badly hurt.

The RFC encountered tremendous criticism. Most of its funds went to large banks, which was hardly surprising since they controlled disproportionately large shares of money-market assets. Critics accused Hoover of taking care of big business while ignoring the poor. In July 1932 Congress passed the Emergency Relief and Construction Act, authorizing the RFC to make $300 million in relief loans and $1.5 billion in public-works loans to states. By early 1933 the RFC had loaned out $300 million for relief and more than $1 billion to banks and railroads, but the economy was collapsing when Hoover left office in March 1933. The RFC—at that point the largest government agency in American history—had failed.

After 1933, President Franklin D. Roosevelt expanded the RFC. The EMERGENCY BANKING ACT (1933) authorized the RFC to invest in the preferred stock of commercial banks. Within two years the RFC owned more than $1 billion in the stock of thousands of banks. The RFC also invested in railroads and other financial institutions to maintain the liquidity of the money markets. Its bank-rescue operation made the RFC one of the more important agencies of the NEW DEAL. During WORLD WAR II, the RFC expanded even more, loaning more than $40 billion through such subsidiary corporations as the Defense Supplies Corporation, the Defense Plants Corporation, and the U.S. Commercial Company. The RFC offered small-business loans after World War II and was dissolved in 1951 as part of a government reorganization plan.

BIBLIOGRAPHY

Olson, James S. *The Reconstruction Finance Corporation and the New Deal, 1933–1940.* 1988.

JAMES S. OLSON

REGAN, DONALD T. (b. 1919), Secretary of the Treasury, White House Chief of Staff. Donald Thomas Regan was born in 1919 in Cambridge, Massachusetts, receiving a degree in English from Harvard University in 1940. He won a scholarship to attend Harvard Law School but joined the Marine Corps's Officer Training program and was sent off to fight in the Pacific theater. In 1945 he resigned his commission and accepted a position with the Wall Street firm of Merrill Lynch. He stayed with Merrill Lynch, assuming the chairmanship in 1971, until asked by President-elect Ronald Reagan to be Secretary of the Treasury.

Regan was a controversial Secretary of the Treasury as he seemed to move freely between the positions of the supply siders and the monetarists. Perhaps his most important economic pronouncement was that he denied any link between budget deficits and inflation. This position was not popular with many Republicans and many in the financial markets.

Regan often criticized Federal Reserve Chairman Paul A. Volcker over the Federal Reserve's unwillingness to ease the grip on the money supply. While this placed him in the supply-side camp, Regan's choice to head the COUNCIL OF ECONOMIC ADVISERS was a committed monetarist, Beryl Sprinkel.

While Regan may have appeared stuck between two economic viewpoints, his style of management was distinct. Many Washington politicians complained about the way in which Regan interacted with them. Regan seemed to have little patience for the backroom political dealing of Congress. He exchanged public words with many on Capitol Hill including Republican Senator Robert Dole.

In January 1985, JAMES A. BAKER, III, and Donald Regan switched jobs—Baker to Secretary of the Treasury and Regan to WHITE HOUSE CHIEF OF STAFF for the President. The announcement was somewhat of a surprise; however, many considered it a move to create more energy in Reagan's second term.

Regan took his corporate approach to the White House and attempted to restructure the nature of the Chief of Staff. He replaced the collective decision-making system with a hierarchical one that placed him directly below the President. He also imposed a more businesslike discipline—what aides referred to as "a structured environment." He added strategic planning as an ongoing way to control the many demands on the executive. He even tried to plan the budget a year in advance the way a corporation would have done it.

As the President's plan for his second term began to stall, many critics pointed the finger at Regan's management style. Regan was criticized for centralizing too much under himself and for his inability, or unwillingness, to play power politics. His seeming control of Reagan's agenda even brought the Chief of Staff in conflict with the President's wife, NANCY REAGAN, and her astrologer.

During the height of the IRAN-CONTRA AFFAIR, Regan resigned from office in November 1987. False reports had surfaced that he had been directly involved in the scandal. Subsequently, the TOWER COMMISSION cleared Regan of any direct responsibility, but blamed him "for the chaos that descended upon the White House." President Reagan appointed former Senator Howard Baker of Tennessee to replace Regan.

BIBLIOGRAPHY

Regan, Donald T. *For the Record.* 1988.
Walczak, Lee, et al. "Regan Inc." *Business Week* (9 September 1985): 76–82.

JEFFREY D. SCHULTZ

REGAN v. WALD 468 U.S. 222 (1984). In *Regan,* the Supreme Court upheld a de facto ban on Americans traveling to CUBA imposed by Treasury Department regulations that prohibited spending money in Cuba. The United States first declared a trade embargo on Cuba in 1963 under the Trading with the Enemy Act (TWEA), which authorized the President to declare trade embargoes in time of war or national emergency. The original embargo included restrictions on travel by Americans, but in 1977 President Jimmy Carter relaxed the embargo to permit such travel. In 1982, President Ronald Reagan reimposed the travel restrictions, prohibiting all travel except by journalists, professional researchers, persons visiting close relatives, or people whose visits were hosted by Cuba.

In the meantime, in 1977, Congress had amended the Trading with the Enemy Act to restrict its invocation by the President to times of war and in 1978 had amended the Passport Act of 1926 to prohibit the executive from imposing geographic restrictions on the use of U.S. passports except in narrowly limited circumstances [*see* TRAVEL, RIGHT TO].

Americans seeking to travel to Cuba brought suit, challenging the reimposition of the ban on the grounds that the President did not have the authority to impose it under the TWEA and that, in any event, the ban was unconstitutional. They argued that when Congress repealed the President's national EMERGENCY POWERS under TWEA in 1977, the grandfather clause preserving aspects of the embargoes then in effect did not include authority to impose a travel ban not in effect at that time.

The appeals court struck down the travel ban as unauthorized, based on earlier Supreme Court decisions requiring a narrow construction of delegated presidential powers restricting the right to travel. The appeals court also reasoned that the 1978 Passport Act amendment prohibiting geographic restrictions on the use of passports would be meaningless if the President could achieve the same result by imposing currency restrictions under the trade embargo laws.

The Supreme Court, with Justice William Rehnquist writing the opinion, reversed the appeals court decision by a 5 to 4 vote. Taking an expansive view of the President's powers in areas affecting FOREIGN AFFAIRS, the Supreme Court read the grandfather clause broadly. The Supreme Court gave short shrift to the citizens' constitutional claims, finding that the right to travel abroad was entitled to less protection than the right to travel inside the United States and that any restriction on international travel was justified in the President's view by "weighty concerns" of foreign policy that would not be questioned by the Court.

In dissent, Justice Harry Blackmun described the history of legislation that has given the President extraordinary emergency powers as a one-way ratchet to enhance the President's discretionary authority over foreign policy. He noted that the TWEA contained no provision to reduce the President's authority to its normal scope when the emergency subsided and that Presidents have historically been slow to terminate declarations of emergency. The 1978 amendments to TWEA and the enactment of a new, more restrictive statute governing peacetime emergencies were meant to curtail the discretionary authority that the "President had accumulated because of past 'emergencies' that no longer fit Congress' conception of that term." He quoted Professor Harold G. Maier to the effect that a "combination of legislative permissiveness and executive assertiveness over the past 40 years has created a significant shift in the functional allocations of constitutional power to regulate foreign commerce." The Supreme Court did not reverse this shift in *Regan*.

BIBLIOGRAPHY

Koh, Harold Hongju. *The National Security Constitution.* 1990.

KATE MARTIN

REGULATORY POLICY. Presidential interest in managing federal regulatory policy dates, not surprisingly, from late in the NEW DEAL, after an explosion in the size and functions of the bureaucracy. Beginning with Franklin D. Roosevelt, Presidents have appointed special commissions or advisers to study administrative problems and to recommend reforms. Over the decades, the perceptions of the nature of regulatory deficiencies and the consequent recommendations have displayed a depressing constancy, focusing on the lack of policy coordination.

In 1937, the report of the BROWNLOW COMMITTEE branded the independent agencies "a headless 'fourth branch' of government." The HOOVER COMMISSION in 1955 and the ASH COUNCIL in 1971 added calls for more separation between prosecuting and adjudicating personnel in agencies. Meanwhile, James Landis prepared a famous report to President-elect John F. Kennedy, pointing out deficiencies in personnel, ethics, timely application, policy coordination, and administrative organization. Landis's litany of regulatory ills was echoed by the American Bar Association's Commission on Law and the Economy in 1979, but was somewhat discounted by the Senate Committee on Government Operations Study on Federal Regulation in 1977. Finally, beginning in the late 1970s and peaking under President Ronald Reagan in the 1980s, a movement for substantive DEREGULATION was pursued through both legislative and administrative initiatives.

Modern Presidents have responded to the need to manage regulatory policy in a number of ways. First, and perhaps most important, a President shapes regulatory statutes through his powers to propose and to veto legislation. Congress rarely enacts a major statute without presidential guidance and support. Passage of such important statutes as those regulating air pollution or deregulating the airlines requires sustained presidential participation, often over the period of several Congresses. During that process, the President's veto power is an often indirect but always potent influence on the final shape of a statute. Because overriding a veto is so difficult, the threat of a veto can allow the President to force major alterations in a pending bill.

Second, ever since the BUDGET AND ACCOUNTING ACT of 1921, Presidents have possessed the power to formulate the federal budget for congressional consideration and passage. Unlike participation in enactment of a particular regulatory statute, the budget process provides an opportunity for policy coordination, since regulation is influenced by funding levels. An agency's funding level is a critical practical determinant of its capacity to regulate. Although the budget does not bind Congress, many of its assumptions and specific provisions invariably find their way into appropriations. In general, the President's OFFICE OF MANAGEMENT AND BUDGET (OMB) controls not only the budget requests of federal agencies, but their legislative requests and congressional testimony as well. Congress has, however, exempted some of the independent agencies from some or all of these requirements.

Third, the President appoints federal regulators, often with the Senate's ADVICE AND CONSENT. (Alternatively, the heads of EXECUTIVE DEPARTMENTS, who reflect the President's policies, appoint them.) Neither the nomination nor the confirmation process has received good reviews over the years. Too often, Presidents have nominated political allies with little ability or experience in regulation, and the Senate has approved them with little critical scrutiny. Heightened interest in regulatory performance on the part of both branches seems to have improved the quality of appointments in recent years. The political appointees at the top of the agencies supervise the much larger CIVIL SERVICE bureaucracy, which stays while Presidents come and go, and which has a reputation for resistance to presidential supervision.

Presidential choice of personnel extends to removal of political appointees whose performance is disappointing. For the independent regulatory agencies, however, Congress restricts presidential removal power, requiring the presence of cause for dismissal. In practice, this has meant substantially greater policy autonomy for the independent than for the executive agencies. Ever since the Supreme Court upheld the constitutionality of congressional restrictions on removal in 1935, Presidents have been reluctant to provoke a confrontation with Congress by removing independent officers or by supervising their formulation of policy.

Fourth, Presidents often possess statutory power to reorganize existing agencies [see REORGANIZATION POWER]. Reorganization plans may, within limits, transfer, consolidate, or abolish agency functions. Because the agencies have differing policy orientations, the placement of a function in one department rather than another can influence its policy importantly.

Fifth, some statutes vest substantive regulatory authority directly in the President. Wage-price control statutes, for example, have typically done so. Under a housekeeping statute enacted to relieve Presidents of direct administrative burdens, the President may subdelegate such powers to any executive agency. This provides him an opportunity to supervise regulation more closely than he otherwise might, while allowing subordinates to craft policy initially.

Sixth, the DEPARTMENT OF JUSTICE controls most federal government litigation. This power allows the President, through his ATTORNEY GENERAL, to set legal policy for the agencies. For example, an agency is sometimes informed that the Attorney General will not defend in court some policy initiative it is contemplating. Within the department, the SOLICITOR GENERAL decides which lower court decisions will be appealed

to the Supreme Court, thus providing another coordinating function. Congress has, however, given some independent agencies the power to represent themselves in court.

Finally, Presidents issue EXECUTIVE ORDERS and other less formal directives to the agencies, stating principles and policies that administrators must follow when regulating. In order to impose a measure of coordination on the sprawling executive establishment, Presidents employ their explicit constitutional powers to ensure faithful execution of the laws and to require department heads to provide opinions in writing on their responsibilities. These presidential powers are limited mainly by explicit statutory boundaries to policy discretion. Statutory delegations of regulatory power ordinarily contain enough latitude to allow compliance with generalized presidential commands.

Prominent executive-order programs have required agencies to consider the inflationary impact of their actions, to follow cost-benefit principles when regulating, and to formulate an agenda for future regulation each year [see EXECUTIVE ORDER 12291 and EXECUTIVE ORDER 12498.]. Others have required agencies to consider the impact of their policy on such topics as federalism and family values. By having the OMB review agencies' compliance with such programs, the President influences policy substantially.

As a result of this congeries of constitutional and statutory powers, Presidents exert important but limited influence over regulatory policy. They provide legislative and personnel leadership, and a measure of overall coordination of policy formation. But Presidents and their relatively small staffs of immediate advisers are too busy to oversee all the details of regulation in the vast federal bureaucracy. The administrators themselves are left with substantial discretion and responsibility in their relations with the American public.

BIBLIOGRAPHY

Fisher, Louis. *Constitutional Conflicts between Congress and the President.* 3d ed. 1991.

National Academy of Public Administration. *Presidential Management of Rulemaking in Regulatory Agencies.* 1987.

Pierce, Richard A., Jr., Sidney A. Shapiro, and Paul R. Verkuil. *Administrative Law and Process.* 2d ed. 1992.

Robinson, Glen O. *American Bureaucracy, Public Choice and Public Law.* 1991.

Shane, Peter M., and Harold H. Bruff. *The Law of Presidential Power.* 1988.

HAROLD H. BRUFF

REID v. COVERT 351 U.S. 487 (1956); 354 U.S. 1 (1957). In *Reid v. Covert,* the Supreme Court held that neither laws nor international agreements could deprive American citizens of such basic constitutional rights as the right to trial by jury. The decision laid to rest many of the concerns about treaties and EXECUTIVE AGREEMENTS that had fueled the drive to enact the BRICKER AMENDMENT, a constitutional amendment proposed in the 1950s to limit the internal effects of international agreements.

Clarice Covert, an American citizen, had killed her husband, an American serviceman stationed in England, and she had been tried and convicted of murder by a court-martial. She later challenged the legitimacy of such proceedings, arguing that she had been deprived of her right to indictment and a jury trial as guaranteed by Article III and the Fifth and Sixth Amendments of the Constitution.

The government argued that Article I, Section 8, of the Constitution specifically authorized Congress to make rules governing and regulating the armed forces, and that Congress had exercised that power in passing the Uniform Code of Military Justice. This statute authorized military trials for civilians accompanying the armed forces overseas if so provided in an agreement with the host country, and the United States had entered into such an agreement with Great Britain—an executive agreement in 1942 that gave American military officials exclusive jurisdiction over offenses committed in England by American soldiers and their dependents. The government now claimed that the statute should be sustained under Congress's delegated powers and as "necessary and proper" to carrying out the agreement with Britain.

When the case first reached the Supreme Court in 1956, the justices upheld Mrs. Covert's conviction, citing *In re Ross* (1891) involving a consular court, and the *Insular Cases* (1901) involving territory acquired by conquest and cession, to show that the right to a jury trial did not extend to Americans overseas even if they were tried by an agency of the United States government.

After a rehearing and further argument and deliberations in 1957, however, the Justices ruled 6 to 2 that Mrs. Covert's trial by military authorities had deprived her of her constitutional rights. Justices Hugo L. Black, William O. Douglas, William J. Brennan, Jr., and Chief Justice Earl Warren dismissed *Ross* and the *Insular Cases*, citing instead the Court's recent decision in *Toth v. Quarles* (1955) that a former soldier could not be tried by court-martial once he had been released from the military. Black emphasized that Congress could not by statute deprive a civilian of her rights under the Constitution, and that "no agreement with a foreign nation can confer power on the Congress or on any other branch of Government which is free from the restraints of the Constitution." Besides resolving the issue at hand, Black hoped that reiterating the Constitution's supremacy over treaties and executive agreements would remove some of the fears that had led people to support the Bricker Amendment.

Justices Felix Frankfurter and John Marshall Harlan concurred in the decision because it involved a capital offense committed during peacetime, but, along with Justices Tom C. Clark and Harold Burton, who dissented, they believed the decision should be based solely on Congress's power to regulate the armed forces. They objected to Black's discussion of the relationship between the Constitution and international agreements, which they viewed as unnecessarily interjecting the Court into the Bricker Amendment controversy.

BIBLIOGRAPHY

Currie, Donald. "Court-Martial Jurisdiction of Civilian Dependents." *Washington and Lee Law Review* 15 (1958): 79–88.
Tananbaum, Duane. *The Bricker Amendment Controversy: A Test of Eisenhower's Political Leadership.* 1988.
Wiener, Frederick Bernays. *Civilians under Military Justice.* 1967.

DUANE TANANBAUM

RELATIVES, PRESIDENTS'. See KINFOLK, PRESIDENTIAL.

RELIGION, POLICY ON. "Of all the dispositions and habits which lead to political prosperity," wrote President George Washington in 1796, "Religion and Morality are indispensible supports. In vain would that man claim the tribute of Patriotism, who should labour to subvert these great Pillars of human happiness." Washington's famous comment set the tone for all future presidential pronouncements on the role of religion in American public life. Regardless of party affiliation or constitutional persuasion, American Presidents have universally recognized the importance of religion to American republicanism in their INAUGURAL ADDRESSES, thanksgiving and prayer day proclamations, letters to church groups, and similar public utterances.

Like Washington, subsequent Presidents believed that republicanism depends in large part on the moral character of the citizenry, and they looked to religion to help supply that character. "The most perfect machinery of government will not keep us as a nation from destruction if there is not within us a soul," declared Theodore Roosevelt. "No abounding material prosperity shall avail us if our spiritual senses atrophy." Calvin Coolidge similarly claimed that "if American democracy is to remain the greatest hope of humanity, it must continue abundantly in the faith of the Bible." And Lyndon Johnson argued that "men of God have taught us that social problems are moral problems on a huge scale. . . . They have preached that the church should be the first to awake to individual suffering and the church should be the bravest in opposing all social wrongs." Along with this presidential recognition of religion's moral role has been an acknowledgment that American government also relies for its success upon what Abraham Lincoln called "the ever-watchful providence of Almighty God."

This rhetorical admiration of the role of religion in American republicanism has been separate and distinct from policy questions about government sponsorship of religion. Presidents have realized that they can acknowledge the nation's ultimate dependence upon God and praise religion's role in the formation of moral character without having the government officially sponsor religious activities. Thus, Thomas Jefferson, who declined to issue thanksgiving proclamations because he thought the Constitution did not authorize them, did not deem it improper in his second inaugural address to ask his fellow citizens to join him in prayers for the government, or to praise in his first inaugural the nation's religious denominations for "inculcating honesty, truth, temperance, gratitude, and the love of man." During most of the nation's history, other Presidents have adopted an approach similar to Jefferson's: rhetorical support for religion's social role even while assuring religious liberty for all and preserving a practical separation between church and state.

Religious Liberty. Presidential efforts in support of religious liberty have been particularly noteworthy in the area of FOREIGN AFFAIRS, where one of the earliest policy questions concerned the persecution of American missionaries abroad. In the nation's formative years, American diplomacy focused chiefly on protecting and promoting commercial interests. As a result, missionaries found little support from American diplomats and often had to rely on British consular officers when they had difficulties. This situation began to change as the American missionary presence abroad began to grow, and in 1842 Secretary of State DANIEL WEBSTER finally instructed the American minister in Constantinople that missionaries should receive the same help and protection from consular officers as merchants. By the latter half of the nineteenth century, the protection of the lives and property of missionaries had become a recognized responsibility of

the diplomatic corps, and during this period Presidents regularly mentioned their efforts to provide redress for persecuted missionaries in their annual messages to Congress.

In the late twentieth century, the presidential concern for religious liberty in other countries has broadened. Notable examples include President Jimmy Carter's vigorous HUMAN RIGHTS policy on behalf of dissidents of all kinds, and the Reagan administration's sheltering of a group of Siberian evangelicals in the American embassy in Moscow until the Soviet government would allow them to emigrate.

In the domestic sphere, presidential policies on behalf of religious liberty have been slower to develop, largely because of the slight role of the federal government in state and local affairs prior to the NEW DEAL. Still, there were a few issues of note that arose early in the nation's history. One of the first, and surely one of the most heated, was Sunday mails. After Congress authorized post offices to be open every day of the week in 1810, thousands of evangelicals began to send in protests, attacking not only open post offices but the operation of mail coaches on Sundays. The protestors regarded Sunday mails as a twofold assault on religious liberty: first, it forced many postal workers to choose between violating their religious beliefs or losing their jobs; and second, it involved the government in openly undercutting a religious belief held by many Americans to be fundamental. While Congress bore the brunt of this campaign, the actual regulations under which Sunday mails were conducted were the responsibility of the executive branch, which generally sought to diminish the controversy as best it could. When Sunday mails were first mandated by Congress during the administration of James Madison, for example, Postmaster General Gideon Granger interpreted the requirement as narrowly as possible. The first Whig administration in 1841 went considerably further. Counting conservative evangelicals as one of its chief constituencies, its Postmaster General, Charles A. Wickliffe, made substantial reductions in the number of Sunday mail routes.

Separation of Church and State. Efforts to curb Sunday mails and to protect the lives and property of American missionaries abroad helped promote religion by securing religious liberty. But Presidents have also acted to curb religion in order to maintain the separation between church and state. Before the CIVIL WAR, the federal government removed MORMON religious leader Brigham Young as Utah's territorial governor in an effort to establish a legitimate secular government there. When resistance ensued, President James Buchanan sent in troops to extinguish the rebellion; his firm resolve in the matter provides a stark contrast with the paralysis he later exhibited when faced by southern seccession. After the Civil War, President Ulysses S. Grant decried "the accumulation of vast amounts of untaxed church property" and urged "the taxation of all property equally, exempting only" cemeteries and "possibly, with proper restrictions, church edifices." Grant further proposed a ban on the distribution of government monies to religious schools, and a constitutional amendment to that effect was later submitted to Congress by Representative JAMES G. BLAINE. This proposal was primarily designed to preclude public funding of Catholic schools.

Though Presidents have universally supported church-state separation, the outer parameters of this principle have sometimes been ambiguous. President Ronald Reagan, for example, periodically called for a constitutional amendment allowing voluntary prayer in the public schools, a proposal many saw as violating the separation between church and state. Perhaps more important, Presidents have differed on whether religious groups should be employed to achieve secular policy ends. James Madison thought not, and this was one reason he vetoed a bill that would have granted a corporate charter to an Episcopal church in the District of Columbia. Part of the charter gave the church the authority to support and educate the poor. Madison opposed the provision because it supplied a "precedent for giving to religious societies as such a legal agency in carrying into effect a public and civil duty."

Other Presidents, however, have adopted a different view, and Madison himself acted inconsistently while President. Surely the most sustained use of religious groups to achieve federal objectives came in American Indian policy during the nineteenth century. From the earliest days of the republic, tax dollars subsidized missionary efforts among the INDIANS in the hope of gaining secure borders and tempering the inevitable problems created by western expansion. These government efforts were sanctioned even by staunch separationists like James Madison and Thomas Jefferson. This general policy probably made good sense given the circumstances. It was in the nation's best interest to cultivate the Indians' friendship and to introduce them to farming, writing, and self-government; and missionaries were likely more trustworthy in performing as educators than many others who came into contact with the Indians. Their benevolent intentions made them the best available candidates to promote harmony between Indians and whites.

Entanglements and Religious Liberty. In the late twentieth century, entanglements between the federal government and religion have become much more frequent, largely because the scope and power of the federal government have expanded dramatically. As the federal government has moved to finance health and social services, the arts, education, child care, and many other activities, the question has arisen whether religiously affiliated charities can be recipients of any of the monies. Restricting federal aid to secular institutions in these areas raises important religious-liberty objections because the federal aid can effectively crowd out religious charities by placing secular education, social services, or childcare at an overwhelming economic advantage. Such a restrictive policy also effectively undermines the traditional presidential support for the positive social role of religion. If religion really is necessary for the maintenance of social order—as most Presidents have publically argued—then undercutting religious charities and educational groups by the discriminatory disbursement of federal funds poses serious difficulties.

Seeking to avoid these difficulties, the administrations of Ronald Reagan and George Bush favored inclusion of religious groups in generally available government programs. With regard to both education and day care, they argued that vouchers or tax credits should be usable at both religious and secular programs. Similarly, the Reagan administration's teen-pregnancy program, run out of the DEPARTMENT OF HEALTH AND HUMAN SERVICES, supplied grants to religious as well as secular social service agencies (a practice provisionally upheld by the Supreme Court in *Bowen v. Kendrick* in 1988).

The ever-expanding jurisdiction of the federal government has also increased the number of possible friction points between the federal government and religious adherents on policy questions. Accordingly, the Reagan and Bush administrations tried to avoid government actions that might undercut the religious beliefs of large groups of Americans—such as the public funding of ABORTION, the promotion of abortion using federal funds earmarked for family planning, or the use of federal funds to distribute contraceptives to teenagers without parental knowledge or consent. The general policy has been that whenever practicable, religious adherents should not have to pay taxes to have the government undermine their religious beliefs.

Religion and Partisan Purpose. Undoubtedly, there is an underside to any connections between the presidency and religion, even rhetorical ones. Throughout human history, unscrupulous rulers have employed religion to sanction whatever policies they happened to be pursuing at any given moment, turning religion into a political tool rather than relying on it as an independent moral force. American Presidents have not been entirely blameless in this area; on occasion they too have sought to employ religion for mere partisan advantage. The fast days proclaimed by John Adams in the 1790s became occasions for Federalist ministers to urge support for both the ALIEN AND SEDITION ACTS and the administration's unpopular tax program. In the late 1820s, the Jackson administration tried to counter missionary opposition to its Indian-removal policy by organizing a front-group of clergymen that would lobby for the administration proposal. President McKinley justified keeping the PHILIPPINES after the SPANISH-AMERICAN WAR by telling a group of clerics that after praying to God, he realized that America must "civilize and Christianize" the Filipinos.

This temptation to manipulate religion for partisan purposes has increased during the twentieth century along with federal power and the sophistication of modern campaign methods. Presidents have hired assistants to cultivate relations with religious groups, and the White House regularly brings in religious leaders to hear the President in order to gain support for administration policies. While such efforts are sometimes sincere, religious groups ought to recognize that the man in the White House may have different purposes than their own for invoking divine sanctions.

BIBLIOGRAPHY

Cord, Robert. *Separation of Church and State: Historical Fact and Current Fiction.* 1982.
Field, Jr., James A. *America and the Mediterranean World, 1776–1882.* 1969.
Grabill, Joseph L. Grabill. *Protestant Diplomacy and the Near East: Missionary Influence on American Policy, 1810–1927.* 1971.
Hutcheson, Richard G., Jr. *God in the White House: How Religion Has Changed the Modern Presidency.* 1988.
John, Richard R. "Taking Sabbatarianism Seriously: The Postal System, the Sabbath, and the Transformation of American Political Culture." *Journal of the Early Republic* 10 (1990): 517–567.
Richardson, James D., ed. *A Compilation of the Messages and Papers of the Presidents.* 1911.
Shepherd, David R., ed. *Ronald Reagan: In God I Trust.* 1984.
Stokes, Anson Phelps. *Church and State in the United States.* 3 vols. 1950.

JOHN G. WEST, JR.

RELIGIONS, PRESIDENTIAL. Beginning with the first President, the personal religious beliefs and practices of the Presidents have ranged from adher-

ence to an evangelical faith that saw politics as a way to serve Christ to nominal adherence to a childhood faith. George Washington was a lifelong Episcopalian, holding vestry membership. Though he belonged to the Episcopal church, which had been the established religion of the colonies under Britain's rule, he is better described as a deist, that is, as someone who believes in a creator of the universe who set in motion the natural laws by which it operates without his intervention.

The nation's second President, John Adams, though raised as a Congregationalist (the Congregationalist church being the established church of Massachusetts), was a moderate Unitarian, that is, someone who rejects the division of God into the Trinity. Nonetheless, he considered himself a Christian.

Thomas Jefferson, perhaps the most interesting President when it comes to religion, was officially an Episcopalian, though he tended to be a freethinking skeptic. Rewriting the New Testament by removing all the references to miracles, he hoped to "demythologize" Christianity. Though his writings contain many references to religion, Jefferson distrusted formal religion. Like Washington, Jefferson can probably be best described as a deist.

Presidents James Madison and James Monroe were both Virginia Episcopalians. There is little to distinguish their personal beliefs as they rarely, if ever, spoke of them. The sixth President, John Quincy Adams, was an independent Congregationalist who read the entire Bible yearly. Much of his correspondence with his children dealt with religion.

Andrew Jackson was the first President not to belong to any formal church, perhaps as a result of his long military career. He was the first President whose home state, Kentucky, never had an established religion. He did, however, build a Presbyterian church on his estate for his wife, Rachel. After her death he faithfully attended services there.

Martin Van Buren, a member of the Dutch Reformed Church, attended St. John's Episcopal Church while President because there was no Dutch Reformed Church in Washington. His funeral was conducted by both Dutch Reformed and Episcopal ministers.

The ninth and tenth Presidents, William Henry Harrison and John Tyler, were both Episcopalians.

James K. Polk was raised a Presbyterian. During his administration, dancing and liquor were banned from the White House and no business was conducted on Sunday. On his deathbed in 1849, Polk asked for a Methodist minister to baptize him. He had become interested in Methodism after attending a camp meeting in 1833.

The twelfth President, Zachary Taylor, did not belong to any church. His funeral was reportedly conducted according to the Episcopal rite.

A charter member of the First Unitarian Society of Buffalo, Millard Fillmore withdrew from the church because of the intense criticism he received on his handling the SLAVERY issue. His funeral services were conducted by a Baptist, an Episcopalian, and a Presbyterian minister.

The Franklin Pierce White House was a melancholy one, its mood colored largely by the religious fanaticism of Pierce's wife and by the loss of their son shortly before the inauguration. Pierce regularly attended both Presbyterian and Congregational services. Pierce later converted to Episcopalianism to avoid political sermons that increasingly inveighed against slavery and commented on the Civil War.

James Buchanan, the fifteenth President, was a lifelong Presbyterian who left the church during his presidency because of the growing political nature of sermons. After retirement, he tried to reenter his church, but radical abolitionists controlling the northern branch refused to readmit him.

Though he was never baptized and was not a member of any church, Abraham Lincoln is considered one of the most religious Presidents. He made constant reference to a civil religion that united the American people. Despite Lincoln's liberal use of the Bible in speeches and writings, Lincoln's law partner, William Herndon, claimed that Lincoln was a skeptic or agnostic.

The seventeenth President, Andrew Johnson, initially attended Methodist services and then Catholic masses at old St. Patrick's parish in Washington in order to avoid political sermons.

Although his personal memoirs ran for two volumes, Ulysses S. Grant did not once mention religion. A clergyman called to Grant's deathbed falsely claimed that Grant had converted and been baptized, but Grant actually refused his pleadings.

Rutherford B. Hayes was consumed with the issue of religion. His wife was a strict Methodist and prohibitionist. While President, Hayes held daily prayers and Bible readings, and on Sunday evenings the family gathered for the singing of hymns.

James Garfield, the twentieth President, was a lay preacher in the Disciples of Christ church. Both Chester A. Arthur's and Grover Cleveland's fathers were ministers (a Baptist and a Presbyterian, respectively). Neither President was particularly religious, however; in fact, Arthur did not even belong to a church.

Serving his church as both an elder and a deacon,

Benjamin Harrison was an evangelical Presbyterian. As a delegate to the Presbyterian General Assembly, he supported the church's progressive wing.

William McKinley, the twenty-fifth President, was an evangelical Methodist who believed that political activity was one path for serving Christ and advancing Christ's message. He adhered to a strict Protestant theology in interpreting the Gospels. His successor, Theodore Roosevelt, used the presidency as a BULLY PULPIT from which to teach ethics and moral behavior. Roosevelt, the second Dutch Reformed President, saw religion as the duty of all educated men. He was skeptical of dogma and thought little was gained by the doctrinal squabbles of various denominations. He was so well versed in the Bible that he lectured at a seminary.

A devout Unitarian, William Howard Taft refused the presidency of Yale University because of its Congregational affiliation. His religion became an issue in the 1908 election because many fundamentalists, who read the Bible literally, were encouraged to vote against him.

The third preacher's son to become President, Woodrow Wilson was a Presbyterian. He applied his critical mind to questions of theology as to his many intellectual interests.

A nominal Baptist, Warren G. Harding was possibly the least religious President. His successor, Calvin Coolidge, a lifelong Congregationalist, considered religion a private matter and was largely silent on the issue. Yet Coolidge inaugurated the traditions of delivering an annual Christmas message and lighting a national Christmas tree.

Herbert Hoover, the first Quaker President, believed religion was an organized form of ethical humanitarianism. His marriage received a dispensation by the Catholic bishop of New York because Hoover wished to be married by a friend who was a priest.

Of Franklin D. Roosevelt's personal religious beliefs, his wife, Eleanor, commented that her husband's Episcopal faith was "simple and direct." His successor, Harry S. Truman, was an outspoken Baptist who once severed his ties with the First Baptist Church of Washington, D.C. because the minister criticized his attempt to establish diplomatic relations with the Vatican.

Unlike previous military men elected President, Dwight D. Eisenhower actively participated in religion. Though raised in a strict River Brethren sect, he joined the Presbyterian church after his inauguration. He opened each Cabinet meeting with a prayer, hoping to establish a tradition.

John F. Kennedy's Roman Catholicism was a major campaign issue in the 1960 election, though his religious practice was largely a private matter. Lyndon B. Johnson, his successor, was a member of the Disciples of Christ church. A practical man, Johnson saw religion in utilitarian terms.

Richard M. Nixon, a California Quaker who became a committed evangelical after a tent rally in the 1920s, held regular religious services in the White House. Religious Heritage of America, a fundamentalist group headed by the evangelist Billy Graham, honored Nixon as "churchman of the year" in 1970. Nixon's successor, Gerald Ford, a lifelong Episcopalian, tended toward evangelicalism.

A committed evangelical Baptist, Jimmy Carter taught Sunday school at Washington's First Baptist Church. His religious zeal was a campaign issue in the 1976 election.

Despite nominal membership in the Disciple of Christ church and irregular attendance of Presbyterian services, Ronald Reagan is often considered one of the most conservative and active evangelicals to have served as President. Reagan espoused a civil religion that included a vision of America as a "city on the hill" and of Americans as a chosen people.

George Bush, the forty-first President, was also the ninth President to be a member of the Episcopal church. His personal religious views remained largely private, though he continued some of the moral/ethical themes from the Reagan presidency.

Bill Clinton was the fourth Baptist to be elected President; his views on religion, however, were not an issue in the 1992 election. Many of the moral themes stressed by his campaign differed markedly from those of the Reagan and Bush presidencies.

As the nation grew and Presidents hailed from states other than Virginia and Massachusetts and came from a wider variety of socioeconomic backgrounds, their personal religious affiliations also diversified. Presidents have been members of nine different denominations, and there have been six religiously unaffiliated Presidents. Neither official membership nor lack of affiliation, however, is an accurate gauge of a President's personal religious beliefs.

BIBLIOGRAPHY

Alley, Robert. *So Help Me God.* 1972.
Fuller, Edward, and David F. Green. *God in the White House: The Faith of American Presidents.* 1986.
Hampton, Vernon. *Religious Background of the White House.* 1932.
Isely, Bliss. *Presidents: Men of Faith.* 1953.
Menendez, Albert J. *Religion and the U.S. Presidency: A Bibliography.* 1986.

JEFFREY D. SCHULTZ

REMOVAL POWER. The power to remove executive-branch officials whose appointments require Senate consent is not mentioned in the Constitution. This silence invites four competing theories. According to the first theory, the power of removal is given to Congress by the necessary and proper clause of Article I, Section 8, clause 18, and may be delegated by Congress to the President or other officials with such conditions or limitations as Congress determines necessary. The second theory says that the power to remove is contained in the APPOINTMENT POWER and therefore requires the Senate's consent. In the third theory, executive-branch offices are expected to serve through the term of the President who appointed them and to resign at the end of that term, subject only to IMPEACHMENT by the House and conviction by the Senate. Finally, according to the fourth theory, the removal power—though not explicitly mentioned—is a functional necessity for the President in the exercise of the EXECUTIVE POWER and therefore exists as one of the INHERENT POWERS.

The Federal Period. In FEDERALIST 77 ALEXANDER HAMILTON argued that the Senate's ADVICE AND CONSENT to presidential nominations also extended to removals, unless Congress legislated otherwise. But James Madison, in the debates in 1789 over a removal clause in the statute creating the Department of Foreign Affairs, argued for an unrestricted removal power for the President. Madison warned that providing the Senate with a share in such power would create a "two-headed monster" superintending the departments [*see* DECISION OF 1789]. Following Madison's argument, the statutes creating the departments of Foreign Affairs, War, and the Treasury acknowledged the removal power of the President.

From the very first, Presidents began to assert their power to remove officials. George Washington secured the resignation of EDMUND RANDOLPH as Secretary of State in 1795 after an intercepted letter implied that Randolph would pursue a pro-French policy in exchange for a bribe. Washington also removed seventeen officials whose appointments had been consented to by the Senate. John Adams was the first President to remove a CABINET secretary without going through the formalities of a resignation: incensed at Secretary of State Timothy Pickering's interference with his French policy and Pickering's failure to support Adams's nomination of his son-in-law for adjutant general, Adams fired him. Adams removed nineteen other civil officers as well. Only one removal, that of Tenche Coxe in 1797 from his post as Commissioner of Revenue, involved party politics.

President Thomas Jefferson removed the Surveyor

General of the United States, Rufus Putnam, who disagreed with the President's policies on western lands. He fired John Adams's son-in-law, Col. William Smith, surveyor of the port of New York, for taking part in a plot against Spanish possessions in South America, a violation of U.S. law. Jefferson removed a total of 109 officers, including Adams's midnight appointments at the end of his term, and several lawyers and collectors of customs. James Madison fired his Secretary of State, Robert Smith, for incompetence, claiming that whatever talents Smith had he did not "possess those adapted to his station." During the WAR OF 1812, he also obtained the resignation under pressure of Gen. John Armstrong as Secretary of War after Armstrong failed to prepare the nation's capital against the arrival of British troops and Washington was occupied and sacked. Madison removed twenty-seven officers altogether, most of them revenue collectors. James Monroe also removed only twenty-seven civil officers, one-third of whom were from the foreign service and one-third of whom were collectors of revenue. President John Quincy Adams removed only twelve.

For the most part removals by the Presidents through the 1820s involved wrongdoing in office and not partisan politics. In 1820, Congress passed a TENURE OF OFFICE ACT (3 Stat. 582) that established four-year terms for officers handling funds. It also made such officers removable "at pleasure," which presumably empowered the President. Officials covered by the 1820 law included U.S. attorneys, collectors of customs, receivers of moneys for public lands, registrars of land offices, paymasters in the army, and commissary officers in the military.

The Jacksonian and Whig Periods. Controversy over the removal power erupted during the administration of Andrew Jackson, who established the principle of rotation in office on partisan grounds. Although Jackson's slogan "to the victor belong the spoils" seems to imply wholesale removals, the historian Erik McKinley Eriksson has calculated that fewer than one-tenth of the lower-ranking officers of the United States had been removed after Jackson's first year in office, with perhaps one-fifth gone by the end of Jackson's term—a total of 180 removals. Jackson, however, also claimed the power to remove Cabinet officials who asserted an independent judgment on the statutory powers given them by Congress. Jackson removed Secretary of the Treasury William J. Duane for refusing to remove the funds from the BANK OF THE UNITED STATES and deposit them in state banks. He then appointed Roger B. Taney during a congressional recess, and Taney implemented Jackson's pol-

icy. When it reconvened, the Senate retaliated by blocking Taney's appointment as Secretary of the Treasury, forcing him to give up his post, and then by rejecting his nomination for Associate Justice of the Supreme Court. (In 1836 a more cooperative Senate approved Jackson's nomination of Taney for Chief Justice of the United States.)

The Whig-dominated Senate passed a resolution of censure against Jackson in 1834, stating that the President had "assumed upon himself authority and power not conferred by the constitution and laws, but in derogation of both." Jackson sent a vigorous rebuttal, claiming that he possessed the right of "removing those officers who are to aid him in the execution of the laws." Three years later the Senate expunged the resolution of censure.

In 1838 the Supreme Court observed in *Ex parte Hennen* (1839) that it had "become the settled and well-understood construction of the Constitution that the power of removal was vested in the President alone," but, since the case involved the removal of a clerk by a federal judge, this statement was an obiter dictum. Abel P. Upshur, in his classic *A Brief Inquiry into the Nature and Character of Our Federal Government* (1840), specifically warned of the "great and alarming defect" that the removal power was held by the President.

The Civil War and After. The removal power became unsettled in the years during and after the CIVIL WAR. The Currency Act of 1863 (12 Stat. 665) established the office of Comptroller of the Currency, giving the officer a five-year term and authorizing his removal only with the consent of the Senate. In 1864 Congress passed the Consular and Diplomatic Appropriation Act (13 Stat. 137), which required the President to submit reasons for removal of consular clerks to Congress.

In the aftermath of the Civil War, Congress passed measures to protect its RECONSTRUCTION policies from President Andrew Johnson. Legislation in 1866 forbade dismissals of military officers in time of peace without sentence by courts martial (14 Stat. 92). The Command of the Army Act of 1867 provided that "the General of the Army shall not be removed, suspended, or relieved from command, or assigned to duty elsewhere than at said headquarters, except at his own request, without the previous approval of the Senate" (14 Stat. 487). The TENURE OF OFFICE ACT of 1867, passed the same day, provided that the heads of certain departments, including the Secretary of War, would hold office during the term of the President by whom they had been appointed and for one month thereafter, subject to removal by consent of the Senate.

It also provided that "every person holding any civil office to which he has been appointed by and with the advice and consent of the Senate . . . shall be entitled to hold such office until a successor shall have been in like manner appointed and duly qualified" (14 Stat. 430). During a Senate recess the President could suspend an official for reason of misconduct in office, criminal activity, incapacity, or legal disqualification, but he would be restored to his office if the Senate refused to endorse the President's action. Both the Command of the Army Act and the Tenure of Office Act were passed over Johnson's veto.

In 1867, after Congress adjourned, Johnson asked Secretary of War EDWIN M. STANTON to resign. When Stanton refused, the President, seemingly acting in accordance with the law, suspended him and authorized Gen. Ulysses S. Grant to act as Secretary of War. Johnson had outmaneuvered Congress, for he used the provision in the law that permitted him to suspend a department secretary until the Senate reconvened. But when the Senate did so, it reinstated Stanton. Now Johnson acted for the first time in apparent violation of the Tenure of Office Act by removing Stanton while the Senate was in session and appointing Gen. Lorenzo Thomas as his Secretary of War. The House thereupon voted articles of IMPEACHMENT against the President in February 1868. At his Senate trial Johnson argued that the Tenure of Office Act was unconstitutional. He also argued that even if the act was constitutional his removal of Stanton did not violate it. Stanton had been appointed by Abraham Lincoln, and Johnson argued that the law covered only those nominations a President himself had made and could not prevent him from removing an official nominated by his predecessor. Johnson escaped removal himself by just one vote in the Senate, and Stanton surrendered his office [see IMPEACHMENT OF ANDREW JOHNSON]. Congress repealed the Tenure of Office Act in 1887 after a confrontation with President Grover Cleveland.

The Twentieth Century. In a series of cases the Supreme Court chipped away at legislative removal powers. In *Shurtleff v. United States* (1903), the Court recognized a presidential removal power in the absence of explicit statutory language controlling removals. In *Wallace v. United States* (1922), Chief Justice William Howard Taft ruled that Senate confirmation of a successor (to the person the President intended to remove) nominated by the President would invalidate legislative restrictions that might otherwise have applied to the removal of an official. Finally, in the landmark case of MYERS V. UNITED STATES (1926) Chief Justice Taft recognized the removal power as an inherent presidential prerogative and declared unconstitu-

tional statutory procedures that gave the Senate authority to review removals and suspensions.

The acts that established regulatory agencies—the INTERSTATE COMMERCE ACT of 1887, the FEDERAL TRADE COMMISSION ACT of 1914, the Federal Tariff Commission Act of 1916, and Federal Power Commission Act of 1920—all provided fixed terms for commissioners, whom the President could remove for "inefficiency, neglect of duty or malfeasance in office." In creating the Railroad Labor Board in 1920, Congress provided that the members should be removable by the President "for neglect of duty or malfeasance in office, but for no other cause" and applied a similar provision to the Board of General Appraisers in 1922 and Board of Tax Appeals in 1924. Such provisions were upheld by the Supreme Court in HUMPHREY'S EXECUTOR V. UNITED STATES (1935), which distinguished between officials performing executive tasks and those engaged in quasi-legislative and quasi-judicial duties. The Court held that the latter could be insulated from the presidential removal power by legislation. Moreover, in WIENER V. UNITED STATES (1958), the Court held that the presidential removal power could be restricted even in the absence of statutory provisions.

Agencies that Congress considered its own were also insulated from the removal power. In establishing the GENERAL ACCOUNTING OFFICE in 1921, Congress provided that the COMPTROLLER GENERAL could be removed only by impeachment or a joint resolution of Congress. While a joint resolution requires the President's signature and can be vetoed, clearly such an officer is accountable to Congress and not to the President. Congress has continued to protect commissioners of certain agencies from presidential removals. The U.S. Commission on Civil Rights, for example, was reconstituted in 1983 when Congress added language to the effect that commissioners could be removed by the President "only for neglect of duty or malfeasance in office."

Courts and Congress have also protected special prosecutors and independent counsels who investigate high-level scandals involving the presidency, such as the WATERGATE AFFAIR. President Richard M. Nixon ordered Attorney General Elliot Richardson to dismiss Special Prosecutor Archibald Cox, who pursued the inquiry further than Nixon wished; Richardson promptly resigned along with Deputy Attorney General William Ruckelshaus. Finally, Solicitor General Robert Bork, who had become Acting Attorney General, did fire Cox. The political activist Ralph Nader and several members of Congress filed suit. In *Nader v. Bork* (1973), a district court agreed that Cox had been illegally removed from office because the removal violated the department's regulations regarding the special prosecutor. The Ethics Act of 1978 prohibited the removal of a special prosecutor (now called the INDEPENDENT COUNSEL) except for cause, and that statutory restriction was upheld by the Supreme Court in *Morrison v. Olson* (1988).

By asserting their prerogative to use the removal power, Presidents throughout the history of the office have transformed their role into that of CHIEF EXECUTIVE, exercising broad control over the administrative establishment. Presidents can make departmental officials do their bidding because they have the ultimate sanction to employ against the officials if they refuse.

BIBLIOGRAPHY

Corwin, Edward S. *The President's Removal Power under the Constitution.* 1927.

Fisher, Louis. *Constitutional Conflicts between President and Congress.* 3d ed. 1991. Chapter 3, "Theory in a Crucible: The Removal Power."

White, Leonard D. *The Federalists: A Study in Administrative History, 1789–1801.* 1948.

White, Leonard D. *The Jacksonians: A Study in Administrative History, 1829–1861.* 1954.

White, Leonard D. *The Jeffersonians: A Study in Administrative History, 1801–1829.* 1951.

White, Leonard D. *The Republican Era: A Study in Administrative History, 1869–1901.* 1958.

RICHARD M. PIOUS

REORGANIZATION POWER.

The delegated authority whereby the President can effect change in executive-branch organization, subject to qualifications imposed by Congress, is known as the reorganization power. Typically, this power has been delegated to Presidents for limited periods. The LEGISLATIVE VETO made its first appearance as a qualification on the delegation of reorganization power to the President. The power and accompanying veto appeared for the first time in the Economy Act of 1932; it ended in 1983 with the Supreme Court case of INS v. CHADHA.

Without reorganization power, the President has little capacity to affect administrative organization. With this power, the President has primary responsibility for organization within the executive branch.

Origin of the Reorganization Powers. In the 1920s President Warren G. Harding and the congressional Joint Committee on Reorganization cooperated in creating a reform plan for government. The joint committee's report proposed that genuine reform would require ongoing executive reorganizations. According to the committee, reorganization was a continuing process of change in which the most important job would remain to be accomplished after the initial wave of organizational reforms.

In 1932 President Herbert Hoover requested that Congress grant him reorganization authority. Congress passed the Economy Act of 1932, which gave the President the power to transfer whole agencies or parts of agencies to departments or independent agencies. The act also initiated a mechanism to check presidential use of reorganization power, the legislative veto. It specified that the President's orders for reorganization were subject to a resolution of disapproval by either house of Congress within sixty days after their issuance.

In early December 1932, Hoover issued eleven orders specifying reorganizations. He had, however, been beaten by Franklin D. Roosevelt in the November election, and the House of Representatives passed a resolution of disapproval for all eleven orders, blocking the LAME-DUCK PRESIDENT's action.

Routinization of the Reorganization Power. As Roosevelt entered office, Congress passed the Economy Act of 1933. The act empowered the President to abolish agencies as well as to reorganize them and also gave the President greater leeway by requiring that congressional disapproval of a presidential reorganization order proceed through a bill that had to pass both houses of Congress and achieve the President's signature. That is, the President could veto the very bill meant to block his reorganization action. Congress did qualify this grant by specifying that it would expire in two years.

Roosevelt gave primary attention to the crisis of the Great Depression and spent relatively little effort trying to fix administrative inefficiencies through reorganization. The lapse of the reorganization authority in 1935 therefore meant little to him. The BROWNLOW COMMITTEE and its 1937 report, however, convinced Roosevelt that executive reorganization could be a tool for managing the executive branch. In 1939, Congress passed a reorganization act renewing the President's reorganization power for two years. The act introduced the concept of the President issuing reorganization plans rather than EXECUTIVE ORDERS as means of implementing reorganization power. The act's legislative veto provision specified that a presidential reorganization plan could be killed by a concurrent resolution in which both houses passed expressions of disapproval (not requiring presidential signature).

In early 1937, the Brownlow Committee had proposed a number of reforms at which Congress had balked. The Reorganization Act of 1939 contained few of those recommendations, but with the reorganization power granted in the act, Roosevelt created the

Brownlow-recommended EXECUTIVE OFFICE OF THE PRESIDENT and transferred agencies to it.

During WORLD WAR II the President gained reorganization powers (as part of his WAR POWERS) through the First War Powers Act of 1941. Peacetime, however, left President Harry S. Truman without reorganization authority, and on 24 May 1945 he sent Congress a message requesting the renewal of reorganization power. Congress was slow to respond to Truman's request, and there were some in Congress who advocated a one-house legislative veto to make it even easier for Congress to block a presidential reorganization plan. Congress, however, ended up retaining the concurrent-resolution requirement for the legislative veto in the Reorganization Act of 1945. The 1945 act renewed the delegation of authority for two years only.

Truman issued three reorganization plans in 1946. Plans nos. 1 and 3 addressed rather small-scale reforms without effecting any interdepartmental shifts of agencies, and both survived legislative veto attempts. In Reorganization Plan No. 2, however, the President attempted to transform the Federal Security Administration into a CABINET-level human services department. That plan was vetoed by Congress.

The postwar years saw increasing recognition of the need for an increased presidential managerial capacity. Many observers saw the reorganization power as a necessary instrument for management. But some members of Congress were increasingly uneasy about both the delegation of legislative authority to Presidents and the constitutional propriety of the legislative veto.

The Reorganization Act of 1949 renewed the reorganization authority but eased the requirements for the legislative veto, making it a one-house resolution of disapproval by a constitutional majority (a majority of all members of the House or of the Senate). The act extended the reorganization power for four years, twice what had become the typical extension period. The first of the two HOOVER COMMISSIONS was the main beneficiary of the 1949 renewal of the reorganization power. President Truman sent forty-one reorganization plans to Congress, most of which implemented the commission's recommendations, saving them from the riskier pathway of statutory implementation.

In 1953 Congress came close to weakening the reorganization power even further by specifying a one-house veto by a simple majority vote. At first it had seemed that President Dwight D. Eisenhower endorsed that change, but the administration quickly clarified its intentions to Congress, and the Reorganization Act of 1953 extended the 1949 act for two years.

In 1955 it was extended for an additional two years. Eisenhower presented twelve reorganization plans to Congress in his first year in office, none of which were vetoed. Several of these effected major changes in departments and one of them created a new department—Health, Education, and Welfare.

A Weakened Reorganization Power. The Reorganization Act of 1957 extended the reorganization power for two years but changed the requirement for the legislative veto to a one-house simple majority. Only two reorganization plans were submitted under the 1957 act, one of which was disapproved by Congress. The reorganization authority was renewed early in the Kennedy administration for a two-year period, with the same one-house, simple-majority veto as the 1957 act. In Reorganization Plan No. 1 of 1962, President John F. Kennedy proposed to establish a department of urban affairs and housing. Congress had rejected a bill to create that department just a year earlier. Kennedy attempted to use the more direct route of a reorganization plan, only to have it killed by legislative veto. In part because of congressional dissatisfaction with the effort to create a new Cabinet department through reorganization, the reorganization power was not renewed during the Kennedy administration, but it was renewed in 1965 at President Lyndon Baines Johnson's behest. Johnson requested permanent renewal, but Congress was only willing to extend the grant of power for four years.

Once it was renewed, Johnson made active use of the reorganization power. In 1965 he sent twelve reorganization plans to Congress, only one of which was vetoed. These addressed diverse subjects, such as shifting all water pollution controls to the DEPARTMENT OF THE INTERIOR, reorganizing the District of Columbia government, and restructuring the Public Health Service. Johnson also created two new Cabinet-level departments through statute during his term: the DEPARTMENT OF HOUSING AND URBAN DEVELOPMENT and the DEPARTMENT OF TRANSPORTATION.

Early in the presidency of Richard M. Nixon the reorganization authority was renewed for a two-year term. Two years later, Congress renewed the authority but added a new restriction on its use. According to the 1971 act the reorganization power could only be used to introduce one reorganization plan within a thirty-day period, and each reorganization plan could deal with only one subject. The restrictions were designed to protect congressional committees from being overwhelmed by presidential reorganization plans. The reorganization authority lapsed on 1 April 1973, in a context of worsening PRESIDENTIAL-CONGRESSIONAL RELATIONS, and it was not extended. Nixon did, however, effect significant changes through the reorganization power. In 1969 he reorganized the Interstate Commerce Commission, giving more power to its presidentially appointed chairperson. In 1970 he reorganized the Bureau of the Budget, renaming it the OFFICE OF MANAGEMENT AND BUDGET. At the same time he also ordered creation of a new Domestic Policy Council within the Executive Office of the President.

The reorganization power was not again granted to a President until 1977, when it was given to Jimmy Carter. Carter requested a grant of reorganization authority for a four-year period and proposed a presidential right of amendment for reorganization plans. In the Reorganization Act of 1977 new requirements for congressional action were specified, aiming to force a vote in each house on every reorganization plan. The act granted the President the right to amend a reorganization plan within thirty days after it was sent to Congress. A new qualification included in this act prohibited reorganization plans from addressing independent regulatory commissions.

Carter actively sought government reorganization. His largest initiatives were enacted through statutes, but he sought some significant reforms through reorganization plans. Among the more important targets of these plans were reorganization of the Executive Office of the President to reduce the size of its staff, the shift of federal personnel functions from the defunct Civil Service Commission to the MERIT SYSTEMS PROTECTION BOARD and the OFFICE OF PERSONNEL MANAGEMENT, and creation of the OFFICE OF THE U.S. TRADE REPRESENTATIVE.

From its beginning in the Economy Act of 1932, the presidential reorganization power depended on the legislative veto. Without that legislative check, Congress could not justify the delegation of its authority to the President. The alternative to this arrangement was the normal constitutional pattern of presidential submission of proposals to Congress for positive legislative action. In 1983, in the case of *INS v. Chadha*, the Supreme Court settled the half-century-old argument about the constitutionality of the legislative veto, ruling that it was unconstitutional in any form and thereby erasing the basis for the delegation of presidential reorganization power. From then on, presidential efforts at reorganizing the executive branch required positive legislative action. Following the Court's decision, Congress passed legislation in 1984 that gave the President reorganization authority subject to congressional approval by joint resolution. The difficulty of gaining the approval of both houses within a fixed period of days resulted in the Ronald Reagan administration not seeking future authority after the 1984 statute expired on 31 December 1984.

BIBLIOGRAPHY

Berg, Clifford L. "Lapse of Reorganization Authority." *Public Administration Review* 35 (1975): 195–199.
Fisher, Louis, and Ronald Moe. "Delegating with Ambivalence: The Legislative Veto and Executive Reorganization." *Studies on the Legislative Veto.* By Committee on Rules, U.S. House of Representatives. 1980.
Seidman, Harold, and Robert Gilmour. *Politics, Position, and Power.* 1986.

PERI E. ARNOLD

REPUBLICAN PARTY. Springing from the national tumult and dissension over the SLAVERY issue that had been building for decades, the Republican Party was founded in 1854. It gained the presidency in 1860—a remarkable achievement for a six-year-old party—and controlled the presidency for eighty-four of the next 132 years, winning twenty-one of the thirty-three presidential contests from 1860 through 1992. Of the twenty-one presidential elections in which they triumphed, Republicans won majorities of the popular vote in sixteen (1864, 1868, 1872, 1896, 1900, 1904, 1908, 1920, 1924, 1928, 1952, 1956, 1980, 1984, 1988) and narrow pluralities in three (1860, 1880, 1968). In two elections (1876, 1888), Republicans lost the popular vote but had enough electoral votes for victory. Of the fifteen Republican Presidents, Abraham Lincoln in 1860 had the smallest percentage of the popular vote (39.8 percent, against three other presidential candidates) and Richard M. Nixon in 1972 had the highest (60.7 percent). Nixon's 1972 margin was the third-highest in American history, outdistanced only by Democrats Lyndon B. Johnson in 1964 (61.1 percent) and Franklin D. Roosevelt in 1936 (60.8 percent). (Republican Warren G. Harding's victory in 1920, with 60.4 percent, falls just behind Nixon's.) As these figures indicate, the Republican Party clearly dominated the American presidency from 1860 to 1992.

Origins. With a history stretching back 140 years, the Republican Party is longer-lived than any other political party in the United States except the DEMOCRATIC PARTY. In its long history it has passed through a number of stages and represented very different political points of view. It began in the 1850s as a crusading reform party whose efforts were directed at the burning issue of the day—the expansion of slavery to the territories. It then saved the Union from the SECESSION crisis of the 1860s through its successful prosecution of the CIVIL WAR. Adding to the moral luster it gained by leading its great antislavery crusade during the decade before the war was the emancipation of American black slaves by Republican President Abraham Lincoln.

In two lengthy periods of ascendancy, during the period from the Civil War to the early 1890s and again from the SPANISH-AMERICAN WAR to the Great Depression, it was identified as the party of big business, but it not only gained the loyalty of most businessmen but of most workers and most African Americans as well.

The Republican Party was almost mortally wounded by the Great Depression of the 1930s, for which it received nearly all the blame, and continued to be weakened by Democratic success in controlling the presidency from 1932 to 1952. Despite its feeble, ineffective opposition to the Democrats during this period, however, the party escaped extinction. Re-emerging as the modern Republican Party, it had adjusted itself to the changes in American life that had taken place under the NEW DEAL and FAIR DEAL. It benefited from the difficulties and handicaps faced by Democratic administrations of the 1960s and 1970s, recapturing control of the presidency in the election of 1980 and maintaining that control until Bill Clinton's defeat of George Bush in 1992.

For a generation before 1854 the divisive and passionately fought issue of the extension of slavery to the territories had been repeatedly, though temporarily, resolved by compromise. Americans in both the North and the South were coming to see, however, that none of these compromises could endure and that the bonds holding the Union together were weakening. Exemplifying this tension, two national church organizations, the Baptists and the Methodists, split over slavery in the mid 1840s, and the Democratic Party and the WHIG PARTY, the two national parties that since the 1830s had been attempting to transcend sectional issues, had begun by the 1850s to fall apart.

The Republican Party's origins, however, are more comprehensive and complex than just the antislavery cause. Economic forces were transforming the country, and demands for free or inexpensive land by northern white farmers moving westward, improved transportation systems to serve the growing population in both the North and the South, and greater opportunities for free labor in the North all played a part in shaping the new party.

In 1854, the KANSAS-NEBRASKA ACT, sponsored by Senator STEPHEN A. DOUGLAS of Illinois, a leading Democrat, sought to resolve the issue of the expansion of slavery into the territories through local determination, or popular sovereignty. The act permitted local voters to decide whether slavery would be allowed in or forbidden from the two new territories of Kansas and Nebraska, and it repealed the MISSOURI COMPROMISE of 1820 by allowing slavery north of the 36°30′ line. Moral indignation over the "atrocious crime" of this legislation swept the north, and longtime ties of party

loyalty were broken. Southern Whigs abstained from voting, while northern Whigs moved their allegiance to new parties. Some joined the nativist KNOW-NOTHING (AMERICAN) PARTY. Many northern Whigs joined with Independent Democrats and with the FREE-SOIL PARTY in an array of antislavery coalitions—among them the Anti-Nebraska, Fusion, and People's parties.

According to Wilfred E. Binkley in his influential study *American Political Parties,* in its infancy the Republican Party was "an aggregation of Free Soilers, Independent Democrats, Conscience Whigs, Know-Nothings, Barn Burners [rural New Yorkers whose revolt against the Democratic Party was directed against the greed of predatory interests], abolitionists, teetotallers." The Whig Party was the major source of the Republican Party, with former Whigs constituting about four-fifths of the new party's membership. The goodwill of former Democrats had to be more carefully courted by the new party combination. In 1854, the new organization finally settled on the name "Republican," recalling the Republican (Democratic-Republican) Party of Thomas Jefferson and James Madison. It was the third American political party to take the name "Republican" (the first was the party of Jefferson and Madison; the second John Quincy Adams's and HENRY CLAY's National Republican Party).

Thus the Republican Party was born of political strife and shifting coalitions. Many towns—including Ripon, Wisconsin; Jackson, Michigan; and Exeter, New Hampshire—have claimed to be the party's birthplace. Actually, a series of anti-Nebraska meetings in different parts of the country prepared the way for the new party's formation. How the party got its name has also generated controversy. Some have credited HORACE GREELEY, editor of the *New York Tribune,* with naming the party, but the name "Republican Party" was first used at anti-Nebraska meetings at Jackson, Michigan, and Madison, Wisconsin, in July 1954.

Despite its almost spontaneous formation and its control of the presidency for sixty of its first one hundred years, the Republican Party had a singularly unimpressive birth. No important politician was involved in its founding in 1854. According to George H. Mayer's standard history of the Republican party (1967) Abraham Lincoln "protested sharply against attempts to use his name in connection with initial attempts to organize the party in Illinois." (No member of his first Cabinet was any more willing to accept the Republican label than Lincoln had been in 1854, and the only one who came forward in 1855, SALMON P. CHASE, thought the word *Democratic* should be placed in front of *Republican.*) Subsequently, the party did attract some notable recruits, but the party's national committee left out the word *Republican* from its calls for nominating conventions in 1856 and 1860, and Edward Bates, one of the leading candidates for the presidency at the latter party gathering, referred to it as the National Union Convention. Some of the initial hesitation about the new Republican Party had to do with its third-party status, given the high mortality rate that THIRD PARTIES had had.

Against the background of "Bleeding Kansas" (the combat in Kansas in 1856 over slavery) and "Bleeding Sumner" (the physical attack on Charles Sumner in the U.S. Senate in 1856), the first Republican national convention met at Philadelphia on 17 June 1856. Following in the Whig tradition, the delegates nominated a military hero (JOHN C. FREMONT) for President. They named Whig Senator William L. Dayton as his running mate. The Whig influence could also be seen in the first Republican platform, which favored a transcontinental railroad and other INTERNAL IMPROVEMENTS. The Republicans also came out against the repeal of the Missouri Compromise, the Democratic policy of expansion into CUBA and Nicaragua, and "those twin relics of barbarism—Polygamy and Slavery." It was the first time a major party had taken an antislavery stand. The Republican campaign slogan was "Free Speech, Free Press, Free Men, Free Labor, Free Territory, and Fremont."

In their first presidential campaign, Republicans used all the electoral techniques and methods of the era—parades, banners, cartoons, pamphlets, books, songs, and such visual aids as transparencies—as well as exceptionally mean tactics.

The Democrats' 1856 campaign was better organized and financed than the Republicans'. Also, many voters were persuaded by the greater public experience of the Democratic candidate, James Buchanan of Pennsylvania, whose public career went back to 1815. Buchanan carried all the slave states except Maryland as well as five free states (Pennsylvania, New Jersey, Indiana, Illinois, and California), accumulating a winning total of 174 electoral votes. Frémont carried eleven states, including New York and all of New England, for 114 electoral votes. (Maryland, with 8 electoral votes, went to former President Millard Fillmore, running on the Know-Nothing ticket.) On its first time out—and running an inexperienced candidate—the Republican Party had done very well, winning one-third of the popular and nearly two-fifths of the electoral vote in an election marked by a voter turnout of 78.9 percent, the sixth-highest voter turnout from 1824 and 1992. The high turnout was also encouraging to the new party.

Civil War and Reconstruction. During the Civil War and RECONSTRUCTION the Republican Party became the majority party in the United States, which it was to remain until the New Deal period. The Republican Party helped save the federal union through its successful prosecution of the war against the southern states that seceded in 1861 to form the Confederate States of America. The party also became known as the party of emanicipation when American black slaves were freed by the EMANCIPATION PROCLAMATION. Freeing the slaves—which was actually accomplished with the Union victory—was a social and economic revolution of great consequence. But the impressive national legislative program enacted by Republicans of the Civil War and postwar period was an even more far-reaching revolution. In redeeming the promises of the 1860 platform, which has been described as the neatest "translation of social pressures into public policies" in American history, the Republicans before 1862 had mandated a protective tariff, a transcontinental railroad, and a long-desired homestead act provided free or cheap land for western settlers. These accomplishments were supplemented by the MORRILL LAND GRANT ACT (1862), which provided federal aid to state colleges of "agriculture and mechanic arts"; the National Bank Act (1863), which established a banking system that lasted until 1913; and the Contract Labor Law (1864), which encouraged the importation of immigrant laborers. All this Republican legislation had longlasting significance.

During the Reconstruction era (1865–1877), the Republican Party was associated with a radical and controversial policy to reconstruct the defeated South as well as with several of the most important constitutional changes in American history. The radical element in the party called itself the National Union Party during the war to broaden support for the war and Lincoln's policies; its supporters in Congress, known as the RADICAL REPUBLICANS, became the dominant group in the national legislature following the Congressional elections of 1866. Through military occupation of the South and national legislation, they sought to determine the conditions under which "all civil and political rights under the constitution" that in their view had been forfeited by the southern states when they seceded might be restored to those states. For a variety of motives ranging from the humanitarian to the vengeful, they forcefully imposed their program, which included black suffrage and civil rights, over the opposition of the President, not shrinking even from the use of the IMPEACHMENT power [*see* IMPEACHMENT OF ANDREW JOHNSON]. The Radical Republican program of Reconstruction, whose results were both beneficial and baneful, was hotly debated at the time and has been hotly debated ever since by students of American political history.

While the Radical Republicans were reconstructing the South they were also putting some of their Reconstruction ideas into the Constitution in three landmark amendments. The Thirteenth Amendment (1865) abolished slavery in the United States. The Fourteenth Amendment (1868), considered by some observers the most important constitutional amendment, included a federal guarantee of citizenship, forbade any state to deny any person "the equal protection of the law," imposed penalties on prominent Confederates, and reduced the congressional representation of any state that deprived any of its citizens' VOTING RIGHTS. And the Fifteenth Amendment (1870) forbade the United States or any state from denying any person the vote on grounds of race, color, or previous condition of servitude.

Republican President Ulysses S. Grant (1869–1877) presided over what are generally considered the worst excesses of Radical Reconstruction. Because of this—and because of incompetence and corruption in the Grant administration—there was an open revolt within the Republican ranks against Grant and his friends. The Liberal Republican movement of 1870 to 1872 attempted to prevent Grant's renomination, and then his reelection, in 1872, but party regulars stood with Grant, who was again chosen by the voters in what was the most sweeping victory the Republicans would have until the election of Theodore Roosevelt in 1904.

The Gilded Age. After the large popular majorities with which Republicans won the presidential elections of 1864, 1868, and 1872, the Republicans entered into a long period (1876–1892) of stalemate with the Democrats. The Republicans won three of the five presidential contests during this period but failed to gain a popular majority in any of them (Rutherford B. Hayes won 48 percent of the popular vote in 1876; James A. Garfield 48.5 percent in 1880; and Benjamin Harrison 47.9 percent in 1988). In only one of these elections (1880) did they manage even to secure a plurality—and that by a mere one-tenth of one percent. During these years the Republicans depended for victory on the small majorities they received in such key states as Indiana and New York, and they never once obtained a plurality of counties in the nation as a whole. In this weakened condition, the Republicans of the Gilded Age were able to control both the presidency and the Congress for only two years (1889–1891).

During this period the Republican Party remained a sectional party with little or no appeal to white southern voters. After President Hayes withdrew the last federal troops from the South, ending military Reconstruction, he and other Republicans laid plans to develop a different kind of Republican South—a southern wing of the party that would have the support of southern whites willing to grant blacks their constitutional rights. But the Republicans were not able to bring this off, and the South remained largely Democratic until the post–WORLD WAR II years, when the Republicans were at long last able to build a southern wing.

Republican Dominance, 1896–1928. From the mid 1890s until the Great Depression, the Republican Party again became the majority party of the United States. Republicans won seven of the nine presidential elections from 1896 through 1928, with substantial popular majorities for William McKinley in 1896 (51.1 percent) and 1900 (51.7 percent), Theodore Roosevelt in 1904 (57.4), William Howard Taft in 1908 (51.6), Warren G. Harding in 1920 (60.4), Calvin Coolidge in 1924 (54), and Herbert Hoover in 1928 (58.2). During these thirty-two years the Republicans lost only two presidential elections, and the Democratic winner on both occasions, Woodrow Wilson, was a minority President, with 41.9 percent of the vote in 1912 and 49.4 percent in 1916. In 1912, the combined popular vote won by Theodore Roosevelt, who ran on the PROGRESSIVE (BULL MOOSE) PARTY ticket, and the regular Republican candidate, Taft, was 1.3 million votes greater than Wilson's.

During these many years when they controlled the presidency, the Republicans built a winning combination of large numbers of farmers, workers, businesspeople, African Americans, and many average Americans. In establishing its position as the majority party after 1894, the Republican Party benefited from the depression of 1893 and from Democratic mistakes. But the Republicans prevailed because they were better at meeting the needs and desires of the mass of American voters and because they provided workable solutions to the problems of economic expansion. During the period of Republican supremacy there was a new, close integration of the legislative and executive branches, giving coherence to the running of the government.

The Republicans had a definite sense of direction. They were the "Expansionists of 1898" who led the United States into the Spanish-American War and, for the first time in American history, the acquisition of an overseas empire, which included the PHILIPPINES and Hawaii. This led, in turn, to the United States' debut as a world power, with the enunciation of the OPEN DOOR policy (1900–1901), one of the cornerstones of modern American foreign policy and the underlying basis of American policy in the Far East in the twentieth century. Added to these moves were the building of the PANAMA CANAL (1904–1914) and deeper American involvement in the Caribbean.

The Republicans were in power when two more

important constitutional amendments with far-reaching effects were enacted: the Sixteenth Amendment (1913), which authorized a federal income tax, and the Seventeenth Amendment (1913), which provided for the direct election of U.S. Senators. They were also in power when some of the most important Progressive reforms of the early twentieth century were realized, among them enforcement of the SHERMAN ANTITRUST ACT against monopolies; the strengthening of the Interstate Commerce Commission's regulation of business, especially railroads; and the enactment of proposals to conserve the nation's natural resources. Among other Republican reforms of these years were the establishment of rural free delivery mail, a Children's Bureau in the federal government, safety measures in mines, a liability law for employers, and the Budget Bureau, the first significant reform of the national budget-making process.

With the advent of Franklin Roosevelt and the New Deal, the Republican Party lost its long-held dominance in national politics and its position as the majority party. From 1932 to 1944 Republicans lost much of their support among what had been their winning coalition of workers, blacks, farmers, and ordinary Americans. In the presidential elections of 1932, 1936, 1940, and 1944 the Republican candidates won a total of only 248 electoral votes—not enough to win even one election. These four losses constituted a major setback, a long period of uncertainty for Republicans, who were divided over how to regain the party's viability.

Modern Republicanism. Then, in 1952, Republican Dwight D. Eisenhower was elected President with 57.6 percent of the popular vote (and an ELECTORAL COLLEGE total that was almost twice the combined total of Republican electoral votes during the New Deal years). Not only did they win back the presidency, they regained control of both houses of Congress for the first time in twenty-two years. Eisenhower was his party's chief asset—remaining the most popular figure in the country regardless of what he said or did—and he easily extended Republican control of the presidency in the election of 1956, winning an even larger margin of popular and electoral votes that year. A century after the party's founding, Republicans were fond of quoting words of Lincoln's, but they subscribed to Eisenhower's idea of modern Republicanism—to be liberal in dealing with people and conservative in handling money, the economy, and the government. This was an effort to alter the image of the Republican Party, which since the 1890s had been perceived as the party of big business and vested interests.

Under Eisenhower, SOCIAL SECURITY and housing programs were extended and there was flexible support for farm prices and an increase in the minimum wage.

An interstate highway program, land conservation projects, and the CIVIL RIGHTS ACT OF 1957 (the first such legislation since 1875) were other landmarks of the Eisenhower years. More importantly, there was no reversal of the New Deal and Fair Deal, whose programs Eisenhower made palatable to modern Republicans.

The TWENTY-SECOND AMENDMENT (1951) prevented Eisenhower from seeking a third term. Richard Nixon, Eisenhower's Vice President for his two terms and ultimately the most controversial of modern Republicans, lost his party's control of the presidency to John F. Kennedy in the election of 1960—by two-tenths of one percent the closest presidential contest since that of 1884.

After their party lost again in 1964, when conservative Senator BARRY GOLDWATER was trounced by Lyndon B. Johnson, and winning only narrowly in 1968, when Richard Nixon received 43.4 percent of the popular vote to HUBERT H. HUMPHREY's 42.7 percent, many Republicans believed that their party needed to broaden its appeal. Despite Eisenhower's two decisive electoral victories—which had been partly a personal tribute to the World War II hero—Republicans had remained a minority party since 1932, which by the early 1980s was a longer period than that in which they had been the majority party before the New Deal.

Though narrow, Nixon's victory in 1968 was the beginning of another era during which the Republicans controlled the presidency (though not the Congress). In 1972 Nixon triumphed overwhelmingly, winning 60.7 percent of the popular vote. Despite his damaging resignation from office in 1974 [see WATERGATE AFFAIR] and the Democratic interlude of Jimmy Carter's presidency (1977–1981), Ronald Reagan and then George Bush went on to win sweeping Republican victories in 1980 (with 50.8 percent of the popular vote), 1984 (59.2 percent), and 1988 (53.3 percent). The new Republican majority (at least in presidential elections) that emerged from the late 1960s onward resulted from the breakup of the worn-out Democratic New Deal coalition and was based on what analysts described as a new middle-class populism and a southern-western alignment in the so-called Sun Belt states. Whether Democrat Bill Clinton's 1992 victory (with only 43 percent of the popular vote) represented an actual end to the Republican presidential majority or merely sidetracked it remained to be seen.

BIBLIOGRAPHY

Binkley, Wilfred E. *American Political Parties: Their Natural History.* Rev. ed. 1945.
Burdette, Franklin L. *The Republican Party: A Short History.* 2d ed. 1972.

Crandall, Andrew Wallace. *The Early History of the Republican Party, 1854–1856.* 1930.

Gienapp, William E. *The Origins of the Republican Party, 1852–1856.* 1987.

Jones, Charles O. *The Republican Party in American Politics.* 1965.

Mayer, George H. *The Republican Party, 1854–1966.* 2d ed. 1967.

Moos, Malcolm. *The Republicans: A History of Their Party.* 1956.

Myers, William Starr. *The Republican Party: A History.* Rev. ed. 1931.

Phillips, Kevin B. *The Emerging Republican Majority.* 1969.

Phillips, Kevin B. *Boiling Point: Republicans, Democrats, and the Decline of Middle-Class Prosperity.* 1992.

Ross, Earl Dudley. *The Liberal Republican Movement.* 1919.

Trefousse, Hans L. *The Radical Republicans: Lincoln's Vanguard for Racial Justice.* 1968.

VINCENT P. DESANTIS

REPUBLICAN PARTY (JEFFERSONIAN). For discussion of the Republican Party of the first decades of the United States, also called the Democratic-Republican Party and the Jeffersonian Republican Party, see DEMOCRATIC PARTY.

RETREATS, PRESIDENTIAL. The need for a presidential retreat arose with the expansion of the presidential office. With the exception of the Adamses, the earliest Presidents had country places—their own homes—where they could find surcease from the WHITE HOUSE and, in the summer, from the heat of Washington, D.C. Those from Virginia had the advantage of being near the capital while they rusticated, and they returned as often as they could to these beloved, sprawling estates, sometimes spending weeks at a time there—George Washington at MOUNT VERNON, Thomas Jefferson at MONTICELLO, James Madison at MONTPELIER, James Monroe at Ash Lawn. Washington once wrote, "I can truly say I had rather be at Mount Vernon with a friend or two about me, than to be attended at the Seat of Government by the Officers of State and the Representatives of every Power in Europe." Andrew Jackson turned the Hermitage, the central-Tennessee home that he had originally built for his wife, into not only a retreat but also a place for the conduct of political affairs. The plantation-owning Presidents were intimately involved in the building of their country seats: Washington, Jefferson, and Jackson had drawn the plans for their houses themselves and had guided their slaves in the making and laying of the bricks. In the public mind, these estates were veritable symbols of their owners' social standing and prestige.

James Buchanan made Wheatland, his sumptuous mansion in Lancaster County, Pennsylvania, a center for the gathering of his aides and allies. In the summer he occasionally retreated from the White House to put himself up at the Soldiers' Home in Washington, a comfortable refuge sometimes also used by the Lincolns. (Abraham Lincoln had departed from his family's well-loved place in Springfield, Illinois, in 1861 with the uncannily prescient words, "I go, not knowing whether or if I shall ever return.")

After the CIVIL WAR Presidents retreated less often as the office become busier and more absorbing, although the Ulysses S. Grants maintained a summer White House, a two-and-a-half-story "cottage" on the water at Long Branch, New Jersey. During his second term (1893–1897), Grover Cleveland and his family spent summers on Buzzards Bay on Cape Cod in Massachusetts in a clapboard cottage they called Gray Gables. They also found occasional summer refuge in a house in Georgetown, one slightly cooler and drier than the White House in Washington's heat and humidity. The William McKinleys spent the summer of 1901 back at their home in Canton, Ohio, which had recently been remodeled.

Theodore Roosevelt relied for relaxation on visits to his house at Oyster Bay, New York, on Long Island Sound, an estate eventually comprising 155 acres commanded by a gracious gabled house. Named Sagamore Hill after Sagamore Mohannis, the Indian who had originally deeded it away, it was the real home of the President and his large and active family, as well as serving as the summer White House during Roosevelt's presidency.

Presidential retreats were inconspicuous in the next two decades. During Calvin Coolidge's presidency he and his wife continued to regard as home the half of the house in Northampton, Massachusetts, that they had rented when they were married in 1906. A special retreat would have been out of the question for them. The Herbert Hoovers, who had traveled the world during the President's earlier career, had lived much of their married life outside the country. In 1920, they had completed the building of a house on the Stanford University campus in Palo Alto, California, which they occupied briefly in the summertime. Being a fisherman, Hoover preferred the group of cabins he built, mostly at his own expense, as a White House retreat on the Rapidan River in Virginia. (He later turned the property over to Shenandoah National Park.)

Franklin D. Roosevelt gloried in his family seat, Springwood, at HYDE PARK, New York, where he was born and to which he loved to return. Even as he began his campaign for a third term in the White House, he declared, "Everything that is within me cries out to go back to my home on the Hudson." The public became intimately familiar with that home as the site from which the President often broadcast his famous FIRE-SIDE CHATS. While President, he maintained a summer office at Springwood; it was there that he received election returns and that he entertained national and international guests (including, in 1939, the king and queen of England). And it was there, in Springwood's Rose Garden, that he was buried in 1945. Because ELEANOR ROOSEVELT had never felt that Springwood was her home, in 1925 Franklin converted a nearby furniture factory into a small cottage for her. She called it Val-Kill, and it became a sanctuary for her and her friends. Today, it is the only National Historic Site dedicated to the memory of a FIRST LADY.

Roosevelt longed for a place near Washington to which he could comfortably escape. Because of his disability he did not enjoy the Hoovers' Camp Rapidan, with its unsuitable terrain. He visited it only once. In 1939, he established a hideaway in the Catoctin Mountains in Maryland. The retreat, comprising 143 acres, was built by the Civilian Conservation Corps and the WORKS PROGRESS ADMINISTRATION. Roosevelt playfully called the camp Shangri-la—in tribute to the Himalayan utopia of James Hilton's novel, *Lost Horizon*. Here Roosevelt conducted some of the most important planning sessions for Allied operations during WORLD WAR II, sometimes with British prime minister Winston Churchill present. This idyllic place has now been institutionalized as the official presidential retreat. Harry S. Truman did not use it much because he and his family did not like to rough it. But Dwight and Mamie Eisenhower enjoyed it so much that they renamed it CAMP DAVID for Eisenhower's father and for their grandson David Eisenhower. Eisenhower's cordial "bull session" there with the Soviet leader Nikita Khrushchev was celebrated for a time as the "Spirit of Camp David." The name of the retreat became truly world-renowned during Jimmy Carter's presidency. Carter brought the Egyptian president, Anwar Sadat, and the Israeli prime minister, Menachem Begin, together at Camp David, where, after days of keen negotiating in seclusion, they reached the CAMP DAVID ACCORDS. Richard M. Nixon had appreciated Camp David as a refuge from what he regarded as the badgering of the media, and his daughter Tricia and her husband spent their honeymoon there. Nixon, who made 120 trips to Camp David, sometimes stayed as long as two weeks there. Gerald Ford did not take to spending time at the retreat, but BETTY FORD was quoted as saying, "The best thing about the White House is Camp David." The Ronald Reagans and then the George Bushes made frequent journeys there, Reagan adding a stable for eight horses. By helicopter, the seventy-mile trip to Camp David from the White House takes only half an hour. Maintained by the National Park Service and staffed by about a hundred U.S. Navy and Marine personnel, it is now one of the most alluring perquisites of the Presidency, as well as one of the most attractive recreational facilities in the world.

Harry and BESS TRUMAN sometimes made the U.S. naval base at Key West, Florida, a vacation White House. The Eisenhowers acquired a farm and house at Gettysburg, Pennsylvania, in 1950, and it became a veritable substitute White House while Eisenhower was recuperating from his heart attack in 1955.

John F. Kennedy turned Hyannisport, on Cape Cod, into a household word. In summer the Kennedys took their leisure at the family compound there. From photos taken at Hyannisport, the public became intimately acquainted with the President as a sportsman, as readily at home on the water as the golf course. Eager to protect the Kennedy children from the constant glare of the press and to provide a relaxing environment for the President and herself, JACQUELINE KENNEDY selected Glen Ora, an elegant four-hundred-acre estate in the Virginia countryside forty-one miles south of Washington. There, only a few miles from James Monroe's Oak Hill (to which Monroe had moved from Ash Lawn just as he was leaving the presidency), the First Lady, an enthusiastic horsewoman, could ride to her heart's content; the children and the President could swim; and the whole family could enjoy the greenhouses. President Kennedy, however, came to think that this home was unnecessary because, as he pointed out, Camp David was available free. When the lease on Glen Ora expired, the Kennedys acquired a thirty-acre estate near Rattlesnake Mountain in Atoka, Virginia. It was mainly used by Jacqueline Kennedy. The President also often retreated alone with friends to the Kennedy family house in Palm Beach, Florida.

Lyndon and LADY BIRD JOHNSON provided a new, Texas-style kind of retreat—the LBJ Ranch in the Perdinales River valley just west of Austin. Foreign and domestic issues were discussed and sometimes settled there, especially at Johnson's favorite time—when the bluebonnets were in bloom. The Nixons established a summer White House at San Clemente, California, whose maintenance costs came under considerable public scrutiny and criticism. The Carters periodically returned to their house in Plains, Georgia; although ROSALYNN CARTER had often spoken of her joy in fleeing Plains, she came to recognize it as a refuge. Ronald and NANCY REAGAN, who remained Californians to the core, retreated for extended vacations to their spread at Rancho del Cielo near Santa Barbara.

George and BARBARA BUSH enjoyed the President's ancestral setting at Kennebunkport, Maine, where Bush could indulge his love of outdoor sports—especially spinning about on his powerboat, *Fidelity*. In the early stages of Iraq's invasion of Kuwait in 1990, Bush held forth from his Kennebunkport home, determined to show that events abroad could not make him a prisoner of the White House. The partial destruction of the house during an Atlantic storm in the middle of his term aroused public sympathy.

When Bill Clinton and HILLARY RODHAM CLINTON entered the White House in 1993 they not only did not have a retreat (other than Camp David), they did not even own a home to return to. But by then instant communications between the White House and everywhere in the world had long since made the word *retreat* a misnomer, and the existence of intercontinental nuclear arms had left the President no way of escaping constant contact with the crises of which he is the steward.

[*See also* HOMES, PRESIDENTIAL.]

BIBLIOGRAPHY

Booth, Edward Townsend. *Country Life in America: As Lived by Ten Presidents of the United States.* 1947. The Presidents are Washington, John Adams, Jefferson, Jackson, Van Buren, William Henry Harrison, Buchanan, Lincoln, Theodore Roosevelt, and Coolidge.

Jones, Cranston. *Homes of the American Presidents.* Photographs by W. H. Schleisner. 1962.

Packard, Jerrold H. "Presidential Outposts." In *American Monarchy: A Social Guide to the Presidency.* 1983. Chap. 4.

HENRY F. GRAFF

RHETORICAL PRESIDENCY. Rhetoric has always been an essential element of executive power. Issuing a command, summoning force, proposing legislation—almost any executive activity requires rhetoric. Although Presidents have always relied on words, the kind of rhetoric they have employed and the audiences to which their words have been directed have changed dramatically over the course of American history.

Throughout the nineteenth century, Presidents directed most of their rhetoric to Congress, and those messages were almost always written, seldom spoken. The relatively few speeches that were directed to the American people rarely defended pending public policies or legislative initiatives. Instead, nineteenth-century public rhetoric is distinctive in its attention to constitutional principle. The one major exception to this norm was Andrew Johnson, who toured the country to campaign for his RECONSTRUCTION legislation. But

Johnson was impeached for that behavior, confirming the power of the norm.

Since the presidencies of Theodore Roosevelt and Woodrow Wilson, Presidents have regularly gone over the heads of Congress, taking their policy proposals directly to the people. What was once exceptional activity has become routine. Political culture now judges Presidents by their capacity to inspire or inform the American people through visual performance. Inspiration and policy specificity are the rhetorical standards that have replaced constitutional acuity as ideals for great presidential speech.

Although most presidential scholars agree that the practice of presidential rhetoric shifted over two centuries, there is disagreement over the causes of this transformation. Prominent among the posited causes of the twentieth-century rhetorical presidency are the breakdown of the party system and the concomitant rise of candidate-centered nomination processes, the development of the mass media, and conscious attempts to alter the constitutional understandings that undergird the presidency.

With the breakdown of the party system for choosing Presidents, the skills imported into the White House have increasingly become those required to secure nomination. These are essentially campaign skills—public relations, media manipulation, and polling (all aspects of successful popular appeals). Because the modern rhetorical presidency can be reasonably conceptualized as an ongoing campaign some have speculated that changes in the selection process have caused changes in the governing process.

The development of modern media technologies—radio, television, satellite communications—have given Presidents the power to speak to enormous audiences. For many students of the presidency, the availability of such power necessitated its use. Moreover, the character of these technologies has affected the form and content of presidential speech. For example, the structure of the evening television news, with its short sound-bites, is echoed in presidential speeches, which are increasingly written as series of phrases to be quoted individually rather than as structured arguments to be read whole.

Perhaps the deepest cause of the modern rhetorical presidency, however, was Wilson's reform of the institution. Wilson was an articulate diagnostician of many of the difficulties of governance—stalemate between the branches, interest-group-driven policy making, and lack of accountability for decision making. Wilson attributed these defects to nineteenth-century constitutional understandings of the SEPARATION OF POWERS, political representation, and the independence of the executive. After failing to generate support for formal amendments to the Constitution designed to make the American policy more like that of the parliamentary systems he admired, Wilson reinterpreted the conceptual pillars of the nineteenth-century constitutional view to accomplish the same objective without formal amendment. In two exceptionally influential books, *Congressional Government* (1884) and *Constitutional Government in the United States* (1908), Wilson constructed an argument to justify routine appeals to public opinion and legitimized the ideals of visionary and policy-specific speech. As President, he acted out this new understanding of the office through a series of public campaigns for his legislative initiatives. The most famous of these campaigns, to secure support for the LEAGUE OF NATIONS, failed to pressure the Senate to support the League, but it set a precedent for presidential conduct that has become as generative of presidential behavior today as the Constitution itself.

BIBLIOGRAPHY

Campbell, Karlyn Kohrs, and Kathleen Hall Jamieson. *Deeds Done in Words: Presidential Rhetoric and the Genres of Governance.* 1990.
Thurow, Glen. *Abraham Lincoln and American Political Religion.* 1976.
Tulis, Jeffrey K. *The Rhetorical Presidency.* 1987.
Wills, Garry. *Lincoln at Gettysburg: The Words that Remade America.* 1992.

JEFFREY K. TULIS

RIO TREATY. Signed at Rio de Janeiro, Brazil, in 1947 and known formally as the Inter-American Treaty of Reciprocal Assistance, the Rio Treaty entered into force on 3 December 1948. The initial parties to the treaty were the United States, Argentina, Bolivia, Brazil, Chile, Colombia, Costa Rica, CUBA, the DOMINICAN REPUBLIC, El Salvador, Guatemala, Haiti, Honduras, Mexico, Nicaragua, PANAMA, Paraguay, Peru, Uruguay, and Venezuela. The Bahamas, Ecuador, and Trinidad and Tobago signed later. Under Article 3, the parties agreed that an armed attack against an American state "shall be considered as an attack against all the American States and, consequently, each one of the said Contracting Parties undertakes to assist in meeting the attack." Unlike the other MUTUAL SECURITY TREATIES to which the United States became a party, this commitment is not qualified by language suggesting that it would be carried out in accordance with the constitutional processes of each party. The commitment in Article 3 is qualified by a provision stating that "each of the Contracting Parties may determine the immediate measures which it may individually take in fulfillment of the obligation" referred to in the treaty. Yet this applies only until the "organ of consultation" meets and agrees upon measures of a collective character. Another qualification appears in Article 20, which provides that "no State shall be required to use armed force without its consent."

In response to questions from the Senate Foreign Relations Committee, the State Department reiterated that the United States would not be required to use force without Congress's consent. In its report, the committee included the statement that the "character and amount of this [armed] assistance would be determined by our Government." Floor debate emphasized that it was left to the discretion of each nation to determine the extent of its commitment and obligation.

BIBLIOGRAPHY

Glennon, Michael J. *Constitutional Diplomacy.* 1990.
Glennon, Michael J. "United States Mutual Security Treaties: The Commitment Myth." *Columbia Journal of Transnational Law* 24 (1986): 509–552.

MICHAEL J. GLENNON

ROCKEFELLER, NELSON A. (1908–1979), governor of New York State, forty-first Vice President of the United States (1974–1977). Nelson Rockefeller's nomination for the vice presidency by President Gerald R. Ford on 20 August 1974 presented a surprising twist in a political career that had failed to take him to the White House as President. Building on service in a variety of positions under Presidents Franklin D. Roosevelt, Harry S. Truman, and Dwight D. Eisenhower, Rockefeller had used his four-term governorship of New York as a springboard to mount three unsuccessful campaigns for the Republican presidential nomination: against Richard M. Nixon, in 1960 and 1968, and against Barry Goldwater in 1964. Thus, despite family wealth, an impressive record as a governor, and his standing as a national political figure, Rockefeller was never able to make his liberal Republicanism acceptable to a party that nationally was becoming increasingly conservative.

Prior to 1974, Rockefeller had twice rejected offers of becoming a vice presidential running mate. The first of these, from Nixon in 1960, had been dismissed out of hand with a refusal to become merely "standby equipment." The second, from Hubert Humphrey in 1968, was firmly declined as improbable at best, envisaging as it did running Rockefeller, a life-long Republican, on the Democratic presidential ticket. By 1974, however, Ford's offer of the vice presidency now presented the sixty-six-year-old former governor with a (possibly) last chance of performing on the center stage of national politics—as such, it was an offer he could not reject.

Rockefeller's vice presidential nomination in 1974 came from a unique set of political circumstances. In October 1973, following the abrupt resignation of Vice President SPIRO AGNEW (in the wake of corruption charges relating to a land deal while governor of Maryland), President Nixon had invoked for the first time the provisions of Article 2 of the TWENTY-FIFTH AMENDMENT to nominate Representative Gerald R. Ford for the vacant vice presidency. On 9 August 1974, Ford had succeeded to the presidency on Nixon's own resignation following the commencement of impeachment proceedings against him stemming from the WATERGATE AFFAIR. Immediately, he was faced with the task of naming his own vice presidential successor and thus establishing the first unelected team of President and Vice President in American history.

Ford's selection of Rockefeller was designed to supply a depth of expertise, experience, and interest in policy planning and implementation that were clearly absent from his own background. In his original telephone soundings with Rockefeller on 17 August, he indicated that he wanted him to take responsibility for developing the administration's domestic policy. However, protracted nomination hearings in the Senate and House (over alleged misuse of his family wealth as governor of New York) delayed Rockefeller's confirmation as Vice President until 19 December. The effect of this was to dent considerably the prospects of establishing his promised role at the center of domestic policy; by the time he was confirmed, the other major administration players were established and had been operating without him for some four months.

As Vice President, Rockefeller attempted to play a dual role in the Ford administration: the conventional role of performing a variety of traditional tasks such as his attendance at funerals of foreign leaders and service on five national commissions (including chairmanship of the Commission on CIA [CENTRAL INTELLIGENCE AGENCY] Activities within the United States); and, an unconventional role of seeking to operate as a staff assistant to the President on domestic policy. His policy endeavors brought him into considerable conflict with key Ford personnel. Besides his evident liberalism, Rockefeller's problems arose from his activist approach, which appeared threatening to the personal or institutional positions of others. In larger measure, conflict stemmed from Ford's failures, first, to communicate to his senior staff his original mandate for

the vice presidential nominee and, subsequently, to revise that mandate in the changed circumstances of the Vice President's delayed entry into the administration.

Nevertheless, Rockefeller produced a variety of policy proposals and initiatives, of which the three most important were a major package of domestic policy reforms (excluded as too liberal from Ford's 1976 state of the union message); a $220 billion energy independence initiative (accepted by Ford at $100 billion, but rejected by Congress); and a proposal to create a White House science advisory unit that led to the creation of the OFFICE OF SCIENCE AND TECHNOLOGY POLICY.

However, Rockefeller's conservative critics both within and outside the administration put President Ford under pressure to drop his Vice President from the ticket in the face of a strong right-wing challenge for the 1976 Republican nomination from Ronald Reagan. Undercut publicly by the President's campaign manager, Howard (Bo) Callaway, Rockefeller spared Ford from political embarrassment by informing him on 3 November 1975 that he did not wish to be considered for the vice presidential nomination in 1976. Although he maintained at the time that Rockefeller's decision was purely voluntary, Ford's autobiography makes clear that it was otherwise with the following admission: "I was angry with myself in not saying to the ultraconservatives, 'It's going to be Ford and Rockefeller, whatever the consequences.' "

Rockefeller's vice presidency showed that it is possible for a Vice President to play a substantive policy role in the White House. Working within what was always for him a highly adverse political environment, he managed to demonstrate that the vice presidency was capable of being more than what Arthur M. Schlesinger, Jr., has termed a "nonjob." Moreover, he created some useful precedents for his successors: first, with his regularly scheduled weekly meetings in private with the President, based on the Vice President's agenda; and, second, with his practice of obtaining express written approval of the President for all of his policy initiatives as Vice President. Such mechanisms were vital safeguards for a Vice President in conflict with senior presidential staff assistants—a conflict by no means peculiar to the Rockefeller experience.

BIBLIOGRAPHY

Casserly, John J. *The Ford White House*. 1977.

Ford, Gerald R. *A Time to Heal*. 1979.

Hartmann, Robert T. *Palace Politics: An Inside Account of the Ford Years*. 1980.

Kramer, Michael, and Sam Roberts. *"I Never Wanted to Be Vice President of Anything!": An Investigative Biography of Nelson Rockefeller.* 1976.

Turner, Michael. *The Vice President as Policy Maker: Rockefeller in the Ford White House.* 1982.

MICHAEL TURNER

ROOSEVELT, ELEANOR (1884–1962), First Lady, political activist, wife of Franklin Delano Roosevelt. Born into a branch of the prominent Roosevelt family (she was Theodore Roosevelt's niece), Anna Eleanor Roosevelt experienced an unhappy childhood, a formative education abroad, and a brief stint teaching in a social settlement in New York City before marrying her third cousin, Franklin D. Roosevelt, in 1905. She devoted the following years to domesticity, bearing six children (five of whom lived), and supporting her husband's career. Her discovery in 1918 of his affair with her social secretary, Lucy Mercer, altered her domestic priorities. Thereafter, her marriage became a "business partnership," and she sought emotional sustenance primarily among a circle of women political friends.

In 1921, Franklin became paralyzed from poliomyelitis. At the urging of Louis Howe, Franklin's mentor and campaign manager, Eleanor Roosevelt joined New York women's political and advocacy groups, ostensibly to keep Franklin's name before the public. The leadership positions she attained in these groups not only brought her new friends but enabled her to pursue important reform issues such as unionization and protective legislation for women. In 1928, during ALFRED E. SMITH's presidential campaign, she headed the women's division of the national Democratic committee. These experiences influenced the evolution of her political views and honed her speaking, writing, and organizational skills.

As the President's wife, Eleanor Roosevelt represented the views of reformers to White House administrators, influenced federal appointments of women, and made certain that NEW DEAL programs included women. In 1936 she began a syndicated newspaper column, "My Day," that reported on her travels to gather support for New Deal programs and collect information for the President. She also went on paid lecture tours.

Some of her activities drew criticism. Called a "busybody," she was told that a proper FIRST LADY should confine herself to White House ceremonial functions. Criticism mounted when she invested her earnings in "Arthurdale," a subsistence homestead scheme for West Virginia miners, and when she took

unpopular stands for free speech or against racial discrimination. During WORLD WAR II, she served as codirector of the Office of Civilian Defense but resigned when the social-service programs she devised were ridiculed. Her travels on the President's behalf to bring comfort to troops were more appreciated although still censured for being costly. Criticism upset her, but it did not deter her public activities. Within the limits imposed by her marital status, she was the most independent, activist of all First Ladies.

After Franklin Roosevelt's death, President Harry S. Truman appointed her a delegate to the UNITED NATIONS. She helped defeat Soviet delegate Andrei Vishinsky's position on refugee repatriation and later led the struggle to hammer out the Universal Declaration of Human Rights. When Dwight D. Eisenhower became President, she resigned but remained politically active: she helped form Americans for Democratic Action, opposed Senator Joseph McCarthy's anticommunist witch-hunts, supported presidential candidate ADLAI E. STEVENSON, and represented the American Association for the United Nations. President John F. Kennedy appointed her chair of his Commission on the Status of Women. Although she died before it completed its work, her role as chair provided fitting closure to a life that had been committed so fully to women's and other social concerns.

BIBLIOGRAPHY

Hoff-Wilson, Joan, and Marjorie Lightman, eds. *Without Precedent: The Life and Career of Eleanor Roosevelt.* 1984.

Lash, Joseph P. *Eleanor and Franklin: The Story of the Relationship Based on Eleanor Roosevelt's Private Papers.* 1971.

Lash, Joseph P. *Eleanor Roosevelt: The Years Alone.* 1972.

Scharf, Lois. *Eleanor Roosevelt: First Lady of American Liberalism.* 1987.

ELISABETH ISRAELS PERRY

ROOSEVELT, FRANKLIN D. (1882–1945), thirty-second President of the United States (1933–1945). Franklin Delano Roosevelt (or FDR, as he became popularly known), was born on 30 January 1882 on his family's estate along the Hudson River at Hyde Park, New York, the only child of James and Sara Delano Roosevelt. Descended from seventeenth-century Dutch immigrants, the Roosevelts were wealthy. James Roosevelt was vice president of the Delaware and Hudson Railroad. He married Sara Delano in 1880; twenty-six at the time, she traced her lineage to Philippe de la Noye of Luxembourg, who had come to Plymouth Colony in 1621. Her father, Warren Delano, had become wealthy in the China trade and coal mining.

Early Career. The major influence on Franklin's upbringing was his strong-willed mother. He was taught at home until 1896, when he was sent to Groton School in Groton, Massachusetts. The Groton years, which reinforced his Episcopalianism, exposed him to the influence of Groton founder and headmaster Endicott Peabody, whose preachments focused on one's Christian duty to improve society.

In 1900, Franklin went on to Harvard College, where he completed the requirements for the A.B. in three years. He entered Columbia University Law School in fall 1904. After passing the New York bar examination in the spring of his third year, he did not bother to finish his courses for the LL.B. degree.

During his last year at Harvard, Franklin became engaged to a distant cousin, ELEANOR ROOSEVELT, the niece of President Theodore Roosevelt. They married in 1905. Six children (one of whom died in infancy) followed. The marriage had its difficulties from the start, and the upshot of the Roosevelts' marital troubles was an informal understanding whereby Eleanor continued to play the supportive wife, while they both went their own ways sexually, emotionally, and intellectually.

Roosevelt's involvement in politics began in 1910, when he was elected to the New York senate. The twenty-nine-year-old newcomer led a revolt by insurgent Democrats in the legislature against the election to the U.S. Senate of the Tammany Hall favorite. When typhoid fever kept Roosevelt bedridden before the 1912 election, direction of his successful reelection campaign was taken over by a newspaperman from nearby Saratoga, LOUIS MCHENRY HOWE, who would go on to play a key role in shaping his political future.

Roosevelt jumped on the Woodrow Wilson presidential bandwagon early, receiving as his reward appointment in 1913 to the post of Assistant Secretary of the Navy, which Theodore Roosevelt had once held. In 1914, he was defeated in the Democratic primary for the U.S. Senate nomination by the Tammany-backed candidate. Within a few months after the outbreak of the war in Europe, he became a strong exponent of preparedness. In 1920, party leaders slated him—more for his name than his achievements—as the Democratic vice presidential nominee on the ticket headed by Governor JAMES M. COX of Ohio.

In 1921 Roosevelt suffered a severe attack of poliomyelitis. Most biographers have seen his illness as a turning point in his life—an experience that matured him and deepened his human sympathies. Searching for a treatment that would restore the use of his legs, in 1924 he discovered the benefits of swimming in the mineral waters at Warm Springs, Georgia. In 1927, he set up the Warm Springs Foundation, which purchased the property and established a treatment center for polio. But he was never again able to walk more than short distances—and then only with the support of leg braces and canes.

Despite his physical infirmity, Roosevelt continued to be active in DEMOCRATIC PARTY affairs. Having made his peace with Tammany Hall, he tied his own political fortunes to its ablest son, New York governor ALFRED E. SMITH. Roosevelt's ties with Smith were more a matter of political expediency than any personal closeness. Despite private doubts about Roosevelt's abilities, Smith named Roosevelt campaign manager for his bid for the 1924 Democratic presidential nomination. After winning that nomination in 1928, Smith asked Roosevelt to run for New York governor in hopes that Roosevelt's gubernatorial candidacy would offset the negative effect Smith's Roman Catholicism would have on the presidential race in New York. While Smith lost the state by a hundred thousand votes, Roosevelt ran sufficiently ahead of the presidential nominee upstate to win his race by the narrow margin of twenty-five thousand votes.

Election of 1932. Aware that his surprise victory had sparked talk about his being possible Democratic presidential nominee in 1932, Roosevelt worked to make his governorship a launching pad for the White House. He kept many of the top Smith appointees on his staff, backed labor and welfare reforms appealing to working-class voters, and continued his truce with Tammany Hall. At the same time, he worked to broaden the base of his support by pushing issues appealing to rural voters and middle-class progressives: tax relief for farmers, public development of hydroelectric power, and stricter regulation of telephone and private utility rates. He neutralized the disruptive PROHIBITION issue by publicly coming out in 1930 in favor of state and local option on legalizing liquor. He won a smashing reelection victory in 1930 with an unprecedented 725,000-vote margin.

As the depression continued to deepen, Roosevelt began to call for more aggressive state action to assist its victims. His major achievement was the establishment in 1931 of a Temporary Emergency Relief Administration, headed by HARRY HOPKINS, which provided assistance to almost 10 percent of New York's families. In early 1932, Roosevelt assembled a group of campaign advisers and speechwriters for his bid for the presidential nomination. The group included three Columbia University professors—economist REXFORD G. TUGWELL, lawyer Adolf A. Berle, Jr., and political scientist RAYMOND MOLEY—whom the newspapers labeled the BRAIN TRUST. Louis Howe, working closely with JAMES A. FARLEY, the chairman of the state Democratic committee, labored to line up local and state party organizations behind Roosevelt. The backbone of Roosevelt's support lay in the South, because party leaders there saw him as the man most likely to avoid a repeat of the battles over religion and prohibition that had so divided the Democratic Party during the 1920s. By contrast, many liberals looked upon Roosevelt as a political trimmer.

When the Democratic convention met at Chicago in June 1932, Roosevelt was more than a hundred votes short of the needed two-thirds majority on the first ballot. The next two roll calls saw no significant gain. Then, Texas Congressman JOHN NANCE GARNER threw his support to Roosevelt to avoid a deadlocked convention that could damage the party. Garner received the vice presidential nomination. To quiet doubts about his health, Roosevelt broke with precedent by flying to Chicago to give his acceptance speech to the assembled delegates. A cartoonist picked up on his closing pledge of "a new deal for the American people," and the term NEW DEAL became identified with Roosevelt and his program. Roosevelt won the election handily, with 57.4 percent of the popular vote to President Herbert Hoover's 39.7 percent.

In Miami, Florida, on the night of 15 February 1933, Roosevelt narrowly missed being shot by a would-be assassin, Joseph Zangara. A woman in the crowd grappled with Zangara and deflected the bullets, which fatally wounded Chicago mayor Anton Cermak.

The New Deal. Hoover and his successor failed to cooperate in trying to deal with the depression. Hoover tried to inveigle Roosevelt into supporting his own goals of reestablishing the gold standard, balancing the budget, and upholding sound money. Roosevelt wanted to keep his options open while making sure that none of Hoover's unpopularity rubbed off on him. And Roosevelt at first failed to grasp the seriousness of the banking crisis that hit the country starting in mid-February 1933, as state after state closed its banks. The forcefulness and optimism of Roosevelt's inaugural address—with its assurance that "the only thing we have to fear is fear itself"—had a tremendous psychological impact, however.

Programs. On 5 March, Roosevelt called Congress into special session to deal with the banking crisis while issuing an EXECUTIVE ORDER declaring a national BANK HOLIDAY and halting transactions in gold. When Congress met, he submitted for its approval legislation that had been drafted by Treasury Department officials during the Hoover administration to provide emergency assistance to the sounder banks. Its swift adop-

tion of the EMERGENCY BANKING ACT restored public confidence in the banks. Buoyed by this triumph, Roosevelt decided to keep Congress in session and to move forward with a broad package of legislative requests. By the time Congress adjourned on 16 June —one hundred days after the beginning of the special session—the lawmakers had approved all his recommendations. (This period has become known as the hundred days.) Included in Roosevelt's package was legislation to promote the future stability of the banking and financial system, to create the Tennessee Valley Authority, and to save farmers and homeowners from mortgage foreclosure. The CIVILIAN CONSERVATION CORPS (CCC) put unemployed young men to work on conservation projects under army supervision. The Federal Emergency Relief Administration (FERA) received one-half billion dollars for grants to the states for relief. Roosevelt placed Harry Hopkins, who had been director of the New York relief program in charge of FERA. The NATIONAL INDUSTRIAL RECOVERY ACT (NIRA) established the PUBLIC WORKS ADMINISTRATION (PWA) with a $3.3 billion appropriation for public works.

Roosevelt and most of his top advisers were convinced that a major cause of the depression had been the drag on the economy exerted by low farm income. The centerpiece of the administration's farm program was the so-called domestic allotment plan embodied in the AGRICULTURAL ADJUSTMENT ACT (AAA) of May 1933. Its aim was to raise farm prices to the level of parity— that is, to give farm products the same purchasing power they had had during agriculture's golden age of 1909 to 1914. The means was to restrict farm acreage and to give benefit payments to farmers who agreed to limit their acreage; money for these payments was to be raised from a tax on the processors of farm products. Aided by droughts, the AAA succeeded in raising the prices of leading farm staples. But the law had major shortcomings, including its adverse impact on southern tenant farmers and sharecroppers and its failure to do much to boost total purchasing power. Since processors passed on the processing tax that funded benefit payments, the AAA simply redistributed income from consumers to commercial farmers.

As with the AAA, the thrust of the industrial recovery program embodied in the NIRA was to raise prices by controlling production. The mechanism allowed businesses, under the aegis of the National Recovery Administration (NRA), to join in drawing up so-called codes of fair practice. The codes were similar to private trade association cartel agreements, but with the backing of federal government enforcement. In return, the codes were to guarantee workers minimum wages, maximum hours, and the right to bargain collectively. Roosevelt's choice of General Hugh Johnson to head the NRA was a mistake. Johnson proved too willing to gain business cooperation by acceding to production-limitation and price-fixing arrangements. As time went on the NRA acquired a large number of critics. Consumer groups blamed the NRA for higher prices. Smaller businesses complained that big business dominated the code-making and enforcement to small businesses' disadvantage. Most businessmen, big and small, were upset over how NRA's guarantee of workers' right to bargain collectively had stimulated union organizing activities.

The major difficulty, however, was that higher prices could stimulate the economy only if there was an accompanying increase in purchasing power. Under the cautious management of Secretary of the Interior HAROLD ICKES, the PWA was slow in doing much to solve the problem. Roosevelt grew so alarmed that, in November 1933, he took some of the PWA funds, set up the Civil Works Administration (CWA) under Hopkins, and directed Hopkins to put as many people to work as fast as possible. Although the CWA kept the country going through the winter of 1933–1934 by pumping a billion dollars of purchasing power into the economy, Roosevelt was alarmed at the high cost—and even more at the danger of ending up with thousands of reliefers permanently upon the government payroll. He accordingly terminated the CWA in spring 1934.

Opposition. The political honeymoon that had marked Roosevelt's first days in office ended in 1934. Businessmen were becoming more and more unhappy about government interference with managerial prerogatives, the rising national debt, and labor unrest. The hostility to Roosevelt from the right found expression in the organization of the American Liberty League in August 1934. Roosevelt's continued popularity with the mass of voters, however, was shown by the Democratic gains in the 1934 elections. But a growing number of Americans were becoming attracted by would-be leaders peddling appealing panaceas. Dr. Francis Townsend's advocacy of a $200-a-month pension for persons over sixty years of age was rallying the nation's elderly. Father Charles Coughlin, a Roman Catholic priest from Michigan, was attracting an enormous following with his nationwide radio broadcasts blaming the depression on a bankers' conspiracy and demanding monetization of silver. The rival who most worried Roosevelt was Louisiana Senator Huey Long. To further his national political ambitions, Long in January 1934 launched his "Share our Wealth" movement, which called for the liquidation of

all large fortunes and the use of the proceeds to give every family a homestead worth $5,000 and a $2,500 annual income.

These pressures contributed to Roosevelt's 1935 shift to the left—what some historians have termed the "Second New Deal." The evident failure of his first recovery program, even before the Supreme Court struck down the NRA in May 1935 in SCHECHTER POULTRY CORP. V. UNITED STATES, also pushed Roosevelt leftward. The break with the administration by the formerly supportive United States Chamber of Commerce removed Roosevelt's last major link with the organized business community. But more than political expediency was at work in Roosevelt's conversion. He did feel a genuine sympathy with the depression's victims. Although he never questioned the system of private enterprise, he thought that government had to play a larger role than before in assuring long-term economic stability and growth, in protecting society's weaker groups from exploitation, and in guaranteeing at least minimum subsistence for all.

Topping Roosevelt's agenda was a massive public works program. Worried about the debilitating moral and psychological effects of subsistence cash payments, Roosevelt wanted to take the federal government out of giving direct relief, except to those who were unemployable. The bulk of the almost $5 billion authorized by the Emergency Relief Appropriation Act of April 1935 went to the newly established WORKS PROGRESS ADMINISTRATION (WPA), which Hopkins was appointed to head. While most WPA enrollees worked on construction projects, some innovative WPA programs combined relief with the promotion of cultural nationalism—the Federal Theatre Project, the Federal Writers' Project, the Federal Art Project, and the Federal Music Project. A WPA offshoot, the National Youth Administration (NYA), provided part-time jobs to allow high school and college students to remain in school. But Hopkins never had sufficient funds to absorb all the able-bodied unemployed. Because the WPA emphasized labor-intensive projects in which the cost of materials was minimal, many WPA projects were make-work expedients that offered inviting targets for Roosevelt's political opponents. The administration of the WPA became deeply entangled in politics.

Of more lasting importance was the Social Security Act. In June 1934, Roosevelt had appointed a Committee on Economic Security chaired by Secretary of Labor FRANCES PERKINS to draw up plans for a comprehensive system of social insurance. The SOCIAL SECURITY package submitted to Congress in January 1935 included no recommendation for health insurance to avoid a battle with the American Medical Association. The legislation imposed a payroll tax on employers and employees, at first 1 percent of the first $3,000 of annual earnings but to be gradually increased to 3 percent in 1949, to go into a trust fund to pay benefits to retired workers sixty-five or older. The second major provision was a federal-state program of unemployment insurance financed by a payroll tax on employers. The last major part consisted of the so-called categorical assistance programs—federal grants to the states on a matching basis for aid to dependent mothers and children, the physically disabled, and the blind, as well as for old-age pensions and public health services.

The National Labor Relations Act (WAGNER ACT) of July 1935 was of similar long-term significance. The adoption of the Wagner Act was the key to the unionization of mass-production industries. Roosevelt gained the support of most unions and their members, but his feelings about unions were more mixed than many of his admirers have recognized. Roosevelt preferred government paternalism to independent worker action, was late in throwing his support behind the measure, and was alarmed at the threat to recovery from the strikes accompanying the rise of the Committee for Industrial Organization (later renamed the Congress of Industrial Organizations, or CIO).

Another 1935 initiative was Roosevelt's creation by executive order of the Rural Electrification Administration to encourage, through low-interest loans, the building of electric power lines into rural areas. Roosevelt's proposed "death sentence" against public utility holding companies sparked strong opposition from the power companies, but Roosevelt won the substance of what he wanted in the Public Utility Holding Company Act of August 1935. The most controversial, and least successful, of his moves were his calls for increased taxes on inheritances, a gift tax, and higher graduated levies on large individual and corporate incomes. Congress watered down this "soak the rich" tax plan. The federal tax burden at the end of the 1930s applied at virtually a flat percentage rate to all except the top one or two percent of income receivers.

Election of 1936. The 1935 reforms succeeded in undercutting the threat to Roosevelt from the left even before Huey Long's assassination in September 1935. The Republicans nominated Governor ALFRED M. LANDON of Kansas. Most Republican leaders warned that Roosevelt's reelection would mean the end of democracy in the United States and talked loudly of wiping the New Deal from the books. Roosevelt replied with a stinging attack on these "economic royal-

ists" who would impose "a new industrial dictatorship." He swept to a landslide victory, outpolling Landon by 27.75 million to 16.68 million votes (with third-party candidate William Lemke drawing under 900,000) and carrying every state except Maine and Vermont. The twin pillars of Roosevelt's extraordinary majority were the so-called solid south and ethnic working- and lower-middle-class voters in the nation's cities. African Americans constituted an important addition to the Democratic coalition. As late as 1932, black voters had remained loyal to the party of Abraham Lincoln, but 1936 a majority had swung behind Roosevelt. The switch largely reflected the dependence of blacks, as the group hardest hit by the depression, on New Deal relief programs. Roosevelt personally shied away from disturbing the racial status quo to avoid alienating southern Democratic Congressmen. His one positive act for blacks as blacks—his issuance in June 1941 of an executive order forbidding racial discrimination by defense contractors and setting up a Fair Employment Practice Committee—he did reluctantly under the threat of a mass march by blacks on Washington.

Second Term. Despite his 1936 mandate, the political climate was dramatically transformed on 5 February 1937, when Roosevelt suddenly proposed what the newspapers termed his COURT-PACKING PLAN: that Congress authorize him to name up to forty-four new federal judges, including as many as six additional members of the Supreme Court if incumbents failed to retire at age seventy. Although his rationale was that age was preventing judges from keeping up with their work, everyone recognized that his purpose was to gain a Court majority favorable to the New Deal. Conservatives were up in arms, and even many liberals worried lest he set a dangerous precedent that would weaken the Court as a protector of CIVIL LIBERTIES. The Court itself struck what was probably the decisive blow when Chief Justice CHARLES EVANS HUGHES lined up majorities to uphold the National Labor Relations and the Social Security acts.

In later years, Roosevelt would claim that although he had lost the battle he had won the war. The Supreme Court no longer presented a barrier against reform legislation. On the other hand, the fight over the Court was the catalyst for the emergence of a bipartisan conservative bloc in Congress to resist such legislation. The political damage done was aggravated by the economic downturn that hit the country in August 1937. Roosevelt had never felt comfortable with deficit spending, and by 1937 he had become worried that the recovery was threatening to turn into a runaway inflation. Yielding to the advice of the champions of fiscal orthodoxy, led by Secretary of the Treasury HENRY MORGENTHAU, JR., he slashed government spending. The outcome was a sharp recession that wiped out much of the gains made since 1933.

In April 1938, Roosevelt moved to resume government spending. But he continued to balk at the massive expenditures that his more Keynesian-minded advisers called for. His halfway measures alienated and frightened business by increasing the national debt without bringing full recovery. As late as 1941, the United States still had six million unemployed workers.

While Roosevelt had worse difficulties with Congress than during his first term, his second-term achievements were still substantial. The Wagner-Steagall Housing Act of 1937 made low-interest loans available to local authorities to build low-income public housing. The Farm Security Administration was established by the Bankhead-Jones Farm Tenancy Act of 1937 to assist poor farmers, tenants and sharecroppers, and migratory agricultural laborers. The FAIR LABOR STANDARDS ACT of 1938 set minimum wages and maximum hours and prohibited child labor for businesses engaged in interstate commerce. Although Roosevelt's ambitious plan to reorganize the executive branch was blocked, his executive order of September 1939 creating the EXECUTIVE OFFICE OF THE PRESIDENT (EOP) laid the institutional basis for the modern presidency by giving the CHIEF EXECUTIVE the nucleus of a personal staff.

By 1938, Roosevelt had become so angry with anti–New Deal Democrats in Congress that he reversed his former hands-off policy and intervened publicly in a number of Democratic primaries against those he stigmatized as "Copperheads." In undertaking what newspapers called his purge, Roosevelt underestimated the built-in advantages of incumbency and the continued strength of localism in the decentralized American party system. Most of those he targeted for defeat won. The fall elections dealt Roosevelt a further blow. Capitalizing on voter disillusionment because of the still-sluggish economy, the Republicans made impressive gains. The 1938 elections marked the end of the New Deal. The reason was not simply the resurgent conservative strength in Congress but Roosevelt's own growing preoccupation with FOREIGN AFFAIRS. He appears even to have made a tacit deal with southern Democrats to drop further reform in return for their support on foreign policy and defense measures.

Foreign Affairs. Roosevelt had, and would retain, an exaggerated opinion of his knowledge about the world outside the United States. There is no question that he intended to be his own Secretary of the State.

The formal holder of that position, CORDELL HULL, did not have a major influence on policy making. Historians have differed sharply in their appraisal of Roosevelt's purposes in foreign affairs. Admirers have pictured him as an internationalist who wished to cooperate with the European democracies against aggression but who found his hands tied, until almost too late, by the strength of American isolationist sentiment. Others have argued that Roosevelt personally shared the isolationist goal of avoiding United States entanglement in any conflict and was only driven hesitantly and reluctantly to involvement in the European conflict by the worsening Axis threat. Isolationist historians have charged that Roosevelt's lip-service to keeping the United States out of war was simply a cover to hide his interventionist plans.

Unclear direction. Advocates of these different interpretations can all find supporting evidence for their positions because of the twists and turns that marked Roosevelt's foreign policies. At first, he looked favorably on the London Economic Conference, scheduled for early summer 1933, whose intent was to foster international cooperation to deal with the depression. But then, without warning, he torpedoed the conference to allow himself freedom for his domestic price-raising efforts. In May 1933, he sought to give the Geneva Disarmament Conference a boost by offering that the United States would not interfere with LEAGUE OF NATIONS sanctions against an aggressor if the European powers agreed to arms reduction. But then he failed to follow through on this proposal. Roosevelt took the initiative in arranging the agreement in November 1933 for United States recognition of the Soviet Union. He was motivated partly by a wish to expand United States exports to the U.S.S.R., and partly by the illusion that the Soviet Union might act as a counterweight to Germany and Japan in world politics. But those expectations never materialized.

Roosevelt's entry into Latin American affairs appeared to be a reversion to heavy-handed United States policing of the Caribbean. After a revolution in August 1933 overthrew the brutal dictatorship of Gerardo Machado in CUBA, Washington's withholding of diplomatic recognition from the left-leaning provisional government opened the door for Fulgencio Batista's rise to power. After this, though, Roosevelt switched to a self-styled GOOD NEIGHBOR POLICY toward Latin America whereby the United States renounced armed intervention south of the border. Later in the decade, alarm over the German and Japanese threats spurred him to draw the countries of Latin America into mutual security arrangements.

From the start of his presidency, Roosevelt approached Far Eastern questions with a pro-Chinese bias. His naval-building program added to frictions with Japan. Although Roosevelt started out favorably disposed toward Italian dictator Benito Mussolini, the Italian invasion of Ethiopia in October 1935 chilled relations. Roosevelt appears to have instinctively regarded Adolf Hitler as a menace, but he shied away from any action that might entangle the United States in war. Protests in defense of the OPEN DOOR irritated Japan without deterring its expansionist ambitions. And as late as September 1938, during the European crisis over German demands on Czechoslovakia that culminated in the Munich Conference, Roosevelt made clear to Hitler that the United States would not become involved.

Preparation for war. There is no way of knowing what Roosevelt would have done if he had been given freer hand. Many—perhaps most—Americans had become convinced that United States intervention in WORLD WAR I had been a tragic mistake, and they opposed foreign commitments. When Roosevelt in January 1935 called for United States membership on the World Court, he suffered an embarrassing defeat in the Senate. More important, congressional isolationists pushed through NEUTRALITY legislation to prevent a repetition of the policies blamed for United States involvement in World War I; the legislation included a mandatory embargo on arms exports to belligerents, bans on loans to belligerents and on American citizens' sailing on belligerent ships, and cash-and-carry for the sale of goods other than arms. When Japan launched a full-scale invasion of northern China in July 1937, Roosevelt took advantage of the absence of a formal DECLARATION OF WAR to refuse invoking an arms embargo and thus allowed China to continue to purchase American weapons. In a speech on 5 October 1937, he spoke publicly of a "quarantine" against aggressors. Whatever he may have had in mind—if in fact there was anything concrete—the outcry from the isolationists was such that at his press conference the next day he denied any thought of sanctions.

In the aftermath of Hitler's triumph at the Munich Conference, Roosevelt moved militarily and psychologically to prepare the United States to counter the aggressors' threat. He had no difficulty in gaining congressional backing for his recommendations to strengthen the armed forces. After the German invasion of Poland in September 1939 he succeeded in winning approval for the sale of arms to the belligerents on a cash-and-carry basis. The German blitzkrieg that swept over Western Europe from April to June 1940 reinforced Roosevelt's commitment to all-out aid

for Britain. To rally bipartisan support, in June 1940 he named two leading Republican backers of aid to Britain to key posts in his Cabinet—HENRY L. STIMSON as Secretary of War and Frank Knox as Secretary of the Navy. In September he announced a deal with Britain, arranged via an EXECUTIVE AGREEMENT that bypassed Congress, to supply fifty American destroyers in return for ninety-nine-year leases on bases in Newfoundland and the Caribbean [see DESTROYERS FOR BASES].

The international situation was responsible for Roosevelt's decision to run for a third term. Roosevelt insisted, to the dismay of many southern Democrats and big-city bosses, on the nomination of Secretary of Agriculture HENRY A. WALLACE as his running mate. The moderate, internationalist wing of the Republican Party succeeded in winning the Republican nomination for WENDELL WILLKIE. Willkie was personally a supporter of aid to Britain. Finding his campaign lagging, however, Willkie switched to attacking the Democrats as the war party and warned that Roosevelt's reelection would mean war within six months. Stung by these attacks and alarmed by Willkie's gains in the polls, Roosevelt responded by flatly pledging that "your boys are not going to be sent into any foreign wars." Although isolationists have cited these words as evidence of Roosevelt's dishonesty, he appears to have sincerely believed that the United States could stop Hitler without becoming directly involved by giving sufficient aid to Britain. Accordingly, he repeatedly overruled his military advisers, who doubted Britain's ability to survive, by continuing to send Britain scarce materials and equipment. The majority of Americans appear to have agreed that the risk of possible United States involvement was preferable to the alternative of a Hitler victory. While Willkie cut into his popular margin, Roosevelt still won, beating Willkie by 27.24 million to 22.30 million votes and an Electoral College margin of 449 votes (38 states) to 82 (10 states).

Immediately after the election, Roosevelt was faced with the disturbing news that Britain was running out of dollars to pay for its purchases. To circumvent the prohibition against cash loans to foreign governments that had not paid their World War I debts, Roosevelt picked up a suggestion made by Secretary of the Interior Ickes for lending military equipment and supplies. After an acrimonious debate, Congress approved the LEND-LEASE ACT in early March 1941 by a surprisingly wide margin. Following Hitler's invasion of Russia in June, Roosevelt extended lend-lease to the Soviet Union. Through 1941, Roosevelt followed a convoluted path, whether from political calculation or simple uncertainty over what he should do. The cumulative result was to bring the United States ever nearer direct involvement. But Roosevelt continued to shrink from the final step of asking Congress to declare war. Perhaps he retained a lingering hope that the United States could stay out; more likely he wished to place the onus of responsibility on Hitler. Roosevelt was rescued from his dilemma by the Japanese attack on PEARL HARBOR on 7 December 1941.

World War II. Roosevelt had initially been reluctant to antagonize Japan because his primary concern was the threat posed by Hitler. He was pushed to tougher action, however, partly because of the pressure of public opinion aroused by stories of Japanese atrocities in China and partly because of Japan's exploitation of the European war to advance its expansionist ambitions. Japan's signing of the Tripartite Pact with Germany and Italy in September 1940 convinced most American officials that Japan was a partner with Hitler in mounting a worldwide threat to the United States and its way of life. Escalation of U.S. economic pressure on Japan culminated in the cutoff of oil supplies at the end of July 1941. Japanese leaders were thus faced with the alternative of coming to terms with the United States or moving or seize the resources of Southeast Asia.

Under pressure from Emperor Hirohito, the Japanese government made a final effort to arrange at least a short-term accommodation with the United States. At the same time, Japan made the decision that if no agreement was reached by 25 November (later postponed to 29 November), it would move southward against Malaya and the Dutch East Indies and attack the U.S. fleet at Pearl Harbor, Hawaii, to eliminate its threat to the Japanese flank. Although doubting that the Japanese would directly attack the United States, Roosevelt appears to have resolved to treat an attack on British and Dutch possessions in Asia as grounds for war. The military still wished to delay war until the United States could strengthen its forces in the Far East. Accordingly, American officials drew up their own proposal for a three-month modus vivendi. But Chinese and British protests—coupled with intelligence reports of Japanese troop movements southward—led Secretary of State Hull to revert to an extreme hard-line position in his talks with the Japanese envoys.

Isolationists have charged that Roosevelt deliberately provoked the Japanese into attacking as a backdoor way of entering the war against Hitler. The more extreme go so far as to accuse Roosevelt of knowing in advance about the coming Japanese assault and purposely failing to warn the military commanders in Hawaii. The weight of the evidence, however, exoner-

ates Roosevelt from advance knowledge of Pearl Harbor. On the other hand, Roosevelt must have realized that the United States' stance would lead to war, given the information he had received about the Japanese deadline for negotiations that had been acquired by the "Magic" intercepts and decipherment of the Japanese diplomatic code. Hitler could have put Roosevelt in a difficult situation if he had kept to his policy of avoiding a showdown with the United States. On 11 December 1941, however, the German leader declared war against the United States.

The domestic front. From spring 1939 on, Roosevelt shuffled and reshuffled the administrative machinery for the mobilization of men and matériel. Confusion and bureaucratic wrangling remained problems until October 1942, when Roosevelt placed former Senator and Supreme Court Justice JAMES F. BYRNES in overall charge of the war effort, first as head of the Office of Economic Stabilization and then, after May 1943, as director of the OFFICE OF WAR MOBILIZATION. Roosevelt was successful in pressuring Congress into giving the Office of Price Administration the requisite powers to prevent runaway inflation. The most politically explosive issue on the domestic side of the war effort was who would pay for the war. Although the Revenue Act of 1942 raised the top bracket of personal income tax to 81 percent, the bulk of new revenues came from a broadening of the income tax to increase the number of persons within the tax net. To expedite tax collections, Congress in 1943 instituted the withholding, or pay-as-you-go, system. In his 1943 budget message, Roosevelt asked for another major tax increase, but Congress balked, failing to pass a new tax bill until February 1944 and then increasing revenues far below the level that Roosevelt had requested. An angry Roosevelt vetoed the bill with a stinging attack on Congress that sparked a revolt among lawmakers. Senate majority leader ALBEN W. BARKLEY of Kentucky resigned his post rather than support the veto. The Senate Democratic caucus unanimously reelected Barkley as majority leader, and then the full Senate, along with the House, overrode the veto.

While WORLD WAR II witnessed fewer violations of civil liberties than had World War I, there also was much less domestic opposition to the war. Roosevelt's personal instincts were to crack down on what he regarded as seditious voices, whether they were black newspapers complaining about Jim Crow laws or right-wing pro-Axis sympathizers. That more prosecutions were not instituted is owed to Attorney General FRANCIS BIDDLE, not Roosevelt. Roosevelt shared in the general hysteria about the west-coast Japanese Americans and fully approved their forced evacuation and internment [see JAPANESE AMERICANS, TREATMENT OF]. He refused to act against the discrimination against blacks practiced by the armed services. And he must be counted an accessory to Hitler's murder of six million European Jews. His refusal to bargain with Hitler to save Jewish lives can be defended in terms of the exigencies of war, but no such exoneration can be made of his failure to open U.S. doors to larger numbers of Jewish refugees.

The war reinforced the conservative reaction against further social reform. Roosevelt himself gave the impression of having lost interest, even announcing at a press conference that "Dr. Win-the-War" had replaced "old Doctor New Deal" for the duration of hostilities. Republican gains in the 1942 elections strengthened the bipartisan conservative coalition in Congress. Although Roosevelt was successful in winning approval of most his war-related policies, lawmakers killed such now-vulnerable New Deal agencies as the Civilian Conservation Corps, National Youth Administration, and National Resources Planning Board. In his annual message to Congress in January 1944, Roosevelt called for adoption of a second, economic bill of rights. Congress turned a deaf ear except for its passage of the Servicemen's Readjustment Act of 1944 (popularly known as the G.I. Bill of Rights) to give returning veterans financial assistance for education, starting businesses and farms, and purchasing homes.

Managing the war. Roosevelt exercised to the full his powers as COMMANDER IN CHIEF. His most important decision, in terms of its long-term ramifications was made before the United States' entry into the war—his launching a research program for the development of an atomic bomb [see MANHATTAN PROJECT]. During the war, Roosevelt wisely left tactical matters to his able senior military advisers—headed by General GEORGE C. MARSHALL, the Army Chief of Staff, and Admiral Ernest J. King, the Chief of Naval Operations. But he personally decided the larger questions of strategy and did not hesitate to overrule his military advisers when differences arose. The keystone of Roosevelt's approach was to give first priority to the defeat of Germany, which he considered the more dangerous enemy. The more difficult question was how. The British favored a war of attrition along the periphery to minimize casualties. American military planners pushed for the concentration of all available resources in Britain for a cross-channel invasion of Europe as early as fall 1942, if possible, and no later than spring 1943.

Bowing to British warnings that a fall 1942 assault was too risky, Roosevelt accepted the British plan (known as TORCH) for an invasion of North Africa in November 1942. Any remaining possibility of a spring

1943 cross-channel invasion was foreclosed by Roosevelt's decision in the wake of the American victory over the Japanese fleet in the battle of Midway in June 1942 to divert sufficient resources from Europe to allow United States forces in the Pacific to undertake limited offensive operations. Roosevelt thus agreed when he met with British prime minister Winston Churchill at the CASABLANCA CONFERENCE in January 1943 to take advantage of the existing Allied troop buildup in the Mediterranean by invading Sicily in the hope of knocking Italy out of the war. At the Trident Conference at Washington in May 1943, Roosevelt and Churchill set 1 May 1944 as the tentative date for the cross-channel invasion. Churchill then had second thoughts and pushed for an invasion of the Balkans to drain German strength further while simultaneously raising a buffer against Soviet expansion into the area. This time Roosevelt stood firm behind the spring 1944 deadline for the cross-channel invasion.

The close personal relationship existing between Roosevelt and Churchill was the bedrock of the wartime Great Alliance. The two did have their frictions, however: Churchill was irritated, for example, by Roosevelt's reflexive anticolonialism. But Roosevelt never carried his complaints about the British empire beyond words, and Churchill yielded gracefully on differences over military strategy as the power balance between the two countries shifted in favor of the United States. In contrast to the respect, even admiration, Roosevelt had for the British, he held France and the French in contempt. Roosevelt paid lip-service to Nationalist China as a great power, at least in potentia. He took pains to flatter Chiang Kai-shek; he even gave in to his demand for removal of the strongly anti-Chiang commander of the American Army forces in the China-India-Burma theater, General Joseph Stilwell. At no time, however, did Roosevelt give China a high priority.

The most controversial aspect of Roosevelt's diplomacy involved his dealings with the Soviet Union. He was convinced that cooperation with the U.S.S.R. was indispensable not simply to defeat Hitler but to maintain a lasting postwar peace. Roosevelt's major source of friction with the Soviet Union in 1942 and 1943 was over the delay in the cross-channel invasion of Europe that Soviet dictator Joseph Stalin was demanding to reduce the German pressure on the Russian front. Roosevelt's surprise announcement, at a press conference after his Casablanca meeting with Churchill, of the policy of unconditional surrender was largely motivated by his wish to reassure Stalin that the United States would not make a separate peace. Exaggerating his ability to charm Stalin, he pushed hard for face-to-face talks. When the "big three"—Roosevelt, Churchill, and Stalin—met at the TEHRAN CONFERENCE at the end of November 1943, Roosevelt made strenuous efforts to win Stalin over, even to the extent of appearing to align himself with the Soviet leader against Churchill.

Their next meeting came at the YALTA CONFERENCE, in the Russian Crimea, in February 1945, at a time when victory in Europe looked near. Because of military intelligence's overestimate of Japanese strength, Roosevelt made a priority of extracting a Soviet promise to enter the war against Japan after the defeat of Hitler. The price he paid was concessions to the Soviets in the Far East. The most troublesome question was over the future of Eastern Europe—most importantly, Poland. Roosevelt granted the legitimacy of the Soviet demand for friendly powers along its borders. He seems not to have fully understood the contradiction between allowing pro-Soviet regimes in Eastern Europe and the American commitment to national self-determination. More realistically, he recognized that Russian military occupation of the area allowed Stalin to do whatever he wanted there, but he hoped to avoid antagonizing Polish American voters by making a patched-up agreement vaguely promising free elections in Poland. In the aftermath of Yalta, he grew sufficiently disturbed by Soviet actions in Eastern Europe that he decided to keep the atomic bomb secret and to delay any commitment on a postwar loan.

Toward peace. From the early days of the war, Roosevelt had grappled with how to ensure a lasting peace. He was temporarily attracted by the plan advanced by Secretary of Treasury Morgenthau for the elimination of German industrial capability to prevent a resurgence of the German threat, but he later backed away from that proposal. The failure of the League of Nations had disillusioned him with the idea of a peacekeeping organization in which all nations would have an equal vote. He thus wished the put responsibility for keeping the peace on the "four policemen"— the United States, Britain, the Soviet Union, and China. Under pressure from a propaganda campaign by latter-day Wilsonians, he accepted the idea of a universally inclusive UNITED NATIONS organization whose members would have each one vote in the assembly but where effective power would be concentrated in a Security Council that would have the big four powers as permanent members, each able to exercise a veto.

Election of 1944. Despite Roosevelt's deteriorating health—which was largely hidden from the public— there was never any doubt about his running for a fourth term in 1944. The important question concerned who his running mate would be. Although

Roosevelt made a public show of continuing to support Wallace, he privately knifed him. After behind-the-scenes wheeling and dealing, the vice presidential nomination went to Senator Harry S. Truman of Missouri. The Republican presidential nominee was the youthful governor of New York, THOMAS E. DEWEY. Dewey did not challenge Roosevelt on the issues. The thrust of his appeal was that the administration had grown old and tired. In newspaper pictures, Roosevelt certainly looked drawn and exhausted. At first, Roosevelt played the role of Commander in Chief in a way that was above limiting himself to brief visits to war plants and military bases. In the last two weeks before the election, however, he threw himself with renewed vigor into an active campaign that did much to quiet questions about his health. He won by a popular vote of 25.6 million to Dewey's 20 million, with a margin of 432 (36 states) to 99 (12 states) in the electoral college.

Overwork and tiredness aggravated his health problems from high blood pressure and its complications. He went to Warm Springs for a vacation at the end of March 1945. He died there, on 12 April 1945, from a cerebral hemorrhage. In accordance with his wishes, he was buried under a plain headstone in the rose garden of his Hyde Park home.

Assessing Roosevelt. Roosevelt's years in the White House witnessed far-reaching changes in American life. How much of this change was due to him personally and how much to larger forces is impossible to disentangle. There is no question that he played a major role in shaping the modern American presidency, in expanding the regulatory power of the federal government over the economy, and in instituting at least the basics of a welfare state. He built the most powerful political coalition in the nation's history—one that would continue to dominate American politics for at least a generation after his death. In recent years, Roosevelt's image has faced sharp assault from the left and the right. The left complains about the New Deal's neglect of blacks, the gaps in its welfare programs, and its subsidizing of the social costs of capitalism out of the public treasury. The right blames the New Deal for undermining the work ethic, destroying the sense of individual responsibility, and spawning what has become an ever-growing list of entitlement programs whose costs threaten to bring the nation to financial ruin.

In foreign affairs, Roosevelt's imperishable achievement was the decisive contribution he made in blocking the monstrous ambitions of Hitler. So evil was Hitler that praise for Roosevelt's role in bringing about his downfall has kept most historians from questioning whether Japanese expansion on the Asian mainland really threatened significant United States interests.

The halo effect of Roosevelt's resistance to Hitler has similarly made historians reluctant to face up to the deviousness, if not dishonesty, with which he often acted. Roosevelt's policy toward the Soviet Union remains more controversial. Critics complain that the defeat of the Axis powers left the United States facing an equally dangerous threat from the Soviet Union. Roosevelt was guilty of miscalculations: he exaggerated the possibilities of cooperation with the Soviets, was overconfident about his ability to charm Stalin, and was naive about the realities of Eastern Europe in the postwar era. In Roosevelt's defense, however, it must be said that the expansion of Soviet power was an inevitable result of the power vacuum left by World War II.

BIBLIOGRAPHY

Burns, James M. *Roosevelt: The Lion and the Fox.* 1956.

Burns, James M. *Roosevelt: The Soldier of Freedom.* 1970.

Dallek, Robert. *Franklin D. Roosevelt and American Foreign Policy, 1932–1945.* 1979.

Freidel, Frank. *Franklin D. Roosevelt.* 4 vols. 1952–1973.

Freidel, Frank. *Franklin D. Roosevelt: A Rendezvous with Destiny.* 1990.

Greenfield, Kent Roberts. *American Strategy in World War II: A Reconsideration.* 1963.

Kimball, Warren F. *The Juggler: Franklin Roosevelt as Wartime Statesman.* 1991.

Leuchtenburg, William E. *Franklin D. Roosevelt and the New Deal, 1932–1940.* 1963.

Polenberg, Richard. *War and Society: The United States, 1941–1945.* 1972.

Schlesinger, Arthur M., Jr. *The Age of Roosevelt.* 3 vols. 1957–1960.

Tugwell, Rexford G. *The Democratic Roosevelt.* 1957.

JOHN BRAEMAN

ROOSEVELT, THEODORE (1858–1919), twenty-third President of the United States (1901–1909). Two salient aspects of Theodore Roosevelt's historical reputation best capture his relationship to the American presidency. First, his appearance and personality have remained more familiar to people than those of most of his predecessors or successors. Instantly identifiable and easily caricatured by his eyeglasses, moustache, and big teeth, Teddy Roosevelt continues to evoke near-universal recognition as a figure of energy, zest, physical vigor, and fun. The demented brother in the popular play *Arsenic and Old Lace* yells "Charge!" whenever he goes upstairs and fantasizes that he, like Roosevelt, is leading his troops up San Juan Hill in the SPANISH-AMERICAN WAR. As late as the 1980s, *Teddy*, a one-man play drawn from Roosevelt's speeches and writings, ran on Broadway and toured the country.

The second salient aspect of Roosevelt's historical reputation is that he does not rank among the greatest Presidents. Historians, political scientists, and other students of American politics have persistently placed him at or near the top of the second tier, the "near-great" Presidents. His placement on Mount Rushmore alongside George Washington, Thomas Jefferson, and Abraham Lincoln testifies more to the personal friendship and admiration of the monument's creator, Gutzon Borglum, than to any widely held estimate that he should stand with them or with his great rival Woodrow Wilson or his distant kinsman Franklin D. Roosevelt in the top rank of American Presidents.

The reason for this comparative downgrading of Theodore Roosevelt is readily apparent. Few great feats in domestic or foreign affairs highlighted his tenancy of the White House. On his own list of achievements, he always placed the beginning of the PANAMA CANAL first, followed by conservation of natural resources, sending the navy on a world cruise, mediation of the Russo-Japanese War in 1905, and some domestic regulation and legislation. These were impressive accomplishments, but they do not compare with the deeds associated with the founding of the American republic; the CIVIL WAR; sweeping reforms in political, economic, and social life; or the President's role in WORLD WAR I or WORLD WAR II. Still, Roosevelt's near-great status is arresting and speaks to his contribution to the evolution of the presidency.

Some critics charge that his familiarity and ranking demonstrate that there was more show than substance to his presidency. Actually, that judgment need not be taken as pejorative, because the primacy of appearance and public effect betokened a pioneering accomplishment. Roosevelt was the first media president. He owed his entire political career, particularly his rapid rise to the White House, to the public dimensions of politics, which had come to be magnified and intensified after the Civil War by the proliferation of popular newspapers and illustrated magazines. These media anticipated the later and larger impact of radio and television on politics, and Roosevelt's career demonstrated how much a truly gifted public performed could do in a preelectronic age. Besides his own vivid personality, Roosevelt owed most in his ability to attract popular attention to what he thought was his greatest political liability—his privileged social background. He was born into a wealthy, socially prominent New York City family and educated by private tutors and at Harvard University, and he chose to enter politics to show that a scion of the upper classes could compete successfully with men of humbler, tougher origins. Ironically, the prepresidential experience that gave him his closest identification with common people—his cowboy days as a rancher and hunter in the Dakota Territory in the 1880s—was really the kind of fashionable pursuit followed by upper-crust East Coast Americans and Europeans (much like the African safari he went on after his presidency).

Early Career. From the moment Roosevelt entered the New York State Assembly, as a dandified, twenty-three-year-old Republican, he never knew an hour of public obscurity. Both his social status and his personality made him good copy for journalists as he followed an unconventional path to the White House. Leaving the state legislature after only three years, he ran unsuccessfully for mayor of New York City in 1886, served on the virtually powerless federal Civil Service Commission for six years, and then returned to his native city as police commissioner in 1895. Meanwhile, he participated in national Republican politics as a convention delegate and campaigner, published books of history and biography, and developed an early interest in naval, military, and foreign affairs. Those interests and the patronage of his close friend and fellow aristocrat-in-politics, Senator Henry Cabot Lodge of Massachusetts, led in 1897 to his appointment as Assistant Secretary of the Navy (the same post that both Franklin D. Roosevelt and his own son, Theodore, Jr., would later hold). The Navy Department offered Roosevelt both a platform for broadcasting his views about military preparedness and assertive, expansionist foreign policy and a chance to demonstrate considerable administrative skill, as he helped upgrade and modernize the navy and prepare it for war in 1898.

Roosevelt's big political break came with the Spanish-American War. Resigning from his civilian post, he raised a cavalry regiment that mixed western cowboys with eastern bluebloods; the troops were soon dubbed the Rough Riders by attentive reporters. On the famous charge up San Juan Hill (which his troops made on foot because their horses never got to CUBA) Roosevelt showed real courage and captured the affections of Americans. Adoration for military heroes was nothing new, but this catapulting of a combat lieutenant colonel, not a commanding general, to the political front rank was unprecedented. Long attention from newspapers and magazines had already made Roosevelt a public figure, and the values that he embodied in his fighting exploit expanded his preexisting fame to outright heroism. Just a little over three years after San Juan Hill, Roosevelt was President of the United States.

Chance obviously intervened to shorten his road to the White House, but not by that much. Needing glamour to rescue a troubled state ticket, New York Republicans at once nominated Roosevelt for governor. When he won that office in November 1898 he was on the fast track to the presidency. In the twenty presidential elections from the end of the Civil War through World War II, thirteen featured a past or present governor of New York as a major-party nominee. Not only Roosevelt's new office but also the huge, adoring crowds that he attracted both in and outside New York ensured him a national political future. That future came faster thanks both to the admirers who promoted him publicly for the Republican vice presidential nomination and to the state bosses who privately wanted to get rid of an unmanageable governor. As the vice presidential nominee, Roosevelt bore the brunt of national campaigning for the Republicans in 1900. He once again attracted crowds and press coverage and gave his party a public performer who could match and even outshine the Democrats' star, their second-time presidential nominee WILLIAM JENNINGS BRYAN. Like other Vice Presidents, Roosevelt chafed at his enforced inactivity, but President William McKinley's death by assassination in September 1901 elevated him to an office that matched his ambitions and absorbed his energies.

Presidency. Theodore Roosevelt's ascent to the presidency created a great apparent contrast to the past. Unlike his immediate predecessors, he was young. At forty-two, he was the youngest man ever to become President, before or since. When Roosevelt left office nearly eight years later, he was still younger than all but four men have been when they entered the office. He had a boisterous, attractive family, with six children ranging downward in age from his society-belle teenage daughter "Princess" Alice to small sons who played ball on the White House lawn. He brought glamour, thanks to his family's social status, and he added intellectual and cultural distinction, through his own literary and cultural attainments as well as his personal and official patronage of science and the arts. Above all, Roosevelt brought a taste and talent for modern publicity. The White House (the name he officially adopted for the executive mansion) became the center of public attention, and he himself became the most famous man in America and the most famous leader in the world. Much of the new public attention sprang from Roosevelt's instincts and background, but a great deal also reflected conscious policy. Roosevelt cultivated reporters, set up the first pressroom in the White House, and was a pioneer in the use of planned leaks and trail balloons. Most of the twentieth-century institutions and practices of the public presidency either began or find precedents in what Roosevelt did between 1901 and 1909.

First term. The apparent contrast between McKinley and Roosevelt—especially the sense of much greater activity in the Roosevelt presidency—masks a strong strain of continuity, particularly in domestic affairs. One story recounts that soon after Roosevelt's succession conservative Republican congressional leaders struck a bargain with the new President in which he agreed to maintain the party's cherished tariff and currency policies and generally probusiness posture in return for a free hand in foreign affairs. The story is apocryphal; no such deal ever occurred. But there is symbolic truth to the story. Much of Roosevelt's activity during his first term was foreign affairs, and he did retain the personnel and continue the domestic policies of the McKinley administration. Members of McKinley's Cabinet stayed in key positions such as Secretary of State (JOHN HAY), Secretary of War (ELIHU ROOT), and Attorney General (PHILANDER KNOX). The most celebrated seeming departure from McKinley's policies, increased antitrust prosecutions (erroneously dubbed "trustbusting"), actually carried forward initiatives begun under McKinley. Likewise, Roosevelt's well-publicized mediation of the anthracite-coal strike in 1902 repeated a feat quietly brought off two years earlier at McKinley's behest by his friend Senator Marcus A. Hanna of Ohio. Roosevelt initiated policy and took bold action in only one domestic field: conservation of natural resources, in which he made vigorous, often high-handed moves and promoted the career and ideas of his friend Gifford Pinchot, who in 1905 became head of the newly created Forest Service.

This continuity at home stemmed equally from Roosevelt's personal preferences and his political circumstances. His reputation for impulsiveness and impetuosity was deceptive. His political views were conservative, and his temperament favored caution and calculation. His zestful, madcap, sometimes slightly comic public postures were rarely spontaneous but were usually planned for political effect. Equally weighty was what he perceived as his precarious prospects for the 1904 Republican presidential nomination. Up to that time, none of the three Vice Presidents who had replaced a fallen chief executive had received his party's nomination in the following presidential campaign. Roosevelt's popularity notwithstanding, he enjoyed few organizational ties to Republican machines and had no major following. In contrast, Senator Hanna enjoyed such ties and had a claim to McKinley's mantle because of his close personal and political friendship with the late President. Roosevelt devoted much of his first term to PATRONAGE and party

affairs. He isolated Hanna (who died unexpectedly early in 1904) and built a Republican presidential steamroller that served him well, both in securing his own nomination in 1904 and in imposing his choice as successor—William Howard Taft—on the party in 1908. As matters stood, conservative skeptics were never likely to try to deny him the nomination, and he received his party's affirmation by acclamation.

Roosevelt's cautious approach to domestic policy did not extend either to his rhetoric or to foreign affairs. Almost as soon as he ascended to what he called the BULLY PULPIT of the presidency, he began to preach. Roosevelt delivered three main, interrelated messages. First, he deplored divisiveness at home, especially along lines of economic class. He heartened conservatives by denouncing radicals and socialists and by dismissing the sensationalist exposé journalism of the time with the pejorative label of muckraking. But his main targets were those whom he dubbed "malefactors of great wealth," greedy tycoons and irresponsible trust magnates who cheated consumers, unfairly crushed competitors, and abused workers. Roosevelt's second message followed from his first: he constantly exhorted Americans to eschew materialism, by which he meant the exaltation of economic self-interest. He railed equally against the "greed of the haves" and the "envy of the have-nots," and he upheld a vision of service to a transcendent national interest, which he later called the NEW NATIONALISM.

Tying together these two messages was Roosevelt's third message, his preachment of national strength and of the United States' role as a great power in the world. Roosevelt was almost unique among Presidents from the 1820s to the 1950s in his previous knowledge and concern about foreign affairs, and in this area he practiced as well as preached from the outset of his presidency. Roosevelt had earlier adopted the African motto "Speak softly and carry a big stick" as his diplomatic watchword, and he proceeded to follow that injunction during his presidency. Roosevelt often spoke so softly, so secretly, that his subtle, involved diplomacy remained unrecognized for years afterward. In 1902 he warned Germany against intervention in Venezuela. In 1904 and 1905 he matched his public mediation of the Russo-Japanese War with private efforts to prevent its spread and the general breakdown of the international balance of power that could have ensued. In 1906 he intervened in the Moroccan crisis to oppose German attempts to upset that balance. His mediation of the Russo-Japanese War earned him the first Nobel Peace Prize awarded to an American. Because Roosevelt was such a frank admirer of military strength, that prize always struck many people as odd, but given his resourceful exercises in international restraint, he deserved the award more than almost anyone knew. Roosevelt really was a great peacemaker.

The "big stick" also characterized his presidency from start to finish. Roosevelt devoted himself tirelessly to the expansion of the armed forces. Each year he sought bigger appropriations for the army and navy, for which he had to struggle against congressional resistance from peace-minded liberal Democrats and economy-minded conservative Republicans. The President was no mindless military expansionist, however. For the navy, he pushed modernization of ships and weaponry and higher educational qualifications for officers. For the army, he aided and abetted Secretary of War Root's reforms, which introduced the general staff system and laid the groundwork for a reserve force. Roosevelt never got all he wanted, either from Congress or from the services, particularly the navy, where entrenched admirals stymied reforms like Root's, but he did preside over significant advances in national defense capabilities. Another feat that Roosevelt rated high among his presidential accomplishments came in 1907, when he ordered the great white fleet on an around-the-world cruise to impress people at home and abroad with America's armed might. One of his last and proudest acts as President came in February 1909, when he reviewed the fleet on its return.

Subtle diplomacy and strong arms did not constitute the whole Roosevelt record in foreign affairs. He sometimes spoke loudly, both in his constant harangues to Americans to wake up to their nation's role as a great power and in his deeds and pronouncements on the world stage. His most famous and controversial diplomatic move came in 1903, when he aided PANAMA's secession from Colombia (with which he may have conspired in advance) and then immediately pressured the new nation into ceding to American rule a strip of territory for the proposed isthmian canal. Roosevelt's superheated defenses of his actions in later years probably betrayed some repressed qualms about his actions. But the Panama Canal stood in his mind as his premier achievement, and in 1906 he became the first sitting President to travel abroad when he visited the construction site and inspected this, then the greatest human engineering project ever undertaken. Offended and frightened as many Latin Americans were by Roosevelt's deeds in Panama in 1903, they were still more deeply chagrined by his words the next year when he proclaimed the Roosevelt corollary to the MONROE DOCTRINE. He asserted that the United States had a duty to punish "chronic wrongdoing" by

its hemispheric neighbors through "the exercise of an international police-power." This was the most baldly imperialistic declaration that any American President ever made.

His performance in foreign affairs starkly exposed the inseparable mixture of light and dark, sweet and sour, noble and bullying elements that made up Roosevelt's political personality. The presidency brought out the best in him. The enormous responsibilities of the office restrained him, and its manifold opportunities channeled his energies constructively. Yet he never ceased to be a frank, unapologetic worshiper of power. That characteristic bred persistent uneasiness about him, even among some of his warmest supporters, and it sowed deep suspicion among critics and opponents, Democrats and fellow Republicans alike. The clearest indication of all these tendencies came as his first term ended and he launched himself into the next four years, when, as he put it, he would be President "in his own right."

Few elections have belonged to a presidential candidate so completely and undisputedly as the 1904 election belonged to Roosevelt. After the Republicans virtually crowned him at their convention, the Democrats obliged him further by coming close to rolling over and playing dead. The twice-beaten Bryan and his reformist followers stood aside and let the party's conservative wing have a turn at bat. The conservative Democrats proceeded to strike out by nominating ALTON B. PARKER, an obscure New York judge. Parker repudiated much of his party's platform and campaigned exclusively against Roosevelt's alleged "executive usurpations." The only time Parker struck any sparks came shortly before the election, when he charged the President with "blackmailing" Wall Street. There was some truth to the charge, because Roosevelt had feared Parker's potential appeal to big business and had authorized his managers to solicit large donations. But Parker got his facts garbled, and Roosevelt blasted back that the charges were "atrociously false." The flap probably had little impact on the election, which Roosevelt won in a landslide. With 336 electoral votes and 57.4 percent of the popular vote, he had gained the greatest victory yet accorded to any contestant for the American presidency.

Second term. Roosevelt responded to his electoral triumph with two actions that revealed the complexity of his political character. First, as soon as he knew the magnitude of his victory, he issued a statement in which he expressed gratitude to the people for their trust and pledged not to seek another term in 1908, following the TWO-TERM TRADITION. When he made that pledge, Roosevelt was not carried away by sentiment.

He had planned the move for a long time, and he privately explained that he justified his belief in a strong executive by ensuring that it was not a permanent executive. In a deeper sense, he was giving the lie to charges of usurpation and combatting misgivings about his hunger for power by voluntarily renouncing power. Some observers wondered whether Roosevelt would keep his promise, and at least once during the next four years he seems to have been tempted to wriggle out of the commitment. But he did abide by his self-denying ordinance. It was one of the noblest gestures Roosevelt ever made. Also, in view of the pain it caused him to keep the promise and the frustrations that dogged him as an ex-President, it was the biggest mistake of his political career.

Before Roosevelt had to face the consequences of his renunciation, he took a second action or rather a series of actions. During his second term, he pursued something much closer to his ideal of the presidency than he had before. He did not cast aside caution or break with Republican conservatives, but he did mount bolder initiatives in domestic affairs and defer less to congressional leaders. The years 1905 and 1906 witnessed the two major legislative accomplishments of his presidency. One was the Hepburn Act, which addressed the increasingly heated issue of railroad regulation by vesting the Interstate Commerce Commission (ICC) with its first rate-making authority. By patient negotiation, implied threats, and willingness to compromise, the President prevailed over opposition from some of the most powerful Republicans on Capitol Hill. In the end, the Hepburn Act disappointed more ardent reformers among Democrats and midwestern and western "progressive" Republicans because the ICC could not initiate rate-making procedures and its decisions were made subject to broad judicial review. Still, this act marked the first significant federal regulation of economic activity and paved the way for further expansion of federal regulatory powers.

The other major legislative move was the Pure Food and Drug Acts. Concern about fraudulent and impure products and unsanitary food-processing plants had led to the introduction of bills in Congress to create a new federal agency to oversee these areas. Conservative opposition stymied this proposed legislation until the President found an excellent opening for the exercise of his publicizing skills. When Upton Sinclair's novel *The Jungle*, with its lurid descriptions of the Chicago stockyards, was published early in 1906, Roosevelt not only egged on the magazines that published corroborating stories, but he also launched his own official investigation. When congressional opponents persisted in blocking action on the bills,

Roosevelt released the first part of his investigators' report and threatened to make public the even more damning second part. Popular reaction to these disclosures, combined with the threat of worse to come, sufficed to bring the bills to votes in both houses, where they passed easily. These acts created the Food and Drug Administration, which, along with the Forest Service, remains the principal governmental legacy of the Roosevelt administration.

These two legislative initiatives showed the President at his most resourceful in domestic affairs. Given the overwhelming power that conservatives held among Republicans in Congress and in the Republican Party's big state branches, getting even modest economic-reform laws passed represented a great accomplishment. To induce this predominantly conservative, probusiness party to approve these measures, Roosevelt pursued several strategies. The patience and persistence he exhibited in pushing for the Hepburn Act and the adroit exploitation of publicity he employed in championing the Pure Food and Drug Acts did not exhaust his political repertoire. When he tried to persuade conservative Republican Senators and Representatives to support these measures, or at least not to oppose them too vigorously, he repeatedly reminded them of growing public discontent with one of their most cherished policies, the protective tariff. In the absence of railroad and food-and-drug regulation, Roosevelt warned, that discontent would inexorably grow and might force him, reluctantly, to seek revision to the tariff. Such threats helped soften conservatives' resistance and get these measures enacted.

Roosevelt's reluctance to tackle the tariff was no pose. More than once he declared that the issue contained "political dynamite" because it was so complicated and so intricately interwoven with the business and labor interests that supported the Republican Party. Furthermore, in that era, tariff making was an exclusively legislative function, which Presidents could influence only through lobbying and vetoes. Advanced reformers were already proposing that an independent agency be established to set and alter tariff rates, particularly in the context of reciprocal trade agreements with other countries. Roosevelt began to support such proposals during his last year in the White House, and he continued to favor creation of a tariff commission as ex-President. In the meantime, however, he preferred to back reform measures in less controversial areas and ones that expanded administrative government by executive agencies, as with the Forest Service, the Food and Drug Administration, and the Interstate Commerce Commission. This kind of expansion of EXECUTIVE POWER would continue through most of the twentieth century. The precedents set by Roosevelt reflected a combination of expert advice, which he eagerly accepted; a desire to minimize the difficulties of dealing with Congress, which seems to be a constant among Presidents; and his own temperament, which sought to aggrandize himself and his office.

Congressional resistance did not provide the only irksome obstacle faced by Roosevelt. The judiciary troubled him even more, particularly because the federal courts had a penchant for interpreting the due process clause of the Fourteenth Amendment as banning governmental intervention in the economy. Roosevelt used the three Supreme Court vacancies that occurred during his presidency to attempt to push constitutional interpretation in a different direction. The first and most distinguished of his appointments went to Oliver Wendell Holmes, Jr., who became one of the greatest jurists in American history. Holmes did not always vote the way Roosevelt wished, especially in antitrust cases, but his dissents in regulatory cases advanced trenchant counterarguments to the dominate due process line. The glacial pace of judicial reconsideration never satisfied Roosevelt, and by his last year in the White House he was openly challenging the Supreme Court's main line of thinking, suggesting that legislative remedies might be necessary to reverse some decisions. He was already on the road to his post-presidential advocacy of recall of judicial decisions, which would be the most radical and controversial stand he ever took in domestic affairs.

Roosevelt's presidency reached its zenith of accomplishment in 1905 and 1906. Domestic reform legislation dovetailed with activist public diplomacy in the Far East and Europe to swell his popularity and raise his stature among sophisticated observers at home and abroad. The trip to Panama at the end of 1906 was a triumphal journey. One of the most famous photographs taken of Roosevelt shows him at the controls of a huge steam shovel helping to dig the canal. That picture epitomized the image of constructive power that he had cultivated so assiduously and so successfully.

From then on, the shadows gathered fast. A financial panic and brief recession in 1907 fanned public discontent, while business leaders and their conservative Republican allies blamed the President's "radical" policies for the downturn. Congressional resistance escalated sharply. Not only did the Republican leaders block any further legislative initiatives, but they also froze appropriations for Roosevelt's favorite agencies and ended the President's power to create forest reserves on public lands.

Roosevelt responded to this newfound adversity in a characteristically activist way. He mounted a vigorous effort to combat the recession, even though he had only limited governmental means available. He stepped up disbursements of contracts and spending and ordered the Treasury to help some threatened banks. He met privately with leading financiers to persuade them to lend and invest in ways that might help stem the panic. He promised to waive antitrust actions against the steel industry so that some apparently endangered firms could be rescued through acquisition. Congressional wing-clipping roused him to a variety of actions. In the face of refusals to fund investigations and publish reports by the presidential commissions that Roosevelt appointed on waterways, natural resources, and country life, he solicited private funds. Because the ending of his authority to create forest reserves was attached to an essential appropriation measure, Roosevelt did not use the VETO. Instead, with energetic help from Pinchot and the Forest Service, he proceeded to sequester more than 7 million acres of public lands just hours before his authority expired. The seizure of these midnight reserves was, arguably, Roosevelt's single most arrogant display of presidential power. It was done in patent defiance of the will of Congress, and it was done for the sake of conservation, which was always Roosevelt's most passionate commitment in domestic affairs.

In foreign affairs, Roosevelt drew back from his earlier involvements. He did send the fleet on its cruise in 1907, intending the move to serve as both a diplomatic warning to Japan and a lesson to the public and Congress about the need for a strong defense and vigorous foreign policy. Otherwise, the President concerned himself less than he had earlier with European rivalries and threats to the balance of power. On the home front, he continued to preach as before, delivering the same three messages. But now he pointed his admonitions against divisiveness and materialism almost exclusively against big business and Republican conservatives, and he added fresh specificity to his preachments. He advocated further railroad regulation measures, new legislation to protect workers' health and safety, and the levying of corporate, income, and inheritance taxes to curtail what he saw as the undue influence of wealth. These exhortations got nowhere in Congress, but they effectively set the agenda for domestic politics for the next decade.

Roosevelt's strongest response to the waning of his presidency was his exercise of the power that he had created himself to try to perpetuate his ideas and approaches. The best revenge that he could have taken on his party foes would have been to run again in

1908. Instead, honoring his pledge not to seek reelection, Roosevelt chose his successor and imposed the choice on a somewhat reluctant Republican Party. The man Roosevelt really wanted was Elihu Root, who had succeeded Hay as Secretary of State in 1905, but Root considered himself too old (he was sixty-three in 1908) and too conservative, and he declined the offer.

Roosevelt then turned to William Howard Taft, Root's successor as Secretary of War. Though well respected and well liked, Taft had never run for office, and everyone knew that he got the inside track for the nomination solely because he was Roosevelt's man. Reformers and progressives readily accepted Taft on the ground that if he was good enough for Roosevelt he was good enough for them. Some conservatives balked and tried to promote the candidacy of the man who now held Roosevelt's old office, Governor CHARLES EVANS HUGHES of New York. (Ironies abounded in this squabble, because Taft later sided with the conservatives in the Republican intraparty conflict, while Hughes established a solid reputation as a reformer.) The effort to nominate Hughes fizzled in part because Hughes gave it no encouragement but more because Roosevelt's presidential steamroller proved as potent for Taft as it had for himself four years earlier.

The Republican convention, platform, and campaign of 1908 simultaneously embodied and concealed the party's deep internal divisions. Roosevelt prevailed in the choice of the nominee, drew fulsome verbal praise at the convention, and virtually ran Taft's campaign against Bryan, whom the Democrats nominated a third time. Roosevelt's party foes chose one of their own, conservative Representative JAMES S. SHERMAN, as the vice presidential nominee and adopted a platform that would have gladdened McKinley and Hanna. In the campaign the conservatives supported Taft without much enthusiasm—on the ground that anybody would be better than Roosevelt. Taft won easily in November, although he fell far short of his predecessor's landslide victory of 1904. As Roosevelt's presidency drew to its close in March 1909, many odd notes jarred the atmosphere of ostensible personal and political success. Privately, Roosevelt made no secret of his unhappiness at leaving office, and he voiced some misgivings about Taft's Cabinet choices. To his credit, Roosevelt chose a singularly effective way of attempting not to upstage his successor. He went on a safari to Africa, which kept him incommunicado for several months. But it was a measure of party disharmony that some conservative Republicans reportedly toasted, "Health to the lions!"

Contributions to the presidency. In sum, Theodore Roosevelt richly earned his historical reputation through his presidency. The vividness with which he is remembered nearly a century later is a tribute to his pioneering development of the most important public dimensions of the office. No successful aspirant to or occupant of the White House could afterward operate outside those dimensions. Roosevelt's augmentation of executive power set precedents and advanced the main course of development of American government in the twentieth century. Withal, however, he remains near great, and that ranking he also earned, partly by his own choice. As the leader of an entrenched conservative party, he enjoyed few options for bold domestic initiatives, even if he had wanted to pursue them. The stalemate and frustration of Roosevelt's last two years in office, as well as the explosive divisions among Republicans afterward, amply testified to that overweening political reality. Perhaps the finest tribute to Roosevelt's character was his restraint and pursuit of peace in foreign affairs. Never once did he foment a crisis or seek to exploit external events for political profit. As a result, he presided over comparatively prosaic times, which, he believed, had failed to call forth his full capacity for leadership. The Roosevelt presidency left, therefore, a legacy that was equally luminous and bittersweet.

Ex-Presidency. No account of his relationship with the presidency would be complete without some consideration of his ex-presidency. Roosevelt remains to this day the most politically active and significant former chief executive in all American history. When he returned to the United States in 1910, after his African safari and a triumphal European tour, he at once plunged into the Republicans' internal conflict, which had intensified during his absence. Now, unlike earlier, Roosevelt sided openly with Progressive insurgents, endorsed a still broader and bolder reform agenda, and adopted the slogan "the New Nationalism" to characterize his program. The ex-President at first spurned the insurgents' entreaties to run for the 1912 nomination against Taft, who had sided with party conservatives. At the beginning of 1912, however, he decided to enter the race, announcing, "My hat is in the ring." The Taft-Roosevelt contest split the Republican Party wide open. The ex-President won most of the primaries, but his own invention, the patronage- and organization-based steamroller, now worked as effectively against him as it had once worked in his behalf. Roosevelt had foreseen this outcome, and he had already decided to bolt the party if he did not win the Republican nomination.

Using the conservatives' "theft" of the nomination as a pretext for bolting, the ex-President admonished his delegates to form a new party. "We stand at Armageddon, and we battle for the Lord," he proclaimed. In

August 1912, a hastily called convention formed the PROGRESSIVE (BULL MOOSE) PARTY and nominated Roosevelt for President and a former Republican insurgent, Governor Hiram Johnson of California, for Vice President. The Progressive Party also adopted a platform of advanced reform measures that included nationwide woman suffrage, thereby making it the first national party to favor giving women the vote. When someone asked Roosevelt how he felt about his candidacy and new party, he asserted that he felt as "fit as a bull moose." The bull moose quickly became the Progressives' symbol, to match the Republican elephant and Democratic donkey.

Roosevelt and his followers initially had high hopes of either winning or at least establishing the Progressives as a strong, enduring party. But those hopes quickly died. The Democrats nominated an attractive reformer of their own, Governor Woodrow Wilson of New Jersey, who countered Roosevelt's New Nationalism with his own luminous reform program and vision, the NEW FREEDOM. This campaign witnessed perhaps the highest level of discussion and virtual debate (the candidates never met face-to-face) in the history of presidential politics. It also witnessed an assassination attempt on Roosevelt in Milwaukee, Wisconsin, in October. He was shot in the chest and severely wounded. Wilson suspended campaigning during most of the remainder of the campaign, while Roosevelt recovered. In the November 1912 election, the ex-President came in second, ahead of Taft but losing badly to Wilson. Progressive candidates for lesser offices also fared poorly.

Theodore Roosevelt spent the rest of his life in opposition and mostly in political exile. No one appreciated the Progressives' weaknesses better than he did, and after their virtual collapse in the 1914 state and congressional elections, he actively conspired to scuttle the party. By that time, his main political concern had reverted to foreign affairs, particularly after the outbreak of World War I. It galled Roosevelt not to be President at such an unquestionably momentous time in world history, and he quickly came to despise what he scorned as Wilson's "spineless neutrality." The depth of his concern and the fury he felt toward the President led him to take increasingly unpopular stands, as he called for ever bigger increases in the army and navy, proposed establishment of a draft, and demanded foreign policies that would have almost certainly plunged the United States into the war against Germany. These unpopular stands and lingering bitterness from 1912 killed any chance that he might rejoin his old party at the head of the ticket in 1916. Instead, Roosevelt supported the Republican nominee, Charles Evans Hughes, and campaigned

vigorously against Wilson. Wilson's narrow reelection came as a bitter blow to Roosevelt, as did Wilson's attempt just after the election to mediate the war and promote "peace without victory."

Thanks to Germany's renewal of submarine warfare, however, the United States did go to war in 1917, and American intervention swiftly resurrected the ex-President's political standing. His formerly unpopular belligerency now became fashionable, and even though President Wilson rejected his request to lead troops, Roosevelt emerged once more as a popular hero and leader. By the end of the war in 1918, former foes among the Republicans had switched to support him, and the 1920 nomination was generally regarded as his for the asking. He had made the most remarkable comeback in American presidential politics. But another Roosevelt presidency also became a haunting might-have-been: He died unexpectedly on 4 January 1919, at the age of sixty. He had packed a remarkable career into a comparatively short lifetime.

Ironically, Roosevelt's ex-presidency probably made a bigger impact on American politics than his presidency. His leadership of the Progressives and his articulation of the New Nationalism unquestionably reshaped the course of domestic politics. His stands on defense and foreign policy during World War I undoubtedly altered the course of American diplomacy at a critical juncture. Even though he did not achieve those results by occupying the White House, he was able to accomplish more on the outside during the last ten years of his life than most Presidents have accomplished from the inside. The ex-presidency of Theodore Roosevelt completed the legacy of his presidency.

BIBLIOGRAPHY

Blum, John M. *The Republican Roosevelt.* 1954.
Cooper, John Milton, Jr. *The Warrior and the Priest: Woodrow Wilson and Theodore Roosevelt.* 1983.
Einstein, Lewis. *Roosevelt: His Mind in Action.* 1930.
Gould, Lewis L., Jr. *The Presidency of Theodore Roosevelt. 1991.*
Harbaugh, William, H. *Power and Responsibility: The Life and Times of Theodore Roosevelt.* 1961.
Marks, Frederick W., III. *Velvet on Iron: The Diplomacy of Theodore Roosevelt.* 1979.
Morris, Edmund. *The Rise of Theodore Roosevelt.* 1979.
Mowry, George. *The Era of Theodore Roosevelt, 1900–1910.* 1958.
Mowry, George. *Theodore Roosevelt and the Progressive Movement.* 1946.
Roosevelt, Theodore. *Autobiography.* 1913.
Wister, Owen, *Roosevelt: The Story of a Friendship.* 1930.

JOHN MILTON COOPER, JR.

ROOT, ELIHU (1845–1937) Secretary of War, Secretary of State, Senator. Elihu Root was born in

Clinton, New York. Son of a Hamilton College mathematics professor, Root himself graduated from Hamilton in 1864. In 1869, he began to practice law in New York City.

By temperament and principle a conservative, Root specialized in corporate law, gaining a strong reputation for defending railroads and banks. A Republican, Root first involved himself in state politics, advising Theodore Roosevelt in his mayoral campaign of 1886 and when Roosevelt became New York police commissioner in the mid 1890s. The two were close friends and political allies.

William McKinley picked Root to become Secretary of War in 1899. Along with Roosevelt, JOHN HAY, Henry Cabot Lodge, and Alfred T. Mahan, Root transformed U.S. foreign policy, helping to define American internationalism and America's initial relationship with its new colonial possessions. As Secretary, Root secured PUERTO RICO's free access to the American market. With General Leonard Wood, he established CUBA's qualified form of independence; Root also drafted much of the Teller Amendment. Root reestablished order in the conquered territory of the PHILIPPINES. The Filipino experience (in which the U.S. military had shown itself inefficient and oftentimes brutal) indirectly led to his reorganization of the WAR DEPARTMENT. He reformed the department's administrative structure, founded the army war college, and centralized access to the national guard.

Root retired from the War Department in 1904, but upon Roosevelt's request, became Secretary of State in 1905, replacing the deceased Hay. Root shared in many of Roosevelt's international triumphs, particularly the informal agreement with Japan limiting Japanese immigration. A tour of Central America in 1906 soothed tensions in that region. In 1912, he received the Nobel Peace Prize for his diplomatic efforts in the western hemisphere.

In 1908, Roosevelt retired and narrowed his choice of successor to Root and William Howard Taft. In part because of Root's reluctance to become involved in electoral politics (he refused to run for the New York governorship in 1904), Roosevelt chose Taft. Root subsequently became a Senator in 1909. Having already endorsed Taft, with much reluctance Root presided over the Republican national convention of 1912 and watched as his friend Roosevelt bolted to the PROGRESSIVE (BULL MOOSE) PARTY.

Root remained in the Senate until 1915 and became a critic of Woodrow Wilson's administration and supported entering WORLD WAR I on the Allied side. In 1917, Wilson appointed Root head of the Russian mission, but ignored Root's reports during that revolutionary year.

In 1918 and 1919, Root lead the so-called LEAGUE OF NATIONS reservationists. He supported the League in principle, but disavowed American compliance with Article X, which could have potentially involved American forces in unspecified international conflicts. During the election of 1920, Root campaigned for Warren G. Harding, hoping that Harding would endorse the reservationist position. In the 1920s, Root played an important role in establishing the World Court. He also served as adviser to Andrew Carnegie.

BIBLIOGRAPHY

Cooper, John Milton, Jr. *Pivotal Decades: The United States, 1900-1920.* 1990.
Keller, Morton. *Affairs of State.* 1977.
Leopold, Richard W. *Elihu Root and the Conservative Tradition.* 1954.
Wiebe, Robert. *The Search for Order.* 1967.

JOHN F. WALSH

ROSENMAN, SAMUEL (1896–1973), speechwriter, political adviser, Special Counsel to the President. Long active in New York state politics, Samuel Irving Rosenman began working for Franklin D. Roosevelt as a political adviser and speechwriter in the 1928 gubernatorial campaign. He became Roosevelt's counsel and played a key role in the 1932 presidential campaign: it was Rosenman who created the idea of the BRAIN TRUST—a group of academics and quasi academics brought together to advise the candidate—and who coined the term NEW DEAL, first used by Roosevelt in his acceptance speech at the 1932 Democratic national convention.

Rosenman became a justice of the New York State Supreme Court in 1933, though he continued to advise Roosevelt on an informal basis until 1943, when he became special counsel to the President. His most important role, particularly after 1936, was as a PRESIDENTIAL SPEECHWRITER and as supervisor of the White House speechwriting corps. He was responsible, at least in part, for such speeches as the FIRESIDE CHAT defending the COURT-PACKING PLAN of 1937; the "Arsenal of Democracy" speech of December 1940; and the FOUR FREEDOMS speech of 1941. During WORLD WAR II Rosenman helped mediate disagreements between the growing number of war agencies and traveled to London to investigate supply problems in the liberated parts of Europe and to negotiate with the British on the pending trials of Nazi war criminals. After Roosevelt's death Rosenman continued to serve President Harry S. Truman as a political adviser and speechwriter. Rosenman also served, at Roosevelt's request, as editor and compiler of *The Public Papers and Addresses of Franklin D. Roosevelt,* a multivolume work

RULEMAKING, CONGRESSIONAL CONTROL OF   1337

published between 1938 and 1950 and still a standard reference tool.

Hand, Samuel B. *Counsel and Advice: A Political Biography of Samuel I. Rosenman.* 1979.
Rosenman, Samuel I. *Working with Roosevelt.* 1952.

WILLIAM LASSER

RULEMAKING, CONGRESSIONAL CONTROL OF. Rulemaking is a major step in the policy-making process as administrative agencies translate statutory provisions into specific mandates that are binding on regulated parties and have the force of law. Rules often reflect major policy choices and, as a consequence, rulemaking is very much a political process. The same political interests that shape legislation also seek to influence the rules agencies issue.

Many regulatory statutes are written in broad and vague language, while others provide detailed, specific mandates. However, in either case, the jurisdiction, authority, and tasks delegated to regulatory agencies often greatly exceed the resources provided. Agency officials must make basic choices in rulemaking as they set priorities and balance competing goals of economic growth and regulatory protection.

The Rulemaking Process. The importance of rulemaking in public policy-making has naturally created strong interest in Congress in controlling the process. Congressional supervision of rulemaking can ensure that congressional intent, or at least the policy views of particular members, guides the formulation of rules. It can ensure that policy goals are achieved, that elected officials hold unelected agency officials accountable for the exercise of public power, and that rule writers are responsive to the concerns of congressional constituents.

Congress can instruct regulatory agency officials through provisions in the legislative history of statutes, including committee reports, hearings, debates on the floor, and statements issued by the bill's sponsors. It has sought to respond to the President's increased power to review regulatory agency actions by creating for itself and its support agencies an extensive set of procedures and mechanisms for overseeing the administrative process.

The Supreme Court's 1983 ruling against the LEGISLATIVE VETO, INS V. CHADHA, which had permitted members of Congress to review and reject regulations proposed by some agencies, limited Congress's use of one of its favorite oversight tools. The Court struck down in BOWSHER V. SYNAR (1986) the Gramm-Rudman-Hollings Acts deficit-reduction trigger mechanism, arguing that the Constitution "does not contemplate an active role for Congress in the supervision of officers charged with the execution of the laws it enacts." Congressional participation in appointing officials to the Federal Election Commission was rejected by the Court in BUCKLEY V. VALEO (1976).

The loss of the legislative veto, the willingness of executive-branch officials to challenge congressional expectations and priorities and statutory provisions, and the great amount of legislation that is in place and that needs to be reviewed periodically have all made the search for means of more effective control over rulemaking an increasingly important challenge confronting Congress. Much of the congressional control of rulemaking takes place informally, through phone calls and meetings between regulation writers and congressional staff members where problems are discussed and differences resolved.

The authorization process provides an important opportunity for members of Congress to review and redirect the implementation of the laws they pass. Congressional committees monitor rulemaking through oversight hearings, reports from the executive branch (more than two thousand reports are required each year), informal meetings with agency staffs, written inquiries, reports prepared by the GENERAL ACCOUNTING OFFICE (GAO), media investigations, and complaints from constituents. Some regulatory agencies must undergo annual reauthorizations and the accompanying oversight proceedings, while others enjoy multiyear or permanent authorization.

The GAO reviews selected agencies and programs to ensure that agency expenditures are consistent with congressional mandates. Because congressional committees lack the staff to monitor agency activity comprehensively, they rely largely on criticisms and concerns raised by affected parties and others to identify areas for oversight investigation. In the House, most committees have established oversight subcommittees to oversee the agencies and programs within the committees' jurisdiction. In the Senate, only a few committees have established investigations subcommittees. The House Government Operations and Senate Governmental Affairs committees have a government-wide responsibility to oversee executive-branch activities, including the rulemaking process.

Appropriations hearings, agency budget submissions, reports, and meetings between agency and appropriations subcommittee staffs provide the fodder for congressional scrutiny of rulemaking. Language in appropriations bills may forbid an agency from using funds to write or implement specific regulations. Appropriations committee reports sometimes contain specific instructions to agencies concerning expendi-

1338   RULEMAKING, CONGRESSIONAL CONTROL OF

tures they are required to make (and some they are prohibited from making). Congress may require agencies to obtain the approval of appropriations committees before issuing or implementing regulations. Report-and-wait provisions require that proposed rules be submitted to committees and not go into effect until a specified date, usually thirty or sixty days, after the proposed regulation is submitted to Congress; the regulation goes into effect unless legislation is enacted rejecting the initiative. Or the provision may require that Congress pass a joint resolution of approval, to be signed by the President, before the proposed rule goes into effect.

The confirmation process has been used by Senate committees to collect information—through hearings, informal meetings, and written inquiries—concerning rulemaking and other agency activities. Confirmation hearings also provide an opportunity for members of Congress to instruct, warn, cajole, and otherwise direct agency activity. Senators and Representatives often extract commitments and promises concerning agency practices and activities from nominees during the confirmation hearings, although it may be difficult for committees to ensure compliance with those informal agreements.

Evaluations of the Process. In 1977 the Senate Government Operations (later renamed Governmental Affairs) Committee issued a major report on the regulatory process. The study found that oversight of regulatory activities was a "low priority for most Members of Congress," that there was "little active coordination between committees for oversight," and that most committees lacked staff with expertise in regulatory issues. The appropriations process was viewed as the most "potent form of oversight in those areas where attention is directed," but it generally worked "haphazardly as an oversight mechanism." Similar criticisms were aimed at the appropriations process as being ad hoc and in response to "a newspaper article, a complaint from a constituent or special interest group, or information from a disgruntled agency employee" rather than stemming from a systematic, regular review.

The committee proposed several recommendations for improving oversight of regulation. All regulatory agencies should be "subject to a periodic authorization process" to ensure thorough scrutiny before being reauthorized. Each regulatory agency should be required to "evaluate its regulatory programs and present its evaluations to congressional authorizing committees annually," to include "a discussion of the agency's goals for the next few years" and "a plan for evaluating agency performance of those goals." Other recommendations emphasized increased use of con-

gressional support agencies, follow-up hearings and inquiries to see if agencies implemented committee recommendations, and the writing of statutes "as narrowly as possible."

Competing Views of Rulemaking. Congressional initiatives to control rulemaking collide with presidential efforts to direct the promulgation of regulations. The differences are rooted in competing views of the nature of rulemaking itself. From one perspective, administrative agencies are arms of Congress and rulemaking, in particular, is an extension of the legislative process. Agencies are delegated part of Congress's legislative power to take advantage of their technical expertise. Rulemaking is understood as a form of lawmaking, since it produces legally binding rules, even though it is not done by members of Congress. Congress can freely intervene in rulemaking decisions and bears primary responsibility for monitoring rulemaking and ensuring that rules are consistent with the statutes that authorized them. The President's role in the regulatory process is a limited one; he is simply to take care that the laws passed by Congress are faithfully executed. In *Myers v. United States* (1926), the Supreme Court provided some support for this view, finding that "there may be duties so peculiarly and specifically committed to the discretion of a particular officer as to raise a question whether the President may overrule or revise the officer's interpretation of his statutory duty in a particular instance." Since most rulemaking authority is delegated to specific agency officials, such as the Administrator of the Environmental Protection agency, the President may not be constitutionally empowered to overrule or revise rules issued by agency officials.

From another view, however, the executive branch is unified and hierarchical, with the President perched on top and all administrative officials arrayed below him. While the President cannot order agencies to act contrary to the law, he has broad powers to direct and shape the execution of the law. He can set priorities, balance competing policy goals, choose among conflicting statutory mandates, and impose his own set of principles on agencies to guide their rulemaking and general policy-making efforts. In *Sierra Club v. Costle* (1981), a federal appellate court concluded that "the authority of the president to control and supervise executive policy-making is derived from the Constitution; the desirability of such control is demonstrable from the practical realities of administrative rulemaking. . . .Single mission agencies do not always have the answer to complex regulatory problems." Others simply define rulemaking as an executive function because it is located in administrative agencies, thus limiting congressional intervention and justifying presidential supervision. An expansive view of the executive power inherent in the presidency envisions a broad supervisory, managerial role for the President in overseeing rulemaking that is independent of any congressional delegation of power.

From yet another view, the creation of independent regulatory agencies was an attempt to insulate agencies from presidential control and sometimes even from congressional intervention. Some agencies, such as the FEDERAL RESERVE SYSTEM, are more independent of both congressional and presidential control than are others. In most cases, agencies find themselves caught between presidential and congressional efforts to monitor and direct their rulemaking efforts. They are torn between the imperatives of managerial efficiency, professional norms, procedural constraints and judicial review, and the oversight efforts of elected officials.

Much of the current controversy surrounding rulemaking results from basic differences between Republican Presidents and Democratic-dominated Congresses. Ideally, efforts to control rulemaking will proceed in an atmosphere of restraint in both branches; both executive and legislative branch officials will be committed to the rule of law; agency heads will faithfully execute the laws; and members of Congress and their staffs will avoid the temptation to become so involved in the details of administration that agency managers cannot function effectively. While it is tempting to use the administrative process to gain what was not achieved in the legislative process, government cannot function without full acceptance of the rule of law and an unqualified commitment of executive branch officials to faithfully execute the laws enacted by Congress. If Congress, the President, and the agencies constantly seek to strike a balance in oversight, then good oversight is possible; if that accommodation is lacking, then no set of structures and procedures will likely be able to channel that interaction into productive activity.

The more the executive branch recognizes and accepts the role of Congress in overseeing rulemaking, the more likely that oversight relations will be productive. Congress can contribute to improved oversight by furnishing the resources and political support for thorough, systematic oversight activities that critically examines the adequacy of existing statutes.

BIBLIOGRAPHY

Fisher, Louis. *The Politics of Shared Power.* 3d ed. 1993.
National Academy of Public Administration. *Congressional Oversight of Regulatory Agencies.* 1988.
National Academy of Public Administration. *Presidential Management of Rulemaking in Regulatory Agencies.* 1987.
Strauss, Peter. "The Place of Agencies in Government: Separation of Powers and the Fourth Branch." *Columbia Law Journal* 84 (April 1984): 573–669.
U.S. Congress. Senate. Committee on Government Operations. *Principal Recommendations and Findings of the Study on Federal Regulation.* 96th Cong., 1st sess., 1977. Committee print.

GARY C. BRYNER

RULEMAKING POWER. Presidents in the late twentieth century have attempted to influence rulemaking in federal agencies in order to achieve overall policy coordination. In doing so, Presidents have asserted their constitutional powers over the executive branch and have taken advantage of certain indirectly related statutory powers. Congress has not enacted a statute specifically controlling this aspect of presidential supervision of the agencies. Nevertheless, Presidents have established some important programs by EXECUTIVE ORDER.

The Administrative Procedure Act of 1946 (APA) established general policy-making procedures for the executive branch but did not discuss the President's relationship with rulemaking agencies. The Supreme Court in *Franklin v. Massachusetts* (1992) held that the APA does not apply directly to the President.

The APA specifies a simple process for federal rulemaking. Agencies must give public notice of proposed rules, receive and consider written comments on the proposals, and then publish final rules in the *Federal Register*. Over the years, this process has become a somewhat more formal interchange with affected interests. The result for most final rules is a record of fact and opinion that undergoes judicial review. The courts seek a reasonable basis for the agency's decision in fact, law, and procedure, but avoid invading the agency's policy-making discretion.

Presidents have a combination of constitutional and statutory powers through which they influence federal rulemaking. First, they have constitutional powers to propose and to veto the statutes that authorize regulation. Second, the Constitution provides that the President or his subordinates, and not Congress, may appoint federal regulators (although often with the Senate's ADVICE AND CONSENT). Third, the President has constitutional powers to ensure the faithful execution of the laws and to require his subordinates to furnish him opinions in writing on the performance of their duties. These powers imply the capacity to remove regulators whose performance is disappointing. The Supreme Court upheld the President's authority to remove subordinate executive officers in MYERS V. UNITED STATES (1926). For the independent regulatory agencies, however, Congress restricts presidential RE-

MOVAL POWER to the presence of cause. In HUMPHREY'S EXECUTOR v. UNITED STATES (1935), the Court upheld the authority of Congress to do so. In practice, this has meant far greater policy autonomy for independent agencies than for executive agencies.

Presidents have statutory power to formulate the federal budget for congressional consideration and passage. This power applies not only to the executive agencies but also to most of the independent ones. An agency's funding level critically affects its capacity to regulate. Because the President's OFFICE OF MANAGEMENT AND BUDGET (OMB) both formulates the budget and exercises most presidential supervision of rulemaking, agencies are reluctant to oppose its preferences. Presidents also often possess statutory power to reorganize existing agencies.

Occasionally a President has taken interest in a particularly important pending regulation and has consulted with the administrator who is responsible for issuing it. The Supreme Court has never decided the permissible extent of this presidential participation in rulemaking. Since a particular regulation of one agency can affect many related policy responsibilities of other agencies, it is important for the President to play some coordinating role. For example, an environmental regulation of power-plant emissions can affect energy and economic policy. The lower courts have struggled to accommodate two competing values. One of these is EXECUTIVE PRIVILEGE—the need for policy debate in the executive branch to be confidential, so that it will be candid. The other is the need to abide by administrative law requirements that rules be based on known administrative records that fully support them. Thus, it may be permissible for the President or his immediate advisers to consult privately with an administrator, as long as the final rule is supported by the agency's record.

More often, Presidents take a generalized interest in the performance of federal rulemaking. They issue executive orders and other less formal directives to the agencies, stating principles and policies that administrators must follow when regulating. Here, Presidents attempt to impose a measure of coordination on the sprawling executive establishment, within statutory limits. Statutory delegations of regulatory power ordinarily contain enough discretion to allow compliance with such presidential commands.

Since the early 1970s, all Presidents have created interagency review procedures that balance health, safety, and environmental goals of statutes with the administration's economic goals. President Richard M. Nixon instituted "quality of life" review of environmental and other health and safety regulations. Pro-posed rules were submitted to OMB and other agencies for review and comment. In practice, this program focused on rules of the Environmental Protection Agency. President Gerald Ford issued an executive order requiring executive agencies to prepare an "inflation impact statement" for each proposed major regulation. These were reviewed by the Council on Wage and Price Stability. Agency compliance with the program was quite uneven. The analyses were performed too late in the rulemaking process to affect policy significantly. President Jimmy Carter sought to remedy these deficiencies by issuing an executive order that required agency heads to prepare agendas of proposed actions, to review their own rules early in the process of formulation, and to assure that the most cost-effective approaches were taken for significant rules. President Carter established a Regulatory Analysis Review Group to review analyses prepared for major rules and to comment on them. He also created a Regulatory Council, composed of the heads of rulemaking agencies, to coordinate policy and to avoid conflict or duplication of effort.

A pair of related executive orders that were issued by President Ronald Reagan have had the most far-reaching impact on rulemaking. EXECUTIVE ORDER 12291 requires executive agencies, to the extent permitted by statute, to observe cost-benefit principles when promulgating regulations. (The order does not apply to the independent agencies.) Proposed rules must be sent to OMB, which reviews them and discusses them with the agencies. This function has been placed partly in the OFFICE OF INFORMATION AND REGULATORY AFFAIRS (OIRA) within OMB and partly in the President's Council on Competitiveness. Executive Order 12291 is not based on statutory authority. It rests on the President's constitutional powers to supervise the executive branch. Congress has repeatedly considered applying statutory controls to the program, but has yet to do so.

EXECUTIVE ORDER 12498, promulgated by President Reagan in 1985, established a "regulatory planning process" to be implemented through formulation of an annual regulatory program for the executive agencies of the federal government. (Again, independent regulatory agencies are not included.) The head of each executive agency must send OMB a draft regulatory program containing a description of all significant regulatory actions to be undertaken in the next year. When these are combined into the federal government's program for the year, a single document exists to give an overview of the direction of federal rulemaking.

Other executive orders have required agencies to

consider the impact of their rules on such values as federalism. Thus, whenever a President regards an issue as important enough to merit special consideration by the executive agencies, he possesses a mechanism to ensure that the bureaucracy will share his sense of priorities.

BIBLIOGRAPHY

Fisher, Louis. *The Constitution between Friends.* 1978.

National Academy of Public Administration. *Presidential Management of Rulemaking in Regulatory Agencies.* 1987.

Pierce, Richard A., Jr., Sidney A. Shapiro, and Paul R. Verkuil. *Administrative Law and Process.* 2d ed. 1992.

Shane, Peter M., and Harold H. Bruff. *The Law of Presidential Power.* 1988.

Strauss, Peter L., and Cass R. Sunstein. "The Role of the President and OMB in Informal Rulemaking." *Administrative Law Review* 38 (1986): 181–207.

Symposium. "Cost-Benefit Analysis and Agency Decision-Making: An Analysis of Executive Order No. 12,291." *Arizona Law Review* 23 (1981): 1195–1298.

HAROLD H. BRUFF

RUSK, DEAN (b. 1909), Secretary of State. Born in Cherokee County, Georgia, Dean Rusk graduated from Davidson College and Oxford University. A professor of political science at Mills College in Oakland, California, as war clouds gathered, he joined the army in 1940 and served in the China-Burma-India theater. After WORLD WAR II, he joined the State Department where he won the admiration of DEAN ACHESON. As Assistant Secretary of State for Far Eastern Affairs from 1950 to 1953, Rusk strenuously opposed the new communist regime in China, helped plan U.S. policy in the KOREAN WAR, and helped negotiate the peace treaty with Japan. He left the Truman administration to become president of the Rockefeller Foundation where he remained until John F. Kennedy selected him as Secretary of State in 1961. He held that position until the end of the Johnson administration in 1969. Relations between Kennedy and Rusk were more correct than close and cordial. The new President relied more on McGeorge Bundy, the national security adviser, and ROBERT S. MCNAMARA, the Secretary of Defense, for foreign policy counsel. A formal man, Rusk preferred to speak directly to the President than to voice his opinions in large meetings, where he feared that his words would be leaked to the press by the many subordinates present. He advised Kennedy against the 1961 BAY OF PIGS INVASION, counseled firmness in the CUBAN MISSILE CRISIS, and advocated greater U.S. involvement in the growing VIETNAM WAR.

Rusk became a more important foreign policy adviser in the Johnson administration. Johnson, himself inexperienced in foreign affairs, valued Rusk's knowledge of U.S. relations with Asia. The Secretary of State constantly recalled what he believed were the lessons of World War II (no appeasement of dictators) and Korea (that the Chinese communists presented a grave threat to the United States). In 1964 and 1965, Rusk urged Johnson to bomb communist positions in North and South Vietnam and to send additional American ground forces in 1965. At the same time he cautioned against provoking Chinese intervention in the war. Rusk advocated the administration's Vietnam policy before Congress, where he was well received by the Senate committee on armed services but greeted with skepticism and eventual scorn by the committee on foreign relations. Rusk advised Johnson to continue to increase American forces in Vietnam in the aftermath of the communists' Tet offensive of 1968, but the President eventually overruled him. Vietnam absorbed so much of Rusk's attention that he had little time to devote to reducing the danger of nuclear war with the Soviet Union, to U.S. relations with the poorer nations of the world, and to long-range planning. Several former aides to President Kennedy, who later broke with the Johnson administration's Vietnam policy, recalled that their superior had wanted to replace Rusk as Secretary of State. Physically and emotionally exhausted by the end of the Johnson administration, Rusk felt wounded that many of his former friends in the foreign policy establishment now shunned him. After 1970 he taught international law at the University of Georgia.

BIBLIOGRAPHY

Cohen, Warren. *Dean Rusk.* 1980.

Rusk, Dean. *As I Saw It.* 1990.

Schoenbaum, Thomas J. *Waging Peace and War: Dean Rusk in the Truman, Kennedy, and Johnson Years.* 1988.

ROBERT D. SCHULZINGER